OXFORD PAPERBACK REFERENCE

The Concise
Oxford Dictionary
of Ballet

The Concise Oxford Dictionary of Ballet

HORST KOEGLER

Second edition
(*Updated, 1987*)

Oxford   New York
OXFORD UNIVERSITY PRESS

Oxford University Press, Walton Street, Oxford OX2 6DP

Oxford New York
Athens Auckland Bangkok Bombay
Calcutta Cape Town Dar es Salaam Delhi
Florence Hong Kong Istanbul Karachi
Kuala Lumpur Madras Madrid Melbourne
Mexico City Nairobi Paris Singapore
Taipei Tokyo Toronto

and associated companies in
Berlin Ibadan

Oxford is a trade mark of Oxford University Press

Original German edition © Friedrich Verlag 1972
English edition and all new material © Oxford University Press 1977
Second edition © Oxford University Press 1982

First published 1977
Second edition published 1982
First issued as an Oxford University Press paperback 1982

British Library Cataloguing in Publication Data
Data available

Library of Congress Cataloging in Publication Data
Koegler, Horst.
Concise Oxford dictionary of ballet—2nd ed.
1. Ballet—dictionaries.
I. Title.
792.8'03'21 GV1787
ISBN 0-19-311330-9 Pbk

7 9 10 8

Printed in Great Britain by
Clays Ltd
Bungay, Suffolk

Foreword to the Second Edition

While the general principles stated in the foreword to the first edition still hold true for this second edition, a great many entries have been deleted and replaced by topical new subjects. This does not mean that what was considered important in 1977 has not stood the test of time. But some names, titles, and events need to be registered only once, and not perpetuated from one edition to another.

In the foreword to the first edition I forgot to mention how much I owed to the invaluable information provided by Monique Babsky, who compiled the 'complete list of roles and activities' I so often quoted for French dancers and choreographers from the magazine *Les Saisons de la danse* in the biographical entries – for which I duly apologize to her.

In the bibliographies of ballets, some references have been retained to *Balanchine's New Complete Stories of the Great Ballets* (1968). These may be taken to refer to the more recent edition, George Balanchine and Francis Mason, *Balanchine's Complete Stories of the Great Ballets* (1977).

Despite the repeated wish of my esteemed new American collaborator, Susan Au, I could not bring myself to include an entry on 'Post-Modern Dance'. The term is currently very much in vogue with American critics (though hardly used as yet by their European colleagues), but so far seems too vague even for them, as nobody has yet come forward with a workable definition.

I am grateful to the many readers who have written to direct my attention to errors or omissions. I have gladly taken up a lot of their suggestions, though not all of them (for instance if I felt there was too personal a bias). I sincerely hope they will come forward with further comments and suggestions for future editions.

While colleagues from all over the world, too numerous to be mentioned here by name, have provided me with welcome advice, help, and facts, for which they have put me deeply in their debt, none has so patiently and diligently answered every individual question as my dear friend Yelizaveta Yakovlevna Souritz, that inexhaustible source of Moscow ballet wisdom.

In the final proofreading stage Susan Au in New York and Noël Goodwin in London have been last-minute saviours. They have spotted not only many errors and misprints I had overlooked, but in addition a number of missing amendments, which had somehow evaded what I had considered up to that time my impeccable ballet bookkeeping. To them my profound gratitude — as to Geoffrey Norris and Anthony Mulgan, my helpful and attentive erstwhile and present Oxford University Press editors.

Stuttgart, January 1982   H.K.

Note to the 1987 Oxford Paperback Reference Edition

In the preparation of this updated impression of *The Concise Oxford Dictionary of Ballet* I was greatly assisted by my English and American collaborators, Nöel Goodwin and Marilyn Hunt. I would like to express my gratitude for their conscientious research and advice, and for the invaluable additional information they have provided.

Stuttgart, 1987   H.K.

Foreword to the First Edition

The Concise Oxford Dictionary of Ballet was originally planned as an Anglo-American adaptation of the German *Friedrichs Ballettlexikon von A-Z*, published in 1972. But while the German version can still be recognized as the point of departure, the final product has turned out to possess an individuality all its own. Not only has matter been cut which was of interest only to German-speaking readers and the focus shifted towards what the Anglo-American reader might be looking for. In addition there has been a general reconsideration of the distribution of emphasis, and a considerable number of new entries have been added.

Like its German predecessor it represents an attempt to cover the whole ballet scene, past and present, its personalities, works, companies, places of performance, and technical terms, with some consideration of modern dance, ethnic dance, and ballroom dance. There are also special entries for cities which have in one way or another played an important role in ballet history, for certain familiar literary subjects (e.g. *Faust* and *Macbeth*), and for dramatists and composers whose works have often been adapted for ballet (e.g. García Lorca, Goldoni, Pushkin, Shakespeare, Bach, Beethoven, and Berio). It is also the first English-language ballet dictionary to provide bibliographical references, supplementing the individual entries.

Such an attempt cannot be undertaken without making full use of the existing standard reference sources, which include the Italian *Enciclopedia dello spettacolo* (9 vols., Rome 1954–62, suppl. 1966), A. Chujoy and P.W. Manchester, *The Dance Encyclopedia* (New York, 1967), G.B.L. Wilson, *A Dictionary of Ballet* (London, 1974), Jacques Baril, *Dictionnaire de danse* (Paris, 1964), and Y.Y. Souritz, *Vse o Balete* (Moscow-Leningrad, 1966), and the German ballet annual from its first volume, *Ballett 1965*, to the most recent. The other main references are listed separately in the Select Bibliography.

The ballet history of individual countries is mostly given in the entry for their capital city — though not always; for instance, Amsterdam stands for the Netherlands (instead of The Hague) and

New York for the United States (instead of Washington, D.C.). However, there are a number of additional entries for individual cities, such as some of the capitals of the Soviet Republics and of the German states.

Titles are entered according to their Anglo-American usage, e.g. *La Fille mal gardée* and *Le Sacre du printemps*, but *The Sleeping Beauty* and *Swan Lake*. In addition all the original titles are given, the Russian ones in transcription. Where there has been any doubt whether the English or foreign versions whould be preferred, cross-references have been given.

Entries are in alphabetical order: German ä, ö, and ü are treated as a, o, and u, and the Danish ø as o. Names preceded by de, van, or von, are listed thus: e.g. Valois, Ninette de; Manen, Hans van.

For Russian names and titles the British standard transliteration has been adopted wherever it seemed practical, unless the bearer prefers a different Western spelling, as in the case of Balanchine and Massine. Russian dates are given, wherever known, according to our Gregorian calendar. St. Petersburg became Petrograd in 1914 and Leningrad in 1924.

My profound gratitude is due to John Percival and his wife Judith Cruickshank, for their countless suggestions on how to improve the manuscript, and for their copious additional information. Once again I must acknowledge my great debt to my friend Alfred Oberzaucher in Vienna, who has proved anew an invaluable and tireless consultant and advisor. My other chief English collaborator has been Noël Goodwin, my closest American collaborators were Jack Anderson and George Dorris, while all the new Soviet information has come from Yelizaveta Yakovlevna Souritz in Moscow. For their generous help and assistance I am deeply grateful.

However, a number of people from all over the world have readily and repeatedly provided new material — those to whom I am especially indebted include Professor Derra de Moroda in Salzburg, Jean-Claude Diénis in Paris, Judith Brin Ingber in Tel Aviv, Jutta Knittl in Vienna, Renée Mandl in Rome, Giora Manor in Tel Aviv, Dr. Henrik Neubauer in Ljubljana, Alica Pastorová in Bratislava, Claire Robilant, formerly of Santiago de Chile, now in London, Dr. Gunhild Schüller in Vienna, Anna Greta Ståhle in Stockholm, and Irena Turska in Warsaw.

I further wish to express my appreciation to Jack Anderson and George Dorris, Prof. Derra de Moroda, Noël Goodwin, Alfred Oberzaucher, and John Percival and Judith Cruickshank who have taken upon themselves the unenviable task of proof-reading and carried it out with patience, diligence, and conscientiousness, and to Anthony Mulgan and Sally Wright of the Oxford University Press for their help and advice in the preparation of this English edition.

I hope that through our common effort the inevitable omissions and errors have been kept to the absolute minimum — those which may still be discovered must be entirely charged to my account. I should be grateful if readers would draw my attention to them, care of Oxford University Press, so that they can be remedied in future editions.

Cologne, March 1976   H.K.

·

Select Bibliography

In addition to the standard reference books listed in the Foreword, and the individual monographs listed in the bibliographical supplements of the individual entries, I have constantly used the following:

G. Balanchine and F. Mason, *Balanchine's Complete Stories of the Great Ballets* (Garden City, N.Y., 1977)

Balet Encyclopedia (Moscow, 1981)

C.W. Beaumont, *Complete Book of Ballets* (London, 1951); *Supplement to Complete Book of Ballets* (London, 1952); *Ballets of Today* (London, 1954); *Ballets Past and Present* (London, 1955)

A. Bland, *The Royal Ballet — The First 50 Years* (London, 1981)

P. Brinson and C. Crisp, *A Guide to the Repertory of Ballet & Dance* (Newton Abbot, 1980)

M. Clarke, *Dancers of the Mercury* (London, 1962)

S. Grigoriev, *The Diaghilev Ballet 1909–1929* (London, 1953)

I. Guest, *The Romantic Ballet in Paris* (London, 1966); *The Ballet of the Second Empire* (London, 1974)

L. Kersley and J. Sinclair, *A Dictionary of Ballet Terms* (London, 1952)

L. Kirstein, *Movement & Metaphor* (New York, 1970)

D. McDonagh, *The Complete Guide to Modern Dance* (Garden City, N.Y., 1976)

The New Grove Dictionary of Music and Musicians (London, 1980)

N. Reynolds, *Repertory in Review – 40 Years of the New York City Ballet* (New York, 1977)

N. Roslavleva, *Era of the Russian Ballet* (London, 1966)

H. M. Winter, *The Pre-Romantic Ballet* (London, 1974)

Annuals, etc.

The Ballet Annual, a Record and Year Book of the Ballet, London 1947–63, 18 vols.

Ballett 1965, Chronik und Bilanz des Ballettjahrs, Velber/Hannover, 17 volumes up to 1981

Dance Index, New York 1942–8 (reprinted in 7 vols., New York, n.d. [1971])

Dance Perspectives, New York, 1958–75, 64 issues

Dance World, New York, 1966–79, 14 vols.

Israel Dance '75, Tel Aviv, 6 vols. up to 1981.

Periodicals

Ballet Review, New York, since 1965
Ballet News, New York, since 1979
Ballett Info, Cologne, since 1978 (since 1982: *Ballett International*)
Dance and Dancers, London, since 1950
Dance Chronicle, New York, since 1977
Dance Magazine, New York, since 1936
Dance News, New York, since 1942
The Dancing Times, London, since 1898
Les Saisons de la danse, Paris, since 1968
Das Tanzarchiv, Hamburg and Cologne, 1953–80
Tanzblätter, Vienna, since 1976

Abbreviations

Amer.	American	Fr.	French
Argent.	Argentinian	Ger.	German
arr.	arranged	ho.	house
art. dir.	artistic director	Hung.	Hungarian
assoc.	associate, associated	incl.	including
asst.	assistant	Ind.	Indian
Austral.	Australian	Inst.	Institute
b.	ballet	intern.	international
b	born	Isr.	Israeli
Belg.	Belgian	Ital.	Italian
bibl.	bibliography	libr.	libretto
Braz.	Brazilian	Lith.	Lithuanian
Brit.	British	Met.	Metropolitan
Can.	Canadian	Mex.	Mexican
ch.	choreography,	Munic.	Municipal
	choreographer,	mus.	music, musical
	choreographed,	Norweg.	Norwegian
	choreographic	N.Y.	New York
Chil.	Chilean	N.Z.	New Zealand
co., cos.	company, companies	op.	opera
comp.	composer, composed	orig.	originally
cond.	conductor	perf.	performance
cost.	costume(s)	Pol.	Polish
Cov. Gdn.	Covent Garden	prod.	produced, production
Cub.	Cuban	Rum.	Rumanian
d.	dance, dancer, danced	Russ.	Russian
d	died	S.A.	South Africa (n)
Dan.	Danish	Sov.	Soviet
déc.	décor	Span.	Spanish
dir.	director	Swed.	Swedish
Egypt.	Egyptian	th.	theatre
Eng.	English	univ.	university
Eur.	Europe, European	Yugosl.	Yugoslav
Finn.	Finnish		

A

Abarca, Lydia (*b* New York, 8 Jan. 1951). Amer. dancer. Studied at Harkness House. Joined D. Th. of Harlem 1968, later becoming principal d.

Abe, Chie (*b* Tokyo, 15 June 1940). Jap. dancer. Studied at Paris Conservatoire 1950–6, d. with B. Paul Goubé 1957—8, joined Tokyo B. 1964, of which now a principal d. and teacher. Prize of Artistry (Japan, 1965).

Abramova, Anastasia Ivanovna (*b* Moscow, 30 June 1902). Russ. dancer. Studied with Tikhomirov (later also with Geltzer and Vazem) at Moscow School 1910–17; member of Bolshoi B. 1918–48. With Lubov Bank, Valentina Kudriavtseva, and Nina Podgoretskaya belonged to the famous quartet of Bolshoi ballerinas during the 1920s.

Abramowitsch, Ruth (also Ruth Sorel; (*b* Halle, Saale, 1907, *d* Warsaw, 1 Apr. 1974). Ger.-Pol. dancer and teacher. Studied with Wigman, d. with Wigman group. Became known as character-soloist during 1927–33 engagement at the Berlin Mun. Op.; Wife of Potiphar in Maudrik's *Legend of Joseph* her biggest success. With Groke as her regular partner appeared in numerous recitals. In 1933 was forced by the Nazis to emigrate to Poland, from where she undertook several tours (still with Groke) to Palestine, South Amer., N.Y., and Can. (where she opened a school in Montreal). Returned to teach in Warsaw. 1st prize International Dancers Competition (Warsaw, 1933).

Abraxas. *Faust ballet in 5 scenes; libr. and mus. Egk; ch. Luipart; déc. Wolfgang Znamenacek. Prod. 6 June 1948, Bavarian State Op., Prinzregenten Th., Munich, with Luipart, Irina Kladivova, Schwarz, Nika Nilanowa-Sanftleben. Based on Heine's d. poem *Der Doctor Faust* (1847). The ageing Faust signs a pact with Bellastriga, a beautiful she-devil, who grants him youth and accompanies him to the arch-courtesan Archisposa, to a black mass in Hell, and then to Helen of Troy. At last he discovers pure love with Marguerite. Tearing up the pact, he becomes his old self again, and he and she are killed by the enraged crowd. Withdrawn after only 5 perfs. because of moral objections, received its 2nd prod. at the Berlin Munic. Op. (ch. Charrat, 1949), after which it became one of the most successful bs. in post-war Ger. in numerous different versions. The only prod. of the short-lived Deutsche B. Th. Kompanie (ch. Helge Pawlinin, Hamburg, 1951). The word *A.* is a cabbalistic symbol.
BIBL.: Various authors, '*A.*', *Die Tanzarchiv-Reihe* 2 (Hamburg, 1964).

Abstract Ballet. A b. without plot, concerned only with the pursuit of ch. aims (as opposed to the story-orientated *Ballet d'action*). A subject, a certain mood or general idea are possible, though not necessary. Robbins's *Moves* dispenses with mus. altogether, Ashton's *Symphonic Variations* is based on Franck's score, Massine's *Choreartium* tries to embody the mus. structures of Brahms's Fourth Symphony, Fokine's *Les Sylphides* strives to evoke the romantic mood of Chopin's piano pieces, and Balanchine's *Four Temperaments*, set to Hindemith's piano concerto, is meant as a realization of man's four basic temperaments in form of character variations. Balanchine and other choreographers reject the term because a b., being performed by human dancers, can never be abstract.

Abstrakter Tanz. Term coined by Schlemmer to designate the d. forms which he started to develop at Stuttgart during the early 1920s and continued at the Bauhaus in Weimar and Dessau. It reduces the function of the d. to the status of an animator of geometric forms, colours, and patterns in a logically structured space. Distinctly anti-illusionist, 'the A.T. is meant as a creation, born from itself and self-sufficient' (Schlemmer, *Abstraktion in Tanz und Kostüm*, 1928). See also *Bauhaus Dances*.

Abyss, The, Ballet in 1 act; ch. Hodes; mus. Marga Richter; cost. André Delfau. Prod. 21 Feb. 1965, Harkness B., Cannes, with Bruhn and Isaksen. 'Alone together in the sunlight of late afternoon, a very young couple become lost and encounter strangers. Then fear, violence, madness . . . the abyss' (programme note). The b., which is based on a story by Leonid N. Andreyev, was later produced by several other cos. An earlier version by Dokoudovsky, mus. Tcherepnine, Jacob's Pillow, 1956.
BIBL.: 'Abyss', in *Balanchine's Complete Stories of the Great Ballets* (Garden City, N.Y., 1977).

Academic Dance. Term coined for the th. d. which developed from the Fr. *Ballet de cour* of the 16th and 17th century and was constantly improved and refined through national schools (especially in Milan and St. Petersburg). Its positions, steps, and movements are strictly codified in the *Danse d'école*, the basis of the classes every b.-d. has to attend regularly to perfect his technique.
BIBL.: 'Danza Accademica' in *Enciclopedia dello spettacolo*.

Académie de musique et de poésie, L'. Founded 1570 by Charles IX and headed by the poet Antoine de Baïf and the comp. de Courville, its theories contributed indirectly to the creation of the *Ballet Comique de la Reine*.

Académie royale de danse, L'. Founded 1661 by Louis XIV in Paris on the advice of Cardinal Mazarin, its aim was the fixing of objective standards for the perfection of the art of d. The A. consisted originally or 1 dir. and 13 d.-masters who regularly met at the 'L'Epée de bois' tavern. Here the court- and character-dances were codified. All public and private employment as a d.-teacher was dependent on a diploma, which the A. bestowed on its students after rigorous examinations. The successful candidate was then appointed Académicien de l'art de la danse. Noverre fiercely attacked the institution in his *Lettres sur la danse*, thus contributing to its closure in 1780. 1856–66' saw an attempted revival as the Société académique de professeurs-artistes du théâtre de l'Opéra (with the teaching of ballroom-dances as its main object).
BIBL.: B. Kochno, *Le Ballet* (Paris, 1954).

Académie royale de musique, L'. Official name of the Paris Opéra since 1671. Founded in 1669 by the Abbé Perrin and the Marquis de Sourdéac as the Académie d'Opéra, it changed its name with the 1st prod. of Robert Cambert's *Pomone*, a mixture of b., pastoral, and opera (ch. Beauchamp). In 1672 Lully became its dir., remaining until his death in 1687. Early in his régime an assoc. d. school was opened, with 12 danseurs, 12 danseuses, a b.-composer, a master of the d.-salon, a designer, and a master-tailor. The institution later changed its name several times. Since 1871 it has been called Théâtre National de l'Opéra.
BIBL.: E. Campardon, *L'A.r.d.m. au XVIIe siècle* (Paris, 1884).

Academies of Dance. Modelled upon the Fr. As. of the 16th and 17th century, these were founded in other countries for the conservation, perfection, and renovation of the art of d. (also of ballroom-d.) One of the most famous was the Imperiale Regia Accademia di Ballo, established in 1812 by Benedetto Ricci in Milan (where it was attached to the Teatro alla Scala). In 1920 the *Royal Academy of Dancing opened in London. Of more recent reputation is the Internationale Sommerakademie des Tanzes, founded 1957 in Krefeld, and based since 1961 in Cologne.

Achcar, Dalal (*b* Rio de Janeiro, *c.* 1935). Braz. dancer, choreographer, and b. director. Studied with Preobrajenska, Egorova, Schwezoff, and Maria Makarova. Artistic dir. and ch. of her own B. Rio de Janeiro, 1960 (assoc. with Rio B. Academy). Temporarily artistic dir. at Rio Teatro Municipal. Has organized various Braz. d. festivals.

Acis and Galatea. Derived from Ovid's *Metamorphoses* and dealing with the love of a shepherd A. and the nymph G., the story has often served as a source for b. librettos—by, among others, Hil-verding (Vienna, 1753), Lauchery (mus. Cannabich, Kassel, 1768), Noverre (mus. Aspelmayr, Vienna, 1772), Onorato Viganò (Venice, 1782), and Fokine (mus. G. Kadletz, St. Petersburg, 1905).

Acrobats of God. Ballet in 1 act; ch. and cost. Graham; mus. Surinach; set Noguchi. Prod. 27 Apr. 1960, Martha Graham D. Co., 54th St. Th., New York, with Graham, Ross, McGehee, Taylor. 'To their contemporary biographers, the early Church Fathers who subjected themselves to the discipline of the desert were *athletae Dei*, the athletes of God.—This is M. Graham's fanfare for d. as an art ... a celebration in honour of the trials and tribulations, the discipline, denials, glories and delights of a dancer's world . . . and of the world of the artist' (programme note).

Adagio (Ital., at ease, i.e. slow, though not so slow as Largo). (1) Any slow d. movement (contrasted with Allegro). (2) The central part of the traditional b.-class, which aims to build up the dancers' feeling for placement, line, and balance. (3) The introductory movement of the traditional four-part pas de deux. (4) The acrobatic display of revue-dancers. Also used in its Fr. version *Adage*.

Adagio Hammerklavier. Ballet in 1 act, ch. Van Manen, mus. Beethoven, déc. Vroom. Prod. 4 Oct. 1973, Dutch National B., Stadsschouwburg, Amsterdam, with Radius, Ebbelaar, Sand, Jurriëns, Marchiolli, Sinceretti. Based on the Adagio from the 'Hammerklavier' sonata, op. 106 (in the gramophone interpretation of Christoph Eschenbach), the b. consists of movement-constructions for 3 couples without any suggestion of story or plot. It can be called a ch. set of variations on the Adagio, 25 minutes of uninterrupted slow-moving d. Revived for Berlin Ger. Op. B. (1975), Royal B. (1976).
BIBL.: 'A.H.' in *Balanchine's Complete Stories of the Great Ballets* (Garden City, N.Y., 1977).

Adam, Adolphe Charles (*b* Paris, 24 July 1803, *d* there, 3 May 1856). Fr. composer. Comp. the mus. to the following bs.: *Faust* (ch. Deshayes, London, 1833), *La Fille du Danube* (ch. F. Taglioni, Paris, 1836), *Les Mohicans* (ch. Guerra, Paris, 1837), *L'Ecumeur de mer* (St. Petersburg, 1840), *Die Hamadryaden* (ch. P. Taglioni, Berlin, 1840), *Giselle ou les Wilis* (ch. Coralli and Perrot, Paris, 1841), *La Jolie Fille de Gand* (ch. Albert, Paris, 1842), *Le Diable à quatre* (ch. Mazilier, Paris, 1845), *The Marble Maiden* (ch. Albert, London, 1845), *Griseldis ou les cinq sens* (ch. Mazilier, Paris, 1848), *La Filleule des fées* (together with H.F. de Saint-Julien, ch. Perrot, Paris, 1849), *Orfa* (ch. Mazilier, Paris, 1852), and *Le Corsaire* (ch. Mazilier, Paris, 1856).
BIBL.: C. W. Beaumont, 'A.A. and the music of *Giselle*, in *The Ballet Called Giselle* (London, 1944); R. Fiske, 'A. and the Romantic Ballet', in *Ballet Music* (London, 1958).

'adame miroir. Ballet in 1 act; libr. Jean Genet; mus. Milhaud; ch. Charrat; sets Paul Delvaux; cost. Jacques Fath. Prod. 2 June 1948, B. de Paris, Th. Marigny, Paris, with Petit, Skouratoff, and Perrault. The b. is set in a labyrinth of mirrors, where a sailor faces death. During the whole b. he is followed by his mirror-image, acting as his double. Later prods. among others by Betty Merck (Gelsenkirchen, 1953) and Furtwängler (Münster, 1964, and Cologne, 1967).

Adams, Carolyn (b New York, 6 Aug. 1943). Amer. dancer. Studied with Mme de Bayser, Nelle Fisher, Graham, Bessie Schönberg, and in Paris with Waehner; joined Waehner's Bs. Contemporains and in 1965 joined the Paul Taylor Co., and became one of its most distinguished soloists; retired 1982. Created parts in Taylor's *Post Meridian, Orbs* (both 1966), *Public Domain* (1968), *Big Bertha, Book of Beasts* (both 1971), 'Noah's Minstrels' section of the evening-length *American Genesis* (1973), *Sports and Follies* (1974), and *Esplanade* (1975).
BIBL.: S. Goodman, 'C.A,', *Dance Magazine* (1970/11).

Adams, David (b Winnipeg, 16 Nov. 1928). Can. dancer. Studied at Winnipeg B. School, Sadler's Wells School, with Volkova and Gontcharov; made his début 1946 with the Royal Winnipeg B., 1946–8 with the Sadler's Wells B., then with International B., and Metropolitan B., became 1st soloist of the National B. of Can. in 1951, soloist with London Festival B. 1961–9, Royal B. 1970–6. Created roles in Taras's *Designs with Strings* (1948), MacMillan's *Anastasia* (London version, 1971), and *The Seven Deadly Sins* (1973 version). Director of *B. for All 1976–7. Brother of the d. Lawrence A. and was married to the d. *Lois Smith.

Adams, Diana (b Stanton, Va., 29 Mar. 1926). Amer. dancer and teacher. Studied with Emily Hadley, Caton, de Mille, and Tudor, made her début 1943, in *Oklahoma!*, joined B.Th. 1943, was promoted soloist 1945 and d. as a leading soloist with the New York City B. 1950–63. Created roles in Robbins's *Facsimile* (1946), de Mille's *Fall River Legend* (1948), Balanchine's *La Valse* (1951), *Caracole* (1952), *Opus 34* (1954), *Agon,* (1957) *Monumentum pro Gesualdo, Liebeslieder Walzer* (both 1960), *Electronics* (1961), Ashton's *Picnic at Tintagel* (1952), et al. Film roles included D. Kaye's *Knock on Wood* (1954) and Kelly's *Invitation to the Dance* (1956). Taught at the School of American B. in New York; now heads school of Kansas City B. Was married to the late Ronald Bates.

Adam Zero. Ballet-allegory in 1 act; libr. Michael Benthall; mus. Bliss; ch. Helpmann; déc. Roger Furse. Prod. 10 Apr. 1946, Sadler's Wells B., Cov. Gdn., London, with Helpmann. The b. shows the creation of a b., which process is supposed to symbolize man's path of life. Other prod.

Wiesbaden, 1953 (ch. Hans Heinz Steinbach, with Luipart).

Addison, Errol (b Heaton, 1903, d Hastings, 10 Aug. 1983). Brit. d. and teacher. Studied with Cecchetti, whom he succeeded as dir. of his London school 1923. D. with Cov. Gdn. Op., Diaghilev's Bs. Russes, continued in musicals, variety, and pantomimes, principal d. of International B. 1947–53, teacher of the Royal B. and Royal B. School 1954–63, then at the Rambert B. School. Retired 1974.

Adelaïde, ou Le Langage des fleurs. Ballet in 1 act; libr. and mus. Ravel (the orchestral version of his *Valses nobles et sentimentales*); ch. Clustine; déc. M. Drésa. Prod. 22 Apr. 1912, Th. du Châtelet, Paris, with Trouhanova. The b. is set in the 1820 drawing-room of a courtesan who expresses her shifting moods through various flowers. A different version, libr. and ch. Lifar, prod. 21 Dec. 1938, Opéra, Paris, with Chauviré, Darsonval, and Lifar.

Adret, Françoise (b Versailles, 7 Aug. 1920). Fr. dancer, choreographer, and b.-mistress. Studied with Rousanne, Kiss, and V. Gsovsky; b.-mistress with various cos., incl. R. Petit's B. de Paris, at the Amsterdam Op. 1954–8, after 1960 several times in Nice, and guest-ch. in Warsaw, Zagreb, and Sofia. Chief ch. of the B.-Th. Contemporain 1968–80, for which she ch. *Aquathème* (mus. Ivo Malec, 1968), *Eonta* (mus. Xenakis, 1969), *Requiem* (mus. Ligeti, 1971), *La follia di Orlando* (mus. Petrassi, 1972). and *7 pour 5* (1973). Since 1980 Art. Dir., Lyon B.
BIBL.: M. Lobet, 'F.A.', in *Le Ballet Français d'aujourd'hui* (Brussels, 1958).

African Dance Company of Ghana. The co. is based on the Dance Department of the Univ. of Ghana, where it was founded in 1963, with J. H. Nketia as its dir. and A. M. Opoku as its artistic dir. Its aim is to preserve and develop in an authentic manner the dances of black Africa. On its numerous tours abroad it has been praised for having the 'taste and good sense to present folk materials without apologies or sugar-coating. The dances are edited for the theatre, of course, but they look unmistakably like the real thing' (*Dance Magazine*).
BIBL.: R. A. Thom, 'Spontaneous and Authentic', *Dance Magazine* (1969/5).

After Eden. Ballet in 1 act; ch. Butler; mus. Lee Hoiby; déc. Ter-Arutunian. Prod. 15 Mar. 1966, Harkness B., Monte Carlo with Isaksen and Rhodes. A b. for 2 people about the 'paradise lost' situation, exploring the emotional landscape of exposure and desperation. Revived for Netherlands D. Th. in 1971 *et al.* Cologne TV prod. with original cast (1969).
BIBL.: 'A.E.' in *Balanchine's Complete Stories of the Great Ballets* (Garden City, N.Y., 1977).

Afternoon of a Faun. Ballet in 1 act; ch. Robbins;

mus. Debussy; set Rosenthal; cost. Sharaff. Prod. 14 May 1953, New York City B., City Center, New York, with LeClercq and Moncion. Based on Debussy's famous *Prélude à l'après-midi d'un faune*, the b. shows the encounter between two dancers practising in a b.-studio, with the proscenium as an imaginary mirror. In the repertoire of various cos.; it was also mounted by the Royal B. in 1971. CBC TV prod. in 1957. For other ch. versions of the same mus. see *Après-midi d'un faune, L'*.
BIBL.: 'A.o.a.F.' in *Balanchine's Complete Stories of the Great Ballets* (Garden City, N.Y., 1977).

Agamemnon Ballets. Ballets based on the mythological King of Mycenae, the husband of Clytemnestra and father of Iphigenia, Orestes, and Electra, who was slaughtered by his wife when he returned from Troy, were ch. by—among others—Noverre (*Der gerächte A.*, mus. Aspelmayr, Vienna, 1772), Clerico (*Il ritorno d'A.*, Florence, 1821), Laban (*A.s Tod*, 1924), and Graham (*Clytemnestra*, mus. El-Dabh, 1958). See also *Clytemnestra Ballets*.

Age of Anxiety, The. Dramatic b. in 6 scenes; libr. and ch. Robbins; mus. Bernstein; sets O. Smith; cost. Sharaff; light. Rosenthal. Prod. 26 Feb. 1950, New York City B., City Center, N.Y., with LeClercq, Moncion, Bolender, Robbins. The b. is based on Bernstein's 2nd Symphony (1949), which in turn was inspired by W. H. Auden's *T.A.o.A.: A Baroque Eclogue* (1946). 'It is a ritual in which four people exorcize their illusions in their search for security. It is an attempt to see what life is about' (Robbins, in *Balanchine's Complete Stories of the Great Ballets* (Garden City, N.Y., 1977). Other prod. by Neumeier (Hamburg, 1979).

Age of Gold, The. See *Golden Age, The*.

Agitanado. Span., meaning (1) the gipsy feeling of a Span. dance or dancer, and (2) the heel-technique in the non-Flamenco Span. dances.

Aglaë, ou l'Elève de l'amour. Ballet divertissement in 1 act; libr. and ch. F. Taglioni; mus. Johann Friedrich Keller. Prod. 22 Jan. 1841, St. Petersburg, with M. Taglioni. The solo roles are shared between the nymph A., who is a pupil of Cupid, Cupid himself, a faun, and a young man. BIBL.: C. W. Beaumont, 'A.'. in *Complete Book of Ballets* (London, 1951).

Agon. Ballet for 12 dancers; mus. Stravinsky; ch. Balanchine; light. Nananne Porcher. Prod. 27 Nov. 1957 (benefit perf.) and 1 Dec. 1957, New York City B., City Center, N.Y., with Adams, Hayden, Mitchell, Bolender. The plotless b. has 3 different sections: Pas de quatre, Double pas de quatre, and Triple pas de quatre; Prelude, First pas de trois (Saraband Step), Gaillarde, Coda, Interlude, Second pas de trois (Bransle Simple), Bransle Gay, and Bransle de Poitou; Interlude, Pas de deux, Coda, Four Duos, and Four Trios. The

Greek title means contest, here a contest of dancers. Stravinsky's score was partly inspired by de Lauze's *Apologie de la danse* and Mersenne's *Musical Examples* (R. Craft, *Stravinsky: The Chronicle of a Friendship*, (New York, 1972)). The b. has been mounted by several other cos. incl. the Stuttgart B. (1970), the Royal B. (1973), and Paris Opéra (1974). TV prod. by R.M. Prods. (Ger., 1973). Prods. with different ch., among others, in Düsseldorf (Otto Krüger, 1958—1st Eur. perf.), London (MacMillan, 1958), Vienna (Georgi, 1958), Berlin (T. Gsovsky, 1958), and Copenhagen (E. Holm, 1967).
BIBL.: 'A.', in *Balanchine's Complete Stories of the Great Ballets* (Garden City, N.Y., 1977); L. Kirstein, 'A.', in *Movement & Metaphor* (New York, 1970).

Agrionia. Ballet in 1 act; libr. and ch. J. Carter; mus. Salzedo; déc. Farmer. Prod. 22 June 1964, London D. Th., Th. Royal, Newcastle, with J. Graeme, Y. Meyer, Kay Elise, N. McDowell, Terence Etheridge. The b. is set during the Great War and shows the feast of A., which is a provocation to savagery, with a young man (a modern Dionysus) inflaming 3 sisters and inciting them to madness, in which they undertake the ritual murder of the eldest sister's son.

Ahonen, Leo (*b* Vyborg, 19 June 1939). Finn. dancer, teacher, and ballet-master. Studied at the b.-school of the Helsinki National Op., and at the Leningrad B. School, also with Vilzak and L. Christensen. Début 1954 with Finnish National B.; d. as a guest with the Kirov and Bolshoi B., later also with the Scandinavian B. Co., Dutch National B., Royal Winnipeg B., San Francisco B., and Houston B. (until 1978). Now in charge of his own Houston-based Texas B. Co. Guest-teacher with various Eur. and Amer. cos. Has developed his own system of d. notation and written a book for b.-teachers. Married to the d. Soili Arvola.

Aiello, Salvatore (*b* New York, 26 Feb. 1944). Amer. dancer. Studied with Danielian, S. Williams, and Hightower. Début with Joffrey B. 1964. D. with the cos. of McKayle, Lang, Ailey, Harkness B., and Royal Winnipeg B. before joining Hamburg State Op. B. as a principal d. 1973. Rejoined Royal Winnipeg B. 1975. Ass. Dir. and b. master of North Carolina D. Th., 1979. Married to the d. *Marina Eglevsky.

Ailes de pigeon (Fr., pigeon-wings). Also called *pistolets*. A b.-step, in which the left leg is thrown up, while the d. leaps off the right, which then is thrown up to beat beneath the left calf—then comes a change of the legs and another beat, followed by one more change and a landing on the right foot, with the left leg extended in the air. Is performed *en avant* and *en arrière*. The step, very difficult to execute, is a feature of the *Blue Bird* variation.

Ailey, Alvin (*b* Rogers, Tex., 5 Jan. 1931). Amer.

The Alvin Ailey American Dance Theater in Ailey's *Revelations*.   Photo Alvin Ailey.

dancer, choreographer, and ballet-director. Studied with Horton in Cal., and with Graham, Holm, and Weidman in New York, classic d. with Shook, and acting with Stella Adler. Début as a d. 1950 with the Horton D. Th., of which he became dir. when Horton died in 1953. Appeared in various musicals (*House of Flowers*, 1954), films (*Carmen Jones*, 1954), and plays (*Tiger, Tiger, Burning Bright*, 1962). Formed his own A.A. Amer. Dance Th. 1958, with which he toured extensively in the U.S.A., and from 1964 also frequently overseas. Since 1972 his co. has been called A.A. City Center D. Th. and is part of the New York City Center for Mus. and Drama organization. In 1979 the school and co. moved to new premises at Minskoff Building. Very prolific ch., whose best works offer a highly individual blend of elements from primitive d., modern d., jazz d., and academic d. His two most famous bs. to traditional mus. are *Blues Suite* (1958) and *Revelations* (1960). Other works for his own co. are: *Knoxville: Summer of 1915* (mus. Barber, 1960), *Hermit Songs* (mus. Barber, 1962), *Reflections in D* (mus. Ellington, 1964), *Masekela Language* (mus. Hugh Masekela, 1969), *Gymnopédies* (mus. Satie, 1970), *Flowers* (mus. Pink Floyd and Janis Joplin, 1971),

Choral Dances (mus. Britten, 1971), *Cry* (mus. Alice Coltrane, 1971), *Archipelago* (mus. André Boucourechliev, 1971), *Mary Lou's Mass* (mus. Williams, 1971), *The Lark Ascending* (mus. Vaughan Williams, 1972), and *Hidden Rites* (mus. Petrice Sciortino, 1973). Since 1975 has been ch. a cycle of bs. to mus. by Ellington. For other cos. and occasions he ch.: *Feast of Ashes* (mus. Surinach, R. Joffrey B., 1962), *Labyrinth* (later called *Ariadne*, mus. Jolivet, R. Joffrey B., 1963), *The River* (mus. Ellington, Amer. B. Th., 1970), *Mass* (mus. Bernstein, Washington, 1971), *Sea Change* (mus. Britten, Amer. B. Th., 1972). TV-portrait in *Memories and Visions* (WNET, 1974). D. Magazine Award (1975). Capezio D. Award (1979).

BIBL.: R. Philip, 'The A. A. American Dance Theatre', portfolio, *Dance Magazine* (1978/10); J. H. Mazo, *The A. A. American Dance Theatre*, (New York, 1978).

Ailian, Dai (b Trinidad, 10 May 1916). Chin. dancer, choreographer, and artistic director. Studied with Craske and Dolin in London, Jooss, and Laban in Dartington. Went to China 1940, appearing in d. recitals and with various groups.

Dir. of Central Song and D. Ensemble 1949–54. Prin. of Peking D. School 1954–64. Dir. of Central B. (Peking) 1963–4. Vice-Dir. of Central Op. and B. Th. 1964–6. Art. Dir. of Central B. 1976–80 and now its Art. Adviser. Vice-Pres. of All-China D. Association. Member of Intern. Council Kinetography/Labanotation. Committee member of Conseil Intern. de la Danse (UNESCO). Has ch. various bs.

Aimez-vous Bach? Ballet in 1 act; ch. Macdonald; mus. Bach. Prod. 6 Aug. 1962, Banff School of Fine Arts, Alberta, Can. Performed to a selection of Bach compositions, the b. develops from a lesson, in which a b.-master corrects a female dancer, via various small ensembles (à la Balanchine's *Concerto Barocco*) to large corps-ensembles, finishing with a section in which the dancers try time and again to break from their classic-academic movements into jazz-d. intermezzi of Jive and Twist. Revived for several other cos.

Air (Fr. and Eng.; Ital. *Aria*). Designates various musical forms from the 16th to the 18th century, mostly based on 16th-century d. songs. In the *b. de cour* the *a.* serves as an episodic couplet. 'In the French b.-opera and -suite of the 17th and 18th century, however, orchestra-airs are often used freely, unconnected with certain types of d. In the b.-opera they often appear with characteristic adjectives (tendre, majestueux, gracieux) or an indication of the performer.' (Riemann).

Air, en l' (Fr., in the air). In b., a succession of movements, executed in the air—for instance *tour en l'air*. Also used for the working of one leg in the air in comparison with the supporting leg. The opposite is *par terre*.

Air for the G String. Ballet in 1 act; ch. Humphrey; mus. Bach. Prod. 24 Mar. 1928, Humphrey-Weidman Group, Little Th., Brooklyn, N.Y. Set for a group of 5 to Bach's 3rd orchestral suite, with a slight Renaissance flavour, the b. develops in processional patterns, 'in which the women are continuously sculpting the space in precise lines and curves' (M. B. Siegel). Filmed 1934. Revived by Ernestine Stodelle for a summer workshop at New York Univ., 1976.
BIBL.: M. B. Siegel, in 'Four Works by Doris Humphrey', *Ballet Review* (vol. 7, no. 1).

Åkesson, Birgit (*b* Malmö, 1908). Swed. dancer and choreographer. Studied with Wigman and joined her group 1931. Solo-début 1934 in Paris. Toured in many Eur. countries and also in the U.S., where she returned for the 1957 Jacob's Pillow Festival. One of the most individual of Europe's modern d. personalities. Her bs. for the Royal Swed. B. incl. *Sisyphus* (mus. Blomdahl, 1957), *The Minotaur* (mus. Blomdahl, 1958), *Rites* (mus. Lidholm 1960), *Play for Eight* (mus. Blomdahl, 1962), *Icaros* (mus. Sven Erik Back, 1963), and *Nausikaa* (mus. Lidholm, 1966). Co-

founded the Stockholm Ch. Institute with B. Haeger in 1964, heading its ch. department until 1968. Has concentrated since on research into Afr. d.

Akhundova, Rafiga (*b* Baku, 7 Aug. 1931). Sov. dancer and choreographer. Graduated from Baku B. School 1952 (pupil of G. Almas-sade) and d. at the Baku op. th., her best roles being Giselle, Zarema (*Fountain of Bakhchisaray*), Shirin (*Legend of Love*), Egina (*Spartacus*), and Gulianak (*The Maiden Tower*). Has ch. (together with her husband M. Mamedov) *The Ballet of the Caspian Sea* (mus. Bakikhanov, 1968), *The Shadows of Kobistan* (mus. F. Karaev, 1969), *Caleidoscope* (mus. Scarlatti and F. Karaev, 1971), *The Path of Thunder* (mus. K. Karaev 1974), and *The Seven Beauties* (mus. K. Karaev, 1977).

Akimov, Boris Borisovich (*b* Vienna, 25 June 1946). Sov. dancer. Studied at Moscow B. School, graduated 1965; since then a member of the Moscow Bolshoi B., where he created Rothbart in Grigorovich's *Swan Lake* (1969) and Prince Kurbsky in *Ivan the Terrible* (1975). Graduated also from the faculty of choreographers at GITIS 1978. Bronze Medal (Varna, 1966).

Ala and Lolly. See *Scythian Suite.*

A la recherche de . . . . Production in 3 parts by Béjart. 1st perf. 26 July 1968, B. of the 20th Century, Avignon. The quest starts with *Cantates*, based on Webern's cantatas op. 29 and 31, a b.-class essay in dry neo-classicism (originally premièred in 1965). It continues with *La Nuit obscure*, in which Maria Césarès recites texts of the Span. mystic Juan de la Cruz in a sort of *cante jondo* style, accompanied by strong **çapateado* rhythms and shouts of a frightening horde of males, one of them being Béjart himself, who finally takes over her role. The 3rd part, *Bhakti*, shows three young men setting off on a quest, during which they meet Rama, Krishna, and Shiva, the objects of their adoration, with whom they identify in an act of love. Solo-parts in the 1st section were danced by Sifnios, Pinet, and Lanner, and in the 3rd section by Bortoluzzi, Asakawa, Donn, Bari, Lommel, and Gielgud. 2nd Ger. Channel TV prod. of *Bhakti* 1971.

Albert, François Decombe (*b* Bordeaux, 15 Apr. 1789, *d* Fontainebleau, 18 July 1865). Fr. dancer and choreographer. Started to study aged 10, broke off and started again after seeing Vestris. Began his career as premier danseur at the Th. de la Gaîté in Paris, where he continued to take classes with Coulon, then d. in Bordeaux and from 1803 at the Paris Opéra, being its premier danseur 1817–35 and one of its choreographers 1829–42. Also worked in London (several times between 1821 and 1845), Naples (1825), Vienna (1830), and Brussels (1838–40). Created roles in Gardel's *Paul et Virginie* (1806), Milon's *Nina* (1813), F. Taglioni's *Aglaë* (London version, 1841), and *The Marble Maiden* (1845). Ch. many bs., incl. *Le Séducteur au village* (mus. Schneitzhoeffer, Paris, 1813), *Cendrillon* (mus. A. Sor, Paris, 1823), *Daphnis and Céphise* (mus. L. de Saint-Lubin, Vienna, 1830), *Le Corsaire* (mus. Nicholas Bochsa, London, 1837), *La jolie fille de Gand* (mus. Adam, Paris, 1842), and the b.-divertissements for Donizetti's opera *La Favorite* (Paris, 1841). Author of *L' art de la danse à la ville et à la cour, manuel à l'usage des maîtres à danser, des mères de famille et maîtresses de pension* (Paris, 1834).

Albertieri, Luigi (*b c*. 1860, *d* New York, 25 Aug. 1930). Ital. dancer and b.-master. Started as a child-d.; when 10 years old became the favourite pupil of Cecchetti, who adopted him; they appeared together in the London 1st perf. of Manzotti's *Excelsior*. Toured with Cecchetti in Russia, 1886, and was then premier danseur of the Empire B. in London (until 1902). Appeared in Amer. 1895; became b.-master of Chicago Lyric Op. 1910–13, b.-master of the New York Met. Op. House 1913–27. In 1915 he opened a school in New York, where Rasch and Astaire were among his most prominent pupils. Author of *The Art of Terpsichore* (New York, 1923).

Albrecht, Angèle (*b* Freiburg, 12 Dec. 1942). Ger. dancer. Studied with Lula von Sachnowsky in Munich and at Royal B. School. D. in Mannheim 1960–61, at the Hamburg State Op. 1961–67, where Balanchine gave her prominent parts in his prods., and B. du XXᵉ Siècle 1967–79, becoming one of the leading dancers. Created parts in Béjart's *Messe pour le temps présent* (1967), *Ni Fleurs, ni couronnes* (1968), *Baudelaire* (1968), *Bhakti* (1968), *Actus tragicus* (1969), *L'Oiseau de feu* (Brussels version, 1970), *Nijinsky, Clown de Dieu* (1971), *Golestan* (1973), *Pli selon pli* (1975), and *Dichterliebe* (1978). Resigned 1979, starting new career as teacher. Has had several exhibitions of her ch. drawings.
BIBL.: N. McLain Stoop, 'A.A.', *Dance Magazine* (1972/11); I. Lidova, 'A.A..', *Les Saisons de la danse* (1976/3).

Alcestis. Ballet in 1 act; ch. and cost. Graham; mus. Vivian Fine; sets Noguchi. Prod. 29 Apr. 1960, M. Graham and Dance Co., 54th Str. Th., New York, with Graham, McDonald, Ross, and Taylor. Graham interprets the journey of A. into the underworld to save her husband as a parallel to the Persephone legend. Former b.-treatments of the same myth in Noverre's *Admète et A.* (Stuttgart, 1761), Gioia's *A.* (Vienna, 1800), Didelot's *A.* (mus. F. Antonolini, St. Petersburg, 1821), and Cortesi's *A.* (Milan, 1827).

Alder, Alan (*b* Canberra, 14 Sep. 1939). Austral. dancer. Studied with B. Todd and at Royal B. School. Joined Cov. Gdn. Op. B. 1957, Touring Royal B. 1958, Austral. B. as a senior soloist 1963, becoming principal d. 1969. Created leading role in Butler's *Threshold* (1968). Married to the d. *Lucette Aldous.

Aldous, Lucette (*b* Auckland, 26 Sep. 1938). N.Z. dancer and teacher. Studied in Sydney and at the Royal B. School 1955–57, was soloist 1957 and ballerina of B. Rambert 1958–63, with London Festival B. 1963–66, with Royal B. 1966–70, and with the Austral. B. 1971–7. Among her best roles were Swanilda, Kitri (also in Nureyev's *Don Quixote* film, 1973), and La Sylphide. Now teacher with Austral B. Married to the d. *Alan Alder.
BIBL.: E. Herf, 'L.A.', *Ballet Today* (1967/12).

Aldridge, Robert (*b c*. 1738, *d* Edinburgh, 1793). Irish dancer and teacher. He ran a very popular d. school in Dublin during the middle of the 18th century, ch. some Irish bs. in London, and finally opened a famous dancing school in Edinburgh. He was the father of the d. Simon Slingsby.

Alegrias. Span. Flamenco-dance in 3/4 or 6/8 time, 'the Queen of Flamenco dances', It is d. with or without castanets and distinguished by its refined elegance and rich display of the arms.

Aleko. Ballet in 1 act, 4 scenes; libr. and ch. Massine; mus. Tchaikovsky; déc. Chagall. Prod. 8 Sep. 1942, B. Th., Mexico City, with Skibine, Markova, Laing, Tudor. Based on Pushkin's poem *The Gipsies* and set to an orchestrated version of Tchaikovsky's Trio in A minor, who the b. tells the story of A., a boy from the city, who is lured to a gipsy camp by the beautiful gipsy girl Zemphira. In a fit of jealousy he kills her gipsy lover and is banned from the camp by Zemphira's father. An earlier Russ. version under the title of *Gipsies*, ch. Kholfin, mus. Vasilenko (Moscow, 1937).

Alenikoff, Frances (*b* New York, 20 Aug. 1930). Amer. dancer, teacher, choreographer, and director. Studied with Graham Horton, Limón, M. Anthony, Sanasardo, Sokolow, Humphrey, Barashkova, and several other teachers (also ethnic d.). Toured as dir., ch., and principal d. of Aviv Th. of D. and Song 1959–66, performing programmes based on ethnic themes. Since 1967 has toured as soloist or with her own co. in a contemporary d.-th. multimedia programme, integrating d. with films, slides, poetry, verbal material, mime, and tape collage. Also reviews for *Dance News*.

Alexander Ballets. There have been numerous bs. about A. the Great, King of Macedon (356–23 B.C.), incl. Noverre's *A.* (Stuttgart, probably after 1761), Angiolini's *A. trionfante nell'Indie* (Verona, 1780), D'Egville's *A. the Great* (London, 1795), Gardel's *A. chez Apelles* (Paris, 1808), Viganò's *A. nell, Indie* (Milan, 1820), and Lifar's *A. le Grand* (mus. Philippe Gaubert, Paris, 1937).

Alexander, Dorothy Moses (*b* Atlanta, 22 Apr. 1904, *d* Atlanta, 17 Nov. 1986). Amer. d., teacher, and ch. Started to take summer d.-classes with Mrs. Dan Noble, later also with Fokine, Duncan, Chamié, Nijinska, Shawn, and at the Sadler's Wells School summer-courses. Guest d. with numerous small groups and leading d. of the

D.A. Concert Group, established 1929. In 1933 wrote and staged *Heirs of All the Ages* for 3000 performers, commemorating Atlanta's Bicentennial Celebration. From her performing group the Atlanta Civic B. developed 1941, for which she ch. a great number of works. Toured widely with it not only in the U.S., but also abroad, performing for U.S. military personnel in the Far East. In 1956 the co. was host to the 1st Southeastern Regional B. Festival, which inspired the regional b. movement in the U.S. In 1963 she was appointed permanent dir. of the National Regional B. Association. Dance Magazine Award (1959), Caperio Award (1981).
BIBL.: 'D.A.', *Dance Magazine* (1960/3); D. Hering, 'D.A.', *Dance Magazine* (1973/5).

Alexandrova, Natalia Donatovna (*b* Leningrad, 22 May 1936). Russ. dancer. Studied at Leningrad B., graduating in 1953. With Kirov B. until 1960, transferred to Novosibirsk 1960–9, where she became prima ballerina. Returned to Kirov B. in 1970.

Alexidze, Georgy Dmitrievitch (*b* Tblisi, 7 Jan. 1941). Sov. dancer and choreographer. Graduated 1960 from Moscow B. School (pupil of A. Messerer) and 1967 from the ch. section of the faculty of stage directors of the Leningrad Conservatory (pupil of F. Lopukhov), to which he returned 1967–8 as a teacher. Started to d. at Tblisi Op. 1961, where he was appointed chief ch. 1972. Ch. for Kirov B. *Oresteia* (mus. Falik, 1968), *The Scythian Suite* (mus. Prokofiev, 1969), *Variations on a Theme by Schumann* (mus. Brahms), *Divertissement* (mus. Mozart), and *Concert in F major* (mus. Vivaldi, all 1970), various programmes of chamber bs. given at Leningrad Philharmonic Hall 1973, and for Tblisi *Variations on a Theme by Mozart* (mus. Chopin), *Classical Symphony* (mus. Prokofiev), *Berikoaba* (mus. Kvernadse, all 1973), *Les petits riens* (mus. Mozart), *Chaconne* (mus. Bach), *Esquisses antiques* (mus. Zinzadse, all 1974), *Coppélia* (1975), *Nutcracker* (1976), *The Svan Suite* (mus. Zinzadse, 1977), and *Medea* (mus. Gabichvadze, 1978). Has taught at Leningrad Conservatory, b. master department, and since 1978 ch. at Tblisi B. School.

Algaroff, Youly (*b* Simferopol, 28 Mar. 1918). Russ.-Fr. dancer and impresario. Studied with Eduardova in Berlin and Paris, continuing with Kniaseff, made his début with Les Bs. de la Jeunesse, d. in Lyons and with the Bs. des Champs-Elysées (1946 and 1948–9), then as a freelance d. and was danseur étoile at the Paris Opéra, 1952–64. Created roles in Charrat's *Jeu de cartes*, and Lifar's *Chota Roustaveli* (1946). Since 1965 has worked as an impresario in Paris.

Algeranoff, Harcourt (orig. Harcourt Essex; *b* London, 1903, *d* Robinvale, Australia, 7 Apr. 1967). Brit. dancer, teacher, and b.-master. Studied with Legat, Tchernicheva, and others, was character soloist of Pavlova's comp., d. with

Markova-Dolin B., Bs. Russes de Monte Carlo, and Inglesby's International B. In 1954 went to Australia, working with the Borovansky B., then actively engaged in the Austral. Children's Th. In his position as examiner at the Austral. National B. School established close links with Van Praagh and the slowly growing Austral. B. One of the pioneer figures of b. in Austral. and wrote *My Years with Pavlova* (London, 1957). He was married to the d. *Claudie Algeranova.

Algeranova, Claudie (née Claudie Leonard; *b* Paris, 24 Apr. 1924). Brit. dancer. Studied at Cone-Ripman School, became a member of International B. 1941, d. during the 1950s with Borovansky's Austral. B., worked with Austral. Children's Th., was ballerina at Lucerne and Graz and lately b.-mistress at the Bavarian State Op. in Munich, where she works now as b.-secretary. She was married to the d. teacher and b.-master *Harcourt Algeranoff.

Algo, Julian (*b* Ulm, 9 Dec. 1899, *d* Stockholm, 24 May 1955). Ger. dancer, choreographer, and b.-master. Studied with Eduardova, Kröller, and Laban, joined the Petz-Kainer B., d. with Georgi in Gera and Hanover 1925–7, b.-master in Duisburg 1927–31, and was then appointed solo-d. and b.-master of the Royal Swed. B. in Stockholm, where he ch. many bs., incl. *Prima Ballerina* (mus. Offenbach-Nilsson), *Casanova* (1937), *Orpheus in the City* (mus. Hilding Rosenberg), and *La Taglioni* (mus. Auber). 1st Prize at the 1945 Competition of the Archives Internationales de la Danse in Copenhagen for his b. *Visions* (mus. Mussorgsky).

Alhambra Ballets. The A. Th. in Leicester Square functioned from 1864 to 1936 as one of London's top music halls, presenting bs. as the main feature of its programmes. Though most works stressed the spectacular, they were not altogether without ch. merit, and they displayed many internationally famous dancers. Especially during the musical directorship of George Jacobi, 1869–98, it enjoyed considerable prestige. Noteworthy choreographers were A. Bertrand, J. Hansen, C. Coppi, and later Gorsky and Berger. Among its most famous ballerinas were Emma Palladino, Bessone, Legnani, and Cerri, and later Geltzer, who appeared together with Tikhomirov. Diaghilev's Bs. Russes premièred here Massine's *La Boutique fantasque* and *The Three-Cornered Hat* (both 1919) and staged here its sumptuous revival of *The Sleeping Princess* (1921).
BIBL.: I. Guest, 'The A.B.', *Dance Perspectives* 4.

Alhanko, Anneli (*b* Bogota, 11 Dec. 1953). Swed. dancer. Studied at Royal Swed. B. School and with Northcote, Besobrasova, Franchetti, and von Bahr. Joined Royal Swed. B. 1971 as a soloist, appointed principal d. 1976. Second Prize (junior category, Varna, 1972).

Alice in Wonderland. Ballet in 2 acts; libr. and

mus. Joseph Horovitz; ch. Charnley; déc. Rowell. Prod. 9 July 1953, London Festival B., Bournemouth, with Wright, Gilpin, Beckett. The b. is based on L. Carroll's book (1865). BBC TV prod. 1953. Other prods. of the same work: Vienna, 1970 (ch. Mitterhuber), and Cassel, 1973 (ch. Doutreval). Earlier pantomime-versions in London 1906, and Chicago 1921. Different b. treatments by Page (*A. in the Garden*, mus. I. Van Grove, Jacob's Pillow, 1971), and E. Virginia Williams (Boston, 1972).

Allan, Maude (also Maud A., *b* Canada, 27 Aug. 1873, *d* Los Angeles, 7 Oct. 1956). Can. dancer. Studied music in San Francisco in her youth, and through her interest in Greek art finally decided to become a d., and thus to revive the d. of ancient Greece. She made her début in Vienna in 1903 with *The Vision of Salome* (the mus. was not, as often stated, by Richard Strauss, but by Marcel Remy). She danced mostly barefoot and in loosely skirted gown, preferably to mus. by Mendelssohn. After touring the whole world, she settled in Eng. where she opened a school 1928. Wrote *My Life and Dancing* (1908).
BIBL.: McDearmon, 'M.A., The Public Record', *Dance Chronicle* (vol. II, no. 2).

Allard, Marie (*b* Marseilles, 14 Aug. 1742, *d* Paris, 14 Jan. 1802). Fr. dancer. She was the mistress of Gaétan Vestris and the mother of August Vestris. As a d. she excelled in comic and character roles. She made her début in Marseilles, whence she proceeded via Lyons to the Paris Opéra (1761–82), where she appeared in the 1st perf. of Mozart and Noverre's *Les petits riens* (1778) and other bs. She retired when she became too fat.
BIBL.: P. Migel, 'M.A.', in *The Ballerinas* (New York, 1972).

Allegro (Ital., merry). As a term for tempo it means quick, lively. Designates (1) every d.-movement combination in fast tempo (as opposed to Adagio); (2) the 3rd part of the b.-class (after the Adagio), serving to improve the attack, vivacity, and the dancer's capability to turn and to leap. Typical A. steps are Déboulés, Pas de bourrée, Sauts, and Batteries.

Allegro Brillante. Ballet in 1 act; ch. Balanchine; mus. Tchaikovsky; cost. Karinska; light. Rosenthal. Prod. 1 Mar. 1956, New York City B., City Center, N.Y. with Maria Tallchief, Magallanes. This is a plotless b., set to the posthumous (unfinished) 3rd piano concerto, op. 75 in E flat, ch. for 2 principals and 4 accompanying couples. Also in the repertory of numerous other cos. (Royal B., 1973).
BIBL.: 'A.B.', in *Balanchine's Complete Stories of the Great Ballets* (Garden City, N.Y., 1977).

Allemande (Fr., German). (1) A serious, though not heavy, generally moderate striding dance, with four beats to the bar, of rather formal character. It consists of simple steps, followed by a leaping d. First described as a couple-d. by *Arbeau in his *L'Orchésographie* (1588). During the 18th century the A. enjoyed renewed popularity in Paris and elsewhere; it was usually performed by four couples in square formation, with richly patterned arm figurations. (2) A peasant d. in slow 3/4 time, still d. in Swabia and Switzerland, which is often said to be a forerunner of the waltz.

Allongé (Fr. lengthened). Designates in b. an elongated line and is mostly used in connection with Arabesque: the horizontal line between the forward and backward stretched arms.

Allumez les étoiles. Ballet in 13 scenes; libr. Petit and Jean Ristat; ch. Petit; mus. Prokofiev, Shostakovich, Mussorgsky, and Georgian folksongs. Prod. 5 May 1972, B. de Marseille, Marseilles, with Petit, Barbara Malinovski, Lowski. The b. gives a free account of the life of the Russ. revolutionary poet Vladimir Mayakovsky (1893–1930), inspired by his 'Listen!—they are lighting up / the stars; / it is because someone needs them' (1913).

Alma Mater. Ballet in 1 act; libr. Edward M. M. Warburg; mus. Kay Swift and Gould; ch. Balanchine; déc. John Held. Prod. 1 Mar. 1935, The Amer. B., Adelphi Th., New York, with Caccialanza, Dollar. The b. is set at the stadium entrance and tells in a humorous way of the antics of football-mad Amer. college boys and their girl-friends.
BIBL.: G. Amberg, in *Ballet* (New York, 1949).

Alma, ou la Fille de feu. Ballet in 4 acts; libr. A. J. J. Deshayes; ch. Cerrito and Perrot; mus. G. Costa; déc. W. Grieve. Prod. 23 June 1842, Her Majesty's Th., London, with Cerrito and Perrot. The b. tells of a marble beauty, who is animated by the hellish spirit Belfegor and starts to seduce a number of men, until she herself falls in love and becomes a statue again. This was one of Cerrito's greatest successes, with her famous *Pas de fascination*, accompanied by a tambourine, as the climax.
BIBL.: C. W. Beaumont, 'A.', in *Complete Book of Ballets* (London, 1951).

Alonso, Alberto (b. Havana, 22 May 1917). Cub. dancer, choreographer, and b.-director. Brother of Fernando A. Started to study with Nikolai Yavorsky in Havana in 1933, later also with Tchernicheva, Preobrajenska, and Idzikowsky. D. with Bs. Russes de Colonel de Basil 1935–40 and 1941–8, with B. Th. 1944–5, with B. Alicia Alonso 1948–9, and since 1966 with National B. of Cuba. Since 1941 also b.-master and ch., choreographing for B. de la Sociedad Pro-Arte Musical *Concerto* (mus. Vivaldi–Bach, 1943), *Sombras* (mus. Sibelius, 1946), and *Antes de Alba* (mus. Hilario Gonzáles, 1947); for National B. of Cuba *Espacio y Movimiento* (mus. Stravinsky,

1966), *El Güije* (mus. Juan Blanco, 1967), *Un retablo para Romeo y Julieta* (mus. Berlioz and P. Henry, 1970), *Conjugaciones* (mus.-collage, 1970), *A Santiago* (mus. Almeida and Ferrer, 1972); for Moscow Bolshoi B. *Carmen* (mus. Bizet–Shchedrin, 1967). Has worked also for Ensemble Experimental de la Danse and for film and television. Best ch. (with *Espacio y Movimiento*), Varna, 1968.

BIBL.: Documentation of activities, *Cuba en el ballet*, (vol. 2, no. 2).

Alonso, Alicia (née Alicia Ernestina de la Caridad dei Cobre Martinez Hoyo; *b* Havana, 21 Dec. 1921). Cuban dancer and b.-director. Studied in Havana, with Vilzak-Schollar and School of Amer. B. in New York, later also with Volkova. Started to d. in Broadway musicals, became member of B. Th. 1940 and temporarily also of the Havana Pro-Arte Musical co. Occasional defects of her eyesight compelled her to interrupt her career. Returned as ballerina to B. Th. 1943 and founded her own co., B.A.A., in Havana, 1948, and a school, 1950. Returned to the now Amer. B. Th. 1950 and appeared as guest with numerous other cos. Since the accession of Fidel Castro in 1959 has been dir. and prima ballerina of the National B. of Cuba, which is associated with the national b.-school. As ballerina she represents the pure classical style, with Giselle as one of her most famous roles, but she has also been very successful in modern roles. Is still the dominant b.-personality in Central Amer. On numerous committees and a regular adjudicator at the Varna and Moscow competitions. Created roles in Tudor's *Undertow* (1945), Balanchine's *Theme and Variations* (1947), de Mille's *Fall River Legend* (1948), Alb. Alonso's *Romeo and Juliet* (1946) and A. Mendez' Marguerite-Gautier-b. *Nous nous verrons hier soir* (1971)—but one of her most fascinating interpretations is undoubtedly the title-role in Alberto Alonso's *Carmen*. Was married to the b.-dir. *Fernando Alonso, now to Pedro Simón. Decoration of Carlos Manuel de Cespedes (1947), *Dance Magazine* Award (1958), Médaille de la Ville de Paris, and Prix Pavlova (1966).

BIBL.: W. Terry, *Alicia and Her Ballet Nacional de Cuba* (Garden City, N.Y., 1981).

Alonso, Fernando (*b* Havana, 27 Dec. 1914). Cub. dancer, teacher, and b.-director. Brother of Alberto A. Studied at Havana and in New York with Mordkin, Vilzak, and at School of Amer. B. Début with Mordkin B., appeared in musicals, d. with B. Caravan and B. Th., and was solo-d. with the Sociedad Pro-Arte Musical in Havana. Dir. of the B. de Cuba, now called National B. of Cuba, 1948–75. He was married to the d. and b.-dir.*Alicia Alonso.

BIBL.: Documentation of activities, *Cuba en el ballet* (vol. 2. no. 1).

Alston, Richard (*b* Stoughton, 30 Oct. 1948). Brit. dancer and choreographer. Studied at London School of Contemporary D. Joined London Contemporary D. Th. 1970 and immediately began to ch. Taught composition at associated school. Received Gulbenkian Award 1972 to form *Strider, of which he was a ch. and d. until 1975, when he went to New York to study with M. Cunningham and others. Returned to London 1978, working at Riverside Studios. Ch. *The Seven Deadly Sins* for Eng. National Op. (1978). Resident ch. of B. Rambert since 1980, art. dir. since 1986. Ch. *Landscape* (mus. Vaughan Williams), 1980, *Sacre du printemps* (mus. Stravinsky), and *Night Music* (mus. Mozart), both 1981.

BIBL.: Interview with R.A., *Dance and Dancers* (1978/5).

Alt, Marlis (*b* Uffenheim, 19 March 1950). Ger. dancer. Studied at Essen Folkwang Hochschule and with Grahan in New York. Soloist Wuppertal D. Th. 1973–8, where she created leading roles in most of P. Bausch's bs., incl. *Fritz* (1973), *Sacre du printemps* (1975), and *Blaubart* (1977).

Alton, Robert (*b* Bennington, 1902, *d* Hollywood, 12 June 1957). Amer. dancer and choreographer. Studied with Mordkin and d. with his co. During the 1930s one of the most sought-after choreographers for Broadway musicals (*Anything Goes, Panama Hattie, Ziegfeld Follies* of 1938, 1940, and 1942, *Du Barry Was a Lady, Hellzapoppin', Pal Joey, Hazel Flagg, Me and Juliet,* and *The Vamp*) and Hollywood films (*Ziegfeld Follies, Easter Parade, Annie Get Your Gun, Show Boat, Call Me Madam, White Christmas, No Business Like Show Business,* and *Daddy Long Legs*). Was also in charge of the Judy Garland show in Las Vegas and at the New York City Palace.

Alum, Manuel (*b* Avezibo, Puerto Rico, 23 Jan. 1943). Puerto Rican dancer, teacher, choreographer, and b.-director. Studied with Neville Black in Chicago, and in New York with Graham, Slavenska, and Sanasardo, of whose co. he became a member and eventually its artistic dir. Has been guest-teacher at various schools and is now dir. of his own M.A. D. Co. Started to ch. in 1966 for the Sanasardo co.: *Storm* (mus. Juliusz Luciuk), *Nightbloom* (mus. Serocki), and *The Offering* (mus. Penderecki), followed by *The Cellar* (mus. W. Kilar, 1967), *Palomas* (mus. P. Oliveros, 1968), *Overleaf* (mus. Messiaen, 1969), *Era* (mus. Penderecki, 1970), *Roly-Poly* (mus. Berio, 1970), *Sextetrahedron* (1972), *Women of Mystic Body, Pray for Us* (1972), *Steps—A Construction* (1973), and *East—to Nijinsky* (1973). Has also worked for Batsheva D. Co. and B. Rambert.

BIBL.: S. Goodman, 'M.A.', *Dance Magazine* (1969/3), interview with M.A., *Dance and Dancers* (Dec. 1974).

Amants magnifiques, Les. Divertissement royal; libr. Molière; mus. Lully; ch. Beauchamp; machinery Gasparo Virgarini. Prod. 4 Feb. 1670, St. Germain-en-Laye. 'The king, who desires only the extraordinary in all he undertakes, proposes to give his court a divertissement which should be composed of all that theatre might offer; to encompass so vast a diversity of elements, His Majesty has chosen as subject two rival princes, who are celebrated the Pythian games, regale a young princess and her mother with all possible gallantry' (Molière, quoted from L. Kirstein, 'L.A.m.', in *Movement & Metaphor*, New York, 1970). These were d. and mimed scenes linked by songs, finishing with a scene that recalled the combat from *Les Noces de Pelée et de Thétis* (1654). This was probably Louis XIV's last public appearance as a d.

Amati, Olga (*b* Milan, 19 Jan. 1924). Ital. dancer and teacher. Studied at La Scala B. School with Ettorina Mazzucchelli, Paula Giussani, Volkova, and Bulnes; became a member of the La Scala B., and in 1942 its prima ballerina. Noted for her *leggerezza*, she had her best roles in bs. by Milloss and Wallmann. She now teaches at the b.-school of the Teatro dell'Opera in Rome.

Amaya, Carmen (*b* Granada, 1913, *d* Bagur, 19 Nov. 1963). Span. dancer. She came from a family of dancers, first appeared in public when 7 years old, d. in Paris the following year, and continued to tour the whole world almost without interruption until the end of her life. Particularly successful in S. Amer.; Buenos Aires named a theatre after her. More and more members of her large family joined her co., but she always remained undisputed chief. She was one of the most inspired, fiery, and passionate gipsy dancers that ever lived. Was married to the guitarist Juan Antonio Aguero. Medal of Isabela la Catolica (1963).

Amberg, George (orig. Georg Amberg; *b* Halle, 1901, *d* New York, 27 July 1971). Ger-Amer. lecturer and writer. Came to the U.S. after a Ger. univ. career 1941, when he was appointed curator of the D. Archives at the Museum of Modern Art in New York, which he reorganized into the Department of D. and Th. Design. He was the editor of *Art in Modern Ballet* (New York, 1946), and wrote the standard *Ballet in America* (New York, 1950).
BIBL.: J. Brin, 'In Memoriam: G.A.', *Ballet Review* (IV/1).

Amboise, Jacques d' (*b* Dedham, 28 July 1934). Amer. dancer. Studied at School of Amer. B., became member, 1950, and soloist, 1953, of the New York City B., of which he was, until he resigned in 1984, one of the most popular stars. Dances leading parts in many Balanchine bs., and created parts in Balanchine's *Western Symphony* (1954), *Ivesiana* (1954), *Gounod Symphony* (1958), *Stars and Stripes* (1958), *Episodes* (1959), *Figure in the Carpet* (1960), *Electronics* (1961), *Raymonda Variations* (1961), *Movements for Piano and Orchestra* (1963), *Meditation* (1964), *Who Cares?* (1970), *Cortège Hongrois* (1973), and *Davidsbündlertänze*

(1980). Has participated in several film prods.—
Carousel, The Best Things in Life are Free, and *Seven Brides for Seven Brothers*—and in the T.V. 1st prod. of Stravinsky and Balanchine's *Noah and the Flood* (1962). At first the incarnation of the typical clean-cut Amer. boy, he developed into one of the finest interpreters of Balanchine's Amer. neo-classicism, with Apollo as one of his best roles. Started ch. with *The Chase or The Vixen's Choice* (mus. Mozart, 1963), and has since done several more bs. Now also teaching at School of Amer. B. and dir. of National Dance Institute.
BIBL.: O. Maynard, 'J. d'A.', *Dance Magazine* (1969/10); S. Goodman, 'An Extraordinary Anniversary', *Dance Magazine* (1970/11).

Ambrose, Kay (*b* Surrey, 1914, *d* London, 1 Dec. 1971). Brit. artist and writer. After studying art, she did the drawings for Haskell's *Ballet* (Pelican, 1938), which she followed with her very successful *Ballet Lover's Pocket Book* (1943), *Ballet Lover's Companion* (1948), and *Beginners, Please* (1953). She collaborated with Haskell once again on *Balletomane's Sketchbook* (1943). After having travelled as art-dir. with the Ram Gopal co., published her standard *Classic Dances and Costumes of India* (1950). Art. Dir. of the National B. of Canada 1952–61, for which she designed about 30 prods.

America. See *United States*.

American Ballet, The. The A.B. derived from the School of Amer. B. which Kirstein and E.M.M. Warburg had founded together with Balanchine and V. Dimitriev at the end of 1933. The S.A.B. opened Jan. 1934 in New York. Students' perf. given June 1934 in White Plains, N.Y. There was a 2-week season, starting 1 March 1935, at the New York Adelphi Th. The programme offered 7 bs., all by Balanchine: *Alma Mater, Dreams, Reminiscences, Serenade, Transcendence, Mozartiana,* and *Errante*. Among the dancers were Boris, Caccialanza, Lyon, Dollar, and Loring, with Geva and Haakon as guest-artists. After a short tour of north-eastern U.S., the co. joined the Metropolitan Op. House in the autumn of 1935 as its resident troupe, strengthened by additional dancers such as Vilzak as premier danseur, Moore, H. and L. Christensen, and E. Hawkins. The co. d. the bs. of its 1st New York season; Balanchine created *The Bat* (based on J. Strauss's *Die Fledermaus*), and ch. the op. bs. There were, however, from the very beginning rather strained relations between the traditionally orientated op.-management and the ambitious young b.-directors. In the spring of 1936 Balanchine produced the Gluck opera *Orpheus and Eurydice*, banishing the singers to the orchestra-pit—a highly controversial prod. The following year saw the climax of the A.B.: on 27 and 28 Apr. 1937 the Met. staged a Stravinsky Festival with Stravinsky himself conducting his 3 bs., *Apollon musagète*, the 1st perf. of *The Card Game (Jeu de cartes)*, and *Le Baiser de la Fée*—all in Balanchine's ch. The spring of 1938 brought the much publicized break between the Met. and the A.B. For 3 years the co. was inactive. During this time Kirstein organized a smaller troupe with different aims (but mostly the same dancers), calling it *Ballet Caravan. At the invitation of Nelson A. Rockefeller, the A.B. reassembled in 1941 for a S. Amer. goodwill tour, during which the co. performed from June to Nov. in various Latin-Amer. countries. Art. dir. was Balanchine, among the dancers were Marie-Jeanne, Caccialanza, Tompkins, L. Christensen, Dollar, Bolender, Kriza, Magallanes, Solov, and Taras. The repertory consisted of *Ballet Imperial, Juke Box, Pastorale, Concerto Barocco, The Bat, Billy the Kid, Charade, Time Table, Filling Station, Errante*, and *Apollon musagète*. After its return to the U.S., the A.B. disbanded. Kirstein and Balanchine then founded the *B. Society 1946, from which emerged in 1948 the *New York City B.

BIBL.: Kirstein, in *The New York City Ballet* (New York, 1973). N. Reynolds, in *Repertory in Review* (New York, 1977).

American Ballet Center. After teaching at various New York b. schools, Joffrey founded his own school in 1953, located in Greenwich Village, sharing its direction with Arpino. It also functions as the headquarters of the (now) Joffrey B. Some of its other best known teachers are D. Lister, M. Baylis, F. Martinet, and B. Thompson.

BIBL.: J. Dunning, 'The A.B.C. School', *Dance Magazine* (1978/6).

American Ballet Company. Originally named A. B. Players, the New York-based co. made its début at the 12th Festival of Two Worlds in Spoleto (Italy). In its 1st programme on 29 June 1969 it offered 3 bs. by Feld: *Harbinger, Cortège burlesque*, and *At Midnight*, plus Ross's *Caprichos*. The co. then started its 1st New York season on 21 Oct. 1969. In due course the repertory was supplemented with some more bs. by Feld; however, mounting financial difficulties led to the disbanding of the co. in the summer of 1971, with Feld and some of his best dancers joining Amer. B. Th. T.V. prods. of *Harbinger, At Midnight*, and *Eliot Feld and the A.B.C.* (Cologne TV, 1970). Feld then reassembled a 2nd co., the E. Feld B., in 1974.

BIBL.: D. Hering, 'Eliot Feld's A.B.C.', *Dance Magazine* (1969/12).

American Ballet Theatre. Founded by some ex-members of the former Mordkin B. under the direction of Chase and Pleasant, the co. then named Ballet Th. gave its 1st perf. on 11 Jan. 1940 at the New York Radio City Center Th., listing 11 choreographers, 85 dancers, and 21 bs. among them 6 world 1st perfs. The aim was to build up a museum of the best works of b.-history, supplemented by an at least equally strong contingent of specially commissioned Amer. creations. The artistic results were rather unsteady in the course of the years, and the co.

was time and again on the verge of bankruptcy. One of the main problems was the lack of clear-sighted and systematic repertory policy. However, the co. thrived on the spontaneous and vital temperament of Chase, whose instinct and whose constant injections of private money steered it past all the obstacles of its turbulent history. There can be no doubt of its role as an ambassador of Amer. b. and as a platform for dozens of internationally renowned dancers as well as for budding young and already established master-choreographers from all over the world. Its lack of individual style is amply compensated for by its wide scale of contrasting personalities and styles, However, there have always been certain focal points within its repertory—originally the Fokine bs., then the Tudor bs., the de Mille bs., the Cullberg bs., and nowadays the prods. of classics. The co. has appeared several times in Europe (1st visit in 1946), as well as in S. Amer. and the Far East; since 1957 it has been known as A.B.Th. Starting with the 1972/73 season an affiliated group, deriving from the associated A.B.Th. School and called Ballet Repertory Co., was established under the direction of Englund. The long list of dancers who have appeared with A.B.Th. over the years incl. Alonso, Arova, Babilée, Baryshnikov, Baronova, Bortoluzzi, Bruhn, Denard, Dolin, Eglevsky, Fracci, Gilpin, Gregory, Haydée, Hayden, Hightower, Kaye, Kirkland, Koesun, Kriza, Laing, T. Lander, Makarova, Markova, Marks, Martin, Mlakar, Nagy, Nureyev, Orlando, Paul, Philippart, Robbins, Serrano, both Tallchiefs, Tetley, Verdy, Wilson, Youskevitch, and Zorina. Among the creations of the co. were Dolin's *Pas de quatre* (1941), Fokine's *Bluebeard* (1941), Tudor's *Pillar of Fire* (1942), Massine's *Aleko* (1942), Fokine's *Helen of Troy* (1942), Tudor's *Romeo and Juliet* and *Dim Lustre* (1943), Massine's *Mam'zelle Angot* (1943), Robbins's *Fancy Free* (1944), Tudor's *Undertow* (1945), Kidd's *On Stage!* (1945), Balanchine's *Theme and Variations* (1947), Tudor's *Shadow of the Wind* (1948), de Mille's *Fall River Legend* (1948) and *The Harvest According* (1952), MacMillan's *Winter's Eve* (1957), Ross's *Paean* and *The Maids* (1957), Cullberg's *Lady from the Sea* (1960), Robbins's *Les Noces* (1965), Feld's *Harbinger* and *At Midnight* (1967), Ailey's *The River* (1970), Tudor's *The Leaves are Fading* (1975), and Tharp's *Push Comes to Shove* (1976). TV prod. of *A.B.Th.: A Close-Up in Time* (National Educational TV, 1973), *A.B.T.: Live from Lincoln Center* (NET, 1978). Since 1980 Baryshnikov has been Art Director.

BIBL.: C. Payne, *A.B.T.* (New York, 1978).

American Dance Festival. The annual series of modern d. perfs., which marked the end of the summer term of the Connecticut College School of D., was first held in 1948. A great number of important modern d. works were premièred here—among them Graham's *Diversion of Angels* (under the title *Wilderness Stair*, 1948) and *Secular*

Games (1962), Limón's *The Moor's Pavane* (1949), *The Traitor* (1954), *A Choreographic Offering* (1964), and *Psalm* (1967), Humphrey's *Night Spell* (1951) and *Ruins and Visions* (1953), Nikolais' *Kaleidoscope* (1956), Nagrin's *Indeterminate Figure* (1957), Cunningham's *Antic Meet* (1958) and *Scramble* (1967), Lang's *Shirah* (1960) and *Shore Bourne* (1964), P. Taylor's *Insects and Heroes* (1961) and *Agathe's Tale* (1967), Hawkins's *Everybody Out There* (1964), Hoving's *Satiana* (1965), Kuch's *The Brood* (1967), and Tharp's *Medley* (1969). Åkesson (1956) and Hoyer (1957) gave their U.S. débuts here as solo-dancers. In 1978 the A.D.F. moved to Durham, N.C.
BIBL.: T. Borek, 'The Connecticut A.D.F..', *Dance Perspectives* 50.

American Dance Machine, The. The New York-based institution, founded in 1976 and thriving on the initiative and energy of Lee Becker Theodore, combines a school, a research facility, and a performing group of about 16 dancers. It is dedicated to the reconstruction and preservation of Amer. th. d.—a 'living archive' of isolated d. numbers, mostly from the hit musical prods. of the last 50 years. The official co. début took place in Feb. 1978 at the historic Ford's Th. in Washington, D.C.
BIBL.: J. Gruen, 'A.D.M.: The Era of Reconstruction', *Dance Magazine* (1978/2).

American Dance Theatre, The. Financially assisted by the New York State Council, this modern dance-based co. was set up in 1964 as a repertory co. with works by various choreographers. Under the artistic direction of Limón it made its début on 18 Nov. of that year at the New York State Th., performing works by Limón, Humphrey, McKayle, and Sokolow. A 2nd series of perfs. with works by Bettis, Cunningham, Draper, Hoving, Humphrey, Lang, Limón, Nikolais, and Sokolow was given in Mar. 1965 in the same th., after which the co. disbanded.

American Document. Ballet with texts in 6 sections; ch. Graham; mus. Ray Green; set Arch Lauterer; cost. Edythe Gilfond. Prod. 6 Aug. 1938, M. Graham and co., Vermont State Armory, Bennington, Verm., with Graham, Hawkins, and Housely Stevens Jr. as Speaker. Graham herself selected the texts from the Declaration of Independence, Jonathan Edwards' sermons, Walt Whitman, and others. The sections were called 'Entrance', 'Declaration', 'Occupation', 'The Puritan', 'Emancipation', and 'Hold Your Hold'. 'A.D. took a theatrical form, the minstrel show, . . . and infused it with Graham's own preoccupation with the formation of the American sensibility . . . a compressed social history of the United States' (D. McDonagh). This was Graham's first group work to include a male soloist.

American Genesis. Ballet in 5 parts; ch. P. Taylor; mus. Bach, Haydn, Martinů, Gottschalk, and John Faley. New York first perf. 14 Mar.

1974, P. Taylor Dance Co., Brooklyn Academy of Mus., Brooklyn, with C. Adams, de Jong, Taylor. This full-length work had previously been tried out on the co.'s Amer. tour. 'It calls for only ten dancers to perform a five part pageant . . . Based on the Bible and the Bill of Rights, G. tells how, in the beginning, all humans were created equal. It explains the fall of man and woman in their inalienable pursuit of happiness. Quite literally, it puts Old Testament stories in New World settings' (G. Jackson).

American in Paris, An. Gershwin's orchestral piece of 1928 has often been ch., and Page's 1936 Cincinnati staging was one of its first b.-versions. None, however, has been more brilliant and famous than Kelly's 1951 film prod.

Amiel, Josette (b Vanves, 19 Nov. 1930). Fr. dancer. Studied at the Conservatoire Français and at Paris Opéra B. School; made her début at the Op. Comique, and then became a member of the Opéra co., appointed première danseuse 1953, and danseuse étoile 1958–71. Danced the ballerina roles of the standard repertory, and has often been a guest with foreign cos. (mostly with Flindt as her partner). Created roles in Lifar's *Chemin de lumière* (1957), Milloss's *Il cimento dell'allegria* (1960), and Flindt's *La Leçon* (1963) and *Le jeune homme à marier* (1965). Chevalier de la Légion d'Honneur (1975).

Amodio, Amedeo (b Milan, 14 Mar. 1940). Ital. dancer and choreographer. Studied at La Scala B. School, with Elide Bonagiunta and Besobrasova, and Span. d. with Antonio Marin in Madrid. After his début 1958 at La Scala has d. at most of the Ital. op.-houses and toured widely with smaller troupes. Is currently considered one of Italy's star b.-performers. Started as a ch. in 1967 with *Escursioni* (mus. Berio) in Spoleto, and followed this with *L'après-midi d'un faune* (mus. Debussy, Spoleto, 1972), *Sequenza V* (mus. Berio), *Discours II* (Globokar, both La Scala, 1973), and *Oggetto Amato* (mus. Busotti, La Scala, 1976). Played his first film role in L. Cavati's *The Night Porter* (1973). Formed Aterballetto 1981.

Amor. Ballet in 2 parts and 16 scenes; libr. and ch. Manzotti; mus. Romualdo Marenco; déc. Alfredo Edel. Prod. 17 Feb. 1886, La Scala, Milan, with Antonietta Bella, Ernestina Operti, Cecchetti. Starting with Chaos, and finishing with the Temple of Love, Manzotti presents here a display of spectacular scenes, among them Parnassus, the Pantheon of Arts in Greece, the Triumph of Caesar, The Destruction of Rome, Barbarossa, and the Battle of Legnano. Together with hundreds of dancers, mimes, children, and extras, there appeared on the stage a live elephant, and several horses and oxen.
BIBL.: C. W. Beaumont, 'A.', in *Complete Book of Ballets* (London, 1951).

Amor and Psyche. See *Amour et son amour, L'*.

Amor brujo, El (Eng. title *Love, the Magician*). Ballet in 1 act; libr. G. Martinez Sierra; mus. de Falla; ch. Imperio. Prod. 15 Apr. 1915, Teatro Lara, Madrid, with Imperio. The action is set on an Andalusian village square. Candelas, a passionate young gipsy, has once been loved by a gipsyboy who was killed in a fight and ever since pursues her as a spectre. When he tries to intervene in her new love-affair with Carmelo, she undergoes a ritual of purification, in which Carmelo dresses like the spectre, after which she is cured of her hallucinations and can now marry Carmelo. The b. became internationally famous through Argentinita's 1928 Paris version, with which she toured half the world; there have since been numerous other versions. The Ritual Fire Dance has often been performed as a solo-recital d. New prod. by P. Wright, Touring Royal B., Edinburgh 1975.

Amors og Balletmesterens Luner. See *Whims of Cupid, The*.

Amour et son amour, L'. Ballet in 2 scenes; libr. and ch. Babilée; mus. Franck; déc. Cocteau. Prod. 13 Dec. 1948, Th. des Champs-Elysées, Paris, with Babilée and Philippart. The b., set to Franck's tone-poem *Psyché* (1888), tells the familiar story of the mythological encounter between Eros and Psyche. A former b.-version by Noverre (*Psyche et l'Amour*, mus. J. J. Rodolphe, Stuttgart, 1762) was performed all over Eur.
BIBL.: C. W. Beaumont, '*L'A.e.s.a.*', in *Ballets Past and Present* (London, 1955).

Amours de Jupiter, Les. Ballet in 1 act and 5 scenes; libr. Kochno; ch. Petit; déc. Jean Hugo. Prod. 5 Mar. 1946, Bs. des Champs-Elysées, Th. des Champs-Elysées, Paris, with Babilée, Pagava, Philippart, Skorik, Petit. Based on the *Metamorphoses* of Ovid, the b. shows the encounters of Jupiter with Europa, Leda, Danaë, Ganymede, and finally his return to Juno.
BIBL.: C. W. Beaumont, '*L.A.d.J.*', in *Ballets Past and Present* (London, 1955).

Amphion. Melodrama, based on a poem by Valéry; mus. Honegger; ch. Massine; déc. Benois. Prod. 23 June 1931, Opéra, Paris, with Rubinstein and Vilzak. This is less a b. than a mimed cantata about A. who played so beautifully on his lyre that the stones were drawn into their places by his mus., thus constructing the walls of Thebes. Prod. by Orlikowsky for the 1962 Basle Honegger Festival.

Amsterdam. First th. opened in 1638; first b. perfs. took place 1642 and 1645 (*Ballet of the Five Senses*). First names of Dutch dancers appeared in the *Ballet of Maidens* (1658 — 23 years before Paris first admitted female dancers, in *Triomphe de l'amour*). While A. cultivated the comic b., The Hague preferred the allegorical genre. The first important A. ch. was Pietro Nieri (1761–9), whose *Peasant Life* (1762) anticipated Dauberval's *Fille*

mal gardée. Gradually A. took to the b. d'action. At the turn of the century b. blossomed under Jean Rochefort who was succeeded by Le Boeuf. Polly de Heus Cunninghamme was prima ballerina 1801–23—she had studied with Gardel—the most popular male d. was Jan van Well. Under Piet Grieve romantic influences gained ground, with *The Golden Magic Rose or Harlequin Freed from Slavery* (1819) his biggest success. Andries Voitus van Hamme (1828–68) created no less than 115 3-act bs. (incl. many harlequin bs.) for his co. of 60 dancers. Also responsible for introd. A. to the main bs. of P. Taglioni, Coralli, and Albert (first local perf. of *Giselle* in 1844). His son Anton also became a much respected ballerino and ch. 1871–87. The Palace for People's Industry had Eduard Witt as ch. collaborating with the composer Coenen. After 1890 b. existed only as an appendix to op., and the few local activities were dwarfed by guest-appearances (Fuller, Duncan, and, mainly, Pavlova). There was a strictly limited audience for Dutch modern dancers like Lilli Green, Darja Collin, Conny Hartong, and Florrie Rodrigo. A troupe emerged from the school of Y. Georgi during the middle 1930s, and in 1941 became the official B. of the A. Stadsschouwburg, functioning as a reservoir for the younger generation of dancers, which took over after 1945: Mascha ter Weeme, Marie Jeanne van der Veen, Nora de Wal, Karel Poons, and Pieter Sloot. The first newly founded co. after the war was Hans Snoek's *Scapino B. for children (1945). In 1947 ter Weeme established the B. der Lage Landen. She was followed in 1949 by Collin with the Netherlands Opera B. (in 1959 they were united in the Amsterdam B.). Also in 1949 Gaskell established her B. Recital, from which the Netherlands B. came in 1954. From the Amsterdam B. and Netherlands B. there emerged in 1961 the *Dutch National B. (though some breakaway dancers had already founded the Netherlands D. Th. in 1959, which, however, is based on The Hague). The independent activity of modern d. ch. K. Stuyf and his wife E. Edinoff is also significant. Today all the 3 Dutch cos. (Dutch National B., Netherlands D. Th., and Scapino B.) have regular seasons in A., which during the annual Holland Festival is also visited by b. cos. and modern d. troupes from abroad.
BIBL.: entry 'Paesi bassi' in *Enciclopedia dello spettacolo*; E. Rebling, *Een Eeuw Danskunst in Nederland* (A., 1950); J. Sinclair, *Ballet der Lage Landen* (Haarlem, 1956); W. Boswinkel, D. Koning, J. Schultink, *Het Nederlands Ballet* (Haarlem, 1958).

Anastasia. Ballet in 3 acts; libr. and ch. MacMillan; mus. Tchaikovsky and Martinů; déc. Kay. Prod. 22 July 1971, Royal B., Cov. Gdn., London, with Seymour, Beriosova, Rencher, Grater, Sibley, Dowell. The first act, set to Tchaikovsky's First Symphony, shows the Tsar and his family at a picnic with their guests, where they are inter-

rupted by the news of the outbreak of the 1914 war. The second act, set to Tchaikovsky's Third Symphony, plays against mounting social unrest at the Winter Palace, where the Tsar gives a ball for his youngest daughter A., with the festivities being disrupted by the outbreak of the October Revolution. The third act, set to electronic mus. (produced by Fritz Winckel and Rüdiger Rüfer) and Martinů's *Fantaisies symphoniques*, shows a woman who believes she is A. and for whom past and present intermingle while she lives in a Berlin hospital. The b. started its life with the 3rd act, first performed 25 June 1967 at the Ger. Op., Berlin, with Seymour, Holz, Derman, and Bohner. MacMillan then extended the work to full length for Cov. Gdn., but revived the orig. version for Stuttgart B. (1976).
BIBL.: 'A.' in *Balanchine's Complete Stories of the Great Ballets* (Garden City, N.Y., 1977).

Anastos, Peter (*b* Schenectady, N.Y., 1948). Amer. dancer and choreographer. Studied with the local civic co., continuing in New York and Leningrad. Started to ch. for the cos. of Eglevsky, San Antonio, Dallas, Garden State, and Pennsylvania B. Dir., ch., and star-performer of Bs. Trockadero (a transvestite co.). Resident ch. of Garden State B. 1979–81. Now freelance ch.

Anatomical & Mechanical Lectures upon Dancing. John Weaver's treatise, published in London in 1721, was the first attempt to explore and define the human anatomical structure in its relationship to the requirements of d.

Anatomy Lesson, The (orig. Dutch title: *De anatomische les*). Ballet in 1 act; ch. Tetley; mus. Marcel Landowsky; déc. Nicolaas Wijnberg. Prod. 28 Jan. 1964, Netherlands D. Th., The Hague, with Flier. 'The b. is based on Rembrandt's famous painting 'The Anatomy Lesson of Dr. Tulp' in the Mauritshuis of the The Hague. It challenged Tetley's sympathy for the man on the doctors' table. The whole life, the desires, and, perhaps, even the ideals the man might have had, set up a strong contrast against the sober and impersonal arguments of science' (programme note). The b. is set to Landowsky's First Symphony, *Jean de la Peur*. BBC TV prod. 1968.
BIBL.: J. Anderson, 'T.A.L.', *Dance Magazine* (1965/6); P. Brinson and C. Crisp, in *Ballet & Dance* (Newton Abbot, 1980).

Anaya, Dulce (orig. Dulce Esperanza Wöhner de Vega; *b* Rancho Boyeros, nr. Havana, 26 Dec. 1933). Cub. dancer. Studied at the Havana Sociedad Pro-Arte Musical school with G. Milenoff and the Alonsos, later also at the School of Amer. B. in New York. D. as D. Wöhner with B. Th. 1947, then as ballerina with B. de Cuba, returned to B. Th. 1951, was ballerina in Stuttgart 1957, and at the Bavarian State Op. in Munich 1958–63. Since 1967 has been ballerina with B. Concerto in Florida. Founded Jacksonville B. Th. 1970, and

since then has been its ch. Dances the ballerina roles of the standard repertory.

Ancient Voices of Children. Ballet in 1 act; ch. Bruce; mus. G. Crumb; déc. Baylis. Prod. 7 July 1975, B. Rambert, Sadler's Wells Th., London, for 7 dancers, set to Crumb's song-cycle to poems by García Lorca. 'The ragged children arise in winding sheets, which serve also as cloaks, playthings, or protective wrappers, and act out their games, their loves, and their fantasies against the harshness of poverty and neglect, and the suddenness and inexplicability—for the young—of death' (David Dougill). Other versions by J. Stripling (Stuttgart, 1971), Sparemblek (Lisbon, 1972), Butler (B. du Rhin, 1972), Tetley (Utah Repertory Th., 1973), and Reiter-Soffer (in *Yerma*, Irish B., 1976).

And Daddy Was a Fireman. Ballet in 1 act; libr., ch., and cost. Weidman; mus. Herbert Haufrecht; déc. Harnley Perkins. Prod. 7 Mar. 1943, Humphrey-Weidman Th., New York. A sequel to Weidman's autobiographical *On My Mother's Side*, the humorous work describes the rise of Fireman Weidman from ordinary ranks to captain of the fire department of the Panama Canal during its construction, and his amorous pursuits.

Andersen Ballets. The Dan. poet and writer Hans Christian Andersen (*b* Odense, 1805, *d* Copenhagen, 1875) made his début as a d. 1821 in C. Dahlén's heroic b. *Armida*. In his later life he closely followed the events of the b. world, and he was a friend of Aug. Bournonville. Many of his fairy-tales have been used for b.-librs., incl. *The Red Shoes* (ch. Hassreiter, mus. Raoul Mader, Vienna, 1898—a later Eng. film version by Helpmann and Massine, 1948), *The Little Mermaid* (ch. Beck, mus. Fini Henriques, Copenhagen, 1909), *Little Ida's Flowers* (ch. Emilie Walbom, mus. Paul von Klenau, Copenhagen, 1916), *Le Baiser de la Fée* (after *The Ice Maiden*, ch. Nijinska, mus. Stravinsky, Paris, 1928), *Les cent baisers* (after *The Swineherd*, ch. Nijinska, mus. Fréderic d'Erlanger, London, 1935—later also as *The Swineherd*, ch. Lander, mus. Johann Hye-Knudsen, Copenhagen, 1936), *Le Roi nu* (after *The Emperor's New Clothes*, ch. Lifar, mus. Français, Paris 1936), and *The Steadfast Tin-Soldier* (ch. Balanchine, mus. Bizet, 1975). Lazzini produced *Andersen cygne Sauvage* (mus. J.-K. Damase, for B. Royal de Wallonie, 1979). For the Amer. film *Hans Christian Andersen* Petit ch. the b.-sequences (1951). A Dan. TV prod. of *The Swineherd* by Flindt (1969).
BIBL.: 'Hans Christian Andersen', *Dance Index* IV/9.

Andersen, Ib (*b* Copenhagen, 14 Dec. 1954). Dan. dancer. Studied at Royal Dan. B. School. Joined Royal Dan. B. 1973, appointed solo d. 1975. Created title-role in Flindt's *Toreador* (1978). Principal d. of N.Y. City B. since 1980, creating roles in Balanchine's *Davidsbündlertänze* (1980) and his revised *Mozartiana* (1981), and in Robbins's *Piano Pieces* (1981).

BIBL.: M. Hunt, 'Breaking Away', *Ballet News* (1980/6).

Anderson, Jack (*b* Milwaukee, 15 June 1935). Amer. dance critic. Educated at Northwestern Univ., Indiana Univ. (M.A.), and Univ. of California at Berkeley. Associate critic of *Dance Magazine*, contributing editor of *Ballet Review*, New York correspondent of *The Dancing Times*. Associate d. critic, *New York Times*, since 1978. Co-founder and -editor (with G. Dorris) of *Dance Chronicle* since 1977. Taught d. history and d. criticism at New School for Social Research, Connecticut College, and Long Beach State Univ. Editor of 'The Dance, The Dancer, and The Poem: An Anthology of Twentieth-Century Dance Poems', *Dance Perspectives* 72. Author of *Dance* (N.Y., 1974), *The Nutcracker Ballet* (N.Y., 1979). Also writes poetry. Bueno Prize for *The One and Only: The B. Russe de M. C.* (1981).

Anderson-Ivantzova, Yelizaveta Yulievna. (*b* Moscow 9 Apr. 1890 (O.S.), *d* New York, 10 Nov. 1973). Russ.-Amer. dancer and teacher. Studied at Moscow Th. School, becoming a member of the Bolshoi B., and a ballerina in 1917. After emigrating to the United States, staged Stravinsky's *Les Noces* at the New York Met. Op. House 1929. Opened her New York b. studio 1937, and taught there until her death. Became known as one of the city's most austere and demanding teachers; Alicia Alonso, Hightower, and Harkarvy were among her pupils.

Anderson, Reid Bryce (*b* New Westminster, B.C., 1 Apr. 1949). Can. dancer. Studied at Dolores Kirkwood Academy of Performing Arts and Royal B. School. Member Stuttgart B. 1965–85, appointed soloist 1972 and principal d. 1974. Created roles in MacMillan's *Requiem* (1976) and *My Brother, My Sisters* (1978), Helliwell's *Mirage* (1977), Forsythe's *Urlicht* (1977), *Dream of Galilei* (1978) and *Orpheus* (1979), and Neumeier's *Lady of the Camellias* (1978). Art. dir. B. British Columbia since 1986.

Andersson, Gerd (*b* Stockholm 1932). Swed. dancer. Studied at Royal Swed. B. School and with Karina; joined the Stockholm co. in 1948; promoted ballerina in 1958. Created parts in Tudor's *Echoing of Trumpets* (1963) and Macdonald's *Ballet Russe* (1966). Retired 1976.

Anderton, Elizabeth (*b* London, 28 May 1938). Brit. dancer. Studied at Sadler's Wells School, joined the Sadler's Wells Op. B. 1955, the Royal B. 1957–74; promoted soloist 1958, principal d. 1961. D. the ballerina-roles of the standard repertory. Created roles in Cranko's *Sweeney Todd* (1959), Ashton's *Les deux pigeons* (1961), Tudor's *Knight Errant* (1968), Cauley's *Lazarus* (1970), and Nureyev's *Romeo and Juliet* (1977). After being assistant to R. Helpmann, 1975, became teacher

and guest d. London Festival B. 1976, and asst. artistic dir. 1979–83, reappointed 1984.

Andrew, Thomas (orig. Edward Thomas Andrulewicz; *b* Mount Carmel, 1932, *d* New York 11 Jan. 1984). Amer. dancer and choreographer. Studied with Douglas Henkel and Schwezoff, started to d. and ch. in the U.S. Army Special Services, was then d. and ch. at the Met. Op. House (1956–62), and then pursued a career mainly as a ch. and dir. for ops., operettas, and musicals. Occasionally appeared with his own co. BIBL.: G. Loney, '48 Opera Ballets in One Year', *Dance Magazine* (1973/3).

Andreyanova, Yelena Ivanovna (*b* St. Petersburg, 13 July 1819, *d* Paris, 26 Oct. 1857). Russ. dancer. Studied at St. Petersburg Th. School, graduated in 1837; one of the first Russ. ballerinas to appear abroad (Paris, 1845, Milan). In 1842 she became Russia's first Giselle.

Angara. Ballet in 2 acts; libr. and ch. Grigorovich; mus. Andrei Eshpai; déc. Virsaladze. Prod. 30 Apr. 1976, Bolshoi B., Moscow, with Bessmertnova, Vassiliev, M. Lavrovsky. Based upon A. Arbuzov's play *The Irkutsk Story* (1960), the b. depicts young Siberian construction workers and their emotional vagaries.
BIBL.: '*Izvestia* on A.', in *Dance News* (1976/10).

Angelo, Ann Marie De. See *De Angelo, Ann Marie*.

Angiolini, Gaspero (sic, not Gasparo, *b* Florence, 9 Feb. 1731, *d* Milan, 6 Feb. 1803). Ital. dancer, choreographer, b.-master, and composer. He came from a family of th. artists and studied first with his father. D. in Venice 1748, then worked at various Ital. ths. and in Turin 1757, where he did some bs. to mus. by R. Gioanetti. In 1758 went to Vienna, where he came under the influence of Hilverding and his theories about the *b. d'action*. Created Gluck's *Don Juan* b. 1761 and was ch. of the first perf. of Gluck's *Orpheus and Eurydice* (1762). His later bs. incl. Gluck's *Semiramide* (1765) and *Alessandro*. St. Petersburg briefly 1762, then returned 1766–72, ch. there and in Moscow about 10 bs., among them *Les Chinoises en Europe* to mus. of his own (1767). Worked in Venice, Padua, and Milan, 1772–3, where he started his polemics against Noverre, in which he accused him of plagiarizing Hilverding and his ideas about the *b. d'action* (*Lettere di G.A. a Mons. Noverre sopra i balli pantomimi.*) In 1774 he was once again in Vienna, creating *L'Orfano della China* (to his own mus., not Gluck's). Returned to St. Petersburg 1776–9 (among other bs. *Thésée et Ariane* to mus. of his own). Worked during the next years in Venice, Milan, Turin, and Verona, and once again and for the last time in St. Petersburg 1782–6. He then returned finally to Italy, where he was imprisoned in 1797 because of his sympathies for the progressive and democratic ideas of the French. In contrast to Noverre, whom he considered his arch-enemy, A. put the greatest emphasis on tauteness and concentration of action and gesture. He abhorred long-winded programme notes and propagated unity of style. For his time he was of extraordinary musical sensibility, and was always striving for a synthesis between mus. and ch. He also tried to develop a system of movement-notation, based on the notation of mus.

BIBL.: entry 'A.,G.', in *Enciclopedia dello spettacolo*; H. M. Winter, in *The Pre-Romantic Ballet* (London, 1974).

Anglaise (Fr., English). During the 18th century the dances performed in Brit. were called thus. Later the term was used for a fast chain-dance in duple time. If used in connection with triple time, it mostly refers to the *Ecossaise.

Anglo-Polish Ballet. The co. was founded by the dancers Czeslow Konarski and Alicja Halama in 1940 in London, later touring the provinces and abroad under the direction of Jan Cobel. Apart from the standard works, the repertory also incl. *Cracow Wedding*, and *Pan Twardowski*. Among its dancers were Gilmour, Kersley, Rassine, and Hamilton. Disbanded after 1947.

Animaux modèles, Les. Ballet in 1 act, prologue, 6 scenes, and epilogue; libr. and ch. Lifar; mus. Poulenc; déc. M. Brianchon. Prod. 8 Aug. 1942, Opéra, Paris, with Lifar, Schwarz, Peretti, Chauviré, Lorcia. The b. is based on the following 6 fables by La Fontaine: L'Ours et les deux compagnons, La Cigale et la Fourmi, Le Lion amoureux, L'Homme entre deux âges et ses deux mâitresses, La Mort et le Bûcheron, Les deux coqs.

Anisimova, Nina Alexandrovna (*b* St. Petersburg, 27 Jan. 1909). Russ. dancer and choreographer. Studied with Romanova, Vaganova, and Shiriaev at the Petrograd-Leningrad B. School, graduated 1926 and became a member of the Leningrad GATOB. In 1932 she created Thérèse in Vainonen's *Flames of Paris*. Started as a ch. 1936 with *Andalusian Wedding* (mus. Chabrier). Ch. in 1942 the revised version of Khatchaturian's *Gayane* for the Kirov, evacuated at that time in Molotov/Perm, and ch. 1944 in Ufa the first national Bashkirian b., *Songs of the Cranes* (mus. Lev B. Stepanov and S. Ismagilov). Has worked several times at the Leningrad Maly Th. Staged 1964 the Copenhagen prod. of *Swan Lake*.

Annabel Lee. Dance B. in 1 act; ch. Skibine; mus. Byron Schiffman; déc. André Delfau. Prod. 26 Aug. 1951, Grand B. du Marquis de Cuevas, Deauville, with Marjorie Tallchief and Skibine. The b. is inspired by Poe's poem. It is really an extended pas de deux for A.L. and her lover, surrounded by symbolic figures, representing death and the sea. The accompanying poem is sung by a tenor.

BIBL.: C. Beaumont, 'A.L.', in *Ballets Past & Present* (London, 1955).

Anna Karenina. Lyric Scenes in 3 acts; libr. Boris Lvov-Anokhin; ch. Plisetskaya, Natalia Ryzhenko, and Victor Smirnov-Golovanov; mus. Shchedrin; déc. Valeri Leventhal (cost. for Plisetskaya by Pierre Cardin). Prod. 10 June 1972, Bolshoi B., Moscow, with Plisetskaya, Liepa, Fadeyechev, Y. Vladimirov. The b. follows closely the main events of Tolstoy's novel (1878), though without the Levin episode. Other prod. by Parlić (Belgrade, 1973), different full-length b. by A. Prokovsky (mus. Tchaikovsky, Australian B., 1979).

BIBL.: 'Plisetskaya on A.K.', *Dance News* (1972/5).

Anouilh, Jean (*b* Bordeaux, 23 June 1910). Fr. playwright. He wrote in 1932 *Le Bal des voleurs* (*Thieves' Carnival*), b. for actors; a b.-version was ch. by Massine (Nervi, 1960), and revived for Royal B. (London, 1963). Later also some librs. for Petit, among them *Les Demoiselles de la nuit* (1948), and (together with Georges Neveux) *Le Loup* (1953).

Ansermet, Ernest (*b* Vevey, 11 Nov. 1883, *d* Geneva, 20 Feb. 1969). Swiss conductor. Diaghilev engaged him in 1915, and he conducted the first prods. of Stravinsky's *L'Histoire du soldat* (1918), *Chant du rossignol* (1920), *Pulcinella* (1920) *Renard* (1922), and *Les Noces* (1923), Satie's *Parade* (1917), de Falla's *Le Tricorne*, and Prokofiev's *Chout* (1923).

Anspannung-Abspannung. Laban used these terms to define the contrasting actions of modern dance. The Graham equivalent is *Contraction-Release*; in Eng. one finds occasionally *Tension-Relaxation*.

Antheil, George (*b* Trenton, 8 July 1900, *d* New York, 12 Feb. 1959). Amer. composer. He composed the mus. for *Ballet Mécanique*, a film planned in collaboration with Fernand Léger (1925), later also the bs. *Dreams* (ch. Balanchine, 1935), and *Capital of the World* (ch. Loring, 1953). Author of *Bad Boy of Music* (New York, 1945).

Antigone. Ballet in 1 act; libr. and ch. Cranko; mus. Theodorakis; déc. Rufino Tamayo. Prod. 19 Oct. 1959, Royal B., Cov. Gdn., London, with Beriosova, Blair, Burne, MacLeary. The b. is freely based on the tragedy by Sophocles (441 B.C.). Revived for Stuttgart B. (1961). Other A. bs. by Gioia (Venice, 1790), G. Galzerani (Milan, 1825), and Sokolow (mus. Chávez, 1940?).

Antonia. Ballet in 1 act; libr. and ch. Gore; mus. Sibelius; déc. Harry Cordwell. Prod. 17 Oct. 1949, B. Rambert, King's Th., London, with Hinton, Paltenghi, and Gore. Set to Sibelius's *The Bard*, incidental mus. for *The Tempest*, and *Scènes historiques*, the b. tells the story of a man who discovers the infidelity of his beloved and of his revenge.

BIBL.: C. Beaumont, 'A.' in *Ballets of Today* (London, 1954).

Antonio (orig. Antonio Ruiz Soler; *b* Seville, 4 Nov. 1922). Span dancer, choreographer, and b.-director. Studied with D. Manuel Real (Realito) and made his début 1928, together with Rosario, his partner for many years. He toured the whole world, and became the most famous Span. d. of his generation. After separating from Rosario in 1953, he established a co. of his own, but his mesmerizing personality as a d. has often since dwarfed his achievements as a ch. A purist in his solo dances, he has tried in his bs. to create a synthesis of classic-academic and Span. d. Dances the leading role in the Span. prods. of *El amor brujo* and *The Three-Cornered Hat* (1974). Has been awarded numerous prizes.

BIBL.: C. Beaumont, *A.* (London, 1952); E. Brunelleschi, *A. and Spanish Dancing* (London, 1958).

Antonio, Juan (*b* Mexico City, 4 May 1945). Mex. dancer. Studied with Xavier Francis and Zaraspe, also at Amer. B. Th. School and Amer. B. Center. Started to d. when 18 years old at the Nuevo Teatro de la Danza Mexico, became member of the B. Clásico de Mexico 1964, with which he toured abroad. D. with the cos. of Lang, Sokolow, de Lavallade, Limón, and Tetley, and has been since 1967 a prominent member of the L. Falco D. Co., of which he is now Associate Dir.

BIBL.: S. Goodman, 'J.A.', *Dance Magazine* (1970/5).

Antony and Cleopatra Ballets. The love between the Egyptian queen and the Roman general has inspired several bs., e.g. Noverre's (Ludwigsburg, 1765), Aumer's (mus. Kreutzer, Paris, 1808), Igor Tchernishov's (mus. E. Lazarev, Leningrad, 1968), and dell'Ara's (mus. Prokofiev, Milan, 1971).

Antuono, Eleanor D'. See *D'Antuono, Eleanor.*

Aplvor, Denis (*b* Collinstown, 14 Apr. 1916). Irish composer. Wrote the mus. for Howard's *A Mirror for Witches* (1952) and *Vis-a-Vis* (1953), Rodrigues's *Blood Wedding* (1953) and *Saudades* (1955), and arranged the Donizetti mus. for Howard's *Veneziana* (1963).

Aplomb (Fr., balance). Defined by Despréaux in *L'Art de la danse* (1806) as '. . . lorsque la tête et les reins sont en ligne perpendiculaire audessus de la partie du pied sur laquelle tout le corps est porté. On peut être en équilibre sans être d'aplomb; mais il n'y a pas d'aplomb sans équilibre.' (When the head and the small of the back are in a straight line and held directly above the supporting foot. One can be in balance without aplomb; but not the reverse.)

Apollo Ballets. Long before Stravinsky's **Apollon musagète* (1928) the god of music had appeared on the b.-stage, for instance in Hilverding's *Apollon et Daphné, ou Le retour d'Apollon au Parnasse* (1763), Noverre's *Apollon et les muses* (1782), Didelot's *Apollon et Daphné* (1802) and *Apollon et Persée* (1803), also later in Kölling's *Apollo und Daphne* (1936), and Nijinska's *Apollon et la belle* (1937).

Apollon musagète. Ballet in 2 scenes; mus. Stravinsky; ch. Bolm; déc. Nicholas Remisoff. Prod. 27 Apr. 1928, Library of Congress, Washington, D.C., with Bolm, Page, Berenice Holmes, Elise Reiman. The b. shows the birth of A. to his mother Leto, and his education through the muses Terpsichore, Calliope, and Polyhymnia, after which he ascends Mount Parnassus. The score was commissioned by Elizabeth Sprague Coolidge. The first Eur. prod. followed on 12 June 1928, ch. Balanchine, déc. André Bauchant, B. Russes de Diaghilev, Th. Sarah Bernhardt, Paris, with Lifar, Nikitina, Tchernicheva, and Doubrovska. This version, which often has been hailed as marking the birth of neoclassicism on the b.-stage, has been constantly revived all over the world (Royal B., 1966). Under the preferred title of *Apollo* it is still one of the key works in the repertory of the New York City B. Individual versions have been choreographed, among others, by Milloss (Rome, 1951), T. Gsovsky (Berlin, 1951), and Georgi (Hanover, 1955).

BIBL.: 'A.', in Balanchine's *Complete Stories of the Great Ballets* (Garden City, New York, 1977); L. Kirstein, 'A.', in *Movement & Metaphor* (New York, 1970).

Aponte, Christopher (*b* New York, 4 May 1950). Amer. dancer. Studied at High School of Performing Arts, then with Thalia Mara and at Harkness Ho.; joined Harkness Youth Dancers and became soloist with Harkness B. 1971. To A. Ailey City Center D. Th. 1974; Amer. B. Th., 1975–6. Joined B. of Emilia Romagna 1978, Boston B. 1983.

BIBL.: S. Goodman, 'C.A.', *Dance Magazine* (1973/2).

Appalachian Spring. Ballet in 1 act; ch. Graham; mus. Copland; sets Noguchi; cost. Edythe Gilfond. Prod. 30 Oct. 1944, Library of Congress, Washington, D.C., with Graham, O'Donnell, Cunningham, E. Hawkins. A newly-wed Amer. couple set up their house in the wilderness; the work is based on the puritan ethos of the Amer. pioneers. Commissioned by the Elizabeth Sprague Coolidge Foundation. Pittsburgh WQET TV prod. 1959, also Nat. Educ. Television, 1976.

BIBL.: D. McDonagh, 'A.S.', in *The Complete Guide to Modern Dance* (Garden City, N.Y., 1976).

Apparitions. Ballet in 5 scenes, incl. a Prologue and Epilogue; libr. Lambert; ch. Ashton; mus. Liszt/Jacob; déc. Beaton. Prod. 11 Feb. 1936, Sadler's Wells B., Sadler's Wells Th., London, with Helpmann, Fonteyn, Turner. The b., for which Gordon Jacob orchestrated several piano-pieces by Liszt, was inspired by Berlioz' *Symphonie Fantastique*. It shows a romantic poet who in the

world of his opium-dreams is searching for a symbol of love, which he wants to express in his poem.
BIBL.: C. W. Beaumont, '*A.*', in *Complete Book of Ballets* (London, 1951).

Appel, Peter (*b* Surabaya, 8 Sep. 1933). Dutch dancer, b.-master, and teacher. Studied at the Kennemer Studio in Haarlem, and with Preobrajenska, joined the Netherlands B. 1955, was solo-d. in Basle, guest b.-master with the co. of Larrain and London Festival B., b.-master of the Hamburg State Op., b.-dir. in Cologne 1969–71, and dir. of the Cologne Inst. for Stage D. (together with K. Peters) until 1976. Returned to Basle in 1977 as b.-master. In great demand as an international guest-teacher.

Apprenti sorcier, L'. See *Sorcerer's Apprentice, The.*

Après-midi d'un faune, L' (Eng. title *The Afternoon of a Faun*). Ballet in 1 act; libr. and ch. Nijinsky; mus. Debussy; déc. Bakst. Prod. 19 May 1912, B. Russes de Diaghilev, Th. du Châtelet, Paris, with Nijinsky. A faun, lazily playing on his flute during a warm summer afternoon, is taken unawares by some nymphs who are on their way to bathe. He becomes amorously entangled with one of them before she, too, leaves the stage, after which he lovingly fondles the scarf she has dropped. The b. is based on Debussy's famous *Prélude à l'a.-m. d'u. f.* (1894), which in itself was inspired by Mallarmé's poem (1876). Though the audience of the first night was scandalized by the b.'s outspoken eroticism, the mus. has often been rechoreographed since—occasionally also in the form of a solo dance (Lifar, 1935). The most famous contemporary version is Robbins's *★Afternoon of a Faun* (1953).
BIBL.: L. Kirstein, '*L'a.-m. d'u f.*', in *Movement & Metaphor* (New York, 1970).

Ara, Ugo dell' (*b* Rome, 13 Apr. 1921). Ital. dancer, choreographer, and b.-master. Studied at Rome Op. B. School, joined the Rome co., becoming its premier danseur, dancing the leads in a number of Milloss bs. Became a member of La Scala in 1946, toured Eur. with the musical *Carosello Napoletano* (which he had also ch.) 1949–50, and returned afterwards to La Scala. Since 1950 has concentrated on a career as ch., working with various ths. and for TV. Among his bs. are revivals of the famous b. of nuns from Meyerbeer's *Robert le Diable* (Palermo, 1966), and Manzotti's *Excelsior* (Palermo, 1967), as well as *Notte egiziane* (mus. Prokofiev, Milan, 1971). Married to the d. Wanda Sciaccaluga.

Arabesque (Fr., ornament). One of the fundamental positions in b. The body is in profile, supported on one leg, the other leg is extended behind at an angle of 90°, while the arms are held in various harmonious positions, striving for the longest direct line from the fingertips to the toes (the shoulders are held square to the line of direction). It was known in the 18th century and codified by Blasis. There are many variations according to the individual schools.

Aradi, Mária (*b* Högyez, 21 Sep. 1944). Hung. d. Studied at Budapest B. Inst., joined Budapest State Op. B. 1960, d. 1963–9 with the B. Sopianae, then returned to Budapest, joined Munich Th. am Gärtnerplatz co. 1970, and was principal d. of the Dutch National B. from 1972. Retired 1983, becoming asst. b. master. Was married to the d. Zoltán Péter. Bronze Medal (Varna, 1966).

Araiz, Oscar (*b* Bahia Blancal, 2 Dec. 1940). Argent. dancer, choreographer, and b.-director. Studied with Elide Locardi, Schottelius, and Hoyer; made his début 1958 at the Teatro Argentino in La Plata, toured with a troupe of his own 1964–7, and was artistic dir. of the B. del Teatro San Martin in Buenos Aires 1968–73, where he was considered one of the major choreographers of the contemporary South Amer. b.-scene. Among his bs. are *El Canto de Orfeo* (mus. Henry, 1964), *La Gorgona y la Manticora* (mus. Chávez, 1964), *Orpheus* (mus. Stravinsky, 1964), *La pazzia senile* (mus. Banchieri, 1965), *Sacre du printemps* (mus. Stravinsky, 1966), *The Miraculous Mandarin* (mus. Bartók, 1967), *Deserts* (mus. Varèse, 1967), *Sinfonia India* (mus. Chávez, 1967), *Sinfonia* (mus. Berio and others, 1968), *Magnificat* (mus. Bach, 1969), *Romeo and Julia* (mus. Prokofiev, 1970), and *In a Gadda Da Vida* (mus. Iron Butterfly, 1970). Has also ch. the 'Dance Around the Golden Calf' for the Buenos Aires *Moses and Aaron* prod. (mus. Schoenberg, 1970), a programme *Family Scenes* (mus. various, Hamburg, 1976), and various TV prods. Since his 1977 *Romeo and Juliet* prod., has ch. for Joffroy B. B. dir. Genève B. since autumn 1980, ch. full-length *Tango* (mus. A. Stampone, 1981).

Araujo, Loipa (*b* Havana, *c.* 1943). Cub. dancer. Studied at the Escuela de la Sociedad Pro-Arte Musical and with the Alonsos, L. Fokine, and Parés; joined National B. of Cuba 1959, appointed prima ballerina 1967. Has often appeared abroad. Created leading role in Petit's *Les Intermittences du coeur* (1974). Participated in the Cuban b. films *Giselle* (Bathilde, 1963), *Grand Pas de quatre* (Grisi, 1968), and *Edipo Rey* (El Oráculo, 1971). Gold Medal (Varna, 1965), Silver Medal (Moscow, 1969), Golden Star (Paris, 1970).
BIBL.: Checklist of activities and roles in *Cuba en el ballet* (III, 1).

Arbeau, Thoinot (orig. Jehan Tabourot; *b* Dijon, 1519, *d* Langres, 1596). Fr. dance writer. Published his famous *L'Orchésographie* in 1588 in Langres, a treatise about 16th-century dancing, fencing, piping, and drumming in the form of a dialogue between A. and his young friend Capriol. Gives a description of various dances with musical notation: Basse danse, Pavane, Gaillarde, Volte, Courante, Allemande, Gavotte, Canaries, Bouffons, Morisque, Pavane d'Espagne, and 23 different versions of the Branle. Positions and steps are precisely defined. C. W. Beaumont's English translation (London, 1925—reprinted in the Amer. D. Horizons series) inspired Ashton's *Capriol Suite* (mus. Warlock, 1930).

Archives Internationales de la Danse (A.I.D.). Founded by de Maré, with Tugal as curator, on 16 June 1931 in Paris in memory of Bs. Suédois and its ch. Börlin. A generously furnished and richly endowed institution, not only housing a vast library with books, magazines, souvenir-programmes, cuttings, models, designs for décors and costumes, and scores, dealing with the d.-history of the whole world, but also presenting lectures, demonstrations, and exhibitions. An important magazine, *A.I.d.l.D.*, was published 1932–6 (20 issues). In 1932 the A.I.D. held its first Ch. Competition in Paris, won by Jooss with *The Green Table*. The competition was resumed in 1947 in Copenhagen. In 1950 the archives were dissolved, the greater part of de Maré's collection being handed over to the Paris Musée de l'Opéra, and the rest to Stockholm Dansmuseet.

Archives of the Dance. Founded in 1945 in London, and housed by the Imperial Society of Teachers of Dancing, it is based on the collection of d.-material of the then B. Guild, and has since acquired further items (manuscripts, scores, photographs, programmes, etc.).

Argentina, La (orig. Antonia Mercé; *b* Buenos Aires, 4 Sep. 1890, *d* Bayonne, 18 July 1936). Span. dancer. Her Span. parents were professional dancers who returned to Spain 2 years after her birth, where Manuel Mercé became b.-master at the Madrid Teatro Real. He educated his daughter strictly as a classic d. She made her début at 6 years old, appointed première danseuse of the Madrid Op. when 11. Three years later she gave up her career as a classic d., and began studying Span. d. with her mother. When 18, she embarked on her first foreign tour, after which she toured the whole world until the end of her life, becoming New York's most celebrated d. (after a very difficult initial season there). She was a tireless worker and literally d. herself to death. Those who saw her are convinced that she was the greatest Span. d. that ever lived. The critic Levinson attributed to her the renaissance of Span. d. in our century. Though all her inspirations came from Span. folklore dancing, through her personality and her brilliant dramatic instinct the traditional forms underwent a subtle metamorphosis, emerging as perfect products of art. She was also famous for the sensitivity with which she played the castanets.
BIBL.: A. Levinson, *La A.* (Paris. 1926).

Argentine. See *Buenos Aires*.

Argentinita, La (orig. Encarnacion Lopez Julves; *b* Buenos Aires, 1895, *d* New York, 24 Sep. 1945). Span. dancer. She was the daughter of Span. parents (and the sister of Pilar Lopez), studied in Spain, made her début at 6 years old in Madrid, and was soon considered one of the greatest exponents of the Span. d. and one of its purest stylists. Toured widely in Eur. and both the Amers. With García Lorca she founded 1932 the B. de Madrid. Her 2 most famous choreographies were *Bolero* (mus. Ravel), and *Goyescas* (mus. Granados).
BIBL.: A. Levinson, in *La danse d'aujourd'hui* (Paris, 1929).

Argyle, Pearl (orig. Pearl Wellman; *b* Johannesburg, 7 Nov. 1910, *d* New York, 29 Jan. 1947). Brit. dancer. Studied with Rambert, made her début 1926 with B. Rambert, also d. with Les Bs. 1933, Camargo Society, and Sadler's Wells B. Was admired as one of the greatest beauties of modern Eng. b. Created roles in Ashton's *Façade* (1931) and *Lady of Shalott* (1931), de Valois's *Bar aux Folies-Bergères* (1934), and Howard's *Mermaid* (1934). Valéry and Vaudoyer have written about her with great admiration.
BIBL.: G. Anthony, 'P.A.', *Dancing Times* (1970/2).

Ari, Carina (orig. Carina Janssen; *b* Stockholm, 14 Apr. 1897, *d* Buenos Aires, 24 Dec. 1970). Swed. dancer. Studied in Stockholm and with Fokine in Copenhagen, was ballerina of the Bs. Suédois 1920–5. Later did several chs. for the Paris Op. Comique (*Sous-Marine*, mus. Honegger, 1925; *Valses de Brahms* 1933), and created the lead in Lifar's *Le Cantique des cantiques* (Opéra, 1938). She established the C.A. Foundation to further the cause of d. in Sweden (scholarships for young dancers, the C.A. Gold Medal, awarded to Ashton 1972, to Tudor and Jooss 1973, to Béjart 1974, and to Flindt and Kragh-Jacobsen 1975).

Ariadne Ballets. The daughter of King Minos, who gave Theseus the thread by which he was able to find his way out of the labyrinth, and who was deserted by him on the island of Naxos, where Dionysos found her and made her his wife, has inspired a great number of bs., incl. those by Deshayes (Paris, 1747), Hilverding (Vienna, 1754), Angiolini (Milan, 1773), Gallet (London, 1797), Reisinger (Moscow, 1875), Lifar (*Bacchus et Ariane*, mus. Roussel, Paris, 1931), John Taras (*The Minotaur*, mus. Elliott Carter, Ballet Society, 1947), Walter (mus. Monteverdi, Wuppertal, 1958), and Ailey (mus. Jolivet, Harkness B., 1965).

Armida Ballets. See *Rinaldo Ballets*.

Armitage, Merle (*b* Mason City, 1893; *d* 1975). Amer. writer, designer, and impresario. After being in charge of the Amer. publicity for Diaghilev's Bs. Russes and Pavlova's troupe, he became actively engaged in promoting Graham and her group on their first transcontinental tours and wrote the first book on her: *Martha Graham, Dancer* (1937).

BIBL.: D. McDonagh, 'M.A. 1893–1975', *Ballet Review* (vol. 5, no. 1).

Armour, Thomas (*b* Tarpon Springs, 7 Mar. 1909). Amer. dancer, teacher, and b. director. Studied with Ines N. Armour, Preobrajenska, and Egorova. D. with co. of Rubinstein 1933–4, Nijinska 1934, Woizikovsky 1935–8, Rio de Janeiro Op. House 1939, B. Russe de Monte Carlo 1931–41. Founded a school in Miami 1949, later becoming dir. of Miami Conservatory of Mus. and D. Founder-Artistic Dir. of Miami B. Co. 1951. Executive vice-president of South-eastern Regional B. Association.

Arnold, Malcolm (*b* Northampton, 21 Oct. 1921). Brit. composer. Wrote the mus. for Ashton's *Homage to the Queen* (1953) and *Rinaldo and Armida* (1955), and for Helpmann's *Elektra* (1963). MacMillan based his *Solitaire* (1956) on A.'s 'English Dances'.

Aroldingen, Karin von (*b* Berlin, 9 Sep. 1941). Ger.-Amer. dancer. Studied in Berlin, d. with Amer. Festival B., was soloist in Frankfurt 1959–61, joined the New York City B. 1961, promoted solo-d. 1967, and principal d. 1972. Created roles in T. Gsovsky's *The Seven Deadly Sins* (1960), Balanchine's *Who Cares?* (1970), *Suite No. 3* (1970), *Violin Concerto* (1972), *Variations pour une Porte et un soupir* (1974), *Vienna Waltzes* (1977), *Kammermusik No. 2* (1978), *Davidsbündlertänze* (1980), and Robbins's *Goldberg Variations* (1972). Retired 1984; Faculty of Sch. of Amer. B. since 1979.
BIBL.: J. Gruen, 'K.v.A.', in *The Private World of Ballet* (New York, 1975).

Arova, Sonia (*b* Sofia, 20 June 1927). Bulg.-Brit. dancer and b.-director. Studied with Anastas Petroff, Preobrajenska, and Lifar; became a member of the Eng. International B. 1946, d. with the Metropolitan B. from 1947 (where she created a part in Taras's *Designs with Strings*, 1948), later with various cos. in Eur. and Amer. Appeared in numerous pas de deux guest-performances with Bruhn and Nureyev, becoming b.-dir. in Oslo 1966–70, where she played an active role in the formation of the Norwegian National B. Was b.-dir. of the Hamburg State Op. 1970–1, Artistic Dir. of San Diego B. and since autumn 1976 Dir. of D. Dpmt., Alabama School of Fine Arts. Married to the d. Thor Sutowski.
BIBL.: 'Olga Maynard Talks to S.A.', *Dance Magazine* (1969/5).

Arpino, Gerald (*b* West Brighton, Staten Island, 14 Jan. 1928). Amer. dancer, teacher, and choreographer. Studied with Mary Ann Wells in Seattle, and in New York at School of Amer. B., with O'Donnell and Shurr. Started to d. on Broadway and with Joffrey's first co. Teaches at the Amer. B. Center in New York and is now Associate Dir. of the City Center Joffrey B., for which he has ch. the majority of its specially created bs., being equally versed in the classical and modern idiom. Among his best known bs. are *Sea Shadow* (mus. Ravel, later replaced by M. Colgrass, 1962), *Viva Vivaldi!* (1965), *Olympics* (mus. T. Mayuzumi, 1966), *The Clowns* (mus. Kay, 1968), *Trinity* (mus. Lee Holdridge, 1971), *Reflections* (mus. Tchaikovsky, 1971), *Valentine* (mus. Jacob Druckman, 1971), *Kettentanz* (mus. Joh. Strauss sen. and Joh. Mayer, 1971), *Chabriesque* (1972), *Sacred Grove on Mount Tamalpais* (mus. Alan Raph, 1972), *Jackpot* (mus. Druckman, 1973), *The Relativity of Icarus* (mus. G. Samuel, 1974). *Orpheus Times Light* (mus. J. Serebrier, 1976), and *Suite Saint-Saëns* (1978). Dance Magazine Award (1974).
BIBL.: J. Gruen, 'G.A.' in *The Private World of Ballet* (New York, 1975); O. Maynard, 'A. and the Berkeley Ballets', *Dance Magazine* (1973/9).

Arqué (Fr., bowed). Bow-legged; the opposite is *Jarreté*.

Arrière, En (Fr., backwards).

Art of Movement Studio. Formed in Manchester in 1946 (the result of R. von Laban's lifelong research into the theory and practice of harmonious movement). It transferred to Addlestone in 1953, becoming incorporated into the Art of Movement Centre, which consists of a Research and Development and an Extra-Mural Department. Its director is Lisa Ullmann. Various courses are offered, all based on the principles and practice of movement and d.: the training of the body as an instrument of action and expression, the study of effort, rhythm, the shape of gesture and carriage, harmony of movement and the dynamic and spatial pattern of action, the study of group relationships, movement observation, methods of movement recording, the theory and practice of movement education, movement and work efficiency, and the adjustment of the individual and his or her social adaptation through movement. These courses serve not only the requirements of d. and th., but also the needs of professional workers in education, industry, and social work who wish to study movement and its specific use in their particular professions. Now incorporated in Laban Centre for Movement and D., Univ. of London, Goldsmiths' College.
BIBL.: A. Turnbull, 'The A.o.M.S.', *Dance and Dancers* (1969/6).

Arthur, Charthel (*b* Los Angeles, 8 Oct. 1946). Amer. dancer. Studied with Eva Lorraine, Nijinska, and at Amer. B. Center in New York. Made her début 1965 with the City Center Joffrey B. and has been a member of this co. ever since.

Asafiev, Boris Vladimirovich (*b* St. Petersburg, 29 July 1884, *d* Moscow, 27 Jan. 1949). Russ. composer. Wrote the mus. for 27 bs., incl. Vainonen's *Flames of Paris* (1932), Zakharov's *Fountain of Bakhchisaray* (1934), and Lavrovsky's *Prisoner of the Caucasus* (1938). Also a much-respected writer on b.

Asakawa, Takako (b Tokyo, 23 Feb. 1938). Jap. dancer. Studied at Komadori D. School. Toured with the musical revue *Holiday in Japan*, which brought her to New York, where she continued to study with Graham and Nemchinova. Joined Graham co. 1962, where she now dances some of the roles created by Graham. Has also appeared with the cos. of Lang, Ross, Ailey, McKayle, Falco, and Lubovich, now mostly with her own group, which she co-directs with her husband *D. Hatch-Walker.
BIBL.: J. Gruen, 'Ritual Union: Asakawalker', *Dance Magazine* (1980/1).

Åsberg, Margaretha (b Stockholm, 1939). Swed. dancer, teacher, and choreographer. Studied at Royal Swed. B. School, dancing with Royal Swed. B. 1957–62. Left the co. to study modern d. with Graham and at Juilliard School in New York. Returned to Stockholm as a teacher at the Ch. Institute 1967. Has also taught modern classes for the Royal Swed. B. Ch. . . . *from one point to any other point* (mus. Lars. Gunnar Bodin, 1969). Since 1973 has been president of Fylkingen Association for avant-garde mus. Teaches at Royal Swed. B. School.

Aschenbrödel. *Cinderella ballet in 3 acts, with orig. music by J. Strauss II, partly orch. by J. Bayer. First perf with ch. by E. Graeb (Berlin Staatsoper, 2 May 1901). Later versions ch. by J. Hassreiter (Vienna, 4 Oct. 1908); for TV by S. Barkóczy (1975), and as *Cinderella* by R. de Warren for Northern B. Th. (Manchester, 17 Dec. 1979). See also *Cinderella*.
BIBL.: P. Kemp, 'Johann Strauss and his Cinderella Stagework', with full historical background (Northern B. Th. prog., Manchester, 1979).

Aschengreen, Erik (b Copenhagen, 31 Aug. 1935). Dan. b. critic. Studied Univ. of Copenhagen and Sorbonne (Paris). D. critic at Berlingske Tidende, Copenhagen, since 1964. Dan. correspondent of *Dance Magazine* and *Les Saisons de la Danse*. Author of *Etudes* (Copenhagen, 1970); 'The Beautiful Danger: Facets of the Romantic Ballet', *Dance Perspectives* 58. Contributor on 'Bournonville, Biedermeier, and French Romanticism' in *Th. Research Studies* (Copenhagen, 1972). Assistant Professor at the Univ. of Copenhagen. Lecturer at the b. school of the Royal Th., Copenhagen.

Asel. Ballet in 3 acts; libr. Boris Khaliulov and Nikolai Kharitonov; mus. Vladimir Vlasov; ch. Vinogradov; déc. Valeri Leventhal. Prod. 7 Feb. 1967, Bolshoi Th., Moscow, with Ryabinkina, Timofeyeva, Fadeyechev, Sekh. The b. is based on Chingiz Aitmatov's romantic novel *My Little Poplar Sapling in a Red Kerchief* (known in Eng. as *To Have and to Lose*). The hero is a truck driver who returns to A., the woman he once left in pursuit of his new love, to find her happily married to a demobilized soldier. Each of the three protagonists tells the story from his or her own perspective.

BIBL.: N. Rene, 'The Cause of Controversy', *Dance and Dancers* (1967/11).

Asensio, Manola (b Lausanne, 7 May 1946). Swiss dancer. Studied at La Scala B. School. D. with Geneva B. 1963–4, Dutch National B. 1964–6, New York City B. 1966–8, Harkness B. 1969–74; principal d. with London Festival B. 1975–86.

Ashbridge, Bryan (b Wellington, 1926). N.Z. dancer. Studied with Kirsova and Borovansky, joined Sadler's Wells B. 1948, promoted soloist 1954, principal d. 1958, leaving the co. 1965. Has since been Associate Dir. of the Australian B.

Ashley, Merrill (b Linda Michelle Merrill, St. Paul, Minn., 2 Dec. 1950). Amer. d. Studied with Sybil de Neergaard, Phyllis Marmein, and at School of Amer. B. Joined N.Y. City B. 1967, appointed soloist 1974, principal d. 1977, creating parts in Robbins's *Requiem Canticles* (1972), Balanchine's *Ballo della Regina* (1977), and *Ballade* (1980). Wrote *Dancing for Balanchine* (1984).
BIBL.: T. Tobias, 'All-American A.', *Dance Magazine* (1979/6).

Ashmole, David (b Cottingham, 31 Oct. 1949). Brit. dancer. Studied at Kilbourn School, Wellingborough, and Royal B. School 1965–8. Joined Royal B. 1968, appointed soloist 1972, principal d. 1975. To Sadler's Wells Royal B. from 1976, where he dances leading roles in classical repertory, and created roles in Wright's *Summertide* (1976), Seymour's *Intimate Letters* (1978), Hynd's *Papillon* (1980), Bintley's *Homage to Chopin* (1980) and *Night Moves* (1981), and Corder's *Three Pictures* (1981). To Australian B. 1984.

Ashton, Sir Frederick (b Guayaquil, Ecuador, 17 Sep. 1904). Brit. d., ch., and b.-director. Studied with Massine and Rambert; started to ch. 1926 with *A Tragedy of Fashion* (for a Hammersmith revue). D. with the Rubinstein co. 1928–9; returned to Rambert and ch. for B. Club and Camargo Society. Became chief ch. of Vic-Wells B. 1935; stayed with the co. when it became the Sadler's Wells and finally the Royal B. Appointed its associate dir. 1952, and dir. 1963–70. Has also been guest ch. for B. Russe de Monte Carlo, Bs. de Paris, London Festival B., New York City B., Royal Danish B., and La Scala B., and film ch. for *Tales of Hoffmann* (with Massine, 1950), and *Tales of Beatrix Potter* (1971). Continues to work as a freelance ch. With his bs. he has led modern Eng. b. to its current world-wide reputation. He has created for it a repertory which shows remarkable versatility, and he has shaped its style of a soft, fluid, lyrical, musically highly sensitive classicism. He is as brilliant in creating new works as he is skilled in adapting historical bs., a ch. of faultless taste and cultivated nobility. Among the important artists who contributed to the shaping of his personality were the designer Fedorovitch and the conductor Lambert. One of his greatest achievements was the building up of Fonteyn's career—a collaboration between ch. and ballerina of rare distinction. Among his more important bs. have been: *Capriol Suite* (mus. Warlock, 1930), *Façade* (mus. Walton, 1931), *Les Rendezvous* (mus. Auber, 1933), *Mephisto Valse* (mus. Liszt, 1934), *Le Baiser de la Fée* (mus. Stravinsky, 1935), *Apparitions* (mus. Liszt-Lambert, 1936), *Les Patineurs* (mus. Meyerbeer-Lambert, 1937), *A Wedding Bouquet* (mus. Lord Berners, 1937), *Dante Sonata* (mus. Liszt-Lambert, 1940), *Symphonic Variations* (mus. Franck, 1946), *Scènes de ballet* (mus. Stravinsky, 1948), *Cinderella* (mus. Prokofiev, 1948), *Illuminations* (mus. Britten, 1950), *Daphnis and Chloë* (mus. Ravel, 1951), *Picnic at Tintagel* (mus. Bax, 1952), *Sylvia* (mus. Delibes, 1952), *Homage to the Queen* (mus. Arnold, 1953), *Romeo and Juliet* (mus. Prokofiev, 1955), *Birthday Offering* (mus. Glazunov, 1956), *La Valse* (mus. Ravel, 1958), *Ondine* (mus. Henze, 1958), *La Fille mal gardée* (mus. Herold-Lanchbery, 1960), *Les deux pigeons* (mus. Messager, 1961), *Persephone* (mus. Stravinsky, 1961), *Marguerite and Armand* (mus. Liszt-Searle, 1963), *The Dream* (mus. Mendelssohn-Lanchbery, 1964), *Monotones* (mus. Satie, 1965 and 1966), *Sinfonietta* (mus. M. Williamson, 1967), *Jazz Calendar* (mus. R. R. Bennett, 1968), *Enigma Variations* (mus. Elgar, 1968), *Lament of the Waves* (mus. Masson, 1970), *Creatures of Prometheus* (mus. Beethoven, 1970), *A Month in the Country* (mus. Chopin-Lanchbery, 1976), *Rhapsody* (mus. Rachmaninov, 1980); also ch. for the op. prods. of *Four Saints in Three Acts* (mus. Thomson, 1934), *The Fairy Queen* (mus. Purcell, 1946), *Orpheus and Eurydice* (mus. Gluck, 1953), and *Death in Venice* (mus. Britten, 1973). C.B.E. (1950). Royal Academy of Dancing Queen Elizabeth II Coronation Award (1959), knighted (1962), Légion d'honneur (1962), Commander of the Order of Dannebrog (1964), D. Magazine Award (1970), Carina Ari Gold Medal (1972). Dr. of Mus., h.c. (Oxford Univ., 1976), C.H. (1974), O.M. (1977).

BIBL.: Z. Dominic and J. S. Gilbert, *F.A.* (London, 1971); D. Vaughan, *F.A. and His Ballets* (London, 1977).

Assemblé (Fr., assembled). Designates the leap from one to both feet, usually landing in the fifth position. There are various sorts of As.: petits, grands, doubles, soutenus, simples, tournés, etc.

Assembly Ball. Ballet in 1 act and 4 movements; ch. and déc. Howard; mus. Bizet. Prod. 8 Apr. 1946, Sadler's Wells Op. B., Sadler's Wells Th., London, with Brae, Kersley, Newman. Based on Bizet's Symphony in C major, the b. deals loosely with the encounters, flirtations, and romances of several people at a ball. (Balanchine ch. the same mus. 1947.)

Association des écrivains et critiques de la danse. A Fr. society of writers on dance, founded 1935 with de Maré as its president. Reorganized after 1945 with Michel Georges as president and Lidova as secretary. Has been responsible for occasional gala performances with young dancers. Since 1951 it has awarded the annual Prix René Blum; some of its recipients have been Palley, Sombert, Seigneuret, Thibon, Piletta, Chaussat, and Pontois. Is now also in charge of the annual critics' prize of the Paris D. Festival, which has been awarded to Makarova, Bosch, Monin, Kirnbauer, Kun, and Rouba, among others.

Association of Dance and Mime Artists (ADMA). A professional association of British artists working in new dance and mime, esp. those independent of other cos. and organizations. Formed in 1977 to represent their common interests in relation to funding, the media, facilities for perfs. and other matters of concern, and to provide exchange of information.

Astafieva, Serafina Alexandrovna (*b* 1876, *d* London, 13 Sep. 1934). Russ. dancer and teacher. Studied at St. Petersburg Th. School, graduating 1895; member of the Maryinsky B. 1895–1905, d. with the Diaghilev co. 1909–11, then opened a school in London, where Markova, Dolin, and Fonteyn were among her students.

Astaire, Fred (orig. Frederick Austerlitz; *b* Omaha, Neb., 10 May 1899, *d* Los Angeles, 22 June 1987). Amer. dancer. One of the most famous tap-dancers of the century, whom Balanchine has called 'the most interesting, inventive, and elegant dancer of our time'. Started to d. in vaudevilles, appeared with his sister Adele in musicals on Broadway and in Shaftesbury Avenue. Later went to Hollywood, where he made some of his most popular films with Rogers (among others *Flying Down to Rio*, 1933; *The Gay Divorcée*, 1934; *Roberta*, 1935; *Top Hat*, 1935; *Swing Time*, 1936; *Shall We Dance*, 1937; *The Story of Vernon and Irene Castle*, 1939). Further films with Eleanor Powell (*Broadway Melody*, 1940), Rita Hayworth (*You'll Never Get Rich*, 1941), Judy Garland (*Easter Parade*, 1948), Leslie Caron (*Daddy Long Legs*, 1955), Audrey Hepburn (*Funny Face*, 1956), and Cyd Charisse (*Silk Stockings*, 1957), concentrating afterwards on acting roles. Various TV prods., the most successful *An Evening with F.A.* (NBC, 1958), and *Another Evening with F.A.* (NBC, 1959). Nine Emmy (TV) Awards, D. Magazine Award (1959). Author of *Steps in Time* (New York, 1959).

BIBL.: A. Croce, *The F.A.–Ginger Rogers Book* (New York, 1972); J. Domarchie, 'F.A.' with complete check-list of roles and activities, *Les Saisons de la danse* (1974/6); D. Harris, 'I Just Dance: F.A.', *Ballet News* (1981/8).

Astarte. Mixed media prod. by Joffrey; mus. Crome Syrcus (Beat Band); déc. and light. Thomas Skelton; film Gardner Compton. Prod. 20 Sep. 1967, City Center Joffrey B., City Center, New York, with Singleton and Zomosa. A young man approaches the stage, strips, dances with an oriental goddess-girl, and leaves again through the backstage door, while the camera follows him through the corridors into the street. Joffrey's first b. since 1963, meant as a shock-prod., bombarding the audience with a multitude of simultaneous impressions of vivid intensity.

BIBL.: 'A.' in *Balanchine's Complete Stories of the Great Ballets* (Garden City, N.Y., 1977).

As Time Goes By. Ballet in 3 parts; ch. Tharp; mus. Haydn; cost. Chester Weinberg. Prod. 24 Oct. 1973, City Center Joffrey B., City Center, New York, with Beatriz Rodriguez, Larry Grenier. Begins with an introductory solo in silence (Rodriguez), continues with the last 2 movements of Haydn's 'Farewell' Symphony; 'most of the time it is as though a fine lace had been laid upon the Haydn score' (J. Anderson).

BIBL.: 'A.T.G.B.' in *Balanchine's Complete Stories of the Great Ballets* (Garden City, N.Y., 1977).

Astuzie femminili, Le. Opera in 3 acts by Cimarosa. Prod. 1794 in Naples. Diaghilev asked Respighi to adapt it as a b.-op., produced with ch. by Massine, déc. by Sert, and his co. (augmented by some singers) on 27 May 1920 at the Paris Opéra, with Karsavina, Tchernicheva, Nemchinova, Massine, Idzikowsky, and Woizikovsky. In spite of its success in Paris and London, Diaghilev was dissatisfied with the prod., and readapted the dances for the b. *Cimarosiana*, which had its première on 8 Jan. 1924 in Monte Carlo.

Atanassoff, Cyril (*b* Puteaux, 30 June 1941). Fr. d. Studied at Paris Opéra B. School, joining the Opéra co. 1957; promoted premier danseur 1962, and danseur étoile 1964. Created roles in Béjart's *La Damnation de Faust* (1964), Descombey's *Sarracenia* (1964), and *Bacchus et Ariane* (1967), Petit's *Notre-Dame de Paris* (1965), Butler's *Intégrales* and *Amériques* (1973), Petit's *Nana* (1976), and Spoerli's *La Fille mal gardée* (1981). Retired 1986.

BIBL.: A.-Ph. Hersin, 'C.A.', with complete list of roles, *Les Saisons de la danse* (1968/11).

Atlanta Ballet, The. The Amer. co. started life in 1929 as Dorothy Alexander Concert Group—the first of the country's regional b. cos., closely connected with the Atlanta B. School. It rapidly extended its activities beyond the city, and became the Atlanta Civic B. 1944, as which it toured the U.S. and abroad, still with Alexander as its Founder-Dir. In 1967 the co. changed its name to the above, and it is now run by Robert Barnett as Art. Dir. In 1978 the co. consisted of a professional touring ensemble of 11 and a regional troupe of 26 dancers.

BIBL.: H. S. Smith, 'The A.B.: Fifty Golden Years, *Dance Magazine* (1979/11).

Atlas, Helen V. (*b* New York, 28 June 1931). Amer. editor and publisher. Studied with Mordkin and Anderson-Ivantzova and at Mount Holyoke College, South Hadley, Mass. (B.A.) After working as Russ. and Fr. interpreter for Hurok Concert, Inc., became ed. and pub. of *Dance News* in 1969 to its demise in 1983.

At Midnight. Ballet in 1 act; ch. Feld; mus. Mahler; sets Leonard Baskin; cost. Stanley Simmons. Prod. 1 Dec. 1967, Amer. B. Th., City Center, New York, with Marks, Sarry, Orr, Gregory. The b. is based on Mahler's four *Rückert Lieder*. Feld prefaces it with a quotation from Thomas Hardy: 'In the ill-judged execution of the well-judged plan, the call seldom produces the comer, the man to love rarely coincides with the hour for loving.' The b. shows the nostalgic agony of love. Also in the repertory of the Royal Swed. B. and the E. Feld B.

BIBL.: 'A.M.' in *Balanchine's Complete Stories of the Great Ballets* (Garden City, N.Y., 1977).

Attack. Denotes the sharp and incisive accentuation of a movement.

Attitude (Fr.). A position of the body inspired by Giovanni da Bologna's statue of Mercury, and codified by Blasis. The body is supported on one leg with the other lifted behind, the knee bent at an angle of 90°, turned out, with the knee higher than the foot. The corresponding arm is raised above the head, while the other arm is extended to the side. The various national schools have developed different variants. It can be executed in several ways: relevée, sautée, en tournant en avant (or en arrière), effacée, croisée, etc.

Aubade. Ballet in 1 act; libr. and mus. Poulenc; ch. Nijinska; déc. J.-M. Franck. Prod. 19 June 1929 at the Vicomte de Noailles, Paris. Poulenc has specified the b. as 'Concerto chorégraphique', asking that the small orchestra (piano and 18 instruments) shall be placed on the stage. The b. shows the encounter of Diana and Actaeon and his metamorphosis into a stag which is torn to pieces by her dogs. Later versions by Balanchine (Paris, 1930), Lifar (Monte Carlo, 1946), and Rosen (Munich, 1961). See *Diana Ballets*.

Auber, Daniel-François-Esprit (*b* Caen, 29 Jan. 1782, *d* Paris, 12/13 May 1871). Fr. composer. Wrote no bs., but the long interludes and divertissements in his grand operas became very important for the development of the romantic b.; for instance in *La Muette de Portici* (ch. Aumer, 1828), *Le Dieu et la Bayadère* (ch. F. Taglioni, 1830), *Gustave* (ch. Taglioni, 1833), *L'Enfant prodigue* (ch. Saint-Léon, 1850), and *Le Cheval de bronze* (ch. L. Petipa, 1857). He adapted the score of *Marco Spada* (ch. Mazilier, 1857) from his mus. for various ops.; it is quite different from his own op. on the subject. Several choreographers have since used mus. of his for their bs., among them Ashton (*Les Rendezvous*, 1937), V. Gsovsky (*Grand Pas Classique*, 1949) and L. Christensen (*Divertissement d'Auber*, 1959).

Audeoud, Susana. (*S.* Janssen, *b* Köniz, 10 Oct. 1919). Swiss dancer and teacher. Studied with Dora Garraux in Berne, Angiola Sartorio in

Florence, Preobrajenska, Volinine, and Kniaseff in Paris, and Span. d. with Estampio, La Quica, and Pericet. Prima ballerina of Madrid Op. in 1947. Gave her first Span. d. recital with Udaeta 1948 in Geneva, after which she became his regular partner, touring the world until 1970. Since her first summer course 1964 in Zurich has been in great demand as a teacher for Span. d. all over Europe and especially at Brussels Mudra School. Married to the composer Antonio Robledo.
BIBL.: G. Zacharias, *Susana y José* (Vienna, 1970).

Aufforderung zum Tanz. See *Spectre de la Rose, Le.*

Augusta, Mlle. (Caroline Augusta Josephine Thérèse Fuchs, Comtesse de Saint-James; *b* 1806, *d* 1901). Fr. dancer. She d. in Brussels in *La Muette de Portici* and *La Sylphide*, then went to the U.S. where she gave her début in *Les Naiades*, enjoying her greatest success in *La Bayadère* (1836) and as New York's first Giselle on 2 Feb. 1846 (though the Amer. Mary Ann Lee had d. the role a month earlier in Boston).

Augustyn, Frank (*b* Hamilton, Ont., 27 June 1953). Can. dancer. Studied at National B. School. Member of National B. of Can. since 1970, appointed soloist 1971, principal 1972. Has appeared with various cos. abroad, often partnering K. Kain. Principal d. of Ger. Op. Berlin since 1980–1. First Prize (Pas de deux category—with Kain), Intern. B. Competition, Moscow 1973. Order of Canada, 1979.
BIBL.: C. Darling and J. Fraser, *Kain and A.* (Toronto, 1978).

Auld, John (*b* Melbourne, 6 Jan. 1925). Austral. dancer and co. manager. Studied with Mme Borovansky, Preobrajenska, Goncharov, A. de Vos, Idzikowsky, and Nordi. Started to d. with Borovansky B., appeared in musicals and revues in London 1951–3, rejoined Borovansky B. as a soloist 1953–8, d. with B. of Two Worlds and with Festival B. 1960–4. Assistant art. dir. of Festival B. 1962–4, also b. master of the Gulbenkian B. 1964–70. Assistant to the directors and co manager of the Royal B. touring co. 1971 and then Assistant Dir. Sadler's Wells Royal B. Resigned in 1981.

Aumer, Jean (*b* Strasbourg, 21 Apr. 1774, *d* Saint-Martin-en-Bosc, July 1833). Fr. dancer and choreographer. Studied with Dauberval and was deeply influenced by his opinions on character d. and the *b. d'action*. Made his début as a d. under the Paris Opéra 1798. B.-master at the Paris Th. de la Porte Saint-Martin 1804–6, mounting several Dauberval bs. and ch. his own first works: *Rosina et Lorenzo* (1805), *Jenny ou Le Mariage secret* (1806), and *Les deux Créoles* (mus. Darondeau, 1806—based on the novel *Paul et Virginie*). His extremely successful *Les Amours d'Antoine et Cléopâtre* (mus. R. Kreutzer, Opéra, 1808) caused Jérôme Bona-

parte, King of Westphalia, to engage him for the Cassel court th. where he stayed until 1814. He then went to Vienna, ch. many bs. and divertissements until 1820, with *Les Pages du Duc de Vandôme* (mus. A. Gyrowetz) as his biggest success. Returning to Paris, he revived Dauberval's *La Fille mal gardée* and *Le Page inconstant* (the title of which refers to Cherubino from *Figaro*), ch. also *La Somnambule* (mus. Herold, 1827), *La Belle au bois dormant* (mus. Herold, 1829), and *Manon Lescaut* (mus. Halévy, 1830). He retired from the Opéra to Normandy in 1831.
BIBL.: I. Guest, in *The Romantic Ballet in Paris* (London, 1966); M. H. Winter, in *The Pre-Romantic Ballet* (London, 1974).

Aureole. Ballet in 1 act; ch. P. Taylor; mus. Handel. Prod. 4 Aug. 1962, Amer. D. Festival, Connecticut College, N.L., with Taylor, Elizabeth Walton, Wagoner, Sharon Kinney, René Kimball. Set to various orchestral pieces by Handel, the b. unfolds as a series of beautifully structured, crystal-clear dances in modern idiom. Revived for Royal Danish B. (1968) and for Paris Opéra (1974).
BIBL.: 'A.' in *Balanchine's Complete Stories of the Great Ballets* (Garden City, N.Y., 1977).

Auric, Georges (*b* Lodève, 15 Feb. 1899, *d* there 23 July 1983). Fr. composer. A member of the group of composers 'Les six'; contributed to the 1921 Cocteau prod. of *Les Mariés de la Tour Eiffel*. Later wrote the mus. for Nijinska's *Les Fâcheux* (1924), Massine's *Les Matelots* (1925), *Le Peintre et son modèle* (1949), and *Bal de voleurs* (1960), Balanchine's *La Concurrence* (1932), Lifar's *Phèdre*, and V. Gsovsky's *Chemin de lumière* (1952).

Aurora's Wedding (also Fr. *Le Mariage de la Belle au Bois dormant*). This is in effect the divertissement of the last act from *The Sleeping Beauty*, supplemented by some additional numbers based on the London Diaghilev prod. of 1921. Prod. 18 May 1922, Bs. Russes de Diaghilev, Opéra, Paris, with Trefilova and P. Vladimirov.

Ausdruckstanz. The general Ger. term for modern d. (literally expressive rather than expressionist d.), though it has been rejected by some of the most famous of its representatives (because they did not want to 'express' anything). Thus Wigman preferred to speak of the *Neue Künstlerische Tanz* (new artistic d.), while Milloss opted for *Freier Tanz* (free d.).

Australia. Individual dances in the course of th. perfs. date back to 1883, in which year a d. school was opened by a Mr Cavendish de Castell from the Paris Conservatoire in Sydney. Mme Velbein was appointed to take care of the d. at the Royal Victoria Th. 1840, and Mme Rosine was appointed b. mistress at the Melbourne Royal Th. By 1841 1-and 3-act bs. were very popular, incl. *The Millers, Freaks of Milor Plump Podin, Cobbler and Tailor, Polinchinelle Vampire, Mountain Ape,*

The Australian Ballet in André Prokovsky's *The Three Musketeers*.   Photo Branco Gaica.

and *Tawny in a Galloping Consumption*. Other bs. were brought by visiting Ital. and Eng. op. cos. (with *La Sylphide* and *La Fille mal gardée* on their programmes). Lola Montez made her sensational appearance 1855 and a little later the country raved about 'Tomato, the three-legged dancer'. For the prod. of *Sinbad the Sailor* 1889, J. C. Williamson of Melbourne engaged a corps de ballet which was then absorbed into the Comic Op. Co., with Mary Weir as ballerina. A school was opened 1897 on the stage of the Melbourne Princess Th. run by Minnie Everett, who followed it with another one in Sydney 1909. Minnie Hooper arranged 'some of the grandest ballets ever seen in this country, receiving praise from Melba herself'—these were for the Royal Comic Op. Cos. and the Melba Op. Co. A. Genée made her first appearance 1913 with a co. of Russ. Imperial Dancers, her bs. incl. *Coppélia, La Camargo,* and *La Danse*, as well as the inevitable *Dying Swan* (danced by Helena Schmolz). The next sensation was caused by Maud Allan, who came 1914. Then Pavlova visited the country 1926 and 1929, creating a deep and lasting impression. During the later 1920s some eminent foreign teachers made their homes here, incl. Errol Addison, Lucie Saronova, and Mischa Burlakov, who, with Louise Lightfoot, started the First Austral. B., even venturing to stage the first native prods. of *Petrushka, Sheherazade,* and *Carnaval*, plus *The Fruit of Forgetfulness* (based upon Gauguin's famous picture, with mus. by

Ramsay Pennycuick). Victor Dandré, Pavlova's husband, returned 1934 with a large co., the Levitoff Russ. B., headed by Spessivtseva and Vilzak. La Meri toured the country 1936; she was competing with de Basil's B. Russes de Monte Carlo, which scored a tremendous success, and returned in 1938 (as Covent Garden co.) and in 1940 (as Original B. Russe) when Lichine premièred his *Graduation Ball* in Sydney. About the same time the B. Contemporain was formed in Adelaide backed by the Univ. Th. Guild, and the South Australian B. Club was founded by Joanne Priest, whose bs. incl. *Lady Augusta* (about the inauguration of the Murray River Trade). Gertrud Bodenwieser came from Vienna in 1939, opening a school and touring with her co. Some members of the de Basil cos. remained: Helene Kirsova, who opened a school in Sydney, from which her co. derived, and Borovansky and his wife Xenia, who opened another school in Melbourne in 1939, which soon started to give studio perfs., and became the Australian B. 1940, managed by J. C. Williamson; from this co. emerged the present *Australian B. Various clubs and guilds were formed during the mid 1940s, generating a lively interest in b. matters. After the Second World War various visiting cos. began to appear, and today the country is regularly visited by famous cos. from all over the world, as well as contributing substantially through its own cos. to the intern. scene. Apart from *the Australian B. and the *Australian D. Th., other

resident cos. incl. the North Fremantle-based West Australian B., dir. by Robin Haig, the Brisbane-based Queensland B., dir. by Harold Collins, and the *Sydney D. Co., dir. by Graeme Murphy. The main schools are the Australian B. School (Melbourne), the Scully-Borovansky School (Sydney), the Lorraine Norton School (Sydney), the Kathleen Gorham B. Academy (Melbourne), and the Bodenwieser D. Centre (Sydney).
BIBL.: E. H. Pask, *Enter the Colonies Dancing—A History of Dance in A. 1835–1940* (Melbourne, 1979).

Australian Ballet, The. The co., the leading classical troupe of its country, is based on Melbourne, where it was founded 1962, absorbing a great number of the ds. from the former Borovansky B., with Van Praagh as its Art. Dir. (later joined by Helpmann). It is closely linked with the Royal B. and its school. With Lanchbery as Mus. Dir., Bryan Ashbridge and Ray Powell as Assoc. Dirs, the co., consisting of 57 dancers in 1979, encompasses the classical tradition: its ds. are equally at home with the divergent ch. styles of Ashton, Balanchine, Bournonville, Butler, Cranko, Fokine, Helpmann, MacMillan, Massine, Nureyev, Petipa, Petit, Tetley, and Tudor. Among its most popular prods. is Nureyev's *Don Quixote* (also filmed in 1973). Specially commissioned bs. have been Helpmann's *The Display* (1964), *Yugen* (1965), and *Sun Music* (1968), Butler's *Threshold* (1968), Tetley's *Gemini* (1973), Hynd's *Merry Widow* (1975), Prokovsky's *Anna Karenina* (1979), and B. Wells's *The Hunchback of Notre Dame* (1981). Since its London début 1965, the co. has toured extensively: Eur. (1965), Can. and South Amer. (1967), the U.S. (1970–1). Helpmann was art. dir. 1974–5, succeeded by A. Woolliams 1976–7. Van Praagh returned 1978–9, since when the co. has been directed by Marilyn Jones, with R. Powell and B. Ashbridge as assoc. dirs., and M. Gielgud since 1983/4.
BIBL.: P. Van Praagh, *Ballet in Australia* (Melbourne, 1965).

Australian Dance Theatre. Modern d.-orientated co. based on Adelaide, founded by Elizabeth Dalman 1965. Reorganized 1977 to serve both Victoria and S. Australia, with J. Taylor as artistic dir. The repertory incl. creations by J. Taylor, N. Morrice etc. and made first Eur. tour to Edin-burgh Festival, Holland and Poland in 1980. J. Taylor replaced by L. Warren as art. dir. 1985.

Austria. Apart from the various cos. based in *Vienna (where during the 1981/2 season the State Op. B. is headed by G. Brunner, the Volksoper by G. Senft, the Th. an der Wien by Matyas Jurkovics, and the Raimund Th. by V. Avratova), the following cities have b. cos. attached to their municipal ths.: Graz (V. Orlikovsky), Klagenfurt (Radomir Krulanovic), Salzburg (Leonard Salaz), Innsbruck (Alexander Meissner), Linz (Alexander Schneider), St. Pölten (Susanne Papez), and Baden (Monika Wiesler).

Autumn Leaves. Ballet in 1 act; libr. and ch. Pavlova; mus. Chopin; déc. Konstantin Korovin. Prod. 1918, B. A. Pavlova, Rio de Janeiro, with Pavlova, Volinine. Set to various piano pieces by Chopin, the b. shows the fate of a chrysanthemum, lovingly tended by a poet in his garden, which is killed by the ruthless north wind.

Avant, En (Fr., forward). Designates all forward-directed movements.

Aveline, Albert (*b* Paris, 1883, *d* Anvières, 3 Feb. 1968). Fr. dancer, choreographer, teacher, and b.-master. Entered Paris Opéra B. School 1894, joining its co. after graduation; became one of its most popular étoiles and 1917 its b.-master. Later appointed dir. of its B. School. Was one of the favourite partners of Spessivtzeva. Staged revivals of some of the bs. by Mérante, Staats, and Clustine. Ch. *La Grisi* (mus. O. Métra, 1935), *Le Festin de l'araignée* (mus. Roussel, 1939), *Jeux d'enfants* (mus. Bizet, 1941), *La grande jatte* (mus. Fred Barlow, 1950), and the prologue for *Les Indes galantes* (mus. Rameau, 1952).

Avrahami, Gideon (*b* Tel Aviv, 31 Oct. 1941). Israeli dancer. Studied with Rina Shenan, Sokolow, and Graham. First d. in the Israel prod. of *My Fair Lady*. Joined Batsheva D. Co. 1966. Member of B. Rambert 1968–74, where he created parts in Chesworth's *Pawn to King 5* (1968), Morrice's *The Empty Suit* (1970) and *Spindrift* (1974), and Bruce's *There Was a Time* (1973). Ch. *Full Circle* (mus. Bartók, 1972). In 1975 became first D. Officer to be appointed by a regional Arts Assoc. in Brit. dir. EMMA D. Co. 1975–81, now dir. of D. Studies, Leicester Polytechnic.

B

Babilée, Jean (orig. J. Gutman; *b* Paris, 2 Feb. 1923). Fr. dancer, choreographer, and actor. Studied at Paris Opéra B. School, and with Kniaseff, Volinine, and V. Gsovsky. Started to d. in the early forties in Cannes and Monte Carlo, joining the corps of the Opéra. Took part in the Paris Soirées de Danse, for which he also did his first ch. (*Sérénité*, mus. Beethoven) 1944. Danseur étoile of the Bs. des Champs-Elysées 1945 and of the Bs. de Paris from 1947. Guest periods with Amer. B. Th., at the Maggio Musicale Fiorentino, the Paris Opéra, and La Scala di Milano. Founded Les Ballets J.B. 1956, with which he has undertaken several foreign tours. Dir. of the B. du Rhin (Strasbourg) 1972–3. Has appeared in several films and as a stage actor. His charismatic personality and his dazzling technique (especially his soaring leaps) made him one of the most admired dancers of his generation, particularly known for his Blue Bird and in *Spectre de la rose*. Some of his most famous role creations were in Charrat's *Jeu de cartes* (1945), Petit's *Le jeune homme et la mort* (1946), Lichine's *Oedipe et le Sphinx* (1948), his own *Till Eulenspiegel* (1949), Massine's *Mario e il mago* (1956), Dick Sanders' *Maratona di danza* (1957), and Lazzini's *Prodigal Son* (1967). Among the better known of the bs. he created were *L'Amour et son amour* (mus. Franck, 1948), *Till Eulenspiegel* (mus. Strauss, 1949), *Balance à trois* (mus. Damase, 1955), *Sable* (mus. Le Roux, 1956), *Caméléopard* (mus. Sauguet, 1956), *La Boucle* (mus. Damase, 1957), and *Haï-Kaï* (mus. Webern, 1969). Acting roles in *Le Balcon* (J. Genet) and *La Reine verte* (Béjart). Was married to the d. Nathalie Philippart. His daughter Isabelle B. made her début as Princess in her father's *The Soldier's Tale* in 1971.
BIBL.: C. Brahms, 'J.B.', in *Dancers and Critics* (London, 1950). N. McLain Stoop, 'B.', *Dance Magazine* (1979/7).

Baby Ballerinas. The nickname of Baronova, Toumanova, and Riabouchinska, who at the foundation of the B. Russe de Monte Carlo (1933) were 13, 14, and 15 years old respectively.

Baby Stork, The. See *Little Stork, The.*

Baccelli, Giovanna (*b* Venice, *c.* 1753, *d* London, 7 May 1801). Ital. dancer. Made her début in 1774 at the London King's Th. and in 1782 became a member of the Paris Opéra. Became famous as partner of A. Vestris and LePicq in Noverre's *Caprices de Galathée* and *Médée et Jason*, also in Gardel's *Ninette à la cour*. She was very popular, and was notorious as the mistress of the

Duke of Dorset: Reynolds and Gainsborough painted portraits of her.
BIBL.: I. Guest, 'The Italian Lady of Knole', in *The Ballet Annual* no. 11.

Bacchanale. (1) Originally the ancient Roman orgies of Dionysus or Bacchus. Very popular in b. in form of a divertissement of character-dances, celebrating the autumn vintage festival. Two of the best known specimens in ops. are to be found in Wagner's *Tannhäuser* (ch. L. Petipa, Paris 1861) and Gounod's *Faust* (ch. Henri Justament, Paris 1869)—both also often performed as individual bs. (2) Ballet in 1 act; libr. and déc. Dali; ch. Massine; mus. Wagner. Prod. 9 Nov. 1939, B. Russe de Monte Carlo, Met. Op. House, New York, with Krassovska, Theilade, Eglevsky, Platoff. Set to the *Tannhäuser* B., the work is a surrealistic phantasmagoria, with Ludwig II of Bavaria as its protagonist who identifies himself with various figures from Wagner's operas. Other ch. treatments of the same mus. by L. Petipa (the opera's Paris 1st prod. in 1861), Duncan (Bayreuth, 1904), Laban and Jooss (Bayreuth, 1930), and Béjart (Bayreuth, 1961—later as a separate b., *Venusberg*, Brussels, 1965).
BIBL.: (Massine version): C. W. Beaumont, 'B.' in *Supplement to Complete Book of Ballets* (London, 1952).

Bacchus and Ariadne (orig. Fr. title: *Bacchus et Ariane*). Ballet in 2 acts; libr. Abel Hernant; mus. Roussel; ch. Lifar; déc. de Chirico. Prod. 22 May 1931, Opéra, Paris, with Lifar, Spessivtzeva, Peretti. The b. retells the famous story of Theseus's return from the labyrinth, the celebration of his victory over the minotaur, Bacchus's enchantment of Ariadne, whom he saves from drowning herself when she thinks herself abandoned by Theseus, the bestowing of immortality on her through Bacchus's kiss, and their final union in a Bacchanale. A later version by Descombey (Paris Opéra, 1967).
BIBL.: D. Mitchell, 'B.a.A.' in *The Decca Book of Ballet* (London, 1958).

Bach, Johann Sebastian (*b* Eisenach, 21 Mar. 1685, *d* Leipzig, 28 July 1750). Ger. composer. Wrote no b.-mus., but his concert and church mus. has been often used for b. purposes. Among the more important Bach bs. are: Nijinska's *Etude* (Paris, 1931), Fokine's *Les Eléments* (Overture in B minor, London, 1937), Balanchine's *Concerto Barocco* (Concerto for 2 Violins in D minor, New York, 1941), Lifar's *Dramma per musica* (Coffee Cantata, Monte Carlo, 1946), Petit's *Le jeune homme et la mort* (Passacaglia in C minor, Paris, 1946),

Charrat's *Diagramme* (Brandenburg Concerto no. 6, Paris, 1957), Gore's *Night and Silence* (various pieces, Edinburgh, 1958), Macdonald's *Aimezvous Bach?* (various pieces, Alberta, 1962), Harkavy's *Recital for Cello and Eight Dancers* (Suite for Solo Cello no. 6, The Hague, 1964), Cranko's *Brandenburg nos. 2 & 4* (London, 1966), Béjart's *Actus tragicus* (Cantatas nos. 106 and 51, Brussels, 1969), Robbins's *The Goldberg Variations* (New York, 1971), Van Manen's *Opus Lemaitre* (Toccata and Fugue in D minor, Paris, 1972), P. Taylor's *Esplanade* (various pieces, New York, 1975), Béjart's *Notre Faust* (B Minor Mass, Brussels, 1975), and Neumeier's *St. Matthew Passion* (Hamburg, 1981).

Badings, Henk (*b* Bandung, Java, 17 Jan. 1907). Dutch composer. Wrote several b.-scores—among them *Kain* (ch. Jan L. Zielstra, The Hague, 1956), *Electronic Ballet* (ch. Georgi, Hanover, 1957), *Evolutions* (ch. Georgi, Hanover, 1958—also used by Van Dantzig for his *Jungle*, Amsterdam, 1961 and by J. Taylor for *Diversities*, B. Rambert, 1966), and *The Woman of Andros* (ch. Georgi, Hanover, 1960).

Bagnolet. The Paris suburb of B. established its annual Concours International de Chorégraphie: Le Ballet pour Demain in 1969. Organized by the municipal cultural service, with subventions from the Fr. Ministry of Culture, and patronized by the Intern. Council of D. as part of the UNESCO, it has since become under the energetic artistic direction of Jacques Chaurand one of the foremost Eur. platforms for aspiring young amateur and professional choreographers to present their works. Awards are distributed in the 'catégorie professionels' and the 'categorie non-professionels' plus an additional 'prix de l'humeur'.

Baignères, Claude Pierre (*b* Clarens, Switzerland, 29 June 1921). Fr. b. critic. Educated at Univs. of Aix-en-Provence and Paris. D. critic of *Le Figaro* since 1957. Author of *Ballets d'hier et d'aujourdhui, Alicia Markova, Yvette Chauviré*.

Baiser de la Fée, Le (also Eng. *The Fairy's Kiss*). Ballet in 1 act and 4 scenes; libr., mus., and cond. Stravinsky; ch. Nijinska; déc. Benois. Prod. 27 Nov. 1928, Bs. I. Rubinstein, Opéra, Paris, with Rubinstein, Schollar, Vilzak. 'A fairy marks a young man with her mysterious kiss while he is still a child . . . She withdraws him from life on the day of his greatest happiness in order to possess him and preserve this happiness for ever. She marks him once more with her kiss' (from the composer's note prefacing the published score). The story is based on Hans Andersen's fairy-tale *The Ice Maiden*. Later versions by Ashton (Sadler's Wells B., 1935), Balanchine (Amer. B., 1937—the Divertissement only in a new version, New York City B., 1972), MacMillan (Royal B., 1960), Hynd (Dutch National B., 1968—also London Festival B., 1974), and Neumeier (also

using mus. by Tchaikovsky, Frankfurt, 1972—also Amer. B. Th., 1974).

BIBL.: G. Balanchine, 'L.B. d.l.F.', in *Balanchine's Complete Stories of the Great Ballets*, (Garden City, N.Y., 1977).

Baker, Josephine (*b* St. Louis, 3 June 1906, *d* Paris, 12 Apr. 1975). Amer.-Fr. revue-dancer and chanteuse. Started as a chorus-girl in a negro revue in Philadelphia, went to Europe 1925, appearing first in the Paris Revue Nègre, after which she reigned for almost 30 years as one of the stars of the Paris music halls. She toured the world; a series of farewell perfs. began in the late fifties but she continued to appear for special occasions. She had a unique blend of singing, reciting, and dancing, combined with inimitable sex-appeal and minimal dress. She spent her last years in South-West France, where she cared for dozens of adopted children from all over the world. Author of *Mémoires* (1927).

Bakhrushin, Yuri Alexeievich (*b* Moscow, 27 Jan. 1896, *d* there, 4 Aug. 1973). Russ. b.-critic and historian. The son of Alexei B. (1865–1929), founder of the famous Moscow B. Theatre Museum; he started to write on b. 1918, continuing to teach, lecture, advise, and write throughout his life. Among his most important publications were 'Tchaikovsky's Ballets and Their Stage History' (in *Tchaikovsky and the Theatre Almanach*, 1940), *A. A. Gorsky* (1946), *Bolshoi Ballet* (1948), and *History of Russian Ballet* (1965), which is the official text-book used at all b.-schools throughout the U.S.S.R.

Bakst, Léon (orig. Lev Semuilovich Rosenberg; *b* Grodno, 10 May 1866, *d* Paris, 28 Dec. 1924). Russ. painter and designer. A co-founder of the magazine *The World of Art (Mir Iskusstva)*, published by Diaghilev 1899; later one of the most influential members of the Diaghilev circle and the Bs. Russes. After designing the 1903 prod. of *The Fairy Doll* for St. Petersburg, he did the déc. for the Diaghilev prods. of *Cléopâtre* (1909), *Carnaval* and *Sheherazade* (1910), *Spectre de la rose* and *Narcisse* (1911), *Le Dieu bleu, Thamar, L'après-midi d'un faune*, and *Daphnis and Chloë* (1912), *Jeux* (1913), *La Légende de Joseph* (cost. only, 1914), *Les Femmes de bonne humeur* (1917), and *The Sleeping Princess* (1921). For Rubinstein he designed *Le Martyre de Saint-Sébastien* (1911).

BIBL.: A. Alexandre, *L'Art décor de L.B.* (Paris, 1913); A. Levinson, *L.B.* (Paris, 1927); C. Spencer, *L.B.* (London, 1973).

Bal, Le. Ballet in 1 act and 2 scenes; libr. Kochno; mus. Rieti; ch. Balanchine; déc. di Chirico. Prod. 7 May 1929, Bs. Russes de Diaghilev, Monte Carlo, with Danilova, Dolin, Doubrovska, Lifar, Balanchine. The b. shows a masked ball, at which a young officer pursues a beautiful woman with his attentions.

Balabina, Feya Ivanovna (*b* Rostov-na-Donu,

11 June 1910). Russ. dancer and teacher. Studied at the Leningrad B. School with Vaganova, joined the Kirov B., and was one of its solo dancers 1931–56, creating Jeanne in Vainonen's *Flames of Paris* 1932. After her active career made Artistic Dir. of her former school; retired 1972.

Balancé (Fr., balanced). Designates in b. a rocking step from one foot to the other, mostly executed in 3/4 time.

Balance à trois. Ballet in 1 act; libr. Constantin Nepo; mus. J.-M. Damase; ch. Babilée; déc. Tom Keogh. Prod. 25 Apr. 1955, Bs. Jean Babilée, Monte Carlo, with Chauviré, Kalioujny, Babilée. The b. is set in a gymnasium, with two athletes parading in front of a girl.

Balanchine, George (orig. Georgi Melitonovich Balanchivadze, *b* St. Petersburg, 22 Jan. 1904, *d* N.Y., 30 Apr. 1983). Russ.-Amer. d., ch., and b.-director. Entered Petrograd B. School in 1914, graduated in 1921, and became a member of the GATOB, simultaneously starting to study mus. Created his first bs. in 1920 for the Evenings of Young B. He ran into considerable trouble with his traditionally-minded superiors by choreographing some very unconventional pieces. Touring Germany with his small co. of Soviet State Dancers in 1924, he auditioned for Diaghilev, who immediately engaged him and, and after some op. chs., promoted him chief ch. of his Bs. Russes in 1925. From this time dates his life-long friendship with Stravinsky. After Diaghilev's death in 1929 he worked temporarily for the Paris Opéra, the Royal Danish B., and R. Blum's B. Russe de Monte Carlo, becoming art. dir. 1933 of Les Bs. 1933. At Kirstein's invitation he went to the U.S. 1933, starting the School of Amer. B. He recruited some of its best student-dancers for his first Amer. co., which as Amer. B. made its New York début 1935 and was then invited by the Met. Op. House to become its resident co. for the 1935–8 seasons, with the Stravinsky Festival of 1937 as climax. The co. then had to be disbanded, while B. continued to teach and choreograph for various groups (among them the B. Russe de Monte Carlo) and for Hollywood films and worked on Broadway musicals. With the reassembled Amer. B., called Amer. B. Caravan, he toured South America in 1941. In 1946 he became one of the co-founders of the B. Society, appearing in 1947 as a guest ch. at the Paris Opéra. In 1948 the B. Society became the New York City B. with the City Center as its permanent home. As its artistic dir., B. created his great corpus of modern ch. In 1950 he and his co. embarked on their first Europ. visit, to London. Retaining NY as his base, he was frequently guest ch. for the leading West-Eur. cos., occasionally also directing op.-prods. (mostly in Hamburg). In 1962 he and his co. visited the U.S.S.R. for the first time. Since 1964 the New York City B. has occupied the New York State Th.

at Lincoln Center, built according to B.'s specifications. The week-long Stravinsky Festival of 1972 set the seal on his intern. reputation. He was undoubtedly one of the greatest choreographers in the history of b. He found his own style with *Apollon musagète* in 1928, becoming one of the dominant forces o' neoclassicism, to which he always returned afte、 is wide-ranging excursions. He was a past master of the plotless b., while most of his action bs. have been controversial. Through him Amer. has established a direct and creative link with the Eur. b.-tradition, reacting on it through the numerous stagings of his bs. by Europ. cos. He married four of his ballerinas: Geva, Zorina, Maria Tallchief, and LeClercq. The following represent a selection from his vast list of works—for Basil B. Russe: *Cotillon* (mus. Prokofiev, 1929);—for Diaghilev's B. Russes: *Le Chant du rossignol* (mus. Stravinsky) and *Barabau* (mus. Rieti, 1925), *Apollon musagète* (mus. Stravinsky, 1928), *Le Bal* (mus. Rieti) and *The Prodigal Son* (mus. Prokofiev, 1929);—for Les Bs. 1933: *Mozartiana* (mus. Tchaikovsky; rev. production NYCB 1981), *The Seven Deadly Sins* (mus. Weill), and *Errante* (mus. Schubert-Liszt);—for Amer. B.: *Serenade* (mus. Tchaikovsky, 1934), *Le Baiser de la Fée* (mus. Stravinsky) and *Jeu de cartes* (mus. Stravinsky, 1937);—for Amer. B. Caravan: *Concerto Barocco* (mus. Bach) and *Ballet Imperial* (mus. Tchaikovsky, 1941);—for B. Russe de Monte Carlo: *Danses concertantes* (mus. Stravinsky, 1944), *Night Shadow* (mus. Bellini-Rieti, 1946), and *Raymonda* (together with Danilova, mus. Glazunov 1946);—for B. Society: *The Four Temperaments* (mus. Hindemith, 1946) and *Orpheus* (mus. Stravinsky, 1948);—for Paris Opéra: *Le Palais de cristal* (alias *Symphony in C*, mus. Bizet, 1947);—for Amer. B. Th.: *Theme and Variations* (mus. Tchaikovsky, 1947);—for New York City B.: *Firebird* (mus. Stravinsky) and *Bourrée fantasque* (mus. Chabrier, 1949), *La Valse* (mus. Ravel, 1951), *Caracole* (mus. Mozart) and *Scotch Symphony* (mus. Mendelssohn, 1952), *Opus 34* (mus. Schoenberg), *Nutcracker* (mus. Tchaikovsky), *Western Symphony* (mus. Kay), *Ivesiana* (all 1954), *Pas de dix* (mus. Glazunov, 1955), *Allegro Brillante* (mus. Tchaikovsky) and *Divertimento no. 15* (mus. Mozart, 1956), *Agon* (mus. Stravinsky, 1957), *Stars and Stripes* (mus. Sousa-Kay) and *The Seven Deadly Sins* (mus. Weill, new version 1958), *Episodes* (mus. Webern, 1959), *Monumentum pro Gesualdo* (mus. Stravinsky) and *Liebeslieder Walzer* (mus. Brahms, 1960), *A Midsummer Night's Dream* (mus. Mendelssohn, 1962), *Bugaku* (mus. Mayuzumi) and *Movements for Piano and Orchestra* (mus. Stravinsky, 1963), *Don Quixote* (mus. Nabokov, 1965), *Variations* (mus. Stravinsky, 1966), *Jewels* (mus. Fauré, Stravinsky, and Tchaikovsky, 1967), *Metastaseis & Pithoprakta* (mus. Xenakis, 1968), *Slaughter on Tenth Avenue* (mus. R. Rodgers, 1968), *Who Cares?* (mus. Gershwin, 1970), *Symphony in Three Movements* (mus. Stravinsky), *Violin Concerto* (mus. Stravinsky), *Duo concer-*

tant (mus. Stravinsky), *Pulcinella* (together with Robbins, mus. Stravinsky, all 1972), *Variations pour une porte et un soupir* (mus. P. Henry), *Coppélia* (with Danilova, 1974), *Sonatine*, and *Tombeau de Couperin* (both mus. Ravel, 1975), *Vienna Waltzes*, (mus. Joh. Strauss, Lehár, R. Strauss, 1977), *Ballo della Regina* (mus. Verdi), *Kammermusik No. 2* (mus. Hindemith, 1978); prod. of *Le Bourgeois gentilhomme* (mus. R. Strauss) and *Dido and Aeneas* (mus. Purcell) for N.Y. City Op. (1979), *Davidsbündlertänze* (mus. Schumann, 1980). In addition he ch. various musicals (*On Your Toes*, 1936; *The Boys from Syracuse*, 1938), films (*The Goldwyn Follies*, 1938; *On Your Toes*, 1939; *A Midsummer Night's Dream*, 1966), and the TV première of Stravinsky's *Noah and the Flood* (1962). Opera prods. by him were Ravel's *L'Enfant et les Sortilèges* (Monte Carlo, 1925), Gluck's *Orpheus and Eurydice* (N.Y., 1936), Stravinsky's *The Rake's Progress* (N.Y., 1953), Tchaikovsky's *Eugene Onegin* (Hamburg, 1962), and Glinka's *Ruslan and Ludmila* (Hamburg, 1969). There are many TV films of his bs., most from the occasion when 15 of his bs. were produced for TV in Berlin. Author (with F. Mason) of *B.'s Complete Stories of the Great Ballets* (Garden City, N.Y., 1977—1st ed. 1954). Dance Magazine Award (1964); Handel Medallion of the city of N.Y. (1970); honorary degrees from several univs.; Légion d'Honneur (1975); Order of Dannebrog (1978); U.S. Medal of Freedom (1983).
BIBL.: B. Taper, *B.* (N. Y., 1984, new edn.); H. Koegler, *B. und das moderne Ballett* (Velber-Hanover, 1964); B. portfolio in *Dance Magazine* (1972/6); *Choreography by B: A Catalogue of Works* (N. Y., 1983); see also *New York City B.*

Balançoir (Fr., swing). A seesaw exercise at the bar, a grand battement with the leg swinging forcefully forward and backward while the body leans in the opposite direction.

Balasaraswati (*b* Madras, *c.* 1919, *d* Madras 9 Feb. 1984). Ind. dancer. When she was four began to study with Kandappa Nattuvanar who remained her mentor when she later continued with Gauri Ammal, Chinnayya Naidu, and Lakshmi Narayana Shastri. Her début took place when she was seven at the Ammanakshi Amman temple in Kanchipuram, from where she progressed to Madras, already astonishing the public everywhere with the eloquence and perfection of her art. Later she toured Eur. and the U.S. and taught at the Music Academy in Madras. Considered the greatest Bharata Natyam d. of the day.
BIBL.: R. Singha and R. Massey, 'B.', in *Indian Dances*, (London, 1967).

Balashova, Alexandra Mikhailovna (*b* 3 May 1887, *d* Chelles, nr. Paris, 8 Jan. 1979). Russ.-Fr. dancer and teacher. Studied at Moscow Th. School, joining Bolshoi B. 1905, eventually appointed ballerina, with her best roles in *La Fille mal gardée*, *Coppélia*, *Swan Lake*, and *La Bayadère*.

Her last creation at the Bolshoi was *Salome*, ch. by Gorsky 1921. Left Moscow 1922 and settled in Fr., where she continued to d. at the Paris Opéra and at numerous galas. Opened a school of her own in Paris 1931. Staged various prods. of *La Fille mal gardée*, incl. Nouveau B. de Monte Carlo (1946).

Bal de blanchisseuses, Le. Ballet in 1 act; libr. Kochno; mus. V. Duke; ch. Petit; déc. Stanislav Lepri. Prod. 19 Dec. 1946, Bs. des Champs-Elysées, Th. des Champs-Elysées, Paris, with Danielle Darmance, Petit. A ball in the streets of Paris is improvised when a handsome young apprentice starts to flirt with a laundress and her colleagues.

Bal des cadets. See *Graduation Ball.*

Baldina, Alexandra Vasilievna (*b* St. Petersburg, 27 Sep. 1885). Russ.-Amer. dancer and teacher. Studied at St. Petersburg Th. School, graduated into the Maryinsky Th. b. co., but soon transferred to the Moscow Bolshoi B., where she became a ballerina. Created Prélude in Fokine's *Les Sylphides* (1909). D. with the Diaghilev co. during its early seasons. Then went with her husband, the d. Theodore Kosloff, to the U.S., where they both taught in Los Angeles.
BIBL.: V. H. Swisher, 'A.B.-K.', *Dance Magazine* (1975/12).

Bales, William (*b* Carnegie, 27 June 1910). Amer. dancer and teacher. Studied at Olive and Amour Studios in Pittsburgh and with Humphrey and Weidman. D. with the Humphrey-Weidman co. 1936–40, also appearing at Radio City Music Hall and on Broadway, and as a member of the Dudley-Maslow-Bales D. Co. 1942–52. Has taught at Humphrey-Weidman Studio, Bennington School of D., Connecticut College, Univ. of Cal. at Los Angeles; Dean of Division of D. at State Univ. of New York, College at Purchase 1967–75. Author of *A Curriculum Statement for a Liberal Arts College.*

Balet Praha. See *Prague Ballet.*

Ballabile (Ital., danceable). (1) The term for a group or corps de ballet d. without solos. It is to be encountered in a great number of bs. of the romantic period, but also in the ops. of the 19th century. (2) Ballet in 1 act and 6 scenes; ch. Petit; mus. Chabrier arr. Lambert; déc. Clavé. Prod. 5 May 1950, Sadler's Wells B., Cov. Gdn., London, with Elvin, Negus, Grant, Chatfield. A loose succession of sketches and impressions without a definite plot: dancers at their exercise, a circus intermezzo, a Sunday on the river, a funeral in the rain, a boisterous Span. fiesta.

Ballerina (Ital., female dancer). A principal female d. in a b. co. See also *Prima ballerina.*

Ballet (1) (Fr., from Ital. balletto, diminutive of ballo, dance). (a) The theatrical d. of occidental culture, presented in artistically stylized form; (b) the work thus presented; (c) a co. performing those works. The term should properly be used only for works based on the *danse d'école*, i.e. the codified academic theatrical d. and its legitimate extensions, but now folklore ensembles and jazz d. groups call themselves b. cos. and even works based on modern d. are termed bs. (2) Eng. magazine, edited by Richard Buckle, published in 2 issues July–Aug. and Sept.–Oct. 1939, resumed in Jan. 1946, and continued on a monthly basis until Oct. 1952 (from Oct. 1948 to Dec. 1949 it appeared as *Ballet and Opera*).

Ballet (History of). The Western form of th. d. sprang from the renaissance festivities of the Ital. courts and the efforts of the 16th-century Fr. Académiciens to reestablish the basic relationship between poetry, mus., and d. as epitomized in the classical Greek th. This brought forth the bs. de cour of the Paris court of Catherine de' Medici, with the *Ballet Comique de la Reine* of 1581 setting an example to be followed by a multitude of lesser achievements. They were executed by members of the nobility only, performed in banquet halls rather than in ths., and accompanied not only by mus. but also by words. At the court of Louis XIV the new art form enjoyed special popularity. The king himself participated in some of the comédie-bs. of Molière, Lully, and Beauchamp, while the Académie Royale de Danse, established 1661, and the school of dancing attached to the Académie Royale de Musique, which opened 1672, embarked on the codification of the approved steps and movements, and the education of professional dancers for the new ths.; the 1st ballerina appeared in *Le Triomphe de l'amour* in 1681. Gradually the b. de cour gave way to the still very formal b. d'action, which emerged from the attempts at telling a story through the marriage of d.-steps and mime gestures—without any spoken words. Foreshadowed in the London works of Weaver, its most famous advocates were Angiolini in Vienna and Noverre in Stuttgart and Vienna during the 1760s and 1770s. 1789 saw the advent of yet another type, aiming for greater realism—the demicaractère b. as exemplified by Dauberval's *La Fille mal gardée*. The pupils of Angiolini, Noverre, and Dauberval spread the gospel of their masters. Viganò and Blasis in Milan, Didelot in St. Petersburg, and Galeotti and Bournonville père in Copenhagen made their cities vie with each other for the perfection of their art. The highest point was undoubtedly reached at the Paris Opéra, with Filippo Tagioni's b. of nuns in Meyerbeer's op. *Robert le Diable* in 1831 and his *La Sylphide* in 1832. With such ballerinas as Taglioni, Elssler, Grisi, and Cerrito the 1830s and 1840s witnessed the Golden Age of b. London actively participated in the international b. boom, and Copenhagen under Bournonville fils developed its own brand of charming middle-class b. romanticism. While Western b. suffered a severe decline during the 2nd half of the 19th century, St. Petersburg came to the fore, under the Fr. M. Petipa, cultivating

its refined yet dramatic form of Tsarist classicism which culminated in the 3 Tchaikovsky bs., *Sleeping Beauty* (1890), *Nutcracker* (1892) and *Swan Lake* (1895); offshoots spread to Moscow, generating a more Russ. coloured variant under Gorsky. From the best dancers of both cities Diaghilev assembled a troupe which he brought to Paris in 1909, where the bs. of the young Fokine created a sensation through their marvellous artistic integrity. For the next 20 years Diaghilev's Bs. Russes dominated the international b. scene, establishing new standards of artistic perfection—supplemented by Pavlova's co., Les Bs. Suédois, and the troupe of Rubinstein. All served to promote the cause of b. against the gradually growing modern dance movement, with the Amer. Duncan and St. Denis as its leading figures and Laban and Wigman almost as important in Europe. While the U.S.S.R. developed its own species of socialist b. realism after 1917, the dispersal of the Bs. Russes after Diaghilev's death in 1929 served to encourage the building up of new national schools. The 1930s thus became formative years: Lifar brought back some of the former splendour to the Paris Opéra, while in London Rambert and de Valois laid the foundation of what was to develop into the B. Rambert and the Royal B., and in Amer. Balanchine started the School of Amer. B., from which the New York City B. was to grow. Through Diaghilev the status of the ch. had been considerably raised, and with artists of the calibre of Fokine, Massine, Nijinska, Balanchine, Ashton, Tudor, and Robbins (and Graham in the modern d. field), the 20th century witnessed the definite arrival of the ch. as the *primus inter pares* among a b.'s authors. Travelling ensembles sprang up everywhere and supplemented the resident cos. attached to the op. houses all over the world. Thus b. gained increasing popularity during the 2nd half of the 20th century, and countries like Belgium, the Netherlands, Ger., Swed., Can., Jap., and Austral. discovered and exploited their b. potentials. There is now a world-wide exchange of ideas, artists, works, and cos. such as has never been experienced before.

BIBL.: M. Clarke and C. Crisp, *Ballet—An Illustrated History* (London, 1973).

Ballet Annual, The. Eng. year book, edited by Arnold Haskell, published from 1947 to 1963. C. W. Swinson and G. B. L. Wilson were Associate Editors for the 2nd volume (1948), Mary Clarke and Ivor Guest for the 7th volume (1954). Clarke became co-editor in 1961.

Ballet aux ambassadeurs polonais (also *Le Ballet des Polonais*). Divertissement commissioned by Catherine de' Medici in honour of the Polish ambassadors and prod. 19 Aug. 1573 at the Palace des Tuileries, Paris. The ch. consisted of strictly geometrical patterns, arranged by B. de Beaujoyeux to mus. by Orlando di Lasso. 16 ladies from the court represented the 16 provinces of France.

As a suite of consecutive dances it is considered one of the seminal predecessors of the *Ballet Comique de la Reine.

BIBL.: L. Kirstein, 'L.B.d.P.', in *Movement & Metaphor* (New York, 1970).

Ballet blanc (Fr. white b.). Designates a b. in the classical style in which the danseuses wear the white tulle skirts introduced by Taglioni in *La Sylphide* in 1832. Typical examples are the 2nd act of *Giselle* and *Les Sylphides*.

Ballet Caravan. L. Kirstein founded this co. in 1936 to function as a platform for young Amer. choreographers. Bs. first performed by it incl. L. Christensen's *Pocahontas* (mus. E. Carter), *Encounter* (mus. Mozart), and *Filling Station* (mus. V. Thomson, 1937), Dollar's *Promenade* (mus. Ravel, all 1936), Loring's *Yankee Clipper* (mus. P. Bowles), and *Billy the Kid* (mus. Copland, 1938). In 1938 the co. changed its name to Amer. Ballet Caravan. Joined with the Amer. B. 1941 for its South Amer. tour; B.C. disbanded after its return Oct. 1941.

Ballet Comique. A short-lived British co. founded in 1954 by George Kirsta, who also designed most of its prods. Its best creation was *Eugene Onegin*, romantic b. in one act, (mus. Tchaikovsky, arr. Hancock; ch. V. Gsovsky). Jack Carter, Peter Darrell, and Michel de Lutry also created bs. for the co. Principal dancers were Irène Skorik, Dominic Callaghan, Xenia Palley, Stanley Williams (also ballet master), Denys Palmer, Bjorn Holmgren, and de Lutry. Disbanded after one tour.

Ballet Comique de la Reine (also *Balet Comique de la Royne*). The prod., a mixture of recitation, singing, and dancing, is generally considered as the first b. It was performed on 15 Oct. 1581 at the Paris Hôtel de Bourbon in the Louvre, on the occasion of the marriage between the Duc de Joyeuse and Mlle. de Vaudemont (Marguerite de Lorraine). The book was written by La Chesnay, the mus. by Lambert de Beaulieu and Jacques Salmon, the déc. was designed by Jacques Patin and the man responsible for the whole prod. was Balthasar de Beaujoyeux (Baldassaro de Belgiojoso). It lasted from 10 p.m. to 3.30 a.m., and showed scenes from the Circe legend. The corps was made up of 12 Naiads, acted by members of the aristocracy. Jupiter, Pallas Athene, Pan, and Mercury were protagonists and there were Dryads, 4 Virtues, and 8 Satyrs. The ch. was strictly geometrical, consisting mainly of circles, spirals, triangles, and squares. The immensely successful spectacle, which included a great number of technical effects and a huge triumphal car, cost more than 3½ million gold francs. Basically it represented a blend of the court allegories and masquerades and the aesthetic principles of the Académie de Poésie et de Musique, which provided for the printing of its book.

BIBL.: L. Kirstein, 'B.-C. d.l.R. Louise', in *Movement & Metaphor* (New York, 1970).

Ballet Contemporaneo de la Ciudad de Buenos Aires. See *San Martin Ballet*.

Ballet d'action (Fr., b. with a story). A b. with a dramatically shaped structure, designed to convey a story. There should be a perfect integration of libr., mus., ch., and déc. The B.d'a. thus represents the opposite of the Divertissement, which has the character of a suite. Though Noverre is generally considered the first representative of the B.d'a., other choreographers such as Weaver, Hilverding, and Angiolini helped to prepare the ground for it.

Ballet de chevaux (Fr., b. on horseback). Performed by knights on horseback; enjoyed special popularity during the 17th century. Menestrier considered 'les pas des chevaux comme des vraies figures de danse, en rapport avec les sons et les airs, qui guident les chevaux au cours du ballet' (the horses' steps as true d. figures, in harmony with the sounds and tunes, which guide the horses during the ballet). In 1606 a *Ballet à cheval des quatre élements* was performed in Paris. In 1608 a *Ballo di persone a cavallo: La Giostra dei Venti* was staged in Florence. In Vienna these 'Ross-Ballette' were particularly popular; the most spectacular was in 1666 for the marriage of Leopold I and Margharita Theresa of Spain: *La Contessa dell'paria e dell'aqua*—succeeded in 1667 by *La Germania esultante*, described as a 'Festa a cavallo'. The Lipizzaner perfs. at the Span. Riding School of Vienna may be considered their late descendants.

Ballet de cour (Fr., court b.). Derived from the court masquerades and allegorical/mythological Trionfi, and performed exclusively by aristocratic amateurs instructed by a professional d.-master. Even the Fr. kings liked to participate. Its most brilliant period was between 1580 and 1660. Vocal and instrumental mus., recitation, d., pantomime, and ceremonial processions had an equal share in it. In addition there were spectacular technical effects and sumptuous décors and costumes. Usually there was a poetic Leitmotiv. Topical references were given a mythological or allegorical disguise. Generally the *Ballet Comique de la Reine* of 1581 is considered the first legitimate B.d.c. Later the amateurs were gradually replaced by professional artists, performing in front of paying audiences. The slowly crystallizing formula consisted of overture, up to 5 entrées, and grand b. The members of the Académie de Poésie et Musique functioned as censors.

BIBL.: H. Prunières, *Le B.d.c. en France avant Benserade et Lully* (Paris, 1914); M. M. McGowan, *L'Art du B.d.c en France 1581–1643* (Paris, 1963); M.-F. Christout, *Le B.d.c. de Louis XIV* (Paris, 1967) and 'The Court Ballet in France', *Dance Perspectives* 20; B. Quirey: 'An Introduction to Baroque Ballet' (English Bach Festival programme book, 1976).

Ballet de Cuba. See *National Ballet of Cuba.*

Ballet de France. The Bs. de Janine Charrat, set up in 1951, first appeared under this name in 1955, when her *Le Massacre des Amazones* was premièred. Later 1st prods. of the co. were her *Herakles* (1953), *Les Liens* (1957), *Chimère* (1958), *Paris* (1964), and *Up to date* (1968).

Ballet de la nuit. One of the representative Bs. de cour. Text de Benserade, mus. Jean de Cambefort and Jean-Baptiste Boësset, ch. Chancy, Mollier, Manuel, Vertpré, and Lully, machinery effects G. Torelli, cost. Henry de Gissey (?). Prod. 23 Feb. 1653, Salle du Petit-Bourbon, Paris. Lasting 13 hours, the b. started at sunset, presenting the mythological figures of the night and some nocturnal episodes, Lully, who arranged the scene at the court of miracles, and himself played Sosias in a mimed Amphitryon episode, was appointed court comp. of the bs. of the King after the performance. Louis XIV, not yet 15 years old, participated in various roles, culminating in his appearance as the sun, whereafter he was called the Sun King.
BIBL.: M.-F. Christout, in *Le B.d.c. de Louis XIV* (Paris, 1967); L. Kirstein, 'Le B. d.l.n.', in *Movement & Metaphor* (New York, 1970).

Ballet del Teatro San Martin. See *San Martin Ballet.*

Ballet des Etoiles de Paris. The co. first appeared as Bs. 1956 de Paris at the Festival of Lyon-Charbonnières, with Miskovitch and Lidova as artistic directors. Later it called itself B. 1958 des Etoiles de Paris; the year in the title was changed annually until 1961 when it was abandoned. Its aim was 'to emphasize the qualities and the style of a *danseur étoile*, and to project with the message of all forms of contemporary dance something of the *esprit* and the taste of Paris' (programme note). A co. of soloists, consisting at its 1st appearances of Miskovitch, Monin, H. Trailine, Mlakar, Sparemblek, and Sulich—later members were Y. Meyer, Pagava, Sifnios, Skorik, and Banovitch. Its most popular bs. were Taras's *Le Rideau rouge*, Lifar's *L'Ecuyère*, Charrat's *La Dryade*, D. Sanders's *L'Echelle*, Béjart's *Prométhée*, and Sparemblek's *Quatuor.*

Ballet des Polonais, Le. See *Ballet aux ambassadeurs polonais.*

Ballet de Wallonie. See *Ballet royal de Wallonie.*

Ballet Director. The term is of fairly recent origin, designating the person who heads a b. co. He or she can be either a manager or an artist, who will then often also act as chief ch. A synthesis of both types has produced some of the most influential people in the ballet world, e.g. Diaghilev, de Maré, Kirstein, and Kochno. He or she is responsible for the definition of the co.'s policy, its general aesthetic outlook, the principles of its repertory policy, the selection of staff-

members as well as the engagement of guest choreographers, dancers, and starring guests. It is he or she who is finally responsible for the image of the co. See also *Ballet Master.*

Ballet du Rhin. The co., based on Strasbourg and performing regularly in Mulhouse and Colmar, was founded in 1972, with Babilée as its dir. After Babilée had left, D. Carey took over for the 1973–4 season. P. van Dyk was dir. 1974–8, succeeded by Jean Sarelli.

Ballet du XXe Siècle. See *Ballet of the 20th Century.*

Ballet Folklorico de Mexico. The co. was founded 1952 by A. Hernandez for the special purpose of producing Mex. folklore dances for TV with some of her students of the department for modern d. at the Instituto Nacional de Bellas Artes in Mexico City. Later the Mex. government became its sponsor, sending the co. abroad. Enormous success everywhere led to its official acknowledgement as the national folklore co.; Hernandez is still its dir. Today considered one of the most artistically gifted folklore cos. in the world. On its tours it has appeared regularly all over Europe and the U.S.

Ballet for All. This offshoot of the Royal B. co., consisting of dir. b.-master, 6 dancers, 2 pianists, and 2 actor-narrators, was founded 1964 with a twofold aim: 'to introduce ballet to those who have not seen it, or who may have lacked the chance to do so; and to extend the knowledge of those who have seen it, but wish to learn more about it.' The man behind it who wrote the specially devised '* ballet-plays' was P. Brinson, its 1st dir. succeeded by A. Grant 1971–6, D. Adams 1976–7, then by b. master O. Symons 1977–9. Its dancers were lent by the Royal B. for a limited stay with the co. Its programmes always centre on a single theme; some of the most successful have been *The World of Giselle*, *Ashton and La Fille mal gardée*, *Two Coppélias*, and *Birth of the Royal Ballet*. Disbanded April 1979. A specifically educational group of the same name under direction of R.A.D. was formed to replace it, but was discontinued in 1979 after one tour.
BIBL.: L. E. Stern, 'B.f.A.', *Dance Magazine* (1973/5).

Ballet Imperial. Ballet in 3 movements; ch. Balanchine; mus. Tchaikovsky; déc. Doboujinsky. Prod. 29 May 1941, Amer. B., Hunter College Playhouse, New York, with Marie-Jeanne, Caccialanza, Dollar. Set to Tchaikovsky's Piano Concerto no. 2 in G Major, this is a rigidly classical, plotless b. tribute to Petipa and the St. Petersburg b. of his time. Revived for Sadler's Wells B., 1950 (déc. Berman) and New York City B., 1964 (déc. Ter-Arutunian). Now called *Tchaikovsky Piano Concerto No. 2.*
BIBL.: G. Balanchine, 'B.I.', in *Balanchine's Complete*

The Ballet of the 20th Century in Béjart's *Les Illuminations*.   Photo Gert Weigelt.

Stories of the Great Ballets (Garden City, N.Y., 1977).

Ballet Internacional de Caracas. The co., based upon the capital of Venezuela, was established in 1975 by the Fundacíon Pro-Artes Coreográficas. It gave its debut perf. on 4 Sep., 1975, at the local Teatro Municipal, since when it has had numerous seasons at home as well as toured widely abroad. Most of the bs. of its repertory have been ch. by its artistic dir., V. Nebrada. The co. numbers about 20 dancers, headed by Z. Rodriguez, A. Filipov, and Z. Wilson.
BIBL.: N. McLain Stoop, 'The B.I.d.C. and Two of Its Dancers', *Dance Magazine* (1978/1).

Ballet International. See *Grand Ballet du Marquis de Cuevas.* Also a short-lived London-based co. with sponsorship of Orange Free State, S. Afr., 1977.

Ballet Master (also Maître de ballet). The term has changed considerably over the centuries. Formerly it designated the man who at the court or the th. was responsible for the arrangement and prod. (sometimes even for the musical composition) of the dances and the well-being of the dancers. Today it most often designates the man who is responsible for setting and controlling the co.'s daily rehearsal schedule, not to be confused with the co.'s dir., ch., or teacher (with the smaller cos., however, the various functions often overlap). He has to arrange the rehearsals and to maintain the quality of execution of a b. after the ch. and his assistants have finished their work. He continues their work, polishes, coaches dancers in their new roles, and prepares everything for an appropriate performance. See also *Ballet Director.*

Ballet mécanique. Composition by Antheil, written in 1925, though not for the th., but for a surrealist film which the painter F. Léger was to design.

Ballet Nacional de Cuba. See *National Ballet of Cuba.*

Ballet National Jeunesses Musicales de France, Le. The co., which enjoyed the official backing of the J.M.d.F., was founded in June 1963, after which it made several tours through France and abroad. Its dir. was P. Lacotte, who contributed the large majority of the repertory's bs.—among them *Gosse de Paris, La Femme et sa fable, Hippolyte et Aricie, Penthesilée, Hamlet,* and

Numéros. Other choreographers who have worked with the co., which gradually faded out during the late sixties, incl. Skibine, Taras, and Descombey.

BIBL.: *Ballet News*, No. 1 (1979/5).

Ballet of Flanders (Ballet van Vlaanderen). The Belg. co. was founded Dec. 1969, with Brabants as dir.; Leclair as chief-ch. Based in Antwerp, it performs as an autonomous ensemble, also appearing in the op. prods. of the op. hos. in Antwerp and Ghent. It also travels to other Belg. cities and has occasionally appeared abroad. The classically based co. has about 50 ds., incl. Patricia Carey, A. de Lignière, S. Schuller, and Ben van Cauwenbergh. The repertory incl. a wide choice of styles and chs., with Bournonville, Jooss, de Valois, Cullberg, Flindt, Van Dantzig, Van Manen, J. Carter, and Butler supplementing the bs. of Leclair and Brabants. Since 1977 the co. has called itself Royal B. of F., with V. Panov as art. dir. 1984–6.

BIBL.: R. Barbier, *Van Operaballet naar Ballet van Vlaanderen* (Antwerp, 1973).

Ballet of the 20th Century (official title: Ballet du XXe Siècle). The co., based in Brussels, where it regularly performs at the Th. Royal de la Monnaie, the Cirque Royal, and the Forest National, was founded in 1960, and has since undertaken world-wide tours, appearing in Great Britain and the U.S. for the 1st time in 1971. The bulk of its repertory was created by its artistic dir. Béjart—other choreographers have occasionally worked for the co., e.g. Sparemblek, Charrat, Milloss, Massine, and Dolin, while the dancers of the co. have also regularly been stimulated to contribute bs. of their own. Its dancers come from all over the globe. From its very beginnings it has had an especially impressive contingent of male dancers. Among its best known members have been A. Albrecht, T. Bari, P. Belda, V. Biagi, P. Bortoluzzi, A. Cano, G. Casado, K. Csarnóy, J. Donn, S. Farrell, M. Gielgud, L. Höfgen, D. Laga, A. Leclair, J. Lefebre, D. Lommel, W. Lowski, I. Marko, M. Martinez, Lorca Massine, S. Mírk, R. Poelvoorde, L. Proença, M. Seigneuret, D. Sifnios, and P. Touron. The co. has gained world-wide popularity with its mass-spectacles, especially with the younger generation, while more sophisticated audiences have often complained about the lack of ch. substance and mus. traducement. A selection of representative prods. must incl. *Sacre du printemps* (mus. Stravinsky, 1959—for an especially assembled co. which provided the kernel of the later co.), *Bolero* (mus. Ravel, 1960), *Les quatre fils Aymon* (1961), *Tales of Hoffmann* (the Offenbach op., 1961), *A la Recherche de Don Juan* (1962), *Les Noces* (mus. Stravinsky, 1962), *The Merry Widow* (the Lehár operetta, 1963), *Ninth Symphony* (mus. Beethoven, 1964), *Mathilde* (mus. Wagner, 1965), *Romeo and Juliet* (mus. Berlioz, 1966), *Messe pour le temps présent* (mus. P. Henry, 1967), *Baudelaire* (1968), *Les Vainqueurs* (mus.

Wagner, 1969), *The Firebird* (1970), *Offrande chorégraphique* (1971), *Nijinsky, Clown de Dieu* (1971), *Stimmung* (mus. Stockhausen, 1972), *Le Marteau sans maître* (mus. Boulez, 1973), *Golestan—Le Jardin des roses* (1973), *Trionfi* (1974), *Pli selon pli* (mus. Boulez, 1975), *Notre Faust* (mus. Bach, 1975), *Le Molière Imaginaire* (mus. div., 1976), *Petrushka* (mus. Stravinsky, 1977), *Gaîté Parisienne* (mus. Offenbach/Rosenthal, 1978), *Dichterliebe* (mus. Schumann, 1978), *Les Illuminations* (mus. div., 1979), and *Magic Flute* (mus. Mozart, 1981). See also *Béjart, Maurice.*

BIBL.: M.-F. Christout, in *Béjart* (Paris, 1972); A. Livio, in *Béjart* (Lausanne and Zurich, n.d. (1972?)); portfolio in *Dance Magazine* (1975/12).

Balletomane. A person suffering from 'balletomania'—a term coined to designate originally the intense form of partisan b. interest of Russian b. audiences during the 19th century, running through all stages of infection, from critical connoisseurship to wild hysteria. In his book *Balletomania* (1934) A. Haskell introduced the term to Western usage.

BIBL.: A. Chujoy, 'Russian Balletomania', *Dance Index* VII, 3.

Ballet Opera. Designates a form of op., in which the d. enjoys an equal, or even a dominating partnership. It incl. the majority of tragédies lyriques by Campra, Lully, and Rameau. Later specimens are Rimsky-Korsakov's *The Golden Cockerel* and Henze's *Boulevard solitude*. Ops. with a large share of d. are often produced as b.o.s— for instance Gluck's *Orpheus and Eurydice*, which has been treated thus by Balanchine, Wigman, de Valois, and Bausch. Occasionally choreographers banish the singers from the stage altogether or place them at the proscenium, entrusting all the action to the dancers; e.g. in Fokine's *The Golden Cockerel*, Walter's *Orfeo* (Monteverdi), Massine's *Il barbiere de Siviglia*, Antonio's *La vida breve* (Falla), and Béjart's *Tales of Hoffmann*. See *Opéra Ballet.*

Ballet Pantomime. (1) The sort of pantomime developed specially for the needs of b., with fixed gestures to express an emotion or to project a concrete story-telling element (the Scène de pantomime roughly resembles the recitative in op.) (2) Bs. which lean heavily on the projection of a dramatic story, where the telling of the content may be more important than the d. proper (the early ballets d'action were thus mostly called B.Ps.—for instance Angiolini-Gluck's *Don Juan*, but even Lengyel-Bartók's *The Miraculous Mandarin* received its 1st prod. as a pantomime). The Danes have developed a special brand of B.P. which still enjoys undiminished popularity at the Copenhagen Tivoli Pantomime Th.

BIBL.: J. Lawson, *Mime* (London, 1957).

Ballet Play. Special form of theatrical programmes, which P. Brinson developed for the perfs. of the Ballet for All group of the Royal B. from 1963. They combine narration and d. in a solid theatrical context (with mus., costumes, props, and sets or projected backdrops) and focus on a single theme: e.g. *The World of Giselle* (1963), Ashton and *La Fille mal gardée* (1964), *Two Coppélias* (1970), *Sun King, Swan Queen* (1971), *Birth of the Royal Ballet* (1972), and *World of Harlequin* (1973).

Ballet Rambert. This, the oldest of existing Eng. b. cos., emerged from individual b. prods. started by Marie Rambert 1926. After 2 short spring seasons 1930, Oct. of that year saw an experimental season at the London Mercury Th., backed by the newly founded Ballet Club. Its regular Sunday matinées became a platform for young Brit. choreographers. Among the first choreographers presented by Rambert were Ashton (*A Tragedy of Fashion*, 1926), Tudor (*Cross-Garter'd*, 1931), and Howard (with Susan Salaman; *Our Lady's Juggler*, 1933). Gradually the traditional classics entered the repertory (though at first only in excerpts). There followed the first visits to the provinces and 1937 to France. Further important prods. of these very creative early years, which continued through the war: Ashton's *Capriol Suite* (1930),

Façade (1931), and *Les Masques* (1932), Tudor's *The Planets* (1934), *Jardin aux lilas* (1936), and *Dark Elegies* (1937), Howard's *Mermaid* (1934) and *Lady into Fox* (1939), Staff's *Peter and the Wolf* and *Enigma Variations* (1940), and Gore's *Simple Symphony* (1944). After the war came the first overseas tours, incl. visits to China (1957) and the U.S. (1959). Rambert now actively furthered the choreographers of the post-war generation: Morrice (*Two Brothers*, 1958; *Hazaña*, 1959; *A Place in the Desert*, 1961; *Conflicts*, 1962; *The Travellers*, 1963; *The Realms of Choice*, 1965) and J. Taylor (*Diversities*, 1966), with Cranko (*Variations on a Theme*, 1954; *La Reja*, 1959) and MacMillan (*Laiderette*, 1955) among her guests. During the early 1960s there were especially successful prods. of *La Sylphide, Night Shadow* and *Don Quixote*. Some of the best known dancers of the co.'s first 3 decades were Argyle, Ashton, Tudor, Turner, Hinton, Gilpin, B. Wright, Paltenghi, Goldwyn, Bennett, Aldous, and Bannerman. In 1955 David Ellis joined as associate dir. Besides its discovery of new choreographers, the co. gradually developed an individual chamber-like style of

The Ballet Rambert in Tetley's *Embrace Tiger and Return to Mountain*.   Photo Anthony Crickmay.

producing the classics. After the co. had run into various crises, a complete reorganization took place in the summer of 1966. The classics were abandoned and from the old repertory little more than the Tudor bs. were kept. Instead the accent shifted to the assimilation of Amer. modern d. techniques. The co. was reduced to 17 dancers, each with solo status. Morrice became associate dir., choreographing *Them and Us* and *1–2–3* (1968), *Pastorale variée* and *Blind Sight* (1969), *That Is the Show* (1971), and *Isolde* (1973). Apart from J. Taylor ('*Tis Goodly Sport*, 1970; *Listen to the Music*, 1972) newly discovered d.-choreographers were Chesworth (*Time Base*, 1966; *Tic-Tack, H,* and *Pawn to King 5,* 1968; *Four According,* 1970; *Pattern for an Escalator,* 1972), Bruce (*George Frideric* and *Living Space,* 1969; . . . *for these who die as cattle,* 1972; *There was a Time, Duets,* 1973, and *Ancient Voices of Children,* 1975; *Black Angels,* 1976; *Cruel Garden,* 1977; *Ghost Dances,* 1981) and some others. The most decisive influence of the 'new B.R.' (for a time mostly performing at the Jeannetta Cochrane Th., but now also frequently at Sadler's Wells Th.), however, has been Tetley, who mounted his *Pierrot lunaire, Ricercare,* and *Freefall* (1967), and created *Ziggurat* (1967), *Embrace Tiger and Return to Mountain* (1968), *Rag Dances* (1971), and *The Tempest* (1979). During workshop seasons collaborations with th. design students of the art academies were started and new ways to break through to the younger generation of audiences explored, resulting in occasional seasons at the Young Vic and the Round House. Of all the established London b. cos. the B.R. now has one of the most open-minded and progressive young publics. J. Chesworth was appointed art. dir. 1974, Bruce assoc. dir. 1975, (from 1979 associate ch.) R. North, art. dir. 1981, with R. Alston as resident ch. R. Alston art. dir. since 1986.

BIBL.: M. Clarke, *Dancers of Mercury* (London, 1962); Interview with N. Morrice on 'Direction Change', *Dance and Dancers* (1968/8); J. Percival, 'B.R.: The Company That Changed Its Mind', *Dance Magazine* (1973/1); complete list of prods up to 1979 in souvenir-programme of *The Tempest,* also in C. Crisp, A. Sainsbury, P. Williams (eds.), *Ballet Rambert: 50 Years and On* (London, 1981).

Ballet Review. An irregular Amer. publication of exceptional intellectual standards, which appeared for the first time as a completely privately run venture during the mid-sixties (undated), with A. Croce as its editor. Its 3rd issue first showed the year of its publication: 1966. Since vol. 3, no. 6 (1971) it has been published by D. Research Foundation, Inc. Apart from Croce its associated and contributing editors have been David Vaughan, Don McDonagh, George Dorris, Jack Anderson, Robert Cornfield, Nancy Reynolds, Francis Mason and Don Daniels. Now edited by Francis Mason.

Ballet Royal de Wallonie. The co., based in Charleroi, was founded Dec. 1966, integrating the former B. du Hainaut of Hanna Vooss, who was appointed artistic dir., with T. Hulbert as chief ch. Classically based, with some 50 dancers, the co. in 1981 has Guy Rassel as dir. général, J. Lefèbre as artistic dir., Jaky Richard as b. mistress, with M. Martinez, Gabriella Cohen, Noelle Taddëi, Annie Savouret, Estale Erman, and Jean-Pierre Laporte, Jacques Dombowski, and John Lohan as first soloists. It regularly tours Belgium and abroad.

Ballet Russe de Monte Carlo. The co. descended from R. Blum's Ballets de Monte Carlo, which itself resulted from Blum's separation from the Ballets Russes de Monte Carlo. At the foundation Massine acted as artistic dir., choreographing *Gaîté Parisienne* and *Seventh Symphony* for the opening season in Monte Carlo (April 1938). June 1938 saw the notorious season at the London Drury Lane Th., when the Colonel de Basil Ballets Russes appeared at the neighbouring Cov. Gdn. Op. House, resulting in a lawsuit between the 2 cos. for the performing rights of the Diaghilev repertory (de Basil was awarded the exclusive rights to perform some Massine bs.). In Oct. the co. went to the U.S. which became its permanent home during the war. Massine stayed until 1945, aiming for a continuation of the original Ballets Russes policy. Dancers during the war years incl. Danilova (prima ballerina 1938–51), Markova, Slavenska, Toumanova, Franklin, Platoff, Youskevitch, and Zoritch, and temporarily also Lifar. During the Second World War (in which Blum died at Auschwitz) more and more young Americans joined the co. 1942 saw the première of de Mille's sensationally successful *Rodeo,* 1944 the Balanchine bs. *Danses concertantes* and *Le Bourgeois gentilhomme,* 1946 his *Night Shadow.* S. Denham became b. dir. 1942. In 1944 Franklin was appointed b. master. The co. performed mostly in the Amer. provinces, relying mainly on the box-office appeal of its old Eur. repertory. New bs. became increasingly rare and were generally of little artistic importance. One of the more ambitious undertakings was Balanchine's and Danilova's 3-act version of *Raymonda* (1946). But the final decline had already started, and in the early 1950s it was disbanded. Refounded in 1954 with Maria Tallchief and Franklin as stars and Novak, Tyven, Chouteau, Borowska and Danielian as soloists, it toured the smaller U.S. cities, gradually disappearing from the scene, until after the 1962–3 season it completely vanished, with a short-lived attempt at reviving it in Monte Carlo. The last repertory additions of some merit were Rosen's *The Lady and the Unicorn* (1953) and Massine's *Harold in Italy* (1954). However, the co. has never been officially dissolved and still runs its own school in New York. See *Ballets de Monte Carlo, Ballets Russes de*

M. C. Nouveaux Ballets de M. C., Original Ballet Russe.
BIBL.: J. Anderson: *The One and Only: The B. Russe de M. C.* (N. Y., 1981).

Ballets Africains de la Republique de Guinée, Les. The co. was founded in 1950 by Keita Fodéba in Conakry. Originally based on male dancers only, it presented 'songs and dances, belonging both to the traditional and colonial Africa of our ancestors and to contemporary Africa, which is assimilating more and more of Western civilization' (Fodéba). Very French in its taste and outlook, its programmes reflect the basic problems Africa is facing today, the fight between tradition and modern achievements. It has successfully toured Europe and the U.S.

Ballet School (orig. Fr. title: *Leçon de Danse*, also *School of Ballet*). Ballet in 1 act; ch. Messerer; mus. Liadov, Glazunov, Rubinstein, Liapunov, and Shostakovich. Prod. 6 May 1961, B. of the 20th Century, Théâtre Royal de la Monnaie, Brussels; definitive version prod. 17 Sep. 1962, Bolshoi B., Met. Op. House, New York, with Plisetskaya, Maximova, Fadeyechev, Vasiliev, Lavrovsky. The b. starts as a display of the classic Moscow school style, expands in technical difficulty and finally erupts in a series of virtuoso stunts. A Soviet equivalent to Lander's *Etudes*. Now performed to Shostakovich's mus. only.
BIBL.: 'B.S.' in *Balanchine's Complete Stories of the Great Ballets* (Garden City, N.Y., 1977).

Ballets de la Jeunesse, Les. The Paris-based co. was founded 1937 by Egorova, J.-L. Vaudoyer, and F. Barette. It only existed for 1 year, but introduced Skibine, Geneviève Moulin, Leskova, Algaroff, and Audran to the public.

Ballets de l'Etoile, Les. Béjart's first co., which he founded together with Jean Laurent, made its début at the Paris Th. de l'Etoile, 21 Aug. 1953, presenting *Hommage à Chopin*, 3 bs. ch. by Béjart. Béjart's *Symphonie pour un homme seul* (1955) became the favourite prod. of the repertory; the other most successful Béjart creations were *Le Teck* (1956) and *Sonate à trois* (1957). In the summer of 1957 it changed its name to *Ballet-Théâtre de Paris.

Ballets de Monte Carlo, Les. The Monte Carlo-based co. was founded by R. Blum in 1936, after he had left Colonel de Basil. Its stars were Nemchinova, Vilzak, and Gollner. Under Fokine's direction *L'Epreuve d'amour* (1936) and *Les Eléments* (1937) received their 1st prod. When Massine became artistic dir. in 1938, the co. changed its name to *Ballet Russe de Monte Carlo.
BIBL.: *Les Ballets de Monte Carlo* (Paris, 1954).

Ballets de Paris. The co. was founded by Petit after his break with the Bs. des Champs-Elysées, making its début at the Paris Th. Marigny, 21 May 1948, with Charrat, Jeanmaire, Marchand, Petit, Skouratoff, Perrault, and Hamilton as soloists and Fonteyn as guest-ballerina. The repertory was dominated by the bs. of Petit: *Les Demoiselles de la nuit* (1948), *Carmen* (1949), *La Croqueuse de diamants* (1950), supplemented by Charrat (*La Femme et son ombre* and '*adame miroir*', 1948), and Dollar (*Le Combat*, 1949). The co. frequently appeared abroad, but disbanded after its visit to the U.S. It was newly assembled for its Mar. 1953 season at the Paris Th. de l'Empire, with Marchand, Hélène Constantine, Ferran, Perrault, Babilée, and Reich as soloists. New Petit bs. were *Le Loup, Deuil en 24 heures, Ciné-Bijou*, and *Lady in the Ice*. Another season in Dec. 1955 saw Verdy, Mlakar, Beaumont, and B. Miller as newly acquired soloists in Petit's *La Chambre* and *Les belles damnées*. In Oct. 1956 there followed a *Revue des B.d.P.* at the Th. de Paris. In Feb. 1958 Petit gave *Contre-Point, La Rose des vents*, and *La Dame dans la lune* at the Th. de l'Alhambra, and on 17 Apr. 1959, at the same th., *Cyrano de Bergerac* with Jeanmaire, Beaumont, Petit, Reich, and Ferran. Succeeding the Bs. des Champs-Elysées, the Bs.d.P. functioned during the fifties as a sort of pace-maker of Parisian b. haute couture.
BIBL.: all Petit prods. listed in *Les Saisons de la danse* (Summer 1968).

Ballets des Champs-Elysées. The foundation of the co. was preceded by the perfs. Lidova had organized with Petit and Charrat 1944 at the Paris Th. Sarah Bernhardt. They became the meeting point of all the young d. talent opposing the official course of the Opéra, under the personal protection of Kochno, Cocteau, and Bérard. In Mar. 1945 they gave their 1st perf. at the Th. des Champs-Elysées, for which Petit ch. *Les Forains*. Among the dancers were Jeanmaire, Pagava, Philippart, Skorik, Algaroff, Foye, Perrault, Vyroubova, and Petit (also Riabouchinska as guest). After its success Roger Eudes invited the co. to make the Th. des Champs-Elysées its home. Here the official début took place on 12 Oct. 1945. In the following years a great number of bs. were created, in which some of the most progressive artists in Paris after the Liberation participated—among them Charrat's *Jeu de cartes* (1945), Nevada's *Los Caprichos* (1946), Babilée's *L'Amour et son amour* (1948), Milloss's *Le Portrait de Don Quichotte* (1947), and from Petit himself *Déjeuner sur l'herbe, Le Rendez-vous, La Fiancée du diable* (1945), *Les Amours de Jupiter, Le jeune homme et la mort* (1946), *Le Bal des blanchisseuses* and *Treize danses* (1947). Through its many foreign tours the co. became the most important ambassador of the Fr. post-war b. In 1948 Petit left the co., but it continued until 1951 under the direction of Jean Robin, V. Gsovsky, and Kochno. New bs. in the repertory were Lichine's *La Création* and *La Rencontre ou Oedipe et le Sphinx* (1948), Massine's *Le Peintre et son modèle* (1949), Babilée's *Till Eulenspiegel* (1949), and Gore's *La Damnée* (1951). New or returning dancers incl. Babilée, Philippart, Marchand, Tcherina, Bon, Skouratoff, Kalioujny, and Caron. In 1950 Eudes withdrew his protection, the co. lost its home and after 1952, ceased to exist. At that time, however, it had fulfilled its aim: to offer a platform for the experiments of the younger generation of Fr. dancers and choreographers, which the traditionally minded Opéra could never provide. It was a co. much admired for its youth, its unconventional appearance, its chic, charm, and sexual attraction—altogether for its eminent Frenchness, and less for any enduring qualities of its bs., which may explain why relatively so few works have survived in the repertory. It was to this co. that the post-war Fr. b. primarily owed its reputation.

Ballets Etorki. The co. was founded in 1954 by Philippe Oyhamburu as Les Ballets et Choeurs basques Etorki to collect and perform Basque songs and dances. It has often toured abroad.

Ballets Jooss. Established 1933 by the members of the former Folkwang Tanzbühne Essen, the co. emigrated 1934 to England, where it was offered a residence first at Dartington Hall and then at the Jooss-Leeder school in Cambridge, from where they toured widely. During the war the co. performed for the Eng. ENSA cultural programme. In 1949 Jooss returned to Essen, where he started to reorganize his co., henceforth called Folkwang Tanz-Theater. After touring Germany, the co. appeared for a season at the London Sadler's Wells Th., 1953, after which it disbanded. During the sixties another attempt at reviving it resulted in the creation of the Folkwang Ballet Essen, consisting of teachers and students of the masterclasses at the Essen Folkwangschule, giving occasional perfs. Centre-piece of the repertory was always Jooss's *The Green Table* (1932), which represents the supreme example of Jooss's aesthetic and stylistic ideas of the 'Neue Bühnentanz'. Among the best known dancers of the B.J. were Leeder, Züllig, Noelle de Mosa, Hertha Thiele, Elsa Kahl, Ulla Soederbaum, Uthoff, Rolf Alexander, and Jooss himself. Apart from the *The Green Table* other important bs. of the repertory were *The Big City* (1932), *Ball in Old Vienna* (1932), *The Prodigal Son* (1933), *Ballade* (1935), *A Spring Tale* (1939), *Chronica* (1939), *Pandora* (1944), and *Dithyrambus* (1948), and Züllig's *Le Bosquet* (1945). See *Folkwang Ballett Essen*.
BIBL.: A. V. Coton, *The New Ballet* (London, 1946).

Ballets 1933, Les. The co., which existed for 1 season only, was founded in 1933 in Paris by Edward James. Experimentally orientated, it was virtually a gift from James to his wife, the d. Tilly Losch. Artistic directors were Balanchine, Kochno, and Vladimir Dimitriev. Among its members were Toumanova, Jasinsky, Lubov Rostova, N. Leslie, Losch, and Lenya. Sauguet, Milhaud, Koechlin, and Weill composed special scores for the new bs. which were designed by Derain,

Tchelitchev, Bérard, and Caspar Neher. The co.'s sole ch. was Balanchine. The programme which was shown in Paris at the Th. des Champs-Elysées and in London at the Savoy Th. offered *Fastes, Songes, L'Errante, Mozartiana,* and *Les Sept Péchés capitaux (The Seven Deadly Sins).*

Ballets Modernes de Paris. The chamber-size co. was founded in 1955 by Françoise Michaud and Dominique Dupuy. For years it has appeared regularly at the Festival de Danse des Baux de Provence, in the ths. of the Paris suburbs, throughout the country, and abroad, presenting its programmes under such collective titles as *Jazz et Ballet contemporain, Nijinsky et les Ballets Russes, Le Folklore et la Danse, Evolution du Ballet contemporain,* and *Cocteau, Marivaux, Lorca, Ionesco, et la Danse.* In addition to Françoise and Dominique (who are generally advertised under their Christian names only) other choreographers who have worked for the co. incl. D. Mendel, Paul d'Arnot, and J. Andrews. The repertory has offered Françoise and Dominique's *L'Arbre* (1959), *Incantation* (1964), *La Femme et son ombre* (1968), *L'Homme et son désir* (1968), Mendel's *Epithalame* (1957) and *Apprendre à marcher* (1960), Andrews's *Le Jour où la terre tremblera* (1959), *Baudelaire* (1972), and the original Nijinsky chs. of *L'après-midi d'un faune* and *Jeux.* Françoise and Dominique are also the chief soloists of the co.

Ballet Society. Founded 1946 in New York by Kirstein and Balanchine as an organization for the encouragement of the lyric th. through the perf. of new works. Functioning on a subscription basis, its activities were restricted to registered members only. B.-master was L. Christensen, technical adviser J. Rosenthal, and dir. of the supplementary literary department, responsible for the publication of the magazine *Dance Index*, Paul Magriel. Among the important events were the Balanchine prods. of Ravel's *L'Enfant et les sortilèges,* Hindemith's *Four Temperaments,* and Stravinsky's *Orpheus* (the last two as world premières). Other choreographers participating were Taras, Bolender, and Christensen. Another 1st prod. was G.-C. Menotti's *The Medium.* The 1948 prod. of *Orpheus* gave rise to an invitation to join the New York City Center of Music and Drama as the New York City Ballet, and this was accepted.

Ballet Sopianae. The co. was founded in 1960 by Imre Eck and is attached to the op. house of the Hung. city of Pécs (called Sopianae in Roman times). Based initially on young dancers, who had just graduated from the Budapest State B. School, it aimed to offer a chamber-size platform for avant-garde ch. Today its director is Sándor Tóth, with Eck acting as artistic adviser and chief ch. 40-odd dancers strong, its repertory consists mainly of bs. by Eck (with his bs. to mus. by Bartók as its backbone). The co. has toured widely abroad.

BIBL.: A. Dallos, *A Pécsi Balett Története* (Budapest, 1969).

Ballets Russes de Monte Carlo. The co. emerged from a fusion of the Ballets de l'Opéra de Monte Carlo and the Ballet de l'Opéra Russe à Paris, with Colonel de Basil as dir., Blum as artistic dir., and S. Grigoriev as stage-dir.; it was founded Jan. 1932 to succeed the Bs. Russes de Diaghilev. From the former members of the Diaghilev co. Kochno, Balanchine, Massine, Doubrovska, and Woizikovsky joined the new co., supplemented by the 3 'baby-ballerinas' Baronova, Riabouchinska, and Toumanova. After its début at Monte Carlo, Apr. 1932, the co. toured Belgium and the Netherlands, enjoyed a sensationally successful season in London, and embarked 1933 for its 1st U.S. tour under the management of Hurok. Later Danilova, Eglevsky, Lichine, and Petroff joined its ranks. Balanchine left 1933 to direct a co. of his own, having contributed to the repertory (which consisted otherwise mostly of bs. from the Diaghilev era) *La Concurrence*, *Cotillon*, and *Le Bourgeois gentilhomme*. He was succeeded as b. master by Massine who ch. *Jeux d'enfants* (1932), *Beau Danube*, *Beach*, *Scuola di ballo*, *Les Présages*, *Choreartium* (1933), *Union Pacific*, and *Jardin public* (1935). Nijinska's *Boléro*, *Variations*, *Etude*, and *Les Comédies jaloux* were also mounted. In 1936 an open quarrel between de Basil and Blum resulted in the latter founding the Ballets de Monte Carlo, while de Basil renamed his co. Ballets Russes du Colonel de Basil. Later the co. changed its name again to Covent Garden Russian Ballet (1938), and *Original Ballet Russe (1939). Creatively the early years, which started the intern. discussion about symphonic bs., were the most important. Other creations were Massine's *Symphonie fantastique* (1936), Lichine's *Francesca da Rimini* (1937), *Protée*, and *Prodigal Son* (1938), and Fokine's *Cendrillon* (1938) and *Paganini* (1939).
BIBL.: K. Sorley Walker, *De Basil's B.R.* (N.Y. and London, 1983).

Ballets Russes de Serge Diaghilev. After the success of his Paris spring season, when he had presented exhibitions of Russ. painters, concerts with Russ. mus., and perfs. of Russ. ops., Diaghilev brought a b. co. to Paris for the 1st time in 1909, consisting of some of the best dancers from the St. Petersburg and Moscow cos. Its début on 18 May 1909 at the Th. du Châtelet, with *Le Pavillon d'Armide*, the Polovtsian Dances from *Prince Igor*, and *Le Festin*, caused a sensational success and ever since has been considered the birthday of modern b. Thereafter Diaghilev and his St. Petersburg circle of friends decided to undertake a return visit to Paris 1910. In 1911 the co. was presented under Diaghilev's own name, and also visited London for the 1st time. Its residence now became Monte Carlo. The 1st World War compelled Diaghilev to sever his bonds with Russia. The Paris seasons and tours were continued and the co. embarked for its 1st visit to America

in 1916–17. These were extremely hard years, with the co. often on the brink of bankruptcy; however, at the last minute someone was always found to underwrite a new season. The influence which the co. had on the European b. scene can hardly be overrated. For 20 years Diaghilev and his collaborators, among whom were some of the most important writers, composers, and painters of the day, not to mention the choreographers and dancers, set the international b. fashion. Through his aesthetics of perfect integration he reformed the b. of his time in all its forms, until his death in 1929, after which the co. dissolved. The last performance took place on 4 Aug. 1929 in Vichy. The soloists of the 1st Paris season in 1909 were Pavlova, Karsavina, Nijinska, Fokine, Bolm, Nijinsky, Mordkin, and Novikov; those of the last 1929 season were Karsavina, Spessivtzeva, Danilova, Tchernicheva, Doubrovska, Sokolova, Dolin, Lifar, Woizikovsky, and Balanchine. Other dancers who temporarily joined the co. were Rubinstein, Lopokova, Nikitina, Nemchinova, Zvereff, Orlov, Cecchetti, Massine, and Vilzak (Rambert and de Valois were also members); S. L. Grigoriev was régisseur while Cecchetti was for many years in charge of the classes. The co.'s successive chief choreographers were: 1909–12 and 1914 Fokine, 1913 Nijinsky, 1915–20 and 1925–8 Massine, 1922–6 Nijinska, and 1926–9 Balanchine. Composers who worked for Diaghilev incl. Stravinsky, Hahn, Ravel, Debussy, Schmitt, R. Strauss, Satie, de Falla, Respighi, Prokofiev, Poulenc, Auric, Milhaud, Rieti, Sauguet, and Nabokov. The co. exerted an important influence not only on b. design, but on stage design generally, owing to its collaboration with such painters as Benois, Bakst, Golovine, Roerich, Soudeikine, Sert, Larionov, Ballo, Picasso, Dérain, Goncharova, Matisse, Gris, Laurencin, Braque, Laurens, Utrillo, M. Ernst, Mirò, Bauchant, di Chirico, and Rouault. In his book on the co. Grigoriev lists 68 prods. The most important creations, as listed by their choreographers, were—from Fokine: *Le Pavillon d'Armide*, the Polovtsian Dances from *Prince Igor*, *Les Sylphides*, *Cléopâtre* (1909), *Le Carnaval*, *Shéhérazade*, *Firebird* (1910), *Le Spectre de la rose*, *Narcisse*, *Petrushka* (1911), *Le Dieu bleu*, *Thamar*, *Daphnis and Chloe* (1912), *Les Papillons*, and *The Legend of Joseph* (1914);—from Nijinsky: *L'après-midi d'un faune* (1912), *Jeux*, and *Sacre du printemps* (1913);—from Massine: *Las Meniñas* (1916), *Les Femmes de bonne humeur*, *Parade* (1917), *La Boutique fantasque*, *The Three Cornered Hat* (1919), *Le Chant du rossignol*, *Pulcinella* (1920, *Cimarosiana* (1924), *Zéphire et Flore*, *Les Matelots* (1925), *Mercure*, *Le Pas d'acier* (1927), and *Ode* (1928);—from Nijinska: *Renard* (1922), *Les Noces* (1923), *Les Biches*, *Les Fâcheux*, *The Night on the Bare Mountain*, *Le Train bleu* (1924), and *Roméo et Juliette* (1926);—from Balanchine: *Barabau* (1925), *La Pastorale*, *Jack-in-the-Box*, *The Triumph of Neptune* (1926), *La Chatte*

(1927), *Apollon musagète, The Gods Go a-Begging* (1928), *Le Bal,* and *Prodigal Son* (1929).

BIBL.: S. L. Grigoriev, *The Diaghilev Ballet 1909–1929* (London, 1953); A. Benois, *Reminiscences of the Russian Ballet* (London, 1941); Prince P. Lieven, *The Birth of Ballets Russes* (London, 1936); C. W. Beaumont, *The Diaghilev Ballet in London* (London, 1937); R. Buckle, *In Search of Diaghilev* (London, 1955); L. Sokolova, *Dancing for Diaghilev* (London, 1960); B. Kochno, *Diaghilev and the Ballets Russes* (Paris and New York, 1970); J. Percival, *The World of Diaghilev* (London, 1971); N. Macdonald, *Diaghilev Observed* (New York, 1975); R. Buckle, *Diaghilev* (London, 1979); complete list of productions in *Les Saisons de la danse* (1972/1).

Ballets Suédois. The co. was founded by R. de Maré in 1920, aiming for an avant-garde repertory. After its début on 25 Oct. 1920 at the Paris Th. des Champs-Elysées it continued until 1925. Its ch. dir. and star soloist was Börlin. It toured all of Europe and the U.S. and contributed considerably to the interest paid by contemporary artists to b. The co. functioned as a sort of platform for the group of composers calling themselves Les Six, with *Les Mariés de la Tour Eiffel* (1921) as their collective showpiece. Milhaud and Honegger comp. for the co.; other composers were Satie, Casella, A. Tansman, and D. Inghelbrecht. Librettists who collaborated incl. B. Cendrars, Claudel, Cocteau, Pirandello, and R. Clair. Like Diaghilev's, this co. was strongly influenced by the painters who collaborated on the déc., incl. Bonnard, Steinlen, Léger, J. Hugo, Picabia, and de Chirico. The main contingent of its dancers came from Scandinavia; apart from Börlin its best known dancers were C. Ari, J. Hasselquist, Kaj Smith, Yolande Figoni, and Ebon Strandin. The list of prods. gives 24 different titles, among them *Jeux, Ibéria, Nuit de Saint-Jean, Le Tombeau de Couperin, El Greco, Les Vierges folles* (1920), *L'Homme et son désir, Les Mariés de la Tour Eiffel* (1921), *Skating Rink* (1922), *La Création du monde* (1923), *La Jarre,* and *Relâche* (1924).

BIBL.: *Les Ballets Suédois dans l'art contemporain* (Paris, 1931); catalogue *Modern Swedish Ballet* (Victoria and Albert Museum, London, 1970).

Ballets: U.S.A. The co. was founded by Robbins in 1958 to perform at the Festival of Two Worlds in Spoleto and at the Brussels World Fair. Its sensational success gave rise to further perfs. in Florence and Trieste, and a return invitation to Spoleto in 1959, after which it toured Eur. Another Eur. tour followed in 1961, but a planned Amer. tour had to be cancelled after a few perfs. The co. had no stars but cast its dancers individually—among them Curley, Mazzo, V. Mlakar, S. Douglas, J. Jones, and Tetley. New bs. created by Robbins were *New York Export: Op. Jazz* (1958), *Moves* (1959), and *Events* (1961), with revivals of *Afternoon of a Faun. The Cage,* and *The Concert.* 'The program ... was planned to show

Europeans the variety of techniques, styles, and theatrical approaches that are America's particular development in the dance' (programme note).

Ballet-Théâtre Contemporain. The co., backed by the Fr. ministry of culture, was founded in the autumn of 1968 in Amiens to function as a place of encounter and to effect a synthesis between the individual arts. It performed in the various Fr. maisons de culture, had regular seasons in Paris and often toured abroad, paying its 1st visit to London 1971, and to New York 1972. Dir. was Jean-Albert Cartier, with F. Adret as chief ch. The co. was 45 dancers strong, and was based in Angers 1972–8. It emphasized a wide choice of choreographers and a close collaboration with leading artists, aiming to create a repertory reflecting the topical tendencies of contemporary art. Among the leading soloists have been M. Parmain, M. Belmondo, T. Thoreux, V. Filatoff, J. Urbain, and I. Lazarov. Choreographers who have worked for the co. were Adret, Lazzini, Descombey, Blaska, Sparemblek, Babilée, Skibine, Butler, and Sanders. An all-Stravinsky programme (several choreographers) and Stockhausen's *Hymns* (collective of choreographers) were particularly successful. The co. dissolved 1978, with Cartier, H. Trailine, and some of the dancers moving to Nancy, where they established the B. Th. Français de Nancy.

BIBL.: R. Baker, 'By Way of Sarlat, Seattle, and Saskatoon', *Dance Magazine* (1972/10).

Ballet-Théâtre de Paris. The co., which derived from the former Les Ballets de l'Etoile, made its début in June 1957 at the Paris Th. Marigny. Co-directors were Béjart and R. Henriques-Pimentel. The first new Béjart prods. were *L'Etranger, Chapeaux,* and *Pulcinella.* The co. immediately started touring, with Béjart's *Orphée, Arcane II* (1958), *Equilibre,* and *La Mer* (1959) supplementing the repertory, for which several of his former bs. were also revived. A Brussels co-prod. with the co. of the Th. Royal de la Monnaie, The Bs. Miskovitch, and the Western Th. B. for Béjart's *Sacre du printemps* resulted in the founding of the *Ballet of the 20th Century, 1960.

Ballett-Info. The Ger. magazine for b. and d. th. started life as a mimeographed information service for the members of the Cologne-based Deutsche Ballett-Bühne, a society to further the interest in and knowledge of th. d. in all its manifestations, in the autumn of 1977. Since Oct. 1978 it has been published in Cologne as a fully-fledged monthly magazine, edited by Rolf Garske, with Hedwig Müller as co-editor and Birgit Kirchner and Norbert Servos as associate editors. Now called *Ballett International.*

Ballett 1965. The 1st volume of the Ger. b. annual, published by Friedrich Verlag, Velber-Hanover, edited by H. Koegler and C. Barnes. It covered the Ger. and international 1964/5 b. season. Subsequent volumes, co-edited by Koegler, Hartmut Regitz, and Jens Wendland, have since always been called after the year of their publication.

Ballet Today. Brit. magazine, which first appeared in March–April 1946 with P. W. Manchester as editor. In April 1951 Estelle Herf took over until the final issue, dated July–Aug. 1970.

Ballet van Vlaanderen. See *Ballet of Flanders*.

Ballet West. The co., emerging from the Utah Civic B., was established on a professional basis 1963, with the Univ. of Utah in Salt Lake City as its base. Artistic dir. and chief ch. was until 1978 W. Christensen, since when he has been succeeded by B. Marks and more recently by John Field. There are 30-odd dancers, occasionally augmented by guest stars such as D'Antuono and d'Amboise. The repertory is dominated by Christensen bs.; other choreographers represented incl. Balanchine, d'Amboise, and Ruud. The co. tours regularly and has occasionally visited Eur.
BIBL.: O. Maynard, 'B.W.: Moving into the Majors', *Dance Magazine* (1979/2).

Ballet Workshop. Organization functioning as a club at the Mercury Th., 1951–5, directed by David and Angela Ellis. Programmes of specially created works (and a few historic revivals like Ashton's original *Mephisto Waltz*) were presented Sunday evenings, each being given several perfs. so that apprentice choreographers had the chance to revise their work. Jack Carter, M. Charnley, P. Darrell, and W. Gore were among the choreographers, Michael Hobson, J. Lanchbery, L. Salzedo, and others wrote special scores and the designers incl. D. Heeley, L. Hurry, K. MacMillan, and N. McDowell.
BIBL.: M. Clarke, in *Dancers of Mercury* (London, 1962).

Ball in Old Vienna, A (orig. Ger. title: *Ein Ball in Alt-Wien*). Ballet in 1 act; ch. Jooss; mus. Lanner-Cohen; déc. A. Siimola. Prod. 21 Nov. 1932, Folkwang Tanzbühne, Cologne. Set to Lanner's *Hofballtänze*, the b. depicts 'the gay and gallant life of the 1840s . . . sentimental intrigues of crinolined ladies and their ardent swains, to the entrancing rhythm of the waltz' (programme note). Revived City Center Joffrey B. and Cologne Dance Forum (1976).

Ballo (Ital., dance). Designates the Ital. standard dances of the 15th and 16th century. By about 1600 it specified a popular, lively d. with regular beat and song-like melodies. From its diminutive 'balletto' the word 'ballet' is derived.

Ballo della Regina. Ballet in 1 act; ch. Balanchine; mus. Verdi, cost. Ben Benson. Prod. 15 Nov. 1977 (benefit preview) and 12 Jan. 1978 (première), New York City B., New York State Th., New York, with M. Ashley, R. Weiss. Set to the b. mus. from Verdi's *Don Carlos*, the b. develops in the form of a divertissement, with a sequence of brilliant solos, radiating unstoppable cheerfulness and zest.

Ballo delle ingrate, Il. Mascherata by O. Rinuccini (text) and Monteverdi (mus.), prod. 4 June 1608, with ch. by Isacchino l'Ebreo at the court of Mantua. It centres on a d. of prudes, procured by Pluto from Hades at the request of Venus and Cupid to demonstrate the consequences to young ladies who have sworn to abstain from love. In the Fr. dances of their time they show the sufferings they have to endure in the underworld.

Ballon (Fr., balloon). Designates in b. the capability of a d. to seem to pause for a moment while jumping in mid-air. Is also used as a general description of a dancer's skill in jumping.

Ballonné (Fr., blown up). Designates in b. a jumping step, during which the d. stretches one leg to the front, the back, or the side, landing on the other leg, with the first closing on the coup-de-pied.

Ballotté (Fr. tossed). Designates in b. a bounding step, with the body leaning forward and backward during each change of weight. Giselle and Albrecht d. it with linked arms after the flower oracle in *Giselle*.

Ballroom Dances. The Eng. term for all sorts of social dances (the Germans call them 'Gesellschaftstänze').

Balon, Jean (*b* Paris 1676, *d* there 1739). Fr. dancer and choreographer. He appeared 1688 in a Chantilly performance of *L'Oronthée* before the royal family, became a member of the Opéra 1691, d. with Pécourt, Blondi, and Mlle Prévost in *Les Saisons*, 1695, participated in Pécourt's *Jeu de cartes*, 1700, and was then appointed compositeur of the bs. of the king. Ch. the intermezzi for Corneille's *L'Inconnue*, for Lalande's *Les Eléments* and for a new prod. of Rebel's *Caractères de la danse* for the début of Camargo 1726. He was famous for the ease of his dancing. Together with Prévost he scored a sensational success in Corneille's *Horace* on the occasion of a fête of the Duchesse de Maine at her castle in Sceaux in 1714—an event considered today as one of the forerunners of the b. d'action.
BIBL.: J. Lawson, in *A History of Ballet and its Makers* (London, 1964).

Balustrade. Ballet in 4 movements; ch. Balanchine; mus. Stravinsky; dec. Tchelitchev. Prod. 22 Jan. 1941, Original B. Russe, 51st St. Th., New York, with Toumanova, Jasinski, Petroff. Set to Stravinsky's violin concerto, the plotless b. received its name from Tchelitchev's déc. Though Stravinsky judged it one of the most satisfactory visualizations of any of his works, it received few perfs. Other b. versions of the same mus. by von Milloss in *Les Jambes savantes* (Vienna, 1965) and by Balanchine in *Violin Concerto* (New York, 1972).

Bannerman, Kenneth (*b* Haddington, 4 Oct. 1936). Scot. dancer. Studied with M. Middleton, continuing at Rambert School. Joined B. Rambert 1958, becoming eventually its leading premier danseur. Appeared in all the co.'s prods. of classics (mostly with L. Aldous as his partner) and created various roles in bs. by N. Morrice. Retired 1966.

Banovitch, Milenko (*b* Zagreb, 1936). Yugosl. dancer, teacher, and choreographer. Studied at Zagreb State B. School. Joined Zagreb State Op. B. 1945, later becoming principal d. Went to Paris 1958, where he d. with the cos. of Charrat and Petit and appeared opposite Tcherina in the film *Les Amants de Teruel* (1962). After freelancing in France, went to the U.S.A. in 1970, where he has worked with the Met. Op. B. and Dallas Civic B. Now Artistic Dir. of Denver Civic B. and Dir. of D. Department at Loretto Heights College.
BIBL.: S. Robin, 'Travels with B.', *Dance Magazine* (1971/6).

Barabau. Ballet in 1 act with choir; libr. and mus. Rieti; ch. Balanchine; déc. Utrillo. Prod. 11 Dec. 1925, Bs. Russes de Diaghilev, Coliseum Th., London, with Woizikovsky, Lifar, Chamié. This is a burlesque, based on an Ital. nursery song, with B., a cunning peasant, feigning death to trick some pillaging soldiers. Later version by de Valois for Sadler's Wells B. (1936).

Bar aux Folies-Bergère. Ballet in 1 act; libr. and ch. de Valois; mus. Chabrier; déc. Chappell. Prod. 15 May 1934, B. Rambert, Mercury Th., London, with Markova, Argyle, Gould, Ashton. The b., based on Chabrier's *Dix pièces pittoresques*, starts and finishes with a group composition representing Manet's famous painting. The characters, however, seem to have been inspired by Toulouse-Lautrec, the b.'s 2 most famous dances being the solo for La Goulue, and the can-can. This was the only b. ever created by de Valois for the Rambert co.

Barbay, Ferenc (*b* Miskolc, 11 June 1943). Hung. dancer. Studied at the Budapest State B. Inst.; graduated 1967, becoming a member of the Budapest State Op. B. Soloist at the Munich State Op. since 1969, creating roles in Charrat's *Casanova in London* (1969), Cranko's *French Suite* (1969) and *Swan Lake* (1970) and Tetley's *Sacre du printemps* (1974). Bronze Medal (Varna, 1968).

Barber, Samuel (*b* Westchester, 9 Mar. 1910 *d* New York, 23 Jan. 1981). Amer. composer. Wrote the mus. for Graham's *Cave of the Heart* (published as *Medea*, 1946). Bolender ch. his *Capricorn Concerto* (1955—later versions by Neumeier in *Separate Journeys*, Schwetzingen, 1968 and MacMillan in 6.6.78, 1978), P. Wright his *Six Short Dance Movements* in *A Blue Rose* (Royal B., 1957), Ailey his *Knoxville, Summer of 1915* (1960) and *Hermit Songs* (1961).

Barberina, La (also Barbarina; *b* Parma, 1721, *d* Barschau, Silesia, 7 June 1799). Ital. dancer. Studied with Rinaldi Fossano and accompanied him as his partner to Paris, where she made her début in Rameau's *Festes de Hébé ou Les Talens lyriques* at the Opéra, 1739. She was a dazzling technician, famous for her pirouettes, jetés battus and entrechats huit. Her most important roles were in *Zaïde, Reine de Grenade, Momus amoureux, Dardanus, L'Empire de l'amour*, and *Les Fêtes grecques et romains*, with guest appearances in London and Dublin. She was also noted for her love affairs with Prince Carignan, Lord Arundel, the Marquis de Thebouville, and the Duke of Durfort. Frederick the Great engaged her for 1744 in Berlin. However, instead of meeting her obligations, she travelled with her latest lover, Lord Stuart Mackenzie, to Venice, from where the King had her brought to Berlin by force. She then seems to have enjoyed a romance with the King, for he granted her extraordinary privileges. She d. at the Berlin Court Op. until 1748, and in 1749 married the privy councillor Cocceji, whom she accompanied to Silesia. After her divorce in 1788, she became Countess de Campanini, spending the rest of her life supervising her estates, which she had converted into a charitable institution for poor noble ladies. Frederick's court-painter Antoine Pesne painted her. In 1935 L. Maudrik ch. a b. *Die Barberina* (mus. Herbert Trantow) for the Berlin State Op.
BIBL.: P. Migel, in *The Ballerinas* (New York, 1972).

Barbieri, Margaret (*b* Durban, S.A., 2 Mar. 1947). Brit. dancer. Studied with Iris Manning and Brownie Sutton, also Royal B. School, graduating 1963, joined Sadler's Wells Royal B. 1965, appointed principal d. 1970. Acclaimed as Giselle, but also shows a notable gift for comedy roles. Created roles in Tudor's *Knight Errant* (1968), Drew's *From Waking Sleep* (1970), *Sacred Circles* (1973), and *Sword of Alsace* (1973), Cauley's *Ante Room* (1971), Layton's *O.W.* (1972), Hynd's *Charlotte Brontë* (1974), Killar's *The Entertainers* (1974), Wright's *Summertide* (1976), Thorpe's *Game Piano* (1978), and Corder's *Day into Night* (1980).
BIBL.: J. Percival, in *The Royal B., A Souvenir* (London, 1979).

Bari, Tania (*b* Rotterdam, 5 July 1936). Dutch dancer. Studied with Kiss, V. Gsovsky, and Messerer, and has collaborated with Béjart since 1955, first as a member of his B. de l'Etoile and from 1960 as one of the chief soloists of the B. of the 20th Century. Has appeared in most of Béjart's bs., with creations in *Sonate à trois* (1957), *Orphée* (1958), *Sacre du printemps* (1959), *Les quatre fils Aymon, Tales of Hoffmann* (1961), *Ninth Symphony* (1964), *Mathilde* (1965), *Bhakti* (1968), and *Les Vainqueurs* (1969). Retired 1973. Married to the d. Günter Kranner.
BIBL.: L. Rossel, 'T.B.', with complete list of her roles, *Les Saisons de la danse* (Summer 1971).

Barishnikov, Mikhail. See *Baryshnikov, Mikhail.*

Barkóczy, Sándor (*b* Szolnok, 1934). Hung. dancer and choreographer. Studied at Budapest State B. School and Moscow. Joined Budapest State Op. B. 1957, eventually becoming one of its choreographers. His bs. include Prokofiev's *Classical Symphony* (1966), Bartók's *Dance Suite* (1968), and Rudolf Maros' *Symphony for Strings* (1971). Also teaches at the State B. School.

Barnard, Scott (*b* Indianapolis, Ind., 17 Oct. 1943). Amer. dancer and b. master. Studied with G. Verdak, M. Saul, Englund, Joffrey, Arpinos, S. Douglas, and others. D. with City Center Joffrey B., creating roles in Arpino's *Clowns* (1968), *Confetti* (1970), *Kettentanz* (1971), and *Chabriesque* (1972). Asst. and b. master to Joffrey and Arpino. BIBL.: S. Goodman, 'S.B.', *Dance Magazine* (1970/12).

Barn Dance. (1) A rural Amer. dance in 4/4 time, originally called *Military Schottische*, introduced in the early 19th century. It got its name, not through being d. in a barn, but because it was accompanied by the song 'Dancing in the barn'. It combines Schottische hops and waltz steps. (2) Ballet in 1 act; libr. and ch. Littlefield; mus. potpourri of Amer. folk-songs; déc. Salvatore Pinto. Prod. 23 Apr. 1937, Littlefield B. Co., Philadelphia, Pa., with Littlefield, Thomas Cannon. A village festival provides the background for a sequence of lively scenes of exuberant dancing. A country girl who has 'gone wrong' reforms, and at last even the Deacon, who at first looked rather indignantly on the proceedings, joins in the finale. Revived for B. Th. in 1944.

Barnes, Clive Alexander (*b* London, 13 May 1927). Anglo-Amer. dance and drama critic. Educated Oxford Univ. Associate Editor of *Dance and Dancers* since 1950. D.-contributor to *New Statesman, The Times, Daily Express,* and *The Spectator.* D. critic of *The New York Times* 1965–77, also its drama critic 1967–77. Since late 1977 d. and drama critic of *New York Post.* Wrote 'Frederick Ashton and his Ballets' (*Dance Perspectives* 9, New York, 1961). Contributor *Ballet in Britain Since the War,* (London, 1953); *Ballet Here and Now,* (London, 1961); *Dance Scene USA* (New York, 1967). C.B.E. (1975). His wife Patricia B. is New York correspondent of *Dance and Dancers.*

Barnett, Robert (*b* Okanogan, Wash., 6 May 1925). Amer. dancer, teacher, and b. director. Studied with Nijinska, Egorova, Preobrajenska, and at School of Amer. B. Début with Original B. Russe. D. 1948, with New York City B. 1950–8, then with Atlanta B., becoming its art. dir. 1963. Has his own school.

Baronova, Irina (*b* Petrograd, 1919). Russ.-Brit. dancer. Studied with Preobrajenska in Paris; appeared 1930 at the Opéra, and was engaged by Balanchine in 1932 as one of the 3 'baby ballerinas' for the Bs. Russes de Monte Carlo, creating roles in Massine's *Les Présages, Jeux d'enfants, Beau Danube* (new version, all 1933), and Nijinska's *Les cent baisers* (1935). In 1940 went to the U.S., becoming ballerina of B. Th., also appearing in films and musicals. Guest ballerina, Original B. Russe, 1946. Returned to Eng., where she still keeps contact with the b. world through her membership of the Royal Academy of Dancing. Contributed 'Dancing for de Basil' to *About the House* (1964/6).

Baron (Baron de V. Nahum; *b* Manchester, 1906, *d* London, Sep. 1956). A leading Brit. b. photographer; published *Baron at the ballet* (1950), *Baron Encore* (1952), and *Baron's Ballet Finale* (1958).

Barra, Ray (orig. Raymond Martin Barallobre; *b* San Francisco, 3 Jan. 1930). Amer. dancer and b. master. Studied at San Francisco School of B. and Amer. B. Th. School; joined San Francisco Op. B. Member of Amer. B. Th. 1953–59. Principal Stuttgart Ballet 1959–66, creating roles in Cranko's *Romeo and Juliet* (1962), *Swan Lake* (1963), *Firebird* (1964), *Onegin* (1965), and MacMillan's *Las Hermanas* (1963), and *Song of the Earth* (1965). B. master Germ. Op. Berlin 1966–70, Frankfurt Op. 1970–3, and Hamburg State Op. 1973–6. Now working as a freelance b. master, mostly for Neumeier revivals.

Barre (Fr., bar). The wooden bar, fastened on the walls of a d. studio, which helps ds. to stabilize their balance while going through the initial exercises of the daily classroom work.

Bart, Patrice (*b* Paris, 30 July 1945). Fr. d. Studied at Paris Opéra B. School. Member of its b. co. since 1959, promoted danseur étoile 1972. Has enjoyed particular success in Béjart's *Bhakti.* Has regularly appeared with London Festival Ballet. B. master Paris Op. B. from 1986. Prix René Blum (Paris, 1963); Gold Medal (Moscow, 1969); Prix Nijinsky (1975).
BIBL.: L. Rossel, 'P.B.', *Les Saisons de la Danse* (1970/5).

Barta, Karoly (*b* Bekescaba, 8 May 1936). Hung.-Amer., dancer, teacher, choreographer, and b. director. Studied at Budapest State B. School and, after going via Vienna to the U.S.A., Metropolitan Op. B. School, School of Amer. B., and Amer. B. Th. School. D. with Budapest State Op B., R. Page's Chicago Op. B., The Washington B., A. Eglevsky's B. Co., and in various Broadway, TV, and nightclub prods. Head of D. for Washington, School and Co. of B.
BIBL.: S. Goodman, 'K.B.', *Dance Magazine* (1966/5).

Bartholin, Birger (*b* Odense, 1 May 1900). Dan. dancer, choreographer, and teacher. Studied with Fokine, N. Legat, and Volinine, danced with Bs. I. Rubinstein, Bs. de Monte Carlo, with Kniaseff, Nemchinova-Oboukov, in some London Cochran revues, and ch. several bs. for the Bs. de la Jeunesse in Paris and the Royal Danish B. 1938–

9. B. master in Helsinki (1954) and Oslo (1955). Runs a renowned b. school in Copenhagen, which has been the centre of an annual International B. Seminar since 1963.

Bartók, Béla (b Nagyszentmiklós, 25 Mar. 1881, d New York, 26 Sep. 1945). Hung. composer. Wrote the mus. for *The Wooden Prince* (ch. Otto Zöbisch, Budapest, 1917) and *The Miraculous Mandarin* (ch. Hans Steinbach, Cologne, 1926). Among his concert compositions which have been adapted for b. purposes are: *Sonata for 2 pianos and percussion* (by D. Hoyer, Hamburg, 1951; also Milloss in *Sonate de l'angoisse,* Rio de Janeiro, 1954; Béjart in *Sonate à trois,* Essen, 1957; MacMillan in *Rituals,* London, 1975); *Contrasts for violin, clarinet and piano* (by Ross in *Caprichos,* New York 1950); *Dance Suite* (by Milloss in *Hungarica,* Rome, 1956; also Barkóczy, Budapest, 1968; Feld, New York, 1969); *Music for Strings, Percussion and Celeste* (by Milloss in *Mystères,* Paris, 1951; also MacMillan in *Journey,* Amer. B. Th., 1957; Darrell in *The Prisoners,* Western Th. B., 1957; Eck, Budapest, 1964; Descombey in *Sarracenia,* Paris Opéra, 1964; Van Manen in *Dualis,* Netherlands Dance Th., 1967; Cullberg in *Revolt,* 1973); *Divertimento for string orchestra* (by Hoyer, Hamburg, 1950; also Van Manen in *Opus 12,* Netherlands Dance Th., 1964); *Concerto for Orchestra* (by Milloss in *Threshold of Time,* Rome, 1951; also Lander in *Concerto aux étoiles,* Paris Opéra, 1956); 2nd Piano Concerto (by Milloss in *Estro barbarico,* Cologne, 1963); 3rd Piano Concerto (by Darrell in *A Wedding Present,* Western Th. B., 1962); String Quartet No. 5 (by Darrell in *Home,* Western Th. B., 1965). Cullberg ch. her *Medea* (Gaevle, 1950) to several pieces from his *Mikrokosmos;* Suite No. 1 for orch. Op. 3, and *Two Pictures,* Op. 10 (second and third movements of Op. 3, No. 1. of Op. 10, both by M. Corder in *Three Pictures,* Sadler's Wells Royal B., 1981); another anthology for B. Wells in *The Hunchback of Notre Dame* (Austral. B., 1981).
BIBL.: R. Sabin, 'B.B. and the Dance', *Dance Magazine* (1961/4).

Baryshnikov, Mikhail Nikolaievich (b Riga, 27 Jan. 1948). Sov. dancer. Studied at Riga B. School and Leningrad B. School with Pushkin, joining Kirov B. 1967. Soon became admired as one of the co.'s most brilliant soloists. Jacobson ch. the solo-d. *Vestris* for him, and he created the title role in Sergeyev's *Hamlet* (1970) and Adam in Kasatkina and Vassiliov's *Creation of the World* (1971). While touring with a group of Sov. dancers in the summer of 1974 he decided to stay in Canada. Has since appeared with various cos., regularly with Amer. B. Th., dancing with G. Kirkland and with many other partners. Joined New York City B., summer 1978. Created roles in Butler's *Medea* (1975), Neumeier's *Hamlet Connotations,* Tharp's *Push Comes to Shove,* Robbins's *Other Dances,* Ailey's *Pas de Duke* (1976), Petit's *Dame de Pique* (1978) Robbins's *Opus 19* (1979),

Ashton's *Rhapsody* (1980) *et al.* Has starred in film *The Turning Point* and in TV prod. *B. on Broadway* (1980). Started as a producer-ch. of classics with *Nutcracker* (Amer. B. Th., 1977), following it with *Don Quixote* (Amer. B. Th., 1978). Since autumn 1980 artistic dir. of Amer. B. Th. Gold Medals (Varna, 1966; Moscow, 1969); D. Magazine Award 1978.
BIBL.: *B. at Work*—*M.B. Discusses His Roles* (text edited by C. Engell France, New York, 1976; G. Smakov, *B.: From Russia to the West* (New York, 1981). Complete list of activities and roles, *Les Saisons de la danse* (1978/12).

Barzel, Ann (b Minneapolis, 26 Dec. 1913). Amer. dance critic. Studied with Bolm, Fokine, Volinine, Humphrey, School of Amer. B., *et al.* Educated Univ. of Chicago. D. with Chicago Op. B. and Berenice Holmes B. Co. D. critic of *Chicago American* and *Chicago Today* since 1951. Contributor to *Dance Magazine, Dance News,* London *Ballet Annual,* and *Dance Encyclopedia.* D. Consultant, Illinois Arts Council. Lecturer on D. at Univ. of Chicago.

Bas, En (Fr., low). Designates a low position (e.g. of the arms).

Basil, Colonel de (orig. Vassili Grigorievich Voskresensky; b Kaunas, 1888, d Paris, 27 July 1951). Russ b. director. Said to have been a Cossack general, in 1925 he became asst. of Prince Zeretelli, who was in charge of the London and Paris seasons of Russ. Op. Founded B. Russe de Monte Carlo with R. Blum 1932 and organized its world-wide tours. After Massine had left 1938 and Blum withdrawn, was sole dir. of the Original B. Russe 1939–48.
BIBL.: A. L. Haskell, 'C. Wassily d.B.', *The Ballet Annual* (1952).

Basilio (b Basilio Esteban S. Villaruz, Manila, 15 Mar. 1940). Philip. dancer, choreographer, teacher, notator, and artistic director. Studied at local schools in Manila, Amer. B. Th. School, Amer. B. Center, Amer. D. Center *et al.* D. with various cos. in Manila, becoming eventually a teacher, b. master (D. Th. Philippines, D. Concert Co., and B. Federation of the Philippines), ch., and founder-dir. of Movement Manila. Continued to study at London Inst. of Choreology. Editor of *Sayaw Silannganan* (bi-monthly Phil. d. magazine).

Basle. Dance traditions at the Municipal Th. of the Swiss city date back to the late 1920s and 30s, when interest centred on contemporary works of the central Eur. school of modern d., with R. Chladek and H. Rosen as its best known representatives. In 1938 B. saw the first prod. of the partly d.-orientated 'oratorio dramatique' *Jeanne d'Arc au Bûcher* (with I. Rubinstein). A total change of orientation took place when V. Orlikovsky became artistic dir. 1955–67. With a much enlarged co. he put emphasis strictly on the classics, supplementing them with some full-length works from the Sov. repertory (with the West Eur. first prods. of *The Stone Flower*, 1962, and *Fountain of Bakhchisaray*, 1965) plus some full-length creations of his own (*Peer Gynt, Dorian Grey*, etc.). During those years B. experienced unprecedented b. enthusiasm. After Orlikovsky left, the b. situation declined again and did not really improve when P. Smok tried to realize his ambitious plans 1970–3. Since then, however, B. has returned to its former creativity and activity under the inspired b.-directorship of H. Spoerli, who over the years has managed to build up an unusually balanced repertory of classics and contemporary works, performed by a co. of promising young dancers, restoring B. to its prime position among the Swiss cities which value b.

BIBL.: S. Enkelmann and R. Liechtenhan, *Ballet in B.* (Basle, in Ger.).

Basque, Pas de (Fr., Basque step). Designates in b. a step of 3 beats, similar to the waltz step of the ballroom dances. It is made up of a dégagé, a rond de jambe, and a glissade at the end.

Basse danse (Fr., low dance). A group of court dances from between 1450 and 1525. Arbeau, who considered them, in his *Orchésographie* (1588), a thing of the past, calls them 'danse par bas ou sans sauter.' They can be traced to Fr., the Netherlands, and Italy. Mostly they were solemn walking dances, with a limited number of steps, without any jumps, most often in duple time. They were often followed by a lively jumping d. Ashton used a B.d. in his *Capriol Suite*.

Bat-Dor Dance Company. The name is Hebrew for contemporary. The Tel Aviv based co. emerged from the Bat-Dor d. studio, which was sponsored by Bethsabee de Rothschild and directed by J. Ordman. It made its début Sep. 1967 under the direction of Ordman and with her as chief-soloist together with 12 dancers. Unlike the modern-d. orientated *Batsheva D. Co., Bat-Dor aims for a repertory of bs. based both on classic-academic and modern techniques. A great number of foreign choreographers have worked for the co., including Tudor, Van Dantzig, J. Sanders, P. Wright, Bolender, Carey, Walker, Lubovitch, and Sanasardo as well as the Brit. trained Reiter-Soffer. The co. has visited Eur. several times (first London visit 1974); since 1971 it performs at the th. of the specially built Tel Aviv Bat-Dor D. Center.

Batsheva Dance Company. Founded 1963 and sponsored by Bethsabee (whose Hebrew name is Batsheva) de Rothschild, the modern d. orientated co. made its début in 1964 in Tel Aviv. Directed by J. Dudley until 1970, the co. was originally 16 dancers strong, most of whom had studied with Graham, who was artistic adviser from the very beginning. Four of her works formed the backbone of the repertory: *Errand into the Maze*,

Embattled Garden, Cave of the Heart, and *Diversion of Angels*, plus the specially created *Dream* (1974). Foreign choreographers who have created new works for the co. incl. Lang, McKayle, Tetley (*Mythical Hunters*, 1965), Morrice, Macdonald, Butler, and Cranko. In addition the dancers themselves have been stimulated to contribute bs. of their own—among them R. Schenfeld, R. Gluck, M. Efrati, and E. Ben-David. After various interim directorships Linda Hodes and Kaj Lothmann were appointed artistic co-directers 1974–77, succeeded by Sanasardo until Moshe Romano was appointed artistic dir. in 1981. The co. has toured widely abroad, making its Brit. début 1968 at the Bath Festival, and its New York début in 1972. Rothschild withdrew her financial support of the co. at the end of 1974, and it is now backed by State funds.

BIBL.: D. Sowden, 'Israel's B.D.C.', *Dance News* (1972/12).

Battement (Fr., beating). Designates in b. a beating movement of the stretched or bent leg. One distinguishes between the *grands battements* and *petits battements*.

Batterie (Fr., beating). Designates in b. all kinds of movements with the legs beating together. One distinguishes between the *grande batterie* and *petite batterie*, according to whether the elevation is large or small.

Baudelaire. Spectacle in 9 scenes; texts from B. adapted by Béjart, who was also in charge of the mus. montage and the ch.; déc. Joëlle Roustan and Roger Bernard. Prod. 9 Feb. 1968, B. of the 20th Century, Grenoble, with Michel Bringuies, Bortoluzzi, Donn, Lowski, Lommel, Albrecht, Bari, Gielgud, Kerendi. For the 9 scenes (Prélude—L'Etranger—La Femme—Wagner—Recueillement—Les Litanies de Satan—Les Amants—Le Poète et la foule—Postlude) Béjart uses poems by Baudelaire, songs by Debussy, and excerpts from Wagner's *Tannhäuser* as the main material for his dance spectacle, which tries to create a connection between Baudelaire's artificial paradises and the drug experiences of the hippies. Other ingredients are jazz, Asian, and psychedelic mus. A new version of the 'Les amants' section was first performed in Vienna under the title *Les Fleurs du mal* in 1971. A different work, *Baudelaire*, ch. J. Andrews, had its first prod. in 1972 at the Paris Espace Cardin.

Bauhaus Dances. After the preparations for his Stuttgart *Triadic Ballet*, the painter O. Schlemmer set out to explore systematically the relationship between man and stage-space, when he joined the Weimar Bauhaus 1920 and also after its transfer to Dessau. During his researches he presented at the Dessau experimental stage his so-called 'Bauhaustänze' 1925. Starting with the space-d., concerned with waiting, striding, and jumping, there followed the d. of forms, relying on such props as sticks, bars, clubs, and balls; the

d. of gestures, based on standing, lying, gesticulating, a fight with furniture, and inarticulate speech; and the exploration of technical materials, embodied in the metal-, glass-, hoop- and scenery-d. These were really studies of movement, performed by dancers in differently coloured tights and masks, accompanied by percussion rhythms. In his d. for women and d. for a choir of masks, however, Schlemmer went beyond these stylistic exercises to include anecdotal incidents. In her film *Mensch und Kunstfigur*, (1968), Margarete Hasting tried to reconstruct some of these dances, following this with a TV film about the *Triadic Ballet* in 1970.
BIBL.: H. Hildebrand, in *Oskar Schlemmer* (Munich, 1952).

Baumann, Art (*b* Philadelphia, 22 Dec. 1939). Amer. dancer, choreographer, and director. Educated at G. Washington Univ., Washington, D.C. Studied at Juilliard School and with Sanasardo. D. in the cos. of Weidman, Hoving, and Sanasardo 1959–65, and since then with D. Th. Workshop of which he is now Assistant Dir. Has ch. many pieces for various contemporary groups.

Bausch, Pina (orig. Philippine B; *b* Solingen, 27 July 1940). Ger. dancer, choreographer, and b.-director. Studied at Essen Folkwang School. D. with Folkwang B., New Amer. B., Metropolitan Op. House. B. dir. Wuppertal D. Th. since 1973–4. Ch. *In the Wind of Time* (mus. M. Dorner, 1969), *Actions for Dancers* (mus. Günther Becker, 1971), *Tannhäuser-Bacchanale* (1972), *Fritz* (mus. Wolfgang Hufschmidt, 1974), entire prods. of Gluck's ops. *Iphigenia in Tauris* (1974) and *Orpheus and Eurydice* (1975), and Stravinsky's *Sacre du Printemps* (1975) *Arien* (1979), *Legend of Chastity* (1979), and *Bandoneon*, (1980). 1st Prize Cologne Ch. Competition (1969). Currently considered the leading exponent of dance-th. in Ger.

Bayadère, La (orig. Russ. title: *Bayaderka*). B. in 4 acts; libr. Sergei Khudekov and M. Petipa (also ch.); mus. Minkus; déc. K. Ivanov, P. Lambin, O. Allegri, and A. Kwapp. Prod. 4 Feb. 1877, Maryinsky Th., St. Petersburg, with Vazem. Based on Kalidasa's *Sakuntala* and *The Carl of Clay*, the b. tells of the bayadère Nikia, who loves Solor and is loved by him in return. Solor, however, gets engaged to Gamzatti, daughter of a Rajah. Gamzatti sends Nikia a basket of flowers, concealing a snake. Bitten by it, Nikia dies. Solor dreams of meeting her in the Kingdom of Shades. At the wedding of Solor and Gamzatti the temple collapses, burying them under the ruins. In later prods. the last act was omitted. Although a full-length prod. is still in the repertory of the Kirov B., only the Kingdom of Shades act, considered one of Petipa's masterpieces, is usually seen today. First performed in the West by the Kirov B. in 1961, it was reproduced by Nureyev for the Royal B. on 27 Nov. 1963, and by Makarova for Amer. B. Th. on 3 July 1974 (other recent prods. at Paris Opéra and in Holland). First complete prod. in the West by Makarova for Amer. B. Th., 1980. An earlier op.-b. version, *Le Dieu et la bayadère*, by F. Taglioni (mus. Auber) at the Paris Opéra in 1830.
BIBL.: P. Brinson and C. Crisp, in *Ballet & Dance* (Newton Abbot, 1980).

Bayanihan Dance Company. The co., consisting of Filipino dancers and musicians, gave its début in Manila 1956. Its name derives from the Tagalog word for 'to collaborate'. Since its first appearance in the West at the Brussels World Fair of 1958, it has gained immense popularity throughout the world. Its chief-ch. is Lucrecia Reyes Urtula. Its programmes are based on Far Eastern, Mohammedan, Span., and Amer. influences.
BIBL.: R. G. Alejandro, in 'The Dance in the Philippines', (*Dance Perspectives* 51).

Bayer, Josef (*b* Vienna, 6 Mar. 1852, *d* there, 12 Mar. 1913). Austrian comp. and conductor. As court op. kapellmeister, he comp. the mus. to 22 bs., most of which were ch. by Hassreiter. His most popular b. was *The Fairy Doll* (1888).

Baylis, Nadine (*b* London, 15 June 1940). Brit. designer. Educated at London Central School of Art. Has designed many of Tetley's bs., including *Ziggurat* (1967), *Embrace Tiger and Return to Mountain* (1968), *Imaginary Film* and *Field Figures* (1970), *Rag Dances* (1971), *Small Parades* and *Threshold* (1972), *Gemini* (1973), *Sacre du printemps* and *Tristan* (1974), *Greening* (1975), *Moveable Garden* (1976), *Praeludium* (1978), and *The Tempest* (1979), also Van Manen's and Tetley's *Mutations* (déc. only, 1970), Morrice's *Realms of Choice* (1965), *Hazard* (1967), *Blind-Sight* (1969), and *That Is the Show* (1971), Bruce's *Living Space* (1969), *There Was a Time* and *Duets* (1973), *Unfamiliar Playground* (1974), *Ancient Voices of Children* (1975), *Girl with a Straw hat*, and *Promenade* (1976).
BIBL.: G. Gow, 'N.B.: Designer', *Dancing Times* (1979/7).

Beach. Ballet in 1 act; libr. René Kerdyck; mus. Français; ch. Massine; déc. Dufy. Prod. 19 Apr. 1933, Bs. Russes de Monte Carlo, Monte Carlo, with Lichine, Riabouchinska, Baronova, Massine. At a fashionable seaside resort, the gods of the sea appear as human bathers—a very slight subject, which presented Massine with the opportunity to borrow from sports, acrobatics, and the ballroom dances of the early thirties.

Beale, Alan (*b* 20 May 1936). Brit. dancer, teacher, and b. master. Studied Sadler's Wells B. School, joined Sadler's Wells B. in 1957. Left the comp. because of an injury in 1965. Appointed asst. b. master Stuttgart B. in 1966; Dir. of the Stuttgart Noverre B. 1971–3, for which he ch. *Coppélia* in 1971. At present b. master of Stuttgart B. Has been guest teacher School of Amer. B. and in Los Angeles and Washington.

Beat. (1) Designates in b. the beating of one leg against the other or their mutual crossing while in the air. One of the virtuoso effects of the *petite batterie*. (2) Designates in jazz and pop mus. the regular, elastic beating of time. From this derive word-combinations like beat mus. and beat movements, also the movement of the so-called Beatniks as representatives of a youth subculture of the sixties and early seventies of our century. The beat mus. and dances inspired some choreographers to embark on beat bs.—among them Darrell in *Mods and Rockers* (Western Th. B., 1963), Van Manen in *Ready-Made* (Netherlands Dance Th., 1967), Béjart in *Mass for Our Time* (B. of the 20th Century, 1967), Joffrey in *Astarte* (City Center Joffrey B., 1967), and Arpino in *Trinity* (City Center Joffrey B., 1971).

Beaton, Sir Cecil (*b* London, 14 Jan. 1904, *d* Salisbury, Wilts., 18 Jan. 1979). Brit. photographer and designer. Designed the scenery and costs. for Ashton's *Apparitions* (Sadler's Wells B., 1936), *Les Sirènes* (Sadler's Wells B., 1946), *Les Patineurs* (B. Th., 1946), *Illuminations* (New York City B., 1950), *Picnic at Tintagel* (New York City B., 1951), *Casse-Noisette* (Sadler's Wells Th. B., 1951), and *Marguerite and Armand* (Royal B., 1963), and Balanchine's *Swan Lake* (New York City B., 1951). C.B.E. (1972).
BIBL.: B. issue, *Dance Index* V, 8; A. Fatt, 'Designers for the Dance', *Dance Magazine* (1967/2).

Beatrix. Ballet in 3 acts; ch. J. Carter; mus. Adam and Horovitz; sets Henry Bardon; cost. David Walker. Prod. 31 Aug. 1966, London Festival B., Festival Hall, London, with D. Richards, Gilpin, Miklosy, Salavisa, Hayworth. The b. is based upon and adapted from *La jolie Fille de Gand*.

Beatty, Talley (*b c.* 1923). Amer. dancer and choreographer. D. first with Dunham in 1940, performed in musicals, started a career as concert-d. in 1947, enjoying special success with his Negro- and jazz-dances. Ch. for his own group *The Road of the Phoebe Snow* (1959), *Come and Get the Beauty of it Hot* (1960), *Powers of Six* (1964)—for other cos. *The Black District* (A. Ailey Amer. D. Th., 1968), *Poème de l'extase* (Cullberg D. Co., 1972), *Caravanserai* (Inner City D. Co., 1973), and *Cathedral of Heaven* (Batsheva D. Co., 1973).

Beauchamp, Pierre (also Beauchamps, though not, as is often stated, Charles-Louis B.; *b* Versailles, 1636, *d* Paris, probably 1705). Fr. dancer, choreographer, and b. master. Descended from a family of Fr. musicians and dancers, and thoroughly educated in both professions. Début in 1650, becoming superintendent of the bs. of the King, with whom he appeared in many bs. de cour. Appointed dir. of the Académie royale de danse. Ch. many bs. including bs. for the ops. by Campra and Lully, and the comédie bs. of Molière. P. Rameau credits him with the invention of the five classic positions, but it is more probable that he just codified them. Designed his

own system of d. notation. Resigned from the Op. at Lully's death (1687), but continued with his theoretical researches. As a d. his nobility and technical virtuosity were impressive. Said to have been one of the first to perform tours en l'air.
BIBL.: P. J. S. Richardson, 'The B. Mystery', *Dancing Times* (March/Apr. 1947); F. Derra de Moroda, in 'Chorégraphie', *The Book Collector* (Winter 1967).

Beau Danube (originally: *Le beau Danube bleu*). Ballet in 1 act; libr. and ch. Massine; mus. Joh., Jos., and E. Strauss, arr. by R. Désormière; set Wladimir Polunin (after Constantin Guys); cost. E. de Beaumont. Prod. 17 May 1924, Soirées de Paris de Comte E. de Beaumont, Th. de la Cigale, Paris, with Lopokova, Massine. A character comedy, the b. is set in the Vienna Prater of the 1860s, where a dapper Hussar, engaged to the elder daughter of a noble family, is surprised by the sudden appearance of his former mistress, a street d.. The last named has always been one of the favourite roles of Danilova, who first d. it when Massine revived the b. in 1933 for the B. Russe de Monte Carlo. There have been numerous later revivals, incl. London Festival B. in 1971 and City Center Joffrey B. in 1972. A similar b. *Straussiana* by Bourmeister, M. Aniryanov, and P. Markov at the Moscow Stanislavsky and Nemirovich-Danchenko Th. (1941).
BIBL.: C. W. Beaumont, 'L.B.D.' in *Complete Book of Ballets* (London, 1951).

Beaugrand, Léontine (*b* Paris, 26 Apr. 1842, *d* there, 27 May 1925). Fr. dancer. Studied at Paris Opéra B. School with Mme Dominique and M. Taglioni, made her début in Taglioni's *Le Papillon* (1860), enjoyed her first success in Saint-Léon's *Diavolino* (1864), and became the second Swanilda in his *Coppélia* after Bozzacchi's premature death (1871). Created principal role in Mérante's *Gretna Green* (1873). Retired 1880. Nestor Roqueplan and Sully-Prud'homme wrote enthusiastically about her, praising her extraordinary élévation.

Beaujoyeux, Balthasar de (orig. Baldassare di Belgiojoso; also Beaujoyeulx; *b* 15??, *d* Paris, *c.* 1587). Ital. violinist, composer, and choreographer. Came to Paris about 1555 with a group of Piedmontese violinists, who were in the service of the Maréchal de Brissac. Thanks to his gifts of organizing fêtes at the royal court, made a rapid career. As personal servant to Catherine de' Medici he participated in the masquerade *Défense du paradis* (1572), arranged the *Ballet aux ambassadeurs polonais* (1573), and his most important work, the *Ballet Comique de la Reine* (1581), considered the first b. de cour. Retired in 1584.
BIBL.: H. Prunières, in *Le Ballet de cour* (Paris, 1914).

Beaumont, Comte Etienne de (*b* 8 Mar. 1883, *d* 1956). Fr. designer. A rich patron of modern art, particularly interested in b. Together with Cocteau, Massine, and some soloists of the Diaghilev comp. he organized the Soirées de Paris at the Th. de la Cigale, in May and June 1924, which saw the first prod. of *Romeo and Juliet* (Cocteau—V. Hugo), *Salade* (Milhaud—Braque), *Mercure* (Satie—Picasso), *Le beau Danube* (Strauss/Désormières—Polunin), *Scuola di ballo* (Boccherini/Françaix—de Beaumont), and *Gaîté Parisienne* (Offenbach/Rosenthal—de Beaumont); all ch. by Massine.

Beaumont, Cyril William (*b* London, 1 Nov. 1891, *d* there, 24 May 1976). Brit. bookseller, writer, and publisher. The owner of a world-renowned b. bookshop in Charing Cross Rd., London, for 55 years until he retired in 1965. As critic, president and member of various London academies and societies, and especially as writer on b. (also often publishing his own books) he was one of the outstanding personalities of the Brit. b. scene and responsible for the recording and preserving of the Cecchetti system. His most important books are *A Manual of the Theory and Practice of Theatrical Dancing* (with Idzikovsky, 1922), *A Bibliography of Dancing* (1929), *Michel Fokine and His Ballets* (1935), *The Complete Book of Ballets* (1937), *The Diaghilev Ballet in London* (1940), *Supplement to the Complete Book of Ballets* (1942), *The Ballet Called Giselle* (1944), *The Sadler's Wells Ballet* (1946), *Ballet Design: Past and Present* (1946), *Dancers Under My Lens* (1949), *The Ballet Called Swan Lake* (1952), *Ballets of Today* (1954), *Ballets Past and Present* (1955), and *A Bookseller at the Ballet* (1975). In addition he has been the translator of several textbooks of b. history by Noverre, P. Rameau, and Gautier. Palmes Académiques (1934); Légion d'honneur (1950); Royal Academy of Dancing's Queen Elizabeth II Coronation Award (1962); O.B.E. (1962), and other awards.
BIBL.: 70th anniversary issue, *Dance and Dancers* (1961/12).

Beaumont, Piers (*b* Barcelona, 1944). Brit. dancer and teacher. Studied at Royal B. School. Joined Cov. Gdn. Op. B. in 1961, Touring Royal B. in 1963, appointed principal d. in 1968 and seen mostly in the danseur noble roles. Then d. with London Festival B. and freelance with the Gothenburg B. Taught the male graduation class of the Royal B. School, 1972–77, then taught in Spain. B. master London City Ballet 1980.
BIBL.: J.P., 'P.B.', *Dance and Dancers*, (1966/2).

Beaumont, Tessa (*b* Paris, 8 Mar. 1938). Fr. Dancer. Studied with Kschessinska, Kiss, Peretti, V. Gsovsky, and Franchetti. Début with Béjart's Bs. de l'Etoile in 1954. D. with the cos. of Charrat, Petit, Larrain, Miskovitch, Grand B. Classique de Fr., *et al.*, creating roles in Béjart's *Le Belle au boa* (1955), *Sonate à trois* (1957), and *Pulcinella* (1957), Sanders' *L'Echelle* (1956), Petit's *Cyrano* (1959), Massine's *The Barber of Seville* (1960), Orlikowsky's *Cinderella* (1963), and Lazzini's *Enea* (1972). Now has a school in Paris. National Order of Merit (1975).
BIBL.: A.-P. Hersin, 'T.B.' (with complete list of roles and activities), *Les Saisons de la danse* (1974/4).

Beauty and the Beast. (1) Ballet in 1 act; ch. Cranko; mus. Ravel; déc. Margaret Kaye. Prod. 20 Dec. 1949, Sadler's Wells Th. B., Sadler's Wells Th., London, with P. Miller, D. Poole. A d. version of the famous fairy-tale in pas de deux form; BBC TV prod. 1953. (2) Ballet in 2 acts; libr. Colin Graham; ch. Darrell; mus. Thea Musgrave; déc. Peter Minshall. Prod. 19 Nov. 1969, Scottish Th.B., Sadler's Wells Th., London, with Tatsuo Sakai, D.D. Washington. In this version, based on the story by Mme de Villeneuve, the b. is a full-length work. A Ger. version of it was ch. by I. Keres in Wiesbaden 1972.
BIBL.: (2) Interview with the authors, *Dance and Dancers* (1969/11).

Beck, Hans (*b* Haderslev, 31 May 1861, *d* Copenhagen, 10 June 1952). Dan. dancer, b. master, and ch. Studied at Royal Danish B. School, joined its co., becoming solo-dancer in 1881 and b. master 1894–1915. He was responsible for the conservation of the Bournonville repertory, supplementing a new prod. of *Napoli* by choreographing the solo variations for the last act. One of his best prods. was *Coppélia* (1896), which is still performed. As a ch. he was most successful with *The Little Mermaid* (mus. Fini Henriques, 1909). After his retirement continued to work as a rehearsal-coach and to advise H. Lander on the new prods. of Bournonville bs.

Beckett, Keith (*b* Bletchley, 1929). Brit. dancer. Studied at Cone-Ripman School. Started his career as an actor. Joined London Festival B. in 1950, eventually becoming soloist. Left the co. in 1959 to become a TV producer. Adeline Genée Silver Medal (1946).

Bedells, Phyllis (*b* Bristol, 9 Aug. 1893, *d* Henley on Thames, 2 May 1985). Brit. d. and teacher. Studied with Bolm, Cecchetti, and Pavlova, made her début in the London 1906 prod. of *Alice in Wonderland* and appeared regularly at the London Empire Th. 1907–17, at first as 2nd ballerina to L. Kyasht, and from 1914 as prima ballerina. Danced with various cos., in revues, in the perfs. of the Camargo Society, and as a guest with the Vic-Wells B. until she gave her farewell perf. in 1935. Opened her Bristol b. school in 1925, transferring it later to London, where she was active as a member of various societies and committees. Author of *My Dancing Years* (London, 1954). Queen Elizabeth II Coronation Award of the R.A.D. (1958); Fellow of the R.A.D. (1971).

Beethoven, Ludwig van (*b* Bonn, prob. 16 Dec. 1770, *d* Vienna, 26 Mar. 1827). Ger. composer. Wrote 2 bs.: *Ritterballett* (ch. Habich, Bonn, 1791) and *The Creatures of Prometheus* (ch. S. Viganò, Vienna, 1801). In addition one finds many individual dances in his oeuvre, which have been used now and again by recital dancers. Choreog-

raphers who have based their bs. on symphonies by B. include Deshayes (*Sixth Symphony*, London, 1829; also in Disney's film, *Fantasia*, 1940; T. Schilling, Com. Op. Bln., 1979) I. Duncan (*Seventh Symphony*, New York, 1908; also Massine, B. Russe de Monte Carlo, 1938; V. Biagi, Lyons, 1971), Lopokov (Fourth Symphony in *Dance Symphony*, Petrograd, 1923), Béjart (*Ninth Symphony*, B. of the 20th Century, 1964; the last movement as *Ode to Peace* by Irma Duncan, New York, 1934). Other bs. to mus. by B.: Jooss' *Company at the Manor* (*Spring Sonata*, Bs. Jooss, 1953; also Walter, Düsseldorf, 1968). Massine's *Moonlight Sonata* (Amer. B. Th., Chicago, 1944; Miskovitch, Genoa, 1970), Tudor's *La Gloire* (overtures *Egmont*, *Coriolanus*, and *Leonora III*, New York City B., 1952), P. Taylor's *Orbs* (Quartets op. 127, 130, and 133, P. Taylor D. Co., 1966), Van Manen's *Grosse Fuge* (op. 133, Netherlands Dance Th., 1971), and *Adagio Hammerklavier* (op. 106, Dutch National B., 1973), J. Thorpe's *Quartet* (op. 130, Northern Dance Th., 1971), and *Triptych* (Piano Sonata No. 23 in F Minor, op. 57 'Appassionata', Northern Dance Th., 1975).
BIBL.: E. Gockel, 'B. und das Ballett', *Tanzarchiv* (1970/9–10).

Beiswanger, George (*b* Baltimore, 1902). Amer. univ. teacher and writer. After receiving a Ph.D. from the State Univ. of Iowa he has taught philosophy and aesthetics at various colleges and univs. D. critic for *Theatre Arts Monthly* 1939–44, contributor of d. articles to many periodicals, d. critic for *The Atlanta Journal* 1967–72. Wrote 'Doing and Viewing Dances: A Perspective for the Practice of Criticism', *Dance Perspectives 55*.

Béjart, Maurice (orig. M. Berger; *b* Marseilles, 1 Jan. 1927; other sources 1924). Fr. dancer, choreographer, and b. director. Studied at the local op. b. school and in Paris with Staats, Egorova, Kiss, Rousanne, and Volkova in London. Made his début 1945 in Vichy. Toured 1945–7 with Schwarz, Charrat, and Petit. D. with Inglesby's International B. 1949–50, Royal Swedish B. 1950–2 (where he did his first film-ch.: *The Firebird*). Founded Les Bs. de l'Etoile with the writer Jean Laurent 1953, becoming its artistic dir. and star-soloist, from which grew 1957 the B.-Th. de Paris. After numerous tours ch. *Sacre du printemps* 1959 in Brussels for a specially assembled co. This became the most successful prod. of the Brussels-based B. of the 20th Century, formed with B. as director in 1960. During the following decade he shaped this co. into one of the world's foremost troupes, with regular seasons in Brussels and continuous tours around the globe. He has attracted huge new and young audiences, but has always been a controversial figure among more discriminating b.-goers. Since 1960 he has created relatively few bs. for other than his own co.—among them *The Journey* (Cologne, 1962) and for the Paris Opéra Berlioz' *Damnation of Faust* (1964), Stravinsky's *Renard*

(1965) and *Firebird* (1970). As ch. he developed from an academically-based idiom, inclining towards neo-expressionism, which culminated in his *Symphony for a Lonely Man* (mus. P. Henry, 1955). After the total-spectacle prods. of his early Brussels years *4 fils Aymon*, 1961; *The Merry Widow*, 1963) he became the ideologist of a highly personal brand of b. mysticism, impregnated with Far Eastern influences in works like *Mass for the Present Time* (1967), *Bakhti* (1968), *Nijinsky, Clown de Dieu* (1971), and *Golestan—Garden of Roses* (1973). In between he has always returned to more choreographically orientated bs. such as *Bolero* (mus. Ravel, 1960), *Suite Viennoise* (mus. Schoenberg, Berg, and Webern, 1962), *Ninth Symphony* (mus. Beethoven, 1964), *Ni Fleurs, ni couronnes* (mus. Tchaikovsky, 1968), *Offrande chorégraphique* (mus. Bach, collective ch., 1971), and *Le Marteau sans maître* (mus. Boulez, 1973). Th. prods. of his have been *la Reine verte* (Paris, 1963) and *Tentation de Saint Antoine* (Paris, 1967). Since 1970 he has also been in charge of the Brussels MUDRA Centre européen de perfectionnement et de recherche des interprètes du spectacle—a school and studio for exploring the possibilities of total th. He has been constantly obsessed by the work of R. Wagner—participating in Wieland Wagner's 1961 Bayreuth prod. of *Tannhäuser*, ch. *Venusberg* (1965), *Mathilde* (1965), *Baudelaire* (1968), and *Les Vainqueurs* (1969), and writing the novel *Mathilde ou le Temps perdu* (1963). Apart from the pieces already mentioned other representative bs. by him have been: *Haut voltage* (mus. Henry, 1956), *Prométhée* (mus. Ohana, 1956), *Sonate à trois* (mus. Bartók, 1957), *Orphée* (mus. Henry, 1958), *The Seven Deadly Sins* (mus. Weill, 1961), *Tales of Hoffmann* (the op. by Offenbach, 1961), *Les Noces* (mus. Stravinsky, 1962), *Romeo and Juliet* (mus. Berlioz, 1966), *A la recherche de . . .* (mus. various, 1968), *Actus tragicus* (mus. Bach, 1969), *Songs of a Wayfarer* (mus. Mahler, 1971), *Stimmung* (mus. Stockhausen, 1972), *La traviata* (the op. by Verdi, 1973), *Mallarmé III* and *Tombeau* (mus. Boulez, 1973), *I Trionfi* (mus. Berio) and *Ce que l'amour me dit* (mus. Mahler, 1974), *Pli selon pli* (mus. Boulez, 1975), *Notre Faust* (mus. Bach, 1975), *Les Illuminations* (mus. diverse, 1979) and *La Flûte enchantée* (mus. Mozart, 1981). Author of *M.B. Un instant dans la vie d'autrui. Memoires* (Paris, 1979) and *B. par B.* (Paris, 1979). Grand Prix of the Paris Th. des Nations (1960 and 1962); Ch. Award of the Paris D. Festival (1965); D. Magazine Award (1974). Erasmus Prize (1974).
BIBL.: A. Livio, *B.* (Lausanne, 1969); M.-F. Christout, *B.* (Paris, 1972); complete list of works in *Les Saisons de la danse* (1968/5, 1970/1 supplement).

Belda, Patrick (*b* 1943, *d* Brussels, 7 Feb. 1967). Fr. dancer. Started to d. with Béjart's co. after having studied for only 6 months, creating the principal role in Béjart's *Voyage au coeur d'un*

enfant when 12 years old in 1955. He stayed with Béjart's various troupes until his death, becoming one of his most popular dancers, creating further roles in *Pulcinella*, *L'Etranger*, and *Haut voltage* (1957), *Orphée* (1958), *Sacre du printemps* (1959), *La Belle au boa* (1960), *4 Fils Aymon* (1961), *Ninth Symphony* (1964), *Renard* and *Les Oiseaux* (1965), *Romeo and Juliet* and *Cygne* (1966). Had just started to ch. when he was killed in a car accident. Was married to the d. Laura Proença.
BIBL.: M. Béjart, *P.B.* (Brussels, 1967).

Belfiore, Liliana (*b* Buenos Aires, 12 Oct. 1952). Arg. dancer. Studied at Institute of Superior Arts. Member of B. Festio Argentina 1967–8, Teatro Colón B. 1971–5, London Festival B. 1976–80. Now has her own co., for which she has ch. *Griselda, a Butterfly's Dream* (mus. Barry J. Drogin).

Belgium. The main Belg. b. developments took place in *Brussels, and the provinces saw very few perfs. until after the 2nd world war. Though Ghent had a small co. attached to the local op. house, which registered b. perfs. between 1835 and 1891—incl. *Giselle* and *Coppélia*—and though Antwerp showed some sort of b. ambition when Sonja Korty took over as b. mistress in 1923, those dancers who were engaged by the op. cos. appeared mainly in op. bs. only, while individual perfs. were taken care of by visiting folklore groups, guest ballerinas, and very occasionally by some modern d. Not until the Charleroi-based *Ballet de Wallonie started to work in 1966 and the *Ballet of Flanders at Antwerp followed suit in 1970 can one talk of regular professional b. cos. outside Brussels, though, of course, both cos. were preceded by various troupes, pursuing individual hopes and ambitions.
BIBL.: R. Barbier, *Van Operaballet naar Ballet van Vlaanderen* (Antwerp, 1973).

Belgrade. After the establishment of its own op. house a small b. group was attached in 1921, consisting of 6 dancers, headed by Claudia Issachenko. One of them, Natalija Boskovič, became the first B. prima ballerina, while the co. soon expanded to 22 members, performing its first separate programme in 1922 with *Sheherazade* and excerpts from the *Nutcracker*. Other important figures in these early years, which also saw the opening of a b. school, were Jelena Poljakova, Nina Kirsanova, Alexander Fortunato, Fyodor Vasiliev, and from 1927 Margaret and Max Froman. With her Russ. training Froman built up a markedly Russ.-orientated repertory, which apart from the usual Diaghilev bs. also offered *The Humpbacked Horse* and *Raymonda*. Her most popular success, however, was the first b. based upon a national subject, *The Gingerbread Heart* (1927). Also in 1927 Pavlova appeared in B. (with Novikov as her partner), and in 1928 Karsavina—2 events which deeply impressed the B. citizens. By about 1930 the co. had grown to 50 members, with Ana Roje as one of its best

soloists. Boris Romanov came in 1930–1, and was succeeded in 1932–4 by Kirsanova, under whom Pia and Pino Mlakar attracted attention; they later acted as ambassadors of Yugosl. b. in Switzerland and Germany. 1934–6 Boris Kniaseff headed the co., and for 1937–8 Froman returned (this season saw the first perf. of the Mlakars' very popular *The Devil in the Village*); Romanov returned in 1939. During the war no perfs. took place, so after 1945 the co. had to be completely reestablished. The first major b. event after the war was the first prod. of the full-length *The Legend of Ohrid* (ch. Froman) in 1947, which has become the most frequently performed of all Yugosl. bs. In 1949 Dimitrije Parlič joined the co. as premier danseur (with Ruth Parnel as ballerina); he also ch. Prokofiev's *Romeo and Juliet* in the same year. After the Mlakars and Froman he became the best internationally known Yugosl. ch.; he has been connected with the comp. ever since (he has several times been b. director), while pursuing his international career on leave of absence. In 1950 the Mlakars prod. *The Ballad of a Medieval Love*, and in 1955 followed Parlič's *A Chinese Tale*. During the later 1950s Lavrovsky mounted his famous *Giselle* prod. Further important premières were *Abbandonate* (a b. based upon García Lorca's *House of Bernarda Alba*, ch. Parlič, 1964), *Ondine* (ch. I. Eck, 1968), *La Fille mal gardée* (ch. Ashton, 1971), *Anna Karenina* (ch. Parlič, 1972), and *Abraxas* (ch. Parlič, 1973). The co. paid its first visit abroad to the Edinburgh Festival in 1951, since when it has regularly conducted foreign tours. One of its major problems is retaining its dancers, who often find more lucrative jobs abroad. After Froman and Roje had left the country early on, some of the best dancers who decided to work abroad included D. Sifnios, M. Miskovitch, M. Sparemblek, V. Sulich, and M. Banovitch. Artistic dir. is currently Vladimir Logunov.
BIBL.: B. Marinković-Rakić and R. Nikolajević, *Yugoslav Ballet* (B., 1958).

Belle au bois dormant, La. See *Sleeping Beauty, The*.

Belle dame sans merci, La. Ballet in 1 act; libr., ch., and déc. A. Howard; mus. Alexander Goehr. Prod. 4 Sep. 1958, Edinburgh International B., Empire Th., Edinburgh, with Y. Meyer, Miskovitch. The b. is based on the poem by Keats, which tells of a knight, held in thrall by a beautiful lady—a fairy's child—whose weeping he silences with kisses. Lulled to sleep, he dreams of pale kings and princes who warn him that he is held by 'La Belle dame sans merci'. He awakens to find himself lying on the cold hillside.

Belle Hélène, La. Ballet in 4 scenes; libr. Marcel Achard and R. Manuel; ch. Cranko; mus. Offenbach, arranged by L. Aubert and M. Rosenthal; déc. M. Vertès. Prod. 6 Apr. 1955,

Opéra, Paris, with Chauviré, Renault, Bozzoni, Bessy. A comic b. about Helen of Troy.

Bells, The. Ballet in 5 episodes; libr. and ch. R. Page; mus. Milhaud; déc. Noguchi. Prod. 26 Apr. 1946, Chicago Univ. Composers Series, Chicago, with Page, J. Andrews, R. Josias. The b. is about a married man who seeks refuge from his broken marriage with a group of homosexuals.
BIBL.: C. Beaumont, 'T.B.' in *Ballets Past & Present* (London, 1955).

Belsky, Igor Dmitrievich (*b* Leningrad, 28 Mar. 1925). Sov. dancer, choreographer, and b. director. Studied at Leningrad Ch. School, graduating in 1943. Joined the Kirov B., where he became a distinguished character soloist, creating roles in Jacobson's *Shuraleh* (1950) and Sergeyev's *Path of Thunder* (1959). Ch. for the Kirov B. *Coast of Hope* (mus. A. Petrov, 1959) and the first movement of Shostakovich's Seventh Symphony (*Leningrad Symphony*, 1961). As chief ch. of the Leningrad Maly Th. 1963–72, he did new versions of *The Humpbacked Horse, Swan Lake,* and *Nutcracker,* creating *Eleventh Symphony* (mus. Shostakovich, 1966), and *Gadfly* (mus. Tchernov, 1967). For some years during the early 1970s artistic dir. of the Kirov B.

Ben-David, Ehud (*b* Tel Aviv, 11 Apr. 1939), *d* Natanya, 22 Mar. 1977). Israeli dancer and teacher. Studied with Graham, L. Hodes, Lang, Tetley, and MacKayle. Joined Batsheva D. Co. in 1964 and became one of its most distinguished soloists. Created numerous roles, incl. Jacob in Graham's *The Dream* (1974). Taught and became head of Tel Aviv D. Centre. Gold Medal (Paris Festival, 1971). Was married to the d. teacher and ch. Linda Hodes.
BIBL.: D. Sowden, 'E.B.-D.: A Home-Grown Star', *Dance Magazine* (1973/5).

Benesh, Rudolf and Joan. Brit. dance notators. Rudolf B. (*b* London, 16 Jan. 1916, *d* there, 3 May 1975) and his wife Joan B. (*née* Rothwell; *b* Liverpool, 24 Mar. 1920) developed the Benesh Dance Notation (copyright 1955). Started to teach their system at the London Royal Academy of Dancing, 1956, then proceeded to the Royal B. School, founding their own Institute of Choreology in 1962. They have educated a great number of notators who are now working with the foremost cos. of the (Western) world. Today all important Royal B. prods. are written down in Benesh Notation. Like musical notation, the Benesh Notation works with a system of 5 lines, into which are written the positions and movements of the body according to the musical development in the symbols developed for this purpose. Together with Labanotation the Benesh D. Notation today represents the most widely used international system of d. notation.
BIBL.: R. and J.B., *An Introduction to B. Dance Notation* (London, 1956).

Bennett, Alexander (*b* Edinburgh, 1930). Brit. dancer, b. master, and teacher. Studied with M. Middleton. D. with Edinburgh B. Club, B. Rambert (rapidly becoming principal d.), and Sadler's Wells Th. B. master Transvaal B. in 1965, Western Th. B. in 1966, Cov. Gdn. Op. B. in 1969, Iceland B. in 1970. Has taught at Arts Educational Schools since 1971.

Bennett, Charles (*b* Wheaton, Ill., 4 Aug. 1934). Amer. dancer, choreographer, and director. Studied with Stone, Camryn, Pereyaslavec, Maracci, and Vladimiroff. D. with R. Page Op. B. 1952–3, Amer. B. Th. 1953–8 (becoming soloist), New York City B. 1960. Was one of the founder members of First Chamber D. Quartet 1961, which became First Chamber D. Co. of New York 1969, of which he is now Director. Founder and Director The Summer D. Laboratory since 1972.

Bennett, Isadora (*b* Canton, Missouri, 21 July 1900, *d* New York, 8 Feb. 1980). Amer. d. publicist. Started as a music critic of *Chicago Daily News*. Had a diverse career, writing for various newspapers and magazines, appearing as an actress, designing décors, writing plays. From the late 1930s until the early 1970s was in charge of the publicity of many Amer. and foreign dancers and cos., including La Argentinita, B. Th., Graham, Limón, Butler, City Center Joffrey B., National B. of Canada, Royal Dan. B. D. Magazine Award (1962); Capezio Award (1973).

Bennett, Michael (*b* Buffalo, N.Y., 8 Apr. 1943). Amer. dancer and choreographer. Studied locally. D. in *West Side Story* and *Subways Are for Sleeping*. Successful ch.-dir. of musicals: *Promises, Promises* (1968), followed by *Coco* (1970), *Company* (1971), *Follies* (1972), and *A Chorus Line* (1975). Has also worked for films and TV. D. Magazine Award (1976).
BIBL.: R. Philp, 'M.B. and the Making of *A Chorus Line*', *Dance Magazine* (1975/6); M. Hodgson, 'B.'s Tribute to the Chorus Line', *Dance News* (1976/2).

Bennington School of the Dance. The summer courses, first held in 1934 at the Bennington College and Undergraduate Liberal Arts College for Women, were destined to become one of the most important platforms for modern d. in the U.S. Until 1938 it presented many first prods. of works by Graham, Humphrey, Holm, Weidman and others. In 1939 a guest-session was held at Mills College, Calif. In 1940 the name was changed to Bennington School of Arts. In 1942 it practically ceased to exist. After the war it was succeeded by the *Connecticut College School of D.

Benois, Alexander Nicolaievich (*b* St. Petersburg, 3 May 1870, *d* Paris, 9 Feb. 1960). Russ. painter and designer. Descended from a famous family of artists; studied law at the univ. of St. Petersburg, started 1899 (with Diaghilev, Bakst, and Nouvel) the art magazine *Mir Iskusstva* (The World of Art), the staff of which was responsible for the Paris exhibitions of Russ. art and for the first Russ. b. season in Paris, 1909, from which emerged the Bs. Russes de Diaghilev. Artistic dir. of Diaghilev's co. until 1911. A man of great knowledge and immaculate taste, he influenced everybody who worked with him. Designed his first b. décors for the St. Petersburg Maryinsky Th. (*Sylvia* and *Cupid's Revenge*, 1901), followed by *Le Pavillon d'Armide* (1907). Became an international celebrity through his décors for Diaghilev: *Les Sylphides* and *Le Festin* (1909), *Giselle* (1910), *Petrushka* (1911), and *Song of the Nightingale* (1914). Further designs—for the co. of Rubinstein: *La Bien-Aimée* and *Les Noces de Psyché et l'Amour* (1928), and *La Valse* (1929); for B. Russe de Monte Carlo: *Graduation Ball* and *Nutcracker* (1940), and *Raymonda* (1946); for the de Cuevas co.: *Le Moulin enchantée* (1949); for London Festival B.: *Nutcracker* and *Graduation Ball* (1957). Author of *Reminiscences of the Russian Ballet* (London, 1941), and *Memoirs* (London, 1960). His son Nicola B. was chief-designer at the Milan La Scala. His niece Nadia B. (the mother of P. Ustinov) designed several bs. for B. Rambert (*Dark Elegies*, 1937, and *Lady Into Fox*, 1939) and Sadler's Wells B. (*The Sleeping Princess*, 1939).

Benserade, Isaac de (*b* Lyons-la-Forêt, 1612, *d* Paris, 19 Oct. 1691). Fr. poet. A favourite of Richelieu, Mazarin, and Louis XIV, he was very popular at the French court, writing poems for the bs. de cour, often set to mus. by Lully—among them *Mascarade en forme de Ballet* (1651), *Ballet de la nuit* (1653), *Ballet royal des noces de Pélée et de Thétis* (1654), *Ballet royal des proverbes* (1654), *Ballet royal des saisons* (1661), *Les Amours déguisés* (1664), and *Le Triomphe de l'amour* (1681). BIBL.: O. Silin, *B. and his Ballets de cour* (London, 1940); M.-F. Christout, in *Le Ballet de cour de Louis XIV* (Paris, 1967).

Bentley, Muriel (*b* New York). Amer. dancer. Studied with Tarasoff, Swoboda, Fokine, St. Denis, and Dolin, début with St. Denis 1931. D. with J. Greco 1936–7, Met. Op. B. 1938–9 and from 1940 for many years with B. Th.; particularly admired for her comic roles.

Bérain, Jean-Louis (*b* Bar-le-Duc, 1638, *d* 1711). Fr. designer. In charge of costumes for the prods. at the Paris Opéra from 1673 until his death, occasionally also designing the sets (*Le Triomphe de l'amour*, 1681). His richly embroidered costumes were much liked by Louis XIV, who wore them in the bs. de cour. He was succeeded by his son Jean B. fils.

Béranger, Anne (*b* Cairo). Fr. b. director. Trained in Paris to become a singer and actress, appearing in the Paris prod. of Menotti's *The Medium* (1958). Then started to work for Fr. TV, becoming O.R.T.F. producer of bs. in 1964. Formed a co. of her own in 1970, with J. Russillo as ch. Though

not a ch. herself, she made the co. a platform for young choreographers; Russillo was succeeded by C. Carlson, M. van Hoecke, J.-M. Marion, and S. Bonnafoux.
BIBL.: L. Rossel, 'Pleins feux sur A.B.', *Les Saisons de la danse* (1970/10).

Bérard, Christian (*b* Paris 1902, *d* there 13 Feb. 1949). Fr. painter and designer. Among his b. designs were Balanchine's *Cotillon* (Bs. Russes de Monte Carlo, 1932) and *Mozartiana* (Les Bs. 1933), Massine's *Symphonie fantastique* (Colonel de Basil's B. Russe, 1936), *Seventh Symphony* (B. Russe de Monte Carlo, 1938), and *Clock Symphony* (Sadler's Wells B., 1948). Co-founder (with Petit and Kochno) of Bs. des Champs-Elysées, for which he designed Petit's *Les Forains* (1945), and Lichine's *La Rencontre* (1948).

Beretta, Caterina (*b* Milan, 1839, *d* there, Jan. 1911). Ital. dancer and teacher. Studied at the school of La Scala, d. in the first prod. of Verdi's *Les Vêpres siciliennes* (Paris, 1853), becoming one of the most famous ballerinas of her time, acclaimed as far away as Russia. Maîtresse de b. at the St. Petersburg Maryinsky Th. (1877), and later also at La Scala 1902–8, where she was considered one of the best teachers. Among her students were Trefilova, Pavlova, Legnani, and Karsavina.

Berg, Alban (*b* Vienna, 9 Feb. 1885, *d* there, 24 Dec. 1935). Austrian composer. Wrote no b. mus. Choreographers who have set bs. to his concert works include Sokolow (*Lyric Suite*, Mexico City 1953; also L. Meyer in *Trial*, Western Th. B., 1966, Van Dyk, B. de Wallonie, 1973, and Ulrich, Bavarian State Op., 1974), Béjart (Pieces for Orchestra, op. 6, in *Matière*, as part of *Suite Viennoise*, B. of the 20th Century, 1961), L. Meyer (String Quartet, op. 3, in *Reconciliations*, Western Th. B., 1963; also Danovschi, Bucharest 1968), I. Eck (*Lulu* suite, B. Sopianae, 1967), and Tetley (Violin Concerto in *Threshold*, Hamburg, 1972).

Bergamasca (also Bergomask, Bergamasco, or Bergamasque). A very old, rustic peasant dance from the district around Bergamo in Lombardy. It is rather fast and usually in duple time. Men and women move in two circles in different directions; when the melody changes they embrace each other and continue as couples. The most popular musical instance is in Mendelssohn's *Midsummer Night's Dream* incidental mus.

Berger, Augustin (*b* Boscovice, 11 Aug. 1861, *d* Prague, 1 June 1945). Czech dancer, choreographer, and b. master. Studied with A. Viscusi, d. at the Dresden and Prague op. houses. B. master Prague National Th. and Metropolitan Op. House, New York (1922–32). Ch. the first non-Russ. prod. of the second act *Swan Lake* (1888), which Tchaikovsky attended in Prague—also Janáček's *Rákoš Rakoszy* (1891). He was the father of Jaroslav B., long-time b. master of the Zurich op. house.

Bergese, Micha (*b* Garmisch, 19 Feb. 1945). Ger.

dancer and choreographer. Studied first mus. and then at Andrew Hardie School and London School of Contemporary D. Joined London Contemporary D. Th. 1970, appointed lead d. in 1973. Created roles in R. Cohan's *Stages* (1973) and *Masque of Separation* (1974). Ch. *Hinterland* (mus. various, London Contemporary D. Th., 1972), *Act of Waiting* (mus. Webern, Junction D. Co., 1977), *Solo Ride* (mus. Douglas Gould, 1978), and *Some Dance and Some Duet* (mus. Stravinsky, 1980) as well as for other cos. and TV. Resigned as a d. to study Arts Administration at London Univ. Now has his own group called Mantis.

Bergsma, Deanne (*née* D. Harrismith; *b* Pretoria, 1941). Brit. dancer. Studied with Marjorie Sturman in S.A. and at Royal B. School. Member of the Royal B. since 1958, promoted soloist in 1962, principal d. in 1967. Created Lady *** in Ashton's *Enigma Variations* (1968), Polish Mother in his bs. for *Death in Venice* (1973), also principal part in Tetley's *Field Figures* (1970). With Royal Opera as Stella in Offenbach's *The Tales of Hoffmann* (1980–81).

Berio, Luciano (*b* Imperia, 24 Oct. 1925). Ital. composer. Wrote the mus. for Béjart's *I trionfi* (Florence, 1974). Choreographers who have used his concert mus. for their purposes include Halprin (*Visage*, Rome 1963—also Milloss, Florence, 1973, and J. Carter in *Pythoness Ascendant*, New London B., 1973), Tetley (*Circles,* Netherlands D. Th., 1968; *Laborintus*, Royal B., 1972—also Cauley, Zurich, 1973), Butler (*Sinfonia in Itinéraire*, B.-Th. Contemporain, 1970)—also Veredon in *Collage,* Cologne, 1970, Lubovitch in *Whirligogs*, Bat-Dor D. Co., 1970, Van Manen in *Keep Going*, Düsseldorf, 1971, Morrice in *That Is the Show*, B. Rambert, 1971, Van Dantzig in *Après Visage*, Dutch National B., 1972, Prokovsky in *Folk Songs*, New London B., 1974, and Kylian in *Dream Dances*, Netherlands Dance Th., 1979. All-Berio programmes have been presented by Descombey at the Opéra Comique, Paris, 1970, and by Blaska in Grenoble, 1974.

Beriosova, Svetlana (*b* Kaunas, Lithuania, 24 Sep. 1932). Brit. dancer. The daughter of b. master N. Beriozoff, she started to study in the U.S. with Schollar and Vilzak 1940, made her début in Ottawa 1947, joining Grand B. de Monte Carlo in the same year. Ballerina of the Eng. Metropolitan B. 1948–49, became soloist of the Sadler's Wells Th. B. 1950, transferred to the Sadler's Wells B. in 1952, promoted ballerina in 1955. Guest ballerina with many cos. throughout the world. Was noted for the immaculate aristocracy of her ballerina roles of the classic repertory and the nobility of her performances in the bs. of the modern repertory. Created roles in Taras's *Designs With Strings* (1948), Balanchine's *Trumpet Concerto* (1950), Cranko's *The Shadow* (1953), *Prince of the Pagodas* (1957), and *Antigone* (1959), Ashton's *Rinaldo and Armida* (1955),

Birthday Offering (1956), *Persephone* (1961), and *Enigma Variations* (1968), MacMillan's *Baiser de la Fée* (1960), *Diversions* (1961), *Images of Love* (1964), *Checkpoint*, and *Anastasia* (1970 version). Officially retired in 1975, but continues coaching with various cos.

BIBL.: A. Franks, *S.B.* (London, 1958).

Beriozoff, Nicholas (*b* Kaunas, Lithuania, 16 May 1906). Lith.-Brit. dancer, choreographer, and b. master. Studied in Prague, started to d. in Kaunas 1930–5, with R. Blum B. de Monte Carlo 1935–8, B. Russe de Monte Carlo 1938–44. B. master of B. International 1944, of Metropolitan B. 1948, La Scala, Milan, 1950–1, London Festival B. 1951–4, returned to Grand B. du Marquis de Cuevas 1956, b. dir. Stuttgart 1957–60, again with Grand B. du Marquis de Cuevas 1961–2, Helsinki 1962–4, Zurich 1964–71, Naples 1971–3. A b. master of the old school, he created a special local b. climate both in Stuttgart (where he preceded Cranko) and Zurich. As ch. he specialized in producing the classics of the 19th century (also *Esmeralda*, mus. Pugni-Corbett, London Festival B., 1954) and the Fokine bs. of the Diaghilev repertory. Has also ch. own versions of *Ondine* (mus. Henze. 1965), *Romeo and Juliet* (mus. Prokofiev, 1966), and *Cinderella* (mus. Prokofiev, 1967). Head of B. Department of Univ. of Indiana, Bloomington, during the late 1970s. He is the father of the d. Svetlana Beriosova. Now married to the d. Doris Catana.

BIBL.: G. B. L. Wilson: 'B. at 75', *Dancing Times* (1981/7).

Berk, Fred (*b* Vienna, 25 Jan. 1911, *d* New York, 26 Feb. 1980). Amer. dancer, choreographer, and teacher. Studied with H. Pfundmayr and G. Kraus. Appeared in Europe in many d. concerts as soloist, and with his group, 1934–8. Member of Cuban Yavorsky B. 1939–41. Co-founded Merry-Go-Rounders in New York, for which he ch. as well as for his own co. of Hebraica Dancers. Became Dir. of the Jewish D. Division at the New York YMHA.

Berkeley, Busby (*b* Los Angeles, 29 Nov. 1895, *d* Palm Springs, 14 Mar. 1976). Amer. director and choreographer, known particularly for his extravagantly staged d.-numbers in Hollywood films of the 1930s. He let the cameras rather than the dancers move within the mostly geometrical patterns he set up, thus becoming one of the innovators of cine-dance. One of Broadway's busiest stage dir. of the twenties, he came to Hollywood for the prod. numbers of *Whoopee* (1930), followed by *Palmy Days* (1931), *The Kid From Spain* (1932), *Roman Scandals* (1933), *42nd Street* (1933), *Gold Diggers of 1933* (also 1935, 1936, and 1938), *Footlight Parade* (1933), *Wonder Bar* (1934), *Caliente* (1935), *Broadway Serenade* (1939), *Lady Be Good* (1941), *Ziegfeld Girl* (1943), *Girl Crazy* (1943) and others. His favourite leading lady was Ruby Keeler.

BIBL.: B. and T. Thomas, *B.B. Book* (New York, 1973).

Berkeley, Michael (*b* London, 29 May 1948). Br. composer. Wrote his String Quartet No. 1 partly for M. Pink's *Attraction* (Northern B. Th., 1981), partly for simultaneous independent concert prèmiere.

Berlin. Ballet started here with the opening of the Royal Op. House in 1742. Completely Fr. orientated, its first b. masters were Michel Poitier, Bartholomé Lany, and Etienne Lauchery; its most famous ballerina was La Barberina (1744–8). Though the National Th. at the Gendarmenmarkt, as the house for Ger. ops. and Singspiele, initially had a co. of its own, from 1792 its bs. were performed by the Court Op. co. Constantin Michel Telle, Monsieur Titus, and Michel-François Houguet were the leading b. masters during the first half of the 19th century, when internationally known works were produced (*La Fille mal gardée*, 1818; *Danina or Jocko the Brazilian Ape*, 1826; *La Sylphide*, 1832; *Giselle*, 1843; *Esmeralda*, 1847; *Le Diable à quatre*, 1849) and ballerinas such as Elssler and Taglioni frequently appeared as guests. B. flourished especially during the reign of Paul Taglioni (1856–83), who had already earlier ch. *Ondine* (1836), *Don Quixote* (1839), and *Satanella* (1852); his successes continued with *Flick and Flock's Adventures* (1858), *Electra or The Stars* (1862), *Fantasca* (1869) up to *Coppélia* (1881). Later on, however, the situation deteriorated; *Sylvia* (1884) and *The Fairy Doll* (1892) were the century's last important premières. Though there were occasional visits by guest cos., regular b.-perfs. only re-started after the First World War when the house became the State Op. Under Heinrich Kröller (1921–3), Max Terpis (1923–30), Rudolf von Laban (1930–4), and Lizzie Maudrik (1934–45) a modern repertory was cultivated, from which only *Joan von Zarissa* (1940) has survived. As the Ger. State Op. the co. continued after the Second World War at the East Berlin Admirals-Palast makeshift th. There Tatjana Gsovsky (1945–51) ch. the repertory—still mainly modern—culminating in the first Ger. prod. of Prokofiev's *Romeo and Juliet* (1948). When the co. returned to its rebuilt house, Unter den Linden in 1955, she was succeeded by Lilo Gruber (1955–70), who ensured a balanced repertory of classics and moderns. After her there have been only temporary b. directorships with guest-choreographers such as L. Seregi and V. Vainonen. The city's second op.-house, the Charlottenburg Op. House, has followed its own b. course since it was opened in 1912. It changed its name several times—the Municipal Op., the German Op. House, and today the German Op. Berlin, which is the West Berlin equivalent of the East Berlin German State Op. It enjoyed an active b. policy under the direction of Rudolf Kölling (1934–45), and particularly after the war, when T. Gsovsky (1957–66) ch. a great number of first prods. including works by B. Blacher and L. Nono; J. Charrat prod. a long-lasting success in 1949 with *Abraxas*, and M. Wigman did a much discussed version of *Sacre du printemps* (1957). When K. MacMillan was b. director 1966–9, he introduced the classics and created such bs. as *Concerto* (1966) and *Anastasia* (1967), which were later revived for other cos. A steady stream of guest-choreographers began during the sixties and still continues with G. Reinholm as the co.'s dir. During recent years Balanchine, Cranko, Taras, Van Manen, Van Dantzig, Panov, Forsythe, and Spoerli have worked here. The city's third b. co. is based on the East Berlin Comic Op., where regular b. performances started in 1947. It was, however, only with the appointment of T. Schilling as its chief ch. in 1965 that the co. began to develop an individuality of its own.

BIBL.: H. Koegler, entry 'B.', in *Friedrichs Ballettlexikon von A-Z* (Velber, 1972).

Berlin Ballet (orig. Ger. name: Berliner Ballett). The co. which T. Gsovsky assembled for the 1955 Berlin Festival, for which she choreographed *Labyrinth, Signals, Souvenirs*, and *Ballade*, with J. P. Ponnelle as designer, and G. Deege, S. Köller, G. Reinholm, and R. Smolik as principal soloists. The co. toured widely with continually changing personnel, though Gsovsky contributed almost all the new bs., and revived some of her works which she had done for other cos.—including *The Lady of the Camellias, Hamlet, The Moor of Venice, Orphée*, and *The Idiot*. Among the dancers performing with the co. were I. Skorik, J. Sassoon, N. Trofimowa, H. Sommerkamp. Y. Chauviré, O. Ferri, J. Cadzow, G. Urbani, and H. Horn. When Gsovsky became b. director of the Berlin Municipal Op., the co. became the touring ensemble of the house.

Berlioz, Louis Hector (*b* Côte-Saint André, 11 Dec. 1803, *d* Paris, 8 Mar. 1869). Fr. composer. Wrote no. bs., but his op. *Les Troyens* (1863) contains substantial b. sequences, which have lately been choreographed by Meriel Evans (Cov. Gdn., London, 1957), Skeaping (Royal Swedish Op., Stockholm, 1958), A. Woolliams (Stuttgart, 1967), G. Lynne and M. Parker (Cov. Gdn., London, 1969), Taras and Wallmann (Opéra, Paris, 1969, and Bolender (Met. Op. House New York, 1973). Ch. who have produced his symphony *Romeo and Juliet*, with soli and choirs, include Skibine (de Cuevas comp., 1955), E. Walter (Wuppertal, 1959), and Béjart (B. of the 20th Century, 1966). Béjart also ch. *Damnation of Faust* (Opéra, Paris, 1964). Many choreographers have tackled his *Symphonie fantastique* since Massine staged it for the B. Russe de Monte Carlo (1936). Other bs. to his mus. have been Massine's *Harold in Italy* (B. Russe de Monte Carlo, 1954—also by H. Spoerli, Ger. Op. Berlin, 1981), Petit's *Palais de Chaillot* (various overtures, Paris, 1962), J. Carter's *The Unknown Island* (to his *Nuits d'été*,

London Festival B., 1969) and F. Howald's *Lélio* (Frankfurt, 1980).

Berman, Eugene (*b* St. Petersburg, 4 Nov. 1899, *d* Rome, 14 Dec. 1972). Russ.-Amer. designer. He came to the U.S. in 1937, and became one of the most respected designers of the Amer. th., collaborating with Ashton in *Devil's Holiday* (1939), Balanchine in *Concerto Barocco* (1941), *Danses concertantes* (1944), *Le Bourgeois gentilhomme* (1944), and *Pulcinella* (1972), Tudor in *Romeo and Juliet* (1953), and designing the 2nd *Giselle* prod. for Amer. B. Th. (1946).
BIBL.: A. Delarue, 'The Stage and Ballet Designs of E.B.', *Dance Index*, vol. 5, no. 2; A. Fatt, 'Designers for the Dance', *Dance Magazine* (1967/3).

Bernadelli, Fortunato. Of unknown descent; his name appears as a dancer and choreographer of the Kobler family troupe when it appeared in Amsterdam in 1812. He went to Paris and Brussels with the Koblers (always advertised individually), and from there to Vienna (1813–14). He brought *La Fille mal gardée* to St. Petersburg in 1818; then he was in Moscow 1819–22, where he ch. a great number of bs., incl. the highly popular *La Flûte enchantée ou les Danseurs involontaires* (1818). He returned there in 1826, and was much acclaimed as a mime and for his short b. comedies, which presented simple people in sympathetic fashion. During his second stay in Moscow he also produced several 'serious' works, as well as some revivals of bs. by Noverre and Viganò.
BIBL.: M. H. Winter, in *The Pre-Romantic Ballet* (London, 1974).

Berners, Lord (Gerald Hugh Tyrwhitt-Wilson) (*b* Bridgnorth, 18 Sep. 1883, *d* London, 19 May 1950). Brit. composer and designer (and diplomat). Wrote the mus. for Balanchine's *The Triumph of Neptune* (1926), and for Ashton's *A Wedding Bouquet* (for which he was also the designer, 1937), *Cupid and Psyché* (1939), and *Les Sirènes* (1946).

Bernstein, Leonard (*b* Lawrence, Mass., 25 Aug. 1918). Amer. composer and conductor. Wrote the mus. for Robbins's *Fancy Free* (1944), *Facsimile* (1946), and *Dybbuk Variations* (1974). Robbins also ch. his second Symphony (*Age of Anxiety*, 1950) as well as all his musicals (*On the Town*, 1944; *Wonderful Town*, 1953; *Candide*, 1956; *West Side Story*, 1957). The dances for his *Mass* were ch. by Ailey (Washington, 1971). Neumeier ch. an all-B. programme, incl. *Age of Anxiety* and *Song fest* (Hamburg, 1979).

Bertram Batell's Side Show. A children's programme, prepared by J. Taylor and P. Cazalet, with additional ch. by P. Curtis, J. Scoglio, P. Law, A. Knott, and others, for a short season of B. Rambert at the Jeannetta Cochrane Th., London, from 28 Mar. 1970; later frequently given on tour. The title is an anagram of the co.'s name, and the programme consisted of a string of short dances and scenes, all highly entertaining.

Beryozhka. A Sov. d. co., founded in 1948 by Nadezhda Nadezhdina, who became its artistic director and chief ch., originally consisting only of women. Its name is Russ. for 'young birch-trees', referring to a round d. from the Kalinin region, in which the women glide round the stage, their feet invisible under long 'sarafan' skirts, carrying birch branches in their hands. In 1961 some men joined the Moscow-based co., which today consists of 70 women and 40 men, most of whom are graduates from the Moscow Bolshoi School, plus an orchestra of 20. The dancers are trained regularly both in academic and character classes, and the co. sees its position as halfway between a folklore ensemble and a character d. troupe, with an extensive repertory of dances and scenes based on Russ. themes and sources. It tours widely abroad, and paid its first visit to England in 1954, and to the U.S. in 1958.
BIBL.: N. Roslavleva, *The 'B.' State Dance Company* (Moscow, 1960).

Besobrasova, Marika (*b* Yalta, 4 Aug. 1918). Russ.-Monegasque dancer and teacher. Studied with Sedova, Egorova, and V. Gsovsky, joined the Bs. de Monte Carlo, in 1935, had a Cannes-based co. of her own 1940–3, was teacher of the Grand B. du Marquis de Cuevas 1947–8 and of the Bs. des Champs-Elysées 1949–50, after which she opened a school in Monte Carlo, where she is also in charge of the bs. at the Opéra. Has been guest-teacher with a great number of cos. (Rome, Copenhagen, Paris, Milan, Zurich, Stuttgart *et al.*).

Bessmertnova, Natalia Igorievna (*b* Moscow, 19 July 1941). Sov. dancer. Studied 1952–61 at Moscow Bolshoi School, joining the Bolshoi B. after graduation. With her soft, lyrical, eminently feminine quality, she is an ideal interpreter of the ballerina roles of the classic repertory; also excels as Kitri, Juliet, Shirin (in *Legend of Love*), Maria (in *Fountain of Bakhchisaray*), and Phrygia (in *Spartacus*). Created Leili in Goleisovsky's *Leili and Medshnun* (1964), Anastasia in her husband Y. Grigorovich's *Ivan the Terrible* (1975), and female lead in his *Angara* (1976). Gold Medal (Varna, 1965); Prix A. Pavlova (Paris, 1970).

Bessmertnova, Tatyana Igorievna (*b* 1947). Sov. dancer. Studied at Moscow Bolshoi B. School, joining the co. after graduation; appointed soloist 1970. D. Giselle in Sov. TV prod. 1975. Sister of Natalia B.; married to the d. M. Gabovich.

Bessone, Emma. Ital. dancer. Studied in Milan. Prima ballerina in St. Petersburg where she created Ivanov's *The Tulip of Harlem* (1887); then moved to Moscow, staying for several years as prima ballerina with the Bolshoi. She was a brilliant technician.

Bessy, Claude (*b* Paris, 20 Oct. 1932). Fr. dancer and teacher. Entered Paris Opéra B. School in 1942, joined its co. in 1945, promoted Danseuse étoile in 1956. Directrice de l'Ecole de Danse de l'Opéra since 1972. D. the ballerina roles of the classic and modern standard repertory, creating parts in Lifar's *Snow White* (1951), *Pas et lignes* (1954), *Les Noces fantastiques* (1955), *Chemin de lumière* (1957), and *Daphnis and Chloe* (1958), Cranko's *La belle Hélène* (1955), G. Kelly's *Pas de dieux* (1960), Descombey's *Sarracenia* (1964), Skibine's *Les Bandar Log* (1969), and N. Schmucki's *Aor* (1971). Retired as an Opéra étoile in 1975. Apart from choreographing a small number of bs., appeared in numerous TV prods. and films (among them Kelly's *Invitation to the Dance*, 1953) and wrote *Danseuse-Etoile* in 1961. Prix A. Pavlova (1961); Legion d'honneur (1973).
BIBL.: A.-Ph. Hersin, 'B.', *Les Saisons de la danse* (1969/3—with complete list of roles).

Bestonso, Roberto (*b* Nice, 27 May 1942). Fr. dancer. Studied at the local Conservatory and Paris Opéra B. School. Danced with Bs. R. Petit 1965–7, joined the Opéra in 1966, and London Festival B. in 1967; appointed principal soloist. Went to South Africa to d. with PACT B. in 1970. R. Blum Prize (1961).
BIBL.: 'R.B.', *Dance and Dancers* (1969/6).

Bettis, Valerie (*b* Houston, 1920, *d* N.Y., 26 Sept. 1982). Amer. dancer and choreographer. Studied in Houston and with Holm and d. in her co. 1938–40. Gave her first solo-perf. in New York in 1941; appeared with her own group from 1944. Her best known works are *Virginia Sampler* (mus. L. Smith, B. Russe de Monte Carlo, 1947), *As I Lay Dying* (after Faulkner, mus. B. Segall, for her own co., 1948), and *A Streetcar Named Desire* (after T. Williams, mus. A. North, Slavenska-Franklin co., 1952). Considered one of the pioneers of TV b. in the States; also appeared in musicals and films, and collaborated on the th. adaptation of J. Joyce's *Ulysses in Nighttown* (1958).

Bewegungschor. R. von Laban coined this term for his mass movement choirs, based mainly on amateurs, for which he ch. such works as *The Rocking Temple* (1922), *Light Turn* (1923), *Agamemnon's Death* (after Noverre, 1924), *Dusky Rhythms* (1925), and *Titan* (1927). This movement had a great influence in the Ger. th., with every ensemble trying to have its own B. for its prods. of plays and ops. (especially for the works of Monteverdi, Handel, and Gluck).

Bewley, Lois (*b* Louisville, 1936). Amer. dancer and choreographer. Studied with Lilias Courtney, subsequently with Schwezoff. Joined B. Russe de Monte Carlo in 1955, Amer. B. Th. in 1958, J. Robbins's Bs.: U.S.A. in 1959, and New York City B. in the same year, before becoming co-founder of First Chamber Dance Quartet in 1961, for which she ch. extensively during the next 9 years, with *Pi R Square* (mus. Varèse, 1961) as her

biggest success. Now working as a freelance ballerina, dir., ch., and designer.
BIBL.: S. Goodman, 'L.B.', *Dance Magazine* (1964/10).

Bey, Hannelore (*b* Leipzig, 6 Nov. 1941). Ger. dancer. Studied at Dresden Palucca School and Leningrad Ch. School; joined the co. of the Dresden State Op. and in 1966 the Berlin Comic Op., rapidly becoming one of its most popular soloists and dancing the ballerina roles in the co.'s repertory. Created roles in Schilling's *Abraxas* (1965), *La Mer* (1968), *Cinderella* (1968), *Ondine* (1970), *Match* (1971), and *Romeo and Juliet* (1973). Married to the d. Frank Bey. Bronze Medal (Varna, 1968).

Bhakti. See *A la recherche de . . .*

Bharata Natyam. A female solo d., over 2000 years old, performed by Hindu devadasis (temple d.), practised today mainly in the region of Madras, South India. Its name derives from *Bharata Natya Shastra*, Bharata's book (written between 200 B.C. and 300 A.D.) on drama for the d.-actor. It is based on clear structures and characterized by great strength and austerity. Its perf. lasts up to 3 hours and has 6 different parts: *Allarippu* (an invocation of the deity and greeting to the audience) and *Tillana* (a pure d. as a coda), between which are placed various examples of *nritya* (the expression of sentiment and mood in d.), and *nritta* (pure d.). The d. wears a brocade blouse and a richly decorated silk sari and is accompanied by musicians playing cymbals and singing.
BIBL.: R. Singha and R. Massey, in *Indian Dances* (London, 1967).

Bhaskar (orig. B. Roy Chowdhury; *b* Madras, Ind., 11 Feb. 1930). Ind. dancer and teacher. Studied with Ellappa Pillai; début with his own group in Madras in 1950. Came to New York in 1956, where he teaches Ind. d. and occasionally appears with a small co. Has also ch. for Broadway.
BIBL.: J. Pikula, 'B., The Boy from Madras', *Dance Magazine* (1975/7).

Biagi, Vittorio (*b* Viareggio, 24 May 1941). Ital. dancer, choreographer, and b. director. Studied with M. Porcile in Genoa and with M. Molina. Member of the Milan La Scala co. 1958–60, and of the B. of the 20th Century 1961–6, where he appeared in numerous Béjart bs. and began to ch. (*Jazz Impressions*, 1964; *L'après-midi d'un faune*, 1964; *Walpurgis Night*, 1965). Joined the Paris Op. Comique as an étoile; ch. Ravel's *L'enfant et les sortilèges* in 1967 in Amsterdam and Rameau's *Platée* in 1968, both in prods. by Louis Erlo, who, after being appointed general manager of the op. in Lyons, engaged him in 1969 as b. dir. Now has his own, Ital.-based group Danza Prospettiva. Many of his bs. created there during recent years are based on mus. by Prokofiev—including *Alexander Nevsky, Scythian Suite,* and *Romeo and*

Juliet. Other prods.: *Requiem* (mus. Berlioz), *7th Symphony* (mus. Beethoven), *Symphonie fantastique* (mus. Berlioz), and *Song of the Earth* (mus. Mahler).

Bias, Fanny (*b* 3 June 1789, *d* Paris, 6 Sep. 1825). Fr. dancer. Entered Paris Opéra B. School as a child, becoming a member of its co. in 1807, and gradually progressing to the post of senior premier sujet. She was noted for her precision, aplomb, lightness, and flexibility and was one of the first dancers to be shown on points, in a lithograph by Waldeck of 1821.
BIBL.: I. Guest, in *The Romantic Ballet in Paris* (London, 1966).

Biches, Les. Ballet in 1 act; ch. Nijinska; mus. Poulenc; déc. Laurencin. Prod. 6 Jan. 1924, Bs. Russes de Diaghilev, Monte Carlo, with Nijinska, Nemtchinova, Tchernicheva, Sokolova, Vilzak, Woizikovsky, Zverev. Eight d. numbers with slight jazz accents, set in S. France at a privileged house party of the 1920s, and showing the flirtations of 3 handsome boys who proudly parade their muscles before their worldly-wise hostess, a sexually ambiguous creature in blue, a group of giggling girls, and 2 young women absorbed in each other. J. Cocteau described it as 'les Fêtes galantes de notre temps'. The Fr. title means 'the hinds', but more colloquially 'the little darlings'. Revived for many cos., incl. Royal B. (1964).
BIBL.: J. Cocteau, *L. B.* (Paris, 1924); F. Poulenc, *L.B.* in *Ballet* (London) 1947/Vol. 2, No. 4; G. Balanchine in *Balanchine's Complete Stories of the Great Ballets* (Garden City, N.Y. 1977).

Bien-Aimée, La. See *Beloved, The*.

Big Bertha. Ballet by P. Taylor; mus. from the collection of band machines in the St. Louis Melody Museum. New York first perf. 9 Feb. 1971, P. Taylor and D. Co., ANTA Th., with de Jong, Eileen Cropley, C. Adams, Taylor. A d. cartoon in Charles Addams style; it shows the disintegration of a typical Amer. middle-class family who visit a fair and become increasingly enthralled by B.B., a huge animated doll on the top of a musical box, which incessantly plays sentimental waltzes and marches. While working on the b., Taylor created a duet version for TV, performed by de Jong and Nureyev.

Big City, The (orig. Ger. title: *Großstadt 1926*). Ballet in 3 scenes; libr. and ch. Jooss; mus. A. Tansman; déc. Heckroth. Prod. 21 Nov. 1932, Folkwang D. Stage, Cologne, with Mascha Lidolt, Leeder, Uthoff. 'In the hurrying throng of a continental city are seen the Young Girl and the Young Workman, her sweetheart, homeward bound after the day's work. The Libertine, in search of new conquests, follows the Young Girl to her home. Dazzled by the promise of adventure she fares forth on his arm to the dance halls, where disillusion awaits her' (programme note).

Revived for Wuppertal D. Th. (1974), City Center Joffrey B. (1975), and Northern B. Th. (1976).

Bigottini, Emilie (*b* Toulouse, 16 Apr. 1784, *d* Paris, 28 Apr. 1858). Fr. dancer. Descended from a family of players, she studied with her brother-in-law Milon, d. at the Paris Théâtre de l'Ambigu-Comique, becoming a member of the Opéra in 1801, where she was much admired because of her dramatic eloquence (in Vienna they later called her 'the ear of the deaf'). She remained there until 1823 and created a great number of roles, her most famous being Nina in Milon's eponymous b. of 1813; she was the fierce rival of Mme. Gardel and counted Napoleon among her many admirers.
BIBL.: I. Guest, in *The Romantic Ballet in Paris* (London, 1966).

Bije, Willy de la. See Bye, Willy de la.

Billy the Kid. Ballet in 1 act; libr. Kirstein; ch. Loring; mus. Copland; déc. Jared French. Prod. 16 Oct. 1938, B. Caravan, Chicago Op. House, Chicago, with Loring, Marie-Jeanne, L. Christensen, Bolender. A. b. western, based on the legendary William H. Bonney (alias B.t.K.), who had killed a man for every year of his life and at the age of 21 was hunted down and shot from ambush by his former friend, the sheriff. One of the most successful bs. based on Amer. folklore. Since 1941 it has enjoyed a favourite place in the repertory of B. Th. Omnibus TV prod. 1953.
BIBL.: G. Balanchine, '*B.t.K.*' in *Balanchine's New Complete Stories of the Great Ballets* (Garden City, N.Y., 1968).

Bintley, David Julian (*b* Huddersfield, 17 Sep. 1957). Brit. d. and ch. Studied with Audrey Spencer, Dorothy Stevens and at Royal B. Upper School (with Walter Trevor, T. Westmoreland, and P. Beaumont). Joined Sadler's Wells Royal B. in 1976, creating roles in bs. by L. Seymour, D. Morse and K. MacMillan and becoming a leading character d. in classical repertory. Started to ch. for S.W. Royal B. in 1978: *The Outsider* (mus. Josef Boháč) and *Take Five* (mus. D. Brubeck, both 1978), *Meadow of Proverbs* (mus. Milhaud, 1979), *Punch and the Street Party* (mus. Lord Berners, S.W. Royal B., 1979), *Homage to Chopin* (mus. Panufnik, S.W. Royal B., 1980), *Adieu* (mus. Panufnik, Royal B., 1980), *Polonia* (mus. Panufnik, S.W. Royal B. 1980), and *Night Moves* (mus. Britten, S.W. Royal B., 1981). Promoted co. ch. S.W. Royal B. 1983, resident ch. R.B. 1985.

Birkmeyer. Viennese family of ds.; Adolf, Toni, and Michael are its most famous members. Adolf B. joined the Vienna Court Op. in 1852, one of its solo-dancers 1870–85. His son Toni B. (*b* Vienna, 25 Apr. 1897, *d* there, 30 Aug. 1973) studied at the sch. of the Court Op., joining its co. in 1912; appointed solo-d. in 1921, and first solo-d. 1938–54, with an interregnum as the co.'s b. master 1931–4. He was in charge of the revivals of bs. by Hassreiter and Kröller. His best roles were in *Legend of Joseph, Sheherazade, Carnaval, The Good-for-Nothing in Vienna,* and *Coppélia.* With G. Wiesenthal and Losch he toured abroad. Taught at the Vienna State Acad. 1948–63. His son Michael B. (*b* Vienna, 20 Oct. 1943) studied at Vienna State Op. B. School, with his father, V. Gsovsky, and Hightower, joining the State Op. co. in 1960; appointed principal d. in 1972. He danced the premier danseur roles of the repertory and was a guest with The Australian B. when it toured Europe in 1965. Dir. B. Sch. Aust. State Ths. from 1985.

Birthday Offering. Ballet in 1 act; ch. Ashton; mus. Glazunov, arr. Irving; déc. A. Levasseur. Prod. 5 May 1956, Sadler's Wells B., Cov. Gdn., London, with Fonteyn, Grey, Elvin, Nerina, Jackson, Beriosova, Fifield, Somes. A virtuoso display in the form of a grand divertissement, created by Ashton on the occasion of the co.'s 25th birthday for its 7 ballerinas.
BIBL.: G. Balanchine, 'B.O.' in *Balanchine's New Complete Stories of the Great Ballets* (Garden City, N.Y., 1968).

Birth of the Royal Ballet. Ballet-Play in 2 parts. Written by P. Brinson, prod. by A. Grant. Prod. 13 Oct. 1972, B. for All, Spa Pavilion, Felixstowe. The play retraces the story of Britain's top co. from its early days in 1930 to its Cov. Gdn. début with *Sleeping Beauty* in 1946, through excerpts from its repertory during these years.

Bischoff, Egon (*b* Gotha, 10 June 1934). Ger. dancer and b. director. Studied at the Dresden Palucca school and at the Leningrad Ch. Institute; then became a member of the East Berlin Germ. State Op., of which he has been b. dir. since 1974.

Bissell, Patrick (*b* Corpus Christi, Tex., 1 Dec. 1957). Amer. dancer. Studied with Bud Kerwin in Toledo, Ohio, then at National Academy of the Arts in Champaign, Ill., and School of Amer. B., before joining Boston B. 1975. Joined Amer. B. Th. 1977, promoted soloist 1978 and principal d. 1979. Created leading male role in Tudor's *The Tiller in the Fields* (1979). Left Amer. B. Th. 1980, cr. title role in P. Darrell's *Chéri* (Scottish B., 1980), returned to Amer. B. Th. 1981.
BIBL.: J. Gruen, 'P.B.', *Dance Magazine* (1979/4).

Bix Pieces, The. Three d. pieces by Tharp; mus. songs from the 1920s and Haydn. Prod. 7 Sept. 1972, T. Tharp and Dancers, Delacorte Dance Festival, New York, with Tharp, Sara Rudner, Rose Marie Wright, Isabel Garcia-Lorca, and Kenneth Rinkler. Referring to the Bix Beiderbecke era, the ch. evokes memories of ballroom dances, chorus-girl routines, baton-twirling parades, and tap dancing. An earlier version under the title of *True Confessions* was premiered on 9 Nov. 1971 at the Th. de la Cité Internationale, Paris.

Bizet, Georges (*b* Paris, 25 Oct. 1938, *d* Bougival,

3 June 1875). Fr. composer. Composed no specific b. mus., apart from individual dances for his ops. Arrangements of his mus. for *Carmen* have often been used for b. purposes—in 1931 for K. Goleizovsky's *Carmen*, by Jerome Moross for Page's *Guns and Castanets* (Chicago, 1939), anon. for Petit's *Carmen* (London, 1969), R. Shchedrin for Alb. Alonso's *Carmen Suite* (Moscow, 1967), and W. Fortner and W. Steinbrenner for Cranko's *Carmen* (Stuttgart, 1971). Among the various ch. versions of his *Jeux d'enfants*, Massine's of 1932 is the most famous. His Symphony in C major served both Howard for her *Assembly Ball* (London, 1946) and Balanchine for his *Palais de cristal* or *Symphony in C* (Paris, 1947). In 1974 the Bs. de Marseille presented an *Hommage à B.,* with G. Vantaggio's *Bizet'isme* (from *Jolie Fille de Perth*) and Petit's *Jeux d'enfants, L'Arlésienne,* and *Carmen.*

Bjørn, Dinna (orig. D. B. Larsen; *b* Copenhagen, 14 Feb. 1947). Dan. d. The daughter of Niels B. Larsen. Studied at Royal Dan B. School and with Besobrasova, M. Surowiak, Hightower, Golovine, and Pereyaslavec. Since 1966 she has been a member of the Royal Dan. B., where she made her début in Robbins's *Afternoon of a Faun.* Apart from appearing in the bs. of the repertory, has d. at the Tivoli Pantomime Th. where she created von Rosen's *Mam-zelle Nitouche* (1970). Has also ch. individual bs. Bronze Medal (Varna, 1968). Now dir. Soloists of Royal Dan. B. and b. master.

Bjørnsson, Fredbjørn (*b* Copenhagen, 10 Sep. 1926). Dan. dancer and teacher. Entered Royal Dan. B. School in 1935, becoming a member of the co. in 1945, appointed solo-d. in 1949. An excellent character d., particularly admired for his interpretations of Bournonville roles. Has ch. smaller pieces at various times and is now much in demand as a teacher. Married to the d. Kirsten Ralov. Knight of the Order of Dannebrog (1961).
BIBL.: S. Kragh-Jacobsen, 'F.B.' in *20 Solo-dancers of The Royal Danish Ballet* (Copenhagen, 1965).

Blache, Jean-Baptiste (*b* Berlin, 17 May 1765, *d* Toulouse, 24 Jan. 1834). Fr. dancer and choreographer. Studied in Berlin and from 1776 with Deshayes in Paris. D. at the Paris Opéra 1781–6, after which he made a very successful career as ch. in Montpellier, Marseilles, Lyons, Bordeaux (where he succeeded Dauberval), and elsewhere; *Daphnis, La Noce villageoise, La Fête indienne, La Folle par amour,* and *La Famille fugitive ou La Laitière polonaise* were his most popular bs. Together with Duport he created for the Paris Opéra *Le Barbier de Séville* (1806) and *Les Filets de Vulcain ou Mars et Vénus* (mus. Schneitzhöffer, 1820). After choreographing the very successful *Almaviva ou Rosine* for Lyons, he retired in 1830. His first son Frédéric Auguste (*b* Marseille, 1791, *d* ?) was b. master at the Paris Th. de la Porte-Saint-Martin, where he produced in 1825 *Jocko ou le Singe du Brésil*; his second son Alexis Scipion (*b* Marseilles, 1792, *d* Bordeaux, 1852) became a much respected b. master in Bordeaux, Paris, Marseilles, and St. Petersburg, where *Malek Adel ou Les Croisés, Don Juan, Gustave Vasa, Amadis de Gaule,* and *La Tarentule* were among his bs.

Blacher, Boris (*b* Newchwang, China, 6 Jan. 1903, *d* Berlin, 30 Jan. 1975). One of the most successful Ger. b. composers. Wrote the mus. for *Hamlet* (ch. V. Gsovsky, Munich, 1950), *Chiarina* (ch. J. Keith, Berlin, 1950), *The First Ball* (ch. Charrat, Berlin, 1950), *Lysistrata* (ch. Blank, Berlin, 1951), the b. op. *Prussian Fairy-Tale* (ch. Blank, Berlin, 1952), *The Moor of Venice* (ch. Hanka, Vienna, 1955), *Demeter* (ch. Georgi, Schwetzingen 1964), and *Tristan* (ch. T. Gsovsky, Berlin, 1965). Several choreographers have set bs. to his *Paganini Variations,* among them Bolender (Cologne, 1963) and Urbani (Florence, 1969).

Black Crook, The. Amer. extravaganza. Prod. 12 Sep. 1866, Niblo's Garden, New York. One of the biggest hit-prods. of the Amer. th., it is considered the main source of later developments in the Amer. music hall, variety th., vaudeville, and mus. th. A Great Parisienne Ballet Troupe from the Grand Opéra, Paris, participated under the direction of David Costa with M. Bonfanti and R. Sangalli as premiers danseurs. During its almost uninterrupted run in New York and on tour until 1909, hundreds of dancers appeared in this show, thus introducing large numbers of Amer. citizens to the art of b.
BIBL.: G. Freeley, 'The B.C. and The White Fawn', *Dance Index* IV, 1.

Black, Maggie (*b* c. 1930). Amer. dancer and teacher. Studied with Tudor and others. D. with Met. Op. B., Amer. B. Th., and other cos. Taught at Juilliard School. Opened her own New York studio in the late 1960s; soon became one of the city's most sought-after teachers.

Black Swan. The grand pas de deux from the 3rd act of *Swan Lake,* where Odile (as the black reflection of the white swan princess Odette) tries to seduce prince Siegfried and thus to make him forget his vow that he will never be unfaithful to Odette.

Black Tights (orig. Fr. title: *Un, deux, trois, quatre*). Fr. film of bs. by Petit, produced in 1960, consisting of shortened versions of his *La Croqueuse de diamants* (Jeanmaire, Dirk Sanders), *Cyrano de Bergerac* (Shearer, Petit), *Deuil en 24 heures* (Charisse, Petit), and *Carmen* (Jeanmaire, Petit, Kronstam).

Blair, David (orig. Butterfield; *b* Halifax, 27 July 1932, *d* London, 1 Apr. 1976). Brit. dancer and b. master. Studied at Sadler's Wells B. School; joined Sadler's Wells Th. B. in 1947, promoted soloist in 1953, and principal d. in 1955. On Somes' retirement in 1961 became for a time Fonteyn's regular partner. D. a wide range of roles, and created parts in Cranko's *Pineapple Poll* (1951), *Harlequin in April* (1951), *Prince of the Pagodas*

(1957), and *Antigone* (1959), Ashton's *La Fille mal gardée* (1960), and MacMillan's *Romeo and Juliet* (1965). Toured widely abroad with various groups from the Royal B. and often appeared on Brit. TV. During the middle sixties he did a number of prods. of the classics for Amer. cos.: *Swan Lake* (1965) and *Sleeping Beauty* (1966) for the Atlanta Civic B., *Swan Lake* (1967) and *Giselle* (1968) for Amer. B. Th. Retired as a d. in 1973, and became freelance teacher and coach. Appointed Artistic Dir. of Norweg. National B. in 1976, but died before taking up the job. C.B.E. (1964). Was married to the d. Maryon Lane.
BIBL.: C. Swinson, in *Six Dancers of Sadler's Wells* (London, 1956), J. Percival, 'Jack of all Ballet Trades', *Dance and Dancers* (1958/3).

Blanche-Neige. See *Snow White Ballets.*

Bland, Alexander. Pseudonym for collaborators Nigel Gosling and *Maude Lloyd (the former dancer, now Mrs. N. Gosling). Gosling was *b* London, 29 Jan. 1909, *d* there, 21 May 1982. Educated at Eton and Oxford Univ. Studied part-time at B. Rambert School 1935–9, participating occasionally in perfs. of B. Rambert. Started to write criticism for *Ballet* magazine in 1948. Ballet critic for *The Observer* since 1955 (also its art critic 1962–75). Author of *The Dancer's World* with M. Peto, London, 1963), *A History of Ballet and Dance* (London, 1976), and *The Royal Ballet—The first 50 years* (London, 1981). Editor of *Nureyev, An Autobiography* (London, 1962).

Blank, Gustav (*b* Altenbögge, 28 Oct. 1908). Ger. dancer, teacher, and b. master. Studied with Laban, Jooss, V. Gsovsky, Eduardova, and Nikolajeva. Member of Berlin State Op. B. 1933–49, b. master of Berlin Municipal Op. 1949–57, and of Hamburg State Op. 1949–57 and 1959–62. Head of b. dept. at Munich Academy of Music 1962–74. In Berlin, Hamburg, and Munich he ran schools of his own, becoming one of the most respected teachers of the Ger. post-war generation of dancers. Ch. the first prod. of Blacher's *Lysistrata* (Berlin, 1951) and *Prussian Fairy-Tale* (Berlin, 1952), as well as the first Ger. perf. of F. Mannino's *Mario and the Magician* (Hamburg, 1957) and Ibert's *Le Chevalier errant* (Hamburg, 1957).

Blankshine, Robert (*b* Syracuse, N.Y., 22 Dec. 1948). Amer. dancer. Studied with Olive McCue in Rochester, at School of Amer. B., and with Joffrey; début 1965 with the Joffrey B., soon becoming one of its virtuoso soloists and remaining with the co. until 1968. He then worked partly freelance and partly as a regular member of the cos. in West Berlin, Geneva, and Frankfurt. Joined Los Angeles B., 1975. His technique is light and delicate; he has created roles in Arpino's *Viva Vivaldi!* (1965), *Olympics* (1965), *A Light Fantastic* (1968), and *The Clowns* (1968), H. Baumann's *3 plus 16* (1971), and J. Clifford's *Gershwin Concert* (1972).

Blanton, Jeremy (*b* Memphis, 1939). Amer. dancer. Studied with Tudor. D. with R. Joffrey B. in 1957, Metropolitan Op. B. 1958–60, and as a soloist with National B. of Canada since 1962.

Blasis, Carlo (*b* Naples, 4 Nov. 1797, *d* Cernobbio, 15 Jan. 1878). Ital. dancer, choreographer, and teacher. Studied with Dauberval and Gardel. Made his début aged 12 in Marseilles, and proceeded to Bordeaux and Paris. Created his first bs. for prods. of ops. by Gluck, Sacchini, and Mozart. Appointed solo-d. at the Milan La Scala, where he worked under Viganò. In 1826–30 he was soloist and ch. at the London King's Th. Later he also appeared in St. Petersburg. In 1837 he became the dir. of the d. academy attached to La Scala, where he also worked as a ch. He continued to teach as a guest in numerous European cities. His *Traité élémentaire, theoretique et pratique de l'art de la danse* appeared in Milan in 1820, his *Code of Terpsichore* in London in 1828, his *Notes Upon Dancing* in London in 1847, and his most ambitious and least known book, *L'Uomo fisico, intellettuale e morale*, in Milan in 1857. All these books contain his theories about the academic d. and the codification of its technique. They established and defined the standards upon which whole generations of dancers have been brought up. He is considered the most important individual b. teacher of the 19th century. Cerrito, Rosati, Maywood, and Andreyanova were among his pupils.
BIBL.: entry B. C., in *Enciclopedia dello spettacolo*.

Blaska, Félix (*b* Gomel, U.S.S.R., 8 May 1941). Fr. dancer, choreographer, and b. director. Studied at Paris Conservatoire, graduating in 1960, after which he danced with the co. of the Marquis de Cuevas, Z. Jeanmaire, and R. Petit, for whose troupe he ch. his first bs. in 1966: *Octandre* (mus. Varèse), and *Les Affinités electives* (based on Goethe's *Die Wahlverwandtschaften*, mus. Patrice Mestral). For the newly founded B. Th. Contemporain in Amiens he created *Danses concertantes* (mus. Stravinsky) and *Equivalences* (mus. Jean-Claude Eloy) in 1968. In 1969 he founded his own troupe, Les Bs. de F.B., which has p rformed regularly in Paris and the provinces and toured successfully abroad, and which has been based since 1972 upon the Maison de la culture de Grenoble. He is a very prolific ch.; he has also worked for the cos. of the Marseilles Op., the Royal Danish B., the Hamburg State Op., and the Paris Opéra. Among his bs. are *Electro-Bach* (mus. Walter Carlos, 1969), *Ballet pour tam-tam et percussion* (mus. J. P. Drouet, 1970), *Deuxième Concerto* (mus. Prokofiev, Marseilles, 1970), *Sonate pour deux pianos et percussion* (mus. Bartok, 1971), *Le Poeme électronique* and *Arcana* (mus. Varèse, Paris Opéra, 1973), and *Spectacle Berio* (1974). Joined Amer. group 'Crowsnest' in 1981.
BIBL.: J.-C. Diénis, 'F.B.', *Les Saisons de la danse* (1969/2).

Blažek, Jiří (*b* Pardubice, 5 July 1923). Czech dancer, choreographer, and b. master. Studied with S. Machov and A. Messerer—later also at the Moscow GITIS Institute under Zakharov and Lavrovsky. After his 1943 début at the Prague Schwanda Th. and dancing at the Th. of the 5th of May 1945–6, he joined the Prague National Th. in 1946, and is today one of its choreographers. As a d. he created a great number of roles in bs. by Machov and J. Němeček. Has ch. many bs. Married to the d. Marta Drottnerová.

Blind-Sight. Ballet in 1 act; ch. Morrice; mus. Bob Downes; déc. Baylis; light. John B. Read. Prod. 28 Nov. 1969, B. Rambert, Jeannetta Cochrane Th., London, with Bruce, Craig, J. Taylor. '. . . the seed in the jungle is blind, yet the plant will grow and the child will have eyes and men must choose to see or to be blind . . .' (programme note). The contrast between blind and sighted characters is used as a metaphor of closed and open minds.

Bliss, Sir Arthur (*b* London, 2 Aug. 1891, *d* 27 Mar. 1975). Brit. composer. Wrote the mus. for de Valois' *Checkmate* (1937), Helpmann's *Miracle in the Gorbals* (1944) and *Adam Zero* (1946). Also *The Lady of Shalott* for San Francisco B. (1958). MacMillan ch. *Diversions* (1961) to his *Music for Strings*, and Neumeier *Frontier* (1969) to his Quintet for Oboe and Strings.

Blondy, Nicolas (*b* 1677, *d* 13 Aug. 1747). Fr. dancer and choreographer. The nephew and pupil of Beauchamp, he became a member of the Opéra in 1691, appearing in many ops. and bs. by Lully and Campra. In 1729 he succeeded Pécourt as compositeur des bs. de l'Académie Royale de Musique, creating in the same year his most famous b. *Les Amours des déesses* (mus. Quinault). Was considered the foremost danseur noble of his time. D. regularly with Prévost. Was the teacher of Sallé and Camargo.

Blood Wedding. Ballet in 1 act; libr. Rodrigues (also ch.) and Aplvor (also mus.); déc. Isabel Lambert. Prod. 5 June 1953, Sadler's Wells Th. B., Sadler's Wells Th., London, with Fifield, Poole, Trecu. Based on Garcia Lorca's *Bodas de sangre* (1933), the b. deals with love, jealousy, and revenge in Spain: on the eve of her wedding to a man she does not love the bride escapes with her youthful lover into the woods, where the two men kill each other in a fight. First Ger. prod. ch. Nika Nilanowa (Düsseldorf, 1960). A different version as *Noces de sang* by J. Giuliano (Paris, 1972).

Bluebeard. Ballet with 2 prologues, 4 acts, 3 interludes; libr. and ch. Fokine; mus. Offenbach/Dorati; déc. Marcel Vertès. Prod. 27 Oct. 1941, B. Th., Palacio de Bellas Artes, Mexico City, with Dolin, Markova, Baronova, Ian Gibson. Based on Offenbach's opéra bouffe *Barbe-bleu* (1866), Count B. kills his wives when out of curiosity they enter a forbidden room. New York first perf. 12 Nov. 1941, 44th St. Th. Other bs. on the same subject by C. Coppi (mus. Jacobi, London, 1895), M. Petipa (mus. P. Schenk, St. Petersburg, 1896), and R. O'Monroy (mus. Lecocq, Paris, 1898). A b. *Bluebeard's Dream* by the Norweg. composer Harald Saeverud received its first Ger. perf. in 1961 in Hanover, ch. by Y. Georgi.

Bluebell Girls. Troupes of cabaret or night-club dancers trained and managed since 1933 by 'Miss Bluebell' (Margaret Kelly, Anglo-Irish d. *b* 1915 who led the d. troupe at the Folies-Bergère, Paris). Tall and well disciplined, they are found at the Paris Lido, Las Vegas Stardust, and elsewhere.

Blue Bird. Pas de deux from the last act of *Sleeping Beauty*, d. by Princess Florine and the B.B. Ch. Petipa and Cecchetti; the latter performed it at the b.'s first prod. in St. Petersburg in 1890 with Nikitina. A virtuoso display in 4 parts, often performed as a concert number at gala occasions. Especially demanding for the male dancer (brisés volés).

Blues Suite. Ballet by Ailey; mus. traditional blues, arr. and sung by Brother John Sellers. Prod. 30 Mar. 1958, A. Ailey and Co., 92nd St. YMHA, New York, with Thompson, Ailey. Framed by Good Morning Blues, d. by the whole co., the individual solo and ensemble numbers deal with mourning over a lost love, despair, protest, and anger. The b. is one of the most popular items in the Ailey repertory.

Blum, Anthony (*b* Mobile, Alab., *c.* 1936). Amer. d. Studied at School of Amer. B.: appeared on Broadway, joined N.Y. City B. as a soloist in 1963, promoted principal d. in 1966. Apptd. asst. b. master 1985. Created roles in Robbins's *Dances at a Gathering* (1969), *In the Night* (1970), *The Goldberg Variations* (1971), and *Dumbarton Oaks* (1972), and in Balanchine's *Suite No. 3* (1970).

Blum, René (*b* Paris, 13 Mar. 1878, *d* Auschwitz, 28 Apr. 1942). Fr. b. impresario. Appointed b. dir. of the Monte Carlo Op. after Diaghilev's death, he inspired the foundation of the Bs. Russes de Monte Carlo, of which he became manager 1932–4 and then its artistic dir. until 1936. After his break with Colonel de Basil he founded the René Blum Bs. de Monte Carlo in 1936, with Fokine as chief ch. 1938–40 he co-directed the B. Russe de Monte Carlo with Massine. During the Ger. occupation of Fr., he was deported to the concentration camp at Auschwitz, and killed. A man of exceptional culture and immaculate taste, it is partly due to him that so much of the Diaghilev heritage has been conserved so faithfully.

Boatwright, Christopher (*b* N.Y., 25 July 1954). Studied at various schools in N.Y. Joined Stuttgart B. 1974, appointed soloist 1978, with Apollo,

Romeo (Cranko), and Orpheus (Forsythe) among his best roles. Now with San Francisco B.

Boccadoro, Vera (*b* Nice, *c.* 1934). Fr. dancer and choreographer. Studied at Paris Op. B. School, joining its co. Went to Moscow B. School 1958. Bourmeister engaged her as his assistant 1960, letting her ch. her first b., *A Day at Montmartre* (mus. Gershwin), for Stanislavsky and Nemirovich-Danchenko Th. 1964. Since 1970 she has been a member of the Bolshoi B., for which she ch. *Mozart and Salieri* (mus. Mozart and Salieri, 1973) and *Love for Love* (mus. Khrennikov, 1976). Also ch. the Moscow prod. of *My Fair Lady* (1973).

Bodenwieser, Gertrud (often misspelt Bodenweiser, *b* Vienna, 3 Feb. 1890, *d* Sydney, 1959). Austrian dancer, teacher, and choreographer. After her début in Vienna 1919 she became a teacher of gymnastics and dance, later also head of the dance department at the Vienna State Academy of Mus. and Th. Formed her own group in 1921, touring Europe extensively. Developed a style, attempting to translate mechanical movements into a genuine dance form. After the 'Anschluss' of 1939 emigrated with her group to Australia, continuing to teach, choreograph, and direct, her co. consisting more and more of Austral. dancers.

Boelzner, Gordon (*b* Los Angeles, *c* 1940). Amer. pianist. Studied at Eastman School of Mus. in Rochester, also with A. Benedetti-Michelangeli. Joined New York City B. as rehearsal pianist 1960, since when he has played the piano in many of the co.'s perfs. inc. Robbins's *Dances at a Gathering* and *Goldberg Variations*. Now assoc. cond.

Boeuf sur le toit, Le. Pantomimic divertissement; libr. and prod. Cocteau; mus. Milhaud; déc. Guy-Pierre Fauconnet and R. Dufy. Prod. 21 Feb. 1920, Comédie des Champs-Elysées, Paris, with the Fratellini brothers. Confronted with Milhaud's Brazilian melodies and rhythms, Cocteau invented a scenario, set in a bar in Amer. during Prohibition. Among its exotic characters are a Negro Dwarf, a Red-headed Woman dressed as a man, a Boxer, and a Barman with a face like that of Antinous. Afer a few incidents and various dances, a Policeman enters, whereupon the scene is immediately transformed into a milk-bar. Originally given as a music-hall spectacle, it was later staged occasionally as a b.
BIBL.: D. Milhaud, in *Notes Without Music* (London, 1952).

Bogatyrev, Alexander Yurievich (*b* Tallinn, 1949). Sov. dancer. Studied at the local Ch. School 1959–65, continued with P. A. Pestov in Moscow, where he entered the Bolshoi B. upon his graduation (1969). Dances the premier danseur roles of the classic and modern repertory. Prix Nijinsky (1967); Bronze Medal (Moscow, 1969); 1st Prize (Tokyo, 1976).

Bogdanov, Konstantin Fedorovich (*b c.* 1809,

d 1877). Russ. dancer, teacher, and régisseur. Studied at Moscow Th. School and then with Didelot in St. Petersburg. Returned to Moscow, where he partnered all the Bolshoi ballerinas of his time, with Gurn in *La Sylphide* in its Moscow first prod. as one of his best roles. Appointed régisseur (manager) of the Bolshoi B. in 1839. Also taught at the Moscow Th. School until 1842 when he opened a private b. school, which he ran until 1849, when he retired to concentrate on furthering the career of his daughter *Nadezhda B. Was married to the d. Tatiana Karpakova.

Bogdanova, Nadezhda Konstantinova (*b* Moscow, 2 Sep. 1836, *d* there, 5 Sept. 1897). Russ. dancer. Trained by her father *Konstantin B., who even organized a small co. around her, where she d. the ballerina roles when she was still in her teens. She continued to study in Paris, later dancing in St. Petersburg and Moscow, where she was much admired as a lyrical ballerina. Later she toured Ger., Hung., and Italy; her last perf. took place in Warsaw in 1867.

Bogomolova, Ludmila Ivanovna (*b* Moscow, 25 Mar. 1932). Sov. dancer. Entered the Bolshoi school in 1945, becoming a member of the Bolshoi B. upon graduation (1951), since when she has been entrusted with the ballerina roles of the standard and modern repertory. Created roles in Lavrosky's *Pages of Life* (1961) and Lapauri's and Tarasova's *Lieutenant Kijé* (1963). Married to the d. Vladimir Nikonov.

Bohner, Gerhard (*b* Karlsruhe, 19 June 1936). Ger. dancer, choreographer, and b. director. Studied at a local b. school. D. in Mannheim 1958–60, Frankfurt 1960–1, and at West Berlin Ger. Op. 1961–71. Headed the Darmstadt D. Th. 1972–5, which under him developed into one of Ger.'s most progressive troupes. After creating many roles in the bs. of T. Gsovsky and MacMillan, started to ch. in 1964—mostly to avant-garde mus. by such composers as Ligeti, Zimmermann, and Xenakis. His two most interesting bs. so far have been *The Torturings of Beatrice Cenci* (1971) and *Lilith* (1972), both to mus. by Gerald Humel. Has also ch. new version of *Triadic Ballet* (Berlin, 1977). 2nd Prize, Choreographers' Competition (Cologne, 1969); Critics' Prize (Berlin, 1972).

Boieru, Marin (*b* Lugoj, 16 Aug. 1952). Ruman. d. Studied at Cluj B. School and in Leningrad with Semionov and Soloviev. Joined Bucharest Op. B. in 1970, promoted soloist. Gold Medal (Varna, 1976), Silver Medal (Moscow, 1977), Special Prize (Tokyo, 1978). Since 1978 a soloist with B. of the 20th Century, creating a role in Béjart's *Les Illuminations* (1979). With Pennsylv. B. from 1982.

Boîte à joujoux. Ballet in 4 scenes; libr., ch., and déc. André Hellé; mus. Debussy. Prod. 10 Dec. 1919, Th. Lyrique du Vaudeville, Paris. The b. tells of a triangular affair between the dolls in a toy-box. It was, however, the prod. of the Bs. Suédois, ch. by Börlin (Paris, 1921), which really introduced the b. to the repertory.

Boldin, Dragutin (*b* Zagreb, 16 Oct. 1930). Yugosl. dancer, choreographer, and b. master. Studied with Olga Orlova in Rijeka, joined Rijeka B. in 1948. Later d. with the cos. in Sarajevo 1951–5, Zagreb 1955–8, Nuremberg 1958–60, Mannheim 1960–1, and Essen 1961–3. B. master in Oldenburg 1963–5, Lübeck 1965–7, and Heidelberg 1968–77. Has since worked in Münster and Bonn. Has ch. many bs. Married to the d. Jennifer Lowe.

Bolender, Todd (*b* Canton, Ohio, 17 Feb. 1914). Amer. dancer, choreographer, and b. director. Studied with Chester Hale, Vilzak, and at School of Amer. B., d. with B. Caravan, Littlefield B., Amer. B. Caravan, B. Th., B. Russe de Monte Carlo, and from 1946 with B. Society and New York City B. B. Dir. in Cologne 1963–6, and Frankfurt 1966–9. Created roles in Balanchine's *Four Temperaments* (1946), *Symphonie Concertante* (1947), and *Agon* (1957), and Robbins's *Age of Anxiety* (1950), *The Pied Piper* (1951), *Fanfare* (1953), and *The Concert* (1956). As a ch. he started in 1943 with *Mother Goose Suite* (mus. Ravel). His bs. include—for New York City B.: *The Miraculous Mandarin* (mus. Bartók, 1951), *Souvenirs* (mus. Barber, 1951), *The Still Point* (mus. Debussy, 1956—an earlier prod. for Dance Drama Co., 1955), *Creation of the World* (mus. Milhaud, 1960), *Serenade in A* (mus. Stravinsky, 1972), and *Piano Rag Music* (mus. Stravinsky, 1972)—for Cologne: *Theme and Variations* (mus. Blacher, 1963), *Contrasts* (mus. Zimmermann, 1964), and *Dance 1—Dance 2* (mus. Copland, 1964)—for Frankfurt: *Time Cycle* (mus. L. Foss, 1967). Artistic Dir. of Kansas City B. since 1980. Has also directed some musicals.

Bolero. (1) Span. d. in leisurely triple time, said to have been introduced about 1780 by Sebastian Zerezo as a variant of the Fandango. The d. accompanies himself by singing and playing castanets, with the instrumental accompaniment provided by guitars and tambourine. (2) B. in 1 act; ch. Nijinska; mus. Ravel; déc. Benois. Prod. 22 Nov. 1928, Bs. I. Rubinstein, Opéra, Paris, with Rubinstein, Vilzak. In its original version the b. is set in a Span. tavern, where a gipsy dancing on a table gradually induces a state of ecstasy in the onlookers. Later versions by Lifar (1941), P. Lopez and Argentinita (1943), Béjart (1960), Lavrovsky (1964), *et al.* Solo versions by Dolin and D. Hoyer.

Bolger, Ray (*b* Boston, 1904, *d* L.A., 15 Jan. 1987). Amer. d. and actor. Appeared in many revues, musicals, film and TV prods., incl. Balanchine's b. *Slaughter on Tenth Avenue*, in *On Your Toes* (1939).

Bolm, Adolph (*b* St. Petersburg, 25 Sep. 1884,

d Hollywood, 16 Apr. 1951). Russ.-Amer. dancer, choreographer, and teacher. Studied with Karsavin and Legat at Imperial B. Academy, entering the Maryinsky Th. upon graduation (1903—not 1904). Toured with Pavlova. Was especially successful as the Chief Warrior in Fokine's *Polovtsian Dances* and as Pierrot in Fokine's *Le Carnaval* during Diaghilev's first Paris seasons. Left the Maryinsky Th. in 1911 to become a regular member of Diaghilev's Bs. Russes. After the second Amer. tour of the co. decided to stay in the U.S., producing and choreographing ops. and bs. at the New York Metrop. Op. House and the Chicago Civic Op. Ch. the first prod. of Stravinsky's *Apollon musagète*, which had been commissioned by the Elizabeth Sprague Coolidge Foundation (Washington, D.C. 1928). Worked in South Amer., later taking up residence in Hollywood, where he did the ch. for several films (*The Mad Genius, The Men in Her Life,* and *Life of Cellini*) and the b. *Iron Foundry* (mus. A. V. Mossolof, 1932). Guest ch. in San Francisco, 1933. Joined the newly established B. Th. in 1939, choreographing a highly successful version of Prokofiev's *Peter and the Wolf* in 1940. During his last years taught in Hollywood and worked on his memoirs. He is considered one of the great pioneer figures of the Amer. b. scene.

BIBL.: J. Dougherty, 'Perspective on A.B.', *Dance Magazine* (1963/1–3).

Bolshakova, Natalia Dimitrievna (*b* Leningrad, 25 Nov. 1943). Sov. dancer. Studied at Leningrad Ch. School, joining the Kirov B. upon her graduation (1963), where she dances the ballerina roles of the traditional and modern repertory. Married to the d. Vadim Gulyayev. Silver Medal (Varna, 1968); Bronze Medal (Moscow, 1969).

Bolshoi Ballet (Ballet of the Great [Bolshoi] Academic Theatre for Opera and Ballet of the USSR in Moscow). 1776 is now considered the beginning of the co., but the first b. class opened at the Moscow orphanage in 1773, providing the dancers for the Petrovsky Th., established in 1780 on the site of the present Bolshoi Th. When it burned down in 1805, the Arbat (New Imperial) Th. served as a makeshift th., until the New Bolshoi Petrovsky Th. (the present Bolshoi Th.) opened on 19 Jan. 1825. Its first important Russ. b. master was Adam Gluszkowski, a pupil of Didelot, who ch. the first Pushkin-inspired bs. During the 1820s and 30s it became the basis of the national Russ. b. movement, with Yekaterina Sankovskaya as its principal figure. In 1850 the co. already numbered 155 dancers. In 1861–4 Blasis worked here and at the affiliated school. 1869 saw the first prod. of Petipa's and Minkus's *Don Quixote*, 1877 the notorious first prod. of Reisinger's and Tchaikovsky's *Swan Lake*. The co. received a fresh impetus under Gorsky, who ch. a great number of prods. from 1898 until his death in 1924, becoming one of the great

reformers of the dramatic b. The most popular ballerina of those years was Geltzer, who together with Gorsky, Mordkin, and Tikhomirov reorganized the co. after the October Revolution. During the early 1920s Messerer, Moiseyev, and Gabovich joined the institute. In 1927 the first new Sov. b. which is still occasionally given entered the repertory: *The Red Poppy*. Semenova and Yermolayev were among the most important dancers of the early 1930s, and Y. Gerdt from Leningrad the most influential teacher. In the later 30s the great dancers were Lepeshinskaya, Preobrajensky, and Koren. These were also the years when the choreographers Vainonen and Zakharov became known. The most important new Sov. bs., however, were created in Leningrad. During the war the co. was evacuated to Kuibyshev. With the first prod. of Zahkarov's and Prokofiev's *Cinderella*, the co. returned in 1943 to its Moscow house. When Ulanova and Lavrovsky were transferred from Leningrad, the discussion about the new Sov. b. aesthetics shifted to Moscow. Apart from Ulanova, ballerinas like Plisetskaya and Struchkova, and later Timofeyeva (from Leningrad) became stars of the post-war generation—and the men Farmanyantz, Fadeyechev, Kokhlov, Liepa, and Sekh. 1954 saw the first prod. of Lavrovsky's and Prokofiev's *The Stone Flower*. In 1956 the co. appeared for the first time in London, and in 1959 in New York. In 1960 there followed a new version of the very popular *The Little Humpbacked Horse* with new mus. by Shchedrin. Some other first prods. of those years were Kasatkina-Vasiliov's *Vanina Vanini* (1962), Goleizovsky's *Scriabiniana* (1962), Lapauri-Tarasova's *Lieutenant Kijé* (1963), Kasatkina-Vasiliov's *Heroic Poem* (1964), Vinogradov's *Asel* (1967), Alb. Alonso's *Carmen* (1967), and Plisetskaya's *Anna Karenina* (1972). In 1964 Grigorovich was appointed chief ch. and some time later he succeeded Lavrovsky as artistic dir. His new version of Khachaturian's *Spartacus* (1968) became one of the biggest hits in the history of the co., after which he embarked on his remarkable new prods. of the classics and, in 1975, *Ivan the Terrible*. Rather than the dramatic expressiveness of the Zakharov-Lavrovsky generation, Grigorovich favours a more d.-orientated style, leaning less heavily on mime and stressing the importance of ch. over prod. The dancers Bessmertnova, Maximova, Pavlova, Sorokina, Vasiliev, M. Lavrovsky, Vladimirov, and Gordeyev are the exponents of the new Bolshoi style. The co. also performs regularly at the Kremlin Palace Th.

BIBL.: various authors, *Bolshoi Theatro SSSR* (Moscow-Leningrad, 1958—in Russ.); Y. Slonimsky, *The B.B.* (Moscow, 1960); in N. Roslavleva, *Era of Russian Ballet* (London, 1966); Bolshoi-issue of *Les Saisons de la Danse* (1971/2).

Bolt (orig. Russ. title). Ballet in 3 acts and 7 scenes; ch. Lopokov; mus. Shostakovich. Prod. 8 Apr. 1931, GATOB, Leningrad. The first

The Bolshoi Ballet in *Swan Lake*.   Photo Novosti Press Agency (A.P.N.)

industrial b. of the USSR; it attempted a satirical presentation of the petty bourgeoisie, the drunken representatives of which try to sabotage the socialist progress by placing a bolt in a machine. However, the Komsomol discovers the treachery and hands over the guilty for punishment. The b. was severely criticized for representing the heroes as primitive grotesques.

Bon, René (*b* Montpellier, 30 Aug. 1924). Fr. dancer, b. master, and teacher. Studied with Staats; a member of the b. at the Paris Opéra Comique 1940–3 and at the Opéra 1943–4. D. with the co. of the Marquis de Cuevas (becoming principal d. 1950), with Charrat 1951–4, and afterwards freelance at the Maggio Musicale Fiorentino, with Massine's Balletto Europeo in Nervi, at the Hamburg State Op., and with Béjart. In 1961 he worked as b. master in Amsterdam and as Assist. at the Vienna State Op. 1963–5. He has since divided his time between teaching in Paris and for various cos. abroad (including the London Royal B. and the Lisbon Gulbenkian B., and often at the Cologne Summer Academy). As a d. he was much admired for his splendid élévation and quicksilver batterie, with his best roles as Blue Bird, and in Charrat's *Massacre des Amazones* (1951) and Massine's *The Good-Humoured Ladies* and *The Barber of Seville* (1960).
BIBL.: E. Herf, 'R.B.', *Ballet Today* (1967/7–8).

Bonfanti, Marietta (also Maria or Marie; *b* Milan, 1847, *d* New York, 26 Jan. 1921). Ital.-Amer. dancer and teacher. Studied with Blasis; became prima ballerina at La Scala in 1851, also d. in London and Madrid, then went to Amer., appearing in *The Black Crook* and *The White Fawn*. Toured the U.S. in 1869/70, returned to New York, where she d. in several operettas and

extravaganzas and in *Sylvia*. Prima ballerina of the Milan Ital. Grand Op. Co. (touring the U.S.), and in 1885–6 at the New York Met. Op. House. Further Amer. and Eur. tours in 1888–94, after which she opened a b. school in New York, where she taught until 1916 (St. Denis was one of her pupils).
BIBL.: entry 'B., M.' *Enciclopedia dello spettacolo*.

Bonino, Luigi (*b* Bra, 4 Oct. 1949). Ital. dancer. Studied with Egri in Turin, joining her group as a soloist in 1965. Has d. with various Ital. cos., in Ital. TV prods. and 1973–5 with Cullberg B., since when he has been d. with R. Petit's B. de Marseille. Positano D. Prize (1973).

Boniuszko, Alicja (*b* Miadziół, 16 Oct. 1937). Pol. dancer. Studied at Gdansk State B. School, graduating in 1956. Joined Gdansk State Op. B., becoming prima ballerina in 1959. Has created many roles in bs. by J. Jarzynówa-Sobczak. Second Prize (Vercelli, 1960); Third Prize (Rio de Janeiro, 1961).

Bonne-Bouche. Ballet in 3 scenes; libr. and ch. Cranko; mus. Arthur Oldham; déc. O. Lancaster. Prod. 4 Apr. 1952, Sadler's Wells B., Cov. Gdn., London, with Clayden, May, Shaw, Grant. The rather farce-like b. is set in Edwardian times in Kensington and in the African jungle, with a mother who marries her daughter to a Cannibal King.
BIBL.: C. Beaumont, 'B.B.', in *Ballets of Today* (London, 1954).

Bonnefoux, Jean-Pierre (*b* Bourg-en-Bresse, 25 Apr. 1943). Fr. dancer. Entered Paris Opéra B. School in 1954, studied with Lorcia, Franchetti, and Mulys; became a member of the co. in 1959, promoted premier danseur in 1964 and danseur étoile in 1965. From 1970 principal d. of the New York City B. Now retired. Created roles in Béjart's *Damnation of Faust* (1964) and *Webern Opus V* (1966), Descombey's *Sarracenia* (1964), *Maratona di Danza* (Frankfurt, 1965), and *Bacchus and Ariadne* (1967), Petit's *Notre-Dame de Paris* (1965), Skibine's *La Péri* (1966), Balanchine's *Violin Concerto* (1972), *Cortège Hongrois* (1973), and *Sonatine* (1975), Robbins's *A Beethoven Pas de deux* (1973) and *An Evening's Waltzes* (1973). Ch. *Othello* (mus. Prokofiev) for Louisville Civic B., 1981. Prix Nijinsky (1965); Silver Medal of the City of Paris (1966). He is married to the d. Patricia McBride.

BIBL.: J.-C. Diénis, 'J.-P.B.', with complete list of activities and roles, *Les Saisons de la danse* (1970/10).

Bonynge, Richard (*b* Sydney, 29 Sep. 1930). Austral. conductor. Though he has so far never conducted a 'live' b. perf., he has recorded a great number of b. excerpts and complete bs. which otherwise would not be available. Among his recordings are *The Art of the Prima Ballerina* (1963), Adam's *Le Diable à quatre* (1965), Burgmüller's *La Péri* (1969), Adam's *Giselle* (first absolutely complete version, 1970), Delibes's *Coppélia* (1971), and *Sylvia* (1974), *Homage to Pavlova* (1972), Offenbach's *Le Papillon* (1973), Auber's *Marco Spada* (1975), and Tchaikovsky's *Swan Lake* (1977).

BIBL.: 'Two Views on R.B.', *Dance Magazine* (1973/3).

Boquet, Louis (also Bosquet). Chief costume designer at the Paris Opéra 1760–82, often collaborating with Noverre, for whom he had designed *Les Fêtes chinoises* in 1754 at the Opéra Comique, and also accompanying him to Stuttgart where he was in charge of *The Death of Lycomedes* in 1764.

Borchsenius, Valborg (*née* Jorgensen; *b* Copenhagen, 19 Nov. 1872, *d* there, 5 Jan. 1949). Dan. dancer and teacher. Studied at Royal Dan. B. School, joined the co., promoted solo-d. in 1895. She enjoyed great popularity throughout her career until she retired in 1918, mostly appearing with H. Beck as her partner. She collaborated with H. Lander on the revival of the Bournonville repertory and was considered one of the foremost Bournonville teachers at the Royal Dan. B. School.

Bordeaux. The local Académie royale de musique was established in 1752, with its b. wing consisting of 2 maîtres de b. (Dubuisson and Ghérardi), 4 prime ballerine (Mmes Arnaud, Humblot, Dorfeuil, and Julie), and 14 corps de b. dancers. These were the dancers participating in the perfs. of the ops. of Rameau. Noverre's *La Toilette de Vénus ou Les Ruses de l'amour* was performed in 1758—21 years before its first Paris prod. The magnificent Grand Théâtre was opened in 1780 and Dauberval, its first resident b. master 1785–91, created here his highly important *La Fille mal gardée* (with his wife, Mlle Théodore, as

Lise) in 1789. Though his successors were of a lesser artistic calibre, b. continued to flourish under Sębastien Gallet and Hus fils. Blasis was primo ballerino 1816–17, and Jean-Antoine Petipa was appointed b. master in 1834, followed by Marius Petipa 1840–5. During the second half of the 19th century, however, b. fell into complete oblivion, to recover only very hesitatingly after 1945 for the rare soirées de b. ventured upon by the b. co. attached to the Grand Th. (mainly for the op. and operetta prods. of the house). Since 1970 it has been under the direction of V. Skouratoff. The general b. apathy of the city is temporarily relieved every spring when the Mai musical de Bordeaux presents specially invited guest-cos. from abroad.

BIBL.: entry 'B.' in *Enciclopedia dello spettacolo*.

Borg, Anne (*b* Oslo, 28 Sept. 1936). Norwegian dancer and b. director. Studied with Gerd Kjølass, Rita Tori, Northcote, Rambert B. School, Leningrad Ch. School, Pereyaslavec, and Zaraspe. Joined Norske B. as soloist 1954–8, Norwegian National B. in 1961, becoming principal d. 1967–71. Dir. of Norwegian National B. 1971–6.

Borg, Conny (*b* Stockholm, 1939). Swed. dancer, choreographer, and b. director. Studied in Stockholm, became a member of the Royal Swed. B., promoted premier danseur in 1963. Left the co. to become b. director in Gothenburg 1967–70, after which he and U. Gadd founded the New Swed. B., with which he visited Paris and London in 1970. B. dir. at the Municipal Th. in Malmö 1972–9.

Boris, Ruthanna (*b* Brooklyn, 1918). Amer. dancer and choreographer. Studied at Met. Op. House B. School, joined its co., and in 1943 the B. Russe de Monte Carlo, where she d. the ballerina roles. As a ch. she started in 1951 with *Cirque de deux* (mus. Gounod, B. Russe de Monte Carlo) but scored her biggest success with *Cakewalk* (mus. Gottschalk-Kay, New York City B., 1951). A hip ailment compelled her to relinquish her th. career, since when she has become a teacher, based on Seattle, Wash.

Borkowski, Witold (*b* Vilno, 26 Oct. 1919). Pol. dancer, choreographer, teacher, and b. director. Studied with Nadiezda Muraszowa, Piotr Zajlich, and Woizikovsky. Began to d. in Vilno 1937, with Polish B. of F. Parnell 1938, Warsaw Revue Th. 1938–9, later with Silesian State Op. Bytom, and State Op. Warsaw 1950–64. Appointed b. dir. and chief ch. of Łódz Teatr Wielki 1964, where he is also in charge of the affiliated b. studio. Has ch. many bs. Staged Minkus' *Don Quixote* for B. Rambert (1962) and London Festival B. (1970).

Börlin, Jean (*b* Haernösand, 13 Mar. 1893, *d* New York, 6 Dec. 1930). Swed. dancer and choreographer. Studied with Gunhild Rosen at the Royal Th. in Stockholm, entered its corps in 1905, then came under the influence of Fokine, appointed

second soloist in 1913, and left the co. in 1918 to continue studying with Fokine in Copenhagen. At about this time he got to know the Swed. patron *de Maré, who financed a d.-recital for him in Paris in Mar. 1920, after which de Maré founded the *Bs. Suédois, of which B. became the star soloist and ch. During the co.'s life until 1924 he ch. a great number of bs.: *Iberia* (mus. Albéniz, 1920), *Les Vierges folles* (mus. Atterberg, 1920), *La Nuit de Saint Jean* (mus. Alfvén, 1920), *Jeux* (mus. Debussy, 1920), *L'Homme et son désir* (mus. Milhaud, 1921), *Les Mariés de la Tour Eiffel* (mus. Tailleferre, Auric, Honegger, Milhaud, Poulenc, 1921), *La Boîte à joujoux* (mus. Debussy, 1921), *Skating Rink* (mus. Honegger, 1922), *La Création du monde* (mus. Milhaud, 1923), *Relâche* (mus. Satie, 1924), and *La Jarre* (mus. Casella, 1924). He also appeared in many solo-recitals. He collaborated both with some of the most interesting composers and with some of the foremost painters of the day, including Léger, Picabia, Bonnard, and di Chirico.
BIBL.: various authors, *Les Ballets Suédois dans l'art contemporain* (Paris, 1931).

Borodin, Alexander Porfirievich (b St. Petersburg, 12 Nov. 1833, d there, 27 Feb. 1887). Russ. composer. Wrote no bs., but the *Polovtsian Dances* from his op. *Prince Igor* (ch. Ivanov, St. Petersburg, 1890) became one of the hit prods. of the Bs. Russes de Diaghilev as ch. by Fokine, since when they have been revived and rechoreographed dozens of times. Individual pieces from his concert works were used by Massine in his *Bogatyri* (1938).

Borovansky, Edouard (b Přerov, 1902, d Sydney, 18 Dec. 1959). Czech dancer, choreographer, and b. director. Studied at the Prague National Th. B. School, joined its co., becoming premier danseur. D. with Pavlova and as a soloist with B. Russe de Colonel de Basil 1932–9, which he left on one of the co.'s Austral. tours. In 1940 he opened a b. school in Melbourne with an affiliated b. club, from which the Borovansky B. derived in 1942, presenting its first professional season in 1944. He himself was in charge of the prods. of the classics, also contributing some modern bs. His co., though often on the verge of bankruptcy, was one of the pioneer forces of b. in Australia, with Peggy Sager, Kathleen Gorham, Paul Hammond, and Paul Grinwis as its best known dancers. After his death his co. was absorbed into the *Australian B.

Borowska, Irina (b Buenos Aires, 9 Jan. 1930). Argent. dancer and teacher. Studied at Teatro Colón B. School and at National Conservatory, d. 1940–54 with the co. of the Teatro Colón (becoming principal d.), 1954–9 as ballerina with the B. Russe de Monte Carlo, with R. Page's Chicago Op. B., and Z. Solov, and 1961–6 with London Festival B. Has taught at the Vienna Academy of Music. Married to the d. Karl Musil.

BIBL.: A. Moss, 'Beauty and the Ballerina', *Dance Magazine* (1961/1), E. Herf, 'I.B.' *Ballet Today* (1963/12).

Borri, Pasquale (b Milan, 1820, d Desio, 20 Apr. 1884). Ital. dancer and choreographer. Studied with Blasis, made his début as premier danseur in 1840 at La Scala, also d. in 1843 in Venice and Vienna, where he was engaged 1844–8 as premier danseur at the Th. am Kärntnertor. Started as a ch. in 1848 in Vienna, returning 1854–6, 1858–9, and 1879–80 as ch. of the Court Op. He ch. most of his bs. for Vienna and La Scala, also worked occasionally for the Paris Opéra, and Her Majesty's Th., London.
BIBL.: entry 'B., P.' in *Enciclopedia dello spettacolo*.

Bortoluzzi, Paolo (b Genoa, 17 May 1938). Ital. dancer. Studied with dell'Ara, Kiss, V. Gsovsky, and Messerer. Made his début in 1957 at the Nervi Festival, joined Massine's Balletto Europeo in 1960 and became a member of Béjart's B. of the 20th Century in the same year, soon being acknowledged as one of its leading soloists. After regular guest appearances with the cos. of La Scala in Milan and the Düsseldorf Ger. Rhine Op., he left the Béjart troupe in 1972, joining Amer. B. Th. as a principal d. With his d.-wife Jaleh Kerendi he opened a b. school in 1973 in Turin. Art. dir. Düsseldorf B. since 1984. Among his role-creations are Béjart's *Bolero* (1960), *Ninth Symphony* (1964), *Cygne* (1965), *Romeo and Juliet* (Berlioz, 1966), *Mass for the Present Time* (1967), *Neither Flowers Nor Wreaths* (1968), *Baudelaire* (1968), *Bhakti* (1968), *Nomos Alpha* (1969), *Firebird* (1970), *Songs of a Wayfarer* (1971), and *Nijinsky, Clown de dieu* (1971). In Düsseldorf he created parts in Walter's *Creatures of Prometheus* (1966), *String Quartet No. 1* (Janáček, 1966), *Cinderella* (1967), *Suite No. 1 for Violoncello* (Bach, 1969), *Daphnis and Chloë* (1973), and *Sleeping Beauty* (1974). At the Vienna State Op. he created roles in Milloss's *Per aspera* (1973) and *Relazioni fragili* (1974). In Brussels he ch. his first bs., including Ravel's *La Valse* (1965), which he revived for Düsseldorf (1969). Cologne TV produced four films with him: *Nomos Alpha* (1971), *Portrait P.B.* (1971), *Apollo* (1974), and *Moment of Memory* (on Nijinsky, 1975).
BIBL.: L. Rossel, 'P.B.' (with complete list of roles), *Les Saisons de la danse* (1969/8).

Bosch, Aurora (b Havana, c. 1940). Cuban dancer and b. mistress. Studied with Alicia and Fernando Alonso and J. Parés, d. with cos. in San Francisco and Los Angeles, joining the National B. of Cuba in 1959, promoted soloist in 1962 and prima ballerina in 1967. Has appeared several times as guest with the Classic B. of Mexico and is now a member of the artistic staff and b. mistress of the National B. of Cuba. In the Cub. *Pas de quatre* film she dances Grahn. Silver Medal (Varna, 1965), Gold Medal (Varna, 1966), Prix A. Pavlova, (Paris, 1966), Critics' Prize (Paris, 1966), Gold Medal (Mexico, 1971).

BIBL.: complete list of activities and roles in *Cuba en el ballet* (vol. 4, no. 1).

Boschetti, Amina (*b* Milan, 1836, *d.* there, 1881). Ital. dancer. Studied with Blasis; made her début in 1848 (*sic*) at La Scala, later became its prima ballerina, and often appeared abroad as guest. In 1862 she created the three top roles in P. Taglioni's *Flick and Flock* at La Scala and in 1864 the title-role in Giuseppe Rota's *La Maschera* at the Paris Opéra. Baudelaire dedicated a sonnet to her in *Les Espaves*.

Bosl, Heinz (*b* Baden-Baden, 21 Nov. 1946, *d* Munich, 12 June 1975). Ger. dancer. Studied at Munich State Op. B. School with de Lutry, L. Gonta, and Blank, joining the co. of the Op. upon graduation (1962), promoted soloist in 1965. Considered one of the best Ger. dancers of the 1970s; he d. the premier danseur roles of the traditional and modern repertory and created roles in H. Rosen's *Symphonie fantastique* (1966), Cranko's *Encounter in Three Colours* (1968), and Charrat's *Casanova in London* (1970). Among his best roles were the title-role in Cranko's *Onegin* and Günther in Neumeier's *Nutcracker* version. From 1973 he undertook several tours abroad as the partner of Fonteyn.
BIBL.: M. Niehaus (ed.), *H.B.* (Munich, 1975).

Boston Ballet. The co. is the successor of the New England Civic B. of Boston. Dir. by E. Virginia Williams, with some financial help from the Ford Foundation, it made its professional début in 1964 at the Boston Arts Festival. Through its close links with the N.Y. City B., the repertory includes a great number of Balanchine bs., in addition to the usual fare of classics, but there are also individual works by Lang, Holder, Beatty, de Mille, and others. Bruce Wells resident ch. from 1979, Violette Verdy joint art. dir. 1980–4. In 1979 the co. consisted of 34 ds. with Elaine Bauer, Anamarie Sarazin, Durine Alinova, Laura Young, David Brown, Tony Catanzaro, Nicolas Pacana, Woytek Lowski, and Augustus Van Herden as principals. Apart from its regular seasons at the Boston Center for the Arts and the Music Hall, the co. tours widely, incl. China, 1980 (first US co. to do so), London, 1981 (European début). Bruce Marks art. dir. since 1985.
BIBL.: I. M. Fanger, 'The Fearsome First Ten Years', *Dance Magazine* (1973/10).

Botta, Bergonzio di. Ital. dance master who arranged the first lavish Ital. b., in 1489 on the occasion of the marriage of Galeazzo Visconti, Duke of Milan, to Isabel of Aragon in Tortona. The individual dances matched the various courses of the dinner—with Jason and the Argonauts serving as the connecting thread. So greatly were people impressed by the b., described by Tristano Calco in his *Nuptiae ducum medionalensium*, that there were many other similar bs., thus preparing the path which eventually led to the *Ballet Comique de la Reine* of 1581.

Boulez, Pierre (*b* Montbrison, 25 Mar. 1925). Fr. composer and conductor. Has not composed any b. mus., but several of his concert pieces have been used for b. purposes, incl. *Le Marteau sans maître* (by P. Taylor in *Meridian*, New York 1960, Stere Popescu, Bucharest Op. B. in Paris, 1965, Béjart, B. of the 20th Century in Milan, 1973), *Improvisations sur Mallarmé* (by D. Mendel, Ger. Op. Berlin, 1961), and *Pli selon pli* (by Béjart, B. of the 20th Century, Brussels, 1975).

Bourgeois gentilhomme, Le. (1) Comédie Ballet by Molière; mus. Lully; ch. Beauchamp; déc. Carlo Vigarani. Prod. 14 Oct. 1670, Chambord. (2) Ballet in 1 act; ch. Balanchine; mus. R. Strauss; déc. Benois. Prod. 3 May 1932, B. Russe de Monte Carlo, Monte Carlo, with Lichine (revived for the same co. in New York 1944, with new déc. by Berman), then in 1979 with Nureyev and New York City Op. Tudor used the same mus. for his *Knight Errant*.

Bourman, Frank (*b* Los Angeles, 6 Jan. 1934). Amer.-Can. dancer, teacher and b. master. Studied with Oboukhoff, Vladimiroff, Doubrovska, Panaieff, and others. D. with Los Angeles City B. 1955–6, Alicia Alonso's Los Angeles B. 1958, Borovansky B. 1959–60, and co. of Z. Solov 1960–1. Associate Director of B. Centre of Buffalo 1967–71. Appointed b. master of Royal Winnipeg B. 1972. Co-Dir. of Dance/B. Division at Banff Centre School of Fine Arts.

Bourke, Walter (*b* Austral., 1945). Austral. dancer. Studied with P. Hammond, Volkova, and others. D. with Australian B.; joined Royal Swed. B. as a soloist in 1968, Royal Winnipeg B. in 1970; returned to Royal Swed. B. in 1972, becoming principal d. in 1974. Guest artist of Austral. B., with his d. wife, Maria Lang, Jan.-Aug. 1975. Ch. *Tarantella* (mus. Gottschalk).

Bourmeister, Vladimir Pavlovich (*b* Vitebsk, 15 July 1904, *d* Moscow, 5 Mar. 1971). Sov. d., ch. and b. master. Studied at Moscow Lunacharsky Th. Technicum, appeared during his student years with the Dramatic B. comp. Joined the Moscow Art Th. of B. in 1930; soon became one of its best known dancers and eventually its b. master when the co. became the Moscow Stanislavsky- and Nemirovich-Danchenko Music Th.; remained there until his death. As a d. he was best in strong character roles. As a ch. he started in 1931 with a new version of Adam's *Le Corsaire*. Of the vast corpus of bs. created by him, the best known are *Straussiana* (1941), *The Merry Wives of Windsor* (mus. V. Oransky, 1942), *Lola* (mus. S. Vasilenko, 1943), *Sheherazade* (mus. Rimsky-Korsakov, 1944), *Carnaval* (mus. Schumann, 1946), *Coast of Happiness* (mus. A. Spadavecchia, 1956), *Jeanne d'Arc* (mus. N. Peiko, 1958), and *The Lonely White Sail* (1970). Of special importance was his prod. of *Swan Lake* (1953), in which he used Tchaikovsky's score in its original sequence; the prod. created quite a stir when the co. showed it on its first Western visit in Paris in 1956. He revived it in 1960 for the co. of the Paris Opéra. He ch. *Snow Maiden* for London Festival B. in 1961, the first instance of a Sov. ch. allowed to work with a western co., using, among other pieces, the mus. which Tchaikovsky wrote for the play of this title by Ostrovsky. Merited Artist of the R.S.F.S.R.

Bournonville, Antoine (*b* Lyons, 1760, *d* Fredesborg, Denmark, 1843). Fr. dancer, choreographer, and b. director. Descended from a family of artists, he studied with Noverre in Vienna and accompanied him to Paris. He went to Stockholm in 1792 and thence to Copenhagen, where he d. in many bs. by Galeotti, succeeding him as b. dir. 1816–23. His most famous b. was *Les Meuniers provençaux* (1785). Father of August B.

Bournonville, August (*b* Copenhagen, 21 Aug. 1805, *d* there 30 Nov. 1879). Dan. dancer, choreographer, and b. director. The son of Antoine B., he studied at the school of the Royal Dan. B., joining the co. when 15 years old. Went to Paris with a scholarship to study with Vestris. He then d. in Copenhagen until his father resigned. With another 2 years' leave of absence he once again went to Paris and became a member of the Opéra for 2 years, where he was the favourite partner of Taglioni, also d. in various other Eur. capitals. On 1 Jan. 1830 he returned to Copenhagen to take up his position as dir. and ch. of the bs. at the Royal Th. After ending his career as a d. in 1848 he continued to work in Copenhagen, except for 1 year at the Vienna Court Op. (1855–6) and 3 years at the Stockholm Op. (1861–4), even after his official retirement in 1877. Since his death his main works have been carefully conserved, thus forming the basis of the Dan. repertory of classics and enjoying worldwide popularity since the Bournonville renaissance started in the 1930s. He was not only one of the greatest personalities of b. history, but also one of the best educated and most cultivated men of the international th. scene of his day, a man of exceptional moral integrity and a strongly developed social sense of duty. He collaborated with almost every Dan. composer of his time who was interested in the th. 'Through his ability to organize and through his discipline he created just the right structure for the Royal Danish Ballet, which still exists today in a somewhat modified form. He lifted the artistic level of Danish ballet to a high plane, and his "children", as he called his pupils, came to be regarded as respectable citizens, the aim he in his extreme youth had set himself to achieve. Under his direction, ballet in Denmark came to a flowering, becoming, in spite of its French origin, a national art with distinct characteristic features. *Joie de vivre* and *beauty* are the corner-stones in Bournon-

ville's conception of ballet . . . August Bournonville, through his life's rich work, occupies the greatest position in the history of Danish ballet. With his artistic and broadminded outlook he was also a citizen of the world, who knew no boundaries for his art. Dancing for him was a religion and the most beautiful and uplifting of all forms of art' (S. Kragh-Jacobsen, in *The Royal Danish Ballet*, Copenhagen and London, 1955). Bs. of his which have been preserved to the present day are *La Sylphide* (mus. H. Lövenskjold, 1836), *Festival in Albano* (mus. J. F. Froehlich, 1839), *Napoli* (mus. H. S. Paulli, E. Helsted, N. W. Gade, and H. C. Lumbye, 1842), *The Dancing School* (*Konservatoriet*, mus. Paulli, 1849), *The Kermesse in Bruges* (mus. Paulli, 1851), *A Folk Tale* (mus. Gade and J. P. E. Hartmann, 1854), *La Ventana* (mus. Lumbye, 1854), *Flower Festival in Genzano* (mus. Helsted and Paulli, 1858), *Far From Denmark* (mus. Jos. Glaeser, L. Gottschalk, Lumbye, Eduard Dupuy, A. F. Lincke, 1860), and *The Life Guards on Amager* (mus. W. Holm, Dupuy, and Lumbye, 1871). Author of *Mit Theaterliv* (1848, 2nd part 1865, 3rd part 1877—Eng. translation as *My Theatre Life*, Middletown, Conn., 1979, and *Efterlade Skrifter*, edited by Charlotte B., 1891). On the occasion of the 100th anniversary of his death a B. Festival was held in Copenhagen, 23–30 Nov. 1979, in Copenhagen, with a 'Salut for B.' exhibition at the local Statens Museum for Kunst.
BIBL.: A. Fridericia, *A.B.* (Copenhagen, 1979 in Dan.); W. Terry, *The King's Ballet Master* (New York, 1979); Kirsten Ralov, ed., *The Bournonville School* (3 parts, New York, 1979).

Bourrée (Fr.). (1) A Fr. folk d., performed in the provinces of Auvergne and Limousin in 3/4 time and in the provinces of Berry and Bournonnais in 2/2 (Alla Breve) time, with a strongly accentuated rhythm and a skipping step. (2) From this derives the pas de bourrée, a series of very fast little steps, with the feet close together, done so evenly that it has been compared to the stitches of a sewing-machine. It can be performed in any direction.

Bourrée fantasque. Ballet in 3 parts; ch. Balanchine; mus. Chabrier; cost. Karinska. Prod. 1 Dec. 1949, New York City B., City Center, New York, with LeClercq, Robbins, Maria Tallchief, Magallanes, Reed, Bliss. Apart from the title-piece, the plotless b. uses the intermezzo from Chabrier's op. *Gwendolyne* and his *Fête Polonaise*. The first part has a humorous and burlesque character, the second offers a lyric and romantic pas de deux, and the third develops as a spectacular crescendo finale. On 18 Aug. 1960 the b. entered the repertory of London Festival B.
BIBL.: G. Balanchine, '*B.F.*', in *Balanchine's New Complete Stories of the Great Ballets* (Garden City, N.Y., 1968).

Boutique fantasque, La (*The Fantastic Toyshop*). Ballet in 1 act; libr. and déc. A. Derain; ch.

The Royal Danish Ballet (Jeppesen and Willumsen) in Bournonville's *La Sylphide*.

Photo John R. Johnsen.

Massine; mus. Rossini, arr. Respighi. Prod. 5 June 1919, Bs. Russes de Diaghilev, Alhambra Th., London, with Cecchetti, Lopokova, Massine, Sokolova, Woizikovsky. The b. is a modernized and dramatically tightened adaptation of *The Fairy Doll*, for which Respighi re-orchestrated several unknown pieces by Rossini, with the Can-Can as its climax. Among the many revivals is that for the Sadler's Wells B. (27 Feb. 1947). BIBL.: C. W. Beaumont, 'L.B.f.' in *Complete Book of Ballets* (London, 1951).

Boven, Arlette van (*b* Antwerp, 12 Aug. 1942). Belg.-Brit. dancer. Studied at J. Brabants's school and with V. Gsovsky, A. Messerer, M. Fay, and H. Plucis; joined Flemish B. in Antwerp in 1960. Member of the B. of the 20th Century 1961–5, of B. for All 1965–7, of Western Th. B. 1967–9; has d. with Netherlands D. Th. 1969–81. Created parts in a number of bs. by Tetley and Van Manen. Now directing Netherlands D. Th's apprentice group. Was m. to d. Tony Hulbert.

Bovt, Violetta Trofimova (*b* Los Angeles, 9 May 1927). Sov. dancer. Born into an Amer. family of Russ. extraction; her parents moved to the USSR in the 1930s, where she entered the Moscow Bolshoi B. School in 1935. Upon her graduation in 1944 she became a member of the Stanislavsky and Nemirovich-Danchenko Th., where she soon became the unofficial prima ballerina, excelling in Bourmeister's version of *Swan Lake*, in his *The Merry Wives of Windsor*, *Lola*, and *Jeanne d'Arc*, and in Tchitchinadze's *Don Juan*.
BIBL.: G. Granovskaya, *V.B.* (Moskow, 1972; in Russ.).

Bowman, Patricia (*b* Washington, D.C., 12 Dec. 1908). Amer. dancer and teacher. Studied with L. Gardiner, N. Legat, Egorova, and Wallmann. Danced as ballerina at the New York Roxy Th. 1937–9, with Mordkin B. in 1939 and with B. Th. in 1940, after which she appeared with many other cos. and in prods. of vaudeville, operetta, and musicals all over the U.S., d. with Bruhn in 1955 in the 15th anniversary Season of B. Th. in *Les Sylphides*. She now has her own studio in New York.

Boyarsky, Konstantin Fyodorovich (*b* Petrograd, 22 Feb. 1915, *d* 14 May 1974). Sov. dancer, choreographer, and b. master. Studied at Leningrad Ch. School, graduating in 1935. Member of Kirov Th. 1935–41, becoming soloist. B. master of Leningrad Musical Comedy Th. 1945–56, Maly Th. 1956–67, then artistic dir. of Leningrad Ice B. until his death. Ch. many bs., including Stravinsky's *Orpheus* and Shostakovich's *The Lady and the Hooligan* (both 1962).

Boyartchikov, Nicolai Nicolaievich (*b* Leningrad, 27 Sept. 1935). Sov. dancer, choreographer, and b. director. Studied at Leningrad Ch. School, graduating in 1954. D. at the Maly Th. 1954–71. Artistic dir. of the b. co. at the State Th. Perm 1971–7. Among his chs. are *The Three Musketeers* (mus. V. Bassner, Maly Th., 1964), *The Woodcut Prince* (mus. Bartók, Maly Th., 1965), *Pique Dame* (mus. Prokofiev, Leningrad Chamber B., 1969), *Romeo and Juliet* (mus. Prokofiev, Perm, 1972—also at the West Berlin German Op., 1974), *The Miraculous Mandarin* (mus. Bartók, Perm, 1973), and *Tsar Boris* (mus. Prokofiev, 1975). Has since returned to Leningrad becoming chief ch. of Maly B. Married to the d. Larissa Klimova.

Bozzacchi, Giuseppina (*b* Milan, 23 Nov. 1853, *d* Paris, 23 Nov. 1870). Ital. dancer. A protégée of the Milan prima ballerina Amina Boschetti, she went to Paris to study with Mme Dominique. She created Swanilda in the Paris prod. of *Coppélia* in 1870. Immensely popular with the Parisian audiences, she danced the role 18 times until she succumbed to a fever during the Ger. siege and died on her 17th birthday.
BIBL.: I. Guest, in *The Ballet of the Second Empire* (London, 1953).

Bozzoni, Max (*b* Paris, 30 May 1917). Fr. dancer and teacher. Studied at Paris Opéra B. School. Joined its co. in 1936, became étoile in 1947, retired in 1963. Appointed b. master Geneva Op. B. in 1964. Now has his own school in Paris, and teaches at Opéra B. School.

Brabants, Jeanne (*b* Antwerp, 25 Jan. 1920). Belg. dancer, choreographer, teacher, and b. director. Studied with Lea Daan, later also with Jooss, Leeder, André van Damme, Preobrajenska, and at Royal B. School. D. with various troupes 1935–59, and started to ch. in 1939—first for the D. Ensembles Brabants, in which she appeared together with her two sisters, later also for the Royal Netherlands Th., the Royal Flemish Op., for Belg. TV and since 1970 as director of the Antwerp-based B. of Flanders. After founding a b. school with her father in 1941, she taught at various institutes and since 1951 at the b. school of Antwerp Royal Flemish Op., which is now attached to the B. of Flanders. She has created a great number of bs. and often appeared as a d. publicist.
BIBL.: R. Barbier, in *Van Operaballet naar Ballet van Vlaanderen* (Antwerp, 1973).

Brada, Ede (*b* Vienna, 11 Mar. 1879, *d* Budapest, 1953). Hung. dancer, choreographer, and teacher. Studied in Vienna, d. at the Court Op. 1895–1902, also in charge of the d. education of the children of Archduke Joseph for 11 years. In 1919 he moved to Budapest, where he was b. master of the State Op. from 1921 until the mid-30s. After retirement he still continued to teach at various Budapest institutes. Among the 54 bs. he ch. for the State Op. the most popular were *Princess Malve* (mus. Raoul Maria Mader), *Prince Argyrus* (mus. István von Gajáry), and *Carnival in Pest* (mus. various rhapsodies by Liszt). He was the father of Rezső B.

Brada, Rezső (*b* Budapest, 1906, *d* 1948). Hung. dancer and b. master. Studied with his father Ede B. and with A. Rasch in New York. Solo-d. of the Budapest State Op., promoted b. master in 1935. He often appeared abroad as a guest. Some of his most popular bs. were *Szent fáklya* (mus. Dohnányi, 1934) and *Kuruc Mese* (in collaboration with Milloss, mus. Kodály, 1935).

Bradley, Lisa (*b* Elizabeth, New Jersey, 1941). Amer. dancer. Studied at School of Amer. B., joined Joffrey B. 1961–6; then became a member of the First Chamber D. Co. Now d. with the Hartford B., returned as a guest artist to Joffrey B., spring 1976. Created roles in Arpino's *Sea Shadow* (1962), *Incubus* (1965), *Viva Vivaldi!* (1965), *Nightwings* (1966), and *Secret Places* (1968), Ailey's *Feast of Ashes* (1962), Joffrey's *Gamelan* (1963), and Bewley's *Death and the Maiden* (1974).
BIBL.: N. Laroche, in 'Hartford Belle', *Dance Magazine* (1975/2).

Brae, June (orig. J. Baer; *b* Ringwood, 1917). Brit.

dancer. Studied with George Goncharov in China, Legat, and Kschessinska, made her début with B. Club, joined Sadler's Wells B. as a principal d. 1936–42, creating leading roles in de Valois's *Checkmate* (1937) and Ashton's *Nocturne* (1936) and *A Wedding Bouquet* (1937). After her retirement she made a short comeback in 1946, creating roles in Helpmann's *Adam Zero* and Howard's *Assembly Ball*. Together with Fonteyn and May, she was one of the three most popular stars of the co. during the 1930s.

BIBL.: G. Anthony, 'J.B.' *Dancing Times* (1970/4).

Brahms, Caryl (*b* Surrey, 1901, *d* London, 4 Dec. 1982). Brit. writer and critic. Editor of *Footnotes to Ballet* (1936), wrote *Robert Helpmann, Choreographer* (1943), *A Seat at the Ballet* (1951), and among her satirical novels (collaborating with S. J. Simon) *A Bullet at the Ballet* (1937—later turned into a musical with Massine and Baronova) and *Six Curtains for Stroganova* (1945).

Brahms, Johannes (*b* Hamburg, 7 May 1833, *d* Vienna, 3 Apr. 1897). Ger. composer. Wrote no b. mus., but some of his compositions have been adapted for b. purposes—especially his Hungarian Dances, often used by recital dancers. Some of the more important bs. ch. to mus. by B. are Massine's *Choreartium* (4th Symphony, 1933), Nijinska's *Brahms Variations* (Variations on Themes by Handel and Paganini, 1944), Balanchine's *Liebeslieder Walzer* (1960) and *Brahms-Schoenberg Quartet* (op. 25, 1966), Feld's *Intermezzo* (various piano pieces, 1969), L. Meyer's *Brahms Sonata* (op. 5, 1969), Walter's *Remembrance* (Sextet for Strings, op. 36, 1969), Nahat's *Brahms Quintet* (op. 111, 1969), Cranko's *Initials R.B.M.E.* (2nd Piano Concerto in B flat major, 1972), Thorpe's *The Wanderer and his Shadow* (4 Serious Songs, 1972), and Veredon's *One Day* . . . (Piano Quartet, op. 25, 1974).

Branle (Fr., swing, shake—also spelt Bransle). A collective term for old Fr. folk dances, often accompanied by singing. Almost every province had its own variant. Best known was the B. de Poitou, d. in an anti-clockwise direction. Arbeau in his *Orchésographie* described no less than 26 kinds of Bs. in 1588. There was the festive striding d. (B. double and B. simple), but also the less stylized, very fast d. (B. gay, B. de Bourgogne). Its popularity is shown by frequent names like B. of the Washerwomen, Clog B., Peas B., and B. of the Hermits. At the court of Louis XIV the B., executed by a solo-couple, served as an introduction to the Bals parés. Because they often contained some mime, they became the forerunners of the b. In modernized form they can be found in Stravinsky's *Agon*.

Braque, Georges (*b* Argenteuil, 13 May 1882, *d* Paris, 31 Aug. 1963). Fr. painter. He was the designer of Nijinska's *Les Fâcheux* (1924), Massine's *Salade* (1924), and *Zéphire et Flore* (1925).

Bratislava (Pressburg). The first local th. opened in 1776 and what is today the Slovakian National Th. (TNS) was inaugurated in 1886. B. came to life here, however, only after the city had become the capital of Slovakia in 1919, and first really flourished when the Ital. Achille Viscusi was appointed b. master during the management of Oskar Nedbal (1923–31); Viscusi was a prolific ch. of bs. (*Coppélia*, Dvořak's *Slavonic Dances*, and *Swan Lake*, 1924; *Giselle*, 1926; *Nutcracker*, 1928; *Sylvia*, 1929). His successors were Ella Fuchsová (*Nikotina* and *Pan Twardowski*, 1931), Vladimir Pirnikov (together with Nikolská, *Raymonda*, 1933), Bohuslav Relský (*Swan Lake*, 1939), and Maximilian Froman (revivals of several Fokine bs.; *Sleeping Beauty*, 1942). After 1945 the co. rapidly expanded and its repertory of classics, contemporary works, and the standard Sov. bs. was built up by such choreographers as Rudolf Macharovský, Stanislav Remar (*Romeo and Juliet*, 1949; *Cinderella*, 1951; *Flames of Paris*, 1952; *Fountain of Bakhchisaray*, 1953), Jozef Zajko (*Gayaneh*, 1957; *Laurencia*, 1959), Milan Herényi, and Karol Tóth, the co.'s b. dir. 1961–72 (*Sacre du printemps*, *Scythian Suite*, and *Hiroshima*, 1964; *Minkus' Don Quixote*, 1970). After an interregnum Boris Slovák was appointed b. dir. in 1973, succeeded by K. Toth, in 1980.

BIBL.: Eva Jaczová, *Balet Slovenského národného divadla* (Bratislava, 1971; in Czech).

Braunsweg, Julian (*b* Warsaw, 1897, *d* London, 26 Mar. 1978). Pol.-Brit. impresario and b. director. Started to arrange various th. perfs. in the Berlin of the 1920s. Manager of the Russ. Romantic B. Was in charge of several individual artists (incl. Karsavina and La Argentina) and cos. (Pavlova, Max Reinhardt, Nijinska's Polish Bs., Nouveau B. de Monte Carlo, Met. B., Original B. Russe, R. Gopal), until he founded the London Festival B. in 1950, being its general dir. until 1965. Has since returned to arranging tours for the Royal B., Vienna State Op. B., and Amer. Classical B. Author of *B.'s Ballet Scandals* (London, 1973).

Bregvadze, Boris Jakovlevich (*b* Saratov, 19 Mar. 1926). Sov. dancer and b. master. Studied at the local b. school and at the Leningrad Ch. School, where upon graduation (1947) he became a member of the Kirov B. He d. the premier danseur roles of the repertory, but his real forte was the heroic roles of the modern Sov. repertory such as Lenny in *Path of Thunder* and the title-roles in Chaboukiani's *Othello* and Jacobson's *Spartacus*. He now works as a b. master. People's Artist of the R.S.F.S.R. His wife Emma B. (*née* E. Minchenok, *b* Leningrad, 29 Aug. 1932) is a solo-d. of the Kirov B.

Brenaa, Hans (*b* Copenhagen, 9 Oct. 1910). Dan. dancer, teacher, and b. master. Studied at Dan. B. School, becoming a member of the co. in 1928; promoted solo-d. in 1943, left in 1955. Is now in worldwide demand as a producer of Bournonville bs.

Breuer, Peter (b Tegernsee, 29 Oct. 1946). Ger. dancer. Studied with Roleff, Blank, L. Gonta, and V. Gsovsky, joined the Munich State Op. B. in 1961. Since 1964 he has been in addition a member of the Düsseldorf Rhine Op. co., promoted solo-d. in 1966. Regular guest-engagements in West Berlin and abroad have made him one of the best intern. known of younger Ger. dancers. Created roles in Walter's *Baiser de la Fée* (1965), *L'Orfeo* (1967), *The Four Seasons* (1970), *Sacre du printemps* (1970), and *Jeux* (1973), Van Manen's *Keep Going* (1971) and Romeo in Boyart-chikov's Berlin prod. of *Romeo and Juliet* (1974). Numerous guest-appearances with London Festival B. to 1978.
BIBL.: M. Nichaus: *P.B.* (Munich, 1978).

Briansky, Oleg (b Brussels, 9 Nov. 1929). Belg. dancer and teacher. Studied in Brussels and with V. Gsovsky, Rousanne, Preobrajenska, and Volkova, made his début in 1945 with a group of his own in Brussels, joined the Bs. des Champs-Elysęs in 1946, then became a member of the B. de Paris, which he left again after an Amer. tour to d. on Broadway. Principal d. London Festival B. 1951–5, after which he pursued a career as a freelance d. with many different cos., until he took up residence in New York during the early 1960s. Had his own small co. in New York, where he teaches as well as at the Saratoga B. Center. Married to Mireille Briane (née Lefevre), who teaches at their school.
BIBL.: L. Chiavaroli, 'Ballet Comes to Binghampton', *Dance Magazine* (1970/6).

Brianza, Carlotta (b Milan, 1867, d Paris, 1930). Ital. dancer. Studied with Blasis; continued when became prima ballerina of La Scala. Toured the U.S. in 1883 and created a sensation when she appeared in 1887 at the St. Petersburg Arcadia Th. in Manzotti's *Excelsior*, subsequently engaged at the Maryinsky Th. She made her début there with Cecchetti in Ivanov's *The Tulip of Haarlem* in 1889 and created Aurora in Petipa's *Sleeping Beauty* (1890) and the leading role in his *Kalkabrino* (1891). In 1891 she returned to Western Europe. After her retirement as a d. continued to teach in Paris. Diaghilev engaged her to d. Carabosse in his London prod. of *The Sleeping Princess* in 1921. Is said to have committed suicide in Paris.

Bright Stream, The (orig. Russ. title: *Svetly ruchey*). Ballet in 3 acts and 4 scenes; libr. and ch. Lopokov; mus. Shostakovich; déc. V. Bobyshev. Prod. 4 Apr. 1935, Maly Th. Leningrad. The title is the name of a collective farm in the Kuban region, where a group of artists arrives. Zina, married to the agronomist, knows the ballerina from her student days. When her husband starts to flirt with the ballerina, Zina and her friends are upset about such unsocialist behaviour. They prepare a plan to expose Pyotr's fickleness, after which he can only beg for pardon. This is granted, so that everything ends in general jubilation. The b. was heavily attacked because of its use of the classic idiom to represent the contemporary world of Russ. peasants and workers. Pravda published a much discussed article, 'Ballet Falsities' and Lopokov was dismissed as b. chief of the Maly Th.
BIBL.: M. G. Swift, in *The Art of the Dance in the U.S.S.R.* (Notre Dame, Ind., 1968).

Brind, Bryony (b Plymouth, 27 May 1960). Eng. dancer. Studied Royal B. School, joined Royal B. at Covent Garden 1978; promoted soloist 1981 and principal d. 1984. Début as Odette-Odile in *Swan Lake*, 1981, while still in corps de ballet. Created role in Ashton's *Rhapsody* (1981).

Brinson, Peter (b Llandudno, 6 Mar. 1923). Brit. lecturer and writer on b. Educated Oxford Univ. Prod. first stereoscopic b. film, *The Black Swan* (1952). Editor of *Pavlova* film (1954). Contributor to *The Dancing Times, Ballet, The Times*, etc. Extension lecturer on b. Oxford, Cambridge, and London Univs. 1954–64. Founder-Dir. of B. for All group 1964, for which he wrote and directed many programmes. Dir. of Royal Academy of D. 1968–9. Dir. of the Brit. and Commonwealth Branch of the Gulbenkian Foundation 1971–82, then Head of Postgraduate Studies, Laban Centre 1982–7, but continues as professor of d. at Univ of Toronto. Chairman of national enquiry into d. in education, 1975–80, and wrote resulting report, *Dance Education and Training in Britain* (London, 1980), the first national study of its kind. Editor of *The Ballet in Britain* (London, 1962). Author of *The Choreographic Art* (with Van Praagh, London, 1963), *The Polite World* (with J. Wildeblood, London, 1965), *Background to European Ballet* (London 1966), and *Ballet for All* (with C. Crisp, London, 1970)—new edition *Ballet & Dance, A Guide to the Repertory* (Newton Abbot, 1980).

Brisé (Fr., broken). Designates a step belonging to the petite batterie—a leap upwards off one foot, 'breaking' the movement in mid-air through light beating of the legs, and landing on both feet. One distinguishes between brisés dessus and brisés dessous. The coda of the Blue Bird pas de deux starts with a diagonal of 24 brisés volés, which are executed alternately to front and back.

Brito, Amparo (b Havana, 1950). Cub. dancer. Studied at Cub. National B. School with Mirta Pla, Ramona de Saa, and Joaquin Banegas. Joined National B. of Cuba in 1968; subsequently appointed soloist. Gold Medal (Moscow, 1973).

Britten, Benjamin (b Lowestoft, 22 Nov. 1913, d 4 Dec. 1976). Brit. composer. Wrote the mus. for the b. *Prince of the Pagodas*, which Cranko ch. in 1957 for the Royal B. There are also several b. sequences in his op. *Death in Venice*, ch. by Ashton at the work's first prod. in 1973. Choreographers have often used his concert mus. for b. purposes—

incl. his *Soirées musicales* (Tudor, 1938; Cranko in *Bouquet garni*, 1965), *Simple Symphony* (Gore, 1944; Dollar, 1961), *Variations on a Theme of Frank Bridge* (L. Christensen in *Jinx* 1942; Ashton in *Le Rêve de Léonor*, 1949; Cranko in *Variations on a Theme*, 1954; A. Carter in *House of Shadows*, 1955; Gore in *Eaters of Darkness*, 1958; Neumeier in *Stages and Reflections*, 1968; Bintley in *Night Moves*, 1981), *The Young Person's Guide to the Orchestra* (Robbins in *Fanfare*, 1953; Ashton in *Variations on a Theme of Purcell*, 1955), *Les Illuminations* (Ashton, 1950; T. Gsovsky, 1961); String Quartet No 1 in D (Cauley in *Last of Three*, 1978); and *Sinfonia da Requiem* (Tetley in *Dances of Albion*, 1980, preceded in the same b. by B.B.'s *Serenade for tenor, horn, and strings*); Kylián in *Forgotten Land* (1981).

Britton, Donald (*b* London, 1929, *d* Birmingham, 31 May 1973). Brit. d. and teacher. Studied in Bristol and at Sadler's Wells School; joined Sadler's Wells Th. B. in 1946. Became a member of the Sadler's Wells B. in 1947, promoted principal d. (after an interruption of his career for military service) in 1951. Created roles in MacMillan's *Danses concertantes* (1955), *The Burrow* (1958), and Cranko's *Sweeney Todd* (1959). Taught at the Royal B. and Arts Educational Schools in London and later in Fr.
BIBL.: J. Percival, 'Ballet's Tough Guy', *Dance and Dancers* (1958/7).

Brno (also known as Brünn). The th. Nahradbách was opened in 1882, but this was the home of the Ger. co., though Czech op. was also performed here, and most of Janáček's ops. were first prod. here. Since 1965 it has been the residence of the city's drama co. The Janáček Th. opened in that year, becoming the home of the city's State Op. and B. Though individual th. perfs. of dances and bs. have been registered, local professional b. activities started only after the First World War, when Achille Viscusi and Jaroslav Hladik were in charge of the co. attached to the op. house. Ivo Váňa Psota was the dominating personality of b. in the city during his three terms of b. directorship 1926–32, 1936–41, and 1947–52, of which the high point was his first prod. of Prokofiev's *Romeo and Juliet* in 1938 (Lavrovsky's Leningrad prod. was not until 1940). He was followed by Rudolf Karhánek, Jiří Nemrut, Věra Vagnerová, and others; Luboš Ogoun was appointed b. director 1961–4, and succeeded in giving the co. and its repertory a marked contemporary profile. When Ogoun left to form the Prague B. with P. Smok, Miroslav Kůra took over, succeeded by J. Němeček 1974–5 and O. Skalová since 1975.
BIBL.: L. Schmidová, *Ceskoslovenský Ballet* (Prague, 1962; in Czech).

Brock, Karena (*b* Los Angeles, 21 Sept. 1942). Amer. dancer. Studied at b. school of Texas-Christian University, Fort Worth, with D. Perkins, Lichine, and Riabouchinska. D. with Lich-

ine's co. 1959–61, Dutch National B. 1962, and Amer. B. Th. since 1963, becoming soloist 1967 and principal d. 1973.

Broken Date, The. See *Rendez-vous manqué, Le.*

Bronze Horseman, The (original Russ. title: *Medny vsadnik*). Ballet with prologue, in 4 acts and 9 scenes; libr. P. Abolimov; ch. Zakharov; mus. Glière; déc. Mikhail Bobyshov. Prod. 14 Mar. 1949, Kirov B., Leningrad, with Sergeyev, Dudinskaya. The b. is based on Pushkin's poem and deals with the tragic love story of Yevgeny and Parasha, set against the historic flood of St. Petersburg in 1824. Parasha is drowned, and Yevgeny goes mad and accuses the statue of the Bronze Horseman—i.e. Peter the Great—of pursuing him. In the Moscow first prod. of the same year (same ch.) the protagonists were Gabovitch and Ulanova.
BIBL.: C. Beaumont 'T.B.H.', in *Ballets Past & Present* (London, 1955); N. Roslayeva, 'T.B.H.', in C. Crisp and M. Clarke, *Making a Ballet* (London, 1975).

Brosset, Yvonne (*b* Stockholm, 1935). Swed. dancer. Studied at Royal Swed. B. School and Sadler's Wells School, joined Royal Swed. B. in 1953, promoted ballerina in 1963. She dances the leading roles of the traditional repertory as well as the bs. of Cullberg, Åkesson, and Cramér.

Brouillards. Ballet in 1 act; ch. Cranko; mus. Debussy. Prod. 8 Mar. 1970, Stuttgart, with Reyn, Hanke, Keil, Madsen, Cragun, Clauss. Set to nine préludes for piano—the opening piece is repeated at the end—the b. develops as a string of sketches, presenting various moods and encounters, all of which end with a question-mark: ch. variations, dealing with uselessness and transitoriness. Generally considered one of Cranko's most personal and intimate statements.

Brown, Carolyn (*née* Rice; *b* Fitchburg, 1927). Amer. dancer and choreographer. Studied at the school of her mother who came from Denishawn. As a child she regularly spent the summer months at Jacob's Pillow. Educated at Wheaton College where she graduated in philosophy. After marrying the comp. Earle B. moved to Denver, where she met Cunningham. Studied with him and with Craske and Tudor in New York, and became one of the founding members of the Cunningham co. at Black Mountain College in 1952 and was Cunningham's foremost female d. throughout her whole active career, up to 1972, collaborating closely with him and Cage in the creation of dozens of works. A d. of striking beauty, a virtuoso technician, and an extremely cultivated artist of great intelligence, she has often stepped forward as a writer, to spread the cause of modern d. Since her retirement as a d. continues to teach and ch. Now Dean of D. at State Univ. of New York at Purchase. D. Magazine Award (1969). Contributed 'On Chance', *Ballet Review* (II, 2).

BIBL.: O. Maynard, 'In Celebration of C.B.' *Dance Magazine* (1971/7).

Brown, Vida (*b* Oak Park, 1922). Amer. dancer and b. mistress. D. with Chicago Op. B., B. de la Jeunesse, and B. Russe de Monte Carlo 1939–48. Joined New York City B. 1950, becoming b. mistress and asst. to Balanchine 1954–8, after which she worked as a freelance producer of Balanchine bs.

Browne, Leslie (*b* New York, 1957). Amer. dancer. The daughter of dancers Isabel Mirrow and Kelly Brown, and the sister of the d. Elizabeth Laing, she started to study with M. Craske, then with her parents in Phoenix, Ariz., continuing after moving back to New York at School of Amer. B. Joined New York City B. and, after performing the juvenile ballerina role in the film *The Turning Point* (1977), was appointed soloist with Amer. B. Th., now principal d.

BIBL.: N. McLain Stoop, 'L.B. of American Ballet Theatre and 'The Turning Point'', *Dance Magazine* (1977/10).

Browne, Louise (*b* Madison, USA, 1906). Brit. dancer and teacher. Studied in New York with Fokine, Kosloff, Tarasoff, and Vladimirov, in London with de Valois and Craske, and in Paris with Preobrajenska. D. in musicals in New York and London. Founded and directed with Gerd Kjølaas New Norwegian B. 1948–50. Returned to U.K. in 1950. Joined Royal Academy of Dancing, becoming one of its administrators and examiners and since 1965 Dir. of the Academy's Intern. B. Summer School in London. Member of Arts Council of Great Britain D. Committee 1970–80. Fellow of the Royal Academy of Dancing. Queen Elizabeth II Coronation Award (1971). O.B.E. (1978).

Bruce, Christopher (*b* Leicester, 3 Oct. 1945). Brit. dancer and choreographer. Studied in Scarborough and at Rambert School, made his début with Gore's London B. Member of the B. Rambert since 1963, he soon became one of its foremost dancers. For it he ch. his first bs.; assoc. dir. 1975–9, assoc. ch. to 1987. Also assoc. ch. London Festival B. 1986. Among his best roles are the Faun in Nijinsky's *L'après-midi d'un faune* and Pierrot in Tetley's *Pierrot lunaire*. Some of his important role creations were in Morrice's *The Realms of Choice* (1965), *Hazard* (1967), *Blind-Sight* (1969), and *That Is the Show* (1971), J. Taylor's *Diversities* (1966), Tetley's *Embrace Tiger and Return to Mountain* (1968), L. Hodes's *The Act* (1968), and Scoglio's *Stop-Over* (1972). Ch. *George Frideric* (mus. Handel, 1969), *Living Space* (texts by Robert Cockburn, 1969), *Wings* (mus. Bob Downes, Cologne, 1970), *... for these who die as cattle* (no mus., 1972), *There was a Time* (mus. Brian Hodgson, 1973), *Duets* (mus. Hodgson, 1973), *Unfamiliar Playground* (mus. Anthony Hymas, Royal B., 1974), *Ancient Voices of Children* (mus. G. Crumb, 1975), *Black Angels* (mus. G.

Crumb, 1976), *Echoes of a Night Sky* (mus. G. Crumb, 1977), *Cruel Garden* (with L. Kemp, mus. C. Miranda and collage of Spanish items, texts Lorca, 1977), *Responses* (no mus., 1977), *Night with Waning Moon* (mus. G. Crumb, 1979), *Preludes and Song* (mus. A. Hymas, 1980), *Dancing Day* (mus. Holst), *Cantata* (mus. Stravinsky), *Ghost Dances* (mus. S. Amer. folk-songs, arr. N. Carr, all 1981). Has also worked for Tanz-Forum, Cologne, Batsheva D. Co., Austral. D. Th., Kent Opera, *et al.*

BIBL.: Interview with C.B., *Dance and Dancers* (1969/12); G. Gow, 'C.B.' *Dancing Times* (1973/3).

Bruel, Michel (*b* Sète, 1944). Fr. dancer. Studied with various teachers in Cannes. Started to d. with Lazzini at Marseilles Op., then with Washington National B., also appearing with National B. of Cuba, Bolshoi B., Kirov B., and Cullberg B. Since 1976 has mainly appeared with various Japanese cos.

Brugnoli, Amalia (*b* before 1810). Ital. dancer. She was prima ballerina of the San Carlo Th. in Naples during the 1820s and some say that she was the first ballerina to d. on points. When she exhibited this feat in Vienna in 1823 she created a sensation, though it cost her a considerable effort. During the early 1830s a fierce rivalry between her and Elssler became the talk of the town. In 1832 she also appeared as a guest in Paris and London. Married to the d. and ch. Paolo Samengo.

Bruhn, Erik (orig, Belton Evers; *b* Copenhagen, 3 Oct. 1928, *d* Toronto, 1 Apr. 1986). Dan. d. and b. dir. He entered the school of the Royal Dan. B. in 1937, becoming a member of the co., in 1947, promoted solo d. in 1949. D. 1947–9 as a guest with the Eng. Metropolitan B., later also with Amer. B. Th., Nat. B. of Canada, N.Y. City B., Royal B., Harkness B., and R. Page B. Dir. of the Royal Swed. B. 1967–71. Assoc. dir. of the Nat. B. of Canada, for which he prod. *La Sylphide* in 1965, *Swan Lake* in 1966, and *Coppélia* in 1975. Art. dir. Nat. B. Canada 1983–6. Throughout his active career he was considered one of the best dancers in the world, an immaculately stylish technician, unsurpassed in his culture and nobility, and of rare intelligence. Though he occasionally did some ch. his real gift seems to have been as a prod. of the classics. He d. all the premier danseur roles of the traditional and the Bournonville repertory. Among his best modern roles were Jean in Cullberg's *Miss Julie* and Don José in Petit's *Carmen*. For a d. of his standing he created relatively few roles—the most important in Taras' *Designs with Strings* (1948), MacMillan's *Journey* (1957), Cullberg's *Lady from the Sea* (1960), Cranko's *Daphnis and Chloe* (1962), and S. Hodes' *The Abyss* (1965). Nijinsky Prize (1963); Knight of Dannebrog (1963); D. Magazine Award (1968). Author (together with L. Moore) of *Bournonville*

and Ballet Technique (London, 1961) and 'Beyond Technique' (*Dance Perspectives* 36).
BIBL.: J. Gruen, E. B.: *Danseur Noble* (N.Y., 1979).

Brunner, Gerhard (*b* Villach, 23 Mar. 1939). Austrian b. director. Educated Univ. of Vienna. After having been mus. and d. critic for various Austrian and Ger. newspapers and artistic advisor of Vienna B. Festival 1969 and Styrian D. Festival (Graz) 1976, was appointed dir. of the Vienna State Op. B. and its affiliated school in the autumn of 1976. Was married to the d. Christl Zimmerl.

Brussels. At the Académie de musique (opened in 1682) and at the Th. sur la Monnaie (1700), dancers, mainly Ital., appeared at first only in ops. by Lully. In 1705 a regular op. co., was founded with a small b. troupe, consisting of 4 male and 5 female dancers plus a singing ballerina. In 1817 a regular b. co., was created, listing 7 soloists, 20 female and 20 male dancers, plus 8 children, who appeared in bs. by Oudar and Hus. In 1819 the present Th. Royal de la Monnaie opened its doors (in 1855 it burned down, but was immediately reconstructed). First prominent b. master was J.-A. Petipa (1819–32, 1833–5, 1841–2, and 1843). He also founded the Conservatoire de la Danse in 1826–7. Choreographing a great number of bs., he saw that the many members of his family got the appropriate roles, but he also invited Elssler, Cerrito, Taglioni, Grisi, and Grahn as guest ballerinas. In the reconstructed house Desplace was appointed b. master in 1858. In 1871 B. saw the first prod. of *Coppélia* outside Fr. (ch. J. Hannsen). L. Petipa, who had been appointed b. master in 1872, was succeeded around the turn of the century by G. G. Saracco and F. Ambrosiny, with Brianza as temporary prima ballerina. The most successful bs. were *Quand les chats sont partis* (1908), *Hopjes*, and *Istar* (1913). After the first world war, Marthe Coeck was appointed as b. mistress, followed by a number of Fr. choreographers until J. J. Etchevery took over in 1953. He was especially successful with a series of bs. based on Fr. paintings of the 19th century (*Les Bals de Paris, Manet, Opéra-Ballets*). B.'s most important b. event, however, was the foundation in 1960 of the *Ballet of the 20th Century with Béjart as its head. At the traditional op. house, the Cirque Royal, the Forest National, and other unconventional places a huge young audience crowds the perfs. of the co., which through its regular tours abroad has brought international b. renown to the city of B. for the first time.
BIBL.: J. Isnardon, *Le Théâtre de la Monnaie* (B., 1890); J. Salès, *Théâtre Royal de la Monnaie 1856–1970* (B., 1971).

Bryans, Rudy (orig. Bernard Godet; *b* Lyons, *c.* 1945). Fr. dancer. Studied in Lyons with Karnetzki. Joined Lille B. in 1963, becoming soloist. D. with the cos. of Charrat and Daydé. Joined Bs. de Marseille as a principal d. in 1973, creating leading roles in Petit's *La Rose malade* (as partner of Plisetskaya, 1973), *L'Arlésienne* and *Les Intermittences du coeur* (1974), *Septentrion* (1975). Married to the d. Dany Maynet. Fr. TV film about him, 1975.
BIBL.: J. Cartier, 'Pleins feux sur R.B.', *Les Saisons de la danse* (1974/12).

Bucharest. It was a long time before b. was on an equal footing with op. in the new Th. of Op. and Ballet in B., which opened its doors in 1953. At first there had been small visiting op. troupes from abroad to which even smaller b. ensembles were attached, performing divertissements only. In 1822 a group appeared from Brasov, performing a b. based upon Rum. folk-dances and celebrating the national heroes Closca and Crisan. In 1833 a School for Mus. and Declamation opened, to which a d.-class was added in 1852. 1869 saw the first classic b. with a Rum. subject: *The Golden Girl* (mus. Ludovic Wiest), ch. by the famous Amer. ballerina A. Maywood (with Gheorge Moceanu) and performed during a season of an Ital. op. ensemble. In 1885 the National Th. at last established a Rum. op. troupe together with a b. co., and b. school, from which came Maria Balanescu, the first prominent Rum. prima ballerina. Before the first world war b. was put on a broader basis, which strengthened when the th. came under state control and a close collaboration materialized with the op. of Cluj. In the repertory of both ths. were the standard classics and the most successful works of the Diaghilev repertory. At the b. schools in B. and Cluj one could find such esteemed teachers as M. Balanescu, A. Romanowski, E. Pienescu-Liciu, and B Kniaseff. Typical Rum. bs. between the 2 world wars were *Ileana Cosinzeana* (mus. Ion Nona- Ottesco), *On the Market* (mus. M. Jora), *A Night in the Carpathian Mountains* (mus. Paul Constantinesco), *The Werewolf* (mus. Zeno Vancea) and the often-ch. *Rumanian Rhapsody* (mus. G. Enescu). After 1945 the B. b. came under the influence of the U.S.S.R., yet it is a remarkable fact that not only the Russ. standard classics, but also most of the bs. of the modern Russ. repertory were ch. in B. by Rum. artists—incl. Oscar Danovschi, Tilde Urseanu, and Vasile Marcu, who were the most prominent post-war choreographers. During the 1960s more Western influences found their way to Rum., and in 1965 the co. mounted one of the very first prods. of a b. set to mus. by Boulez: *Le Marteau sans maître* (ch. Stere Popescu). Today Octav Enigarescu is b. dir. of the B. State Op., with Cornel Trailescu, Gheorge Cotovela, Urseanu, Marcu, Valentina Massini, and Ion Tugearu as members of his staff and Irinel Liciu, Alexandra Mezinescu, Ileana Iliescu, M. Popa, Sergiu Stefanschi, and D. Moïse as its best known dancers (some of them have also regularly appeared in the West). Apart from the prods. of the standard classics, the repertory offers several bs. set to mus. by Enescu and Dinu Lipatti, plus the usual fare of bs. from Stravinsky and

Prokofiev to A. Petrov and Shchedrin and a certain number of home-made works, of which Danovschi's *Prince and Beggar* (mus. Laurentiu Profeta) and *Return from the Depths* (mus. Jora) enjoy special popularity.

Buckle, Richard (*b* Warcop, 6 Aug. 1916). Brit. writer on b. B. critic of the *Observer* 1948–55, of *Sunday Times* 1959–75. Founded magazine *Ballet* in 1939 (appearing, with a war-time interruption, until 1952). Organized the Edinburgh Diaghilev exhibition in 1954. Contributor to various d. magazines and publications. Author of *Adventures of a Ballet Critic* (London, 1953), *In Search of Diaghilev* (London, 1955), *Modern Ballet Design* (London, 1955), *Dancing for Diaghilev* (The Memoirs of Lydia Sokolova; London, 1960), *The French Romantic Movement as a Background to the Ballet Giselle* (limited ed., 1966), *Nijinsky* (London, 1971), *Diaghilev* (1979), and *B. at the Ballet* (London, 1980). C.B.E. (1979).

Budapest. Before the State Op. moved to its present house in 1884, b. perfs. took place at the Ofen Court Th. and at the National Th. There the bs. of the Romantic repertory were prod.— among them *La Fille mal gardée* (1839), *Ondine* (1846), *Giselle* (1847), *Paquita* (1847), *La Péri* (1851), *Esmeralda* (1856), *La Sylphide* (1858), *Coppélia* (1877), and *Naïla* (1881), with occasional appearances of famous ballerinas from abroad. There were also, however, pantomimes and bs. by such Hung. choreographers as Szöllösy, Farkas, Kaczér, Veszter, Kilányi, and Tóth, though most of the choreographers (and teachers) came from abroad, among them the Ital. Friedrich Campilli. About the middle of the century Emila Aranyvári became the first Hung. prima ballerina. At the Royal Op. Luigi Mazzantini and Cesar Smeraldi worked as b. masters. The b. co. enjoyed its first flowering when N. Guerra became b. dir. 1902–15 (with short interruptions), choreographing such bs. as *Adventures of Love* (mus. Mader, 1902), *Carnival of Venice* (mus. Berté, 1903), *The Lilliputian Grenadier* (mus. Szikla, 1903), *Gemma* (mus. Zichy, 1904), *Hungarian Dance Suite* (mus. Liszt and Szikla, 1907), *The Veil of Pierette* (mus. Dohnányi, 1910), *Prometheus* (mus. Beethoven, 1913), and *Games of Amor* (mus. Mozart, 1913). Among his pupils were Emilia Nirschy, Anna Palley, and F. Nádasi. He was succeeded by E. Brada and Otto Zöbisch (first prod. of Bartók's *The Wooden Prince*, 1917), after whom came J. Czieplinsky, whose *Bolero* (mus. Ravel) and dances from Goldmark's *Queen of Sheba* are still performed today. Main soloists were then Carola Szalay, Bella Bordy, Ferenc Köszegi, László Scányi, and Zoltán Sallay. The 1930s were dominated by G. Oláh, who engaged G. Harangozó in 1936 and F. Nádasi in 1937, who eventually became b. directors. While Harangozó laid the basis of the cos. repertory (for his bs. see *Harangozó*), Nádasi became the country's most important teacher, training such excellent dancers as Melinda Ottrubay, Ilona

Vera, György Tatár, Hedvig Hidas, Kató Patócs, and Ernö Vashegyi. A. von Milloss was invited twice and mounted his *Creatures of Prometheus* (mus. Beethoven) in 1942. After the second world war, the second generation of Nádasi pupils included such eminent soloists as N. Kovács, I. Rab (later known as Rabovsky), Vera Pásztor, Dora Csinády, V. Fülöp, and G. Lakatos. In 1948 Charrat mounted Stravinsky's *Jeu de cartes*. In 1950 the B. State Ch. Institute was founded. Close collaboration with Russ. guest choreographers and b. masters started with Vainonen's *Nutcracker* and *Flames of Paris* (1950), continuing with Messerer, Zakharov, Lavrovsky, Anisimova, Boyarski, Gusev, Chaboukiani, Kasatkina-Vasiliov, and N. Baltacheyeva. Apart from Harangozó the most important Hung. choreographers of the 1960s and 70s incl. I. Eck, L. Seregi, and A. Fodor. During the 1970s the co. opened up considerably to western influences, inviting choreographers like Ashton, Lander, Béjart, Balanchine, and Ailey. After 1950 some more Nádasi pupils came to the fore, incl. Z. Kun, K. Ugray, F. Havas, A. Orosz, V. Roná, and L. Sipeki—later succeeded by J. Menyhárt, M. Kékesi, V. Szurák, I. Dózsa, and J. Forgach. Since 1977 Seregi has succeeded György Lörinc as artistic dir. The co., whose last soloist recruits incl. L. Partay, M. Metzger, K. Czarnoy, I. Pongor, N. Szöny, and G. Keveházi, regularly tours abroad, appearing for the first time at the Edinburgh Festival 1963. In B. it performs both at the Op. House and the Erkel Th.

BIBL.: G. Körtvélyes and G. Lörinc, *B. Ballet* (in Eng., B., 1971).

Budarin, Vadim Andreyevich (*b* Kovrov, 2 Aug. 1942). Sov. dancer. Studied at the Leningrad Ch. School, joining the Kirov B. upon graduation (1961); dances the leading roles of the traditional and modern repertory. Bronze Medal (Varna, 1970).

Buenos Aires. There were perfs. of individual dances in the op. seasons given at the Th. at the Rio Plata, but the first professional couple of dancers were the Fr. Toussaints in 1823 at the Teatro Coliseo. In 1829 José (father) and Juana (daughter) Cañete enjoyed some sort of success; they were succeeded in 1832 by Philippe and Caroline Caton, who liked to d. small bs. and pantomimes, based on Napoleonic subjects, to Rossini overtures. Later a small co. of 19 dancers was established, with La Toussaint and Caroline Caton among its members; however the very cold winters and political instability prevented a consequent b. policy. In 1844 the Ital. Guglielma and Enrico Priggioni came as guests, and 1845 B.A. went polka-mad upon the appearance of the 14-year-old Irene Ramirez with Teodoro Rousseau. The Span. d. Dolores Gonzales Gambin came in 1847, and the co. of Gonzales Gambin, with the Finarts as premier couple, in 1849. When the Teatro Colón opened in 1857 B.A. got its first impression of traditional b. from a co. which was headed by Jean Rousset and based mainly on the members of his large family, performing *Giselle, Catalina,* and *Satanella or The Triumph of Virtue,* and others bs. after Montplaisir and Perrot. In 1860 came the co. of Thierry with *Almea or An Oriental Dream* and *The English in Spain,* with the technically prodigious Celestine Thierry scoring a special success. The co. also performed *La Sylphide* and returned in 1861 with *Esmeralda, The God and the Bayadère, Zéphir and Flore,* and *Don Quixote de la Mancha.* From 1861 the Bouffes Parisiens enjoyed great popularity for 12 years, with special dances added to their normal programmes. In 1868 Josephine Lecerf had a great success in *Robert the Devil.* Giovanni Pratesi, who made his début here in 1865, opened B.A.'s first b. school in 1879. In the same year Angelo Ferrari staged an extremely successful prod. of Manzotti's *Excelsior;* a cigarette was named after it and sold with the pictures of the ballerinas. Ferrari returned in 1886, offering the spectacular *Brahma.* 1903 saw the first B.A. perf. of *Coppélia,* d. by the co. of Ludovico Saracco. In 1908 the new Teatro Colón opened with a co. listing 40 dancers, most of whom were Itals. Since 1912 the city has seen an almost uninterrupted flow of guest ballerinas and cos. of every kind—among them in 1912 Preobrajenska, in 1914 Mazzuchelli, in 1915 Fornaroli, and in 1916 Zucchi; in 1913 and 1917 the Bs. Russes de Diaghilev, in 1915 the troupe of Argentina, in 1916 Duncan and for the first time the co. of Pavlova, and in 1921 Massine and Vera Savina. In 1922 Pierre Michailowsky was appointed b. master at the Colón, with Maria Olenewa as prima ballerina 1923–4. In 1925 the co. was completely reorganized, with R. Page and A. Ludmila as prima ballerinas and for the first time a considerable contingent of Argent. dancers. In the following years many guest choreographers from abroad mounted their bs., occasionally creating new ones. The following are only a small selection: Bolm, Kyasht, Nijinska (who returned several times), Fokine, Romanoff, Lifar, Cieplinsky, Wallman (frequently between 1937 and 1948), Balanchine, and Psota. They were succeeded after 1945 by Lichine, Milloss, T. Gsovsky, Borovsky, Rosen, Massine, J. Carter, Nureyev, Skibine, and Georgi. Today the repertory of the Teatro Colón is completely internationally orientated, without showing any particularly individual profile. In 1968 the co. embarked on its first visit to Europe (Paris Festival). Since 1973 the direction of the co. is shared between Antonio Truyol, Olga Ferri, Enrique Lommi, and Bruno D'Astoli—with Esmeraldá Agoglia, Liliana Belfiore, Ferri, Violeta Janeiro, Nancy López, Rubén Chayan, Rodolfo Fontán, Lommi, Gustavo Mollajoli, and Truyol as principal dancers. Since 1968 the city has had a second more modern-orientated

b. co., at the Teatro San Martín (Balletto Contemporaneo de la Ciudad de B.A.).
BIBL.: entry 'B.A.' in *Enciclopedia dello spettacolo.*

Bugaku. Ballet in 1 act; ch. Balanchine; mus. Toshiro Mayuzumi; scenery and light. Hays; cost. Karinska. Prod. 20 Mar. 1963, New York City B., City Center, New York, with Kent, Villella. The visit of Gagaku to New York inspired Balanchine to create this b. in 3 parts, which presents a purely fictitious Jap. marriage ceremony.
BIBL.: G. Balanchine, 'B.' in *Balanchine's New Complete Stories of the Great Ballets* Garden City, N.Y. 1977).

Buirge, Susan (*b* Minneapolis, Minn., 19 June 1940). Amer. dancer, teacher, and choreographer. Studied at Univ. of Minnesota, with Limón, Jones, Corvino, and Horst at Juilliard School, and with Nikolais and Louis at Henry Street Playhouse. D. with A. Nikolais D. Th. 1963–7, also with M. Louis D. Co., and since 1975 as d., ch., and artistic dir. of her own Danse Théâtre Susan Buirge, based on Paris, where she has lived since 1970. Has taught at many schools in New York, Paris (where she opened her school Pour Un Lieu de Création in 1975), and various cities of Fr., Switzerland, and Ger. Started to ch. in 1961, since when she has created numerous ch. events.

Bujones, Fernando (*b* Miami, 9 Mar. 1955). Amer. dancer. Studied at School of Amer. B., Juilliard School and with Zeida Cecilia Méndez. Began to dance with comp. of Eglevsky in 1970. Joined Amer. B. Th. 1972 becoming principal dancer in 1974. Has since danced with many cos. all over the world. With Amer. B. Th. to 1985.
BIBL.: H. Bruback, 'F.B. Interviewed', *Ballet News* (1980/10).

Bulerias. Part of the Span. flamenco dances, also called Chuflas (boasting), very fast, with mime and humorous accents and many syncopations. They are mostly danced at the end of flamenco perfs.

Bulnes, Esmée (*b* Rockferry, 6 June 1900, *d* Rimini, 3 Mar. 1986). Brit. dancer, b. mistress and teacher. Studied with Cecchetti, Nijinska, Egorova, Smirnova, and B. Romanow. Teacher at the Teatro Colón 1931–49 (and temporarily also asst. to Fokine), where she reorganized the b. school. Then went to Milan, where she was dir. of the b. school 1951–4, b. dir. of the co. up to 1962, after which she returned to directing the school 1962–9.

Burgmüller, Friedrich (*b* Regensburg, 1804, *d* Paris, 1874). Ger. composer. Wrote *La Péri* for Coralli in 1843, followed the next year by *Lady Henriette, ou la Servante de Greenwich* (collaborating with F. Von Flotow) for Mazilier (this inspired Flotow later on to comp. his op. *Martha*). His best known piece of d. mus., however is the Peasant pas de deux, which he comp. in 1841 for the first prod. of *Giselle.*

Burke, Dermot (*b* Dublin, 8 Jan. 1948). Amer. dancer. He grew up in Orlando, Fl., and studied b., jazz-d. tap, and gymnastics, incl. tumbling, and was in all-star football and baseball teams. However, he took up a scholarship at the Joffrey School, after which he became one of the most prominent dancers of the Joffrey B. 1966–72, creating roles in Arpino's *Secret Places* (1968), *A Light Fantastic* (1968), *Animus* (1969), and *Trinity* (1971), and in Layton's *Double Exposure* (1972). After quitting the b. world for a while, he returned in 1974, starting a career as freelance d.

Burr, Marilyn (*b* Parramatta, 20 Nov. 1933). Austral. dancer. Studied at the Austral. B. School with L. Kellaway, made her début in 1948 with the National B. Co., joined London Festival B. as a soloist in 1952, promoted ballerina 1953–63, same position 1963–5 at the Hamburg State Op., and 1966–72 with the National B. of Washington, D.C. D. the ballerina roles and created roles in Charnley's *Alice in Wonderland* (1953), Beriozoff's *Esmeralda* (1954), and Bourmeister's *Snow Maiden* (1961). B. mistress, B. de Santiago, 1982. Is now retired. Married to the d. Ivan Nagy.
BIBL.: E. Herf, 'M.B.' *Ballet Today* (1965/5–8).

Burra, Edward (*b* London, 1905). Brit. painter. Designed for Ashton *Rio Grande* (1932) and *Don Juan* (1948), for de Valois *Barabau* (1936) and *Don Quixote* (1950), and for Helpmann *Miracle in the Gorbals* (1944).

Burrow, The. Ballet in 1 act; libr. and ch. MacMillan; mus. F. Martin; déc. Georgiadis. Prod. 2 Jan. 1958, Royal B., Cov. Gdn, London, with Heaton, Britton, Seymour, MacLeary. The b., set to Martin's Concerto for 7 Wind Instruments, Timpani, Percussion, and Strings, deals with the relationships of a group of people, living together in a small room, obviously hiding from something which threatens them. At the time of its first perf. it was automatically linked to the recently premièred stage version of the *Diary of Anne Frank*, though MacMillan categorically denied having been inspired by it. Revived for Royal Dan. B. in 1962. The same mus. was used by P. Darrell for *The Scarlet Pastorale* (1975).

Burth, Jürg (*b* Zurich, 28 Feb. 1944). Swiss dancer and choreographer. Studied at Zurich Op. House B. School and later with Hightower and Graham, joined Basle B. in 1964 and Cologne B. 1968–75 (with a New York season in between, when he d. with Lubovitch and the Graham Workshop Co., 1970–1). Co-founder (with Baumann, Ulrich, Veredon) of the Cologne D. Forum in 1971. Ch. and asst. b. dir. of Zurich Op. House 1975–8, where he ch. a number of bs.

Bush, Noreen (*b* Nottingham, 1905). Brit. dancer and teacher. Studied with Edouard Espinosa. D. at London Gaiety Th. and Daly's Th. 1924–7. Taught at Espinosa School. Took charge of her mother's school in Nottingham 1930. Founded the Noreen Bush School with her husband Victor Leopold in London, which became Bush Davies School in 1939. An additional branch opened at Charters Towers, East Grinstead, 1945, and its school grounds have housed the Adeline Genée Th. since 1967.
BIBL.: M. Clarke, 'Bush Davies Diamond Jubilee 1974', *Dancing Times* (1974/10).

Butler, John (*b* Memphis, 29 Sep. 1920). Amer. dancer and choreographer. Studied at the Graham School and School of Amer. B., d. with Graham co. 1945–55, also in musicals and on TV. Then founded his own J.B. D. Th., with which he also toured Europe. Has worked ever since as a freelance ch. staging his bs. for cos. all over the world—among them New York Met. Op. B., New York City Op. B., New York City B., Harkness B., Pennsylvania B., Australian B., Netherlands D. Th., B. Th. Contemporain, B. of the Paris Opéra, B. du Rhin, and Frankfurt B. Though trained in modern d. he has assimilated many elements of the academic technique, so that he is as able to collaborate with modern-d.-based ensembles as with classically orientated cos. Among the many bs. he ch. are *The Unicorn, The Gorgon, and the Manticore* (mus. Menotti, Washington, 1956), *The Sybil* (mus. Surinach, Spoleto, 1959), *Carmina Burana* (mus. Orff, New York, 1959), *Sebastian* (mus. Menotti, The Hague, 1963), *After Eden* (mus. Lee Hoiby, Cannes 1966), *Catulli Carmina* (mus. Orff, Caramoor Festival, 1964), *A Season in Hell* (mus. P. Glanville-Hicks, New York, 1967), *Threshold* (mus. Zsolt Durko and Gracyna Bacewicz, Sydney, 1968), *Transitions* (mus. Webern, Cologne, 1969), *Itinéraire* (mus. Berio, Amiens, 1970), *La Voix* (mus. G. Crumb, B. du Rhin, 1972), *Intégrales* and *Ameriques* (mus. Varèse, Paris, 1973). D. Magazine Award (1964).
BIBL.: G. Loney, 'Busy J.B.', *Dance Magazine* (1974/1).

Butsova, Hilda (orig. Boot; *b* Nottingham, *c*. 1897, *d* 21 Mar. 1976). Brit. dancer. Studied with Volinine and Cecchetti. Made her début in pantomime in *Alice in Wonderland* at 13 years old and then joined the co. of Pavlova, becoming her understudy and eventually appointed ballerina. Stayed with the Pavlova co. until her marriage in 1926, and returned for 1 season in 1928. Also toured with Mordkin and Dolin. Settled in the U.S. in 1930, becoming ballerina of the New York Capitol Th. Continued to teach for many years after giving up her dancing career.

Bye, Willy de la (*b* Leiden, 1 June 1934). Dutch dancer. Studied with Gaskell and Harkarvy, made her début in 1953 with B. Recital Group. Transferred to the Netherlands B. (becoming ballerina); member of the Netherlands D. Th. 1959–70, where she created roles in Tetley's *Anatomy Lesson* (1964), *Circles* (1968), and *Imaginary Film* (1970), Harkarvy's *Recital for Cello and 8 Dancers* (1964), Sokolow's *Dreams* (1966), J. Sanders' *Impressions* (1976), and Van Manen's *Variomatic* (1968). Resident teacher and rehearsal dir. of Austral D. Th. 1973–5, when she and her husband, the d. and ch. J. Flier, returned to Eur.

C

Cabriole (Fr., from Ital. capriola, leap of a goat). Designates a leaping step in which the stretched legs are beaten in the air, with the lower leg beating against the upper one, so that it is sent even higher, after which the landing is made on the lower leg.

Caccialanza, Gisella (*b* San Diego, 17 Sep. 1914). Amer. dancer. Studied with Cecchetti, at School of Amer. B., and San Francisco B. School, d. with B. Caravan, B. Society, and San Francisco B. Created roles in Balanchine's *Serenade* (1934), *Alma Mater* (1934), *Le Baiser de la Fée* (1937), *The Spellbound Child* (1946), and *Four Temperaments* (1946). Now lives in San Francisco, married to Lew Christensen, artistic dir. of the San Francisco B.
BIBL.: 'Letters from the Maestro: Enrico Cecchetti to G.C.' (*Dance Perspectives 45*).

Cachucha. Graceful Span. dance in 3/4 or 3/8 time, not unlike the bolero. It is performed by a single d. with castanets. Especially popular during the middle of the 19th century, when Elssler caused a real c. fever with her own arrangement of the c. in Coralli's *Le Diable boiteux* (1836). F. A. Zorn notated a version and in 1967 it was recreated by A. Hutchinson for Philippa Heale for the B. for All group of the Royal B., and filmed with Margaret Barbieri, 1981, as *Fanny Elssler's Cachucha*, dir. N. Morrice.
BIBL.: I. Guest, *Fanny Elssler's Cachucha*, with orig. Zorn notation and Labanotation (London/New York, 1981).

Caciuleanu, Gheorge (*b* Bucharest, 13 May 1947). Rum. dancer, choreographer and b. director. Studied at Bucharest State Op B. School, entering its co., upon graduation. After twice winning the 1st prize at the Cologne Competition for Young Choreographers (in 1971 for *Voices*, mus. collage, and in 1972 for *Shadow of Candles*, set to Ravel's *Bolero*), stayed in the West, working with the Essen Folkwang B. and becoming b. master and subsequently b. dir. of the Nancy B. 1974–8, since when he has been artistic dir. of Th. Chorégraphique de Rennes—Centre National.

Cadzow, Joan (*b* Melbourne, 17 July 1929). Austral. dancer. Studied in Melbourne with Jennie Brennan and at Sadler's Wells School. Made her début in 1947 with the Sadler's Wells Th. B., where she stayed until 1952. Continued to d. with various small Fr. cos., the Netherlands B., in Frankfurt, and West Berlin, until she joined the B. of the Düsseldorf Rhine Op. in 1966. Created roles in numerous bs. by E. Walter. Critics' Prize and Pavlova Prize (Paris, 1961).

Cage, John (*b* Los Angeles, 15 Sep. 1912). Amer. composer. Has collaborated closely with M. Cunningham ever since he became mus. dir. of his co., in 1944. Among the very many pieces which he comp. for Cunningham, or Cunningham used, are *Root of an Unfocus* (1944), *Four Walls* (1944), *The Seasons* (1947), *Sixteen Dances for Soloist and Company of Three* (1951), *Suite for Two* (1958), *Antic Meet* (1958), *Music With Dancers* (1960), *Aeon* (1961), *Field Dances* (1963), *Museum Event no. 1 and 2* (1964 – this is a continuing series), *How to Pass, Kick, Fall and Run* (1965), *Second Hand* (1970), and *Un jour ou deux* (for Paris Opéra, 1973). Van Manen ch. his *Solo for Voice 1* (1969) and *Twilight* (to *Perilous Night*, 1972). Author of *A Year from Monday* (Middletown, Conn., 1967).
BIBL.: 'J.C.' in a Symposium on Comp./Ch. in *Dance Perspectives 16*.

Cage, The. Ballet in 1 act; libr. and ch. Robbins; mus. Stravinsky; set and light. Rosenthal; cost. Ruth Sobotka. Prod. 14 June 1951, New York City B., City Center, N.Y., with Kaye, Magallanes, Mounsey, Maule. The b. is set to Stravinsky's Concerto in D and tells the story of two male intruders into a female society, where they are considered as prey, to be castrated and killed after copulation. Other b. versions to the same mus. (but without the Robbins plot) by D. Hoyer (Hamburg, 1950), W. Ulbrich (Stuttgart, 1959), and Van Manen (in *Tilt,* Netherlands D. Th., 1972).
BIBL.: G. Balanchine, 'T.C.' in *Balanchine's New Complete Stories of the Great Ballets* (Garden City, N.Y., 1977).

Cain and Abel. Ballet in 1 act; ch. MacMillan; mus. Panufnik; déc. Kay. Prod. 1 Nov. 1968, Ger. Op. Berlin, with Frey, Daniel Job, Bohner. Set to Panufnik's *Sinfonia Sacra* and *Tragic Overture*, the b. shows Cain's murder of his brother Abel as motivated by his rejected love, with the snake (performed by a male d.) as the agent provocateur. Other contemporary versions of the same Bible story by J. Carter in *Cage of God* mus. Rawsthorne, 1967) and M. Efrati in *Sin Lieth at the Door* (mus. Noam Sheriff, 1969).

Cahusac, Louis de (*b* Montauban, 1700, *d* Paris, 1759). Fr. b. librettist and dance historian. Wrote the libr. to many op. bs. which were performed at the Académie Royale. Rameau comp. the mus. to his *Les Fêtes de Polymnie* (1745), *Les Fêtes de l'Hymen et de l'Amour* (1747), *Naïs* (1749), and

Zoroastre (1749). In his 3-volume treatise *La danse ancienne et moderne, ou traité historique sur la danse*, published in 1754 in The Hague, he pleaded for the dramatic mission of the mimed d. so that one can see in him a precursor of Noverre and his theories about the b. d'action.

Cakewalk. (1) A d. of the North Amer. Negro, strongly syncopated, the execution of which is left to the imagination of the performer. It derives from the custom of giving a piece of cake to the d. who performed the most virtuoso and intricate steps. At the end of the 19th century it reached the height of its popularity and was absorbed into the minstrel shows and vaudeville, from where it was adapted for revue and mus. comedy purposes. (2) B. in 3 parts; libr. and ch. R. Boris; mus. L.M. Gottschalk (arr. by H. Kay); déc. Robert Drew. Prod. 12 June 1951, New York City B., City Center, N.Y., with Hobi, LeClercq, Tompkins, Reed, Wilde, Mounsey, Bliss. A witty and vivacious, but nostalgic, d.-parody of the old-time minstrel show, which ends with the whole co., strutting across the stage in a cakewalk.
BIBL.: G. Balanchine, 'C.' in *Balanchine's New Complete Stories of the Great Ballets* (Garden City, N.Y., 1968).

Calzada, Alba (*b* San Juan, 28 Jan. 1945). Puerto Rican dancer. Studied with Ana García, Zaraspe, School of Amer. B., and Harkarvy. Joined B. de San Juan as principal d. 1963–7, Pennsylvania B. 1969.
BIBL.: S. Goodman, 'A.C.', *Dance Magazine* (1972/6).

Camargo, Marie (orig. M.-Anne de Cupis de Camargo; baptized Brussels, 15 Apr. 1710, *d* Paris, 28 Apr. 1770). Fr. dancer of Span./Ital. descent. The daughter of a musician, she made her début in Brussels, continuing her studies with Prévost and Blondi in Paris; became a member of the Opéra in 1726, where she soon became a fierce rival of Sallé. Retired in 1734 to live as the mistress of the Comte de Clermont, but returned 1741–51, dancing in 78 bs. with undiminished success. She was an excellent brio d. with brillant batterie, and was the first to manage steps which so far had been considered the prerogative of the male d., such as entrechats and cabrioles. Even Noverre, who did not like her, had to admit: 'Mlle Carmargo had intelligence and she made use of it in choosing a style which was lively and quick.' She is credited with shortening the skirt of the traditional costume, thus allowing the performer more liberty during the execution of allegro movements. She was a star performer, and the ladies of her time tried to emulate her, wearing shoes 'à la Camargo', while the cooks offered Bombe Camargo, Filet de Boeuf Camargo, Ris de Veau grillé Camargo, and Soufflé Camargo. Nicolas Lancret did two famous paintings of her, and Petipa and Minkus created a *Camargo* b. for St. Petersburg in 1872. Ops. about her were

written by Enrico de Leva and Charles Lecocq, and in London the Camargo Society was founded in 1930.
BIBL.: P. Migel, 'M.-A. C.d.C.' in *The Ballerinas* (New York, 1972).

Camargo Society. Founded in 1930 in London to further the cause of b., after Richardson and Haskell had advocated it for a year. Its 1st subscription perf. took place on 19 Oct. 1930 at the Cambridge Th., with bs. by Genée, N. Legat, de Valois, and Ashton. The dancers for these and later perfs. came mainly from the schools of de Valois and Rambert, with such stars as Dolin, Markova, Lopokova, and Spessivtzeva contributing extra glamour. These were the occasions which saw the 1st Brit. prods. of abbreviated versions of *Giselle* and *Swan Lake*. Here de Valois' *Job* (1931) and *Création du monde* (1931), Ashton's *Façade* (1931), and Tudor's *Adam and Eve* (1932) received their 1st prods. After 2 special perfs. at Cov. Gdn. in the summer of 1933 the society was dissolved, its aims having been achieved and the basis laid for the development of Brit. b., which was carried on afterwards by the Vic-Wells B. and the B. Rambert.
BIBL.: J. Percival, 'The C.S.', *Dance and Dancers* (1961/1–3).

Cambré (Fr., curved, arched). Designates the bending of the body from the waist, either backwards or sideways.

Campanini, Barbara. See *Barberina, La*.

Campra, André (*b* Aix-en-Provence, baptized 4 Dec. 1660, *d* Versailles, 29 June 1744). Fr. composer. In 1697 his b. op. *L'Europe galante* received its anonymous 1st prod. in Paris and in 1699 there followed his b. *Le Carnaval de Venise*, announced under the name of his brother Joseph C. He was appointed chef d'orchestre royale et directeur de pages de musique in 1723, composing about 25 bs. and b. ops. for the Paris Opéra, incl. *Les Ages* (1718). His b. op. *Les Fêtes vénitiennes* (1710) was revived for the 1970 Schwetzingen Festival (ch. I. Sertić) and *Le Carnaval de Venise* for the 1975 Aix-en-Provence Festival (ch. Schmucki).

Camryn, Walter (*b* Helena, Mont., 22 July 1903, *d* Chicago, 29 Feb. 1984). Amer. dancer, teacher, and choreographer. Studied with Bolm, Maximova, Swoboda, Novikoff, and M. Stuart; d. with Chicago Civic B., Page-Stone B., and Federal Th. for which he also ch. occasionally. Together with *B. Stone opened Stone-C. School of B. in Chicago 1941, where he taught until his death.
BIBL.: M. Finitzo, 'A Chicago Landmark', *Dancing Times* (1977/1).

Canada. Ballet in C. is a 20th-century development, starting from small b. schools in the big cities, which sent performing troupes to the Can. B. Festival established in 1948 and continuing in various cities until 1954. The 1st professional co., the *Royal Winnipeg B. (then The Winnipeg B.), started to function in 1939, followed in 1951 by the *National B. of C. in Toronto, and in 1952 by the *Grands Bs. Canadiens of Montreal. These are still the 3 major cos., of the country, which have since grown enormously, performing to ever widening audiences. Prominent modern-d. troupes include Winnipeg Contemporary Dancers (founded 1964); *Toronto D. Th. (1968) and Anna Wyman D. Th., Vancouver (1971). There is also much TV b. activity. Today C. regularly sends cos., abroad, and plays host to all the big cos. on the international circuit.

BIBL.: special issue 'Dance in C.', *Dance Magazine* (1971/4).

Canada, National Ballet of. See *National Ballet of Canada*.

Canaries (also Canarie, or Canary). A sprightly d. in 3/8 or 6/8 time, similar to the jig and the gigue. It may have come from the Canary Islands via Spain to Fr., where the 1st mus. examples are to be found in the harpsichord suites of de Chambonnière and Couperin. Shakespeare mentions it in *All's Well That Ends Well*: 'Make you dance Canary with sprightly fire and motion.' It strongly accentuates the tapping of toes and heels but has nothing to do with the heel-technique of the Span. d.

Cancan (also Can-Can or Chahut). Originally a decent and measured social dance, invented by Monsieur Masarié in 1830 as a variant of the quadrille, it appeared after 1844 in the Fr. music halls, developing there an increasingly uninhibited emphasis on the throwing up of the legs of the danseuses and the display of their underwear so that it was soon forbidden by the authorities. It is an immensely electrifying and lively d. in 2/4 time, considered by some to be a successor of the fandango. The most thrilling cancans can be found in the *Offenbach* operettas (for instance in *Orpheus in the Underworld*). Henri de Toulouse-Lautrec made countless drawings of the c. as performed at the Moulin Rouge. Massine uses it as a climax in his bs. *Boutique fantasque* and *Gaîté Parisienne*; Tudor did a more down-to-earth version in *Offenbach in the Underworld*.

Candide. Among the bs. inspired by Voltaire's *Candide ou l'optimisme* (1758) are C. Weidman's (mus. W. Riegger, New York, 1933) and M. Marceau's C. (mus. M. Constant, Hamburg, 1971).

Canfield. Ballet by M. Cunningham; mus. Pauline Oliveros; déc. Robert Morris. 1st perf. New York, 15 Apr. 1969, M. Cunningham and D. Co., Brooklyn Academy. The piece is dedicated to Nikola Testa, Cosmic Engineer and derives its title from the game of c., or solitaire. Due to a strike it was performed on its 1st night without sound. Throughout its duration of about 80 minutes a suspended pillar containing a set of lamps travels back and forth along the front of the stage, while 12 dancers perform their

individual actions, cool, very distant, and without any emotions or plot.

Cannabich, Johann Christian (*b* Mannheim, baptized 28 Dec. 1731, *d* Frankfurt, 20 Jan. 1798). Ger. composer. He was concert master of the Mannheim court orchestra, with which he later moved to Munich, composing the mus. to more than 40 bs., some of which seem to have been strongly influenced by Noverre. He worked closely with the ch. *Etienne Lauchery.

BIBL.: R. Kleiber, *Die dramatischen Ballette von C.C.* (dissertation, 1928).

Canticle for Innocent Comedians. Ballet in 1 act; ch. and cost. Graham; mus. Thomas Ribbink; scenery Frederick Kiesler; light. Rosenthal. Prod. 22 Apr. 1952, M. Graham D. Co., Juilliard School of Mus., New York. 'A dance of joy, in praise of the world as it turns' (programme note); solos for Sun, Earth, Wind, Water, Fire, Moon, Stars, and Death join with other celebrants within 'an elaborate series of curved panels in and out of which they danced' (D. McDonagh).

CAPAB Ballet. The b. co., based on Cape Town, South Africa, named after the Cape Performing Arts Board, the State organization which finances it. It emerged from the Univ. of Cape Town B. Co., and assumed its present name in 1965, though it still calls itself U.C.T. B. Co., when dancing in Cape Town. The co. performs all over S.A.; its original dir. was *Dulcie Howes, with D. Poole as b. master, who took over the directorship when Howes resigned in 1969. Headed by Phyllis Spira, the co., has over 30 full-time dancers and regularly imports guest stars from abroad (often from the Royal B.). Frank Staff was resident ch. until he died in 1971. Its repertory is classically based.

BIBL.: P. Williams, 'The Awakening Peninsula', *Dance and Dancers* (1975/5).

Cape Town Ballet. See *CAPAB Ballet*.

Capezio Award. The prize was established by the famous Amer. firm of b. shoe makers in 1952 'for the purpose of contributing to public awareness of the progress of dance in the U.S.' Its recipients have so far been: Z. Solov (1952), L. Kirstein (1953), D. Humphrey (1954), L. Horst (1955), G. Oswald (1956), T. Shawn (1957), A. Danilova (1958), S. Hurok (1959), M. Graham (1960), R. St.Denis (1961), B. Karinska (1962), D. McKayle (1963), J. Limón (1964), Maria Tallchief (1965), A. de Mille (1966), P. Taylor (1967), L. Chase (1968), J. Martin (1969), W. Kolodney (1970), A. Mitchell (1971), La Meri and the Laubins (1972), I. Bennett (1973), R. Joffrey (1974), R. Irving (1975), J. Robbins (1976), W. Terry (1980), Dorothy Alexander (1981).

BIBL.: B. Como, 'A Diamond for C.', *Dance Magazine* (1962/10).

Capriccio Espagnol. Ballet in 1 act; libr. and ch. Massine in collaboration with Argentinita; mus.

Rimsky-Korsakov; déc. Mariano Andreù. Prod. 4 May 1939, B. Russe de Monte Carlo, Monte Carlo, with Argentinita, Massine, Danilova, Panaieff. A sequence of 5 dances, without any continuous plot, the b. develops as a grand Span. divertissement, based upon individual characters: a gipsy fortune teller, a young gipsy boy, a girl from the country and a peasant. The déc. was originally designed for Fokine's *Jota Aragonesa*. This version was filmed in 1941 by Warner Brothers under the title of *Spanish Fiesta*. Fokine made an earlier version in 1924 for his own co., in New York under the title *Olé Toro*.
BIBL.: G. Balanchine, 'C.E.' in *Balanchine's New Complete Stories of the Great Ballets* (Garden City, N.Y., 1968).

Caprices du Cupidon, Les. See *Whims of Cupid, The*.

Capriole (Fr., from Ital. capriola, leap of a goat). Carosio da Sermoneta describes this d. in his d. treatise, published in 1581 in Venice. He subdivides it into terzo, quarto, and quinto, which seem to be identical with our entrechats. Special variants are the c.intrecciata (an intermingled c.) and the c. spezzata.

Capriol Suite. Ballet in 1 act; ch. Ashton; mus. Peter Warlock; déc. W. Chappell. Prod. 25 Feb. 1930, Rambert Dancers, Lyric Th., London, with Howard, Gould, Turner, Ashton, Chappell. Based musically upon the airs from Arbeau's *Orchésographie*, the original Fr. dances were shifted by Ashton to an Eng. Elizabethan setting. Ashton's 1st fully successful b.; it remained in the repertory for 20-odd years.
BIBL.: G. Balanchine, 'C.S.' in *Balanchine's New Complete Stories of the Great Ballets* (Garden City, N.Y., 1968).

Caracole. See *Divertimento No. 15*.

Carbone, Giuseppe (*b* Messina, 7 Feb. 1939). Ital. dancer and choreographer. Studied at the Rome Accademia Nazionale di Danza, made his début in 1960, d. in Bonn, where he also started to ch. until 1970, and has since been working as a ch. for various Ital. cos., (mostly for the Venice Teatro Fenice). Since 1980 has been artistic dir. of La Scala B.

Card Game. See *Jeu de cartes*.

Carey, Denis (*b* London, 31 Dec. 1926). Brit. dancer, choreographer, and b. master. Studied at Sadler's Wells School and with Volkova, Northcote, Leeder, M. Cunningham, and Limón. D. with Sadler's Wells B. 1945–6, in the *Red Shoes* film, with Metropolitan B., B. der Lage Landen, in the *La petite Ballerina* film and the Massine prod. of *Bullet in the Ballet*. B. master of Guatemala National B. 1956–9, National B. of Chile 1965–8. Has since worked as a ch. of cos. in Marseilles, Amsterdam (Scapino B.), Tel Aviv (Bat-Dor), Lisbon (Gulbenkian), Zurich, and Strasburg. Has

taught at Essen Folkwang School and Zurich B. Academy.

Carlson, Carolyn (*b* Oakland, 7 Mar. 1943). Amer. dancer and choreographer. Studied at Utah Univ., San Francisco B. School, and with Nikolais, with whose co., she d. 1965–71, afterwards joining the co., of Béranger. She was then based in Paris, and appeared and ch. at various places (Avignon, Hamburg, Milan, Bordeaux) until her appointment as danseuse étoile chorégraphique (specially invented title) at the Paris Opéra in 1974, for which she ch. *Densité, 21.5* (mus. Varèse), *L'Or des fous* (mus. G. Arrigo) and *Les Fous d'or* (mus. I. Wakhevitch, 1973), *Sablier prison* (mus. various), *Il y a juste un instant* (mus. Barre Phillips, 1974), and *Wind, Water, Sand* (1976). Created leading female role in Tetley's *Tristan* (1974). Moved to Venice 1980 to direct her own group at Teatro Fenice.

Carmagnole, La. 'Originally the name of sort of short coat, worn in the north Ital. district of Carmagnola, and brought into France by workmen from that district. The insurgents of Marseilles in 1792 ... introduced it to Paris, where it became identified with the Revolution. A round dance of the time was given the name and a song with the refrain, "Dansons la Carmagnole, vive le son du canon", to a very catchy air, became identified with revolutionary festivities such as executions. The authorship of both words and music is unknown' (*The Concise Oxford Dictionary of Music*, 1972). A b. C. was ch. by Moiseyev 1930 in Odessa (mus. V. Femilidi). In the 3rd act of Vainonen's *Flames of Paris* (1932) the revolutionaries d. a c. at the climax of their festivities.

Carmen. Ballet in 5 scenes; libr. and ch. Petit; mus. Bizet; déc. Clavé. Prod. 21 Feb. 1949, B. de Paris, Prince's Th., London, with Jeanmaire, Petit, Perrault, Hamilton. The b. follows roughly the plot of Prosper Mérimée's story (1845) and Bizet's op. (1875). Petit later revived it for several cos. one of the best prods. being the one for the Royal Dan. B. in 1960. A film version of this and some other Petit bs. was produced in 1960 under the title of *Un-deux-trois-quatre ou 'Les Collants noirs'* (Eng. title: *Black Tights*). Other b. treatments of the same subject by Petipa (*C. et son Toréro*, Madrid, 1845), Goleizovsky (1931), Page (*Guns and Castanets*, Chicago, 1939), Alb. Alonso (*Carmen*, mus. Shchedrin after Bizet, Moscow, 1967), and Cranko (mus. W. Fortner and W. Steinbrenner after Bizet, Stuttgart, 1971).
BIBL.: G. Balanchine and F. Mason, in *Balanchine's Complete Stories of the Great Ballets* (Garden City, N.Y. 1977).

Carmina Burana. Scenic cantata by C. Orff to Latin texts of worldly songs from the Benediktbeuern Monastery. Prod. 8 June 1937, Frankfurt (ch. Inge Härtling). Orff's highly popular work has often ben prod. with an emphasis on ch. and d. e.g. by Maudrik (Berlin State Op., 1941), Hanka (La Scala, Milan, 1943), Rosen (Bavarian State Op., Munich, 1959), Butler (New York City Op., 1959, and many revivals elsewhere, making it the most widely known version), Nault (Les Grand Bs. Canadiens, 1967), and Darrell (Ger. Op. Berlin, 1968). Bavarian TV prod., 1976.

Carnaval, Le. Ballet in 1 act; libr. and ch. Fokine; mus. Schumann, orchestrated by Glazunov, Rimsky-Korsakov, Liadov, Tcherepnin, and Arensky; déc. Bakst. Prod. 5 Mar. 1910, Pavlov Hall, St. Petersburg, on the occasion of a ball of the magazine Satyricon, with Karsavina, Leontiev. Fokina, Schollar, Nijinska, Nijinsky, Meyerhold. D. of an assembly of simple people in commedia dell'arte costumes and masks, loosely strung together. It is considered one of Fokine's masterworks and after its th. première on 20 May 1910 by the Bs. Russes of Diaghilev in Berlin was often revived by Fokine himself as well as by others—also for Camargo Society, London 1933; B. Th., New York, 1940; Western Th., B., 1963; Scottish B. (mus. orig. piano version), 1967 and subsequently.

BIBL.: C. W. Beaumont, 'L.C.' in *Complete Book of Ballets* (London, 1951).

Carnival of Animals. Ballet in 1 act; ch. and déc. A. Howard; mus. Saint-Saëns. Prod. 26 Mar. 1943, B. Rambert, Mercury Th., London, with Elisabeth Schooling, Gilmour, Harrold, Holmes. Howard's b. version of Saint-Saëns' Grand Zoological Fantasy shows a Victorian child, meeting all the different animals (but not the most famous of the suite's 14 numbers, Le Cygne). Revived for Scapino B, 1967 (with Le Cygne included).

Caron, Leslie (b Paris, 1 July 1931). Fr.-Amer. dancer and actress. Studied with Jeanne Schwarz at the Paris Conservatoire; made her début in 1948 with the Bs. des Champs-Elysées, where she created the Sphinx in Lichine's La Rencontre in the same year. G. Kelly engaged her in 1951 for his film An American in Paris. In 1954 she returned for a short time to Petit's B. de Paris, creating his La Belle au bois dormant in London, after which she pursued a career as an actress.

Caroso, Fabritio (orig. F.C. de Sermoneta; b Sermoneta, near Rome, about 1553). Ital. dancer, choreographer, dance-theoretician, and composer. He was the d.-teacher of Rome's high nobility and published a treatise about the d. Il Ballarino, in 1581 in Venice, reprinted several times (in 1600 under the title Nobiltà di Dame, and in 1630 as Raccolta di varii balli). Its 1st part describes the d. steps and rules, and the 2nd part the topical balli from Italy, Fr., and Spain, with some balletti, providing the mus. in lute tablature with many illustrations.

Carroll, Elisabeth (née E. Pfister; b Paris, 19 Jan. 1937). Amer. dancer and teacher. Studied with

Sedova and Besobrasova d. with the op. b. in Monte Carlo 1951–3, then with Amer. B. Th., Joffrey, and with Harkness B. 1964–70, creating roles in Macdonald's Time Out of Mind (1962), de Mille's Golden Age (1967), and Harkarvy's La Favorita (1969). Now teaches at New York Harkness School.

Carter, Alan (b London, 24 Dec. 1920). Brit. dancer, choreographer, and b. director. Studied with Astafieva and N. Legat; d. with Sadler's Wells B. 1938–40 and after his military service with Sadler's Wells Th. B., 1946–7, for which he ch. his 1st b. (The Catch). Appeared in the films The Red Shoes, Tales of Hoffmann, and Invitation to the Dance. Later also dir. of St. James' B. and London Empire Th. B. dir. at the Bavarian State Op. in Munich 1954–9, Wuppertal 1964–8, Bordeaux 1968–70, Helsinki 1971–2, Icelandic B. 1973–5; artistic co-dir. of Elmhurst B. School 1976–80. Among the many bs. he has ch. are the 1st Ger. prods. of Britten's The Prince of the Pagodas (1958) and Henze's Ondine (1959). Married to the d. Julia Claire.

Carter, Jack (b Shrivenham, 8 Aug. 1923). Brit. dancer and choreographer. Studied at Sadler's Wells School and with Preobrajenska; d. with B. Guild in 1946, then with M. Lake's Continental B. (where he made his 1st bs.), Original B. Russe, B. Rambert, and London Festival B. Ch. of the B. der Lage Landen in Amsterdam in 1954–7 (1st prod. of The Witch Boy, mus. L. Salzedo, 1956). Then worked in Sweden, Buenos Aires, Geneva, and for various Brit. cos. Chief ch. London Festival B. 1965–70. Has since also worked in Japan. Other important bs.: Agrionia (mus. Salzedo, 1964), Beatrix (or La jolie fille de Gand, 1966), Cage of God (mus. A. Rawsthorne, 1967), Pythoness Ascendant (mus. Berio, 1973), Three Dances to Japanese Music (1973), Shukumei (mus. Stomu Yamash'ta, Royal B., 1975), and Lulu (mus. Milhaud, Royal B., 1976). Among his prods. of classics Swan Lake (Buenos Aires and London Festival B.) and Coppélia (London Festival B.) have been widely discussed.

BIBL.: E. Herf, 'J.C.', Ballet Today (1960/4).

Carter, William (b Durant, Okla., 1936). Amer. d. Studied with Coralane Duane and Maracci. Joined Amer. B. Th. in 1957, N.Y. City B. in 1959. Founder member of First Chamber Dance Co., in 1961. To Graham co., in 1972. Rejoined Amer. B. Th. in 1972, but also appeared as a guest artist with modern cos. Dir. Rome Op. B. from 1986.

BIBL.: T. Tobias, 'Bill C., An Interview', Dance Magazine (1975/6).

Cartier, Jean-Albert (b Marseille, 15 May 1930). Fr. art publicist and b. director. Studied at L'Ecole du Louvre in Paris. Art critic of Le Combat. Organized various exhibitions of contemporary art. Founder-dir. of Ballet Théâtre Contemporain, 1968. Directeur du Centre Chorégraphique et Lyrique National in Angers, 1972–78, after which he was in charge of the Ballet Théâtre Français de Nancy. Directeur Général of the Grand Théâtre de Nancy 1979–80. Now in charge of b. at Th. du Châtelet, Paris.

Carvajal, Carlos (*b* San Francisco, 3 June 1931). Amer. dancer, choreographer, and b. director. Studied at San Francisco State College and with W. Harzold, L. Christensen, Caccialanza, and A. Girard. D. with San Francisco B. 1952–5, then with Grand B. du Marquis de Cuevas, in Bremen, Bordeaux and Caracas, returning to the San Francisco B. as b. master and associate ch. 1965–70. In June 1970 he opened a b. school in San Francisco and established the D. Spectrum, for which he has ch. a number of full-length prods.

Casado, Germinal (*b* Casablanca, 6 Aug. 1934). Moroccan dancer, designer, and th. director. Studied with Nina Leontiev, Zverev, and V. Gsovsky. D. in Wuppertal and with Grand B. du Marquis de Cuevas, joined the Béjart co., in 1957 and was one of the top soloists of the B. of the 20th Century from 1959 until early 1970s, creating roles in Béjart's *Sacre du printemps* (1959), *A la recherche de Don Juan* (1962), *Mathilde* (1964), *Ninth Symphony* (1964), and *Romeo and Juliet* (1966). He designed for Béjart *Les 4 Fils Aymon* (1961), *Tales of Hoffmann* (1961), *A la recherche de Don Juan* (1962), *The Merry Widow* (1963), *The Damnation of Faust* (Paris Ópéra, 1964), *Renard* (Paris Opéra, 1965), *Les Oiseaux* (1965), *Romeo and Juliet* (1966), *The Temptation of Saint Anthony* (Paris, 1967), *La Nuit obscure* (1968), and *Bhakti* (1968). Since 1977 artistic dir. of Karlsruhe State Th. b.
BIBL.: L. Rossel, 'G.C.', *Les Saisons de la danse* (1970/1).

Casanova Ballets. Bs. dealing with Giacomo Girolamo C. (1725–98), the famous Ital. adventurer, were ch. by Laban (1923), Kröller (1929), Algo (1937), and Charrat (*C. in London*, mus. W. Egk, Munich, 1969).
BIBL.: O. Marmin, 'C. et la danse', *Les Saisons de la danse* (1973/1).

Casati, Giovanni (*b* Milan, 1811, *d* there, 20 July 1895). Ital. dancer, choreographer, and teacher. Studied at La Scala B. School and with A. Vestris, d. at La Scala 1821–33, worked as a ch. in various Ital. cities as well as at Cov. Gdn. in London, Vienna Court Op., and the São Carlos of Lisbon. Later became the director of the b. school at La Scala. Married to Margherita Wuthier, a favourite pupil of Blasis.
BIBL.: entry 'C.,G.' in *Enciclopedia dello spettacolo*.

Casella, Alfredo (*b* Turin, 25 July 1883, *d* Rome, 5 Mar. 1947). Ital. composer. Wrote the mus. for the bs. *The Jar* (ch. Börlin, 1924) and *Il convento veneziano* (ch. N. Guerra, 1925). His concert mus. *Scarlattiana* was used by Nijinska (in *Les Comédiens*, 1932) and Milloss (in *Deliciae populi*, 1943), and his *Paganiniana* by Milloss (in *La rosa del sogno*, 1943).

Casenave, Roland (*b* Bordeaux, 26 July 1923, *d* 17 Feb. 1980). Fr. dancer and b. master. Studied with Preobrajenska, Egorova, Kiss, V. Gsovsky, Volkova, and Taras. D. with Ballets des Champs–Elysées, Grand B. du Marquis de Cuevas, Op. B. Amsterdam, and Charrat's B. de France. Has worked as a teacher and b. master with many, mainly Eur. cos., incl. Dutch National B., London Festival B., New London B., Scottish B., Gulbenkian B., and the op. houses of Stockholm, Munich, Rome, Florence, Strasbourg, Lyon, and Marseille.

Cassandre, Alexandre M. (*b* Kharkov, 21 Jan. 1901, *d* Versailles, 1967). Russ.-Fr. painter and designer. Designed the Lifar bs. *Le Chevalier et la Damoiselle* (Paris, 1941), *Les Mirages* (Paris, 1944), *Dramma per musica* (Monte Carlo, 1946), and *Chemin de lumière* (Paris, 1957; 1st prod. ch. by V. Gsovsky, Munich, 1952).

Casse-Noisette. See *Nutcracker, The.*

Castelli, Victor (*b* Montclair, N.Y., 9 Oct. 1952). Amer. dancer. Studied at Garden State B. School and School of Amer. B. Joined New York C. B. 1971, appointed soloist 1980, creating parts in Balanchine's *PAMTGG* (1971), *Le Tombeau de Couperin* and *Gaspard de la nuit* (both 1975), and *Union Jack* (1976), Robbins's *Watermill* (1972) and *Dybbuk Variations* (1974).

Castil-Blaze (orig. François-Henri-Joseph B.; *b* Cavaillon, 1 Dec. 1784, *d* Paris, 11 Dec. 1857). Fr. mus. and b. critic. As critic of the *Journal des débats* he followed closely and described minutely the events of the Paris b. scene from the early 1820s until 1832. His *La Danse et le ballet depuis Bacchus jusqu'à Mlle Taglioni* (1832) *L'Académie Impériale de Musique . . . de 1645 à 1855* (3 vols., 1847–55), and *L'Opéra Italien 1548–1856* (Paris, 1856) have become standard reference works on the history of d. and especially of dance in Paris.

Castle, Irene and Vernon. Exhibition ballroom dancers and teachers. Vernon C. (orig. V. Blyth) came from Norwich, Eng., Irene C. (*née* Foote) from New Rochelle (N.Y.). They were married in 1911 and became a great success in Paris, London, and the U.S. for the unsurpassed elegance of their ballroom dancing. Their most famous numbers were the Maxixe, the Castle Walk, the Castle Polka, the Tango, and the Hesitation Waltz. In 1914 they wrote *The Modern Dance*. He was killed in an air-crash in 1918, after which she retired from dancing, and wrote *My Husband* in 1919 and later *Castles in the Air* in 1958. In 1939 RKO Radio Pictures released the film *The Story of Vernon and Irene Castle*, starring F. Astaire and G. Rogers.

Catá, Alfonso (*b* Havana, 3 Oct. 1937). Cub.-Amer. dancer, choreographer, and b. director. Studied at School of Amer. B., d. with the cos. of Petit and Joffrey, Grand B. du Marquis de Cuevas, Stuttgart B., and with N.Y. City B. B. Dir. in Geneva 1969–73 and 1973–6 in Frankfurt.

Among the bs. he ch. are *Images 60/70* (mus. Jacques Guyonnet, 1970), *Nuit de mai* (mus. Rimsky-Korsakov, 1970), *Schubertiana* (1970), *Transfigured Night* (mus. Schönberg, 1973), *Ragtime* (mus. various, 1973), *Sleeping Beauty* (mus. Tchaikovsky, 1973), and *Sweet Carmen* (mus. Bizet-Shchedrin, Frankfurt, 1975). Art. dir. of Baltimore B. 1980–1. Dir. B. du Nord, Roubaix, France from 1983.

Catanzaro, Tony (*b* Brooklyn, 10 Nov. 1946). Amer. dancer. Studied at High School of Performing Arts, dancing in many school prods. and as a guest with Juilliard D. Th. Appeared in a touring prod. of *West Side Story*, then in various musical prods. all over the country and with Alabama B., Dallas Civic Op., before joining Boston B. for the 1969–70 season, creating title role in Butler's *The Minotaur*. Soloist member of the City Center Joffrey B., since 1970.
BIBL.: S. Goodman, 'T.C.', *Dance Magazine* (1972/12).

Catarina, ou La Fille du bandit. Ballet in 3 acts and 5 scenes; libr. and ch. Perrot; mus. Pugni; déc. Charles Marshall. Prod. 3 Mar. 1846, Her Majesty's Th., London, with Grahn, Perrot. The b. tells the story of the painter Salvator Rosa, who falls in love with C., the chief of the bandits, who is also loved by her lieutenant Diavolino. The title role was one of Elssler's biggest successes when she d. it in Milan and St. Petersburg.
BIBL.: C. W. Beaumont, 'C.' in *Complete Book of Ballets* (London, 1951).

Caton, Edward (*b* St. Petersburg, 3 Apr. 1900, *d* New York, 22 Oct. 1981). Amer. dancer, b. master, choreographer, and teacher. Studied with Lydia Nelidova in Moscow and privately with Vaganova in Petrograd, d. with Pavlova 1924–5, then with the op. in Chicago, Littlefield co., Mordkin B., and with B. Th. 1940–2. B. master with B. Russe de Monte Carlo in 1943, with B. Th. and from 1944 with the co. of the Marquis de Cuevas, to which he returned several times. Has taught widely in U.S. and Europe (especially at Hightower's school in Cannes). Joined the Sansardo co. in 1974 as b. master. Ch. the bs. *Sebastian* (mus. Menotti, 1944) and *Lola Montez* (mus. Fred Witt, 1946).
BIBL.: R. D. Fletcher, 'The Then and Now of E.C.', *Dance Magazine* (1968/10).

Catulli Carmina. Scenic cantata by C. Orff to Latin texts from Catullus. Prod. 6 Nov. 1943, Leipzig (ch. T. Gsovsky). The work, which deals with the unhappy love of Catullus for Lesbia, has often been produced with the emphasis on d. e.g. by Wigman (Mannheim, 1955), Hanka (Vienna, 1957), Rosen (Munich, 1959), Butler (Caramoor Festival, 1964), and Darrell (Ger. Op. Berlin, 1968).

Cauley, Geoffrey (*b* Somerset, Bermuda, 1942). Brit. dancer, choreographer, and b. director.

Studied with Geraldine Lamb in Plymouth and at Sadler's Wells School, d. with the Op. B. of Cov. Gdn. and Royal B. until 1971 when he left to assist Field at La Scala. B. dir. of the Zurich op. 1973–5, chief ch. of Teatro Comunale, Florence, during the later seventies. Bs. he ch. include *Lazarus* (mus. Bloch, 1968), *In the Beginning* (mus. Poulenc, 1969), *La Symphonie pastorale* (mus. Martinů. 1970), *Ante-Room* (mus. B. Hermann, 1971), *Transfigured Night* (mus. Schönberg, 1972), *Laborinthus II* (mus. Berio, 1973), *Swan Lake* 1974), *Last of Three* (mus. Britten, 1978), *Metamorphoses* (mus. Strauss, 1980), *The Wooden Prince* (mus. Bartók, 1981).
BIBL.: G. Dow, 'Emergent Choreographer', *Dancing Times* (1970/5).

Cauwenbergh, Thomas van (*b* Antwerp, 25 Sep. 1954). Belg. dancer. Studied at Municipal B. Inst. 1965–73 and with numerous teachers abroad. Joined Royal B. of Flanders in 1973, appointed soloist in 1974. D. with Joffrey B. 1976–7 and as a principal d. with London Festival B. since 1977. Created Andrei Bolkonsky in Panov's *War and Peace* (Berlin, 1981). Brother of the d. Ben van C. Bronze Medal (Varna, 1972), Gold Medal (Lausanne, 1973).

Cavallazzi, Malvina (*d* Ravenna, 1924). Ital. dancer and teacher. Studied at La Scala B. School, made her London début in 1879, d. at the Alhambra and Empire Ths., and was the 1st ballerina when the New York Met. Op. Ho. opened in 1883. Had a school in London, where Bedells was among her pupils. Was summoned to New York in 1909 to open a b. school at the Met. which she dir. until 1914.

Cave of the Heart. Ballet in 1 act; ch. Graham; mus. Barber; set Noguchi; cost. Edythe Gilfond; light. Rosenthal. Prod. 10 May 1946, M. Graham and Co., McMillin Th., Columbia Univ., New York, with Graham, Hawkins, Yuriko, O'Donnell. Based on the legend of Medea and Jason, the work was originally called *Serpent Heart*, changing its title to the above for its New York perf. on 27 Feb. 1947.

Cazalet, Peter (*b* Kitwe, North Rhodesia, 1934). Brit. dancer and designer. Studied architecture at Univ. of Cape Town and d. with Howes and Pamela Chrimes. Joined Edinburgh International B. in 1958, London Festival B. in 1959, Western Th. B. in 1960, remaining with the co., when it became Scottish Th. B., until 1972 (designed several prods. for this co., incl. *La Sylphide*). Regularly contributed cartoons on b. to *Dance and Dancers*. Now works as a designer for op. and b. in Cape Town.

Cébron, Jean (*b* Paris, 1938). Fr. dancer, choreographer, and teacher. Studied with his mother Mauricette C., (a d. at the Paris Opéra 1911–36 and a teacher at its school 1934–56) and later at the London Leeder school as well as several Far

Eastern styles. After his London début in 1956 with a group of his own, went to the Essen Folkwang school, where he continues to teach. Has also d. with the Folkwang B. and with the troupe of Goslar. Also teaches regularly in Rome and occasionally in London and the U.S.

Cecchetti, Enrico (*b* Rome, 21 June 1850, *d* Milan, 13 Nov. 1928). Ital. dancer, b. master, and teacher. The son of two dancers, he made his début when 5 years old in Genoa, studied with Blasis' pupil Lepri in Florence, toured the U.S. with a small troupe, made his adult début in 1879 at La Scala in *Gods from Valhalla*, then appeared as guest premier danseur in the European capitals and made his St. Petersburg début in 1887 in *The Tulip from Haarlem*. In 1890 he became 2nd b. master of the Imperial Ths. in St. Petersburg, and from 1892 he taught at the attached school, where he contributed considerably to the improvement of the technical standard of the dancers. Among his pupils here were Trefilova, Egorova, Pavlova, Sedova, Vaganova, Kschessinska, Preobrajenska, Karsavina, Gorsky, Legat, Fokine, Oboukhoff, and Nijinsky—later also Massine, Bolm, Lopokova, de Valois, Danilova, Markova, Dolin, and Lifar. In 1902 he moved to the b. school of the Warsaw op. house, but returned to St. Petersburg to open a school of his own until Diaghilev engaged him in 1910 as b. master for his co. In 1918 he opened a b. school in London with his wife, and was in charge of the Milan La Scala B. School 1925–8. He ch. some bs., none of which have survived, however. His real importance has been as one of the greatest teachers of b. history. For the strict conservation of his system the C. Society was founded in 1922 in London; it was incorporated into the Imperial Society of Teachers of Dancing in 1924. In the U.S. a C. Council of Amer. has existed since 1939. Among the roles he created were Carabosse and Blue Bird in *Sleeping Beauty* (1890), the Chief Eunuch in *Sheherazade* (1910), and the Showman in *Petrushka* (1911).
BIBL.: O. Racster, *The Master of Russian Ballet* (London, 1922); C. W. Beaumont, *E.C.* (London, 1929); V. Celli, *E.C.* (Dance Index V, 7); 'Letters from the Maestro: E.C. to Gisella Caccialanza' (*Dance Perspectives* 45).

Cech, Gisela (*b* Vienna, 29 Aug. 1945). Austrian dancer. Studied at the Vienna State Op. B. School; joined the co. in 1961, promoted soloist in 1970, principal in 1972. Married to the d. Paul Vondrak.

Celeste, Mme. (*née* C. Keppler; *b* Paris, 1811, *d* there 1882). Fr. dancer. Toured U.S. in the late 1820s and 30s; was the 1st ballerina to perform *La Sylphide* there. Was also very successful in Europe, where she often appeared in London and co-leased the Adelphi Th. in 1843, presenting bs. and b.-burlesques for 16 years.

Celli, Vincenzo (*b* Salerno, 1905). It.-Amer. dancer, choreographer, and teacher. As a boy

emigrated with his parents to Chicago. Started in the straight th. and only then went into d. collaborating with Bolm. To Italy, where he studied with Cecchetti, becoming his last favourite pupil, graduating 1928, though he had already d. at La Scala in 1923, eventually appointed primo ballerino, staying with the co. until 1931, choreographing in addition numerous op. bs. After touring in Eur. transferred to the U.S. 1935, where he has taught ever since. B. master of B. Russe de Monte Carlo 1938–40. Has his own studio in New York, where he has been responsible for the careers of many star dancers, inc. Slavenska, Serrano, Maria Tallchief, and R. Fernandez. Considers himself *the* Amer. authority on the Cecchetti method.
BIBL.: C. J. Sroufe, 'V.C.', *Dance Magazine* (1980/6).

Cendrillon. See *Cinderella*.

Cent Baisers, Les (*The Hundred Kisses*). Ballet in 1 act; libr. Kochno; ch. Nijinska; mus. Frederic d'Erlanger; set J. Hugo. Prod. 18 July 1935, Colonel de Basil's B. Russe, Cov. Gdn., London with Baronova, Lichine. The b. is based on the Andersen fairy-tale of the swineherd who is rejected by a princess, though he is really a prince, and rejects her in his turn, when she wants to possess his magic bowl which makes everyone d.

Ce que l'amour me dit (Eng. title: *What Love Tells Me*). Ballet in 3 scenes; libr. and ch. Béjart; mus. Mahler; cost. Judith Gombar. Prod. 24 Dec. 1974, B. of the 20th Century, Monte Carlo, with Donn, Savignano, Michel Gascard. Set to the 4th, 5th, and 6th movements of Mahler's 3rd Symphony (the last of which gave the b. its title), the b. shows a young man in quest of himself, finding happiness and love at last with a boy. A different version of the complete symphony by Neumeier (Hamburg, 1975).

Černá, Michaela (*b* Brno, 24 Aug 1958). Czech dancer. Studied at Prague Conservatory and Leningrad Ch. School. Appointed solo d. at Slovakian National Th., Bratislava, in 1977. Guest ballerina, Prague National Th. Appeared in the Film *The Children of Theatre Street* (1977). Laureate at various competitions (Prague, 1975, Lausanne, 1976, etc.).

Cerrito, Fanny (*b* Naples, 11 May 1817, *d* Paris, 6 May 1909). Ital. dancer. Studied with Perrot, Blasis, and Saint-Léon (to whom she was married 1845–51). One of the most famous ballerinas of the Romantic age; she made her début in 1832 in Naples, and during the following years conquered the ths. of almost all the Eur. capitals: Vienna (1836), Milan (1838), London (1840), Paris (1847), St. Petersburg (1855), and Moscow (1856). She was gifted with unusual strength and considered a dancer of distinct brio, with a tempestuous temperament and much erotic appeal. She created the leading roles in *Alma ou*

La Fille de Feu (1842), *Ondine* (1843), *La Vivandière* (1844), *Lalla Rookh* (1846), and *Gemma* (1854)—in some of which she collaborated as a ch.—and participated in the 1st prods. of the famous *Pas de quatre* (1845) and the *Pas des Déesses* (or *Le Jugement de Pâris*, 1846). She retired at the end of the 1850s.
BIBL.: I. Guest, *F.C.* (London, 1956).

Chaboukiani, Vakhtang Mikhailovich (*b* Tiflis, 12 Mar. 1910). Sov. dancer, choreographer, b. master, and teacher. Studied in Tiflis with Maria Perrini and from 1926 at the evening courses of the Leningrad Choreographic School, where his progress was so stunning that he was soon transferred to the normal classes, graduating in 1929. Entering the co. of the GATOB, he became its leading soloist within 2 years. Through his athletic physique, his dynamic personality, and his forceful virtuoso technique, he became the ideal representative of the new Sov. hero, creating a number of important roles, e.g. in Vainonen's, Jacobson's, and Chesnakov's *The Age of Gold* (1930), Vainonen's *Flames of Paris* (1932) and *Partisans' Days* (1937), Zakharov's *Fountain of Bakhchisaray* (1934) and *Lost Illusions* (1935), and in his own bs. *The Heart of the Hills* (mus. Andrei Balanchivadze, 1938) and *Laurencia* (mus. A. Krein, 1939). Returned to Tiflis in 1941, continuing at its Paliashvili op. house as d. ch. dir. and teacher (until 1972). He also ch. for the co. *Sinatle* (mus. V. Kiladze, 1947), *Gorda* (mus. D. A. Toradze, 1950), *Othello* (mus. A. D. Matchavariani, 1957), and *The Demon* (mus. S. Sinadze, 1961). He participated in various films: *Stars of Ballet* (in *Flames of Paris*, 1946) and *Othello* (1960). In 1934 he became the 1st Sov. d. to tour the U.S. (with T. Vetcheslova). In 1958 he brought the Tiflis co., to Vienna and in 1966 to Paris.
BIBL.: V. Krasovskaya, *V.A.* (Moscow, 1956; in Russ.).

Chabrier, Alexis Emmanuel (*b* Ambert, 18 Jan. 1841, *d* Paris, 13 Sep. 1894). Fr. composer. Wrote no b. mus., but some of his concert mus. was used for b. purposes—by Bolm in *Foyer de la danse* (1927), Balanchine in *Cotillon* (1932) and *Bourrée Fantasque* (1949), de Valois in *Bar aux Folies-Bergère* (1934), Petit in *Ballabile* (1950), Joffrey in *Chabriana* (1957), Gore in *Light Fantastic* (1963), Feld in *Cortège Burlesque* (1970) and Arpino in *Chabriesque* (1972).

Chaconne (Fr.; also Ital. ciaccona, Span. chacona). A triple-time d. probably from Spain (possibly originally Arabic) where it was known as a very sensuous couple-d. It then came to Italy and Fr. and found its way in a much refined form into the B. de cour and bs. ops. of Lully, Rameau, and Gluck, who often liked to finish their works with a majestic chaconne (or passacaglia). Musically it develops on a ground bass.

Chadwick, Fiona (*b* Morecambe, 13 May 1960). Eng. dancer. Studied Royal B. School and joined

Royal B. 1978, touring first with Ballet for All group. To Covent Garden Royal B. from 1979. Debuts in title roles of *The Firebird* and *Isadora*, 1981, while still in corps de ballet; promoted soloist 1981 and principal d. 1984.

Chaffee, George (*b* Oakland, 1907, *d* N.Y. 19 Oct. 1984). Amer. dancer, teacher, collector, and writer. Studied with a great many teachers in the U.S. and in Europe. D. with Fokine's B., Mordkin B., and B. Russe de Monte Carlo. Internationally known as the owner of one of the world's foremost collections of lithographs, drawings, paintings, sculptures, and books on b. Some of his valuable possessions were published in *Dance Index*: 'American Lithographs of the Romantic Ballet' (Feb. 1942), 'American Music Prints of the Romantic Ballet' (Dec. 1942), 'The Romantic Ballet in London' (Sep./Dec. 1943), and 'Three or Four Graces' (Sep./Nov. 1944). A picture-spread of his collection appeared in *Dance Magazine* (1962/10).

Chagall, Marc (*b* Vitebsk, 7 July 1887, *d* St. Paul de Vence, 28 Mar. 1985). Russ.-Fr. painter. Designed *Aleko* (1942) for Massine, *The Firebird* (1949—now in the repertory of the New York City B.) for Bolm/Fokine, and *Daphnis and Chloe* (1958) for Lifar.
BIBL.: Chagall issue of *Dance Index* (Nov. 1945); J. Lassaigne, *M.C.: Drawings & Water Colors for the Ballet* (1969).

Chahut. An especially free and sprightly variant of the quadrille, very popular in the Paris of the 1830s, which rapidly turned into the *Cancan.

Chaîné (Fr., chained). Should really be termed Tours chaînés déboulés. A sequence of fast, seamless turns from one foot to the other, executed in a straight line.

Chalif, Louis H. (*b* Odessa, 1876, *d* New York, 1948). Russ.-Amer. dancer and teacher. Studied at Odessa B. School under Alfred Bekefi, Ivan Savitsky, and Thomas (father of Vaslav) Nijinsky, graduating in 1893 and joining the co., of the local op. house, eventually becoming premier danseur. Left in 1904 for the U.S. D. with the Met. Op. B. in 1904–5, opening the C. Russian Normal School of D. in 1907, which became one of the pioneer b. schools in the U.S. Published a great number of textbooks on dance.

Chalon, Alfred Edouard (*b* Geneva, 1780, *d* 1860). Swiss-Brit. painter and illustrator. His lithographs and illustrations give an impression of what romantic b. looked like. He became famous as the portraitist of Taglioni and especially through his lithograph of the *Pas de quatre* from 1845.
BIBL.: G. Chaffee, in 'Three or Four Graces', *Dance Index* (1944/9–11).

Chamié, Tatiana, Collection. Given to the D. Collection of the New York Public Library in

1953 by the estate of T. Chamié, a d. and teacher, who had collected photographs, programmes, clippings, and other memorabilia of the late Diaghilev years, also covering the cos. of R. Blum and Colonel de Basil and the Amer. start of B. Russe de Monte Carlo.

Champion, Gower (b Geneva, Ill., 22 June 1920, d New York 25 Aug. 1980). Amer. dancer, choreographer, and director. Studied with L. Fokine, Holm, and Nick Castle; d. in night-clubs and on Broadway, choreographing his 1st prod. of a musical in 1948 (*Lend an Ear*), after which he became one of the most sought-after directors on Broadway and in Hollywood, creating *Bye Bye Birdie* (1960), *Carnival* (1961), *Hello Dolly* (1964), *I Do! I Do!* (1966), and *42nd Street* (1980). D. Magazine Award (1963). Was married to his d. partner Marge Champion (*née* Marjorie Belcher).

Changement de pieds (Fr., changing feet). Designates a jump, during which the position of the feet is changed.

Chant du compagnon errant. See *Song of the Wayfarer*.

Chant du rossignol, Le (*Song of the Nightingale*). Ballet in 1 act; ch. Massine; mus. Stravinsky; déc. Matisse. Prod. 2 Feb. 1920, Bs. Russes de Diaghilev, Opéra, Paris, with Karsavina, Sokolova, Idzikovsky. The b., based on Andersen's fairy-tale, tells the story of the Emperor of China who bans the real nightingale when he is presented with a bejewelled mechanical one. When he falls so ill that he seems at death's door, the mechanical nightingale keeps silent, so the real nightingale has to be brought back, and it is she who charms Death and sings the Emperor back to life. The b. is based on the symphonic poem which Stravinsky extracted from his op. *Le Rossignol*, which Diaghilev had 1st produced in 1914. When Diaghilev wanted the b. to be revived in 1925, he commissioned the young Balanchine to do the ch., which became his 1st b. for the troupe. Later versions by Cranko (Munich, 1968) and Taras (New York City B., 1972). A different musical treatment of the same subject by Egk in *The Chinese Nightingale* (ch. T. Gsovsky, Munich, 1953). BIBL.: G. Balanchine, 'S.o.t.N.' in *Balanchine's New Complete Stories of the Great Ballets* (Garden City, N.Y., 1968).

Chappell, Annette (b Liverpool, 1929). Brit. dancer and teacher. Studied with Judith Espinosa. D. with B. Rambert 1944–8, appeared in musicals 1949–55, joined Munich State Op. B. in 1955 as ballerina, eventually becoming a teacher at its associated school. Moved to Stuttgart in 1970, where she has been a teacher of the J. Cranko B. school ever since.

Chappell, William (b 1908). Brit. dancer and designer. He was one of the 1st members of the B. Rambert, dancing also with the co. of Rubinstein and the Vic-Wells B., creating roles in de Valois' *Job* (1931), *The Rake's Progress* (1935), and *Checkmate* (1937). Designed *Cephalus and Procris* (1931) for de Valois, *Les Rendezvous* (1933), *Les Patineurs* (1937), and *Rhapsody* (1980) for Ashton, *The Judgment of Paris* (1938) for Tudor, *Giselle* (1935) and *Coppélia* (1940) for Sadler's Wells B., and *Swan Lake* (1948) for International B. Published *Studies in Ballet* in 1948, and *Margot Fonteyn* in 1951. Has since worked mainly as a director of plays, musicals, and revues.
BIBL.: G. Anthony, 'W.C.', *Dancing Times* (1970/5).

Character Dance. General term for all kinds of th. d. outside the bounds of the classic-academic d., deriving from traditional, national, or folklore sources—also the d. of the artisans and guilds, the comic d. and the d. which is representative of a certain type of character. Dancers who are not tall enough, or in technical respects are not ideally gifted for the academic d. often prefer the character d. B. also knows the demi-caractère d. which includes 'the performer of great academic virtuosity, as opposed to the grace and lyrical qualities of the purest classical type' (N. de Valois, *Invitation to the Ballet*, London, 1937)—e.g. The Blue Bird.

Charisse, Cyd. (orig. Tula Ellice Finklea; b Amarillo, Tex., 1923). Amer. dancer and show-business personality. Studied with Bolm, Nico Charisse (who became her 1st husband), and Nijinska; made her début in 1939 with Colonel de Basil's B. Russe (under the name of Felia Sidorova), and from 1946 onwards became a very popular star-performer of the Amer. musical, film, TV and nightclub scene, appearing in *The Band Wagon, Singing in the Rain, Brigadoon, Silk Stockings*, and in Petit's film *Black Tights* (as the widow in *Deuil en vingt-quatre heures*).

Charles, Lynne Roberta (b New York, 17 Jan. 1955). Amer. dancer. Studied at Harkness School of B., Amer. School of B. and B. Th. School. D. with Amer. B. Th. Repertory Co. 1972–4, Geneva B. 1974–5, now principal d. of Hamburg State Op. B. Created roles in Neumeier's *Schubert Streich-quintett* (1977) and Aurora in his *Sleeping Beauty* (1978), et al. 3rd Prize (Bronze Medal), Varna 1976, Berlin Art Prize 1977.

Charleston. Amer. social d. named after the city of C. in South Carolina. Originally a Negro solo-d. it became immensely popular as part of the big Negro revues in the New York of the 1920s, and then became accepted in 1926 as a ballroom d. It is a sort of speeded-up fox-trot which is strongly syncopated. One of its most famous performers was J. Baker.

Charlip, Remy (b Brooklyn, 10 Jan. 1929). Amer. dancer and choreographer. D. with the co. of M. Cunningham, acted with and ch. for Living Th. Founder member of The Paper Bag Players. Has written and illustrated many picture books. Ch.

for London Contemporary D. Th., Scottish Th. B., City Center Joffrey B., and The National Th. of the Deaf. Has taught at many schools and colleges throughout the U.S.A.
BIBL.: G. Gow, 'The Versatile Talents of R.C.', *Dancing Times* (1974/4); interview with R.C., *Dance and Dancers* (1974/4); M. Pierpont, 'A Conversation with R.C.', *Dance Magazine* (1980/4).

Charrat, Janine (*b* Grenoble, 24 July 1924). Fr. dancer, choreographer, and b. director. Studied with Jeanne Ronsay, Egorova, and Volinine; made her début as the dancing child star of the film *La Mort du cygne* in 1937. D. in many perfs. with Petit 1941–4, enjoying her 1st success as a ch. with Stravinsky's *Jeu de cartes* (Bs. des Champs-Elysées, 1945). Continued to d. and ch. for various cos. Her next important bs. were *Concerto No. 3* (mus. Prokofiev, Opéra Comique, 1947), *'adame miroir* (mus. Milhaud, Bs. de Paris, 1948), and *Abraxas* (mus. Egk, Berlin Municipal Op., 1949). In 1951 Les Bs., J.C. made their Paris début, her new bs. being *Concerto* (mus. Grieg) and *Le Massacre des Amazones* (mus. Y. Semenoff). She also ch. Egk's *Columbus* in Berlin in 1951. In 1953 her co. was renamed Le B. de France, with her new *Les Algues* (mus. Guy Bernard) as its hit prod. In 1956 she created *The Seven Deadly Sins* (mus. Veretti) for Milan's La Scala. During the following years she ch. *Les Liens* (mus. Semenoff, B. de France, 1957), *Diagramme* (mus. Bach, Grand B. du Marquis de Cuevas, 1957), *Electre* (mus. Pousseur, Brussels, 1960), the Paris prod. of Honegger's op. *Le Roi David* (1960), and co-ch. with Béjart *Les 4 Fils Aymon* (mus. F. Schirren, Brussels, 1961). Very severe burns, suffered in a TV studio, compelled her to relinquish all work for almost a year. She led the b. co. in Geneva 1962–4, creating *Tu auras nom . . . Tristan* (mus. Jef Maes), *Pour le temps présent* (mus. A. Schibler). and *Alerte . . . puis 21* (mus. P. Wissmer). At the Vienna Volksoper she ch. Ravel's *L'Enfant et les sortilèges* (1964) and Stravinsky's *Firebird* (1969), for her co. in Paris *Pâris* (mus. Sauguet, 1964), in Gelsenkirchen *Persephone* (mus. Stravinsky, 1968), in Munich *Casanova in London* (mus. Egk, 1969), for the Opéra Comique *Les Collectioneurs* (mus. Y. Malec, 1972), and for the Opéra *Offrandes and Hyperprism* (mus. Varèse, 1973). She has revived her co. several times, creating new works for it. In 1970 she opened a school in Paris. D. Dir. at the Centre Pompidou since 1980. Légion d'honneur (1973).
BIBL.: M. Humbert, *J.C.-Antigone de la danse* (Paris, 1970); I. Lidova, 'J.C.' with complete list of roles and activities, *Les Saisons de la danse* (1970/8).

Chase, Lucia (*b* Waterbury, 24 Mar. 1897, *d* N.Y., 9 Jan. 1986). Amer. d. and b. director. Studied with Mordkin, Fokine, Tudor, Vilzak, and Nijinska, d. as ballerina with the Mordkin B. 1938–9, and a founder of B. Th. in which she repeatedly invested large sums from her private fortune. With indefatigable zest and energy she moulded B. Th. and later *Amer. B. Th. into one of the 2 top Amer. b. cos. She created the Eldest Sister in Tudor's *Pillar of Fire* in 1942 and appeared in special mime roles (*Fall River Legend, Swan Lake*). Handel Medallion (1975). Resigned 1980.
BIBL.: O. Maynard, 'L.C.: First Lady of American Ballet', *Dance Magazine* (1971/8); J. Gruen 'Close-up: L.C.', *Dance Magazine* (1975/1); W. Terry, 'Make Way for Lucia', *Ballet News* (1979/9).

Chassé (Fr. hunted). A sliding step, in which one foot displaces the other as if by chasing it.

Chat, Pas de (Fr., step of the cat). It derives its name from its likeness to the movement of a leaping cat. Starts from 5th position, right foot back, right leg stretched, followed by an upward leap from the left foot, with the left knee bent—while the body is suspended in the air, the torso bends backward—followed by the landing on the right foot, while the left foot closes in the 5th position front, bending the knee.

Chatfield, Philip (*b* Eastleigh, 1927). Brit. dancer. Studied at Sadler's Wells School, joining Sadler's Wells B. in 1946; appointed principal d. in 1955. Created roles in Howard's *Mirror for Witches* (1952), Cranko's *The Shadow* (1953), and had one of his best roles as Moondog in Cranko's *The Lady and the Fool*. Retired in 1959, since when he has been active in New Zealand. Since 1972 joint dir. of National School of B. in Wellington, N.Z. Married to the d. Rowena Jackson.
BIBL.: J. Percival, 'A Dancer for Leading Roles', *Dance and Dancers* (1958/3); C. Swinson, *Rowena Jackson and P.C.* (London, 1958).

Chatte, La. Ballet in 1 act; libr. Sobeka (alias Kochno); mus. Sauguet; ch. Balanchine; déc. Naum Gabo and Antoine Pevsner. Prod. 30 Apr. 1927, Bs. Russes de Diaghilev, Monte Carlo, with Spessivtzeva, Lifar. Based upon the fable by Aesop, in which a young man asks Aphrodite to change the cat, with which he has fallen in love, into a young girl—a wish that is fulfilled, until the girl becomes more interested in a mouse and becomes her old cat-self again, when the young man dies. The b. had an extravagantly original constructivist décor of transparent materials reflecting the lights in a dazzling display of rays. Another version by R. Hynd with modified story to the same mus. (London Festival B., 1978).
BIBL.: C. W. Beaumont, 'L.C.' in *Complete Book of Ballets* (London, 1951).

Chaussat, Geneviève (*b* Mexico City, 22 Nov. 1941). Swiss dancer. Studied at the conservatory in Mexico City and with Besobrasova and Golovine; made her début at the op. in Nice, d. with the co. of Golovine, joining Munich State Op. B. in 1968 as a soloist. To Dusseldorf B. in 1975. Prix René Blum (1962).

Chausson, Ernest (*b* Paris, 21 Jan. 1855, *d* Limay, 10 June 1899). Fr. composer. Though he wrote no b. mus., his very popular *Poème* has often been used by chs., the best known b. version being Tudor's *Lilac Garden* (1936). H. Ross used his Concerto for Violin, Piano, and String Quartet for *Paean* (1957).

Chauviré, Yvette (*b* Paris, 22 Apr. 1917). Fr. dancer and teacher. Studied at Paris Opéra B. School and with Kniaseff and V. Gsovsky. Entered the co. of the Opéra, creating her 1st solo role in Lifar's *Le Roi nu* in 1936; appeared in the film *La Mort du cygne* in 1937, promoted première danseuse étoile in 1941, continued—with minor interruptions—until she retired in 1972. Appeared as a guest ballerina with cos. all over the world; she was admired for the beauty, elegance, and finesse of her interpretations in the great ballerina roles. Created roles in Lifar's *David triomphant* (1937), *Alexandre le Grand* (1937), *Le Chevalier et la Damoiselle* (1941), *Istar* (1941), *Joan de Zarissa* (1942), *Suite en blanc* (1943), *Dramma per musica* (1946), *Chota Roustaveli* (1946), *Nauteos* (1947), *Mirages* (1947), *La Péri* (1957), and *Constellations* (1969), in Cranko's *La Belle Hélène* (1955), and L. Gai's *The Seagull* (1968). Was then in charge of the Académie Internationale de Danse in Paris and also teaches at the Opéra. Chevalier de la Légion d'Honneur (1964), Officier de la Légion d'Honneur (1974), Author of *Je suis ballerine* (Paris, 1960).
BIBL.: L. Nemenschousky, *A Day with Y.C.* (London, 1960); I. Lidova, 'Y.C.' with complete list of roles. *Les Saisons de la danse* (1968/2).

Checkmate. Ballet in 1 act with prologue; libr. and mus. Bliss; ch. de Valois; déc. E. McKnight Kauffer. Prod. 15 June 1937, Sadler's Wells B., Th. des Champs-Elysées, Paris, with Brae, May, Helpmann, Turner. A game of love and death, acted out according to the rules of a game of chess. It is finally won by the Black Queen, who first captures the Red Queen, then defeats the Red Knight and at the end delivers the tottering Red King to her warriors who kill him. The London première took place on 15 Oct. 1937 at the Sadler's Wells Th. The b. has been revived several times (also by the Vienna State Op. in 1964). BBC TV prod. (1963).
BIBL.: C. W. Beaumont, 'C.' in *Supplement to Complete Book of Ballets* (London, 1952)

Chenchikova, Olga (*b* Moscow, 1956). Sov. dancer. Studied with L. Sakharova at Perm State B. School: graduated in 1974 and subsequently joined the Perm B. 1st appeared in the West at Bregenz Festival in 1973. Silver Medal (Moscow, 1973).

Chesworth, John (*b* Manchester, 1930). Brit. dancer. choreographer, and b. director. Studied at Rambert School, joining the co. after only 18 months, and later its Artistic Dir. Created roles in Morrice's *Two Brothers* (1958) and *Hazaña* (1959), J. Taylor's *Diversities* (1966), and Tetley's *Ziggurat* (1967). Choreographed *Time Base* (mus. Lutos-

ławski, 1966), *Tic-Tack* (mus. F. Kreisler, 1967), *H* (mus. Penderecki, 1968), *Pawn to King 5* (mus. The Pink Floyd, 1968), *Four According* (mus. G. Bačewicz, 1970), *Games for Five Players* (mus. Toru Takemitsu, Northern D. Th., 1971), *Pattern for an Escalator* (mus. J. Harvey and G. Newson, 1972), *Project 634/9116Mk2*(1974). Left B. Rambert 1980.

Chevalier et la Damoiselle, Le. Ballet in 2 acts; libr. and ch. Lifar; mus. Philippe Gaubert; déc. Cassandre. Prod. 2 July 1941, Opéra, Paris, with Schwarz, Chauviré, Lifar. The b. is based on a medieval Burgundian legend, in which during the night a knight errant meets a white-antlered hind, which changes into a young girl when he stabs her heart. Only in the 2nd act does she reveal her real identity: she is a Princess, and after the knight has won a tournament he is finally granted her hand.
BIBL.: C. Beaumont, 'L.C.e.l.D' in *Ballets Past and Present* (London, 1955).

Chicago. Though touring cos. (Genée, Pavlova, *et al.*) occasionally visited the city, no real local b. initiatives existed until the C. Opéra B. was established in 1910, which had a rapid turnover of b.-masters and dancers; the best-known during its early years were Serge Oukrainsky and particularly Bolm, who ch. the 1st prod. of J. A. Carpenter's *The Birthday of the Infanta* in 1919. A touring co., the Pavley-Oukrainsky B., functioned during the mid-1920s, and Bolm founded the C. Allied Arts, which existed 1924–7, with Ruth Page as prima ballerina, who was to become city's most important b. personality during the next 5 decades. Having been in charge of the b. activities at the Ravinia Park Festival in 1929–33, she was appointed ch. and prima ballerina of the C. Grand Op. Co., 1934–7, and again 1944–7 (when she did the 1st prods. of *The Bells* and *Billy Sunday*). From the school of B. Stone and W. Camryn came most of the dancers of the Page-Stone B. which existed 1938–41 (and continued until the late 1970s as the Stone-Camryn B., giving perfs. with its pupils). Other important b. schools were those of B. Holmes, E. McRae, and R. Ellis, while modern d. activities centred around S. Shearer who still works at her own nearby Winnetka Community Th. and other institutions. Ch. who maintained a close connection with C. for several years included C. Littlefield, K. Dunham, and T. Beatty. However Page was and is the city's most prolific b. promoter as the head of various cos. (including *C. Opera B. and R. Page Bs.). These have at times been closely connected with the C. Lyric Opera since 1955, while at other times they have been run on a more private basis, constantly being newly assembled, touring extensively, and thus introducing some of the internationally most coveted dancers to Amer. audiences, and disbanding again after the end of the tour. Maria Tallchief's C. City B. gave its first season in June 1981.

BIBL.: entry 'C.—Balletto' in *Enciclopedia dello spettacolo*.

Chicago Opera Ballet. Founded by R. Page, the co. made its début on 16 Nov. 1955 at the Chicago Lyric Op. with *The Merry Widow*, starring Markova. At its New York perfs. in Dec. changed its name to Ruth Page Bs. During the following years appeared under various names, but always headed by Page, whose bs. were the basis of the repertory, with special emphasis on bs. derived from ops., e.g. *Camille* (i.e. *La traviata*), *Die Fledermaus*, and *Carmen*. On its wide annual tours it has introduced many Eur. dancers to Amer. audiences, incl. Amiel, Simone, Flindt, Kronstam, and Nureyev (Amer. début with the co., 1962, Brooklyn Academy).

Children of Theatre Street, The. A Sov.-Amer. film co-prod., released in the west by Columbia-EMI-Warner, 1978. Directed by Robert Dornhelm, with a commentary spoken in the Eng. version by Princess Grace of Monaco, it shows the working of the famous Leningrad B. School with glimpses into its glorious past and a graduation performance as its climax. A picture book about the film with an introduction by Earle Mack who made it and a text by Patricia Barnes has been published by Phaidon Press.

Childs, Lucinda (*b* New York, 1940). Amer. dancer and choreographer. Graduated as a d. major at Sarah Lawrence College 1962. Continued to study at Amer. B. Center and with M. Cunningham. Became a member of the Judson D. Th. Mostly appears as a solo performer. Her dances are characterized by unremitting repetition and perpetual motion, radiating a strange and aloof ritualist quality.
BIBL.: S. Banes, 'L.C.: The Act of Seeing', in *Terpsichore in Sneakers* (Boston, 1980).

Chile. See *Santiago de Chile*.

China. The country has a centuries-old tradition of variety and acrobatic d. culminating in the dazzling display of virtuosity in the danced and mimed numbers of the Peking Opera, which created a sensation when it first appeared in the West in the mid-1950s. Though there have been individual b. schools, b. did not really catch on until well after the Liberation, when Russ. teachers such as Viktor Tsaplin from the Bolshoi and Gusev from the Kirov helped to establish the Peking D. School in 1954 and the Shanghai D. School in 1960, and to build up a repertory of standard classics and a few Russ. bs. During these years China was regularly visited by the big cos. from the Sov. bloc, but also by the B. Rambert and individual dancers such as B. Grey. The estrangement between China and the U.S.S.R and the cultural revolution severed these bonds, and the Chinese went their own way. The schools, however, continued to function (though no longer controlled by foreigners, of course), and

they were the basis of the two leading cos., the China D. Drama Troupe (Peking) and the Shanghai D. School (also the name of the performing co.). In 1964 2 full-length bs. were premièred, based on national revolutionary subjects: *The Red Detachment of Women* and *The White-Haired Girl*. Technically they use the classic-academic vocabulary, embellished with the virtuoso feats of traditional mime and acrobatics. Both have been filmed and shown in the West. They were considered the prime examples of the new revolutionary Chinese b. After the cultural revolution ended, classic b. was reintroduced, based mainly on the Central Peking B. and the Shanghai Classical B.
BIBL.: B. Grey, *Through the Bamboo Curtain* (London, 1965); H. Atlas, 'China Dances to Revolutionary Tune', *Dance News* (1972/9–10).

Chinese Orphan Boy, The (original Ital. title: *L'Orfano della China*). Ballet by Angiolini after Voltaire's *L'Orphelin de la Chine*. Prod. Vienna, 1774. For a long time it was believed that Gluck was the composer, and the score is included in the Gluck Collected Edition. However, at the time of its 1st perf. Gluck was already in Paris. Nowadays some scholars (incl. Gerhard Winkler in his thesis *Das Wiener Ballett von Noverre bis Fanny Elssler*, Vienna, 1967) are convinced that Angiolini himself composed the mus. The story centres on the faithful mandarin Xamti, who sacrifices his own son to save the heir of the throne when Genghis Khan and his Tartars conquer Peking. The Mlakars revived it for the Bayreuth Baroque Week in 1954.

Chiriaeff, Ludmilla (*b* Riga, 1924). Latvian-Can. dancer and b. director. Studied in Berlin with Alexandra Nikolajeva; d. 1936–7 with Colonel de Basil's B. Russe, then worked with Fokine and Massine; d. at the Berlin State Op. 1939–44. After the 2nd world war she became b. mistress and solo-d. in Lausanne; opened a school in 1948 in Geneva, and then went to Canada, where she prod. several bs. for TV. From her group of dancers Les Bs. Chiriaeff emerged in 1955, which became Les Grands Bs. Canadiens in 1957, for which she has ch. several bs. She retired as dir. of the co. in 1974, but continues as head of the attached b. academy. Order of Canada (1969, Companion, 1984).
BIBL.: O. Maynard, 'L.C.', *Dance Magazine* (1971/4).

Chirico, Giorgio di (*b* Volo, Greece, 10 July 1888, *d* Rome, 19 Nov. 1978). Greek-Ital. painter. He designed the bs. *The Jar* (ch. Börlin, 1924), *Le Bal* (ch. Balanchine, 1929), *Bacchus and Ariadne* (ch. Lifar, 1931), *Protée* (ch. Lichine, 1938), *Amphion* (ch. Milloss, 1944), *Dances from Galanta* (ch. Milloss, 1945), *The Legend of Joseph* (ch. Wallmann, 1951), and *Apollon musagète* (ch. Lifar, 1956).

Chladek, Rosalia (*b* Brno, 21 May 1905).

Austrian dancer, choreographer, and teacher. Studied at Hellerau 1921–4, dancing with the group of V. Kratina, made her début as a recital d. in Dresden in 1924. Started to teach in Hellerau in 1924, continuing in Laxenburg, then in Basle, where she also ch. for the Municipal Th. She headed the d.-education department and the d.-group of Hellerau-Laxenburg 1930–8, developing her own system of modern d. training. Taught in Berlin 1940–1, after which she returned to Vienna, where she was in charge of the d. department of the conservatory 1942–52 and at the Academy for Music and Performing Arts 1952–70. One of the most interesting dancers of the European modern d. scene, she undertook extensive tours abroad. As a ch. she worked for her own group, in various Ital. open-air prods. of classical dramas (mainly in Sicily), for the Salzburg and Vienna Festivals, and at the Vienna State Op. She also ch. the d.-film *Symphonie Wien* (1952). Continues as a guest teacher in Vienna as well as abroad; an international R.C. society was founded in 1971 in Strasbourg to spread her system of teaching. 2nd prize Choreographers' Competition (Paris, 1932); 2nd prize Dancers' Competition (Warsaw, 1933); Professor, Honorary Medal of the City of Vienna (1971).
BIBL.: G. Alexander and H. Groll, *Tänzerin-Choreographin-Pädagogin R.C.* (Vienna, 1965).

Chopin Concerto. Ballet in 3 movements; ch. Nijinska; mus. Chopin; déc. W. Borowskij. Prod. 20 Nov. 1937, Bs. Polonais, Th. de Mogador, Paris, with Olga Slawska, Nina Yuszkiewicz, Zbigniew Kilinski. Set to Chopin's Concerto for Piano and Orchestra in E minor, the b. follows no plot but tries to reflect the shifting moods of the mus. Revived for B. Russe de Monte Carlo (New York, 1942) and on various later occasions.

Chopin, Fryderyk Frantizek (*b* Zelezow-Wola, 1 Mar. 1810, *d* Paris, 17 Oct. 1849). Pol. composer. Wrote no b. mus., but his piano pieces and concertos have often been used by choreographers—e.g. by Fokine in *Chopiniana* (1907, definitive version as *Les Sylphides*, 1909), Pavlova in *Autumn Leaves* (1918), Nijinska in *Chopin Concerto* (1937), Dollar in *Constantia*, Robbins in *The Concert* (1956), *Dances at a Gathering* (1969), and *In the Night* (1970), Ashton in *A Month in the Country* (1976), and Neumeier in *Lady of the Camellias* (1978).

Chopiniana. See *Sylphides, Les*.

Choreartium. Ballet in 4 movements; ch. Massine; mus. Brahms; déc. Constantine Terechkovich and Eugène Lourié. Prod. 24 Oct. 1933, B. Russe de Monte Carlo, Alhambra Th., London, with Baronova, Danilova, Riabouchinska, Verchinina, Zorina, Jasinski, Lichine, Petroff, Shabelevski. Set to Brahms's 4th Symphony in E minor, the b. represents an abstract ch. interpretation of the mus., stressing the interplay between mascu-

line and feminine movements. This was Massine's 2nd symphonic b. (after *Les Présages*).
BIBL.: C. W. Beaumont, 'C.' in *Complete Book of Ballets* (London, 1951).

Choreographer. The person in charge of the ch.—i.e. the author or composer of a d. who arranges the steps and patterns so that they add up to an integrated work of art. In his *Manifeste du Chorégraphe*, published 1935, Lifar argued that the term choréauteur should be preferred.

Choreographer's Workshop. Founded in New York in 1946 and active until 1954, it served as a platform for young choreographers. Among the bs. receiving their 1st prod. here were Bettis's *As I Lay Dying* (1948), Ross's *Caprichos* (1950), and Joffrey's *Persephone* (1952). Other choreographers presenting new bs. included Beatty, Charmoli, Erdman, Johnson, Koner, Nikolais, and Tetley.

Choreography (Greek, d. writing). Feuillet and Beauchamp, who wrote down the movement of the feet in graphic symbols about 1700, called their system of d. notation chorégraphie. In his treatise *Die Kunst nach der Choregraphie zu tanzen und Tänze zu Schreiben* (The Art of dancing from ch. and writing dances), published in 1777 in Brunswick, J. C. Feldstein used the term for the art of inventing and composing dances. In this sense it is used today to describe the art of composing a d. or a b.
BIBL.: L. Kirstein, 'Choreography: Materials and Structure' in *Movement & Metaphor* (New York, 1970).

Choreology (Greek, science of the d.). Laban used the term for the group of sciences connected with the d. In Eng. it is now used by the Beneshs for their system of d. notation, though this is etymologically not quite correct. See also *Institute of Choreology*.

Choreomania. (Greek, desire to d.). A somewhat different meaning is expressed in the word *balletomane.

Choreutic (Greek, concerned with d.). The word choreut, a d. is derived from it. Laban used the term as a description of the analysis of d. forms and movements.

Choros. The Greek word has 3 different meanings: (1) the round d.; (2) the 'choir' which performs the round-dance; (3) the place where the round dance is performed. In modern Greek it also means a lively folk-d., involving leaps in a circle.

Chota Roustaveli. Georgian choreographic epic in 4 acts; libr. and ch. Lifar; mus. Honegger, Tcherepnin, and Tibor Harsányi; déc. Prince A. Schervachidze and C. Nepo. Prod. 5 May 1946, Nouveau B. de Monte Carlo, Monte Carlo, with Lifar, Chauviré, Charrat, Algaroff. Based upon the Georgian poem *A Hero in a Leopard's Skin*, the b. tells of the adventures of the poet C.R. and

Queen Thamar, who is both his inspiration and his love.

BIBL.: C. Beaumont, 'C.R.' in *Ballets Past & Present* (London, 1955).

Chout, Le (orig. Russ. title: *Ska{zka pro shuta*; Eng. *The Buffoon*). Ballet in 6 scenes: libr. and mus. Prokofiev; ch. Tadeusz Slavinsky and M. Larionov. Prod. 17 May 1921, Bs. Russes de Diaghilev, Th. Gaîté-Lyrique, Paris, with Katharina Devillier, Slavinsky, Jazvinsky. The story, of the buffoon who fools seven of his colleagues, comes from Afanasyev's collection of Russ. fairytales. He pretends to kill his wife and then restore her to life with a magic whip. He then sells the whip to the other buffoons for a great sum, who try it on their wives—so successfully that they fail to return from the other world. Not a success at its first prod., the b. has been very rarely revived since, one of its more successful versions being that by Gertrud Steinweg at the Berlin Comic Op. in 1957. Czech TV prod. (ch. E. Gabzdyl) 1967.

Chouteau, Yvonne (b Vinita, Okl., 7 Mar. 1929). Amer. dancer and teacher. Studied with Veronine Vestoff, D. Perkins, E. Belcher, Bolm, Vilzak-Schollar, and at School of Amer. B. Joined B. Russe de Monte Carlo in 1943, appointed ballerina in 1949; she stayed with the co. until 1957. Is now Artist in Residence at Univ. of Oklahoma at Norman and Dir. (with her husband, Miguel Terekhov) of her Academy of B. in Oklahoma City. Honorary doctor of Humanities (Phillips Univ., 1974).

Christensen Brothers. Willam C. (b. 1902), Harold C. (b 1904), and Lew C. (b 1909). Together won the D. Magazine Award 1973.

BIBL.: B. Como and R. Philp, 'The Christensen Brothers', portfolio in *Dance Magazine* (1973/6).

Christensen, Harold (b Brigham City, Utah, 25 Dec. 1904). Amer. dancer and teacher. Studied with his uncle Peter C. in Salt Lake City, with Stefano Mascagno and L. Albertieri in New York, and at School of Amer. B.; joined Amer. B., B. Caravan, San Francisco Op. B., and San Francisco B. Retired as a d. in 1946, then in charge of the San Francisco B. School to 1975? (Present dir. apptd. 1975). Married to the d. Ruby Asquith.

BIBL.: see *Christensen Brothers.*

Christensen, Lew (b Brigham City, Utah, 9 May 1909, d Burlingame, Cal., 9 Oct. 1984). Amer. dancer, choreographer, and b. director. Studied with his uncle Peter C. in Salt Lake City, with Stefano Mascagno and L. Albertieri in New York, and at the School of Amer. B. Toured the vaudeville circuit, joined the Amer. B., becoming Balanchine's first Amer. Apollo, and widely considered Amer.'s first legitimate premier danseur of the 20th century. Ch. *Filling Station* (mus. V. Thomson) in 1938 for B. Caravan, of which he was b. master, and *Jinx* (mus. Britten) in 1942 for

D. Players, of which he was associate dir. Joined the faculty of the School of Amer. B. in 1946, also becoming b. master of B. Society and eventually of the New York City B. In 1951 he went to San Francisco to become dir. and chief-ch. of the San Francisco B. Among the best known bs. he ch. are *Pocahontas* (mus. E. Carter, 1936), *Con Amore* (mus. Rossini, 1953), *Nutcracker* (1954), *Beauty and the Beast* (1958), *Jest of Cards* (mus. Křenek, 1962). *Divertissement d'Auber* (1959). Was married to the d. Gisella Caccialanza.

BIBL.: see *Christensen Brothers.*

Christensen, Willam (orig. William C.; b Brigham City, Utah, 27 Aug. 1902). Amer. dancer, choreographer, teacher, and b. director. Studied with his uncle Peter C. in Salt Lake City, with Stefano Mascagno and L. Albertieri in New York, and with Novikoff, Julietta Mendes, and Fokine. Toured the vaudeville circuit. Opened a b. school in Portland, Oreg., in 1932, from which came the Portland B.; danced with the co. of Fokine and from 1937 with the San Francisco Op. B., of which he became b. master and ch. in 1938. Ch. the first Amer. full-length versions of *Coppélia, Nutcracker,* and *Swan Lake.* In 1951 he went to the Univ. of Utah, where he chairs the d. department; established the Utah b., which is now called the B. West. Has ch. many bs. for the various cos. he has worked with.

BIBL.: see *Christensen Brothers.*

Christmas Eve (orig. Russ. title: *Noch pered ro{zhdestvom*). Ballet in 3 acts and 7 scenes; libr. Slonimsky; ch. V. A. Varkovitsky; mus. Asafiev; déc. A. A. Kolomoytsev. Prod. 15 June 1938, Kirov Th., Leningrad, with L. Goncharova, N. Serebrennikov, C. Sheina, N. Nevdachina. Based on the story by Gogol, the b. tells of fair Oksana and the blacksmith Vakula, who brings her the Tsarina's slippers to win her favour—also involved are the Devil and the witch Solokha. The b. was produced in honour of the 200th anniversary of the founding of the Imperial School of the Th.

BIBL.: C. W. Beaumont, 'C.E.' in *Supplement to Complete Book of Ballets London, 1952).*

Christout, Marie-Françoise (b Neuilly-sur-Seine, 1925). Fr. writer on dance and th. Educated at Sorbonne Univ. Librarian of the d. collection of the Paris Bibliothèque de l'Arsenal since 1960. Fr. correspondent of *Dance Magazine* and *Dance and Dancers*, regular contributor to *Les Saisons de la danse.* Her books on d. include *Histoire du Ballet* (Paris, 1965), *Le Ballet de cour de Louis XIV* (Paris, 1967), and *Maurice Béjart* (Paris, 1972). Author of 'The Court Ballet in France 1615–1641', *Dance Perspectives* 20.

Chronica. Ballet in 3 acts; libr. and ch. Jooss; mus. Berthold Goldschmidt; déc. D. Bouchène. Prod. 14 Feb. 1939, Bs. Jooss, Arts Th., Cambridge. Against an Ital. renaissance background, the b. tells of the condottiere Fortunato's achievement of power, how he used it, and the evil that followed from it.

BIBL.: A. V. Coton, in *The New Ballet* (London, 1946).

Chryst, Gary (*b* La Jolla, Cal., 1949). Amer. dancer. Studied at New York High School of Performing Arts with Schurr, Walker, and D. Wood, also with Matteo, Jaime Rogers, and at Amer. B. Center. D. with the co., of Walker, then with the Utah B. and since 1967 with the Joffrey co., Created roles in Arpino's *The Puppet* (1969) and *Trinity* (1970), Sappington's *Weewis* (1971), Layton's *Double Exposure* (1972), and Tharp's *Deuce Coupe* (1973).
BIBL.: O. Maynard, 'G.C.', *Dance Magazine* (1974/11).

Chujoy, Anatole (*b* Riga, 1894, *d* New York, 24 Feb. 1969). Latvian-Amer. writer, editor, and critic. Educated at the univs. of Riga, Warsaw, and St. Petersburg-Petrograd (from which he held a law degree), he came to the U.S. in the early 1920s. Contributed to the magazine *American Dancer*, became co-founder and managing editor of *Dance Magazine* in 1936. He founded *Dance News*, in 1942, which he edited and published until his death. Wrote, edited, and translated a great number of dance books and individual publications, the most important being *Dance Encyclopedia* (New York, 1949—second, completely rewritten edition, with P. W. Manchester as co-author, in 1967), *The New York City Ballet* (New York, 1953), and *Fokine, Memoirs of a Ballet Master* (ed., New York, 1961).
BIBL.: A.C., 'A.C.' in *Dance Encyclopedia* (New York, 1967); P. W. Manchester, 'A. C.', *Dance News* (1969/4).

Ciceri, Pierre (*b* 1782, *d* 1868). Fr. designer and chief decorator of the Paris Opéra. He designed the sets—occasionally collaborating with one of his colleagues—for Didelot's *Flore et Zéphyre* (1815), Albert's *Cendrillon* (1823), Aumer's *La Somnambule* (1827) and *La Belle au bois dormant* (1829), Taglioni's *La Sylphide* (1832) and *La Fille du Danube* (1836), Coralli's *Giselle* (1841), and Mazilier's *Le Diable à quatre* (1845). In 1822 he introduced gas lighting for the first time to light the stage.

Cieplinski, Jan (*b* Warsaw, 1900, *d* Brooklyn, 17 Apr. 1972). Pol. dancer, choreographer, and teacher. Studied at Warsaw B. School; became a member of the op. house where he soon started to ch. He made an international career, working for many cos. abroad; returned to Warsaw from time to time. Cos. with which he has been assoc. include Pavlova's, Bs. Russes de Diaghilev (1925–7), Royal Swed. B. (1927–31), Budapest State Op. B. (1932–5), B. of the Teatro Colón, B. Polonais, and Anglo-Pol. B. From London, where he opened a studio in 1950 at the Legat school, he went to New York in 1959, heading his own b. school. As a ch. he became known through his bs. to mus.

by such Pol. composers as Moniuszko, Moszkowski, and Szymanowski.

Cimarosiana. Divertissement; ch. Massine; mus. Cimarosa; déc. Sert. Prod. 8 Jan. 1924, Bs. Russes de Diaghilev, Monte Carlo, with Nemchinova, Tchernicheva, Sokolova, Idzikovsky, Woizikovsky, Vilzak. This is the final divertissement from Cimarosa's op. *Le Astuzie femminili*, which Diaghilev had presented complete at the Paris Opéra in 1920.

Cincinnati Ballet Company, The. Founded in 1962 as a regional non-professional co., now called Cincinnati/New Orleans B. Since 1971 it has been run as a fully professional troupe, serving as the city's resident repertory b. co. Its ds. perform a repertory of bs., most of which have been specially ch. by McLain, Sabline, Truitte, and Jasinski. The co. works closely with its b. school, which is part of The Univ. of Cincinnati College-Conservatory of Music, whose faculty is headed by Markova, Manchester, Truitte, Sabline, and others. David McLain was art. dir. to 1984, then Frederick Franklin was acting dir. Ivan Nagy art. dir. from 1986.

Cinderella (orig. Russ. title *Zolushka*—also Fr. *Cendrillon*, Ital. *Cenerentola*, Ger. *Aschenbrödel*). B. in 3 acts and 7 scenes; libr. Nicolai Volkov; mus. Prokofiev; ch. Zakharov; déc. Pyotr Williams; cond. Fayer. Prod. 21 Nov. 1945, Bolshoi Th., Moscow, with Lepeshinskaya and Gabovich. Based on Perrault's famous fairytale. Other prods. of the b. with different ch. by K. Sergeyev (Leningrad, 1946), Ashton (déc. J.-D. Malclès, 23 Dec. 1948, Sadler's Wells Ballet, Cov. Gdn., London, with Shearer and Somes), Orlikowsky (co., of R. de Larrain, Paris, 1963), Vinogradov (Novosibirsk, 1964), Stevenson (National B. of Washington, 1970, London Festival B., 1973), *et al.* Film prod. of the Bolshoi version 1961. Different b. treatments by Duport (Vienna, 1813), Reisinger (Moscow, 1871), Petipa (mus. Baron Schell, St. Petersburg, 1893), E. Graeb (mus. J. Strauss, Berlin, 1901), J. Hassreiter (mus. J. Strauss, Vienna, 1908), A. Howard (mus. Weber, B. Rambert, 1935), Fokine (mus. F. d'Erlanger, B. Russe de Colonel de Basil, London, 1938), de Warren (mus. J. Strauss, Northern B. Th., 1979), and Darrell (mus. Rossini, The Scottish B., 1979). See also *Aschenbrödel*.

Cintolesi, Ottavio (*b* Santiago de Chile, 14 Apr. 1924). Chilean dancer, choreographer, and b. director. Studied at the D. Conservatory of Univ. of Chile with Uthoff, Jooss, Poliakova, and V. Sulima. Joined National B. of Chile in 1946, becoming principal d. and ch. in 1948, b. master in 1950. Has taught at D. Conservatory of Univ. of Chile 1948–52, later also in Paris, Washington, New York, Chicago, San Francisco, etc. B. master and ch. of Charrat's co., 1954–6. Founder dir. and chief ch. of Santiago Municipal B. 1958–66. Then worked in Florence, Zurich, and with B. Th.

Contemporain before becoming b. dir. of Bonn Municipal Th. in 1973. Since 1979 again with Santiago Municipal B. Has ch. many bs. Married to the d. Irena Milovan.

Circe. Ballet in 1 act; libr. and ch. Graham; mus. Hovhaness; set Noguchi; light. Rosenthal. Prod. 6 Sep. 1963, M. Graham and D. Co., Prince of Wales Th., London, with Hinkson, Ross, Clive Thompson. 'The world Ulysses sees, in Martha Graham's adaptation of the myth of Circe, is his own: that inner world of bestialities and enchantments where one discovers what it costs to choose to be human' (programme note). The work was created as a homage to Robin Howard. Other b. versions of the same myth in *Ballet comique de la reine* (1581), a b. de cour of the Comte de Savoy (1627), Joseph Salomon's *L'isola incantata di Circe la Maga* (Venice, 1764), and W. Egk's b. op. *C.* (Berlin, 1948).

Circus Polka. For a young elephant; mus. Stravinsky; ch. Balanchine; cost. Norman Bel Geddes. Prod. Spring 1942, Barnum and Bailey Circus, Madison Square Garden, New York. The leading elephant's name was Modoc. Balanchine arranged this circus number for 50 elephants and 50 beautiful girls as an 'original ch. tour de force'. It received no fewer than 425 perfs. Later versions by A. Carter (Munich, 1957), P. Taylor (Spoleto, 1960), and Robbins (New York City B., 1972).
BIBL.: E. W. White, 'C.P.' in *Stravinsky* (London, 1966); G. Balanchine and F. Mason, *Balanchine's Complete Stories of the Great Ballets* (Garden City, N.Y., 1977).

Ciseaux (Fr., scissors). More correctly pas ciseaux. A scissor-like movement, during which the feet open to a wide second position sur les pointes, or during a jump the opening of both legs to the 2nd position en l'air. Not to be confused with *sissonne.

City Center Joffrey Ballet. See *Joffrey Ballet.*

Civic Ballet. See *Regional Ballet Movement.*

Clarke, Mary (*b* London, 23 Aug. 1923). Brit. writer on b. Editor of *The Dancing Times* since 1963. London correspondent of *Dance Magazine* 1943–55, then of *Dance News* 1955–70. Assistant Editor and contributor to *The Ballet Annual* 1952–63. Has written for various London newspapers and weeklies. Author of *The Sadler's Wells Ballet—A History and an Appreciation* (London, 1955), *Dancers of Mercury, the Story of Ballet Rambert* (London, 1962), *Ballet, An Illustrated History* (with C. Crisp, London, 1973), *Making a Ballet* (with Crisp, London, 1974), *The Encyclopedia of Dance & Ballet* (with D. Vaughan, 1977), *Design for Ballet* (with Crisp, 1978), and *The History of Dance* (with Crisp, 1981). Sections on d. in *Man the Artist* (1964) and *Encyclopedia Britannica* (1974).

Clarke, Paul (*b* Byfleet, 10 Aug. 1947, *d* London, 12 Sep. 1976). Brit. dancer. Studied at Royal B.

School, joining Royal B. in 1964; promoted soloist in 1966 and principal d. in 1968. D. the premier danseur roles of the standard repertory. Left the Royal B. at the end of 1973 for London Festival B., where Moreland ch. *Prodigal Son* for him (1974).

Clauss, Heinz (*b* Esslingen, 17 Feb. 1935). Ger. dancer and b. school director. Studied with Robert Mayer in Stuttgart and with Kiss, entered Stuttgart B. in 1951, transferred to Zurich in 1957, d. as soloist at the Hamburg State Op. 1959–67, when he returned to Stuttgart. Dir. of Stuttgart Cranko B. School since 1976. Created leading parts in Cranko's *Onegin* (new version 1967), *Présence* (1968), *Taming of the Shrew* (1969), *Brouillards* (1970), and MacMillan's *Miss Julie* (1970). He was a splendid Balanchine stylist, with Apollo as one of his very best roles, and has occasionally been asked to reproduce Balanchine bs. for other cos.
BIBL.: E. Herf, 'H. C.', *Ballet Today* (1966/1–2); K. Geitel, 'H. C.' in *Ballet 1967* (Velber, 1967).

Clavé, Antoni (*b* Barcelona, 5 Apr. 1913). Span. painter. Created the designs for Nevada's *Los Caprichos* (1946), Petit's *Carmen* (1949), *Ballabile* (1950), and *Deuil en 24 heures* (1957), and Page's *Revanche* (1951).

Clayden, Pauline (*b* London, 1922). Brit. dancer. Studied at Cone B. School; d. with London B., B. Rambert, and as a soloist with Sadler's Wells B. 1942–56, sharing many of Fonteyn's modern parts and creating roles in de Valois' *Promenade* (1943), Helpmann's *Miracle in the Gorbals* (1944), Ashton's *Cinderella* (1948), Cranko's *Bonne-Bouche* (1952), and Howard's *Veneziana* (1953). Now with Inner London Educ. Authority youth service. Her son, Paul C., is also a dancer.

Cléopâtre (orig. called *Une Nuit d'Egypte*, or Russ. *Egipetskiye nochi*). Ballet in 1 act; libr. and ch. Fokine; mus. Arensky; set O. Allegri; cost. M. Zandin. Prod. 21 Mar. 1908, Maryinsky Th., St. Petersburg, with Pavlova, Gerdt, Preobrajenska, Nijinsky. An Egyptian romance between Cleopatra and the slave Amoûn, who must inevitably die, once she has yielded to his desire. An extended version with additional pieces of mus. by Taneyev, Rimsky-Korsakov, Glinka, and Glazunov, newly designed by Bakst, was given by the co., of Diaghilev on 2 June 1909, Th. du Châtelet, Paris with Rubinstein, Pavlova, Fokine, Karsavina, Nijinsky.
BIBL.: C. W. Beaumont, 'C.' in *Complete Book of Ballets* (London, 1951).

Clerc, Florence (*b* Paris, 1951). Fr. dancer. Studied at Paris Op. B. School, joining its co., 1967, appointed danseuse étoile 1975. Bronze Medal (Tokyo, 1976). Married to the d. Ch. Jude.

Clerico, Francesco (*b c.* 1755, *d* after 1833). Ital. dancer, choreographer, and composer. He was a pupil of Noverre, working mainly in Vienna,

Venice, and Milan, ch. a great number of mythological bs., for some of which he himself composed the mus.

BIBL.: entry 'C., F.' in *Enciclopedia dello spettacolo.*

Clifford, John (*b* Hollywood, 12 June 1947). Amer. dancer and choreographer. Studied with Irina Kosmovska, Loring, and at School of Amer. B.; joined New York City B. in 1967, promoted principal d. in 1973. Created roles in Balanchine's *Glinkiana* (1967) and *Variations pour une porte et un soupir* (1974), Robbins' *Dances at a Gathering* (1969), and Bolender's *Piano-Rag-Music* (1972). Ch. a Los Angeles summer stock prod. of *West Side Story* when only 16 years old, then for New York City B. *Stravinsky Symphony* (in C, 1968), *Fantasies* (mus. Vaughan Williams, 1969—also for Ger. Op. Berlin, 1972), *Prelude, Fugue and Riffs* (mus. Bernstein, 1969), *Sarabande and Dance* (mus. Debussy, 1970), *Symphony in E flat* (mus. Stravinsky, 1972), and *Bartok No. 3* (Piano concerto, 1974); for Royal Winnipeg B. *Concert Fantasy* mus. Tchaikovsky, 1971); and for Ger. Op. Berlin *Gershwin Concerto* (1972). Founded Los Angeles B. 1973.

Cloud Gate Dance Theatre. The Taiwan co. of about 25 dancers was established by Lin Hwai-min, who functions as its artistic dir. and chief ch., in 1973. Its name derives from the oldest existing Chin. dance and it aims for a synthesis of trad. Chin. dancing (incl. that of the classic Peking Op.) and contemporary dance techniques. It also tours abroad and appeared first in the U.S. in 1979 and in Eur. in 1981.

Clog Dance. A rustic d. in wooden-soled shoes, originating from Ireland and Lancashire. A very popular b. example occurs in Ashton's *La Fille mal gardée*, where it is performed by Mother Simone.

Clouser, James (*b* Rochester, N.Y., 1935). Amer. dancer, b. master, and choreographer. Studied with Caton, Schwezoff, and Vilzak; started to d. in summer stock in 1956, joining Amer. B. Th. in 1957 and royal Winnipeg B. in 1959; appointed soloist and eventually b. master of the co., Today pursues a freelance career, with his wife Sonja Zarek. Ch. Orff's *Carmina Burana* for Houston B. in 1974; artistic dir. 1975–6. Began a Texas trilogy with *Allen's Landing* (mus. Fisher Tull, 1975).

Clowns, The. Ballet in 1 act; ch. Arpino; mus. H. Kay; cost. Edith Bel Geddes. Prod. 28 Feb. 1968, City Center Joffrey B., with Blankshine, Goodman, Zomosa. Clowns act out the duality of man: his urge to destruction of himself and others, and his fierce will to survive.

Clustine, Ivan (*b* Moscow, 10 Aug. 1862, *d* Nice, 21 Nov. 1941). Russ. dancer, b. master, and choreographer. Studied at Bolshoi B. School, joining Bolshoi B. in 1878; promoted premier danseur in 1886 and b. master in 1898. Opened a b. school in Paris in 1903; promoted b. master of

the Opéra 1909–14, then with Pavlova 1914–31, after which he pursued a career as teacher and freelance b. master and ch. Ch. some of the favourite bs. of the Pavlova repertory; *The Fairy Doll*, excerpts from *Sleeping Beauty* and *Raymonda*, and the famous *Gavotte Pavlova.*

BIBL.: S. Sarabelle, 'A la mémoire d'I.C.', with list of bs. and activities, *Les Saisons de la danse* (1973/12).

Clytemnestra. Ballet in 2 acts, with prologue and epilogue; libr., ch., and cost Graham; mus. Halim El-Dabh; sets Noguchi; light. Rosenthal. Prod. 1 Apr. 1958, M. Graham and D. Group Co., Adelphi Th., New York, with Graham, Ross, Paul Taylor, Yuriko. A full-length work, based on Aeschylus' *Oresteia*, it develops as a re-enactment of the famous events in Mycenae, while C. waits in the Underworld for the decision of the gods about her eternal fate. Other bs. dealing with the same subject were Noverre's *Agamemnon Revenged* (mus. Aspelmayer, Vienna, 1772), T. Gsovsky's *Black Sun* (mus. H. F. Harting, Munic. Op. Berlin, 1959), Charrat's *Electre* (mus. Pousseur, 1960), Helpmann's *Elektra* (mus. M. Arnold, Royal B., 1963), and Dolgushin's *C.* (mus. Gluck, Maly B., 1972). See also *Elektra.*

Coast of Happiness (also *Shore of Happiness* or *The Happy Coast*, orig. Russ. title: *Bereg schastya*). Ballet in 4 acts; libr. P. Abolimov; ch. Bourmeister and I. Kurilov; mus. A. Spadavecchia; déc. B. Volkov and E. Archangelskaya. Prod. 6 Nov. 1948, Stanislavsky and Nemirovich-Danchenko Music Th., Moscow. The b. tells of the growing up of Natasha and the three pioneers Petia, Kostia, and Tolia and their heroism during the Great Patriotic War.

BIBL.: M. G. Swift, in *The Art of the Dance in the U.S.S.R.* (Notre Dame, Ind., 1968).

Coast of Hope (also *Shore of Hope*, orig. Russ. title; *Bereg nadezhdy*). Ballet in 3 acts; libr. Slonimsky; ch. Belsky; mus. A. Petrov; déc. V. Dorrer. Prod. 16 June 1959, Kirov Th., Leningrad, with A. Makarov, Osipenko. The b. shows two different fishing villages, the one on the Sov. side of the sea, friendly, happy, and full of solidarity, the one on the other side, unfriendly, hostile, and oppressive. A Sov. fisherman is shipwrecked on the other shore, where the people imprison him and try to win him over. But he remains steadfast to his own people, and so one day the walls of his prison miraculously burst apart and he finds himself home with his comrades on the right side of the shore.

BIBL.: M. G. Swift, in *The Art of the Dance in the U.S.S.R.* (Notre Dame, Ind., 1968).

Cocteau, Jean (*b* Maison-Lafitte, near Paris, 5 July 1889, *d* Milly-le-Forêt, 11 Oct. 1963). Fr. writer and designer. He met Diaghilev when very young, and designed posters and wrote scenarios and publicity handouts for his co. Contributed the librs. for Fokine's *Le Dieu bleu* (1912), Massine's

Parade (1917), and Nijinska's *Le Train bleu* (1924)—and for other occasions *Le Boeuf sur le toit* (Fratellini Brothers, 1920), *Les Mariés de la Tour Eiffel* (ch. Börlin, 1921), *Le jeune homme et la mort* (ch. Petit, 1946), *L'Amour et son amour* (ch. Babilée, 1948), *Phèdre* (ch. Lifar, 1950), and *The Lady and the Unicorn* (ch. Rosen, 1953); for the 2 last he also created the décor. Wrote a great number of essays and articles dealing with all kinds of d. and was one of the most inspiring figures of the international b. scene of his time. In 1955 he became a member of the Académie Française. A prod. *Cocteau et la Danse* (with *Le Fils d'air*, *L'Ange Heurtebise*, and *Les Mariés de la Tour Eiffel*) was staged by the Mudra Institute and B. of the 20th Century in 1972 at the Brussels Cirque Royal—another b. prod. about C.'s life, *Poppy*, by G. Murphy (Sydney Dance Th., 1979).
BIBL.: C. Wildmann, 'J.C. and the Ballet', *Dancing Times* (1973/10).

Code of Terpsichore. Book by Blasis, first published in London in 1828 (only very few copies, because the publisher went bankrupt), 1830 in Paris under the title *Manuel complet de la danse*, 1831 edition in London (as *The Art of Dancing*); considered throughout the 19th century the standard work on classic-academic d. technique. In addition it offered a history of the d. and general essays on d. and mime.

Coe, Kelvin (*b* Melbourne, 1946). Austral. dancer. Studied with Downes and Rex Reid. Joined Austral. B. 1962, becoming soloist in 1966 and principal d. in 1968. Has also appeared as a guest with London Festival B. With Sydney Dance Co. from 1982. Silver Medal (Moscow, 1973); O.B.E. (1980).

Cohan, Robert (*b* New York, 1925). Amer. dancer, choreographer, teacher, and b. director. Studied with Graham, dancing with her co., 1946–57 and 1962–9, becoming her co-dir. in 1966. In 1958 he opened a school in Boston, also teaching at Graham School, Juilliard School, Connecticut College, and New York Univ. Appeared occasionally on Broadway and in films and from 1959 with his own group, for which he did several chs. Art. dir. London Contemp. D. Th. and assoc. with Lond. Sch. Contemp. D. 1967–83, then member of directorate and art. adviser, Contemp. D. Trust. He ch. *Eclipse*, *Sky* (both mus. Eugene Lester, 1967), *Hunter of Angels* (mus. B. Maderna, 1967), *Cell* (mus. Ronald Lloyd, 1969), *Stages* (mus. A. Nordheim and B. Downes, 1971), *People Alone* (mus. Downes, 1972), *Mass* (mus. Vladimir Rodzianko, 1973, rev. 1977 with mus. J. Weir), *Waterless Method of Swimming Instruction* (mus. Downes, 1974), *Myth* (mus. Burt Alcantara, 1975, renamed *Masque of Separation*), and *Stabat Mater* (mus. Vivaldi, 1975), *Class* (mus. J. Keliehor, 1975), *Nympheas* (mus. Debussy, 1976), *Khamsin* (mus. Downes, 1976), *Forest* (mus. B. Hodgson, 1977), *Ice* (mus. M. Subotnick, 1978),

Eos (mus. B. Guy, 1978), *Rondo* (mus. J. H. McDowell, 1979), *Songs, Lamentations and Praises* (mus. G. Burgon, 1979), *Field* (mus. Hodgson, 1980), *Dances of Love and Death* (mus. C. Davis and C. Nancarrow, 1981). Dir. Gulbenkian Nat. Ch. Summer School, Guildford, 1977, 1978. Artistic adviser, Batsheva D. Co. 1980.
BIBL.: Interviews with R. C., *Dance and Dancers* (1967/9, 1972/2, and 1976/4).

Cohen, Frederic (orig. Fritz C.; *b* Bonn, 1904, *d* New York, 9 Mar. 1967). Ger.-Amer. conductor and composer. After his univ. studies he became a repetiteur for Georgi in Hanover in 1924 and eventually musical dir. of the Jooss co., 1932–42, writing or adapting the mus. for *The Green Table* (1932), *Ball in Old Vienna* (after Lanner, 1932), *Seven Heroes* (after Purcell, 1933), *The Mirror* (1935), *Johann Strauss, To-night!* (1935), and *A Spring Tale* (1939).
BIBL.: A. Chujoy, 'C., Dr.F.' in *Dance Encyclopedia* (New York, 1967).

Cohen, Selma Jeanne (*b* Chicago, 18 Sep. 1920). Amer. writer on the dance. Educated Univ. of Chicago. Studied with McRae, Loring, Graham, Holm, and Limón. Has taught d. history and aesthetics at many schools and colleges throughout the U.S.A. Contributor on d. to a great number of Amer. and foreign publications. Editor of *Dance Perspectives* 1959–75. Editor of *The Modern Dance: Seven Statements of Belief* (Middletown, Conn. 1966), *Doris Humphrey: An Artist First* (Middletown, 1972) and *Dance as a Theatre Art: Source Readings in Dance History* (New York, 1974). Now preparing the forthcoming *International Encyclopedia of the Dance*. Dance Magazine Award 1981.

Cohen, Ze'eva (*b* Tel Aviv, 15 Aug. 1940). Amer. dancer, teacher, and choreographer. Studied with G. Kraus, R. Gluck, Sokolow, and at Juilliard School of Music. Performed with Juilliard D. Ensemble, and the cos. of Sokolow and Lang. Started to give solo concerts in New York 1971, touring with her programme in the U.S.A., Europe, and Israel. Now lectures on modern d. at Princeton Univ.
BIBL.: I. M. Fanger, 'Z.: A Close-Up', *Dance Magazine* (1976/3).

Cole, Jack (*b* New Brunswick, 1913, *d* Los Angeles, 17 Feb. 1974). Amer. dancer and choreographer. Studied with St. Denis and T. Shawn, dancing with Shawn's Men D. in 1933, later also with Humphrey-Weidman. Toured the nightclub circuit with his own group 1936–7, after which he worked as a ch. on Broadway and for Hollywood (*Kismet*, 1953; *Jamaica*, 1957; *Foxy*, 1964; *Man of La Mancha*, 1965; *Mata Hari*, 1967). For Harkness B. he ch. *Requiem for Jimmy Dean* (mus. Ronald Herder, 1968).

Coleman, Michael (*b* Beacontree, 10 June 1940). Brit. dancer. Started to study tap d., then at Royal

B. School. Became a member of the touring co., of the Royal B. in 1959; joined the main co., in 1965, promoted principal d. in 1969. A splendid technician, he dances mainly demicaractère roles of the standard repertory; his best parts are in Robbins's *Dances at a Gathering* and *The Concert*, Blue Bird, in Ashton's *La Fille mal gardée* and *Symphonic Variations*, and Nureyev's *La Bayadère*. Created roles in MacMillan's *Elite Syncopations, Anastasia, Mayerling*, and other bs.
BIBL.: J. Gruen, in *The Private World of Ballet* (New York,1975).

Collier, Lesley (*b* Orpington, 13 Mar. 1947). Brit. dancer. Studied with Irene Ayres, at Royal Academy of Dancing and Royal B. School. Joined Royal B. in 1965, promoted principal d. in 1972, and dances all the ballerina roles in the classical repertory, incl. Princess Aurora in *Sleeping Beauty* at the Royal B.'s 50th anniversary perf., 1981. Created roles incl. MacMillan's *Anastasia* (1971) and *Four Seasons* (1975), van Manen's *Four Schumann Pieces* (1975), Ashton's *Rhapsody* and Tetley's *Dances of Albion* (both 1980). Married to the d. critic N. Dromgoole.
BIBL.: S. Goodman, 'L. C.', *Dance Magazine* (1972/8).

Collin, Darja (*b* Amsterdam, 19 Nov. 1902, *d* Florence, 28 Mar. 1967). Dutch dancer, b. director, and teacher. Studied with Preobrajenska, Wigman, and with Trümpy in Berlin, d. in Ger. and with the Ital. Op. in Amsterdam. During the 1930s she became known as a modern recital d. touring widely, occasionally appearing with von Swaine as her partner. In 1949 she founded the Netherlands Op. B., from which grew the present Dutch National B. Moved to Florence in 1952 where she opened a school.

Collins, Janet (*b* New Orleans, 2 Mar. 1917). Amer. dancer and teacher. Studied with Craske, Maracci, Slavenska, Bolm, Tudor, Holm, Horton, and Humphrey. Gave her first solo recitals in Los Angeles. Came to New York in 1949, appearing in the Cole Porter musical *Out of this World*. Prima ballerina of Met. Op. House 1951–4. Solo concert tours throughout the U.S. and Canada 1952–5. Has taught at Marymount Manhattan College, Harkness House, School of Amer. B., and San Francisco B. School. Dance Magazine Award (1959); Donaldson Award (1950–1).

Cologne. Though d. plays an important role in the city's carnival revelries, with every carnival association maintaining its own d.-corps to perform at its official ceremonies, th. d. in former times hardly ventured beyond the confines of op. and operetta. The occasional 'Ballettabende' were insignificant, with 1 or 2 exceptions: the world premiere of Bartók's *Miraculous Mandarin* was given here in 1926 (produced rather than ch. by Hans Strohbach) and immediately taken off again because of moral objections from the Lord Mayor, Konrad Adenauer—and the first Europ. prod. of Stravinsky's *Sacre du printemps* outside the Diaghilev orbit took place here in 1930 (ch. by Lazar Galpern). Things improved somewhat after 1945, and during the b. directorship of Milloss in 1960–3 and under his successor T. Bolender in 1963–6 C. attracted international attention for the first time. With the transfer of the Krefeld International Summer Academy of D. (founded in 1957) to C. and with the establishment of the Institut für Bühnentanz (Institute for Th. Dance) and the acquisition of the previously Hamburg-based Tanzarchiv (which is a library and d. collection, connected through its dir. Kurt Peters, with the magazine *Tanzarchiv*, of which he was chief editor) in 1961, C. gradually became one of the focal points of the Ger. d. scene, with the Summer Academy regularly drawing some 500 students, who come from many countries to study here for a fortnight with the best teachers from all over the world. For the 1971–2 season, the b. co., of the C. Municipal Stages was completely reorganized, taking the new name Tanz-Forum Köln, with a collective directorship, now solely controlled by Jochen Ulrich. The dancers are trained in both academic and modern classes, but the accent is clearly on modern d. and the repertory is exclusively given over to contemporary works. To emphasize the city's modern d. orientation—which has spread from here to other cities such as Bremen, Darmstadt, and Wuppertal—a Week of Modern D. is held annually in connection with the Summer Academy, with perfs. by the Tanz-Forum as well as by specially invited guest cos.
BIBL.: N McLain Stoop, 'They have the nail: a C. diary', *Dance Magazine* (1975/5).

Colombo, Vera (*b* Milan, 10 Aug. 1931). Ital. dancer. Studied at La Scala B. School and with Volkova and Tchernicheva; made her début at La Scala in 1953, since when she has become one of the best known dancers of the co., dancing the ballerina roles of the standard repertory, and often appearing on TV and as a guest abroad.

Colón, Teatro. See *Buenos Aires*.

Combat, Le. Ballet in 1 act; libr. ch. Dollar; mus. R. de Banfield; déc. Vicomtesse Marie-Laure de Noailles. Prod. 24 Feb. 1949 B. de Paris, Princes Th., London, with Charrat and Skouratoff. The b. is based on Tasso's *Jerusalem Delivered* and tells of Tancredi, a Christian knight, and Clorinda, a Saracen girl, who fights in male armour and reveals her identity only when she is dying. At first only an extended pas de deux; Dollar added 3 more knights for the New York City B. prod. of 1950, under the title *The Duel*. A different version to the same mus. by D. Parlić (Vienna, 1959).

Combattimento di Tancredi e Clorinda, Il. Scenic cantata by Claudio Monteverdi. Prod. Venice, 1624. Based on the same episode from Tasso as **Le Combat* and nowadays often performed as a b. Versions have been ch. by Gore (Ballet Workshop, 1951), Walter (Düsseldorf, 1965), Sparemblek (Paris, 1967), J. Thorpe (Northern Dance Th., 1970), Forsythe (Stuttgart, 1981), and C. Bruce (Kent Opera, Venice, 1981).

Combes, Jean (b Paris, 10 Nov. 1904). Fr. dancer, choreographer, b. master, and teacher. Studied at Paris Opéra B. School and with N. Guerra and Egorova, d. with the cos. in Bordeaux, Vichy, and Marseilles; had his first engagement as a ch. and b. master in 1936 in Rouen, from where he proceeded to Aix-les-Bains, Lausanne, Geneva, Toulouse, and the Bs. de Monte Carlo. Became b. chief of the Strasburg Opéra in 1945, and also directed the attached b. school. Has ch. about 70 bs. for the Strasbourg co. Now retired.

Comédie-Ballet. The type of comedy with a strong inclination towards b. Especially popular in the 17th and 18th century, its founders and perfectionists were Molière and Lully, with *Le Bourgeois gentilhomme* (1670) as the most famous work of their collaboration.

Comelin, Jean-Paul (b Vannes, 10 Sep. 1939). Fr. dancer, balletmaster, and choreographer. Studied with Brieux, made his début at the Paris Opéra, d. with London Festival B., at Hamburg State Op., with National B. of Washington (D.C.), Pennsylvania B., Wisconsin B. 1974. Since 1981 b. master, Stuttgart B. Has ch. individual bs.

Commedia dell'arte. The popular Ital. type of improvised comedy, with stock characters such as Harlequin, Columbine, Pantaloon, etc., which flourished from the 16th to the 18th century, has often provided the plots for b. librs., e.g. M. Petipa's *Les Millions de Harlequin* (1900), Fokine's *Carnaval* (1910), Massine's *Pulcinella* (1920), Lifar's *Salade* (1935), Tetley's *Pierrot lunaire* (1962), and MacMillan's *The Poltroon* (1972). A d.-play *The World of Harlequin* was staged by B. for All in 1973.

Communauté. Society of Fr. d.-masters and violinists founded in 1659 by Louis XIV. Its first dir. was G. Dumenoir, whose official title was Le Roi de danse et des violons. The *Académie royale de danse derived from it in 1662.

Como, William (b Williamstown, Mass., 10 Nov. 1925). Amer. writer and editor. Educated Amer. Academy of Dramatic Arts. Joined staff of *Dance Magazine* in 1954, becoming editor-in-chief in 1969—also editor of *Ballroom Dance Magazine*, which he transformed into *After Dark* in 1968. Author of 2-volume *Anatomy for the Dance* (with Raoul Gelabert).

Compan, Le Sieur. He published a very important treatise on d. in Paris in 1787, which he dedicated to Mlle Guimard: *Dictionnaire de danse, contenant l'histoire, les régles et les principes de cet art.*

Comus. B. in 2 scenes; ch. Helpmann; mus.

Purcell (arr. C. Lambert); déc. O. Messel. Prod. 14 Jan. 1942, Sadler's Wells B., New Th., London, with Helpmann, Fonteyn, J. Hart, Paltenghi. Based on Milton's Masque, it was a mimed play (with 2 of the original speeches retained) with incidental dances, in which the magician C., the son of Bacchus and Circe, tries to seduce the Lady, who has lost her way in the forest, but is defeated by the strength of her chastity. A revival of Milton's original masque with long dance sequences was staged by Leslie French in 1946 for International B.

Con Amore. Ballet in 1 act and 3 scenes; libr. James Graham Luján; ch. L. Christensen; mus. Rossini; déc. James Bodrero. Prod. 10 Mar. 1953, San Francisco B., San Francisco, with Sally Bailey, Nancy Johnson, Danielian. The b., which is set to three overtures by Rossini, tells of a bandit, who is captured by some Amazons and who has great difficulty in resisting their amorous advances. Revived for several cos.
BIBL.: G. Balanchine, 'C. A.' in *Balanchine's New Complete Stories of the Great Ballets* (Garden City, N.Y., 1968).

Concert, The. Ballet in 1 act; ch. Robbins; mus. Chopin (partly orchestrated by H. Kay); cost I. Sharaff. Prod. 6 Mar. 1956, New York City B., City Center, N.Y. with LeClercq, Mounsey, Curley, Bolender. A sequence of humorous sketches, in which the members of a group of concert-goers enact their flights of fancy while they are listening to a recital of piano pieces by Chopin. A revised version which Robbins mounted for the Spoleto Festival of 1958 had 2 specially designed act-drops by Saul Steinberg. Revived for Royal B. in 1975 with new act-drops by Edward Gorey.
BIBL.: P. Brinson and C. Crisp, in *Ballet & Dance* (Newton Abbot, 1980).

Concert Champêtre. Poulenc's Concerto for Harpsichord and Orchestra (1938) has been ch. several times; e.g. by Walter (Düsseldorf, 1965), Adama (Bremen, 1965), and Lazzini (Paris, 1967).

Concerto. Ballet in 3 movements; ch. MacMillan; mus. Shostakovich; déc. J. Rose. Prod. 30 Nov. 1966, Ger. Op. Berlin, with Carli, Kapuste, Seymour, Holz, Kesselheim. The plotless b. reflects the various moods of Shostakovich's second Piano Concerto, op. 102. MacMillan staged it as his first new b. when he became b. dir. of the Berlin co. Revived for Amer. B. Th. (18 May 1967) and Royal B. Touring Section (26 May 1967) as well as for several other cos.
BIBL.: P. Brinson and C. Crisp, in *Ballet & Dance* (Newton Abbot, 1980).

Concerto Barocco. Ballet in 3 movements; ch. Balanchine; mus. Bach; déc. Berman. Prod. 29 May 1941, Amer. B. Caravan, Hunter College Th., New York, with Marie Jeanne, Mary Jane Shea, Dollar. Set to Bach's Concerto in D minor for Two Violins, the plotless b. develops as a visual comment upon and ornamentation of the mus. It has very often been revived, mostly without any décor, d. in practice clothes (first prod. New York City B.: 11 Oct. 1948).

BIBL.: G. Balanchine, 'C. B.' in *Balanchine's New Complete Stories of the Great Ballets* (Garden City, N.Y., 1968).

Concurrence, La. Ballet in 1 act; libr. and déc. A. Derain; ch. Balanchine; mus. Auric. Prod. 12 Apr. 1932, B. Russe de Monte Carlo, Monte Carlo, with Stepanova, Toumanova, Woizikovsky. The b. tells of the competition of 2 tailors, who quarrel in the street to attract customers.

Cone Ripman Schools. Emerged in 1944 from the schools which Grace Cone had founded in 1919 in Brighton and Olive Ripman in 1922 in Croydon and London. Both schools had already started to cooperate somewhat earlier, establishing an affiliated institute in Tring, north of London, during the Second World War for those pupils who had been evacuated. Among their pupils were Gilpin, G. Lynne, K. Beckett, J. Andrews, Arova, and Algeranova. In 1962 the Arts Educational Trust was established and the school, which today operates in Golden Lane House in the City of London, was renamed The Arts Educational Schools.

Confessional. Ballet in 1 act; ch. Gore; mus. Sibelius; déc. A. Howard. Prod. 9 May 1941, Oxford B. Club, Oxford, with S. Gilmour, Gore. Based on Robert Browning's poem and on Sibelius's Suite from *Pelléas,* the b. tells of the despair of a girl who betrays her lover in the confessional only to discover that as a result he is executed by the Inquisition. It was later included in the B. Rambert repertory.

Confetti. Ballet in 1 act, ch. Arpino; mus. Rossini. Prod. 3 Mar. 1970, City Center Joffrey Ballet, City Center, New York, with Corkle, Barnard, R. Wright. A bravura pas de six, performed to the overture from *Semiramide.*

Conley, Sandra (*b* Hatfield, 24 Oct. 1943). Brit. dancer. Studied with Stella Wallace at the Sutton School of Dancing and Royal B. School, made her début with the Royal B. Touring Co., in 1962, eventually promoted soloist, and transferred to larger co., in 1970, appointed principal d. 1980. Dances leading roles in the standard repertory and created leading parts in Tudor's *Knight Errant* (1968), Ashton's *Creatures of Prometheus* (1969), Cauley's *Symphonie pastorale* (1970), MacMillan's *Manon* (1974), and Neumeier's *The Fourth Symphony* (1977). Married to the d. Adrian Grater.

Connecticut College School of Dance. The 6-week summer d. courses which have regularly been held every year since 1948 at Connecticut College in New England have become one of the foremost platforms of modern d. in the U.S. For years Humphrey was the leading spirit of the enterprise, though most of the top personalities of the Amer. modern d. scene have been connected with it at one time or another. Special emphasis is put on close working contacts between teachers and students, the results were shown in the annual perfs. of the *Amer. D. Festival.

BIBL.: T. Borek, 'The Connecticut College Amer. Dance Festival' (*Dance Perspectives* 50).

Connor, Laura (*b* Portsmouth, 1946). Brit. dancer. Studied with Dugan and Butler and at Royal B. School. Joined Royal B., becoming soloist in 1971 and principal d. in 1973. Created roles in MacMillan's *Manon* (1974), *Mayerling* (1978), and *Isadora* (1981). Left Royal B. 1982.

Conservatory, or a Proposal of Marriage Through a Newspaper (orig. Dan. title: *Konservatoriet eller Et Avisfrieri*). Vaudeville Ballet in 2 acts; ch. Bournonville; mus. H. S. Paulli. Prod. 6 May 1849, Royal Dan. B., Copenhagen. The b. incl. a dancing class of the Paris Conservatory, showing a typical Vestris class, originally against the background of a complex plot of amorous intrigues. A revised version, of the classroom scene only, by H. Lander and V. Borchsenius was given in Copenhagen in 1941 and this has occasionally been revived in recent years (also in the repertory of the Joffrey B. since 1969, London Festival B. since 1973). A new ch. for the orig. plot was staged by N.B. Larsen at Tivoli Pantomime Th.

BIBL.: P. Brinson and C. Crisp, in *Ballet & Dance* (Newton Abbot, 1980).

Constant, Marius (*b* Bucharest, 7 Feb. 1925). Fr. composer and conductor. Wrote the mus. for Béjart's *Haut Voltage* (1956), Petit's *La Peur* (1956), *Contre-pointe* (1956), *Cyrano de Bergerac* (1956), *Eloge de la folie* (1966), *Paradise Lost* (1967), *24 Préludes* (1967), *Nana* (1976), and Marceau's *Candide* (1971). Was musical dir. of Petit's Bs. de Paris and is now Directeur mus. de la danse at the Paris Opéra.

BIBL.: L. Gordon, 'Rencontre avec M.C.', *Les Saisons de la danse* (1973/3).

Constantia. Ballet in 3 movements; ch. Dollar; mus. Chopin; set Armistead; cost. Grace Houston. Prod. 31 Oct. 1944, B. International, International Th., New York, with Marie Jeanne, Dollar, Yvonne Patterson. Set to Chopin's Piano Concerto No. 2 in F minor, the b. is tinged with the fervour of Chopin's feeling for the singer Constantia Gladowska, to whom he dedicated the Larghetto movement. Has been revived for several cos. The b. is a revision of Dollar's first ch. work, *Classic B.* (first and third movements ch. Dollar, second ch. Balanchine), created 1937 for Amer. B. at Met. Op. Ho.

BIBL.: G. Balanchine, 'C.' in *Balanchine's New Complete Stories of the Great Ballets* (Garden City, N.Y., 1968).

Contract improvisation. Improvised movement system based on 'the communication between two moving bodies and their combined relationship to the physical laws that govern their motion: gravity, momentum, friction and inertia'. Initiated in New York, 1972, by *S. Paxton, former d. with M. Cunningham, who brought professional co. to London, 1981. Publishes *Contact Quarterly* (ed. N. Stark Smith).

Contemporary Ballet Trust. Set up by Robin Howard in 1964 to subsidize Eng. dancers wishing to study at the Graham School in New York. Renamed Contemporary Dance Trust in 1971 after establishing the *London Contemporary D. Th. and the London School of Contemporary D. with a London headquarters at The Place, a former army drill-hall converted into studios and a studio theatre, of which the freehold is now owned by the Trust.

BIBL.: 'The C.B.T.—The Background to a New Venture', *Dancing Times* (1969/9).

Contemporary Dance Theatre. See *London Contemporary Dance Theatre.*

Contes Russes. Ballet with prologue and 4 scenes; ch. Massine; mus. Liadov; déc. Larionov. Prod. 11 May 1917, Bs. Russes de Diaghilev, Th. du Châtelet, Paris, with Sokolova, Idzikowsky, Tchernicheva, Massine. The b. develops as a sequence of episodes from Russ. fairy-tales and folklore. Its central Kikimora scene was premièred on 25 Aug. 1916 in San Sebastian.

BIBL.: C. W. Beaumont, 'C. R.' in *Complete Book of Ballets* (London, 1951).

Contraction—Release. Terms from the Graham technique of modern d. defining the moments of complete inhalation of breath (contraction) and of utter exhalation (release). The Central Eur. school of Laban and his followers preferred the Ger. pair of contrasts *Anspannung and Abspannung.

Contredanse. Probably derived from the Eng. country d. which was originally a folk d. from before 1600, and developed into a social d. which is described in 1659 in John Playford's *The English Dancing Master* as existing in 2 different types: (1) Longways, in which the couples face each other in rows, and (2) Rounds, which are d. in circles. Both aim for rich variations of the basic patterns. At about 1685 the Eng. form appeared on the continent, where it became known as C. or Contretanz, and also as Kontertanz and Kontratanz. It was especially popular during the 18th century when it developed five variants: *quadrille, *cotillon, *anglaise, the Ger. Contretanz (Haydn, Mozart, and Beethoven), and the Fr. C. (Rameau).

Contreras, Gloria (orig. Carmen G. C. Roeniger; b. Mexico City, 15 Nov. 1934). Mex. dancer, choreographer, and teacher. Studied with Nelsy Dambre in Mexico, at School of Amer. B., and

with Carola Trier and Slavenska. D. with B. de N. Dambre, B. Concierto, formed her own G. C. D. co., in 1962 in New York, which regularly appeared during the next 8 years. Since 1970 has been dir. ch. and d. at the Taller Coreográfico de la Universidad Nacional Autónoma de México. Created many chs. for her own group as well as for other cos. and TV. Her d.-method has been taught at B. Margarita & G. C. School in Mexico City since 1950. Prize of the Union Mexicana de Cronistas de Musica (1970), Gold Medal (Guadalajara, 1972).

Cook, Bart (b Ogden, Utah, 7 June 1949). Amer. dancer. Studied with W. Christensen, P. Keeler, and at School of Amer. B. D. with B. West; joined New York City B. 1971, later became soloist, principal 1979, and asst. b. master 1981. Created leading parts in Robbins's *Scherzo fantastique* (1972), *An Evening's Waltzes* (1973), *Dybbuk Variations* (1974) and *The Four Seasons* (1979) and in Balanchine's *Vienna Waltzes* (1977).

Cooke, Kerrison (b Bournemouth, 19 Dec. 1943). Brit. dancer. Studied at the local Wessex School with Elizabeth Collins and Ida Stewart, and with E. Addison and Turner at Royal B. School; made his début in 1962 with Royal B., eventually being promoted soloist (1965) and principal d. (1968) and creating roles in Ashton's *Sinfonietta* (1967), *Creatures of Prometheus* (1970), and Layton's *O.W.* (1972). Left the co. 1973 for London Festival B. until 1979; returned as b. master to London Festival B., 1983.

Coolidge, Elizabeth Sprague (b Chicago, 20 Oct. 1864, d Cambridge, Mass., 4 Nov. 1953). Amer. pianist, composer, and patron. Established the E.S.C. Foundation at the Library of Congress in Washington, D.C. in 1925, to further the cause of contemporary mus. B. scores specially commissioned include Stravinsky's *Apollon musagète* (ch. Bolm, 1928), Hindemith's *Herodiade* (ch. Graham, 1944), Copland's *Appalachian Spring* (ch. Graham, 1944), and Chávez' *Dark Meadow* (ch. Graham, 1946).

Copenhagen. See *Royal Danish Ballet.*

Copland, Aaron (b Brooklyn, 14 Nov. 1900). Amer. composer. Wrote the mus. for the following bs.: *Hear Ye! Hear Ye!* (ch. Page, 1934), *Billy the Kid* (ch. Loring, 1938), *Rodeo* (ch. de Mille, 1942), *Appalachian Spring* (ch. Graham, 1944), and *Dance Panels in Seven Movements* (ch. Rosen, 1963). Other bs. set to his concert mus. include Tudor's *Time Table* (based on *Music for Theatre*, 1941—also used by Darrell in *Lessons in Love*, 1966, and by Ulrich in *Ballet for a Theatre*, 1973), Humphrey's *El Salon Mexico* (1943), Robbins's *The Pied Piper* (based on his Concerto for Clarinet and String Orchestra, 1951), J. Carter's *Improvisations* (based on *El Salon Mexico*, and *Danzan Cuban*, 1962), T. Ruud's *Polyandrion* (based on his *Dance Symphony*, 1973), and J. Neumeier's *Hamlet:*

Connotations (based on his *Connotations for Orchestra*, 1976).

Coppélia, ou La Fille aux yeux d'émail. Ballet in 3 acts; libr. Charles Nuitter and Saint-Léon; ch. Saint-Léon; mus. Delibes; scenery Cambon, Despléchin, Lavastre; cost. Paul Lormier. Prod. 25 May 1870, Opéra, Paris, with Bozzacchi (Swanilda) and Eugénie Fiocre (Franz). Based on E.T.A. Hoffmann's *Der Sandmann*, the b. combines the romance between Swanilda and Franz with the story of the doll-maker Coppelius, whose greatest desire is to create a doll with a soul. Franz promptly falls in love with Coppélia, whom he thinks alive, but eventually recognizes that she is just a doll and returns to Swanilda, after which the final grand divertissement sees everyone reconciled. With its touch of East European folklore (csárdás) the b. continues to enjoy undimished world-wide popularity. 1st prod. in London in a one-act version at the Empire Th. on 8 Nov. 1884 and in full-length form on the same stage on 14 May 1906 (with Genée as Swanilda in one of her very best roles). 1st New York prod. given by the Amer. Op. at the Met. Op. House on 11 Mar. 1887, with Marie Giuri and Felicita Carozzi. Other famous early versions: Telle in Vienna (1876), P. Taglioni in Berlin (1881), M. Petipa in St. Petersburg (1884), Alexander Genée in Munich (1896), and G. Glasemann and H. Beck in Copenhagen (1896). The b. has since been revived in countless versions, in most of which the role of Franz has been d. by a man (though the Paris Opéra maintained the *en travestie* casting of Franz well into the 1950s). Some of the more important recent prods. have been P. Lacotte's for the Paris Opéra (1973), Balanchine and Danilova's for the New York City B. (1974), and Petit's for Bs. de Marseille (1975). An interesting attempt at tracing the b.'s development from its original prod. to the Royal B. version of today was made in Brinson's b.-play *Two Coppélias* (Ballet for All, 1967—entirely new prod. in 1970). In 1964 BBC TV produced a studio adaptation of the prod. performed by the Royal B.
BIBL.: I. Guest, *Two Coppélias* (London, 1970).

Coq d'or, Le. See *Golden Cockerel.*

Coralli, Jean (orig. J. C. Peracini; *b* Paris 15 Jan. 1779, *d* there, 1 May 1854). Ital. dancer and choreographer. Coming from a Bolognese family he studied at Paris Opéra B. School, making his début in 1802. Ch. his 1st bs. for Vienna, Milan, Lisbon, and Marseilles. Appointed b. master at Paris Th. de Porte-Saint-Martin in 1825, he moved to the Opéra in 1831, where he created some of the most famous bs. of his time,—incl. *L'Orgie* (mus. M. E. Carafa, 1831), *La Tempête, ou L'Ile des génies* (mus. Schneitzhoeffer, 1834), *Le Diable boîteux* (mus. C. Gide, 1836), *La Chatte métamorphosée en femme* (mus. A. de Montfort, 1837), *La Tarentule* (mus. Gide, 1839), *Giselle* (in collaboration with Perrot, mus. Adam, 1841), *La Péri* (mus.

Burgmüller, 1843), *Eucharis* (mus. E. Deldevez, 1844), and *Ozai, ou L'Insulaire* (mus. Gide, 1847); also the ch. for the 1st prod. of Cherubini's op. *Ali-Baba* (1833). He was married to Teresa C., a solo-d. of the Vienna Kärntnertor Th. during his Vienna engagement.
BIBL.: I. Guest, in *The Romantic Ballet in Paris* (London, 1966).

Coralli, Vera. See *Karalli.*

Corder, Michael (*b* London, 17 Mar. 1955). Brit. dancer and choreographer. Studied Royal B. School, joined Royal B. 1973. Began to ch. for Royal B. Ch. Group from 1974, one of which bs. became his first professional prod. by Sadler's Wells Royal B. as *Rhyme nor Reason* (mus. Stravinsky), 1978. Left to join Dutch Nat. B. 1978–9, where he ch. *Lexicon.* Returned to Sadler's Wells Royal B. 1979 as soloist, and ch. *Day into Night* (mus. Martinů, 1980), and *Three Pictures* (mus. Bartók, 1981). Left co. 1981 and joined Joffrey B. in New York.

Cordua, Beatrice (*b* Hamburg, 12 Mar. 1943). Ger. dancer. Studied in Hamburg and at Royal B. School; made her début in 1959 at the Hamburg State Op., d. as a soloist in Cologne 1962–6, Frankfurt 1966–73, and since 1973 again as a principal d. at the Hamburg State Op. Has been guest-ballerina with Royal Winnipeg B.

Corelli, Juan (*b* Barcelona, 1 Nov. 1934). Span.-Fr. dancer and choreographer. Studied with Idzikowsky and Preobrajenska, d. with the Liceo Op. B. in Barcelona, B. Russe de Colonel de Basil, and Grand B. du Marquis de Cuevas, after which he pursued a career as a ch. of TV bs., occasionally also working for th. cos. (in Washington, D.C., East Berlin, and Sofia).
BIBL.: E. Herf, 'J. C.', *Ballet Today* (1961/2).

Corkle, Francesca (*b* Seattle, 2 Aug. 1952). Amer. dancer. Studied with Virginia Ryan Corkle and at Amer. B. Center. Joined City Center Joffrey B. 1967; became principal d. and created roles in Arpino's *Confetti* (1970) and *Kettentanz* (1971), and Joffrey's *Remembrances* (1974).
BIBL.: S. Goodman, 'F. C.', *Dance Magazine* (1972/4).

Cornazano, Antonio (*b* Piacenza, 1431, *d* Ferrara, *c.* 1500). Ital. dance master. Wrote his *Libro dell'arte del danzare* in 1465 (1455?), which exists only in manuscript (Codex Capponiano no. 203, Vatican Library).

Corps de ballet. Orig. the whole body of d. of a b. co., and still used in that sense at Paris Opéra. Elsewhere now indicates the group members of a b. co., (as opposed to the solo dancers). It appears in the standard classics mostly as a group, while modern bs. often use the members individually (for instance the visitors to the fair in *Petrushka*). It fulfils a function like that of the chorus in an op.

Corsaire, Le. Ballet in 3 acts and 5 scenes; libr. H. Vernoy de Saint-Georges and Mazilier; ch. Mazilier; mus. Adam and others; sets Martin, Despléchin, Cambon, and Thierry; cost. A. Albert. Prod. 23 Jan. 1856, Opéra, Paris, with Rosati, D. Segarelli. The b. is based on Lord Byron's poem *The Corsair*. Its very complicated plot centres on a Greek girl, Medora, sold into slavery; she is miraculously saved by the pirate Conrad, who becomes her lover. They have to face almost insuperable hardship, culminating in the final shipwreck—a spectacular technical feat, for which due credit was paid to the chief-machinist of the Opéra, Victor Sacré. An earlier version, ch. by F. D. Albert to mus. by Robert Bochsa, was premièred at the King's Th. London, in 1837. However, it was in the Mazilier version that the b. gained world-wide popularity. M. Petipa completely rech. it for the 1899 prod. at the St. Petersburg Maryinsky Th., for which additional mus. was used by Drigo, Minkus, and Pugni, and it is from this prod., that the perfs. derive which one can see today in the U.S.S.R. In the West only the spectacular pas de deux to mus. by Drigo is still performed—mostly credited 'after Petipa'. A film version of it in *An Evening with the Royal Ballet*, where it is d. by Fonteyn and Nureyev (British Home Entertainment, 1965). Orlikowsky staged the complete b. for the Lake Stage of the Bregenz Festival in 1975 with the Zagreb B.
BIBL.: C. W. Beaumont, 'L. C.' in *Complete Book of Ballets* (London, 1951.)

Cortesi, Antonio (*b* Pavia, Dec. 1796, *d* Florence, Apr. 1879). Ital. dancer, choreographer, and teacher. Started his career *c.* 1811; d. with various Ital. cos. Went to Lisbon as a ch. in 1823; later also worked in London and Vienna, though mainly in Italy. He is said to have been an unusually fertile ch., some sources crediting him with up to 100 bs. At the Milan La Scala he was responsible for the first prods. of *La Sylphide* (1841), *Giselle* (in a new 5 act version, with additional mus. by N. Bajetti, 1843), and *Beatrice di Gand* (1845).
BIBL.: entry 'C., A.' in *Enciclopedia dello spettacolo*.

Coryphée (Fr., from Greek, leader of the chorus). In the classical Fr. and Russ. hierarchy the term designates a minor soloist. An incorrect form 'coryphaae', has been used in England, apparently under the misapprehension that the French word can apply only to female dancers.

Cosi, Liliana (*b* Milan, 15 Aug. 1941). Ital. dancer. Studied at the b. school of La Scala and continued in Moscow with Vasilyeva, Tikhomirova, Jordan, Messerer, and Gerdt. Upon her graduation in 1958 she became a member of the La Scala co., where she now dances the ballerina roles of the standard repertory. Guest ballerina with numerous cos. abroad (London Festival B., Bolshoi B., etc.).

Cotillon. (1) A very popular ballroom d. derived from the *contredanse, known by *c.* 1796 and mostly d. as a finale to conclude a ball. It has a leading couple, who choose their figures from a large number of available forms. During its execution there is a continual change of partners. As mus. waltzes and mazurkas are preferred. One of its most popular examples is in the second act of Tchaikovsky's op. *Eugene Onegin.* (2) Ballet 1 act; libr. Kochno; ch. Balanchine; mus. Chabrier; déc. Bérard. Prod. 12 Apr. 1932, B. Russe de Monte Carlo, Monte Carlo, with Toumanova, Lichine, Woizikovsky. 'Cotillon was a heartbreak ball which seemed to express, for all its tenderness, the insecurity and desperate gaiety of one moment of time over which hovered a sense of fatality and doom' (B. Taper).

Coton, A. V. (orig. Edward Haddakin; *b* York, 1906, *d* Blackheath, 7 July 1969). Brit. b. critic and writer. Worked as a volunteer to help Tudor form The London B. in 1938. B. critic of *The Daily Telegraph* 1954–69. London correspondent of *Dance News*, New York, 1943–56. Occasional contributor to *Dancing Times* and *Dance and Dancers*. Wrote *A Prejudice for Ballet* (London, 1938), *The New Ballet: Kurt Jooss and His Work* (London, 1946), and *Writings on Dance 1938–68* (ed. posthumously; London, 1975). Contributed to *Ballet Here and Now* (London, 1961).
BIBL.: C. Beaumont, 'Mr. A. V. C.', *Dancing Times* (1969/8).

Cou-de-Pied (Fr., ankle). Sur le cou-de-pied: the position of one foot placed on the ankle of the other foot.

Coulon. Famous Fr. family of dancers during the last quarter of the 18th and the first half of the 19th century. Anne-Jacqueline C. was a d. at the Opéra 1778–1802, appearing with Dauberval, Gardel, and Vestris. Her brother Jean-François C. (1764–1836) entered the Opéra in 1787, becoming one of the most prominent Paris teachers 1808–30. His son Antoine-Louis C. (1796–1849) made his career at the Opéra, but often appeared as a guest at London's Her Majesty's Th., where he was appointed b. regisseur in 1844. His son Eugene C. was in great demand as a ballroom d. teacher in England.

Council for Dance Education and Training. Independent institution representing d. and academic professions in Eng. estab. in 1979 to sustain standards, approve teaching methods and schools, provide centre for exchange of information, and to represent d. and d. teaching at national level. Chmn. M. Wood, 1979–81, Lord Vaizey from 1981; Dir. J. Ranger. Sep. councils also set up for Scotland and Wales.

Country Dance. See *Contredanse*.

Coupé (Fr., cut). The pas coupé is an intermediary step as a preparation for some other step: one foot 'cuts' the other away to take up its place.

Couperin, François (*b* Paris, 10 Nov. 1668, *d* there, 12 Sep. 1733). Fr. composer. Did not write any b. mus., but his harpsichord and chamber mus. have often been used for d. purposes. R. Strauss based his Couperin Suite on various of his pieces, and this was performed as a b. by Kröller (*Höfische Tänze im Stil Ludwigs XIV*, Vienna, 1923—an extended version, ch. by P. and P. Mlakar, as *Verklungene Feste*, Munich, 1941). Another adaptation of his mus. which has occasionally been ch. is Ravel's *Le Tombeau de Couperin* (1917)—e.g. by Balanchine, New York City B., 1975.

Courante (Fr., running d.). An old Fr. court d. from the 16th century in compound time. Originally a d. with emphasis on mime, it later became the rapid triple-time sequel to the allemande.

Cournand, Gilberte (*b* Gérardmer, 25 Sep. 1913). Fr. b. critic and bookseller. Founder and dir. of the Paris bookshop and gallery 'La Danse' (originally at Place Dauphine, now in Rue de Beaune). D. critic of *Parisien Libéré* in 1965 and for *Carrefour* since 1973. Author of *Les Premières Bases de la Danse* (with Maryelle Kempf). Set up a series of gramophone records for d. education. Has organized many exhibitions and given lectures on various aspects of d. Chevalier dans l'ordre national des Arts et Lettres (1973).

Couronne, En (Fr., like a crown). Designates the curved holding of the arms as if to frame the head.

Court Ballet. See *Ballet de cour*.

Couru (Fr., run). The pas couru is a running step as a preparation for a jump.

Cova, Fiorella (*b* Milan, 1936). Ital. dancer. Studied at La Scala B. School, graduating in 1954. Joined La Scala B., becoming soloist in 1958. Married to the d. Mario Pistoni.

Covent Garden, Royal Opera House. London's op. house opened in 1732 as a dramatic th. Destroyed by fire in 1809, it was rebuilt the following year. In 1847 it became the Royal Italian Opera. Again destroyed by fire in 1856; the present building opened in 1858. It reopened after the second world war in 1946, becoming the permanent home of the Covent Garden Opera (now the Royal Opera) and the (then) Sadler's Wells Ballet (the present Royal B.), and has been a host to many famous cos. from abroad.

Cox, Patricia (*b* Edgware, 1936). Brit. dancer. Studied at Sadler's Wells School, joining Sadler's Wells B. in 1953, where she had her biggest success in Cranko's *Pineapple Poll*. In 1960 she went to the Borovansky B. and has been a soloist of the Austral. B. since 1966.

Cragun, Richard Allan (*b* Sacramento, 5 Oct. 1944). Amer. dancer. Studied tap dance and later b. with Barbara Briggs and at the Can. Banff School of Fine Arts and Royal B. School, whence he went to Stuttgart in 1962; promoted principal in 1965. A d. of robust virtuosity, he created roles in Cranko's *L'Estro Armonico* (1963), *Opus 1* (1965), *Mozart Concerto* (1966), *Présence* (1968), *Taming of the Shrew* (1969), *Brouillards* (1970), *Poème de l'extase* (1970), *Carmen* (1971), *Initials R.B.M.E.* (1972), and *Traces* (1973), P. Wright's *The Mirror Walkers* (1963) and *Namouna* (1967), MacMillan's *Song of the Earth* (1965), Tetley's *Voluntaries* (1974) and *Daphnis and Chloe* (1975), Neumeier's *Lady of the Camellias* (1978), Forsythe's *Orpheus* (1979), and Kylián's *Forgotten Land* (1981).
BIBL.: J. Gruen, 'Stuttgart Profiles: Marcia Haydée and R. C.', *Dance Magazine* (1975/8).

Craig, Sandra (*b* Adelaide, 7 Dec. 1942). Austral. dancer. Studied with Dorothy Noye, at Royal B. School and Rambert School; joined B. Rambert in 1962, promoted soloist in 1964. Created roles in Morrice's *Hazard* (1966), *Blind Sight* (1970), *Solo* (1971), and *That Is the Show* (1971), Tetley's *Ziggurat* (1967) and *Embrace Tiger* (1968), Chesworth's *Pawn to King 5* (1968) and *Four According* (1970), Bruce's *George Frideric* (1969) and *Living Space* (1970). Retired in 1972.

Cramér, Ivo (*b* Gothenburg, 5 Mar. 1921). Swed. dancer, choreographer, and b. director. Studied with Cullberg and Leeder; d. in 1944 with Cullberg. Toured Swed. with a troupe of his own; co-dir. Svenska Dansteatern with Cullberg in 1946, which toured the continent. Appointed b. master of the Lisbon Verde Gaio co., 1948–9. Freelance ch. and operetta dir. in Scandinavia with various jobs in Oslo, Gothenburg, Malmö, and the Royal Swed. B., of which he became b. dir. 1975–80, and for which he ch. in 1958 his most successful b. so far, a folklore version of *The Prodigal Son* (mus. H. Alfvén—an earlier version in 1947). He founded the Cramérballetten in Stockholm with his ch. wife Tyyne Talvo in 1968, for which he has ch. a great number of bs., incl. *Good Evening, Beautiful Mask* (about the assassination of Gustav III, 1971), and—among many other bs. based on religious subjects—*Peasant Gospel* (1972).
BIBL.: A. G. Stahle, Interview with I. C., *Dans* (No. 8, Eng. summary).

Cranko, John (*b* Rustenburg, S.A., 15 Aug. 1927, *d* Dublin, 26 June 1973). Brit. dancer, choreographer, and b. director. Studied at the Cape Town Univ. B. School, where he ch. his first b. in 1942, the suite from Stravinsky's *The Soldier's Tale*. Went on to study at Sadler's Wells School in 1946, joining Sadler's Wells B., where it soon became clear that he was interested in ch. rather than dancing. Ch. a great number of bs. during his years with the Sadler's Wells and Royal B. incl. *Tritsch-Tratsch* (mus. J. Strauss, 1946), *Children's Corner* (mus. Debussy, 1947), *Beauty and the Beast* (mus. Ravel, 1949), *Pineapple Poll* (mus. Sullivan/

Mackerras, 1951), *Harlequin in April* (mus. R. Arnell, 1951), *Bonne-Bouche* (mus. A. Oldham, 1953), *The Shadow* (mus. E. von Dohnányi, 1953), *The Lady and the Fool* (mus. Verdi/Mackerras, 1954), *The Prince of the Pagodas* (mus. Britten, 1957), and *Antigone* (mus. Theodorakis, 1960), and for other cos. *School for Nightingales* (mus. Couperin, St. James's B., 1949), *The Witch* (mus. Ravel, New York City B., 1950), *Variations on a Theme* (mus. Britten, B. Rambert, 1954), *La Belle Hélène* (mus. Offenbach/Rosenthal, Paris Opéra, 1955), *La Reja* (mus. Scarlatti, B. Rambert, 1959), *Romeo and Juliet* (mus. Prokofiev, La Scala di Milano in Venice, 1958), the 2 revues *Cranks* (1955) and *New Cranks* (1960); also dir. of the first prod. of Britten's op. *A Midsummer Night's Dream* (Aldeburgh, 1960). After a Stuttgart prod. of his *Prince of the Pagodas* in 1960 he left the Royal B. to become b. dir. in Stuttgart in 1961. Within a very few years he achieved the 'Stuttgart Ballet Miracle', building up the Stuttgart Ballet into one of the most vigorous cos. of the world, moulding a marvellous troupe of dancers, creating an unusually large and diversified repertory, and leading the co. on its extensive foreign tours. He was also chief ch. of the Bavarian State Op. in Munich 1968–71. His influence on the Ger. b. scene can hardly be over-estimated. He died on the return flight from an Amer. tour of his co., As a ch. he was at home in many different styles, though his forte was undoubtedly full-length dramatic works. Of the bs. he created after 1960 the following represent his major output: *The Catalyst* (mus. Shostakovich, 1961), *Daphnis and Chloe* (mus. Ravel, 1962), Stuttgart version of *Romeo and Juliet* (mus. Prokofiev, 1962), *L'estro armonico* (mus. Vivaldi, 1963), *Swan Lake* (1963—also various later versions), *The Firebird* (mus. Stravinsky, 1964—prod. for the Ger. Op. Berlin), *Jeu de cartes* (mus. Stravinsky, 1965), *Onegin* (mus. Tchaikovsky/Stolze, 1965), *Opus 1* (mus. Webern, 1965), *Mozart Concerto* (1966), *The Nutcracker* (1966), *The Interrogation* (mus. B. A. Zimmermann, 1967), *Quatre Images* (mus. Ravel, 1968), *Présence* (mus. Zimmermann, 1968), *Taming of the Shrew* (mus. Scarlatti/Stolze, 1969), *Brouillards* (mus. Debussy, 1970), *Poème de l'extase* (mus. Scriabin, 1970), *Ebony Concerto* (mus. Stravinsky, 1970—for Munich), *Carmen* (mus. Bizet/Fortner-Steinbrenner, 1971), *Initials R.B.M.E.* (mus. Brahms, 1972), and *Traces* (mus. Mahler, 1973). TV film *Cranko's Castle* (BBC, 1967); several Ger. TV prods. of some of his bs.
BIBL.: Various authors, *J. C.* (Stuttgart, 1973); J. C. and W. E. Schäfer, *Gespräche über den Tanz* (Frankfurt, 1974); and various authors, *J. C. und das Stuttgarter Ballett 1961–1973* (Pfullingen, 1975). J. Percival, *Theatre in my Blood* (London, 1983).

Craske, Margaret (*b* Norfolk, 26 Nov. 1892). Brit. dancer and teacher. Briefly a member of the Diaghilev co., she started to teach in London as an authority on the Cecchetti system and moved to the U.S in 1946, where she was at first b. mistress of Amer. B. Th., and began to teach at the Metropolitan Op. B. School in 1950. Co-author (with C. W. Beaumont) of *The Theory and Practice of Allegro in Classical Ballet (Cecchetti Method)* (1930) and (with F. Derra de Moroda) *Practice of Advanced Allegro in Classical Ballet* (Cecchetti Method) (1956).

Création, La. Ballet in 1 act; ch. Lichine. Prod. 26 Sep. 1948, Bs. des Champs-Elysées, Prince's Th., London, with Lichine, Caron, Philippart, Riabouchinska. Without any mus., d. between black curtains and in practice dress, the b. shows a ch. in the process of creating a b. An earlier version to C. Franck's Symphonic Variations had its première at the Buenos Aires Teatro Colón.
BIBL.: C. Beaumont, '*L. C.*' in *Ballets Past & Present* (London, 1955).

Creation of the World, The (orig. Fr. title: *La Création du monde*). Ballet in 1 act; libr. Blaise Cendrars; ch. Börlin; mus. Milhaud; déc. Léger. Prod. 25 Oct. 1923, Bs. Suédois, Th. des Champs-Elysées, Paris, with Börlin, Ebon Strandin. The b., which has been termed 'ballet Nègre', shows the story of the creation as the imagination of an Afr. Negro might conceive it. It has often been revived with new ch., e.g. by de Valois (Camargo Society, 1931), MacMillan (Royal B., 1964), Bolender (New York City B., 1964), and J. Taylor (in *Almost an Echo*, B. Rambert, 1974). A completely different b., with a comic, parody approach, inspired by the drawings of Jean Effel, under the same title by N. Kasatkina and V. Vasiliov, mus. A. Petrov, déc. E. Stenberg, on 23 Mar. 1971, Kirov B., Leningrad, with Y. Soloviev, Baryshnikov, Panov, Kolpakova, Ragozina.
BIBL.: C. W. Beaumont, '*L.C.d.m.*' in *Complete Book of Ballets* (London, 1951). D. Milhaud, *Notes sans musique* (Paris, 1951; Eng. version as *Notes without Music*).

Creatures of Prometheus, The (orig. Ital. title: *Gli uomini di Prometeo*; Ger. title: *Die Geschöpfe des Prometheus*). Heroic-allegorical ballet in 2 acts; ch. S. Viganò; mus. Beethoven. Prod. 28 Mar. 1801, Burg Th., Vienna, with Cesari, Mme Brendl. The libr. is lost, but the th. bill gives a rough outline of the plot, which has been treated in a different way by every ch. since. Beethoven's score consists of overture, introduction, and 16 numbers. Viganò himself ch. a new version for Milan's La Scala in 1813, in which he used only 4 of the original Beethoven numbers, substituting for the rest various pieces by himself, J. Weigl, and Haydn. The b. has never been long out of the Ger. repertory, and there have continually been new versions, including those by Knust (Dessau, 1927), Milloss (Ausburg, 1933) and Walter (Düsseldorf, 1966). Lifar ch. a prod. for the Paris Opéra in 1929. There have been 2 noteworthy Eng. stagings of the b.—a) by de Valois, déc. John Banting, 13 Oct. 1936, Sadler's Wells B., Sadler's

Wells Th., London; b) by Ashton, déc. Ottowerner Meyer, 6 June 1970, Royal B. (Touring Group), Bonn, with Wells, Cooke, Thorogood, Last, Davel. BIBL.: R. Lawrence, in *The Victor Book of Ballets and Ballet Music* (New York, 1950).

Crickmay, Anthony (b Woking, 20 May 1937). Brit. b. and th. photographer. Works with Royal B., London Festival B., B. Rambert, Netherlands D. Th., National B. of Canada, and many other cos. Regular contributor to *Times, Financial Times, Sunday Telegraph,* and *Vogue.*

Crimson Sails (also *Red Sails*; orig. Russ. title: *Alye parusa*). Ballet in 3 acts with prologue; ch. Radunsky, Popko, and Pospekhin; mus. V. Yurovsky; déc. P. Williams. Prod. 30 Dec. 1942, Bolshoi B., House of Culture, Kuibyshev, with Tikhomirnova, Preobrajensky, Messerer. Based on a story by Alexander Green, the b. tells of the little girl Assol, whose dream—of the day when a ship with red sails will appear, out of which a strong seaman will step to lead her away to a faraway happy land—is fulfilled. The b. stimulated a great controversy because of its romanticism and reactionary philosophy. BIBL.: M. G. Swift, in *The Art of the Dance in the U.S.S.R.* (Notre Dame, Ind., 1968).

Crisp, Clement (b Romford, 21 Sep. 1931). Brit. b. critic. Educated Bordeaux and Oxford Univs. B. critic of *The Financial Times* since 1957. Librarian and Archivist of Royal Academy of Dancing since 1968. Editor of *Covent Garden Books* nos. 14 and 15. Author of *Ballet for All* (with P. Brinson, London, 1970), *Dance, An Illustrated History* (with M. Clarke, London, 1973), *Making a Ballet* (with Clarke, London, 1974), *Ballerina* (portraits and impressions of Nerina; London, 1975), *Design for Ballet* (with Clarke, London 1978), *Lynn Seymour* (London, 1980), *The History of Dance* (with Clarke, London, 1981), and *Ballet & Dance—A Guide to the Repertory* (with P. Brinson, Newton Abbot, 1980).

Croce, Arlene (b Providence, R.I., 5 May 1934). Amer. writer on dance. Founder of *Ballet Review* and Editor 1965–78. D. critic of *The New Yorker* since 1974. Author of *The Fred Astaire & Ginger Rogers Book* (New York, 1972), *Afterimages* (New York, 1979).

Crofton, Kathleen (b Fyzabad, India, 1902, d Rochester, N.Y., 30 Nov. 1979). Brit. dancer, teacher., and b. mistress. Studied with Novikov, Preobrajenska, Legat, and Trefilova; d. with Pavlova 1923–7, later also in Chicago, with Nijinska, B. Russe de Colonel de Basil, and Markova-Dolin. Opened her own studio in London in 1951, where she also taught for the Royal B. Her Amer. activities were mainly based upon Buffalo, N.Y., where she was dir. of the Niagara Frontier B. Artistic Dir. of Maryland B. Co., 1974–80.

Croisée (Fr., crossed). A position of the body at an oblique angle to the spectator, with the working leg crossing the line of the body (either en avant or en arrière).

Croqueuse de diamants, La. Ballet in 4 scenes; libr. Petit and Alfred Adam, with couplets by Raymond Queneau; ch. Petit; mus. J.-M. Damase; déc. Wakhevitch. Prod. 25 Sep. 1950, Bs. de Paris, Th. de Marigny, Paris, with Jeanmaire, Petit, Hamilton. A 'b. chantant', in which Jeanmaire had not only to dance but also to sing. She is a member of a gang at Les Halles who steals diamonds—to eat them with relish. A special adaptation in the film *Un—deux—trois—quatre* (Eng. title: *Black Tights,* 1960). BIBL.: G. Balanchine, 'L.C.d.d.' in *Balanchine's New Complete Stories of the Great Ballets* (Garden City, N.Y., 1968).

Crumb, George (b Charleston, W. Va., 24 Oct. 1929). Amer. composer. His *Ancient Voices of Children* is one of the contemporary scores which has most often been used by ch. for b. purposes, incl. J. Stripling (Stuttgart, 1971), Sparemblek (Lisbon, 1972), Butler (in *La Voix,* B. du Rhin, 1972), and Bruce (B. Rambert, 1975). Bruce ch. also *Black Angels* (B. Rambert, 1976) *Echoes in Autumn for Stationary Flying* (Utah Rep. Dance Th., 1973) *Echoes of a Night Sky* (B. Rambert, 1977), and *Night with Waning Moon* (B. Rambert, 1979). Hamburg did a first trilogy of bs. to his mus., called *Makrokosmos,* incl. *The Echo* (*Voice of the Whale,* ch. Sergej Handzic), *The Cry* (*Ancient Voices,* ch. Howald), and *The Silence* (*Makrokosmos,* vol. 1, ch. Neumeier), 1975. L. Houlton finished a G. C. trilogy for Minnesota D. Th. in 1978, incl. her *Ancient Air* (*Ancient Voices,* 1973), *Diabolus* (*Black Angels,* 1974) and *Contemporary Aire—Discontinued Spaces* (*Dream Sequence,* 1978).

Csárdás also czardas; Hung., pub). It derives from Hajdútanz, the dance of the Heiducks. Appeared in Hung. ballrooms about 1835, enjoying its main popularity 1845–80. The steps are not fixed, but it is in 2 parts—a slow and melancholy Lassu and a rapid Friss or Friszka, with many turns and leaps. Its characteristic is the en dedans of many of its steps. The most famous b. examples are in *Coppélia,* the ballroom act of *Swan Lake,* and the divertissement in *Raymonda.*

Csarnoy, Katalin (b Szolnok, 26 Dec. 1948). Hung. dancer. Studied at Budapest State B. Inst., graduating in 1967. Joined Budapest State Op.B. in 1967, becoming soloist in 1971. Created Diana in Seregi's *Sylvia* (second première, 1972) and Black Lady in *The Cedar* (second première, 1975). Joined B. of the 20th Century 1975, on temporary leave of absence from the Budapest co. Created roles in Béjart's *Dichterliebe* (1978) and *Variations 'Don Giovanni'* (1979). Second prize, junior category Varna, 1968).

Cuadro Flamenco. Literally a gipsy picture, it

designates a divertissement of gipsy songs and dances of mounting excitement. It was also the title of a d.-scene which Diaghilev presented on 17 May 1921 at the Paris Th. Gaîté-Lyrique, designed by Picasso, and d. by such Spaniards as Maria Delbaicin, La Rubia de Jerez, La Gabrielita del Garrotin, La Lopez, El Tejero, and El Moreno.

Cuba. There were occasional perfs. of individual Span. dances during the seasons given by visiting th. cos. in Havana, but it was not until 1842 that Cub. audiences saw traditional b., when Elsser appeared with her sister and partner at the Tacón Th. Later very occasional perfs. were given by touring cos. including some by Pavlova in 1917. B. evenings were started by the Sociedad Pro-Arte Mus. in 1931, which also housed the conservatory with a b. class, which produced the Alonsos. The B. Alicia Alonso was started in 1948, and became *National B. of Cuba in 1959—soon growing into a co., attracting worldwide attention, not at least for its brilliantly gifted generation of young dancers, who collected medals at all the important international competitions. Since the Revolution in 1959 b. has enjoyed an ever widening popularity with Cub. audiences. There now exists a 2nd classically orientated co., the B. da Camagüey as well as a Conjunto Nacional de Danza Moderna and a Conjunto Folklórico Nacional.
BIBL.: various articles in *Cuba en el ballet*, a magazine which started to appear in 1970.

Cucchi, Claudina (*b* Monza, 6 Mar. 1834 [according to I. Guest: 20 Mar. 1838], *d* Milan, 8 [Guest: 10] Mar. 1913). Ital. dancer. Studied with Blasis, made her début in the Paris first prod. of Verdi's *Les Vêpres Siciliennes* in 1855, created a role in Mazilier's *Le Corsaire* (1856), appointed prima ballerina at the Vienna Kärntertor Th. 1857–68. Was also very popular in London, St. Petersburg, and Warsaw, with Catarina and Esmeralda as her most successful roles.

Cuevas, Marquis George de (orig. Marquis de Peidrablanca de Guana de Cuevas; *b* Santiago de Chile, 26 May 1885 [not 1886], *d* Cannes, 22 Feb. 1961). Chil.-Amer. patron and b. director. With his wife's money (she was a Rockefeller heiress), he founded the B. Institute and B. International in 1943, which made its début in New York in 1944. In the summer of 1947 he took over the Nouveau B. de Monte Carlo, running it as the Grand B. de Marquis de Cuevas, with Nijinska as b. mistress. This was the first European b. co., with a strong contingent of Amer. dancers (incl. Hightower, Marjorie Tallchief, Dollar, and Skibine) and bs. by Amer. choreographers (Dollar's *Constantia*, Caton's *Sebastian*, Skibine's *Tragedy in Verona*). The success of the first Paris season in 1947 marked the beginning of the extensive touring programme, which took the co. to most countries of the western world. The taste and caprices of the Marquis determined the policy of

the co., which relied on the box-office appeal of big star names. The artistic output became negligible in the later years, but until the death of the Marquis the co., continued as a platform for interesting dancers, incl. Nureyev, who found his first western refuge here. It was dissolved in June 1962, after attempts at continuing the co., under the direction of the Marquis' nephew Raymundo de Larrain had proved futile. Apart from Nijinska the list of b. masters included Dollar, Beriozoff, and Taras. Among the dancers appearing at various times with the co., were Markova, Toumanova, Massine, Lichine, Bruhn, Moreau, Skouratoff, Vyroubova, Golovine, Melikova, Polajenko, Consuelo, Dale, Prokovsky, and Goviloff. Some of its more successful prods. were Skibine's *Annabel Lee* (1951), *The Prisoner of the Caucasus* (1951), and *Idylle* (1954), Ricardo's *Doña Inez de Castro* (1952), Taras' *Piège de lumière* (1952), and Nijinska-Helpmann's *The Sleeping Beauty* (1960).
BIBL.: P. Daguerre, *Le Marquis de Cuevas* (Paris, 1954).

Cullberg, Birgit (*b* Nyköping, 3 Aug. 1908). Swed. dancer, choreographer, and b. director. Read literature at Stockholm Univ., studied with Jooss-Leeder 1935–9 and with Lillian Karina, later also with Graham in New York. Appeared with her own group in 1939. Founded the Svenska Dansteater with Cramér in 1946, with which she also toured the continent. Worked 1952–7 as a ch. for the Royal Swed. B. and as a freelance ch. in Scandinavia, Ger., and for Amer. B. Th. Has also ch. many TV bs., of which *The Evil Queen* (mus. Dag Wirén) won the Prix d'Italia in 1961. Since 1967 she has been dir. of the State subsidized Cullberg-Balletten. Has frequently appeared as a lecturer and also as a writer. Her bs. are mostly based on strong dramatic subjects and they have become more and more orientated to modern d.—with her special interest concentrated on psychological problems. Among her best known bs. are *Miss Julie* (mus. T. Rangström, 1950—revived for several cos., *Medea* (mus. Bartók/Sandberg, 1950), *The Moon Reindeer* (mus. K. Riisager, 1957), *Lady from the Sea* (mus. Riisager, 1960), *Eden* (mus. H. Rosenberg, 1961), *I Am Not You* (mus. B. Brustad, first prod. as a TV b., 1966), *Romeo and Juliet* (mus. Prokofiev, 1969), *Bellman* (mus. Beethoven, 1971), *Revolte* (mus. Bartók, 1973), and *War Dances* (mus. A. Petterson, 1979). Contributed 'Television Ballet' to *The Dance Has Many Faces* (second ed., New York, 1966); 'Ballet: Flight and Reality' to *Dance Perspectives 59*.
BIBL.: E. Näslund, *B.C.* (Stockholm, 1978).

Cunningham, James (*b* Toronto, 1 Apr. 1938). Can. dancer and choreographer. Educated at Toronto Univ. Studied at Graham School. Has had his own co., since 1967, for which he has ch. extensively, including *Lauren's Dream, Skating to*

Siam, The Sea of Tranquility Motel, and *The Junior Birdsmen.*
BIBL.: M. B. Siegel, in *At the Vanishing Point* (New York, 1972).

Cunningham, Merce (*b* Centralia, Wash., 16 Apr. 1919). Amer. d., ch., b. dir., and teacher. Started to study tap, folk, and ballroom d., continued at the Cornish School of Fine Arts in Seattle and at the Bennington School of D. Member of the Graham co., 1939–45, where he created roles in Graham's *Every Soul is a Circus* (1939), *El Penitente* (1940), *Letter to the World* (1940), and *Appalachian Spring* (1944). As a ch. he worked independently at first, and since 1952 with his own group. A very important step was the start of his collaboration in the 1940s with J. Cage, who still functions as his mus. dir. Hardly less important were his working contacts with such painters as R. Rauschenberg, A. Warhol, F. Stella, and J. Johns. As a ch. he also works with isolated movements, far from the academic d. He has occasionally experimented with aleatory elements. Since the mid–1950s he has maintained his position as one of the foremost personalities of the Amer. avant-garde. His list of works is very long—some of its best known titles are *The Seasons* (mus. Cage, B. Society, 1947), *Antic Meet*

(mus. Cage, 1958), *Summerspace* (mus. M. Feldman, 1958), *Field Dances* (mus. Cage, 1963), *Winterbranch* (mus. LaMonte Young, 1964), *How to Pass, Kick, Fall and Run* (mus. Cage, 1965), *Scramble* (mus. Ichiyanagi, 1967), *Rain Forest* (mus. D. Tudor, 1968), *Walkaround Time* (mus. D. Behrman, 1968), *Canfield* (mus. P. Oliveros, 1969), *Landrover* (mus. Cage, 1972), *Un jour ou deux* (mus. Cage, Paris Opéra, 1973), *Locale, Roadrunners* and *Duets* (all 1980). Started series of *Events* in 1964—at first consecutively numbered. Dir. (with J. Cage) Intern. D. Course for chs. and composers, Guildford, 1981. Film: *498 Third Avenue* (1968), CBS 2 part TV prod. on C. and his co., *Video Event* (1974). List of his films in *Dance Magazine* (July 1975). Contributed 'A Technique for Dance' to *The Dance Has Many Faces* (New York, 1951). Author of *Changes: Notes on Choreography* (N.Y., 1970); L'Ordre des Arts et des Lettres (1983).
BIBL.: various authors on M. C. in *Dance Perspectives 34*; J. Klosty, *M. C.* (New York, 1975).

Cuoco, Joyce (*b* Boston, 7 May 1953). Amer. dancer. Started to study tap d. continuing with H. Hoctor, Roje, V. E. Williams, and Lee Daniels. Appeared on stage as an extra at the Boston perfs. of such guest-cos. as the Bolshoi and the Royal

The Merce Cunningham Dance Company in Cunningham's *Sounddance.*   Photo Johan Elbers.

Danish B. When her family moved to Hollywood in 1965, she appeared on the D. Kaye Show, and with Ed Sullivan in 1966—becoming known as a prodigy ballerina who could spin endless pirouettes. D. on Radio City Music Hall and other TV shows, also with R. Page, and continued to study with Riabouchinska and Lichine. Became a member of the Stuttgart B. in 1970, since when she has matured considerably, dancing the ballerina roles of the standard repertory. Joined Munich State Op. B. in 1976.

Curley, Wilma (*b* Brooklyn, 1 Apr. 1937). Amer. dancer and choreographer. Studied with G. Chaffee and School of Amer. B. D. with New York City B. 1955–7, created Graziella in Robbins' *West Side Story* in 1957, toured with Bs. U.S.A. 1958–61. Created roles in Robbins' *The Concert* (1956), *New York Export: Op. Jazz* (1958) and *Moves* (1959), and Butler's *The Unicorn, the Gorgon and the Manticore* (1957). Has since worked mainly for TV and re-created prods. of some Robbins bs. for various cos. Ch. for Alabama State B., Harkness B., and *Mother's Mozart '73* for Joffrey II in 1973.

Currier, Ruth (*née* Miller; *b* Ashland, Ohio, 1926). Amer. dancer, choreographer, teacher, and b. director. Studied with Humphrey and Limón, becoming a member of his co., in 1949. Created a great number of roles in his works—*Night Spell* (1951), *The Exiles* (1953), *Ritmo Jondo* (1953), *Missa Brevis* (1958). She worked as an assistant of Humphrey 1952–8, also appearing with her own group for which she ch. several pieces. Teaches at the Ohio State Univ. in Columbus and has been artistic dir. of the Limón co., 1953–79.
BIBL.: M. Hodgson, 'R. C. Views the Limón Co., *Dance News* (1976/3).

Curry, John (*b* Birmingham, 9 Sep. 1949). Brit. ice skater and creator of Dance Th. of Skating. Trained with Carlo Fassi and studied d. with J. Graeme. Impressed audiences and critics at the international contests through the genuine musicality, technical expertise and artistic refinement of his virtuoso perfs., winning both the Olympic Gold Medal and the World Championship in 1976. Started to build up his D. Th. of Skating with perfs. at the London Cambridge Th. late in 1976. Since his début at New York in 1978 calls his troupe Ice Dancing. Choreographers like Norman Maen, T. Tharp, K. MacMillan, P. Darrell, P. Martins, J. P. Bonnefous and R. Hynd have created special solos and bs. for him and his co. Has recently started to appear as a musical performer.
BIBL.: J. C. and K. Money, *J. C.* (London, 1978).

Cygne, Le. See *Dying Swan, The.*

Cyrano de Bergerac. Ballet in 3 acts; libr. and ch. Petit, mus. Constant; sets Basarte; cost. Saint-Laurent. Prod. 17 Apr. 1959, Bs. de Paris, Alhambra Th. Paris, with Petit, Jeanmaire, Reich. The b. follows closely the plot of Edmond Rostand's heroic comedy (1897) about the famous hero with the long nose who loves his beautiful cousin Roxane but is rejected in favour of the rather bland but handsome Christian. Revived for Royal Dan. B. in 1961. A specially adapted version in the film *Un-deux-trois-quatre* (Eng. title *Black Tights*, 1960).

Czardas. See Csárdás.

Czarny, Charles (*b* Chicago, 4 Jan. 1931). Dutch d., ch., and teacher. Studied with Graham, Dudley, Bales, Limón, Humphrey, and Harkarvy. Started to d. with the N.Y. City Op. Co., in 1952, then with Dudley-Maslow-Bales Co., Royal Winnipeg B., Netherlands D. Th., also on Broadway and in Amer. TV prods. Worked as a ch. for Netherlands D. Th., Scapino B., North Carolina D. Th., Northern D. Th., Norwegian National G., Bat-Dor D. Co., and B. of Flanders. Has taught at Royal Conservatory of The Hague and for Netherlands D. Th. 1959–67; teaches now at Rotterdam D. Academy.

Czechoslovakia. See the individual entries on *Bratislava, Brno,* and *Prague.* Apart from these 3 cities the following State Ths. have b. cos. of their own: Ostravá (dir. in 1981: Albert Janíček), Košice (Marilena Halászová), Plzeň (František Tichý), and Liberec (František Pokorný), České Budějovice (Milan Hojdys), Banská Bystrica (Jozef Zajko), Opava (František Vychodil), Ustí nad Labem (Hana Machová), and Olomouc (Karel Jurčík).
BIBL.: L. Schmidová, *Ceskoslovenský Balet* (Prague, 1962; in Czech).

Czernyana. Ballet in 1 act; ch. Staff; mus. Czerny; déc. Eve Swinstead Smith. Prod. 5 Dec. 1939, B. Rambert, Duchess Th., London, with Gilmour, E. Schooling, Gore, Staff. A string of unrelated dances, gently poking fun at the foibles of the b. world. A sequel, *Czerny II*, had its first prod. in 1941. Later revivals include some dances from each of these prods.

Czobel, Lisa (*b* Bamberg, 2 Apr. 1906). Hung.-Ger. dancer. Studied at the Berlin Trümpy school, and with Preobrajenska and Egorova; d. with Skoronel's group and with the Essen Folkwang D. Th., where she created the Young Girl in Jooss' *The Green Table.* She emigrated with the co., and later embarked on a career as a freelance modern dancer, appearing mainly in Switzerland and Italy. Returned to Ger. after the second world war, where she d. with several th. cos. and from where she undertook several extensive overseas tours with A. von Swaine as her partner. Married to the ch. Karl Bergeest.

D

Dalcroze, Jaques. See *Jaques-Dalcroze*.

Dale, Margaret (*b* Newcastle-upon-Tyne, 30 Dec. 1922). Brit. dancer and TV producer. Studied at Sadler's Wells School, becoming a member of the Corp.; created roles in de Valois' *The Prospect Before Us* (1940) and Helpmann's *Comus* (1942). Started to ch. with *The Great Detective*—her only stage b.—and for TV, joining the BBC in 1954, becoming one of the most internationally respected producers of TV bs. Left the BBC in 1976 to do teaching and research in Canada, Britain, and elsewhere.
BIBL.: M. Harriton: 'M.D.: TV Ambassador', *Dance Magazine* (1969/11).

Dali, Salvador (*b* Figueras, 11 Mar. 1904). Span. painter. Designed Massine's *Bacchanale* (1939), *Labyrinth* (1941), *Mad Tristan* (1944), and Eglevsky's *Sentimental Colloquy* (1944), Argentinita's *Café de Chinitas* (1944), and Béjart's *Gala* (1961) and *Le Chevalier romain et la dame espagnole* (1961).
BIBL.: A. Fatt, 'Designers for the Dance', *Dance Magazine* (1967/3).

Dallas Ballet. The co. was founded, as the Dallas Civic B., as a civic, non-profit-making educational organization in 1957. After the appointment of G. Skibine and Marjorie Tallchief, as Dir. and Assoc. Dir. respectively, in 1969 the co. vastly extended its activities and scope, and the assoc. Dallas Civic B. Academy was opened in 1971. The repertory is based on the standard classics, with in addition numerous Skibine bs., and individual contributions by such choreographers as Balanchine, Dolin, Taras, Miskovitch, and Banovitch. After Skibine's death F. Flindt became artistic dir. in 1981. The civic co. is now called the Dallas B. Youth Dancers.

Dalman, Elizabeth Cameron (*b* Adelaide, 23 Jan. 1934). Austral. dancer, teacher, choreographer and director. Studied with Nora Stewart, later also in London, Stockholm, Essen, Amsterdam, and New York. D. with B. der Lage Landen 1958–9, in Dutch and Austral. prods of *My Fair Lady*, and with the co. of E. Pomare. Opened her own school in Adelaide 1964, from which the Australian D. Th. emerged in 1965, of which she is now dir. and one of the choreographers. Has taught at various Dutch schools and academies.

D'Amboise, Jacques. See *Amboise, Jacques d'*.

Dame à la licorne, La. See *Lady and the Unicorn, The*.

Dame aux camélias, La. Ballets based on the novel by A. Dumas fils (1848) exist in a great number—incl. those by F. Termanini (*Rita Gauthier*, mus. Verdi, Turin, 1857), Taras (*Camille*, mus. Schubert-Rieti, Original B. Russe, 1946), Tudor (*Lady of the Camellias*, mus. Verdi, New York City B., 1951), Page (*Camille*, mus. Verdi, Chicago, 1957), T. Gsovsky (*Die Kameliendame*, mus. Sauguet, Berlin, 1957), Ashton (**Marguerite and Armand*, mus. Liszt-Searle, Royal B., 1963), Alberto Mendez (*Nous nous verrons hier soir*, National B. of Cuba, 1971), Neumeier (**Lady of the Camellias* mus. Chopin, Stuttgart, 1978), and Lefèbre (mus. Verdi, B. Royal de Wallonie, 1980).

Dame de Pique, La. Ballet in 6 scenes; libr. and ch. Petit; mus. Tchaikovsky, arr. by Laurent Petitgirard; sets A. Beaurepaire; cost. J. Schmidt and E. Peduzzi. Prod. 11 Nov. 1978, Bs. de Marseille, Th. des Champs-Elysées, Paris, with Baryshnikov, Evelyne Desutter, J. Rayet. The b., which uses a potpourri arr. from Tchaikovsky's op., follows closely the plot of Pushkin's short story *Pikovaya dama* (1834). An earlier version by Lifar (mus. Tchaikovsky, arr. Annenkov, Monte Carlo, 1960).

Dance and Dancers. Brit. monthly magazine devoted to all kinds of theatrical dancing, published in London Jan. 1950–June/July 1980. P. Williams was its editor throughout this period, originally with C. Barnes as assoc. editor, who then became New York editor. Barnes' London post was taken over by J. Percival and N. Goodwin. Publication resumed Sept. 1981, edited by Percival, and with Goodwin, H. Koegler, and D. Dougill as assoc. editors; Barnes continues as N.Y. editor.

Dance Archives Museum of Modern Art. The basis of these Archives, founded in New York in 1940, was Kirstein's private collection of d. memorabilia. Its historical possessions became part of the Harvard College Th. Collection in 1947, while the rest, dealing with d. in the 20th century, went to the D. Collection of the New York Public Library in 1961.
BIBL.: entry 'D.A.M.o.M.A., N.Y.' in *Dance Encyclopedia* (New York, 1967).

Dance Centre. A former school building in Floral St., Cov. Gdn., London, acquired by Gary Cockrell and converted by him into a complex of d. studios with the appropriate changing rooms, showers, etc., and opened under the above name in 1959. In the following years many of the leading London teachers moved in, renting studios to give their classes, so that it increasingly became the London equivalent of the former Paris *Studio Wacker.

Dance Chronicle. The Amer. magazine, subtitled 'Studies in D. and the Related Arts', considers itself 'as a journal of d. research', that 'will offer the best writing on d.-related subjects, carefully researched and authoritatively presented.' Its editors are G. Dorris and J. Anderson. The first issue was published in the fall of 1977; appears quarterly.

Dance Collection of the New York Public Library, The. Established in 1944 as part of the institute's Music Division, it acquired its own curator in 1947, since when it has developed into the world's foremost library and museum of the d., 'devoted to the literature and iconography of the d., stressing historical, theatrical, educational, therapeutic, and socio-economic aspects and covering every form of d.: ballet, modern, "expressionist", social, ethnic, primitive, folk, and national' (G. Oswald). One of its fastest expanding sections is the Jerome Robbins Film Archive.
BIBL.: G. Oswald, 'D.C., The N.Y.P.L. in *Dance Encyclopedia* (New York, 1967).

Dance Horizons. A New York series of paperback reprints of d. classics, founded in 1965, including authors from Arbeau, Pécour, Feuillet, Lambranzi, and Noverre, to St. Denis, Shawn, Laban, and Beaumont.

Dance Index. The 'new magazine devoted to dancing', published by D. Index, Ballet Caravan, Inc., first appeared in New York in January 1942. Edited by Baird Hastings, L. Kirstein, and Paul Magriel, it was originally planned as a monthly, but soon appeared at irregular intervals and eventually became a series of monographs on all kinds of theatrical d., pursuing a strictly scholarly approach. Its contribution to b. literature can hardly be overestimated. Its last issue was listed as vol. VII, nos. 7, 8, 1948. A reprint appeared in 1971.

Dance Magazine. Amer. monthly magazine devoted to all kinds of theatrical dancing. It emerged in 1926 from the *Dance Lovers Magazine* (itself based on the former *Denishawn Magazine*), but ceased publication in the Depression of 1932. In 1941 it was acquired by Rudolf Orthwine, who built it up into 'the world's largest d. publication'. Its present editor-in-chief is William Como.

Dance Magazine Award. The first D.M.As. were presented in 1955 for the year 1954. This practice continued until 1970. No As. were presented in 1971. From 1972 presentations have been made for the current year. Recipients have been—1954: Max Liebman, *Omnibus*, Tony Charmoli, *Adventure*; 1955: M. Shearer, J. Cole, G. Nelson; 1956: Graham, de Mille; 1957: Markova, Chase, Robbins, Limón; 1958: Humphrey, G. Kelly, Youskevitch, Alicia Alonso; 1959: D. Alexander, F. Astaire, Balanchine; 1960: M. Cunningham, Moiseyev, Maria Tallchief; 1961:

M. Hayden, Gwen Verdon, Sokolow; 1962: Fonteyn, B. Fosse, I. Bennett; 1963: G. Champion, Joffrey, Koner; 1964: Villella, Butler, Gennaro; 1965: M. H'Doubler, Denby, Plisetskaya; 1966: Hurok, de Lavallade, Wesleyan University Press; 1967: Nikolais, Verdy, Loring; 1968: Fracci, Bruhn, Dunham; 1969: Ashton, C. Brown, Shawn; 1972: Jamison, Dowell; 1973: The Christensen Brothers, Nureyev; 1974: Tudor, Arpino, Béjart; 1975: Ailey, C. Gregory, A. Mitchell; 1976: M. Bennett, S. Farrell, E. V. Williams; 1977: M. Louis, N. Makarova, P. Martins; 1978: M. Baryshnikov, B. Lewitzky, R. Gelabert; 1979: A. Copland, J. Donn, E. Hawkins; 1980: P. Taylor, R. Page, P. McBride; 1981: S. J. Cohen, A. Dolin, T. Tharp, S. Williams.

Dance Masters of America. The 'professional organization for d. teachers only' was established in 1884, but its present name dates from 1926 when a merger took place between the Amer. National Association of Masters of Dancing and the International Association of Masters of Dancing. It is today the largest organization of its kind in the U.S. with a Ballroom Division, a Performing Arts Division, and a Business Administration Division.

Dance Museum. The Stockholm based Dansmuseet opened in 1953 at the Royal Th. as a display of R. de Maré's unique collection of costumes, masks, instruments and other d. attributes from Asia. It quickly extended its scope and today houses all sorts of d. memorabilia—incl. the most comprehensive collection of documents from Les Ballets Suédois. Early in 1981 it moved to its own building.

Dance News. A monthly Amer. newspaper (not published during July and Aug.) devoted to all kinds of theatrical d. Founded by S. Chujoy in 1942 and run by him up to his death in 1969 (for years with P. W. Manchester as its managing editor), since when Helen V. Atlas acted as its publisher and editor; ceased publication with Feb. 1983 issue.

Dance Notation. Attempts at recording individual dances and complete bs. by graphic symbols can be traced back for several centuries. The municipal archives of Cervera hold two mid-15th-century manuscripts with letter-symbols for certain step-sequences. In Margherita d'Austria's *Livre des Basses Danses* (c. 1460) and the *Art de instruction de bien dancer* (c. 1488) word-abbreviations are used, while Arbeau's *Orchésographie* (1588) provides very accurate descriptions of contemporary dances. A much more differentiated system of d. notation is offered by Feuillet's *Chorégraphie ou l'art d'ecrire la danse par caractères, figures et signes démonstratifs* (1700). The necessity of notating not only individual steps but also the carriage of the body and the use of the arms was first met by Saint-Léon in his *Sténochorégraphie* (1852) and by A. Zorn in his *Grammatik der*

Tanzkunst (1887). After B. Klemm's attempt to develop graphic symbols derived from the notes of musical notation in 1855, V. Stepanov in St. Petersburg worked out a special stave to hold the movement symbols, while the floor patterns were written above. This was taught at the Imperial B. Academy and in 1892 he published it in Paris as his *Alphabet des mouvements du corps humain*. N. Sergeyev used the Stepanov notation to notate the Petipa and Ivanov bs. which he later mounted in Western Europe. During the 20th century the desire for a more scientifically based d. notation inspired Laban to develop another set of symbols, which are arranged in 3 vertical lines (representing the centre, the left, and the right side of the body), running parallel with the musical stave. He published them first in 1926 in his *Choreographie*, but preferred later to call his system *Kinetographie*, while it is generally known outside Ger. as *Labanotation*. With Jooss and Knust as his closest collaborators Laban made it possible to record any kind of human movement, so that it is now acknowledge as a means for the copyright protection of ch. In New York a special *D. Notation Bureau was founded in 1940. While Knust became its most persuasive spokesman in Ger. speaking countries, A. Hutchinson functioned as the system's best advocate in the Eng. speaking countries. Since the mid-50s it has had strong competition from a system which R. and J. Benesh developed in Eng. and which they call *Choreology*, (commonly referred to as *Benesh Notation*). Less complicated than Laban's method, it derives from a five-line music stave, running horizontally across the page, with the movements of the dancers written into it in special symbols. Through now being officially taught at the Royal B. School and accepted by the Royal B. for the notation of its bs. it has gained world-wide distribution. There are, of course, many other individual systems (one of the more recent developments is the Eshkol-Wachman Movement Notation), but the ones in widest use now are *Labanotation* and *Choreology*.

BIBL.: A. Hutchinson, 'Dance Notation, History of' in *Dance Encyclopedia* (New York, 1967); a series of articles on D.N. appeared in *The Dancing Times* (1968/2–9).

Dance Notation Bureau. The New York centre for movement research and analysis was formed in 1940. It provides a library, research centre, training programmes, and services to the d. profession for most systems of recording, notation, and reconstruction of d. works. Its prime concern, however, has always been to cultivate and further the cause of Labanotation.

Dance Observer. An Amer. magazine founded in 1933 and run almost single-handed by L. Horst to propagate the cause of modern d.; it ceased to exist when Horst died in Jan. 1964.

Dance Perspectives. The New York based series

of quarterly monographs dedicated to all aspects of dance was founded in 1958, quickly developing under the editorship of S. J. Cohen into one of the world's most respected and best designed publications on d. and all related topics. Last issue no. 66 (1976).

Dancers. The chamber ensemble b. co. grew from the group which d. Dennis Wayne had assembled around himself while still a member of Amer. B. Th., 'designed for better communication with the public and greater satisfaction to its dancers.' At its New York debut-season, starting 17 Nov, 1977, at Roundabout Stage One, it consisted of 12 dancers, performing 18 works by 12 different choreographers, incl. works by Béjart, B. MacDonald, C. Keuter, Van Dantzig, N. Vesak, and N. Walker.

Dancer's World, A. A black and white 30-minute documentary film, starring Graham and her co., commissioned by WQED, the Pittsburgh TV station, prod. and internationally released 1957. Though Graham does not d. in the film, she serves as guide and commentator, explaining her approach to d. and showing how she trains and rehearses her dancers. The script was published in *Dance and Dancers* (1962/8).

Dances at a Gathering. Ballet in 1 act; ch. Robbins; mus. Chopin; cost. J. Eula; pianist Gordon Boelzner. Prod. 8 (preview gala) and 22 May 1969, New York City B., State Th., New York, with Kent, Leland, Mazzo, Bride, Verdy, Blum, Clifford, Maiorano, Prinz, Villella. This is a b. for 5 male and 5 female dancers set to a string of Chopin etudes, waltzes, mazurkas, one nocturne, and one scherzo with no plot, yet full of atmospheric nuances; a b. about the feeling of togetherness. Robbins dedicated it to the memory of J. Rosenthal, who died on 1 May 1969. Revived for Royal B. in 1970.

BIBL.: E. Denby, 'Jerome Robbins Discusses *D.a.a.G*', *Dance Magazine* (1969); G. Balanchine and F. Mason, in *Balanchine's Complete Stories of the Great Ballets* (Garden City, N.Y., 1977).

Dances of Love and Death. Ballet in 2 acts; ch. Cohan; mus. C. Davis and C. Nancarrow; dec. N. Chiesa. Prod. 31 Aug. 1981, London Contemporary D. Th., Moray House, Edinburgh. Commissioned for the 35th Edinburgh International Festival with the second Tennent-Caledonian award (given annually to different performing arts for a new festival work), it depicts Love and Death symbolically contending over figures of classical myth and popular legend: Pluto and Persephone; Tristan and Iseult; The Sleeping Beauty; Cathy and Heathcliff; Marilyn Monroe. These are framed and separated by unrelated divertissements for supporting ensemble.

Dance Symphony, The Greatness of Creation (also *The Magnificence of the Universe*, orig. Russ. title: *Tants simfoniya—Velichiye myrozdaniya*). Bal-

let in 4 movements; ch. Lopokov; mus. Beethoven; cost. Pavel Goncharov. Prod. 7 Mar. 1923, GATOB, Leningrad, with Balanchivadze (Balanchine), Gusev, Lavrovsky, Mikhailov, Danilova. Set to Beethoven's Fourth Symphony, for 18 dancers, the individual movements deal with the Birth of Light, Triumph of Life Over Death, Awakening of Nature in the Sun of Spring, and The Cosmogonic Spiral. Closely wedded to the score, the b. develops from strictly academic to completely free forms. The first really large-scale attempt at a symphonic b. (though there had been other such bs. before, for instance by Gorsky), it was instantly rejected at its one and only perf. and accused by the critics of obscenity. Its influence, though, can hardly be overestimated.
BIBL.: L. Kirstein, 'Tanzsynfonia' in Movement & Metaphor (New York, 1970).

Dance Theatre of Harlem. The co., directed by A. Mitchell and K. Shook, is the first long-lived classically orientated b. co. of the U.S. with almost entirely black dancers. The decision to found it dates back to 1968. Initially a school was established, and the co. made its official début on 8 Jan. 1971 at the N.Y. Guggenheim Museum with 3 bs. by Mitchell. During the same season the repertory was supplemented by several bs. from Balanchine and Robbins. In June 1971 the co. made its Eur. début at the Spoleto Festival, after which it also appeared in the Netherlands. In 1974 it had its first regular New York and London seasons. First black b. co. to have a season at Cov. Gd. in 1981, when its principal dancers incl. Stephanie Baxter, Elena Carter, Lorraine Graves, Virginia Johnson, Joseph Cippola, Eddie Shellman, Lowell Smith, Mel Tomlinson, and Donald Williams. An Amer. TV film, 'The D.T.o.H. with Arthur Mitchell', was first shown in 1973; also on TV series Dance in America (Nat. Educ. Television, 1977).
BIBL.: M. Steinbrink, 'Dream Factory', Ballet News (1981/2).

Dancing Times, The. The oldest of the existing monthly magazines dedicated to d. was founded in London in 1894. In 1910 P. J. S. Richardson became its editor, vehemently campaigning for 'better teaching' and 'better dancing' but it did not concentrate on the theatrical forms of d. until 1956 and it still devotes much space to the reporting of what happens 'Round the Classes'. Richardson was succeeded in 1958 by A. H. Franks as dir. and managing editor, from whom the magazine passed to M. Clarke, who had been its editor since 1963.

Dandré, Victor E. (b 1870, d London 1944). Russ. b. impresario. A rich landowner and balletomane, he associated himself in 1914 with Pavlova, becoming her manager and possibly her husband, though no official marriage document has been discovered so far. He organized her

world-wide tours. After her death in 1931 he sent a co. of his own to Europe, South Amer., India, and Austral. He took over the B. Russe de Colonel de Basil in 1938, renaming it Royal Cov. Gdn. Russ. B. and later Original B. Russe. Author of Anna Pavlova in Art and Life (London, 1932).

Danias, Starr (b New York, 18 Mar. 1949). Amer. dancer. Studied at School of Amer. B., d. with London Festival B. 1968–70 and with City Center Joffrey B., where she has created roles in Arpino's Trinity (1970), Reflections (1971), Kettentanz (1971), Chabriesque (1972), and Sacred Grove on Mount Tamalpais (1972). Headed Pavlova Celebration, 1980.

Danieli, Fred (b New York, 17 July 1917). Amer. d., teacher, and b. director. Studied at School of Amer. B. and with Fokine, Mordkin, Vilzak, Fedorova, Schollar, and Tudor. D. with Mordkin B., B. Caravan, B. Th., Chicago Civic Op. Comp., also appeared on Broadway and TV. Established School of the Garden State B. 1949. Now art. dir. of Garden State B. Co.

Danielian, Leon (b New York, 31 Oct. 1920). Amer. dancer and teacher. Studied with Mordkin, Fokine, Dolin, and Tudor; made his début in 1937 with Mordkin B. Appeared on Broadway, d. as a soloist with B. Th. 1939–41 and as premier danseur with B. Russe de Monte Carlo 1943–61, also making guest appearances with other cos. (Bs. des Champs-Elysées, San Francisco B., etc.). Has been dir. of Amer. B. Th. School since 1968. Assistant Dean of D., Purchase State Univ. of N.Y., 1980. Now Prof. of D., Univ. of Texas.
BIBL.: R. Gold, 'L.D. and the American Ballet Theatre School', Dance Magazine (1975/1).

Daniels, Danny (b Albany, 25 Oct. 1924). Amer. dancer and choreographer. Studied with Thomas Sternfield, Edith Jane, Jack Potteiger, V. Celli, Anderson-Ivantzova, and Vilzak; made his Broadway début in 1941, since when he has appeared in dozens of musicals and TV prods., with A. de Mille's D. Th., and as a solo performer (creating M. Gould's Tap Dance Concerto in 1952), eventually becoming a ch. for musicals and TV. Opened own school in Santa Monica, Cal., in 1974.

Danilova, Alexandra Dionysievna (b Peterhof, 20 Nov. 1903). Russ.-Amer. dancer and teacher. Studied at Imperial and State B. School in St. Petersburg/Petrograd, becoming a member of the GATOB upon graduation, where she soon appeared in solo roles. In 1924 she was one of the Soviet State Dancers (together with Balanchine) who embarked on a tour of Western Europe. While there she was engaged by Diaghilev for his Bs. Russes, being promoted ballerina in 1927. D. as ballerina with the B. Russe de Colonel de Basil 1933–8 and as prima ballerina with B. Russe de Monte Carlo 1938–52. Guest appearances with many other cos. In 1954–6 she toured with her

own group, giving her farewell perf. in New York in 1957. Occasionally she did some ch.—op. bs. for the New York Met. Op. House—and also joint ' prods. with Balanchine (*Raymonda*, 1946; *Coppélia*, 1974). She now teaches at the School of Amer. B. and occasionally in Europe. As a ballerina she was one of the most popular dancers of her time, extremely versatile, of irresistible charm and glitter, elegant and distinguished, a lady of the world. She danced all the great ballerina roles and created leading parts in Balanchine's *The Triumph of Neptune* (1926), *Le Bal* (1929), *Danses concertantes* (1944), and *Night Shadow* (1946). Apart from Odette and Swanilda she enjoyed her greatest triumphs in Massine's *Beau Danube* and *Gaîté Parisienne*.
BIBL.: A. E. Twsyden, *A.D.* (London, 1945); anon. 'A Conversation with A.D.' *Ballet Review* (vol. 4, no. 4/5).

Danilova, Maria (*b* 1793, *d* 20 Jan. 1810). Russ. dancer. Studied at the Imperial B. School in St. Petersburg, where she proved such an extraordinarily gifted pupil that Didelot had her dancing in several of his bs. She enjoyed an enormous success when she appeared, aged 15, in *Les Amours de Vénus et d'Adonis ou La Vengeance de Mars*, together with Duport with whom she had a short and unhappy love-affair which undermined her delicate constitution, so that she died of consumption when she was only 17, just after she had graduated. She was considered the brightest hope of the Russ. b. Several poets (N. M. Karamsin, N. I. Gnedich) have immortalized her in verse.
BIBL.: M. G. Swift, in *A Loftier Flight* (Middletown, Conn., 1924).

Danina, or Jocko the Brazilian Ape. Ballet in 4 acts; libr. and ch. F. Taglioni; mus. Peter von Lindpaintner. Prod. 12 Mar. 1826, Stuttgart, with M. Taglioni, Stuhlmüller, J. Briol. Based on a Fr. melodrama the b. tells of D., a beautiful Brazilian. One day she saves the ape Jocko from being bitten by a snake. Later on Jocko returns her kindness by protecting D.'s son from kidnapping. The b. was very popular, receiving 33 perfs. during its first two seasons in Stuttgart alone—after which it travelled around the world, being given many individual prods. With the advent of the romantic movement it lost its appeal, but was revived in 1940 by the Mlakars in Munich.

Danish Ballet. See *Royal Danish Ballet*.

Danovschi, Oleg (*b* Voznesensk, 9 Feb. 1917). Rum. dancer, choreographer, and b. director. Studied with Kniaseff in Bucharest, d. at the local Alhambra Th. 1932–40, since when he has been a member of the Bucharest State Op., being its chief ch. up to 1970. In recent years he has mainly worked at the State Op. of Cluj.

Dans. A. Swed. quarterly, first published in November 1973 in Stockholm. Its chief editor is Bengt Häger and its assistant editor Erik Näslund.

Each number contains a study in depth of a special subject.

Danse d'école (Fr., school dance). Designates the academic school style of classic b., the system of which was first formulated by Beauchamp at about 1700 and has been gradually perfected ever since; Blasis' *Traité élémentaire théoretique et pratique de l'art de la danse* of 1818 (antedating his more famous *Code of Terpsichore* by 12 years) is one of its foremost textbooks.

Danse macabre. The idea of death as a dancer before whom all men are equal is of ancient origin and can be found on Etruscan tombstones. It culminated in the literature and paintings of the 14th and 15th century. One of its most famous representations is a Lübeck fresco of 1463, marking the beginning of the Ger. development, which culminated in the series of etchings by Hans Holbein jr. in 1538. Recent d. adaptations of the idea can be found in Jooss' *The Green Table* (1932), Wallmann in Honegger's *La Danse des morts* (Salzburg, 1954), and in the Jooss prod. of Cavalieri's *Rappresentatione di anima et di corpo* (Salzburg, 1968).

Danses Concertantes. Ballet in 5 movements; ch. Balanchine; mus. Stravinsky; déc. Berman, Prod. 10 Sep. 1944, B. Russe de Monte Carlo, City Center, New York, with Danilova, Franklin. Commissioned by the Werner Janssen Orchestra of Los Angeles and first performed by it in 1942, the mus. was intended for concert and not for stage perf. Since Balanchine's version (he reworked it for the Stravinsky Festival of the New York City B. in 1972), the score has often been ch.; e.g. MacMillan (London, 1955) and Blaska (Amiens, 1968).
BIBL.: G. Balanchine, 'D.C.' in *Balanchine's New Complete Stories of the Great Ballets* (Garden City, N.Y., 1968).

Danseur, Danseuse. (Fr., male and female dancer). Often used with an adjective—for instance as d. étoile (the d. who stands at the top of the hierarchy of the Paris Opéra B.), d. caractère (a character d.), or d. noble (a d. of 'princely' roles).

Danseuses Viennoises. The Viennese co. of Josephine Weiss, consisting of 48 very young girls, who toured Europe and the U.S. 1845–8, enjoying great success everywhere. There had been troupes of child dancers in Vienna before, for whom Hilverding had ch. in 1765 and Noverre established a th. d. school in 1771, creating special bs. for its pupils. The Horschelt Children's Bs. were very popular at the Th. an der Wien 1815–7—counting among their members such future stars as Therese Heberle, Wilhelmine Schröder-Devrient (the Wagner singer), and Anton Stuhlmüller (though F. Elssler denied that she ever had anything to do with it). Later on the co. had to be disbanded because of moral objections.

BIBL.: on the Horschelt co., see I. Guest, *Fanny Elssler* (London, 1970); on the co. of Mme Weiss, see Guest, *The Romantic Ballet in England* (London, 1966), and F. Crisp, 'Scandalous and Delightful', *Dance Magazine* (1969/8)

Dansmuseet. See *Dance Museum*.

Dante Sonata. Ballet in 1 act; ch. Ashton; mus. Liszt-Lambert; déc Fedorovitch. Prod. 23 Jan. 1940, Sadler's Wells B., Sadler's Wells Th. London, with Fonteyn, May, Brae, Helpmann, Somes. Based on Liszt's 'D'après une lecture de Dante' and inspired by John Flaxman's illustrations of Dante's *Divina commedia*, the b. shows the fight of the Children of Light against the Children of Darkness. At the time of its first prod. it was generally interpreted as Ashton's personal commentary on the onset of the Second World War.
BIBL.: C. W. Beaumont, '*D.S.*' in *Supplement to Complete Book of Ballets* (London, 1952).

D'Antuono, Eleanor (*b* Cambridge, Mass., 1939). Amer. dancer. Studied with Maria Papporello and V. Williams in Boston, made her début with the New England Civic B., joined B. Russe de Monte Carlo in 1954, d. with the Joffrey B. 1960–61, then with Amer. B. Th.; appointed ballerina in 1963. Created roles in Nahat's *Brahms Quintet* (1969) and Ailey's *River* (1970).
BIBL.: O. Maynard, 'Eleanor, Eleanor', *Dance Magazine* (1975/1).

Dantzig, Rudi van (*b* Amsterdam, 4 Aug. 1933). Dutch dancer, choreographer, and b. director. Studied with Gaskell, but later strongly influenced by Graham. Made his début in 1952 with the B. Recital co.; d, and ch. of Het Nederlands B. 1954–9, became one of the founder members of the Netherlands D. Th. 1959–60, since when he has returned to the (now) Dutch National B., becoming co-dir. 1969, sole art. dir. 1971. Has also worked as a guest-ch. for B. Rambert, Harkness B., Royal B., Royal Danish B., Amer. B. Th., Bat-Dor D. Co., and some other cos. His bs.— most of which were created in close collaboration with *Van Schayk as his designer and often also his leading soloist—show a marked preference for subjects inspired by personal experience and feeling. Though fundamentally based on the academic vocabulary he frequently also uses modern d. movements. His bs. include *Night Island* (mus. Debussy, 1955—revived for B. Rambert, 1966), *The Family Circle* (mus. Bartók, 1958), *Jungle* (mus. Badings, 1961), *Monument for a Dead Boy* (Jan Boerman, 1965—revived for Harkness B., 1969; Amer. B. Th., 1973; and others), *Moments* (mus. Webern, 1968), *Epitaph* (mus. Ligeti, 1969), *On the Way* (mus. Isang Yun, 1970), *The Ropes of Time* (mus. Boerman, Royal B., 1970), *Coloured Birds* (mus. Niccolò Castiglioni and Bach, 1971), *Here Rests: A Summer Day* (mus. Schubert's Unfinished Symphony 1973), *Ramifications* (mus. Ligeti-Purcell, 1973), *Blown in a Gentle Wind* (mus. R. Strauss, Death and Transfig-

uration, 1975), *Four Last Songs* (mus. Strauss, 1977), and *Life* (mus. diverse, 1979). Dutch TV portrait 1974. Prix des critics (Paris, 1961).
BIBL.: Interview with R.v.D., *Dance and Dancers* (1966/5 and 1974/9); N. Goodwin, 'R.v.D.', in *About the House* (1970/3); G. Loney, 'R.v.d.', *Dance Magazine* (1974/3).

Daphnis and Chloe (orig. Fr. title: *Daphnis et Chloé*). Ch. symphony in 3 scenes; libr. and ch. Fokine; mus. Ravel; déc. Bakst, cond. Monteux. Prod. 8 June 1912, Bs. Russes de Diaghilev, Th. du Châtelet, Paris, with Karsavina, Nijinsky, Bolm. Based upon the famous antique pastoral by Longus, the b. tells of the love of the young shepherd D. for beautiful C., who is captured by pirates and led away but finally restored to D. after Pan himself has intervened. Later versions by Ashton (déc. John Craxton, Sadler's Wells B., London, 5 Apr. 1951, with Fonteyn, Somes, Elvin, Field, Grant), Lifar (déc. Chagall, Paris, 1958), Cranko (déc. Georgiadis, Stuttgart, 1962), Neumeier (déc. Rose, Frankfurt, 1972), Van Manen (second suite only; déc. Vroom, Dutch National B., 1972), and Tetley (Stuttgart, 1975).
BIBL.: C. W. Beaumont, '*D.a.C.*' in *Complete Book of Ballets* (London, 1951).

Darius, Adam (*b* New York, 10 May 1930). Amer. mime artist. Studied d. at B. Arts, School of Amer. B., New D. Group and with Preobrajenska. D. with B. der Lage Landen, Malmö B., International B., Royal Winnipeg B., Scandinavian B., and Israeli B. Ch. various bs. for cos. in Holland, Sweden, and Israel and *The Anne Frank B.* (traditional Jewish mus., originally for Stora Teatern, Sweden, 1961), which he has revived several times since (also for TV). Has worked as a mime instructor for many cos., teaching in London since 1974. Continues to perform as a mime artist all over the world. Author of *Dance Naked in the Sun* (London, 1973).
BIBL.: G. Loney, 'A.D.: A Mime Without a Country', *After Dark* (1975/3).

Dark Elegies. Ballet in 1 act; libr. and ch. Tudor; mus. Mahler; déc. Nadia Benois. Prod. 19 Feb. 1937, B. Rambert, Duchess Th., London, with van Praagh, de Mille, Lloyd, Tudor, Laing. Based upon Mahler's *Kindertotenlieder*, which are sung by a baritone (sometimes a contralto) on stage while a group of villagers d. their grief and finally their resignation about a disaster that has struck them. Revived for B. Th. in 1940, and for Royal B. in 1980.
BIBL.: G. Balanchine, in *Complete Stories of the Great Ballets* (Garden City, N.Y., 1977).

Dark Meadow. Ballet in 4 sections; ch. Graham; mus. Chávez; scenery Noguchi; cost. Edythe Gilfond; light. Rosenthal. Prod. 23 Jan. 1946, M. Graham and Co., Plymouth Th., New York, with Graham, Hawkins. This 'is a re-enactment of the Mysteries which attend the eternal adventure of seeking' (Graham).

Darrell, Peter (*b* Richmond, Surrey, 16 Sep. 1929). Brit. dancer, choreographer, and b. director. Studied at Sadler's Wells School. One of the first members of the Sadler's Wells Th. B., which he left to work in musicals and abroad; then with London Festival B., ch. his first bs. there and for B. Workshop. He founded Western Th. B. with E. West in 1957, becoming its sole dir. when West died in 1962, and staying with the co. as b. dir. and chief-ch. when it became Scottish Th. B. (now Scottish B.) and moved to Glasgow. His bs. for Western Th. B. and Scottish B. incl. *The Prisoners* (mus. Bartók, 1957), *Chiaroscuro* (mus. Milhaud, 1959), *A Wedding Present* (mus. Bartók, 1962), *Jeux* (mus. Debussy, 1963), *Mods and Rockers* (mus. The Beatles, 1963), *Sun Into Darkness* (mus. M. Williamson, 1966), *Beauty and the Beast* (mus. T. Musgrave, 1969), *Tales of Hoffmann* (mus. Offenbach-Lanchbery, 1972—revived for Amer. B. Th. in 1973), *The Scarlet Pastorale* (mus. Martin, 1975), *Mary, Queen of Scots* (mus. J. McCabe, 1976), *Five Rückert Songs* (mus. Mahler, 1978), *Cheri* (mus. Dav. Earl, 1980) and prods. of *Giselle* (1971), *Nutcracker* (first act in 1972, second act in 1973) and *Swan Lake* (1977), reverting to Tchaikovsky's original music sequence. For other cos. he ch. *Lessons in Love* (mus. Copland, Zurich, 1966), *Catulli Carmina and Carmina Burana* (mus. Orff, West Berlin, 1968), *Othello* (mus. Liszt, New London B., 1971), and *La Péri* (mus. Dukas, London Festival B., 1973); C.B.E. (1984).

BIBL.: Interview, *Dance and Dancers* (1963/6 and 1979/6); N. Goodwin, *A Ballet for Scotland* (Edinburgh, 1979).

Darsonval, Lycette (*b* Coutances, 12 Feb. 1912). Fr. dancer and teacher. Studied at Paris Opéra B. School; made her début at the Opéra in 1930. Left for foreign tours and returned to the Opéra in 1936, promoted étoile in 1940; stayed with the co. until 1953. During her career as a ballerina she toured extensively with a small group of dancers, for which she did some ch.—not only in Fr., but also abroad and in the U.S.; she thus became one of the most active ambassadresses of Fr. b. She d. the ballerina roles and created leading parts in Lifar's *David triomphant* (1937), *Oriane et le Prince d'amour* (1938), *Adélaide* (1938) and *Sylvia* (1941). She was dir. of the school of the Opéra 1957–9. Continues to teach at the Nice Conservatory. Sister of the d. Serge Perrault.

Dauberval, Jean (orig. J. Bercher; *b.* Montpellier, 19 Aug. 1742, *d.* Tours, 14 Feb. 1806). Fr. dancer, b. master, and choreographer. Studied at Paris Opéra B. School, joining its co. in 1761, promoted premier danseur demi-caractère in 1763, premier danseur noble in 1770, and maître de b. in 1771. He worked in Bordeaux 1785–91, where *La Fille mal gardée*, his most famous b., was premièred in 1789. Strongly influenced by Noverre and his theories about the b. d'action, he became one of the first choreographers to produce bs. about ordinary people and proved especially skilled in handling sentimental and amusing subjects. Other very popular bs. of his were *Le Déserteur*, *Psiché et l'Amour*, *Télémaque*, and *Le Page inconstant* (after Beaumarchais' *Le Mariage de Figaro*). Among his best known pupils were Didelot, Aumer, and S. Viganò. Married to the d. Mlle Théodore, a pupil of Lany.

BIBL.: in *La Fille mal gardée*, ed. by I. Guest (London, 1960).

Daughter of Castile, A. (orig. Russ. title: *Doch kastilii*). Ballet in 4 acts and 6 scenes; libr. and ch. A. V. Tchitchinadze; mus. Glière; déc. M. Shikovani. Prod. 28 May 1955, Stanislavsky and Nemirovich-Danchenko Lyric Th., Moscow, with E. Vlassova. The b. derives—like Chaboukiani's *Laurencia*—from L. de Vega's *Fuente ovejuna* (*The Sheep Well*) and tells of the rising of the peasants of a village in Castile. Led by Laurencia and her fiancé Frondoso, they storm the palace of the Commander who tried to seduce her, and kill him.

Daukaev, Marat (*b* Ufa, 1952). Sov. dancer. Studied at Leningrad Ch. School 1964–8, later also at the Perm Ch. School. Member of the Bashkir Th. for Op. and B. 1968–70 and soloist of the Perm Th. for Op. and B. since 1973, where he dances the premier danseur roles of the standard repertory, with Romeo as one of his best parts. Bronze Medal (Varna, 1972).

Davel, Hendrik (*b* Reitz, 28 Sep. 1940). S.A. dancer. Studied in Pretoria with Gwynne Ashton. Came to London in 1960, making his début with London Festival B. D. with Gore's London B., N. McDowell's London D. Th., and with the Royal B. 1964–72; appointed principal d. in 1970. Created roles in A. Howard's *The Tempest* (1964), Charrat's *Phaedra* (1964), Tudor's *Knight Errant* (1968), Cauley's *Symphonie pastorale* (1970), Ashton's *The Creatures of Prometheus* (1970), and Layton's *The Grand Tour* (1971). Returned to S.A. with his d. wife Vicki Karras in 1972.

Davidsbündlertänze. Ballet in 1 act; ch. Balanchine; mus. Schumann; déc. Ter-Arutunian. Prod. 12 (gala preview) and 19 June 1980, N.Y. City B., N.Y. State Th., N.Y., with Farrell, von Aroldingen, H. Watts, Mazzo, d'Amboise, Lüders, Martins, and Ib Andersen. With the piano on stage of a ballroom with suggestion of wintry desolation, the b., set to Schumann's famous piano cycle op. 6, deals with 4 couples on the edge of heartbreak. There are some slight references and parallels to Schumann's own oscillation between desperate mirth and unrestrained melancholy.

David triomphant. Ballet in 2 acts and 3 scenes; ch. Lifar; mus. V. Rieti; déc. F. Léger. Prod. 15 May 1936, Th. de la Maison Internationale des Etudiants, Paris, with Lifar, Slavinska; then 21 June 1937, Opéra, Paris, with Lifar, Chauviré, Darsonval. One of Lifar's 'ballets de rhythmes', it tells the story of David and Goliath and of King Saul and his jealousy of David's deeds. A different version, *David and Goliath*, ch. R. North and W. Sleep, mus. C. Davis, London 1975.

Davies, Sir Peter Maxwell (*b* Manchester, 8 Sep. 1934). Brit. composer. Wrote the mus. for W. Louther's *Vesalii Icones* (London, 1969) and for Flindt's *Salome* (Copenhagen, 1978). His concert mus. has been used by D. Drew in *St Thomas's Wake* (Royal B. touring co., 1971), B. Moreland in *In nomine* (1973, *First Fantasia on an 'In nomine' of John Taverner*) and *Journey to Avalon* (1980, *Missa super L'Homme armé*), both for London Festival B., and R. Alston in *Bell High* (1980, on both *Stedman Doubles* and *Hymnos*) for B. Rambert. Knighted 1987.

Davies, Siobhan (orig. Sue Davies; *b* London, 18 Sep. 1950). Brit. d., teacher and ch. Studied at Hammersmith College of Art and Building 1966–7, and with Robert Cohan at London School of Contemporary D. 1967–71. D. with Ballet For All 1971, and with London Contemporary D. Th. since its inception, originally as student and now as soloist. Became assoc. ch. 1974, member of the directorate and resident ch. 1983; has ch. *Relay* (1972), *Pilot* (1974), *The Calm* (1974), *Diary* (1975) and other works for the co., and *Celebrations* (1979) for B. Rambert. Was involved in the creation of early Richard Alston pieces and several works of Robert Cohan, incl. *No Man's Land* and *Masque of Separation*; d. the Moon in his *Eclipse* and the Goddess in *Stages*. Teacher at London School of Contemporary D. and guest teacher with Ballet Moderne de Paris. Formed her own group of ds. 1981 for which she ch. *Plain Song* and *Standing Waves*.

Day, Mary (*b* Washington, D.C.). Amer. d., teacher, and ch. Studied with Lisa Gardiner, co-founding the Washington School of B. with her in 1944, from which the Washington B. (later National B. of Washington) developed, for which she ch. several bs.

Daydé, Bernard (*b* Paris, 3 Feb. 1921). Fr. th. designer. Among his many b. designs are those for Béjart's *L'Etranger* (1957) and *Pulcinella* (1957), Charrat's *Les Liens* (1957), and *Rencontres* (1966), Lander's *Etudes* (London Festival B., 1956), *Qarrtsiluni* (Paris Opéra, 1960), and *The Sorcerer's Apprentice* (Copenhagen, 1970), Lazzini's *La Valse* (1959), *Les Illuminations* (1962), and *Prodigal Son* (1965), Flindt's *La Leçon* (1964) and *The Three Musketeers* (1966); and the Paris Opéra's *Hommages à Varèse* (1973).
BIBL.: L. Rossel, 'B.D.', *Les Saisons de la danse* (1972/4).

Daydé, Liane (*b* Paris, 27 Feb. 1932). Fr. dancer. Studied at Paris Opéra B. School, joining its co. when only 13 years old; promoted danseuse étoile in 1951. Left the Opéra in 1959 to d. with the Grand B. du Marquis de Cuevas, after which she continued as a guest ballerina with various cos. and since 1963 as prima ballerina of the Grand B. Classique de France, directed by her husband Claude Giraud. Apart from dancing the traditional ballerina roles, created leading parts in Lifar's *Snow White* (1951), *Fourberies* (1952), and *Romeo and Juliet* (1955), Lander's *Printemps à Vienne* (1954), and Rosen's *Dance Panels in Seven Movements* (Munich, 1963).

Dean, Laura (*b* Staten Island, 3 Dec. 1945). Amer. dancer, choreographer, and teacher. Studied at High School of Performing Arts, School of Amer. B., and with Hoving, Sanasardo, M. Cunningham and Slavenska. D. with P. Taylor Sanasardo, Monk, K. King, and worked with R. Wilson. Formed L.D. D. Co. in 1971 and began to collaborate with Steve Reich and Musicians; works include *Square Dance* (1972), *Circle Dance* (1972), *Jumping Dance* (1972), *Walking Dance* (1973), *Changing Pattern Steady Pulse* (1973), *Spinning Dance* (1974), *Response Dance* (1974), *Music* (1980). Ch. *Night* (mus. Dean) for City Center Joffrey B., 1980. Taught Univ. of Texas, Univ. of Rhode Island, Pratt Institute.

De Angelo, Ann Marie (*b* Pittston, Pa., 1 Oct. 1952). Amer. dancer. Studied with Vilzak and Schollar at San Francisco B. School. Joined San Francisco B. 1970, then Joffrey B. 1972–82. Has also d. with Amer. B. Th. and numerous cos. abroad. Has her own programme *Tribute to Pavlova* (1981). Awards: Varna (1976) and Jackson, Miss. (1979).

Death and the Maiden. Ballet in 1 act; ch. and cost. A. Howard; mus. Schubert. Prod. 23 Feb. 1937, B. Rambert, Duchess Th., London, with Howard. The b. uses the Andante con moto from Schubert's String Quartet in D minor, D 810, showing how a young and happy girl is overcome but finally reconciled with Death. Revived for B. Th., 1940; Northern D. Th., 1969. The complete quartet was ch. by Walter (Wuppertal, 1964).

Deaths and Entrances. Ballet in 1 act; ch. Graham; mus. Hunter Johnson; set Arch Lauterer; cost. Edythe Gilfond; light. Rosenthal. Prod. 26 Dec. 1943, M. Graham and co., 46th St. Th., New York, with Graham, Dudley, Maslow, Hawkins, Cunningham. Based on the life of the Brontë sisters, this is 'the story of the relationships of three sisters who live with their memories in a large gloomy house. At times the sight, or handling, of symbolic objects . . . sets off trains of memories in which the past replaces the present and whole sets of relationships are acted out with incredible intensity' (D. McDonagh). A preview perf. with improvised costs. and piano accompaniment, 18 July 1943, Bennington College Th. Another b. by R. Hynd, *Charlotte Brontë* (mus. D. Young), for Royal B. touring co. 1974.

Déboulé (Fr. suddenly running away). Designates a turn from one foot to the other, with the feet held very close together in first position, executed as quickly as possible. Is performed either in a straight line (chainé) or in a circle (en manège).

Debussy, Claude (b St-Germain-en-Laye, 22 Aug. 1862, d Paris, 25 [not 26] Mar. 1918). Fr. composer. He occasionally composed for the d. th.: his *Masques et Bergamasques* of 1910 did not grow beyond the scenario stage, but in 1911 he composed *Le Martyre de Saint-Sébastien* (ch. Fokine, commissioned by Rubinstein), and in 1912, *Khamma*, commissioned by Maud Allan, a légende dansée (scenic first prod. in the instrumentation of Koechlin at the Paris Opéra Comique in 1947, ch. Etchevery); then *Jeux* (ch. Nijinsky, 1913) for Diaghilev and *La Boîte à joujoux* for the Th. Lyrique de Vaudeville (first prod. in the instrumentation of André Chaplet in 1919, ch. André Hellé). Later versions of *Jeux* by Darrell (Western Th. B., 1963), and other chs. Apart from these works his concert mus. has often been used by choreographers—L. Fuller in *Nuages* and *Sirènes* (1913), Nijinsky in *L'Après-midi d'un faune* (1912)—and many other versions, Bolender in *The Still Point* (the first 3 movements of the String Quartet, 1955), Van Dantzig in *Night Island* (*Six Epigraphes antiques*, orch. Ansermet, 1955; revived B. Rambert, 1966), Walter in *La Damoiselle élue* (Düsseldorf, 1966), Sequoio in *Wind's Bride* (String Quartet, 1967), Schilling in *La Mer* (Varna, 1968), Cauley in *Chansons de Bilitis* (1970), Cranko in *Brouillards* (several of his préludes for piano, Stuttgart, 1970), and Kylián in *Cathédrale engloutie* (The Hague, 1975).

Dedans (Fr., inside). Designates the inward turning of the legs or arms (en d.) as opposed to en dehors.

Défilé (Fr. march past). Designates the spectacular presentation of an entire co., e.g. on the stage of the Paris Opéra, from the élèves to the étoiles in strict observance of the hierarchical grading. In rigorously symmetrical formations the co. parades to the sounds of the march from Berlioz' *The Trojans* (ch. Aveline). Originally (and again in 1975) mus. from *Tannhäuser* was used.

Dégagé (Fr. disengaged). The shifting of weight from one foot to the other.

Degas, Edgar Hilaire Germain (b Paris, 19 July 1834, d Paris, 26 Sep. 1917). Fr. painter. He drew, painted, and modelled many dancers during their work in the studio and on the stage; he was less interested in their personalities than in the sensuous play of light and shadow in their movements. His genre drawings and paintings have inspired various bs., incl. Ashton's *Foyer de la danse* (1932) and Lifar's *Entre deux rondes* (1940).

D'Egville, James Harvey (b c. 1770, d c. 1836). Brit. dancer and choreographer. The son of Pierre D'E., b. master at the London Drury Lane and Sadler's Wells. Th., he appeared in 1783 as a child

d. at the King's Th. He d. at the Paris Opéra 1784–5. Dauberval had a very high opinion of him. From 1793 onwards he worked in London again, becoming a close collaborator of Noverre; became ch. at the King's Th. 1799–1809, and composed the mus. for many of his bs. In response to the shortage of imported dancers during the Napoleonic Wars, he founded an Academy of D. for the training of Eng. dancers.
BIBL.: entry 'D'E.' in *Enciclopedia dello spettacolo*.

De Hesse, Jean-Baptiste François (also Des-Haies, Dezaies, or Deshayes; b The Hague, 1705, d Paris, 22 May 1779). Fr. dancer, choreographer, and b. master; it has not yet been established whether he was a member of the famous Deshayes family. Trained by his Fr. actor parents, with whom he toured Holland, Belgium, and Fr., became a noted d. in comic, grotesque, and character parts. He then embarked on a career as a ch., and became one of the most influential pioneers of the b. d'action. B. master of Le Th. des petits appartements at Versailles 1747–51, where he built up a children's troupe and ch. all the bs., for perf. by a mixed group of professional and non-professional artists. He then worked for the Paris Opéra Comique, until he retired in 1768. Much respected by his contemporaries as 'the most excellent composer of ballets in Europe' and 'the greatest ballet-master in all Europe before Noverre's advent'; his best known bs. included *La Vallée de Montmorency* (1745), *Le Pédant* (1748), and *Divertissement pantomime, la Guinguette* (1750).
BIBL.: M. H. Winter, in *The Pre-Romantic Ballet* (London, 1974).

Dehors (Fr., outside). Designates the outward turning of the legs or arms (en d.) as opposite to en dedans.

Dejanow, Bisser (b Swoge, 11 Mar. 1949). Bulg. dancer. Studied at Sofia State B. School, graduating 1965. Continued to study at Leningrad Ch. School 1965–8. Joined Sofia State Op. B. 1968, becoming principal d. First Prize (junior category, Varna, 1968); Gold Medal (Varna, 1974).

De Jong, Bettie (b Sumatra, Indonesia, 5 May 1933). Dutch dancer, teacher, and b. mistress. Studied with Max Dooyes, Jan Bronk, Graham, Limón, and D. Farnworth. D. with the cos. of Graham, Lang, Hoving, Butler, and since 1962 P. Taylor, creating many roles in his works and becoming b. mistress of his co. in 1973. Has also taught at Graham School, London Contemporary School of D., Rambert B. School, and P. Taylor master-classes.
BIBL.: S. Goodman, 'B.D.J.', *Dance Magazine* (1964/11).

Delibes, Clément Philibert Léo (b St-Germain-du-Val, 21 Feb. 1836, d Paris, 16 Jan. 1891). Fr. composer. He composed the b. *La Source* (second and third scene, ch. Saint-Léon, Paris Opéra) with Minkus in 1866 followed by *Coppélia ou La Fille* *aux yeux d'email* (ch. Saint-Léon, Paris Opéra, 1870), and *Sylvia ou La Nymphe de Diane* (ch. Mérante, Paris Opéra, 1876).

Deller, Florian (baptized Drosendorf, 2 May 1729), *d* Munich, 19 Apr. 1773). Austrian violinist and composer. In 1751 he became a member of the Stuttgart court orchestra and was later one of Noverre's closest collaborators, composing for him *Orfeo ed Euridice* (1763), *Der Sieg des Neptun* (1763), *La Morte di Licomede* (1764), the dances for Jommelli's ops. *La Schiava liberata* (1768), *Ballo polonese* and *La Costanza*—probably also *La Mort d'Hercule* (1762). Some of his b. compositions were also ch. by Lauchery in Kassel.

Dello Joio, Norman (*b* New York, 24 Jan. 1913). Amer. composer. Wrote the mus for Loring's *Prairie* (1942), Kidd's *On Stage!* (1945), Graham's *Diversion of Angels* (1948), *Seraphic Dialogue* (orig. *Triumph of St. Joan*, 1951), and *A Time of Snow* (1968), and Limón's *There Is A Time* (1956).

Delsarte, François (*b* Solesmes, 11 Nov. 1811, *d* Paris, 20 July 1871). Fr. mus. teacher and theoretician. He analysed the gestures and expressions of the human body, dividing the movements into 3 categories (eccentric, concentric, and normal) and the expressions into 3 zones (head, torso, and limbs), formulating from them his system of teaching the control of body movements. Through his pupils and spokesmen—among them Jaques-Dalcroze and Shawn—his theories have strongly influenced the pioneers of modern d.
BIBL.: T. Shawn in *Every Little Movement* (New York, 1954); O. Maynard, 'In Homage to F.D.': 1811–1871' *Dance Magazine* (1971/8).

Demi (Fr., half). Designates a movement, position, or pose, executed in half measure only (or hinted at)—e.g. demi-plié. As demi-caractère it means a type of dancer or dancing, adding character flavour to a basically academic technique.

Demoiselles de la nuit, Les. Ballet in 1 act and 3 scenes; libr. J. Anouilh; ch. Petit; mus. J. Françaix; déc. Fini. Prod. 22 May 1948, Bs. de Paris, Th. Marigny, Paris, with Fonteyn, Petit, Hamilton. A young musician falls in love with Agathe, the cat; she tries very hard to be his faithful wife, but cannot resist the wailing of the tom-cats, so she leaps back to freedom and he falls to his death from the rooftops as he tries to get hold of her, whereupon she decides to follow him.
BIBL.: C. Beaumont, 'L.D.d.l.n.' in *Ballets of Today* (London, 1954).

Demon, The (orig. Ger. title: *Der Dämon*). D.-pantomime in 2 scenes; libr. Max Krell; mus. Hindemith; dir. Albrecht Joseph; déc T. C. Pilartz. Prod. 1 Dec. 1923, Darmstadt, with Nini Willenz, Aenne Osterborn, and Gillis von Rappard. A demon subjugates two sisters in succession

and then turns to his next victim. Later prods. by Jooss (Münster, 1925), Keith (Berlin Munic. Op., 1949), Chladek (Austrian TV, 1959), and Limón (New York, 1963).

Denard, Michaël (*b* Dresden, 5 Nov. 1944). Fr. dancer. Studied with Golovina, Peretti, and Franchetti; made his début in Toulouse. Came via Nancy to the Paris Opéra Comique, where he first appeared as an extra; d. with the cos. of Golovine D. Sanders, Lorca Massine, and Lacotte, eventually joining the Paris Opéra, promoted étoile in 1971. Also a regular guest soloist with Amer. B. Th. He dances the premier danseur roles of the standard repertory and created leading parts in Lifar's *Istar* (1967 version), Béjart's *Firebird* (1970), Descombey's *Visage* (1970), Lacotte's *La Sylphide* TV prod. (1972), M. Cunningham's *Un jour ou deux* (1973), Petit's *Shéhérazade*, B. Macdonald's *Variations on a Simple Theme*, Tetley's *Tristan* (1974), and Petit's *Symphonie fantastique* (1975). Nijinsky Prize (1971). TV Portrait d'une étoile (ORTF, 1975).
BIBL.: A.-P. Hersin, 'M.D.' with complete checklist of roles and activities, *Les Saisons de la danse* (1974/11).

Denby, Edwin (*b* Tientsin, China, 1903, *d* Searsport, Maine, 12 July 1983). Amer. writer and critic. Studied at Harvard Univ., in Vienna, and at Hellerau-Laxenburg, d. during the early 1930s with the Darmstadt co. D. critic of *Modern Music* 1936–42 and of *New York Herald Tribune* 1942–5. Contributor to many d. magazines. Author of *Looking at the Dance* (New York, 1949) and *Dancers, Buildings and People in the Streets* (New York, 1965).
BIBL.: Portfolio E.D., *Dance Magazine* (1969/1); interview with E.D. *Ballet Review* (vol. 2, nos. 5 and 6).

Denham, Sergei I. (*b* Moscow, 1897, *d* New York, 30 Jan. 1970). Russ.-Amer. b. impresario. Interested in b. from his student days; he became vice-president of the Amer. corporation which ran the B. Russe de Monte Carlo in 1938 (after Massine's departure from Colonel de Basil's B. Russe had brought about a complete reorganization of the co.). He directed it for 24 years and in 1954 founded the B. Russe School in New York (taking over the Swoboda-Yurieva School).

Denishawn. The school, named after and directed by *Ruth St. Denis and *Ted Shawn, opened in Los Angeles in 1915. Though all kinds of d. were taught, its main attention was concentrated on modern d. Branches all over the U.S. were soon established. Many of the leading personalities of the modern d. scene have at one time or another studied at D.—among them Graham, Humphrey, Shurr, Weidman, and Cole. For several years L. Horst was its mus. dir. In 1931, when St. Denis and Shawn separated, D. and its performing co. (which had toured the U.S. extensively) ceased to function.

BIBL.: B. Hastings, 'The D. Era'. *Dance Index* (vol. 1, no. 6), J. Sherman, *The Drama of Denishawn Dance* (Middleton, Conn., 1979).

Denmark. See *Royal Danish Ballet.*

Derain, André (*b* Chatou, 10 June 1880, *d* Chambourcy, 11 Sep. 1954). Fr. painter. Designed the déc. for Massine's *La Boutique fantasque* (1919), Balanchine's *Jack in the Box* (1926), *La Concurrence* (1932), *Les Songes* (1933), and *Les Fastes* (1933), Lifar's *Salade* (1935), Fokine's *L'Epreuve d'amour* (1936), Ashton's *Harlequin in the Street* (1938), and Petit's *Que le Diable l'emporte* (1948), Massine's *Mam'zelle Angot* (1947), *Les Femmes de bonne humeur* (prod. Grand B. du Marquis de Cuevas, 1949), and *La Valse* (1950).
BIBL.: H. Rischbieter (ed.), 'A.D.' in *Art and Stage in the 20th Century* (New York, 1971).

Derevianko, Vladimir Ilich (*b* Omsk, 15 Jan. 1959). Sov. dancer. Studied at Novosibirsk B. School 1970–1 and at Moscow Bolshoi B. School 1971–7. Joined Bolshoi B. in 1977. Bronze Medal (Moscow, 1977), Special Prize (Varna, 1978). Since 1983 has d. with various western cos.

Derman, Vergie (*b* Johannesburg, 18 Sep. 1942). Brit. dancer. Studied with Arnold Dover and at Royal B. School. D. with the Royal B. 1962–6, at the Ger. Op. Berlin 1966–7. Returned to the Royal B. 1967–83; promoted soloist in 1968 and principal d. in 1972. Created leading parts in MacMillan's *Valses nobles et sentimentales* (1966), *Anastasia* (1967, extended version 1971), *The Seven Deadly Sins* (1973), *Manon* and *Elite Syncopations* (1974), *Four Seasons* and *Rituals* (1975), Ashton's *The Dream* (1964) and *Jazz Calendar* (1968), Tetley's *Field Figures* (1971) and *Laborintus* (1972).

Deroc, Jean (*b* Zurich, 5 May 1925). Swiss dancer, choreographer, b. director, and teacher. Studied with Mario Volkart, Kniaseff, Preobrajenska, and Egorova. D. with various cos. in Basle, Malmö, Lyons, Berlin, and Zurich. B. master in St. Gall, Lucerne, Graz, and Bremen. Now dir. of Swiss Chamber B.

Derp, Clothilde von (née C. von der Planitz; *b* Berlin, 1892, *d* Rome, 11 Jan. 1974). Ger. dancer and teacher. She made her début in Munich 1912; d. in M. Reinhardt's London prods. and toured widely with her d. husband Alexander Sakharoff in what they called 'abstract pantomime'—their very individual, rather statuesque, and highly mannered variant of modern d. In 1953 they opened a school in Rome, also conducting regular summer courses in Siena.

Derra de Moroda, Friderica (*b* Pozsony [now Bratislava], Hung., 2 June 1897, *d* Salzburg, 19 June 1978). Greek-Brit. dancer, teacher, b. mistress, and writer. Studied in Munich with Flora Jungmann, various other teachers, and intensively with Cecchetti, graduating as a master pupil. Made her début at the Vienna Secession in 1912,

toured Ger. and Russia as a recital d. From 1913 she concentrated on London, where she appeared in music halls and pantomime, ch. for several troupes, became a co-founder of the Cecchetti Society, and eventually a Life Member of the Imperial Society of Teachers of Dancing. She was dir. of the Berlin based KDF Ballet 1940–4. After 1945 lived in Salzburg, where she had her own school 1952–67. She owned one of the largest private d. collections in the world. As a writer she became known through her publications on d. notation in the 18th century and as an internationally acknowledged authority on Cecchetti. In 1936 she rediscovered the original manuscript of Lambranzi's *Theatralische Tantz-Schul* (1715), which she had earlier translated into Eng. In 1932 she contributed to the second edition of *A Manual of the Theory of Classical Theatrical Dancing*. Co-author (with M. Craske) of *The Theory and Practice of Advanced Allegro in Classical Ballet* (1953). Professor (1972); O.B.E. (1974).

Descombey, Michel (*b* Bois-Colombes, 28 Oct. 1930). Fr. dancer, choreographer, and b. director. Studied with Egorova and at Paris Opéra B. School, joining its co. in 1947; promoted premier danseur in 1959 and b. master 1963–9. B. dir. in Zurich 1971–3. Started to ch. in 1958 for the Opéra comique—among his many creations were *L'Enfant et les sortilèges* (mus. Ravel, 1960), *Symphonie concertante* (mus. F. Martin, 1962), *Sarracenia* (mus. Bartók, 1964), *Coppélia* (mus. Delibes, 1966), *Bacchus and Ariadne* (mus. Roussel, 1967), *Déserts* (mus. Varèse, 1968), *Spectacle Berio* (1970), *Hymnen* (with several other choreographers, mus. Stockhausen, 1970), *Mandala* (mus. Toshiro Mayuzumi (1970), *The Miraculous Mandarin* (mus. Bartók 1971), *Messe en jazz* (mus. L. Schifrin, 1972), *ES, le 8ème jour* (mus. Stockhausen, 1973). Since 1975 has worked in Mexico, appointed associate dir. and chief ch. B. Th. del Espacio de Mexico in 1977. Married to the d. Martine Parmain.

Deserts. Ballet in 1 act; ch. Sokolow; mus. Varèse. Prod. 10 Mar. 1967, Anna Sokolow D. Co., Hunter College Playhouse, New York, with Ze'eva Cohen, Chester Wolenski. A co. work about bareness, aloofness, timelessness, and loneliness. Revived 25 July 1967, B. Rambert, Jeannetta Cochrane Th., London, with J. Taylor, C. Roope, Bruce, Curtis. Other versions by Milloss (Vienna, 1965), and Descombey (B. Th. Contemporain, 1968).

Deshayes, André Jean-Jacques (*b* Paris 1777, *d.* there, 1846). Fr. dancer and choreographer. Descended from a famous Fr. family of artists; he worked under Gardel at the Paris Opéra and then came via Madrid and Milan to London, where he first appeared as a d. at the King's Th. and later also at her Majesty's Th., becoming a much respected ch. up to 1842. He ch. Beethoven's Sixth Symphony and *Masaniello* there in 1829.

Other bs. of his were *Kenilworth* (1831), *Faust* (1833), *Beniowsky* (1836), and *Le Brigand de Terracina* (1837). In 1842 he staged the London first prod. of *Giselle* with Perrot and wrote the libr. for *Alma ou La Fille de feu* for Cerrito. His wife was as Mme Deshayes one of the most respected London dancers of her time.
BIBL.: I. Guest, in *The Romantic Ballet in England* (London, 1954).

Designs with Strings. Ballet in 1 act; ch. Taras, mus. Tchaikovsky; déc. George Krista. Prod. 6 Feb. 1948, Metropolitan B., Edinburgh, with Beriosova, Arova, Franca, Delysia Blake, Bruhn and David Adams Set to the second movement of Tchaikovsky's Trio in A major, the b. has no definite plot, but reflects the vagaries of young love. Revived for B. Th. in 1950 (and for many other cos.—often under variations of the orig. title).
BIBL.: G. Balanchine, 'D.w.S.' in *Balanchine's New Complete Stories of the Great Ballets* (Garden City, N.Y., 1968).

Despréaux, Jean-Etienne (*b* Paris, 1748, *d* there, 1820). Fr. musician, dancer, b. master, and poet. Started as an extra at the Paris Opéra, had to resign as a d. after he injured his foot, and became a violinist; promoted b. master. In 1789, upon his marriage to the d. Madeleine Guimard, he relinquished his th. career, continuing as a poet and satirist. In 1806 he wrote *Mes Passe-Temps: Chansons, suivies de l'art de la danse, poème en quatre chants, calqué sur l'art Poetique de Boileau Despréaux.*
BIBL.: P. Migel, in *The Ballerinas* (New York, 1972).

Dessous (Fr., under). Designates a movement in which the working foot passes behind the supporting foot—as opposed to dessus.

Dessus (Fr., over). Designates a movement in which the working foot passes in front of the supporting foot—as opposed to dessous.

Deuce Coupe. Ballet in 1 act; ch. Tharp; mus. Beach Boys; déc. Graffiti. N.Y. prem. 1 Mar. 1973, City Center Joffrey Ballet and Tharp and her dancers, City Center, New York, with Goodman, Chryst, Tharp. An ambiguous set of dances, with classical steps performed in alphabetical order, while around them the ensemble explodes with eccentric pop movement, until a kind of fusion of pop and b. finally emerges. Revised version *Deuce Coupe II* for the Joffrey dancers only, with new déc. by pop artist James Rosenquist, 1975.

Deuil en 24 heures. Ballet in 1 act and 5 scenes; libr. and ch. Petit; mus. M. Thiriet; déc. Clavé. Prod. 17 Mar. 1953, Bs. de Paris, Th. de l'Empire, Paris, with Marchand, Perrault, Reich. A music-hall farce in the style of the early silent movies, with a beautiful blonde lady, who adores black dresses. When her husband dies of fright at facing his wife's suspected lover in a duel, she is delighted to be able to celebrate her widowhood at Maxim's

in an elegant black dress. Film prod. in *Un-deux-trois-quatre* (Eng. title: *Black Tights*, 1960).
BIBL.: C. Beaumont, 'D.e.24h.' in *Ballets of Today* (London, 1954).

Deutscher (also Deutscher Tanz). A popular, rather fast d. for individual turning couples in 3/4 or 3/8 time—popular in the South of Ger. and Austria during the 18th and early 19th century. Ital. and Fr. called it Tedesco or Allemande (not to be confused with the A. of the baroque). It is a rather rustic d. (Leporello and Masetto perform it in *Don Giovanni*, while their superiors d. the menuet). Its tempo was speeded up so that it approached the waltz. Sometimes also called Ländler. Mozart, Beethoven, and Schubert wrote Deutsche (Tänze).

Deux pigeons, Les (Eng., *The Two Pigeons*). Ballet in 3 acts; libr. Henry Régnier and Mérante (also ch.); mus. Messager; sets Rubé, Chaperon, and J. B. Lavastre; cost. Bianchini. Prod. 18 Oct 1886, Paris Opéra, with Mauri, Marie Sanlaville. The b. is based on Lafontaine's fable of the 2 pigeons: Pepino (originally an en travestie role) dreams of a life of adventure with the gipsies and leaves his fiancée Gourouli. Gourouli follows him disguised as a gipsy and makes him return to her. A 1-act version by Aveline for Zambelli at the Opéra in 1919. A very successful new version by Ashton, déc. J. Dupont, 14 Feb. 1961, Touring Royal B., Cov. Gdn., London, with Seymour, Gable, Ánderton.
BIBL.: C. W. Beaumont, 'L.d.P.' in *Complete Book of Ballets* (London, 1951); P. Brinson and C. Crisp, in *Ballet & Dance* (Newton Abbot, 1980).

De Valois, Ninette. See *Valois, Ninette de*.

Devant (Fr., in front). Designates a movement executed in front of the body.

Développé (Fr. developed). Designates the unfolding of the working leg into an open position in the air, where it is held with perfect control.

Devi, Ritha (*b* Baroda, 6 Dec. 1934). Ind. dancer and teacher. Studied Manipuri, Bharata Natyam, Kathakali, Mohiniattam, Kuchipudi, Opissi, and Satriya Nritya with some of India's most famous gurus. Has been touring as a solo d. continually since 1958, being acclaimed all over the world as India's most versatile d. Has taught at London's The Place and Jacob's Pillow. Now teacher of Indian d.-technique at New York Univ.

Devil in the Village, The (orig. Croatian title: *Davo u selu*). Ballet in 3 acts and 8 scenes; libr. and ch. P. and P. Mlakar; mus. F. Lhotka; sets Roman Clemens. Prod. 18 Feb. 1935, Zurich, with the Mlakars, Mischa Panajew, Maja Kübler. The b. tells of the young peasant Mirko who loves Jela but in his simplemindedness is ensnared by the devil, who seduces him to all kinds of vice and takes him to hell. Mirko's robust moral health finally triumphs over the devil's artifices, and he returns to Jela to save her at the last moment from marrying a wealthy simpleton. The b. has been constantly revived in the Mlakars' and other ch. versions in the Ger. speaking countries and in Yugoslavia, where it still enjoys great popularity.

Devil's Holiday. Ballet with prologue, in 3 scenes and 2 entr'actes; libr. and mus. V. Tommasini; ch. Ashton; déc. Berman. Prod. 26 Oct. 1939, B. Russe de Monte Carlo, Met. Op. House, New York, with Semenoff, Danilova, Franklin, Zoritch, Platoff. Arranged to themes from Paganini, the b. tells of the love affair between the daughter of an impoverished lord and a poor young man. Her father wants her to marry a rich man, and so the devil has to play some tricks during carnival to straighten things out.

Devil's Violin, The. See *Violon du diable, Le*.

Diable amoureux, Le. Ballet in 3 acts and 8 scenes; libr. Vernoy de Saint-Georges; ch. Mazilier; mus. François Benoist and Napoléon-Henri Reber; sets Humanité-René Philastre and Charles-Antoine Cambon; cost. Paul Lormier. Prod. 23 Sep. 1840, Paris Opéra, with Leroux, Noblet, Mazilier. The amorous devil of the title is Urielle, a female demon, who in the guise of a page tries to win the soul of the impoverished count Frédéric. When Urielle's body finally bursts into flames, only the intervention of an angel can stop the demons of Beelzebub from tearing their former colleague into pieces.
BIBL.: C. W. Beaumont, 'L.D.a.' in *Complete Book of Ballets* (London, 1951).

Diable à quatre, Le (Eng. title: *The Devil to Pay or The Wives Metamorphosed*). Ballet in 3 acts; libr. Adolphe de Leuven; ch. Mazilier; mus. Adam; sets P. L. C. Ciceri, E. D. J. Despléchin, and C. Séchan; cost. P. Lormier. Prod. 11 Aug. 1845, Paris Opéra, with Grisi, L. Petipa, Mazilier. The b. is set in Poland and has two leading couples: the Count and Countess, and the basketmaker Mazurki and his wife Mazurka. In addition there is a blind violinist, whose instrument is broken by the Countess, whereupon he reveals himself as a Magician. She is punished by having to play the role of the basketmaker's wife for a day, being roughly treated by Mazurki, while Mazurka as the Countess astonishes everybody at the castle by her unaccustomed kindness. At the end the Countess and Mazurki solemnly promise to behave more humanely in the future. First London prod., Princess's Th., 1845; first New York prod., Broadway Th., 1848.
BIBL.: C. W. Beaumont, 'L.D.à q.' in *Complete Book of Ballets* (London, 1951).

Diable boîteux, Le (Eng. title: *The Devil on Two Sticks*). Pantomimic ballet in 3 acts; libr. Butat de Gurguy and A. Nourrit; ch. Coralli; mus. Casimir Gide; sets Feuchères, C. Séchan, J.-P.-M. Diéterle, and H.-R. Philastre; cost. E. Lami. Prod. 1 June

1836, Opéra, Paris with Elssler, Mazilier. The b. is based on Lesage's novel on the same title. The student Cléophas helps the demon Asmodée to escape from a bottle in which he is imprisoned and is rewarded by the conjuring up of 3 beautiful ladies. He falls passionately in love with the d. Florinda (this was the occasion of Elssler's famous cachucha), loses all his money through gambling in Dorothea's house, and finally meets his true love in the poor Paquita. First London prod. Drury Lane Th., 1836.
BIBL.: C. W. Beaumont, 'L.D.b.' in *Complete Book of Ballets* (London, 1951).

Diaghilev, Sergei Pavlovich (b Selistchev barracks, province of Novgorod, 31 Mar. 1872, d Venice, 19 Aug. 1929). Russ. b. impresario. He came to St. Petersburg in 1890 as a law-student, and soon became a member of the circle of young musicians, painters, and writers assembled around A. Benois and L. Bakst. Co-founder of the progressively orientated art magazine *Mir Iskosstva* (The World of Art) in 1899. In the same year he was appointed artistic adviser to the Maryinsky Th., where he was in charge of the publication of the th. annual and of the highly successful prods. of *Sadko* and *Sylvia*. He resigned from this post in 1901. After the magazine stopped appearing in 1904, concentrated on organizing exhibitions of Russ. art in St. Petersburg and Paris. In 1908 he brought a prod. of *Boris Godunov* to Paris with Chaliapin. From this came an invitation to present a Paris season of Russ. op. and b. in 1909. With some of the best dancers from St. Petersburg and Moscow he scored a unique triumph in May and June 1909 in Paris. Repeat visits during the following years led to the gradual formation of his Bs. Russes, which became an independent private co. when Nijinsky, his friend and male star, resigned from the Maryinsky Th. He directed his Bs. Russes until he died in 1929, and effected a complete reformation of the Eur. b. scene. His co. was often on the verge of bankruptcy, and never returned to Russia after the October Revolution (nor indeed ever performed there); it was a pure product of the Eur. financial aristocracy. With his infallible flair for young and rising talent, his immaculate taste, and his singular gift of integrating various interests and people, he exerted a marked influence on the b. scene of his day, the aftermath of which can be seen even today. Thanks to him b. regained its artistic integrity and seriousness. Thus he became a catalyst of all the most important artistic trends and developments during the 1910s and 1920s. Contrary to what one occasionally reads, he never ch. a b. himself. The long list of his collaborators includes some of the foremost artistic personalities of those two decades—as dancers: Karsavina, Tchernicheva, Lopokova, Spessivtzeva, Sokolova, Danilova, Doubrovska, Nijinsky, Bolm, Woizikovsky, Dolin, and Lifar—as choreographers: Fokine, Nijinsky, Massine, Nijinska, and Balan-

chine—as designers: Benois, Bakst, Roerich, Picasso, Matisse, Laurencin, Derain, Braque, Utrillo, and de Chirico—as composers: Stravinsky, Prokofiev, Ravel, Debussy, Satie, de Falla, Milhaud, and Poulenc. There can be no question that D. was one of the major personalities of the artistic scene of the 20th century. For a list of the bs. he produced see *Ballets Russes de Diaghilev*, two BBC TV films on D. by John Drummond, 1968.
BIBL.: R. Buckle, *D.* (London, 1979).

Diana Ballets. There are many bs. about the goddess of the moon (also called Artemis), who was also the goddess of hunting and chastity. Noverre's *Diane et Endymion* (mus. Starzer, Vienna, 1772), Giuseppe Fabiani's *Diana ed Endimione* (Venice, 1765), Onorato Viganò's *Diana sorpresa* (Venice, 1774), Mme Rossi's *La Surprise de Diane* (mus. Joseph Wölfl, London, 1805), and Nijinska's *Aubade* (mus. Poulenc, 1929). Heine published in 1854 a b. libr., *Die Göttin Diana*, which seems never to have been produced; nor has the b. *Das Wunder der Diana*, composed by E. Wellesz in 1924. For the Diana and Actaeon pas de deux see *Esmeralda*.

Dichterliebe-Amor di poeta. Ballet by Béjart; mus. R. Schumann and N. Rota; poems and texts by H. Heine and Ch. Baudelaire; set and light. Alan Burett; cost. T. Bosquet. Prod. 4 Dec. 1978, B. of the 20th Century, Palais des Beaux Arts, Brussels, with Béjart, Donn, Y. le Gac, C. Verneuil, R. Poelvoorde, M. Gascard, P. Touron. With Béjart himself in the central role of Le Poète, and with Donn as Le Héros de l'histoire, the ch. has here created an autobiographical alfresco revue à la Fellini (based upon Schumann's famous songcycle, with additional mus. by Rota), which he has peopled with Les Amis (Les Muses, Un Chat, Elle), Les Forces de la mort (L'homme en noir, La Femme en blanc, Le Motard), Les Personnages mythologiques (Pegase, Dionysos, Zarathoustra), and La Poésie de derisoire (Le Cirque).
BIBL.: N. McLain Stoop, 'The Creator and the Interpreters', *Dance Magazine* (1979/3).

Dickson, Charles (*b* Bellwood, Pa., 30 June 1921). Amer. dancer, teacher, choreographer, and b. director. Studied with Ruth Barnes, Fokine, Massine, Balanchine, Vilzak, Vladimiroff, and others. D. with B. Russe de Monte Carlo 1938–40, B. Th. 1940–2, later also on broadway. B. master of Bs. Alicia Alonso 1952–5, Borovansky B. 1955–8, London Festival B. 1958–62, National B. of Chile 1962–6. Currently teaching at Met. Academy of B., Bethesda, Maryland, and Dir. of Met. B. Co.

Didelot, Charles-Louis (*b* Stockholm, 1767, *d* Kiev, 7 Nov. 1837). Fr. dancer, choreographer, and teacher. Studied with his father at the Royal Th. in Stockholm, continuing with Dauberval and Lany in Paris and Bordeaux, later also with Noverre and Vestris. Made his début under Noverre in London in 1788; came via Bordeaux

in 1790 to the Paris Opéra, where he was the partner of M. Guimard. Then worked in London, where he ch. his most famous b. *Flore et Zéphyre* for the King's Th. in 1796. He was b. master, ch., and teacher in St. Petersburg 1801–11, where he completely reorganized the whole system of b. teaching, thus laying the foundation for the famous St. Petersburg school style. The following 5 years he spent reviving his bs. for Paris and London, before finally returning to St. Petersburg in 1816, continuing his b. reforms at the Imperial Ths. After his wife Rose Pole (or Paul) died in St. Petersburg in 1803, he married the d. Rose Colinette in 1807/8, who was a great favourite with her contemporaries. A faithful pupil of Noverre and Dauberval, D. was very influential in spreading the gospel of the b. d'action, becoming a much respected man: Pushkin said 'there is more poetry in his bs. than in the whole Fr. literature of his times'. He created a great number of bs., incl.: *Apollo and Daphne* (1802), *Cupid and Psyche* (mus. C. Cavos, 1810), *Telemachus on the Island of Calypso* (1807), *The Hungarian Hut* (mus. F. M. A. Venua, 1813), *Nicette and Lucas or the Young Milkmaid* (1817), *Raoul de Créquis or The Return from the Crusade* (mus. Cavos, 1819), and *The Prisoner of the Caucasus* (mus. Cavos, 1823). He was also in charge of the first Russ. prod. of Dauberval's *La Fille mal gardée*.
BIBL.: M. G. Swift, *A Loftier Flight: The Life and Accomplishments of C.-L.D.* (Middletown, Conn., 1975).

Dienes, Gedeon (*b* Budapest, 16 Dec. 1914). Hung. dance publicist. The son of Valeria D. Lived in Raymond Duncan's Paris and Nice colony 1921–2, appearing in his Greek D. group of children. Graduated in Bewegungskunst and as a teacher of ballroom dancing in Budapest, 1936. Taught and arranged dances in his mother's 'orchestic school'. Joined Ministry of Foreign Affairs 1946–52. Editor for Eng. and Russ. publications at Publishing House of Hung. Academy of Sciences. Dr. jur. (Pécs, 1948). Created Library and Documentation for Hung. Inst. of Cultural Relations 1964–73. As Head of Intern. Dept. at the Inst. for Culture since 1973 has participated in numerous intern. conferences of UNESCO etc. Also a member for Hung. on the D. Committee of the Intern. Th. Inst. since its foundation. Editor (and sometimes author) of Hung. Studies of D. Science 1959–75. Contributor to various intern. d. encyclopedias and dictionaries.

Dienes, Valeria (*b* Szekszárd, 25 May 1879, *d* Budapest, 8 June 1978). Hung. dance publicist, choreographer and dance theoretician. Studied philosophy and mathematics at Budapest univ. (doctor of philosophy, mathematics and esthetics, Budapest 1905), then with Henri Bergson at the Paris College de France. After attending some I. Duncan perfs. in Paris and participating in Raymond Duncan's courses of Greek callisthenics, concentrated in Budapest on her systematic research of human movements, starting 1912 with a course of Greek gymnastics, from which developed her 'Orchestic School'—her individual system of teaching and choreographing, which she also took abroad and spread through books and other publications. Started to give perfs. 1917, culminating in her great ch. movement-dramas of the 1920s and 30s like *Waiting for the Dawn* (1925), *The Eight Beatitudes* (1926), *Wedding of the Ten Virgins* (1934), *Mystery Play of St. Emeric or Hungarian Fate* (1930), *The Children's Road* (1935), and *The Mother* (1937)—most of them with Lajos Bárdos as musical collaborator). Her institute existed until 1944. Her system of 'Orchestic' is based upon the 4 criteria of human movement: space, time, power, and meaning—corresponding with sculpture, rhythm, dynamics, and symbolism. She was the mother of the d. publicist Gedeon D.

Diénis, Jean-Claude (*b* Paris, 22 Oct. 1941). Fr. writer on b. Secretary and critic of *Les Saisons de la danse* since its inception in 1968. Fr. correspondent of Ger. b. annual *Ballett* since 1972. Editor of special Béjart issue of *Les Saisons de la danse* (1973).

Dieu bleu, Le. Ballet in 1 act; libr. Cocteau and Frédéric de Madrazo; ch. Fokine; mus. R. Hahn; déc. Bakst. Prod. 13 May 1912, Bs. Russes de Diaghilev, Th. du Châtelet, Paris, with Nijinsky, Karsavina. The b. depicts a Hindu legend of the love of a young couple, against a background of temple rituals.

Dieu et la Bayadère, Le. Ballet divertissement from the op. of the same title by Auber; ch. F. Taglioni. Prod. 13 Oct. 1830, Paris Opéra, with Taglioni, Noblet. This is really a b. op., based upon Goethe's ballad *Der Gott und die Bajadere*. The heavily mime-orientated role of the bayadère Zoloé was one of Taglioni's greatest triumphs. A different treatment of a similar story was Petipa's *La Bayadère* (St. Petersburg, 1877).

Dieux mendiants, Les. See *Gods Go a-Begging, The.*

Dijk, Peter van. See *Dyk, Peter van.*

Dim Lustre. Ballet in 1 act; libr. and ch. Tudor; mus. R. Strauss; déc. Motley. Prod. 20 Oct. 1943, B. Th., Met. Op. House, New York, with Kaye, Laing. Set to Strauss's Burlesque in D minor for piano and orchestra, the b. centres upon 'a whiff of perfume, the touch of a hand, a stolen kiss, releasing whirls of memories which take the rememberers back briefly to other moments and leave them not exactly as they were before' (programme note). Revived for New York City B. (1964).
BIBL.: G. Balanchine, '*D.L.*' in *Balanchine's New Complete Stories of the Great Ballets* (Garden City, N.Y., 1968).

Diversion of Angels. Ballet in 1 act; ch. Graham; mus. Dello Joio; set Noguchi. Prod. 13 Aug. 1948, M. Graham D. Co., Conn. College, New London, with O'Donnell, Lang, McGehee, Hawkins, Cohan. The title (originally *Wilderness Stair*) comes from a poem by Ben Bellitt; the b. is 'a lyric ballet about the loveliness of youth, the pleasure and playfulness, quick joy and quick sadness of being in love for the first time. It tells no story but, like a lyric poem, simply explores its theme' (programme note).

Diversions. Ballet in 1 act; ch. MacMillan; mus. Bliss; déc. Philip Prowse. Prod. 15 Sep. 1961, Royal B., Cov. Gdn., London with Lane, Beriosova, MacLeary, Usher. Set to Bliss's *Music for Strings*, this is a plotless b. for 2 contrasting solo couples and 8 female dancers. Revived for Stuttgart (1964) and Ger. Op. Berlin (1967).

Divertimento. Ballet in 5 parts; ch. Balanchine; mus. A. Haieff; light. Rosenthal. Prod. 13 Jan. 1947, B. Society, Hunter College Playhouse, New York, with Moylan, Moncion. This is a plotless b., built around a girl going from one party to another.
BIBL.: G. Balanchine, '*D*' in *Balanchine's New Complete Stories of the Great Ballets* (Garden City, N.Y., 1968).

Divertimento No. 15. Ballet in 5 movements; ch. Balanchine; mus. Mozart; set Hays; cost. Karinska. Prod. 31 May 1956, New York City B., Amer. Shakespeare Festival Th., Stratford, Conn., with LeClercq, Magallanes. This is a plotless b., set to Mozart's Divertimento in B flat major, KV 287, and d. by 5 girls, 3 boys, and a corps of 8 girls, reflecting the serene mood of the individual movements. An earlier version under the title *Caracole* was first performed in 1952 at the City Center Th. of New York. Revived for various cos.
BIBL.: G. Balanchine, '*D. No. 15*' in *Balanchine's Complete Stories of the Great Ballets* (Garden City, N.Y., 1968).

Divertissement (Fr., entertainment). Originally used for dances and songs inserted in a stage spectacle of the 18th century. They usually occur between single acts or at the end of the work, but also as special episodes loosely connected with the main plot. As b. inserts they are to be encountered in many Fr. ops. (Rameau's *Platée*, Gluck's *Iphigénie en Aulide*, Gounod's *Faust*, Saint-Saëns' *Samson et Dalila*), while the major action bs of the 19th century prefer to introduce them as a kind of dance-suite in the last act (e.g. in *Coppélia* and *Sleeping Beauty*). The term is also used for an arrangement of soli, pas de deux, and smaller group dances within a concert programme of dances.

Dixon, Norman (*b* Northampton, 1926). Brit. dancer, choreographer, and b. master. Studied at a local school and from 1947 at Sadler's Wells and later at Rambert B. School; joined B. Rambert in 1949, also d. with Gore's co. B. master and ch. at the Welsh National Op. in 1959. Went to Lisbon in 1960, to Rijeka (Yugosl.) in 1967, to Santiago de Chile in 1968, to Montevideo in 1970; since 1972 he has pursued a career as a freelance ch. and dir., mainly working in Yugoslavia. Artistic Dir., Rijeka National Th. B. since 1975. One of his most frequently revived prods. is *La Fille mal gardée*.

Doboujinsky, Mstislav (*b* Novgorod, 2 Aug. 1875, *d* New York, 1957). Russ. painter. Diaghilev commissioned him to do the designs for Fokine's *Papillons* (1914) and *Midas* (1914). Later designs of his were *The Fairy Doll* (Pavlova co., 1915), *Coppélia* (B. de Monte Carlo, 1935, and B. Rambert, 1956), *The Nutcracker* (Sadler's Wells B., 1937), *Ballet Imperial* (Amer. B., 1941), *Russian Soldier* (B. Th., 1942), *Mam'zelle Angot* (B. Th., 1943), *Graduation Ball* (B. Th., 1944), and *Prisonnier du Caucase* (Grand B. du Marquis de Cuevas, 1951).

Dobrievich, Pierre (*b* Veles, 27 Dec. 1931). Yugosl. dancer and b. master. Studied at Zagreb State B. School. Début with Zagreb State Op. B. in 1955; then d. with B. Th. de Paris, co. of Tcherina, Les Etoiles de Paris, and from 1960 with B. of the 20th Century; b. master until 1975. B. Director La Scala, Milan, 1975–81, and from 1981 at Munich State Op. Married to the d. Louba Dobrievich.

Docherty, Peter (*b* Blackpool, 21 June 1944). Brit. designer. Educated at Regent St. Poly, Central School of Arts and Crafts, and Slade School of Fine Art. Designed Darrell's *Ephemeron* (Western Th. B., 1968), *Four Portraits* (Scottish Th. B., 1971), *Tales of Hoffmann* (Amer. B. Th. prod., 1973), and *Mary, Queen of Scots* (1976), Hynd's *Dvořák Variations* (London Festival B., 1970), *Le Baiser de la fée* (Munich State Op. B., 1971), *In a Summer Garden* (Royal B., 1972), *Mozartiana* (London Festival B., 1973), and *Charlotte Brontë* (Royal B., 1974), *The Sanguine Fan* and *Nutcracker* (both London Festival B., 1976), *La Chatte* (London Festival B., 1977), *Rosalinda* (PACT B., 1977; London Festival B., 1979), *Papillon* (Houston B., 1979; Sadler's Wells Royal B., 1980), *Les Valses* (Grands Bs. Canadiens) and *The Seasons* (Houston B., both 1980), and W. Dollar's *Francesca da Rimini* (Asami Maki B., 1978).

Dokoudovsky, Vladimir (*b* Monte Carlo, 31 May 1919). Amer. dancer, teacher, and choreographer. Studied with Preobrajenska. D. with Monte Carlo Op. B. 1934–5, B. Russe de Paris 1936, Nijinska's B. Polonais, 1937, B. Russe de Monte Carlo 1938, Mordkin B. 1939–40, B. Th. 1940–1, Original B. Russe 1942–50. Teacher of B. Arts at Carnegie Hall since 1950, Amer. B. Th. School since 1965, and Amer. B. Th. co. since 1966, Has ch. many bs. Now Dir. of N.Y. Conservatory of D. Married to the d. Patricia Heyes.

Dolgushin, Nikita Alexandrovich (*b* Leningrad, 8 Nov. 1938). Sov. dancer and choreographer. Studied at the Leningrad Ch. School, graduating in 1959; became a member of the Kirov B. 1959–61, dancing at Novosibirsk 1961–6 and with Moiseyev's State Concert Ensemble 1966–8; then returned to Leningrad, where he is now one of the top soloists at the Maly Th., but also appears at the Kirov Th. He dances the premier danseur roles of the standard repertory. Created Prince Igor in Vinogradov's *Yaroslavna* (1974). Among the bs. he has ch. so far are *Concert in White* (mus. Tchaikovsky, 1969), *Mozartiana* (mus. Tchaikovsky, 1970), and *Clytemnesstra* (mus. Gluck, 1972). Gold Medal (Varna, 1964).

Dolin, Sir Anton (orig. Sydney Francis Patrick Chippendall Healey-Kay; *b* Slinfold, 27 July 1904, *d* Paris, 25 Nov. 1983). Brit. dancer, choreographer, and teacher. Started to study in Brighton, then with Astafieva and Nijinska. Appeared as a child actor. Joined the Diaghilev *Sleeping Princess* prod. in London 1921 as a corps member; rejoined and promoted soloist in 1924. Created roles in Nijinska's *Le Train bleu* (1924) and Balanchine's *The Prodigal Son* (1929) and *Le Bal* (1929). Appeared with a group of his own (and Nemtchinova's) in 1927, for which he ch. Gershwin's *Rhapsody in Blue* and Chopin's *Revolutionary Etude*. After Diaghilev's death he appeared in various revues; became a co-founder of the Camargo Society in 1930, for which he created Satan in de Valois' *Job* in 1931, and appeared as a soloist with Vic-Wells B. 1931–5. Founded the Markova-D.B. with Markova in 1935 and was its dir. and first soloist until 1938. In 1940 he joined the newly established B. Th. in New York, later dancing with it as a guest-soloist until 1946—here he was also in charge of some prods. of classics and of the reconstructed *Pas de quatre* (1941). Created the title-role in Fokine's *Bluebeard* (1941). With the New York *Seven Lively Arts* revue 1944–5, for which he ch. the first prod. of Stravinsky's *Scènes de ballet*. Dir. and toured with the new Markova-D. Co. 1945–8 and then d. as a guest-soloist with Original B. Russe, Sadler's Wells B., and B. Russe de Monte Carlo. From another newly formed troupe with Markova the London Festival B. emerged in 1950, of which he became artistic dir. and first soloist until 1961. In more recent years he pursued a world-wide freelance career as a teacher, b. master, and ch., which took him as far afield as Leningrad, Tokyo, Venezuela, and Canada. He is one of the great pioneer personalities of Brit. b. and was one of its first genuine danseurs nobles. Author of *Divertissement* (London, 1931), *Ballet Go Round* (London, 1938), *Pas de deux: the Art of Partnering* (London, 1949) *Alicia Markova* (London, 1953), *Autobiography* (London, 1960), and *The Sleeping Ballerina—The Story of Olga Spessivtzeva* (London, 1966). Queen Elizabeth Coronation Award (1957). Knighted 1981. D. Magazine Award (1981).

BIBL.: J. Selby-Lowndes, *The Blue Train: the Story of A.D.* (London, 1953); G. Anthony, 'Pioneers of the Royal Ballet: A.D.' *Dancing Times* (1970/6).

Dollar, William (*b* East St. Louis, Ill., 20 Apr. 1907, *d* Flourtown, Penn., 28 Feb. 1986). Amer. d., ch., b. master, and teacher. Studied with Fokine, Mordkin, Balanchine, Vladimirov, and Volinine. D. with Philadelphia Op. B., with Amer. B. 1936–7, then with B. Caravan, New Op. Co., and in 1944 with B. International. Became b. master of Amer. Concert B. in 1943, then with B. Society, Grand B. de Monte Carlo, and Grand B. du Marquis de Cuevas. The best known bs. he ch. are *Constantia* (mus. Chopin, 1944) and *Le Combat* (mus. R. de Banfield, 1949). Was highly regarded as a teacher.

Domenico de Piacenza (also D. da Ferrara; *b* Piacenza, late 14th century, *d* after 1462). Ital. d. master and theoretician. He worked at the d'Este court in Ferrara and assembled his theories about the art of d. at about 1460 in the codex *De arte saltandi et choreas ducendi* (with the subtitle: *De la Arte di ballare at danzare*) which is now in the Paris National Library. Descriptions of his balli and balletti exist written by him and by his pupils Guglielmo Ebreo and Antonio Cornazano.
BIBL.: entry 'D.d.'P.' in *Enciclopedia dello spettacolo*.

Dominic, Zoë (*b* London). Brit. b. photographer. Works with the Royal B., Bolshoi B., New York City B., Stuttgart B. Contributor to *John Cranko und das Stuttgarter Ballett* (Pfullingen, 1969) and *Frederick Ashton* (London, 1971).

Dominique et Françoise. See *Dupuy, Dominique et Françoise.*

Doña Ines de Castro. Ballet in 1 act and 5 scenes; libr. and ch. Ricarda; mus. Joaquin Serra; déc. Celia Hubbard. Prod. 1 Mar. 1952, Grand B. du Marquis de Cuevas, Cannes, with Hightower, Skibine, Taras. The b. tells of the tragic love of the Portuguese Infant Don Pedro for Doña Ines, whom his father murders so that he can marry the Infanta of Navarra. After the King's death, when Don Pedro himself becomes King, he arranges for the dead body of Doña Ines to be laid out in the Throne Room, where he crowns her as Queen and then dances with her into madness and death.
BIBL.: C. Beaumont, 'D.I.d.C.' in *Ballets of Today* (London, 1954).

Donizetti, Gaetano (*b* Bergamo, 29 Nov. 1797, *d* there, 8 Apr. 1848). Ital. composer. Wrote no bs., but some of his ops., especially those he wrote for Paris, contain more or less elaborate b. divertissements (complete recording of these published 1980); e.g. *Les Martyrs* (ch. Coralli, 1840), *La Favorite* (ch. Albert, 1840), and *Dom Sébastien de Portugal* (ch. Albert, 1843). Some of these compositions were later used individually for b. purposes, e.g. by Howard in *Veneziana* (1953), Balanchine in *Donizetti Variations* (1960), Bolender

in *Donizettiana* (1967), and Harkarvy in *La Favorita* (1969).

Donizetti Variations. Ballet in 1 act; ch. Balanchine; mus. Donizetti; cost. Karinska; light. Hays. Prod. 16 Nov. 1960, New York City B., City Center, N.Y., with Hayden, Watts. Set to the b. mus. from Donizetti's op. *Dom Sébastien de Portugal*, 'the b. features a central pas de deux for a ballerina and her partner—entrée, adagio, two variations and coda, plus variations and ensembles for the corps of six girls and three boys' (Balanchine). The b. was originally called 'Variations from *Don Sebastian*'. Revived Hamburg State Op. in 1967.

Don Juan ou Le Festin de pierre. Ballet Pantomime in 1 act and 3 scenes; libr. and ch. Angiolini; mus. Gluck. Prod. 17 Oct 1761, Burg Th., Vienna. 28 years before Mozart's *Don Giovanni*, Angiolini, who with Noverre was the most important representative of the b. d'action, simplified the story of the notorious seducer to include only 3 protagonists (Don Juan, Donna Elvira, and the Commendatore) plus the servant Sganarello. The end is tragic: furies and demons take Don Juan with them to hell. Angiolini has here created a representative example of the classic b. d'action, the importance of which is increased by Gluck's score. It was very popular at the time, and was kept in the repertory for more than 40 years. Later revivals mostly adapted the libr., e.g. Kröller in 1924 in Vienna and Laban in 1925 in his 3 *D.J. Reigen.* A prod. which drew worldwide attention was Fokine's in 1936 for R. Blum's B. Russe in London. Other more recent revivals by Walter (Düsseldorf, 1965), Adama (Vienna, 1969), and Neumeier (Frankfurt, 1972—revived for National B. of Canada, 1974). Other b. treatments of the same subject were O. Viganò's *Il convitato di pietra* (Venice. 1787), T. Gsovsky's *D.J.* (mus. R. Strauss, Berlin, 1938—also by Ashton, London, 1948), V. Kašlik's *D.J.* (mus. by himself, ch. Nina Jirsíková, Prague, 1941), and L. Christensen, *D.J.* (mus. Rodrigo, San Francisco, 1973).
BIBL.: L. Kirstein, '*D.J.*' in *Movement & Metaphor* (New York, 1970).

Donn, Jorge (*b* Buenos Aires, 28 Feb. 1947). Argent. dancer. Studied at Teatro Colón B. School; appeared in smaller parts and on TV. Joined the B. of the 20th Century in 1963; soon became one of its top soloists. Created roles in Béjart's *Ninth Symphony* (1964), *Cygne* (1965), *Romeo and Juliet* (1966), *Mass for the Present Time* (1967), *Baudelaire* (1968), *Les Vainqueurs* (1969), *Serait-ce la mort?* (1970), *Nijinsky, Clown de dieu* (1971), *L'Ange Heurtebise* (1972), *Stimmung, Marteau sans maître,* and *Golestan* (1973), *I trionfi* and *Ce que l'amour me dit* (1974), *Notre Faust* (1975), *Dichterliebe, Leda* (1978), *Les Illuminations* (1978), and *Magic Flute* (1981). Belg. TV produced a film on him, *Le Danseur* (1972), and he has had leading parts in a

number of films on Béjart's bs. (e.g. *Romeo and Juliet, Firebird*). Appointed Artistic Dir. of Yantra co. in 1976, and Artistic Dir. of B. of the 20th Century 1980. Critics' Prize (Buenos Aires, 1968).
BIBL.: A.-P. Hersin, 'J.D.' with complete list of roles, *Les Saisons de la danse* (1974/2).

Don Quixote. Ballet with prologue, in 4 acts and 8 scenes; libr. and ch. M. Petipa; mus. Minkus. Prod. 26 Dec. 1869, Bolshoi Th., Moscow with Sobeshanskaya, S. Sokolov, W. Wanner. In Petipa's first version the b. was a rather robust comedy, following roughly the love affair between Quiteria (she becomes Kitri in the b.) and Basil from the second volume of the novel by Cervantes. D.Q. and his servant Sancho Panza only provide the thread to hold together the individual episodes (among them the encounter with a troupe of travelling comedians, and also the fight against the windmills). A drastically revised version which also contained much new ch. was prepared by Petipa for St. Petersburg in 1871. In 1900 Gorsky produced a new version at the Moscow Bolshoi Th., which caused an uproar by its unaccustomed character realism. It served as the basis for the new prod. by Zakharov in 1940, which is still kept in the repertory of the Bolshoi B. The first prod. of the complete b. for a western co. was that staged by Witold Borkowski for B. Rambert in 1962 (also based on Gorsky). Nureyev, however, who first did *D.Q.* for the Vienna State Op. B. in 1966 (revived for The Australian B. in 1970; a film of this prod. was premièred in 1973), kept to the St. Petersburg–Leningrad tradition. Other *D.Q.* bs., more or less based on Cervantes, by Hilverding (Vienna, 1740), Noverre (mus. Starzer, Vienna. 1768—a satire on Angiolini), Milon (Paris, 1801), Didelot (St. Petersburg, 1808), D'Egville (mus. Venua, London, 1809), P. Taglioni (mus. Strebinger, Berlin, 1850), Milloss (in *Portrait de D.Q.*, mus. Petrassi, Paris, 1947), T. Gsovsky (mus. L. Spies, Ger. State Op., Berlin, 1949), de Valois (mus. R. Gerhard, déc. E. Burra, 20 Feb. 1950, Sadler's Wells B., Cov. Gdn., London, with Helpmann, Fonteyn, A. Grant), Lifar (in *Le Chevalier errant*, mus. Ibert, Paris, 1950), and Balanchine (mus. Nabokov, déc. E. Francés, 28 May 1965, New York City B., State Th., N.Y., with Richard Rapp, Farrell, Deni Lamont).
BIBL.: C. W. Beaumont, 'D.Q.' in *Complete Book of Ballets* (London, 1951); and (on the Balanchine b.) in *Balanchine's New Complete Stories of the Great Ballets* (Garden City, N.Y., 1968).

Dorati, Antal (*b* Budapest, 9 Apr. 1906). Hung.-Amer. conductor. After his apprentice years in Budapest, Dresden, Munich, and Frankfurt, he was appointed second conductor of the B. Russe de Monte Carlo (1935–7), conductor of the Original B. Russe (1938–41), and mus. dir. of the newly founded B. Th. (1941–5). In these positions he arranged the mus. for several bs., incl. Lichine's *Graduation Ball* (after J. Strauss, 1940), Fokine's

Bluebeard (after Offenbach, 1941) and *Helen of Troy* (after Offenbach, 1942), and Lichine's *Fair at Sorochinsk* (after Mussorgsky, 1943). Conducted the first complete recordings of the 3 Tchaikovsky bs. in the 1950s. Author of *Notes of Seven Decades* (London, 1979).

Dorris, George (*b* Eugene, Oreg., 3 Aug. 1930). Amer. teacher, writer and editor. Studied at Univ. of Oregon (B.A., 1951) and Northwestern Univ. (M.A., Ph.D., 1957). Associate Editor, *Ballet Review*, 1967–78. US correspondent of Ger. *Ballett* (annual, since 1976). Contributor to *Ballet Today* and *The Dancing Times*. Founder and co-editor (with J. Anderson) of *Dance Chronicle: Studies in Dance and the Related Arts* (1977). Secretary and Member of Board of D. Perspectives Foundation since 1975. Has taught d. history at various colleges and univs.

Doubrovska, Felia (*b* St Petersburg, 1896, *d* New York, 17 Sept. 1981). Russ.-Amer. dancer and teacher. Studied at St. Petersburg Imperial Academy, graduating in 1913, upon which she became a member of the Maryinsky Th. In 1920 she joined Diaghilev's co., creating roles in Nijinska's *Les Noces* (1923) and Balanchine's *Apollon musagète* (1928) and *Prodigal Son* (1929). She d. with the Met. Op. B. in New York 1938–9, and has for years been one of the most respected teachers of the School of Amer. b. She was married to the d. Pierre Vladimirov.
BIBL.: M. Horosko, 'In the Shadow of Russian Tradition', *Dance Magazine* (1971/2); G. S. Ackerman and S. Cook, 'Doubrovska Remembers', *Ballet News* (1980/8).

Dougill, David Arthur (*b* Blackpool, Lancs., 10 Jan. 1944). Brit. dance critic. Studied at King's College, Univ. of London, and London Univ. Inst. of Education. Research assistant to R. Buckle, 1968–75. D. Critic of *Sunday Times* since 1975; assoc. ed. *Dance and Dancers* since 1980. Teacher of history of b., Royal B. School, since 1978.

Douglas, Scott (*b* El Paso, Tex., 16 June 1927). Amer. dancer, teacher, and choreographer. Perf. when only 9 years old as a tap dancer. Studied after his military service with St. Denis, Horton, and W. Christensen. Joined San Francisco B. in 1948; member of Amer. B. Th. 1950–62. Performed as guest with the Met. Op. B. and with N. Kaye in Spoleto; became a member of the Bs.: U.S.A. D. with Dutch National B. 1963–4, returned to Amer. B. Th. in 1964. Joined Tetley's group and was b. master of the Netherlands D. Th. in 1969/70; he has since pursued a career as a freelance teacher and ch. (returning occasionally to Amer. B. Th. as b. master), creating bs. for— among others—the Hamburg State Op. B. and the Norwegian National B. Created roles in e.g. Loring's *Capital of the World* (1953), Bettis' *A Streetcar Named Desire* (1954), and Ross's *Paean* (1957) and *Angel Head* (1959).

Doutreval, André (*b* Vienna, 5 Jan. 1942). Austrian dancer, choreographer, and b. director. Studied at Vienna State Op. B. School, made his début there 1958–9. D. with the cos. in Klagenfurt, Cologne, Bern, Wuppertal, Düsseldorf, Ger. Op. Berlin, and Frankfurt; b. dir. in Kassel 1970–6, where he has created a great number of bs. for his co. Now has a school in Kassel.

Douvillier, Suzanne Théodore (*née* Vallande; *b* Dole, *d* New Orleans, 30 Aug. 1826). Fr dancer and choreographer. She probably studied at Paris Opéra B. School and came to New York with her partner and companion Alexandre Placide in 1792, after which they toured Amer., finally settling in Charleston, where she appeared in bs. by Gardel and Noverre and ch. *Echo and Narcissus* in 1796. After a duel between Placide and the singer Louis Douvillier she married Douvillier and moved with him to New Orleans, where she was not only very popular as a ballerina, but ch. many bs., for which she also designed and painted the scenery.

Dowell, Anthony (*b* London, 16 Feb. 1943). Brit. d. Studied with June Hampshire and from 1953 at the Sadler's Wells and Royal B. School; became a member of the Cov. Gdn. Op. B. in 1960, moved to Royal B. in 1961, dancing his first leading part in Bruhn's 1962 prod. of the *Napoli pas de six*; promoted principal d. in 1966, since when he has become one of the very first danseurs nobles of his generation—a d. of unusual lightness, smoothness, and elegance, and an immaculate technician and stylist: the born aristocrat among today's b. princes. Apart from dancing the premier danseur roles of the standard repertory, he created roles in Ashton's *The Dream* (1964), *Monotones* (1965), *Jazz Calendar* (1968), *Enigma Variations* (1968), *Meditation* (1971), and *A Month in the Country* (1976), Tudor's *Shadowplay* (1967), MacMillan's *Anastasia* (version 1971), *Triad* (1972), and *Manon* (1974), and Van Manen's *Four Schumann Pieces* (1975). Also a principal d. of Amer. B. Th. 1978–80; art. dir. of Royal B. since 1986/7. Dance Magazine Award (1972); C.B.E. (1973).
BIBL.: D. Harris, 'Spreading His Wings,' *Ballet News* (1979/9).

Doyle, Desmond (*b* Cape Town, 16 June 1932). S.A. dancer and b. master. Studied with Dulcie Howes, joined Univ. B. of Cape Town and in 1951 Sadler's Wells B.; promoted soloist in 1953. Created roles in Ashton's *Madame Chrysanthème* (1955), *Jazz Calendar* (1968), and *Enigma Variations* (1968), Cranko's *Lady and the Fool* (1955) and *Sweeney Todd* (1960), MacMillan's *Noctambules* (1956), *The Invitation* (1960), *Symphony* (1963), and *Romeo and Juliet* (1965). B. master of the Royal B. 1970–5.

Dózsa, Imre (*b* Budapest, 9 Nov. 1941). Hung. dancer. Studied at Budapest State B. Inst.; joined the State Op. B. permanently upon graduation in

1959, and became one of its leading soloists. Since 1971 he has also often appeared with the Royal Swedish B. and other cos. abroad. He dances the premier danseur roles of the standard repertory and created leading parts in Seregi's *Spartacus* (1969), *The Woodcut Prince* (1970), *Sylvia* (1972), and *The Cedar* (1975). Liszt Award (1964). Married to the d. Vera Szumrák.

Draper, Paul (*b* Florence, 1909). Amer. dancer, teacher, and photographer. Became known as a brilliant tap d. (though he had also studied with Vilzak and Oboukoff), and created his own tap style, incorporating more and more b. elements. His most ambitious piece is the *Sonata for Tap Dancer*, which he performed without any mus. Many tours have made him known throughout the world. Is also a much respected teacher, and works as a photographer. Now teaches at Carnegie-Mellon Univ.
BIBL.: 'A Conversation with P.D.', *Ballet Review* (Vol. 5, No. 1).

Dream, The. Ballet in 1 act; libr. and ch. Ashton; mus. Mendelssohn (arr. Lanchbery); sets Henry Bardon; cost. David Walker. Prod. 2 Apr. 1964, Royal B., Cov. Gdn., London, with Sibley, Dowell, Martin, A. Grant. The b. follows broadly the main plot of Shakespeare's *A Midsummer Night's Dream*. New déc. by P. Farmer for Royal B. Touring Comp. (1966). BBC TV prod. (1967). Revived for City Center Joffrey B. and Royal Swed. B. in 1975. Other versions of the same plot and mus. by M. Petipa (St. Petersburg, 1877), Fokine (St. Petersburg, 1906), and Balanchine (New York City B., 1962), Neumeier (Hamburg, 1977; revived for Royal Danish B., 1981), and de Warren (Northern B. Th., 1981).
BIBL.: P. Brinson and C. Crisp, in *Ballet & Dance* (Newton Abbot, 1980).

Dreher. South Ger. and Austrian folk d. in 3/4 or 3/8 time from the 18th century, with the dancers holding each other's hips and turning. The origin of the Ländler (and later the waltz).

Dresden. B. origins date back to the founding of the famous Hofkapelle; the first b. master, Adrian Rothbein, is mentioned in 1612. One of the subsequent b. masters was Gabriel Möhlich, who ch. two bs. to mus. by Schütz—*Ballet von dem Orpheo und der Euridice* (1638) and *Ballet von dem Paris und der Helena* (1650). In 1678 one of the most spectacular baroque bs. was performed; *Musikalische Oper und Ballett von Wirkung der Sieben Planeten*. During all these early years, until the middle of the 18th century, it was mostly Fr. b. masters who were in charge of the rather ambitious court b. Most of the documents of the later developments were destroyed during the Second World War. During the 19th century the D. b. scene seems to have been rather dull. A new initiative dates from the years after 1910 when Jaques-Dalcroze established his school in the garden suburb of Hellerau, which produced

many of the protagonists of the continental modern d. movement. During the 1920s and early 1930s modern d. flourished around the schools of Wigman and Palucca. Ch. by the State Op.'s b. director V. Kratina, Stravinsky's *Jeu de cartes* received its first Eur. prod. in 1937, von Einem's *Prinzessin Turandot* (ch. T. Gsovsky) in 1944. After the second world war, D.'s b. activities were severely hampered through the loss of the op. house. There has been a rapid turnover of b. masters, until the State Op.'s present chief ch., H. Wandtke, was appointed in 1980. Bs. which received their first Ger. perf. here were Prokofiev's *Cinderella* (ch. Bernhard Wosien, 1950) and *The Stone Flower* (ch. Schilling, 1960). A second b. co., occasionally giving individual perfs. (and otherwise appearing in op. perfs.) is connected with the Landesbühnen Sachsen (b. master is Günter Buch). In matters of d. education, however, D. enjoys a very good reputation due to its Palucca School and its intern. renowned summer courses.
BIBL.: H. Koegler, 'D.' in *Friedrichs Ballettlexikon von A-Z* (Velber, 1972).

Drew, David (b London, 12 Mar. 1938). Brit. dancer and choreographer. Studied at Westbury School of Dancing in Bristol and Royal B. School; made his début at Cov. Gdn. in 1955, rejoining Royal B. after his military service; promoted soloist in 1961 and principal d. in 1974. Created roles in Ashton's *The Dream* (1964), Tudor's *Shadowplay* (1967), Layton's *The Grand Tour* (1971), MacMillan's *Manon* (1974), *Rituals* (1975), *Mayerling* (1978), and *Isadora* (1981). Started as a ch. with *Intrusion* (mus. Schubert) for the Royal B. in 1969. More recent bs. of his are *From Waking Sleep* (mus. Hovhaness, 1970), *St. Thomas' Wake* (mus. Maxwell Davies, 1971), *Sacred Circles* (mus. Shostakovich, 1973), and *Sword of Alsace* (mus. J. Raff, 1973). Also ch. the London prod. of the musical *Canterbury Tales* (1968).

Dreyer, Bernd (b Berlin, 5 Sep. 1946). Ger. Dancer. Studied at East Berlin State B. School and Leningrad Ch. School, joining the Berlin State Op. in 1967; promoted soloist in 1971.

Drigo, Riccardo (b Padua, 30 June 1846, d there, 1 Oct. 1930). Ital. composer and conductor. Became kapellmeister of the St. Petersburg op. in 1878; chief conductor of the Maryinsky Th. 1886–1917. His b. compositions included *The Talisman* (ch. M. Petipa, 1889), *The Magic Flute* (ch. Ivanov, 1893), and *Les Millions d'Arlequin* (ch. Petipa, 1900).

Driver, Senta (b Greenwich, Conn., 5 Sep. 1942). Amer. dancer, choreographer, and artistic director. Studied at Bryn Mawr College and Ohio State Univ. (MA in D., 1966), with M. Graham, M. Cunningham, Conn. College School of D., D. Farnworth, and M. Black. Worked at D. Faculty, Ohio State Univ., 1966–7, with P. Taylor co. 1967–73. Since 1974 artistic dir. of HARRY, for which she has regularly ch. since 1975.

Dromgoole, Nicholas (b Maranham, 3 Dec. 1927). Brit. b. critic. Educated Oxford Univ., Sorbonne (Paris). B. critic, *Sunday Telegraph* since 1965. Chairman, Institute of Choreology. Member for Ballet of the Drama Advisory Committee of the Brit. Council 1968–80. Member of the D. Panel of Southern Arts Association. Married to the d. L. Collier.

Drottnerová, Marta (b Gottwaldov, 26 Aug. 1941). Czech dancer. Studied with E. Gabzdyl in Ostrava, later also with Gerdt in Moscow; made her début as Katerina in *The Stone Flower* in Ostrava in 1957. Became a member of the Prague National Th. in 1959, of which she is now its leading ballerina. Has participated in various films and often appears abroad. First prize (Rio de Janeiro, 1961), Silver Medal (Varna, 1964), Gold Medal (Varna, 1966). Married to the d. and ch. Jiří Blažek.

Drozdova, Margarita Sergeyevna (b Moscow, 1948). Sov. dancer. Studied at Moscow B. School 1958–67, becoming a member of the Stanislavsky and Nemirovich-Danchenko Music Th. upon graduation. Now its leading ballerina, with Odette-Odile and Esmeralda as her best roles. Prix Pavlova (Paris, 1968), Silver Medal (Varna, 1972), Bronze Medal (Moscow, 1973).

Drzewiecki, Conrad (b Poznań, 14 Oct. 1926). Pol. dancer, choreographer, and b. director. Studied with M. Kopiński, J. Kapliński, Woizikovsky, T. Piankova, J. Andrews, F. and D. Dupuy, and others. Started to d. 1948; joined Poznań Op. B. 1950, later becoming soloist and (after dancing abroad with Th. d'Art du B., co. of Tcherina, and Grand B. du Marquis de Cuevas 1958–63) b. master and ch. 1963–73. Since 1973 Artistic Dir. and chief ch. of the Poznań-based Polish D. Th. (also of Poznań B. School since 1971).
BIBL.: P. Chynowski, 'C.D. and his Polish D. Theatra', *Dance Magazine* (1975/8).

Dublin. Though the city enjoyed a short Golden Age of B. when Taglioni, Elssler, and Grisi visited Mr. Calcraft's Th. Royal between 1833 and 1846, the b. activities which took place here were for much of the 19th and 20th century the concern only of the local b. schools. Before the Second world war the only memorable visits of cos. from abroad were those of Pavlova, the Bs. Jooss, and the Sadler's Wells B. in 1938. After 1945 things improved somewhat, and there have been irregular visits by foreign cos. ever since, but for the founding of a native professional full-time b. co., the country had to wait until 1974, when the Irish B. was established—and this is based in Cork. D. City B. was established in 1980 with Janet Lewis as Artistic Dir. until 1981.
BIBL.: I. Guest, 'Romantic Ballerinas in Dublin', *Dance and Dancers* (1960/3–6).

Dubreuil, Alain (b Monte Carlo, 4 Mar. 1944).

Monégasque-Brit. dancer. Studied at his mother's school and from 1960 at Arts Educational School in London. Joined London Festival B. in 1964 and Royal B. as a principal d. in 1973. Returned to London Festival B. in 1976; rejoined Sadler's Wells Royal B. in 1977, where he dances both noble and character roles, and cr. roles in L. Seymour's *Intimate Letters* (1978), D. Bintley's *Meadow of Proverbs* (1979) and *Polonia* (1981), and M. Corder's *Day into Night* (1980).

BIBL.: R. Scale, 'A.D.', *Dancing Times* (1967/4).

Dubrovska, Felia See *Doubrovska, Felia.*

Dudinskaya, Natalia Mikhailovna (*b* Kharkov, 21 Aug. 1912). Sov. dancer and b. mistress. Studied at her mother's studio and from 1923 at the Petrograd State B. School, where she graduated as a pupil of Vaganova in 1931. Made her début as Princess Florine before leaving school, and d. Odette-Odile six months after joining the GATOB. She d. all the ballerina roles of the traditional repertory, much admired because of her stupendous technique, but was hardly less successful in the modern Sov. repertory, for which she created roles in Chaboukiani's *Laurencia* (her most famous part, 1939), Anisimova's *Gayane* (new version, 1945), K. Sergeyev's *Cinderella* (1946) and *Path of Thunder* (1957), Zakharov's *The Bronze Horseman* (1949), Jacobson's *Shuraleh* (1950), and Fenster's *Taras Bulba* (1955). After her retirement she became b. mistress of the perfection classes of the Kirov B. In the Sov. film *Trio Ballet* she d. Odile in *Swan Lake* (1953) and in a later film Carabosse in *Sleeping Beauty* (1964). She was awarded the Stalin Prize four times; Order of the Red Banner (1973). Married to the d. and ch. Konstantin Sergeyev.

BIBL.: N.D., 'My Life Is Dance', *Dance and Dancers* (1970/10).

Dudley, Jane (*b* New York, 1912). Amer. dancer, teacher, and b. director. Studied with Holm, Graham, and Horst, d. with the Graham co. 1937–44, also with Maslow and Bales in the D. Trio 1942–54, for which she ch. several pieces, including *Family Portrait* (1954). She then worked as a teacher, continuing to appear occasionally as a d. with Graham up to 1970. In the late 1960s she was dir. of the Batsheva D. co. Since 1971 she has been in charge of the Graham classes at the London School of Contemporary D.

BIBL.: interview with J.D., *Dance and Dancers* (1971/5–6).

Duell, Daniel (*b* Rochester, N.Y., 17 Aug. 1952). Amer. dancer. Started to study with David McLain in Dayton, continuing at School of Amer. B. Joined New York City B. as an apprentice 1972, appointed soloist 1977 and principal 1979. Created roles in P. Martins's *Calcium Light Night* (1977) and in Robbins's *The Four Seasons*. He is the brother of Joseph D. Ch. for various groups since 1983.

BIBL.: L. Draegin, 'The Balanchine Man', *Dance Magazine* (1979/1).

Duell, Joseph (*b* Dayton, Ohio, 30 April, 1956, *d* N.Y. 16 Feb. 1986). Amer. d. Studied at School of Amer. B. Joined New York City B. 1975, appointed soloist 1980 and principal d. 1984. Started to ch. 1980 and then did some bs. for workshop perfs. and New York City B. He was the brother of Daniel D.

BIBL.: S. Flatow, 'Duells in the Sun'; *Ballet News* (1981/5).

Dukas, Paul (*b* Paris, 1 Oct. 1865, *d* there, 17 May 1935). Fr. composer. Wrote the d. poem *La Péri* in 1911, which was first ch. by Clustine in Paris in 1912 and has since been revived in many different versions. His symphonic poem *The Sorcerer's Apprentice* was first ch. by Fokine (Petrograd, 1916).

Duke, Vernon (orig. Vladimir Dukelsky; *b* Pskov, 10 Oct. 1903). Russ.-Amer. composer. Wrote the mus. for Massine's *Zéphire et Flore* (1924) and *Jardin public* (1934), Petit's *Le Bal des blanchisseuses* (1946), and L. Christensen's *Emperor Norton* 1957). Also composed the scores for the bs. in the musicals *Ziegfeld Follies* (1935), *Cabin in the Sky* (1940), and *Lady Comes Across* (1941), and the film *Goldwyn Follies* (1938), all ch. by Balanchine.

Dumilâtre, Adèle (*b* Paris, 30 June 1821, *d* there, 4 May 1909). Fr. dancer. A member of the Paris Opéra 1840–8, she created Myrtha in *Giselle* (1841) and Fatma (the title-role) in a guest appearance in the London prod. of *La Fille de marbre* (1845). Her sister, Sophie, was also a d. at the Opéra 1838–45.

BIBL.: I. Guest, in *The Romantic Ballet in Paris* (London, 1966).

Dumoulin, David. Fr. Dancer. The youngest and most famous of the 3 D. brothers, François, Pierre, and D., all dancers; d. at the Paris Opéra 1705–51, often as a partner of Camargo, Prévost, and Sallé.

Dunas, William A. (*b* New York, 1 May 1947). Amer. dancer, choreographer, and teacher. Studied with Sanasardo, M. Cunningham, Nagrin, Slavenska, Corvino, and Farnworth. Started performing in 1968, since when he has appeared in many solo demonstrations of his work. Taught ch. at New York Univ. Artistic Dir., The Trust, 1971. President of Ambrose Arts Foundation since 1972. Brandeis Univ. Creative Arts Award (1974).

BIBL.: R. Baker, 'D.'s Götterdämmerung', *Dance Magazine* (1974/6).

Duncan, Elizabeth (*b* San Francisco, 1874, *d* Tübingen, 1 Dec. 1948). Amer. teacher. The sister of Isadora D., with whom she founded a boarding school for girls in Berlin-Grunewald in 1904, where the development of bodily and dancing abilities and the education of the mind were considered equally important. Moved to Darmstadt where she opened her own school with Max Merz in 1911, the results of which were widely acclaimed when its performing group appeared at the Dresden health exhibition in the same year. During the first world war she returned to Amer. but came back to Ger. in 1920, working in Potsdam until 1925, at Schloss Klessheim near Salzburg 1925–33. In 1921 she opened a New York branch of her school, which she transferred to Prague 1933–5 and from there to Munich. She is also said to have taught in special courses (with Merz) in Stuttgart. An offshoot of her former school still exists in Schloss Mörlbach on Lake Starnberg (near Munich). The educational system of the E.D. schools aimed for 'the harmony of the inner and exterior education of man' and for the 'unification of the spiritual, physical and artistic education'.

BIBL.: H. Brandenburg, 'Die E.D.-Schule' in *Der moderne Tanz* (Munich, 1931).

Duncan, Irma (orig. I. Dorette Henriette Ehrich-Grimme; *b* Schleswig-Holstein, 26 Feb. 1897, *d* Santa Barbara, Cal., 20 Sept. 1977). Ger.-Amer. dancer and teacher. One of the first of Isadora's pupils at the school in Berlin-Grunewald; made her début at the Berlin Kroll Op. in 1905, toured with the children's group, which she led to St. Petersburg in 1908. Started to teach at the Elizabeth D. School in Darmstadt in 1911, moving to Isadora's school in Bellevue-sur-Seine near Paris in 1914. A first visit to New York in 1914 resulted in a return invitation for 1918–20, when she appeared as one of the 6 D. girls. She then d. with Isadora in Paris, and founded the Moscow school with her in 1921, of which she became dir. upon Isadora's death in 1927. She toured the U.S. and China with her Moscow pupils in 1928, and, after another tour in the U.S., decided to live there in 1930. Gave her farewell perf. in New York with the prod. of *Ode to Peace* to the last movement from Beethoven's Ninth Symphony in 1934. Continued to teach and to paint, but gradually withdrew from the public scene. Author of *Isadora Duncan's Russian Days* (with A. Ross Macdougall, New York, 1929), *The Technique of Isadora Duncan* (New York, 1937), and *Duncan Dancer* (Middletown, Conn., 1966).

Duncan, Isadora (*b* San Francisco, 26 May 1877, *d* Nice, 14 Sep. 1927). Amer. dancer and teacher. After very few b. classes, which she considered an intolerable constraint, started to develop her own, anti-b.-orientated philosophy and dances. These lacked any systematic basis, but were inspired by purely emotional-expressive sources, which she considered a revival of the Greek d. of antiquity; her decision to abandon tights and dance instead clad in a loosely falling tunic also goes back to her ideas of classic Greek d. Performed as an actress in small roles with the troupe of Augustin Daly, New York début 1896. To London 1897, starting

to perform in various homes and art-galleries as a recital d.—also in Paris from 1900. Toured Ger. with some L. Fuller dances. Professional breakthrough in Budapest 1902. Legitimate Paris th. début at Th. S. Bernhardt 1903. To Greece with her whole family 1903, where they built a house at Hymettus. Toured Russia for the first time 1904—she possibly influenced Fokine in his efforts to reform b. To Berlin, where she opened a school with her sister Elizabeth 1905. Making Paris her residence 1908, she toured continuously all over Eur., acclaimed by an enormous multitude of admirers and followers, whereas she had a chilly reception in Amer. where she returned 1909, 1911, 1917, and—after setting up another school in Moscow 1921–22, not least for moral and political reasons (due to her much publicized love-affairs with the th. reformer E. G. Craig, the sewing-machine millionaire Paris Singer, and the Russ. poet S. Esenin, and her repeated declarations of sympathy for the young Sov. state). In spite of her preference for dancing to great classical mus., and her massed chs. for her pupils (incl. an appearance at the 1904 Bayreuth Festival), her importance seems to rest less on her artistic achievements than on her activity as a representative and spokesman of a new liberty of movement according to man's natural impulses. She was a dominating and influential phenomenon of her time, whose appearance, work, and effect have been registered in many literary and pictorial documents. She ended in genuine 'roaring twenties' style: during a drive along the Côte d'Azur in an open car, her trailing scarf got entangled in the spokes of one of the wheels and strangled her. Her autobiography, covering the years up to 1921, *My Life*, much tampered with by her editor, appeared 1928; a planned sequel, *My Two Years in Bolshevik Russia*, never materialized. After a successful TV documentary on I.D. by Ken Russell (1966) a highly controversial film, *Isadora*, appeared 1969 (Amer. title: *The Loves of Isadora*, dir: Karel Reisz, title-role: Vanessa Redgrave). Ashton ch. *Five Brahms Waltzes in the Manner of I.D.* for L. Seymour (first version of 2 waltzes only, Hamburg 1975; complete version B. Rambert, London 1976), Béjart a solo *Isadora* for Plisetskaya (Brussels, 1976), and MacMillan a 2-act b. *Isadora* (mus. R. R. Bennett, London, 1981).

BIBL.: Irma Duncan, *The Technique of I.D.* (New York, 1937); A. Ross Macdougall, *Isadora—A Revolutionary in Art and Love* (New York, 1960); I. I. Schneider, *I.D.—The Russian Years* (London, 1968); V. Seroff, *The Real Isadora* (New York, 1971); N. Macdonald, 'Isadora Re-examined': Lesser-Known Aspects of the Great Dancer's Life', *Dance Magazine* (1977/7–12); G. McVay, *Isadora and Esenin* (Ann Arbor, 1980).

Duncan, Jeff (*b* Cisco, Tex., 4 Feb. 1930). Amer. dancer, teacher, and ch. Studied with Holm, Nikolais, Limón, M. Cunningham, and Schwezoff. Made his début at Henry St. Playhouse in

1952; worked as an assistant with Humphrey and Sokolow, and d. with various cos., and with his own J.D. D. Co. and in Broadway musicals, before becoming founder and dir. of the New York D. Th. Workshop. His best known chs. include *Antique Epigrams, Four Preludes, Frames, Terrestrial Figure* (solo dances), and *Three Fictitious Games, Winesburg Portraits, Outdoors Suite,* and *View* (ensemble dances).

BIBL.: J. Dunning, 'Dance Theater Workshop Grows Up', *Dance Magazine* (1976/3).

Duncan, Maria-Theresa (orig. Theresa Krüger; *b* Dresden, *c.* 1896). Ger.-Amer. dancer. Chosen by Isadora D. for her first school in Berlin-Grunewald, she became one of the original Isadorables, dancing in her many tours, incl. those to Russia. Left Isadora in 1921, and, under the name of Maria-Theresa, began a long independent career as a recital-d. which lasted well into the 1960s. J. Martin admired her for 'the integrity of her emotional experience and her extraordinary musical sensitivity'.

Dunham, Katherine (*b* Chicago, 22 June 1912). Amer. dancer, teacher choreographer, and director. Studied anthropology at the Univ. of Chicago, graduating as a Ph.D.; her M.A. thesis was *The Dances of Haiti.* Took cl. classes with Ludmila Speranza and Mark Turbyfill, dancing her first leading part in Page's *La Guiablesse* in 1933. After an extensive period of research in anthropology and especially Negro d. in the West Indies, appointed d. dir. for the Negro Unit of the Chicago branch of the Federal Th. Project in 1938 and d. dir. of the New York Labor Stage in 1939 (ch. dances for the plays *Emperor Jones, Run Li'l Chillun,* and the musical *Pins and Needles*). A programme *Tropics and Le Jazz Hot—From Haiti to Harlem,* given by her specially assembled co. in New York in 1940, launched her career as one of the most sought-after choreographers for Afro-Amer. dances. In 1940 she did her first Broadway musical, *Cabin in the Sky,* after which she moved to Hollywood to appear in and/or ch. various films—the most important being *Carnival of Rhythm* (1942). During the following years she developed her extremely successful formula of black revues, designed by her husband John Pratt. Her Dunham School of D. in New York became the cradle of Amer. black d. 1945–55. During the 1950s she was mostly on tour with her troupe, which proved an instant success with Eur. audiences. Ch. the New York Met. Op. House prod. of *Aida* in 1963; technical cultural adviser to both the President and the Minister of Cultural Affairs in Dakar, Senegal, 1965–6. Now dir. of the Performing Arts Training Center at Southern Illinois Univ., East St. Louis branch. 'Her innate sense of th. and mus., the glorious costumes and the wonderful dancers in her co., as well as her own ch. and dancing, put Negro dancing on the map once and for all and her work has since had enormous influence' (A. Todd). Wrote *K.D.'s*

Journey to Accompong (New York, 1946) *A Touch of Innocence* (New York, 1959), and *Island Possessed* (Garden City, N.Y., 1969). Honorary Citizen of Port-au-Prince; Laureate of the Lincoln Academy; Professional Achievement Award of Univ. of Chicago Alumni Assoc.; D. Magazine Award (1968).

BIBL.: T. Harman, *African Rhythm—American Dance* (New York, 1974); R. Beckford, *K.D.* (New York, 1979).

Dunn, Douglas (*b* Palo Alto, Cal., 1942). Amer. dancer and choreographer. Studied with Princeton Regional Ballet Co. 1964–5, Yvonne Rainer and Group 1968–70, Merce Cunningham and Co. 1969–73 and Grand Union 1970–76. Appears now mostly as a soloist performer or with his own group. Ch. *Time Out* (1973), *Four for Nothing* (1974), *Gestures in Red* (1975), *Solo Film & Dance* (1977), *Rille, Relief, Coquina* (all 1978), and *Pulcinella* (mus. Stravinsky, Paris Opéra, 1980).

BIBL.: S. Banes, in *Terpsichore in Sneakers* (Boston, 1980).

Duo Concertant. Ballet in 1 act and 5 movements; ch. Balanchine; mus. Stravinsky; light. Ronald Bates. Prod. 22 June 1972, New York City Ballet, State Th., N.Y., with Mazzo and Martins, plus Lamar Alsop (violin) and Gordon Boelzner (piano). A piece for 2 dancers who relate to the musicians on the left-hand side of the stage. There is no real plot, though a kind of love seems to develop. TV prod., Ger. second channel, 1973.

Dupond, Patrick (*b* Paris, 14 Mar. 1959). Fr. dancer. Studied at Paris Opéra B. School, joining its co. 1974 (1 year in advance); promoted premier danseur 1978, étoile 1980. Created roles in Petit's *Fantôme de l'Opéra* (1980) and Spoerli's *Fille mal gardée* (1981). Gold Medal (junior category, Varna, 1976).

Dupont, Jacques (*b* Chatou, 16 Jan. 1909, *d* Paris, 21 Apr. 1978). Fr. designer. Designed the sets and costumes for the prologue (ch. Aveline) and epilogue (ch. Lifar) of *Les Indes galantes* (Paris, 1952), Sparemblek's *Les Amants de Teruel* (Paris 1959), T. Gsovsky's *La Dame aux camélias* (Paris, 1960), Ashton's *The Two Pigeons* (Royal B., 1961), Skibine's *Romeo and Juliet* (Buenos Aires, 1970), Hightower's *The Sleeping Beauty* (Marseilles, 1970), Cranko's *Carmen* (Stuttgart, 1971), and Labis' *Coppélia* (Charleroi, 1975).

Duport, Louis Antoine (*b* Paris, 1781 or 1783, *d* there, 19 Oct. 1853). Fr. dancer, choreographer, and b. master. One of the most famous dancers of his time, he enjoyed a phenomenal success at the Paris Opéra 1797–1808, becoming a serious rival to Vestris, who was 20 years his senior. Much admired because of his légèreté and the virtuosity of his pirouettes, he soon started to ch. as well, proving no less successful. When even Napoleon tried in vain to curb his staggering demands, he had to leave Paris in female disguise (with a former mistress of Napoleon), fleeing via Vienna (where he produced *Figaro or The Barber of Seville* in 1808) to St. Petersburg, where he dazzled audiences in the bs. of Didelot. Returned to Vienna in 1812, ch. many bs. for the Th. am Kärntnertor during the following years, appearing in Naples and London, and co-directing the Th. am Kärntnertor with the famous op. impresario Barbaia 1821–36. He then returned to Paris, and withdrew from public life. In the U.S. a dancing child prodigy called L.D. drew wide attention during the first half of the 1790s, completely disappearing in 1796, but it has never been clearly established whether he had anything to do with his Fr. namesake.

BIBL.: L. Moore, 'The Duport Mystery', *Dance Perspectives* 7.

Dupré, Louis (*b* 1697, *d* 1774). Fr. dancer and teacher. Started as a dance teacher in Mans, proceeding to Paris where he was a much acclaimed solo d. at the Opéra 1715–51, being called Le Grand D. Even in his sixties, audiences admired his gracefulness and his splendid physique. Until 1743 he was in charge of the Opéra's b. school, where Vestris and Noverre were among his pupils. Casanova was one of his many admirers.

BIBL.: M. H. Winter, in *The Pre-Romantic Ballet* (London, 1974).

Dupuy, Dominique et Françoise (F.D. [*née* Michaud]; *b* Lyons, 6 Feb 1925–D.D., *b* Paris, 31 Oct. 1930). Fr. married couple of dancers, choreographers, and teachers. Studied with M. Cunningham, McGehee, J. Andrews, *et al.*, d. with B. des Arts 1947–9 and in several drama prods. After their marriage in 1951 embarked on a career as modern recital dancers, founding their Académie de Danse Contemporaine à Paris in 1955, from which Les Bs. Modernes de Paris emerged, with which they toured widely and appeared regularly at the Festival de Danse de Baux de Provence. In their individual dances and whole programmes they show a marked predilection for connections between literature and d. (Valéry, Cocteau, Claudel).

Durang, John (*b* York, Pa., 6 Jan. 1768, *d* Philadelphia, 1822). Amer. dancer and choreographer. Became the first native Amer. d. to gain widespread recognition, especially for his hornpipes and harlequinades. A member of the Old Amer. Co. of Lewis Hallam in Philadelphia and New York 1784–96, then a dir. for pantomimes for the circus troupe at Ricketts' Amphith. in Philadelphia, and in 1800–19 at the Chestnut Th. His pantomime bs. included *The Country Frolic, or The Merry Haymakers* (1796) and *The Western Exhibition, or The Whiskey Boy's Liberty Pole* (1797). He raised a large family and saw that all of his children were trained as dancers; his son Charles D. (1794–1870) followed most directly in his father's footsteps as actor, b. master, stage

manager, writer, critic, and author of several guides to dancing.

BIBL.: L. Moore, 'J.D.', *Dance Index* (vol. 1, no. 8); A. S. Downer (ed.), *The Memoirs of J.D.* (Pittsburgh, 1966).

Duse, Riccardo (Rome, 1 Aug. 1937). Swiss dancer, choreographer and b. director. Studied with Mara Dousse, B. Kniaseff and N. Zvereff. D. with Teatro alla Scala 1955–8, Compagnia del balletto italiano 1958–9, Het Nederlands B. 1960, Cologne B. 1961–6, New York City B. 1967, Frankfurt B. 1967–72. B. master and ch. Luzerne Munic. Th. 1972–6, same position Freiburg since 1976. B. master at Bayreuth Festival since 1972.

Düsseldorf. First mentions of d. at courtly occasions date from the early 16th century. Under various b. masters imported from Fr., b. flourished here under the reign of Duke Jan Wellem and especially 1687–1716, when D. was seen as a sort of suburb of Paris. Later b. fared rather badly as an individual art form. When the Neues Stadttheater am Hofgarten opened in 1875, b.'s only contribution was in op. perfs. Not until the 1930s did some b. ambition develop in D., and under Milloss (1934–6) there was suddenly enormous b. activity, which, however, died down again when he left. After the second world war there was the usual coming and going of b. masters, though Georgi managed to draw some national attention during her stay (1951–4), when she staged Stravinsky's *Sacre du printemps*, and so did Jooss, who remained for only 2 seasons (1954–6). With the formal establishment of the city's op. house as Ger. Op. on the Rhine in 1956 things improved somewhat and b. master Otto Krüger tackled the Eur. first prod. of Stravinsky's *Agon* in 1958. However, it was not until *Erich Walter took over as b. dir. in 1964 that the Ger. Op. on the Rhine started to build up a major co. with a solid repertory of classical and contemporary bs., most of which are made up by Walter's own contributions with carefully selected works by other choreographers (including Balanchine, Massine, Nijinska, Cranko, and Van Manen). In recent years the co. has developed an identity of its own (with a musically highly demanding repertory) and is now in the forefront of Ger. b. cos. It plays regularly in its two houses in D. and Duisburg and tours widely abroad. The number of perfs. has risen so steeply that a second co. had to be established in 1971 to fulfil the necessary op. functions. Since 1973 the so-called Ballet Days of the Ger. Op. on the Rhine serve to provide a concentrated survey of the co's. activities, while specially invited cos. offer complementary fare.

BIBL.: G. Barfuss, K. Geitel, and H. Koegler, *Ein Ballett in Deutschland* (D., 1971); H. Riemenschneider, 'Tanz und Hofoper in der Residenz D.', *Die Tanzarchiv-Reihe* 13/14.

Dutch National Ballet (Dutch title: Het Nationale Ballet). The Amsterdam-based co. is the

The Dutch National Ballet in Van Dantzig's *Four Last Songs*.   Photo Jorge Fatauros.

product of the 1961 merger of Gaskell's Netherlands B. and ter Weeme's Amsterdam B.; these ladies shared the direction, later Gaskell became the sole dir. (until 1969—she shared responsiblities during her last years with Van Dantzig and Kaesen). In its early years its repertory was so extensive that it has been likened to a supermarket of ch. With Van Dantzig's advance as a ch., however, the co. started to develop a profile of its own, which is today complemented by the Van Manen bs., some Van Schayk bs. and a choice selection of classics and 20th-century works, especially the masterworks of Balanchine. Van Dantzig's *Night Island* (1955) and *De Disgenoten* (1958) were taken over from the previous cos.—the other signs of the co's. development were Van Dantzig's *Monument for a Dead Boy* (1965), *Moments* (1968), *Epitaph* (1969), *Coloured Birds* (1971), and *Ramifications* (1973), and Van Manen's *Daphnis and Chloe* (1972), *Adagio Hammerklavier* (1973), *Le Sacre du printemps* (1974), and Van Manen's and Van Dantzig's joint prod. of *Live/Life* (1979). The co. performs regularly in all the Netherlands' major cities and often tours abroad. BIBL.: G. Loney, 'Rudi van Dantzig on the National Ballet of Holland', *Dance Magazine* (1974/3).

Duvernay, Pauline (*b* Paris, 1813, *d* Mundford, Norfolk, 2 Sep. 1894). Fr. dancer. Studied with Vestris and F. Taglioni at Paris Opéra B. School; made her début in *Mars et Vénus* in 1831 and d. in London in *La Belle au bois dormant* in the same year. Her career was extremely erratic, with many private conflicts. Like Elssler, had one of her greatest successes with the Cachucha. Retired in 1837, marrying an Eng. banker, and dedicating her further life to charity.

Dvořák, Antonín (*b* Nehalozeves, 8 Sep. 1841, *d* Prague, 1 may 1904). Czech composer. He did not write any b. mus., but several of his compositions have been used for b. purposes—most often his *Slavonic Dances* op. 46 and 72, which have become a standard part of Czech b. repertoires, but also his *Symphonic Variations* (ch. Hynd, London Festival B., 1970), his *Symphony from the New World* (ch. Lefèbre, B. de Wallonie, 1971), various pieces for *The Leaves are Fading* (ch. Tudor, Amer. B. Th., 1975), and his String Quartet in F (ch. Thorpe, Northern D. Th., 1976).

Dvorak Variations. Ballet in 1 act; ch. Hynd; mus. Dvořák (*Symphonic Variations*); déc. Peter Docherty. Prod. 7 May 1970, London Festival B., Grand Teatro del Liceo, Barcelona, with Samsova, Prokovsky. A plotless suite of dances, reflecting the changing moods of the individual variations. Revived for Munich State Op. B. (1970) and for Dutch National B. (1973).

Dybbuk Variations. Ballet in 1 act; ch. Robbins; mus. Bernstein; set: Ter-Arutunian; cost. Patricia Zipprodt. Prod. 15/16 May 1974, New York City B., State Th., N.Y. with McBride, Tomasson. The b. takes the Jewish play by S. Ansky (about the demonic possession of a girl by the soul of her lover to whom she had been betrothed at birth) as a departure point for a series of dances on the essences, moods, spirit, and sources of its atmosphere and relationships. An earlier b. version of the play by Ross (mus. Robert Starer, Bs. of Two

Worlds, Berlin, 1960). Another full-length version, *The Possessed* by P. Lang (mus. Meyer Kupferman and Joel Spiegelman, New York, 1975).

Dying Swan, The (orig. Russ. title: *Umirayushchy lebed*— also Fr. *La Mort du cygne* or *Le Cygne*). Solo d. ch. by Fokine to mus. by Saint-Saëns for Pavlova. First per. at a gala perf. on 22 Dec. 1907 at the Hall of Noblemen, St. Petersburg. Set to *Le Cygne* from Saint-Saëns' *La Carnaval des animaux*, the d. is a poignant poem about the final struggle for life of a dying bird. It became identified with Pavlova (whose interpretation has been conserved fragmentarily in an old film, which despite its poor quality gives a valid impression of her uniqueness), and is the most famous solo d. ever created, representing for many people still the very essence of b. dancing. Other famous interpreters of the now somewhat hackneyed piece incl. Markova, Ulanova, Chauviré, and Plisetskaya. BIBL.: O. Kerensky, in *Anna Pavlova* (London, 1973).

Dyk, Peter van (also Dijk; *b* Bremen, 21 Aug. 1929). Ger. dancer, choreographer, and b. director. Studied with T. Gsovsky, Kniaseff, and Lifar; made his début at East Berlin State Op. in 1946. D. with the Berlin Munic. Op. 1950–1. B. dir. at Wiesbaden 1951–2. D. with the co. of Charrat 1952–4 and from 1955 as an étoile (the first Ger. to ever hold this title) at the Paris Opéra. B. dir. of the Hamburg State Op. 1962–70, Hanover State Op. 1973–4, B. du Rhin (Strasbourg) 1974–8, Geneva 1978–80 and since 1981 Bonn. Started as a ch. Wiesbaden, 1952. Has created numerous bs. since, incl. *Unfinished Symphony* (mus. Schubert, 1957).

Dynalix, Paulette (*b* Grenoble, 10 Mar. 1917). Fr. dancer and teacher. Studied with Zambelli at the Paris Opéra B. School, joining the co. upon graduation; promoted étoile in 1943. Her most famous role was Franz in *Coppélia*. Retired in 1957, since when she has become a teacher. Artistic adviser of the B. for All's *Two Coppélias* prod.

E

Eagling, Wayne (*b* Montreal, 1950). Can. dancer. Studied with Patricia Webster and at Royal B. School. Joined Royal B. in 1969, becoming soloist in 1972 and principal d. in 1975. Created leading roles in MacMillan's *Triad* (1972), *Elite Syncopations* (1974), *Rituals* (1975), and *Gloria* (1980) and Van Manen's *Four Schumann Pieces* (1975). He appears in the main *danseur noble* and other roles of the classical repertory with impressive versatility and presence.
BIBL.: M. Leech, 'Spotlight on W. E.', *Dance Magazine* (1976/8).

Early, Fergus (*b* Worthing, 4 Aug. 1946). Brit. dancer, b. master, and teacher. Studied at Royal B. School; joined Royal B. 1964–8; became assist. b. master for B. for All (until 1971), choreographing *A Yorkshire Marriage* and *The Ballet of the Twelfth Rose*. Has since concentrated on a career as a teacher, working mainly for London School of Contemporary D. Mounted *History of Coppélia* for Norwegian National B. Now an independent d., dir. and ch.

Eaters of Darkness (original Ger. title: *Die im Schatten leben*). Ballet in 1 act; libr. and ch. Gore; mus. Britten; déc. Heckroth. Prod. 29 Jan. 1958, Frankfurt, with Hinton, Paul Herbinger, Wolfgang Winter. Set to Britten's *Variations on a theme of Frank Bridge*, the b. shows how a young bride, though completely normal, is committed by her husband to an asylum, where her encounters with the inmates finally drive her mad. Revived for several cos., e.g. Harkness B. (1970—this prod. also for Ger. second channel TV), and Northern B. Th. (1980).

Ebbelaar, Han (*b* Hoorn, 16 Apr. 1943). Dutch d. Studied with Harkarvy, Hanny Bouman, Zaraspe, and P. Wilde. D. with Netherlands D. Th. 1959–69, Amer. B. Th. 1969–70, and since then with Dutch National B., of which he was one of the top soloists. Created parts in Van Manen's *Symphony in Three Movements* (1963), *Essay in Silence* (1965), *Metaforen* (1965), *Five Sketches* (1966), *Dualis* (1967), *Twilight* (1972), *Daphnis and Chloe* (1972), *Adagio Hammerklavier* (1973), and *Sacre du printemps* (1974), and Van Dantzig's *On the Way* (1970), *Painted Birds* (1971), and *Ramifications* (1973). Married to the d. Alexandra Radius. Retired 1987.
BIBL.: E. Huf, *Alexandra Radius, H. E. Dancing* (Haarlem, 1979).

Ebony Concerto. Stravinsky's Concerto for Jazz band in 3 movements, which he wrote in 1946 for Woody Herman, has been ch. several times—e.g. by A. Carter (in *Feuilleton*, Munich, 1957),

Taras (New York City B., 1960), Cranko (Munich, 1970), and Van Manen (Dutch National B., 1976).

Ebreo, Guglielmo (also Guillaume le Juif, or William the Jew of Pesaro; *b* before 1440). Ital. dance master. Came from Pesaro, studied with Domenico da Piacenza; taught social d. at various Ital. courts and prod. dances and balli for court festivities, e.g. with Domenico for the wedding of Costanzo Sforza and Camilla d'Aragon in Pesaro, 1475). Author of *Trattato della danza* and *De Praticha seu arte tripudii vulghare opusculum*, in which he described the necessary qualifications of a d. (musicality, memory, style, posture, etc.) and the dances he had created.
BIBL.: O. Kinkeldey, *A Jewish Dancing Master of the Renaissance: G. E.* (New York, 1929; repr. Dance Horizons, 1966).

Ecart, Grand (Fr., large step aside). Designates in b. the splits.

Ecarté (Fr., wide apart). Designates a b. pose with one leg raised at an oblique angle to the body which in itself is at an oblique angle to the spectators.

Echappé (Fr., escaped). Designates a movement from a closed to an open position.

Echoing of Trumpets (also *Echo of T.*, orig. Swed. title: *Ekon av Trumpeter*). Ballet in 1 act; libr. and ch. Tudor; mus. Martinů; déc. Birger Bergling. Prod. 28 Sep. 1963, Royal Swed. B., Stockholm, with G. Andersson, Svante Lindberg, A. Wiedersheim-Paul, M. Mengarelli. Set to Martinů's *Fantaisies Symphoniques* (his Sixth Symphony), the b. tells of a partisan who returns to his war-ravaged village, where he is hidden by his wife but is finally discovered by the occupants and executed. Though often said to have been inspired by the total destruction of Lidice in Czechoslovakia in the Second World War, Tudor has denied this and stated that he was rather thinking of incidents which had taken place in Poland, near Łódz. Revived for Met. Op. B. (New York, 1966) and for London Festival B. (1973). MacMillan used the same mus. for the third act of his *Anastasia*.
BIBL.: G. Balanchine, 'E.o.T.' in *Balanchine's New Complete Stories of the Great Ballets* (Garden City, N.Y., 1968).

Eck, Imre (*b* Budapest, 2 Dec. 1930). Hung. dancer, choreographer, and b. director. Studied with Nádasi, joining the Budapest State Op. B. in 1947. Started to ch. in the 1950s, creating his first major b. in 1958 (*Csonger and Tünde*, mus. Leo Weiner). Other important bs. of his for the State

Op. have been *Sacre du printemps* (mus. Stravinsky, 1963), *Music for Strings, Celesta and Percussion* (mus. Bartók, 1964), and *Ondine* (mus. Henze, 1969). In 1960 he became the founder-dir. of the *B. Sopianae, based upon Pécs, for which he ch. the majority of its bs., many of them to mus. by Bartók and other Hung. composers, incl. the first prod. of W. Bukový's *Hiroshima* (1962). Has also ch. for Finn. National B.

BIBL.: A. Dallos, *A Pécsi Balett Története* (Budapest, 1969; in Hung.).

Ecole de Danse de l'Opéra de Paris, L'. The b. school of the Paris Opéra dates back to 1713, since when it has seen an uninterrupted continuation of great teachers and brilliantly gifted pupils who became the famous étoiles of the assoc. co. Entrance age is 8–12 years (13 for the boys), and the ballet curriculum (based upon 5 years of training) is supplemented by academic school tuition. Directrice of the school from 1981 C. Bessy, with the classe de perfectionnement (style and interpretation) taught by Y. Chauviré.

Ecossaise. A Brit. country d. of obscure origin. It was d. *c.* 1600, accompanied by bagpipes, and in triple time. When it became popular in the ballrooms of Fr. and Eng. in the late 18th and early 19th centuries it changed its rhythm to 3/2 or 2/4 time. Schubert and Beethoven comp. in this form.

Edinburgh International Ballet. For the 1958 Edinburgh Festival a b. co. was established under the direction of Van Praagh, which, it was hoped, would become a permanent organization. An announced London season was cancelled, and the Edinburgh appearances in Aug. and Sep. of that year remained the only ones, after which the co. was disbanded. From the bs. created by Cullberg, Cranko, Toye, Skibine, Taras, Parlić, Mendel, and A. Carter, only Holmgren's *Midsummer Vigil*, Wright's *The Great Peacock*, Gore's *Night and Silence*, and Howard's *La belle dame sans merci* were eventually revived for other cos.

Edinoff, Ellen (*b* 20 Dec. 1942, New York). Amer. dancer and teacher. Studied at Graham School, Juilliard School, and with Cunningham. Co-founded the Contemporary D. Th. and School of Contemporary D. in Amsterdam with her husband Koert Stuyf in 1962. Performed in Stuyf's prods. (also occasionally with other cos. such as the Dutch National B., for which she also taught).

Eduardova, Eugenia Platonovna (*b* St. Petersburg 1882, *d* New York, 10 Dec. 1960). Russ. dancer and teacher. Studied at the St. Petersburg Imperial B. Academy, graduating in 1901, after which she joined the Maryinsky Th., becoming one of its most brilliant demi-caractère ballerinas. Stayed with the co. until 1917, then toured with Pavlova and settled in 1920 in Berlin where she opened a b. school, which soon flourished, her co.

of pupils often performing at the Berlin Winter Garden. Married the d. critic and editor Joseph Levitan; she left Berlin in 1938 for Paris where she opened another school, which she maintained until 1947, after which she and her husband moved to New York. Her pupils included Zorina, Ress, Trofimowa, Leskova, von Swaine, Skibine, and Algaroff.

Education of the Girlchild. Opera in 2 parts by M. Monk; solo version prod. 22 Apr. 1972, The House Loft, New York; various other versions; final version prod. 8 Nov. 1973, 70 Grand Street, New York. 'A strikingly imaginative theater piece, visually stunning and a model of integration of sounds, pictorial imagery and movement ... Its first section consists of detailed episodes, literary in their associations, in which she and six female "companions", who may represent either a family or a composite of the heroine, take a walk through life—often wittily' (A. Kisselgoff). 'The second act contains the original solo out of which everything else arose ... traces a specific life—but backwards, Monk appearing as an old lady, then turning progressively energetic until she is almost ecstatic' (J. Anderson).

BIBL.: R. Baker, 'Landscapes and Telescopes', *Dance Magazine* (1976/4).

Edwards, Leslie (*b* Teddington, 6 Aug. 1916). Brit. dancer and b. master. Studied with Rambert and at Sadler's Wells B. School, making his début in 1933 with the Vic-Wells B. Apart from his 2 years with the B. Rambert 1935–7, his career has been entirely within the Sadler's Wells and Royal B. organization, which he served for many years as a distinguished character d. and since 1958 as Dir. of the Royal B. Ch. Group and B. Master to The Royal Op. Has also taught at Royal B. School and abroad. Created roles in de Valois' *The Rake's Progress* (1935), Ashton's *The Quest* (1943) and *Enigma Variations* (1968), Helpmann's *Miracle in the Gorbals* (1944), Massine's *Donald of the Burthens* (1951), MacMillan's *Noctambules* (1956), and Cranko's *Prince of the Pagodas* (1957) and *Antigone* (1959). O.B.E. (1975).

BIBL.: C. Swinson, 'L. E.' in *Six Dancers of Sadler's Wells* (London, 1956); G. Anthony, 'L. E.', *Dancing Times* (1970/7).

Effacé (Fr., obscured). Designates a position of the body at an oblique angle to the audience, from whom it is partly hidden.

Efimoff, Nicholas. Russ. dancer. Was one of the Sov. State Dancers who, together with Balanchine, Danilova and Gevergeyeva, came to Western Europe in 1924 and was eventually engaged by Diaghilev. After the disbanding of the Bs. Russes, joined the Paris Opéra as premier danseur, later becoming its principal mime.

Efrati, Moshe (*b* Jerusalem, 24 Dec. 1934). Isr. dancer and choreographer. Studied at the Jerusalem Academy, with Graham, J. Taylor, and Horst,

made his début in 1956 in Jerusalem and became one of the founder members of the Batsheva D. Co. in 1964, creating roles in Tetley's *Mythical Hunters* (1965), Lang's *Voices of Fire* (1967), Morrice's *Side Show* (1966) and *Percussion Concerto* (1970). Among his chs. are *Sin Lieth at the Door* (mus. Noam Sheriff, 1969), *Ein-Dor* (mus. Zvi Avni, 1970), and *Paths* (mus. K. Serocki, 1973). Has also worked for Ger. Op. Berlin and B. of Flanders. Is at present working with deaf-mutes in Israel and has a group of his own.
BIBL.: G. Manor, 'The Very Articulate Demana', *Dance News* (1975/11).

Egk, Werner (*b* Auchsesheim, 17 May 1901, *d* Inning, 10 July 1983). Ger. composer. Wrote the mus. for Maudrik's *Joan von Zarissa* (1940), Luipart's *Abraxas* (1948), Charrat's *Ein Sommertag* (1950), T. Gsovsky's *The Chinese Nightingale* (1953), Rosen's *Danza* (1960), and Charrat's *Casanova in London* (1969). His *French Suite* has also often been ch.—e.g. by Cranko (in *Une Fête galante*, Munich, 1969). Author of *Musik—Wort—Bild* (with various articles on b.; Munich, 1960).

Eglevsky, André (*b* Moscow, 21 Dec. 1917, *d* Elmira, N.Y. 4 Dec. 1977). Russ.-Amer. d. and teacher. Studied with Egorova, Kschessinska, Volinine, N. Legat, and at School of Amer. B. Joined B. Russe de Colonel de Basil in 1933, the Woizikovsky comp. in 1935, R. Blum's B. de Monte Carlo in 1936, Amer. B. 1937–8, B. Russe de Monte Carlo 1939–42, B. Th. 1942–3 and 1945; also d. with B. International, Original B. Russe, Grand B. du Marquis de Cuevas, and with N.Y. City B. 1951–8. Taught for many years at the School of Amer. B. and then was dir. of his own school in Massapequa (L.I.) and the Eglevsky Ballet. As a premier danseur he was much admired for his technical virtuosity and for his noble bearing. Created roles in Fokine's *L'Epreuve d'amour* (1936) and *Don Juan* (1936), Lichine's *Helen of Troy* (1942), his own *Sentimental Colloquy* (mus. P. Bowles, 1944), Balanchine's *Pas de trois* (1951), *Capriccio Brillante* (1951), *Swan Lake* (1951), *Caracole* (1952), *Scotch Symphony* (1952), *Harlequinade Pas de deux* (1952), *Western Symphony* (1954), *Pas de dix* (1954), and *Waltz Scherzo* (1958). Father of the d. Marina E.

Eglevsky, Marina (*b* 1951). Amer. d. The daughter of André E., she studied with her mother, Leda Anchutina. D. in her father's co., and then with Harkness B. and Royal Winnipeg B., before joining the Hamburg State Op. B. as a principal d. in 1973, creating Clara in Neumeier's *Schumann* (1974). Rejoined Royal Winnipeg B. in 1975.
BIBL.: O. Maynard, 'The New Generation: M. E.', *Dance Magazine* (1973/11).

Egorova, Lubov Nicolayevna (Princess Nikita Troubetzkoy; *b* St. Petersburg, 8 Aug. 1880, *d* Paris, 18 July 1972). Russ. d. and teacher. Studied at the Imperial B. Academy, graduating in 1898,

after which she joined the Maryinsky Th., promoted ballerina in 1912. In 1918 she moved to Paris, d. with Diaghilev's Bs. Russes, opened a school in Paris in 1923, and founded the B. de la Jeunesse in 1937. Among her pupils were S. Schwarz, Charrat, and Pagava. Married to Prince Troubetzkoy. Chevalier de l'Ordre des Arts et Lettres (1964).
BIBL.: N. Milford, in *Zelda Fitzgerald* (New York, 1970).

Egri, Susanna (*b* Budapest, 18 Feb. 1926). Ital. dancer, teacher, and choreographer. Studied with F. Nádasi and Sári Berczik in Budapest. Graduate of Hung. State Inst. for Ch. and Teaching in 1946. Appeared in many solo-recitals in Budapest, Italy, and Paris. Prima ballerina of various Ital. op. houses, often also appearing on Ital. TV. Started to ch. and to teach at her own Turin-based B. Academy in 1950. Dir. of I Balletti di S. E. Ch. of the Turin op. house (and for many TV b. prods.). Vice-president of Ital. B. Teachers' Association. Prix d'Italia for her TV b. *Cavalleria Rusticana* (1963).

Egypt. The country has only recently adopted b. A government sponsored B. Institute opened 1958 under the tutelage of the former Moscow Bolshoi soloist Alexei Zhukov, with its 9 year curriculum modelled upon Soviet patterns. It is now part of the complex of the Academy of Arts in Cairo, with most of the initially Sov. teachers being replaced now by Sov. trained Egyptian teachers. From the B. Inst. grew the Cairo B. Co., which had its inaugural perf. (*The Fountain of Bakhtchisaray*) 1966. Performing at the Cairo op. house until it burned down 1971 and since existing on a somewhat haphazard base, its rep. incl. as well some of the classics, a Lifar programme, and as the first attempts of indigenous national bs. *The Difficult Days* (inspired by the events of the 1967 Arab-Israeli war; ch. Abd el Moneim Kamel, mus. Mukhtar Ashrafi) and *Baheyya's Eyes* (imbued with political-nationalistic symbolism; ch. Moneim Kamel and Esmat Ali, mus. Gamal Salama). First tourings abroad brought the co. to the U.S.S.R. (1972), Yugosl. and Bulgaria (1975), and Syria and Japan (1977).
BIBL.: M. Saleh, 'The Rise of the Egyptian Ballet', *Dance News* (1979/4).

Eifman, Boris Yakovlevich (*b* Rubtsovsk, 22 July 1946). Sov. dancer, choreographer and b. director. Studied at Kishinev B. and Mus. College, graduating 1964, then at ch. faculty of Leningrad conservatory. D. at Kishinev Op. and B. Th., eventually appointed soloist. Now artistic dir. and b. master of Leningrad B. Co. Started to ch. 1970, his bs. incl. *Gayane* (mus. Khatchaturian, Maly Th., Leningrad 1972), *Firebird* (mus. Stravinsky, Kirov B., Leningrad 1975) and for Leningrad B. Co. *Love Alone* (mus. Shchedrin), *Bivocality* (mus. Pink Floyd) and *The Broken Song* (mus. Kalnynsh, all 1977). Has also ch. for various films.

Einem, Gottfried von (*b* Bern, 24 Jan. 1918). Austrian composer. Wrote the mus. for T. Gsovsky's *Princess Turandot* (1944), Swedlund's *Rondo of the Golden Calf* (1952), V. Gsovsky's *Pas de coeur* (1952), Georgi's *Happiness, Death and Dream* (1954), and Hanka's *Medusa* (1957).

Ek, Mats (*b* Malmö, 18 Apr. 1945). Swed. dancer and choreographer. Son of Birgit Cullberg and actor Anders Ek, and brother of d. Niklas Ek. Started as an actor, studying d. at Stockholm B. Academy only from 1972. D. with Cullberg B. 1973–4, Düsseldorf B. 1974–5 and since then again with Cullberg B. Started to ch. with *The Batman* (mus. Bartók), succeeding it with *St. George and the Dragon* (collage of pop and folk mus., both 1976), *Soweto* (collage of contemporary mus., 1977), *The House of Bernarda Alba* (collage of Span. and organ mus. by Bach), and *The Four Seasons* (mus. Vivaldi, both 1978, all for Cullberg B.) Has also d. with Netherlands D. Th.

Ek, Niklas (*b* Stockholm, 16 June 1943). Swed. dancer. Son of Birgit Cullberg and actor Anders Ek, and brother of d. Mats Ek; started to train as a d. after military service. Studied with D. Feuer in Stockholm and in New York with Graham and Cunningham; d. with the Cunningham co., with the Cullberg B. 1967–72, with the B. of the 20th Century 1972–5, since when he has returned to the Cullberg B. Created roles in his mother's *Dionysos* (1965), *I am not You* (1966), *Coppelius* (1968), *Romeo and Juliet* (1969), and *Bellmann* (1971), and Béjart's *Stimmung* (1972), *Marteau sans Maître* (1973), *Golestan* (1973), and '*I trionfi' di Petrarca* (1974). Prize for best d. (Paris, 1969). Married to the d. Sighilt Pahl.
BIBL.: G. Loney, 'Sons and Mothers, N. E. and Birgit Cullberg', *Dance Magazine* (1970/4).

Elektra. Ballet in 1 act; ch. Helpmann; mus. Arnold; déc. Arthur Boyd. Prod. 26 Mar. 1963, Royal B., Cov. Gdn., London, with Nerina, Blair, Mason, Rencher. A melodramatic retelling of the homecoming of Orestes to Mycenae, 10 years after his mother Clytemnestra and her lover Aegisthus have murdered his father, King Agamemnon. A different b., *Electre*, by Charrat (mus. Pousseur, Brussels, 1960)—also *E.–Study about Hysteria* by M. Taubert (mus. Stockhausen, Brunswick, 1972), and *E.* by Bolender (for E. Frankel, mus. Henze's Fifth Symphony, Hong Kong, 1972). A remarkable feature film by Miklós Jancsó, *Elektreia*, is ch. throughout by Károly Szigeti (Hungary, 1974).

Eléments, Les. (1) Ballet in 1 act; ch. Perrot; mus. Bajetti. Prod. 26 June 1847, Her Majesty's Th., London, with Grisi, Rosati, Cerrito. This was a divertissement which tried to repeat the sensational success of the *Pas de quatre*, with the 3 ballerinas representing water, fire, and air, after an initial ensemble as the earth. (2) Ballet in 1 act; ch. Fokine; mus. Bach; déc. Bouchène. Prod. 1 Apr. 1937 (according to Fokine's *Memoirs*), B. de

Monte Carlo de R. Blum, Alhambra Th., London, with Theilade, Eglevsky. Set to Bach's Overture in B minor, this is a plotless b. with solo numbers for Flora, Zephyr, Vulcan, and the Tritons, and group dances for Water, Flowers, Air, and Flames.

Elévation (Fr., height). Designates the capacity of a d. to attain height in springing steps (but Lifar uses it to indicate 'the flight of the soul' as expressed in bodily movement).

Elève (Fr., pupil). Designates the apprentice dancers at the Paris Opéra, where they are also known as 'les petits rats'.

XI. Symphony (orig. Russ. title: *Odinnadtsataya simfoniya*). Ballet in 4 scenes; libr. and ch. Belsky; mus. Shostakovich; déc. M. Smirnov and M. Tcheglov. Prod. 7 May 1966, Maly Th., Leningrad. Shostakovich called his symphony *The Year 1905*, reflecting the events of the first Russ. revolution; Belsky, too, shows the happenings on 9 Jan. 1905, when the Tsarist militia fired at the demonstrators on the square in front of the St. Petersburg Winter Palace. The 4 movements are: The Palace Square; the 9th of January; Eternal Memory; the Tocsin. The protagonists are 4 symbolic figures: Freedom; Hope; Despair; Youth.

Elfes, Les. (1) Ballet in 3 acts; libr. J.-H. V. de Saint Georges; ch. Mazilier; mus. Nicolo Gabrielli; sets Despléchin, Nolau, Rubé, Thierry, and Martin; cost. A. Albert. Prod. 11 Aug. 1856, Opéra, Paris, with Ferraris, L. Petipa, Segarelli. The b. tells of a Count who falls in love with a statue of Sylvia, which the Queen of the Elves brings to life. This marked the Paris début of Ferraris who scored a sensational success as Sylvia. (2) Ballet in 1 act; ch. Fokine; mus. Mendelssohn; déc. Kairansy and Fokine. Prod. 26 Feb. 1924, Fokine's Amer. B., Met. Op. House, New York. Set to the overture from *A Midsummer Night's Dream* and the Andante and Allegro movements from the violin concerto, this is a plotless b. which attempts to embody the atmosphere of the mus.
BIBL.: G. Balanchine, '*L. E.*' in *Balanchine's New Complete Stories of the Great Ballets* (Garden City, N.Y., 1968).

Elgar, Sir Edward (*b* Broadheath, Worcs., 2 June 1857, *d* Worcester, 23 Feb. 1934). Brit. composer. Wrote a single b. score, *The Sanguine Fan*, which was performed as a mimed play at London's Chelsea Palace in aid of war charities 1917, but did not receive a legitimate b. prod. until R. Hynd ch. it under the title *L'Eventail* for London Festival B. at the occasion of its appearance at the Monte Carlo 1976 Intern. Festival of Arts (for later perfs. the original Eng. title was restored). F. Staff was the first to choreograph E.'s *Enigma Variations* (Cambridge, 1940), later also used by Ashton for his homonymous b. (Royal B., 1968).

Other bs. to his mus. incl. Tomon Ruud's *Introduction and Allegro* (San Francisco B., 1980).

El Greco. Ballet in 1 act; libr., ch., and cost. Börlin; mus. D.E. Inghelbrecht; sets after El Greco by Mouveau. Prod. 18 Nov. 1920, Bs. Suédois, Th. des Champs-Elysées, Paris, with Jolanda Figoni, Torborg Stjener, Börlin. The b. develops as a succession of mimed scenes, inspired by El Greco's paintings, culminating in *The Entombment of Count Orgaz*.

Eliasen, Johnny (*b* Copenhagen, 1949). Dan. d. Studied at Royal Dan. B. School. Joined Scandinavian B. as a soloist in 1964 and Royal Dan. B. in 1967, becoming solo-d. 1972. Created leading roles in Flindt's *Felix Luna* and *Trio* (1973), and Holm's TV prod. of *Firebird* (1974). B. master London Fest. B., 1987.

Elite Syncopations. Ballet in 1 act; ch. Mac-Millan; mus. S. Joplin and others; déc. I. Spurling. Prod. 7 Oct. 1974, Royal B., Cov. Gdn., London, with Derman, Mason, Park, Penney, Coleman, Eagling, Macleary, Sleep, Wall. A ragtime b. in a d.-hall, with a costumed band at the back and a number of dancers in carnival costumes in front. BBC TV prod. in 1975.

Ellis, Angela (née A. Dukes; *b* London, 1920). Brit. dancer and teacher. The daughter of Rambert and Ashley Dukes, she studied with her mother, Volkova, V. Gsovsky, and Craske. D. with B. Rambert 1943–7, since when she has become a teacher. Founded the London B. Workshop with her husband David Ellis in 1951. Is now dir. of the Rambert School of B.

Ellis, David (*b* London, 1921). Brit. dancer, choreographer, and teacher. Studied at Oxford Univ. and with Volkova, Rambert, and V. Gsovsky. Member of B. Rambert from 1946, eventually becoming Associate Dir. (until 1966). Ch. for B. Guild and Anglo-Russ. B. Founded the London B. Workshop with his wife Angela E. (Rambert's daughter) in 1951. Dir. of the Mercury Th. Trust until he returned to medical research.

Ellis, Richard (*b* London, 19 Feb. 1918). Brit. dancer and teacher. Studied with Grace and Lillie Cone, de Valois, Craske, Idzikowski, Dolin, and Volkova. D. with Anton Dolin B. and Camargo Society in 1933, Vic-Wells and Sadler's Wells B. 1933–40 and 1945–52. Started to teach in Chicago 1952, opening own school 1954. Co-director with his wife Christine Du Boulay of the School and of the Illinois B. (founded 1959), which performs extensively in the Chicago area, the Mid-West, and for Chicago Educational TV.

Ellis, Wendy (*b* Risaton, Lancs., 6 Dec. 1951). Brit. dancer. Studied at White Lodge Junior Royal B. School. Joined Royal B. in 1970, promoted soloist in 1975, and principal in 1979. Created Princess Stephanie in MacMillan's *Mayerling* (1978) and role in *Gloria* (1980).

Elssler, Fanny (orig. Franziska E.; *b* Gumpendorf, 23 June 1810, *d.* Vienna, 27 Nov. 1884). Austrian d. The daughter of Jos. Haydn's valet and copyist, she studied with her sister Therese E. (1808–78) at the b. school of Horschelt at the Th. an der Wien. (It has never been established beyond doubt whether she was a member of Horschelt's controversial children's b.) In 1818 both sisters joined the Kärntnertor Th., where their older sister Anna E. (1804–63) was already dancing. Fanny was acclaimed in bs. by F. Taglioni, L. Henry, and A. Vestris and charmed all Naples in 1825 through her temperament and her sensual appeal. Made her Berlin début in 1830, London in 1833, and Paris in 1834, where Taglioni viewed her meteoric career with some jealousy. After having impressed her public everywhere with her Fenella in *La Muette de Portici*, Zoloë in *Le Dieu et la Bayadère*, and Lise in *La Fille mal gardée*, she scored one of her greatest triumphs with her Cachucha solo in Coralli's *Le Diable boiteux* in 1836. She was much admired by Gautier who called her a pagan ballerina (compared to Taglioni as a Christian ballerina); her next big successes came in Mazilier's *La Gypsy* (1839) and Coralli's *La Tarentule* (1839). After complicated negotiations she embarked on an Amer. tour in 1840, which brought her as far South as Havana. She earned a fortune and extended her leave of absence from the Paris Opéra by more than one year, for which she was made to pay a large sum for breach of contract. In 1842 she returned to Europe, dancing in Vienna, Berlin, Brussels, Dublin, and Hamburg, and her first Giselle in London in 1843. Though her Milan perfs. in 1844 were not successful (due to the political estrangement between Italy and Austria), she was fêted in Budapest and again in London in Perrot's *Esmeralda*. She returned to Italy in 1846–7 and visited Russ. twice in 1848–50, where she had an unprecedented reception in St. Petersburg and especially Moscow. In 1851 she gave 12 farewell perfs. at the Vienna Kärntnertor Th., mainly in the bs. *La Esmeralda, Catarina,* and *Faust*. Her last appearance was on 21st June 1851. She lived with her daughter in Hamburg for several years but returned to Vienna in 1855, where she stayed in close contact with the th. life of the city. She was one of the greatest ballerinas of the romantic b., and charmed her contemporaries with her sensual temperament and her dramatic projection. Her sister Therese E., who had devised most of the ch. for her early bs., often appeared with her in *en travestie* roles, and suffered ridicule because of her excessive height.
BIBL.: I. Guest, *F. E.* (London, 1970).

Elvin, Violetta (*née* V. Prokhorova; *b* Moscow, 3 Nov. 1925). Sov.-Brit. d. Studied with Maria Kozhukhova at Bolshoi B. School, graduating in 1942, after which she joined the State Th. in Tashkent, becoming a member of the Bolshoi B.

at its war-time location in Kuibyshev in 1944, promoted soloist in 1945 upon the co's. return to Moscow. With her husband Harold Elvin she emigrated to England, made her début as Princess Florine with Sadler's Wells B. in 1946, after which she soon appeared in the other ballerina roles of the co's. repertory, creating parts in Ashton's *Cinderella* (Summer Fairy, 1948), *Daphnis and Chloe* (Lykanion, 1951), *Homage to the Queen* (1953), and *Birthday Offering* (1956), Petit's *Ballabile* (1950), and Howard's *Veneziana* (1953). Retired in 1956; b. dir. Teatro San Carlo, Naples, 1985–6.

BIBL.: C. Swinson, *V. E.* (London, 1953).

Embattled Garden. Ballet in 1 act; ch. Graham; mus. Surinach; set Noguchi; light. Rosenthal. Prod. 3 Apr. 1958, M. Graham and D. Co., Adelphi Th., New York, with Turney, Yuriko, Ross, Tetley. 'Love, it has been said, does not obey the rules of love but yields to some more ancient and ruder law. The Garden of Love seems always to be threatened by the Stranger's knowledge of the world outside and by the old knowledge of those like Lilith (according to legend, Adam's wife before Eve) who lived there first' (programme note).

Emblen, Ronald (*b* Port Said, Egypt, 14 Oct. 1933). Brit. dancer. Studied with Northcote, Perretti, Egorova, Volkova, Addison, and Royal B. School. D. with International B. 1951–3, Walter Gore's B. 1953, London Festival B. 1954–60 (and 1961–2), Western Th. B. 1960–1, and Royal B. since 1962; appointed principal d. in 1964. Now a freelance teacher.

Emboîté (Fr., boxed in). Designates a boxed-in step. Usually a series of steps with interlocking feet.

Embrace Tiger and Return to Mountain. Ballet in 1 act; ch. Tetley; mus. Morton Subotnick; déc. Baylis. Prod. 21 Nov. 1968, B. Rambert, J. Cochrane Th., London, with S. Craig, Bruce, J. Taylor, M. Willis. Set to Subotnick's *Silver Apples of the Moon*, the b. was inspired by the Chinese system of shadow-boxing known as *T'ai-chi*. 'Its 37 movements, of which *Embrace Tiger and Return to Mountain* is the 17th, are non-aggressive and attempt by a concentration of stillness and centred balance to offset the opponent' (programme note). Also in the repertory of the Netherlands D. Th., the Royal Swed. B., and the E. Feld co.

BIBL.: P. Brinson and C. Crisp, in *Ballet & Dance* (Newton Abbot, 1980).

Emperor Jones. Ballet in 1 act; ch. Limón; mus. Villa-Lobos; set Kim Swados; cost. P. Lawrence. Prod. 12 July 1956, J. Limón D. Co., Ellenville (N.Y.), with Limón, Hoving. Inspired by E. O'Neill's one act play of the same title, the b. shows the downfall of E.J., self-appointed ruler of a Caribbean island, who remembers his former days of misery and triumph as he flees in terror

into the jungle from the beating of the drums. Filmed in 1972.

Empire Ballets. Together with the *Alhambra Th., the E. Th. functioned as the main platform for b. perfs. in London at the turn of the last century, enjoying its biggest popularity 1887–1914. Its b. mistress was the Austrian Katti Lanner and one of its first premier danseurs was Cecchetti. Genée was prima ballerina 1897–1907, succeeded by Kyasht and Bedells. It also saw the London début of Bolm.

BIBL.: I. Guest, *The E. B.* (London, 1962).

Enchaînement (Fr., linking). Designates a combination of steps or movements constituting a phrase.

Endicott, Josephine Ann (*b* Sydney, 14 Mar. 1950). Austral. dancer. Studied at Austral. B. School and D. Centre London. D. with Austral. B. Co., 1969–72 and since 1973 with Wuppertal D. Th., creating roles in P. Bausch's *Fritz* (1973), *Orpheus and Eurydice* (1975), *Seven Deadly Sins* (1976), *Come Dance With Me, Renate Emigrates* (1977), and *Contact Court* (1978). Young Artists Prize of Northrhine Westfalia (1976).

Enfant et les sortilèges, L' (Eng. title: *The Spellbound Child*). Fantaisie lyrique in 2 parts; libr. Colette; mus. Ravel. Prod. 21 Mar. 1925, Monte Carlo, ch. Balanchine. 'Toys, books, and furniture rebel against a bad child who has ill-used them; fleeing to the garden he finds the trees and animals equally hostile. They relent when he bandages the paw of a baby squirrel hurt in the rumpus. The child runs back to the comforting figure of his mother' (*Concise Oxford Dictionary of Opera*). The op. has occasionally been staged by choreographers, incl. Balanchine (New York, 1946 and 1975), Descombey (Paris, 1960), and Charrat (Vienna, 1964). TV prod. by Balanchine, Nat. Educ. Television, 1981.

England. See Great Britain.

English Folk Dance and Song Society. See *Folk Dance and Song Society, English.*

Englund, Richard (*b* 1931, Seattle). Amer. dancer and teacher. Educated Harvard Univ. Studied with Tudor, Graham, Volkova. D. with the co. of Limón, Met. Op. B., National B. of Can., and Amer. B. Th. In charge of B. Repertory Co. (second co. of Amer. B. Th.) from 1972 and Joffrey II from 1985.

Englund, Sorella (*b* Helsinki, 1945). Finn dancer. Studied with Elsa Sylverston at local op. b. school; became a member of the State Op. B., where Blondelaine in *Scaramouche* was one of her first solo roles. She has been a member of the Royal Dan. B. since 1967, appointed soloist in 1970. Created roles in Flindt's *Triumph of Death* (1971), Marks' *Dichterliebe* (1972), and Holm's *Firebird* (1972—TV prod. 1974).

Enigma Variations. Ballet in 1 act; ch. Ashton; mus. Elgar; déc. Julia Trevelyan Oman. Prod. 25 Oct. 1968, Royal B., Cov. Gdn., London, with Rencher, Beriosova, Doyle. 'Some time before the action of the ballet takes place, Elgar had sent the score of the E.V. to the famous conductor Richter in the hope of interesting him in the work. The characters, intimates and friends of the composer, dance their individual variations, at the end of which a telegram arrives from Richter, addressed to their mutual friend Jaeger, agreeing to conduct the first performance. The action of the ballet takes place in Worcestershire in 1898' (Ashton). The b. was filmed for Argo Record Co. in 1969. An earlier abstract b. to this mus. by F. Staff (Cambridge, 1940).
BIBL.: D. Vaughan: *Frederick Ashton and his Ballets* (London, 1977).

Enters, Angna (*b* New York, 1907). Amer. dancer-mime, choreographer, painter, writer. Has developed her highly individual form of d. and pantomime: *The Theatre of A. E.*, consisting of nearly 300 different characters, with which she has toured the whole world, herself designing and executing all her costs. and props. Master teacher at various Amer. collegs and univs. Has also held several exhibitions of her own paintings and written various books.

Entrechat (Fr., caper). Designates a criss-crossing of the legs before and behind each other while the d. is in the air. They are numbered from deux to dix according to the number of movements performed—with each crossing counted as 2 movements (one out, one in). Even-numbered entrechats are finished by landing on both feet, while the odd-numbered land on one foot. Camargo is said to have first executed an e. quatre on stage, for the better execution of which she slightly shortened her skirt.

Entrée (Fr., entrance). Designates the entry on the stage of a single d. or a group of dancers. Also the individual number of a divertissement.

Eoline, ou la Dryade. Ballet in 6 scenes; libr. and ch. Perrot; mus. Pugni. Prod. 8 Mar. 1845, Her Majesty's Th. London, with Grahn, Perrot. Based on the story of *Libussa* by Musäus, which it connects with Rübezahl, the gnome from the Riesengebirge. The b. is set in the Bohemian forest, where the wood nymph Eoline must die on her wedding day, because Rübezahl sets on fire the oak-tree which is her home.
BIBL.: C. W. Beaumont, '*E.o.l.D.*' in *Complete Book of Ballets* (London, 1951).

Epaulement (Fr., shoulder). Designates the placing of the torso from the waist upward. Apart from its technical implications it has become a term of qualification for the correctness of the placing of the shoulders.

Episodes. Ballet in 2 parts; ch. Graham and Balanchine; mus. Webern; set and light. David Hays; cost. Karinska. Prod. 14 May 1959, M. Graham and D. Co., and New York City B., City Center, N.Y., with Graham, Ross, McGehee, Winter, S. Wilson; Verdy, Watts, D. Adams, d'Amboise, Kent, Magallanes, Hayden, Moncion, P. Taylor. Originally a close collaboration of the 2 choreographers was intended. However it was decided to let Graham and her co. stage the first part, performed to Webern's Passacaglia, op. 1, and Six Pieces for Orchestra, op. 6, with Mary Stuart (Graham), remembering some moments of her life (incl. a tennis game between her and Queen Elizabeth) on her way to the scaffold. Balanchine and his co. then did the plotless second part, set to Webern's Symphony, op. 21 (ensemble), Five Pieces for Orchestra, op. 10 (pas de deux), Concerto, op. 24 (pas de deux plus 4 female dancers), Variations for Orchestra, op. 30 (solo for Paul Taylor), and Ricercar for Six Voices from Bach's *Musical Offering* (ensemble). The first part was soon dropped from the repertory and so was the Taylor number of the second part. Today E. consists of the 4 Balanchine movements, and in this form the b. is also in the repertory of the Ger. Op. Berlin (1969) and the Dutch National B. (1973). TV prod., second Ger. Channel (1973).
BIBL.: G. Balanchine, '*E.*' in *Balanchine's New Complete Stories of the Great Ballets* (Garden City, N.Y., 1968).

Epitaph. Ballet in 1 act; ch. Van Dantzig; mus. Ligeti; déc. Van Schayk. Prod. 26 June 1969, Dutch National B., Stadsschouwburg, Amsterdam, with Guus Wijnoogst, Van Schayk, Clyde Geldorp. The b. is a personal confession of the difficulties of communication in modern society. It is d. to Ligeti's *Atmosphères* and *Volumina*. Revived for Munich (1972).

Epreuve d'amour, L'. Ballet in 1 act; libr. Fokine (also ch.) and Derain (also déc.). Prod. 4 Apr. 1936, R. Blum's B. Russe, Monte Carlo, with Nemchinova, Eglevsky, Yazvinsky, Oboukhov, Kirsova. Based on a Korean fairy-tale, the b. tells of the daughter of a Mandarin who is to marry a rich Ambassador. She, however, loves a poor young man, who, disguised as a dragon, steals the Ambassador's treasure, whereupon the Mandarin is no longer interested in the marriage, so that the girl gets her true-love after all. The mus. for the b. was discovered in 1928 in the collection of the Graz Musikverein in Austria, and at first believed to be by Mozart (who is still named as the comp.); A. Einstein, however, is convinced that it is Effisio Catte's *Der Rekrut (The Recruit)*, a divertissement in 3 tableaux, with mus. by various composers, which was first performed at the Vienna Kärntnertor Th. in 1838. After its rediscovery the b. was first prod. in Karlsruhe in 1930 (ch. H. J. Fürstenau). The Fokine version as staged by G.Gé in 1956 was kept until recently in the repertory of the Finnish National B.

Equilibre (Fr., balance). Designates the ability to balance or hold a pose.

Era, Antonietta dell' (*b* Milan, 16 Dec. 1861, *d* ?). Ital. dancer. Prima ballerina of the Berlin Court Op. 1879–1909. She came to St. Petersburg in 1886 where she first appeared in operetta entr'actes during the open air perfs. in the summer. She then became a guest ballerina at the Maryinsky Th., where she was very popular, creating the Sugar Plum Fairy in Ivanov's *Nutcracker* (1892).

Erdman, Jean (*b* 20 Feb., 1917 Honolulu). Amer. dancer, choreographer, and teacher. Studied with Graham, Bennington Summer School, and School of Amer. B. as well as with several teachers of Far Eastern d. styles; d. with Graham 1938–43 (also later as a guest), and founded her own troupe in 1944, for which she ch. extensively, and toured the U.S. She then became interested in doing ch. for several experimental play prods., writing, choreographing, and directing *The Coach with the Six Insides* in 1963 (after J. Joyce's *Finnegans Wake*), with which she also toured Europe. Until 1972 she was director of the D. Th. programme of the New York Univ. School of Arts, after which she opened in New York The Open Eye, a base for total th., where she prod. 3 plays by Yeats under the title of *Moon Mysteries*. A more recent prod. by her was *The Shining House* (1980). Contributed 'A Contemporary Dancer Looks at Her Heritage', *Dance Magazine* (Oct. 1960).
BIBL.: J. Meredith, 'On with the Dance at NYU', *Dance Magazine* (1970/4).

Errand into the Maze. Ballet in 1 act; ch. Graham; mus. Menotti; set Noguchi; cost. Edythe Gilfond. Prod. 28 Feb. 1947, M. Graham and D. Co., Ziegfeld Th., New York, with Graham and Mark Ryder. Based upon the Theseus legend and his fight against the Minotaur, the duo b. enacts victory over one's innermost fears. Also in the repertory of the Batsheva D. Co.

Errante. Ballet in 1 act; libr. Balanchine and Tchelitchev, and ch. Balanchine; mus. Schubert, arr. Liszt; déc. Tchelitchev. Prod. 10 June 1933, Les Bs. 1933, Th. des Champs-Elysées, Paris, with Losch. The b. is centred around an enigmatic woman who desperately fights against obviously very pressing though totally obscure emotional problems. Revived for Amer. B. (1935) and B. Th. (1943). Also under the title *The Wanderer*.

Escudero, Vicente (*b* Valladolid, 27 Oct. 1892, *d* Barcelona, 4 Dec. 1980). Span. dancer. D. as a child in cafés and cabarets in Spain. Made his Paris début with his long-time partner Carmita García in 1920. World-wide tours as a recital d. and with his own group earned him the reputation of being the most aristocratic Span. d. in the world. Retired from dancing 1961.
BIBL.: A. V. Krinkin, 'Vincente, Esto Es!', *Dance Magazine* (1955/2).

Eshkol, Noa (*b* Safad, 28 Feb. 1924). Israeli dance notator. Directed all perfs. (public, studio, lecture-demonstrations) of own Chamber D. Group from 1954 to the present. The co. performs dances comp. by N. E., all of which use E.-Wachman Movement Notation. The Group constitutes one framework among a number of overlapping working groups concerned with the development and application of E.-Wachman Movement Notation in tuition, research, folklore, etc. Author and co-author of various books on the system of movement notation she developed with Abraham Wachman, one of her earliest students, 1952–8, including *Movement Notation* (London, 1958).

Esmeralda, La. Ballet in 3 acts and 5 scenes; libr. and ch. Perrot; mus. Pugni; sets W. Grieve; cost. Mme Copère. Prod. 9 Mar. 1844, Her Majesty's Th., London, with Grisi, Perrot, Antoine Louis Coulon. The b. is based upon V. Hugo's novel *Notre-Dame de Paris* (1831), showing the hopeless love of the deaf and hunchbacked Quasimodo for the gipsy girl E., who is also pursued by Frollo, an evil priest. Further protagonists of the very complicated plot are Phoebus, a captain, and Gringoire, a poet. E. falls the victim of an intrigue and is awaiting execution when Quasimodo exposes Frollo as the real villain. In this early version the b. had a happy ending. It enjoyed immense popularity in Russ., where Elssler scored one of her biggest triumphs in the title role. It was repeatedly revived and adapted. For the Petipa prod. of 1886 in St. Petersburg Drigo comp. several new numbers, including the Diana and Actaeon pas de deux, which is still performed today (though in a ch. based upon the later Vaganova version). A completely new version, libr. V. Tikhomirov and V. Bourmeister (also ch.) mus. Glière and S. Vasilenko, was premièred on 14 Oct. 1950 at the Moscow Stanislavsky and Nemirovich-Danchenko Lyric Th. This had a tragic ending. Another different version was ch. by Beriozoff in 1954 for London Festival B. (mus. arr. by G. Corbett). A new b., **Notre-Dame de Paris*, by Petit, had its first prod. at the Paris Opéra in 1965, and another, *The Hunchback of Notre Dame*, by B. Wells (mus. Bartók) for the National B., 1981. An earlier version was by Antonio Monticioni at La Scala di Milano in 1839.
BIBL.: L. Kirstein, 'L. E.' in *Movement & Metaphor* (New York, 1970).

Espinosa. Famous family of dancers and teachers of Span. extraction. Léon E. (1825–1904) studied at the school of the Paris Opéra; d. at the Th. de la Porte-Saint-Martin, toured U.S. then became a member of the Moscow Bolshoi B. (as a premier danseur de contraste, because he was so very small), until he settled in 1872 in London where he opened a school. His wife and their daughter Lea both specialized in tap as well as 'operatic' (i.e. ballet) dancing. Léon's son Edouard E. (1871–1950) became one of the founders of the Royal Academy of Dancing in 1920 and of the Brit. B.

Organization in 1930. He was a much admired teacher and wrote several books. Edouard's son Edward Kelland-Espinosa became the head of the Brit. B. Organization. Bridget E. (née Kelly; *b* 1928), d. of the Embassy B. (1947) and International B. (1948), artistic dir. of the Elmhurst School since 1966, is the wife of Geoffrey E., a nephew of Edouard E.

Esquivel, Jorge (*b* Havana, 1950). Cuban dancer. Studied with F. Alonso, Joaquín Banegas, Anna Leontieva, Michel Gurov, and A. Plisetski, graduating in 1968, when he became a full-time member of the National B. of Cuba (with which he had already d.), appointed principal d. in 1972. Created roles in J. Lefèbre's *Edipo Rey* (1970), A. Mendez' *La Dame aux camélias* (1971), and Alb. Alonso's *Viet Nam: la lección* (1973). Bronze Medal (Varna, 1970).
BIBL.: complete list of activities and roles, *Cuba en el ballet* (1973/5).

Estampio, Juan Sanchez-Valencia (*b* Jerez de la Frontera, 1883, *d* Madrid, 1957). Span. dancer and teacher. Started to d. in cafés and cabarets, and was soon acknowledged as one of the best flamenco dancers of his generation. In 1921 he appeared in Diaghilev's *Cuadro flamenco* prod. Later he opened a school, becoming one of the most sought after teachers of flamenco d.

Estro Armonico. Ballet in 3 movements; ch. Cranko; mus. Vivaldi. Prod. 27 Apr. 1963, Stuttgart, with Barra, Delavalle, Cardus, Cragun. For this plotless b. K.-H. Stolze, the conductor, chose three from the 12 concertos of Vivaldi's op. 3. The subjects Cranko states in the first and second movements are resumed and developed in the third.

Etchevery, Jean-Jacques (*b* Paris, 1916). Fr. dancer and choreographer. Studied with Karpova, Ricaux, Zverev. D. with Nouveau B. de Monte Carlo 1941–4, when he founded his own co., Bs. de l'Oiseau Bleu. Appointed b. master at the Paris Opéra Comique 1946–53 and at the Brussels Th. de la Monnaie 1954–9. Many of the bs. he ch. received their inspiration from famous paintings. His best known bs. include *Ballade de la geôle de Reading* (mus. Ibert, 1947) and *Pelléas et Mélisande* (mus. Fauré, 1953).

Etoile (Fr., star). The highest title a danseuse or danseur can aspire to within the hierarchy of the Paris Opéra. The Eng. equivalent would be star d.

Etorki (Les Ballets et Choeurs Basques Etorki). The co., based on St Jean de Luz (on the Fr. side of the Pyrenees), was founded in 1954 for the conservation and development of Basque folk song and d. It has often toured abroad.

Etrange farandole, L'. Ballet in 4 movements; ch. Massine; mus. Shostakovich; déc. Matisse. Prod. 11 May 1939, B. Russe de Monte Carlo,

M. C., with Markova, Youskevitch, Franklin, Krassovska. The b., originally called *Le Rouge et le noir* and set to Shostakovich's First Symphony, belongs to Massine's symphonic bs. The 4 movements represent: Aggression—City and Country—Loneliness—Fate.
BIBL.: C. W. Beaumont, '*R.e.N.*' in *Supplement to Complete Book of Ballets* (London, 1952).

Etude. Ballet in 6 movements; ch. Nijinska; mus. Bach. First version as *Holy Etudes*, 3 Aug. 1925, Th. Chorégraphique Nijinska, Margate, Eng. Second version *Un Estudio religioso*, 27 Aug. 1926, Teatro Colón Buenos Aires. A plotless b. which tries to translate the mus. into visual terms. Revived for several cos.—best known in its 1931 version (with Nijinska and Lichine) for the Op. Russe de Paris.

Etudes (original Dan. title: *Etude*). Ballet in 1 act; ch. Lander; mus. Riisager (after Czerny); déc. Erik Nordgren. Prod. 15 Jan. 1948, Royal Dan. B., Copenhagen, with M. Lander, Brenaa, Svend Erik Jensen. Revised version in 1951 with T. Pils (later T. Lander), Bruhn, and Jensen. The b. develops as a demonstration of the academic school style, starting with the plié at the barre, via the adagio work au milieu through the allegro and batterie exercises. The whole b. is propelled by an irresistible escalation of technical difficulties, with a pas de deux à la *La Sylphide* interrupting its drive. It is the best known of Lander's bs. and an international success. Also in the repertory of many other cos. including Paris Opéra (1952), London Festival B. (1955), and Amer. B. Th. (1961). Dan. TV prod. 1969.
BIBL.: E. Aschengreen, *E.* (Copenhagen, 1970).

Eugen Onegin. See *Onegin*.

Eulenspiegel. See *Till Eulenspiegel*.

Eurythmics (also Fr. *Eurythmie*). Eurhythmia meant rhythmic order in classical Greece, and also movement and gracefulness. From the renaissance it designated the uniformity of the single parts and the good proportions of the parts to the whole. The term was applied by Rudolf Steiner to movements striving to express the content of poems and mus.—different from pantomime as well as from d. i.e. visible language and visible song.

Evans, Bill (*b* Lehi, Utah, 11 Apr. 1946). Amer. dancer, choreographer, and teacher. Studied at Univ. of Utah. D. with Harkness Youth Dancers, R. Page's Chicago Op. B. Since 1967 d. ch. teacher, and chairman of the Repertory D. Th. at Univ. of Utah, for which he has created a number of bs., including *Interim* (mus. Badings, 1968), *Tropic Passion* (mus. Milhaud, 1969), *When Summoned* (mus. Subotnick—first performed by the Ger. Op. Berlin, 1969), *For Betty* (mus. Vivaldi, 1970), and *Praise* (mus. Stanley Sussman, 1973).

Evdokimova, Eva (*b* Geneva, 1 Dec. 1948).

Amer. dancer. Studied at Munich State Op. B. School, then at Royal B. School, with M. Fay, also in Copenhagen and Leningrad. Made her début in 1966 with Royal Dan. B. Has been a member of the Ger. Op. Berlin since 1969, appointed prima ballerina in 1973. Often appears with other cos.—now also a principal d. with London Festival B. Dances the ballerina roles of the traditional repertory. Among her few modern roles is Juliet both in Cranko's and in Boyarchikov's version of *Romeo and Juliet*. Created the central role in Luipart's *Scarecrows* (1970), and Louise, the ballerina role in R. Hynd's *Nutcracker* (1976) for London Festival B. Gold Medal (Varna, 1970); Critics' Prize (Berlin, 1974).
BIBL.: K. Geitel, 'Alles über Eva' in *Ballett 1971* (Velber, 1971).

Event. M. Cunningham started the series of his events with *Museum Event 1* in Vienna in 1964. This offered a selection of excerpts from several of his works. Subsequent perfs. (with the same or different excerpts) were numbered accordingly; he started a series of Gymnasium Events in 1968. Today he prefers to call them just Events.

Eventail de Jeanne, L'. Ballet in 10 numbers; ch. Yvonne Franck and Alice Bourgat; mus. various composers; sets Pierre Legrain and René Moulaert; cost. Laurencin. Prod. 16 June 1928 in the Salon de Mme Jeanne Dubost—revived for Opéra, Paris, on 4 Mar. 1929, with Toumanova and other petits rats of the Opéra's b. school. The b. started as a caprice of Mme Dubost who gave the 10 leaves of her fan to 10 composers, asking each of them to compose one d. number. Participating were Ravel (Fanfare), Pierre-Octave Ferroud (March), Ibert (Valse), Roland-Manuel (Canarie), M. Delannoy (Bourrée), Roussel (Sarabande), Milhaud (Polka), Poulenc (Pastourelle), and F. Schmitt (Finale); the 10th comp. is unkown. At its private première the b. was so favourably received that it was decided to take it into the repertory of the Opéra. In the Polka and the Valse the technical virtuosity of the 8-year-old Toumanova impressed the audience.

Events. Ballet in 1 act; ch. Robbins; mus. Robert Prince; sets Ben Shahn; cost. Ray Diffen. Prod. 12 July 1961, Bs.: U.S.A., with Patricia Dunn, Verso, Tetley, Gain. A b. about 'happenings, attempts, and recoveries' (Robbins), dealing with the manifold threats imposed on modern man by contemporary society.
BIBL.: G. Balanchine, 'E.' in *Balanchine's New Complete Stories of the Great Ballets* (Garden City, N.Y., 1968).

Everett, Ellen (*b* Springfield, In., 19 June 1942). Amer. dancer. Studied with B. Holmes, School of Amer. B., Amer. B. Th. School, R. Thomas, and B. Fallis. D. with R. Page's Chicago Op. B. 1958–64 and Amer. B. Th. since 1964; appointed

principal d. in 1973. Created lead in Smuin's *Pulcinella Variations* (1968).

Every Soul Is a Circus. Ballet in 1 act; ch. Graham; mus. Paul Nordhoff; scenery Philip Stapp; cost. Edythe Gilfond. Prod. 27 Dec. 1939, M. Graham and Co., St James Th., New York, N.Y., with Graham, Hawkins, Cunningham. Based on a poem by Vachel Lindsay, the b. centres on the split personality of a woman, who watches the reactions of her partners while she flirts with a domineering ringmaster and a puckish acrobat. A light and humorous self-portrait of Graham, it introduced Cunningham to her co.

Evil Queen, The (also *The Wicked Queen*). TV ballet film by Cullberg, mus. Dag Wirén, directed by Arne Arnbom for Swed. TV 1961, with G. Andersson, Orlando, F. Schaufuss, Selling. A TV retelling of Grimm's *Snow White and the Seven Dwarfs*, which won the Prix d'Italia of that year.

Evteyeva, Elena. See *Yevteyeva, Yelena*.

Excelsior. Ballet in 6 parts and 12 scenes; libr. and ch. Manzotti; mus. Romualdo Marenco; déc. Alfredo Edel. Prod. 11 Jan. 1881, Teatro alla Scala, Milan, with Bice Vergani, Carlo Montanara. The extraordinarily successful b. showed the rise of human civilization and the stormy progress of technical development as an embittered struggle between the Spirits of Darkness and Light. After the invention of the steam ship, the iron bridge, electricity, telegraphy, the building of the Suez Canal and the Mont Cenis tunnel, the Spirit of Darkness admits defeat, and a Grand Festival of Nations is celebrated, with an apotheosis of light and peace. The b. enjoyed immense popularity and was constantly revived all over Europe. After its Vienna première in 1885 it remained in the repertory for 29 years, receiving 329 perfs. More recent stagings by U. dell'Ara for the Maggio Musicale Fiorentino in 1967 and at La Scala di Milano in 1974.
BIBL.: C. W. Beaumont, 'E.' in *Complete Book of Ballets* (London, 1951).

Exercice (Fr., exercise). Designates the daily class of the b. d.

Extemporary Dance Theatre. Br. modern-d. group. Formed as professional co. in 1976 by graduates of London School of Contemporary D. after they appeared at 1975 Edinburgh Festival under G. Powell as artistic dir. He was succeeded by P. Taras in 1978, and by E. Claid in 1981 (with S. Giles as assoc. dir.). Co. numbers six ds. and since 1978 undertakes regular touring of smaller ths. with Arts Council funding.

Extension. Designates the capability of a d. to raise and hold the extended leg in the air. A d. is said to have 'a good extension' if, in the process of a développé à la seconde, she is able to raise and hold her leg above shoulder level.

F

Fabbri, Flora (*b* Florence). Ital. dancer of the nineteenth century. A pupil of Blasis, she was one of the 6 dancers called 'Pleiades of Blasis'. After making her début at the Teatro Fenice in Venice, she d. in Rome and Bologna. She married the Fr. ch. Louis Bretin in 1842, and was a member of the Paris Opéra 1844–51.
BIBL.: I. Guest, in *The Romantic Ballet in Paris* (London, 1966).

Fables for Our Time. Ballet in 4 parts; ch. Weidman; mus. Freda Miller. Prod. 11 July 1947, Charles Weidman D. Th. Co., Jacob's Pillow D. Festival, with Weidman, Betty Osgood. The b. retells the 4 James Thurber fables, *The Unicorn in the Garden, The Shrike and the Chipmunk, The Owl Who Was God,* and *The Courtship of Al and Arthur.* This was one of Weidman's most popular works. The New York première took place on 18 Apr. 1948 at the Mansfield Th.

Façade. Ballet in 1 act; ch. Ashton; mus. Walton; déc. John Armstrong. Prod. 26 Apr. 1931, Camargo Society, Cambridge Th., London, with Lopokova, Markova, Ashton. The b. is freely adapted to mus. originally written as a setting for the poems by Edith Sitwell. It consists of a string of satirical character sketches: *Scotch Rhapsody, Yodelling Song, Polka, Foxtrot, Waltz, Popular Song, Tango, Tarantella, Finale.* An instant success, the b. was immediately taken into the repertory of the B. Rambert and in 1935 into the repertory of the Vic-Wells B. BBC TV prod. of Sadler's Wells B. prod. 1953. It is still one of the most popular bs. in the Royal B. repertory and has been revived for several other ocas. An earlier version by Günter Hess in Hagen (Ger.)
BIBL.: D. Vaughan, *Frederick Ashton and his Bs.* (London, 1977).

Face, en (Fr., facing). Designates a position of the d. facing the audience directly.

Fâcheux, Les. (1) Comédie-Ballet by Molière; ch. and mus. Beauchamp. Prod. 17 Aug. 1661 at a special perf. for Louis XIV at Vaux as one of the first bs. of its kind. (2) Ballet in 1 act; libr. Kochno (based on Molière); ch. Nijinska; mus. Auric; déc. Braque. Prod. 19 Jan. 1924, Bs. Russes de Diaghilev, Monte Carlo, with Tchernicheva, Vilzak, Dolin. A lover, on his way to a rendezvous, constantly runs into annoying people (the 'fâcheux' of the title), who compel him to participate in their whimsicalities. The strongly mime-orientated b. was not a success. Diaghilev, however, liked it so much that he commissioned Massine to rechoreograph it in 1927.

Facsimile. Ch. observation in 1 scene; ch. Robbins; mus. Bernstein; set O. Smith; cost. I. Sharaff. Prod. 24 Oct. 1946, B. Th., Broadway Th., New York, with Kaye, Robbins, Kriza. 'Small inward treasure does he possess who, to feel alive, needs every hour the tumult of the street, the emotion of the Theatre, and the small talk of society' (programme note). A triangular affair between a woman and 2 men on the beach.
BIBL.: G. Balanchine, '*F.*' in *Balanchine's New Complete Stories of the Great Ballets* (Garden City, N.Y., 1968).

Fadetta. Ballet in 3 acts and 4 scenes; libr. Slonimsky; ch. Lavrovsky; mus. Delibes; déc. N. Nikiforov. Prod. 21 Mar. 1934, GATOB, Leningrad. Using the mus. of Delibes' *Sylvia*, the b. is based on G. Sand's novel *La petite Fadette* (1849), telling of the love between the son of rich peasants and the grand-daughter of an old woman who is ostracized as a witch, and how they both overcome bourgeois prejudice. Lavrovsky originally created the b. for a graduation perf.

Fadeyechev, Nicolai Borisovich (*b* Moscow, 27 Jan. 1933). Sov. dancer. Entered the Bolshoi B. School in 1943, graduating in 1952, when he became a member of the Bolshoi B.; promoted soloist in 1953. He soon became the favourite partner of Plisetskaya. D. the premier danseur roles of the standard repertory, and also created roles in Vinogradov's *Asel* (1967), Alonso's *Carmen Suite* (1967), Kasatkina-Vasiliov's *Preludes and Fugues* (1968), Grigorovich's *Swan Lake* (1969), and Plisetskaya's *Anna Karenina* (1972). In the Eng. *Giselle* film with Ulanova he d. Albrecht (1956). Honoured Artist of the R.S.F.S.R. Married to the d. Irina Kholina.

Faier, Yuri Fedorovich (*b* 17 Jan. 1890 *d* Moscow, 3 Aug. 1971). Sov. conductor. As the Moscow Bolshoi B.'s conductor 1923–63, he was one of the most liked and admired b. conductors of all time. Wrote *Notes of a Ballet Conductor* (1960).

Faigel, Eva Maria. See *Violette, Eva Maria.*

Failli (Fr., failed). Designates a spring into the air with both feet close together in fifth position. While in the air the body is turned with the left shoulder coming forward, the head turning to the left, then the left leg opens, the landing is made on the right foot, with the left foot sliding through the first into the fourth position, finishing in demi-plié with the body slightly inclined to the left.

Fairy Doll, The (orig. Ger. title: *Die Puppenfee*).

Pantomimic divertissement in 1 act; libr. Hassreiter (also ch.) and F. Gaul; mus. Jos. Bayer; déc. A. Brioschi. Prod. 4 Oct. 1888, Court Op., Vienna, with C. Pagliero. The b. is set in a toy shop, the owner of which shows his dolls to a visiting Eng. family. After the shop is closed, the dolls come to life and d. individually and with each other, led by the Fairy Doll, to whom they all pay homage in the final procession. In its original version the title role was mimed. The b. has constantly been revived in Vienna, with Hassreiter's ch. more or less intact. It is still in the repertory of the Vienna State Op., where it received its 750th perf. in 1973. It has been staged in numerous versions all over the world (N. and S. Legat in St. Petersburg, 1903; K. Lanner in London, 1903; I. Clustine for the Pavlova co., 1914). Austrian TV prod. of the Hassreiter version 1971. Massine's *La Boutique fantasque* of 1919 is a dramatically and musically improved adaptation of the b.

Fairy's Kiss, The. See *Baiser de la Fée, Le.*

Faison, George (*b* Washington, D.C., 21 Dec. 1945). Amer. dancer and choreographer. Studied with L. Johnson, C. Thompson, Ailey, D. Williams, and E. Hodes. D. on Broadway and with G.F. Universal D. Experience which he founded in 1971, before choreographing for Broadway, *The Wiz* (1975) being his biggest success so far. Has also ch. for A. Ailey Amer. D. Th.

Falco, Louis (*b* New York, 2 Aug. 1942). Amer. dancer. choreographer, and b. director. Studied with Limón, Weidman, Graham, and at the Amer. B. Th. School, making his début with the Limón co. in 1960. Started to choreograph in 1967. Has had his own group since 1968, with which he regularly appears in New York and the U.S. Toured Eur. with his co. for the first time in 1973. His best known bs. for his own group incl. *Caviar* (1970), *Sleepers* (1971), *Twopenny Portrait* (1973), *Escargot* (1978), and *Kate's Rag* (1980). He ch. *Journal* (1971) and *Eclipse* (1974) for Netherlands D. Th., *Tutti-frutti* (1973) for B. Rambert, and *The Eagle's Nest* (1980) for La Scala B. Almost all his bs. are d. to mus. by Burt Alcantara. Has also ch. for the film *Fame* (1980).
BIBL.: P. Meinertz Shapiro, 'Innovator for Tomorrow', *Dance Magazine* (1971/2); interview 'Creative Togetherness', *Dance and Dancers* (1973/10).

Falla, Manuel de (*b* Cadiz, 23 Nov. 1876, *d* Alta Gracia, Argent., 14 Nov. 1946). Span. composer. Wrote the mus. for P. Imperio's *El amor brujo* (*Love, the Magician*, 1915; new version by P. Wright for Royal B. touring Co., 1975) and Massine's *Le Tricorne* (*The Three-Cornered Hat*, 1919). His posthumous op. *Atlantida* also contains several d.-numbers (prod. M. Wallmann, Scala di Milano, 1962).

Fall-Recovery. These contrasting-dynamics are the basis of Humphrey's teaching system of modern d. It corresponds with Graham's *Contraction—Release, and to the Central European school's *Anspannung-Abspannung.

Fallis, Barbara (*b* Denver, 1924, *d* New York, 5 Sep. 1980). Amer. dancer and teacher. Studied at Mona Clague B. School and Vic-Wells B. School. D. with Vic-Wells B. 1938–40. Returned to U.S., and d. with B. Th. 1941–7, becoming soloist. Joined B. Alicia Alonso as ballerina 1948–52, later dancing with New York City B. and the Rabovskys. Was co-director New York School of B. with Richard Thomas.

Fall River Legend. Ballet in 1 act and 8 scenes; libr. and ch. de Mille; mus. Gould; sets O. Smith; cost. Miles White. Prod. 22 Apr. 1948, B.Th., Met. Op. Ho., New York, with Alonso, Bentley, Kriza. The b. was suggested by the case of Lizzie Borden, who in 1892 was accused of murdering her parents with an axe. 'While in no way attempting to tell the fearful story factually, in fact departing radically from history, it explores the passions that lead to a violent resolution of the oppressions and turmoils that can beset an ordinary life' (programme note). Lizzie became one of the most famous roles of N. Kaye.
BIBL.: G. Balanchine, 'F.R.L.' in *Balanchine's New Complete Stories of the Great Ballets* (Garden City, N.Y., 1968); A. de Mille, *Lizzie Borden: A Dance of Death* (Boston, 1968).

Fancy Free. Ballet in 1 act; libr. and ch. Robbins; mus. Bernstein; set O. Smith; cost. Kermit Love. Prod. 18 Apr. 1944, B.Th., Met. Op. Ho., New York, with Lang, Kriza, Robbins, Bentley, Reed. Robbins's first b. tells what happens to 3 sailors on leave who visit a Manhattan bar and become involved with some girls. An instant hit, the b. became the point of departure for the Robbins-Bernstein musical *On the Town* (1944). Revived for N.Y. City B. (1980). Individually ch. prods. by Marteny (Graz, Austria, 1969) and Schilling (Comic Op., East Berlin, 1971).
BIBL.: G. Balanchine, 'F.F.' in *Balanchine's New Complete Stories of the Great Ballets* (Garden City, N.Y., 1968); L. Kirstein, 'F.F.' in *Movement & Metaphor* (New York, 1970).

Fandango. A lively Span. d. possibly of South Amer. origin, in triple or compound duple time, accompanied by guitars and castanets. One of its first b. appearances was in Angiolini and Gluck's *Don Juan* in 1761, the same melody repeated for the wedding d. in Mozart's *Le Nozze di Figaro*, 1786. A b. of the same name by Tudor for the National B. of Canada (mus. Padre Soler, 1972).

Fanfare. Ballet in 1 act; ch. Robbins; mus. Britten; déc. I. Sharaff. Prod. 2 June 1953, New York City B., City Center, N.Y., with Mounsey, Larsson, Jillana, d'Amboise, Bolender, Bliss, Hobi. Based on Britten's *Young Person's Guide to the Orchestra* (Purcell Variations), the b. sets out to depict the characters of the individual orchestral instruments in d. terms. Revived for Royal Dan. B. in 1956.

BIBL.: G. Balanchine, 'F.' in *Balanchine's New Complete Stories of the Great Ballets* (Garden City, N.Y., 1968).

Farandole. A very old Fr. d. in compound duple time from Provence. It is d. by couples in a chain who hold hands, moving in spirals through the town. It is accompanied by the galoubet and tambourin. In b. it occurs at the beginning of the vision scene in *Sleeping Beauty* and in *Flames of Paris*.

Farber, Viola (b Heidelberg, 25 Feb. 1931). Amer. dancer and choreographer. Studied with Litz, M. Cunningham, Craske, and Corvino. Began to d. with Cunningham co. 1952, later also with P. Taylor and Litz. Now has her own co. Art. dir. Centre Nationale de Danse Contemporaine, Angers, France, 1981.

Farewell, The. Solo d. ch. and cost; Koner; mus. Mahler. Prod. 9 Feb. 1962, Virginia Mus. Th., with Koner; official première 28 Feb. 1962, Hartford (Conn.) Symphony; New York première 30 Apr. 1962, YM-YWHA. D. to the last movement from Mahler's *Song of the Earth*, this was Koner's tribute to the memory of Humphrey, for many years her friend, teacher, and collaborator. For b. versions of the complete symphony see *Song of the Earth*.

Far from Denmark (orig. Dan. title: *Fjernt fra Danmark eller Et Costumeball ombord*). Vaudeville Ballet in 2 acts; libr. and ch. Aug. Bournonville; mus. Jos. Glaeser (plus additional numbers by L. Gottschalk, Lumbye, Dupuy, and A. F. Lincke). Prod. 20 Apr. 1860, Royal Dan. B., Copenhagen. The b. shows what happens when a Dan. frigate anchors in an Argent. harbour. The inevitable romance involves a Dan. naval lieutenant, the daughter of the consul, and her fiancé. A big masked ball aboard the ship becomes the pretext for a lavish divertissement of character dances. The b. has always been kept in the co's. repertory, its latest revival dating from 1973.

BIBL.: C. W. Beaumont, '*Loin du Danemark*' in *Supplement to Complete Book of Ballets* (London, 1952).

Farha, Clint (b Kansas, Mo., 21 Dec. 1953). Amer. dancer. Studied at various US schools, then with M. Day in Washington. Joined Dutch National B. 1973, appointed principal d. 1978. Created leading role in Van Manen's *5 Tangos* (1977) and *Klaviervariationen I* (1980).

Farmanyantz, Georgi Karapetovich (b 4 Nov. 1921). Sov. dancer and teacher. Studied at the Moscow Bolshoi School 1929–40; then became a member of the Bolshoi B., where he was soon admired as a brilliant character d. His Gopak for *Taras Bulba* was a favourite concert number. Retired in 1963, he continues to teach. Honoured Artist of the R.S.F.S.R. (1951).

Farmer, Peter (b Luton, 3 Nov. 1941). Brit. designer. His first b. design was J. Carter's *Agrionia* (1964). He then became known through designing P. Wright's Stuttgart *Giselle* in 1966, which he later did also for several other cos. (Royal B. Touring Co. in 1968). Also designed Wright's *Namouna* (Stuttgart, 1967), *Sleeping Beauty* (Cologne, 1968—also the MacMillan prod. of the Royal B., 1973), and *Dance Macabre* (Western Th.B., 1968), Ashton's *The Dream* (Royal B. Touring Co., 1967), Feld's *Meadow Lark* (London Festival B., 1969), J. Carter's *Coppélia* (London Festival B., 1969), Cohan's *Stages* (London Contemporary D. Th., 1971), Stevenson's *Cinderella* (Festival B., 1973), de Warren's *Cinderella* (Northern B. Th., 1979), Prokovsky's *Anna Karenina* (Austral. B., 1979), *The Three Musketeers* (Austral. B., 1980) and *Nutcracker* (Northern B. Th., 1980).

Farnworth, Don (b Carey, Ida., 20 May 1927). Amer. dancer, teacher, and b. master. Studied with Anderson-Ivantzova, Vilzak, Caton, Swoboda, and others. Toured with F. & Dell 1951–4, then d. as a soloist at Radio City Music Hall. B. master of various cos. including Batsheva D, Co., Bat-Dor B. Co., Netherlands D. Th., Scapino B., P. Taylor D. Co. Now Artistic Dir. of F. and Hauer School in New York.

BIBL.: N. McLain Stoop, 'Main Street on Broadway', *Dance Magazine* (July 1970).

Farrell, Suzanne (b Cincinnati, 16 Aug. 1945). Amer. dancer. Studied at a local b. school, then at the School of Amer. B., becoming a member of the New York City B. in 1961; promoted soloist in 1965. Married the d. Paul Mejia in 1969, after which she left the co. with great éclat. During her years with the co. she had become the Balanchine ballerina par excellence, creating roles in his *Movements for Piano and Orchestra* (1963), *Meditation* (1964), *Don Quixote* (1965), *Variations* (1966), *Jewels* (1967), *Metastaseis & Pithoprakta* (1968), and *Slaughter on Tenth Avenue* (1968 version). From 1970 she became the top ballerina of the B. of the 20th Century, creating roles in Béjart's *Sonate* (1970), *Les Fleurs du mal* (1971), *Nijinsky, Clown de Dieu* (1971), *Ah, vous dirais-je Maman* (1972), *Golestan* (1973), *Farah* (1973), and *I Trionfi* (1974). Returned to New York City B. in 1975, and created roles in Balanchine's *Tzigane* (1975), Robbins's *Piano Concerto in G* (1975), Balanchine's *Union Jack* (1976), *Vienna Waltzes* (1977), *Davidsbündlertänze* (1980), and new version of *Mozartiana* (1981). D. Magazine Award 1976.

BIBL.: Interview in *Dance News* (1970/11); R. Sealy, 'Paul and Suzanne', *Ballet Review* (vol. 3, no. 1); complete check-list of roles and activities in *Les Saisons de la Danse* (1975/12); D. Daniel, 'A Conversation with S.F.', *Ballet Review* (Vol. 7, no. 1); O. Maynard, 'The Metamorphosis of a Balanchine Ballerina', *Dance Magazine* (1979/1).

Farron, Julia (b London, 1922). Brit. d. and

teacher. Studied at the Cone-Ripman and Vic-Wells B. Schools, joining the Sadler's Wells B. in 1936 and dancing with the co. until 1961 (she continued to appear in some mime roles). Created roles in Ashton's *A Wedding Bouquet* (1937), *Cupid and Psyche* (1939), and *Ondine* (1958), Howard's *A Mirror for Witches* (1952), Cranko's *Prince of the Pagodas* (1957) and *Antigone* (1959), and Mac-Millan's *Romeo and Juliet* (1965). Then on the teaching staff of the Royal B. School; dir. Royal Academy of Dancing from 1983. Married to the ch. Alfred Rodrigues.

BIBL.: C. Swinson, 'J.F.' in *Six Dancers of Sadler's Wells* (London, 1956); G. Anthony, 'J.F.', *Dancing Times* (1970/8).

Farruca. A very lively Andalusian d. of gipsy origin. The Miller dances a F. in Massine's *Le Tricorne*.

Fascilla, Roberto (*b* Milan, 27 Dec. 1937). Ital. dancer. Studied at La Scala B. School. Joined La Scala B. in 1956, promoted soloist in 1960 and primo ballerino in 1965. Has occasionally ch. and taught at various Ital. ths. Often tours with the Fracci co.

Fastes. Ballet in 1 act; libr. and déc. Derain; ch. Balanchine; mus. Sauguet. Prod. 10 June 1933, Les Bs. 1933, Th. des Champs-Elysées, Paris, with Toumanova and Jasinsky. The b. shows a pagan ritual on a sun-baked Ital. market square, with the participants wearing grotesque masks.

Fatauros, Jorge (*b* Buenos Aires, 8 Jan. 1940). Argent. photographer. Studied d. with H. Zaraspe in Buenos Aires and at Amer. B. Center. D. with the cos. of Joffrey, Petit, Stuttgart B., Netherlands D. Th., and Dutch National B. Now official photographer of Dutch National B. but works for numerous other cos. in addition.

Fauré, Gabriel (*b* Pamiers, 12 May 1845, *d* Paris, 4 Nov. 1924). Fr. composer. Wrote no b. mus., but his concert mus. has been often adapted for b. purposes, incl. A. Howard in *La Fête étrange* (various piano pieces and songs, London B., 1940), J. J. Etcheverry in *Pelléas et Mélisande* (the eponymous suite for orchestra, Brussels, 1953—also used by many other choreographers), Balanchine in the 'Emeralds' section of *Jewels* (also *Pelléas et Mélisande* plus the *Shylock* overture, New York City B., 1967)—also *Ballads for Piano and Orchestra* (New York City B., 1980), A. Prokovsky in *Soft Blue Shadows* (various instrumental pieces and songs, New London B., 1976), and MacMillan in *Pavane* (Royal B., 1973) and *Requiem* (Stuttgart B., 1976—in the same year also by G. Casado and J. Russillo).

Faust Ballets. In 1723 John Rich presented a b. pantomime, *The Necromancer or the History of Dr. Faustus*, at the London Th. of Lincolns Inn Fields. Aug. Bournonville ch. a F. b. for the Royal Dan. B. in 1832 to a mus. arrangement by Ph. L. Keck. Deshayes's *F.* followed in 1833 at the London King's Th.—the mus. was by Adam (who later borrowed some of its numbers for *Giselle*). Heinrich Heine, commissioned by dir. Lumley of the London Her Majesty's Th., wrote the libr. for a b. pantomime *Der Doktor Faust* in 1847, which, however, was never staged in its original form. After its publication in Fr. and Ger., however, it inspired several other F. bs. In Berlin P. Taglioni ch. a b. *Satanella oder Metamorphosen* in 1852, which was based on Jacques Cazotte's *Diable amoureux*, with the she-devil Biondetta as protagonist. The most successful F. b. of the 19th century was, however, the one by Perrot, which he ch. with Elssler as Gretchen in 1848 for Milan. Reisinger staged a b. *Mephistophelia* to mus. by Kredler for Hamburg in 1856. Another F. by Lanner with mus. by M. Lutz and E. Ford had its first prod. at the London Empire Th. in 1895. Remislav Remislavský's *F.* was derived from Heine's libr. with mus. by František Skvor for the Prague National Th. in 1926—as was Kirsanova's *F.* to mus. by Henry Krips for the Austral. National B. in 1941. In 1948 W. Egk's *Abraxas* appeared in Munich (ch. Luipart), which enjoyed great popularity in the Ger. of the 1950s and 1960s. There have also been several ch. stagings of Berlioz' *La Damnation de Faust*, incl. Béjart's for the Paris Opéra in 1964. Also Béjart, *Notre Faust* (mus. Bach's B Minor Mass, Brussels, 1975). For a Pol. F. version see *Pan Twardowski*.

BIBL.: M. Niehaus, *Himmel, Hölle und Trikot* (Munich, 1959); 'Abraxas' in *Die Tanzarchiv Reihe*, no. 2.

Feast in Albano (original Dan. title: *Festen i Albano*). Idyllic ballet in 1 act; ch. Aug. Bournonville; mus. J. F. Frölich. Prod. 28 Oct. 1839, Royal Dan. B., Copenhagen. The b. was created to celebrate the return of the sculptor Bertel Thorvaldsen to Copenhagen. It is modelled around several of his best known statues.

Feast of Ashes. Ballet in 1 act; ch. Ailey; mus. Surinach; déc. Jack Venza. Prod. 30 Sep. 1962, R. Joffrey B., Fashion Institute of Technology, New York, with Françoise Martinet, Bradley, P. Sutherland. Set to Surinach's *Doppio Concertino* and part of his *Ritmo Jondo*, the b. is based on García Lorca's *The House of Bernarda Alba*: the son of a wealthy family is supposed to marry the oldest daughter of the widowed Bernarda Alba, but he loves her youngest sister, who tries to escape with him but has to pay for this moral outrage with her life. Other b. versions based upon the same source include MacMillan's *Las Hermanas* (1963), I. Sertić's *Abbandonate* (1964), and E. Pomare's *Desenamoradas* (1967).

BIBL.: G. Balanchine, 'F.o.A.' in *Balanchine's New Complete Stories of the Great Ballets* (Garden City, N.Y., 1968).

Fedicheva, Kaleria Ivanovna (*b* Ust-Ijory, 20 July 1936). Sov. dancer. Studied at Leningrad Ch. School, graduating in 1955, and becoming a member of the Kirov B. She excelled as a ballerina in the character roles of the modern repertory, but is also much admired for her Odette-Odile, Kitri, and Nikia. Created roles in Belsky's *Leningrad Symphony* (second première, 1961), K. Sergeyev's *The Distant Planet* (1963) and *Hamlet* (1970), K. Boyarsky's *The Pearl* (1965), Alexidze's *Orestie* (1968), and Vinogradov's *Prince of the Pagodas* (1972). Left the U.S.S.R. in 1975 to join her Amer. d.-husband Martin Freedman. Staged pas d'action from second act of *La Bayadère* for U.S. Terpsichore (1975). People's Artist of the R.S.F.S.R. (1967).

Fedjanin, Vladimir (*b* Schachty, 12 Apr. 1946). Sov. dancer. Studied at Leningrad B. School. Upon graduation in 1967 joined Kirov B. Has also d. in Odessa and with Moscow Bolshoi B., before joining East Berlin Comic Op. B. as a principal d. 1976, since when he has created leading roles in Schilling's *Black Birds* (1976) and *Swan Lake* (1978). Also works as a teacher and b. master. Gold Medal (Varna, 1972).

Fedorova, Alexandra Alexandrovna (*b* St. Petersburg, 12 Oct. 1884, *d* New York, 20 Aug. 1972). Russ.-Amer. dancer and teacher. Studied at St. Petersburg Imperial B. Academy, graduating in 1902, after which she joined the Maryinsky Th., appointed first soloist in 1906. Married Alexander Fokine, the brother of Mikhail F., and became prima ballerina of the Troitzky Th., of which she was dir. In 1925 she moved to Riga as b. mistress of the Latvian State Th. In 1937 she moved to New York, where she taught at her own school until 1965. Mother of the d. and teacher Leon Fokine.
BIBL.: M. Horosko, 'A.F.', *Dance Magazine* (1971/5).

Fedorova, Sophia Vasilievna (*b* Moscow, 28 Sep. 1879, *d* there 3 Jan. 1963). Russ. dancer. Studied at the Moscow Bolshoi School, graduating in 1899, after which she joined the Bolshoi B., becoming one of its most admired character ballerinas, and dancing with the co. until 1919. She lived in Paris 1922–8, dancing with the cos. of Diaghilev and Pavlova.

Fedorovitch, Sophie (*b* Minsk, 15 Dec. 1893, *d* London, 25 Jan. 1953). Russ.-Brit. stage designer. Came to London in 1920, where she became one of Ashton's closest collaborators. Designed for him *A Tragedy of Fashion* (his first b., 1926), *Les Masques* (1933), *Mephisto Valse* (1934), *Le Baiser de la Fée* (1935), *Nocturne* (1936), *Horoscope* (1938), *Dante Sonata* (1940), *Symphonic Variations* (1946), *Valses nobles et sentimentales* (1947), and his prod. of Gluck's *Orpheus and Eurydice* (1953), and for Howard *La Fête étrange* (1940) and *Veneziana* (1953).

Fehl, Fred (*b* nr. Vienna, 21 Jan. 1906). Amer. b. photographer. Works for many Amer. and international d. cos. and regularly with New York City B. Contributor to *Melissa Hayden Off Stage and On* (New York, 1963) and E. Bruhn's 'Beyond Technique' (*Dance Perspectives* 36).
BIBL.: O. Maynard, 'F.F.: The Eye Behind the Image', *Dance Magazine* (1972/7); J. Pikula, 'The F. View', *Dance Magazine* (1976/4).

Feld, Eliot (*b* Brooklyn, 5 July 1942). Amer. dancer, choreographer, and b. director. Studied at the New York School of Amer. B. with Richard Thomas; d. in the *West Side Story* prod., joined Amer. B. Th. in 1963, where he ch. his first b., *Harbinger* (mus. Prokofiev) in 1967, an immediate success, followed in the same year by *At Midnight* (mus. Mahler). In 1969 he founded his own *Amer. B. Co., which made its début in Spoleto, presenting his *Cortège Burlesque* (mus. Chabrier), *Intermezzo* (mus. Brahms), and *Meadow Lark* (mus. Haydn). His next bs. were *Pagan Spring* (mus. Bartók, 1969), *Early Songs* (mus. R. Strauss, 1970), *A Poem Forgotten* (mus. W. Riegger, 1970), *Cortège Parisien* (mus. Chabrier, 1970), *The Consort* (mus. Dowland, Morley, and others, 1970), *Theatre* (mus. R. Strauss, 1971), *The Gods Amused* (mus. Debussy, 1971), and *A Soldier's Tale* (mus. Stravinsky, 1972). After financial reasons compelled him to dissolve his co., returned to Amer. B. Th. 1971–2. Also worked as a guest ch. for other cos. (Royal Winnipeg B., London Festival B., Royal Swed. B., Royal Dan. B.—for City Center Joffrey B.: *Jive*, mus. Gould, 1973). A new co., the E.F.B., made its début in June 1974 in New York, presenting his *Seraphic Songs* and *The Tzaddik* (mus. Copland); *Mazurka* (mus. Chopin, 1975). More recent bs. of his have been *Excursions* (mus. Barber, 1975), *Impromptu* (mus. Roussel, 1976), *Variations on America* (mus. Ives and Schumann, 1977), *Santa Fé Saga* (mus. Gould, 1978). Remodelled the Elgin Theatre, New York as a dance theatre (renamed Joyce Theatre). A TV portrait of him, *E.F. and the Amer. B. Comp.* (Cologne TV, 1970—also his *Harbinger* and *At Midnight*).
BIBL.: Interview with E.F. in *Dance and Dancers* (1969/1); M. B. Siegel, 'F. Re-Fielded', *Dance Magazine* (1974/3).

Felix (orig. F. Fernandez García; *b c.* 1896, *d* Epsom, Eng., 1941). Span. dancer. Diaghilev, who saw him dancing in the streets of Seville, was so fascinated that he engaged him to help Massine with the Span. d. of *Le Tricorne*. Convinced that he would d. the role of the Miller at the b.'s 1919 première, when the b. was first performed with Massine he suffered a shock from which he never recovered. After he had been found dancing on the altar of a London church, was put into an asylum.

Femmes de bonne humeur, Les. See *Good-Humoured Ladies, The*.

Fenster, Boris Alexandrovich (*b* Petrograd, 17 Apr. 1916, *d* Leningrad, 29 Dec. 1960). Sov. dancer, choreographer, and b. master. Studied at

Leningrad B. School, graduating in 1936; joined the Maly B. where he soon became a ch. asst. of Lavrovsky. Chief ch. of the co. 1945–53, after which he moved to the Kirov B. Ch. *Ashik-Kerib* (mus. Asafiev, 1940), *The False Bridegroom* (after Goldoni's *The Servant of Two Masters*, mus. Chulaki, 1946), *Youth* (mus. Chulaki, 1949), *Taras Bulba* (mus. Solovyov-Sedoy, 1955), and *Masquerade* (mus. Laputin, 1960).

Fermé (Fr., closed), Designates a closed position of the feet (as against ouvert).

Fernandez, Royes (*b* New Orleans, 15 Aug. 1929 *d* New York, 3 Mar. 1980). Amer. dancer and teacher. Studied with Lelia Haller, Danilova, and Celli; made his début with de Basil's Original B. Russe in 1946. D. with the Markova and Dolin cos., B. Alicia Alonso, Borovansky B. 1951–4 and Amer. B. Th. 1957–73. Has also appeared with San Francisco B., London Festival B., and with Fonteyn on a world tour. Was asst. professor of d. at the Univ. of South Florida at Tampa.

Ferran, José (*b* Barcelona, 2 Jan. 1924). Span. dancer, choreographer, and b. master. Studied with Juan Magrina, Preobrajenska, Kiss, and Caton. Made his début at the Barcelona Teatro du Liceo in 1942. Joined Original B. Russe in 1948, Grand B. du Marquis de Cuevas in 1949. D. in Rio de Janeiro in 1952, with Petit 1952–60; returned to the Cuevas co. in 1960. Since 1962 he has been Hightower's chief asst. at her Cannes school.

Ferraris, Amalia (*b* Voghera, 1830, *d* Florence, 8 Feb. 1904). Ital. dancer. Studied with Blasis, making her début in Turin in 1844; went to London in 1849, to the Paris Opéra in 1856 (in *Les Elfes*), and to Russ. in 1858. Was much admired as a prodigious technician. Created roles in Mazilier's *Marco Spada* (1857), L. Petipa's *Sacountala* (1861), and *Graziosa* (1861), Borri's *L'Etoile de Messine* (1861), and Monplaisir's *La Camargo* (1868) and *Brahma* (1868). One of the 6 dancers of Blasis's 'Pleiade', she retired in 1868.

Ferri, Olga (*b* Buenos Aires, 1928). Argent. dancer, teacher, and b. director. Studied at Teatro Colón B. School, d. with its co. as a child and joined it upon graduation, eventually becoming its prima ballerina and in 1973 a member of its b. directorate. Has also d. with several Eur. cos. (Miskovitch, Munich State Op., London Festival B., Berliner B., Royal Swed. B.). Appeared in the title-role of J. Carter's film *The Life and Loves of Fanny Elssler* (1961). With her husband, the d. Enrique Lommi, opened a school in Buenos Aires in 1971.

Festin de l'Araignée, Le (Eng. title: *The Spider's Banquet*). Ballet-pantomime; libr. Gilbert de Voisins; ch. Staats; mus. Roussel; déc. Maxime Dethomas. Prod. 3 Apr. 1913, Th. des Arts, Paris, with Sarah Djeli. A spider catches ants, a pair of praying mantises, and a mayfly in her net, until one of the praying mantises succeeds in freeing itself and kills the spider. Later versions by Aveline (Opéra, Paris, 1940) and Howard (Sadler's Wells B., 1944).

Festival Ballet. See *London Festival Ballet.*

Fête étrange, La. Ballet in 2 scenes; libr. Ronald Crichton; ch. Howard; mus. Fauré; déc. Fedorovitch. Prod. 23 May 1940, London B., Arts Th., London, with Lloyd, Staff, Paltenghi. Inspired by Alain-Fournier's novel *Le grand Meaulnes* (1913), and d. to a selection of piano pieces and 2 songs. 'Wandering in the forest at the break of a winter's day, a country boy meets some children, who lead him to a château where the approaching marriage of the young Châtelaine is being celebrated. The boy becomes infatuated with his hostess and thus innocently causes an estrangement between her and her fiancé. Joy and happiness are changed to sorrow. After trying in vain to console the young girl, the boy returns to the forest' (from programme note). Revival for Royal B. in 1957 and for Scottish Th. B. in 1971. BIBL.: C. W. Beaumont, 'F.E.' in *Supplement to Complete Book of Ballets* (London, 1952).

Fêtes Chinoises, Les. This b. was Noverre's first big success. According to Chujoy it was first performed at the Foire St. Laurent, Paris, in 1749. (Lynham says 1751 or earlier, probably in Marseilles or Strasburg). Given in Lyons in 1751–2, at the Paris Opéra Comique in 1754, and at the Drury Lane Th. in London in 1755. Also performed under the title *Les Métamorphoses Chinoises.* BIBL.: L. Kirstein, 'L.F.C.' in *Movement and Metaphor* (New York, 1970).

Feuer, Donya (*b* Philadelphia, 1934). Amer. dancer, teacher, choreographer, and director. Studied with Nadia Chilkovsky, then at Juilliard School and with Graham, whose co. she joined; toured the Far East with the co. in 1955. Formed her own New York-based co., Studio for D., with P. Sanasardo in 1956. To Stockholm in 1963 as a teacher at Lia Schubert's B. Academy. Joined Stockholm Dramatic Th. as a ch. for plays in 1963, collaborating on many I. Bergman prods. (including his *Magic Flute* film in 1975). Has also ch. for Cullberg B. and Oslo's Norske B., as well as producing some 10 TV films, including her 2 Nijinsky films *A Life* and *Requiem for a Dancer*. BIBL.: M. Kats, 'Stirring Up a Commotion', *Dance Magazine* (1969/5).

Feuillet, Raoul-Auger (*b c.* 1675, *d* 1710). Fr. dancer and choreographer. He became a member of the Académie Royale de Danse and claimed to have invented a system of d. notation, which he published as *Chorégraphie ou L'Art d'écrire La Dance par Caractères, Figures et signes demonstratifs* in 1700—but it seems that it was Beauchamp who really 'invented' it. In his *Recueil de Danses,* (1704) some of the dances for the Opéra were notated. Translated into Eng. by P. Siris as *The Art of Dancing* (1706).

Fewster, Barbara. Brit. dancer and teacher. Studied at Wessex School in Bournemouth and at Sadler's Wells School, joining the Sadler's Wells B. and becoming a founder member of the Sadler's Wells Th. B. in 1946. Appointed asst. b. mistress in 1947, b. mistress 1951–4. Toured as b. mistress of the Old Vic's *A Midsummer Night's Dream* prod. 1954–5. Joined Royal B. School as a teacher in 1955, appointed deputy principal in 1967, principal in 1968, and assoc. dir. in 1983.

Field, John (orig. J. Greenfield; *b* Doncaster, 22 Oct. 1921). Brit. dancer and b. director. Studied with Shelagh Elliott-Clarke and Edna Slocombe; made his début at the Liverpool B. Club in 1938, joining Sadler's Wells B. in 1939 and becoming one of its principal dancers. Appointed dir. of the Sadler's Wells Th. B. in 1956. In 1970 he became co-dir. (with MacMillan) of the Royal B., but resigned in 1971. B. Dir. at La Scala di Milano 1971–4. Became Artistic Dir. of the Royal Academy of Dancing in 1975. Appointed Artistic Dir. London Festival B. in 1979. C.B.E. (1967). Married to the d. Anne Heaton.

Field Figures. Ballet in 1 act; ch. Tetley; mus. Stockhausen; déc. Baylis. Prod. 9 Nov. 1970, Royal B., Th. Royal, Nottingham, with Bergsma, Kelly, Derman, O'Conaire, Clarke, Johnson, O'Brien. Set to Stockhausen's *Setz die Segel zur Sonne* and *Verbindung* (from *Aus den sieben Tagen*), this is a free-form pas de deux, continually interrupted by the 5 accompanying dancers. Later Nureyev took over the Kelly part and an excerpt from the ballet with him became part of the film *I Am a Dancer* (1972).

Fifield, Elaine (*b* Sydney, 28 Oct. 1930). Austral. dancer. Studied with Elizabeth Scully and at Sadler's Wells School, joining Sadler's Wells Th. B. in 1947 and becoming principal d. In 1954 she moved to the Sadler's Wells B., promoted ballerina in 1956. Left the co. to d. with Borovansky B. She retired in 1958, but returned to the Austral. B. in 1964, dancing with it on its European tour in 1965. Left again in 1966 and returned in 1969. Created roles in Cranko's *Pineapple Poll* (1951), Ashton's *Madame Chrysanthème* (1955) and *Birthday Offering* (1956). Author of *In My Shoes* (London, 1967). Now retired. She was married to the conductor John Lanchbery.

Filatoff, Vera (*b* Paris, 20 Feb. 1945). Fr. dancer. Studied at Paris Conservatory and with Kniaseff, made her début with Petit's Bs. de Paris, d. with London Festival B., B. Th. Contemporain, and (since 1971) with Blaska's co. Created roles in D. Sander's *Hopop* (1969), Butler's *Itinéraires* (1970) and *Hymnen* (1970).
BIBL.: I. Lidova, 'V.F.', *Les Saisons de la danse* (1970/3).

Filipov, Alexander (*b* Moscow, 19 Mar. 1947).

Sov. dancer. Studied at Leningrad Ch. School 1957–65, d. with Moiseyev's Young Classical B. 1970–2, then as a guest artist with various cos.; principal d. with San Francisco B. since 1974.
BIBL.: N. McLain Stoop, 'From Russia With Love—A.F.', *Dance Magazine*, (1970/12).

Filipova, Natalia Victorovna (*b* Moscow, 11 Jan. 1935). Russ. dancer. Studied at Moscow Bolshoi School, graduating in 1953; she has since become a member of the Bolshoi B., dancing the ballerina roles of the standard repertory.

Fille de marbre, La. Ballet in 2 acts and 3 scenes; libr. and ch. Saint-Léon; mus. Pugni; sets C. A. Cambon and J. Thierry; cost. P. Lormier. Prod. 20 Oct. 1847, Opéra, Paris, with Cerrito, Saint-Léon, Desplaches. The marble girl of the title is a statue, with whom the sculptor falls in love. He asks the devil to grant her life, which he agrees to do, asking only that she may never fall in love herself. When she does so, she becomes marble once again. The b. has a remarkable likeness to Perrot's *Alma*, which had been one of Cerrito's greatest successes in London in 1842.
BIBL.: C. W. Beaumont, 'L.F.d.M.' *Complete Book of Ballets* (London, 1952).

Fille du Danube, La. Ballet in 2 acts and 4 scenes; libr. and ch. F. Taglioni; mus. Adam; sets Ciceri, Despléchin, Diéterle, Feuchère, Séchan; cost. H. d'Orschwiller. Prod. 21 Sep. 1836, Opéra, Paris, with M. Taglioni, Legallois, Leroux, Mazilier. An orphan girl, found as a child on the embankment of the river, and the son of the Baron fall in love with each other. When the Baron himself wants to marry her, she flings herself from the castle's balcony into the river. Her true-love follows her. They die; but after severe ordeals the two lovers are allowed to return to earth.
BIBL.: C. W. Beaumont, 'F.d.D.' in *Complete Book of Ballets* (London, 1952).

Fille du Pharaon, La (orig. Russ. title: *Doch faraona*). Ballet in 3 acts and 9 scenes, with prologue and epilogue; libr. Vernoy de Saint-Georges and M. Petipa (also ch.); mus. Pugni; sets A. Roller and Wagner; cost. Kelwer and Stolyakov. Prod. 30 Jan. 1862, Bolshoi Th., St. Petersburg, with Rosati, Nicholas Glotz, Petipa, Ivanov. The b. was inspired by Gautier's *Le Roman de la Momie*, telling of the adventures of an Eng. lord and his servant who get involved in opium dreams in a pyramid. The b. lasted over 4 hours and had a cast of almost 400; it was so successful that Petipa was appointed asst. b. master after its première. This was Rosati's last appearance in Russ.
BIBL.: C. W. Beaumont, 'L.F.d.P.' in *Complete Book of Ballets* (London, 1952).

Fille mal gardée, La (Eng. title: *Vain Precautions*—also *The Unchaperoned Daughter*). Ballet in 2 acts and 3 scenes; libr. and ch. Dauberval; mus. a potpourri of popular Fr. songs and airs. Prod.

1 July 1789, Grand Th., Bordeaux, with Mlle Théodore (Dauberval's wife) as Lise—then under the title *Le Ballet de la Paille, ou Il n'est qu'un pas du mal au bien*. The b. tells of the rural romance between Lise and Colas; how her mother, the Widow Simone, wants to marry her to the wealthy simpleton Alain; and how Lise and Colas compel Widow Simone to agree to their marriage by hiding in the bedroom, where they are promptly discovered. The b. was given its present title when Dauberval prod. it at the London Pantheon Th. in 1791. It quickly made the circuit of the Eur. stages, but not until 1803 was it seen in Paris at the Opéra. In 1828 Dauberval's pupil Aumer revived it for the Opéra, for which Hérold created a new musical arrangement, partly consisting of the earlier Bordeaux melodies, partly taken from Rossini's ops., and partly comp. by himself. This prod. became one of Elssler's biggest Paris successes in 1837, and it was kept in the repertory until 1854. It was first produced in St. Petersburg in 1818 and again in 1828 by Didelot, who had himself been coached by Dauberval as Colas. Here and in Moscow the b. had a new wave of popularity when Elssler d. it in 1848 and 1850. In 1864 P. Taglioni prod. a new version for Berlin—with new mus. by Peter Ludwig Hertel. When Petipa and Ivanov staged their new St. Petersburg prod. in 1885 they based it on the Hertel score; Zucchi was cheered as one of the greatest Lises of all time. Since the turn of the century the individual versions have been combined. Russ. saw several new prods., including those by Gorsky (Moscow, 1901 and 1918), Messerer and Moiseyev (Moscow, 1930), Lavrovsky (Leningrad, 1937), and Vinogradov (the Hérold version, Maly Th., Leningrad, 1971). In Western Europe several small cos., including those of Pavlova and Kyasht, kept the b. in their repertory. In Amer. the most important prod. was Nijinska's for B. Th. in 1940 (incorporating elements of Mordkin's prod. for The Mordkin B., forerunner of B. Th.). In 1946 the former Bolshoi ballerina Alexandra Balashova revived it for the Nouveau B. de Monte Carlo, and this was later taken into the repertory of the Grand B. du Marquis de Cuevas. But the most important new prod. was undoubtedly Ashton's on 28 Jan. 1960 for the Royal B., Covent Gdn., London, with Nerina, Blair, Grant, Holden—this had a new arrangement of the Hérold mus. by Lanchbery with much additional material and was designed by O. Lancaster. Ashton or his representatives revived it for many cos., incl. Royal Dan. B. (1964), Austral. B. (1967), Budapest State Op. B. (1971), Munich State Op. B. (1971), Royal Swed. B. (1972), and Ankara State Op. B. (1973). BBC TV. prod. (1962). A more recent prod. was ch. by H. Spoerli for Paris Opéra (mus. adapt. by J.-M. Damase, 1981).

BIBL.: ed. I. Guest, *L.F.m.g.* (London, 1960); L. Kirstein, '*L.F.m.g.*' in *Movement & Metaphor* (New York, 1970); D. Vaughan, *Frederick Ashton and his Bs.* (London, 1977).

Filleule de fées, La. Ballet in 3 acts, prologue and 7 scenes; libr. V. de Saint Georges; ch. Perrot; mus. Adam and H. F. de Saint-Julien; sets Cambon, Thierry, Despléchin; cost. P. Lormier and H. d'Orschwiller. Prod. 8 Oct. 1849, Opéra, Paris, with Grisi, L. Petipa, Perrot. The b. is about Ysaure who is at the mercy of friendly and wicked fairies; her lover Hugues has to undergo a severe test before their marriage can be celebrated in the palace of the fairies. The b. was admired, both for Grisi's light-footed perf., and for the spectacular machinery effects, designed by Victor Sacré.

BIBL.: C. W. Beaumont, '*L.F.d.f.*', in *Complete Book of Ballets* (London, 1952).

Filling Station. Ballet-document in 1 act; libr. Kirstein; ch. L. Christensen; mus. V. Thomson; déc. Paul Cadmus. Prod. 6 Jan. 1938, B. Caravan, Avery Memorial Th., Hartford, Conn., with Christensen, Marie-Jeanne, E. Hawkins, Kidd, Bolender. This was one of the very first all-Amer. bs.; the filling station attendant, Mac, was the hero. The characters are drawn as cartoon figures, with truck drivers, a motorist in knickerbockers, an intoxicated young couple, and the inevitable gangster; he shoots the girl, but she mysteriously revives when her body is carried off in procession. Revived for New York City B. in 1953. NBC TV prod. 1954.

BIBL.: G. Balanchine, '*F.S.*' in *Balanchine's New Complete Stories of the Great Ballets* (Garden City, N.Y., 1968).

Film. Though very early films exist of dancers such as Pavlova, Spessivtzeva, and Geltzer, d. only came into its own on the screen in the 1930s, through the film musicals of Busby Berkeley, Fred Astaire (with Ginger Rogers) and, somewhat later, Gene Kelly. One of the first attempts at a feature b. film was *La Mort du cygne* (1938), ch. by Lifar, featuring Slavenska, Chauviré, and the very young Charrat. Cartoon ch. was exploited to the full in Disney's *Fantasia* in 1940. *Capriccio Espagnol* and *Gaîté Parisienne* were filmed in Hollywood in 1941. The most popular b. film of all time was *The Red Shoes* of 1948, ch. by Helpmann and Massine and starring Shearer. Other feature films with strong b. leanings were Georgi's *Ballerina* (introducing Verdy, 1950), Kelly's *An American in Paris* (with Caron, 1951) and Petit's *Hans Christian Andersen* (with Jeanmaire and Bruhn, 1951)—also the strongly b. orientated op. film of *Tales of Hoffmann*, ch. Massine and Ashton (1951). Kelly then produced *Invitation to the Dance*, a triptych of b. episodes, featuring Sombert, Toumanova, Diana Adams, Bessy, Youskevitch, Rall, and himself, in 1952, but this was not released until 1956. From Russia came *Trio Ballet* (1953) with excerpts from *Swan Lake* (Ulanova, Dudinskaya, Sergeyev), *Fountain of Bakhchisaray* (Ulanova, Plisetskaya, Gusev), and

Flames of Paris (Chaboukiani), and Lavrovsky's *Romeo and Juliet* (1954) with Ulanova and Zhdanov. 1954 was also the year of Massine's strongly d.-orientated *Carosello napoletano* and of Tomsky's Czech-produced *The Red Poppy* (with Kura, Mansingerová, and J. Zajko). Ulanova and Fadeyechev appeared with the Bolshoi B. in the Brit. film of *Giselle* in 1956. A Bolshoi *Swan Lake* with Plisetskaya and Fadeyechev was produced in 1957, then came the Bolshoi *Cinderella* with Struchkova and Lediakh of 1961. *The Royal Ballet*, presenting Fonteyn in excerpts from *Swan Lake* (2nd act), *Firebird*, and *Ondine*, was released 1959. Chaboukiani's *Othello* followed in 1960 from Tiflis, and Petit's *Black Tights* (with condensed versions of his *Carmen*, *Cyrano de Bergerac*, *La Croqueuse de diamants*, and *Deuil en 24 heures*). The new Russ. version of *The Little Humpbacked Horse* in 1961, featuring Vasilyev and Plisetskaya, was followed by the Kirov's *Sleeping Beauty* in 1964, starring Sizova, Dudinskaya, and Soloviev. *An Evening with the Royal Ballet* had its première in 1965, with Ashton's *La Valse*, *Les Sylphides*, the *Corsaire* pas de deux, and *Aurora's Wedding*, relying mainly on the box-office appeal of Fonteyn and Nureyev. A full-length feature *Plisetskaya Dances* was released in 1966, and this was followed in 1967 by *Secret of Success* (Bolshoi B.) showing the school, with excerpts from *The Stone Flower*, *Paganini*, and *Bolero*—also the MacMillan *Romeo and Juliet* with Fonteyn and Nureyev and Balanchine's *A Midsummer Night's Dream*. Feature films of 1966 with much d. in them were Disney's *Ballerina* (with Mette Hønningen) and Karel Reisz's *Isadora* (with Vanessa Redgrave). Two more *Swan Lake* films were Nureyev's Vienna State Op. prod., filmed in 1966 with Fonteyn and himself, and Sergeyev's Kirov version of 1968 with Yevteyeva and Markovsky. Another *Giselle* was released in 1969, featuring Fracci and Bruhn in the Amer. B. Th. prod. The Chinese filmed their rousing *Red Detachment of Women* in 1970 (an earlier film version received a prize at the Moscow Film Festival in 1961) and followed it with *The White Haired Girl* in 1972. A rather different kind of b. film was Ashton's *Tales of Beatrix Potter* in 1971. Nureyev's *I Am a Dancer*, made in 1972, showed him in excerpts from *La Sylphide* (with Fracci), *Marguerite and Armand* (with Fonteyn), *Field Figures* (with Bergsma), and *Sleeping Beauty* (with Seymour)—and in 1973 there followed his *Don Quixote* prod. for the Australian B., with Helpmann, Aldous, and himself. More recent d.-orientated films were *The Turning Point* (1977), *The Children of Theater Street* (Sov.-Amer., 1978), *Nijinsky* (1980), and *Fame* (1980).
BIBL.: entry 'Danza—La Danza nel cinema' in *Enciclopedia dello spettacolo*; catalogue *Ten Years of Films on Ballet and Classical Dance 1955–65*, published by UNESCO in 1968; film issue of *Dance Magazine* (1969/4). A monthly film column

by J. Mueller in *Dance Magazine* since Sep. 1974; film issue of *Ballet News* (1981/8).

Fils prodigue, Le. See *Prodigal Son, The*.

Fin du jour, La. Ballet in 1 act; ch. MacMillan; mus. Ravel; déc. Ian Spurling. Prod. 15 Mar. 1979, Royal B., Cov. Gdn., London, with Park, Penney, Hosking, Eagling. 'A cheerful and elegant pleasantry set to Ravel's Piano Concerto in G . . . MacMillan has translated its spry, rhythmical mood into a set of dances derived from fashionplates of the period, the thirties' (A. Bland).
BIBL.: MacMillan comment, *Dance and Dancers* (1979/4).

Fini, Leonor (*b* Buenos Aires, 3 Aug. 1908). Argent.-Ital. painter and th. designer. Designed the déc. for Milloss' *La Dame aux camélias* (Rome, 1945), Balanchine's *Le Palais de cristal* (Paris, 1947), Ashton's *Le Rêve de Léonor* (also libr.; London, 1949), and Charrat's *Orfeo* (Venice, 1952).

Finland, National Ballet of. The co. of the Finn. State Op. in Helsinki, with a b. school attached. When the house opened in 1879 a group of dancers was established to serve in op. and operetta—with very occasional b. perfs., for which the soloists were mostly imported from St. Petersburg. The first real b. co. was formed under *George Gé, from St. Petersburg, who was b. master 1921–35. In 1922 he prod. the first Finn. *Swan Lake*. He was succeeded by the Russ. Alexander Saxelin. The first Finn. ch. was Irja Koskinen, who prod. Sibelius' *Scaramouche* in 1955. After 1945 the co. was reorganized with a more international outlook. The great classics were staged, and guest choreographers included Bartholin, Skeaping, Zakharov, Cullberg, Lifar, Lander, Beriozoff, Parlić, and A. Carter—some of them staying for a longer term. Close contact is still maintained with Leningrad, and Leningrad dancers frequently work in Helsinki. Since the late 1950s the co. has occasionally toured abroad, making its début at the Edinburgh Festival in 1959, and in London in 1979. Dancers who have gained international acknowledgement include Margareta von Bahr, Doris Laine, Klaus Salin, Matti Tikkanen, and Leo Ahonen. During recent years there has been a rapid turnover of b. directors, with D. Laine appointed 1984.

Finney, Truman (*b* Quincy, 13 Oct. 1944). Amer. dancer. Studied at Stone-Camryn School in Chicago and School of Amer. B.; made his début in 1963 with New York City B. D. with the Stuttgart B. and in Cologne and Frankfurt, and with the Hamburg State Op. B. 1973–6. Created roles in Neumeier's *Romeo and Juliet* (1971), *Daphnis and Chloe* (1972), *Le Sacre* (1972), and *Schumann* (1974). Now a b. master of the Hamburg co.

Fiocre, Eugénie (*b* Paris, 2 July 1845, *d* 1908). Fr. dancer. Was première danseuse of the Paris

Opéra 1864–75, a much admired beauty, especially in her many travesty roles. Created Frantz in *Coppélia* (1870).

Firebird (orig. Russ. title: *Zhar-ptitsa*—also Fr. *L'Oiseau de feu*). Ballet in 1 act and 2 scenes; libr. and ch. Fokine; mus. Stravinsky; déc. Golovine (with the cost. for the Firebird and the Tsarevna designed by Bakst); cond. Gabriel Pierné. Prod. 25 June 1910, co. of Diaghilev, Opéra, Paris, with Karsavina, Fokine, Fokina, Bulgakov. Based on motives from various Russ. fairy tales, the b. tells of Prince Ivan who captures the mysterious Firebird. To gain her release the Firebird gives Ivan a feather, with which he can call her in moments of danger. This happens when Ivan falls in love with the beautiful Tsarevna, who is imprisoned by the monster Kastchei. With the assistance of the Firebird Ivan kills Kastchei, after which the marriage between Ivan and the Tsarevna is celebrated with a grand procession. One of the most successful bs. of the 20th century, it has frequently been revived, e.g. by Diaghilev (with new costumes by Goncharova) in 1926 and for the Sadler's Wells B. in 1954. This version is part of *The Royal Ballet* (film, 1959—also BBC TV prod., 1965). Individual versions by Bolm (for B. Th., déc. Chagall, 1945), Balanchine (New York City B., using the Chagall déc., 1949, and a later version with Robbins), Lifar (Opéra, Paris, 1954), Cranko (Stuttgart, 1964), Skibine (Harkness B., 1965) Brian Macdonald (Harkness B., New York, 1967), Béjart (a suite only, Paris and Brussels, 1970, second Ger. Channel TV prod. 1973), and Holm (Copenhagen, 1972, Dan. TV prod. 1974).
BIBL.: C. W. Beaumont, *'L'O.d.f.'* in *Complete Book of Ballets* (London, 1952); A Chujoy (ed.), F., *Memoirs of a Ballet Master* (Boston, 1961); O. Maynard *'T.F.'*, *Dance Magazine* (1970/8).

First Chamber Dance Company of New York, The. The co. grew from 4 dancers, Charles Bennett, Nadine Revene, Lois Bewley, and William Carter, who banded together in 1961 to form the First Chamber D. Quartet. This developed into a chamber-size b., and toured widely. In 1969, with additional dancers, they became the Chamber D. Co., of New York. After taking up temporary residence in Seattle they returned to New York. There are now 9 dancers, and their repertory consists mainly of bs. by Bennett, Bewley, and M. Uthoff.
BIBL.: J. Gale, 'With, a Little Bit of Luck . . .' *Dance Magazine* (1970/3).

Fish Dive. The position in which the partner holds the ballerina almost vertically upside down, diving towards the floor. A very effective final position for a pas de deux (e.g. in *Sleeping Beauty*, act iii).

Fitzjames, Louise and Nathalie. Fr. dancer sisters. (1) Louise F., *b* Paris, 1809. D. at the Opéra 1832–46, where her biggest success was the Abbess in *Robert the Devil*, whom she d. in some 230 perfs. Another role which she took over from Taglioni was in *Le Dieu et la Bayadère*. In 1842 she participated in the first prod. of Albert's *La Jolie fille de Gand*. (2) Nathalie F., *b* 1819. D. at the Opéra 1837–42. Created the peasant pas de deux in *Giselle* with Mabillé in 1841. Later toured Ital. and Amer. A very versatile artist, she appeared as a singer in an act from *Lucia di Lammermoor*, as a mime in 2 scenes from *La Muette de Portici*, and as a d. in the *Giselle* pas de deux, all in the same perf. at Versailles in 1842.
BIBL.: I. Guest, in *The Romantic Ballet in Paris* (London, 1966).

Five Positions. The basic positions of the feet in b., dating back to the times of Beauchamp. Most of the steps in classical b. start and end with one of these. In the first position the feet ideally form a straight line, with the heels touching each other. In the second position the feet are again in a straight line, but approximately a small step apart. In the third position the feet (parallel) are placed one in front of the other, so that the heel of the front foot fits into the hollow of the instep of the back foot. In the fourth position one foot is placed in front of the other, separated by a distance of one step. In the fifth position the feet (parallel) are placed one immediately in front of but touching the other, so that the big toe of the back foot just protrudes beyond the heel of the front foot. Lifar tried to introduce a sixth and seventh position, but these were not generally accepted.

5 Tangos. Ballet in 5 parts; ch. Van Manen; mus. Astor Piazzolla; déc. Vroom. Prod. 3 Nov. 1977, Dutch National B., Stadsschouwburg, Amsterdam, with S. Marchiolli, C. Farha. Ch. to Piazzolla's 5 Tangos for Bandoneon for 7 couples, its 5 parts are entitled 'Todo Buenos Aires', 'Mort', 'Vayamos al Diablo', 'Resurreccion del Angel', and 'Buenos Aires, Hora O'. Revived West Berlin Ger. Op. B. (1979), Stuttgart B. (1981) *et al.*

Flamenco. The word designates a gipsy from Seville, and also their dances. Such f. dances are Alegrias, Soleares, Bulerias, Farruca, Zapateado, Tango, and Zambra. They also show Moorish and Arabian influences. Initially they were d. only to the accompaniment of songs and clapping hands. Later guitars were added. There is always a fixed basic rhythm, to which variants, new steps, and counter-rhythms are invented. Its vigour comes from the contrast between the fixed rules and the individuality of the interpretation. A f. d. must possess 'duende', the demon who inspires him, to really grip the audience. From the cafés chantants the f. found its way into the ths.

Flames of Paris, The (orig. Russ. title: *Plamya Parizha*). Ballet in 4 acts and 5 scenes; libr. N. Volkov and V. Dmitriev (also déc); ch. Vainonen; mus. Asafiev. Prod. 7 Nov. 1932, GATOB, Leningrad, with Chaboukiani, Balabina, Ulanova, Anisimova. The b. is set in the post revolutionary

Fr. of 1792, showing the march of the rebellious people of Marseilles, led to Paris by Philippe, and the storming of the Tuileries. The pas de deux from the last act is often performed separately on gala occasions. An abbreviated form of the b. was part of the Sov. film *Trio Ballet* (1953).

BIBL.: C. W. Beaumont, 'F.o.P' in *Complete Book of Ballets* (London, 1952).

Fledermaus. See *Chauve-Souris, La.*

Fletcher, John (*b* Masjed-de-Sullimain, Persia, 21 Dec. 1950). Brit. dancer. Studied at Arts Educational School, joined London Festival B. in 1967, Northern D. Th. in 1969, and Scottish Th. B. in 1973. Also d. as a guest with the New London B., in 1971. Created roles in S. Hywel's *The Clear Light*, Thorpe's *Tancredi and Clorinda, Quartet*, and *The Wanderer and His Shadow*, Chesworth's *Games for Five Players*, L. Meyer's *Schubert Variations* and *Cinderella*, S. Mottram's *Tchaikovsky Suite*, Darrell's *Othello*, and Gore's *Embers of Glencoe*. Gave up dancing in 1974. A. Genée Gold Medal (1968).

Flexmore, Richard (*b* Kensington, 1824, d. Lambeth, 1860). Brit. dancer and mime. The son of a d. from Sadler's Wells, he excelled in dancing in serious bs. and then in comic versions of them. He appeared with his wife Francisca Auriol.

Flic-Flac (Fr., crack of a whip). Designates a lashing movement, related to the fouetté.

Flick und Flock's Abenteuer (Eng. title *Flik and Flok*). Comedy ballet in 3 acts and 6 scenes; libr. and ch. P. Taglioni; mus. Hertel. Prod. 20 Sep. 1858, Court Op., Berlin. An adventure story of 2 friends who undergo the most improbable magical experiences. Up to 1885 the b. was performed no fewer than 419 times in Berlin. Revived for Milan (1862) and Vienna (1865).

BIBL.: C. W. Beaumont, 'F.a.F.' in *Complete Book of Ballets* (London, 1952).

Flier, Jaap (*b* Scheveningen, 27 Feb. 1934). Dutch dancer, choreographer, and b. director: Studied with Gaskell; made his début with B. Recital in 1950. D. with Netherlands B.; one of the founder members of the Netherlands D. Th. in 1959 (with his d. wife Willy de la Bye), becoming one of the principal dancers of the co. and artistic adviser, then artistic dir. 1970–3. Has then worked as artistic dir. of the Australian D. Th. 1973–5. Created many roles, including the leading roles in Tetley's *The Anatomy Lesson* (1964) and *Arena* (1969). Started to choreograph in 1955; his bs. include *Nouvelles Aventures* (mus. Ligeti, 1968), *Hi-Kyò* (mus. Kazuo Fukushima, 1971), and *Four Stages* (mus. Vivaldi, 1974). Now again working in Eur. Knight of Order of Orange, Nassau (1968).

BIBL.: Interview in *Dance and Dancers* (1971/1).

Flindt, Flemming (*b* Copenhagen, 30 June 1936). Dan. dancer. choreographer, and b. director Studied at Royal Dan. B. School, joining the co. in 1955; promoted solo d. in 1957. On leave of absence for several years, he d. with London Festival B., at the Paris Opéra (where he became étoile in 1960), with R. Page, and with the Royal B. From 1962 he occasionally d. again in Copenhagen, returning when he was appointed dir. of the Royal Dan. B. in 1966. As a d. he was much admired both in the traditional classics and in the Bournonville bs. and more modern works by Lander, Cullberg, and Petit. Started to choreograph for TV in 1963—a b. adaptation of Ionesco's *La Leçon*, (mus. Delerue), which he then staged at the Paris Op. Comique, reviving it for many cos. afterwards. His other bs. (some of them also orig. done for TV) incl. *The Three Musketeers* (mus. Delerue, 1966), *The Miraculous Mandarin* (mus. Bartók, 1967), *The Young Man Must Marry* (mus. Per Nørgåd, 1968), *Swan Lake* (1969), *Nutcracker* (1971), *Triumph of Death* (mus. Thomas Koppel, 1971), *Felix Luna* (mus. Ole Buck, 1973), and *Dreamland* (mus. Koppel, 1974). After resigning in 1978 had his own co., for which he choreographed *Salome* (mus. P. M. Davies, 1978). Appointed artistic dir. of Dallas B. 1981. Knight of Dannebrog (1974). Carina Ari Medal (1975). Married to the d. Vivi Gelker.

BIBL.: E. Aschengreen, 'F.F.' (with complete checklist of roles and activities), *Les Saisons de la danse* (1970/12).

Flindt, Vivi (née Gelker; *b* Copenhagen, 22 Feb. 1943). Dan. dancer. Studied at Royal Dan. B. School, joining the co. after her graduation; promoted soloist in 1967. Created roles in her husband Flemming F.'s *The Miraculous Mandarin* (1967), *Tango Chicane* (1967), *Sacre du printemps* (1968), *Triumph of Death* (1971), *Trio* (1973), *Felix Luna* (1973), and *Salome* (1978).

Floor-Work. Designates the modern d. exercises done on the floor.

Flore et Zéphire. Ballet-Divertissement in 1 act; libr. and ch. Didelot; mus. Cesare Bossi; déc. Liparotti. Prod. 7 July 1796, King's Th., London, with Mmes Hilligsberg and Rose Didelot. A pastoral comedy, the b. tells of Zéphire, who loves Chloris but is punished for his fickleness until he vows eternal fidelity. The b. enjoyed immense popularity, not least because of its use of a flying machine. It quickly spread all over Europe. In 1830 M. Taglioni made her London début in it. A different b. of the same title by Massine, mus. V. Dukelsky, for Diaghilev's Bs. Russes in 1925.

BIBL.: C. W. Beaumont, 'F.e.Z.' in *Complete Book of Ballets* (London, 1952); L. Kirstein, 'F.e.Z.' in *Movement & Metaphor* (New York, 1970).

Florestan and his Sisters. A pas de trois introduced by Diaghilev into his *Aurora's Wedding* prod. of 1923. It is d. to the mus. which was originally destined for the pas de quatre of the Diamond, Gold, Silver, and Sapphire Fairies.

Flower Festival in Genzano (Orig. Dan. title:

Blomsterfesten i Genzano). Ballet in 1 act; ch. A. Bournonville; mus. E. Helsted and H. S. Paulli. Prod. 19 Dec. 1858, Royal Dan. B., Copenhagen. The b. is based on a real event from the early 19th century; it deals with the love and trials of a young couple, Rosa and the sniper Paolo. A pas de deux, (extracted from an ensemble d. only rarely given today) survives and is one of the most popular items of the whole Bournonville repertory, often with additional dances from Bournonville's *Napoli*.

Fodor, Antal (*b* Báránd, 1 Jan. 1941). Hung. dancer and choreographer. Studied at Budapest State B. Inst. 1954–59. Member of Sopianae B. 1959–68, where he ch. his first bs. Joined Budapest State Op. B. 1968 appointed b. master 1971. Has ch. many bs., incl. *Ballo concertant* (mus. Vivaldi, 1966), *E Major Violinconcerto* (mus. Bach, 1974), *Metamorphosis* (mus. Monteverdi, 1975), *Don Juan* (mus. Strauss), *Bolero* (mus. Ravel, both 1977), and *VIII. Ecloga* (mus. Iñ Székely, 1978).

Fokina, Vera Petrovna (*née* Antonova; *b* 3 Aug. 1886, *d* New York, 29 July 1958). Russ. dancer. Studied at the St. Petersburg Imperial B. Academy, joining the Maryinsky Th. after her graduation in 1904. In 1905 she married Mikhail Fokine, becoming one of his best interpreters during his stay with the Diaghilev co. and after they emigrated to the U.S. Created roles in *Carnaval* (1910) and *Firebird* (1910).

Fokine, Mikhail Mikhailovich (in the West he called himself Michel F.; *b* St. Petersburg, 5 May 1880, *d* New York, 22 Aug. 1942). Russ. dancer and choreographer. Studied at Imperial B. Academy, graduating in 1898 and becoming a member of Maryinsky Th.; promoted first soloist in 1904. Started to teach in 1902. Ch. his first b. *Acis and Galatea* for a pupils' perf. in 1905, and *The Dying Swan* for Pavlova in 1907. In 1904 he submitted a b. scenario *Daphnis and Chloe* to the th. authorities in which he formulated for the first time his ideas about the necessary reforms for a greater dramatic, stylistic, and directional unity of b. and a better integration of libr., mus., d. and déc. Ch. his first big b. for the Maryinsky Th., *Le Pavillon d'Armide* (mus. N. Tcherepnin), in 1907 and (for an external perf.) his first version of *Chopiniana* (later *Les Sylphides*). Though he was an excellent, very expressive, and technically strong d. his most important contribution to b. history was as a ch. and he was one of the greatest b. reformers; in his constant search for truth and integrity he may be compared to men of the calibre of Noverre and Viganò. When Diaghilev assembled a troupe of Russ. dancers for a Paris season in 1909, he engaged F. as his chief ch. and he was thus enabled to put his ideas into practice in such prods. as *Le Pavillon d'Armide*, the *Polovtsian Dances*, *Les Sylphides*, and *Cléopâtre*—which not only became great successes for him, but indicated for b. the direction towards a new seriousness. He followed

this with *Le Carnaval* (mus. Schumann, 1910), *Sheherazade* (mus. Rimsky-Korsakov, 1910), *Firebird* (mus. Stravinsky, 1910), *Le Spectre de la rose* (mus. Weber, 1911), *Narcisse* (mus. Tcherepnin, 1911), *Petrushka* (mus. Stravinsky, 1911), *Le Dieu bleu* (mus. Hahn, 1912), *Thamar* (mus. Balakirev, 1912), *Daphnis and Chloe* (mus. Ravel, 1912), *Papillons* (mus. Schumann, 1914), *The Legend of Joseph* (mus. R. Strauss, 1914), and *The Golden Cockerel* (mus. Rimsky-Korsakov, 1914). Apart from these bs., which he created for the Diaghilev co., he continued to work for the Imperial Ths.; but he never returned to Russ. after 1918. After his break with Diaghilev (due to Diaghilev's decision to build up Nijinsky as a ch.), he pursued a career as a freelance ch. (apart from a short stay as chief ch. for R. Blum's B. Russe de Monte Carlo in 1936). In the early years after the first world war he worked mainly in Scandinavia, before settling in New York in 1923. From there he undertook frequent journeys to revive his masterworks from the Diaghilev era, and also created numerous new bs., few of which, however, could compare with his earlier work. His oeuvre comprises more than 60 titles—some of his later bs. were *The Sorcerer's Apprentice* (mus. Dukas, Petrograd, 1916), *Jota Aragonesa* (mus. Glinka, Petrograd, 1916), *Les Elfes* (mus. Mendelssohn, New York, 1924), *L'Épreuve d'amour* (mus. wrongly attributed to Mozart, Monte Carlo, 1936), *Don Juan* (mus. Gluck, London, 1936), *Les Eléments* (mus. Bach, London, 1937), *Paganini* (mus. Rachmaninov, London, 1939), *Bluebeard* (mus. Offenbach-Dorati, Mexico City, 1941), and *Russian Soldier* (mus. Prokofiev, Boston, 1942). In a letter, published on 6 July 1914 in *The Times*, he stated his 5 basic artistic principles: first, to create for every new b. a new form of movement, according to the subject matter, the time, and the character of the mus., rather than to cling to already fixed steps and phrases of movement; second, d. and mime have no meaning in b. unless they become an expression of a dramatic situation; third, conventional gestures are allowed only if necessitated by the style of the b.; in all other cases the hand gestures are to be replaced by movements of the whole body, the d. must be expressive from head to foot; fourth, the group is more than just an ornament—the new b. starts with the expressiveness of the face and hands until the whole body has become a means of expression, proceeding from there to the expressiveness of groups of bodies and the expressiveness of the collective d. of a group; fifth, the relationship of d. to the other arts—the new b. refuses categorically to become a slave of mus. or déc., and strives for perfect equality with the other contributing arts. He was married to the d. Vera Antonova, and their son Vitale F. was a b. teacher in New York, while Vitale's daughter Isabelle (*b* 1958) dances with the Pittsburgh B.

BIBL.: *F.—Memoirs of a Ballet Master* (Boston, 1961); C. W. Beaumont, *M.F. and his Ballets*

(London, 1935); complete documentation in *Les Saisons de la danse* (1973/2).

Folia (Port., madness). A wild Port. d. in triple time from the end of the 15th century. It is accompanied by castanets, etc., and executed in masks. A Madrid document from 1611 says that all the participants seemed 'to have lost their mind'.

Folk Dance. Designates a type of d. which has grown by itself, without any intervention by a ch. or organizer, and in functional connection with the traditional life of the people. The term was coined in the 18th century to mark the difference between the dances of the people and those of the higher social classes. This distinction dates back to the 15th and 16th centuries, when the ballroom d. started to develop from the f.d. It has constantly influenced the ballroom as well as the th. d. One of the earliest forms was the round d. The f.d. was passed from one generation to the next without any fixed form, simply as an idea and a set of rules, undergoing many changes. The orig. f.ds. have remained purer in South-East and East Europe than in central and Western Europe. It was there that the f.d. renaissance started in 1945, generating many specialized ensembles which since have toured the world.
BIBL.: J. Lawson, *European Folk Dancing* (London, 1953).

Folk Dance and Song Society, English. Founded by Cecil Sharp in 1911 in London, its aim is to preserve and propagate Eng. folk dances and folk mus. In the d. section it is mainly concerned with Country Dancing, Morris Dancing, and Sword Dancing. It has a large membership, and has branches all over Eng.

Folk Tale, A (orig. Dan. title: *Et Folkesagn*). Ballet in 3 acts and 14 scenes; libr. and ch. Aug. Bournonville; mus. Gade and J. P. E. Hartmann; sets Christensen and Lund; cost. E. Lehmann. Prod. 20 Mar. 1854, Royal Dan. B., Copenhagen, with J. Price. A Dan. fairy-tale, set in Jutland in the early 16th century, centred on the girl Hilda, who lives in the mountain with the witch Muri and her trolls. It is still in the repertory of the co.
BIBL.: C. Beaumont, 'A.F.T.' in *Ballets Past & Present* (London, 1955).

Folkwang Ballett Essen. In 1927 the Ger. city of Essen in the Ruhr district founded a school of applied arts. From this the Folkwang-Tanztheater-Studio emerged in 1928, headed by Leeder, Siimola, Cohen, Kahl, and Jooss. It was closed again in 1929 and became part of the Essen op. house, later calling itself Folkwang Tanzbühne. Between 1929 and its emigration in 1933 the co. presented a great number of bs., all ch. by Jooss, culminating in *The Green Table* of 1932. The co. then continued its work, based upon Dartington Hall in Devon, now calling itself Bs. Jooss. After Jooss returned to Essen in 1949 there was an attempt to re-establish the Folkwang-Tanztheater, which undertook several tours until it was disbanded in 1953. It was revived for the 1963–4 season in the form of a masterclass of students from the school, as which it still exists—not so much as an independent co., but as an ensemble which is assembled *ad hoc* for individual perfs., consisting of advanced students ex-students, and teachers from the F. School.
BIBL.: A. V. Coton, *The New Ballet* (London, 1946).

Fominych. Lubov Nicolaevna (*b* Kurgan, 20 Aug. 1952). Sov. dancer. Studied at Perm Ch. School 1963–70. Joined Perm Th. for Op. and B. in 1970. where she dances the ballerina roles of the standard repertory.

Fonaroff, Nina (*b* New York, 1914). Amer. dancer, choreographer, and teacher. Studied with Graham and at School of Amer. B. D. with Graham co. 1937–46. Formed her own group in 1945. Taught at various universities and colleges, apptd. Dir. of Ch., London School of Contemporary D. from 1972.

Fondu (Fr. sunk). Designates a sinking step—the lowering of the body by bending the knee of the supporting leg (Saint-Léon: 'Fondu is on one leg what a plié is on two').

Fonteyn, Dame Margot (orig. Peggy Hookham; *b* Reigate, 18 May 1919). Brit. dancer. Studied in Shanghai with George Goncharov and in London with Astafieva and at Sadler's Wells School. Made her début in the *Nutcracker* prod. of Vic-Wells B. in 1934, creating her first major role in Ashton's *Le Baiser de la Fée* (1935). She d. all the ballerina roles of the standard classics and created many roles in Ashton's bs., becoming the representative ballerina of the Sadler's Wells and later Royal B. Since 1959 she has appeared with the Royal B. as guest-ballerina, also dancing regularly with cos. all over the world. President of the Royal Academy of Dancing since 1954. With her beautiful physique, exquisite line, innate musicality, and refined artistry she is one of the greatest ballerinas the 20th century has prod. Some of her important role creations were in Ashton's *Apparitions* (1936), *A Wedding Bouquet* (1937), *Dante Sonata* (1940), *Symphonic Variations* (1946), *Scènes de ballet* (1948), *Cinderella* (alternately with Shearer, 1948), *Daphnis and Chloé* (1951), *Sylvia* (1952), *Homage to the Queen* (1953), *Birthday Offering* (1956), *Ondine* (1958), and *Marguerite and Armand* (1963); Helpmann's *Hamlet* (1942); Petit's *Les Demoiselles de la nuit* (1948), *Paradis perdu* (1962), and *Pelléas et Mélisande* (1969); Nureyev's *Swan Lake* (Vienna, 1964); MacMillan's *Romeo and Juliet* (1965); Cranko's *Poème de l'extase* (Stuttgart, 1970); Graham's *Lucifer* (1975); and Darrell's *The Scarlet Pastorale* (1975). Some of her interpretations have been filmed in *The Royal B.* (*Ondine* and *Firebird*, 1959), *An Evening with the Royal B.* (*Les Sylphides*, *Le Corsaire*, and *Aurora's Wedding*, 1965), *Romeo and Juliet* (1966), and Nureyev's *I am a Dancer*

(*Marguerite and Armand*, 1972). BBC TV prods.:
Nutcracker (1958), *The Sleeping Beauty* (1958), and
Firebird (1965). Granada TV prod.: *Cinderella*
(1960). Hosted TV. series *The Magic of Dance*
(1979). Married to Dr Roberto Arias, former
Panamanian Ambassador in London. C.B.E.
(1950), D.B.E. (1956), several honorary doctorates,
D. Magazine Award (1962), Prima ballerina
assoluta (1979). Author of *M.F.: An Autobiography*
(London, 1975).
BIBL.: J. Monahan, *F.* (London, 1957); K. Money,
The Art of M.F. (London, 1965); Money, *F.—The
Making of a Legend* (London, 1973); C. Crisp,
'M.F.' (with complete list of roles and activities),
Les Saisons de la danse (1968/12); portfolio on F.,
Dance Magazine (1973/7).

Footballer, The (orig. Russ. title: *Futbolist*). Ballet
in 3 acts; libr. V. Kurdyumov; ch. Lashchilin and
Moiseyev; mus. V. Oransky; déc. L. F. Fedorov.
Prod. 30 Mar. 1930, Bolshoi Th., Moscow. The b.
shows the conflicts between a middle-class dandy
and lady and a working-class female scavenger
and footballer, when each falls in love with a
representative of the wrong class. A different
comic sketch *Football* (mus. A. Tsafsman) by
Moiseyev for his co. in 1948.

Forains, Les. Ballet in 1 act; libr. Kochno; ch.
Petit; mus. Sauguet; déc. Bérard. Prod. 2 Mar.
1945, Bs. des Champs-Elysées, Th. des Champs-
Elysées, Paris, with Charrat, Pagava, Petit. The b.
shows a troupe of strolling comedians giving a
perf. on a street square, after which they depart,
disappointed with their audience's meanness.
BIBL.: C. Beaumont, 'L.F.' in *Ballets of Today*
(London, 1954).

Foregger, Nikolai Mikhailovich (*b* 18 Apr.
1892, *d* Kuibyshev, 8 June 1939). Russ. drama
director and b. master. Taught Tafiatrenazh—his
own system of a new culture of body-move-
ments—at the Moscow Proletkult Studio
1920–1. Dir. of his Mastfor Stage 1921–5 (Mast
for master, For for Foregger), where he created a
great stir with his *Dance of Machines*. He rigorously
fought the conventional d., pleading for 'dances
of the pavement, of rushing motor-cars, the
accuracy of machine work, the speed of the
present-day crowd, the grandeur of skyscrapers
...'. Sov. th. historians criticize him for body
fetishism. Chief régisseur in Kharkov (1929–34),
Kiev (1934–6), and Kuibyshev (1938–9).
BIBL.: M. G. Swift, in *The Art of the Dance in the
USSR* (Notre Dame, Ind., 1968); M. Gordon, 'F.
and the Dance of Machines', *The Drama Review*
(1975/3).

Forgách, József (*b* Ozd, 11 Sep. 1941). Hung.
dancer. Studied at Budapest State B. Inst., graduating in 1959. Joined Budapest State Op. B. in
1959, later becoming soloist. Created roles in
Seregi's *The Woodcut Prince* (1970) and *Sylvia*
(1972). Silver Medal (Varna, 1964); Liszt Prize
(1970).

Forlana (also Forlane, Furlana, or Furlano). A
lively Ital. d. from the province of Friuli for 2
couples in 6/8 time. It was especially popular with
Venetian gondoliers in the 18th century.

Fornaroli, Cia (*b* Milan, 16 Oct. 1888, *d* New
York, 16 Aug. 1954). Ital. dancer and teacher.
Studied at La Scala B. School and with Cecchetti,
becoming première danseuse of the New York
Met. Op. House 1910–14. She then undertook
world-wide tours as a guest-ballerina; d. with the
Pavlova co. and as prima ballerina assoluta at La
Scala 1921–32, being considered the greatest Ital.
dancer of her generation. Among her many
admirers was G. d'Annunzio. In 1929 she
succeeded Cecchetti as dir. of the La Scala school.
She experimented as a ch. in 1933 with symphonic
forms (*La Primavera* and *Concerto dell'estate*). Due
to the Fascist attacks against her husband, Dr
Walter Toscanini, they left in 1933 for New York,
where she conducted her own school 1943–50.
In 1955 Dr Toscanini handed over a great part of
their collection of d. memorabilia to the D.
Collection of the New York Public Library.
BIBL.: entry 'F.,C.' in *Enciclopedia dello spettacolo*;
V. Celli, 'Serata d'onore—C.F.', *Dance Magazine*
(1955/1).

Forsythe, William (*b* New York, 30 Dec. 1949).
Amer. dancer and choreographer. Studied with J.
Watts, M. Black and F. Jhung. D. with Joffrey B.
1971–73. Joined Stuttgart B. 1971, choreographing his first b. *Urlicht* (mus. Mahler) 1976, since
when he has become a resident ch. of the co.;
further bs. of his incl. *Flore subsimplici* (mus.
Vivaldi, 1977), *Dream of Galilei* (mus. Penderecki,
1978), *Orpheus* (mus. Henze, 1979), *Time Cycle*
(mus. L. Foss, 1979), and *Whisper Moon* (mus. W.
Bolcom, 1981). Director of Frankfurt B. since
1984/5. Married to the former d. Eileen Brady.

... for these who die as cattle. Ballet in 1 act;
ch. Bruce; no mus.; déc. Baylis. Prod. 9 Mar.
1972, B. Rambert, Young Vic Th., London, with
Bruce, Craig, Scoglio, Avrahami. A modern d. of
death. BBC TV prod. 1972.

Forti, Simone (*b*. Florence, 1935). Ital.-Amer.
dancer and choreographer. Studied with A.
Halprin, Rob. Dunn, also with Graham and M.
Cunningham. Started to perform with her then
husband, painter and d. Robert Morris, in the
early 1960s at galleries, lofts, and other places,
with happenings, games, and plays, exploring all
sorts of natural movements, commonplace human as well as animal or plants, so as to make her
ds. 'another instrument in the ideology of organic
living' (S. Banes).
BIBL.: S. Banes, in *Terpsichore in Sneakers* (Boston,
1980).

Fortner, Wolfgang (*b* Leipzig, 12 Oct. 1907).
Ger. composer. Wrote the b. *The White Rose* (based
on O. Wilde's *The Birthday of the Infanta*; ch. Jens
Keith, Berlin Municipal Op., 1951) and (with W.

Steinbrenner) the Bizet collage for Cranko's *Carmen* (Stuttgart, 1971). Several Ger. cos. have performed bs. to his concert mus., e.g. Cranko's *Triplum* (Munich, 1969).

Fosse, Bob (*b* Chicago, 23 June 1927). Amer. choreographer and producer. Studied with Frederick Weaver. Formed a night club team with Charles Gross, calling themselves The Riff Brothers, 1940. Started to ch. for amateur prods. Appeared in several Broadway musical prods. during the late 1940s; later became one of the most sought-after choreographers and directors of musicals and films such as *The Pajama Game* (1953), *Damn Yankees* (1955), *My Sister Eileen* (1955), *How to Succeed in Business Without Really Trying* (1963), *Sweet Charity* (1966), *Cabaret* (film prod. 1971), *Chicago* (1975), and *Dancin'* (1978); ch. and dir. *All that Jazz* (1980).
BIBL.: 'The B.F. Scrapbook', *Dance Magazine* (1955/10); V. H. Swisher, 'B.F. Translates Sweet Charity from Stage to Screen', *Dance Magazine* (1969/2); R. Philp, 'B.F's Chicago', *Dance Magazine* (1955/11).

Fouetté (Fr., whipped). Designates a whipping movement of the working leg to the side and in to the knee while performing a slight circle. Legnani introduced a series of 32 fs. in the coda of the *Black Swan* pas de deux.

Fountain of Bakhchisaray, The (orig. Russ. title: *Bakhchisaraysky fontan*). Ballet in 4 acts; libr. N. Volkov; ch. Zakharov; mus. Asafiev; déc. Khodasevich. Prod. 28 Sep. 1934, GATOB, Leningrad, with Ulanova, Vetcheslova, Mikhail Dudko. Based on Pushkin's poem of the same title, the b. tells of Maria, a Pol. princess, who is abducted by Khan Girei. He tries in vain to win her love, but this inflames the jealousy of his former lover Zarema who finally stabs Maria. The b. is still in the repertory of many Sov. and East Bloc cos. West European first prod. by Orlikowsky in Basle in 1965. An earlier version of the same subject under the title *A Victim of Jealousy* by Foma (the father of Vaslav) Nijinsky in Kiev in 1892.
BIBL.: C. W. Beaumont, '*T.F.o.B.*' in *Complete Book of Ballets* (London, 1952).

Four Last Songs (orig. Dutch-Ger. title: *Vier letzte Lieder*). Ballet in 4 parts; ch. Van Dantzig; mus. R. Strauss; déc. Van Schayk. Prod. 16 May 1977, Dutch National B., Stadsschouwburg, Amsterdam, with Farha, Sand, Sinceretti, Marchiolli, Jurriëns, Radius, Ebbelaar. The b. is performed to the record, conducted by von Karajan and sung by Gundula Janowitz. It embellishes the autumnal moods of the Hesse and Eichendorff texts, with Death as the omnipresent figure, but soothing rather than frightening. Revived for Vienna State Op. B. (1979). TV prod. by Frankfurt 3rd Channel and NOS TV. Earlier b. version of the same set of Lieder by Macdonald (Stockholm,

1966) and Béjart (in *Serait-ce la mort?*, Marseilles 1970).

Four Schumann Pieces. Ballet in 4 movements ch. Van Manen; mus. Schumann; déc Vroom. Prod. 31 Jan. 1975, Royal B., Cov. Gdn., London, with Dowell, Penney, Collier, Eagling. A plotless b., set to Schumann's string quartet in A major, op. 41, no. 3, centred on Dowell. Revived for Dutch National B. and National B. of Canada in 1976.

Four Seasons, The. 1) Ballet in 4 parts; ch. MacMillan; mus. Verdi; déc. Peter Rice. Prod. 5 Mar. 1975, Royal B., Cov. Gdn., London, with Derman, Parkinson, MacLeary, Collier, Coleman, Ashmole, Eagling, Mason, Wall, Dowell, Penney, Sleep. Based on the b. mus. Verdi wrote for the first Paris prod. of *Les Vêpres siciliennes* (ch. L. Petipa, 1855) and other b. mus. from his *Jérusalem* and *Don Carlos*. A gay and frolicsome divertissement, with some distinctly Ital. accents. Revived prod. with new déc. by B. Kay for Paris Opéra, 1978.—2) Ballet in 4 parts; ch. Robbins; mus. Verdi; cost. Santo Loquasto. Prod. 18 Jan. 1979, New York City B., State Th., New York, with K. Nichols, D. Duell, St. Saland, B. Cook, J.-P. Frohlich, McBride, Baryshnikov. Set to the same mus. as the above mentioned b. from Verdi's op. plus excerpts from the b. mus. for *I Lombardi* and *Il Trovatore*, the b. develops as a suite of classical dances celebrating the changing seasons, with many little jokes. There have been various other b. prods. to the *Vêpres* mus. incl. those by J. Carter (Ambassador B., 1950) and Prokovsky (New London B., 1973). Other bs. dealing with the seasons incl. those by Hilverding (Vienna, *c.* 1750), Perrot (mus. Pugni, London, 1848), Petipa's *Les Saisons* (mus. Glazunov, St. Petersburg, 1900—many other versions), Hassreiter (mus. Schubert-Lehner, Vienna, 1911), Cunningham (mus. Cage, New York, 1947), and Walter (mus. Vivaldi, Düsseldorf, 1970—many other versions).

Four Temperaments, The. Ballet in 5 parts; ch. Balanchine; mus. Hindemith; déc. Kurt Seligmann, light. Rosenthal. Prod. 20 Nov. 1946, B. Society, Central High School of Needle Trades, New York, with Dollar, Moylan, Danieli, Bolender, LeClercq. 'A Dance Ballet without Plot', it deals in an almost abstract way with the melancholic, sanguine, phlegmatic, and choleric 'temperaments'. Revived for New York City B. without déc. in 1951. Now in the repertory of many cos. all over the world (Royal B. prod. 1973).
BIBL.: G. Balanchine, in *Balanchine's Complete Stories of the Great Ballets* (Garden City, N.Y., 1977).

Fourth Symphony, The. Ballet in 4 movements; ch. Neumeier; mus. Mahler; déc. Marco Arturo Marelli. Prod. 31 March 1977, Royal B., Cov. Gdn., London, with W. Sleep, Seymour, Wall,

Coleman. Beginning—Shadows—Evening—Epilogue: The Lost Paradise, these are the titles of the 4 individual movements, corresponding with the 4 movements of Mahler's symphony, in which Neumeier shows the growing up pains of a boy who finally decides to leave his parents and embark on a path of his own. Revived for Hamburg B., same year. A different version by Araiz under the title of *Eternity Is Now* for Royal Winnipeg B.

Foxtrot. 'An Amer. ballroom dance to music of a sort of march-like ragtime, slow or quick. From about 1913 it spread to all the world's ballrooms. The Charleston and Black Bottom are varieties of it' (*Concise Oxford Dictionary of Music*).

Foyer de la Danse. A backstage room of the Paris Opéra, with mirrors and barres. Under Dr Véron it became a notorious salon, where the members of the Jockey Club could meet the dancers. It is now used as a rehearsal stage and for occasional receptions. The barrier between it and the stage is lifted in some prods. (e.g. the défilé of Balanchine's *Triumph of Love*), revealing one large area visible to the audience.

Fracci, Carla (*b* Milan, 20 Aug. 1936). Ital. dancer. Studied at La Scala B. School, graduating in 1954, since when she has been a member of the La Scala co.; promoted solo d. in 1956 and prima ballerina in 1958. Has also d. with many other cos.; principal d. of Amer. B. Th. since 1967. Has had her greatest success in the ballerina roles of the romantic repertory and is often compared with Taglioni. Married to the theatre dir. Beppe Menegatti, who has prod. many bs. with and for her (collaborating with the ch. Loris Gai), incl. *The Seagull* (after Chekhov, 1968), *Macbeth* (1969), and *The Stone Flower* (1973). She dances the title role in the Amer B. Th. film prod. of *Giselle* (1969), and Karsavina in the *Nijinsky* film (1980). Her TV film *Serata con C.F.* won the Golden Rose of Montreux in 1973. Leopardo d'oro (1959); D. Magazine Award (1968).
BIBL.: I. Lidova, 'C.F.' (with complete list of roles and activities), *Les Saisons de la danse* (1972/6); V. Ottolenghi, Madonna of the Dance', *Ballet News* (1981/7).

F.R.A.D. Fellow of the Royal Academy of Dancing.

Fränzl, Willy (*b* Vienna, 5 June 1898). Austrian dancer, b. master, and teacher. He is descended from a famous Viennese family of dancers. Studied at Court Op. B. School, joining its co. in 1914; eventually promoted first solo-d. Teacher at its b. school 1931–62, b. master 1935–62. Thanks to him Hassreiter's *Puppenfee* has been conserved, and he is considered one of the greatest authorities on the waltz. With his wife, the former d. Lucia Bräuer, he conducts one of the most respected Viennese schools for b. and

ballroom d. His daughter Elisabeth F. is a member of the State Op. B.

Franca, Celia (*b* London, 25 June 1921). Brit. dancer, choreographer, and b. director. Studied at London Guildhall School of Mus., and Royal Academy of Dancing, with Tudor and Idzikovsky. Début with B. Rambert in 1937; d. with International B., Sadler's Wells B. 1941–6 (creating roles in Helpmann's *Hamlet*, 1942, and *Miracle in the Gorbals*, 1944), Metropolitan B. in 1948, returning to B. Rambert in 1950. Ch. *Khadra* (mus. Sibelius, 1946) and *Bailemos* (mus. Massenet, 1947) for Sadler's Wells Th. B. Went to Canada in 1951 to found the National Ballet of Canada and assoc. school. Was dir. of the co. until 1974. Co-author (with Ken Bell) of *The National Ballet of Canada* (Toronto, 1979).
BIBL.: O. Maynard, 'C.F.', *Dance Magazine* (1971/4).

Françaix, Jean (*b* Le Mans, 23 May 1912). Fr. composer. Wrote the mus. for Massine's *Scuola di ballo* (1933), and *Beach* (1933), S. Korty's *La Luthérie enchantée* (1936), Lifar's *Le Roi nu* (1936), and Petit's *Les Demoiselles de la nuit* (1948). Balanchine used his *Serenade for String Orchestra* for his b. *A la Françaix* (1951).

France. A typical renaissance product, b. grew here from the allegorical court entertainments and the efforts of the Académiciens to reestablish the basic relationship between poetry, mus., and d. as it was epitomized in the classical Greek th. Catherine de Medici actively furthered these ambitions when she came to Paris from Florence, and the *Ballet Comique de la Reine* in 1581 set an example from which the b. de cour. developed. The Académie Française formulated the literary rules for b. libretti in 1635, but only with the founding of the Académie Royale de Danse in 1661 and the opening of a dancing school attached to the Académie Royale de Musique in 1672 did systematic research for objective standards for the perfection of the art of d. begin. The same year, 1661, was the climax of the comédie b., with *Les Fâcheux* by Molière and Beauchamp. With the appointment of Lully as dir. of the Académie Royale de Musique in 1672 the status of d. improved considerably, and in his *Triomphe de l'amour* (1681) Mlle Lafontaine became the first professional female d. to appear at the Palais Royal. Not until 1758, however, was the first b. without words performed—Noverre's *Caprices de Galatée* in Lyons. With Dauberval's *La Fille mal gardée*, created in Bordeaux in 1789, the first demi-caractère b. was introduced. In 1831 the b. of nuns in Meyerbeer's *Robert the Devil* offered a glimpse of the direction b. would take during its somewhat belated romantic era, the highlights of which were to be Taglioni's *La Sylphide* of 1832 and Coralli-Perrot's *Giselle* of 1841. This was the golden age of ballerinas, when Taglioni, Elssler, Grisi, and Cerrito competed for the public's favour. The general decline of Fr. b. during the second half of the 19th century was temporarily relieved when Saint-Léon's *Coppélia* was premiered in 1870—the first character b. to appear. Not even the opening of the splendid Palais Garnier with Mérante's *Sylvia* in 1876 could conceal the fact that Fr. had lost its most important ch. to Russia: Petipa. Only in the 1910s and 1920s did Paris regain its reputation as the b. capital of the world—and this was due not to any indigenous Fr. contributions, but to the regular appearances of Diaghilev's Bs. Russes. After these ended in 1929, b. at the Paris Opéra regained some life of its own during the long-term directorship of Lifar, but its influence hardly spread beyond the capital. After 1945 the situation changed completely, and Fr. b. became a fashionable export article through small, chic, and versatile cos. such as those of Petit, Charrat, Babilée, and, a little later, Miskovitch and Béjart. At the Opéra Lifar repeatedly resigned and came back, and there was a rapid turnover of directors. Fr. once again lost its most prolific ch. when Béjart went to Brussels to build up his B. of the 20th century. Though Fr. has experienced an ever-increasing influx of d. cos. from all over the world since the 1960s its own creative contribution to d. history has remained slight, although its schools continue to produce an astonishing amount of highly accomplished dancers. In the later 1960s there were more ambitious b. activities outside Paris—Lazzini's work in Marseilles (which became Petit's domain in 1973), the founding of the B. Th. Contemporain in Amiens in 1968, Biagi's installation as b. dir. in Lyons, Blaska's move to Grenoble, and the début of the Strasbourg-based B. du Rhin in 1972. Since the early 1970s the Fr. b. scene has been increasingly influenced by modern d. which received its final approbation when the Opéra invited Cunningham as a ch. in 1973 and Carlson was appointed étoile chorégraphe 1974–81. Fr. now has a multitude of d. cos. of all sizes and types and is constantly visited by the most important troupes from abroad (with Paris and Avignon heading the list of festival facilities), but the Fr. contribution to the d. history of the 1970s continues to be negligible.

BIBL.: for the period up to 1945 see entry 'Francia—III. Balletto' in *Enciclopedia dello spettacolo*; for the years 1945–63 see the appropriate volumes of the Eng. *Ballet Annual*; more recent events have been chronicled in the magazine *Les Saisons de la danse*, which started to appear in Feb. 1968.

Francés, Esteban (*b* 1915, *d*. Barcelona, 22 Sep. 1976). Span. painter and designer. Designed the déc. for Balanchine's *Tyl Ulenspiegel* (1951), *Figure in the Carpet* (1960), *Don Quixote* (1965), and *Glinkiana* (1967), L. Christensen's *Con Amore* (the New York City B. prod., 1953), Loring's *The

Capital of the World* (1954), Solov's *Vittorio* (1954), and Moncion's *Jeux d'enfants* (1955).

Francesca da Rimini. Ballet in 1 act and 2 scenes; libr. Henry Clifford and Lichine (also ch.); mus. Tchaikovsky; déc. Messel. Prod. 15 July 1937, B. Russe de Colonel de Basil, Cov. Gdn., London, with Tchernicheva, Petroff, Platoff, Danilova, Jasinski. Based on the story which Dante tells in his *Divina commedia* of Paolo and F. who love each other. F. is engaged to P.'s older and uglier brother Malatesta, who discovers them both reading a love-story, and kills Paolo; they die together. Other versions of the same story, using the same symphonic fantasy by Tchaikovsky, by Fokine (Petrograd, 1915), Tshitshinadze (Moscow, 1950), and Dollar (1961).

Franchetti, Jean-Pierre (*b* Paris, 27 Apr. 1944). Fr. dancer. The son of Raymond F.; he studied with Mme Cébron and then with his father. Joined the co. of the Opéra; promoted étoile in 1971. Particularly good in character roles. Created parts in Béjart's *Firebird* (1970), Blaska's *Poème électronique* (1973), and Butler's *Amériques* (1973). Married to the d. Emilia Gobin.

BIBL.: 'J.-C. Diénis, 'J.-P.F.', *Les Saisons de la danse* (1968/4).

Franchetti, Raymond (*b* Auberviliers, 1921). Fr. dancer, teacher, and b. master. Studied with Ricaux, Egorova, and Preobrajenska; made his début with B. Jeunesse in 1937. D. with B. de Monte Carlo in 1938 and 1943–5, with the Cuevas co. 1946–7, and from 1947 at the Paris Opéra, where he was especially admired in character roles. Teacher at the school of the Opéra since 1963, but also has his own Académie d'art chorégraphique. Has been guest teacher for Royal B. and Royal B. School. Deputy b. dir. of the Paris Opéra 1971–80. Father of Jean-Pierre F.

Franck, César (*b* Liège, 10 Dec. 1822, *d* Paris 8 Nov. 1890). Belg. composer. He wrote no b. mus., but his concert mus. has often been used for b. purposes, including I. Duncan's *Redemption* (Paris, 1915), Ashton's *Symphonic Variations* (Sadler's Wells B., 1946—also by Lichine in *Evolución del movimiento*, Buenos Aires, 1947), Babilée's *Psyché* (Bs. des Champs-Elysées, 1948), Lazzini's *Le Chasseur maudit* (Liège, 1955), and Russillo's *Samson François* (the piano quintet, Paris, 1971).

Françoise et Dominique. See *Dupuy, Dominique et Françoise*.

Frandsen, Edite (*née* E. Feifere; *b* Riga, 20 Jan. 1914). Latvian-Dan. dancer and teacher. Studied with Fedorova; joined the Riga b. co. in 1927; prima ballerina 1934–44. She then went to Denmark and opened a school of her own in 1951, with a spell as b. mistress in Malmö in 1952. Taught at the Royal Dan. B. school 1961–72; her pupils included Laerkesen, Isaksen, and D. Bjørn; professor at the Vienna State Academy

1972–5. Now b. mistress Düsseldorf Ger. Op. on the Rhine.

Frankel, Emily (*b* New York, *c*. 1930). Amer. dancer. Studied with Craske, Tudor, M. Stuart, Hitchins, Graham, Humphrey, Weidman, Holm. Founded her own Amer. D. Drama Co. in 1955, with which she toured until 1964, dancing in works she had commissioned from Bolender (incl. *Still Point*), Solov, Maslow, and Weidman. After an interruption, she returned in 1970, performing as a recital d. to concert mus., including *Four Seasons* (mus. Vivaldi, own ch.), *Elektra* (mus. Henze's Fifth Symphony, ch. Bolender), *Mahler Fifth Symphony* (ch. N. Walker), *Medea* (mus. Berg's 3 Pieces for Orchestra, ch. Walker). She was married to the d. Mark Ryder.
BIBL.: E. Jacob, 'E.F.: Coming Back for Good', *Dance Magazine* (1970/10).

Frankie and Johnny. Ballet in 1 act; libr. Michael Blandford and Jerome Moross (also mus.); ch. Page and Stone; déc. Paul Dupont. Prod. 19 June 1938, Page-Stone B., Great Northern Th., Chicago, with Page, Stone. The b. is based on the very popular Amer. ballad of F., who is a prostitute in the Chicago of the 1890s, and her faithless pimp J., whom she eventually shoots down. Revived for B. Russe de Monte Carlo in 1945, for Pittsburgh B. Th. in 1976, and for Dance Th. of Harlem (1981).
BIBL.: C. W. Beaumont, 'F.aJ.' in *Supplement to Complete Book of Ballets* (London, 1952).

Franklin, Frederic (*b* Liverpool, 13 June 1914). Brit.-Amer. dancer, choreographer, teacher, and b. director. Studied with Elliott-Clarke in Liverpool, then with Kyasht, N. Legat, and Egorova. Début at Casino de Paris 1931. D. in London music-halls, cabarets, etc., and with Markova-Dolin 1935–7. Joined B. Russe de Monte Carlo as premier danseur in 1938, becoming b. master in 1944. Later worked with various cos. including Sadler's Wells B., Slavenska-Franklin B., La Scala di Milano, and Amer. B. Th. Created roles in Massine's *Gaîté Parisienne* (1938), *Seventh Symphony* (1938), and *L'Etrange Farandole* (1939), Ashton's *The Devil's Holiday* (1939), and de Mille's *Rodeo* (1942). Dir. of the Washington D.C., National B. and its affiliated school 1962–4. Active in staging the classics and the Ballet Russe repertoire.
BIBL.: O. Maynard, 'F.F.: A Life in the Theatre', *Dance Magazine* (1974/6).

Franks, Arthur Henry (*b* Blackheath, 1907, *d* London, 25 Sep. 1963). Brit. writer on b. Joined the staff of *Dancing Times* in 1946; dir. and managing editor 1958–63. Wrote *Approach to the Ballet* (London, 1948), *Ballet for Film and Television* (London, 1950), *Twentieth Century Ballet* (London, 1954), *Svetlana Beriosova* (London, 1958), and *Social Dance* (London, 1963). Editor of *Girl's Book of Ballet* (London, 1953), *Ballet: A Decade of Endeavour* (London, 1955), *Pavlova* (London, 1956).

Frantz, Patrick (*b* Paris, 31 July 1943). Fr. dancer, choreographer, and teacher. Studied at Paris Opéra B. School and Paris Conservatoire. Joined Paris Opéra B. 1960, becoming soloist. Joined Pennsylvania B. 1971, later becoming principal d. Formed his own The New City B. Co. 1973. Then artistic dir. of Tucson Civic B., Ariz.; art. dir. Pittsburgh B. Th. 1978–82.

Freefall. Ballet in 1 act; ch. and déc. Tetley, mus. Max Schubel. Prod. 13 Apr. 1967, Repertory D. Th., Univ. of Utah. Set to Schubel's concerto for 5 instruments (*Insected Surfaces*), the b. explores the mind in limbo, its shifts of balance and attempts to readjust to the changing patterns of the environment. Revived for B. Rambert on 13 Nov. 1967, and, with new déc. by N. Baylis, in 1975.
BIBL.: P. Brinson and C. Crisp, 'F.' in *Ballet for All* (London, 1970).

Fridericia, Allan (*b* Copenhagen, 1921). Danish b. critic, th. designer, and director. Educated Copenhagen and Stockholm Univ. Designed the orig. prod. of Cullberg's *Miss Julie* (1950), and later *Swan Lake, Napoli*, and *Portrait of a Girl* for the prods. of E. M. von Rosen (his wife) at Gothenburg. B. critic of *Information* since 1951. Manager of Scandinavian B. 1960–5, of Aarhus Th. 1963–6. Author of *Harald Lander og hans balletter* (Copenhagen, 1951; in Dan.), *Elsa Marianne von Rosen* (1953; in Dan.), and *August Bournonville* (Copenhagen, 1979; in Dan.). Contributed 'Bournonville's Ballet "Napoli"' to *Theatre Research Studies* (Copenhagen, 1972).

Frolich, Jean-Pierre (*b.* New York, *c* 1954). Amer. dancer. Studied at School of Amer. B., appearing while a student in small roles in *Don Quixote* and *Nutcracker*. Regular member of New York City B. since 1972, appointed soloist in 1980. Excels in bs. by Robbins.
BIBL.: S. Reiter, 'J.-P. F.', in *Dance News* (1979/12).

Froman, Margarita Petrovna (*b* Moscow, 8 Nov, 1890, *d* Boston, 24 Mar. 1970). Russ.-Yugosl. dancer, choreographer, teacher, and b. mistress. Studied at Bolshoi B. School, graduating in 1915; joined the Diaghilev co.; returned to the Bolshoi as ballerina in 1917. In 1921 she moved to Yugosl., where she built up b. cos. and schools first in Zagreb and then in Belgrade; among her pupils were Mia Corak (Slavenska) and Roje. Ch. and prod. many bs., from the standard classics and the Diaghilev repertory to such national bs. as *The Gingerbread Heart* (mus. K. Baranovič, 1924) and *The Legend of Ochrid* (mus. S. Hristić, 1947). In the early 1950s she moved to Connecticut, where she continued to teach.

Frontier. Solo d.; ch. and cost. Graham; mus. Horst, scenery Noguchi. Prod. 28 Apr. 1935, Guild Th., New York, N.Y., with Graham. Originally the first of a two-part piece called *Perspectives No. 1 and 2*, its second part, 'Marching Song' (mus. Lehman Engel—this part incorporated the group), was soon dropped, leaving *F.* as a solo, dealing with 'the conquering of space, the mastering of the frontier', celebrating 'the vigor, the tenacity, and the character of the settlers of the West' (D. McDonagh).

Fuente, Luis (*b* Madrid, 2 Jan. 1946). Span. dancer. Studied Span. d. and then with Zaraspe. Joined the co. of Antonio when 15 years old, touring with him for 2½ years. Joined City Center Joffrey B. in 1965, creating roles in Arpino's *Viva Vivaldi!* (1965), *Olympics* (1966), and *Fanfarita* (1968). D. with Washington National B., Dutch National B., and 1973–4 with London Festival B. Has since d. with various cos. Contributor to *Dance Perspectives* 40 on 'The Male Image'. Married to the d. Zelma Bustillo.
BIBL.: S. Goodman, 'L.F.', *Dance Magazine* (1969/9).

Fuerstner, Fiona (*b* Rio de Janeiro, 24 Apr. 1936). Amer. dancer and b. mistress. Studied at San Francisco B. School. D. with San Francisco B. 1952–64; principal d. Les Grands Bs. Canadiens, 1963–4. Joined Pennsylvania B. in 1965, becoming b. mistress in 1968.

Fukagawa, Hideo (*b* Nagoya, 23 Aug. 1949). Jap. dancer. Studied with Minoru Ochi and with J. Schneider in East Berlin. Début with the Asami Maki B. in Tokyo; joined East Berlin Comic Op. in 1969, Stuttgart B. in 1971, Munich State Op. B. in 1973. Now has a school in Tokyo. Bronze Medal (Varna, 1965); Silver Medal (Moscow, 1969); Nijinsky Prize (1969); Silver Medal (Varna, 1970).

Fuller, Loie (*b* Fullersburg, Ill., 22 Jan. 1862, *d* Paris, 21 Jan. 1928). Amer. dancer. She never had a regular d. education, but started in show-business prods., appearing in 1890 in her *Serpentine Dance*, based mainly on the effect of flowing trains of silk. She then concentrated on the presentation of solo acts, which had little to do with d. but fascinated audiences all over the world and especially in Europe, where she made her début at the Paris Folies-Bergère in 1892. For the Paris World Fair in 1900 a special th. was erected for her, where she could experiment with new lighting effects, new transparent clothes, and new mechanical means (for instance with sticks to extend her arms). She had no technique at all, but improvised, relying on a nebulous 'indefinite force'. Her most successful numbers were *Serpentine Dance, Fire Dance, The Butterfly,* and *Dance of Joy.* She does not really belong among the pioneers of the modern d. movement, but her contemporaries, including such men as Anatole France and Rodin, were great admirers of her art. Author of *Quinze ans de ma vie* in 1908.
BIBL.: C. de Morinni, 'L.F.', *Dance Index* I, 3; S. Sommer, 'L.F.', *The Drama Review* (1975/3).

Fülöp, Viktor (*b* Budapest, 9 Feb. 1929). Hung. dancer and b. master. Studied with Nádasi and in Moscow with Messerer and Rudenko, also ch. with Yermolayev and Varlamov. Joined Budapest State Op. B. in 1947, creating roles in Seregi's *Spartacus* (1968) and *The Miraculous Mandarin* (1970). D. as a guest with London Festival B. in 1961 and 1963. Is now a b. master of the Budapest co. Liszt Prize (1960); Kossuth Prize (1962); Merited Artist (1968).

Fulton, Gaye (*b* Manchester, 15 Oct. 1939). Brit. dancer. Studied at Arts Educational School in London, joined London Festival B. in 1958, promoted soloist in 1960. Prima ballerina in Zurich 1964–78. Guest ballerina Washington National B. in 1970, London Festival B. 1970–1, rejoined London Festival B. in 1972. An excellent interpreter of the traditional ballerina roles, she created roles in Beriozoff's *Romeo and Juliet* (1966), *Cinderella* (1967), and *Nutcracker*, and in Stevenson's *Cinderella* (1969). Married to the conductor Karl Rickenbacher.

Fuoco, Sofia (orig. Maria Brambilla; *b* Milan, 16 Jan. 1830, *d* Carate Lario, 4 June 1916). Ital. dancer. Studied with Blasis, becoming one of his 'Pleiades'. Début at La Scala in 1839; promoted ballerina in 1843, becoming in the same year the first Giselle there. Created Perrot's Milan version of the *Pas de quatre* with Taglioni, Rosati, and Carolina Vente in 1846. D. at the Paris Opéra 1846–50, where she was known as 'La Pointue' because of her skill on points. Very successful guest appearances in Madrid, Barcelona, and London. Retired in the late 1850s.
BIBL.: I. Guest, in *The Romantic Ballet in Paris* (London, 1966).

Furiant. A tempestuous and vivacious Bohemian d. of decided strong but irregular rhythm (3 bars 2/4, 2 bars 3/4 time). Fine examples in Dvořák's *Slavonic Dances* and Smetana's *The Bartered Bride.*

Furlana. See *Forlana.*

Fuzelier, Louis (*b* 1677, *d* 1752). Fr. writer. A member of the Académie Royale, he wrote the libr. for the bs. *Les Amours des dieux* (1727), *Les Indes galantes* (1727), and *Les Amours désguisés.*

G

Gable, Christopher (*b* London, 1940). Brit. d. and actor. Studied Royal B. School; joined touring section of the Royal B. in 1957, becoming soloist in 1959, principal d. in 1961, then soloist of the Cov. Gdn. section 1963–7, after which he resigned. One of the most popular ds. of the co., he created roles in MacMillan's *The Invitation* (1960) and *Images of Love* (1964), and Ashton's *The Two Pigeons* (1961); MacMillan ch. the role of Romeo for him, but it was eventually premiered by Nureyev. He has since pursued a career as an actor, often appearing in films by Ken Russell (he performed the title-role in *The Boy Friend*, 1972). He opened Central School of B., London, 1982.

Gabovich, Mikhail Markovich (*b* Verchnie Gouliaki, Kiev Province, 7 Dec. 1905, *d* Moscow, 12 July 1965). Russ. d. and teacher. After studying privately, he joined the Bolshoi B. School, graduating in 1924. He then became a member of the Bolshoi B., and was soon one of its most admired premier danseurs—not only in the roles of the traditional repertory, but also in such modern bs. as *Fountain of Bakhchisaray, Prisoner of the Caucasus, Romeo and Juliet, The Bronze Horseman*, and *Cinderella*. From 1954–8 he was dir. of the Moscow Bolshoi B. School, where he taught until his death. Has written many articles on topical b. questions. He was the father of the d. Mikhail Mikhailovich G. Merited Artist of the U.S.S.R. (1937); People's Artist (1951); Stalin Prize (1946 and 1950).

Gabovich, Mikhail Mikhailovich (*b* Moscow, 27 May 1948). Sov. dancer. The son of Mikhail Markovich G., he studied at the Moscow Bolshoi School, graduating in 1967, since when he has been a member of the Bolshoi B., excelling in character roles. Married to the d. Tatyana Bessmertnova.

Gadd, Ulf (*b* Gothenburg, 8 Mar. 1943). Swed. dancer, choreographer, and b. master. Studied with Mila Gardemeister and Royal Swed. B. School, joined Royal Swed. B. in 1960, appointed soloist in 1965. D. with Harkness B. and at Gothenburg 1968–70, where he ch. Bartók's *The Miraculous Mandarin*, after which he founded the New Swed. B. with C. Borg, with which they toured widely. Since 1972 he has been b. master and principal d. in Gothenburg, but also choreographs for various other cos. his bs. include *Tratto* (mus. Zimmermann, 1972), *Gemini Suite* (mus. Jon Lord, 1972), *Choreographic Etudes* (mus. Ohana, Cullberg B., 1973), *Sleeping Beauty* (with B. Holmgren, Royal Swed. B., 1974), and *Kalevala*

(mus. Sibelius, Gothenburg, 1975). Artistic Dir. of Gothenburg B. since 1976.

Gades, Antonio (*b* Madrid, 1936). Span. dancer. Performed when only 13 years old at the Circo Price; d. for 9 years with P. Lopez. Worked during the early 1960s mainly in Italy; formed a co., of his own for the New York World's Fair of 1964, which was a sensational success. Has toured ever since. London début 1970. Has also appeared in various films; considered one of the most fascinating Span. dancers of the 1970s.

Gai, Loris (*b* Pistoia, 1928). Ital. dancer and choreographer. Studied at La Scala B. School; member of its b. co., until 1960. Became known as a ch. for the co., of Fracci and Menegatti; his bs. include *Pantea* (1964), *The Seagull* (mus. R. Vlad, 1968), *Baiser de la Fée* and *Pulcinella* (mus. Stravinsky, 1971), *The Stone Flower* and *Cinderella* (mus. Prokofiev, 1973), *Nobilissima Visione* (mus. Hindemith) and *Tragedy of Salome* (mus. R. Strauss, 1974).

Gain, Richard (*b* Belleville, 24 Jan. 1939). Amer. dancer. Studied with Lalla Baumann in St. Louis and with Graham; started to d. at St. Louis Municipal Op., then on Broadway and for TV, with the cos. of Butler, Robbins, and Graham, R. Joffrey B. in 1964, and Amer. B. Th. in 1967, since when he has pursued a career as a freelance d. occasionally appearing with his own group. Created roles in Graham's *Phaedra* (1962), *Secular Games* (1962), and *Circe* (1963), Arpino's *Sea Shadow* (1962), *Olympics* (1966), and *Incubus* (1966), Ch. *If I Never Saw Another Butterfly* (mus. Ger. folk songs, Contemporary Dancers, Winnipeg, 1972).
BIBL.: S. Goodman, 'R.G.', *Dance Magazine* (1966/6).

Gaîté Parisienne. Ballet in 1 act; libr. and déc. Comte Etienne de Beaumont; ch. Massine; mus. Offenbach arr. by Rosenthal. Prod. 5 Apr. 1938, B. Russe de Monte Carlo, M.C., with Tarakanova, Eugenia Delarova, Massine, Franklin, Youskevitch. The b. takes some of the characters from Offenbach's *La Vie Parisienne*—a rich Peruvian, a Glove-Seller, a Flower-Girl, and an Officer—and shows their amorous flirtations in a Paris nightclub. Tarakanova's original role of the Glove-Seller later became one of Danilova's greatest successes. Filmed for Warner Brothers in 1941 as *The Gay Parisian*. Revived for various cos. (Amer. B. Th., 1970; London Festival B., 1973).
BIBL.: C. W. Beaumont, 'G.P.' in *Supplement to Complete Book of Ballets* (London, 1952).

Gala Performance. Ballet in 1 act and 2 scenes; libr. and ch. Tudor; mus. Prokofiev; déc. Hugh Stevenson. Prod. 5 Dec. 1938, London B., Toynbee Hall, London, with Van Praagh, Lloyd, Larsen, Tudor, Laing. The preparations for a b. gala are shown to the first movement of Prokofiev's Piano Concerto no. 3; the gala itself then follows to his Classical Symphony. Three ballerinas, La Reine de la danse from Moscow, La Déesse de la danse from Milan, and La Fille de Terpsichore from Paris outdo each other in competing for the audience's acclaim. Revived for many cos. (B. Rambert, 1940; B.Th., 1941; Ger. Op. Berlin, 1963.) BBC TV prod. 1960.

BIBL.: C. W. Beaumont, 'G.P.' in *Supplement to Complete Book of Ballets* (London, 1952).

Galeotti, Vincenzo (orig. V. Tomazelli; *b* Florence, 5 Mar. 1733, *d* Copenhagen, 1816). Ital. dancer, choreographer teacher, and b. master. Studied in Italy, d. with many Eur. cos. before he concentrated on working in Venice 1765–9, where he ch. his first op. bs. and divertissements. D. at London King's Th. 1769–70. Returned to Venice as b. master of the San Moise Th. 1770–5, after which he spent the rest of his life in Copenhagen, where he laid the foundations of the Royal Dan. B. He was strongly influenced by the b. d'action of Noverre and Angiolini, and was the first to tackle romantic subjects in Scandinavian b. Angiolini's influence is still strong in his *Dido Abandoned* (1777), *Don Juan* (1781), and *Semiramis* (1787)—later bs. of his included *Telemachus on the Island of Calypso* (1792), *Annette and Lubin* (1797), *Lagertha* (1801), *Inez de Castro* (1804), *Romeo and Juliet* (1811), and *Macbeth* (1816–most of his bs. had mus. by Claus Schall). His most popular b. was *The Whims of Cupid and the Ballet Master* (mus. J. Lolle) of 1786, the ch. of which is the oldest to survive and is still in the repertory of the Royal Dan. B.

BIBL.: entry 'G., V.' in *Enciclopedia dello spettacolo*; S. Kragh-Jacobsen, in *The Royal Danish Ballet* (Copenhagen, 1955); M. H. Winter, in *The Pre-Romantic Ballet* (London, 1974).

Gallea, Christina (*b* Sydney, 11 Dec., 1940). Austral. dancer. Studied with Danetree, Idzikowsky, and Northcote. D. with Austral. Th. B. in 1955, Frankfurt B. in 1958, B. der Lage Landen in 1959, Amer. Festival B. in 1960, Amsterdam B. in 1961, Teatro del Balletto in 1962. With her husband A. Roy founded International B. Caravan in 1965 (known since 1976 as Alexander Roy London B. Th.), of which she is ballerina.

Gallet, Sébastien (*b* 1753, *d* Vienna, 10 June 1807). Fr. dancer and choreographer. A pupil of Noverre, he was a fierce adversary of Angiolini. Début at Paris Opéra in 1782. After his engagements in Venice, Turin, Milan, Naples, and London, he worked in Vienna 1803–5, where he ch. many bs.

Galli, Rosina (*b* 1896, *d* Milan, 1940). Ital. dancer

and b. mistress. Studied at La Scala B. School, d. with Chicago Op. B. in 1912; joined New York Met. Op. House in 1914; b. mistress 1919–35. In 1930 she married Giulio Gatti-Casazza, General Manager of the Met. Op. House.

Galliard (also Gaillard). A gay and sprightly court d. in triple time, originating in Lombardy, mostly d. after a pavane. It was full of complicated steps and surprising movements, and became increasingly lascivious during the 17th century. It was especially popular at the Elizabethan court, which developed its own variant, the Volta.

Galop. A lively North Ger. round d. in 2/4 time, which developed during the mid-1820s and spread from there to Fr. and Eng., where it was incorporated in the quadrille. Its characteristic is a change of step, or hop, at the end of every phrase of the mus. An especially electrifying example is the G. infernal from Offenbach's *Orphée aux enfers* (1858).

Galstyan, Vilen Shmavodovich (*b* Yerevan, 12 Feb. 1941). Sov. dancer. Studied at the local Ch. School, graduating in 1959, after which he joined the Yerevan and then the Tiflis b. co., becoming one of the principal dancers. Gold Medal (Varna, 1968).

Gamelan. Ballet in 1 act, ch. Joffrey; mus. Lou Harrison; déc. Willa Kim. Prod. 15 Oct. 1963, Joffrey B., Kirov Th., Leningrad, with Bradley, Ruiz, Arpino, Rhodes. 'Inspired by Japanese haiku, G. is a succession of eight ch. vignettes . . . the conflict of warriors; the idea of pursuit, pursued, and protector; the fragile movement of a butterfly' (programme note).

BIBL.: P. Brinson and C. Crisp, 'G.' in *Ballet for all* (London, 1970).

Games. Ballet in 1 act; ch. McKayle; mus. trad. songs; set Paul Bertelsen; cost. Charlip. Prod. 25 May 1951, Hunter College Playhouse, New York, with McKayle, Charlip. Children of a city's slum district play their games, always conscious of being watched by 'the cops'. Revived on many later occasions.

Gamson, Annabelle (*b* New York, *c*. 1930). Amer. dancer. Studied with J. Levien, M. O'Donnell, H. Platonova, at High School of Mus. and Art, and with K. Dunham, occasionally appearing with Dunham's co. First recital as a solo d. under the name of A. Gold at New York Henry Street Playhouse 1955. Then went for 2½ years to Eur. with her husband, opera conductor Arnold G. Back in New York, she took b. lessons and studied with Nikolais. Doing lecture demonstrations on I. Duncan, she became more and more interested in Duncan's work and had a surprise success when she presented some revived Duncan dances at Amer. Th. Lab 1974, since when she has concentrated on appearing as a solo performer mainly of Duncan dances, but also of some Wigman pieces plus dances of her own.

Contributed 'On Dancing Isadora's Dances', *Ballet Review* (vol. 6, no. 4).

BIBL.: J. Dunning: 'A.G.', *Dance Magazine* (1977/2).

Ganibalova, Vazira Mikhailovna (*b* Tash-kent, 7 Mar. 1948). Sov. dancer. Studied at the local Ch. Institute, graduating in 1966; continued to study with Dudinskaya. Joined Kirov B. in 1968, where she dances the ballerina roles of the traditional and modern repertory, creating roles in V. Katayev's and A. Lifshitz's *The Bagpiper from Strakonitz* (1969) and G. Alexidze's *Ala and Lolly* (1969).

Ganio, Denys (*b* Villeneuve-les-Avignon, 25 Apr. 1950). Fr. dancer. Studied at Paris Opéra B. School. Joined Opéra B. in 1965: later soloist with Bs. de Marseille, creating roles in Petit's *Les Intermittences du coeur* (1974), *Coppélia* (1975), *Transfigured Night* (1976), *Nutcracker* (1976), *La Chauve Souris* (1979), and *L'Arlésienne* (1981).

BIBL.: J.-C. Diénis, 'Plein Feu sur D.G.', *Les Saisons de la danse* (1976/1).

García, Marta (*b* Havana, *c.* 1945). Cub. dancer. Studied at the school of the Alonsos, with Eugenia Klemenskaia and at Escuela Provincial de B., joining National B. of Cuba in 1965, where she dances the ballerina roles. Created roles in A. Vaquez's *Dias que fueron noches (1967) and Parés's Bach × 11 = 4 × A* (1970). Silver Medal (Varna, 1970).

García Lorca, Federico (*b* Fuentevaqueros, 5 June 1898, *d* Viznar, 19 Aug. 1936). Span. poet and dramatist. His poems and plays have often inspired individual dances and bs., including Humphrey's *Lament for Ignacio Sánchez Mejías* (mus. N. Lloyd, 1947), Gaskell's *The Love of Don Perlimplin and Belisa* (mus. Villa-Lobos, 1952; also T. Gsovsky's *The Red Coat*, mus. Nono, 1954), Rodrigues' *Blood Wedding* (mus. ApIvor, 1953), Tomaszewski's *After Five Years Passed* (mus. Juliusz Luciuk, 1972), Pilato's *The Withered Twig* (after *Yerma*, mus. Kelemen, 1974, also Reiter Soffer's *Yerma*, mus. G. Crumb, 1976), and C. Bruce's *Ancient Voices of Children* (mus. G. Crumb, 1975—numerous other versions of the same mus.), and *Cruel Garden* (mus. C. Miranda, 1977). But his most frequently used play is undoubtedly *The House of Bernarda Alba* (1936); e.g. bs. by Ailey (*Feast of Ashes*, mus. Surinach, 1962), MacMillan (*Las Hermanas*, mus. Martin, 1963), Sertić (*Las Apasionadas*, also under the title *Abbandonate*, mus. Kelemen, 1964), and Pomare (*Las Desenamoradas*, mus. Coltrane, 1967). A *Spectacle F.G.L.* (with *Amours de Don Perlimplin, Noces de sang,* and *Ignazio Sánchez Mejías*) was ch. by J. Giuliano for the Th. des Hauts-de-Seine in 1972.

Gardel, Maximilien (*b* Mannheim, 18. Dec. 1741, *d* Paris, 11 Mar. 1787). Fr. dancer and choreographer. The son of a b. master at the court of King Stanislas of Poland (and brother of Pierre G.), he made his début at the Paris Opéra in 1755. He caused a major uproar when he became the first dancer to appear without a mask, in *Castor et Pollux* in 1772 (to avoid being mistaken for Vestris, who had originally been announced for his role). In 1773 he was appointed b. master (together with Dauberval). He is considered one of the pioneers of the b. pantomime. His most successful bs. included *Ninette à la cour* (1778), *Mirza et Lindor* (mus. Gossec, 1779), *Le Déserteur* (1784), *Le premier navigateur* (mus. Grétry, 1785), and *Le Coq du village* (mus. Favart, 1787).

Gardel, Pierre (*b* Nancy, 4 Feb. 1758, *d* Paris, 18 Oct. 1840). Fr. dancer, teacher, ch. and b. master. The brother of Maximilien G. and his pupil, he became soloist of the Paris Opéra in 1780 and succeeded him in 1787 as chief maître de b. and ch.—his bs. include *Télémaque* (mus. Miller, 1790), *Psyché* (1790), *Le Jugement de Pâris* (1793), *La Dansomanie* (mus. Méhul, 1800), *Achille à Scyros* (mus. Cherubini), and *Paul et Virginie* (mus. Kreutzer, 1806). He was also dir. of the affiliated b. school 1799–1815, and a much respected teacher; one of his pupils was Blasis. He was married to the d. Marie Miller.

BIBL.: H. M. Winter, 'P.G.' in *The Pre-Romantic Ballet* (London, 1974).

Gaskell, Sonia (*b* Vilkaviškis, Lithuania, 14 Apr. 1904, *d* Paris, 9 July 1974). Russ.-Dutch dancer, teacher, choreographer, and b. director. After teaching in Paris 1936–9, went to Amsterdam, where she taught and after the war founded the B. Recital group. In 1954 she became dir. of the Netherlands B., founded the Netherlands B. Academy in The Hague, and in 1959 was appointed dir. of the Amsterdam B., which developed into the Dutch National B. in 1961, of which she was artistic dir. until 1969. She ch. many bs., but her real importance was as a teacher and organizer. She is considered one of the most important pioneers of b. in Holland.

BIBL.: C. van de Weetering and L. Utrecht, *S.G.* (Zutphen, 1976); G. Loney, 'Evolution of an Ensemble', *Dance Magazine* (1974/3).

GATOB. Abbreviation for Gosudarstvenny Akademichesky Teatr Opery i Baleta (State Academic Th. for Op. and B.)—the name of the former St. Petersburg-Petrograd Maryinsky Th., from after the October Revolution of 1917. Since 1935 known as the Kirov Theatre.

Gautier, Théophile (*b* Tarbes, 30 Aug. 1811, *d* Neuilly, 23 Oct. 1872). Fr. poet and writer. One of the leading figures of the Fr. romantic movement; he exerted tremendous influence on the course of b. in the Paris of the late 1830s and the 1840s as the critic of *La Presse*. He was a supreme stylist and formalist, and coined the phrase *l'art pour l'art* (art for art's sake). He was a very great admirer of Carlotta Grisi, whose sister he married, and (together with Vernoy de Saint-Georges) wrote the libr. of *Giselle* for her. Thanks to his detailed and precise descriptions we have a very lively impression of what the dancers and bs. were like during the heyday of the Fr. romantic b. His b. writings were collected by C. W. Beaumont and published as *The Romantic Ballet As Seen by T.G.* (London, 1932; reprint Dance Books, 1973).

BIBL.: E. Binney, *Les Ballets de T.G.* (Paris, 1963); I. Guest, 'G.'s Centenary', *Dancing Times* (1972/10).

Gavotte. A gay d. in 4/4 time and steady rhythm, deriving from the Pays de Gap in Fr., whose inhabitants were called Gavots. Originally a folk d. it became a court d. under Marie Antoinette, developing more and more complicated steps, especially when Vestris and P. Gardel took possession of it, until only professional dancers were able to perform it correctly. It was often preceded by a minuet and followed by a musette.

Gawlik, Roland (*b* Grossenhain, 15 Sep. 1944). Ger. dancer. Studied at Dresden State Op. B. School and later also with Pushkin in Leningrad. Joined Dresden Stated Op. B. in 1962 and East Berlin Comic Op. B. in 1966, where he is now the leading male d. creating roles in many Schilling bs. Also dances Spartacus in the East Berlin State Op. prod. of the Seregi version. Bronze Medal (Varna, 1968).

Gayané (orig. Russ. title—also *Gayaneh*). Ballet in 4 acts and 6 scenes; libr. Konstantin Derzhavin; ch. Anisimova; mus. Khachaturian; sets Natan Altman; cost. T. Bruni. Prod. 9 Dec. 1942, Kirov B., Molotov-Perm. The b. is set in an Armenian cotton co-operative. Gayané, a cotton picker, is married to Giko, a drunkard who later reveals himself as an incendiary and is duly imprisoned; but she loves the cooperative chairman Kasakov, whom after Giko's imprisonment she is finally able to marry—the occasion for a lavish divertissement, with the Sabre D. as its most famous individual number. Under the title *Happiness* an earlier version had been ch. by Ilya Arbatov at Yerevan in 1939. In its revised and definitive form the b. received its Leningrad Kirov B. première on 20 Feb. 1945, ch. by Anisimova, with Dudinskaya, Balabina, Anisimova, Nikolai Zubkovsky, and K. Sergeyev. The West European first prod. was ch. by Keres at the Wiesbaden State Th. in 1972, but much of the mus. had already been used by Skibine in his *Prisoner of the Caucasus* in 1951.

Gé, George (orig. G. Grönfeldt; *b* St. Petersburg, 1893, *d* Helsinki, 19 Nov. 1962). Finn. dancer, choreographer, and b. master. Studied with Legat; first Finn. b. master of the Helsinki Suomalainen Op. 1921–35, mounting *Swan Lake* in 1922 as its first prod. He became the formative personality of the young Finn. b. In 1935 moved to Fr., working with Fokine and B. Russe de Monte Carlo, also in Paris at the Th. Mogador and the Folies-Bergère. B. master of Royal Swed. B. 1939–45, after which he returned to Helsinki in 1955

to become b. dir. of the Finn. National B. again. Attracted international attention with his reconstruction of Fokine's *L'Epreuve d'amour*.

Geitel, Klaus (*b* Berlin, 14 Aug. 1924). Ger. b. critic and writer. Studied at the univs. of Halle, Berlin, and Paris. Ballet critic of *Die Welt* since 1959. Author of *Ballettzentrum Paris* (Berlin, 1960), *Ballett vor der Premiere* (Berlin, 1961), *Stars auf Spitze* (Berlin, 1963), *Der Tänzer Nurejew* (Berlin, 1967), *Hans Werner Henze* (Berlin, 1968), and *Das Abenteuer Béjart* (Berlin, 1970). Contributor to *Internationales Ballett auf deutschen Bühnen* (Munich, 1968) and *Ein Ballett in Deutschland* (Düsseldorf, 1971).

Gelabert, Raoul (*b* Santiago de Cuba). Cub.-Amer. dancer and teacher. Studied with N. Verchinina, O. Preobrajenka, J. Barashkova, B. Romanoff and mime with Decroux. D. with B. Pro-Arte Mus. Havana Opera B., N. Verchinina D. Group, R. Segovia Spanish Dances, Metropolitan Op. B. and various other groups. Opened b. studio in New York in 1951 as first school to offer the 'anatomical approach' as therapy for dancers, from which he developed his programme of 'Kinesiology for Dancers', which he has taught since at various univs., d. schools, and summer seminars throughout the U.S. and Europe. Founder-dir. of D. Kinetic Education Inst. Inc., 1974. Author of a series of *Dance Magazine* articles later compiled into *R.G.'s Anatomy for the Dancer*, vol 1 and 2; series of articles related to dancers' injuries, *Dance Magazine* 1976–7: Education films on the G. method, 1968, See-do Productions. D. Magazine Award 1978.

BIBL.: W. Como, 'Therapy for Dancers', *Dance Magazine* (1962/11).

Gelker, Vivi. See *Flindt, Vivi*.

Geltzer, Yekaterina Vassilyevna (*b* Moscow, 14 Nov. 1876, *d* there, 12 Dec. 1962). Russ. dancer. Daughter of Vassily G., a very popular mime and b. master of the Bolshoi B. Studied at Bolshoi School, graduating in 1894, after which she joined Bolshoi B. Continued to study for 2 more years with Johansson in St. Petersburg, acquiring an unusually strong and harmonious technique for her time, which she combined with an exceptional dramatic and expressive talent. She became the Gorsky ballerina, a d. of rare personality. Though appearing in the traditional ballerina roles, her real gift showed in such demi-caractère parts as Kitri, Esmeralda, and Salammbô. In 1910 she d. with the Diaghilev co., in Paris, in 1911 at the Alhambra Th. in London, and later at the New York Met. Op. House. Was fêted by the Soviet cultural minister Anatoly Lunacharsky in an important address on the occasion of her 25th th. anniversary in 1921. Created Tao-Hoa, the chief character of what was to become the first Soviet b. classic, *The Red Poppy*, in 1927. Considered the first ballerina of the new Soviet State, she toured until well into the 1930s.

People's Artist of the U.S.S.R. (1925). She was married to her partner, Vladimir Tikhomirov.

BIBL.: N. Roslavleva, in *Era of the Russian Ballet* (London, 1966).

Gelvan, Vladimir (*b* Riga, 20 Oct. 1946). Sov. dancer. Studied at Riga B. School and Moscow B. School. D. with Riga B. 1964–74, Amer. B. Th 1975–6 and since 1976–7 as a principal d. with the West Berlin Ger. Op. B. Created prince in Panov's *Cinderella* (1977) and title-role in L. Houlton's *Tristan* (1979) and Panov's *The Idiot* (1979).

Gemini. Ballet in 3 movements; ch. Tetley; mus. Henze; déc. Baylis. Prod. 6 Apr. 1973, The Australian B., Elizabethan Th., Sydney, with Rowe, Carolyn Rappel, John Meehan, G. Norman, A plotless b. to Henze's third Symphony ('Anrufung Apolls'), it deals with the relationships of two couples of dancers. Revived for Stuttgart B. in 1974, Amer. B. Th. in 1975, Sadler's Wells Royal B. in 1977.

Genée, Dame Adeline (orig. Anina Jensen; *b* Hinnerup, 6 Jan. 1878, *d* Esher, 23 Apr. 1970). Dan.-Brit. dancer. Studied with her aunt and her uncle, Alexandre G., made her début when only 10 years old in Christiania (Oslo). Joined Central-hallen Th., Stettin, in 1893, Berlin Court Op. in 1895, and Munich Court Op. in 1896, where she d. for the first time what was to become her most famous role: Swanilda in *Coppélia*. From 1897–1907 she reigned as the most popular d. of the London Empire Th., also occasionally appearing as a guest with H. Beck in Copenhagen. In 1907 she embarked on the first of her many Amer. tours. In London she d. from 1911 at the Coliseum and Alhambra Th., touring Austral. and N.Z. in between. A d. of contagious vivacity, charm, and lightness, and an irresistible Swanilda, she gave her farewell perf. in 1917 but returned occasionally to d. in charity perfs. President of the London Association of Operatic Dancing (which became the Royal Academy of Dancing in 1935) 1920–54. She was also a founder-member of the Camargo Society. One of the most respected personalities of the young Brit. b. in 1931 she established the A.G. Gold Medal, the highest award given to a d. by the R.A.D. In 1967 the Genée Th. at East Grinstead was named after her. D.B.E. (1950); various Dan. decorations; Hon. D. Mus. (London).

BIBL.: I. Guest, *A.G.—A Lifetime of Ballet Under Six Reigns* (London, 1958).

Geneva. Apart from occasional d. divertissements by op. and operetta prods., the Swiss city has no b. tradition of its own. During the first World War occasional perfs. of the pupils of the G. based Jaques-Dalcroze, of I. Duncan (exiled in Lausanne) and her pupils, and the Sakharoffs stimulated some quickly fading interest. Regular b. perfs. started only with the opening of the rebuilt Grand Th., with its assoc. co. directed by J. Charrat

(1962–4), S. Golovine (1964–9), A. Catá (who based the repertory mainly on Balachine revivals, 1969–73), P. Neary (continuing the Balachine orientation, 1973–8), P. van Dyk 1978–80, and since O. Araiz.

BIBL.: R. de Candolle, *Histoire du Théâtre de Genève* (G., 1978).

Gennaro, Peter (*b* Metairie, La., 1924). Amer. dancer and choreographer. Studied for a short time with Dunham; made his début on the Amer. tour of the San Carlo Op. in 1948, D. mainly on Broadway, becoming Robbins' asst. for *West Side Story* in 1957, since when he has pursued a career as one of Amer.'s top choreographers for musicals and TV, where he has been in charge of the *Perry Como Show* and the *Ed Sullivan Show.*

BIBL.: H. Stern, 'The Master of Jazz Forms Turns to TV: P.G.', *Dance Magazine* (1970/6).

Gensler, Irina Georgievna (*b* Leningrad, 22 July 1930). Sov. dancer. Studied with Vaganova at the Ch. School, graduating in 1948, since when she has been a member of the Kirov B., creating the Gipsy in Grigorovich's *The Stone Flower* (1957) and many solo character-dances. Her best roles are Teresa (*Flames of Paris*), Aisha (*Gayané*), and Fanny (*Path of Thunder*). Married to the d. Oleg Sokolov. Merited Artist of the R.S.F.S.R. (1960).

Genzano, Flower Festival in. See *Flower Festival in Genzano.*

Geologists, The. See *Heroic Poem.*

Georgi, Yvonne (*b* Leipzig, 29 Oct. 1903, *d* Hanover, 25 Jan. 1975). Ger.-Dutch dancer, choreographer, b. director, and teacher. Studied in Leipzig, at the Hellerau Dalcroze Institute and from 1921 at the Dresden Wigman School, appearing with the Wigman group. Toured extensively as a recital d. after her Leipzig début in 1923. Joined Jooss in Münster in 1924. B. mistress in Gera in 1925 and in Hanover 1926–31, where she opened a school. From Hanover she embarked on many tours with Kreutzberg, her first soloist. Married to an Amsterdam journalist, she moved to that city 1931–2, but returned to Hanover 1932–6, collaborating with V. Gsovsky. From 1936 she appeared with her Dutch b. co., in Scheveningen, also taking it to the U.S.; she continued her b. work in Amsterdam and the Netherlands through the second World War. She ch. the film *Ballerina* in Paris in 1950, starring Verdy. She then returned to Ger. as b. mistress of the *Abraxas* co., in 1951, and of Düsseldorf Op. 1951–4, b. dir. Hanover 1954–70, and dir. of the d. department of the city's Academy of Mus. until 1973. One of the most prominent of Ger.'s modern dancers, she also became one of the most active ch. producing many of the standard works of the classical and modern repertory, and creating a great number of bs. to specially commissioned mus.: e.g. by

Badings, Blacher, Burt, Karetnikov. Under her direction b. in Hanover enjoyed an unprecendented flowering.
BIBL.: H. Koegler, *Y.G.* (Velber, 1963).

Georgiadis, Nicholas (*b* Athens, 1925). Greek th. designer. He became internationally known as the designer of MacMillan's *Danses concertantes* (1955), *House of Birds* (1955), *Noctambules* (1956), *The Burrow* (1958), *Agon* (1958), *The Invitation* (1960), *Las Hermanas* (1963), *Romeo and Juliet* (1965), *Swan Lake* (Berlin, 1969), *Manon* (1974) and *Mayerling* (1978). He also designed Cranko's *Daphnis and Chloe* (Stuttgart, 1962), and Nureyev's *Swan Lake* (Vienna, 1964), *Sleeping Beauty* (Milan, 1966; London Festival B., 1975), *Nutcracker* (London, 1968), and *Raymonda* (Zurich, 1972); C.B.E. (1984).
BIBL.: R. Crichton, 'Romeo's Designer: N.G.', *Dancing Times* (1965/4); interview with N.G., *Opera News* (1973/5).

Gerber, Judith (*b* Vienna, 24 July 1946). Austrian dancer. Studied at Vienna State Op. B. School and with T. Birkmeyer, E. Vondrak, V. Denisova, and Pereyaslavec. Joined the State Op. B. in 1961; promoted soloist in 1973.

Gerdt, Pavel Andreyevich (orig. Paul Friedrich G.; b nr. St. Petersburg, 4 Dec. 1844, *d* Vamaloki, Finnland, 12 Aug. 1917). Russ. dancer and teacher. Studied at Imperial B. School with Petipa and Johansson, graduating in 1864. Joined the co., of the Imperial Th. and became the most famous Russ. d. of his time – a premier danseur of such distinction that every ballerina felt honoured to appear with him. His unique gifts as a mime enabled him to continue his active career long after he had passed his prime as a d. He himself considered Rudolf, in Petipa's new prod. of *La Fille du Danube*, his greatest role. Created the leading parts in Petipa's *Sleeping Beauty* (1890), *Kalkabrino* (1891), *Cinderella* (1893), *Halte de Cavalerie* (1896), and *Raymonda* (1898), Petipa's and Ivanov's *Swan Lake* (1895), and Ivanov's *Nutcracker* (1892). He gave his farewell perf. as Don Gamache in *Don Quixote* in 1916. Started to teach in 1909; his mime and pas de deux classes were especially sought after by such dancers as Pavlova, Karsavina, Kyasht, Fokine, Legat, Tikhomirov, and his daughter Yelisaveta G.

Gerdt, Yelisaveta Pavlovna (*b* St Petersburg, 29 Apr. 1891, *d* Moscow, 5 Nov. 1975). Russ. dancer and teacher. The daughter of Pavel G., she studied with her father and at the Imperial B. School, graduating in 1908. Joined the Maryinsky Th. and d. her first ballerina roles in 1910; appointed ballerina in 1919, and d. all the great traditional roles until the late 1920s. Started to teach co., classes in 1928; moved to Moscow in 1935, where she was one of the top teachers at the Bolshoi B. School until 1960, with Plisetskaya, Struchkova,

Maximova, and Bovt among her pupils. Merited Artist R.S.F.S.R. (1951).

Gerhard, Roberto (*b* Valls, 25 Sep. 1896, *d* Cambridge, 5 Jan. 1970). Span.-Brit. composer; settled in Eng. in 1938 and became Brit. citizen. Wrote mus. for bs. *Ariel* (1934), *Soirées de Barcelone* (1936–8), *Don Quixote* (1941; ch. de Valois, Sadler's Wells B., 1950), *Alegrias* (1942), *Pandora* (1944, ch. Kurt Jooss; later version ch. David Morse, 1976, for Royal B. Touring Co., with additional mus. arr. David Atherton). His Symphony No. 3, *Collages*, ch. MacMillan as *Checkpoint* (Royal B. Touring Co., 1970).
BIBL.: Special G. issue of *The Score and IMA Magazine* (1956/9).

German Dance. The Amer. term for what was called 'deutscher Ausdruckstanz' in Ger. during the 1920s, i.e. the modern d. originating from the Central European schools of Laban and Wigman.

Germany. B. started its life in Ger. at the many aristocratic courts; Darmstadt, Brunswick, Mannheim, Hanover, Stuttgart, Düsseldorf, Berlin, Dresden, and Munich competed with each other. One of its very first examples was Darmstadt's *Die Befreiung des Friedens* (*The Liberation of Peace*) in 1600—a 'sung b.', like so many others during these early years (e.g. Heinrich Schütz's *Ballett von dem Orpheo und der Euridice*, Dresden, 1638). The b. masters often came from Fr., occasionally from Italy—but from the very beginning there was also a strong contingent of Ger. b. masters. Gottfried Taubert's *Der rechtschaffene Tantzmeister*, published in Leipzig in 1717, was the first Ger. d. treatise to be compared with the standard works by Feuillet and Weaver. The development gathered momentum when Noverre worked in Stuttgart 1760–7, creating a platform to propagate his reforms concerning the b. d'action. While Vienna pursued a steady b. course throughout the 18th and 19th century, b. interest and activity in Ger. shifted from one city to another according to the attitude of the local potentate and, of course, the personal talent and initiative of the b. masters, as for example when Filippo Taglioni and his young daughter Marie worked in Stuttgart 1824–8. They created *Danina oder Jocko der brasilianische Affe* in 1826, one of the most popular bs. of the pre-romantic era. Marie's brother Paul Taglioni was in charge of the Berlin Court Op. B. 1856–83, and during this era (and under his predecessor Michel-François Hoguet) Berlin enjoyed a considerable b. boom, with the international top choreographers and dancers regularly appearing for guest-prods. and perfs. Equally, ballet flourished in Hamburg under Katti Lanner's reign during the early 1860s, and in Munich when Lucile Grahn was b. mistress 1869–75. During the 1890s and early 1900s Ger. b. was completely overwhelmed by the sensationally successful *The Fairy Doll*. The only really important Ger. b. personality to emerge was Heinrich Kröller who worked in Dresden, Frankfurt, Munich, Berlin, and Vienna—at times shared between 2 houses—proving a rock of traditionally based b. amidst the raging sea of modern d. during the 1910s and 1920s. Modern d. gained an ever-increasing following after I. Duncan and St. Denis first appeared in Ger. in 1902 and 1906 respectively, and Jaques-Dalcroze opened his institute for applied rhythm in 1911 in Hellerau (a suburb of Dresden). When Rudolf von Laban and Mary Wigman returned from Switzerland after the first World War, they became the leading personalities of the Ger. movement of 'Ausdruckstanz' (the Ger. equivalent of modern d.); Laban established schools everywhere and Wigman concentrated on Dresden. This movement brought forth such very contrasting personalities as Yvonne Georgi, Gret Palucca, Dore Hoyer, Kurt Jooss, Albrecht Knust, Sigurd Leeder, Max Terpis, and Harald Kreutzberg. It had its climax during the mid-1920s and then slowly faded out or was usurped by the Nazis in 1933; significantly, the most important co., work of the movement, Jooss's *Green Table*, had its first perf. by the Essen Folkwang B. in Paris in 1932—after which Jooss and his troupe decided to leave Ger. for good. Apart from occasional guest visits by cos. such as those of Diaghilev or Pavlova, legitimate b. fared extremely badly during those years, surviving mainly through schools like those of Eugenia Eduardova and the Gsovskys in Berlin. After 1945 Ger. was for a long time undecided whether to resume its modern d. activities or to build anew from a classical basis, though the East Berlin State Op. under Tatjana Gsovsky developed a native form of modern b. When she left East Berlin in 1952, b. there and in E. Ger. came more and more under the influence of the Sov. school of b. The cos. in East Berlin (the State and the Comic Op.) and those attached to the op. houses in Leipzig and Dresden spearheaded the movement towards socialist realism. Tom Schilling of the Berlin Comic Op. emerged as the most creative among the East Ger. choreographers. The 3 central institutes for the education of dancers in E. Ger. are the State B. School Berlin, the Dresden Palucca School, and the B. School Leipzig. There are close links between E. Ger. and leading Sov. b. schools and cos. While b. in E. Ger. is today strictly controlled by East Berlin, b. in W. Ger. is of extreme diversity. Every op house has its own b. co., staging its 1 or 2 'Ballettabend' premières each season. Most of them are classically based, but there is also a growing tendency towards modern-d.-orientated cos. such as those attached to the ths. in Cologne, Wuppertal, and Bremen. Since the later 1950s Brit. and Amer. influences have been dominant, due to the import of such b. directors as Alan Carter (Munich), Walter Gore (Frankfurt), and Todd Bolender (Cologne and Frankfurt). Thanks to the pioneering work of Nicholas Beriozoff and the genius of

John Cranko, Stuttgart has once again become the foremost Ger. b. city, its co., enjoying international acclaim. Also in the forefront of Ger. cos. are those of Cologne, Hamburg, Düsseldorf, Munich, West Berlin, and Wuppertal. The repertory is completely international, with a fair balance of classics, revivals, and new creations. The most interesting Ger. choreographers of the early eighties are Erich Walter (Düsseldorf), Jochen Ulrich (Cologne), Pina Bausch (Wuppertal), and Reinhild Hoffmann (Bremen). The most interesting foreign choreographer working in Ger. is John Neumeier (Hamburg). The 3 most productive schools are Stuttgart J. Cranko School, the Cologne Institute for Th. Dance (closely connected with the Cologne International Summer Academy of D. which has gained a worldwide reputation), and the Essen Folkwang School, but many of the young dancers still come from private schools or from abroad. Generally it can be said that b. now flourishes in Ger. on a much more solid and broader basis than at any other time.

BIBL.: See the above-mentioned cities and individual names in H. Koegler, *Friedrichs Ballettlexikon von A–Z* (Velber, 1972).

Gershunova, Lubov Vasilevna (*b* Novosibirsk, 5 Aug. 1947). Sov. dancer. Studied at Novosibirsk B. School, graduating 1967 into Novosibirsk B. co., soon becoming soloist and now dancing all the ballerina roles of the repertory. Bronze Medal (Varna, 1972).

Gershwin, George (*b* Brooklyn, 26 Sep. 1898, *d* Hollywood, 11 July 1937). Amer. composer. Wrote no b. mus., but his concert mus. and songs have often been used for b. purposes, especially his *Rhapsody in Blue* (Dolin, Milloss, Verchinina, Němeček, Rodham, and others), *An American in Paris* (Page—film by G. Kelly, 1951), and his piano concerto (Kelly in *Pas de dieux*, Paris Opéra, 1960; Robbins in *The Gershwin Concerto*, N.Y. City B., 1982). Massine ch. *The New Yorker* to various pieces by G. in 1940. Balanchine based *Who Cares?* on various G. songs in 1970, followed by Feld's *The Real McCoy* in 1974.

Gerster, Joachim (*b* Perleberg, 7 Jan. 1936). Ger. dancer, choreographer, and b. director. Studied with Hoyer, Klütz, T. Gsovsky, and Kiss. Member of Mannheim Th. 1958–60, Ger. Op. Berlin 1960–3, Salzburg Th. 1963–4, Brunswick 1964–78, appointed artistic dir. in 1974). Now b. dir. in Mannheim. Started to ch. in 1968. Was married to the d. Vreni Wohlschlegel.

Gert, Valeska (*b* Berlin, 11 Jan. 1892, *d* Kampen/ Sylt, 15 Mar. 1978). Ger. dancer, cabaret artist, and actress. Self-taught, she was much discussed when she appeared as a recital d. in Berlin in 1920s. Her numbers were grotesque, satirical, or critical of society, and always heavily mime-orientated. She toured extensively, and emigrated to the U.S.A. when the Nazis came to power, after which she continued as a film-actress.

Geschöpfe des Prometheus, Die. See *Creatures of Prometheus, The.*

Gesellschaftstanz. Ger., ballroom d.

Geva, Tamara (orig. T. Gevergeyeva; *b* St. Petersburg, 1908). Russ.-Amer. dancer and actress. Studied at the Petrograd B. Institute and joined the GATOB as a d. Married Balanchine and went to the West with him and other colleagues in 1924 as the Sov. State Dancers, where they were all engaged by Diaghilev. Left his co., later d. with B. Russe de Monte Carlo and with Chauve Souris, which brought her to Amer., where she appeared in the *Ziegfeld Follies.* Starred in *On Your Toes* (1936). Further career as an actress in musicals, plays, and films. Author of *Split Seconds* (New York, 1972).
BIBL.: G. Loney, 'G. Talks About Yesterday, Today and Tamara, too', *Dance Magazine* (1973/1).

Giara, La. See *Jarre, La.*

Gielgud, Maina (*b* London, 14 Jan. 1945). Brit. d. The niece of the actor Sir John G., she studied at the London Hampshire School and with Karsavina, Idzikovsky, V. Gsovsky, Egorova, and Hightower. Made her début with Petit's co., in 1961; joined the Cuevas co., in 1962, Grand B. Classique de Fr. 1964–7, B. of the 20th Century 1967–71, Ger. Op. Berlin 1971–2. Ballerina of London Festival B. 1972–5; then freelance, with recurrent guest appearances with Royal B. Touring Co. Many guest appearances abroad (Marseilles, Budapest). Created parts in Béjart's *Ni Fleurs, ni couronnes, Baudelaire, Bhakti* (all 1968), and *Serait-ce la mort?* (1970). Toured with her own prod. of *Steps, Notes and Squeaks* from 1978. Began to ch. with *The Soldier's Tale* (Stravinsky), 1980. Apptd. rehearsal dir., London City B., 1981. Apptd. art. dir. Austral. B. 1983.
BIBL.: P. Combescat, 'M.G.', *Les Saisons de la danse* (1969/1).

Gigue. A lively d. in 6/8 or 12/8 time, especially popular in Fr. in the early 1700s. It may have come from the Eng.-Scot.-Ir. Jig.

Gil, Jean-Charles (*b* Spain, 1959). Fr. dancer. Studied in Lausanne. Joined B. de Marseille in 1976, where he has become since one of the most successful soloists. Now with San Francisco B.

Gilmour, Sally (*b* Malaya, 1921). Brit. dancer. Studied with Karsavina and Rambert. Joined B. Rambert, eventually becoming its leading ballerina, excelling in the dramatic truth of her interpretations. Her greatest role creation was Silvia in Howard's *Lady into Fox* (1939)—further creations in Howard's *The Fugitive* (1944) and *Sailor's Return* (1947), Staff's *Peter and the Wolf* (1940), and Gore's *Confessional* (1941) and *Winter Night* (1948). She retired in 1953.

Gilpin, John (*b* Southsea, 10 Feb. 1930, *d* London, 5 Sept. 1983). Brit. d. Studied at Cone-Ripman and Rambert Schools. Appeared as a child actor. Joined B. Rambert in 1945, becoming a principal d. D. with the Petit co., in its 1949 season. Joined London Festival B. in 1950, becoming its premier danseur, appointed asst. art. dir. in 1959, and art. dir. 1962–5. A brilliant and noble technician, he d. with many cos. all over the world. Created roles in Howard's *The Sailor's Return* (1947), Ashton's *Le Rêve de Léonor* (1949), Charnley's *Symphony for Fun* (1952) and *Alice in Wonderland* (1953), Beriozoff's *Esmeralda* (1954), Dolin's Variations for Four (1957), J. Carter's *Beatrix* (1966), and Darrell's *La Vida* (1970). Worked in Copenhagen, Tokyo, and Ankara as teacher, b. master, and also actor.
BIBL.: C. Swinson, *J.G.* (London, 1957); J. Percival, 'Britain's Great Virtuoso', *Dance and Dancers* (1958/1); I. Lidova, 'G.G.' (with complete list of roles and activities), *Les Saisons de la danse* (1972/12).

Gingerbread Heart, The (orig. Serbo-Croat title, *Licitarsko scre*). Ballet in 3 acts; ch. Froman; mus. K. Baranović; sets A. Augustinić; cost. Inges Kostincer-Bregovač. Prod. 17 June 1924, Zagreb. A young man presents a gingerbread heart to his beloved. In a dream sequence the gingerbread figures of the fair come alive and the hearts of the boy and the girl join in a classic pas de deux. The b. enjoys enormous popularity in Yugosl.; it has constantly been revived and reproduced and is often shown abroad by the cos. from Belgrade and Zagreb.

Ginner, Ruby (*b* Cannes, 8 May 1886, *d* Newbury, 13 Feb. 1978). Brit. dance teacher and authority on ancient Greek dance. Studied b. for a short time, afterwards concentrating on her research into ancient Greek d. Established her troupe The Grecian Dancers in 1913 which performed in London. Founded the Ruby Ginner School of D. during the first World War; it later became the Ginner-Mawer School of D. and Drama. In 1923 she established the Association of Teachers of the Revived Greek D. from which the Greek D. Association later emerged, which became part of the Imperial Society of Teachers of Dancing in 1951. Author of *The Revived Greek Dance* (London, 1933) and *Gateway to Dance* (1960).
BIBL.: anon., 'Greek Dance Golden Jubilee', *Dancing Times* (1973/6).

Gioia, Gaetano (in Vienna also Gioja; *b* Naples, 1768, *d* there, 30 Mar. 1826). Ital. dancer and choreographer. Studied with Traffieri, made his début in 1787 in Rome (in a female role), ch. the first of his 221 bs., *Sofonisba*, for Vicenza in 1789. He was a great admirer of S. Viganò and a splendid mime, being known as the 'Sophocles of the Dance'. Worked in Venice in 1790, in Milan 1793–4, in Naples in 1795, in Vienna 1800–1, and afterwards in Turin and again in Naples. He wrote most of the mus. for his bs. himself. His ch. seems to have been frequently plagiarized. His most popular bs. included *Antigone* (Venice, 1790), *Alceste* (Vienna, 1800), *Zulima und Azem* (Vienna, 1800), *Das Urteil des Paris* (Vienna, 1801), *Il ritorno d'Ulisse* (Naples, 1804); his most famous b. (much admired by Viganò) was *Cesare in Egitto* (Milan, 1815).

BIBL.: entry 'G.,G.' in *Enciclopedia dello spettacolo*.

Giordano, Gus (*b* St. Louis, 10 July 1930). Amer. dancer, choreographer, and teacher. Educated Univ. of Missouri. Started to d. at New York Roxy Th. in 1948. Appeared in many musicals and TV prods., before forming the G.G. D. Co. and Studio, based in Evanston, Ill. One of the leading jazz d. teachers in the U.S.

BIBL.: N. McLain Stoop, 'G.G. and his Jazz Dance Chicago', *Dance Magazine* (1981/2).

Gipsy, La. *See Gypsy, La.*

Giselle, ou Les Wilis. Fantastic ballet in 2 acts; libr. Vernoy de Saint-Georges, Gautier, and Coralli; mus. Adam; sets Pierre Ciceri; cost. Paul Lormier. Prod. 28 June 1841, Opéra, Paris, with Grisi, L. Petipa, Dumilâtre. Inspired by H. Heine's *Zur Geschichte der neueren schönen Literatur in Deutschland*, the b. is set in the Rhine Valley. Giselle, a peasant girl, loves Albert (in most versions Albrecht), unaware that he is a Count and engaged to Bathilde, daughter of the Duke of Courland. Albert loves Giselle in return, which arouses the jealousy of the gamekeeper Hilarion, whose love for Giselle is unrequited. At a hunting picnic of the Duke and his entourage, Hilarion reveals Albert's identity, whereupon Giselle goes mad and dies. In the second act both Hilarion and Albert come to worship at the tomb of Giselle. At the stroke of midnight the Wilis appear, led by their Queen Myrtha. They are the embodiments of the spirits of dance-loving brides who died before their wedding day. They perform their ghostly rites, discover Hilarion, and drive him into the lake. Albert, too, almost meets his death, but Giselle intervenes by dancing with him until dawn breaks, when the Wilis must return to their graves and Albert is saved. The b. is still considered the very essence of the romantic b. movement. From the very first prod.—in which all the Grisi numbers seem to have been ch. by Perrot—the peasant pas de deux has usually been inserted, d. on that occasion by Fitzjames and Mabille to mus. by Burgmüller. The b. was rapidly seen all over the world, and was first prod. in London, St. Petersburg, and Vienna in 1842, in Berlin and Milan in 1843 (in Milan it was given in a 5-act version, with additional mus. by Giovanni Bajetti, ch. by A. Cortesi), and in Boston in 1846. It became the display piece par excellence for the ballerinas of all future generations. The original Paris prod. was last performed in 1868; modern versions are based on the St. Petersburg tradition—mainly on M. Petipa's last prod. of 1884. It was this prod. which served as the basis for the prod. of the Diaghilev co., which brought the b.

The London Festival Ballet (Ruanne and Jolley) in *Giselle*.   Photo Anthony Crickmay.

back to W. Eur. in 1911. Most of the later prods. make some reference to the Diaghilev—e.g. those of the Paris Opéra in 1924, the Vic-Wells B. in 1934, and the various prods. of the Sadler's Wells B., the Royal B., and the London Festival B. A b. play, *The World of Giselle*, was staged by the B. for All group of the Royal B. in 1963. There have been various films of the complete b., the most noteworthy being the one of the Bolshoi prod., with Ulanova and Fadeyechev, in 1956, and the one of the Amer. B. Th. prod., with Fracci and Bruhn, in 1969.
BIBL.: C. W. Beaumont, *The Ballet Called G.* (London, 1944—Dance Horizons reprint, 1970); portfolio on *G., Dance Magazine* (1969/12); portfolio by Frank W. D. Ries, *Dance Magazine* (1979/8).

Gitana, La. Ballet with prologue, in 3 acts and 5 scenes; libr. and ch. F. Taglioni; mus. Schmidt and Auber. Prod. 5 Dec. 1838, Bolshoi Th., St. Petersburg, with M. Taglioni, N. O. Glotz. The b. tells the story of Lauretta, the daughter of a Duke, who is abducted when only 7 years old and brought up by a tribe of gipsies, and of Ivan, son of the Governor of Nishni Novgorod, who falls in love with her. The title role became one of Taglioni's biggest successes when she d. it in London in 1839. A different b. *La Gypsy with ch. by Mazilier and mus. by Benoist, Thomas, and Marliani, was first perf. on 28 Jan. 1839 at the Paris Opéra with Elssler in the title role.
BIBL.: C. W. Beaumont, 'L.G.' in *Complete Book of Ballets* (London, 1951).

GITIS. The Russ. abbreviation for Gosudarstvenny Institut Teatralnovo Iskusstva (State Institute for Theatre Arts), the name of the Moscow Lunacharsky State Institute for Theatre Art. It derives from the school for actors, existing with numerous changes of titles since 1878. Since 1930 it has added a faculty of critics and historians, and some of the ballet critics have studied there. In 1946 a faculty of choreographers was added and in 1958 another faculty of teachers of d.

Giuliano, Juan (*b* Cordova, 26 Dec. 1930). Argent. d. and ch. Studied at the school of the Teatro Colón. Made his début with SODRE B. (Montevideo) in 1950; d. with many cos. incl. those of T. Grigorieva, Milloss in São Paulo, Grand B. du Marquis de Cuevas, Charrat, Maggio Musicale Fiorentino, Grand B. Classique de France. Started to ch. in 1965, creating bs. for B. Th. Contemporain and Paris Opéra Comique. Appointed b. dir. of the National B. of Venezuela in 1974 and of Th. des Arts, Rouen, in 1976. Married to the d. Hélène Trailine.
BIBL.: J.-C. Diénis, 'Pleins feux sur J.G.' (with check-list of activities), *Les Saisons de la danse* (1974/1).

Gladstein, Robert (*b* Berkeley, Cal., 16 Jan. 1943). Amer. d. and ch. Studied at San Francisco B. School. Joined San Francisco B. in 1959, promoted

soloist. D. with Amer. B. Th. 1967–70, after which he returned to San Francisco B., for which he has also ch. a number of bs. Became principal d., resident ch. and rehearsal asst. of San Francisco B. Retired as a d. 1975; to become b. master and asst. dir., San Francisco B. B. master Dallas B. from 1986.

Glassman, William (*b* Boston, 15 Feb. 1945). Amer. d. and teacher. Studied with E. Virginia Williams, School of Amer. B., Stanley Williams, R. Thomas, and B. Fallis. Started to d. in musicals, member of Amer. B. Th. 1963–8, where he created roles in Robbins' *Les Noces* and de Mille's *The Wind in the Mountains* (both in 1965). Also d. with Niagara Frontier Ballet. Asst. professor of B. at State Univ. of New York at Purchase during the 1970s.
BIBL.: S. Goodman, 'W.G.', *Dance Magazine* (1967/5).

Glasstone, Richard (*b* Elisabethville, Belg. Congo, 1935). Brit. d., ch., and teacher. Studied at Cape Town B. School and in London with Rambert and de Vos. D. with Univ. of Cape Town B. and with Scapino B., for which he ch., various bs. Appointed resident ch. dir. and principal teacher of Turk. National B. of Ankara 1965–9. Joined staff of Royal B. School in 1969. Has also ch. for Royal B. Ch. Group, B. of Flanders and *Sylvia* (Delibes) for Northern B. Th., 1981. Administrator, Cecchetti Soc. 1983.

Glauber, Lynn (*b* Buffalo, N.Y., 1 Jan. 1954). Amer. dancer. Studied at Buffalo B. Center and Amer. B. Center. Joined B. of the 20th Century in 1971, later becoming soloist. Created leading role in Béjart's *Seraphita* (1974).
BIBL.: N. McLain Stoop, 'L.G.', *Dance Magazine* (1975/12).

Glazunov, Alexander Konstantinovich (*b* St. Petersburg, 10 Aug. 1865, *d* Paris, 21 Mar. 1936). Russ. composer. Wrote the mus. for M. Petipa's *Raymonda* (1898), *Ruses d'amour* (1900), and *Les Saisons* (1900). Balanchine used parts of *Raymonda* in his *Pas de dix* (1955), *Raymonda Variations* (1961), and *Cortège Hongrois* (1973); Ashton had various pieces specially arranged for his *Birthday Offering* (1956) as did L. Christensen in *Variations de B.* (San Francisco B., 1960). Gorsky ch. his *Fifth Symphony* in 1916 (this was one of the very first symphonic bs.) and Fokine his *Stenka Razin* in the same year.

Glière, Reinhold Moritzovich (*b* Kiev, 11 Jan. 1876, *d* Moscow, 23 June 1956). Russ. composer. Wrote the mus. for *Chrysis* (ch. N. Mill, 1912), *Egyptian Nights* (ch. Nemirovich-Danchenko, 1926), *The Red Poppy* (ch. Lastchilin and V. Tikhomirov, 1927), *The Comedians* (ch. Chekrygin, 1931—this became later *A Daughter of Castille*, ch. Chichinadze, 1955), and *The Bronze Horseman* (ch. Zakharov, 1949).

Glinka, Mikhail Ivanovich (*b* Novo-Spasskoye,

nr. Smolensk, 1 June 1804, d Berlin, 15 Feb. 1857). Russ. composer. Wrote no b. mus., but some of his concert and op. pieces have been used by choreographers: Zakharov's Polonaise and Krakowiak from *Ivan Susanin* became the favourite opening piece for the Bolshoi B.'s concert programmes. Fokine did a b. to his *Jota Aragonesa* (Petrograd, 1916), Cranko ch. a *Pas de quatre* to the overture from *Ruslan and Ludmila* (Stuttgart, 1966), and Balanchine created a b. *Glinkiana* to various compositions (New York City B., 1967).

Glissade (Fr., glide). Designates a sliding step, which can be executed in any direction, and is mostly used as a joining step.

Gloria. Ballet in 1 act; ch. MacMillan; mus. Poulenc; déc. Andy Klunder. Prod. 13 Mar. 1980, Royal B., Cov. Gdn., London, with Eagling, Penney, Hosking, Ellis *et al*. D. to composer's Gloria in G Major, the b. is inspired by Vera Brittain's *Testament of Youth*, where she speaks of the dreams of happiness 'we thought secure; while, imminent and fierce outside the door, watching a generation grow to flower, The fate that held our youth within its power, Waited its hour'. With great compassion and commitment it mourns the waste of youth which perished in the trenches of the First World War.

Gluck, Christoph Willibald (b Erasbach, 2 July 1714, d Vienna, 15 Nov. 1787). Ger. comp. Wrote the mus. for Angiolini's *Don Juan* (1761), *Alessandro* (1765) and *Semiramis* (1765). Some of his ops. are also strongly b.-orientated, incl. *Alkestis* (Vienna, 1761; Paris, 1776), *Orpheus and Eurydice* (Vienna, 1762; Paris, 1774) and *Iphigenia in Aulis* (Paris, 1774); and there have been occasional prods. with the singers seated either at the proscenium or in the orchestra pit and the stage handed over completely to dancers—e.g. Balanchine's *Orpheus and Eurydice* (Met. Op. Ho., New York, 1936—also by Wigman, Leipzig, 1947; Bausch, Wuppertal, 1975), Wigman's *Alkestis* (Mannheim, 1958), and Bausch's *Iphigenie auf Tauris* (Wuppertal, 1974).

Gluck, Rena (b New York, 14 Jan. 1933). Amer. dancer, teacher, and choreographer. Studied at Blanche Evan School of Creative D, High School of Performing Arts, Juilliard School, and with Graham. Founder-member of Batsheva D. Co. 1964, of which she is still a principal d. and for which she has ch. several bs., including *Women in a Tent* (1966), *Reflections* (1968), *Time of Waiting* (1971), and *Journey* (1973). Teaches at her own school in Tel Aviv and for Inbal D. Th. and Batsheva D. Co.

Gluszkovsky, Adam Pavlovich (b St. Petersburg, 1793, d c. 1870). Russ. dancer, teacher, and choreographer. A favourite pupil of Didelot, he also studied abroad with Duport. Came to Moscow in 1811 to stage some Didelot bs. and his own *Ruslan and Ludmila*. Principal d. and b. master of

the Moscow Bolshoi B. 1812–39; he also taught at the newly founded Moscow B. School, contributing considerably to its great reputation. Author of *Memoirs of a Ballet Master 1812–68*. He was married to the d. Tatiana G.

BIBL.: N. Roslavleva, in *Era of the Russian Ballet*. (London, 1966).

Gnatt, Poul (b Baden, Austria, 24 Mar. 1923). Dan. dancer, choreographer, and b. master. The brother of the d. Kirsten Ralov. Studied at the Royal Dan. B. School, joining the Royal Dan. B.; promoted solo d. in 1952. He then d. with various cos., abroad (Metropolitan B., Bs. des Champs-Elysées, Royal Swed. B., Borovansky B., Original B. Russe). Founded N.Z. B. in 1953. Dir. of Victoria B. Co., (Austral.) in 1967. Asst. b. master Norweg. National B. 1971–2.

Godfrey, Louis (b Johannesburg, 1930). S.A. dancer and b. master. Studied with Ivy Conmee, Marjorie Sturman, and in London with Volkova, Idzikowski, and at Sadler's Wells B. School. D. with Johannesburg Festival B. Society. Joined Markova-Dolin B. in 1949 and London Festival B. as a principal on its foundation in 1950; left 1964. Appeared in musicals in London and returned to S.A. in 1970 to become b. master of the PACT B. in Johannesburg; appointed joint artistic dir. in 1973. Now b. master at Ballet West.

Godounov, Alexander. See *Godunov, Alexander*.

Godreau, Miguel (b Ponce, 17 Oct. 1946). Puerto Rican dancer. Studied at New York High School of Performing Arts, School of Amer. B. and Joffrey's Amer. B. Center. Appeared in musicals; d. with Ailey's co. 1965–70, to which he has returned several times after dancing with other troupes (Harkness B., D. McKayle, Cullberg B.). His most famous role is G. Holder's *Prodigal Prince* (1967). In between has appeared in various Broadway and Shaftesbury Av. shows.

Gods Go a-Begging, The, or Les dieux mendiants. Ballet in 1 act; libr. Sobeka (Kochno); ch. Balanchine; mus. Handel, arr. Beecham; sets Bakst (the first scene from *Daphnis and Chloe*); cost. J. Gris (partly from *Les Tentations de la Bergère*). Prod. 16 July 1928, Bs. Russes de Diaghilev, Her Majesty's Th., London, with Danilova, Woizikovsky. The b. tells of a young shepherd who joins a picnic of young aristocrats and falls in love with a pretty maid. When the other guests are making fun of the two lovers, he suddenly reveals himself and his beloved as gods. Later versions by de Valois (Sadler's Wells B., 1936) and Lichine (B. Russe de Monte Carlo, 1937).

Godunov, Alexander (b Riga, 1949). Sov. dancer. Studied at the local Ch. School and Moscow Bolshoi School, graduating in 1967. Has d. with Moiseyev's Young B. and as a soloist of the Moscow Bolshoi B. after 1967, creating Karenin in Plisetskaya's *Anna Karenina* (second premiere, 1972) and leading role in Boccadoro's *Love for Love* (1976). Gold Medal (Moscow, 1973). Defected Bolshoi B. in Aug. 1979 in New York. Joined American B. Theatre in Dec. 1979. Married to the d. Ludmila Vlasova, who decided to return to Moscow after her husband's defection.

BIBL.: O. Maynard, 'A.G. Speaks about his art', *Dance Magazine* (1979/11).

Goethe Ballets. The works of Johann Wolfgang von Goethe (1749–1832) have inspired several bs., incl. *The Sorrows of Young Werther* (ch. Joseph Schmalögger, Bratislava, 1777—later versions by Piet Greive, Amsterdam, 1816; Zoltan Imre, Cologne, 1974), *The God and the Bayadère* (the b.-op. by Auber, ch. F. Taglioni, Paris, 1830, with M. Taglioni as Zoloé), *The Countess of Egmont* (ch. Rota, Milan, 1861), *The Sorcerer's Apprentice* (ch. Fokine, Petrograd, 1916; a later version by H. Lander, Copenhagen, 1940), and *Les Affinités électives* (ch. Blaska, Paris, 1966).

Goh, Choo San (*b* Singapore, 1948). Chin. dancer, teacher, and choreographer. Studied locally with his brother and sister. D. with Scapino B. and Dutch National B. before joining Washington B. in 1976, of which he is now ch. and asst. dir., also teaching at Washington School of B. Has ch. a great number of bs., also working for other Amer. cos. Asst. art. dir. Washington B. 1985.

BIBL.: D. Cleveland, 'C.S.G.'s Dynamic Challenge to Dance', *Dance Magazine* (1980/7).

Goldberg Variations, The. Ballet in 2 parts; ch. Robbins; mus. Bach; cost. Joe Eula; pianist Gordon Boelzner. Prod. 27 May 1971, New York City B., State Th., N.Y., with Kirkland, Leland, Clifford, Maiorano, von Aroldingen, Blum, McBride, Tomasson, Martins. A plotless b., set to Bach's famous set of variations, with occasional slight 18th-century overtones.

BIBL.: E. Binova, 'The World of G.V.', *Ballet Review* (III, 6).

Golden Age, The (orig. Russ. title: *Zolotoi vek*). Ballet in 3 acts and 5 scenes; libr. A. Ivanovsky; ch. E. Kaplan and Vainonen (with V. Tchesnakov and Jacobson as collaborators); mus. Shostakovich; déc. V. Khodasevich. Prod, 26 Oct. 1930, GATOB, Leningrad. The title refers to an exhibition in a capitalist city, where a fight takes place between some Fascists and a Sov. football team. In the end the capitalist workers join the Sov. footballers in a d. symbolizing the joy of work. The b. was the result of a competition for new b. librs. The prod., however, was accused of minimizing the conflicts of class war and of ideological destructiveness, and soon removed from the repertory.

BIBL.: M. G. Swift, in *The Art of the Dance in the U.S.S.R.* (Notre Dame, Indiana, 1968).

Golden Cockerel, The (orig. Russ. title: *Zolotoi petushok*—also Fr. *Le Coq d'or*). Opera in 3 acts; libr. V. Byelsky, after Pushkin's poem; mus.

Rimsky-Korsakov. Prod. 7 Oct. 1909, Bolshoi Th., Moscow. It was, however, the prod. staged by Diaghilev's Bs. Russes on 24 May 1914 at the Paris Opéra which established the work's world reputation. For this Fokine had all the roles acted by dancers, while the singers sat at the sides of the stage; the déc. was by Goncharova, and the main roles were d. by Karsavina, Bulgakov, and Cecchetti. A later 1-act b. prod. by Fokine without singers for de Basil's B. Russe in 1937. Skibine produced it for B. de Wallonie in 1975, Beriozoff for London Festival B. (as *Le Coq d'or*) in 1976.

Goldner, Nancy (*b* New York, 19 Mar. 1943). Amer. b. critic. B. critic of *Christian Science Monitor, Dance News, The Nation.* U.S. correspondent for *Les Saisons de la danse.* Author of *The Stravinsky Festival of the New York City Ballet* (New York, 1974). Now d. critic of *Philadelphia Inquirer.*

Goldoni Ballets. Several plays by this Ital. dramatist (1707–93) have inspired bs.—e.g. *The Good-Humoured Ladies* (ch. Massine, 1917), *Scuola di ballo* (ch. Massine, 1924), *The False Bridegroom* (alias *The Servant of Two Masters*, ch. Fenster 1946), *Mirandolina* (ch. Vainonen, 1949), and *The Servant of Two Masters* (ch. Němeček, 1958).

Goldwyn, Beryl (*b* Pinner, 1930). Brit. dancer. Studied at Sadler's Wells B. School and Rambert School. Joined B. Rambert in 1949; appointed principal d. in 1953. She was especially admired as Giselle. Retired in 1955.

Goleizovsky, Kasyan Yaroslavovich (*b* Moscow, 5 Mar. 1892, *d* there, 2 May 1970). Russ. dancer and choreographer. Studied in Moscow and St. Petersburg, graduating in 1909. Joined the co., of the Maryinsky Th. and Moscow Bolshoi B. in 1910. Often worked for N. Balyev's cabaret *Chauve Souris*, drawing wide attention with his grotesque miniatures. He was a thoroughly experiméntal ch. who at first tried out his ideas at his Moscow studio, but soon began to influence young Leningrad choreographers such as Balanchivadze. In the early 1920s had his own Moscow Camera B. for which he ch. such miniatures as *Faune* (mus. Debussy), *Salome* (mus. Strauss), and various pieces by Scriabin and Prokofiev. Most of his bs. were controversial, incl. *Joseph the Beautiful* (mus. S. Vasilenko, Bolshoi Filial Th., 1925) and *The Whirlwind* (mus. B. Ber, 1927), which led to his resignation, but he always returned as a ch. on various occasions, for instance during the late 1920s and early 30s with G.'s Thirty Girls in Moscow music-halls. Other bs. of his included *Polovtsian Dances* (Moscow, 1933), *Sleeping Beauty* (Kharkhov, 1935), *Fountain of Bakhchisaray* (Minsk, 1939), *Two Roses* (mus. A. Lenski, Dushanbe, 1940), *Scriabiniana* (Bolshoi Th., Moscow, 1962), *Leili and Mejnun* (mus. S. Balasabian, Moscow, 1964). Author of *Forms of Russian National Ch.* (1964).

BIBL.: L. Joffe, 'K.G.', *Les Saisons de la danse* (1973/3).

Golestan, Le Jardin des roses. Ballet in 4 scenes; ch. Béjart; traditional Iranian mus.; déc. Joëlle Roustan and Roger Bernard. Prod. 30 Aug. 1973, B. of the 20th Century, Persepolis, with Alain Louafi, Farrell, Donn. Inspired by poems by the Persian 13th century poet Sa'adi, the b.'s individual scenes are entitled: Chant des hommes dans le désert; Vision du jardin; Apparition de la lumière—La Rose mystique; Ritual—Le Voile et le miroir.

Golikova, Tatyana Nikolaievna (*b* Vyborg, 14 Oct. 1945). Sov. dancer. Studied at Moscow Bolshoi B. School, graduating in 1965. Joined the Bolshoi B., where her best roles are Odette-Odile, Mehmene-Banu (in *Legend of Love*) and Aegina (in *Spartacus*); created leading role in Boccadoro's *Love for Love* (1976).
BIBL.: N. Arkina, 'T.G.', *Les Saisons de la danse* (1969/4).

Golinelli, Giovanni (*d* Brunswick, 15 Dec. 1884). Ital. mime and choreographer. Worked at the Vienna Court Op. 1836–59; appointed b. régisseur in 1855. B. master in Hamburg 1860–1, Th. an der Wien 1861–3, and in Munich 1864–9. Among his many bs. were *Manon Lescaut* (mus. Strebinger, 1852) and *Don Quixote* (mus. Strebinger, 1855).

Gollner, Nana (*b* El Paso, Tex., 1920, *d* Antwerp, 30 Aug. 1980). Amer. dancer. Studied with Kosloff. D. with de Basil's B. Russe 1935–6, as ballerina with Blum's Bs. Russes de Monte Carlo 1936–7, as prima ballerina with Original B. Russe 1941–3, and with B. Th. 1943–5. Guest ballerina with International B. London in 1947. She then undertook several tours with her d. husband Paul Petroff. Taught in Los Angeles.

Golovin, Alexander Jacovlevich (*b* Moscow, 1 Mar. 1863, *d* Pushkin, 1930). Russ. painter. Designed ops. and bs. for the Russ. Imperial Ths. in St. Petersburg and Moscow, Fokine's original *Firebird* of 1910, the second act *Swan Lake* prod. of the Diaghilev co., with K. Korovin in 1911, Fokine's *Jota Aragonesa* in 1916, and Lopokov's *Solveig* in 1927.

Golovine, Serge (*b* Monaco, 20 Nov. 1924). Fr. dancer and teacher. Studied with Sedova and Ricaux. D. with the Op. B. of Monte Carlo during the war; joined Nouveau B. de Monte Carlo in 1946, Paris Opéra in 1947, and Grand B. du Marquis de Cuevas in 1950, becoming one of its star dancers, much admired for his lightness and batterie. Two of his most famous roles were Blue Bird and Spectre de la rose. Founded his own group in 1962. B. master of the Geneva Op. 1964–9. Now has a school in Geneva. He is the brother of the dancers Solange Golovina and Georges Goviloff.
BIBL.: I. Lidova, 'S.G.', with complete check-list of roles and activities, *Les Saisons de la Danse* (1976/4).

Golovkina, Sophia Nikolaievna (*b* Moscow, 13 Oct. 1915). Sov. dancer and teacher. Studied at Moscow Bolshoi B. School, graduating in 1933. Joined the Bolshoi B., where she d. until 1959. Dir. of the Bolshoi B. School since 1960. Merited Artist of the R.S.F.S.R.; Order of Red Banner of Labour.
BIBL.: M. Horosko. 'S.G.', *Dance Magazine* (1973/11).

Goncharov, George (*b* St. Petersburg, 1904, *d* London, 1954). Russ. dancer, choreographer, and teacher. Studied in St. Petersburg, after which he toured Russ. with a small group of dancers. Had a school in Shanghai during the 1920s and 30s (Volkova was teaching there), where Fonteyn studied in 1933. Came to London in 1945 and taught at Sadler's Wells B. School. He subsequently taught in Italy and Cuba and then returned to London and took over Volkova's school, where Elvin and Beriosova studied with him.

Goncharova, Nathalia Sergeievna (*b* Ladyschino, 3 June 1881, *d* Paris, 18 Oct. 1962). Russ. painter and designer. For the Diaghilev co., she designed Fokine's *Le Coq d'or* (1914), *Liturgie* (not realised, 1915), Nijinska's *Renard* (with her husband Larionov, 1922), *Les Noces* (1923) and *Une Nuit sur le Mont Chauve* (1924), and the 1926 revival of Fokine's *Firebird* (reproduced for the 1954 Sadler's Wells B. prod.). Also designed Fokine's *Ygrouchka* (New York, 1921) and *Cendrillon* (London, 1938), Lifar's *Sur le Borsythène* (with Larionov, Paris, 1932), and Massine's *Bogatyri* (New York, 1938).
BIBL.: H. Rischbieter, in *Bühne und bildende Kunst im XX. Jahrhundert* (Velber, 1968).

Gonzáles, Ofelia (*b* Camagüey, 1953). Cub. dancer. Studied with Vicente de la Torre and at Cub. National B. School with Ramona de Saa, A. Bosch, and Joaquin Banegas. Joined National B. of Cuba in 1970; became soloist in 1972.

Good-Humoured Ladies, The (orig. Fr. title: *Les Femmes de bonne humeur*). Ch. Comedy in 1 act; libr. and ch. massine; mus. D. Scarlatti, arr. V. Tommasini; déc. Bakst. Prod. 12 Apr. 1917, Bs. Russses de Diaghilev, Teatro Costanzi, Rome, with Lopokova, Tchernicheva, Massine, Cecchetti, Idzikowsky, Woizikowsky. The b. is based on Goldoni's *Le donne di buon umore* and tells of the extremely complicated love-affair between Costanza and Rinaldo, who have to overcome many obstacles and the scheming opposition of their parents. Massine revived it for various cos. incl. the Royal B. prod. of 1962.
BIBL.: C. W. Beaumont, 'L.F.d.b.h.' in *Complete Book of Ballets* (London, 1951).

Goodman, Erika (*b* Philadelphia, 9 Oct. 1947). Amer. dancer. Studied with N. Chilkovsky, M. Stuart, Doubrovska, Williams, Eglevsky, L. Moore, Joffrey, Watts, and Griffith. Joined New

York City B. in 1965; d. with Pennsylvania B. and Boston B. and since 1967 with Joffrey B., creating roles in Arpino's *Cello Concerto* (1967), *The Clowns* (1968), *Fanfarita* (1968), *Reflections* (1971), and *Jackpot* (1973).

Goodwin, Noël (*b* Fowey, 25 Dec. 1927). Brit. mus. and dance critic. Educated in Fr. and at London Univ. (B.A.). Music and d. critic for *Daily Express* 1956–78, London d. critic, *Int. Herald Tribune* 1978–84 and *Ballet News* (N.Y.) 1979–86. Regular contributor to *Dance and Dancers* since 1956, Music Editor from 1964, Associate Editor from 1972. Frequent broadcaster. Contributor to *Encyclopedia Britannica* (1974) and other works of reference. Editor, Royal B. Souvenir Yearbooks, 1978, 79, 80. Specializes in the relationship of d. and mus. Librettist *Mary, Queen of Scots* (ch. Darrell, Scottish B., 1976). Author of Scottish B. history, *A Ballet for Scotland* (Edinburgh, 1979). Apptd. Arts Council of G.B. member, 1979–81, and chairman of Dance Advisory Panel, 1980/1.

Gopak (also Hopak). A lively d. from the Ukraine in duple time. Originally d. by men only. An especially popular example is the G. from *Taras Bulba*, ch. by Zakharov to mus. by Soloviev-Sedoy.

Gopal, Ram (*b* Bangalore, 20 Nov. 1920). Ind. dancer, choreographer, and teacher. Studied Kathakali with Kunju Kunrup, Bharata Natya with Sundaram, Kathak with Misra, and Manipuri with Nabakumar. Opened a school of classical Ind. dancing in Bangalore in 1935. Started to appear in public with La Meri in 1937. First came to Europe in 1938, performing in London with his own co., in 1939, after which he undertook several world tours, before finally settling in London, where he opened his Academy for Ind. D. and Mus. in 1962. His best known bs. were *Dances of India, Legend of the Taj Mahal*, and *Dance of the Setting Sun*. Author of *Rhythm in the Heavens* (London, 1957).

Gorbaniev, Gennady Nicolaievich (*b* Riga, 1 Dec. 1950). Sov. dancer. Studied at Riga B. School, graduating 1968, joining the Riga co., and subsequently appointed soloist. Silver Medal (Varna, 1972).

Gorda. Ballet in 4 acts and 10 scenes; ch. Chaboukiani; mus. D. Toradze; déc. L. Lapiashvili. Prod. 30 Dec. 1949, Tiflis, with V. Tsignadze, Z. Kikaleishvili, I. Alexidze, M. Bauer. The Georgian bp. tells of a young sculptor who loves the Tsarevna and turns into an ardent warrior to defend his country against the invading Arabs.
BIBL.: M. G. Swift, in the *The Art of the Dance in the U.S.S.R.* (Notre Dame, Indiana, 1968).

Gordeyev. Vatcheslav Mikhailovich (*b* Moscow, 3 Aug. 1948). Sov. dancer. Studied at Moscow Bolshoi School, graduating in 1968. Joined the Bolshoi B., where he dances the premier danseur

roles of the standard repertory. Contributed 'The Fourth Spartacus', *Dancing Times* (Apr. 1975). Gold Medal (Moscow, 1973). Married to the d. Nadeshda Pavlova.
BIBL.: T. Tobias, 'Bolshoi Profiles: V.G.', *Dance Magazine* (1975/8). K. Sandler 'Moscow's Favorites N. Pavlova and V.G.'. *Ballet News*, (1979/11).

Gore, Walter (*b* Waterside, Scotland, 8 Aug. 1910, *d* Pamplona, 15 Apr. 1979). Brit. dancer and choreographer. Studied at Italia Conti School and with Massine. D. in the first season of Rambert Dancers in 1930 and with B. Rambert until 1935. Joined Vic-Wells B. in 1935, creating title-role in de Valois' *The Rake's Progress*; left the co., during the same year to ch. for musicals. Returned to B. Rambert as a soloist, creating his first bs. for the co. in 1938: *Valse finale* (mus. Ravel) and *Paris Soir* (mus. Poulenc, 1939)—later also *Confessional* (mus. Sibelius, 1941) and *Bartlemas Dances* (mus. Holst, 1941). After war service he once again returned to B. Rambert, choreographing *Simple Symphony* (mus. Britten, 1944), *Mr. Punch* (mus. Oldham, 1946), *Concerto Burlesco* (mus. Bartók, 1946), *Winter Night* (mus. Rachmaninov, 1948), and *Antonia* (mus. Sibelius, 1949). For New B. Co., he ch. *Street Games* (mus. Ibert) in 1952 and for Bs. des Champs-Elysées *La Damnée* (same year). With his d. wife Paula Hinton, he then went to Austral.; returned to Eng. to ch. *Carte Blanche* (mus. J. Addinson) for Sadler's Wells Th. B. in 1953. Formed his own co., (the W.G.B.) in 1954, with which he toured Austral. 1955–6. Guest ch. of B. der Lage Landen in Amsterdam, and of the Miskovitch co., B. master in Frankfurt 1957–9, creating *Eaters of Darkness* (mus. Britten, 1958). He created *The Night and the Silence* (mus. Bach, arr, Mackerras) for Edinburgh Festival B. in 1958. Formed London B. in 1961. His later bs. were *Sweet Dancer* (mus. F. Martin, B. Rambert, 1964) and *The Maskers* (mus. Foss, Western Th. B., 1965). B. master Norweg. National B. 1963–5, Gulbenkian B. (Lisbon) 1965–9, Augsburg (Ger.) 1971–2. Also worked for Northern D. Th. His last bs. incl. *Embers of Glencoe* (mus. Tom Wilson, Scottish Th. B., 1973).
BIBL.: C. Beaumont, in *Ballets of Today* (London, 1954); A. H. Franks, in *Twentieth Century Ballet* (London, 1954).

Gorham, Kathleen (*b* Sydney, 20 Dec. 1932, *d* Melbourne, 30 Apr. 1983). Austral. dancer. Studied with Lorraine Norton and Leon Kellaway, joined Borovansky B. in 1947 and B. Rambert (in Austral.) in 1948. Came to Eng. in 1949, continued to study at Sadler's Wells B. School, joined Sadler's Wells Th. B. 1951–2 and Grand B. du Marquis de Cuevas in 1953. Returned to Austral. to d. with Borovansky 1954–9. Guest ballerina with various Eur. cos. 1959–62. Ballerina of Austral. B. 1962–6. Since her retirement as a dancer ran her own school in Melbourne. O.B.E. (1968).

Gorianka, The Girl from the Mountains. Ballet in 3 acts; ch. Vinogradov; mus. Murad Kashlaev; déc Marina Sokolova. Prod. 20 Mar. 1968, Kirov Th., Leningrad, with Komleva, Panov, Baryshnikov. A girl from the country leaves her family and fiancé to lead a life of her own in the city, where she falls in love, but sees her new lover killed by her old fiancé.

Gorsky, Alexander Alexeievich (b St. Petersburg, 18 Aug. 1871, d Moscow, 20 Oct. 1924). Russ. dancer, choreographer, b. master, and teacher. Entered St. Petersburg Imperial B. School in 1880, graduating in 1889. Joined Maryinsky Th.; appointed soloist in 1895. Started to teach as an asst. of P. Gerdt in 1896. A friend of V. Stepanoff, he saw that his method of notation was introduced into the syllabus of the b. school. Was sent to Moscow in 1898 to mount *Sleeping Beauty* at the Bolshoi, based on the notation of the St. Petersburg prod. For a St. Petersburg school matinée he ch. *Clorinda, Queen of the Mountain Fairies* in 1899, the ch. of which he had already notated before starting rehearsals. In the autumn of 1900 he finally moved to Moscow, becoming premier danseur and régisseur of the Bolshoi B. The same year he prod. his own version of Minkus's *Don Quixote*—his first chance to realize his ideas of a dramatically conceived action b. on a grand scale. His revised versions of *Swan Lake* and *The Little Humpbacked Horse* followed in 1901, and in 1902 he ch. *Gudule's Daughter* (his version of the former *Esmeralda* b., later called *Notre Dame de Paris*). Other important bs. of his included *The Magic Mirror* (mus. Arseny Koreshenko, 1905), *Pharaoh's Daughter* (mus. Pugni, 1905), *Raymonda* (1908), *Etudes* (mus. Robin Stein, and others, 1908) *Salammbô* (mus. A. Arensky, 1910), *Giselle* (1911), *The Corsair* (mus. Adam, 1912), *Love is Quick* (mus. Grieg, 1913), *Eunice and Petronius* (mus. Chopin, 1915), *Fifth Symphony* (mus. Glazunov, 1916), *La Bayadère* (mus. Minkus, 1917), *Stenka Razin* (mus. Glazunov, 1918), *Nutcracker* (1919), *Salome's Dance* (mus. R. Strauss, 1921), *Les petits riens* (mus. Mozart, 1922), and *The Venus Grotto* (mus. Wagner, 1923). In 1911 he staged the b. *The Dance Dream* at the London Alhambra Th. for the Coronation. Recent Sov. writers claim him as a pioneer of a dramatically orientated b. realism and a reformer of no less rank than Fokine.
BIBL.: N. Roslavleva, in *Era of the Russian Ballet* (London, 1966).

Goslar, Lotte (b Dresden). Ger.-Amer. dancer and mime. Studied with Wigman and Palucca; appeared in Berlin cabarets. Left Ger. in 1933, joining Erika Mann's Zurich cabaret The Pepper Mill, with which she undertook several tours; visited the U.S. in 1937. Went to Hollywood in 1943, where she formed her own group to tour the States and occasionally Eur. She has also taught; Marilyn Monroe and G. Champion are her two most famous pupils. Developed an individual form of dance-mime; her prods. include *For Humans Only* (1954) and *Clowns and Other Fools* (1966). Still performs, and is much loved by Amer. audiences for her smiling clown figures.
BIBL.: M. Robertson, 'L.G.', *Dance Magazine* (1980/12).

Gosling, Nigel. See *Bland, Alexander*.

Goss, Peter (b Johannesburg, 30 Jan. 1946). Brit. dancer, teacher, and choreographer. Studied mainly modern d. in S.A., London, and New York. To Paris, where he opened a school and established a co., in 1973 with which he has performed–mostly jazz bs.–on Fr. TV, at Espace Cardin, and for Festival de Marais.

Gosschalk, Käthy (b Amsterdam, 30 Aug. 1941). Dutch dancer. Studied at Scapino D. Academy and New York Juilliard School. Joined Scapino B. in 1957; with Netherlands D. Th. 1962–72, becoming one of its leading soloists and creating roles in Van Manen's *Essay in Silence* (1965), *Dualis* (1967), *Three Pieces* (1968), and *Situation* (1970), and in Van Manen's and Tetley's *Mutations* (1970). Her occasional chs. include *9 Movements* (mus. Brahms, 1967) and *Graffiti* (mus. Roger Reynolds, 1969). Retired from dancing 1972, to become an actress, but ch. *Interviews* (to her own tape collage) for Scapino B. (1975), and was apptd. artistic dir. Werkcentrum Dans, Rotterdam, from 1975.

Gosselin, Geneviève (b 1791, d 1818). Fr. dancer. The sister of Louis G., she studied at Paris Opéra B. School, making her début in 1809. Had her best role in *L'Enfant prodigue*. Though rather plump, she was so supple that people called her 'The Boneless'. Her younger sister also became a d. appearing under the name of Madame Anatole (Petit).

Gosselin, Louis F. (b Paris, 1800, d there, 1860). Fr. dancer and teacher. D. at the Paris Opéra and at the London King's Th. 1827–52, after which he became chief professor at the Opéra, where he taught Cerrito, Rosati, Bogdanova, and others. He was the brother of Geneviève and Anatole G.

Gothenburg. Up to 1920 there were only guest perfs. of individual dancers and cos. from elsewhere. But in 1920 the local Stora Teater became a full-time op. house with a b. co., attached, though it had mainly to appear in the operetta, mus. and op. prods. Individual b. perfs. were rare: G. Gé staged the second act of *Swan Lake* in 1943, also *Coppélia* and some Fokine bs. During the 1950s I. Cramér, Cullberg, and Massine were occasional guests, and Cullberg and Lifar mounted some works during the mid-1960s. But when C. Borg was appointed b. dir. 1967–70, he and U. Gadd turned the co., into a platform of intense ch. creativity, as well as inviting guest-choreographers such as Cullberg, Cramér, Gore, Lander, and Petit. Borg was succeeded by E.M. von Rosen in 1970, since

when the co., has progressed enormously; it first visited London in 1975. The repertory is now firmly based upon such audience favourites as *Napoli, La Sylphide, Swan Lake*, and Prokofiev's *Romeo and Juliet* (all staged by von Rosen) and a number of shorter works by von Rosen, Gadd, and Flindt. Gadd became Artistic Dir. in 1976.
BIBL.: various articles in *Dans* (1974/11).

Goubé, Paul (*b* Paris, 1912 *d* Paris, 30 Mar. 1979). Fr. dancer, choreographer, and teacher. Studied at the Paris Opéra School under Ricaux, joining its co., promoted premier danseur in 1933. Became chief d. and choreographer of the newly founded Bs. de Monte Carlo in 1941. Formed his own Bs. de la Méditerranée at Nice in 1955. His bs. included *Le Lien* (mus. C. Franck, 1952), *Ad Alta* (mus. Britten, 1953) and *Duo* (mus. Scriabin, 1954). Founded his Centre de Danse de Paris at the Salle Pleyel, Paris with himself and his wife Yvonne as chief teachers.

Gould, Diana (*b* London, 1913). Brit. dancer. Studied with Rambert and Egorova and became one of the most prominent soloists of the early Rambert years, after which she d. for a short while with de Basil's B. Russe and the Markova-Dolin co. Created roles in Ashton's *Leda and the Swan* (1928) and *Capriol Suite* (1930). Retired after her marriage to Yehudi Menuhin.

Gould, Morton (*b* Richmond Hill, 10 Dec. 1913). Amer. composer. Wrote the mus. for de Mille's *Fall River Legend* (1948) and E. Martinez' *Fiesta* (1957). His concert mus. was used in Robbins' *Interplay* (based upon his *American Concertette*, 1945), Georgi's *Human Variations* (1955), M. Goddard's *Symphonette* (based on his *Latin-American Symphonette*, 1963), and Balanchine's *Clarinade* (based upon his *Derivations for Clarinet and Jazz Band*, 1964—E. Feld used the same mus. for his *Jive*, 1973).

Gounod Symphony. Ballet in 4 movements; ch. Balanchine; mus. Gounod; set Horace Armistead; cost. Karinska. Prod. 8 Jan. 1958, New York City B., City Center, N.Y., with Maria Tallchief, d'Amboise. Set to Gounod's Symphony no. 1 in D Major, this is a plotless b. for 2 soloists and a corps, whose pattern of movement follows the score. Revived for Paris Opéra in 1959.
BIBL.: G. Balanchine, '*G.S.*' in *Balanchine's New Complete Stories of the Great Ballets* (Garden City, N.Y., 1968).

Govrin, Gloria (*b* Newark, N.J., 10 Sep. 1942). Amer. dancer. Studied at the Tarasoff School, with Danieli and School of Amer. B. Joined New York City B. in 1959; promoted soloist in 1963. Created roles in Balanchine's *Raymonda Variations* (1961), *A Midsummer Night's Dream* (1962), *Don Quixote* (1965), *Harlequinade* (1965), and *Brahms-Schoenberg-Quartet* (1966), and in Bolender's *Piano-Rag-Music* (1972).

Goyescas. There are various d. versions of this set of piano pieces (often orchestrated) by E. Granados; e.g. by Georgi (Hanover, 1935), T. Gsovsky (Berlin, 1940) and Tudor (B. Th., New York, 1940).

Graduation Ball. Ballet in 1 act; libr. and ch. Lichine; mus. J. Strauss, arr, Dorati; déc. Benois. Prod. 28 Feb. 1940, Original B. Russe, Th. Royal, Sydney, with Riabouchinska, Lichine, Orloff, Runanine. The b. is set in a Viennese boarding school, where the young girls put on a ball with the cadets of the city's military academy. There are several divertissements and a secret romance. Revived for many cos. incl. Royal Dan. B. in 1953 and London Festival B. in 1957. BBC TV prod. 1960.
BIBL.: C. W. Beaumont, '*G.B.*' in *Supplement to Complete Book of Ballets* (London, 1952).

Graeme, Joyce (*b* Leeds, 1918). Brit. dancer and teacher. Studied with Idzikowsky, Craske, Volkova, Rambert, and at Sadler's Wells School. Joined Sadler's Wells B. in 1937, d. with International B. 1941–3, and B. Rambert 1945–8, where she was much admired for her Myrtha. Dir. of Austral. National B. 1948–51. Has since worked primarily on short-term engagements, mostly as b. mistress or teacher, with B. Rambert, at La Scala, with London Festival B., Scapino B., and Scottish Th. B.

Graff, Jens (*b* Ger. 1942). Norwegian dancer and b. director. Studied at Oslo. Danced with Bordeaux B. and in London, as a principal with Hamburg B. 1965–8, Cullberg B. 1968–70, and Royal Swed. B. 1970–80, since when he has been artistic dir. of the Norwegian B.

Graham, Martha (*b* Allegheny, Pa., 11 May 1894). Amer. dancer, choreographer, teacher, and director of her co. Began studying at Denishawn in 1916; a member of the Denishawn Dancers until 1923. After appearing for a short while with the *Greenwich Village Follies*, started to teach at the Eastman School of Music in Rochester. Gave her first solo recital in New York in 1926. Founded the M.G. School of Contemporary D. in 1927, which subsequently became the foremost institute of its kind in the U.S. and the world. From her pupils she recruited the members of her co., with which she began to perform in 1929, later touring the States and, after 1950, Eur. (London début 1954) and the Near and Far East. She developed her own technique and became the greatest exponent of modern d. in U.S., creating 'dance plays', in which she explored the mythical landscapes of Eur. and U.S., always viewed from an unmistakable Amer. perspective. Her closest collaborators have been Louis Horst as her mus. advisor and Isamu Noguchi as her designer. The long list of eminent dancers who have emerged from her school includes Ethel Winter, Yuriko, Linda Hodes, Helen McGehee, Pearl Lang, Bertram Ross, Erick Hawkins, Merce Cunningham, and Robert Cohan. Many of her pieces have been filmed, but her most personal film is undoubtedly *A Dancer's World* (1957), in which she talks of her philosophy and demonstrates her system of teaching. Her complete oeuvre comprised in 1981 more than 160 different titles, incl. her best known works: *Primitive Mysteries* (mus. Horst, 1931), *American Document* (mus. Ray Green, 1938), *Every Soul Is a Circus* (Mus. Paul Nordoff, 1939), *El Penitente* (mus. Horst, 1940), *Letter to the World* (mus. Hunter Johnson, 1940), *Punch and Judy* (mus. Robert McBride, 1941), *Deaths and Entrances* (mus. Johnson, 1943), *Hérodiade* (mus. Hindemith, 1944), *Appalachian Spring* (mus. Copland, 1944), *Dark Meadow* (mus. Chávez, 1946), *Cave of the Heart* (mus. Barber, 1946), *Errand Into the Maze* (mus. Menotti 1947), *Night Journey* (mus. William Schuman, 1947), *Diversion of Angels* (mus. Dello Joio, 1948), *Judith* (mus. Schuman, 1950), *Canticle for Innocent Comedians* (mus. Thomas Ribbink, 1952), *Seraphic Dialogue* (mus. Dello Joio, 1955), *Clytemnestra* (mus. Halim El-Dabh, 1958), *Embattled Garden* (mus. Surinach, 1958), *Episodes: Part 1* (mus. Webern, 1959), *Acrobats of God* (mus. Surinach, 1960), *Alcestis* (mus. Vivian Fine, 1960), *Phaedra* (mus. Robert Starer, 1962), *Secular Games* (mus. Starer, 1962), *Circe* (mus. Hovhaness, 1963), *The Witch of Endor* (mus. Schuman, 1965), *Cortege of Eagles* (mus. Eugene Lester, 1967), *A Time of Snow* (mus. Dello Joio, 1968), *The Lady of the House of Sleep* (mus. Starer, 1968), *The Archaic Hours* (mus. Lester, 1969), *Mendicants of Evening* (mus. David Walker, 1973), *Myth of a Voyage* (mus. Hovhaness, 1973), *Holy Jungle* (mus. Starer), *Dream* (mus. M. Seter, for Batsheva D. Co., 1974), *Lucifer* (mus. El-Dabh, 1975), *Frescoes* (mus. S. Barber, 1978), *Acts' of Light* (mus. C. Nielsen, 1981). Author of *The Notebooks of M.G.* (New York, 1973). Among her many awards are the D. Magazine Award (1956), Capezio Award (1960), Aspen Award (1965), Hon. Dr. of Arts (Harvard Univ., 1966), Award of Merit (1970), the first S. H. Scripps American Dance Festival Award (1981).

BIBL.: L. Leatherman, *M.G.* (New York, 1961); D. McDonagh, *M.G.—A Biography* (New York, 1974).

Grahame, Shirley (*b* Teddington, 1936). Brit. dancer. Studied at Sadler's Wells B. School. Joined Sadler's Wells B. in 1954; promoted soloist in 1958 and principal d. of Touring Royal B. 1961–70. D. with London Festival B. 1970–1. Retired; now teaching in Britain.

Grahn, Lucile (*b* Copenhagen, 30 June 1819, *d* Munich, 4 Apr. 1907). Dan. dancer. Studied with Bournonville; appeared when only 7 years old. Made her official début in 1834; created Astrid in Bournonville's *Valdemar* in 1835 and became his first La Sylphide in 1836 and Quiteria in his *Don Quixote* in 1837. To escape Bournonville's attentions she left Copenhagen, made her Paris début in *Le Carnaval de Venise* in 1838, and d. for a short while in Hamburg. After her final break with Copenhagen she accepted a 3-year contract

for the Paris Opéra in 1839, where she competed with Elssler, enjoying particular success as La Sylphide. St. Petersburg saw her first in 1843. She then participated in the London creation of Perrot's *Pas de quatre* and the title-role in Perrot's *Eoline* in 1845, followed by *Catarina ou La Fille du bandit* in 1846. Her pro-Ger. sympathies in the Ger.-Dan. war of 1848–9 offended her many Dan. friends. After resigning as a d. in 1856, she continued as a b. mistress in Leipzig 1858–61, and at the Munich Court Op. 1869–75, where she ch. Wagner's *Tannhäuser* bacchanale and helped Wagner stage *Das Rheingold* and *Die Meistersinger von Nürnberg*. She left her fortune to the city of Munich, which named a street after her.

BIBL.: P. Migel, in *The Ballerinas* (New York, 1972).

Grand Ballet du Marquis de Cuevas. See *Cuevas, Marquis George de.*

Grand Pas. Designates a series of individual d.-numbers, consisting of an Entrée for ballerina, premier danseur, and corps—Adagio—several variations—Coda. Best known are the G.P. from *Paquita* and *Raymonda*.

Grand Pas Classique. Pas de deux; ch. V. Gsovsky; mus. Auber. Prod. 12 Nov. 1949, Th. des Champs-Elysées, Paris, with Chauviré and Skouratoff. A brilliant display of virtuosity, it is still occasionally performed by dancers all over the world.

Grands Ballets Canadiens, Les. The Montreal-based co., was orig. the Bs. Chiriaeff, which participated in the Montreal Festival of 1956 and started to perform under its new name in 1957. In the same year the assoc. Académie des G.B.C. was founded as its permanent school. Both were headed by Ludmilla Chiriaeff, with Fernand Nault as art. co-dir. and Dolin as art. adviser. The co., tours widely; it visited the U.S. for the first time in 1959 and Eur. in 1969. Its repertory consists of a choice of classics (Dolin's *Giselle* and *Pas de quatre*, Nault's *La Fille mal gardée* and *Nutcracker*) and the main body of creations contributed by Nault: his rock b. *Tommy* is its biggest success so far. Another speciality of the repertory is the complete Orff trilogy, consisting of *Carmina Burana* (ch. Nault), *Catulli Carmina* (ch. Butler), and *Trionfo di Afrodite* (ch. N. Walker). Macdonald was appointed art. dir. in 1974, with Nault as resident ch. Linda Stearns and Jeanne Renaud joint art. dirs. 1985.

BIBL.: O. Maynard, 'L. Chiriaeff and L.G.B.C.', *Dance Magazine* (1971/4).

Grand Trio. Ballet in 4 movements; ch. Van Manen; mus. Schubert; déc. Vroom. Prod. 31 May 1979, Vienna State Op., Th. an der Wien, Vienna, with G. Cech, G. Dirtl. Set to Schubert's piano trio in B. major, op. 99, the b. deals very lightheartedly with an affair between a society lady and an adult youth. Revived for Dutch National B. (1979).

Grand Union. The New York-based improvisatory d. co., formed in the autumn of 1970, derived from Yvonne Rainer's group. It performs irregularly, with differing sets of dancers. Some of its most active members have been Trisha Brown, Barbara Lloyd, David Gordon, and Steve Paxton. It has been called imaginist th., group therapy, conceptual d. etc. One of its statements defines it as 'a kind of human community. We provide a kind of collective psyche that individual—and very individualistic—artists can identify with. We are objects of curiosity and fascination. Every audience member experiences G.U. individually, just the way every G.U. member himself experiences the group individually. There is no easy description of who we are.'
BIBL.: R. Baker, 'G.U.: Taking a Chance on Dance', *Dance Magazine* (1973/10).

Grant, Alexander (*b* Wellington, 22 Feb, 1925). N.Z. d. and b. dir. Studied with Kathleen O'Brien and Jean Horne and Sadler's Wells B. School. Joined Sadler's Wells B. in 1946, having his first major success in Massine's *Mam'zelle Angot* in 1947. Apptd. soloist 1949, he developed into the co.'s most distinguished character d. creating a great number of roles—mostly in bs. by Ashton (*Cinderella*, 1948; *Daphnis and Chloe*, 1951; *Ondine*, 1958; *La Fille mal gardée*, 1960; *Persephone*, 1961; *The Dream*, 1964; *Jazz Calendar*, 1968; *Enigma Variations*, 1968; *A Month in the Country*, 1976). Another of his best roles was Petrushka. Dir. of the B. for All group of the Royal B. 1971–5; artistic dir. National B. of Canada, 1976–83. Joined London Festival B. as principal d. and coach, 1985. He is the brother of Garry G. C.B.E. (1965).
BIBL.: C. Swinson, 'A.G.' in *Six Dancers of Sadler's Wells* (London, 1956).

Grant, Carol (*b* Stockport, 1942). Brit. d. Studied with Doreen Bird and Royal B. School. D. with Gore's London B. in 1961, with London D. Th. in 1963, and with London Festival B. 1967–70. Has since appeared as a guest artist with various cos.

Grant, Garry (*b* Wellington, 1940). N.Z. d. The brother of Alexander G., he studied with Jean Horne, Trevor, and Neil, and Royal B. School. Joined Royal B. in 1962, promoted soloist in 1967.

Grant, Pauline (*b* Birmingham, 1915, *d* London, 22 Oct. 1986). Brit. d., ch., and b. mistress. Studied at Ginner-Mawer School and with Tudor and Volkova. Has ch. for musicals, ice shows, drama and op. prods, incl. Royal Shakespeare Co., Glyndebourne Op., Sadler's Wells Op., and Cov. Gdn. Op. Appointed b. mistress of Movement Group of Sadler's Wells Op. in 1969, now d. and movement consultant, Eng. National Op.

BIBL.: P. G., 'Movement in Opera', *Dance and Dancers* (1972/10).

Grantzeva, Tatiana (*b* St. Petersburg), Russ.-Amer.-Fr. dancer, b. mistress, and teacher. Studied with Egorova and Preobrajenska, later also with Pereyaslavec and Anderson-Ivantzova; d. with B. Russe de Monte Carlo 1938–44, then in U.S. with B. for Amer., at the New York Met. Op. House and Cincinnati Summer Op. Festival. Returned as b. mistress to B. Russe de Monte Carlo until 1962. Taught in New York and since 1965 in Paris. Guest b. mistress of the cos. of Béjart and Petit.
BIBL.: N. McLain Stoop, 'In Paris and Many Other Places It's G.', *Dance Magazine* (1971/7).

Grantzow, Adele (*b* Brunswick, 1 Jan. 1845, *d* Berlin, 7 June 1877). Ger. dancer. The daughter of the Brunswick b. master Gustav G., she studied with her father and in Paris with Mme Dominique and became première danseuse in Hanover, where Saint-Léon saw her. He later took her to Moscow as a première danseuse, where she made her début in his *Fiammetta*, with *La Fille mal gardée* and Diavolina as her other great successes. In Paris she made her début as Giselle in 1866, and the role became exclusively hers until the b. was taken out of the repertory in 1868. Saint-Léon created Naila in *La Source* for her, but she had to withdraw because of a foot injury–the first of many accidents which brought her career to a premature end. In St. Petersburg she created Saint-Léon's *Le Lys* (1869), and Petipa's *Camargo* (1872), but in Paris she again had to withdraw from rehearsals of *Coppélia*. She died after one of her legs had been amputated.
BIBL.: I. Guest, in *The Ballet of the Second Empire* (London, 1953).

Grass, Günter (*b* Danzig, 16 Oct. 1927). Ger. writer. He wrote the libr. for 3 bs., all first ch. by Luipart: *Les Cuisiniers méchants* (Aix-les-Bains, 1957), *Stoffreste* (Essen, 1959), and *Die Vogelscheuchen* (Ger. Op. Berlin, 1970).

Grater, Adrian (*b* London, 20 Nov. 1941). Brit. dancer. Studied with Kathleen Hughes and at Bush Davies and Royal B. School. Joined Touring Royal B. 1959, becoming soloist 1964, and moving to Cov. Gdn. Royal B. until 1976. Retired from dancing and is now asst. dir., Inst. of Choreology, since 1981. Married to the d. Sandra Conley.

Great Britain. The mime scenes of dramas and the court masques of the Tudors and Stuarts were the precursors of classical b. in G.B. John Weaver's first comic b. d'action *The Tavern Bilkers* was given in 1702, to be followed by his *The Loves of Mars and Venus* in 1717, the first serious b. d'action. During the 1730s Handel collaborated with Marie Sallé, and Noverre came over to work for David Garrick in 1754. Didelot's *Zéphyre et Flore* was first prod. in London in 1796, and Blasis published his *Code of Terpsichore* in London in 1828. During the 1840s romantic b. finally conquered London; Perrot staged *Ondine* in 1843, *La Esmeralda* in 1844, and *Pas de quatre* in 1845, all three for Lumley. During the last decades of the 19th century the main b. activity shifted to the London Alhambra (from 1871) and the London Empire (from 1884), both continuing to 1914; Adeline Genée became the great attraction of the Empire in 1897. When she went to the U.S. in 1908, her place was taken by Lydia Kyasht. The *Dancing Times* was founded in 1910, and in 1911 Diaghilev's Bs. Russes paid their first visit to Cov. Gdn. In 1912 Pavlova made London her home. Phyllis Bedells was the first Eng. prima ballerina at the Empire from 1914. Seraphina Astafieva began to teach in London in 1916, and she was followed by Marie Rambert in 1919, the year when Massine's *La Boutique fantasque* and *Le Tricorne* were first prod. in London. The Association of Operatic Dancing, founded in 1920, became the present Royal Academy of Dancing. Diaghilev prod. his *Sleeping Princess* in 1921 at the Alhambra, and the Cecchetti Society was founded in 1922. Another school was opened by Ninette de Valois in 1926—the year in which Frederick Ashton's first b., *A Tragedy of Fashion*, was performed by the Rambert Dancers at the Lyric Th., Hammersmith. The Camargo Society started to function in 1930, with Ashton's *Façade* and de Valois' *Job* (1931) as its major creations. The Vic-Wells B. gave its first performance in 1931. In 1933 Ashton prod. *Les Rendezvous* as his first b. for Sadler's Wells, and Massine provoked new discussions about the symphonic b. with his *Choreartium*. The Sadler's Wells B. embarked on its first West End season with de Valois' *The Rake's Progress* in 1935; during the 1930s they also staged the major classics. The second half of the 1930s was dominated by Tudor, who premiered *Lilac Garden* in 1936, *Dark Elegies* in 1937, and founded his London B. in 1938 (lasting until 1941). The war of 1939–45 inevitably caused a setback, but b. activities continued, though necessarily on a smaller scale. In 1940 Ashton's *Dante Sonata* and Andrée Howard's *La Fête étrange* were first performed, and exiled Pol. and other Brit. dancers formed the Anglo-Polish B. (lasting until 1947). Mona Inglesby founded her International B. in 1941 (lasting until 1953). The Sadler's Wells B. took up residence at Cov. Gdn. with a new prod. of *The Sleeping Beauty* in 1946, crowning its first season there with Ashton's *Symphonic Variations*, and The Sadler's Wells Th. B. was set up at the Sadler's Wells Th. The first visiting cos. after the war were the Bs. des Champs-Elysées and B. Th. of New York. In 1947 the Met B. appeared. The end of the 1940s brought the return of Markova and Dolin, who set up the London Festival B. in 1950, and the Sadler's Wells B. made its first visit to New York in 1949. *Ballet Imperial* (1950) was the first Brit. Balanchine prod., and in the same year the New York City B.

paid its first visit to London. John Cranko had his breakthrough during the early 1950s. London earned the title of World Capital of the Span. dancers. Apart from the continuing activity of the Sadler's Wells cos. London Festival B., and B. Rambert, the most discussed foreign visitors were Petit's Bs. de Paris, the Royal Dan. B., the Paris Opéra B., Charrat's Bs. de France, and Graham's co. The next Brit. ch. to emerge was Kenneth MacMillan in 1955. The following year the Sadler's Wells B. and Sadler's Wells Th. B. became the Royal B. The Bolshoi B.'s first visit in 1956 made a tremendous impression. Elizabeth West and Peter Darrell founded the Bristol-based Western Th. B. in 1957; this moved to Glasgow as the Scottish Th. B. in 1969 and became Scottish B. 1974. Earlier attempts by Marjory Middleton, Margaret Morris, and others to form a permanent co. in Scotland had failed, as had a would-be intern. co., formed by the Edinburgh Festival 1958. Ashton's *La Fille mal gardée* was one of the Royal B.'s greatest box-office hits in 1960, closely followed by MacMillan's then very daring *The Invitation* and by London's first impression of Béjart in his *Sacre du printemps*. In 1961 the Kirov co., paid its first visit to London, and Rudolf Nureyev made his first London appearance at Dame Margot Fonteyn's RAD Gala. Walter Gore's London B. was short-lived. On de Valois' retirement in 1963 Ashton took over the Royal B., and strengthened its repertory with Nijinska's *Les Biches* and *Les Noces* and some of Tudor's creations and revivals. Modern d. was finally established in London with the return visit of the Graham co., followed by the appearance of the Cunningham and Taylor cos. and the opening of the London Contemporary D. School. In 1965 Norman McDowell attempted to create an independent small touring co., in the London Dance Th., and Peter Brinson's B. for All embarked on its highly successful enterprise of presenting its b. plays. B. Rambert underwent a complete reorganization in 1966, from which it emerged as the leading London platform for contemporary b., with most of its formative works contributed by Glen Tetley. 1969 was an unusually busy year for non-establishment activities: the London Contemporary D. Th. embarked on its first season at The Place, complemented by the emergence of Geoff Moore's Moving Being, and Laverne Meyer's Northern D. Th. was set up in Manchester. Norman Morrice and John Chesworth were joined by Christopher Bruce as B. Rambert choreographer. At the Royal B. Macmillan succeeded Ashton as dir. (with Peter Wright as his assoc.) in 1970; he invited Robbins, Tetley, and Van Manen to be guest choreographers. Galina Samsova's and André Prokovsky's New London B. was established in 1972 as a chamber b. touring unit, lasting until 1979, when its touring function was largely subsumed by Harold King's London City B. The 1970s showed an increasing tendency to build up new provincial cos.: Moore's Moving Being moved to Cardiff in 1972 (it ceased its activities in 1976), and 1974 saw the start of the short-lived Welsh D. Th. followed by other attempts to build an audience for d. in the Principality. During the later 1970s, concern over a shortage of suitable large ths. for classical b. led to some rebuilding in the regions, proposals for the improvement and extension of Cov. Gdn., and experiments with a movable tent auditorium. The increasing no. of graduates from the London School of Contemporary D. led to a proliferation of small modern d. groups, several of them now based in regional centres. N. Morrice succeeded MacMillan as dir. of the Royal B., 1977, the latter becoming principal ch., and A. Dowell succeeded Morrice 1986.

BIBL.: J. Lawson, 'Charts for the History of Dance in Society and in the Theatre as Ballet', a series which started in *Dancing Times* (1969/4); P. Williams, 'The 21 Years That Changed British Ballet', a series which started in *Dance and Dancers* (1970/12).

Great Fugue. See *Grosse Fuge*.

Greatness of Creation, The. See Dance Symphony.

Greco, Jose (*b* Montorio-nei-Fretani, 23 Dec. 1919). Span.-Ital. d. Studied with Mme Veola in N.Y. and with Argentinita and La Quica. Argentinita's last partner 1943–5 and P. Lopez's partner 1946–8. Formed his own Span. group in 1949, with which he toured the world, first appearing in London in 1951. Has participated in many films and TV prods., becoming one of the most glamorous show personalities of Span. d. Awarded Span. Cross of the Knight of Civil Merit (1962). BIBL.: S. J. Cohen, 'T.G.' in *Twenty-five Years of American Dance* (New York, 1956).

Greek Dance Association. Founded in 1923 by *Ruby Ginner at Stratford-on-Avon for the teachers of her system of Revived Greek Dancing, to standardize its teaching and promote its use in schools. in 1951 it was incorporated in the Imperial Society of Teachers of Dancing.

Greening. Ballet in 1 act; ch. Tetley; mus. A. Nordheim; déc. Baylis. Prod. 29 Nov. 1975, Stuttgart, with Keil, Kage, Kimball, Boatwright. The b. deals with people waiting on the brink of something they are unable to define, encountering emotional storms they don't really understand. Revived for London Festival B. (1978), Royal Dan. B. (1979), and D. Th. of Harlem (1981).

Green Table, The (orig. Ger. title: *Der grüne Tisch*). A d. of death in 8 scenes; libr. and ch. Jooss; mus. Cohen; déc. Heckroth. Prod. 3 July 1932, Folkwang Tanzbühne, Th. des Champs-Elysées, Paris, with Jooss, Uthoff, Kahl, Czobel. Starting and ending with the fruitless discussions of diplomats around the green table, the b. shows the horrors of war as they affect ordinary people.

First prize at the first ch. competition organized by Rolf de Maré and Les Archives Internationales de la Danse in Paris. The prod. became the trademark of the Bs. Jooss when they had to leave Ger. in 1933. Jooss has revived it time and again for his various cos., and also staged it for other cos. incl. Joffrey B. (1967) and Northern D. Th. (1973). Cologne TV prod. 1963.

BIBL.: A. V. Coton, in *The New Ballet* (London, 1946).

Gregory, Cynthia (*b* Los Angeles, 8 July 1946). Amer. dancer. Studied with Maracci, Panaieff, and Rosselat. Joined San Francisco B. in 1961 and Amer. B. Th. as principal d. in 1965, dancing the ballerina roles and creating parts in Smuin's *The Eternal Idol* (1970), Nahat's *Brahms Quintet* (1970), Ailey's *The River* (1971), and title-role in Nureyev's Amer. B. Th. prod. of *Raymonda* (1975). D. Magazine Award (1975). Has at various times since 1975 stopped d.—only to return a little later to d. Was married to the d. Terry Orr.

BIBL.: M. Hodgson, 'C.G. In Search of Siegfried', *Dance News* (1975/3); O. Maynard, 'Conversations with C.G.', *Dance Magazine* (1975/4). W. Terry, *Ballet News* (1979/5).

Gregory, Jill (*b* Bristol, 10 Oct. 1918). Brit. dancer and b. mistress. Studied with de Valois, Sergeyev, Idzikowsky, Egorova, and Craske. Joined Vic-Wells B. in 1934, eventually appointed soloist and b. mistress in 1953—a post she still holds today with the Royal B.

Gregory, John (*b* Norwich, 15 Apr. 1914). Brit. dancer, teacher, and b. director. Studied with Schwezoff, N. Legat, and Idzikowsky. D. with Anglo-Polish B., Jay Pomeroy's Russian B., Bs. Jooss, and de Basil's Original B. Russe. Opened a school with his wife Barbara Vernon in 1949. Founded Federation of Russ. Classical B. in 1950. Formed Harlequin B. in 1959 as a small troupe to bring b. to places where normal cos. cannot perform. Has contributed many b. articles to various magazines. Now teaching at Accademia Filarmonica in Messina, Sicily.

Grey, Beryl (orig B. Groom; *b* Highgate, 11 June 1927). Brit. dancer and b. director. Studied with Madeline Sharp, Audrey de Vos, and Sadler's Wells School. Joined Sadler's Wells B. as its youngest member in 1941, dancing her first ballerina role in 1942 (Odette-Odile). Created roles in Ashton's *The Quest* (1943), *Les Sirènes* (1946), *Cinderella* (1948), *Homage to the Queen* (1953), and *Birthday Offering* (1956), de Valois' *Promenade* (1943) and Massine's *Donald of the Burthens* (1951). Made the first stereoscopic b. film, *Black Swan*, in 1952. Resigned from Royal B. in 1957 to pursue a career as a freelance ballerina, travelling as far afield as Tiflis and Peking. Appointed Dir.-General of Arts Educational Trust b. school in 1966. Artistic Dir. of London Festival B. 1968–1979. Author of *Red Curtain Up* (1958), *Through the Bamboo Curtain*

(1965). Hon. Doctor of Music, Leicester Univ. (1970), Doctor of Lit. (London, 1974). C.B.E. (1973).

BIBL.: H. Fisher, *B.G.* (London, 1955).

Greyling, Eduard (*b* Germiston, Transvaal, 1948). S. Afr. dancer. Studied with Jennifer Louw and at Univ. of Cape Town B. School. Joined CAPAB B. co. 1967. D. with Dutch National B. 1974–5, before returning to CAPAB, of which he is now one of the leading soloists, often appearing together with Phyllis Spira, with whom he stars in the SABC TV film *The Dancer* (1978). Has also appeared with M. Gielgud's *Steps, Notes and Squeaks* prod.

Gribov, Alexander Ivanovich (*b* Leningrad, 17 June 1934). Sov. dancer. Studied at Leningrad Ch. School, graduating in 1953. Joined the Kirov B., creating roles in Grigorovich's *The Stone Flower* (1957) and *Legend of Love* (1961), and Belsky's *Coast of Hope* (1959).

Gridin, Anatoli Vasilyevich (*b* Novosibirsk, 20 Oct. 1929). Sov. dancer. Studied at Leningrad Ch. School, graduating in 1952. Joined the Kirov B., becoming one of its best character dancers. Created roles in Grigorovich's *The Stone Flower* (1957) and *Legend of Love* (1961), and in Sergeyev's *The Path of Thunder* (1958). Married to the d. Irina Bashenova.

Grieg, Edvard Hagerup (*b* Bergen, 15 June 1843, *d* there, 4 Sep. 1907). Norwegian composer. Wrote no b. mus., but his concert mus. has often been used for b. purposes, including his piano concerto (Charrat, 1951; V. Lambrinos, 1953), *Peer Gynt* Suite (Lopokov in *Snow Maiden*, 1927; Orlikowsky in *P.G.*, 1956), and *Holberg Suite* (Cranko, 1967; Mitchell, 1970). A. Howard used various pieces of his for her *Twelfth Night* (1942).

Grieg Concerto. Ballet in 1 act (pas de deux); ch. Charrat; mus. Grieg. Prod. 19 Mar. 1951, Palais de Chaillot, Paris, with Charrat and Perrault. Set to Grieg's piano concerto, the b. reflects the changing moods of the mus.

Grigoriev, Serge Leonidovich (*b* Tichvin, 5 Oct. 1883, *d* London, 28 June 1968). Russ. d. and b. master. Studied at St. Petersburg Imperial B. School, graduating in 1900. Became a member of the Maryinsky Th. Diaghilev appointed him b. master for his Paris season in 1909, and he was Diaghilev's régisseur for the next 20 years. Among his many role creations were Shah Shariar in Fokine's *Scheherazade* (1910) and the Russian Merchant in Massine's *La Boutique fantasque* (1919). After Diaghilev's death he joined de Basil's B. Russe de Monte Carlo, with his wife, the d. Lubov Tchernicheva—and they remained with the co., until it disbanded in 1952. Mounted Fokine's *Firebird* for Sadler's Wells B. in 1954 and *Petrushka* in 1957. Author of *The Diaghilev Ballet* (London, 1953).

Grigorieva, Tamara (*b* Petrograd, 1918). Russ.-Argent. dancer, choreographer, and b. mistress. Studied with Preobrajenska, Balanchine, Vilzak, Tchernicheva, Kniaseff, and Sacharov. Joined Les Bs. 1933 and de Basil's B. Russe de Monte Carlo, promoted ballerina in 1938. Since 1944 she has worked in South Amer. as b. mistress in Montevideo and of the Buenos Aires Teatro Colón (1947–8, 1956–7, and since 1961).

Grigorova, Romayne (orig. R. Austin; b. Kenilworth, 1926). Brit. dancer and b. mistress. Studied with Volkova, de Valois, Goncharov, and A. Philips. D. with B. Rambert (1946), Metropolitan B. (1947), and Sadler's Wells Th. B. (1951–5). B. mistress for the film *Can-Can* in 1955. B. mistress of the op. bs. at Cov. Gdn. Op., since 1957.

Grigorovich, Yuri Nikolaievich (*b* Leningrad, 2 Jan. 1927). Sov. dancer, choreographer, and b. director. Studied at Leningrad Ch. School, graduating in 1946. Joined the Kirov B., where he excelled in demi-caractère parts. After some smaller works for students, ch. Prokofiev's *The Stone Flower* for the Kirov B. in 1957, which became such a success that he had to remount it for the Moscow Bolshoi B. in 1959. He followed this with Melikov's *Legend of Love* for the Kirov B. in 1961, after which he was appointed b. master in 1962. In 1964 he became chief ch. and artistic dir. of the Bolshoi B. His first prod. there was *Sleeping Beauty* in 1965, followed by *Nutcracker* in 1966, Khachaturian's *Spartacus* in 1968, *Swan Lake* in 1969, a new version of *Sleeping Beauty* in 1973, *Ivan the Terrible* (mus. Prokofiev) in 1975), *Angara* (mus. Andrei Eshpai) in 1976, and *Romeo and Juliet* (mus. Prokofiev) in 1979. He is a brilliant classicist and an immensely gifted producer, under whose skilled guidance the Bolshoi B. has shed its former athletic muscularity for a much slimmer and more elegant look. People's Artist of the R.S.F.S.R. (1966), Lenin Prize (1970). Married to the d. Nathalia Bessmertnova.

BIBL.: V. Vanslov, *Baleti Grigorovicha i problemi choreografi* (Moscow, 1971—in Russ.); interview with Y.G., *Dance and Dancers* (1966/9 and 1974/8).

Grisi, Carlotta (*b* Visinada, 28 June 1819, *d* St. Jean, Switzerland, 20 May 1899). Ital. dancer. Studied with Guillet in Milan, entering the corps of La Scala in 1829, though not yet completely decided whether she should concentrate on a career as a d. or a singer. While touring Italy she met Perrot in Naples in 1833, becoming his pupil and mistress (they never married though for some time she called herself Mme Perrot). She d. in Paris in 1836 and 1837, attracting little attention, but was more favourably received when she reappeared with Perrot in the character dances of the op. *Zingaro* in 1840. She got her wished-for Opéra contract in 1841, and created the b. divertissement in Donizetti's op. *La Favorite*

with L. Petipa, and the title role in Coralli-Perrot's *Giselle* in the summer of the same year. During the following years she created the ballerina roles in Albert's *La jolie fille de Gand* (1842), Coralli's *La Péri* (1843), Perrot's *La Esmeralda* (1844), *Pas de quatre* (1845) and *La Filleule de fées* (1849), and Mazilier's *Le Diable à quatre* (1845), *Paquita* (1846), and *Grisélidis* (1848). Made her London début in 1836, and returned there regularly between 1842 and 1851, also appearing repeatedly in Vienna, Milan, Munich, and St. Petersburg. She retired in 1853 and settled in Switzerland with her daughter. One of the greatest ballerinas of the romantic b. Gautier, whom she had met in 1841, who wrote the *Giselle* libr. for her, and whose life-long inspiration and eternal love she was (though she preferred L. Petipa), declared that 'she is possessed of a strength, lightness, suppleness, and originality which at once places her between Elssler and Taglioni'.
BIBL.: P. Migel, 'C.G.' in *The Ballerinas* (New York, 1972).

Grjebina, Irina (*b* St. Petersburg, 9 Sep. 1909). Russ.-Fr. dancer, choreographer, b. director, and teacher. The daughter of an art publisher, she studied with Ossipovna, Preobrajenska, N. Legat, and Nijinska. Started to d. at Geneva Opéra in 1926, then with Opéra Russe de Paris 1929–36. Opened the Ecole Chorégraphique in Paris with her sister Lya G., from which the B. Russe I.G. developed, for which she has ch. extensively and with which she has toured in Fr. and abroad. A specialist in Russ. character dances, she has often been invited to teach in other countries and collaborated in many th. prods. and films. Prix de la meilleur compagnie privée en France (1966).

Grosse Fuge. Ballet in 1 act; ch. and cost. Van Manen; mus. Beethoven; set Jean Paul Vroom. Prod. 8 Apr. 1971, Netherlands D. Th., Scheveningen, with Sarstädt, Benoit, Venema, Vervenne, Westerdijk, Christe, Waterbolk, Koning. Set to an orchestrated version of Beethoven's op. 133 and the cavatina from his string quartet op. 130, the b. explores the contrasting female-male relationships between 4 couples, finally resolving them in mutual harmony and equality. Revived for Royal B. New Group in 1972. TV prod. by Granada in 1974. An earlier version by J. Erdman in *Song of the Turning World* (New York, 1953).
BIBL.: P. Brinson and C. Crisp, in *Ballet & Dance* (Newton Abbot, 1980).

Grossman, Daniel Williams (*b* Daniel Williams, San Francisco, 1943). Amer. dancer, teacher, choreographer, and director. Studied with W. Lathrop, M. O'Donnell, G. Shurr, N. Fonaroff, P. Taylor *et al.* D. with P. Taylor co., 1963–73. Then joined Toronto D. Th., of which he became d. teacher, ch. and dir. Now has his own Danny Grossman D. Co.

Grossstadt 1926. See *Big City, The.*

Grossvatertanz (Grandfather Dance). A 17th century Ger. d. performed to the melody 'Und als der Grossvater die Grossmutter nahm' to conclude a wedding party in polonaise style through the whole house. It can be found in Schumann's *Papillons* and the first act of Tchaikovsky's *Nutcracker.*

Gruca, Witold (*b* Krakow, 15 Aug. 1928). Pol. dancer and choreographer. Studied at Warsaw State B. School of the Great Th. of Op. and B. Member of Poznań Op. B. 1950–2, then Warsaw Great Th. of Op. and B., where he eventually became principal d. and ch. Has ch. many bs., and for op., plays, films, and TV.

Grüne Tisch, Der. See *Green Table, The.*

Gsovsky, Tatjana (née T. Issatchenko; b. Moscow, 18 Mar. 1901). Russ.-Ger. b. mistress, choreographer, and teacher. The daughter of an actress, she was educated in Petrograd; studied at the Duncan studio, later also with Novikov, Matyatin, Kirsanova, Preobrajenska, and at Hellerau. Appointed b. mistress in Krasnodar after the October Revolution, where she met and married the d. and teacher Victor Gsovsky. Together they went to Berlin, where they opened a school in 1928. As a ch. she worked first in Ger. varietés and with various ths.; she was in charge of the first prods. of Orff's *Catulli Carmina* in Leipzig in 1943, and von Einem's *Prinzessin Turandot* in Dresden in 1944. Appointed b. mistress at East Berlin State Op. 1945–52, Buenos Aires Teatro Colón 1952–3, West Berlin Municipal Op. 1954–66 (from 1961 the Ger. Op. Berlin), and also the Frankfurt Op. 1959–66. Founder of the Berlin B. in 1955, with which she undertook many tours abroad. Has been one of the most influential teachers of the Ger. post-war generation of dancers. In her various positions she ch. a great number of bs., incl. the first prods. of L. Spies' *Don Quixote* (Berlin, 1949), Henze's *Der Idiot* (Berlin, 1952) Orff's *Trionfo di Afrodite* (Milan, 1953), Egk's *Die chinesische Nachtigall* (Munich, 1953), Nono's *Der rote Mantel* (Berlin, 1954), Sauguet's *Die Kameliendame* (Berlin, 1957), Klebe's *Menagerie* (Berlin, 1958), Gassmann's *Paean* (Berlin, 1960), and Blacher's *Tristan* (Berlin, 1965), as well as the first Ger. prods. of Prokofiev's *Romeo and Juliet* (1948), Blacher's *The Moor of Venice* (1956), and Weill's *The Seven Deadly Sins* (1960). She is one of the great personalities of Ger. b. history. Author of *Ballett in Deutschland* (with S. Enkelmann, Berlin, 1954).
BIBL.: K. Geitel, 'Hommage à T.G.' in *Ballett 1966* (Velber, 1966).

Gsovsky, Victor (*b* St. Petersburg, 12 Jan. 1902, *d* Hamburg, 14 Mar. 1974). Russ. dancer, teacher, choreographer, and b. master. Studied with Eugenie Sokolova; started to teach at a very early age. Married his colleague Tatjana Issatchenko in Krasnodar, moving with her to Berlin in 1924, where he was appointed b. master at the State

Op. in 1925 and opened a school in 1928. Ch. for the UFA film co. 1930–33 and b. master of Markova-Dolin co., from 1937. Started to teach in Paris in 1938; appointed b. master at the Opéra in 1945, for the Bs. des Champs-Elysées 1946–7 and again in 1948, after a spell with Met. B. B. dir. of the Munich State Op. 1950–2, then worked mainly as a private teacher in Paris. B. master in Düsseldorf 1964–7 and at the Hamburg State Op. 1967–73. As a ch. he was in charge of the first post-war prod. of La Sylphide (Bs. de Champs-Elysées, 1945) and of the first prods. of Blacher's Hamlet (Munich, 1950) and Auric's Chemin de la lumière (Munich, 1952), but his best known work is the Grand Pas Classique (mus. Auber, 1949). He was one of the most internationally respected teachers of his generation.

BIBL.: Y. Chauviré, 'Hommage à V.G.', Les Saisons de la danse (1974/5).

Guerra, Antonio (b Naples, 30 Dec. 1810, d Neuwaldegg, nr. Vienna, 20 July 1846). Ital. dancer, choreographer, and b. master. Studied in Naples with Pietro Hus. D. at the San Carlo Th. in a Duport prod. of La Fille mal gardée in 1816, acquiring the nickname 'le petit Duport'. Ch. his first bs. in Vienna (1826–7) and Naples; d. as Taglioni's partner in La Sylphide in Paris in 1836. Ch. Les Mohicans (mus. Adam) in Paris in 1837; principal d. and b. master at London's Her Majesty's Th. 1838–41, where he was Elssler's partner in his version of La Gitana in 1839, and ch. Le Lac des Fées for Cerrito in 1840. B. master of the Vienna Court Op. 1841–6.

Guerra, Nicola (b Naples, 2 May 1865, d Cernobbio, 5 Feb. 1942). Ital. dancer, choreographer, and b. master. Studied at the school of the San Carlo Th., appointed principal d. of La Scala in 1879. D. in St. Petersburg, Paris, London, and New York. Principal d. of the Vienna Court Op. 1896–1902. B. master of the Budapest Op. 1902–15, where he created 19 bs. Ch. Rameau's Castor et Pollux for Paris Opéra in 1918, F. Schmitt's La Tragédie de Salomé for Rubinstein in 1919, and P. Paray's Artémis troublée in 1922. Dir. of Paris Opéra B. School 1927–9. Continued to work in Milan, Rome, and Paris, until he retired to Cernobbio.

BIBL.: entry 'G., N.' in Enciclopedia dello spettacolo.

Guest, Ivor (b Chislehurst, 14 Apr. 1920). Brit. b. historian. Author of a great number of books dealing with the history of d. in the 18th and particularly the 19th century, incl. The Ballet of the Second Empire 1858–70 (London, 1953), The Romantic Ballet in England (London, 1954), The Ballet of the Second Empire 1847–58 (London, 1955), Fanny Cerrito (London, 1956), Victorian Ballet Girl (Clara Webster, London, 1957), Adeline Genée (London, 1958), The Alhambra Ballet (New York, 1959), La Fille mal gardée (editor, London, 1960), The Dancer's Heritage (London, 1960), The Empire Ballet (London, 1962), The Romantic Ballet

in Paris (London, 1966), Two Coppélias (London, 1970), Fanny Elssler London, 1970), and Le Ballet de l'Opéra de Paris (Paris, 1976). Contributor to many publications. Editorial Adviser of The Dancing Times since 1963. Member of the Executive Committee of the Royal Academy of Dancing since 1965 and Chairman since 1969. A solicitor by profession; he is married to the d. notator Ann Hutchinson.

Guglielmo Ebreo. See Ebreo, Guglielmo.

Guimard, Marie-Madeleine (baptized Paris, 27 Dec. 1743, d there, 4 May 1816). Fr. dancer. Joined the corps of the Comédie Française when only 15 years old and the Opéra in 1763; appointed première danseuse noble in 1763. She appeared in many bs. by Noverre and Gardel, usually as a naïve shepherdess—in marked contrast to her notorious love-life with such prominent men as Jean Benjamin de la Borde and the Prince de Soubise. She was so slim that she was called 'le squelette des grâces'. A typical terre à terre d. she was much admired for her expressive features. In 1772 she opened her Paris villa at the Chaussée d'Antin, with its own small th., called the Temple of Terpsichore, painted by Fragonard, where startlingly obscene bs. and plays were staged. She married the ex-d. and poet Jean-Etienne Despréaux in 1789, and retired into private life.

BIBL.: P. Migel, 'M.-M.G.' in The Ballerinas (New York, 1972).

Guizerix, Jean (b Paris, 27 Oct, 1945). Fr. dancer. Studied with Denise Bazet and Marguerite Guillaumin. Joined the corps of the Opéra in 1964, appointed premier danseur in 1971 and étoile in 1972. Created roles in bs. by Schmucki, Frantz, Garnier, and in Butler's Intégrales and Amériques, Cunningham's Un jour ou deux (all 1973), Macdonald's Variations on a Simple Theme, Tetley's Tristan (1974), and Nureyev's Manfred (1979). Married to the d. Wilfride Piollet.

BIBL.: A.-P. Hersin, 'Profil de J.G.', Les Saisons de la danse (1970/11) and J.G. complete list, Les Saisons de la danse (1979/5).

Gulbenkian Ballet (Grupo Gulbenkian de Bailado). The Portuguese Gulbenkian Foundation established its own b. co., in Lisbon in 1965, where it has its own studios and th. in the institute's luxurious building, opened in 1970. Founding b. master was W. Gore. From 1970–5 the co. was run by Sparemblek on a primarily modern basis; its repertory included bs. by Butler, Lubovitch, Trincheiras, Sparemblek, and Van Manen. Was run by a collective directorate 1975–7, J. Salavisa art. dir. since. Carlos Trincheiras is chief ch. London début 1973.

Guliaiev, Vadim Nicolaievich (b Lomonossov, 2 May 1947). Sov. dancer. Studied at Leningrad Ch. School 1957–66, joining the Kirov B. upon graduation; dances the premier danseur roles of the standard repertory. Silver Medal (Varna, 1968). Married to the d. Natalia Bolshakova.

Guns and Castanets. Ballet in 1 act; libr. R. Page; ch. Page and B. Stone; mus. Bizet; sets Clive Rickabaugh, cost. John Pratt. Prod. 1 Mar. 1939, Page-Stone B., Great Northern Th., Chicago, with Page, Stone, Camryn. This is an updated *Carmen* version, using poems by García Lorca, set against the background of the Span. civil war. There is a film of the original prod.

Gusev, Pyotr Andreievich (*b* St. Petersburg, 29 Dec. 1904). Sov. dancer, teacher, and b. master. Studied with V. Ponomarev and A. Shiriaev, graduating in 1922. Member of GATOB until 1934. Often appeared with his partner Olga Mungalova in stunningly acrobatic pas de deux. Joined the Moscow Bolshoi School as a teacher in 1935; dir. 1937–40 and in 1950. In between he returned to the Kirov B. as a d. 1945–51. Was b. master of the Moscow Stanislavsky and Nemirovich-Danchenko Music Th. at various times between 1935 and 1957. Has often been sent abroad as a teacher and b. master (Peking 1957–60). Dir. of the Maly B. 1960–1. Retired in 1961, but continues to work as a ch. and b. master. Prod. *Raymonda* for Novosibirsk in 1964 and *Sleeping Beauty* for Budapest in 1967. Now head of the ch. faculty of the Leningrad Conservatory.

Gymnopédies. 3 piano pieces by Satie, comp. in 1888, later orchestrated by Debussy and A. Roland-Manuel. They have often been used for b. purposes (occasionally combined with Satie's *Trois*

Gnossiennes of 1890), including Ashton's *Monotones* (Royal B., 1965) and Van Manen's *Squares* (Netherlands Dance Th., 1969).

Gypsy, La. Ballet in 3 acts and 5 scenes; libr. H. Vernoy de Saint-Georges and Mazilier; ch. Mazilier; mus. Benoist, Thomas, and Marliani; sets Philastre and Cambon; cost. Paul Lormier. Prod. 28 Jan. 1839, Opéra, Paris, with Elssler, Mazilier. Based upon Cervantes' *Novelas Exemplares*, the b. is about Sarah, the daughter of a Scottish Lord, who is abducted from the castle of her parents and grows up among the gypsies. She falls in love with the refugee Stenio, who finally reveals that he is of noble birth, whereupon Sarah's rival shoots him, only to be stabbed by Sarah in an act of true gypsy revenge. This is the b. in which Elssler d. her famous Cracovienne, enjoying a popularity similar to that of her earlier Cachucha. It must not be confused, however, with F. Taglioni's *La Gitana*, in which M. Taglioni appeared simultaneously in St. Petersburg. The immense popularity of *L.G.* inspired W. Balfe to compose his op. *The Bohemian Girl* (1843).

BIBL.: C. W. Beaumont, '*L.G.*' in *Complete Book of Ballets* (London, 1951).

Gyrowetz, Adalbert (*b* Budweis, 19 Feb. 1763, *d* Vienna, 19 Mar. 1850). Bohemian composer. Compositeur and kapellmeister of the Vienna Court Th. 1804–31; he wrote the mus. for about 40 bs., incl. Aumer's *Der flatterhafte Page oder Figaros Hochzeit* (1819) and F. Taglioni's *Das Schweizer Milchmädchen* (1821).

H

Haakon, Paul (*b* Denmark, 1914). Dan.-Amer. dancer and b. master. Studied at Royal Dan. B. School and in the U.S. with Fokine, Mordkin, and School of Amer. B. D. in the co., of Pavlova, as premier danseur with Amer. B. in 1935, on Broadway, and in night-clubs. Became b. master and instructor of the J. Greco Span. B. in the 1960s.

Haas, Olga de (*b* Amsterdam, 9 Sep. 1944, *d* Amsterdam, 1 Sep. 1978) Dutch dancer. Studied with Gaskell, later also with E. Tsikvaidze, Belsky, and Casenave. Joined Dutch National B. in 1962, eventually becoming one of its principal dancers. BIBL.: van Dantzig, *O.d.H.Een Herinnering* (Zutphen, 1981).

Habanera. A slow Cuban d. in simple duple time and dotted rhythm, not unlike the Tango. Possibly of Afr. origin, it came to Spain via Havana during the late 19th century, where it became very popular. One of the most famous examples is Yradier's *La Paloma*: it also appears in Bizet's *Carmen*, Ravel's *L'heure espagnole*, and in the works of Chabrier.

Häger, Bengt (*b* Malmö, 27 Apr. 1916). Swed. museum director. Educated Univ. of Stockholm. Worked as impresario or touring manager for various d. cos. President of Swed. D. Association 1944–64. General Secretary of Parisian Les Archives internationales de la danse 1947–9. Dir. of the Stockholm D. Museum since 1952. Founder-dir. of the Swed. State D. School 1963–71. D. adviser for various Swed. and UNESCO boards and for Swed. TV. President of the Carina Ari Foundation and general secretary and treasurer of the C. Ari Memorial Foundation. Author of various books and TV prods. on d. Hon. Member Association des écrivains et critiques de la danse (Paris, 1947); C. Ari Gold Medal (1964). Married to the d. Lilavati.

Häggbom, Nils Åke (*b* Stockholm, 20 Apr. 1942). Swed. dancer. Studied at Royal Swed. B. School; joined Royal Swed. B. in 1959, appointed soloist in 1966. Guest d. with The First Chamber D. Co., in 1971.

Hague, The. Though a number of Fr. bs. de cour were performed here during the reign of William III of Orange in the late 1690s, and though there was occasionally a Fr. orientated co., appearing at the Fr. Th. during the 18th century, the development of Dutch b. took place in Amsterdam rather than in The Hague Pavlova died here at the Hotel des Indes in 1931. Schwezoff established the first important b. school in 1933, which produced the co., with which he toured during the next few years. It was, however, only after the Second World War that The Hague showed any b. initiative of its own, when it became the home of the newly established Netherlands B. in 1954, and even more so when the Netherlands D. Th. took up residence here in 1959; the co., performs regularly at the Royal Th. and at the Circus Th. nearby in Scheveningen.

Haieff, Alexei (*b* Blagovestshensk, 25 Aug. 1914). Russ.-Amer. composer. Wrote the bs. *Zandilda and her Entourage* (ch. M. Cunningham, 1946) and *Beauty and the Beast* in 1947 (which apparently never had a stage prod.). Balanchine used his Divertimento for Small Orchestra in *Divertimento* (1947).

Haigen, Kevin (*b* K. Higgenbotham, Miami, Fla., 6 Nov. 1954). Amer. d. Studied at Sch. of Amer. B. and Amer. B. Th. Sch. D. with Amer. B. Th., Stuttgart B. and as a soloist with Hamburg B. 1976–83. Created Joseph in Neumeier's *Legend of Joseph* (Vienna, 1977) and Puck in his *Midsummer Night's Dream* (1977). D. and teacher, B. de M.C., 1984–5; London Fest. Ballet, 1986. BIBL.: A. Barzel, 'Prince Désiré in Blue Jeans', *Dance Magazine* (1978/11).

Haig, Robin (*b* Perth, 1937). Austral. dancer. Studied with Linley Wilson. Joined Austral. b. in 1955. Further studies at Sadler's Wells B. School. Joined Royal B. in 1957, Gore's London B. in 1961; principal with Western Th. B. 1963–9, Scottish B. 1968–70. Also concert tours with Fonteyn. Soloist of Austral. B. 1973–5; rejoined Scottish B. as d. and asst. to the dir. in 1975-6. Created roles in Darrell's *Mods and Rockers* (1963), *Francesca*, and *Mary, Queen of Scots* (1976), and J. Carter's *Cage of God* (1967). Returned to Australia, 1976.

Halby, Flemming (*b* Copenhagen, 16 Nov. 1940). Dan. dancer. Studied at Royal Dan. B. School. Joined Royal Dan. B., and became soloist in 1966. Now also a soloist of the Amer. First Chamber D. Co.

Hall, Fernau (*b* Victoria, 1915). Can. dancer and critic. Studied with Nesta Brooking, Craske, Volkova, Sokolova, H. Turner, Rosandro, and Ernest Berk. D. with many cos., including Sakuntala, D. Th., and B. Russe de Col. de Basil. Became one of the pioneers of school TV in U.K. Was in charge of many TV d. prods. at Associated Rediffusion and Thames. Started to write on d. for *Dancing Times* in 1937. Chief critic of *Ballet*

Today 1958–70. B. critic of *Daily Telegraph* since 1969. Author of *Ballet* (London, 1948), *Modern English Ballet* (London, 1950), *An Anatomy of Ballet* (London, 1953), *The World of Ballet and Dance* (London, 1972).

Halprin, Anna (*née* A. Shumann, *b* Winnetka, Ill., 13 July 1920). Amer. dancer, choreographer, and teacher. Studied with Margaret H'Doubler and at Harvard School of Design. D. with Humphrey and Weidman in *Sing Out Sweet Land* in 1945. Established a studio with Walland Lathrop in San Francisco, where she taught 1948–55. Founded Dancer's Workshop in 1955, collaborating with painters, architects, musicians, teachers, and dancers. Started her Summer Workshops in 1959, appearing with a group incl. Terry Riley, LaMonte Young, Y. Rainer, and M. Monk in *Birds of America* and *Flowerburger*. From 1963 she drew increasing attention at Eur. avant-garde festivals (Venice, Rome, Zagreb). Premiered her *Parades and Changes* in 1965. New York début in 1967, when the police intervened because of a nude scene. Established a Summer Workshop for architects in 1969 and a Multi-Racial Communal Workshop with her husband, Lawrence H., San Francisco city planning architect. Premiered her *BO'ULU BO'ICI BO'EE* at the Connecticut Amer. Festival of D. in 1971 and in New York, in the same year, *Animal Ritual* and *Initiations and Transformations*. She is one of the most active pioneers of dance happenings.

BIBL.: Interview with A. H., *Dance and Dancers* (1970/3); M. B. Siegel, in *At the Vanishing Point* (New York, 1972); B. Hartman, 'Talking with A.H.', *Dance Scope* (vol. 12, no.1); C. Egan, 'Honors for West Coast Innovator A.H.' (interview), *Dance Magazine* (1980/7).

Halte de Cavalerie. Ballet in 1 act; libr. and ch. M. Petipa; mus. Johann Arnsheimer; set Levogt; cost. Ponomarev. Prod. 2 Feb. 1896, Maryinsky Th., St. Petersburg, with Legnani, Gerdt. Set in an Austrian village, the b. is about Marie, daughter of the most important man in the village, who loves the peasant Pierre, and the amorous pursuits and entanglements when a troop of hussars and lancers appears.

BIBL.: C. W. Beaumont, 'H.d.c.' in *Complete Book of Ballets* (London, 1951).

Hamburg. There has been some b. activity at the op. house from its very beginnings in the 17th century, and various visiting cos. During the late 1830s and 1840s ballerinas such as Taglioni, Grahn, Cerrito, Grisi, and Elssler appeared, the last enjoying such popularity that she made H. her home for several years after her retirement. K. Lanner ch. her first bs. here in the early 1880s. At the turn of the century few bs. other than *Coppélia, The Fairy Doll*, and *Dresden China* were seen, but the city started to attract more attention in the field of d. when Laban and Knust worked here after the First World War; interest in

The Hamburg State Opera Ballet (Scott and Klaus) in Neumeier's *Mahler's Fourth Symphony*.
Photo J. Flügel.

modern d. was centred around the school of Lola Rogge, which still functions. From the 1930s to the 1950s the b. dir. of the State Op. was Helga Swedlund, apart from short periods when E. Hanka and D. Hoyer took over. When Rolf Liebermann became general manager of the house in 1959 he appointed P. van Dyk as b. dir., but put particular emphasis on close collaboration with Balanchine, who revived many of his bs. for the H. co., and also directed some op. prods. Since 1973 J. Neumeier has been b. dir. and through his creativity H. has become one of the most active Ger. b. cities.

BIBL.: H. Koegler, entry 'H.' in *Friedrichs Ballettlexikon von A-Z* (Velber, 1972).

Hamel, Martine van (*b* Brussels, 16 Nov. 1945). Dutch-Amer. dancer. The daughter of a diplomat, she studied, from her childhood, at b. schools in Copenhagen, Java, The Hague, Caracas, and for a longer period, with B. Oliphant in Toronto. Joined National B. of Canada as a soloist in 1963; moved to City Center Joffrey B. in 1970, and to Amer. B. Th. in 1971; appointed principal d. in 1973. Gold Medal (Varna, 1966).

BIBL.: T. Tobias, 'M.v.H.', *Dance Magazine* (1975/10).

Hamilton, Gordon (*b* Sydney, 1918, *d* Paris, 14 Feb. 1959). Austral. dancer and b. master. Studied with Egorova, Preobrajenska, and Rambert. Joined B. de la Jeunesse in 1939. Danced with B. Rambert and Anglo-Pol. B., and with S. Wells B. 1941–6, creating Polonius in Helpmann's *Hamlet* (1942). Member of the Bs. des Champs-Elysées 1946–7. Returned to Sadler's Wells B. 1947–9. With B. de Paris 1949–50, creating roles in Petit's *Carmen* (1949) and *La Croqueuse de diamants* (1949). Appeared in Amer. musicals. Appointed b. master of the Vienna State Op. in 1954, where he contributed greatly to the comp.'s and the school's classical revival; he mounted *Giselle* in 1955, the first prod. of a b. classic at the reopened op. house at the Ringstrasse.

Hamlet. Ballet in 1 scene; libr. and ch. Helpmann; mus. Tchaikovsky; déc. Leslie Hurry. Prod. 19 May 1942, Sadler's Wells B., New Th., London, with Helpmann, Fonteyn, Franca, Paltenghi. Based on Shakespeare's tragedy, the b. shows the last thoughts of the dying H., reliving some of the climactic events of his life. Revived for Royal B. in 1964 and 1981. Other b. treatments of the same subject by Francesco Clerico (own mus., Venice, 1788), L. Henry (mus. Gallenberg, Vienna, 1822), Nijinska (with herself in the title-role, mus. Liszt, Paris, 1934), T. and V. Gsovsky (mus. Blacher, Munich 1950), Sergeyev (mus. Nicolai Chervinsky, Leningrad, 1970), Chaboukiani (mus. Ravaz Gabichvadze, Tiflis, 1971), L. Monreal (mus. Shostakovich, Boston, 1975), and J. Neumeier (*H.: Connotations*; mus. Copland, Amer. B. Th., 1976).

BIBL.: on the Helpmann version in C. Beaumont,

Ballets Past and Present (London, 1955); on the 2 recent Sov. versions in N. Roslavleva, 'Two Hamlets in Russia', *Dancing Times* (1972/7).

Handel, George Frideric (orig. Georg Friedrich Händel, *b* Halle, Ger., 23 Feb. 1685, *d* London, 14 Apr. 1759). Ger.-Brit. composer. Wrote no bs., but some of his ops. contain bs. e.g. *Almira* (Hamburg, 1705). Through his acquaintance with M. Sallé in London, dance featured prominently in some of his works of the 1730s (*Il Pastor fido*, with a *Terpsichore* prologue, 1734; *Ariodante*, 1735; *Alcina*, 1735). Some of his concert works have often been used for b. purposes, predominantly his *Fireworks Music* and *Water Music*, though none of the chs. to these gained international currency (not even Balanchine's *The Figure in the Carpet*, 1960). Beecham arranged several of H.'s pieces for Balanchine's *The Gods Go a-Begging* (1928) and for *The Great Elopement* (1945; later retitled *Love in Bath*), a b. on the elopement of Sheridan and Elizabeth Linley, which was never staged. Other choreographers who used H.'s mus. include P. Taylor (*Aureole*, 1962), Cranko (*Concerti grossi*, 1964), and Bruce (*George Frideric*, 1969). Wigman ch. a prod. of H.'s *Saul* for Mannheim in 1954.

BIBL.: in P. Nettl, *The Dance in Classical Music* (New York, 1963).

Hanka, Erika (*b* Vincovci, Croatia, 18 June 1905, *d* Vienna, 15 May 1958). Austrian dancer, choreographer, and b. director. Studied at the Vienna Academy with Bodenwieser and with Jooss in Essen. Joined the Folkwang B. in 1933. Soloist and assistant b. mistress in Düsseldorf 1936–9. She came as a guest-ch. to the Vienna State Op. (via Cologne, Essen, and Hamburg) in 1941, where her prod. of Egk's *Joan von Zarissa* was so successful that she was appointed b. mistress of the house in 1942, later becoming its b. director—a position she held until her death. During the very difficult war and post-war years and during the first seasons in the rebuilt house, she distinguished herself by keeping up the co.'s morale and creating a solid repertory of strongly drama-orientated bs.; her biggest successes included *Titus Feuerfuchs* (after Nestroy, mus. J. Strauss, Hamburg, 1941), *Höllische G'schicht'* (mus. Strauss, 1949), *Homerische Sinfonie* (mus. Theodor Berger, 1950), *Der Mohr von Venedig* (mus. Blacher, 1955), *Hotel Sacher* (mus. Hellmesberger/Schönherr, 1957), and *Medusa* (mus. von Einem, 1957).

Hanke, Susanne (*b* Altdöbern, 30 Mar. 1948). Ger. dancer. Studied at Stuttgart B. School and Royal B. School. Member Stuttgart B. 1966–74; appointed soloist in 1969, creating roles in Cranko's *Taming of the Shrew* (1969), *Brouillards* (1970), and *The Seasons* (1971).

BIBL.: S. Goodman, 'S.H.', *Dance Magazine* (1969/10).

Hanover. The b. tradition of the city dates back to 1636, when splendid court bs. were arranged by the b. masters Jemmes, Le Conte, and Desnoyer. Later on bs. were performed by visiting cos. of comedians, usually after the perf. of a play. During the 1840s and 1850s H. became acquainted with the internationally established bs. of the romantic era, with such ballerinas as Cerrito, Grisi, Grantzow, and the younger Marie Taglioni appearing in them. The Kobler family and Franz Degen, the Court Th. 's b. master in 1860–98, were prominent in the city's b. history in the 19th century. After the first World War, H. became one of the most active Ger. cities in dance. Y. Georgi was resident here—with short interruptions—1926–70, during which period H. witnessed a flowering b. culture, with many first prods. (Georgi ch. the first Ger. bs. to electronic mus.) and first Ger prods. She was succeeded by R. Adama, P. van Dyk, G. Furtwängler, and, since 1978, L. Höfgen.
BIBL.: H. Koegler, entry 'H.' In *Friedrichs Ballettlexikon von A-Z* (Velber, 1972).

Hansen, Emil (*b* 1843, *d* 1927). Dan. dancer and b. master. Studied with Aug. Bournonville. Became noted danseur noble of the Royal Dan. B., and its b. master 1881–93, during which time he ch. several bs., of which *Aditi* (mus. Rung) was the most outstanding. Developed his own system of dance notation, in which he wrote down the original ch. of *Toreadoren*, *Far from Denmark*, *La Muette de Portici*, and *Napoli*. His memoirs are conserved in manuscript form at the Th. History Museum at Christiansborg.

Hansen, Joseph (*b* 1842, *d* Asnières, 1907). Belg. dancer, b. master and choreographer. B. director of the Moscow Bolshoi Th. 1879–82, during which time he revived *Swan Lake* in 1880, but no more successfully than Reisinger had in 1877. B. master of the London Alhambra Th. 1884–7, and of the Paris Opéra 1889–1907; *La Maladetta* (mus. Paul Vidal, 1893) was his most successful creation. Was in charge of the first prods. of *Coppélia* in Brussels (1871) and Russia (Moscow, 1882).

Happy Coast. See *Coast of Happiness.*

Harangozó, Gyula (*b* Budapest, 18 Apr. 1908, *d* there, 10 Nov. 1974). Hung. dancer, choreographer and b. master. Studied at the Budapest State Op. B. School; joined the co., in 1926,. He became internationally known through his bs. to mus. by Bartók: *The Wooden Prince* (first version 1939) and *The Miraculous Mandarin* (first version 1945), but his long list of works contains all sorts of genres; his most popular bs. include *Coppélia, Scene in the Csárdás* (mus. J. Hubay and J. Kenessey, 1936), *Jankó in Boots* (mus. Kenessey, 1937), *Romeo and Juliet* (mus. Tchaikovsky, 1939), *Liebesträume* (mus. Liszt, 1942), *Promenade Concert* (mus. J. Strauss, 1948), *Mischievous Students* (mus. F. Farkas, 1949), *Kerchief* (mus. Kenessey, 1951), and *Mattie the Gooseboy* (mus. F. Szabó, 1960). Has also

frequently ch. for film and TV. Kossuth Prize (1956), Eminent Artist (1957), Gold Medal of Socialist Labour (1966).
BIBL.: G. Kórtvélyes and G. Lórinc, in *The Budapest Ballet* (Budapest, 1971).

Harangozó, Gyula (*b* Budapest, 1956). Hung. dancer. The son of Gyula Harangozó sen. and b. mistress Irén Hamala, he studied at Budapest State B. Inst. and Moscow B. School. Joined Budapest State Oper. B. 1971, appointed soloist 1977. Guest artist The Scottish B. in 1978–9. Created role in Seregi's *Variations on a Children's Rhyme* (1977).

Harapes, Vlastimil (*b* Chomutov, 24 July 1946). Czech dancer. Studied at Prague conservatory and with Pushkin in Leningrad. Joined Prague National Th. in 1966; subsequently appointed principal dancer. Created Mercutio in Kura-Weigl's TV prod. of *Romeo and Juliet* (1971).

Harbinger. Ballet in 5 movements; ch. Feld; mus. Prokofiev; set O. Smith; cost. Stanley Simmons; light. Rosenthal. Prod. 11 May 1967, Amer. B. Th., New York Th., N.Y., with E. Verso, C. Sarry, P. Tracy, Feld. Set to Prokofiev's Piano Concerto in G major, op. 55, this was Feld's first b. It reflects the generally carefree mood of the mus. Revived for Feld's Amer. B. Co. in 1969—a TV prod. of this version by Cologne TV (1970)—and for the E. Feld B.
BIBL.: G. Balanchine, 'H.' in Balanchine's *New Complete Stories of the Great Ballets* (Garden City, 1968).

Hardie, Andrew (*b* Edinburgh, 1909, *d* London, 21 Feb. 1980). Brit. dancer and teacher. Studied with M. Middleton, Idzikowsky, Sokolova, Craske, and N. Legat. Appeared in Cov. Gdn. op. prods. 1936–7. Danced in Inglesby's group and later in her International B. Taught at Judith Espinosa's school until he opened his own London school in 1958. Author of *Ballet Exercises for Athletes.*

Harkarvy, Benjamin (*b* New York, 16 Dec. 1930). Amer. dancer, choreographer, and b. master. Studied with Chaffee, Caton, School of Amer. B., Anderson-Ivantzova, Tudor, and Craske. Danced with Brooklyn Lyric Op. 1949-50, then in summer stock. Taught at Fokine School 1951–5; opened his own school in 1955. Director, ch., and b. master of Royal Winnipeg B. 1957–8. B. master of the Netherlands B. in 1958. Established Netherlands Dance Th. in 1959; artistic co-director until 1969. Artistic joint director of Harkness B. 1969-70, of Dutch National B. 1970–1 and of Pennsylvania B. 1972-82. His best known bs. include *Septet* (mus. Saint Saëns, 1959), *Grand pas espagnol* (mus. Moszkowski, 1962), *Madrigalesco* (mus. Vivaldi, 1963), *Recital for Cello and Eight Dancers* (mus. Bach, 1964), *La Favorita* (mus. Donizetti, 1969), and *Time Passed Summer* (mus. Tchaikovsky, 1974).

BIBL.: A. Fatt, 'Reintroducing B.H.', *Dance Magazine* (1972/11).

Harkness Ballet. The Amer. co., was named after*Rebekah H., who as the president of the Harkness Foundation repeatedly injected considerable amounts of money into various Amer. d. enterprises. She decided to found a co., of her own in 1964, which gave its début in Cannes in the spring of 1965. It was intended as a platform of young Amer. talents and was first directed by Skibine, later followed by B. Macdonald and Harkarvy. The co., was often blamed for lack of artistic integrity, but much admired for the vitality of its dancers; they toured continuously, but only appeared 3 times in New York. The comp. was recalled from a Eur. tour in 1970 and disbanded. At the same time the Youth Co., mostly consisting of pupils from the Harkness House for B. Arts. established in 1965, was granted senior status and accepted the name of the former co. This co., continued to tour, at first with B. Stevenson as its dir., followed by V. Nebrada, and the specially refurbished Harkness Th. was opened in New York in 1974; this co. also disbanded in 1975. Though many choreographers were recruited for the co., including Butler, S. Hodes, Van Dantzig, Neumeier, and Sappington, it lacked an individual artistic profile, but many talented dancers, including L. Isaksen, B. Ruiz, F. Jhung, H. Tomasson, L. Rhodes, and C. Aponte, emerged from its members.
BIBL.: portfolio on H.B., *Dance Magazine* (1973/11).

Harkness, Rebekah (*b* St. Louis, Mo., 17 Apr. 1915, *d* N.Y., 17 June 1982). Amer. composer and president of the Harkness Foundation. Studied mus. with N. Boulanger and dance with L. Fokine. Established the Harkness Foundation in 1961, through which she gave financial assistance to the cos. of Joffrey, Robbins, and others. Founded her Harkness B. in 1964. Opened the Harkness House for B. Arts in N.Y. in 1965, and the Harkness Th. on Broadway in 1974.

Harlem, Dance Theatre of. See *Dance Theatre of Harlem.*

Harlequinade. Ballet in 2 acts; ch. Balanchine; mus. Drigo; déc. Ter-Arutunian. Prod. 4 Feb. 1965, New York City B., State Th., N.Y., with McBride, Villella. Set to the mus. of Drigo's *Les Millions d'Arlequin*, the b. shows how the Good Fairy provides Harlequin with enough gold to impress the rich merchant Cassandre, the father of his beloved Columbine. Extended prod. on 14 Jan. 1973.
BIBL.: Balanchine, 'H.' in *Balanchine's New Complete Stories of the Great Ballets* (Garden City, N.Y., 1968).

Harlequin Ballet. The small Eng. co., was founded by John Gregory and Barbara Vernon in the autumn of 1959 to tour cities, colleges, and schools which were never visited by bigger cos. Continued until the late 1960s.

Harlequin in April. Ballet in 2 acts; libr. and ch. Cranko; mus. R. Arnell, déc. J. Piper. Prod. 8 May 1951, Sadler's Wells B., Sadler's Wells Th., London, with Blair, Holden, P. Miller. The symbolic b. shows how Harlequin is born out of chaos, devastation, and fire to new life. He aspires to Columbine, the unobtainable ideal love. Between the two stands Pierrot, the perpetual fool and stumbling-block who eternally separates the seeker and his dream.
BIBL.: C. Beaumont, 'H.i.A.' in *Ballets of Today* (London, 1954).

Härm, Tiit (*b* 19 Mar. 1946). Sov. dancer. Studied at Leningrad B. School, graduating 1966. D. with Moscow Young B. ensemble 1967–71 and since then as a principal d. at Estonia State Op. and B. Th. in Reval.

Harnasie. Ballet in 3 scenes; libr. K. Szymanowski. Prod. 1935, National Th., Prague. The b. deals with the Polish Highlanders and the legendary robbers of the Tatra district. After further prods. in Paris (ch. Lifar, 1936) and Hamburg (ch. Swedlund, 1937), H. entered the Pol. b. repertory at Poznan (ch. M. Statkiewicz, 1938), since when it has become a favourite among Pol. contemporary bs.

Harold in Italy. Ballet in 4 movements; ch. Massine; mus. Berlioz; déc. Bernard Lamotte. Prod. 14 Oct. 1954, B. Russe de Monte Carlo, Op. House, Boston, with Danielian, Borowska, Chouteau. The b. follows closely the programme of Berlioz's symphony, which itself received its inspiration from Byron's *Childe Harold's Pilgrimage.* Also used by Spoerli for *Childe Harold* (West Berlin, 1981).

Harris, Joan (*b* London, 26 Mar. 1920). Brit. dancer, teacher, and b. mistress. Studied with Grandison Clark, Sadler's Wells School, and Idzikowsky. D. with Anglo-Pol. B. in 1941, International B. 1941–5, and Sadler's Wells Th. B. 1945–7—also in musicals and films (assistant b. mistress for *The Red Shoes, Tales of Hoffmann,* and *Invitation to the D*). B. mistress of the Munich State Op. 1954–61. Director of Norwegian National B. 1961–6 and since 1965 in charge of the co.'s associated school.

Harrold, Robert (*b* Wolverhampton, 4 June 1923). Brit. dancer and teacher. Studied with Rambert, Preobrajenska, Volinine, and Brunelleschi. Danced with Anglo Pol. B. in 1940, as principal d. with B. Rambert 1941–4, and after the war in films, musicals, and on TV. Ch. of Glyndebourne Op. 1959–67. Taught at Rambert School, Bellairs Studio (Guildford), Legat School, London College, and since 1968 at his own London studio. Fellow and Examiner of the Imperial Society of Teachers of D. since 1964.

Contributor to *Dancing Times*. Author of *Regional Dances of Europe* and *Spanish Dancing*.

Hart, John (*b* London 4 July 1921). Brit. dancer and b. director. Studied with Judith Espinosa. Joined Vic-Wells B. in 1938, becoming one of its principal d. early in the war and b. master in 1955. Created roles in de Valois' *The Prospect Before Us*, Helpmann's *Comus* and *Hamlet*, Howard's *A Mirror for Witches*, Ashton's *Sylvia* and *Homage to the Queen*. Asst. dir. of Royal B. 1963–70. B. dir. at the U.S. International Univ. of Performing Arts in San Diego, Calif., 1970–74. In charge of PACT B. 1974–5; B. Administrator of Royal B. 1975–7. Has published 2 books of b. photos: *Ballet and Camera*, and *The Royal Ballet*. Married to the d. Ann Howard. C.B.E. (1971).

Harvest According, The. Ballet in 3 parts; ch. de Mille; mus. V. Thomson; déc. Lemuel Ayres. Prod. 1 Oct. 1952, B. Th., Met. Op. House, New York, with de Lappe, Koesun, Jenny Workman, K. Brown. A d. panorama of life as seen by a woman, taking its inspiration from W. Whiteman's 'Life, life is the tillage/ and death is the harvest according'.
BIBL.: G. Balanchine, 'T.H.A.' in *Balanchine's New Complete Stories of the Great Ballets* (Garden City, N.Y., 1968).

Harwood, Vanessa (*b* Cheltenham, 1947). Can. d. Studied with B. Oliphant at School of National B. of Canada, joining the co., in 1965; appointed soloist in 1967 and principal d. in 1970; left Nat. B. Canada, 1986. Order of Canada (1984).

Haskell, Arnold Lionel (*b* London, 19 July 1903, *d* Bath, 14 Nov. 1980). Brit. b. writer. Educated Westminster and Trinity Hall, Cambridge. One of the co-founders of the Camargo Society in 1930; participated actively in the preparations which led to the foundation of the Vic-Wells B. School. As a critic he started to write for the *Daily Telegraph* in 1935; later also wrote for other papers. Director of the Sadler's Wells and Royal B. School 1947–65. Governor of the Royal B. School 1947–65. Governor of the Royal B. since 1956. Editor of *The Ballet Annual* from 1947 to 1963. His Pelican *Ballet* (1938) introduced hundreds of thousands of Eng.-speaking people to the appreciation of the art of d. Other books of his have been *Some Studies in Ballet* (London, 1928), *Balletomania* (London, 1934), *Diaghileff* (London, 1935), *In His True Centre* (autobiography; London, 1951), and *Balletomane at Large* (London, 1972). He was vice-president of the R.A.D., has been sent abroad by the British Council to advise on b. matters, and has several times been a member of the jury at the Varna and Moscow dancers' competitions. Legion of Honour (1951); C.B.E. (1954).

Hasselquist, Jenny (*b* Stockholm, 31 July 1894). Swed. dancer, actress, and teacher. Studied at the Royal Swed. B. School, joining the co., in 1910,

appointed soloist in 1915. Left to become ballerina of de Maré's Bs. Suédois 1920–5, where she created leading parts in Börlin's *Jeux, Iberia, Nuit de Saint Jean, Les Vierges folles*, and *Maison du fou*. Then toured Eur. as a concert d., returning to Stockholm in 1932, where she opened a school and also taught at the Royal Swed. B. School until the mid-1950s. She appeared in her first film role (*Prima Ballerina*) in 1916, followed by several other films and plays.

Hassreiter, Joseph. (*b* Vienna, 30 Dec. 1845, *d* there, 8 Feb 1940). Austrian dancer, choreographer, teacher, and b. master. Studied at the Court Op. B. School and in Ger. Joined the Vienna Court Op. B. as a soloist in 1870; b. régisseur, b. master, head of the b. school, and teacher of the soloists 1891–1920. Occasionally he also taught the members of the Imperial family. His first b., *The Fairy Doll* (1888), was to become his most popular work; it is still in the repertory of the State Op. He created 48 bs., many of them to mus. by J. Bayer. His other most popular bs. were *Sonne und Erde, Rouge et Noir, Rund um Wien* (1894), and *Jahreszeiten der Liebe* (1911). Appointed honorary member of the Court Op. in 1918.

Hatch-Walker, David (*b* Edmonton, Alberta, 14 Mar. 1949). Can. dancer and teacher. Studied at National B. School of Can. 1964–68 and at M. Graham School. Joined B. Rambert 1969, then M. Graham D. Co. 1970–76, since when he has appeared with S. Maslow, B. Ross and L. Lubovitch. Artistic dir. and co.-ch. of Asakawalker D. Co. since 1977. Has also taught at Graham School since 1976, at Asakawalker D. Studio and various other schools through the US and in Europe. Married to Takako Asakawa.
BIBL.: J. Gruen, 'Ritual Union: Asakawalker', *Dance Magazine* (1980/1).

Haunted Ballroom, The. Ballet in 1 act and 2 scenes; libr. and mus. Geoffrey Toy; ch. de Valois; déc. Motley. Prod. 3 Apr. 1934, Vic-Wells B., Sadler's Wells Th., London, with Helpmann, Markova, Moreton, Appleyard. The b. tells of the Masters of Tregennis who are condemned to dance themselves to death in the gloomy room where the faded portraits of the family's ancestors hang. Revived for Sadler's Wells Th. B. in 1947 and London Festival B. in 1965. BBC TV prod. in 1957.
BIBL.: C. W. Beaumont, 'T.H.B.' in *Complete Book of Ballets* (London, 1951).

Haut, En (Fr., high up). Designates the position of the arms above the head.

Haut Voltage. Ballet in 1 act; libr. P. Rhallys; ch. Béjart; mus. M. Constant and P. Henry; déc. Rilliard. Prod. 27 Mar. 1956, Les Bs. de l'Etoile, Metz, with H. Trailine, Miskovitch. A woman with supernatural powers causes the electrocution of a couple of young lovers, but the boy revives and kills her. Revived for Massine's Nervi co., and Béjart's own co.

Havana. See *Cuba.*

Havas, Ferenc (*b* Budapest, 12 Mar. 1935). Hung. dancer. Studied with Nádasi at the State B. Institute. Joined the Budapest State Op. B. in 1952; appointed principal d. in 1953. D. as a guest with London Festival B. 1960–4. Liszt Prize (1963), Kossuth Prize (1965).

Hawkins, Erick (*b* Trinidad, Col., 1909). Amer. dancer and choreographer. Studied at School of Amer. B. and with Kreutzberg. D. with Amer. B. 1935–7, B. Caravan 1936–9; member of M. Graham Co., 1938–51, creating roles in Graham's *American Document* (1938), *Every Soul is a Circus* (1939), *Letter to the World* (1940), *Punch and Judy* (1941), *Deaths and Entrances* (1943), *Appalachian Spring* (1944), *Dark Meadow* (1945), *Cave of the Heart* (1947), *Night Journey* (1947), and *Diversion of Angels* (1948). Then formed his own group of dancers, which he co-directs with the composer Lucia Dlugoszewski and the sculptor Ralph Dorazio. First London season in 1980. Teaches his Normative Theory of Movement at his New York studio. His mostly experimental and abstract bs. include *Sudden Snake-Bird, Inner Feet of a Summer Fly* (1957), *Here and Now with Watchers* (1957), *8 Clear Places* (1960), *Cantilever* (1963), *Geography of Noon* (1964), *Naked Leopard* (1965), *Angels of the Inmost Heaven* (1971), and *Greek Dreams with Flute* (1973). Author of 'Pure Poetry' in *The Modern Dance* (Middletown, 1965). The philosopher F.S.C. Northrop has described his way of dancing as 'unique butterfly poetry'. He was married to M. Graham.

BIBL.: J. Baril, 'Rencontre avec E.H.', with complete check-list of activities, *Les Saisons de la danse* (1973/12); A. B. Grausam, 'E.H.: Choreographer as Sculptor', *Dance Magazine* (1974/11).

Hay, Deborah (*b* New York, 18 Dec. 1941). Amer. dancer and choreographer. Studied with her mother, then at Henry St. Playhouse and with M. Cunningham. D. with the cos. of Limón and Cunningham. In 1964 she broke with standard practices of technique and perf., concentrated on Tai Chi ritual exercises, and became an initial member of the Judson Memorial Church movement, dealing in communication between people and individuals with their own special capabilities' (D. McDonagh). Now works with non-technically trained dancers on streets, in parks, gymnasiums, and museums. Her work includes *Rain Fur* (1962), *Elephant Footprints in the Cheesecake* (1963), *Would They or Wouldn't They* (1963), *Victory 14* (1964), *20 Permutations of 2 Sets of 3 Equal Parts in a Linear Order* (1969), *Deborah Hay with a Large Group Outdoors* (1970). Author of *Moving Through the Universe in Bare Feet—Ten Circle Dances for Everybody* (together with Donna Jean Rogers, New York, 1974). She is married to the painter Alex Hay, who through her influence

has become a part-time dancer; 'has never shown any particular concern for music or any other rhythmical structure and has relied on the precise aperçu rather than an enveloping web of motion to carry his kinetic ideas' (McDonagh).
BIBL.: S. Banes, 'D.H.', in *Terpsichore in Sneakers* (Boston, 1980).

Haydée, Marcia (née M. H. Salaverry Pereira de Silva; *b* Niteroi, 18 Apr. 1937). Braz. dancer and b. director. Studied with Vaslav Veltchek, T. Leskova, and at Sadler's Wells School, having previously d. at the Rio de Janeiro Teatro Municipal. After further studies with Egorova and Preobrajenska joined Grand B. de Marquis de Cuevas in 1957, then Stuttgart B. in 1961; appointed prima ballerina in 1962. She became the Cranko ballerina par excellence and one of the greatest dance-actresses of the 1960s and 1970s. Has appeared with many other cos. Created roles in Cranko's *Romeo and Juliet* (1962), *Onegin* (1965), *Présence* (1968), *The Taming of the Shrew* (1969), *Carmen* (1971), *Initials R.B.M.E.* (1972), and *Traces* (1973), in MacMillan's *Las Hermanas* (1963), *Song of the Earth* (1965), *Miss Julie* (1970), and *Requiem* (1977), Tetley's *Voluntaries* (1973) and *Daphnis and Chloe* (1975), and Neumeier's *Hamlet: Connotations* (1976) and *Lady of the Camellias* (1978). Also dances the ballerina roles of the classics. Appointed artistic dir. of Stuttgart B. in 1976. Etoile d'or (Paris, 1967), Deutscher Kritik-erpreis (1971).
BIBL.: J. Gruen, 'Stuttgart Profiles: M. H. and Richard Cragun', *Dance Magazine* (1975/8); H. Kilian, *M.H.* (Sigmaringen, 1975); H. Koegler, 'M.H.', with complete check-list of roles and activities, *Les Saisons de la danse* (1976/6).

Hayden, Melissa (orig. Mildred Herman; *b* Toronto, 25 Apr. 1923). Can.-Amer. d. and teacher. Studied with B. Volkov, Vilzak, and Schollar. D. at Radio City Music Hall. Joined B. Th. in 1945. D. with various other comps., but became internationally known as a principal d. of the N.Y. City B., to which she belonged from 1950 until her retirement in 1973 (with only one short interruption). She had a sch. of her own in N.Y. City until 1983. Now on faculty of the N. Carolina Sch. of the Arts. Created roles in Robbins' *Age of Anxiety* (1950), *The Pied Piper* (1951) and *In the Night* (1970), Ashton's *Illuminations* (1950), Bolender's *The Miraculous Mandarin* (1951), Balanchine's *Caracole* (1952), *Valse fantaisie* (1953), *Divertimento No. 15* (1956), *Agon* (1957), *Stars and Stripes* (1958), *Episodes* (1959), *Liebeslieder Walzer* (1960), *A Midsummer Night's Dream* (1962), *Brahms-Schoenberg Quartet* (1966), *Glinkiana* (1966), and *Cortège Hongrois* (1973). Performed the ballerina role in Chaplin's film *Limelight* (1953). Author of *M.H.—Off Stage and On* (N.Y., 1963), *Dancer to Dancer* (Garden City, N.Y., 1981). Dance Magazine Award (1961); Handel Medallion of the City of N.Y. (1973).

BIBL.: S. Goodman, 'An Extraordinary Anniversary', *Dance Magazine* (1970/11); L. Kirstein, 'M.H.: A Tribute', *Dance Magazine* (1973/8).

Haydn, Franz Joseph (*b* Rohrau, prob. 31 Mar. (baptized 1 Apr.) 1732, *d* Vienna, 31 May 1809). Austrian composer. He wrote no bs. His copyist and faithful servant was Johann Florian Elssler, the father of Fanny Elssler. Concert compositions of his have frequently been used for b. purposes— beginning with S. Viganò's Milan prod. of *The Creatures of Prometheus* (also using part of Beethoven's original mus., 1813). More recent bs. to mus. by H. include M. Terpis' *The Miser* (Berlin State Op., 1928), Massine's *Clock Symphony* (Sadler's Wells B., 1948), Balanchine's *Trumpet Concerto* (same co., 1950), Wright's *Ballet to This Music* (Western Th. B., 1965), Taras' *Haydn Concerto* (New York City B., 1968), Feld's *Meadowlark* (Royal Winnipeg B., 1968), and Tharp's *As Time Goes By* (Joffrey City Center B., 1973) and *Push Comes to Shove* (Symphony No. 82 in C, Amer. B. Th., 1976), and Kylián's *Symphony in D* (1976).

Hays, David (*b* New York, 1930). Amer. th. designer. Has designed the sets for many New York City B. prods., incl. Balanchine's *Stars and Stripes* (1958), *Episodes* (1959), *Liebeslieder Walzer* (1960), *Monumentum pro Gesualdo* (1960), *Electronics* (1961), *A Midsummer Night's Dream* (1962), *Bugaku* (1963), and a new version of *Divertimento No. 15* (1966).
BIBL.: A. Fatt, 'Designers for the Dance: D.H.', *Dance Magazine* (1967/2).

Haythorne, Harry (*b* Adelaide, 1926). Austral. dancer and b. master. Studied with Idzikowsky, Northcote, Leeder, and de Vos. Member of Metropolitan B. in 1949, International B. 1950–1. B. master London Coliseum 1955, Drury Lane Th. 1956. Then worked for TV. B. master of Massine's B. Europeo in 1960, then of Gore's London B. 1962–3. Guest with the Royal B. in 1963. D. Ugly Sister in Larrain's *Cinderella* prod. 1963–4. B. master Sadler's Wells Op. in 1965 and of Western (Scottish) Th. B. 1967–71. Prod. coordinator of Scottish Th. B. 1972–4. Artistic Dir. of Queensland B. since 1975.

Hayworth, Terry (*b* Burnley, 1926). Brit. dancer. Studied with Nicolaeva, Legat, and Preobrajenska. Started as a child actor. D. with Anglo-Pol. B. in 1943, B. des Trois Arts in 1944, Metropolitan B. 1947–9, Massine's B. in 1950, B. de R. Petit in 1951, then in Bordeaux, Brussels, and Antwerp, with Gore's London B. in 1963, and with London Festival B. 1966–84, with Coppelius as one of his best roles.

Heart of the Hills, The (orig. Russ. title: *Serdtse gor*). Ballet in 3 acts and 5 scenes; libr. G. Leonidze and N. Volkov; ch. Chaboukiani; mus. A. Balanchivadze; déc. S. Virsaladze. Prod. 28 June 1938, Kirov Th., Leningrad, with Chaboukiani, Vecheslova, Koren. Based on an episode in the history of Georgia; rebels, led by Djardje, rise against their overlord, to free the community from its heavy tax burdens. The comp. is the brother of G. Balanchine.
BIBL.: C. W. Beaumont, 'T.H.o.t.H.' in *Supplement to Complete Book of Ballets* (London, 1952).

Hear Ye! Hear Ye! Ballet in 1 act; libr. R. Page (also ch.) and N. Remisoff (also déc.); mus. Copland. Prod. 30 Nov. 1934, R. Page B. Co., Op House, Chicago, with Page and B. Stone. After a murder in a night club, the witnesses in the court room give their contrasting evidence of what happened.
BIBL.: C. W. Beaumont, 'H.Y.! H.Y.!' in *Complete Book of Ballets* (London, 1951).

Heaton, Anne (*b* Rawalpindi, 19 Nov. 1930). Brit. dancer and teacher. Studied with Janet Cranmore in Birmingham and at Sadler's Wells School. Joined Sadler's Wells Th. B. in 1945, creating roles in Howard's *Mardi Gras* and Ashton's *Valses nobles et sentimentales* (both 1947). Soloist (later principal), Sadler's Wells B. 1948–59, creating roles in Massine's *Clock Symphony* (1948), Howard's *A Mirror for Witches* (1952), MacMillan's *The Burrow* (1958), and *The Invitation* (1960). Continued to d. as guest with Royal B. until 1962. Teacher at Arts Educational School. She is married to John Field.

Heberle, Therese (*b* Vienna, 1806, *d* Naples, 5 Feb. 1840). Austrian dancer. She was one of Horschelt's most talented Children's Dancers at the Th. an der Wien. D. in Vienna 1813–26, then at London's Ital. Opera. In Naples she married a banker who lost all her money, after which she had to return to dancing, which she did with outstanding success at La Scala (appearing in L. Henry's *La Silfide* in 1828), gaining such popularity that in Milan Grisi was called 'la piccola Heberle'. Grillparzer wrote about her and dedicated his poem *Vorzeichen* to her.

Heiden, Heino (*b* Wuppertal, 6 Oct. 1923). Ger.-Can. dancer, choreographer, b. master, and teacher. Studied with T. and V. Gsovsky, S. Ress, Preobrajenska, and Tudor. D. at East Berlin State Op. 1945–7, Dresden State Op. 1947–8, East Berlin Comic Op. 1947–50, *Abraxas* co., 1950–1, and Munich Th. am Gärtnerplatz 1951–2. He then went to Canada, working in Vancouver and for Montreal TV. Returned to Ger. as B. master in Mannheim 1960–3, then Antwerp 1965–6, and Kiel-Lübeck 1967–9. Guest ch. Washington B., Royal Winnipeg B., Vancouver B., National B. of Canada, and Scapino B. His many bs. included the first Ger. prod. after the Second World War of *La Fille mal gardée* (mus. adaptation by Hans Georg Gitschel, Mannheim, 1962). Opened his own school in Lübeck in 1970.
BIBL.: E. Herf, 'H.H.', *Ballet Today* (1964/3).

Heine, Heinrich (*b* Düsseldorf, 13 Dec. 1797, *d* Paris, 17 Feb. 1856). Ger. poet and writer. His

Wilis story, contained in his *Geschichte der neueren schönen Literatur in Deutschland* (1833); Fr. version *De L'Allemagne*, Paris 1835), provided Gautier with the basic inspiration for his *Giselle* libr. (1841). H. himself wrote the b. libr. *Die Göttin Diana* for Lumley in 1846, hoping that he would produce it at London's Her Majesty's Th., but this never happened. Commissioned by Lumley, he wrote another b. libr. *Der Doctor Faust, Ein Tanzpoem* in 1847; however, this too came to nothing, though later **Faust* bs. made use of some of its ideas. Bs. inspired by some of Heine's verses were R. Page's *Adonis* (based on his *Frühlingsfeier*, mus. Lehmann Engel, Chicago, 1944) and B. Marks' *Dichterliebe* (mus. Schumann, Royal Dan. B., 1972).

BIBL.: M. Niehaus, *Himmel, Hölle und Trikot—H.H. und das Ballett* (Munich, 1959); W. Sorell, 'H.H.'s Unproduced Faust Ballet', *Dance Magazine* (1961/1).

Heinel, Anna Friedrike (*b* Bayreuth, 4 Oct. 1753, *d* Paris, 17 Mar. 1808). Ger. dancer. Studied with Lépy and Noverre, making her début in Stuttgart in 1767 and in Paris in 1768, where she was called 'La Reine de la danse'. Became a fierce rival of Vestris because of her exceptional virtuosity (she is said to have invented the pirouette à la seconde), but she was also a great tragedienne, and Noverre admired the nobility of her style. Appeared in London in 1772, returning occasionally in later years. Returned to Paris in 1773, where she made up her quarrel with Vestris, becoming his mistress and the mother of his son Adolphe in 1791; they married in 1792. She participated in the first Paris prods. of Gluck's *Orpheus and Eurydice* (1774) and *Iphigénie en Tauride* (1779). Retired in 1782.

BIBL.: P. Migel, 'A.H.' in *The Ballerinas* (New York, 1972).

Helen of Troy. Comic ballet in 3 scenes, with prologue; libr. Lichine (also ch.) and Dorati (also adaptor of Offenbach's mus.); déc. Marcel Vertès. Prod. 29 Nov. 1942, B. Th., Detroit, Mich., with Baronova, Eglevsky, Robbins, Semenov. The b. follows the course of Offenbach's operetta *La Belle Hélène*. It was originally planned by Fokine, who died 3 months before its première. A different version by Cranko (*La Belle Hélène*, Paris Opéra, 1955).

BIBL.: G. Balanchine, 'H.o.T.' in *Balanchine's New Complete Stories of the Great Ballets* (Garden City, 1968).

Héliogabale ou L'Anarchiste couronné. Spectacle in 2 parts after a text by Antonin Artaud; ch. and dir. Béjart; mus. Verdi, Bach, ritual Afr. mus. *et al*; déc. Groupe Yantra. Brussels first prod. 14 Jan. 1977 (after earlier perfs. at the Shiraz-Persepolis Festival, the Festival de Flandre à Gand, the Athens Festival, and La Scala of Milan—all in the summer and autumn of 1976), B. of the 20th Century and Yantra, Th. Royal de la Monnaie,

with N. Ek, Y. Le Gac, M. Marin, L. Savignano. Another one of Béjart's théatre total prods., dealing with the ambiguous mysteries of the Near-Eastern cult of the sun which celebrates the mystic union of man and woman in the figure of the hermaphrodite.

Hellerau-Laxenburg. In the garden suburb of H. near Dresden Dalcroze opened his Insitute for Applied Rhythm as a new style of mus. school in 1911, with M. Rambert and Wigman as 2 of its most famous pupils. It was closed in 1914, but reopened in 1915, when a department for dance education was added, headed by Christine H. Baer-Frissell, V. Kratina, and Ernst Ferand. From this developed the H. Tanzgruppe, which staged the first Ger. prods. of Bartók's *The Wooden Prince* and Milhaud's *L'homme et son désir* (both in 1923). During the 1920s many of Ger.'s leading 'Ausdruckstänzer' trained here, including Georgi, Holm, and Chladek. After a particularly successful perf. of its d. group, the city of Vienna invited the school in 1925 to transfer its headquarters to the castle of Laxenburg, nr. Vienna, from where the so-called Hellerau Trio, consisting of the dancers Kratina, Mary Houbergh, and Anssi Bergh, toured widely. Chladek directed the school 1930–8; it abandoned all its activities when the Gers. occupied Austria in 1938.

Helliwell, Rosemary Anne (*b* London 28 July 1955). Brit. dancer and choreographer. Studied at Doreen Bird School of Th. D. and John Cranko B. School. Joined Stuttgart B. in 1976. Appointed resident ch. in 1977. Ch. *Mirage* (mus. F. Martin, 1977), *Ebb Tide* (mus. Fauré) and *Concertino* (mus. Janáček, 1978), *Hedda Gabler* (mus. J. Skrowaczewski, 1981) *et al.*

Hellmesberger, Josef (jr.; *b* Vienna, 9 Apr. 1855, *d* there, 26 Apr. 1907). Austrian composer. Appointed court kapellmeister for b. and concert in 1886. Apart from many individual dances, he composed the mus. for J. Price's *Harlekin als Elektriker* (1884), K. Telle's *Die verwandelte Katze* (1887), Hassreiter's *Die Perle von Iberien* (1902) and *Dresden China* (1903). K. Schönherr based his b. mus. for Hanka's *Hotel Sacher* (1957) on various melodies by H.

Helpmann, Sir Robert (*b* Mount Gambier, 9 Apr. 1909, *d* Sydney, 28 Sep. 1986). Austral. dancer, choreographer, b. director, and actor. Studied with the Pavlova co., while it toured Austral. Came to London in 1933, joined Vic-Wells B. in the same year. Became its chief male d. and partner of Fonteyn, and stayed with the co., until 1950, with a few later guest appearances. His most important role creations were in de Valois' *The Haunted Ballroom* (1934), *Checkmate* (1937), *The Prospect Before Us* (1940), and *Don Quixote* (1950), Ashton's *Apparitions* (1936), *Nocturne* (1936), *A Wedding Bouquet* (1937), *Dante Sonata* (1940), *The Wanderer* (1941), *Don Juan* and *Cinderella* (both 1948). His first ch. was a workshop

prod. of *La Valse* (mus. Ravel, Royal Academy of Dancing, 1939), followed by *Comus* (mus. Purcell-Lambert, 1942), *Hamlet* (mus. Tchaikovsky, 1942), *Miracle in the Gorbals* (mus. Bliss, 1944), and *Adam Zero* (mus. Bliss, 1946), all strongly dramatic works, in which he also created the leading male roles. He appeared occasionally as an actor and op. producer, and acted in the films *The Red Shoes* (1948) and *Tales of Hoffmann* (1951). He collaborated with Nijinska in the de Cuevas prod. of *The Sleeping Beauty* (1960), with Ashton in the Royal B. prod. of *Swan Lake* in 1963, and with Hynd in the Austral. B. prod. of *The Merry Widow* (1975); also in 1963 he ch. *Elektra* (mus. M. Arnold) for the Royal B. He then returned to Austral., becoming joint Dir. with van Praagh of the Austral. B. in 1965, for which he ch. *The Display* (mus. M. Williamson, 1964), *Yugen* (mus. Y. Toyama, 1965), *Sun Music* (mus. P. Sculthorpe, 1968), and *Perisynthion* (mus. Williamson, 1974). Retired in 1976 after producing the co.'s biggest hit, *The Merry Widow* (ch. Hynd). He played the title role in Nureyev's film *Don Quixote* (1973). Queen Elizabeth II Award of the RAD (1961); C.B.E. (1964); knighted in 1968.
BIBL.: C. Brahms, *R.H.— Choreographer* (London, 1943); G. Gow, 'H. and the Australian Ballet', *Dancing Times* (1973/10).

Helsinki. See *Finland, National Ballet of.*

Hendel, Henriette (*née* Johanne H. Rosine Schüler; *b* Döbeln, 13 Feb. 1772, *d* Köslin, 4 Mar. 1849). Ger. dancer, mime, and actress. The daughter of travelling comedians, she received her early d. training from the b. masters of the ths. where her parents were appearing (Mereau in Gotha, Weininger in Breslau, etc.); a strong impression was made on her by J. J. Engel's book *Ideas on Mime*, Rehberg's drawings of Lady Hamilton's 'attitudes', and her meeting with Galeotti in Copenhagen. Starting as an actress, she specialized more and more in the presentation of 'living pictures', i.e. sculptural dances, the subjects of which she took from mythology, ancient sculpture, and Ger. and Ital. renaissance painting, 'developing her studies into a full-length professional evening's entertainment, with which she toured Germany, Scandinavia and even Russia for more than a decade. She might even be said to have given the first concerts of modern expressionistic dance' (L. Moore). Goethe and Schiller were among her admirers.
BIBL.: L. Moore, 'Eighteenth-Century Isadora', *Dance Magazine* (1956/6); M. H. Winter, in *The Pre-Romantic Ballet* (London, 1974).

Henry, Louis-Xavier-Stanislas (*b* Versailles, 7 Mar. 1784, *d* Naples, 4 Nov. 1836). Fr. dancer and choreographer. Studied at Paris Opéra School with Deshayes, Gardel, and Coulon: made his début in 1803. Much admired for the energy of his style. Started to ch. at the Th. de la Porte-St.-Martin in 1805. Went to Italy in 1807, where he

came under the influence of Viganò and Gioja; enjoyed great success in Milan and Naples, and later in Vienna and after his return to Paris in 1816. Ch. over 125 bs., incl. *Otello* (mus. Gallenberg, Naples, 1808), *Hamlet* (mus. Gallenberg, Th. de la Porte-St.-Martin, 1816), *La Silfide* (mus. Carlini, Milan, 1828), and *William Tell* (mus. Pugni, Rossini, *et al.*, Milan, 1833).
BIBL.: entry 'H., L.' in *Enciclopedia dello spettacolo*; M.H. Winter, in *The Pre-Romantic Ballet* (London, 1974).

Henry, Pierre (*b* Paris, 9 Dec. 1927). Fr. composer. One of the pioneers of 'musique concrète'. Wrote (with Pierre Schaeffer) *Symphonie pour un homme seul* in 1950—part of which was used by M. Cunningham in 1952, and the whole by Béjart in 1955. Béjart and H. have often collaborated since, creating *Le Voyage au coeur d'enfant* (1955), *Arcane I* (1955), *Haut Voltage* (with M. Constant, 1956), *The Journey* (1956), *Orphée* (1958), *La Reine verte* (1963), *Variations pour une porte et un soupir* (1965—also Balanchine, 1974), *La Tentation de Saint Antoine* (1967), *Messe pour le temps present* (1967), and *Nijinsky, Clown de dieu* (1971), comp. for G. Pick *Les Noces chymiques* (Paris, 1980) and *Woyzeck* (Augsburg, 1981).

Henry Street Settlement Playhouse. The New York th. was founded as an actors' school in 1915. It housed the D. Th., of A. Nikolais 1948–70, and became one of the outstanding platforms for experimental d. in New York.

Henze, Hans Werner (*b* Gütersloh, 1 July 1926). Ger. composer. He has always been strongly interested in the dance, and his oeuvre shows a perpetual interaction of instrumental, vocal, dance, and pantomime elements, so that the category of the individual work sometimes cannot be clearly defined. His publisher's catalogue lists the following bs.: *Anrufung Apolls* (3rd Symphony, 1949—prod. P. van Dyk, Wiesbaden, 1949, also E. Walter, Wuppertal, 1961, and G. Tetley in *Gemini*, Sydney, 1973), *Jack Pudding* (1949—prod. E. von Pelchrzim, Wiesbaden, 1951), *Ballett-Variationen* (1949—prod. Walter, Wuppertal, 1958), *Rosa Silber* (1950—prod. L. Kretschmar, Cologne, 1958), *Die schlafende Prinzessin* (after Tchaikovsky's *The Sleeping Beauty*, 1951—prod. A. Bortoluzzi, Essen, 1954), *Der Idiot* (prod. T. Gsovsky, Berlin, 1952), *Maratona di danza* (prod. D. Sanders, Berlin, 1957), *Ondine* (prod. Ashton, London, 1958), *Des Kaisers Nachtigall* (pantomime—Venice, 1959), *Tancredi* (first version: *Pas d'action*, prod. V. Gsovsky, Munich, 1954—second version: *T.*, prod. Nureyev, Vienna, 1966), and *Tristan* (prod. Tetley, Paris, 1974). His *Das Wundertheater*, op. for actors, was ch. by M. Luipart in its Heidelberg first prod. in 1949; his op. *Boulevard Solitude* was ch. by Otto Krüger in its Hanover first prod. in 1952. J. Gerster ch. his second Symphony for Brunswick in 1970, T. Bolender his fifth Symphony for E. Frankel (as

Elektra) in Hong Kong in 1972, G. Tetley his third Symphony as *Gemini* (Austral. B. 1973, also Sadler's Wells Royal B., 1977). Author of *Undine—Tagebuch eines Balletts* (Munich, 1959).
BIBL.: K. Geitel, *H.W.H.* (Berlin, 1968).

Herczog, István (*b* Budapest, 18 Nov. 1943). Hung. dancer. Studied at Budapest State B. Inst. Joined Budapest State Op. B. in 1962. Went to Ger. in 1966. D. in Regensburg, Stuttgart, Freiburg, and Munich Th. am Gärtnerplatz before joining Munich State Op. B. as a soloist 1972–4 and Düsseldorf Op. B. in 1974.

Hering, Doris (*b* New York, 11 Apr. 1920). Amer. writer on dance and administrator. Educated at Hunter College and Fordham Univ. Assoc. editor and principal critic of *Dance Magazine* 1950–70 and then its critic-at-large. Has taught d. history at various schools, colleges, and univs. She has been actively engaged in the Amer. Regional B. Movement from its earliest days, and is now Executive Director of the National Association for Regional Ballet. Author and editor of *25 Years of American Dance* (1950), *Wild Grass, The Memoirs of Rudolf Orthwine*, and *Dance in America*. Capezio Award (1985); Dance Magazine Award (1986).

Heritage Dance Theatre. Based upon the North Carolina School of the Arts, the co., gave some preview perfs. in Winston-Salem in Apr. 1973 and launched its initial tour the following Oct. with 32 dancers and 2 different programmes, prod. and ch. by A. de Mille. It tries to conserve and present in authentic and theatrically valid form the traditions of Amer. folklore dancing.
BIBL.: J. Gale, 'Spirit of '76: The Agnes de Mille H.D.T.', *Dance Magazine* (1974/6).

Hermanas, Las. Ballet in 1 act; libr. and ch. MacMillan; mus. F. Martin; déc. Georgiadis. Prod. 13 July 1963, Stuttgart, with R. Papendick, Haydée, Keil, Barra. Set to Martin's Concerto for Harpsichord and Small Orchestra, the b., the Span. title of which means 'The Sisters', derives from F. García Lorca's *The House of Bernarda Alba*. Revived for Western Th. B. (1966), West Berlin Ger. Op. (1967), Amer. B. Th. (1967), and Touring Royal B. (1971). Other treatments of the same subject by A. Ailey (*Feast of Ashes*, mus. Surinach, 1962), I. Sertić (*Las Apasionadas*, mus. Kelemen, Lübeck, 1964) and E. Pomare (*Las Desenamoradas*, mus. M. Coltrane, New York, 1967).
BIBL.: P. Brinson and C. Crisp, 'L.H.' in *Ballet for all* (London, 1970).

Hernandez, Amalia (*b* Mexico City). Mex. dancer, choreographer, teacher, and b. director. Studied with Sybine of the Pavlova co., with Argentinita, and modern d. with Waldseen. Started to work as a teacher and ch. of modern d. at the Institute of Arts in Mexico. Founded her own folklore co., in 1952, which grew rapidly and soon travelled abroad. Has ch. and produced many programmes since 1960. Today her B.

Folklorico de Mexico, which is now State subsidized, lists 200 members, based upon its own th. and a vast complex of studios. Her most recent achievement is the formation of the B. Clasico 70 co.
BIBL.: D. Hering, 'Donna Amalia's At It Again', *Dance Magazine* (1971/6).

Herodiade. Ballet in 1 act; ch. Graham; mus. Hindemith; set Noguchi; cost. E. Gilfond. Prod. 28 Oct. 1944, Library of Congress, Washington, D.C., with Graham and May O'Donnell. Commissioned by the Elizabeth Sprague Coolidge Foundation and first given under the title *Mirror Before Me*, the piece follows closely Mallarmé's poem: Herodiade is confronted in a mirror with her past and her future and thus led to accept her fate. The New York première took place on 15 May 1945 at the National Th. Eur. first prod. by H. Heiden (Mannheim, 1961). Another treatment of the same subject in Darrell's *Herodias* (Scottish Th. B., 1970).

Heroic Poem (The Geologists) (orig. Russ. title: *Geroicheskaya poema (Geologi)*). B. in 1 act; libr. and ch. N. Kasatkina and V. Vasiliov; mus. N. Karetnikov; déc. E. Stenberg. Prod. 26 Jan. 1964, Bolshoi Th., Moscow, with Sorokina, Vladimirov, Koshelev. The b. deals with 3 geologists, two men and one woman, who start on an exploration of the Taiga, where they have to overcome almost unbearable sufferings, but through the steadfastness of the woman finally succeed in reaching their destination.
BIBL.: M. G. Swift, in *The Art of the Dance in the U.S.S.R.* (Notre Dame, Ind., 1968).

Hérold, Louis-Joseph-Ferdinand (*b* Paris, 28 Jan. 1791, *d* there, 19 Jan. 1833). Fr. composer. As a répétiteur at the Opéra he comp. a number of bs., all of which were ch. by J. Aumer: *Astolphe et Joconde* (1827), *La Somnambule* (1827), *Lydie* (1828), a new version of *La Fille mal gardée* (1828), and *La Belle au bois dormant* (1829).
BIBL.: J. Lanchbery, 'The Music of "La Fille mal gardée"' in *La Fille mal gardée* (London, 1960).

Hersin, André-Philippe (*b* Paris, 29 Sep. 1934). Fr. writer on ballet. Publishing Director and chief editor of *Les Saisons de la danse* since 1968. D. Organizer of Festival d'Avignon since 1972.

Hertel, Peter Ludwig (*b* Berlin, 21 Apr. 1817, d. there, 13 June 1899). Ger. composer. He worked at the Berlin Court Op., composing the mus. for P. Taglioni's *Satanella* (1852), *The Adventures of Flick and Flock* (1858), *Sardanapal* (1865), and *Fantasca* (1869), and for the 1864 Berlin prod. of *La Fille mal gardée*.

Het Nationale Ballet. See *Dutch National Ballet*.

Hesse, Jean-Baptiste François de. See *De Hesse, J.-B.F.*

High School of Performing Arts. Established as an annexe of New York's Metropolitan Vocational

High School in 1948 and part of the High School of Music and Arts since 1961. Its D. Department, dir. for many years by Dr. Rachael Yocom and frequented by more than 200 students, offers a full academic curriculum plus several daily periods in the various dance studios. With its diploma graduates may either go straight into show business or on to college. Many of Amer.'s leading dancers of the younger generation have received their basic training here; teachers have included G. Shurr, A. Hutchinson, N. Walker, B. Malinka. The school featured prominently in the film *Fame* (1980).

BIBL.: D. Boroff, 'High School with a Flair', *Dance Magazine* (1962/2).

Hightower, Rosella (*b* Ardmore, Okla., 30 Jan. 1920). Amer. dancer and teacher. Studied with D. Perkins in Kansas City. D. with B. Russe de Monte Carlo 1938–41, as a soloist with B. Th. 1941–5, then with Massine's B. Russe Highlights and Original B. Russe 1945–6. Joined Nouveau B. de Monte Carlo in 1947; became its star ballerina and stayed with the co., later the Grand B. du Marquis de Cuevas, until the Marquis' death in 1961, though she often appeared as a guest with other cos. Founded the Centre de Danse Classique in Cannes in 1962, which soon became the centre of all sorts of d. activities on the Côte d'Azur. B. dir. of the Marseilles Opéra 1969–72, and of the Nancy Grand Théâtre 1973–4. She has often taught abroad, regularly for the B. of the 20th Century, of which her daughter, Dominique Robier, is a member. A dazzling technician, she was much admired in the ballerina roles of the classics and created roles in a great number of bs., including Massine's *Mam'zelle Angot* (1943), A. Ricarda's *Doña Ines de Castro* (1952), Taras' *Piège de lumière* (1952), H. Lander's *La Sylphide* (in the Cuevas prod., 1953), Lichine's *Corrida* (1957), and Béjart's *Variations* (1969). Art. dir. of Paris Opéra B. 1981–3 and of La Scala di Milano 1983–6. Grand Prix des critiques de danse (1949); Gold Medal of the Univ. of the D. (1967); Chevalier de la Légion d'honneur (1975).

BIBL.: Lidova, 'R.H.' with complete check-list of activities, *Les Saisons de la danse* (1968/4); D. Harris, 'Modest Maîtresse', *Ballet News* (1980/12); B. Merrill, 'B.H.', *Dance Magazine* (1981/7).

Highwood, June (*b* Woking, *c*. 1951). Brit. dancer. Studied at Royal B. School, graduating into Royal B. 1969, also dancing with B. for all and joining touring co., 1974, promoted soloist 1975 and principal 1977. Created roles in L. Seymour's *Rashomon* (1976) and D. Bintley's *Meadow of Proverbs* (1979).

Hilferding. See *Hilverding, Franz Anton Christoph*.

Hill, Carole (*b* Cambridge, 5 Jan, 1945). Brit. dancer. Studied with Vera Vintsec and at Royal B. School. Member of Royal B. 1962–72, appointed soloist 1966. Joined London Festival B. as

a principal d. in 1972. Guest ballerina with National B. of Rhodesia.

Hill, Martha (*b* East Palestine, Ohio, *c*.1900). Amer. dancer and teacher. Studied mus., Dalcroze technique, academic and modern d. at Columbia and New York Univ. D. with Graham 1929–31. Taught in Kansas City, Chicago, Bennington School of the D. New York Univ. Founder Connecticut College School of the D. and the affiliated American D. Festival in 1948. Dir. of the D. Department at New York's Juilliard School since 1951; retired 1985. D. advisor on many boards and panels. Honorary Doctorate of Humane letters of Adelphi Univ. (1965).

Hilverding, Franz Anton Christoph (also Franz· Hilferding van Wewen; baptized Vienna, 17 Nov. 1710, *d* there, 29 May 1768). Austrian dancer, choreographer, b. master and teacher. He came from a famous family of comedians, his stepfather being the very popular Viennese Hanswurst Gottfried Prehauser. Studied probably in Brno and with Blondi in Paris. Appointed court d. in Vienna in 1735 and court D.-master in 1749. His first bs. date from 1744. Created more than 30 bs. for various Viennese ths. between 1752 and 1757, in which he showed himself to be a pioneer of the b. d'action. He then went to Russ. where he was in charge of the b. in St. Petersburg and Moscow 1758–64. Returned to Vienna in 1765. Among his pupils were Angiolini and E. M. Veigl, who called herself Violetti (later the wife of D. Garrick).

BIBL.: F. Derra de Moroda, 'A Neglected Choreographer: H.', *Dancing Times*(1968/6); M. H. Winter, in *The Pre-Romantic Ballet* (London, 1974).

Hindberg, Linda (*b* Wiesbaden, 5 Feb. 1955). Dan. dancer. Studied at Royal Dan. B. School. Joined Royal Dan. B. at graduation, appointed solo d. 1977.

Hindemith, Paul (*b* Hanau, 16 Nov. 1895, *d* Frankfurt, 28 Dec. 1958). Ger. composer. Wrote the mus. for Albrecht Joseph's *Der Dämon* (Darmstadt, 1923), Massine's *Nobilissima Visione* (London, 1938), Graham's *Herodiade* (Washington, 1944; new version by Darrell, Scottish Th. B., 1970), and Balanchine's *The Four Temperaments* (New York, 1946), and the mus. for mechanical organ for Schlemmer's *Triadisches Ballett* (Donaueschingen, 1926). Bs. to unidentified mus. by H. were Georgi's *Das seltsame Haus* (Hanover, 1928) and S. Korty's *Der Antiquar* (Antwerp, 1933). Bs. to concert mus. by H. include Balanchine's *Metamorphoses* (New York, 1952), L. Meyer's *Sextet* (Kleine Kammermusik, Op. 24, Western Th. B., 1964), Van Manen's *Five Sketches* (5 Pieces for String Orchestra, op. 44, The Hague, 1966), Harkarvy's *Aswingto* (Concert Music for String Orchestra and Woodwind, op. 50, The Hague, 1969), and Balanchine's *Kammermusik No. 2* (N.Y. City B., 1978).

Hinkson, Mary (*b* Philadelphia, 16 Mar. 1930). Amer. dancer and teacher. Studied with Graham, Horst, Shook, J. Taylor, and Schwezoff. Joined Graham's co., in 1952, becoming one of her most prominent soloists; created roles in *Canticle for Innocent Comedians* (1952), *Seraphic Dialogue* (1955), *Acrobats of God* (1960), and *Circe* (1963). Started to teach at Graham School in 1951, later also Juilliard School. Now works as a freelance teacher. Staff member of the Cologne Summer Academy since 1971. Professor of Modern D, Gulbenkian National Ch. Summer School, Eng., 1975–6 and 1979.

Hinton, Paula (*b* Ilford, 1924). Brit. dancer. Studied with H. Delamere-Wright in Liverpool, joining B. Rambert in 1944. D. in the co., of W. Gore, whom she married, in Austral.—also with Bs. des Champs-Elysées, Original B. Russe, London Festival B., and P. Lopez. Ballerina Frankfurt Municipal Stages 1956–8, Edinburgh Festival B., Gore's London B. in 1961, and Gulbenkian B. 1965–9. Guest artist of Western Th. B. in 1965, Harkness B. in 1970, Northern D. Th. 1971–2 and 1976. A highly expressive d., she created roles in Gore's *Antonia* (1949), *The Night and the Silence* (1958), *Eaters of Darkness* (1958), *Sweet Dancer* (1964), and *Dance Pictures* (1971).
BIBL.: M. Clarke, 'P.H.'s Return and Northern Dance Th.', *Dancing Times* (1972/10).

Hiroshima (orig. Czech title: *A paráncs*). Ballet in 5 scenes; libr. V. Vašut; mus. V. Bukový; ch. Eck. Prod. 21 Dec. 1962, Pécs, with Boldozsár Veöreös, Gabriella Stimácz. The b. shows the conflict of the Amer. pilot who dropped the first atom bomb. It has been frequently given in new prods. throughout the Eastern bloc—especially successful versions have been those of J. Němeček at the Prague National Th. and of L. Ogoun for B. Praha (both 1964). Austrian TV prod. (of Studion B. Praha version, 1965).

Histoire du soldat, L' (*The Soldier's Tale*). To be read, played and d., in 2 parts; libr. C. F. Ramuz; mus. Stravinsky; direction and ch. Georges Pitoëff; déc. René Auberjonois; cond. Ansermet. Prod. 28 Sep. 1918, Lausanne, with Elie Gagnebin, Gabriel Rosset, Jean Villard-Gilles, G. Pitoëff, Ludmila Pitoëff. A narrative b., in which the soldier and the devil try to out-trick each other, but the devil finally wins. The work has received all kinds of prods.— some of the more d.-orientated ones include G. Rennert's and R. Helpmann's Edinburgh Festival prod. of 1954 (with Helpmann and Shearer—later filmed with Beriosova) and J. Babilée's Spoleto prod. of 1967 (with Babilée and G. Daum). There have also been pure b. versions of the concert suite, including those by Cranko (Cape Town, 1942), Feld (Amer. B. Th., 1971), and P. Martins (New York City B., 1981).
BIBL.: G. Balanchine, 'L'H.d.s.' in *Balanchine's New Complete Stories of the Great Ballets* (Garden City, N.Y., 1968).

Hitchins, Aubrey (*b* Cheltenham, 1906, *d* New York, 16 Dec. 1969). Brit. dancer and teacher. Studied with Cecchetti, N. Legat, and Egorova. Became Pavlova's partner 1925–30. D. then with Le Chauve Souris and with Nemchinova and Oboukhoff. Founded his own co., in 1943. Taught in New York from 1947, during his last years at Harkness House.

Hodes, Linda (*née* L. Margolies; *b* New York). Amer. dancer, teacher, choreographer, and b. director. Entered Graham School when 9 years old and joined the co., in 1953. Created roles in Graham's *Seraphic Dialogue* (1955), *Clytemnestra* (1958), *Acrobats of God* (1960), and *Phaedra* (1962). Also d. with P. Taylor and Tetley, for TV, and on Broadway. Teacher of Graham technique for Batsheva D. Co., in 1964, for which she ch. *The Act* (mus. B. Page and B. Johnson, 1967—revived for B. Rambert, 1968). B. mistress of Netherlands D. Th. and artistic dir. of Batsheva co. She was married to Stuart Hodes and to the d. Ehud Ben-David.
BIBL.: S. Goodman, 'Meet L. and S. Hodes', *Dance Magazine* (1962/7).

Hodes, Stuart (*b* New York, 1924). Amer. dancer, choreographer, and teacher. Studied at Graham School and School of Amer. B., also with L. Christensen and Ella Daganova. D. with Graham co., 1947–58, in own recitals, and on Broadway. Taught at Graham School and High School of Performing Arts. Worked as assistant producer for various musicals and for Santa Fe Op. Ch. *The Abyss* (mus. Marga Richter) for Harkness B. in 1965 (revived for several cos.). Has dir. the d. programme of New York Univ. since 1972. He was married to Linda Hodes (Margolies).
BIBL.: S. Goodman, 'Meet L. and S. Hodes', *Dance Magazine* (1962/7).

Hodgson, Brian (*b* Liverpool, 11 Feb. 1938). Brit. composer. Worked as an actor, then with BBC Radiophonic Workshop. Comp. electronic scores for J. Chesworth's *Time Base* B. Rambert, 1966), C. Bruce's *There was a time* and *Duets* (both B. Rambert, 1973), and *Weekend* (B. Rambert, 1974), R. Cohan's *Forest* (1977) and *Field* (1980), both for London Contemporary D. Th.

Hoecke, Micha van (*b* 1945). Belg. dancer and choreographer. Studied with Preobrajenska. Appeared as an actor in several film and th. prods. Joined B. of the 20th Century in 1962, where he soon became one of the most prominent character soloists. His first ch. was *Le Fou* (after Gogol's *Diary of a Madman*, mus. Stravinsky and M. Hadjidakis, 1971), followed by *Les Mariés de la Tour Eiffel* (mus. Groupe des Six, 1972) and other bs. Has also worked for Avignon Festival and Cullberg B.

BIBL.: M. Aranias, 'Pleins Feux sur M.v.H.', *Les Saisons de la danse* (Summer, 1972).

Hoffmann, Ernst Theodor Amadeus (*b* Königsberg, 24 Jan. 1776, *d* Berlin, 25 June 1822). Ger. writer and composer. Some of his stories have been used for b. purposes—for instance *Der Sandmann* for *Coppélia* (ch. Saint-Léon, Paris, 1870), *Nussknacker und Mäusekönig* for *The Nutcracker* (ch. Ivanov, St. Petersburg, 1892), *Elixiere des Teufels* (ch. Ellen Petz, Dresden, 1925), and *Klein Zaches genannt Zinnober* (ch. Georgi, Hanover, 1970). A ch. prod. of the op. *Tales of Hoffmann* was mounted by Béjart for his B. of the 20th Century in 1961. A b. version of this op. by Darrell for Scottish Th. B. in 1972. E. Walter's b. *Klavierkonzert Nr. 2, Es-dur* (mus. Weber, Düsseldorf, 1971) is based on 'associations to the world of E.T.A.H.'

Hoffmann, Reinhild (*b* Sorau, 1 Nov. 1943). Ger. d. and ch. Studied at Essen Folkwang School. D. with Folkwang D. Studio, Bremen B. Co-dir. and co-ch. (together with G. Bohner) of Bremen B. 1978–86; to Bochum 1986. Her bs. inc. *Solo with Sofa* (mus. Cage, 1977), *Five Days, Five Nights* (mus. Ligeti, 1979), and *Unkrautgarten* (mus. G. Barry, 1980).

Höfgen, Lothar (*b* Wiesbaden, 27 May 1936). Ger. Dancer, choreographer, and b. master. Studied with P. Roleff and van Dyk. D. with the cos. in Nuremberg, Mannheim, Lübeck, and Mainz. Principal d. Cologne Op. 1959–64, B. of the 20th Century from 1964. Created roles in Béjart's *The Journey* (1962) *Ninth Symphony* (1964), and *Cygne* (1965). B. master Karlsruhe 1966–9, Bonn 1970–3, Mannheim 1973–8 and Hannover since. Has ch. many bs., the most successful being *Polymorphia* (mus. Penderecki, Bonn, 1966).

Hoguet, Michael-François (*b* Paris, 1793, *d* Berlin, 5 Apr. 1871). Fr. dancer, choreographer, and b. master. Studied with Coulon. Came to Berlin as premier danseur in 1817, where he stayed until his retirement in 1856, becoming 2nd ch., dir. of the b. school, and b. master. Ch. a great number of bs.; his most successful were *Der Geburtstag* (1833), *Robert und Bertrand* (1841), and *Aladin* (1845).
BIBL.: H. Koegler, 'H., M.F.' in *Friedrichs Ballettlexikon von A–Z* (Velber, 1972).

Holden, Stanley (*b* London, 27 Jan. 1928). Brit. dancer and teacher. Studied at Bush-Davies School and Sadler's Wells School. Joined Sadler's Wells B. in 1944. Returned to Sadler's Wells Th. B. after military service in 1948. Left to teach in South Africa in 1954. Returned to Touring Royal B. in 1957. Soloist of Royal B. 1958–60, principal 1960–9. Gained special popularity as a character d. in humorous roles. Created parts in Howard's *Selina* (1948), Cranko's *Harlequin in April* (1951), Ashton's *La Fille mal gardée* (Mother Simone, 1960) and *Enigma Variations* (1968). Dir. of the D. Academy of the Performing Arts Council of The Music Center in Los Angeles since 1970.

BIBL.: V. H. Swisher, '"Sleeping Beauty" May Awake in Los Angeles', *Dance Magazine* (1970/2).

Holder, Christian (*b* Trinidad, 18 June 1949). Brit. dancer. Started to d. in the folklore troupe of his father Bosco. Studied at Corona School, with Graham, and at High School of Performing Arts. Joined City Center Joffrey B. in 1966, soon becoming one of its most prominent soloists; two of his best roles were in Joffrey's *Astarte* and Arpino's *Trinity*.

Holder, Geoffrey (*b* Port-of-Spain, 1 Aug. 1930). Brit. dancer and choreographer. Started to d. in the folklore co., of his brother Bosco, with which he came to New York in 1953. Taught at Dunham School. D. in various Broadway shows and at Met. Op. Ho., with the co., of J. Butler, and with a group of his own. Ch. *Prodigal Prince* for Ailey co., (1967), *Dougla* for D. Th. of Harlem (1974), and for the film *Live and Let Die* (1973). Has also had exhibitions of his own paintings. He is married to the d. Carmen de Lavallade.
BIBL.: A. Moss, 'Who is G.H.?', *Dance Magazine* (1958/8).

Holland. See *Amsterdam, Dutch National B., The Hague, Netherlands D. Th., Scapino B.*

Holm, Eske (*b* Copenhagen, 19 Mar. 1940). Dan. dancer and choreographer. Studied at Royal Dan. B. School, joining the co., in 1958; appointed solo d. in 1965. Started to ch. in 1964. For a while worked for Cullberg B., but returned to Royal Dan. B. Has been especially successful as a choreographer of TV bs. His bs. include Stravinsky's *Agon* (1967) and *Firebird* (1972; TV prod. 1974), Georg Riedel's *Orestes* (1968), and *Chronic* (mus. by his brother Mogens Winkel, 1974). Started his own experimental co., Pakhus 13, based in Copenhagen, in 1975.

Holm, Hanya (*née* Johanna Eckert; *b.* Worms, 3 Mar. 1893). Ger.-Amer. d., teacher, and ch. Studied at Dalcroze school in Hellerau; started to teach there. Joined Wigman in 1921, becoming a teacher in her school and a d. in her group. D. in the premières of Wigman's *Feier* (1928) and *Totenmal* (1930), and was then sent to New York to open the Amer. branch of the Wigman School in 1931. From this her own H.H. Studio developed in 1936, which became one of the city's foremost modern d. schools until its closure in 1967. V. Bettis, J. Moore, Tetley, Redlich, and Nikolais were among her students. Formed a group of her own in 1936, with which she premiered *Trend* (mus. Varèse, 1937), *Metropolitan Day* (mus. Gregory Tucker, 1938), and *Tragic Exodus* (mus. Vivian Fine, 1939), all works very strongly orientated towards social criticism. Started her Center of the D. in the West in Colorado Springs in 1941, to which she returned every year to hold summer courses. Gained great popularity as a ch. of musicals—including *Kiss me, Kate* (1948), *My Fair Lady* (1956), and *Camelot* (1960). Appointed

head of the d. department of the New York Musical Th. Academy in 1961.
BIBL.: W. Sorell, H.H.—*The Biography of an Artist* (Middleton, 1969); M. Siegel, 'Conversation with H.H.', *Ballet Review* (IX/1).

Holmes, Anna-Marie (*née* A.-M. Ellerbeck; *b* Mission City, B.C., 1943). Can. dancer. Studied with H. Heiden, L. Karpova, and Wynne Shaw, later also with Dudinskaya in Leningrad. D. with her then husband, David Holmes, with Royal Winnipeg B. 1960–2, Kirov B. 1962–3, London Festival B. 1963–4, Grands Bs. Canadiens 1964–5, Dutch National b. 1965–7, R. Page's Chicago B. 1968–9, and since then as a guest with various cos. They excelled in virtuoso pas de deux of the Sov. acrobatic school. Both appeared in the film *Ballet Adagio* (1973). Now b. mistress, Boston B.
BIBL.: D. Jowitt, 'A.M. and D.H.—From Winnipeg to the World', *Dance Magazine* (1969/2).

Holmes, David (*b* Vancouver, 1928). Can. dancer. Studied with L. Karpova, des Vos, Addison, later also with Pushkin in Leningrad. For further details see previous entry.

Holmgren, Björn (*b* Stockholm, 1920). Swed. dancer and teacher. Studied at Royal Swed. B. School and with Rousanne, Kniaseff, and Skeaping. Joined Royal Swed. B. in 1939; appointed solo d. in 1946. D. as a guest with International B. in 1949. Created roles in Akesson's *Sisyphus* (1957), *Minotaurus* (1958), and *Ikarus* (1963). Retired in 1965. Has ch. a few bs. Now a teacher at the Stockholm Swed. State D. School and Royal Swed. B.

Homage to the Queen. Ballet in 1 act; ch. Ashton; mus. M. Arnold; déc. Messel. Prod. 2 June 1953, Sadler's Wells B., Cov. Gdn., London, with Fonteyn, Somes, Nerina, Rassine, Elvin, Hart, Grey, Field. The b. was a pièce d'occasion for the coronation of Elizabeth II, with the elements paying their tribute to the Queen.
BIBL.: C. Beaumont, 'H.t.t.Q.' in *Ballets of Today* (London, 1954); D. Vaughan, *Frederick Ashton and his Ballets* (London, 1977).

Homme et son desir, L' (*Man and His Desire*). Ballet in 3 scenes; libr. Claudel; ch. Börlin; mus. Milhaud; déc. Andrée Parr. Prod. 6 June 1921, Bs. Suédois, Th. des Champs-Elysées, Paris, with M. Johanson, Börlin, T. Stejermer, C. Ari. 'Man starts to move in his dream . . . And what he dances, is the eternal d. of longing, of desire and of exile, of his prisoners and of his abandoned lovers' (Claudel).
BIBL.: C. W. Beaumont, 'L'H.e.s.d.' in *Complete Book of Ballets* London, 1951).

Honegger, Arthur (*b* Le Havre, 10 Mar. 1892, *d* Paris, 27 Nov. 1955). Swiss composer. Wrote the mus. for Börlin's *Les Mariés de la Tour Eiffel* (together with the other members of the Groupe des Six, 1921) and *Skating Rink* (1922), Nijinska's *Les Noces de l'amour et de Psyché* (after Bach, 1928),

Massine's *Amphion* (1934), Fokine's *Semiramis* (1934), Lifar's *Cantique des cantiques* (1938), *Chota Roustaveli* (together with Tcherepnin and Harsanyi, 1946) and *La Naissance des couleurs* (1949), and Peretti's *L'Appel de la montagne* (1945). T. Shawn ch. H.'s *Pacific 231* for his Male Dancers in 1933. A selection of his piano pieces was adapted by Charles Lynch for Howard's *Lady into Fox* (1939). Wallmann ch. a prod. of his *Danse des morts* for the Salzburg Festival of 1955.

Hønningen, Mette (*b* Copenhagen, 3 Oct. 1944). Dan. dancer. Studied at Royal Dan. B. School, joining the co., in 1963; appointed solo d. in 1967. An unusually versatile d.; she stars in Disney's film *Ballerina* (1966). Created role in Flindt's *Dreamland* (1974).

Hopak. see *Gopak*.

Hopps, Stuart Gary (*b* London, 2 Dec. 1942). Brit. dancer, teacher, and choreographer. Studied at Hettie Loman School, London School of Contemporary D., and with M. Cunningham. D. with H. Loman Comp. 1962–5, M. Anthony in 1968, and M. Monk in 1969. Has taught at various colleges. Started to ch. for Scottish Th. B. in 1970, becoming founder-dir. of its Movable Workshop (the co.'s modern d. group) 1974–5, since when he has been a freelance ch. working extensively in the theatre as well as d.

Hornpipe. A peculiarly Eng. d., orig. performed to the accompaniment of a now obsolete instrument of that name, consisting of a wooden or horn pipe with a reed mouthpiece. Early examples were in simple triple time, but later, when the d. was chiefly kept up amongst sailors, this changed to simple duple. Purcell (in *Dido and Aeneas*) and Handel are among the comps. who have written hornpipes.

Horoscope. Ballet in 1 act; libr. and mus. C. Lambert; ch. Ashton; déc. Fedorovich. Prod. 27 Jan. 1938, Vic-Wells B., Sadler's Wells Th., London, with Fonteyn, Somes. The signs of the zodiac govern the experiences of two young lovers.
BIBL.: D. Vaughan, *Frederick Ashton and his Ballets* (London, 1977).

Horschelt, Friedrich (*b* Cologne, 13 Apr. 1793, *d* Munich, 9 Dec. 1876). Ger. dancer, choreographer, and b. master. He was b. master of the Th. an der Wien 1815–21, where his Children's Dancers (incl. such later famous artists as Heberle, Angioletta Mayer, Wilhelmine Schröder-Devrient, and perhaps F. Elssler) gained such notoriety that they were disbanded by the Emperor's decree in 1821. He then went to Munich, where he ch. many successful bs. until 1848.
BIBL.: A. H. Winter, in *The Pre-Romantic Ballet* (London, 1974).

Horst, Louis (*b* Kansas City, 12 Jan. 1884, *d* New

York, 23 Jan. 1964). Amer. pianist, composer, teacher, and writer. After his studies in San Francisco and Vienna he became a close musical collaborator of St. Denis 1915–25 and then of Graham 1926–48; eventually became the mus. dir. of her co., for which he comp. *Primitive Mysteries* (1931), *Frontier* (1935), and *El Penitente* (1940). Taught d. comp. at the Neighborhood Playhouse School of Th. in New York 1928–64, at the summer courses of Bennington College 1935–45, at Connecticut College Summer School 1948–63, and at the d. department of the Juilliard School 1958–63. Founded the modern-d.-orientated-magazine *Dance Observer* in 1934, remaining its editor until his death. Author of *Pre-Classic Dance Forms* (1937) and *Modern Dance Forms* (1960). Capezio D. Award (1955); Dr. *honoris causa* of Wayne State Univ. as 'the illustrious dean of American dance' (1963).
BIBL.: P. W. Manchester, 'L.H.: In Memoriam', *Dance News* (1964/3).

Horton, Lester (*b* Indianapolis, 23 Jan. 1906, *d* Los Angeles, 2 Nov. 1953). Amer dancer, choreographer, and teacher. Studied with Bolm, but was greatly influenced by the Jap. d.-actor Michio Ito and by Red Indian dancing. Started with the Indianapolis Civic Th., transferring to Cal. in 1928, where he staged d. festivals, in which he participated as a d. Formed the L.H. Dancers in 1934, for which he ch. extensively, appearing with them regularly in seasons on the West Coast, and occasionally also in New York and Jacob's Pillow. Opened a th. of his own in Los Angeles in 1948. His most important—often revised—works include *Salome* (percussion accompaniment, 1934), *Sacre du printemps* (1937), *Conquest* (mus. Lou Harrison, 1938), *Totem Incantation* (mus. Judith Hamilton, 1948), and *A Touch of Klee and Delightful Two* (mus. Camargo Guarnieri, 1949). He was a very important teacher, gaining wide influence through such students as J. Collins, C. de Lavallade, B. Lewitzky, J. Trisler, Ailey, and J. Truitte.
BIBL.: various authors, 'The Dance Theatre of L.H.', *Dance Perspectives 31*; interview with J. Truitte about L.H., *Dance and Dancers* (1971/12); L. Warren, *L.H.* (New York, 1977).

Horvath, Ian (*b* Cleveland, 3 June 1945). Amer. dancer. Studied with Charles Nicoll and Amer. B. Th. School. Appeared on Broadway and TV; joined City Center Joffrey B. in 1965, creating parts in Arpino's *Viva Vivaldi!* (1965) and *Olympics* (1966). Moved to Amer. B. Th. in 1967, appointed soloist in 1969. Artistic director of Cleveland B. 1974–84.
BIBL.: S. Goodman, 'I.H.', *Dance Magazine* (1971/9).

Houlton, Loyce J. (*b* Duluth, Minn., 13 June 1926). Amer. dancer, choreographer, teacher, and b. director. Studied with Eleanor King, Horst, Graham, Humphrey, Limón, Fonaroff, Hill and

School of Amer. B. Carleton College (B.A., 1946), New York Univ. (M.A. in D., 1950). D. with N. Fonaroff Co., Eve Gentry Co., Nona Shurman Co., D. Humphrey Repertory Group, 1947–51. Artistic director and ch. of Minnesota D. Th. since 1962, has choreographed many bs. Teaches at associated school as well as all over the U.S. Has written articles on d. in numerous publications.

House of Bernarda Alba. For bs. based on the play by F. García Lorca see *Feast of Ashes* and *Hermanas, Las*.

House of Birds. Ballet in 1 act; libr. and ch. MacMillan; mus. Federico Mompou, arr. Lanchbery; déc Georgiadis. Prod. 26 May 1955, Sadler's Wells Th. B., Sadler's Wells Th., London, with D. Tempest, M. Layne, D. Poole. Based on Grimm's *Jorinda and Joringel*, the b. tells of a Bird Woman, who catches young boys and girls and turns them into birds. When she tries to catch two young lovers, the boy resists and frees the birds from their cages; they than attack their oppressor, peck her to death, and thus regain their human form. Revived for Stuttgart B. in 1963. BBC TV prod. 1956.

Houston Ballet. A Houston B. Foundation was formed in 1955; it sponsored a local B. Academy, with Tatiana Semenova as its dir., and arranged occasional perfs. for its pupils. Nina Popova was invited to mount a *Giselle* prod. in 1967; this was so successful that the Foundation decided to back a new b. co. with Popova as its artistic dir. This was to be the H.B., which gave its first perf. in the fall of 1968, with 16 dancers in the co. and 5 bs. in the repertory (1 Balanchine and 1 Ross b. were incl. in the opening programme). The co., has now grown to 30 dancers, with a repertory of 35 bs., incl. works by Balanchine, Dolin, Lichine, Franklin, Taras, Hynd, and several by J. Clouser, resident ch. for the 1974–5 season. B. master is N. Polajenko, and the dancers are headed by L. Ahonen and S. Arvola. The co. maintains a close working relationship with the H.B. Academy. Popova was succeeded by Clouser as artistic dir. 1975–6, and Ben Stevenson from 1976.
BIBL.: S. Shelton, 'H.B.: Brainchild of a Community', *Dance Magazine* (1975/2); A. Holmes, 'Boom Town Ballet,' *Ballet News* (1979/9).

Hovhaness, Alan (*b* Somerville, Mass., 8 Mar. 1911). Amer. composer. Wrote the mus. for Graham's *Ardent Song* (1954) and *Circe* (1963), P. Lang's *Black Marigolds* (1959) and *Shirah* (1960), and J. Erdman's *Dawn Song* (1952). Much of his concert mus. has been adapted for d. use.

Hoving, Lukas (*b* Groningen, 5 Sep. 1912). Dutch-Amer. dancer choreographer, and teacher. Studied with Florrie Rodrigo and Georgi, then with Jooss in Dartington; joined Jooss's co. Went to Amer., d. with the cos. of Graham and Bettis, and (principally) with Limón, creating roles in his *Le Malinche* (1949), *The Moor's Pavane* (1949),

The Traitor (1954), and *Emperor Jones* (1956), and in Humphrey's *Night Spell* (1951) and *Ruins and Visions* (1953). Formed his own co., in the early 1960s, for which he ch. *Icarus* (mus. Shin-Ichi Matsushita, 1963—revived for many other cos.). Has taught at Juilliard School, Essen Folkwang School, Swed. State D. School, and various other institutes. Dir. of Rotterdam D. Academy 1971–8.
BIBL.: N. Stahl. 'Conversation with L.H.', *Dance Magazine* (1955/8).

Howald, Fred (*b* Bern, 16 Oct. 1946). Swiss dancer and choreographer. Studied locally, then at Stuttgart B. School. Member of Stuttgart B. 1968–70, Frankfurt B. 1970–3 (eventually as soloist; a soloist with the Hamburg B. 1973–7. Created numerous roles in bs. by J. Neumeier. Artistic dir. of Frankfurt B. 1977–80. Has ch. many bs. Married to the d. Silvia Winterhalder.

Howard, Alan (*b* Chicago, 7 Aug. 1930). Amer. dancer and teacher. Studied with E. McRae. Joined B. Russe de Monte Carlo in 1949; eventually appointed premier danseur. Stayed with the co., until 1960. Also d. with M. Slavenska B., New York City B., and Radio City Music Hall. Founded his own Pacific B. Academy in San Francisco, from which came the Pacific B., for which he has ch. a number of bs. Guest teacher of various cos. Has taught at the Hanover Academy of Mus. since 1974.

Howard, Andrée (*b* London, 3 Oct. 1910, d. there, 18 Mar. 1968). Brit. dancer, choreographer, and designer. Studied with Rambert, Egorova, Preobrajenska, Trefilova. Founder-member of the B. Club, for which she ch. (with Susan Salaman) *Our Lady's Juggler* (mus. Respighi, 1930) and *The Mermaid* (mus. Ravel, 1934); later chs. for B. Rambert *Cinderella* (mus. Weber, 1935), *Death and the Maiden* (mus. Schubert, 1937), and *Lady into Fox* (mus. Honegger, 1939), most of which she designed herself. Created *La Fête étrange* (mus. Fauré) for London B. in 1940, which immediately went into the B. Rambert repertory (revived for Royal B., 1957; Scottish Th. B., 1971); also for B. Rambert she ch. *Carnival of Animals* (mus. Saint-Saëns, 1943), *the Fugitive* (mus. Salzedo, 1944), and *The Sailor's Return* (mus. Oldham, 1947). Her other bs. include *Twelfth Night* (mus. Grieg, International B., 1942), *Assembly Ball* (mus. Bizet, Sadler's Wells Th. B., 1946), *Mardi Gras* (mus. Salzedo, same co., 1946), *Selina* (mus. Rossini, same co., 1948), *A Mirror for Witches* (mus. Aplvor, Sadler's Wells B., 1952), *Veneziana* (mus. Donizetti, same co., 1953), and *La Belle Dame sans merci* (mus. A. Goehr, Edinburgh Festival B., 1958). During her last years she worked mainly in Turkey and concentrated increasingly on painting.
BIBL.: A. H. Franks, in *Twentieth Century Ballet* (London, 1954).

Howard, David (*b* London). Brit. dancer and teacher. Studied at Arts Education School with G. Cone, O. Ripman, M. Knight, E. Pettinger, and G. Goncharov. D. at London Palladium 1955–7, Sadler's Wells Th. and Royal B. 1957–63, appointed soloist in 1959, National B. of Canada 1963–4 and in various musicals, films and TV prods. 1964–5. Started to teach at Arts Educational School 1965–6, then at Harkness School in 1966. B. master Harkness B. 1967–70, co-director of Harkness B. School in 1970 and dir. of Harkness B. School 1975–7. Has worked as a guest teacher with numerous cos. and schools in Canada and throughout the US. Opened D.H. School of B. in New York in 1977.

Howard, Robin (*b* London, 21 May 1924). Brit. founder of London Contemporary Dance Th. Educated Cambridge Univ. A longtime admirer of d., he met Graham in 1962 and became her most ardent Brit. spokesman. Arranged her 1963 London season, assisted Eng. ds. who went over to New York to study with her, encouraged the start of Graham teaching in London in 1965. Opened a school in 1966 which grew into the London School of Contemporary D., from which emerged the London Contemporary D. Th. in 1967. Estab. the Contemporary B. Trust (from 1971, Contemporary D. Trust) as the controlling agency, which acquired *The Place in 1969 and turned it into the school's and co.'s headquarters. Must be considered the most influential Brit. personality to have promoted the cause of Graham-based modern d. C.B.E. (1976).
BIBL.: 'Trans-Atlantic Influence', an interview with R.H., *Dance and Dancers* (1966/10).

Howes, Dulcie (*b* Cape Province, 1910), S.A. dancer and teacher. Studied with Webb, Crask, Karsavina, and Brunelleschi. D. with Pavlova. Returned to S.A. in 1930. Founded Univ. of Cape Town School of B. in 1932; its performing group became the Univ. of Cape Town B., which, since it was subsidized by the Cape Performing Arts Board in 1965, has become the *Capab B. One of the pioneering women of b. in S.A. Many of her pupils have joined the Sadler's Wells and Royal B., incl. Cranko, Rodrigues, Doyle, Bosman, and Mosaval. Contributed 'Pioneering in Cape Town', *Dance and Dancers* (1958/3).

How Long, Brethren? Ballet in 7 episodes; ch. and dir. Tamiris; mus. Genevieve Pitôt, based on *Negro Songs of Protest* (Siegmeister-Gellert collection); cost. James Cochrane. Prod. 6 May 1937, Federal D. Th., Nora Bayes Th., New York, with Tamiris and group. Preceded by some solo spirituals, 'the plaintive songs of slavery, songs of resignation and hope only in Heaven' (Margaret Lloyd), the work gathers momentum and launches into an indignant group protest about the plight of the Negro in contemporary society.

Hoyer, Dore (*b* 12 Dec. 1911, *d* Berlin, 30(?) Dec. 1967). Ger. dancer and choreographer. Studied at Hellerau and with Palucca (though not with

Wigman). D. with various Ger. th. cos. and groups; gave solo-recitals from 1933. After 1945 she toured with a group in her *Dances for Käthe Kollwitz* and with solo-programmes. B. mistress Hamburg State Op. 1949–51. She was throughout her career the representative of the Ger. Ausdruckstanz tradition; her greatest successes were in very austere and forbidding dances, mostly accompanied by her regular pianist-percussionist Dimitri Wiatowitsch. In her last years she performed mostly in South Amer. Her best known d. was the *Bolero*; she was in charge of the ch. of the Berlin prod of Schoenberg's *Moses und Aron* (1959). Committed suicide.

BIBL.: K. Peters, 'D.H.', *Die Tanzarchiv-Reihe* no. 4; H. Koegler, 'Introducing D.H.', *Dance Magazine* (1957/8).

Huang, Al (*b* Shanghai, 14 Aug. 1937). Chinese-Amer. dancer, teacher, and choreographer. Studied at Peking Op. School, with T' ai Chi and Kung-fu masters in China, then Perry Mansfield School and with Maracci. Appeared with L. Goslar and as a solo artist all over the U.S. and in Can., ch. many dances for various cos., and his own group. Has taught at Bennington College, Univ. of Cal. at Los Angeles, Univ. of Illinois, York Univ., Can., etc. Author of *Embrace Tiger, Return to Mountain* (Moab, Utah, 1973). Specializes as performer-lecturer-author on d. and the oriental th.

Hulbert, Tony (*b* London, 24 May 1944). Brit. dancer, choreographer, and b. master. Studied at Barbara Speake School of Dancing, Royal B. School, and with A. Hardie. D. with Welsh National Op. and Sadler's Wells Op., as a soloist with B. of the 20th Century 1961, London Festival B. 1965, Western Th. B. 1967, Netherlands D. Th. 1968, Royal Winnipeg B. 1970. Started to ch. for Netherlands D. Th. 1969. Has created various bs. for Niagara Frontier B., Eng ITV, and since 1970 for B. de Wallonie, of which he is now b. master and ch. Married to the d. Mitsuyo Kishibe.

Humel, Gerald (*b* Cleveland, 7 Nov. 1931). Amer. composer, living in Berlin. Wrote the mus. for V. Gsovsky's Turgenyev-based *Young Love* (not perf.), M. Taubert's *Herodias* (Brunswick, 1967), G. Bohner's *The Torturings of Beatrice Cenci* (Berlin, 1971), *Lilith* (Berlin, 1972), and *Two Giraffes Dancing Tango* (Bremen, 1980).

Humpbacked Horse, The (original Russ. title: *Konyok-gorbunok*). Ballet in 5 acts and 10 scenes; libr. and ch. Saint-Léon; mus. Pugni. Prod. 15 Dec. 1864, Bolshoi Th., St. Petersburg, with Marfa Muravieva, Nikolai Troitzky. Based upon the popular fairy-tale by P. P. Yershov, the b. tells of the spectacular deeds of Ivanushka with the help of the H.H., through which he finally wins the Tsar-Maiden, after which a grand divertissement of all the different nations living together in Russ. crowns the marriage celebrations. In spite of its

absurd plot, poor mus., and confused folklore, the b. proved an instant hit with the audience. It has often been reproduced in different versions—e.g. by Petipa (St. Petersburg, 1895) and Gorsky (Moscow, 1901). A new b. of the same title, libr. Vainonen and P. Maliarevsky, mus. Shchedrin, was premiered on 4 Mar. 1960 at the Moscow Bolshoi Th. (ch. Radunsky, individual versions, Leningrad Maly Th., ch. Belsky, and Palace of Culture, Leningrad, both in 1963). Sov. film prod. of the Radunsky-Shchedrin version (with Plisetskaya and Vasiliev, 1961).

BIBL.: L. Kirstein, '*Konjok Gorbunok*' in *Movement & Metaphor* (New York, 1970).

Humphrey, Doris (*b* Oak Park, Ill., 17 Oct. 1895, *d* New York, 29 Dec. 1958). Amer. dancer, choreographer, and teacher. Studied at Francis W. Parker School in Chicago. Started to teach ballroom d. in 1913. D. with Denishawn Co., 1917–28. Started to ch. in 1920. Formed performing group with Weidman in 1928, which started with *Color Harmony* and *Air for the G String*, followed by *Air on a Ground Bass* in 1929, *Drama of Motion* (no mus.), prod. of Schoenberg's *Die glückliche Hand* (Met. Op. House, both 1930), *The Dance of the Chosen* (later *The Shakers*, mus. traditional, harmonized D. Jahn, arr. P. Lawrence, 1931), ch. for the plays *Run, Little Chillun!* (Hall Johnson) and *School for Husbands* (Molière, both 1933). Joined staff of Bennington School of D. in 1934. Ch. the trilogy *New Dance, Theatre Piece,* and *With My Red Fires* (mus. W. Riegger, 1935–6), *Passacaglia in C Minor* (mus. Bach, 1938), *El Salon Mexico* (mus. Copland, 1943), and *Inquest* (mus. N. Lloyd, 1944). Owing to a hip-ailment had to abandon her career as a d. but continued as a teacher and as artistic director of the J. Limón co., for which she ch. *Lament for Ignacio Sánchez Mejías* (mus. Lloyd, 1946), *Day on Earth* (mus. Copland, 1947), *Quartet No. 1* (*Night Spell*, mus. P. Rainier, 1951), *Deep Rhythm* (mus. Surinach, 1953), *Ruins and Visions* (mus. Britten, 1953), *Theatre Piece No. 2* (mus. Luening, 1956), and *Brandenburg Concerto No. 4* (finished by R. Currier, mus. Bach, 1959). Author of *The Art of Making Dances* (New York, 1959) and 'New Dance' (*Dance Perspectives* 25). She was one of the most important personalities of the Amer. modern d. movement, equally influential as a d., ch. and teacher.

BIBL.: S. J. Cohen, *D.H.: An Artist First* (Middletown, Conn., 1972); E. Stodelle, *The Dance Technique of D.H. and its Creative Potential* (Princeton, 1978).

Hundred Kisses, The. See *Cent Baisers, Les.*

Hungary. Apart from the Hung. State Op. B. based upon *Budapest and the *Ballet Sopianae from Pécs, the only other co., to gain international acclaim has been the Hung. State Folk Ensemble.

Hurok, Solomon Israelevich (*b* Pogar, 9 Apr. 1888, *d* New York, 5 Mar. 1974). Russ.-Amer. impresario. Came to the U.S. in 1906, where he

started to organize concerts in 1910. A great many individual dancers and cos. have been managed by him, including Pavlova, Duncan, Wigman, Escudero, Argentinita, Graham, B. Russe de Monte Carlo, Original B. Russe, B. Th., Sadler's Wells and Royal B., Moscow Bolshoi B., Leningrad Kirov B., National B. of Canada, and Stuttgart B. Author of *Impresario* (New York, 1947) and *S. Hurok Presents* (New York, 1955).
BIBL.: O. Maynard, 'S.H. at 85', *Dance Magazine* (1973/5); H. Kupferberg, 'S.H. Dead at 85', *Dance News* (1974/4).

Hurry, Leslie (*b* London, 1909, *d* London, 20 Nov. 1978). Brit. painter and designer. Designed Helpmann's *Hamlet* (1942) and the Sadler's Wells B. *Swan Lake* prods. of 1943 and 1952.

Hus Family. A widely travelled family of dancers, b. masters, choreographers, and teachers, whose names appear all over Europe during the 18th and 19th century. Jérôme H. was registered as Maître de danse in Lyons in 1763. Pietro H. was installed as dir. of the Naples San Carlo B. School when it was established in 1812, with S. Taglioni and L. Henry as his associates. Jean-Baptiste H. (1733–1805) was a pupil of L. Dupré; he became a d. and ch. at the Paris Opéra and then b. master at the Th. Français. Best known of all was Eugène H. (H. jeune), who was born Pierre-Louis Stapleton in Brussels in 1758 (*d* there, 1823); he took the name of his teacher, and became the founder-dir. of the b. co., at the Brussels Th. de la Monnaie in 1815.
BIBL.: M. H. Winter, in *The Pre-Romantic Ballet* (London, 1974).

Hutchinson, Ann (*b* New York, 1918). Amer. dancer and authority of dance notation. Studied with Jooss and Leeder at Dartington Hall, and with Holm, Graham, Limón, Tudor, Craske, and Caton in New York, also ballroom d., folk, Span., and Indian d. Appeared in modern d. programmes and on Broadway, before concentrating on research into the various d. notation systems, specializing in Labanotation (which she had started to study under Laban in Dartington). Co-founder and president of the New York Dance Notation Bureau 1940-61. Co-founder of International Council of Kinetography Laban in 1961. Has also taught notation at New York School of Performing Arts and Juilliard School. Lives in London since 1962, where she teaches notation. She is married to the b. writer Ivor Guest. Author of *Labanotation* (New York, revised ed. 1970).

Hynd, Ronald (orig. R. Hens; *b*. London, 22 Apr. 1931). Brit. dancer, choreographer and b. director. Studied with Rambert. Danced with B. Rambert 1949–52, S. Wells and Royal B. 1952–70. Appointed soloist in 1954; created roles in Cranko's *Prince of the Pagodas* (1957) and *Antigone* (1959). First ch. Stravinsky's *Baiser de la Fée* for Dutch National B. in 1968 (revived London Festival B., 1974). Appointed b. dir. Munich State Op. 1970–3 and 1984–6. Other bs. include *Pasiphae* (mus. D. Young, Royal Choreographic Group, 1969), *Dvorak Variations* (London Festival B., 1970), *In a Summer Garden* (mus. Delius, Touring Royal B., 1972), *Mozartiana* (mus. Tchaikovsky, London Festival B., 1973), *Charlotte Brontë* (mus. Young, Royal B. New Group, 1974), *The Merry Widow* (mus. Lehár, arr. Lanchbery, The Austral. B., 1975), *The Sanguine Fan* (mus. Elgar) and *The Nutcracker* (mus. Tchaikovsky, both 1976), *La Chatte* (mus. Sauguet, 1978), all for London Festival B., *Rosalinda* (mus. J. Strauss, PACT B. 1978, London Festival B. 1979), and *Papillon* (mus. Offenbach, Houston B., 1979, Sadler's Wells Royal B., 1980). Married to the former d. Annette Page.

Hywell, Suzanne (*b* Tunbridge Wells, 15 Feb. 1944). Brit. dancer and choreographer. Studied at Bush-Davies School and Royal B. School. Joined Western Th. B. in 1962 and Northern D. Th. in 1968, for which she ch. *The Clear Light* (mus. Messiaen, 1970), and *Teachings of Don Juan* (mus. J. McCabe, 1973). Second Prize Cologne Young Choreographers' Competition (1969). Now working in London.

I

Ibert, Jacques (*b* Paris, 15 Aug. 1890, *d* there, 6 Feb. 1960). Fr. composer. Wrote the mus. for Nijinska's *Les Rencontres* (Paris, 1925), R. Page's *Gold Standard* (Chicago, 1934), Fokine's *Diane de Poitiers,* (Paris, 1934), Petit's *Les Amours de Jupiter* (Paris, 1946), Etcheverry's *La Ballade de la Geôle de Reading* (Paris, 1947), and Lifar's *Escales* (Paris, 1948) and *Le Chevalier errant* (Paris, 1950)—also the *Circus* episode for G. Kelly's film *Invitation to the dance* (1952). There have also been various b. versions of his *Divertissement,* incl. those by Page (Paris, 1951), W. Gore (*Street Games*; New B. Co., 1952), Milloss (Rio de Janeiro, 1954), A. Carter (Wuppertal, 1965) and M. Pink (London Festival B., 1981). P. Wright ch. his *Quintet* for woodwind (Stuttgart, 1963).

Ibéria. Ballet in 3 scenes; ch. Börlin; mus. Albeniz, orchestrated by D. E. Inghelbrecht; déc. Steinlen. Prod. 25 Oct. 1920, Bs. Suédois, Th. des Champs-Elysées, Paris, with C. Ari, M. Johanson, Börlin. The b. presents some typical Span. scenes: a seaside village with an architecture of mastheads—the blue sky of Albaicin—a square in Seville with a procession of monks dressed in white.

Icare. Ballet in 1 act; libr., ch., and rhythms Lifar; instrumentation J. E. Szyfer; déc. P. R. Larthe. Prod. 9 July 1935, Opéra, Paris, with Lifar. The b. shows how Icarus attempts to fly with the wings constructed by his father Daedalus, and becomes a victim of his ambitions when the sun's rays melt the wax of his wings and he crashes down. The b. is really a big solo with the accompaniment of a group. It was performed to rhythms, distributed over a wide selection of percussion instruments, thus trying to free the 'choréauteur' (Lifar) from the dictatorship of the comp. Revived with new déc. by Picasso in 1962. Other d. treatments of the same myth by L. Hoving (mus. Shin-Ichi Matsushita, 1963), V. Vasilyev (mus. S. Slonimsky, Bolshoi B., 1971), Milloss (in *Daidalos,* mus. G. Turchi, Florence, 1972), and Arpino (in *The Relativity of Icarus,* mus. G. Samuel, 1974).
BIBL.: C. W. Beaumont, 'I' in *Complete Book of Ballets* (London, 1951).

Ice Maiden, The (orig. Russ. title: *Ledyanaya deva*). Ballet in 3 acts, 5 scenes, with prologue and epilogue; ch. Lopokov; mus. Grieg, arranged by Asafiev; déc. A. Golovin. Prod. 27 Apr. 1927, GATOB, Leningrad, with Mungalova, Gusev. The b. tells the story of the I.M. who, in the disguise of a beautiful girl, attracts young men and brings them death. The mus. comes mainly from Grieg's

Peer Gynt. The b. caused considerable controversy through its daring acrobatic ch. An earlier version by P. Petrov under the title *Solveig* (same mus., same déc.), GATOB, 1922.
BIBL.: N. Roslavleva, in *Era of the Russian Ballet* (London, 1966).

Idiot, The. There have been 2 bs. after Dostoievsky's novel: 1st a b. pantomime in 7 scenes with prologue and epilogue by T. Gsovsky (mus. Henze, Berlin B., 1952)—and 2nd by V. Panov (mus. Shostakovich, Ger. Op. Berlin, 1979).

Idylle. Ballet in 1 act and 3 scenes; libr. and déc. Alwyn Camble; ch. Skibine; mus. François Serette. Prod. 2 Jan. 1954, Grand B. du Marquis de Cuevas, Th. de l'Empire, Paris, with Marjorie Tallchief, Skibine, Skouratoff. The b. tells of a white mare who lives quite happily with a black stallion until a grey circus horse appears, elaborately dressed up—but she soon becomes disillusioned with his fine feathers and gladly returns to her first love.
BIBL.: C. Beaumont, 'I.' in *Ballets Past & Present* (London, 1955).

Idzikowsky, Stanislas (*b* Warsaw, 1894, *d* London, 12 Feb. 1977). Pol.-Brit. dancer and teacher. Studied with Cecchetti. Made his début with the London Empire Th. B., then d. with Pavlova and with Diaghilev's Bs. Russes 1914–26 (and again 1928–9). Created roles in Massine's *The Good-Humoured Ladies* (1917), *Les Contes Russes* (1917), *Boutique fantasque* (1919), *Le Tricorne* (1919), *Pulcinella* (1920), and Balanchine's *Jack in the Box* (1926), but his most famous role was the Blue Bird in *The Sleeping Princess* prod. of 1921. Continued to d. as a guest with Vic-Wells B., creating a further role in Ashton's *Les Rendezvous* (1933). As a d. he was much admired for his phenomenal elevation and dazzling technique. He then taught for many years in London. Co-author (with C. W. Beaumont) of *A Manual of Classical Theatrical Dancing* (London, 1922).

Illuminations. Dramatic ballet in 1 act; ch. Ashton; mus. Britten; déc. Beaton; light. Rosenthal. Prod. 2 Mar. 1950, New York City B., City Center, New York, with Magallanes, Hayden, LeClerq. The b. develops as a sequence of pictures from a poet's imagination, dealing loosely with the texts of Rimbaud on which Britten based his song-cycle. Revived for Joffrey B. 1980 and Royal B., Cov. Gdn., 1981. Other b. treatments of the same mus. by T. Gsovsky (Ger. Op. Berlin, 1961) and N. Walker (Ger. Op. Berlin, 1969).
BIBL.: G. Balanchine, 'I.' in *Balanchine's New*

Complete Stories of the Great Ballets (Garden City, N.Y., 1968).

Images of Love. Ballet in 9 parts; ch. MacMillan; mus. Peter Tranchell; déc. B. Kay. Prod. 2 Apr. 1964, Royal B., Cov. Gdn., London, with Beriosova, Seymour, MacLeary, Nureyev. The individual episodes are based on speeches from Shakespeare's plays and the Sonnet CXLIV. The b. was part of the triple bill premiered on the occasion of the Shakespeare Quatercentenary (together with Helpmann's *Hamlet* and Ashton's *The Dream*).
BIBL.: G. Balanchine, '*I.o.L.*' in *Balanchine's New Complete Stories of the Great Ballets* (Garden City, N.Y., 1968).

Impekoven, Niddy (*b* Berlin, 2 Nov. 1904). Ger. dancer. A child prodigy d., who later studied with Kröller; she appeared for the first time when only 6 years old and continued to charm her audiences until the 1930s with her unique mixture of spontaneity, naïveté and gossamer lightness, epitomized in her d. performed to mus. by Mozart. She now lives in Basle. Author of *N.I.— Die Geschichte eines Wunderkindes* (Zurich, 1955).

Imperiale Accademia di Ballo. The official name of the b. school attached to La Scala di Milano. Founded by Benedetto Ricci in 1812, it was completely reformed by Blasis when he became dir. in 1837, after which it became one of Europe's most famous institutes. It prod. such ballerinas as Grisi, Cerrito, Fuoco, Legnani, and Zucchi. Cecchetti, who was also one of its pupils, became dir. in 1925; his successors include C. Fornaroli 1928–33, Ettorina Mazzuchelli 1933–50, Volkova 1950–1, E. Bulnes 1951–4 and 1962–9, and Elide Bonagiunta since 1969.

Imperial Society of Teachers of Dancing. Founded in London in 1904 for teachers of ballroom and other types of dancing from the whole Brit. Empire, it is the largest organization of its kind in the world. It conducts its own examinations and issues diplomas, which entitle the recipients to add M. (for Member) I.S.T.D. or F. (for Fellow) I.S.T.D. to their names. The Cecchetti Society was incorporated in 1924 and the Greek D. Association in 1951.

Imperio, Pastora (née P. Rojas; *b* Seville 1894—according to G. B. L. Wilson, Granada, *c.* 1885—*d* 1961). Span. dancer. The daughter of the famous gypsy d. and singer La Mejorana, she first performed in the tavernas and cafés of Seville, then appeared with her guitar-playing brother Victor Rojas in ths. and music-halls. She became one of the foremost representatives of Andalusian dancing between 1908 and 1925, and was called La Emperaora. With her co. she gave the first perf. of de Falla's *El amor brujo* (Madrid, 1915). Later on she became the owner of the Madrid nightclub El Duende, where she continued to

perform for many years. She was married to the bullfighter El Gallo.

Inbal. The National B. and D. Th. of Israel, founded by S. Levi-Tanai in 1950 and originally intended to conserve the songs and dances of the Yemenite minority; *The Yemenite Wedding* is its most popular prod. The name means in Hebrew the clapper of a bell. Later on other folkloristic forms were absorbed. It first appeared in London 1957 and in New York in 1958. Shlomo Haziz was appointed Co. Dir. in 1976.
BIBL.: J. B. Ingber, 'I. Dance Theatre', *Dance Magazine* (Nov. 1973); G. Manor, *I—Quest for a Movement Language* (Israel, 1975).

Indes galantes, Les. Ballet héroique with prologue, 3 entrées, and epilogue; libr. Louis Fuzelier; mus. Rameau; déc. Servandoni. Prod. 23 Aug. 1735, Opéra, Paris—a fourth entrée added in 1736. This is an op.-b., presenting 4 different love-stories from different parts of the world: Le Turc généreux, Les Incas du Pérou, Les Fleurs, and Les Sauvages. It was Rameau's third op., which was a great success with his contemporaries; nonetheless it was dropped from the repertory in 1773. Its present fame dates from the new extremely lavish prod. which Maurice Lehmann mounted at the Opéra in 1952, presenting: prologue—Le Palais d'Hébé (ch. Aveline, déc. Dupont), first entrée—Le Turc généreux (ch. Aveline, déc. Wakhevitch), second entrée—Les Incas (ch. Lifar, déc. Carzou), third entrée—Les Fleurs (ch. H. Lander, déc. Fost and Moulène), fourth entrée—Les Sauvages (ch. Lifar, déc. Chapelain-Midy).

Indrani, Rehman (*b* Madras). Ind. dancer. The daughter of the Amer. Ragini Devi who went to South India to learn its dances, she studied with Chokkalingam Pillai and later with other teachers, becoming a specialist of the Opissi style, which had previously been considered an advanced form of folk d., and which through her gained new artistic eminence. Her tours abroad won her a reputation as one of the foremost representatives of classical Ind. dancing.

Ines de Castro. See *Doña Ines de Castro*.

Inglesby, Mona (*b* London, 1918). Studied with Rambert, Craske, and Egorova. D. with B. Club, B. Rambert, and V. Dandré's Russian B. in 1939. Founded her own *International B. in 1940, becoming its dir., chief ch., and ballerina. Ch. *Endymion* (mus. Moszkowski, 1941), *Everyman* (mus. R. Strauss, 1943), and *The Masque of Comus* (mus. Handel-Irving). Retired in 1953.
BIBL.: A. Franks 'The I. Legend—International Ballet' in *Ballet Annual* (IV, 1950).

Initials R.B.M.E. Ballet in 4 movements; ch. Cranko; mus. Brahms; déc. Rose. Prod. 18 Jan. 1972, Stuttgart. This is a concert b., set to Brahms' second Piano Concerto in B flat, op. 83, which Cranko dedicated to 4 top soloists of the Stuttgart

B., who d. the leads at the première; the initials refer to Richard (Cragun), Birgit (Keil), Marcia (Haydée), and Egon (Madsen).

Inquest. Ballet in 1 act; libr. and ch. Humphrey; mus. N. Lloyd; cost. P. Lawrence. Prod. 3 Mar. 1944, Humphrey-Weidman Studio Th., New York, with Humphrey, Weidman, Peter Hamilton. Based on a chapter in Ruskin's *Sesame and Lilies* ('Of King's Treasuries'), with a coroner's report on the death from starvation of a poor cobbler in the Eng. of 1865 (this is read aloud by a narrator). Its perf. on 26 May 1944 was Humphrey's last appearance as a d.

Institute of Choreology. Founded in London in 1962 by Rudolf and Joan Benesh for the teaching of their Benesh System of d. notation (also called 'choreology'; 'choreology' is strictly the collective term for the sciences connected with the d.). It awards various diplomas and has placed resident 'choreologists' with leading d. cos. in Brit. and abroad.

Intermezzo. Ballet in 1 act; ch. E. Feld; mus. Brahms; cost. Stanley Simmons. Prod. 29 June 1969, The Amer. B. Co., Spoleto, with Sarry, Lee, Stirling, Sowinski, Figueroa, and Coll. A romantic b., set to Brahms' op. 39, op. 117/3, and op. 118/3, performed by 3 couples in a ballroom, with the pianist being part of the setting. Revived for National B. of Canada and Amer. B. Th. (both in 1972), and Stuttgart B. (1975).

Intermittences du coeur, Les (Eng. title: *The Vagaries of the Human Heart*). Ballet in 2 parts; ch. Petit; mus. C. Franck, Saint-Saëns, Debussy, Beethoven, Fauré, Wagner, and Hahn; sets René Allio; cost. Christine Laurent. Prod. 24 Aug. 1974, Les Bs. de Marseille, Monte Carlo, with Araujo, Bryans, Kain, Ganio, Duquenoy. The b. is a free treatment of some key episodes from Proust's *A la recherche du temps perdu*. Paris first perf. on 14 Nov. 1974, Th. des Champs-Elysées. Renamed *Marcel Proust Remembered* for New York perfs. 1980.
BIBL.: R. Petit, 'Why Proust?', *Dance and Dancers* (1975/2—a translation of the programme notes).

International Ballet. The co. was founded by *M. Inglesby in 1940, with herself as dir. chief ch., and ballerina. It made its début in Glasgow on 19 May 1941, appeared regularly each year for a guest-season in London, and toured Eng., Scot., and Ireland, with occasional visits to the continent. The repertory was based on prods. of the classics, mounted by N. Sergeyev, the former régisseur of the St. Petersburg Maryinsky Th., who had emigrated with his notations of the Petipa and Ivanov bs.: *Swan Lake, Sleeping Beauty, Coppélia*, and *Polovtsian Dances*. Other bs. included Fokine's *Les Sylphides* and *Carnaval*, Howard's *Twelfth Night*, Turner's *Fête en Bohème*, and works by Inglesby. Among the early dancers of the co., which existed until 1953, were Turner, Shearer,

Algeranoff, de Lutry, Franca, and Arova, with Gollner and Petroff as guest artists. Hélène Armfelt, Claudie Algeranova, and Anne Suren later d. the ballerina roles. A different Co. to *B. International.
BIBL.: A. Franks, 'The Inglesby Legend—I.B.' in *Ballet Annual* (IV, 1950).

International Ballet Caravan. The small, chamber-size touring co. was founded in Paris in 1965, but has been London-based since 1966. Its dir. is Alexander Roy, who is responsible for most of the ch., with his wife Christina Gallea as ballerina. It has toured the Brit. Isles extensively, but often also performs in other European countries and has toured in the Far East. In 1976 it took the new name of Alexander Roy London B. Th.

International Dance Council. Founded under the auspices of UNESCO in Paris in 1973 'to encourage international displays of ch. in the field of classic, popular, modern dancing, but more especially to develop a policy for the protection and expansion of the world heritage in the field of ch. through studies, information, research work and also to protect all forms of interest in the field of dancing (as for example problems of copyright)'.

International Dance Course for Professional Chs. and Composers. Successor to the *Nat. Ch. Summer School from 1979, when the scope was broadened to include participants and financial support from the Commission of European Communities. Continues as primarily a creative collaboration between chs. and composers at the Univ. of Surrey, Guildford, where the Course dir. for 1979 was G. Tetley, and for 1981 (after a year's suspension), M. Cunningham with J. Cage. Now operated by Creative Dance Artists Ltd., an independent charitable trust with P. Williams as chmn., G. Law as sec. and administrative dir.

International Summer Academy of Dance. Founded in Krefeld (Ger.) in 1957, it moved to Cologne in 1961, where it has become the foremost of Europe's summer d. schools, offering for a fortnight every year (mostly in July) a great number of classes in academic, modern, historic, folk, and jazz d., d.-composition, and mime, with eminent teachers from all over the world. Connected with the Competition for Young Choreographers, established in 1968 and with the Week of Modern D. of the Cologne Tanz.-Forum.
BIBL.: 'Zehn Jahre Internationale Sommerakademie des Tanzes', *Tanzarchiv-Reihe* (no. 12).

Interplay. Ballet in 4 movements; ch. Robbins; mus. Gould; déc. Carl Kent. Prod. 1 June 1945, Concert Varieties, Ziegfeld Th., New York, with J. Reed, Kriza, Kidd, Robbins. The 4 movements, performed to Gould's *American Concertette*, arranged for 4 plus 4 dancers, are entitled: Free Play—Horseplay—Byplay—Teamplay. A very carefree and youthful b., it was immediately

taken into the repertory of B. Th. (newly designed by O. Smith) in Oct. 1945. Revived for New York City B. in 1952.
BIBL.: G. Balanchine, 'I,' in *Balanchine's New Complete Stories of the Great Ballets* (Garden City, N.Y, 1968).

Interrogation, The. See *Die Befragung*.

In the Night. Ballet in 4 movements; ch. Robbins; mus. Chopin; cost. Joe Eula; light. Thomas Skelton; pianist Gordon Boelzner. Prod. 29 Jan. 1970, New York City B., State Th., N.Y., with Mazzo, Verdy, McBride, Blum, Martins, Moncion. Set to Chopin's nocturnes op. 27/1, 55/1 and 2, and 9/2, the b. shows 3 couples establishing very different relationships, before coming together and drifting apart again. In a sense, an afterthought to his *Dances at a Gathering*. Revived for Royal B. in 1973.
BIBL.: R. Sealy, 'Mr. Robbins, Mr. Balanchine, Mr. Boelzner', *Ballet Review* (vol. 3, no. 3).

Intimate Letters. Ballets to Janáček's Second String Quartet have been ch. by G. Furtwängler (with A. Cardus, H. Baumann, H. Troester, and J. Watts, Cologne, 1968), P. Smok (with Petr Koželuh and Marcella Martiniková, B. Praha, 1968), H. King (Scottish B., 1975) and L. Seymour (Sadler's Wells Royal B., 1978). A special TV prod. by J. Kylián with members of the Royal Swed. B. for Swed. TV (1980).

Invitation, The. Ballet in 1 act; libr. and ch. MacMillan; mus. Matyas Seiber; déc. Georgiadis. Prod. 10 Nov. 1960, Touring Royal B., New Th., Oxford, with Seymour, Gable, Heaton, Doyle. Inspired by Beatriz Guido's *The House of the Angel* and Colette's *Le Blé en herbe*, the b. shows the effect on a young and innocent girl and her boy cousin of their encounters with a quarrelling husband and wife at a house party, and their sexual initiation by them. Revived for Ger. Op. Berlin in 1966.
BIBL.: P. Brinson and C. Crisp, 'T.I.' in *Ballet & Dance* (Newton Abbot, 1980).

Invitation to the Dance. Ballet-film in 3 parts by G. Kelly, produced in 1952, released in 1956. Its 3 parts are: *Circus* (mus. Ibert, with Sombert, Kelly, and Youskevitch), *Ring Around the Rosy* (mus. A. Previn, with Paltenghi, Dale, Youskevitch, Bessy, Tommy Rall, Belita, Diana Adams, and Toumanova), and *Sinbad the Sailor* (a combination of cartoon and live d., mus. Rimsky-Korsakov's *Sheherazade*, adapted by Roger Eden, with Kelly and David Kasday).
BIBL.: A. Knight, 'I.t.t.D.', *Dance Magazine* (1956/6).

Iran. On the invitation of the Ministry of Culture and Arts, N. de Valois went to Teheran in 1958 to establish a classical b. co., to which she then sent Ann Cock, M. Zolan, his wife Sandra Vane, and Marion English to teach and stage b. prods. In 1966 R. de Warren was appointed dir. of the

Iranian National B., which performs at Rudaki Hall, the city's op. house, inaugurated in 1967. When de Warren left in 1971 to study the national folk-dances and later form the *Mahalli Dancers of Iran co., prima ballerina Aida Ahmadzadeh succeeded him as dir. Later guest-producers have incl. Heaton, Chaboukiani, and Zolan. Last artistic dir. was A. Pourfarrokh, until the co. dissolved after the revolution of 1979.

Iranian National Ballet. The resident d. co. of Roudaki Hall Op. House in Teheran was founded 1967 by Nejad Ahmadzadeh. Sponsored partially by the Iranian Ministry of Culture and Arts it grew steadily from about a dozen dancers to 46 dancers in 1978, one third being Iranian. The repertory incl. both the classics and contemporary works, with recent additions by Ailey, Beriozoff, Butler, and Cullberg, and by Ali Pourfarrokh, the artistic dir. of the co. 1976–9.

Irish Ballet Company (Irish National Ballet since 1983). The country's first professional co., based on Cork, was founded in 1974, with Joan Denise Moriarty (who had for 25 years run the semi-amateur Cork B.) as its artistic dir., Domy Reiter-Soffer as ch. and art. adviser, and David Gordon as b. master. A. Vourenjuuri-Robinson art. dir. since 1986.

Irving, Robert (b Winchester, 28 Aug. 1913). Brit. b. conductor. Was musical dir. of Sadler's Wells and Royal B. 1949–58. Musical dir. of N.Y. City B. since 1958. Also conducts for Graham co. Contributor to *The Decca Book of Ballet* (London, 1958). Wrote 'The Conductor Speaks', *Dance and Dancers* (Mar., 1963). Capezio Award (1975).
BIBL.: R.I. interviewed, *Ballet News* (1981/8).

Isadora. Ballet in 2 acts; libr. Gillian Freeman, ch. MacMillan, mus. Richard Rodney Bennett, déc. B. Kay. First perf. 30 Apr. 1981, Royal B., Cov. Gdn., London, with M. Park/Mary Miller, L. Connor, J. Hosking, D. Rencher, Ross MacGibbon, S. Jefferies. The b. retells the tempestuous life and loves of I. Duncan with the title role being divided between an actress (with quotations from I.'s memoirs and other sources) and a d.

Ismailova, Galya Bayasetovna (b Tomsk, 12 Feb. 1925). Sov. dancer and b. mistress. Studied at Tashkent b. school, joining the b. co. of the op. house in 1941, and eventually becoming its prima ballerina and in 1962 its b. mistress. Created title role in Baranovsky's and Litvinova's *Ballerina* (1952), the story of which was based upon an incident from her life. D. in London in 1953, performing Uzbek folk dances. Stalin Prize (1950).

Israel. Stage d. began in Isr. (then Palestine, under the Brit. mandate) in the late 1920s when Rina Nikova, a Russ. emigré ballerina, founded her b. group in Jerusalem. She attempted to create biblical bs. which combined oriental subjects with classical style. During the 1930s several choreographers, mainly from central Eur., settled there, incl. Gertrud Kraus, Tilla Rössler, and the Ohrenstein sisters; they brought with them the expressionistic d. style then popular in Eur. At the same time a folk d. movement was started by Rivka Sturman, Gurit Kadman, and others; they used Arab and Druze d. steps (e.g. the Debka) and others of their own invention to create dances which became popular among the members of the new agricultural settlements, symbolizing the renewed bond between the Jewish immigrants and the land. Choreographers and dancers such as Jardena Cohen tried to establish d. cos. in which their pupils could perform. Attempts were made to create a distinct middle-eastern style, by incorporating typical oriental modes of movement, mus., and rhythm into their d. This attempt, however, was only partly successful; only Sara Levi-Tanai, a ch. of Jewish-Yemenite stock, who founded the *Inbal D. Th, in 1949, developed a style in which there is a real fusion of modern b. technique with the soft, implosive oriental style she prefers to call 'Yemenite Gothic' because of its dominant up-and-down movement executed in nearly constant demi-plié. Soon after the creation of the State of Isr. young Amer. dancers arrived in the country and some 'sabra' (Isr. born) dancers went to study in the U.S., mainly at Juilliard School and with Graham. G. Kraus and T. Beatty founded the short-lived Israel B. Th. in 1951. In the late 1950s A. Sokolow visited the country frequently and staged some of her works for the Lyrical Th. Most of the dancers of this group later joined the *Batsheva D. Co., which was founded by Betsabee de Rothschild in 1964. It became the first permanent professional modern d. co. in Isr., based firmly on the Graham technique. Choreographers who created works for it include Graham, Sokolow, Cranko, Tetley, Robbins, Cohan, Butler, and Morrice (since 1974 it has been government-sponsored). In 1968 a new co. was founded by B. de Rothschild, the *Bat-Dor D. Co., with J. Ordman as its Artistic Dir, while in the year before B. Yampolsky and Hillel Markman started the Classical B. Co. (now *The Israel B.). The main d. studios are the Rubin Academy of Mus. in Jerusalem, the Bat-Dor studio in Tel-Aviv, and the Center for D. in Haifa. The kibbutz movement maintains several regional studios and a permanent semi-professional d. co. A d. annual is now being published, starting with *Israel Dance 1975* (ed. Giora Manor and Judith Brin Ingber, Tel Aviv). (*Information kindly provided by the Isr. dance-critic G. Manor*.)

BIBL.: J. Brin Ingber, 'Shorashim: The Roots of Israeli Folk Dance', *Dance Perspectives 59*.

Istar. Ballet in 1 act; libr. and mus. V. d'Indy; ch. Clustine; déc. G. Desvalière. Prod. Paris, 1912, with Trouhanova, M. de Carva. The goddess I. is the Babylonian equivalent of the Greek Persephone, awaiting the arrival of the Son of Life, i.e.

Spring. A new version by Lifar, déc. Bakst, 31 Dec. 1941, Opéra, Paris, with Chauviré.

Israel Ballet, The. The co. was started as the chamber-size Classical B. Co. in 1968 under the direction of Berta Yampolsky and Hillel Markman, two former dancers from the B. Russe de Monte Carlo. Based upon Tel Aviv and still under the direction of Yampolsky/Markman, it consists now of about 25 intern. recruited dancers, offering a repertory which ranges from the classics through Balanchine, Bolender, Lazøini, Charrat, Blaska, and Spoerli. The co. also tours regularly abroad, and has several times been to the U.S.

Istomina. Avdotia Ilyinitshna (b St. Petersburg, 17 Jan. 1799, d. there, 8 July 1848). Russ. dancer. Studied with Didelot; appeared in 1815, in his *Acis and Galathea*. Became a brilliant première danseuse mime, especially admired for her interpretations in Didelot's *Zéphire et Flore, The African Lion or Heroism of a Mother, The Caliph of Baghdad, Ruslan and Ludmila*, and *The Prisoner of the Caucasus*. She combined highly expressive talents with dazzling virtuosity, marvellous aplomb, elevation, and pirouette technique. Pushkin has immortalized her in the first chapter of *Eugene Onegin*: 'Obedient to the magic strings, Brilliant, ethereal, there springs / Forth from the crowd of nymphs surrounding / Istomina the nimbly-bounding. / With one foot resting on its tip / Slow circling round its fellow swings / And now she skips and now she springs / Like down from Aelous's lip, / Now her lithe form she arches o'er / And beats with rapid foot the floor.' Retired after a foot injury in 1836. Died of cholera.

BIBL.: P. Migel, in *The Ballerinas* (New York, 1972).

Italy. Each of the country's many renaissance courts tried to have its own professional dancing-master to arrange and oversee the endless succession of spectacular festivities—some of whom became quite famous, such as Domenico da Piacenza, Antonio Cornazano, and Guglielmo Ebreo, while Bergonzio di Botta's 'dinner-ballet', which he staged at Tortona in 1489, was acclaimed far beyond the city's walls. But the really decisive developments in b. history took place in Paris—though even there they were at first in the hands of such Itals. as Balazarini di Belgiojoso (alias Balthasar de Beaujoyeux) who staged the epoch-making *Ballet Comique de la Reine* in 1581. Italy's most important contribution to the history of b. took place almost exclusively in *Milan—with lesser activity in *Naples and *Rome. Of course, there were occasional b. perfs. in other cities like Venice, Turin, and Florence, and some internationally famous b. master always took up residence there for one or two seasons, while the touring ballerine and ballerini appeared for some hastily assembled star-perfs., but there was hardly any continuity, let alone tradition. In more recent times Palermo, too, has occasionally shown some b. ambition of its own, but this has mostly been rather short-lived. Small Ital. cos. have often toured the country—the best known being those of Menegatti-Gai-Fracci and of Turin's Susanna Egri—but they are usually short-lived, after which they are disbanded, to be reassembled—often with changed personnel—if some new fixtures are offered. For foreign cos. the summer festivals of Florence, Genoa-Nervi, and Spoleto (and even Verona) have provided sympathetic and interested platforms, to which Venice was added in 1981, where the American-born Carolyn Carlson, previously at Paris, formed a new modern d. co. that year.

BIBL.: entry 'Italia—III. Balletto' in *Enciclopedia dello spettacolo*; F. Pitt, *Capriccio Italien* in *Ballet News* (1981/6).

Itelman, Ana (*b* Santiago de Chile, 1932). Argent. dancer and choreographer. Studied with Miriam Winslow, Graham, Holm, Limón, Horst, and Fornaroff. Formed her own group in 1954, based on Buenos Aires, where she has also done ch. for musicals. Worked for the b. co. of the Teatro San Martin.

Ito, Michio (*b* Tokyo, 13 Apr. 1892?, *d* there, 6 Nov. 1961). Jap. dancer. Coming from a highly cultivated family, he went to Eur. to study art. Deeply impressed by Nijinsky and Duncan in 1911, he studied with Dalcroze in Hellerau-Dresden 1912–4, then went to London to continue his studies, making his début as a professional d. at the Coliseum Th. 1915. 1916–29 he lived and worked in New York, 1929–42 in Los Angeles; after the war he returned to Tokyo. Profoundly influenced by his close collaboration with W. B. Yeats and E. Pound, he developed his own, highly poetic d. style, marked by Noh ideals and described as 'a happy marriage of East and West' (H. Caldwell).

BIBL.: H. Caldwell, *M.I.—The Dancer and His Dances* (Berkeley, Cal. 1977).

'I trionfi' di Petrarca—'per la dolce memoria di quel giorno'. Ballet in 6 trionfi, inspired by Petrarch's 'Triumphs', by Béjart (idea, ch., and direction); mus. Berio; déc. Roger Bernard and Joëlle Roustand. Prod. 7 July 1974, B. of the 20th Century, Boboli Gardens, Florence, with Donn, Farrell, B. Pie, A. Ziemski, A. Albrecht, C. Verneuil, R. Poelvoorde, D. Lommel. The 6 triumphs of the spectacle are: The Triumph of Love, of Chastity, of Death, of Fame, of Time, and of Eternity. The Maggio Musicale Fiorentino prod. was televised by Radiotelevisione Italiana.

Ivanov, Lev Ivanovich (*b* Moscow, 18 Feb. 1834, *d* St. Petersburg, 11 Dec. 1901). Russ. dancer, b. master, choreographer, and teacher. Studied in Moscow and St. Petersburg. Joined corps of Maryinsky Th. in 1850, though not graduating until 1852; appointed régisseur in 1882 and second b. master in 1885, continuing as character d. as which he had been much admired by Bournonville. His first ch. was a new version of

the Hertel *La Fille mal gardée* in 1885, followed by *The Enchanted Forest* (mus. Drigo, 1887), *The Tulip of Harlem* (mus. Schel, 1887), some smaller works, and the dances for Borodin's op. *Prince Igor* (1890) and Rimsky-Korsakov's op. *Mlada* (1892). In the same year he ch. the first prod. of Tchaikovsky's *Nutcracker* for Petipa, who had fallen ill. Subsequently made a new version of Bernardelli's *The Magic Flute* (mus. Drigo, 1893), and, with Cecchetti, *Cinderella* (mus. Vitingov-Schel, 1893). He then ch. the second act of *Swan Lake* for a Tchaikovsky memorial matinée in 1894, which was so successful that his chief, M. Petipa, decided to stage the whole b., which had been dropped from the Moscow repertory after its first two prodns. (1877 and 1882). Thus the famous Petipa-Ivanov *Swan Lake* of 1895 materialized; I. was responsible for the two white acts (2 and 4). Another collaboration with Petipa was *The Awakening of Flora* (mus. Drigo, 1894). His last bs. were *Acis and Galathea* (mus. A. Kadletz, 1896), *The Daughter of the Mikado* (mus. Vrangel, 1897), and new versions of Perrot's *Marco Bomba* and Saint-Léon's *Graziella* (both in 1899). He died while collaborating with P. Gerdt on Delibes' *Sylvia*. During all his life he thought himself misunderstood and repressed—and this is the picture which history has drawn of him: a man of extreme sensitivity and exceptional musicality, who never dared to step out of the shadow of his superiors, for the simple reason that at his time no native Russian was thought to be able to head the Imperial B. of St. Petersburg. He was certainly a more musical ch. than Petipa, he definitely matched him in the poetry and imagery of his spatial groups, and today we see him, in his two *Swan Lake* acts, as the pioneer of the symphonic b. Nonetheless we have come to think that I., in spite of his exceptional ch. gifts, would always have been, even under a less dominating personality than Petipa, the second man at the top of the Maryinsky B.

BIBL.: Y. Slonimsky, 'Writings on L.I.', *Dance Perspectives* 2.

Ivan the Terrible (orig. Russ. title: *Ivan Grozny*). Ballet in 2 acts; libr. and ch. Grigorovich; mus. Prokofiev, arr. M. Chulaki; déc. Virsaladse. Prod. 20 Feb. 1975, Bolshoi B., Moscow, with Y. Vladimirov, N. Bessmertnova, B. Akimov. Based on Prokofiev's mus. for Eisenstein's film of the same title, and excerpts from his Third Symphony and *Alexander Nevsky*. The story of the cruel Russ. tsar is retold from the perspective of Ivan's love for his wife Anastasia; it is after she is poisoned that he sets out on his path of terrorism.

Ivanovsky, Nikolai Pavlovich (*b* St. Petersburg, 3 Aug. 1893, *d* Leningrad, 28 Nov. 1961). Russ. dancer and teacher. One of Fokine's most talented pupils, belonging to the famous graduation class of 1911, together with P. Vladimirov, A. Gavrilov and S. Litavkin; he then joined Maryinsky Th. D. with Diaghilev's Bs. Russes 1912–5, with the

Troitzky Miniature Th., and again from the end of 1915 to the end of the 1930s at the Maryinsky Th. Started to teach during the 1920s, eventually becoming professor of d. pedagogy. Dir. of the Vaganova Ch. School 1945–61. Author of *Ballroom Dance of the 16th to the 19th Century* (Leningrad, 1948).

Ives, Charles (*b* Danbury, Con., 20 Oct. 1874, *d* New York, 19 May 1954). Amer. composer. Wrote no b. mus., but his concert pieces have repeatedly been used for b. purposes, incl. by Balanchine in *Ivesiana* (New York City B., first version 1954), H. Spoerli in *Flowing Landscapes* (Basle, 1975), J. Burth in *Years After* (Zurich, 1976), and P. Martins in *Calcium Light Night* (New York City B., 1977).

Ivesiana. Ballet in 6 episodes; ch. Balanchine; mus. Ives; light. Rosenthal. Prod. 14 Sep. 1954, New York City B., City Center, N.Y., with Reed, Moncion, Wilde, d'Amboise, Kent, Bolender, D. Adams, Bliss, LeClercq. Balanchine has ch. the individual pieces according to their title, without any connecting thread—originally *Central Park in the Dark, Hallowe'en, The Unanswered Question, Over the Pavements, In the Inn,* and *In the Night.* Since the première of the revised version on 16 Mar. 1961, the b. consists only of 4 pieces: *Central Park in the Dark, The Unanswered Question, In the Inn,* and *In the Night.* Revived for Dutch National B. in 1968 and Ger. Op. Berlin in 1971.

BIBL.: G. Balanchine, '*I.*' in *Balanchine's New Complete Stories of the Great Ballets* (Garden City, N.Y., 1968).

Izmailova, Galya Bayazetovna. See *Ismailova, Galya Bayasetovna.*

J

Jack-in-the-Box. Ballet in 3 dances; ch. Balanchine; mus. Satie; déc. Derain. Prod. 3 July 1926, Bs. Russes de Diaghilev, Th. S. Bernhardt, Paris, with Danilova, Tchernicheva, Doubrovska, Idzikowsky. A divertissement, with a rubber-balllike mischievous jumping jack, who is pushed about and played with by 3 ballerinas who spin like tops in front of movable cardboard clouds.

Jack Pudding (also *Jacques Pudding*). Ballet in 3 parts; libr. and mus. Henze; ch. Edgar von Pelchrzim; déc. Ponnelle. Prod. 30 Dec. 1950, Wiesbaden, with Pelchrzim. The b. is based on Molière's *Georges Dandin*, showing the miseries of a repeatedly deceived and cuckolded husband.

Jackson, George (*b* Vienna, 10 Dec. 1931). Amer. dance critic. Educated Univ. of Chicago. Studied d. with various teachers in Chicago and New York. Has written for *Dance News* since 1970, Correspondent for *Ballet Today* 1954–70. U.S. correspondent for Ger. *Ballett* annual (during the 1970s).

Jackson, Rowena (*b* Invercargill, 1926). N.Z. dancer and teacher. Studied with Powell and Lawson in N.Z. and at Sadler's Wells School from 1946. Joined Sadler's Wells B. in 1947, appointed principal d. in 1954; created roles in Ashton's *Variations on a Theme of Purcell* (1955) and *Birthday Offering* (1956). Returned to N.Z. with her d. husband Philip Chatfield in 1958, where they are now in charge of the Wellington National School of B. Adeline Genée Gold Medal (1947); M.B.E. (1961).
BIBL.: C. Swinson, *R.J. and Philip Chatfield* (London, 1958).

Jacobi, Georges (*b* Berlin, 1840, *d* London, 1906). Ger. conductor and composer. Mus. dir. of the London Alhambra Th. 1872–98, during which period he comp. the scores for 45 bs. and additional mus. for some other prods. 'Without question he was the most important b. comp. working in London in his day' (I. Guest).
BIBL.: I. Guest, in 'The Alhambra Ballet', *Dance Perspectives* 4.

Jacobsen, Palle (*b* Copenhagen, 3 Dec. 1940). Dan. d. Studied at Royal Dan. B. School; joined the co. but left in 1960 to d. with the cos. in Graz, Basle, Düsseldorf, and Johannesburg. Returned to the Royal Dan. B. in 1967, becoming solo d. in 1969. Has occasionally ch. some TV and other bs., especially for Kirsten Simone. Now teacher of co. and dir. Copenhagen Pantomime Th.

Jacobson, Leonid Venjaminovich (*b* St. Petersburg, 15 Jan. 1904, *d* Moscow, 18 Oct. 1975). Sov. d., ch., and b. master. Studied in the evening courses of the Leningrad B. School with Ponomarev; then continued with the normal training, graduating in 1926. Joined the GATOB, where he excelled in character and grotesque roles. Soon began to ch., collaborating with Kaplan, Vainonen, and Tchesnokov in the first prod. of Shostakovich's *The Golden Age* in 1930. Unusually gifted in grotesque and acrobatic pieces, he was in great demand for concert numbers; *The Bird and the Hunter* and *The Blind Girl* were two of his earliest successes. B. master Moscow Bolshoi B. 1933–42, Kirov B. 1942–69. Began work on F. Yarullin's *Shurale* in Kasan in 1941, which, due to the war, was not premiered until 1950 in Leningrad. Later bs. of his have been *Solveig* (mus. Grieg, Maly Th., 1952), *Spartacus* (mus. Khatchaturian, first prod., Kirov B., 1956), *The Bedbug* (after Mayakovsky, mus. F. Otkazov, Kirov B., 1962), *New Love* (mus. Ravel, Kirov B., 1963), *The Twelve* (after A. Blok, mus. B. Tistchenko, Kirov B., 1963), and *Land of Miracles* (mus. I. Stern, Kirov B., 1967); also many concert pieces, incl. a complete evening of *Choreographic Miniatures* (1938). Owing to his unconventional movements and pantomime almost all his new bs. caused great controversies. Formed his own co., also called Ch. Miniatures, in 1970, based on Leningrad; it first appeared in W. Europe at Venice and Reggio Emilia, 1981, as the Jacobson B. He was married to the d. Irina Pevsner.
BIBL.: M. G. Swift, in *The Art of the Dance in the U.S.S.R.* (Notre Dame, Ind., 1968).

Jacob's Pillow. T. Shawn bought the farm of this name nr. Lee, Mass., in 1930, turning it into a summer th. and making it the residence of his All-Male Dancers co. From 1933 summer d.-courses were held, until 1941, when the farm was acquired by a group of interested people who established the J.P. D. Festival with Shawn as dir. A special d. th. for an audience of 500 was built, which, after a thorough renovation and extension in 1959, was called Ted Shawn Th. With only a short interruption Shawn was in charge of the Festival from 1942 until his death in 1972; it is one of the top summer d. attractions in the U.S.A., distinguished by its open-mindedness to all kinds of d.—classical, modern, jazz, and ethnic. Many Eur. dancers and cos. have made their U.S. débuts here. Since Shawn's death the Festival has been directed by various people, incl. C. Reinhart, W. Terry, N. Walker, and now Liz Thompson.
BIBL.: T. Shawn, 'Remember: J.P. was a Stone', *Dance Magazine* (1970/7).

Jago, Mary (*b* Henfield, 1946), Brit. dancer. Studied at Royal B. School. Joined Cov. Gdn. Op. B. in 1965, then National B. of Canada in 1966, becoming soloist in 1968 and principal d. in 1970. Retired to staff appt. 1984.

Jahn, Wilfried (*b* Berlin, 25 Nov. 1943). Ger. dancer. Studied at East Berlin State B. School. Joined East Berlin Ger. State Op. in 1964, eventually appointed soloist. One of his best roles is in Kasatkina—Vasilyov's *Sacre du printemps*.

Jamaican Dance Theatre. Started by Eddy Thomas and Rex Nettleford as an amateur group, based on Kingston, in 1962. Originally only performed folk-dances (e.g. *Bongo, Banadana Dance, Santa Foulle*), but has since moved increasingly in the direction of modern-d.-based bs. such as *The King Must Die, Desperate Silences,* and *Misa Criola*. London début in 1972, New York in 1973.

Jamison, Judith (*b* Philadelphia, 10 May 1944). Amer. dancer. Studied at Judimar School of D. and Philadelphia D. Academy. D. in de Mille's *The Four Marys* in 1964. Joined Ailey's co. in 1965, of which she became one of the top soloists (occasionally dancing with other cos. such as the Harkness B.). Ailey ch. the solo-d. *Cry* for her (1971), Neumeier *Legend of Joseph* (Vienna, 1977). Starred in the McKayle ch. musical *Sophisticated Ladies* (1981). Dance Magazine Award (1972).
BIBL.: O. Maynard, 'J.J.', *Dance Magazine* (1972/11).

Janáček, Leoš (*b* Hukvaldy, 3 July 1854, *d* Ostrava, 12 Aug. 1928). Czech composer. His compositions have often been adapted to d. purposes; e.g. *Lachian Dances* (first as part of the folk-song play *Rákocz Rákoczy*, ch. Augustin Berger, Prague, 1891; later versions by S. Machov, Prague, 1947, and E. Gabzdyl, Ostrava, 1948), *Taras Bulba* (ch. L. Ogoun, Brno, 1963), *First String Quartet* (ch. E. Walter, Düsseldorf, 1966; also by Tudor, Juilliard School, New York, 1971), *Intimate Letters* (ch. P. Smok, Prague B., and G. Furtwängler, Cologne, both 1968; also H. King, Scottish B., 1975; L. Seymour, Sadler's Wells Royal B. 1978, and Kylián, Swedish TV, 1980), *Glagolitic Mass* (ch. Smok, Brno, 1969, also by Kylián for NDT, 1979, *Sinfonietta* (ch. Smok, Basle, 1971 ; also by Kylián, NDT 1978), *Concertino, In the Mists,* and No. 7 from *From an Overgrown Path* for piano in A. Killar's *Arriving Bellevue Sunday* (Scottish Th. B., Edinburgh, 1971), and various piano pieces in *Return to a Foreign Country* (ch. J. Kylián, Stuttgart, 1975).

Janin, Jules-Gabriel (*b* Saint-Etienne, 16 Feb. 1804, *d* Passy, 20 June 1874). Fr. writer and th. critic. As the dramatic critic of the *Journal des Débats*, a post he held from 1836 until his death, he proved one of the most exacting and knowledgeable b. critics of his day.
BIBL.: I. Guest, in *The Romantic Ballet in Paris* (London, 1966)—also in *The Ballet of the Second*

Empire (vol. 1, London, 1953; vol. 2, London, 1955).

Janotta, Monique (*b* Paris, 3 Mar. 1945). Fr. dancer. Studied at Paris Opéra School and with Golovina, Besobrasova, Hightower, and Golovine. D. with Geneva co. and Grand B. Classique de Fr. Joined Düsseldorf B. as principal d. in 1970, creating roles in many bs. by Walter.
BIBL.: J.-C. Diénis, 'M.J.', *Les Saisons de la danse* (1966/3).

Japan. Though the country possesses an age-old th. d. tradition of its own, as exemplified in the highly stylized prods. of Kabuki and Gagaku, academic d. only entered Jap. tentatively in the 1910s, when the first courses were held at the Imperial Th. Op. Department by Miss Mix and Mr. and Mrs. G. V. Rosi from London. As performers, Yelena Smirnova and Boris Romanov were followed by the Pavlova co. in 1921, which created a tremendous impression, and this newly discovered enthusiasm for d. was strengthened through the visits of the Denishawn Dancers in 1925, the R. Page co. in 1926, and Argentina and her troupe in 1927. However, a special Jap. variant of modern d. came to the fore during the 1930s, headed by Baku Ishii and Masao Takada. After the second world war, various foreign classical and modern d. cos. toured the country, and numerous b. schools sprang up in the larger cities, from which the first Jap. classical b. cos. emerged, most of them operating on a semi-professional basis and hardly any managing to exist long enough to build up a homogeneous troupe and a solid repertory. Thus there are about 50 different cos. operating all over the country, which one reads about occasionally in the d. magazines. Only one co., however, works on a permanent and truly professional basis, and this is the *Tokyo B. Co., founded in 1960 and somewhat Sov.-orientated in its teachers, b. masters, choreographers and repertory. Other cos. which have shown at least some continuity in their work are the Tokyo City B., the Tokyo Th. B. (for which Roy Tobias revived some Balanchine bs.), and the Star Dancers B. (for which Tudor worked for a while).
BIBL.: S. Ogura, 'Ballet in J.', *Ballet Today* (1970/3–4).

Jaques-Dalcroze, Emile (orig. Jakob Dalkes; *b* Vienna, 6 July 1865, *d* Geneva, 1 July 1950). Swiss mus. teacher and theoretician, who developed, as a professor in Geneva, a system of training musical sensibility through the translation of rhythm into bodily movements, called gymnastique rhythmique. Established his Institute for Applied Rhythm in *Hellerau nr. Dresden in 1911, where he trained many of the dancers who later became prominent in the Ger. modern d. movement—incl. Wigman, and Georgi (Rambert also studied with him). During World War I he returned to Switzerland. His school later moved to Laxenburg, nr. Vienna, but he continued with his teaching and research in Geneva, where he had thousands of pupils, who spread his teachings throughout the world.

BIBL.: M. Rambert, in *Quicksilver* (London, 1972).

Jardin aux lilas (also *Lilac Garden*). Ballet in 1 act; libr. and ch. Tudor; mus. Chausson; déc. Hugh Stevenson (who collaborated on the libr.). Prod. 21 Jan. 1936, B. Rambert, Mercury Th., London, with M. Lloyd, Laing, Tudor, van Praagh. 'Caroline, about to enter upon a marriage of convenience, tenders a farewell party to precede the ceremony. Among the guests are the man she really loved and the woman who, unknown to her, has been her fiancé's mistress. Quick meetings, interrupted confidences culminate with Caroline leaving on the arm of her betrothed, never having satisfied the desperate longings for the final kiss' (programme note). Set to Chausson's *Poème*. Tudor has revived the b. for many cos., incl. B. Th. in 1940, National B. of Canada in 1954, and Royal B. in 1968.

BIBL.: C. W. Beaumont, 'J.a.l.' in *Complete Book of Ballets* (London, 1951); L. Kirstein, 'J.a.l.' in *Movement & Metaphor* (New York, 1970).

Jaroslavna. See *Yaroslavna*.

Jarre, La (also *La Giara* and *The Jar*). Ballet in 1 act; libr. Pirandello; ch. Börlin; mus. Casella; déc. di Chirico. Prod. 19 Nov. 1924, Bs. Suédois, Th. des Champs-Elysées, Paris, with Börlin, Inger Fris, Eric Viber. A comedy b. about a broken jar which is repaired by the village tinker, who only discovers after finishing the job that he cannot get out of the jar, until its owner in a moment of rage knocks it over and breaks it again. Different versions by R. Galli (Met. Op. House, New York, 1927), Nijinska (Buenos Aires, 1927), de Valois (Vic-Wells B., London, 1934), and Milloss (Rome, 1939).

Jarreté (Fr.) A knock-kneed type of d. (opposite of *arqué*).

Jasinski, Roman (*b* Warsaw, 1912). Pol.-Amer. dancer and teacher. Studied at Warsaw Op. B. School. D. with Rubinstein's co. in 1928, then with Lifar in some recital programmes, Les Bs. 1933, and B. Russe de Monte Carlo 1933–50. Opened a b. school in Tulsa, Okl. with his wife Moscelyne Larkin, where they are now directors of Tulsa Ballet Th.

Jazz Calendar. Ballet in 7 parts; ch. Ashton; mus. Richard Rodney Bennett; déc. Derek Jarman; light. W. Bundy. Prod. 9 Jan. 1968, Royal B., Cov. Gdn., London, with Derman (Monday), Park (Tuesday; with Dowell and Mead), Lorrayne (Wednesday), Grant (Thursday), Sibley and Nureyev (Friday), Doyle (Saturday), and Trounson (Sunday). Based on the children's rhyme 'Monday's child is fair of face, Tuesday's child is full of grace, Wednesday's child is full of woe, Thursday's child has far to go, Friday's child is loving and giving, Saturday's child works hard for his living, And the child that is born on the Sabbath day is bonny and blithe, and good and gay.'

Jazz Dance. Developed—like jazz mus.—by the Amer. Negroes, who took African d.-techniques, based on polycentrism and the isolation of individually moving parts of the human body, and adapted them to the needs of their new social surroundings. The name first appeared about 1917. During the 1920s it was eagerly taken up by the whites, who introduced it into their various forms of show-business. Today so-called 'jazz ballets' such as Robbins' *New York Export: Op. Jazz* (1958) or Ailey's *Revelations* (1960), mostly use a synthesis of Afro-Amer., academic, and modern d. techniques.

BIBL.: M. and J. Stearns, *J.D.—The Story of American Vernacular Dance* (New York, 1968).

Jeanmaire, Renée (called Zizi; *b* Paris, 29 Apr. 1924). Fr. dancer and revue-star. Studied at Paris Opéra School; joined its co. in 1939. Appeared in the Soirées de la danse, organized by Lidova and Claude Giraud at the Paris Th. S. Bernhardt in 1944, where she met Petit, whom she married in 1954. Joined Nouveau B. de Monte Carlo in 1946 and d. ballerina roles with de Basil's B. Russe for its last London season in 1947, after which she became the top star of Petit's B. de Paris, creating many of his bs., including *Carmen* (1949), her most famous role, and *La Croqueuse de diamants* (1950), where she had her first singing role. She then went to Hollywood to appear in Petit's film *Hans Christian Andersen* (1951), and starred on Broadway in *The Girl in Pink Tights* (1953). Petit ch. all her subsequent shows and revues. She also appeared in his film *Black Tights* (1960). Together they bought the Casino de Paris in 1970, where she first starred in *La Revue*, directed and ch. by Petit, followed by *Zizi, je t'aime* (1972). Comeback at Paris Opéra in Petit's *Symphonie Fantastique* (1975), then *La Chauve souris* (1979). Chevalier de la légion d'Honneur (1974).

BIBL.: A. Livio, 'Z.J.' in *Etoiles et Ballerines* (Paris, 1965); I. Lidova, 'Z.J.', with complete list of roles and activities, *Le Saisons de la danse* (1975/1).

Jefferies, Stephen (*b* Reintelm, W. Ger., 24 June 1951). Brit. dancer. Studied at Royal B. School, joined Royal B. in 1969, appointed principal d. in 1973. Created roles in Layton's *The Grand Tour* (1971), D. Drew's *St. Thomas' Wake* (1971) and *Sword of Alsace* (1973), MacMillan's *Ballade* (1972), *The Poltroon* (1972), P. Wright's *El Amor Brujo* (1975), and D. Morse's *Pandora* (1976). Joined Nat. B. of Canada, 1976–7, then returned to Royal B., since when he has continued to d. both noble and character roles, and cr. roles in Tetley's *Dances of Albion* (1980) and MacMillan's *Isadora* (1981). He also created leading mime role of Yukinojo in Minoru Miki's opera, *An Actor's Revenge* for Eng.

Mus. Th. Co. (London, 1979). Married to the d. Rashna Homji.

BIBL.: 'A Man for All Seasons'; interview with S. J., *Dance and Dancers* (1975/12).

Jenner, Ann (*b* Ewell, 8 Mar. 1944). Brit. d. Studied with Marjorie Shrimpton and at Royal B. School. Joined Royal B. in 1961; appointed principal d. in 1970. Left 1978 and joined Austral. B. Joined San Francisco B. and school staff 1985. Married to the d. Dale Baker.

BIBL.: S. Goodman, 'A.J.', *Dance Magazine* (1969/7); J. Gruen, 'A.J.', in *The Private World of Ballet* (New York, 1975).

Jensen, Chris (*b* Los Angeles, 24 Jan. 1952). Amer. dancer. Studied with Albert Ruiz, Harriet De Rea, C. Maracci and at School of Amer. B. Danced with Geneva B. 1971–3, as a soloist with Harkness B. 1973–5, Joffrey B. 1975–6, Basle B. 1977–9, Netherlands D. Th. 1979–81, since when he has returned to Basle.

Jensen, Svend Erik (*b* Copenhagen, 1 Sep. 1913). Dan. dancer and teacher. Studied at Royal Dan. B. School. Joined Royal Dan. B. in 1933; appointed solo d. in 1942. Created roles in Lander's *The Sorcerer's Apprentice* (1940) and *Etudes* (1948). Has taught at the Royal Dan. Conservatory since 1958. Knight of Dannebrog (1951).

BIBL.: S. Kragh-Jacobsen, 'S.E.J.' in *20 Solo dancers of The Royal Danish Ballet* (Copenhagen, 1965).

Jesuit Ballets. (also called *Bs. de collège*). Th. perfs. have always played an important role in the spreading of the Jesuit message, and their elaborate b. prods. were especially popular in the 17th century, particularly those put on by the College of Louis-le-Grand in Paris. They were, however, always a matter of controversy, and when they tried to answer their critics in P.C. Porée's b. *L'homme instruit par les spectacles* (Paris, 1726) they failed miserably. Ménéstrier and P. Le Jay were Jesuit priests who wrote important treaties on b.

Je t'aime, tu danses. Ballet film by François Weyerganss, prod. in 1973 for Belg. and Cologne TV; ch. Béjart. A long and highly intimate portrait of Béjart; a pas de deux, to mus. by Boulez, for Rita Poelvoorde and Béjart himself.

BIBL.: N. McLain Stoop, 'Béjart's "J.t'a., t.d."— Choreography as Cinema', *Dance Magazine* (1974/2).

Jeté or Pas jeté (Fr., thrown). Designates a jump from one leg to the other, in which the working leg seems to be thrown forwards, sideways, or backwards. There is a wide variety of j., and they may be executed in all directions.

Jeu de cartes (also *The Card Game* or *The Card Party*). Ballet in 3 deals; libr. and mus. Stravinsky; ch. Balanchine; déc. I. Sharaff. Prod. 27 Apr. 1937, Amer. B., Met. Op. House, New York, with Dollar. 'In *Card Game*, Stravinsky and I attempted to show that the highest cards—the kings, queens, and jacks—in reality have nothing on the other side. They are big people, but they can easily be beaten by small cards. Seemingly powerful figures, they are actually mere silhouettes' (Balanchine). The central figure is the Joker. Other versions by Charrat (Bs. de Champs-Elysées, 1945) and Cranko (Stuttgart, 1965; revived for Royal B., 1966). Ménéstrier mentions a *Ballet du J.d.c.*, performed at Turin in 1653.

BIBL.: G. Balanchine, 'C.G.' in *Balanchine's New Complete Stories of the Great Ballets*.

Jeune homme à marier (orig. Dan. title: *Den unge mand skal giftes*—also *The Young Man Must Marry*). TV Ballet; libr. E. Ionesco; ch. Flindt; mus. Per Nøgaard; déc. J. Noël. Prod. Dan. TV,1965, with Flindt, Amiel. Stage prod. as a b. in 1 act, 15 Oct. 1967, Royal Dan. B., Copenhagen, with P. Martins, M. Hønningen. Ionesco based the libr. on his play *Jacques, ou la soumission*. It tells of a young man who very reluctantly agrees to marry, but refuses all the different brides the family presents to him, until he meets a bride with three faces. At last he agrees. After a long kiss, however, she disappears above the stage and the bridegroom sinks dead to the floor. Revived for Western Th. B. and Th. an der Wien (both in 1968).

Jeune homme et la mort, Le. Ballet in 2 scenes; libr., cost., and prod. Cocteau; ch. Petit; mus. Bach; set Wakhevitch. Prod. 25 June 1946, Bs. des Champs-Elysées, Th. des Champs-Elysées, Paris, with Babilée and Philippart. Performed to an orchestrated version of Bach's Passacaglia in C minor (but without the Fugue), repeated three times, the b. shows a young Parisian painter waiting in his attic for his girl. She enters and taunts him, driving him to hang himself, after which she returns wearing a death-mask, which she places on his face and leads him away over the rooftops of the city. The b. was long considered the archetype of Fr. post-war b., and became Babilée's most famous role. A TV prod. with Nureyev and Jeanmaire was never released. Revived in 1975 for Amer. B. Th., with Baryshnikov.

BIBL.: C. Beaumont, 'L.j.h.e.l.m.' in *Ballets of Today* (London, 1954).

Jeux. Poème dansée in 1 act; ch. Nijinsky; mus. Debussy; déc. Bakst; cond. Monteux. Prod. 15 May 1913, Bs. Russes de Diaghilev, Th. des Champs-Elysées, Paris, with Nijinsky, Karsavina, Shollar. This was the first contemporary subject in the repertory of Diaghilev's co. Three tennis-players, a boy and two girls, meet by chance in a garden. He flirts with both of them, but cannot make up his mind which one to choose; they depart in different directions. Other versions by Börlin (Bs. Suédois, 1920), Darrell (Western Th. B., 1963), Taras (New York City B., 1966), Walter

(Düsseldorf, 1973), and Van Schayk (Dutch National B., 1977).
BIBL.: L. Kirstein, 'J.' in *Movement & Metaphor* (New York, 1970); R. Buckle, in *Nijinsky* (London, 1971).

Jeux d'enfants. Ballet in 1 act; libr. Kochno; ch. Massine; mus. Bizet; déc. J. Miró. Prod. 14 Apr. 1932, Col. de Basil's B. Russe, Monte Carlo, with Riabouchinska, Toumanova, Lichine. A girl plays with her toys; they come alive, and she falls in love with the Traveller. Later versions by Aveline (Paris Opéra, 1941) and Balanchine (New York City B., 1959; also a second version, *The Steadfast Tin Soldier*, 1975).
BIBL.: C. W. Beaumont, *'J.d'e.'* in *Complete Book of Ballets* (London 1951).

Jewels. Ballet in 3 parts; ch. Balanchine; mus. Fauré, Stravinsky, Tchaikovsky; cost. Karinska; sets Peter Harvey; light. R. Bates. Prod. 13 Apr. 1967, New York City B., State Th., N.Y., with Verdy, Ludlow, Paul, Moncion, McBride, Villella, P. Neary, Farrell, d'Amboise. 3 plotless divertissements: first, 'Emeralds', to Fauré's *Pelléas et Mélisande* and *Shylock*; second, 'Rubies', to Stravinsky's Capriccio for Piano and Orchestra; third, 'Diamonds', to Tchaikovsky's Symphony No. 3 in D major (without the first movement).
BIBL.: G. Balanchine, 'J.' in *Balanchine's New Complete Stories of the Great Ballets* (Garden City, N.Y., 1968).

Jhung, Finis (*b* Honolulu, 28 May 1937). Korean-Amer. d. Studied in Honolulu, then with W. Christensen and Pereyaslavec. Joined San Francisco B. in 1960, Joffrey B. in 1962; member of Harkness B. 1964–70, since when he has taught in N.Y. Formed own co., Chamber Ballets U.S.A. 1982–6.
BIBL.: S. Goodman, 'F.J.', *Dance Magazine* (1966/8).

Jig. A very old folk d. of the Brit. Isles, believed by some to be derived from the Fr. *Gigue or the Ital. Giga. By the mid–17th century it was also d. on the Continent. It is usually in 6/8 or 12/8 time and has a binary form. During the late 16th and 17th centuries it also designated the lively song and d. entertainment which terminated many theatrical perfs. Tchaikovsky composed a j., which he called 'English Dance', as a supplementary number for *The Nutcracker*.

Jillana (orig. J. Zimmermann; *b*. Hackensack, N.J., 1934). Amer. dancer. Studied with Emily Hadley and at School of Amer. B. Joined B. Society in 1948; became a soloist of the New York City B. in 1955, and stayed with the co. until 1966 (dancing for one season in 1957–8 with Amer. B. Th.). Created roles in Robbins' *The Pied Piper* (1951), Balanchine's *Liebeslieder Waltzer* (1960) and *A Midsummer Night's Dream* (1962). Now teaches at Univ. of California at Irvine.

Jinx. Ballet in 1 act; ch. L. Christensen; mus.

Britten; set James Stewart Morcom; cost. Felipe Fiocca. Prod. 24 Apr. 1942, D. Players, National Th., New York, with Reed, L. Christensen, Conrad Linden. This is a dramatic b. about superstition; the protagonist is a clown who is shunned by everybody for constantly causing mishaps, and is finally beaten to death by the crowd. However, he mysteriously rises again, for a jinx can never be killed. Revived for New York City B. in 1949.
BIBL.: G. Balanchine, 'J.' in *Balanchine's New Complete Stories of the Great Ballets* (Garden City, N.Y., 1968).

Joan of Arc. Ballet in 3 acts; libr. V. Pletneva; ch. Bourmeister; mus. N. Peiko; déc. V. Ryndin. Prod. 29 Dec. 1957, Stanislavsky and Nemirovich-Danchenko Mus. Th., Moscow, with Bovt, Kuzmin. The b. follows the story of the life of the Maid of Orleans. Other b. treatments of the same story by S. Viganò (Milan, 1821), J. Aumer (mus. W. R. Gallenberg, Vienna, 1821), Graham (in *Seraphic Dialogue*, mus. Dello Joio, New York, 1955).
BIBL.: N. René, 'J.o.A.', *Dance and Dancers* (1958/9).

Joan von Zarissa. Ballet with prologue, 4 scenes, and epilogue; libr. and mus. Egk; direction Heinz Tietjen; ch. Maudrik, déc. J. Fenneker. Prod. 20 Jan. 1940, State Op., Berlin, with B. Woisien, I. Meudtner, R. Jahnke. The b. tells of the amorous adventures of a 15th–century Burgundian knight. Egk took his inspiration from a painting by Jean Fouquet in Antwerp, and the text for the linking madrigals are from the chansons of Charles d'Orléans. The b. was frequently prod. in Ger. up to the 1960s. Other versions by Hanka (Vienna, 1942), Lifar (Paris Opéra, 1942), T. Gsovsky (Buenos Aires, 1950), H. Rosen (Munich, 1960).

Job. A Masque for Dancing in 8 scenes; libr. Geoffrey Keynes; ch. de Valois; mus. Vaughan Williams; déc. Gwendolen Raverat; wigs and masks Hedley Briggs. Prod. 5 July 1931, Camargo Society, Cambridge Th., London, with Dolin, Stanley Judson. Based on William Blake's *Book of Job*, the heavily mime-orientated scenes depict the challenges and steadfastness of Job's unshakeable belief in God, against which even Satan is bound to fail. Revived for Vic-Wells B. in 1931, new déc. by J. Piper in 1948, revived again for Royal B., 1970 and later.
BIBL.: C. W. Beaumont, 'J.' in *Complete Book of Ballets* (London, 1951).

Jocko the Brazilian Ape. See *Danina, or Jocko the Brazilian Ape.*

Joel, Lydia (*b* New York, 1914). Amer, dancer, editor and school director. Studied at School of Amer. B., with H. Holm and at Bennington College. D. under the name of Lydia Tarnower with Kreutzberg, H. Holm co., in M. Reinhardt's *Eternal Road* prod. and with her own concert co. Editor in chief of *Dance Magazine* 1952–71. Since

1973 Chairwoman of D. Department High School of Performing Arts in New York. Has written many articles on d. for various magazines, founding member of Association of Amer. D. Cos.

Joffrey, Robert (orig. Abdulla Jaffa Anver Bey Khan; *b* Seattle, Wash., 24 Dec. 1930). Amer. dancer, choreographer, teacher, and b. director. Studied with Mary Ann Wells and at School of Amer. B., also modern d. at High School of Performing Arts, where he started to teach in 1950, having already appeared with Petit's Bs. de Paris. Ch. his first b., *Persephone* (mus. R. Silverman), for a workshop programme in 1952. Formed his own group, R.J. B. Concert, in 1954, and ch. *Pas de Déesses* (mus. J. Field—revived for B. Rambert in 1955 together with his *Persephone* with different mus. by Vivaldi) and *Le Bal masqué* (mus. Poulenc), for its New York opening, followed by *Harpsichord Concerto* (mus. de Falla) and *Pierrot lunaire* (mus. Schoenberg) in 1955. Founded his R.J.B. in 1956, with *Arpino, who became his chief ch.; most of the dancers came from his Amer. B. Center. The R.J.B. became the *City Center J.B. in 1966. Further bs. of his were *Gamelan* (mus. Lou Harrison, 1962), *Astarte* (mus. Crome Syrcus Band, 1967) *Remembrances* (mus. Wagner, 1973), and *Postcards* (mus. Satie, 1980). D. Magazine Award (1963); Capezio Award (1974).
BIBL.: A. Fatt, 'The Capricorn Combine', *Dance Magazine* (1970/10); O. Maynard, 'The Joffrey', *Dance Magazine* (1974/11).

Joffrey Ballet. The Amer. co. descends from the Robert Joffrey B. Concert, which gave its first New York perf. in 1954 at the YM-YWHA. The dancers came mainly from the Amer. B. Center, directed by Joffrey and Arpino. In 1956 the co. toured for the first time as R. Joffrey's Th. Dancers. There followed many other tours until it became the R. Joffrey B. in 1960. 1962–4 it was supported generously by R. Harkness, who not only provided the means for a widening of the repertory but also took the co. on its first visit to the U.S.S.R. At this time the repertory included, apart from the bs. by Joffrey and Arpino, works by Macdonald, Ailey, and L. Christensen, d. by L. Bradley, L. Isaksen, B. Ruiz, R. Gain, F. Jhung, L. Rhodes, and H. Tomasson as leading soloists. After a disagreement between Joffrey and Mrs Harkness, most of the repertory and dancers were taken over into the newly founded Harkness B. Assisted by the Ford Foundation Joffrey started to build up a new co. which made its début at the 1965 Jacob's Pillow Festival, scoring a tremendous success when it first appeared at the New York City Center in 1966. It was invited by M. Baum to become the resident b. co. at that th.—with Joffrey as artistic dir. and Arpino as chief ch. and associate dir. In 1969 the co. appeared at the Vienna Festival, and in 1971 for the first time in London. During the mid-1970s the repertory has

been firmly based on the bs. by Arpino—incl. *Olympics, Sea Shadow, Viva Vivaldi!, Fanfarita, Cello Concerto, Trinity, Sacred Grove on Mount Tamalpais,* and *The Relativity of Icarus,* and supplemented by bs. by Joffrey (*Astarte, Gamelan, Remembrances*) and some standard works by Bournonville, Fokine, Massine, Ashton, Jooss, Tudor, Ashton, and Robbins, and some experimental ch. by Sappington and Tharp. The co. does not distinguish between soloists and corps dancers; C. Arthur, F. Corkle, S. Danias, E. Goodman, R. Wright, G. Chryst, C. Holder, and D. Wayne are among the better known ones. The co. became known as Joffrey B. 1976. A City Center Joffrey II co. was est. in 1970 as an apprentice co. for students of the assoc. Amer. B. Center school— with J. Watts as its dir. An Omnibus educational film, *Dance: Robert Joffrey Ballet,* was made in 1965, and a television prog. in 1976 (WNET-TV).
BIBL.: A. Fatt, 'The Capricorn Combine', *Dance Magazine* (1970/10); O. Maynard, 'The Joffrey', *Dance Magazine* (1974/11).

Johansson, Anna (*b* 1860, *d* St. Petersburg, 1917). Swed. dancer. Studied with her father *Christian J. at the Imperial B. School in St. Petersburg, graduating in 1878; became a member of the Maryinsky Th. and a ballerina, much admired for her brilliant though rather cold technique. Retired in 1899, and became a teacher of the Class of Perfection.

Johansson, Christian (*b* Stockholm, 20 May 1817, *d* St. Petersburg, 12 Dec. 1903). Swed. dancer and teacher. Studied at Royal Swed. B. School and with Bournonville in Copenhagen; became premier danseur in Stockholm in 1837, where he often appeared with M. Taglioni. Went to St. Petersburg in 1841, where he made his début in *La Gitana,* after which he was appointed premier danseur. A much admired d.; his career continued until 1869. Started to teach in 1860; after his retirement became chief teacher of the Imperial B. School, where Kschessinska, Preobrajenska, P. Gerdt, and his daughter Anna were among his pupils. Considered one of the chief architects of the Russ. school of dancing.

Johns, Jasper (*b* Alandale, S. C., 1930). Amer. painter and designer. Artistic director of the M. Cunningham D. Co. for some years. Collaborated with Cunningham on *Walkaround Time* (1968), *Second Hand, Landrover, TV Re-Run* (all 1970), *Borst Park* (1972), and *Un jour ou deux* (1973).

Johnson, Louis (*b* Statesville, N.C., 1930). Amer. dancer and choreographer. Studied with Doris Jones and Claire Haywood in Washington, D.C., and at School of Amer. B. Joined New York City B. in 1952. Left the co. to appear on Broadway. Started to ch. in 1953 with *Lament.* Formed his own group, with which he has appeared regularly in New York and on tour. Has also ch. for Modern Jazz Quartet and D. Th. of Harlem.

Johnson, Nicholas (b London, 12 Sep. 1947). Brit. dancer. Studied at Royal B. School. Joined Royal B. Touring Group in 1965; appointed soloist in 1968 and principal d. in 1970. Created roles in D. Drew's *From Waking Sleep* (1970) and *Sacred Circles* (1973), Tetley's *Field Figures* (1970), and Layton's *Grand Tour* (1971) and *O.W.* (1972). Joined London Festival B. as principal d., 1975.
BIBL.: 'N.J.', *Dance and Dancers* (1968/6).

Jolie fille de Gand, La. Pantomime ballet in 3 acts and 9 scenes; libr. V. de Saint-Georges and Albert (also ch.); mus. Adam; déc. Ciceri, Philastre, Gambon, and Lormier. Prod. 22 June 1842, Opéra, Paris, with Grisi, Fitzjames, L. Petipa, Mazilier. The b. tells of Beatrix, a girl from Ghent, who is about to marry Benedict, but is also ardently courted by the Marquis de San Lucar. She cannot make up her mind between them, but then she has a nightmare, in which she sees herself in the most complicated situations, until she finally hurls herself into an abyss—to awake knowing that it is Benedict she really loves; then the marriage celebrations start. A new version under the title of *Beatrix by J. Carter (mus. arr. Horovitz) for London Festival B. (London, 1966).
BIBL.: C. W. Beaumont, 'L.j.f.d.G.' in *Complete Book of Ballets* (London, 1951.)

Jolivet, André (b Paris, 8 May 1905). Fr. Composer. Wrote the mus. for Lifar's *Guignol et Pandore* (Paris, 1944). His concert mus. has occasionally been used for b. purposes— repeatedly by Skibine (the piano concerto in *Concerto,*' Strasbourg, 1957; *Ombres lunaires*, Opéra, Paris, 1960; *Marines*, Op. Comique, Paris, 1961), and also by E. Walter (*Delphic Suite,* Wuppertal, 1963), Lazzini (*Suite transocéan*, Marseilles, 1963) and Kylián (*Incantations*, Stuttgart, 1971).

Jones, Betty (b Meadville, Pa., 1926). Amer. dancer and teacher. Studied with Limón, Shawn, Markova, and La Meri. First appeared in a touring prod. of *Oklahoma!* Joined Limón co. in 1947; stayed until Limón's death, creating a great number of roles, including Desdemona in *The Moor's Pavane* (1949). She now appears mostly in recital programmes, with Fritz Lüdin as her partner. Has taught for Limón and at Connecticut College Summer School, Juilliard School, and various colleges; has own school in Honolulu, Hawaii.

Jones, John (b Philadelphia, 1937). Amer. dancer and choreographer. Studied at Metropolitan B. School, School of Amer. B., and Amer. B. Center. Started to d. with the co. of K. Dunham, then with Bs. U.S.A., R. Joffrey B., Harkness B., New York City B., and D. Th. of Harlem. Has ch. for Jamaican D. Th. and for Pennsylvania B. Co. Is now associate dir. of Contemporary D. Co. of Philadelphia.

Jones, Marilyn (b Newcastle, N.S.W., 14 Feb. 1940). Austral. dancer. Studied with Norton, van Praagh, and at Royal B. School. Joined Royal B. in 1957, Borovansky B. as a soloist in 1959, and Grand B. du Marquis de Cuevas as prima ballerina in 1961, where she stayed until the co's closure. Returned to Austral. B. in 1962, later becoming prima ballerina and now artistic dir. Guest artist London Festival B. in 1963. O.B.E. (1972). Married to the d. Garth Welch.

Jones Beach. Ballet in 4 parts; ch. Balanchine and Robbins; mus. J. Andriessen; light. Rosenthal. Prod. 9 Mar. 1950, New York City B., City Center, N.Y., with Maria Tallchief, LeClercq, Hayden, Magallanes, Bliss, Robbins, Bolender. The b. shows episodes from a typical summer's day at New York's most famous beach.
BIBL.: G. Balanchine, 'J.B.' in *Balanchine's New Complete Stories of the Great Ballets* (Garden City, N.Y., 1968).

Jong, Bettie de. See *De Jong, Bettie.*

Jooss, Kurt (b Wasseralfingen, 12 Jan. 1901, d Heilbronn, 22 May 1979). Ger. dancer, choreographer, teacher, and b. director. Studied at Stuttgart Academy of Mus. where he met Laban, with whom he collaborated in Mannheim and Hamburg 1922–3. Appointed b. master in Münster in 1924; founded the Neue Tanzbühne, with the Estonian d. Aino Siimola (whom he married in 1929), S. Leeder, and Heckroth, for which he ch. his first bs. 1924–6: *Ein persisches Märchen* (mus. Wellesz, 1924), *Der Dämon* (mus. Hindemith, 1925), *Die Brautfahrt* (mus. Rameau-Couperin, 1925), etc. Continued to study academic d. in Vienna and Paris. Appointed dir. of the d. department at the Essen Folkwang School in 1927, from which the Folkwang Tanztheater developed in 1928, for which he ch. *Drosselbart* (mus. Mozart, 1929), *Zimmer Nr. 13* (mus. Cohen, 1929), *Pavane* (mus. Ravel, 1929), *Petrushka* (mus. Stravinsky, 1930), and *Gaukelei* (mus. Cohen, 1930). B. master of the Essen Municipal Th. in 1930; his co. became the Folkwang Tanzbühne, producing his *Le Bal* (mus. Rieti, 1930), *Polovtsian Dances* (mus. Borodin, 1930), *Coppélia* (1931), *Prodigal Son* (mus. Prokofiev, 1931), *Pulcinella* (mus. Stravinsky, 1932), and his most lasting work, *The Green Table* (mus. Cohen, 1932), followed by *Big City* (mus. Tansman) and *Ball in Old Vienna* (mus. Lanner, both 1932). The pressures of the Nazis forced him to leave Ger. in 1933, with his co., which changed its name to *Bs. Jooss, and took up residence in Dartington, Eng., from where they toured the world. New bs. of his were *Seven Heroes* (mus. Purcell-Cohen, 1933), *The Prodigal Son* (mus. Cohen, 1933), *Ballade* (mus. J. Colman, 1935), *The Mirror* (mus. Cohen, 1935), *Johann Strauss, Tonight!* (1935), *A Spring Tale* (mus. Cohen, 1939), *Chronica* (mus. B. Goldschmidt, 1939), *Company at the Manor* (mus. Beethoven-Cook, 1943), and *Pandora* (mus. R. Gerhard, 1944). The co. disbanded in 1947. He

then went to Santiago de Chile, where he ch. *Juventud* (mus. Handel, 1948—also a revival of *Dithyrambus*). Returned to Essen in 1949 and began to reestablish the Folkwang School and the Folkwang B., with the new bs. *Colombinade* (mus. Strauss-Montijn, 1951), *Weg im Nebel* (mus. Montijn), and *Nachtzug* (mus. Tansman, both 1952). In addition he was b. master of the Düsseldorf Op. House 1954–6, for which he ch. Stravinsky's *Persephone* (he had already been in charge of the work's first prod. in Paris, 1934) and Orff's *Catulli Carmina*. For the Schwetzingen Festival he ch. Purcell's *Fairy Queen* (1959), Rameau's *Castor and Pollux* (1962), and Purcell's *Dido and Aeneas* (1966), and for the Salzburg Festival Cavalieri's *Rappresentatione di anima et di corpo* (1968). Retired from his Essen position in 1968, but continued to control personally, with the assistance of his daughter Anna Markard-J., the prods. of his *Green Table* etc. all over the world. He was the first ch. of international renown to attempt a synthesis of classical and modern dance, in strongly theatrical bs. with contemporary ideas. His daughter Anna Markard-J. (*b*. Essen, 1931) has specialized as a producer of her father's bs.
BIBL.: A. V. Coton, in *The New Ballet* (London, 1946); J. Baril, 'K.J.', with complete checklist of bs., *Les Saisons de la danse* (1975/11), R. Joffrey, 'Remembrances of K.J.', *Ballet News* (1979/9).

Joplin, Scott (*b* Texarkana, Tex., 24 Nov. 1868. *d* New York, 1 Apr. 1917). Amer. ragtime pianist. The sudden international craze for ragtime during the early 1970s encouraged a number of choreographers to use his mus. (often in orchestral arrangements) for b. purposes. Such bs. include J. Waring's *Eternity Bounce* (1973), A. Catá's *Ragtime* (also mus. by Stravinsky and G. Schuller, Frankfurt, 1973), G. Veredon's *The Ragtime Dance Company* (Cologne, 1974), B. Moreland's *Prodigal Son* (also mus. by Grant Hossack and others, London Festival B., 1974), and MacMillan's *Elite Syncopations* (also mus. by other composers, Royal B., 1974).
BIBL.: N. Goodwin, 'Ragtime Reckoning', *About the House* (vol. 4, no. 7).

Jordan, Olga Genrichovna (*b* St. Petersburg, 18 May 1907, *d* Leningrad, 27 May 1971). Sov. dancer and teacher. Studied at Leningrad B. School with Vaganova, graduating in 1926; joined GATOB and became one of the ballerinas of the Kirov Th., where she stayed until 1950. Was one of the few Kirov dancers who stayed in Leningrad when the co. was evacuated to Molotov/Perm, and she continued to give b. recitals in the besieged city. Teacher of the Leningrad Ch. School 1946–63, after which she moved to Moscow.

Joseph the Beautiful (orig. Russ. title: *Iosif prekrasny*). Ballet in 2 acts and 5 scenes; ch. Goleizovsky; mus. S. Vasilenko; déc. B. Erdman.

Prod. 3 Mar. 1925, Experimental Th., Moscow. The b. tells of how the boy J. was sold into Egyptian slavery, where he became the object of the amorous pursuits of Pharaoh's wife. Its unrestrained eroticism and purely constructivist poses and patterns caused considerable controversy.
BIBL.: M. G. Swift, in *The Art of the Dance in the U.S.S.R.* (Notre Dame, Ind., 1968).

Josephslegende. See *Legend of Joseph*.

Jota. A traditional d. from Northern Spain, performed by one or several couples in rapid triple time, accompanied by a guitar player who also sings, while the dancers play their castanets. A famous example can be found in Massine's and de Falla's *Three-Cornered Hat*.

Jota Aragonesa. Ballet in 1 act; ch. Fokine; mus. Glinka; déc. Golovin. Prod. 29 Jan. 1916, Maryinsky Th., Petrograd. The b. presents a rather sinister view of the Spaniards.

Journey, The (orig. Ger. title: *Die Reise*, also Fr. *Le Voyage*). Ch. Action; libr. and ch. Béjart; mus. P. Henry; film projections Thierry Vincens; cost. G. Casado. Prod. 29 Apr. 1962, Cologne, with L. Höfgen, T. Söffing, R. Duse. Based on the Tibetan Book of the Dead, the b. shows the way of life, which is the journey to death, from which man is reborn. Revived for B. of the 20th Century (1968).

Jovita ou les Boucaniers. Pantomime ballet in 3 scenes; libr. and ch. Mazilier; mus. Théodore Labarre; sets. Despléchin, Thierry, and Cambon; cost. Lormier. Prod. 11 Nov. 1853, Opéra, Paris, with Rosati, Mérante, L. Petipa. the b. is set in Mexico; J., the daughter of a rich farmer, loves the naval officer Don Altamirano, who is captured by the notorious Zubillaga, chief of the buccaneers. She then enters the camp of the buccaneers dressed as a gipsy, frees Altamirano, and finally blows up the whole camp—an effect, ingeniously prepared by the chief machinist Sacré, which caused an enthusiastic uproar at every performance.
BIBL.: C. W. Beaumont, 'J.o.l.B.' in *Complete Book of Ballets* (London, 1951).

Jowitt, Deborah (*b* Los Angeles, 8 Feb. 1934). Amer. dancer, choreographer, and writer on dance. Educated at various colleges. Studied with Graham, Perry-Mansfield, Amer. B. Center, and Limón. Has performed with Juilliard D. Th., M. Anthony, V. Bettis, J. Duncan, P. Lang, C. Weidman, and S. Maslow. Since 1965 has worked mostly with D. Th. Workshop, presenting her own dances and performing for J. Duncan, J. Moore, J. Wilson, A. Bauman, and F. Alenikoff. Her most frequent dances include *Road Signs* (1965), *Troy VIIa* (1967), *Black & White and True Blue* (1968), *Palimpsest* (1969), *Green River Road, Summer* (1970), *Arrangement* (1973), *Water Pieces*, and *Journey* (1974). As a teacher she has mostly worked with children. D. critic of *The Village Voice* since 1967. Dir. of the Critics' Conference (a course in d. criticism) in New London, Conn., since 1973. Author of *Dance Beat* (collected reviews) (N.Y., 1977) and *The Dance in Mind* (N.Y., 1985).

Jude, Charles (*b* Mytho, South Vietnam, 25 July 1953). Fr. dancer. Studied with A. Kalioujny, S. Peretti, and at Nice Concervatory 1968–71. Joined Paris Opéra B. in 1971, promoted danseur étoile in 1977. Created Romeo in Grigorovich's *Romeo and Juliet* (1978). Third Prize (Tokyo, 1976). Married to the d. Florence Clerc.

Judgment of Paris. Ballet in 1 act; libr. and cost. H. Laing; ch. Tudor; mus. Weill. Prod. 15 June 1938, London B., Westminster Th., London, with Langfield, de Mille, Bidmead, Tudor, Laing. Set to Weill's Suite from the *Dreigroschenoper*, the b. parallels the famous classical story in the contemporary setting of a sordid night bar. Revived for B. Rambert in 1940.
BIBL.: G. Balanchine, 'The J.o.P.' in *Balanchine's New Complete Stories of the Great Ballets* (Garden City, N.Y., 1968).

Jugement de Pâris, Le. Ballet Divertissement in 1 act; ch. Perrot; mus. Pugni. Prod. 23 July 1846, Her Majesty's Th., London, with M. Taglioni, Grahn, Cerrito, Saint-Léon. The enormous success of the *Pas de quatre* of 1845 stimulated Lumley and Perrot to put on another divertissement, which they tried to structure more firmly by adding some additional parts (Graces, Nymphs, Cupid, Mercury, etc.); the centrepiece was the *Pas des Déesses*, where Juno, Pallas, and Venus try

in vain to win the favours of Paris. It was in this b. that Taglioni gave her farewell perf. on 21 Aug. 1847.
BIBL.: C. W. Beaumont, 'L.J.d.P.' in *Complete Book of Ballets* (London, 1951).

Juilliard School of Music, Dance Department. Instituted in 1952, with M. Hill as its dir. Staff members have incl. de Mille, Graham, Humphrey, Limón, Robbins, Tudor, Horst, and Hutchinson. It offers a full d. education, granting diplomas upon graduation. The perfs. of its prod. group have become regular dates of the New York d. scene. Since 1964 it has operated in Lincoln Center, under the same roof as the School of Amer. Ballet. Dir. now Muriel Topaz.

Jungle. Ballet in 4 scenes; ch. Van Dantzig; mus. Badings; déc. Van Schayk. Prod. 20 Dec. 1961, Dutch National B., Stadsschouwburg, Amsterdam, with Koppers, Campbell. 'When night comes, we don't know whether it is a natural darkness that falls over us, or a darkness created by people around us—ourselves' (programme note). A parable, which mirrors man's beastly behaviour through the social attitudes of animals in a jungle. Revived for London D. Th. (1965) and National B. of Washington, D.C. (1972).

Jurriëns, Henny (*b* Arnhem, 21 Feb. 1949). Dutch dancer. Studied with Winja Marova, later also with Arova, Franchetti, Bon, and Kramar. Member of Norwegian National B. 1966–70, eventually becoming soloist; soloist (now principal d.) of the Dutch National B. since 1970. Has created roles in numerous bs. by Van Dantzig and Van Manen.

K

Kabuki. The Jap. word means song-d.-skill. It designates the popular form of Jap. d. drama which forms a contrast to the more rigid and stylized form of the aristocratic Noh. K. originated in the perfs., around 1600, of the d. and lay-priestess O-Kuni from Izumo, with her troupe of female dancers, first in Kyoto and then in Tokyo; they created a synthesis of the styles of prayer dances, peasant dances, comic interludes, mimes, and erotic dances. From this, small d.-dramas developed which gradually conquered the larger stages; the participants entered by a long path of flowers, called Hamanichi, running right through the auditorium. The appearance of women was forbidden in 1629, and no boys were permitted after 1652. Since then therefore, all roles have been performed by men in the K. th.; there have been very important families of performers. In the K. d., however, women may appear, and they have often played an important role as directors of the K.D. School. Today K. is a highly stylized, integrated work of art, with d. and ch. contributing considerably to its timeless beauty. The d. always fulfils an anecdotal function. There are now also pure K.D. troupes, made up of members of both sexes. Make-up, costumes, and props are just as important as the movement.
BIBL.: E. Ashihara, in *The Japanese Dance* (Tokyo, 1964).

Kafka, Lubomír (*b* Jablonec, 23 Apr. 1956). Czech. dancer. Studied at Prague State Conservatory 1968–74 and Leningrad B. School 1974–5. Joined National Th. of Prague B. as a soloist in 1975. Silver Medal (Varna, 1974, junior category; Tokyo, 1976 and 1978), Gold Medal (Varna, 1978, senior category).

Kåge, Jonas (*b* Lidingö, 1950). Swed. dancer. Studied at Royal Swed. B. School and with Hightower; joined Royal Swed. B. in 1967. D. Romeo in MacMillan's prod. of 1969; appointed soloist in 1970. Joined Amer. B. Th. in 1971; appointed soloist in 1972 and principal d. 1973–5; Stuttgart B. 1975–6; Geneva B. 1976–8 and of Zurich B. 1978–85. Created role in Tetley's *Greening* (1975). Married to the d. Deborah Dobson.

Kai, Una (*b* Glenridge, N.J., 7 Mar. 1928). Amer. dancer, b. mistress, and b. director. Studied with Swoboda, Nemchinova, Oboukhoff, and Balanchine. Joined B. Society in 1948; remained with New York City B. until 1960, having been appointed asst. b. mistress in 1956, then b. mistresss and b. master. Has staged many Balanchine bs. in Europe, U.S., Can., and Austral.

B. mistress of R. Joffrey B. in the early 1960s. Dir. of New Zealand B. Co. 1973–6. Now teaching in Copenhagen.
BIBL.: S. Goodman, 'Meet U.K.', *Dance Magazine* (1963/10).

Kain, Karen (*b* Hamilton, Ont., 28 Mar. 1951). Can. dancer. Studied at Can. National B. School. Joined National B. of Can. in 1969; appointed principal d. in 1970. Dances the leading ballerina roles of the classical repertory. Has often d. with Nureyev when he appears with the co. Guest soloist with Bs. de Marseille, where she created a leading role in Petit's *Les Intermittences du coeur* (1974) and *Nana* (Paris Opéra, 1976). Silver Medal (Moscow, 1973). Order of Canada, 1976.
BIBL.: C. Darling and J. Fraser, *K.K. and Frank Augustyn* (Toronto, 1978).

Kalioujny, Alexandre (*b* Prague, 15 Apr. 1923). Fr. dancer and teacher. Studied with Preobrajenska; joined Nouveau B. de Monte Carlo in 1946, and Paris Opéra as an étoile in 1947, where he created a part in Balanchine's *Palais de cristal* (1947). Had his biggest success in *Prince Igor*. Left the co. in 1953 to appear on Broadway (with Jeanmaire, in *The Girl in Pink Tights*). Returned to Fr. in 1955, dancing occasionally at the Opéra, and also with Babilée's co. Retired in 1961, since when he has taught at his Nice studio.
BIBL.: I. Lidova, in *Ballet Annual* (no. 4, 1950).

Kalkabrino. Fantastic ballet in 3 acts; lib. Modeste Tchaikovsky; ch. M. Petipa; mus. Minkus. Prod. 25 Feb. 1891, Maryinsky Th., St. Petersburg, with Brianza, Gerdt, Legat. Set in Provence; the hero is a smuggler captain who is captivated by a peasant girl but falls prey to evil spirits, who finally take him down to hell.
BIBL.: C. W. Beaumont, 'K.' in *Complete Book of Ballets* (London, 1951).

Kammermusik No. 2. Ballet in 4 movements; ch. Balanchine; mus. Hindemith; cost. Ben Benson. Prod. 26 Jan. 1978, New York City B., State Th., New York, with K. von Aroldingen, C. Neary, A. Lüders, S. Lavery. Set to Hindemith's op. 36, no. 1, for piano and 12 solo instruments, the b. confronts 2 couples of soloists with an all-male corps of 8 in a string of tense, rather intriguing encounters.

Kaplan, Semyon Shlyomovich (*b* St. Petersburg, 25 Dec. 1911). Sov. dancer and teacher. Studied at Leningrad B. School 1921–30. D. with Kirov B. 1930–59. Taught at Leningrad B. School, 1936–8, and, with breaks, from 1946 to the present day. Also worked with Kirov and Maly

cos. from 1959. Wrote the libr. for the Lopukhov/ Soloviev-Sedoy b. *Taras Bulba* (1940).
BIBL.: V. Panov and G. Feifer, in *To Dance* (New York, 1978).

Kapuste, Falco (*b* Oels, 12 Dec. 1943). Ger. dancer. Studied with Georgi and Jan de Ruiter. Joined Wiesbaden B. in 1963, Hamburg State Op. B. in 1964, Ger. Op. Berlin as a soloist in 1965, and Düsseldorf B. as a principal d. in 1970. Has created many roles in bs. by MacMillan and Walter.

Karalli, Vera Alexeyevna (also Coralli or Koralli; *b* Moscow, 8 Aug. 1889, *d* Baden nr. Vienna, 16 Nov. 1972). Russ. dancer. Studied with Gorsky, joining Bolshoi B. in 1906, appointed ballerina in 1914. D. with Diaghilev's co. in 1909 and 1919–20, appearing mainly in *Le Pavillon d'Armide*, *Thamar*, and *Prince Igor*. Became one of the first Russ. film-stars; her most popular role was in *The Dying Swan*. B. mistress in Bucharest 1930–7; lived in Paris 1938–41, then in Vienna for the rest of her life.

Karelskaya, Rimma Klavdiyevna (*b* Kaluga, 16 Apr. 1927). Sov. dancer and b. mistress. Studied at Moscow Bolshoi B. School; joined Bolshoi B. in 1946, where she created the chief role in Radunsky's *Humpbacked Horse* (1960). Her best roles were Odette-Odile, Raymonda, and Myrtha. Was b. mistress of Moscow Classic B.

Karetnikov, Nicolai Nicolayevich (*b* Moscow, 28 June 1930). Sov. composer. Wrote the mus. for Kasatkina-Vasiliov's *Vanina Vanini* (Bolshoi B., 1962) and *Heroic Poem* (Bolshoi B., 1964), and for Georgi's *Klein Zack, genannt Zinnober* (Hanover, 1970).

Karinska, Barbara (orig. Varvara Zhmoudsky; *b* Kharkhov, 3 Oct. 1886, *d*, N.Y., 18 Oct. 1983). Russ.-Amer. designer and maker of costumes. Left Russ. after the October Revolution, and worked in Paris for Bérard, Derain, Dali, and Beaton. Went to New York in 1938, where she designed the costumes for Balanchine's *Bourrée fantasque* (1949), and became the New York City B.'s top costume-maker. Capezio Award (1962). BIBL.: J. Alleman Rubin, 'Costumes by K.', *Dance Magazine* (1967/6).

Karnilova, Maria (*b* Hartford, 3 Aug. 1920). Amer. dancer and actress. Studied at Met. Op. B. School and with Fokine, Mordkin, Fedorova, Tudor, and Dolin. D. with Met. Op. Children's B., with various op. cos., and on Broadway. Soloist with B. Th. 1939–48, later a ballerina with Met. Op. House and Bs.: U.S.A. Has since appeared in several musicals (*Gypsy, Fiddler on the Roof, Zorba*, etc.).

Karsavina, Tamara Platonovna (*b* St. Petersburg, 9 Mar. 1885, *d* Beaconsfield, 26 May 1978). Russ.-Brit. dancer. Daughter of the Maryinsky Th. d. and teacher Platon Karsavin. Studied at the Imperial B. School with Gerdt, Kosloff, Johansson, and Cecchetti. Gave her début at the Maryinsky Th. in *Javotte* in 1902; stayed with the co. until 1918; appointed ballerina in 1909. A member of the Diaghilev co. from its formation in 1909; became its outstanding ballerina, much admired for her vintage perfs. in the traditional classics and even more so for her many creations, incl. Fokine's *Les Sylphides* (1908), *Cléopâtre* (1909), *Carnaval, Firebird* (both 1910), *Spectre de la rose, Narcisse, Petrushka* (all 1911), *Le Dieu bleu, Thamar, Daphnis and Chloe* (all 1912), *Papillons*, and *Le Coq d'or* (both 1914), Nijinsky's *Jeux* (1913), and Massine's *Le Tricorne* (1919) and *Pulcinella* (1920). With her second husband, the Brit. diplomat Henry J. Bruce, she left Russ. in 1918, after which she lived in London. She continued as a guest-ballerina with Diaghilev's Bs. Russes and d. with B. Rambert 1930–1. For many years after the end of her career as a ballerina she actively participated in the formation of the present Brit. b. as Vice-President of the Royal Academy of Dancing until 1955, as an occasional teacher of mime-classes, and as an adviser for many revivals of the Diaghilev prods. and other bs., incl. *The Nutcracker, Giselle*, and *La Fille mal gardée*. Author of *Theatre Street* (her autobiography, London, 1930); *Ballet Technique* (London, 1956), and *Classical Ballet: The Flow of Movement* (London, 1962—both reprints of articles originally written for *Dancing Times*). One of the greatest and most intelligent ballerinas of b. history; her influence on the b. of the 20th century has been outstanding.
BIBL.: L. Moore, 'T.K.' in *Artists of the Dance* (New York, 1938); N. Macdonald, 'T.K.', *Ballet Review* (Vol. VII, 2 and 3).

Karstens, Gerda (*b* Copenhagen, 9 July 1903). Dan. dancer and teacher. Studied at The Royal Dan. B. School, joining the co. in 1921. Appointed solo d. in 1942; remained with the co. until 1956. She excelled in mime-roles, with Madge in *La Sylphide* as her greatest part. She now teaches mime.

Kasatkina, Natalia Dmitrievna (*b* Moscow, 7 June 1934). Sov. dancer and choreographer. Studied at Moscow Bolshoi B. School; joined Bolshoi B. in 1954, becoming one of its most distinguished character-soloists. Started to choreograph with her husband V. Vasiliov in 1962; their 1st b. was *Vanina Vanini* (mus. Karetnikov), followed by *Heroic Poem/The Geologists* (mus. Karetnikov, 1964), *Le Sacre du printemps* (mus. Stravinsky, 1965), *Preludes and Fugues* (mus. Bach, 1968), *Creation of the World* (mus. Petrov, Kirov B., 1971), *Seeing the Light* (mus. Y. Buzko, Stanislavsky and Nemirovich-Danchenko Mus. Th., 1974).

Kastl, Sonja (*b* Zagreb, 14 July 1929). Yugosl. dancer, choreographer, and b. director. Studied with Froman, Roje, Preobrajenska, Kiss, and Skeaping. Joined Zagreb National B. in 1945, eventually becoming its prima ballerina and, in 1965, its dir. Has ch. many bs., frequently in collaboration with Nevenka Bidjin.

Katalyse (also Eng. *The Catalyst*). Ballet in 3 movements; ch. Cranko; mus. Shostakovich. Prod. 8 Nov. 1961, Stuttgart B., with M. Faure, M. Morena, Barra, Delavalle, G. Burne. The b., set to Shostakovich's first Piano Concerto, shows the effect of the appearance of the catalyst, a male d., on two contrasting groups of dancers dressed in black and white. Revived for various cos.

Katarina. Ballet in 3 acts and 7 scenes; lib. and ch. Lavrovsky; mus. A. Rubinstein and Adam; déc. B. Erbstein. Prod. 25 May 1935 as graduation perf. of the Leningrad Ch. School. the b. is based—like Lopokhov's earlier *The Serf Ballerina*—on a story from the history of the Russ. serf th. A piece by Didelot is presented as a b. within the b.; however, the happy ending of this is contradicted by reality; K., the serf ballerina, commits suicide to escape the pursuits of the governor. Taken into the repertory of the Kirov Th. in 1936.
BIBL.: C. W. Beaumont, 'K,' in *Complete Book of Ballets* (London, 1951).

Kathak. Derived from the same two Ind. words, Katha for story and Kathaka for storyteller, as is the vastly different *Kathakali. One of the 4 main styles of Ind. d. (the others being Bharata Natya, Kathakali, and Manipuri). It emerged as a restoration of Hindu arts by the Muslims. Performed on a floor (not a raised platform) amidst the seated audience, it is mainly concerned with mus. and rhythm, while the story elements are of secondary importance. The feet, adorned with ankle bells, act as percussion instruments—not unlike their function in the zapateados of the Span. gypsy d.

Kathakali. Derived from the same two Ind. words, Katha for story and Kathaka for storyteller, as is the very different *Kathak. One of the 4 main styles of Ind. d. (the others being Bharata Natya, Kathak, and Manipuri); now the general term for the heavily mime-orientated d. drama which has become the embodiment of Ind. th. It comes from the Malabar coast in the extreme South of India and achieved its perfection 300 years ago. It combines the traditions of the ancient rituals of pre-Aryan origin with the forms of d., mime, and drama as they have been registered in the Natyashastra, materializing as a perfectly integrated art-form incl. d., drama, singing, and instrumental mus. with a refined, very complicated, and highly stylized vocabulary of gestures. Masks and makeup play a very important role, and its various characters are represented by faces of different colours. The stories come from mythology. Perfs. take place in the court of a temple or in a square after dusk, and can last the whole night.

BIBL.: C. R. and B. T. Jones, *K.* (San Francisco, 1970).

Kay, Barry. (b Melbourne, 1932, d London, 16 Apr. 1985). Austral. designer. Came to Eng. in 1957; designed Darrell's *The Prisoners* (1957); *Chiaroscuro* (1957), and *Salade* (1961), Nureyev's *Don Quixote* (both for Vienna, 1966, and Austral. B., 1970), and MacMillan's *Anastasia* (for Berlin, 1967, and Royal B., 1971), *Sleeping Beauty* (1973), and *Isadora* (1981), and other bs. (e.g. MacMillan's *Images of Love* and the Royal B.'s *Raymonda*, Act III).

Kay, Hershy (b Philadelphia, 17 Nov. 1919, d Danbury, Conn., 2 Dec. 1981). Amer. composer. Wrote or adapted the mus. for Balanchine's *Western Symphony* (1954), *Stars and Stripes* (after Sousa, 1958) and *Who Cares?* (after Gershwin, 1970), Robbins' *The Concert* (after Chopin, 1956), Layton's *The Grand Tour* (after Coward, 1971) and Balanchine's *Union Jack* (1976).

Kay, Lisan (b Conneaut, Ohio, 4 May 1910). Amer. dancer and teacher. Studied with Andreas Pavley, S. Oukrainsky, and later with Nimura, Trefilova, Nemchinova, and Dolin. Began to d. with Chicago Civic Op. B. 1926–7. Toured with Pavley and Oukrainsky B. for 5 years. Established partnership with Nimura in 1931, touring with him in concert perfs. all over the world until 1940. Continued to give solo concerts until 1943, also appearing occasionally in mus. prods. Associate and instructor at B. Arts School in New York from its inception in 1940.

Kayan, Orrin (b Chicago, 12 July 1935). Amer. dancer and b. master. Studied with C. Bockman, E. McRae, and L. Long. Joined Lyric Op. of Chicago as a soloist in 1956; was long a principal d. of the various cos. of R. Page. Appointed b. master of Chicago B. in 1975.
BIBL.: S. Goodman, 'Patricia Klekovic and O.K.', *Dance Magazine* (1962/5).

Kaye, Nora (orig. N. Koreff; b New York, 17 Jan. 1920, d Los Angeles, 28 Feb. 1987). Amer. dancer. Studied with Fokine, Vilzak, Schollar, at Met. Op. B. School, and School of Amer. B. Appeared with Children's B. of Met. Op.; became a regular member of the Amer. B. in 1935. Was one of the dancers at the inception of B. Th. in 1939; soon became its outstanding dramatic ballerina, creating role in Tudor's *Pillar of Fire* (1942), and was cast as Lizzie Borden in de Mille's *Fall River Legend* (1948), which, however, she had to relinquish at its première owing to a sudden ailment. Equally admired in the ballerina roles of the classics, being called the 'Duse of the Dance'. Member of New York City B. 1951–4; created further roles in Robbins' *The Cage* (1951) and Tudor's *La Gloire* (1952). Returned to Amer. B. Th. 1954–9, creating roles in MacMillan's *Winter's Eve* and *Journey*, and in Ross's *Paean* (all 1957). Married Ross and founded the B. of Two Worlds with him in 1960; became its prima ballerina, appearing in her husband's new bs., e.g. *Angel Head, Rashomon Suite*, and *The Dybbuk*. Retired in 1961, but continued to work occasionally as an assistant in Ross's film and mus. prods. Joined Amer. B. Th.'s board of dirs. in 1977.

Kchessinska, Mathilda. See *Kschessinska, Mathilda.*

Keeler, Ruby (*b* Halifax, N.S., 25 Aug. 1910). Amer. dancer, film and musical actress. Studied with Helen Guest; appeared as a member of the Eastside Sextette in 1920. Continued to study rhythm and tap with Jack Blue, performing in clubs and on Broadway and becoming a star of the Ziegfeld shows in the late 1920s (when she married Al Jolson). Her Hollywood breakthrough came with *42nd Street* (1933), which introduced her to B. Berkeley, with whom she collaborated on many other films. Had a great comeback in the 1970 Broadway revival of *No, No, Nanette*.
BIBL.: R. C. Roman, 'R.K.: Back to Broadway After 40 Years', *Dance Magazine* (1970/12).

Keen, Elizabeth. Amer. dancer, choreographer, and teacher. Has performed as a soloist with the cos. of P. Taylor, Tamiris-Nagrin, and K. Litz and at some of the early Judson Memorial Church concerts. Taught at Pratt Institute 1966–9, Juilliard School 1969–71, and Sarah Lawrence College since 1972. After choreographing for film and TV, established her own d. co. in 1970, with which she has appeared at Judson Memorial Church, D. Th. Workshop, Manhattan School of Music, Th. of the Riverside Church, and Amer. Th. Laboratory.

Kehlet, Niels (*b* Copenhagen, 6 Sep. 1938). Dan. dancer. Studied at Royal Dan. B. School. Joined Royal Dan. B. in 1957; appointed solo d. in 1961. A demicaractère virtuoso, equally outstanding in the Bournonville classics and modern roles. Created roles in Flindt's *The Three Musketeers* (1965) and *The Miraculous Mandarin* (1967), von Rosen's *Don Juan* (1967), and Tomaszewski's *Bagage* (1969). Has often appeared as a guest-d. abroad, frequently with the Ital. co. of Fracci-Menegatti-Gai; created title-role in Gai's *Pulcinella* (1971). Many TV appearances in Denmark and abroad.
BIBL.: E. Aschengreen, 'N.K.' (with complete check-list of roles and activities), *Les Saisons de la danse* (1970/3).

Keil, Birgit (*b* Kowarschen, 22 Sep. 1944). Ger. dancer. Studied Stuttgart B. School and Royal B. School. Joined Stuttgart B. in 1961; appointed soloist in 1965, becoming one of its outstanding ballerinas. Created roles in MacMillan's *Las Hermanas* (1963), *Miss Julie* (1970), and *My Brother, My Sisters* (1978); Cranko's *Opus 1, Jeu de cartes* (1965), *Brouillards* (1970), *The Seasons* (1971), and *Initials R.B.M.E.* (1972); P. Wright's *Namouna* (1967), Tetley's *Voluntaries* (1973), *Greening*, and

Daphnis and Chloe (1975), Spoerli's *Dreams* (1980), and Kylián's *Forgotten Land* (1981).
BIBL.: Various authors, *B.K.* (Pfullingen, 1980).

Kékesi, Maria (*b* Budapest, 1941). Hung. dancer. Studied at Budapest State B. Inst., also with Dudinskaya; joined Budapest State B. in 1962, later becoming one of its ballerinas. Created roles in second première of Eck's *Ondine* (1967) and Seregi's *The Wooden Prince* (1970 and *The Cedar* (1975). Bronze Medal (Varna, 1964); Liszt Prize (1970).

Kellaway, Leon (orig. Jan Kowsky; *b* London). Studied with Astafieva and N. Legat. Danced 2 years with Pavlova's co., then with Kyasht in London and Spessivtzeva in Australia. B. master of the Borovansky B. 1940–55. Has a school in Sydney. Associate b. master of the Austral. B. in its early years.

Kelly, Desmond (*b* Penhalonga, S. Rhodesia, 13 Jan. 1942). Brit. dancer. Studied with Elaine Archibald and Ruth French. Joined London Festival B. in 1959; appointed soloist in 1962, principal d. in 1964. D. with his wife, Denise LeComte, with New Zealand B., Washington National B., and in Zurich. Joined Royal B. as a principal d. in 1970, creating roles in Tetley's *Field Figures* (1970) and *Laborintus* (1972), J. Carter's *Shukumei* (1957), L. Seymour's *Rashomon* (1976), and MacMillan's *Playground* (1979). Now b. master of Sadlers' Wells Royal B which he joined in 1977 and where he continued to d. most principal roles. Gave up principal roles in 1984, but continues to dance.
BIBL.: S. Goodman, 'D.K.', *Dance Magazine* (1970/1); R. Davies, 'D.K.' in *Royal Ballet Yearbook, 1979–80.*

Kelly, Gene (*b* Pittsburg, 3 Aug. 1912). Amer. actor, dancer, choreographer, and film director. Studied at his mother's d.-school and at Pittsburgh Univ., where he directed the annual Cap and Gown Shows. Went to New York in 1939, where he appeared in musicals until his decisive breakthrough in *Pal Joey* (1941), which was immediately repeated for Hollywood. His most ambitious d. prods. have been the films *An American in Paris* (1952) and *Invitation to the Dance* (1956), his TV show *Dancing is a Man's Game* (1958), and his b. *Pas de Dieux* (mus. Gershwin, Paris Opéra, 1960). D. Magazine Award (1958); Légion d'honneur (1960); Hon. Dr. of Fine Arts (Univ. of Pittsburgh, 1961).
BIBL.: Complete check-list of activities in *Les Saisons de la danse* (1973/3 and 1975/3); C. Hirschhorn, *G.K.* (London, 1975).

Kemp, Lindsay (*b* Isle of Lewis, 1939). Brit. mime, actor, dancer, director, and teacher. Studied at Bradford Art College and Rambert B. School. First performed at the Edinburgh Festival in 1964. Prod. David Bowie's Ziggy Stardust concerts at the Rainbow in London. Appeared in

K. Russell's film *Savage Messiah*. Formed his own group, whose first success was his prod. of *Flowers*, based on J. Genet's *Our Lady of the Flowers*, in London in 1974 and *Salome* (1977). Ch. *The Parade's Gone By* (mus. arr. C. Miranda, B. Rambert, 1975) and *Cruel Garden* (together with C. Bruce, B. Rambert, 1977). When in London, teaches mime at the D. Centre.
BIBL.: P. Born, 'L.K.'s Psychological Striptease', *After Dark* (1975/5).

Kemp, William. Brit. actor and dancer, who performed in Shakespeare's co., where he was listed as 'head master of Morrice dancers'. Is reputed to have d. all the way from London to Norwich in 1599.

Kennedy, James. See *Monahan, James.*

Kent, Allegra (*b* Los Angeles, 11 Aug. 1938). Amer. dancer. Studied with Nijinska and at School of Amer. B. Joined New York City B. in 1953; appointed principal d. in 1957. Created parts in Balanchine's *Ivesiana* (1954), *Agon* (1957), *Seven Deadly Sins* (1958 version), *Stars and Stripes* (1958), *Episodes* (1959), *Bugaku* (1963), and *Brahms-Schoenberg Quartet* (1966), and Robbins's *Dances at a Gathering* (1969) and *Dumbarton Oaks* (1972).
BIBL.: R. Greskovic, in 'Some Artists of the New York City Ballet', *Ballet Review* (vol. 4, no. 4).

Kerensky, Oleg (*b* London, 9 Jan. 1930). Brit. b. critic. Educated Christ Church, Oxford. B. critic of *Daily Mail* 1957–71, *New Statesman* 1968–78, and *International Herald Tribune* 1971–8. Frequent broadcaster on the arts. Contributor to *Encyclopedia Britannica* (1974). Author of *Ballet Scene* (London, 1970), *Anna Pavlova* (London, 1973), *The New British Drama* (London, 1977), and *The Guinness Guide to Ballet* (London, 1981).

Keres, Imre (*b* Szeged, 1 June 1930). Hung. dancer, choreographer, and b. director. Studied at Budapest State Op. B. Inst. D. at Szeged State Th. 1947–8 and Budapest State Op. 1948–56. Georgi's assistant in Hanover 1958–62. B. master in Lübeck, b. dir. Wiesbaden 1962–76, where he mounted many prods. of the classics and ch. a great number of contemporary bs. Has often worked at Munich's Th. am Gärtnerplatz. B. dir. Brunswick since 1979.
BIBL.: in 'Ballett im Hessischen Staatsheater Wiesbaden' (*Die Tanzarchiv Reihe*, no. 9).

Kermesse in Bruges, The, or The Three Gifts (orig. Dan. title: *Kermessen i Brügge eller De tre Gaver*). Romantic ballet in 3 acts; ch. Bournonville; mus. Paulli. Prod. 4 Apr. 1851, Royal Dan. B., Copenhagen. The b. was inspired by the paintings of Jan Steen and D. Teniers and is set at the Holy Fair in Bruges, where three brothers undergo the most fantastic adventures.

Kershaw, Stewart (*b* Oxford, 11 Apr. 1941). Brit. conductor. Educated Royal Academy of Music, London and Conservatoire de Paris. B. conductor

of Royal B. 1966–9, Opéra de Lyon 1970–1, Munich State Op. 1971–4, and Stuttgart B. 1972–79.

Kersley, Leo (*b* Watford, 1920). Brit. dancer and teacher. Studied with Idzikowsky and Rambert. D. with B. Rambert (1936–9 and 1940–1), Sadler's Wells B. (1941–2), Anglo-Polish B. (1942–3), and Sadler's Wells Th. B. (1946–51). He then taught in U.S. and Holland, and opened a school in Harlow, Essex, with his wife Janet Sinclair in 1959. Author (with Sinclair) of *A Dictionary of Ballet Terms* (London, 1952).

Kessler, Dagmar (*b* Merchantville, N.J., 30 Dec. 1946). Amer dancer. Studied at School of Pennsylvania B. with Frano Jelincik (whom she married). Joined Pennsylvania B. in 1965, Hamburg State Op. B. in 1966, London Festival B. in 1968, and Pittsburgh B. Th. in 1972.
BIBL.: S. Goodman, 'D.K.', *Dance Magazine* (1967/11).

Kettentanz. Ballet in 9 dances; ch. Arpino; mus. Joh. Strauss and Joh. Simon Mayer; cost. Joe Eula. Prod. 20 Oct. 1971, City Center Joffrey B., City Center, New York. The Eng. equivalent would be 'Chain Dance'. The b. unfolds in an unbroken chain of dances for 6 couples as a display of virtuoso zest and energy. Revived for National B. of Can.
BIBL.: G. Balanchine, 'K.' in *Balanchine's Complete Stories of the Great Ballets* (Garden City, N.Y., 1977).

Keuten, Serge (*b* Paris, 25 Nov. 1947). Fr. dancer. choreographer, and b. director. Studied at Paris Opéra B. School. Member of Opéra B. 1963–1973. Also d. with Petit's co. Started Association des Jeunes Artistes Chorégraphiques in 1971 and Groupe des Recherches de Paris Opéra B. in 1973. Has had his own Atelier Chorégraphique de S.K. since 1975.

Keuter, Cliff (*b* Boise, Ida., 1940). Amer. dancer and choreographer. Studied with Welland Lathrop, Graham, Farnworth, Slavenska, and Sanasardo. Started to d. with Tamiris–Nagrin Co. in 1962. Established his own co. in 1969; choreographs for this and other troupes.
BIBL.: Herbert M. Simpson, 'C.K.', *Dance Magazine* (1979/8).

Keveházi, Gábor (*b* Budapest, 25 Feb. 1953). Hung. dancer. Studied at Budapest State B. Inst. and Leningrad Ch. School. Joined Budapest State Op. B. in 1972; created role in second première of Seregi's *The Cedar* (1975). First Prize (Junior class, Varna, 1972); Silver Medal (Varna, 1974).

Khadra. Ballet in 1 act; ch. C. Franca; mus. Sibelius; déc. Honor Frost. Prod. 27 May 1946, Sadler's Wells Th. B., Sadler's Wells Th., London, with O'Reilly, Heaton Kersley, A. Grant. Based on Sibelius' incidental mus. to *Belshazzar's Feast*, the b. enfolds as a series of Persian miniatures around K., a young girl, who is full of wondering astonishment at what life holds for her.

BIBL.: G. Balanchine, 'K.' in *Balanchine's New Complete Stories of the Great Ballets* (Garden City, N.Y., 1968.

Khachaturian, Aram Ilyich (*b* Tiflis, 6 June 1903, *d*. Moscow, 1 May 1978). Sov. composer. Wrote the mus. for Ilya Arbatov's *Happiness* (Yerevan, 1939), which, completely rewritten, became *Gayane* (ch. Anisimova, Kirov B., Molotov-Perm, 1942), and for Jacobson's *Spartacus* (Kirov B., 1956).

Khalfouni, Dominique (*b* Paris, 23 June 1951). Fr. dancer. After studying at some private schools entered Paris Op. B. School aged 9, joining the co. 1967, promoted danseuse étoile 1976. Created central role in MacMillan's *Metaboles* (1978). Resigned Paris Op. B. 1980 for freelancing activities. Married to the d. Jean-Marc Torrès.

Khilko, Raissa Alexeievna (*b* Dnepropetrovsk, 21 Sep. 1950). Sov. dancer. Studied at Kiev B. School, graduating 1968 and joining Kiev B. co., eventually becoming prima ballerina. Gold Medal (Varna, 1978).

Khokhlov, Boris Ivanovich (*b* 1932). Sov. dancer. Studied at Moscow Bolshoi B. School, graduating in 1951, since when he has been a member of the Bolshoi B., dancing the premier danseur roles of the standard repertory, and creating a leading part in Lavrosky's *Pages of Life* (1961). Gold Medal (Moscow, 1957), People's Artist of the R.S.F.S.R. (1969).

BIBL.: J. Sinclair, 'B.K.' in *Ballet Today* (1960/11).

Kholfin, Nicolai Sergeyevich (*b* 23 Nov. 1903, *d* 8 July 1979). Sov. dancer, choreographer, and b. master. Worked for the Moscow Art Th. B., ch. a radical new version of *La Fille mal gardée* in 1933 under the title of *The Rivals*; the prod. became a lasting success of the co. In 1937 he created the Pushkin-based b. *The Gipsies* (mus. S. Vasilenko). He then worked in Kirgisia and Turkmenia, mainly dealing with folklore subjects. In 1947 he ch. Asafiev's *Francesca da Rimini* for the Moscow Stanislavsky and Nemirovich-Danchenko Mus. Th., then for the same co. Igor Morosov's *Doctor Aibolit* (1948), and the first prod. of Alexander Raitschev's *The Song of the Heiducks* in Sofia in 1953.

Kidd, Michael (*b* Brooklyn, 12 Aug. 1919). Amer. dancer, choreographer, and director. Studied with Vilzak and Schollar. Appeared on Broadway in 1937; d. with Amer. B., B. Caravan 1937–40, D. Players 1941–2, B. Th. 1942–7. Created a role in Robbins' *Interplay* (1945), and ch. *On Stage!* (mus. Dello Joio, 1945). Then became a very popular ch. for Broadway and Hollywood; his successes include *Finian's Rainbow* (1947), *Guys and Dolls* (1951), *Can-Can* (1953), *Seven Brides for Seven Brothers* (1954), *Destry Rides Again* (1959), *Ben Franklin in Paris* (1964), *Hello Dolly!* (1969 film version), and *The Rothschilds* (1970).

Kiev. The capital of Ukraine has a rich tradition of folklore and amateur dancing. One of the first professional local choreographers was V. Verchovinetz, and the first professional b. troupe is mentioned in 1816. During the next decades private th. cos. catered for the b. interests of the locals, until the Russ. Op. House opened in 1867, with a resident b. troupe under S. Lentchevsky, offering such bs. as *Harvest in Ukraine*, *Holiday on the Sea*, *The Fairy Doll* (1893), *Coppélia* etc. Occasionally there were guest-visits by dancers of the Bolshoi or Maryinsky Th., including J. Geltzer, L. Egorova, and Mordkin. Like Lentchevsky, the b. masters (F. Vittich, N. Novakovsky, A. Romanovsky) came from the Warsaw Th. Academy. After 1915 the co. was headed by A. Kotchetkovsky from Moscow and then by Nijinska from Petrograd. The th. was nationalized in 1919 and renamed Kiev Liebknecht Op. Th., then State Academic Op. Th. in 1926 and Academic Op. and B. Th. T. G. Tsevtshenko in 1934. Its first post-revolutionary dir. was M. Diskovsky (1924), then L. Shukov and Maria Reizen. An associated b. studio was started in 1918, led by T. Shistyakov; it produced such dancers as A. Gavrilova, A. Berdovsky, N. Ivastchenko, and V. Schechtman. the first Sov. b. given was *Red Poppy* (1928), followed by *Chout* and *The Golden Age*. One of the first national bs. was *Pan Konovsky*. During the 1930s the co. grew to 80 members. Bs. from the 1940s included *The Fountain of Bakhchisaray*, *Laurencia*, *The Prisoner of the Caucasus*, etc. During the war the co. was evacuated to Ufa and then to Irkutsk, where it combined with the Kharkov Th. Among the better known b. masters who worked here in more recent times were S. Sergeyev and V. Vronsky. The co. is now headed by Alexander Shekero, whose bs. include *Stone Ruler* (mus. V. Gubarenko), a new version of *Romeo and Juliet* (mus. Prokofiev), and *Kameniari* (mus. M. Skorik)—other bs. have been ch. by G. Maiorov, incl. *Dawn Poem* (mus. V. Kossenko) and *Cippolino* (mus. by Karen Khatchaturian). Principal dancers are Ludmila Tcherednichenko, Ludmila Smorgacheva, Tatiana Tayakina, Valery Kovtun, and Yevgeny Kosmenko. A Ch. School was opened in 1935, headed by G. Beriosova.

Kikaleishvili, Zurab Malakievy (*b* Tiflis 25 Oct. 1924). Sov. dancer, b. master, and teacher. Studied with Chaboukiani in Tiflis; became a member of the city's b. co. and succeeded Chaboukiani in his roles. Now teaches at Tiflis Ch. School.

Kikimora. Ballet in 1 act; ch. Massine; mus. Liadov; déc. Larionov. Prod. 25 Aug. 1916, Diaghilev's Bs. Russes, San Sebastian, with Shabelska, Idzikowsky. The protagonist is the ugliest and most repulsive of all the Russ. fairy-tale witches. Later it became one episode in Massine's *Contes Russes* (1917).

Killar, Ashley (*b* London, 18 June 1944). Brit. dancer and choreographer. Studied at Royal B. School and Graham School. Member of Stuttgart B. 1963–7, Western (Scottish) Th. B. 1967–71, Royal B. New Group from 1971. Started to ch. for the Stuttgart Noverre matinées, continuing with *Journey* (mus. Janáček, 1970), *Arriving Bellevue Sunday* (mus. Janáček, 1971), *Migration* (mus. Franck, 1973), *The Entertainers* (mus. Pergolesi), *Renard* (mus. Stravinsky, both 1974). Resident ch. of Pact B., Johannesburg since 1979.

Kinch, Myra (*b* Los Angeles, *d.* Bonita Springs, Fla., 19 Nov. 1981). Amer. dancer, choreographer, and teacher. Studied with M. Stuart, La Meri, and Eduardova. Made her début in Berlin. Became known through her many Amer. tours as a solo performer, with her husband Manuel Galea at the piano. Her most popular pieces were satires, e.g. *Giselle's Revenge, Tomb for Two* (inspired by *Aida*), and *A Waltz is a Waltz is a Waltz*. Often appeared at Jacob's Pillow.

Kinderballett. See *Vienna Children's Ballet*.

Kinetic Molpai. Ballet in 11 sections; ch. T. Shawn; mus. Jess Meeker. Prod. 5 Oct. 1935, T. Shawn and his Men Dancers, Goshen, N.Y. A spectacular succession of individual dances about man's power of self-assertion—a piece of relentless drive and male energy. The sections are called Strife, Oppositions, Solvent, Dynamic Contrasts, Resilience, Successions, Unfolding and Folding, Dirge, Limbo, Surge, and Apotheosis. Revived for A. Ailey City Center D. Th. in 1972.

Kinetographie. This is the official name of the system of d. notation developed by von Laban—in Eng.-speaking countries mostly referred to as Labanotation, or occasionally as Kinetography Laban.

King, Bruce (*b* Oakland, Cal., 10 Feb. 1925). Amer. d., ch., and teacher. Studied with Holm, Nikolais, M. Cunningham, Graham, Craske, Tudor. Appeared with the cos. of Henry Street Playhouse, M. Cunningham, Litz, Tamiris, and E. Gentry. Established B.K. Concert (performing group) in 1959, for which he has ch. numerous works. Started to teach in 1951; mainly concerned with creative d. for children. Has been artist in residence at various univs.

King, Kenneth. Amer. dancer and choreographer. Started to perform while still majoring in philosophy at Antioch College during the mid-1960s. Perhaps the most cerebral of today's chs., whose references to Descartes, Kant, Nietzsche, Freud, *et al.*, and whose use of all sorts of media combine with improvisation which breaks down movements like the elements in a chemical analysis. He also likes to work with alter egos and offers a unique brand of highly charged rapid movements which he relates to technical and scientific progresses—some of his more recent titles incl. *RAdeoA.C.tiv(ID)ty, t-e-l-e-g-r-a-p-h-i-c s-o-n-g-s, The Telaxix Synapsulator,* and *The Phi Project.* J. Anderson called him 'a thinking man's choreographer'.

BIBL.: S. Banes, in *Terpsichore in Sneakers* (Boston, 1980).

King's Theatre. The original th. in the Haymarket, London, was built 1704–5 as the city's principal th. for op. and b. It was burnt down in 1789, and a new th. opened in 1793. Under Lumley it attracted all the stars of the romantic b. era. In 1837 it changed its name to Her Majesty's Th., but was often referred to as the Ital. Op. House (not to be confused with the Royal Ital. Op. of Cov. Gdn.). The th. serves as the background for the b. *The Prospect Before Us.*

King's Voluntary Corps on Amager, The. See *Life Guards on Amager, The.*

Kirkland, Gelsey (*b* Bethlehem, Penn., 29 Dec. 1952). Amer. d. Studied at Sch. of Amer. B. Joined N.Y. City B. in 1968; apptd. soloist in 1969 and principal d. in 1972. Created roles in Balanchine's *Firebird* (version 1970) and *Suite No. 3,* Robbins's *The Goldberg Variations* (1971), *Scherzo fantastique* (1972), and *An Evening's Waltzes* (1973). Left N.Y. City B. in 1974 to become a b. with Amer. B. Th., often appearing with Baryshnikov and Nureyev. Further role creations in Tudor's *The Leaves are Fading* and Neumeier's *Hamlet: Connotations* (1976). Has been with the co. on and off ever since. Guest d. with Royal B. in 1980 and 1986. Wrote *Dancing on my Grave: An Autobiography,* with husband Greg Lawrence (N.Y. 1986).

BIBL.: S. Goodman, 'G.K.', *Dance Magazine* (1971/12); K. Sandler, 'Her Own Best Friend', *Ballet News* (1981/10).

Kirnbauer, Susanne (*b* Vienna, 27 July 1942). Austrian d. Studied at Vienna State Op. B. School and with Kiss, Hightower, Peretti, and Franchetti. Joined Vienna State Op. B. in 1956, appointed soloist in 1967 and principal in 1972. Has appeared on leave of absence with Charrat's B. de France, co. of Charrat-Miskovitch, and Grand B. de Paris. Critics Prize (Paris, 1968).

BIBL.: E. Herf. 'S.K.', *Ballet Today* (1967/1–2).

Kirov Ballet. The Leningrad Academic Th. for Op. and B. S. M. Kirov, Order of Lenin. Its forerunners were the Bolshoi Th. of St. Petersburg, which housed the city's op. and b. co. 1783–1860, and the Maryinsky Th., which opened in 1860, though b. perfs. were not given there until 1880, and not regularly until 1889 (individual perfs. were also given at the Th. of the Hermitage and at the Th. of Tsarskoye Selo (now Pushkin). After the October Revolution in 1917 the name was changed to State Academic Th. for Op. and B. (for which the Russ. abbreviation is GATOB); it received its present name in 1935, one year

The Kirov Ballet in Act 1 of Lavrovsky's *Romeo and Juliet*, 1940.

Photo Novosti Press Agency (A.P.N.).

after the assassination of the head of the Leningrad Communist Party after whom it is named. The Frenchman J.-B. Landé was commissioned in 1738 to found a b. school for the children of the servants at the Tsar's court. This became the basis from which the St. Petersburg—Petrograd—Leningrad school and b. tradition developed. Early choreographers included Hilverding, R. Fossano, and Angiolini, followed by Didelot, who ch. the first bs. based on subjects by Pushkin and thoroughly reformed the school, thus achieving a remarkable expansion of the city's b. culture during the first quarter of the 19th century. The earliest well-known Russ. artists from this period are the b. master I. Valberkh, and the dancers A. I. Istomina, Y. I. Kolossova, and A. Glushkovsky. All the international star dancers of the romantic b. appeared in St. Petersburg, where they had to compete against such Russ. artists as Y. Andreyanova, Y. Teleshova, and N. Goltz. In 1847 M. Petipa became solo d., and eventually the co.'s dir.; he led it to the climax of its Tsarist history between 1862 and 1903. Most of its dancers came from the B. Academy at Th. Street (the present State Vaganova Institute for Ch. at Rossi Street). Petipa's brilliant prods. in the 1890s of *Sleeping Beauty, Nutcracker, Swan Lake*, and *Raymonda* were the product of collaboration with Ivanov, the b. master, and such composers as Tchaikovsky and Glazunov. The best known dancers at about the turn of the century included P. Gerdt, O. Preobrajenska, M. Kschessinska. V. Trefilova, A. Vaganova, N. and S. Legat, A. Pavlova, T. Karsavina, A. Bolm, and V. Nijinsky. They caused a sensation when they appeared in the West, individually and with the troupe Diaghilev assembled for his Paris seasons from 1909. They also introduced western audiences to the art of Fokine, another member of the co., who reformed the whole concept of the art of b. After a certain period of instability, due to the October Revolution and its aftermath, the GATOB became a tremendously lively platform of experimental Sov. b. during the 1920s under such choreographers as F. Lopokhov, and Balanchine was first seen in the Evenings of Young B. (not held in the th., but with members of the co.). During the 1930s the most important new Sov. bs. had their first prod. here: Vainonen's *Flames of Paris* (1932), Zakharov's *Fountain of Bakhchisaray* (1934), Chaboukiani's *Laurencia* (1939), and the Lavrovsky version of *Romeo and Juliet* (1940). In this prod. Ulanova made her startling rise to fame. The co. was evacuated to Molotov-Perm 1941–4, while a small contingent of dancers continued to appear in besieged Leningrad. After 1945 the emphasis of Sov. b. shifted to Moscow, but the co. continued to enjoy world-wide acclaim as one of the supreme classic troupes; its reputation was enhanced when it first visited Paris, London, and New York in 1961. Most of these visits were headed by K. Sergeyev and N. Dudinskaya, who had been the co.'s leading couple during the 1950s, and who still hold varying directorial positions in the co. (due to the shifting political climate). Under Sergeyev the co. put its main emphasis on the conservation of the classics; such choreographers as Jacobson and the young Grigorovich provided compatible new material. The most important dancers during the first visits to the west incl. A. Shelest, I. Kolpakova, N. Makarova, A. Sisova, G. Komleva, V. Semyonov, Y. Soloviev, R. Nureyev, M. Baryshnikov, and V. Panov; Nureyev, Makarova, and Baryshnikov decided to stay in the West while Panov, after 2 years' widely publicised struggle, finally succeeded in emigrating to Isr. This mass exodus of the co.'s leading dancers has mainly been caused by the artistic sterility of the repertory, which still offers some of the best prods. of classics one can see anywhere in the world, but is a ch. desert as far as contemporary b. is concerned. The co.'s present Artistic Dir. is O. Vinogradov. The city's second b. co. is attached to the Maly Th.

BIBL.: N. Roslavleva, in *Era of the Russian Ballet* (London, 1966).

Kirova, Vera Lazarevna (*b* Sofia, 1 Jan. 1940). Bulg. dancer. Studied with Vailia Verbeva in Sofia, also with M. Semenova and Naima Baltatcheyeva. Joined Sofia State Op. B. in 1958; appointed prima ballerina in 1961. Has often appeared abroad, mainly with B. de Wallonie, where she was prima ballerina until 1973.

Kirsanova, Nina (*b* Moscow, 1899). Russ.-Yugosl. dancer, teacher and b. director. Studied at Moscow B. School with L. Nelidova, A. Alexandrova, V. Mazalova, Goleizovsky and Novikov. D. at Petrograd Maly Th. and with Moscow Bolshoi B. Left USSR 1921 via Lvov for Yugoslavia, where she became one of the pioneers of b. Artistic dir. of Belgrade B. 1924–6, and again, after dancing with Pavlova and in Monte Carlo, 1931–4 and 1939–41.

Kirsova, Helene (*née* Ellen Wittrup; *b* c. 1911, *d* London, 22 Feb. 1962). Dan. dancer, teacher, choreographer, and b. director. Studied with Egorova. Was for years a member of the Bs. Russes. Stayed in Austral. after one of the co.'s visits, opening a b. school in Sydney in 1940 and founding Kirsova B. in 1941, for which she ch. *Faust* after Heine (mus. H. Krips, 1941). Retired in 1947. Author of *Ballet in Moscow Today* (London, 1956).

Kirstein, Lincoln (*b* Rochester, N.Y., 4 May 1907). Amer. writer and b. director. Educated Harvard Univ. A young man from a wealthy family, he succeeded in bringing Balanchine to the U.S., and founded the School of Amer. B. with him and Dr. E. M. M. Warburg in 1934. Co-founder of Amer. B. in 1935. Founded Ballet Caravan, 1936. Editor of *Dance Index* 1942–8. Established B. Society in 1946, from which the New York City B. developed, of which he has been the General Director since 1948. Through his close connection with Balanchine and the co., became one of the most influential men in the Amer. (and international) b. scene. He was a ghost-writer of part of R. Nijinsky's Nijinsky biography 1932–3. His most important publications include *Dance* (New York, 1935), *Blast at Ballet, a Corrective for the American Audience* (New York, 1938), *The Classic Ballet, Basic Technique and Terminology* (with M. Stuart, New York, 1952), *Movement & Metaphor* (New York, 1970), *The New York City Ballet* (New York, 1974), and *Nijinsky Dancing* (New York, 1975). U.S. Medal of Freedom (1984).

Kiss, Nora (*b* Piatigorsk, 1908). Sov.-Fr. dancer and teacher. Studied with Alexandrova, Brianza, Volinin, and Sarkisian. D. in various Fr. and Russ. cos. (Romanov, Balanchine) 1929–35. Started to teach in Paris in 1938; opened her own studio there in 1946, and became one of the most sought-after teachers of the post-war generation of Fr. dancers. Has often taught abroad (Rome, Cologne, Brussels, Copenhagen, Toronto, etc.).

Kisselgoff, Anna (*b* Paris, 12 Jan. 1938). Amer. writer on d. Educated at Bryn Mawr College and Columbia Univ. Studied b. with V. Belova and J. Yazvinsky. D. critic and reporter, *The New York Times*, since 1968 and its principal critic since 1977.

Kistler, Darci (*b* 1964). Amer. dancer. Studied at School of Amer. B. Joined corps of New York City B. in 1980, where she immediately attracted attention when appearing increasingly in solo roles. Created roles in Robbins's Pas de deux from Tchaikovsky's 1st piano concerto and in P. Martins's *Symphony No. 1* (both 1981).
BIBL.: R. Greskovic, 'The Arrival of D.K.', *Ballet Review* (IX/2).

Kitahara, Hideteru (*b* Isesaki-shi, 12 Nov. 1940). Jap. dancer, choreographer, and b. director. Studied at the school of the Tchaikovsky Memorial Tokyo B. Co., also with Danilova, Franklin, Messerer, and Varlamov. Made his début with Tokyo B. in 1961; became its leading premier danseur and eventually its artistic dir. Mounted the co.'s prods. of *Sleeping Beauty* and *Cinderella*. Prize of the Minister of Education (Tokyo, 1963); Prize for the best classic b. master (Paris, 1970).

Kivitt, Ted (*b* Miami, 21 Dec. 1942). Amer. dancer. Studied with A. Gavriloff, T. Armour, J. A. Kneeland, and G. Milenoff. Appeared in night-clubs and musicals; joined Amer. B. Th. in 1961, appointed soloist in 1964. Created roles in Robbins's *Les Noces* (1965) and Smuin's *Gartenfest* (1968). Married to the d. Karena Brock. Artistic dir. of Milwaukee B., 1980–6.
BIBL.: J. Gruen, 'T.K.' in *The Private World of Ballet* (New York, 1975).

Klamt, Jutta (*b* Striegau, 23 Feb. 1890, *d* Aarau, Switzerland, 26 May 1970). Ger. dancer and teacher. She was self-taught, and gave her first d.-recital in Berlin in 1919. Founded a school in Berlin in 1920, from which a group of dancers was formed, with whom she toured widely. One of the key figures of the Ger. modern d. movement; she and her husband Gustav Vischer were the first to adapt modern d. to the teachings of Nazi ideology.

Klaus, François (*b* Cannes, 10 Nov. 1947). Fr. dancer. Studied with Besobrasova. D. with B. Classique de France and Stuttgart B., Munich State Op. B., principal d. with Hamburg State Op. B. since 1973. Created the leading roles in Neumeier's *Schumann* (1974) and *Third Symphony by Gustav Mahler* (1975). Married to the d. Robyn White.

Klebe, Giselher (*b* Mannheim, 28 June 1925). Ger. composer. Wrote the mus. for T. Gsovsky's *Signale* (1955), *Fleurenville* (1956), and *Menagerie* (based on Wedekind's *Luly*, 1958), and for Keres' *Villons Testament* (1971).

Klekovic, Patricia (*b* Chicago *c*. 1935). Amer. dancer. Studied with E. McRae, appeared with the E. McRae Dancers, the Fine Arts B., and the Chicago Symphony. Joined Chicago Lyric Op. B. in 1955; later one of the principal dancers of R. Page's various cos. until 1972.
BIBL.: S. Goodman, 'P.K. and Orrin Kayan', *Dance Magazine* (1962/5).

Klos, Vladimír (*b* Prague, 1 July 1946). Czech dancer. Studied at School of the National Th. and Conservatoire; joined the Prague Studio B. upon graduation. To Stuttgart B. in 1968; appointed soloist in 1973. Created roles in Cranko's *Brouillards* and *Orpheus* (both 1970).

Kniaseff, Boris (*b* St. Petersburg, 1 July 1900, *d* Paris, 7 Oct. 1975). Russ.-Fr. dancer and teacher. Studied with Mordkin, Nelidova, and Goleizovsky. Left Russia in 1917. B. master Sofia. D. with various emigré Russ. and Fr. cos. in 1921–32—often as a partner of Spessivtzeva, to whom he was married. B. master Paris Opéra Comique 1932–4. Opened his own studio in Paris in 1937; later also in Lausanne, Geneva, Rome, and Athens. Returned to Paris where he taught his world-famous system of 'barre par terre' (with the pupils lying on the floor) at the Académie Internationale de Danse.

Knight Errant. Ballet in 1 act; libr. and ch. Tudor; mus. R. Strauss; déc. Stefanos Lazarides. Prod. 25 Nov. 1968, Touring Royal B., Op. House, Manchester, with Davel, Landon, Anderton, Barbieri, Thorogood. The b., set to Strauss's incidental mus. for *Le Bourgeois gentilhomme* and the prelude to *Ariadne auf Naxos*, is based on an episode from the 79th letter of *Les Liaisons dangereuses* by Choderlos de Laclos (1782); the hero seduces three women during the course of one night and betrays them to their husbands, after which he in turn is betrayed by the Woman

of Consequence. The b. was originally made for D. Wall, who fell ill just before the première.
BIBL.: P. Brinson and C. Crisp., 'K.E.' in *Ballet for All* (London 1970).

Knill, Hans (*b* Schaffhausen, 18 Feb. 1941). Swiss dancer and b. master. Studied with H. Bamert, Plucis, F. Stebler, Casenave, and Harkarvy. D. with Charrat's co. in Geneva in 1963, Dutch National B. 1963–7, and Netherlands D. Th. since 1967 (appointed b. master in 1973), then artistic co-dir. (with Kylián) 1975–7; now régisseur. Has created roles in bs. by Van Manen and Tetley.

Knust, Albrecht (*b* Hamburg, 5 Oct. 1896, *d* Essen, 19 Mar. 1978). Ger. dancer, choreographer, teacher, and dance-notator. Studied with Laban, becoming a member of his Tanzbühne in 1922. Dir. of Hamburg Laban School 1924–5. B. master in Dessau in 1926. Returned to Hamburg, where he concentrated on the further development of 'Kinetographie Laban' (Labanotation). Head of the d. department at Essen Folkwang School in 1934. D. notator at Munich State Op. 1939–45. Teacher and dir. of Kinetographisches Institut at Essen Folkwang School since 1951. Author of *Abriss der Kinetographie Laban* (Munich, 1942—new version Hamburg, 1956). Became a leading international authority on Labanotation.

Kobler Family. An Austro-Ger. th. family, which can be traced back to the mid-18th century; they performed mostly on Austro-Ger. territory, but also in Amsterdam (1812) and then in Paris and Brussels, where they were billed as 'I Grotteschi' or 'Les Grotesques', 'The Kobler family was a highly trained travelling unit, with occasional gifted outsiders incorporated in the troupe. They seem to be the earliest case of a travelling company which presented *only* ballets, thus differently constituted from the children's troupes, which had repertoires of plays, pantomimes, operas *and* ballets. Nor can they be compared to the travelling dancers who played all over Europe in different theatres. They toured as a self-sufficient dance group and were booked as a unit from theatre to theatre' (M. H. Winter).
BIBL.: M. H. Winter, in *The Pre-Romantic Ballet* (London, 1974).

Köchermann, Rainer (*b* Chemnitz, 3 Feb. 1930). Ger. dancer and b. master. Studied with T. Gsovsky, G. Blank, V. Gsovsky, and W. Gore. D. with the cos. in East Berlin (1949–51), West Berlin (1951–5, Frankfurt (1955–9), and Hamburg (1950–73). Has created many roles in bs. by T. Gsovsky, G. Blank, Gore, Rosen, and van Dyk. B. master in Osnabrück 1974–6 and 1976–81 in Saarbrücken.

Kochno, Boris (*b* Moscow, 3 Jan. 1904). Russ-Fr. b. librettist and writer on b. The friend and secretary of Diaghilev, whom he joined in 1923; wrote the libr. for *Les Fâcheux* (1924), *Zéphire et Flore, Les Matelots* (both 1925), *La Pastorale* (1926),

La Chatte (1927), *Ode, The Gods Go a-Begging* (both 1928), *Le Bal,* and *Prodigal Son* (both 1929). Became artistic advisor of the B. Russe de Monte Carlo; wrote librs. for *Cotillon* and *Jeux d'enfants* (1932). Co-founder (with Balanchine) of Les Bs. 1933. After 1945 he collaborated with Petit and co-founded the Bs. des Champs-Elysées. Wrote further librs. for *Les Forains* (1945), *Les Amours de Jupiter, Le Bal des blanchisseuses* (both 1946), and *Pâris* (1964). Author of *Le Ballet* (Paris, 1954) and *Diaghilev et Les Ballets Russes* (Paris, 1970). Some of his b. librs. were published under the penname Sobeka.

Kodály, Zoltán (*b* Kecskemét, 16 Dec. 1882, *d* Budapest, 6 Mar. 1967). Hung. composer. Wrote no b. mus., but his concert mus. has often been adapted for d. purposes; e.g. Graham's *Lamentation* (New York, 1930), Milloss's *Kurucz Mese* (the *Dances of Galanta* and *Dances of Maroszek*, Budapest, 1935), Limón's *Missa brevis in tempore belli* (New York, 1958), and Eck's *Peacock Variations* (B. Sopianae, 1971).

Koegler, Horst (*b* Neuruppin, 22 Mar. 1927). Ger. critic and writer on b. Educated Kiel Univ. and Halle/Saale Academy of Th. B. critic of *Die Welt* 1957–9, *Stuttgarter Zeitung* since 1959 (mus. editor since 1977). Ger. correspondent of *Dance and Dancers, Ballet News,* and *Les Saisons de la danse.* Author of *Ballet international* (Berlin, 1960), *Yvonne Georgi* (Velber, 1963), *Balanchine und das moderne Ballett* (Velber, 1964), *Friedrichs Ballettlexikon von A–Z* (Velber, 1972), 'In the Shadow of the Swastika—Dance in Germany, 1927–1936' (*Dance Perspectives* 57), etc. Editor of the Ger. annual *Ballett 1965* onwards. Wrote 'Dance, Western' for *Encyclopedia Britannica* (1974).

Koesun, Ruth Ann (*b* Chicago, 15 May 1928). Amer. dancer. Studied with Stone-Camryn and V. Swoboda. Joined B. Th. in 1946, becoming one of its principal dancers; created roles in Tudor's *Shadow of the Wind* (1948), de Mille's *Fall River Legend* (1948) and *The Harvest According* (1952), Ross's *Caprichos* (1950) and *Paean* (1957), and Nijinska's *Schumann Concerto* (1951). Retired in 1969. Was married to the d. Eric Braun.

Köhler-Richter, Emmy (*b* Gera, 9 Feb. 1918). Ger. dancer, choreographer, and b. director. Studied with Wigman and T. Gsovsky. D. with the cos. in Bonn, Berlin, Strasbourg, and Leipzig. B. mistress Cologne 1947–51, Basle 1953–5, Weimar 1956–8; b. dir. Leipzig Op. House 1958–78. Has mounted highly individual versions of the classics and ch. a great number of bs. Art prize of the GDR (1964).

Kolo. A Yugosl. national d. form (equivalent to the Rum. Hora and the Bulg. Horo), characterized by an open or closed chain, with a leader who directs movements and steps. Its accent is on rhythm and the coordination of the dancers who move as one unit. It is also the name of the

National Folk B. Co. of Yugosl., founded in Belgrade in 1948, which visited London for the first time in 1952.

Kolosova, Eugenia Ivanovna (*b* 15 Dec. 1780, *d* St. Petersburg, 30 Mar. 1869). Russ. dancer and teacher. A protegée of I. Valberkh, she became Didelot's favourite ballerina during his years in St. Petersburg, especially admired for her dramatic expressiveness and her national dances in *The Hungarian Hut* and *Raoul de Créquis*. When Didelot left Russ. for a while, he left the school in her charge, and actually found it improved on his return.

Kolpakova, Irina Alexandrovna (*b* Leningrad, 22 May 1933). Sov. dancer. Studied at Leningrad Ch. School with Vaganova, graduating in 1951; then joined the Kirov B. and later became its outstanding ballerina. Created roles in Grigorovich's *The Stone Flower* (1957) and *Legend of Love* (1961), Belsky's *Coast of Hope* (1959), G. Alexidze's *Ala and Lolly* (1969) and Kasatkina-Vasilyov's *Creation of the World* (1971). Her most famous roles are Giselle, Masha, Raymonda, and Aurora. For a 1969 gala-perf., dedicated to her, Alexidze, I. Tchernychov, and Vinogradov ch. new bs. for her. Married to the d. Vladilen Semyonov. People's Artist of the R.S.F.S.R. (1960) and of the U.S.S.R. (1965).

Komaki Ballet. Originally called Tokyo B. Co.; founded in 1947 by Masahide Komaki, who had d. with the Shanghai B. Russe. It was the first Jap. co. to offer a prod. of *Swan Lake*, and toured the country with Momoko Tani (and later Sakiko Hirose) as ballerina. Arova and Kaye appeared with the co.

Komleva, Gabriella Trofimovna (*b* Leningrad, 27 Dec. 1938). Sov. dancer. Studied at Leningrad Ch. School, graduating in 1957, after which she joined the Kirov B., and later became one of its ballerinas. Created the title-role in Vinogradov's *Goryanka* (1968). Her best roles were Aurora, Raymonda, Nikya (*La Bayadère*), and the Girl in *Leningrad Symphony*. Silver Medal (Varna, 1966). Merited Artist of the R.S.F.S.R. (1970).

Kondratieva, Marina Victorovna (*b* Leningrad, 1 Feb. 1934). Sov. dancer. Studied at Moscow Bolshoi B. School, graduating in 1952, after which she joined the Bolshoi B., and later became one of its ballerinas. Created roles in Lavrovsky's *Paganini* (1960) and the title-role in Plisetskaya's *Anna Karenina* (second première, 1972). Her best roles were Giselle, Aurora, Cinderella, and Maria (*Fountain of Bakhchisaray*). Merited Artist of the R.S.F.S.R. (1965).

Kondratov, Yuri Grigorievich (*b* 6 Feb. 1921, *d* Moscow, 15 July 1967). Sov. dancer and teacher. Studied at Moscow Bolshoi B. School with Gusev, graduating in 1940, after which he joined the Bolshoi B., and later became one of its principal dancers; he partnered Lepeshinskaya and Ulanova

(also on her first Ital. tour in 1951). Retired in 1959, and became Artistic Dir. of the Bolshoi B. School and later of the State Ice B. of the U.S.S.R. Stalin Prize (1950).

Koner, Pauline (*b* New York, 1912). Amer. dancer, choreographer, and teacher. Studied with Fokine, Michio Ito, and Angelo Cansino. Started to d. in Fokine's co. in 1926; toured with M. Ito. Gave her first solo-recital in New York in 1930, after which she made her career as a solo concert d. Joined Limón's co. in 1946, later becoming his principal d., and remained until 1960; created roles in Limón's *La Malinche* and *The Moor's Pavane* (both 1949) and Humphrey's *Ruins and Visions* (1953). Established her own co. in 1947, with which she has toured widely, also performing in Eur. and Asia. Her best known solo d. is *The Farewell*, which she ch. in 1962 to the last movement from Mahler's *Song of the Earth*. Now lectures and teaches. Wrote 'Intrinsic Dance' for *The Modern Dance—Seven Statements of Belief* (Middletown, Conn., 1965). Was married to the conductor Fritz Mahler.

BIBL.: M. B. Marks, 'P.K. Speaking', *Dance Magazine* (1961/9–11); O. Maynard, portfolio on P.K., *Dance Magazine* (1973/4).

Konservatoriet. See *Conservatory, or a Proposal of Marriage Through a Newspaper*.

Koren, Serge Gavrilovich (*b* Petersburg, 6 Sep. 1907, *d* Moscow, 17 June 1969). Sov. dancer and b. master. Started to study at the Evening Courses, then Ch. School; graduated into the GATOB in 1932 and became an outstanding character d. Moved to Moscow Bolshoi B. in 1942 and continued to d. until 1960, when he was appointed b. master. His best roles were Zaal (*Heart of the Hills*), Ostap (*Taras Bulba*), Mercutio (also in the *Romeo and Juliet* film of 1954), Li Shan-Fu (*Red Poppy*), Ripafratta (*Mirandolina*), and Gert (*Path of Thunder*). Merited Artist of the R.S.F.S.R. (1939).

Korrigane, La. Fantastic ballet in 2 acts; lib. François Coppé and Mérante (also ch.); mus. Ch. M. Widor; set Lavastre, Rubé, and Chaperon; cost. Eugène Lacoste. Prod. 1 Dec. 1880, Paris Opéra, with Mauri, Sanlaville, Mérante. The b. is set in Brittany in the 17th century, and tells of a poor girl who is bewitched; her lover finds her, recognizes her, and rescues her. The second act of the enormously successful b. somewhat resembles that of *Giselle*.

BIBL.: C. W. Beaumont, 'L.K.' in *Complete Book of Ballets* (London, 1951).

Körtvélyes, Géza (*b* Budapest, 7 Feb. 1926). Hung. critic and writer on b. General Secretary of the Hung. Dancers Association. Author of *The Miraculous Mandarin at the Budapest Opera* (1961), *Towards a Modern Ballet* (1970), *The Budapest Ballet* (with G. Lörinc, 1971).

Kosak, Igor (*b* Ljubljana, 15 Dec. 1947). Yugosl.

dancer. Studied with Lidija Vissiakova, High-tower, Kiss, Dolin, Volkova. Started to d. in Ljubljana in 1965, then with Harkness B., Guatemala B., Royal Dan. B. and as soloist of the Ger. Op. Berlin 1972–81, since when he has been b. master in Essen. Married to the d. and artistic dir. H. Schwaarz.

Koshelev, Vladimir Arkadievich (*b* Moscow, 24 Jan. 1938). Sov. dancer. Studied Moscow Bolshoi B. School; joined Bolshoi B. in 1956 and later became one of the co.'s best demi-caractère soloists. Created roles in Kasatkina-Vasiliov's *Vanina Vanini* (1962) and *Heroic Poem* (1964) and the Jester in Grigorovich's *Swan Lake* (1969).

Koslovski, Albert (*b* Libau, 1902, *d* 16 Sep. 1974). Latvian dancer and teacher. Studied in Moscow. D. in Riga and Paris. B. master of the Latvian National Op. 1932–44. Went to Stockholm with his wife Nina (*b* Libau 1908—a pupil of Fedorova), where they started to teach. B. master of the Royal Swed. B. in 1949. In charge of Royal Swed. B. School until 1968.

Kovach, Nóra (orig. N. Kováts; *b* Satoraljaujhely, 1931). Hung.-Amer. dancer. Studied with Nádasi at Budapest State B. School; joined Budapest State Op. B. in 1948, made headlines when she escaped with her husband *I. Rabovsky from East Berlin to the West in 1953. Appeared with London Festival B. and then went to the U.S., where they toured widely with a small co., presenting their virtuoso display-pieces, later also in night-clubs and luxury hotels. They now have a school in Beechhurst, N.Y. Authors of *Leap through the Curtain* (London, 1955).
BIBL.: L. Clandon, 'N.K. and Istvan Rabovsky', *Dance Magazine* (1958/11).

Kovács, Rosalia (*b* 14 Jan. 1945). Ital. dancer. Studied at La Scala B. School. Joined La Scala B. in 1964, of which she is now prima ballerina. Created roles in Petit's *L'estasi* (1970) and Massine's *Pulcinella* (new version 1971). Noce d'oro prize (1970); Positano prize (1971).

Kovtun, Valery Petrovich (*b* Donetsk, 22 Oct. 1944). Sov. d. Studied at Kiev B. School, graduating 1965. Joined Kharkov co. and since 1968 Kiev B. as a soloist. Silver Medal (Moscow, 1973).

Koželuh, Leopold Anton (*b* Welwarn, 9 Dec. 1752, *d* Vienna, 7 May 1818). Bohemian composer. Began to write mus. for pantomimes and bs. in Prague in 1771, and in Vienna from 1778, where he collaborated with chs. Muzarelli and Clerici.

Kozlov, Leonid and Valentina (L., *b* 1947, V., *b* 1955). Sov. ds. Married, both were soloists with the Moscow Bolshoi b. when they defected Sep. 1979 in Los Angeles co.'s U.S. tour. Performed widely with various cos. before joining N.Y. City B. 1983 as principals. Since divorced.

Kragh-Jacobsen, Svend (*b* Copenhagen, 4 Sep. 1909, *d* there, 5 May 1984). Dan. critic and writer on b. Educated Univ. of Copenhagen. B. (and dramatic) critic of *Berlingske Tidende* since 1938. *Balletaftener*, a collection of his reviews, was published in Copenhagen in 1969. Author of *Ballettens Blomstring* (1945), *Margot Lander* (1947), *Ballet-Bogen* (1954), *The Royal Danish Ballet* (1955), *Erik Bruhn* (1965), *20 Solo dancers of The Royal Danish Ballet* (1965), etc. Associate editor (with T. Krogh) of *Den Kongelige Danske Ballet* (1952). Contributor to *Dance Encyclopedia* (1967). Wote 'August Bournonville—Who and What?' for *Theatre Research Studies* II (1972). Carina Ari Medal (1975).

Krakowiak (also Fr., Cracovienne). A lively Pol. d. in 2/4 time, from the district of Krakow, performed by couples, with syncopated rhythm and clicked heels. Very popular in the bs. of the romantic era, especially as d. by Elssler in *La Gypsy* (1839).

Kramar, Ivan (*b* Cehovec, 1942). Yugosl. dancer and b. master. Studied at Zagreb B. School, joining Zagreb B. upon graduation. Joined Dutch National B. in 1966; appointed b. master in 1970. Left the co. in 1981 to become b. master at Netherlands D. Th. Married to the d. Sonia Marchiolli.

Krassovska, Nathalie (orig. Natasha Leslie; *b* Petrograd, 3 June 1919). Sov.-Amer. dancer and teacher. The daughter of the Diaghilev d. Lydia K., she studied in Russ., then with Preobrajenska, Legat, and at School of Amer. B. D. with the cos. of Nijinska, Les Bs. 1933, with Lifar in South Amer., B. Russe de Monte Carlo as ballerina 1936–50, London Festival B. 1950–9. Now teaches in Dallas, Tex.

Krassovskaya, Vera Mikhailovna (*b* Petrograd, 11 Sep. 1915). Sov. writer on b. Studied at Leningrad Ch. School; d. with GATOB and Kirov B. 1933–41. Now works at the Leningrad Th. Institute. Author of *V. Chaboukiani* (1956), *Russian Ballet Theatre from the Beginning to the Middle of the 19th Century* (1958), *Leningrad Ballet* (1961), *Russian Ballet Theatre of the Second Half of the 19th Century* (1963), *Anna Pavlova* (1964), *Russian Ballet Theatre at the Beginning of the 20th Century* (first part: Choreographers, 1971—second part: Dancers, 1972), 'Marius Petipa and The Sleeping Beauty' (*Dance Perspectives* 49), and *Nijinsky* (1974—Eng. version 1979).

Krätke, Grita (*b* Leipzig, 11 June 1907). Ger. dancer, choreographer, and teacher. Studied at Kiel and Essen. Began to d. in Kiel in 1925. Had her own schools in Wuppertal and Schwerin. B. mistress Schwerin 1945–51. Teacher at E. Berlin State B. School 1951–62. B. mistress E. Berlin State Op. 1963–71. Has ch. many bs. Art Prize of the G.D.R. (1967).

Kraus, Gertrud (*b* Vienna, 6 May 1903 *d* Tel Aviv 23 Nov. 1977). Austrian-Isr. dancer, and

choreographer, and teacher. Trained as a d. and pianist at Vienna State Academy. Performed as a recital d. throughout Eur., Egypt, Tel Aviv, Haifa, and Jerusalem 1928–50. Dir., d., and ch. of G.K. D. Co. in Vienna until 1934 and in Israel 1935–51. Had her own school in Vienna and then a studio in Tel Aviv 1935–73, where almost all the country's best-known dancers have trained with her. Much respected also a painter and musician; appointed d. professor at the Rubin Academy for Mus. and D. in Jerusalem. Israel Prize in 1963.
BIBL.: G. Manor, *The Life and Dance of G.K.* (Hakkibutz, 1978).

Kresnik, Johann (*b* Bleiburg, 12 Dec. 1939). Austrian d., choreographer, and b. master. Studied with Rein Esté, J. Deroc, W. Nicks, Woizikovsky, and P. Appel. Danced with the cos. in Gráz, Bremen, and Cologne (1961–8). Began to ch. in Cologne. Went to Bremen as b. master 1968–79 and to Heidelberg since, where he has ch. a great number of fiercely socially committed b. prods. Has also worked as a guest ch. for Ger. Op. Berlin, Th. an der Wien, and Nuremberg Op. Ho.

Kreutzberg, Harald (*b* Reichenberg, 11 Dec. 1902, *d* Muri, Switzerland, 25 Apr. 1968). Ger. dancer, choreographer, and teacher. Studied with Wigman and Terpis. Joined Hanover B. in 1922 and became Georgi's partner; made many tours with her in Ger. and abroad, incl. U.S. Temporarily engaged at various Ger. ths. (Berlin State Op., Brunswick, Leipzig, Düsseldorf, also Salzburg Festival); became intern. known as the leading male exponent of modern d. in Ger. and toured frequently with Friedrich Wilckens as accompanist. Opened a school in Bern in 1955; stopped dancing in 1959, but continued to work as a teacher and occasional ch.
BIBL.: E. Pirchan, *H.K.* (Vienna, 1941).

Krieger, Victorina Vladimirovna (*b* St. Petersburg, 9 Apr. 1893 *d* Moscow, 23 Dec. 1978). Russ. dancer. Daughter of actor-playwright parents. Studied at Moscow Bolshoi B. School; graduated in 1910 and joined the Bolshoi B., where she became the leading Gorsky ballerina, excelling in dramatic roles such as Lise, Swanilda, and Kitri. D. with Pavlova's co. in 1921; toured U.S. with Mordkin 1923–5. On returning to Moscow established a small group of dancers in 1927, with which she appeared in chamber-sized new versions of popular bs.; in her prods. she attempted to apply the teachings of the Stanislavsky system to d. From this the Moscow Art Th. B. derived in 1929, which was succeeded by the co. at the *Stanislavsky and Nemirovich-Danchenko Mus. Th. Had her best roles in *The Rivals* (new version of *La Fille mal gardée*), *La Carmagnole*, and as Zarema in the try-out prod. of *Fountain of Bakhchisaray*. Later returned to Bolshoi B., where she created the stepmother in Zakharov's *Cinderella* (1945). Appointed Dir. of the Bolshoi Th. Museum in 1958. Author of *My Notes* (1930).

Has written many articles on topical b. questions. People's Artist of the R.S.F.S.R. (1951).

Kriza, John (*b* Berwyn, Ill., 15 Jan. 1919, *d* Naples, Fla., 18 Aug. 1975). Amer. dancer. Studied at Stone-Camryn School. Joined B. Th. in 1940, and later became one of its most popular principals; created roles in Robbins's *Fancy Free* (1944), *Interplay* (1945), Kidd's *On Stage!* (1945), de Mille's *Fall River Legend* (1948), and Ross's *Caprichos* (1950). Retired in 1966 and became assistant to the directors.

Kröller, Heinrich (*b* Munich, 25 July 1880, *d* Würzburg, 25 July 1930). Ger. dancer, choreographer, and b. master. Studied Munich Op. B. School and with Zambelli and Staats. Joined Munich Court Op. B.; appointed soloist in 1901. To Dresden as principal d. B. master Frankfurt, Munich State Op. in 1917, Berlin State Op. 1919–22, Vienna State Op. 1922–28. Ch. many bs., incl. first Ger. prod. of Strauss's *Legend of Joseph* (Berlin, 1921) and first prod. of *Strauss's Couperin Suite* (Vienna, 1923) and *Schlagobers* (Vienna, 1924).

Kronstam, Henning (*b* Copenhagen, 29 June 1934). Dan. dancer, teacher, and artistic dir. Studied Royal Dan. B. School. Joined Royal Dan. B. in 1952; appointed solo d. in 1956. Created roles in Ashton's *Romeo and Juliet* (1955), Flindt's *The Three Musketeers* (1966) and *Dreamland* (1974), and von Rosen's *Don Juan* (1967). An outstanding premier danseur in the classics and in the Bournonville repertory; some of his greatest successes were Balanchine's Apollo, and Petit's Cyrano and Toreador. Has often appeared abroad. Art. dir. of the Royal Dan. B. in 1979–85; now b. master. Knight of Dannebrog (1964).
BIBL.: S. Kragh-Jacobsen, 'H.K.' in *20 Solo dancers of The Royal Danish Ballet* (Copenhagen, 1965).

Krupska, Dania (*b* Fall River, Mass. 13 Aug. 1923). Amer. dancer and choreographer. Studied with Ethel Phillips and at Mordkin B. School. D. with C. Littlefield B. Co. and Amer. B. Co. Now a ch. for musicals.

Kruuse, Marianne (*b* Copenhagen, 30 Oct. 1942). Dan. dancer. Studied with Edith Dam and Bartholin. Member of Scandinavian B. 1959–61, co. of A. Galina 1961–2, Mulhouse B. 1962–3, Stuttgart B. 1965–70, principal d. at Frankfurt 1970–3, Hamburg State Op. since 1973. Created roles in Neumeier's *Romeo and Juliet*, *Nutcracker* (both 1971), *Baiser de la Fée*, *Daphnis and Chloe* (both 1972), *Meyerbeer-Schumann* (1974), *Streichquintett C-dur* (1977), and *Songfest* (1979).

Krzyszkowska, Maria (*b* 11 Nov. 1927). Pol. dancer and b. director. Studied with Woizikovsky in Warsaw. D. in Nowogo and Poznan; prima ballerina of Warsaw Grand Th. 1953–70; b. dir. of the co. until 1981.

Kschessinska, Mathilda Maria-Felixovna (also Kschessinskaya; *b* Ligova, 31 Aug. 1872, *d* Paris,

6 Dec. 1971). Russ. dancer and teacher. Daughter of the very popular Pol. character d. Felix Kschessinsky. Studied at St. Petersburg Imperial B. School with Ivanov, Vazem, and Johansson; graduated in 1890. Joined Maryinsky Th.; appointed ballerina in 1892, prima ballerina in 1893, and prima ballerina assoluta in 1895 (the only d. apart from Legnani ever to be officially awarded that title). After 1904 she appeared only as a guest-ballerina but continued to d. frequently at the Maryinsky Th., and also occasionally in the West (with Diaghilev's co. 1911–12). One of the greatest Russ. ballerinas; an unusually brilliant technician—the first Russ. to execute 32 fouettés. Enjoyed her greatest successes in demi-caractère roles such as Kitri and Esmeralda. Created roles in Petipa's *Le Reveil de Flore* (1894), *Les Saisons*, and *Les Millions d'Arlequin* (both 1900). As the mistress of the Tsarevich Nikolai (the later Tsar Nikolai II) and later the morganatic wife of Grand Duke Andrei of Russia (whom she married in France in 1921) she wielded immense influence, and her palais at the St. Petersburg Kronversky Prospect (from the balcony of which Lenin addressed the citizens of Petrograd after his return from exile in 1917) became one of the focal points of the city's social life. Left Russ. in 1920 to live on the Côte d'Azur. Opened a school in Paris in 1929. Appeared for the last time on stage at a London charity gala in 1936. Author of *Souvenirs de la K.* (Paris, 1970; Eng. version *Dancing in St. Petersburg*, London and New York, 1970).
BIBL.: O. Maynard, 'K. at Ninety-Nine', *Dance Magazine* (1971/11).

Kudelka, James (*b* Newmarket, Ont., 10 Sep. 1955). Can. d. and ch. Studied at National B. School, joining National B. 1972, appointed soloist 1976 and co. ch. 1980. His bs. so far include *A Party* (mus. Britten, 1976), *Washington Square* (mus. Michael Conway Baker, 1979), and *Playhouse* (mus. Shostakovich, 1980). Has been invited to participate in Amer. B. Th. ch. workshop. Resident ch. Les Grands Bs. Canadiens, 1984.

Kumudini (orig. K. Lakhia; *b* Bombay, 1930). Ind. dancer. Studied with Radhelal Misra, Shambu Maharaj, Brijju Maharaj, and Sunder Prasad. Went to England in 1948, and became principal d. in the co. of R. Gopal, creating Mumtaz Mahal in his *Legend of the Taj Mahal* (1956).

Kun, Zsuzsa (*b* Budapest, 9 Dec. 1934). Hung. dancer. Studied at Budapest State Op. B. School, then in Moscow with Gerdt and Messerer. Joined Budapest State Op. B. in 1949; appointed soloist in 1952, and later became one of the co.'s most popular ballerinas. Created roles in Eck's *Csongor and Tünde* (1959), *Sacre du printemps* (1963), *Music for Strings, Percussion, and Celeste* (1965), and Seregi's *Spartacus* (1968) and *Sylvia* (1972). Has often appeared abroad (London Festival B., 1961–5). Is now dir. of the Budapest State B. Institute. Married to the d. Levente Sipeki. Liszt Prize

(1962); Kossuth Prize (1968); Critics' Prize (Paris, 1969)
BIBL.: E. Herf. 'Z.K.', *Ballet Today* (1964/3).

Kunakova, Lubov (*b* Izhevsk, 8 Aug. 1951). Sov. dancer. Studied at Perm B. School; joined the Perm co. in 1970 and later became its prima ballerina. Gold Medal (Varna, 1972)

Kůra, Miroslav (*b* Brno, 26 May 1924). Czech dancer, choreographer, and b. director. Studied with I. V. Psota and in Leningrad. Started to d. in Brno in 1939. Has d. with many Czech cos. After 1945, when he appeared in all the classics and modern bs. at Prague's National Th., became the most admired Czech d. Began to ch. in 1948. Has collaborated with film dir. Petr Weigl on many film and TV adaptations of bs. (*Giselle*, *Swan Lake*, *Romeo and Juliet*, etc.). Appointed b. dir. of Prague National Th. in 1973. Married to the d. Jarmila Manšingrová.

Kurgapkina, Ninel Alexandrovna (*b* Leningrad, 13 Feb. 1929). Sov. dancer. Studied at Leningrad Ch. School; graduated in 1947. Joined Kirov B. and later became one of its ballerinas. Resigned in 1972; appointed Dir. of the Leningrad Ch. School. Merited Artist of the R.S.F.S.R. (1966).

Kůrová, Jana (*b* Prague, 18 June 1959). Czech dancer. The daughter of the d. J. Mansingrová and the b. dir. M. Kůra, she studied at b. dept. of Prague State Conservatory and Moscow B. School. Joined Prague National Th. b. as a soloist 1976. First Prize B. Competition Prague 1975, Gold Medal (Lausanne, 1976), Silver Medal (Varna, 1978).

Kusnetsov, Sviatoslav Petrovich (*b* Leningrad, 10 June 1930). Sov. dancer. Studied at Leningrad Ch. School; graduated in 1950. Joined Kirov B. and later became one of its outstanding character soloists; Jago, Andrei (*Taras Bulba*), Vazlav (*Fountain of Bakchisaray*), and Frondoso (*Laurencia*) were his best roles. Retired in 1970. Is now a teacher of scenic movement at the Leningrad Institute of Th., Mus., and Cinema. Married to the d. I. Zubkovskaya.

Kyasht, Lydia Georgievna (also Kyaksht; *b* St Petersburg, 25 Mar. 1885, *d* London, 11 Jan. 1959). Russ.-Brit. dancer and teacher. Studied at St. Petersburg Imperial B. School with Gerdt; joined Maryinsky Th. in 1902 and later became soloist (she always claimed to have been the first d. to perform Fokine's *Dying Swan*). Went to London in 1908, where she succeeded Genée as prima ballerina at the Empire Th. Also appeared in U.S. and with Diaghilev's Bs. Russes. Taught in London and Cirencester, and had her own co. B. de la Jeunesse Anglaise during the 1940s. Author of *Romantic Recollections* (London, 1929). Sister of Georgi Georgevich K. (1873–1936), a soloist at the Maryinsky Th. and later b. master in Buenos Aires, Kaunas, and Vienna State Op.

241 KYLIÁN

BIBL.: E. C. Mason, 'L.K.', *Dance and Dancers* (1959/3).

Kylián, Jiří (*b* Prague, 21 Mar. 1947). Czech dancer and choreographer. Studied at Prague Conservatory and Royal B. School. Joined Stuttgart B. 1968, began to ch. in 1970 and became the co.'s most prolific junior ch. After working occasionally for Netherlands D. Th. was appointed art. co-dir. 1975, then sole art. dir. 1977, since when the co. has enjoyed an enormous boost in intern. reputation. His bs. for the co. incl. *Transfigured Night* (mus. Schoenberg, 1975), *Symphony in D* (mus. Haydn, 1976), *Children's Games* (mus. Mahler and Gary Carpenter, 1978), *Sinfonietta* (mus. Janáček, 1978), *Symphony of Psalms* (mus. Stravinsky, 1978), *Msa Glagolskaja* (Janáček, 1979), *Dream Dances* (mus. Berio, 1979), *Field Mass* (mus. Martinů, 1980), and *Forgotten Land* (mus. Britten, for Stuttgart B., 1981).

BIBL.: N. McLain Stoop, 'J.K. of the Netherlands Dance Theatre', *Dance Magazine* (1979/10).

L

Laban, Rudolf von (orig. R. L. de Varaljas; *b* Pozsony (now Bratislava), 15 Dec. 1879, *d* Weybridge, 1 July 1958). Hung. dancer, choreographer, b. master, and dance theoretician. Studied painting, acting and dancing in Paris. Toured North Afr. with a revue troupe, where he came across Afr. and Arab dances. D. in many Ger. cities, and in Vienna 1907–10. Founded a school in Munich in 1910, where Wigman was one of his pupils. Worked in Zurich and Ascona during the First World War. Returned to Ger. in 1919, working in Nuremberg, Stuttgart (where Jooss became his pupil), and Mannheim; b. dir. in Hamburg 1923–5, where he founded his Kammertanz Th. Established an Institute of Ch. in Würzburg in 1925. B. dir. of the Berlin State Op. 1930–4. Organized the d. contributions to the Berlin 1936 Olympic Games. Went to England in 1938; continued his old collaboration with Jooss (now based on Dartington Hall), and then formed the ★Art of Movement Studio with Lisa Ullmann in Manchester in 1946—it moved to Addlestone in Surrey in 1953. He was the leader of the Central European school of modern d., of far greater importance as an intellectual and theoretician than as a ch. His greatest contribution was Kinetographie L., his system of d. notation, which was further developed by his pupils, incl. A. Knust and Jooss. He started the amateur movement of 'Bewegungschöre' (movement choirs), which had a vast following in the Ger. of the 1920s and 1930s—the purest expression of his philosophy of man's participation in the d. of the cosmos. After his emigration, concentrated on modern educational d., and on research into movement and movement notation in industrial processes. Author of *Die Welt des Tänzers* (Stuttgart, 1920), *Choreographie* (Jena, 1926), *Schrifttanz* (Vienna-Leipzig, 1928), *Ein Leben für den Tanz* (Dresden, 1935; Eng. version, *A Life for Dance*, London, 1975), *Modern Educational Dance* (London, 1948), *The Mastery of Movement on the Stage* (London, 1950), *Principles of Dance and Movement Notation* (London, 1956), *Choreutics* (London, 1966), etc.
BIBL.: S. Thornton, *A Movement Perspective of R.L.* (London, 1971).

Labanotation. The Eng.-Amer. term for Kinetographie Laban, the system of d. notation developed by R. von Laban and his pupils, incl. A. Knust and Jooss. The Kinetographic Institute at the Essen Folkwang School and the D. Notation Bureau in New York are its two main centres.
BIBL.: A. Hutchinson, *Labanotation: The System of Analysing and Recording Movement* (New York, 1954; second ed. 1970).

Labis, Attilio (*b* Vincennes, 5 Sep. 1936). Fr. dancer and choreographer. Studied at Paris Opéra School; joined the Opéra co. in 1954. Became premier danseur in 1959 and étoile in 1960. Since the end of 1972 he has appeared only as a guest at the Opéra; he now works as a freelance d. and occasional ch. Has created roles in Kelly's *Pas de dieux* (1960), Lifar's *Icare* (1962 version), Béjart's *Renard* (1963), and in his own *Arcades* (mus. Berlioz, 1964) and *Romeo and Juliet* (mus. Prokofiev, 1968). Married to the d. Christiane Vlassi.
BIBL.: I. Lidova, 'A.L.' (with complete check-list of roles and activities), *Les Saisons de la Danse* (1971/4).

Laborintus. Ballet in 1 act; ch. Tetley; mus. Berio; déc. Ter-Arutunian. Prod. 26 July 1972, Royal B., Cov. Gdn., London, with Seymour, Nureyev, Bergsma, D. Kelly, Derman, Wall, Hosking, Ashmole. Set to Berio's *Laborintus II.* 'A commentary on life, trapped in a labyrinth from which the only way out leads to death' (J. Percival). Revived for Stuttgart B. 1975.

Labyrinth. Ballet in 4 scenes; libr. and déc. Dali; ch. Massine; mus. Schubert. Prod. 8 Oct. 1941, B. Russe de Monte Carlo, Met. Op. Ho., New York, with Eglevsky, Toumanova, Franklin. Set to Schubert's Seventh Symphony, the b. explores 'the eternal myth of the aesthetic and ideological confusion which characterizes romanticism, and especially, in the highest degree, that of our epoch. The "thread of Ariadne", by which Theseus succeeds in finding the exit from the Labyrinth, symbolizes the thread of continuity of classicism—the saviour. All romanticism merely seeks more or less dramatically its "thread of Ariadne", of classicism' (programme note).
BIBL.: R. Lawrence, 'L.' in *The Victor Book of Ballets and Ballet Music* (New York, 1950).

Lac des cygnes, Le. See *Swan Lake*.

Lacotte, Pierre (*b* Chatou, 3 Feb. 1932). Fr. dancer, choreographer, and teacher. Studied at Paris Opéra School. D. at the Opéra 1946–55, then founded his own co., B. de la Tour Eiffel, with which he toured widely and ch. many bs. Went to New York as premier danseur of the Met. Op. House 1956–7. Re-founded his B. de la Tour Eiffel in 1959, and became Dir. of the newly established B. National Jeunesses Musicales de France in 1963, with his wife, G. Thesmar, as ballerina. He ch. a great number of bs. (incl. *Intermede*, mus. Vivaldi, 1966, for B. Rambert) and a TV prod. of Schneitzhoeffer's *La Sylphide* in 1971, which he then repeated for the Opéra in 1972, followed by *Coppélia* in 1973. Acknowledged as an authority on reviving historic bs., he continued with F. Taglioni's *Nathalie* (Moscow Classic B., 1980) and Mazilier's *Marco Spada* (Rome, 1981). Joint dir. B. de Monte Carlo, 1985.

Lady and the Fool, The. Ballet in 1 act and 3 scenes; libr. and ch. Cranko; mus. Verdi (arranged by Mackerras); déc. Richard Beer. Prod. 25 Feb. 1954, Sadler's Wells Th. B., New Th., Oxford, with P. Miller, MacMillan, Mosaval. Set to a potpourri of melodies from Verdi's lesser known operas, the b. tells of a beauty, La Capricciosa, who is courted by some socially glittering suitors, but prefers two shabby clowns, Moondog and Bootface, who accept her even when she has dropped her mask and revealed herself as a young, disillusioned girl. A revised version was taken into the repertory of the Sadler's Wells B. in 1955. BBC TV prod. in 1959. Revived for several cos. (Stuttgart, 1961; Ger. Op. Berlin, 1965; Royal Dan. B., 1971).
BIBL.: C. Beaumont, 'T.L.a.t.F.' in *Ballets Past & Present* (London, 1955).

Lady and the Hooligan, The (orig. Russ. title: *Baryshnya i khuligan*). Ch. short story in 7 episodes; libr. A. A. Belinsky; ch. K. Boyarski; mus. Shostakovich; déc, V. Dorrer. Prod. 28 Dec. 1962, Maly Th., Leningrad with V. Zimin, L. Klimova (second première V. Panov, G. Pokryshkina). Inspired by Mayakovsky's film-scenario of the same title, and set to Shostakovich's *Suite for Orchestra*, the b. tells of a member of a teenage gang, who falls in love with a teacher but is rejected by her, and finally dies in her arms after being fatally stabbed by his former friends when he tries to protect her against their attack. Revived for various Sov. cos.

Lady and the Unicorn (orig. Fr. title: *La Dame et la licorne*). Ballet in 1 act; libr. and déc. Cocteau; ch. Rosen; mus. J. Chailley. Prod. 9 May 1953, Th. am Gärtnerplatz, Munich, with G. Lespagnol, B. Trailine, V. Mlakar. Inspired by the 15th-century tapestries of the Paris Musée de Cluny, the b. tells of the unicorn which eats only from the hand of a virgin, and must die when its lady yields to the amorous desire of a knight. Revived for Berlin Municipal Op. (1954), Munich State Op. (1958), and B. Russe de Monte Carlo (1955).

Lady from the Sea. Ballet in 1 act and 5 scenes; libr. and ch. Cullberg; mus. K. Riisager; déc. Kerstin Hedeby. Prod. 21 Apr. 1960, Amer. B. Th., Met. Op. House, New York, with Serrano, Bruhn, Tetley. The b. is based on Ibsen's play of the same title; it tells of the conflict of Ellida, who is torn between her love for a sailor, who left her and returned to sea, and the security of her life with an unloved husband. Revived for Royal Swed. B. in 1961 (Swed. TV prod. in 1963), also for Royal Dan. B. and in Bergen. Another, earlier, version, ch. E. Leese, mus. S. Honigman, for National B. of Can. (1955).

Lady into Fox. Ballet in 1 act and 3 scenes; libr. and ch. A. Howard; mus. Honegger (arranged by Charles Lynch); déc. Nadia Benois. Prod. 15 May 1939, B. Rambert, Mercury Th., London, with S. Gilmour, C. Boyd. The b., inspired by David Garnett's novel of the same title and set to a collection of orchestrated piano pieces by Honegger, tells of a gracious hostess who is really a vixen, torn between her love for her husband and her natural instincts which finally make her escape. Revived for B. Th. in 1940.
BIBL.: C. W. Beaumont, 'L.i.F.' in *Supplement to Complete Stories of Ballets* (London, 1952).

Lady of the Camellias (orig. Ger. title: *Die Kameliendame*). Ballet with prologue, in 3 acts; libr. and ch. Neumeier; mus. Chopin; déc. Rose. Prod. 4 Nov. 1978, Stuttgart, with Haydée, Madsen, Keil, Cragun, R. Anderson. Starting with the auction, the b. follows closely the plot of A. Dumas fils' novel *La Dame aux camélias* (1848), closely integrating the characters of Manon Lescaut and Des Grieux, who are encountered first by Marguerite Gautier and Armand in a b. perf. of *Manon Lescaut*. The b. uses only original, unarranged Chopin mus., incl. the complete second piano concerto, the Romanze from the first piano concerto, the Grande Fantaisie sur des airs polonais, the Grande Polonaise as well as some individual piano pieces. Revived for Hamburg B. in 1980. Earlier b. versions of the novel and play by Dumas incl. F. Termanini's *Rita Gauthier* (mus. Verdi, Turin, 1857), Taras's *Camille* (mus. Schubert-Rieti, Original B. Russe, 1946), Tudor's *L.o.t.C.* (mus. Verdi, New York City B., 1951), Page's *Camille* (mus. Verdi, Chicago, 1957), T. Gsovsky's *Die Kameliendame* (mus. Sauguet, Berlin, 1957), Ashton's *Marguerite and Armand* (mus. Liszt, arr. Searle, Royal B., 1963), Alberto Mendez' *Nous nous verrons hier soir* (mus. Sauguet, National B. of Cuba, 1971)—also J. Lefèbre's *D.a.c.* (mus. Verdi, Charlerois, 1980).

Laerkesen, Anna (*b* Copenhagen, 2 Mar. 1942). Dan. dancer. Studied with E. Frandsen and at Royal Dan. B. School. Joined Royal Dan. B. in 1960, became solo d. in 1964 and first solo d. in 1966. Has become internationally known through her interpretation of the title-role in *La Sylphide*.
BIBL.: S. Kragh-Jacobsen, 'A.L.' in *20 Solo dancers of The Royal Danish Ballet* (Copenhagen, 1965).

Lafontaine, Mlle de (also La Fontaine; *b c.* 1655, *d c.* 1738). Fr. dancer. The first professional female d.; made her début at the Paris Opéra in Lully's *Le Triomphe de l'amour* in 1681. Created the leading roles in further Lully bs., incl. *Persée* (1682), *Phaéton* (1683), *Amadis de Gaule* (1684), *Roland* (1685), *Le Temple de la paix* (1685), *Armide* (1686), *Acis et Galathée* (1686), Colasse's *Achille et Polixène* (1687), and Desmaret's *Didon* (1693). Was much admired for the elegance of her style. She later became a nun.

BIBL.: P. Migel, 'L.F.' in *The Ballerinas* (New York, 1972).

Lagerborg, Anne-Marie (*b* Stockholm, 1919). Swed. dancer, choreographer, and b. mistress. Studied at Royal Swed. B. School. Joined Royal Swed. B. in 1937; appointed soloist in 1947 and associate dir. and b. mistress in 1957. Has dir. the Cullberg B. with Cullberg since 1967 and has revived some Cullberg works for various cos. Created the title-role in Cullberg's *Medea* (1950).

Lagertha. Ballet in 3 acts; libr. after Saxo; ch. Galeotti; mus. Schall; déc. L. Chipart and C. Lerneur. Prod. 30 Jan. 1801, Royal Dan. B., Copenhagen, with Mme Bjørn, Antoine Bournonville. The first b. to be based on an incident from Dan. history, derived from Book IX of the *Gesta Danorum,* written *c.* 1200 by Saxo Grammaticus; the b. includes many songs.

BIBL.: C. Beaumont, 'L.' in *Ballets Past & Present* (London, 1955).

Laiderette. Ballet in 1 act; libr. and ch. MacMillan; mus. F. Martin; déc. K. Rowell. Prod. 24 Jan. 1954, Sadler's Wells Choreographers Group, Sadler's Wells Th., London, with M. Lane, D. Poole. MacMillan's second b., set to Martin's Petite Symphonie Concertante. An ugly, bald girl, abandoned by her parents, masked, on a rich man's doorstep, is taken up by him but rejected by society when her real appearance is unmasked. Revived for B. Rambert in 1955.

Laine, Doris (*b* Helsinki, 15 Feb. 1931). Finn. dancer. Studied in Helsinki, Moscow, and with A. Northcote. Joined Finn. National B. in 1947; became prima ballerina in 1956. Has often appeared abroad (with Festival B. in 1964). Dir. Nat. B. of Finland 1984. Pro Finlandia Award.

Laing, Hugh (*b* Barbados, 1911). Brit dancer. Studied with Craske, Rambert, and Preobrajenska. Appeared with London B. Club in 1932; later d. with B. Rambert, where he created many roles in Tudor bs., including *The Planets* (1934), *The Descent of Hebe* (1935), *Jardin aux lilas* (1936), *Gallant Assembly* (1936), *Dark Elegies* (1937), then *Judgment of Paris, Gala Performance,* and *Soirée musicale* (all for Tudor's London B. in 1938). Went to U.S.A. with Tudor in 1939 to join B. Th. and created further roles in Fokine's *Bluebeard* (1941), Massine's *Aleko,* de Mille's *Tally-Ho* (both 1944), Tudor's *Pillar of Fire* (1942), *Romeo and Juliet, Dim Lustre* (both 1943), *Undertow* (1945), *Shadow of the Wind* (1948), and *Nimbus* (1950). Moved to New York City B. in 1950; created roles in Tudor's *Lady of the Camellias* (1951) and *La Gloire* (1952), Bolender's *The Miraculous Mandarin* (1951) and Balanchine's *Bayou* (1952). He was the ideal Tudor d., but excelled also as Balanchine's *Prodigal Son.* Became a fashion photographer in New York. Was married to the d. D. Adams.

Lakatos, Gabriella (*b* Budapest, 18 Oct. 1927). Hung. dancer. Studied at Budapest State B. School. Joined Budapest State Op. B. in 1943; appointed principal d. in 1947. Excelled in dramatic roles; especially admired as the Girl in Harangozó's *The Miraculous Mandarin.* Appeared with London Festival B. in 1960. TV Portrait of G.L. (Hung. TV, 1965). Kossuth Prize (1958); Merited Artist (1971).

Lake, Molly (*b* Cornwall, 1900, *d* 2 Oct. 1986). Brit. dancer and teacher. Studied with Astafieva and Cecchetti. D. in the cos. of Pavlova and Markova-Dolin. Established the Embassy B. with her husband, Travis Kemp, and M. Honer in 1945; it later became Continental B. Went to Ankara in 1954 as Dir. of the Conservatoire. Contributed article about the quality needed for the classics to *Dance and Dancers* (1962/9).

Lalla Rookh or The Rose of Lahore. Ballet in 4 scenes; libr. and ch. Perrot; mus. Pugni, déc. Charles Marshall. Prod. 11 June 1846, Her Majesty's Th., London, with Cerrito, Perrot, Saint-Léon. The b. is inspired by Thomas Moore's oriental romance about the beautiful daughter of the Emperor of Hindustan; she is promised to Aliris, the young King of Bucharia, but he first tests her affections in the disguise of a simple minstrel.

BIBL.: C. W. Beaumont, 'L.R.o.T.R.o.L.' in *Complete Book of Ballets* (London, 1951).

Lambert, Constant (*b* London, 23 Aug. 1905, *d* there, 21 Aug. 1951). Brit. conductor and composer. Became conductor of the Camargo Society and mus. dir. of the Vic-Wells and Sadler's Wells B. in 1930; with de Valois and Ashton he was one of the chief architects of the young Brit. b. Wrote his first b. score, *Romeo and Juliet,* for Diaghilev (ch. Nijinska, 1926), followed by Ashton's *Pomona* (1930), *Rio Grande* (1932), *Horoscope* (1938), and *Tiresias* (1951). Arranged the mus. for Ashton's *Les Rendezvous* (from Auber, 1933) and *Les Patineurs* (from Meyerbeer, 1937), de Valois' *The Prospect Before Us* (from W. Boyce, 1940), Helpmann's *Comus* (from Purcell, 1942), and Petit's *Ballabile* (from Chabrier, 1950), and wrote the libr. and chose the mus. for *Apparitions* (ch. Ashton, mus. Liszt, 1936). Author of *Music Ho! A Study of Music in Decline* (London, 1934). His wife Isabel L. designed the déc. for Ashton's *Tiresias* and *Madame Chrysanthème.*

BIBL.: R. Shead, *C.L.* (London, 1973).

Lambranzi, Gregorio. Venetian choreographer and b. master, whose book *Neue und Curieuse Theatralische Tantz-Schul* was published in Nuremberg in 1716. It describes 50 contemporary dances, giving the melody, a drawing, and a verbal description for each. Such dances as Sarabande, Folie d'Espagna, Bourrée, Rigaudon, and Minuet, and also military, sport, and trade dances are included. Translated into Eng. in 1928 by F. Derra de Moroda, who discovered the original manuscript in 1936 in the Munich State Library; it was published in a luxurious facsimile edition by D. Horizons, New York, in 1972.

Lamentation. Solo dance; ch. and cost. Graham; mus. Kodály. Prod. 8 Jan. 1930, Maxine Elliott's Th., New York, with Graham. Set to Kodály's Piano Piece op. 3, no. 2; the d. was performed sitting on a bench throughout. 'In a sense L. is another of Graham's "outsider" works: a portrait of an isolated, solitary sufferer' (D. McDonagh). Film prod. (1943).

Lament of the Waves. Ballet in 1 act; libr. and ch. Ashton; mus. Gerard Masson; cost. D. Rencher. Prod. 9 Feb. 1970, Royal B., Cov. Gdn., London, with M. Trounson and C. Myers. Set to Masson's *Dans le deuil des vagues II*, the b. is an extended duo for two lovers, who relive their moment of happiness while drowning in the sea. BIBL.: D. Vaughan, *Frederick Ashton and his Bs* (London, 1977).

La Meri (orig. Russell Meriwether Hughes; *b* Louisville, 13 May 1899). Amer. dancer, teacher, ethnologist, and writer. Studied all kinds of d. cultures in Amer. and the Far East. Toured extensively as a d. of ethnic dances. Founded the New York School of Natya with St. Denis in 1938 (it became the Ethnologic D. Center in 1942) and assembled her Exotic B. from its pupils. Has taught at many colleges and univs. Is considered one of the leading Amer. authorities on ethnic dancing. Wrote *Principles of the Dance Art* (London, 1933), *Dance as an Art Form* (New York, 1933), *Gesture Language of the Hindu Dance* (New York, 1941), *Spanish Dancing* (New York, 1948), and *The Basic Elements of Dance Composition* (Jacob's Pillow, 1965). Capezio Award (1965).

Lamhut, Phyllis (*b* New York, 14 Nov. 1933). Amer. dancer and choreographer. Studied with A. Nikolais at Henry St. Playhouse, with M. Cunningham, and at Amer. B. Center. Was one of the leading dancers of Nikolais' co. until 1969. Also appeared with M. Louis' co. Founded P.L. D. Co. in 1969, for which she has ch. extensively. Staff-member of the Louis-Nikolais D. Th. Laboratory. BIBL.: J. Anderson, 'P.L.', *Dance Magazine* (1975/2).

Lancaster, Sir Osbert (*b* 1908, *d* London, 27 July 1986). Brit. painter, cartoonist, author, and b. designer. Designed the déc. for Cranko's *Pineapple Poll* (1951) and *Bonne-Bouche* (1952), de Valois's *Coppélia* (1954), Ashton's *La Fille mal gardée* (1960), and Lander's *Napoli* prod. (London Festival B., 1954). Knighted 1975.

Lanchbery, John (*b* London, 15 May 1923). Brit. conductor and composer. Mus. dir. Met. B. 1947–9; joined Sadler's Wells Th. B. in 1951. Principal conductor, Royal B., 1960–72. Mus. dir. Austral. B., 1972–8, and of American B. Th., 1978–80. Arranged mus. for several bs., incl. MacMillan's *House of Birds* (1955) and *Mayerling* (1978); Ashton's *La Fille mal gardée* (1960), *The Dream* (1964), *Creatures of Prometheus* (1970), *Tales of Beatrix Potter* (film, 1971), and *A Month in the Country* (1976); Nureyev's *Don Quixote* (1966); P. Darrell's *Tales of Hoffmann* (1972); Hynd's *The Merry Widow* (1975), and *Rosalinda* (1978). Mus. dir. *The Turning Point* (film, 1977). BIBL.: 'J.L.', *About the House*; interview in *Dance and Dancers* (1978/3).

Landé, Jean-Baptiste (*d* St Petersburg, 26 Feb. 1748). Fr. dancer and b. master. After dancing in Paris and Dresden and with a Fr. co. in Stockholm, went to St. Petersburg in 1734, where Rinaldi Fossano had established a dancing school for the daughters of the aristocracy. He arranged a school perf. for them which was so successful that it inspired the foundation in 1738 of a larger school for the children of the orphanage, which was to be the basis for the St. Petersburg Imperial B. School. Here the first Russ. solo-dancers received their basic training: Afanasi Toporkov, André Nesterov, Avdotia Timofeyeva, Yelisaveta Zorina, and others. He was also in charge of the b. divertissements which took place in the course of the op. perfs.

Lander, Harald (orig. Alfred Bernhardt Stevnsborg; *b* Copenhagen, 25 Feb. 1905, *d* there, 14 Sep. 1971). Dan.-Fr. dancer, choreographer, b. master, director, and teacher. Studied at Royal Dan. B. School under Christian Christiansen, H. Beck, and Gustav Uhlendorff. Joined Royal Dan. B. in 1923 and became one of its most distinguished character soloists. Studied Russ. folk d. in the U.S.S.R. on leave of absence 1926–7, and with Fokine, I. Tarasoff, and Juan de Baucaire in the U.S. and Mexico 1927–9; he returned to Copenhagen as a solo d. in 1929. Appointed b. master in 1930, and dir. of the Royal Dan. B. School in 1932. Stayed with the co. until 1951; under him it experienced a period of extraordinary creativity, and the beginning of the Bournonville renaissance. He ch. about 30 bs., including *Football* (mus. Poulenc, 1933), *Bolero* (mus. Ravel, 1934), *The Little Mermaid* (mus. Fini Henriques), *The Seven Deadly Sins* (mus. Weill, both 1936), *Thorvaldsen* (mus. J. Hye-Knudsen, 1938), *The Denmark Ballet* (mus. Hye-Knudsen, 1939), *The Sorcerer's Apprentice* (mus. Dukas, 1940), *Qarrtsiluni* (mus. K. Riisager, 1942), *Etude* (mus. Czerny-Riisager, 1948), and *Salute for August Bournonville* (mus. arr. Reesen, 1949). After a disagreement with the directors of the Royal Th., went to Paris in 1952, where he staged Galeotti's *The Whims of Cupid,* the flowers act from *Les Indes galantes,* and his *Etudes* at the Opéra. Dir. of the Paris Opéra School 1956–7 and 1959–63. During these years he worked as a guest-ch. with many cos. in Eur. and N. and S. Amer., frequently reviving *Etudes,* mounting the bs. of Galeotti and Bournonville, and creating many bs., incl. *Printemps à Vienne* (mus. Schubert's Second Symphony, Opéra, Paris, 1954), *Concerto aux étoiles* (mus. Bartók's *Concerto for Orchestra*, Paris, Opéra, 1956), *Vita Eterna* (mus. Dvořák's *Slavonic Dances*, London Festival B., 1958). Returned to Copenhagen in 1962, choreographing *Les Victoires de l'amour* (mus. Lully) and reinstating his old bs. in the repertory. There are various TV prods. of his most successful bs. Was married to the d. Margot L. 1932–50 and to Toni L. 1950–65. Knight of the Dannebrog.

BIBL.: E. Aschengreen, *Etudes* (Copenhagen, 1970).

Lander, Margot (*née* M. Florentz-Gerhardt; *b* Copenhagen, 2 Aug. 1910, *d* there, 19 July 1961). Dan. dancer. Studied at Royal Dan. B. School. Joined Royal Dan. B. in 1925; appointed solo d. in 1931 and prima ballerina (the only Dan. d. officially to be so called) in 1942. Apart from the Bournonville and Lander bs., she was especially admired for her Swanilda. Retired in 1950. Was married to Harald L. 1932–50.

Lander, Toni (*née* T. Pihl Petersen; *b* Copenhagen, 19 June 1931, *d* Salt Lake City, 19 May 1985). Dan. d. Studied at Royal Dan. B. School. Joined Royal Dan. B. in 1948; appointed solo d. in 1950. Married Harald L. in 1950 and accompanied him to Paris, where she continued to study with Egorova and Preobrajenska. Guest ballerina Original B. Russe in London 1951–2; a regular member of London Festival B. 1954–9; also appeared with the co. of the *Le Rendez-vous manqué* prod. in 1958. Member of Amer. B. Th. 1961–71; frequent guest with other cos., incl. Royal Dan. B., to which she returned as a soloist and teacher in 1971. Knight of the Dannebrog (1957). After divorce from Harald L., married the d. Bruce Marks in 1966.

BIBL.: B. Coffey, 'T.L. and Bruce Marks On and Off Stage', *Dance Magazine* (1969/8).

Ländler. An Austrian d. for couples, named after Land ob der Enns. It is a quiet turning d. in 3/4 or 3/8 time, and was very popular during the times of Mozart, Beethoven, and Schubert, who all comp. L. Later it was succeeded by the *Waltz. The Tyrolienne is a Fr. variant.

Landon, Jane (orig. Frances J. Leach; *b* Perth, 4 Jan. 1947). Austral. dancer. Studied with M. Beresowska and at Royal B. School. Joined Touring Royal B. in 1964; appointed principal d. in 1968, creating a role in Tudor's *Knight Errant* (1968). Soloist in Stuttgart 1968–72; now a teacher. A. Genée Gold Medal (1964).

Landrover. Ballet in 4 parts; ch. M. Cunningham; sound-arrangement Cage, G. Mumma, and D. Tudor; cost. J. Johns; light. R. Nelson. Prod. 1 Feb. 1972, M. Cunningham and D. Co., Brooklyn Academy, Brooklyn. 'A peculiarity of the work is that it can be presented either as a four-part ballet lasting nearly an hour, or two of its parts may be presented independently—a programming device consonant with Cun-ningham's principles of indeterminacy. . . . Much of Landrover eats up space in great leaps and bounds. The dance radiates friendliness and good humour . . . pauses which convey a sense of alert calm' (J. Anderson).

Lane, Maryon (*b* Zululand, 15 Feb. 1931). S.A. dancer, and teacher. Studied in Johannesburg and at Sadler's Wells School. Joined Sadler's Wells Th. B. in 1947; became principal d. in 1948, and created roles in Ashton's *Valses nobles et sentimentales* (1947), Balanchine's *Trumpet Concerto* (1950), Ashton's *Casse-Noisette* (1951), Gore's *Carte Blanche* (1953), Rodrigues' *Café des sports* (1954), and MacMillan's *Laiderette* (1954), *Danses concertantes* and *House of Birds* (both 1955). Moved to Royal B. as a soloist 1955–68, creating further roles in MacMillan's *Noctambules* (1956), *Agon* (1958), and *Diversions* (1961), Cranko's *Prince of the Pagodas* (1957), and Ashton's *Ondine* (1958). Also d. with B. Rambert in 1966. Has taught at the London B. Centre since 1970 and also at Royal B. School. Was married to the d. and b. master David Blair.

BIBL.: A. Turnbull, 'Ballet Centre, Director: M.L.', *Dance and Dancers* (1970/11).

Lang, Harold (*b* Daly City, Cal., 21 Dec. 1920, *d* Chico, Calif. 26 July 1985). Amer. dancer and actor. Studied with Kosloff and W. Christensen. D. with San Francisco Op. B., B. Russe de Monte Carlo 1941–3, Am. B. Th. 1943–5; created roles in Robbins's *Fancy Free* (1944) and *Interplay* (1945). Then concentrated on a Broadway career, performing in musicals and straight comedies as well as on numerous TV shows.

Lang, Maria (*b* Stockholm, 21 Mar. 1948). Swed. dancer. Studied at Royal Swed. B. School and with Hightower, Franchetti, and Volkova. Joined Royal Swed. B. in 1965; appointed soloist in 1972. Has also d. with Royal Winnipeg B. and Austral. B. Married to the d. Walter Bourke.

Lang, Pearl (*b* Chicago, 29 May 1922). Amer. dancer, choreographer, and teacher. Studied with Graham, Horst, and M. Stuart. Joined Graham co. in 1942, and later became one of its principal dancers; remained until 1952 and occasionally returned afterwards. Created roles in *Diversion of Angels* (1948), *Canticle for Innocent Comedians* (1952), and *Ardent Song* (1954). Formed her own co. in 1952; her chs. include *And Joy is My Witness*, *Shirah*, *Apasionada*, and *The Possessed—The Dybbuk*. Appeared in several musicals, and worked as guest-ch. with various cos., including Dutch National B. and Batsheva D. Co. Has taught at many univs. and colleges.

BIBL.: T. Tobias, 'Two Essays for P.L.', *Dance Magazine* (1974/9); 'Intrinsics', *Dance Magazine* (1975/3).

Lanner, Katti (orig. Katharina L.; *b* Vienna, 14 Sep. 1829, *d* London, 15 Nov. 1908). Austrian dancer, choreographer, b. mistress, and teacher. Daughter of the famous waltz-comp. Joseph L.

Studied at the Vienna Court Op. School and made her début at the Th. am Kärntnertor in 1845; Fenella was one of her best roles. After the death of her family she went to Berlin, Dresden, and Munich; b. mistress in Hamburg 1862–3, where she ch. 10 bs. Then toured Scandinavia, Russia, and W. Eur.; went to New York in 1872, dancing at Niblo's Garden and touring the country. To London in 1876; became dir. of the National Training School of Dancing, and ch. the bs. for the Ital. op. seasons at Her Majesty's Th. 1877–81. She also worked at several other London ths.; b. mistress of the Empire Th. 1887–97 (she occasionally returned afterwards), which she made one of London's most active b. platforms, with added glamour from the engagement of A. Genée as ballerina. A selection from the 33 bs. she ch. for the th. shows clearly the wide range of her interests: *The Sports of England* (1877), *Cleopatra, The Paris Exhibition* (both 1889), *Orfeo* (1891), *Versailles* (1892), *Round the Town* (1893), *On Brighton Pier* (1894), *Faust, Monte Cristo* (both 1896), *The Press, Alaska* (both 1898), *The Milliner Duchess* (1903), *The Dancing Doll* (alias *The Fairy Doll*, 1905), and *Sir Roger de Coverley* (1907); most of her bs. had mus. by either Hervé or Leopold Wenzel.

BIBL.: I. Guest, in *The Empire Ballet* (London, 1962).

Lany, Jean-Barthélemy (*b* Paris, 24 Mar. 1718, *d* there, 29 Mar. 1786). Fr. dancer, choreographer, and b. master. Son of the b. master Jean L. Became solo d. at the Opéra in 1740, appearing in the b. ops. by Destouches, Rameau, and Boismortier. Went to Berlin in 1743, where he ch. many bs.; Noverre was one of his dancers. Returned to Paris in 1747 and became very popular as a d. of comic roles; made b. master, and ch. the first prods. of Rameau's *Les Fêtes d'Amour et de l'Hymen* (1748), *Platée, Zoroastre* (both 1749), *La Guirlande ou Les Fleurs enchantées* (1751), *Les Surprises de l'amour* (1757), and *Les Paladins* (1760). Later worked in Turin and London. When he returned to Paris he became a much respected teacher; his pupils included M. Gardel and Dauberval. Brother of the d. Louise-Madeleine L. Thérèse Vestris, the sister of Gaetano V., was his mistress.

Lany, Louise-Madeleine (*b* Paris, 1733, *d* there 1777). Fr. dancer. Daughter of the b. master Jean L. and the sister of Jean-Barthélemy L. Made her début at the Opéra in 1744; remained with the co. until 1767. She was admired as one of its outstanding virtuosos, and is said to have been the first danseuse to execute the entrechat six and huit. Noverre called her 'the greatest dancer in the world, who has eclipsed all others by the beauty, precision, and boldness of her execution'. She was, however, overshadowed by M. Sallé.

Lapauri, Alexander Alexandrovich (*b* Moscow, 15 June 1926, *d* there, 6 Aug. 1975). Sov. dancer, choreographer, and teacher. Studied at Moscow

Bolshoi B. School; graduated in 1944. Became a member of the Bolshoi B. and one of its outstanding character dancers; his best roles were Hilarion and Khan Girei, and also in *Walpurgis Night*. A d. of strong personality, athletic power, and virile projection; he excelled in virtuoso pas de deux with his wife R. Strutchkova, e.g. *Moszkowski Waltz* and *Spring Waters*. As a ch. he collaborated with his fellow student Olga Tarasova in *Song of the Woods* (mus. G. Zhukovsky, 1961) and *Lieutenant Kijé* (mus. Prokofiev, 1963). Also taught at the Bolshoi School. Merited Artist of the R.S.F.S.R.

Lappe, Gemze de (*b* Portsmouth, Va., 1921). Amer. dancer. Studied at Baltimore Peabody Conservatory, then with Irma Duncan and Fokine, whose co. she joined when only 9 years old. D. with A. Th. 1953–4 and subsequently with various cos., but became widely known as an A. de Mille d., appearing with de Mille's co. and in her prods. of *Oklahoma!, Paint Your Wagon, Carousel,* and *Brigadoon*; one of her best roles was Emily in *A Rose for Miss Emily*. Resident ch. of the Wolf Trap Co. at Filene Center, Vienna, Va.

Lapzeson, Noemi (*b* Buenos Aires, 28 June 1940). Argent. dancer, teacher, and choreographer. Studied at Juilliard School, Graham School, Amer. B. Center, and with Nikolais. D. with Graham co. and 1967–72 principal d. with London Contemporary D. Th.; also occasionally with other cos. Has ch. several pieces (some in collaboration with R. North) and taught at London Contemporary D. School. Working in Amer. since 1972.

Larionov, Mikhail Fedorovich (*b* Tiraspol, 25 May 1881, *d* Fontenay-aux-Roses, 10 Apr. 1969). Russ. painter and designer. To Paris in 1914, where he designed several of the Diaghilev prods., incl. Massine's *Soleil de nuit* (1915), *Kikimora* (1916), and *Les Contes Russes* (1917), Slavinsky's *Chout* (1921; he also supervised the prod.), and Nijinska's *Renard* (1922—also the Lifar version of 1929), and later Lifar's *Sur la Borsythène* (1932). Was married to the painter Nathalia Goncharova.

Larkin, Moscelyne (*b* Miami, 1925). Amer. dancer and teacher. Studied with her mother Eva Matlagova in Tulsa and later with V. Celli, Mordkin, Vilzak, and Schollar. D. with Orig. B. Russe (as Moussia Larkina) 1941–7, then with B. Russe de Monte Carlo 1948–53. Since 1954 she has taught in Tulsa with her husband Roman Jasinski; they founded and direct the Tulsa Civic B (now Tulsa B. Th).

Larsen, Gerd (*b* Oslo, 20 Feb. 1921). Norweg.-Brit. dancer, teacher, and b. mistress. Studied with Craske and Tudor. D. with Tudor's London B., creating French Ballerina in *Gala Performance*. Then with B. Rambert, International B., and Sadler's Wells B.; became soloist in 1954, later principal mime of the Royal B. Is now the co's.

senior teacher. She was married to the d. H. Turner.

BIBL.: J. Gruen, 'G.L.', in *The Private World of Ballet* (New York, 1975).

Larsen, Niels Bjørn (*b* Copenhagen., 5 Oct. 1913). Dan. dancer, choreographer, and b. master. Studied at Royal Dan. B. School, joining Royal Dan. B. in 1933. Appeared with T. Schoop 1935–7. Returned to Copenhagen: appointed solo d. in 1942; became the co.'s most distinguished mime. Formed his own co. in 1946 with which he toured Scandinavia, but continued to teach at Royal Dan. B. School. Appointed b. master when Lander left the co. in 1951. Dir. of the Tivoli Th. in 1955. Artistic dir. of Royal Dan. B. 1961–5. Continued to teach and to work as a ch. and producer until recent retirement. He is the father of the d. Dinna Bjørn. Knight of the Dannebrog.
BIBL.: S. Kragh-Jacobsen, 'N.B.L.' in *20 Solo dancers of the Royal Danish Ballet* (Copenhagen, 1965).

Lashchilin, Lev Alexandrovich (*b* 29 Nov. 1888, *d* Sep. 1955). Sov. dancer, choreographer, and b. master. Studied at Moscow Bolshoi B. School; member of Bolshoi B. 1906–40. He ch. the first and third act for the first prod. of Glière's *Red Poppy* (1927) and (with Moiseyev) Oransky's *The Footballer* (1930).

Last, Brenda (*b* London, 17 Apr. 1938). Brit. dancer and b. mistress. Studied with Biddy Pinchard, Volkova, and at Royal B. School. Joined Western Th. B. in 1957, creating roles in E. West's *Peter and the Wolf* (1957) and Darrell's *A Wedding Present* (1962), and Touring Co. of Royal B. in 1963; appointed principal d. 1965; created roles in D. Drew's *Intrusion* (1969), Ashton's *Creatures of Prometheus* (1970), Layton's *The Grand Tour* (1971), MacMillan's *The Poltroon* (1972), and P. Wright's *Arpège* (1975). Appointed b. mistress New Group of Royal B. in 1974, while continuing to d. leading roles; and continued with Sadler's Wells Royal B. until 1977, when she became dir. of Norwegian Nat. B., Oslo (1977–80), then returned to London. Now teaching. A. Genée Gold Medal (1955).
BIBL.: checklist in *Dance and Dancers* (1979/6).

Laubin, Reginald and Gladys (Gladys L., née Tortoiseshell, *b* Paterson, N.J.; Reginald L., *b* Detroit, Mich.). Amer. dancers and choreographers. For 20 years they lived and researched among Indians on reservations, and were the first to give concert perfs. of early Indian dances. They have performed as a duo since 1936, and have occasionally appeared with a troupe of Crow Indians. As authorities on American Indian d. they have contributed to *Dance Encyclopedia* and other publications; authors of *Indian Dances of North America* (Oklahoma, 1975).

Lauchery, Albert (*b* Mannheim, 19 Sep. 1779, *d* Berlin, 26 Mar. 1853). Ger. dancer and teacher. Studied with his father, the b. master Etienne L.,

in Berlin, later also in Paris; solo d. at Berlin Court Op. 1803–26. Appointed dir. of the b. school in 1815; a much respected teacher. He celebrated his 50th year with the co. in 1846.

Lauchery, Etienne (also Ger. Stephan; *b* Lyons, Sep. 1732, *d* Berlin, 5 Jan. 1820). Fr. dancer, choreographer, and b. master. To Mannheim in 1746, becoming court d.-master in 1756. B. master in Kassel 1764–72; *Recueil des Ballets*, published in 1768, lists no fewer than 37 bs. of his. Later worked in Mannheim, Kassel, and Munich, then in Berlin 1788–1813. Father of Albert L.

Laurencia (orig. Russ. title). Ballet in 3 acts and 5 scenes; libr. Eugen Mandelberg; ch. Chaboukiani; mus. A. Krein; déc. S. Virsaladze. Prod. 22 Mar. 1939, Kirov Th., Leningrad, with Dudinskaya, Chaboukiani. The b., based on Lope de Vega's *The Sheep Well*, tells of the rising of the peasants of a village in Castile; led by L. and her fiancé Frondoso, they storm the palace of the Commander who tried to seduce L., and kill him. Frequently revived throughout the Eastern Bloc—the pas de six also by Nureyev for Royal B. in 1965. An earlier b. on the same plot, Alexander Chekrygin's *Comedians* (mus. Glière, Bolshoi B., Moscow, 1931), was later revised and became *A Daughter of Castile* (ch. Alexei Tchitchinadze, Stanislavsky and Nemirovich-Danchenko Music Th., Moscow, 1955).
BIBL.: C. W. Beaumont, 'L.' in *Supplement to Complete Book of Ballets* (London, 1952).

Laurencin (*b* Paris 1885, *d* there, 9 June 1956). Fr. painter and designer. Designed Nijinska's *Les Biches*, Massine's *Les Roses* (both 1924), Y. Franck and A. Bourgat's *L'Eventail de Jeanne* (1927), and Petit's *Le Déjeuner sur l'Herbe* (1945).

Lausanne, Prix de. Though not possessing a b. co. of its own, thanks to the Festival de L. the wealthy city on the shore of Lake Geneva for years been Switzerland's main platform for b. and d. cos. from abroad. Through the initiative of some culturally minded industrialists the P.d.L. was established 1973 for young dancers of the 16–19 age group who have not yet started their professional career. It is awarded every year by an intern. jury of about 10 well-known b. personalities to the winners of the 4 day concours and consists of a one-year scholarship of free tuition plus expenses at one of the top b. schools of the Western World. In addition a special prize is awarded to the best Swiss contestant.

Lavallade, Carmen de (*b* Los Angeles, 6 Mar. 1931). Amer. dancer. Studied with Melissa Blake and C. Maracci. D. with L. Horton's co. Appeared in various films (*Carmen Jones*) and on Broadway (*House of Flowers*), where she met and married the d. and ch. G. Holder. Started to work with J. Butler in 1956, dancing in his various cos., creating roles in his *Carmina Burana* (1959),

Portrait of Billie (1962), and *Catulli Carmina* (1964). Has also d. with the cos. of Ailey, Tetley, McKayle, New York City Op., and Amer. B. Th. Holder ch. a programme for her, *Theatre of Dance*. D. Magazine Award (1966).
BIBL.: 'C.d.L.', *Dance Magazine* (1967/3—see also 1967/5, pp. 83–86).

Lavery, Sean (*b* Harrisburg, Penn., 16 Aug. 1956). Amer. dancer. Studied with R. Thomas and B. Fallis 1966–72. D. with San Francisco B. 1972–4, Frankfurt B. 1974–6, as guest artist with Chicago B. 1976, and since 1977 with New York City B., promoted principal d. 1978. Cr. roles in Taras's *Souvenir de Florence*, and Martins's *Symphony No. 1* (both 1981).
BIBL.: L. Draegin, 'The Balanchine Man', *Dance Magazine* (1979/1).

Lavreniuk, Alexander Alexandrovich (*b* 6 June 1939). Sov. dancer. Studied at Moscow Bolshoi B. School. Joined Bolshoi B. upon graduation and became one of its best demicaractère soloists.

Lavrovsky, Leonid Mikhailovich (*b* St. Petersburg, 18 June 1905, *d* Paris, 26 Nov. 1967). Sov. dancer, choreographer, b. director, and teacher. Studied at Petrograd B. School, graduating in 1922. Joined the GATOB, where he d. the premier danseur roles of the repertory and participated in the Evenings of Young B. (also in the prod. of Lopokov's controversial *Dance Symphony* in 1923). Started to teach in 1922. Created his first ch. with some pupils in 1930, followed by his full-length *Fadetta* (Delibes' *Sylvia*, 1934) and *Katerina* (mus. A. Rubinstein and Adam, 1935). B. dir, Maly Th. 1935–8, Kirov Th. 1938–44; his new bs. included *La Fille mal gardée* (1937), Asafiev's *Prisoner of the Caucasus* (1938), and the first Sov. prod. of Prokofiev's *Romeo and Juliet* (1940). During the later years of the Second World War he worked mainly in Yerevan. B. dir. of the Moscow Bolshoi B. 1944–56 and 1960–64, where his most important prods. included *Giselle* (1944), *Raymonda* (1945), *Romeo and Juliet* (1946), Glière's *The Red Poppy* (1949), Prokofiev's *The Stone Flower* (first prod., 1954), Rachmaninov's *Paganini* (1960), Bartók's *Night City* (*The Miraculous Mandarin*), and Balanchivadze's *Pages of Life* (both 1961). Appointed dir. of the Moscow Bolshoi B. School in 1964. Has also taught at the ch. faculty of the Moscow Th. Institute. One of the outstanding personalities of the new Sov. b. Was married to the d. Yelena Chikvaidze; father of the d. Mikhail L. Stalin Prize (1946, 1947, and 1950); People's Artist of the U.S.S.R. (1965).
BIBL.: N. Roslavleva, in *Era of the Russian Ballet* (London, 1966); M. G. Swift, in *The Art of the Dance in the U.S.S.R.* (Notre Dame, Ind., 1968).

Lavrovsky, Mikhail Leonidovich (*b* Tiflis, 29 Sep. 1941). Sov. dancer. Son of the ch. Leonid L.; studied at the Moscow Bolshoi B. School, graduating in 1961. Joined the Bolshoi B., of which he is now one of the leading principal dancers; created Prince in Grigorovich's *Nutcracker* (1966). Apptd. art. dir. Tbilisi B. 1983, for whom ch. *Porgy and Bess* as a b. (1985). Gold Medal (Varna, 1965).
BIBL.: N. René, 'M.L.', *Dance and Dancers* (1968/3).

Lawrence, Ashley (*b* Hamilton, N.Z., 5 June 1934). Brit. conductor. Studied at Royal College of Music. Conductor of Touring Royal B. 1962–6. B. conductor Ger. Op. Berlin 1966–72 and Stuttgart B. 1970–72. Rejoined Royal B. in 1972, appointed music dir. in 1973. Also principal conductor of BBC Concert Orchestra since 1971.

Lawrence, Pauline (*b* Los Angeles, 1900, *d* Stockton, N.J., 16 July 1971). Amer. pianist and costume designer. Joined Denishawn co. as a pianist in 1917. Then played for Graham and became pianist of the Humphrey-Weidman co. and Limón co. Married Limón; designed costumes for many of his prods. and acted as his personal representative.

Lawson, Joan (*b* London, 1907). Brit. dancer, teacher, and writer. Studied with Margaret Morris and Astafieva. D. in Carl Rosa Op. prods., revues, and with Nemchinova-Dolin co. Studied further in Moscow and Leningrad. Teacher at Royal B. School 1963–71. Contributor to *Dancing Times*. Author of *European Folk Dance* (London, 1953), *Dressing for Ballet* (with P. Revitt, London, 1958), *Classical Ballet, its Theory and Technique* (London, 1960), and *A History of Ballet and its Makers* (London, 1964).

Layton, Joe (*b* New York, 3 May 1931). Amer. dancer and choreographer. Studied with J. Levinoff and at Manhattan High School of Mus. and Art. Made his début in *Oklahoma!* in 1947; appeared in many musicals and with G. Reich's Ballet Ho in Paris. Began to ch. in Amer. summerstock prods.; then on Broadway and in London (*Mattress, The Sound of Music, Greenwillow, Tenderloin, Sail Away, No Strings, The Girl Who Came to Supper, Dear World, Barnum*, etc.). To Royal B., for which he ch. *Grand Tour* (mus. Coward/Kay), *Overture* (mus. Bernstein, both 1971), and *O.W.* (about Oscar Wilde; mus. Walton, 1972)—also *Double Exposure* (mus. Scriabin and Pousseur, City Center Joffrey B., 1972).
BIBL.: 'A Talent to Entertain', interview with J.L., *Dance and Dancers* (1971/3).

Lazarov, Itchko (*b* Sofia, 23 Sep. 1937). Bulg. dancer and artistic director. Studied at Sofia Op. B. School and in Leningrad with Pushkin and Balabina. Joined Op. B. of Sofia in 1958, becoming principal d. Has regularly appeared with B. Th. Contemporain since 1968. Appointed artistic dir. of Chorédrame Hellénique, Athens, in 1977.

Lazowski, Yurek (*b* Warsaw, 1917, *d* Los Angeles, 6 July 1980). Pol.-Amer. dancer and teacher. Studied at Warsaw Op. B. School, joining its co. D. with Rubenstein's co. in 1934, in

Antwerp, and with Bs. Russes de Monte Carlo 1935–41. First character d. and régisseur of B. Th. 1941–3. B. Russe de Monte Carlo again 1944–6, also appearing with Massine's B. Russe Highlights.

Lazzini, Joseph (b Marseilles, 1927). Fr. dancer, choreographer, and b. director. Studied with F. Meylach in Nice, joined Nice Op. B. in 1945. D. with various Ital. cos. B. dir., Liège, 1954–7, Toulouse 1958, Marseilles 1959–68 (where b. activity greatly increased under his direction). Formed his own co., Th. Française de la Danse, in 1968; however it was as short-lived as many of his other activities since. Has also quite often worked for TV. His bs. are mostly either spectacular or sensational, often relying on a star performer (Babilée) or designer (Alexander Calder, René Allio, B. Daydé, Michel Raffaelli); they include *Hommage à Jérôme Bosch* (mus. J. Meyrowitz, 1961), $E=MC^2$ (mus. A. Mossolov, 1964), *Lascaux* (mus. J. Antill), *Eppur si muove* (mus. F. Miroglio, both 1965), and *Ecce Homo* (mus. Berghmans, 1968). Has also ch. for Met. Op. House, La Scala, and Paris Opéra. Best ch. (Paris, 1963); Prix de l'Université de la Danse (Paris, 1965).
BIBL.: L. Rossel, 'J.L.' (with complete check list of bs. and activities), *Les Saisons de la danse* (1969/4).

Leaves are Fading, The. Ballet in 1 act; chs. Tudor; mus. Dvořák; set Ming Cho Lee; cost. P. Zipprodt, Prod. 17 July 1975, Amer. B. Th., New York State Th. New York, with M. Tcherkassky, G. Kirkland, C. Tippet, C. Ward, J. Kage. Set to a selection of little known pieces by Dvořák (incl. the string quartets op. 77 and 80 and part of his trio), the b. has been described by A. Bland as 'gently charming and lyrical in a wistful English way. To a tuneful Dvořák score young people meet and flirt and part,'
BIBL.: G. Balanchine, 'T.L.a.F.' in *Balanchine's Complete Stories of the Great Ballets* (Garden City, N.Y., 1977).

Leclair, André (b Brussels, 29 Jan. 1930). Belg. dancer, choreographer, and b. director. Studied with Monique Querida and V. Gsovsky. D. with Bs. des Champs-Elysées in 1947. Joined Brussels Th. de la Monnaie as danseur étoile in 1949, and remained with the co. when it became B. of the 20th Century (until 1966). Began to ch. in 1956. Appointed b. master Royal Op. Antwerp 1966, b. dir. 1968. Chief ch. of B. of Flanders since 1970; has ch. many bs. for the co.

LeClercq, Tanaquil (b Paris, 2 Oct. 1929). Amer. dancer. Studied at School of Amer. B. Joined B. Society in 1946; remained with the co. when it became New York City B., and eventually became one of its most individual soloists and a marvellous Balanchine stylist. Contracted polio on a Eur. tour of the co. in 1956, which abruptly ended her career. The long list of bs. in which she created leading parts incl. Balanchine's *Four Temperaments* (1946), *Divertimento* (1947), *Orpheus* (1948), *Bour-*

rée fantasque (1949), *La Valse* (1951), *Caracole* (1952), *Western Symphony* and *Ivesiana* (both 1954), Ashton's *Illuminations* (1950), and Robbins' *Age of Anxiety* (1950), *The Pied Piper* (1951), *Afternoon of a Faun* (1953), and *The Concert* (1956). Author of *Mourka, the Autobiography of a Cat* (New York, 1964) and *Ballet Cookbook* (New York, 1967). Married to Balanchine 1952–69.

Leçon, La. See *Lesson, The.*

Lee, Mary Ann (b Philadelphia, 1823, d 1899). Amer. dancer. Studied with Paul H. Hazard in Philadelphia; made her début in the local prod. of *The Maid of Kashmir* in 1837 (an Eng. version of *Le Dieu et la Bayadère*); appeared there and in Baltimore in *La Sylphide*, and in New York in *La Bayadère* and *The Sisters* in 1839. From James Sylvain, Elssler's partner, she learned Elssler's most successful pieces; studied with Perrot in Paris in 1844. Formed a small Amer. troupe with G. Washington Smith in 1845, with which she toured the U.S. 1845–7, presenting such bs. as *La jolie fille de Gand*, *La Fille du Danube*, and *Giselle* (first Amer. prod., Boston, 1846). Returned to the th. for a couple of perfs. as Fenella in *La Muette de Portici*, 1852–3. The first Amer. ballerina to gain international renown.
BIBL.: L. Moore, 'M.A.L.—First American Giselle', *Dance Index* (II,5).

Leeder, Sigurd (b Hamburg, 14 Aug. 1902, d Herisau, 20 June 1981). Ger. dancer, choreographer, b. master, and teacher. Studied with Laban in Hamburg, where he already had his own group. Joined the Münster Neue Tanzbühne in 1924, where he became one of Jooss's closest collaborators. Toured with him in a solo programme, called Two Male Dancers; accompanied him to Essen, where he also taught at the Folkwang School. When the Folkwang B. emigrated in 1934, he became co-dir. of the B. Jooss and its schools in Dartington and Cambridge. Since the disbanding of the co. he taught in London, Santiago de Chile and (from 1965) in Herisau, Switzerland.

Lees, Michelle (b Virginia, 18 Mar. 1947). Amer. dancer. Studied with O. Tupine and at Washington School of B. Joined Washington National B. in 1964 and eventually became principal d. (until the co. disbanded in 1974). D. with Amer. Classical B. when it toured Eur. in 1971. To Chicago B. as principal d. in 1974. Prize for the best couple (with Dennis Poole, Varna, 1972).

Lefèbre, Jorge. Cub. dancer, choreographer, and artistic dir. Studied with the Alonsos in Havana, later also with Dollar, Mattox, and Luigi. D. with K. Dunham's Co. Joined B. of the 20th Century in 1963; created the leading role in Béjart's *Actus tragicus* (1969). Has also ch. for B. de Wallonie, East Berlin Ger. State Op., and National B. of Cuba; his most successful b. so far is *Edipe Roi* (mus. B. Maderna, 1970). Artistic dir. of B. Royal de Wallonie since 1980. Married to the d. Menia Martinez.

BIBL.: N. McLain Stoop, 'J.L.', *Dance Magazine* (1971/8).

Legat, Nicolai Gustavovich (*b* St. Petersburg, 27 Dec. 1869, *d* London, 24 Jan. 1937). Russ. dancer, b. master, choreographer, and teacher. Studied with his father Gustav L. and at Imperial B. School with Gerdt and Johansson, graduating in 1888. Joined Maryinsky Th. and later became one of its most respected principal dancers. A brilliant technician; appeared in 70 bs. in 20 years, incl. the first prods. of Petipa's *Kalkabrino* (1891) and Ivanov's *Nutcracker* (1892). He was the favourite partner of Kschessinska, Pavlova, and Trefilova. With his brother Sergei L. he succeeded Petipa as b. master in 1903; he ch. several bs., but concentrated increasingly on teaching, and eventually became dir. of the Imperial B. School (where he succeeded Johansson). Among his many distinguished pupils were Egorova, Preobrajenska, Sedova, Vaganova, Karsavina, Fokine, Nijinsky, and Bolm. Left the U.S.S.R. with his wife, Nadine Nicolayeva L., in 1923; succeeded Cecchetti as b. master of Diaghilev's co. Settled in London in 1926, and opened a school at Colet Gardens, where Nemchinova, Danilova, Lopokova, Inglesby, Fonteyn, de Valois, Dolin, and Lifar studied with him. After his death the school continued under the direction of his wife and is now headed in its new premises at Mark Cross, Sussex, by Eunice Bartell. Apart from being one of the outstanding representatives of the traditional Russ. school of dancing, he was a skilled caricaturist. He published *Russian Ballet* in St. Petersburg (Eng. edition in 1939).

BIBL.: A. Turnbull, 'The L. School', *Dance and Dancers* (1970/8).

Legat, Sergei Gustavovich (*b* St. Petersburg, 27 Sep. 1875, *d* there 1 Nov. 1905). Russ. dancer. Son of Gustav L.; studied at the Imperial B. School with Johansson and Gerdt, and subsequently with his brother Nicolai, graduating in 1894. Joined the Maryinsky Th. and eventually became a soloist, much admired for his stylish perfs. He soon started to teach and was one of the influential teachers of Nijinsky. Committed suicide at the age of 29, possibly because of political or family reasons (he was married to Maria, the daughter of M. Petipa). Like his brother, he was a gifted caricaturist, and seems to have been the more talented ch. of the two.

Legend of Joseph (orig. Ger. title: *Die Josephslegende*; title of Paris first prod.: *La Légende de Joseph*). Action in 1 act; libr. Harry Graf Kessler and H. von Hofmannsthal; mus. R. Strauss (also cond.); ch. Fokine; set J. M. Sert; cost. Bakst. Prod. 14 May 1914, B. Russe de Diaghilev, Opéra, Paris, with Massine, M. Kousnetzova. The authors set the biblical story, of the shepherd J. and his rejection of the wife of Potiphar, in the Venice of

Paolo Veronese *c.* 1530, stressing the contrast between oriental voluptuousness and boyish chastity. At the end J. is led towards an apotheosis, while the Wife of Potiphar strangles herself with her rope of pearls. This marked Massine's début with the Diaghilev co. Later versions by Kröller (Berlin State Op., 1921), Balanchine (Copenhagen, 1931), Tudor (Teatro Colón, 1958), Rosen (Munich State Op., 1958), Neumeier (Vienna, 1977), and others.

BIBL.: C. W. Beaumont, 'L.L.d.J.' in *Complete Book of Ballets* London 1951).

Legend of Judith. Ballet in 1 act; ch. Graham; mus. Mordecai Seter; déc. Dani Karavan. Prod. 25 Oct. 1962, M. Graham D. Co., Habima Th., Tel Aviv, with Graham, L. Hodes, Ross, Yuriko. 'The action of *Legend of Judith* takes place entirely within the "unknown landscape of the mind" of a woman, a kind of Judith. . . . The human soul, besieged by memory and by the powers of imagination confronts the past in its true, mythic dimensions and accepts the consequences of love and brutality and violence' (programme note).

Legend of Love (original Russ. title: *Legenda o lyubi*). Ballet in 3 acts and 7 scenes; libr. Nazim Hikmet; ch. Grigorovich; mus. Arif Melikov; déc. S. Virsaladze. Prod. 23 Mar. 1961, Kirov Th., Leningrad, with Kolpakova, Moisseyeva, Gribov, Gridin. Inspired by Hikmet's play of the same title, the b. tells of Queen Mekhmeneh Bahnu, who sacrifices her beauty to save the life of her sick sister, Princess Shyrin, and of Ferkhad, a young painter and the lover of Shyrin, who heroically sacrifices his love to help the thirsty people to find new water supplies. Revived for Moscow Bolshoi B. in 1965, the b. soon reached the Eastern Bloc countries.

BIBL.: N. René, 'A L.o.L.', *Dance and Dancers* (1962/11); G. Balanchine, 'L.o.L.' in *Balanchine's New Complete Stories of the Great Ballets* (Garden City, N.Y., 1968).

Legend of Ochrid, The (orig. Yugosl. title: *Ohridska Legenda*). Ballet in 4 acts and 5 scenes; libr. and mus. Stevan Hristić; ch. Froman; sets S. Beložanski; cost. M. Babić-Jovanović. Prod. 28 Nov. 1947, Belgrade Op., with M. Sanjina, Parlić. The b. is based on a Macedonian fairy-tale. It tells of the love of Marco and Biljana, and how Marco, with the help of the nymphs from the lake, wins back Biljana and her friends, who have been abducted by invading Turkish soldiers. The Belgrade co. brought it to the Edinburgh Festival in 1951. Later prods. by the Mlakars (Ljubljana, 1948), Bourmeister (Moscow, 1958), and Parlić (Belgrade, 1966).

Léger, Fernand (*b* Argentan, 4 Feb. 1881, *d* Gif-sur-Yvette, 17 Aug. 1955). Fr. painter and designer. Designed the déc. for Börlin's *Skating Rink* and *La Création du monde* (both 1923), Lifar's *David triomphant* (1937), and Charrat's *Léonard de Vinci* (1952).

Legerton, Henry (*b* Melbourne, 1917). Austral. dancer and b. master. Studied with Idzikowsky, Kirsova, and Volkova. Joined London B. in 1940. After the war d. with the Borovansky B., then understudied Massine in *A Bullet in the Ballet* before joining Sadler's Wells B.; became b. master of Touring Royal B. in 1957, then régisseur of the Royal B.; retired 1982.

Legnani, Pierina (*b* 1863, *d* 1923). Ital. dancer. Studied with Beretta in Milan. Joined the co. of La Scala and became prima ballerina in 1892. Also appeared in Paris, London, and Madrid. Went to St. Petersburg in 1893, where in Petipa's *Cinderella* her celebrated 32 fouettés, which had already been seen the year before in London in *Aladdin*, and which she incorporated into the 1895 prod. of *Swan Lake*, dazzled the audiences and encouraged the Russ. dancers to emulate her incredible virtuoso feats. She returned to St. Petersburg every year until 1901. She was appointed prima ballerina assoluta (apart from Kschessinska the only official holder of this title) and created Odette-Odile in Petipa-Ivanov's *Swan Lake* of 1895, and further leading roles in Petipa's *The Talisman* (1895), *Halte de cavalerie*, *La Perle*, *Barbe-Bleu* (all 1896), *Raymonda* (1898), and *Ruses d'amour* (1900); she gave her farewell perf. there in *La Camargo* in 1901. In London she d. at the Alhambra Th. 1888–90. After her retirement she was for many years an adjudicator of the La Scala examinations.
BIBL.: P. San-Francisco, 'Tea-Time with P.L.', *Dance Magazine* (1955/11); P. Migel, in *The Ballerinas* (New York, 1972).

Leili and Mejnun. Ballet in 4 acts and 6 scenes; libr. S. Zenin; ch. G. Valamatzade; mus. S. Balasanyan; déc. J. Chemodurov. Prod. 7 Nov. 1947, Dushanbe. The b. is inspired by the 1188 verse epic of the same name by the Pers. poet Nizwami and tells of the Romeo-and-Juliet-like love story of the nomad poet Kais and the daughter of the cruel ruler of the town. The co. scored a great success when the b. was shown at the Moscow 1957 Decade. Goleizovsky then ch. it for the Moscow Bolshoi B. in 1964 (with Bessmertnova and Vasiliev). A film prod. of the b., with the Tadzhik Op. B. of Stalinabad, was released in 1960.
BIBL.: M. G. Swift, in *The Art of the Dance in the U.S.S.R.* (Notre Dame, Ind., 1968).

Leipzig B. enjoyed some popularity here in the aftermath of the romantic era (*La Fille mal gardée*, 1830; *La Péri*, 1848; *Esmeralda*, 1849; *Le Diable à quatre*, 1850; *Paquita*, 1850–1; *Ondine*, 1856; *Giselle*, 1860; *La Sylphide*, 1865), and Reisinger worked here as a ch. in the 1860s and 1870s. But during the rest of the 19th century and the first decades of the 20th there was little or no ballet. T. Gsovsky ch. the first prod. of Orff's *Catulli Carmina* here in 1943 (as a double bill with Wigman's ch. of *Carmina Burana*), and Wigman

drew wide attention when she ch. Gluck's op. *Orpheus and Eurydice* in 1947. But it was not until E. Köhler-Richter became b. dir. at the L. Op. House, in 1958, that a really continuous b. policy started to develop, culminating in her highly idiosyncratic prods. of the classics. Artistic dir. in 1981 is Klaus Tews, with D. Seyffert as chief ch.

Leistikow, Gertrud (*b* Bückeburg, 21 Sep. 1885, *d* Amsterdam, 9 Nov. 1948). Ger.-Dutch dancer, choreographer, and teacher. Studied in Berlin with Hade Kallmayer. Gave her first solo recital in Berlin in 1910, after which she toured extensively (Ger., Russia, Switzerland) as an early pioneer of the Central Eur. modern d. movement. Then she settled in Holland in 1921, and later opened schools in the Hague and Amsterdam.
BIBL.: H. Brandenburg, 'G.L.' in *Der moderne Tanz* (Munich, 1931).

Leland, Sara (orig. Sally Harrington; b. Melrose, Mass., 2 Aug. 1941). Amer. d. Studied with E. V. Williams in Boston and d. with her New England Civic B. Member of Joffrey B. 1959–60 and New York City B. since 1960; apptd. soloist in 1963 and principal d. in 1972. Created parts in Robbins's *Dances at a Gathering* (1969) and *An Evening's Waltzes* (1973), and Balanchine's *Symphony in Three Movements* (1972). Frequent guest with the Boston B. Asst. b. master N.Y. City B. 1981.
BIBL.: O. Maynard, 'In the Light of Twelve Candles, S.L. of the New York City Ballet', *Dance Magazine* (1972/8); J. Gruen, 'S.L.', in *The Private World of Ballet* (New York, 1975).

Lemaitre, Gérard (*b* Paris, 8 Dec. 1936). Fr. dancer. Studied at Châtelet Th. School and d. with its co.; then with B. Marigny, Petit's Bs. de Paris, co. of G. Reich, and Marquis de Cuevas. Joined Netherlands D. Th. in 1960 and eventually became one of its principal dancers. Created numerous parts, mainly in bs. by Van Manen, but also in those of Harkarvy, Butler, Tetley, and J. Muller. Van Manen ch. *Opus Lemaitre* for him in 1972. Became b. master Scapino B. 1983

Leningrad. The former St. Petersburg became Petrograd in 1914 and received its present name in 1924. For its b. history see the entries on *Kirov Ballet* and *Maly Ballet*.

Leningrad Ballet School. The origins of what many people consider the world's foremost b. school date back to 1738 when the Fr. b. master Landé was granted permission to start the training of professional dancers for the St. Petersburg court performances. It became then part of St. Petersburg's famous Th. School and is still located at its time-honoured precincts at Rossi (former Theatre) Street. It was there that Petipa and Johansson formed the brilliant generation of Russ. dancers who burst upon the West in Diaghilev's Paris seasons of Russ. op. and b., starting 1909. An uninterrupted succession of great teachers reached its peak when A. Vaganova became the school's dir. in 1934, developing her teaching system, which became obligatory for all b. education in the USSR (and many Eastern bloc countries). In 1957 the school was named after her. Today dir. by Sergeyev, it continues to turn out every year a great number of excellently trained dancers, most of whom have studied there the full 8 years curriculum of d. and general education. A film about the school, *Children of Theatre Street,* was prod. 1977.

Leningrad Symphony (orig. Russ. title *Sedmaya simfoniya*). Ballet in 1 act; libr. and ch. Belsky; mus. Shostakovich; déc. M. Gordon. Prod. 14 Apr. 1961, Kirov Th., Leningrad, with Sizova, Soloviev. Set to the first movement of Shostakovich's Seventh ('Leningrad') Symphony, the b. expresses the months of sacrifice endured when the city was besieged by the Ger. invaders in 1942. An earlier version by Massine (B. Russe Highlights, New York, 1945), a later one by L. Ogoun, Brno, 1962.

Leonova, Marina Konstantinovna (*b* Moscow, 18 Feb. 1949). Sov. dancer. Studied at Bolshoi B. School; graduated in 1968. Joined Bolshoi B. in 1969, and later became soloist.

Leotard. A tight-fitting practice and stage garment, invented by the Fr. acrobat Jules L. (1830–70), resembling a sleeveless one-piece bathing suit (also a long-sleeved version).

Lepeshinskaya, Olga Vasilievna (*b* Kiev, 28 Sep. 1916). Sov. ballerina and teacher. Studied at Moscow Bolshoi B. School. Joined Bolshoi B. in 1933; subsequently appointed principal d. Remained with the co. until 1963, and became one of its most popular ballerinas, much admired for her virtuoso technique and almost masculine strength. Created roles in Moiseyev's *The Three Fat Men* (1935), Popko-Pospekhin-Radunsky's *Svetlana* (1939), and Zakharov's *Cinderella* (1945). Toured frequently with a concert programme of virtuoso pieces. Now teaches (often in East Berlin). Stalin Prize (1941, 1946, 1947, and 1950). Merited Artist of the R.S.F.S.R. (1942); People's Artist (1947). Temporary member of the Supreme Soviet.

Le Picq, Charles (also Lepic, Pick, or Lepij; *b* Naples, 1744, *d* St. Petersburg, 1806). Fr. dancer and choreographer. Studied and d. with Noverre in Stuttgart 1761–4. Subsequently staged Noverre's bs. in many Eur. cities, frequently with his wife, the d. Anna Binetti. Went to London as b. master at King's Th. in 1783 and 1785. B. dir. in St. Petersburg 1786–98, where he married prima ballerina Gertruda Rossi; staged many bs. by Dauberval, Gardel, and Noverre, and himself ch. *Bergère* (1790), *Didone abbandonata, La Belle Arsène, Les deux Savoyards* (all 1795), *Les Amours de Bayard,* and *Tancrède* (both 1798). He was one of Noverre's most loyal pupils, and was responsible for the

Naples and St. Petersburg editions of Noverre's *Lettres sur la danse.*

Leroux, Pauline (*b* Paris, 20 Aug. 1809, *d* 1891). Fr. dancer. D. at the Paris Opéra 1826–37 and 1840–44; created roles in F. Taglioni's *Nathalie, ou la Laitière suisse* (1832), *La Révolte au sérail* (1833), Coralli's *Le Diable boîteux* (1836), and many op. bs. Also appeared in London 1824–33.

Leskova, Tatiana (*b* Paris, 1922). Fr.-Braz. dancer, choreographer, and b. mistress. Studied with Egorova, Kniaseff, and Oboukhoff. Began to d. at Paris Opéra Comique in 1937; joined B. de la Jeunesse in 1938. Member of Original B. Russe 1939–45. Settled in Rio de Janeiro in 1945 and appeared with various cos. Formed her own B. Society in 1948. B. mistress and ch. (later also dir.) of Rio de Janeiro Teatro Municipal 1950–71.

Leslie, Nathalie. See *Krassovska, Nathalie.*

Lesson, The (orig. Dan. title: *Enetime*—often also Fr. *La Leçon*). TV ballet; ch. Flindt; mus. G. Delerue; déc. Daydé. Prod. 16 Sep. 1963, Dan. TV, with Flindt, Amiel, and Tsilla Chelton. Inspired by Ionesco's play of the same name, the b. tells of a professor who is so carried away by his work that he finally murders his pupil. This was Flindt's first b. prod., and received the Italia Prize. The first stage prod. took place on 6 Apr. 1964 at the Paris Opéra Comique (with Flindt, Amiel, and Lyna Garden). Revived for many cos. (Copenhagen, 1964; Western Th. B., 1967; City Center Joffrey B., 1968).
BIBL.: G. Balanchine, 'The Private L.' in *Balanchine's New Complete Stories of the Great Ballets* (Garden City, N.Y., 1968).

Lester, Keith (*b* Guildford, 9 Apr. 1904). Eng. dancer, choreographer, b. master, and teacher. Studied with Dolin, Astafieva, Legat, and Fokine. Début in London 1923. D. with Kyasht, Karsavina, Spessivtseva, and Rubinstein. Joined Markova-Dolin B. in 1935, where he ch. *David* (mus. M. Jacobson), *Pas de quatre* (mus. Pugni, 1936), and other bs. Joined London B. in 1939 and ch. *Pas des déesses* (mus. Pugni). Formed Art Th. B. in 1940 with H. Turner, for which he ch. several new bs. Joined London Windmill Th. in 1945, where he did more than 150 show bs. and also ch. the fan dances which were a speciality of the th. Appointed principal teacher of the London Royal Academy of Dancing in 1965.

Letter to the World. Ballet in 1 act; ch. Graham; mus. H. Johnson; set Arch Lauterer; cost. E. Gilfond. Prod. 11 Aug. 1940, M. Graham and D. Co., Bennington College Th., Verm., with Graham, Dudley, Hawkins, M. Cunningham. This was Graham's first piece for a larger group, dealing with the inner life of the New England poet Emily Dickinson, who is represented by two performers: One Who Dances and One Who Speaks. New York première 1941.

Levans, Daniel (formerly Levins: *b* Ticonderoga, N.Y., 7 Oct. 1953). Amer. dancer. Studied at High School of Performing Arts and New York School of B. Début with Amer. B. Co., 1969. Joined Amer. B. Th. 1971, appointed soloist 1973, principal 1974. Since 1975 member of U.S. Terpsichore; has also ch.
BIBL.: R. Baker, 'Spotlight on D.L.', *Dance Magazine* (1973/10).

Levashev, Vladimir Alexandrovich (*b* Moscow, 16 Jan. 1923). Sov. dancer. Studied at Moscow Bolshoi B. School, graduating in 1941; joined Bolshoi B. and became one of its leading character dancers. and mimes. Created a role in Lavrovsky's *Night City* (1961); Shuraleh and Severyan (in *Stone Flower*) were his most impressive roles. People's Artist of the R.S.F.S.R. (1965).
BIBL.: S. Iwanowa, 'V.L.', *Ballet Today* (1963/11).

Levasseur, André (*b* Paris, 18 Aug. 1927). Fr. designer. Designed Ashton's *Birthday Offering* (1956), *La Péri* (1957), and *La Valse* (1958), Balanchine's *La Somnambule* (Cuevas prod., 1957) and *Theme and Variations* (Amer. B. Th., 1958), Taras' *Piège de lumière* (New York City B. prod., 1964), and Lazzini's *Coppélia* (1965).

Levinson, Andre Jacovlevich (*b* St. Petersburg, 1 Jan. 1887, *d* Paris, 3 Dec. 1933). Russ. critic and writer on the dance. A professor of Romance languages at St. Petersburg Univ., he defended the ideals of the pure academic d., and strongly opposed the reforms of people such as Fokine and Diaghilev. Left Russia in 1918 and settled in Paris as a journalist. Author of *Ballet romantique* (1919), *L'Oeuvre de Léon Bakst* (1921), *Meister des Balletts* (1923), *La Danse au théâtre* (1924), *La Vie de Noverre* (1925), *Paul Valéry, philosophe de la danse* (1927), *La Argentina, Anna Pavlova* (both 1928), *Marie Taglioni, La Danse d'aujourd'hui* (both 1929), *Les Visages de la danse* (1933), and *Serge Lifar* (1934).

Levi-Tanai, Sara (*b* Jerusalem, 1911). Israeli dancer, choreographer, and b. director. She was self-taught, and founded the Inbal D. Th. in 1949, for which she created more than 40 dances, including *Sabbath Peace* (mus. Ovadia Tuvia, 1953), *Yemenite Wedding* (mus. traditional songs, 1954), *Story of Ruth* (mus. Tuvia, 1961), *Wild Rose* (mus. Tuvia, 1967), and *Jacob* (mus. Mar-Haim, 1973). Ch. Prize of the Th. of Nations (Paris, 1962); Israel Prize (1973).
BIBL.: L.J., 'S. L.-T.: Dreamer and Doer', *Dance Magazine* (1960/1); J. Brin Ingber, in 'Shorashim', *Dance Perspectives* 59.

Lewitzky, Bella (*b* Los Angeles, 13 Jan. 1916). Amer. dancer, choreographer, and teacher. Studied with L. Horton; member of his D. Group and D. Th. until 1950. Created leading parts in his *Sacre du printemps* (1937) and *Salome* (1938). Taught at various schools and institutes, then established D. Associates Foundation and her own

co., both based on Los Angeles. Has become the leading exponent of modern d. on the W. Coast. New York début of her group 1971; and in Brit. at Torquay only, 1980. Contributed 'A Vision of Total Theatre' to *Dance Perspectives* 31 (issue dedicated to Horton).
BIBL.: R. Renouf, 'Direction-Oriented B.L.', *Dance News* (1971/9–10); E. Moore, 'B.L.: A Legend Turned Real', *Dance Chronicle* (Vol. 2, no. 1).

Lezginka. A Russ. folk-d. from the Lezghis (a tribe from Daghestan, on the Caspian Sea) in fast 6/8 time, usually performed as a male solo, but also by couples. It is an exhibition of stamina and skill, occasionally executed between fixed daggers. It appears in Glinka's *Life for the Tsar*, and is one of the most effective numbers in Khachaturian's *Gayane*.

Lichine, David (orig. D. Liechtenstein; *b* Rostov-on-Don, 25 Oct. 1910, *d* Los Angeles, 26 June 1972). Russ.-Amer. dancer and choreographer. Studied with Egorova and Nijinska. D. with Ida Rubinstein's co. in 1928, with Pavlova in 1930, and as principal with Bs. Russes de Monte Carlo 1932–45, creating roles in Balanchine's *Cotillon* and *Le Bourgeois gentilhomme*, Massine's *Jeux d'enfants, Le beau Danube, Beach* (all 1932), *Choreartium, Les Présages* (both 1933), and *Union Pacific* (1934). Began to ch. in 1933, his many bs. including *Francesca da Rimini* (mus. Tchaikovsky, 1937), *Prodigal Son* (mus. Prokofiev, 1938), and *Graduation Ball* (mus. Strauss-Dorati, 1940). Joined B. Th. with his wife T. Riabouchinska in 1941, where he completed Fokine's unfinished b. *Helen of Troy* (mus. Offenbach-Dorati, 1942); he then ch. *Fair at Sorochinsk* (mus. Mussorgsky, 1943). Worked on Broadway; joined Buenos Aires Teatro Colón in 1947, where he ch. *Evolución del movimento* (mus. C. Franck's *Symphonic Variations*). He ch. *La Création* (a silent re-working of *Evolución del movimento*) and *La Rencontre ou Œdipe le Sphinx* (mus. Sauguet) for Bs. des Champs-Elysées in 1948. He then worked in Los Angeles as a teacher and freelance ch. (Grand B. du Marquis de Cuevas, London Festival B., Borovansky B., Ger. Op. Berlin, etc.).
BIBL.: G. Anthony, 'A Hero of the 1930s', *Dancing Times* (1972/11).

Lido, Serge orig. S. Lidoff; *b* Moscow, 28 Jan. 1906, *d* Paris, 6 Mar. 1984). Russ.-Fr. b. photographer. Based in Paris, has become the outstanding Fr. b. photographer of our time, and his photographs have been published by leading magazines all over the world. Author of many b. photo albums, from *Danse* (1947) to *Les Etoiles de la Danse dans le Monde* (1975), with texts by his wife Irène Lidova. Chevalier des Arts et Lettres (1976).

Lidova, Irène (*b* Moscow, 7 Jan. 1907). Russ.-Fr. critic and writer on dance, educated Sorbonne. Established the Soirées de la danse at the Paris Th. S. Bernhardt in 1944, where she presented young

Fr. dancers. This became Les Bs. des Champs-Elysées in 1945. Critic, correspondent, and contributor to various magazines (*Ballet Annual, Dance News, Les Saisons de la danse,* etc). Author of *Roland Petit* and *17 Visages de la danse française* (1953). Wrote the text for the albums of photos by her husband, Serge Lido. General Secretary of Fr. Association of Ballet Critics and Writers. Chevalier dans l'Ordre des Arts et Lettres, 1979.

Lidström, Kerstin (*b* Stockholm, 24 May 1946). Swed. dancer. Studied Royal Swed. B. School and Royal B. School. Joined Royal Swed. B. in 1963, and later became soloist. D. with Netherlands D. Th. 1970–71, then returned to her home co., where she was promoted principal d.

Liebeslieder Walzer. Ballet in 2 scenes; ch. Balanchine; mus. Brahms; sets D. Hays; cost. Karinska. Prod. 22 Nov. 1960, New York City B., City Center, N.Y., with D. Adams, Hayden, Jillana, Verdy, B. Carter, Ludlow, Magallanes, Watts. The b. is based on Brahms' 2 sets of waltzes (op. 52 and 65) for piano duet and vocal quartet; the musicians perform on the left-hand side of the stage, which shows for the first set a Viennese ballroom in which 4 couples d. various kinds of waltzes; the second set is treated more abstractly. TV prod. second Ger. channel in 1975. Revived for Royal B., Cov. Gdn., 1979.
BIBL.: G. Balanchine, 'L.W.' in *Balanchine's New Complete Stories of the Great Ballets* (Garden City, N.Y., 1968).

Lieder eines fahrenden Gesellen. See *Songs of a Wayfarer.*

Lieder ohne Worte. Ballet in 10 dances; ch. Van Manen; mus. Mendelssohn; déc. Vroom. Prod. 18 June 1977, Netherlands D. Th., Circustheater, Scheveningen, with Van Boven, E. Hampton, G. Lemaitre. To a selection from Mendelssohn's piano pieces of the same name, Van Manen explores the human relationships between 4 couples who are acquaintances, without any stronger dramatic accents. Revived for Vienna State Op. B. (1978).

Lied von der Erde. See *Song of the Earth.*

Liepa, Maris-Rudolph Eduardovich (*b* Riga, 27 July 1936). Sov. dancer. Studied in Riga and at Moscow Bolshoi B. School, graduating in 1955. Member of Riga B. 1955–6, moved to Moscow Stanislavsky and Nemirovich-Danchenko Mus. Th. as a soloist at the end of 1956. Joined Bolshoi B. in 1960 as a principal d.; Crassus (in *Spartacus*) and Vronsky (in *Anna Karenina*) were two of his many outstanding interpretations. Revived Fokine's *Spectre de la rose* for himself and Bessmertnova in 1967. Teaches at Bolshoi B. School. People's Artist (1969); Lenin Prize (1969); Merited Artist of the R.S.F.S.R. (1976).
BIBL.: A. Avdeyenko, 'M.L.', *Dancing Times* (1973/1).

Lieutenant Kijé (orig. Russ. title: *Podporuchik Kizhe*). Ballet in 1 act; libr. A. Veitsler; ch. O. Tarasova and A. Lapauri; mus. Prokofiev; déc. Boris Messerer. Prod. 10 Feb. 1963, Bolshoi Th., Moscow, with Bogomolova, Struchkova. The b. is based on the concert suite of the mus. Prokofiev wrote for Yuri Tynianov's film of the same title. It tells of a non-existent lieutenant who by an error got into the list and enjoyed a fabulous career at the court of Tsar Paul. Fokine used the same mus. for the heroic b. *Russian Soldier* (New York 1942), dedicated to the dead of World War II.
BIBL.: G. Balanchine, 'L.K.' in *Balanchine's New Complete Stories of the Great Ballets* (Garden City, N.Y., 1968).

Lifar, Serge (*b* Kiev, 2 Apr. 1905, *d* Lausanne, 15 Dec. 1986). Russ.-Fr. dancer, choreographer, b. director, and author. Studied with Nijinska in Kiev. Joined Diaghilev's Bs. Russes in 1923, but continued to study with Cecchetti, Legat, and Vladimirov. Appointed premier danseur in 1925; created roles in Nijinska's *Les Fâcheux* and *Le Train bleu* (both 1924), Massine's *Zéphire et Flore, Les Matelots* (both 1925), *Pas d'acier* (1927), and *Ode* (1928), and Balanchine's *Barabau* (1925), *La Chatte* (1927), *Apollon musagète* (1928), *Le Bal,* and *Prodigal Son* (both 1929). His first ch. was a new version of Stravinsky's *Renard* (1929). During these years with Diaghilev, emerged as the outstanding d. of his generation. B. dir. (and premier danseur étoile) of the Paris Opéra 1929–45, during which time the b. co. of the house was completely reorganized, and flourished in consequence. The many bs. he ch. during this period (mostly with himself in the leading male role) incl. *Creatures of Prometheus* (mus. Beethoven, 1929), *Bacchus and Ariadne* (mus. Roussel, 1931), *Salade* (mus. Milhaud), *L'après-midi d'un faune* (mus. Debussy), *Icare* (all 1935), *Harnasie* (mus. Szymanowski), *Le Roi nu* (mus. Françaix, both 1936), *David triomphant* (mus. Rieti), *Alexandre le Grand* (mus. P. Gaubert, both 1937), *Oriane et le Prince d'amour* (mus. F. Schmitt), *Le Cantique des cantiques* (mus. Honegger, both 1938), *Entre deux rondes* (mus. M. Samuel-Rousseau, 1940), *Le Chevalier et la damoiselle* (mus. Gaubert), *Istar* (mus. d'Indy), *Boléro* (mus. Ravel, all 1941), *Joan de Zarissa* (mus. Egk), *Les animaux modèles* (mus. Poulenc, both 1942), *Suite en blanc* (mus. Lalo, 1943), *Guignol et Pandore* (mus. Jolivet), and *Les Mirages* (mus. Sauguet, both 1944). Accused of collaboration during World War II; left Paris in 1944 to form Nouveau B. de Monte Carlo, for which he ch. *Aubade* (mus. Poulenc), *Dramma per musica* (mus. Bach), *Chota Roustaveli* (mus. Honegger and others), *La Péri* (mus. Dukas), *A Night on the Bare Mountain* (mus. Mussorgsky, all 1946), and *Nautéos* (mus. J. Leleu, 1947). Returned to Paris Opéra 1947–58, simultaneously working as guest-ch. in France and abroad. His new bs. for Paris Opéra incl. *Le Chevalier errant* (mus. Ibert), *Phèdre* (mus. Auric, both 1950), *Snow*

White (mus. M. Yvain, 1951), Firebird (mus. Stravinsky, 1954), Les Noces fantastiques (mus. Delannoy), and Romeo and Juliet (mus. Prokofiev, both 1955); also Daphnis and Chloe (mus. Ravel, Milan, 1948). Founded Paris Institut Chorégraphique in 1947 and Université de la Danse in 1957. Since 1959 worked freelance, occasionally returning to the Opéra. Was on many committees and juries. Undoubtedly the chief architect of modern Fr. b.; also a very outspoken author, publishing more than 25 books between 1935 and 1967, incl. Le Manifeste du Chorégraphe (1935), Diaghilev, History of Russian Ballet (both 1939), Traité de danse académique (1949), Vestris, Dieu de la danse (1950), Traité de chorégraphie (1952), Les trois grâces du XXe siècle (1957), and Ma Vie (1965). Though most of his bs. have fallen out of favour with today's audiences, he continued to play an important and influential role in Fr. b. circles. Member of the Académie des Beaux Arts (1968); Carina Ari Medal (1974).

BIBL.: 'Hommage à S.L.' (with check-list of roles and activities), Les Saisons de la danse (1970/2); J. Gruen, 'S.L.', in The Private World of Ballet (New York, 1975).

Life Guards on Amager, The (orig. Dan. title: Livjaegerne på Amager, also Eng. The King's Voluntary Corps on Amager). Ballet in 2 acts; ch. A. Bournonville; mus. W. Holm. Prod. 19 Feb. 1871, Royal Dan. B., Copenhagen. The b. is set at carnival time in 1808 on the island of Amager, near Copenhagen, where the voluntary corps is on duty awaiting an attack by the English; all kinds of flirtation take place between the locals and the soldiers. The protagonist is Edouard, a musician and lieutenant—obviously inspired by E. du Puy, a notorious Copenhagen singer, comp., and rake. Most recent revival in 1971.

Life of the Bee. Ballet in 1 act; ch. Humphrey; accompanied by offstage humming and only later by Hindemith's Kammermusik no. 1. Prod. 31 Mar. 1929, Humphrey-Weidman Group, Guild Th., New York. 'The dance falls without pause into four sections: the nurturing and birth of the new queen; the queen's coming to life; the battle between the new queen and the old, with the challenger victorious; and a dance of celebration presided over by the new queen ... Humphrey seemed to want the dancers not to look like people; the movement and the characteristic uses of the body in this dance are strange, distorted, often exaggeratedly large or abnormally fast and small' (M. B. Siegel). Revived for Juilliard D. Th., 1958, and by J. Trisler for Dans Co., 1975.

BIBL.: M. B. Siegel, in 'Four Works by Doris Humphrey', Ballet Review (vol. 7, no. 1).

Lifschitz, Alexander. See Livschitz.

Ligeti, György (b Dicsöszentmarton, 28 May 1923). Hung. composer. Has written no b. mus., but his concert mus. has often been used for d. purposes, incl. J. Flier's Nouvelles Aventures (1969),

Van Dantzig's Epitaph (Atmosphères and Volumina, 1969) and Ramifications (1973—also by Milloss in Per aspera, 1973), F. Adret's Requiem (1971), and Van Schayk's Past Imperfect (Lontano, 1971).

Light Fantastic. Ballet in 1 act; ch. Gore; mus. Chabrier; déc. Rowell. Prod. 25 May 1953, W. Gore B., Festival Th., Malvern, with Gore, de Lutry, Hinton. Using much of the same mus. as in Balanchine's Cotillon, the b. shows how a Go-getter, a Moon-gazer, and Three Hopefuls ruminate on what young men's fancy turns to in springtime; the objects of their dreams are large dolls suspended in mid-air. Often revived, also for Scottish Th. B. in 1970.

Light Up the Stars. See Allumez les étoiles.

Lilavati, Devi (b Calcutta, c. 1926). Indian dancer. Studied Bharata natyam with various gurus, incl. Krishna Rao and R. Gopal, whose co. she joined in 1947. Married Bengt Häger and now lives in Stockholm, from where her tours as a solo performer of classical Indian dances have taken her all over the world. Continued to study ch. at Stockholm Institute for Ch.; ch. Indian version of Rimsky-Korsakov's Sheherazade for Malmö Th. in 1969, and several contemporary bs. for Swed. TV. Carina Ari Gold Medal (1969); Indian Government Award (1973).

BIBL.: J. Pikula, 'Kurt Jooss's Dixit Dominus for L.', Dance Magazine (1981/8).

Limón, José (b Culiacán, 12 Jan. 1908, d Flemington, N.J., 2 Dec. 1972). Mex.-Amer. dancer, choreographer, and teacher. Studied with Humphrey and Weidman and d. with their co. 1930–40. Began to ch. in 1931. Toured with M. O'Donnell during the next few years. Married his cost. designer P. Lawrence in 1942. Appeared in recitals with B. Seckler and N. Charisse. Founded his J.L. Amer. D. Co. in 1947, which was immediately recognized as one of the outstanding modern d. troupes. Humphrey was artistic co-dir., and J. L., Koner, Currier, B. Jones, and Hoving the leading soloists. His most important works include The Moor's Pavane (mus. Purcell—also staged for numerous other cos.), La Malinche (mus. N. Lloyd, both 1949), The Exiles (mus. Schoenberg, 1950), The Traitor (mus. G. Schuller, 1954), There Is a Time (mus. Dello Joio), Emperor Jones (mus. Villa-Lobos, both 1956), Missa Brevis (mus. Kodály, 1958), I, Odysseus (mus. H. Aitken, 1962), and Carlota (no mus., 1972). Taught at Juilliard School and various colleges. Contributed 'An American Accent' to The Modern Dance (Middletown, Conn., 1965). One of the most distinguished personalities of the Amer. (and international) modern d. scene. After his death the co. continued on a co-operative basis, and is now under the artistic direction of C. Maxwell; it is now resident at the New York YM-YWHA.

BIBL.: S. J. Cohen (ed.), The Modern Dance: Seven Statements of Belief (Middletown, Conn., 1966);

S. J. Cohen, in *Doris Humphrey: An Artist First* (Middletown, Conn., 1972).

Linden, Anya (*née* Eltenton; *b* Manchester, 2 Jan. 1933). Brit. dancer. Studied with Koslov in Hollywood and at Sadler's Wells School. Joined Sadler's Wells B. in 1951, appointed soloist in 1954 and principal d. in 1958. Created roles in Ashton's *Variations on a Theme of Purcell* (1955), MacMillan's *Noctambules* (1956) and *Agon* (1958), and Cranko's *Prince of the Pagodas* (1957). Retired in 1965, but has since organized occasional b. galas for charity. Now Lady Sainsbury. Ed. (with C. Crisp and P. Williams), *Ballet Rambert: 50 Years and On* (London, 1981).

Lindgren, Robert (*b* Vancouver, 1923). Can.-Amer. dancer and teacher. Studied in Vancouver and with Vilzak, Swoboda, Schwezoff, and Preobrajenska. D. with B. Russe de Monte Carlo, Danilova's co., and New York City B. 1957–9. He and his wife, Sonya Tyven, then founded a school in Phoenix, Ariz. Is now dir. of the d. department at N. Carolina School of Arts in Winston-Salem, where he is also in charge of the N. Carolina D. Th.

Linke, Susanne (*b* Lüneburg, 19 June 1944). Ger. dancer and choreographer. Studied at Berlin Mary Wigman Studio 1964–7 and at Folkwang School Essen 1967–70. D. with Folkwang D. Studio 1970–3, collaborating with P. Bausch, G. Cébron, G. Caciuleanu, and G. Bohner. Now a ch. of the Folkwang D. Studio, her bs. incl. *L'histoire obscure* (var. mus., 1975), *Satie* (1977), *The Next One, Please!* (pop mus., 1978), and *Ballet of Women* (medieval mus., 1981). Third Prize (Bagnolet, 1975), Prize of Jury (Cologne, 1975), Folkwang Prize (Essen, 1978).

Linn, Bambi (*b* Brooklyn, 26 Apr. 1926). Amer. dancer and actress. Studied with Mordkin, Anderson-Ivantzova, Platova, Holm, and B. Arts School. Created Aggie in *Oklahoma!* (1943) and Louise in *Carousel* (1945). Appeared and toured with her first husband Rod Alexander. D. as a guest soloist with Amer. B. Th. in 1959. Has since appeared on Broadway and in TV shows.

Lippincott, Gertrude (*b* St. Paul, 1913). Amer. dancer, choreographer, and teacher. Studied with Jan Veen, Leslie Burrowes, Graham, Humphrey, Weidman, Holm, Horst and Daganova. Joined Univ. of Minnesota D. Group in the early 1930s. Toured the country giving solo-recitals and lectures. Founded her Modern D. Center in Minneapolis in 1937.

Lisbon. Dance was very popular here with the Portug. kings of the 15th and 16th century; 16 d. schools were listed in 1550. During the Span. occupation, d. was restricted to Jesuit th. perfs. In the 1730s and 40s b. perfs. were given by guests from Paris and Vienna, but after the earthquake of 1755 all such th. activities were restricted, though some Noverre bs. were staged by his pupils at individual op. perfs. The San Carlos op. house opened in 1793, with 2 bs. by G. Gioja: *La Felicita Lusitana* and *Gli Dispetti amorosi.* Pietro Angiolini and Giuseppe Cagiani later became b. masters, ch. bs. with real soldiers on stage. Local first prods. of *La Sylphide* (1838) and *Giselle* (with A. Maywood, 1843) were not successful; *Giselle* was only accepted when K. Lanner and her troupe came to L. in 1870. Saint-Léon, who worked here 1854–6 (giving the première of his *Il Saltarello*), fared better, but neither C. Blasis nor Cecchetti enjoyed much success. In the 20th century L. was increasingly visited by foreign cos.; but even the Diaghilev co. had some difficulty in surviving when it had to spend 1917–18 in L. because of the First World War. The Verde-Gaio was founded with government aid in 1940; it started as a folklore troupe and later worked under I. Cramér, though it never gained any real importance. The *Gulbenkian B. (founded in 1965) pursued a traditional, rather Eng.-orientated course under the dir. of W. Gore; M. Sparemblek was its dir. 1970–75, and greater emphasis is now placed on the modern d. element of the repertory. Though the city is regularly visited by leading foreign b. cos. and modern d. troupes, they have stimulated little local creativity.

BIBL.: J. Sasportes, 'Feasts and Folias: The Dance in Portugal', *Dance Perspectives* 42; Sasportes, *História da Dança em Portugal* (L., 1970).

Liška, Ivan (*b* Prague, 8 Nov. 1950). Czech dancer. Studied at d. dept. of Prague Conservatory 1964–9. D. with Düsseldorf B. 1969–74, Munich State Op. B. as a soloist 1974–7 and since 1977 as a principal d. with Hamburg State Op. B. Created roles in Neumeier's *Midsummer Night's Dream,* Bohner's *Triadic Ballet* (both 1977), and *St. Matthew Passion* (1981). Married to the d. Colleen Scott.

Liszt, Ferenc (or Franz; *b* Raiding, 22 Oct. 1811, *d* Bayreuth, 31 July 1886). Hung. composer. Wrote no b. mus., but his concert mus. has often been used for d. purposes, incl. Fokine's *Les Préludes* (for Pavlova co., 1913—also by St. Denis, 1928), Nijinska's *Hamlet* (1934), E. Brada's *Carnival in Pest* (the *Hung. Rhapsodies*, 1930), T. Gsovsky's *Orphée* (1955—also by Milloss, 1966), and P. Darrell's *Othello* (first movement of *Faust Symphony*, 1973). Special arrangements of his mus. were made for Nijinska's *Le Bien-aimée* (1928), Ashton's *Mephisto Waltz* (1934), *Apparitions* (1936), *Dante Sonata* (1940), *Vision of Marguerite* (1952) and *Marguerite and Armand* (1963), and for MacMillan's *Mayerling* (1978).

Littlefield, Catherine (*b* Philadelphia, 1905, *d* Chicago, 19 Nov. 1951). Amer. dancer. choreographer, teacher, and b. director. Studied with her mother Caroline L. in Philadelphia, then with Kobeleff, L. Albertieri, Staats, and Egorova. Début on Broadway 1920. Started to teach at her mother's school and d. in local perfs. of the Grand

Op. Co. Founded C.L. B. Co. in 1934, from which the Philadelphia B. emerged in 1936 (the first b. co. exclusively made up of Amer. dancers). She was ballerina and ch., and presented the first Amer. full-length prod. of *Sleeping Beauty* (1937). Took the co. to Paris, Brussels, and London in 1937. From 1938 until it disbanded in 1942 it was the resident b. co. of the Chicago Civic Op. Co. She continued to teach, and is considered one of the pioneers of b. in Amer.; *Barn Dance* (traditional Amer. mus., 1937) is her most successful b. Her many pupils included K. Conrad, D. Krupska, Z. Solov, and E. Caton. Also ch. Sonja Henje's ice revues 1942–8.

Little Humpbacked Horse, The. See *Humpbacked Horse, The.*

Little Mermaid, The (orig. Dan. title: *Den lille Havfrue*). Fairy Ballet in 3 acts; libr. J. Lehmann; ch. Beck; mus. Fini Henriques; déc. T. Petersen. Prod. 26 Dec. 1909, Royal Dan. B., Copenhagen, with E. Price. The b. is based on Andersen's fairy-tale. New version by H. Lander (1936).

Little Stork, The (orig. Russ. title: *Aistyonok*— also Eng. *The Baby Stork*). Ballet in 3 acts; ch. A Radunsky, Lev Pospekhin, and N. Popko; mus. Dmitry Klebanov; déc. R. Makarov, T. Diakova, and V. Zimin. Prod. 6 June 1937 as graduation perf. of Bolshoi B. School, Bolshoi Filial Th., Moscow. The b. tells of how a lost baby stork is rescued and brought up by some pioneers, and how an African Negro boy escapes the exploiters at home and comes to the U.S.S.R. where he finds shelter, love, and kindness. In the first perf. Plisetskaya created the role of the cat. The b. has often been revived in different versions (also by Grigorovich, 1948).
BIBL.: M. G. Swift, in *The Art of the Dance in the U.S.S.R.* (Notre Dame, Ind., 1968).

Liturgie. A ballet planned by Massine for the Diaghilev co. in 1914–5, but never performed. Stravinsky was asked to compose the mus., but never did; Diaghilev then experimented with Filippo Marinetti's Futurist Orchestra, which was to have accompanied 6 or 7 parts of the Byzantine Mass, with Sokolova as Mary and Massine as Archangel Gabriel. Only Goncharova's marvellous icon-derived costume designs survive.
BIBL.: L. Massine, in *My Life in Ballet* (London, 1968).

Litz, Katherine (*b* Denver, 1918, *d* New York, 19 Dec. 1978). Amer. dancer, choreographer, and teacher. Studied with Humphrey, Weidman, Horst, Platonova, and Richard Thomas. Began dancing with Humphrey and Weidman in 1936, then with de Mille and on Broadway. Embarked on a career as teacher and ch. in 1948. In her solo dances she showed a rare gift for satire. Contributed 'Thought and Inner Harangue' to *Dance Perspectives* 38.
BIBL.: M. B. Siegel, in *At the Vanishing Point* (New York, 1972); E. Kendall, 'K.L.: Daughter of Virtue', *Ballet Review* (vol. VII, 2 and 3).

Livio, Antoine (*b* Lausanne, 10 Apr. 1937). Swiss writer on dance. Educated at Lausanne univ. and Sorbonne. D. critic of *Art et Danse* since 1963 and of *Tribune de Lausanne* since 1965. Producer of d. programmes for Radio Suisse and RTF. Chief editor of the short-lived *Danse Perspective*. Author of *Etoiles et Ballerines* (Biel, 1965), *Béjart* (Lausanne, 1969).

Livjaegerne på Amager. See *Life Guards on Amager, The.*

Livry, Emma (orig. E.-Marie Emarot; *b* Paris, 24 Sep. 1842, *d* Neuilly, 26 July 1863). Fr. dancer. Studied with Mme Dominique and became the special protegée of M. Taglioni, who hoped to make E.L. her successor; she d. in *La Sylphide* in 1858. Taglioni commissioned Offenbach's *Le Papillon* and ch. it for her in 1860. At the dress-rehearsal of a new prod. of *La Muette de Portici* in 1862 her dress caught fire and she was severely burned, and died 8 months later.
BIBL.: I. Guest, in *The Ballet of the Second Empire 1858–70* (London, 1953).

Livschitz, Alexander Grigorievich (*b* Leningrad, 5 Aug. 1932). Sov. dancer. Studied at Leningrad Ch. School, graduating in 1954. Joined Kirov B. and became one of the outstanding character soloists. Jacobson ch. *Dance of Baba Yaga* for him. Emigrated to Israel 1980.

Ljung, Viveka (*b* Stockholm, 1935). Swed. dancer. Studied at Royal Swed. B. School; joined Royal Swed. B. in 1952, and became soloist. D. with Amer. B. Th. in 1961 and Dutch National B. in 1962, after which she returned to her home co.

Lland, Michael (*b* Bishopville, S.C., *c.* 1925). Amer. dancer and b. master. Studied with Schwezoff, Craske, and School of Amer. B. Début on Broadway in *Song of Norway*. D. with Teatro Municipal in Rio de Janeiro; joined Amer. B. Th. as a soloist in 1949, becoming principal d. in 1956 and b. master in 1971.

Lloyd, Gweneth (*b* Eccles, 1901). Brit. teacher and choreographer. Studied at Ginner-Mawer School of D. in London. Went to Can., where she and Betty Farrally founded the Can. School of B. in Winnipeg and the Winnipeg B. (now the Royal Winnipeg B.) in 1938, for which she ch. many bs. until 1958. Opened another school in Toronto in 1950.

Lloyd, Margaret (*b* South Braintree, Mass., 1887, *d* Brookline, Mass., 29 Feb. 1960). Amer. critic and writer on the dance. D. critic of the *Christian Science Monitor* from 1936 until her death. Author of *Borzoi Book of Modern Dance* (1949), which has become one of the classics of Amer. d. literature.
BIBL.: D. Hering, 'M.L.: A Search for Human Values', *Dance Magazine* (1969/9–10).

Lloyd, Maude (*b* Cape Town, 16 Aug. 1908). Brit. dancer and critic. Studied with H. Webb and Rambert, and became one of the first Rambert dancers in 1927. Promoted ballerina, and remained with B. Rambert until 1938, when she became co-dir. of Tudor's London B. Created roles in Tudor's *Cross-Gartered* (1931), *The Descent of Hebe* (1935), *Jardin aux lilas* (1936), *Dark Elegies* (1937), and *Gala Performance* (1938), and Howard's *La Fête étrange* (1940). Has also d. with Markova-Dolin B. Wrote, with her husband Nigel Gosling, under the pseudonym Alexander Bland, for *Ballet* and as d. critic for *The Observer* since 1955.

Loggenburg, Dudley von (*b* Port Elizabeth, S.A., 13 Jan. 1945). Brit. dancer. Studied with Dawn Somerton, N. Kiss, and at Arts Educational School. Joined London Festival B. in 1962, becoming soloist in 1964 and principal d. in 1970. Has also taught in Rhodesia and at local schools in London and the regions. Married to the former d. Christine J. M. Hughes.

Lommel, Daniel (*b* Paris, 26 Mar. 1943). Fr. dancer. Studied with Kiss. Started to d. with Charrat in 1962. Joined Hamburg State Op. in 1964 and B. of the 20th Century in 1967 and later became one of its outstanding soloists. Created roles in Béjart's *Bhakti, Mass for the Present Time* (both 1967), *Baudelaire* (1968), *Les Vainqueurs, Actus tragicus* (both 1969), *Nijinsky, Clown de dieu* (1971), *Tombeau* (1973), *'I Trionfi' di Petrarca* (1974), and *Pli selon pli* (1975). Has done occasional ch. Artistic Dir. of Aenon D. Th. in Athens since 1980.
BIBL.: S. Goodman, 'D.L.', *Dance Magazine* (1972/3).

London. Ballet was brought to L. by Fr. and Ital. dancers and d.-masters in the 17th and 18th centuries. John Weaver, a d.-master and writer from Shrewsbury, and John Rich, whose Harlequin pantomimes at the Th. of Lincoln's Inn Fields were very popular, were the earliest b. personalities in L. Rich brought Marie Sallé and her brother to L. in 1725, and Handel was very impressed by their art. A. Vestris and Noverre were very successful at the King's Th. and Drury Lane, and Didelot worked at the King's 1796–1800. But an attempt to have an Eng. b. master, Louis D'Egville, and Eng. dancers and to establish an Eng. Academy of dancing at the King's Th. failed and foreign artists continued to be used. Blasis was b. master at the King's Th. 1830–40. M. Taglioni's 1830 début brought romantic b. to L., and it eventually became one of the world capitals of b. Perrot was b. master at Her Majesty's Th. under B. Lumley 1842–8; he created his famous *Pas de quatre* for Taglioni, Cerrito, Grisi, and Grahn there in 1845. After Lumley's resignation b. suffered a severe setback. During the later decades of the 19th century d. enthusiasts were restricted to the music-hall fare of the Alhambra and Empire Ths. K. Lanner and Genée

were very successful. At the turn of the century Russ.-orientated cos. started to arrive; the climax was the regular seasons of the Diaghilev co. and its various successors. This proved a lasting stimulus to Brit. b., and in 1930 the Camargo Society (a club) was founded, commissioning many creations and drawing its dancers largely from the newly formed co. of Marie Rambert and from the school and troupe established by N. de Valois at the Old Vic, which became successively the Vic-Wells, Sadler's Wells, and now the Royal B. During and after the Second World War local activities increased considerably. Numerous new cos. were formed, and although many were short-lived, they made L. one of the most creative d.-cities of the world. B. cos. and modern d. troupes from all over the world were eager to appear in L., and in the early 1980s it is clearly the most vital and sophisticated b. capital of Eur., if not of the world. For the history of the individual cos. see the entries *Alhambra Ballets, Camargo Society, Ballet Rambert, Empire Ballets, London Festival Ballet, International Ballet, Metropolitan Ballet, New London Ballet,* and *Royal Ballet,* and the various entries under *London*.
BIBL.: I. Guest, *The Romantic Ballet in England* (London, 1954); Guest, *The Alhambra Ballet* (New York, 1959); Guest, *The Empire Ballet* (London, 1962); C. W. Beaumont, *The Diaghilev Ballet in London* (London, 1940); M. Clarke, *Dancers of the Mercury* (London, 1962); J. Percival, *Modern Ballet* (London, 1970—covering the period from 1956); P. Williams, 'The 21 Years That Changed British Ballet', covering 1950–71, *Dance and Dancers* (1970/12 to 1972/3); A. Bland, *The Royal Ballet* (London, 1981).

London Ballet (W. Gore). The comp., founded by Gore, with Hinton as ballerina, gave its first perf. on 28 July 1961 at Hintlesham Hall, nr. Ipswich, and then appeared at the Edinburgh Festival, after which it toured extensively in Britain and abroad. The repertory consisted of such classics as *Giselle*, second act *Swan Lake, Nutcracker,* and *Les Sylphides* (mounted by Gore), and *Eaters of Darkness, The Night and the Silence, The Fair Maid, Light Fantastic, Peepshow, Shindig,* and *Rencontre* (ch. Gore). It disbanded in 1963.

London Ballet, The (A. Tudor). After Tudor had left B. Rambert, he joined de Mille to form D. Th., which performed at Oxford Playhouse. This became The London B. in Dec. 1938, and appeared in London at Toynbee Hall with a number of bs. which Tudor had ch. for B. Rambert, incl. *Jardin aux lilas* and *Dark Elegies,* and new works such as *Judgment of Paris, Soirée musicale,* and *Gala Performance.* Among the better known dancers were P. Clayden, G. Larsen, M. Lloyd, P. van Praagh, H. Laing, and D. Paltenghi. When Tudor and Laing left for New York, Lloyd and van Praagh became co-directors, and under them Lester's *Pas des déesses* and Howard's *La Fête* *étrange* entered the repertory. In June 1940 the co. merged with the B. Rambert.

London City Ballet. A classically based co. with Harold King as artistic dir., formed in 1978 with eight ds. for lunch-time perfs., extended by 1981 to about 20 ds. touring Britain for much of year. M. St. Claire and M. Beare are principal ds., with frequent guests for short engagements, and with a repertory of excerpts from classics (taught by Beriosova and others) and some original works. M. Gielgud, formerly guest d. and artistic adviser, became rehearsal dir. from 1981.

London Contemporary Dance Theatre. The co., which is governed by the *Contemporary D. Trust, gave its first perf. in East Grinstead in Oct. 1967 as the C.D. Group. Its London headquarters is The Place, where most of its early perfs. were given from 1969, and which also houses the L. Contemp. Dance School. It is modern-d. orientated, and enjoys a close connection with the New York M. Graham School and co. Artistic dir. is R. Cohan, and its dancers have incl. N. Lapzeson, R. Powell, W. Louther, and R. North. The repertory has incl. works by Graham, Sokolow, P. Taylor, and Ailey, and has brought a new generation of creative talent to professionalism in the work of R. Alston, S. Davies, R. North, and others. American debut at Amer. D. Festival, New London, 1977.

BIBL.: J. Percival, 'L.C.D.T.', *Dance Magazine* (1975/11).

London Dance Theatre. The co., founded by the d.-designer N. McDowell, made its début on 22 June 1964 at the Newcastle Th. Royal. Its repertory of specially created bs. incl. J. Carter's *Agrionia*, Charrat's *La Répétition de Phèdre*, Howard's *The Tempest*, and T. Gilbert's *Rave Britannia*. Among its dancers were B. Wright, J. Graeme, Y. Meyer, V. Karras, G. Sibbrit, I. Dragadze, and H. Davel. It disbanded about a year later after a London season.

London Festival Ballet. Originally called just Festival B., the London-based co. changed its name first to London's F.B. and in 1968 to London F.B. It came from a co. Markova and Dolin assembled around themselves upon their return from Amer. in 1949. Under the direction of Dr Julian Braunsweg with Dolin as art. dir. it made its début on 24 Oct. 1950 at the London Stoll Th., with Markova, Dolin, Gilpin, Krassov-

The London Contemporary Dance Theatre (Giraudeau) in North's *Troy Game*.
Photo Anthony Crickmay.

ska, Cheselka, Landa, Dale, and Godfrey as the top soloists and Massine, Lichine, and Riabouchinska as guest stars. From its very beginning the co. aimed for popular appeal, based on a repertory of box-office hits and guest stars. With its regular seasons in London (mostly at the Royal Festival Hall, but also at the Coliseum and the New Victoria Th.), its extensive regional tours, and its long continental and overseas tours, it gradually acquired a very wide following. It repeatedly faced bankruptcy, but was always saved at the last minute by various changes of its ownership status. Dolin resigned the artistic direction in 1962, being succeeded by Gilpin 1962–4, after which Braunsweg continued alone until 1965, when he was forced to resign. Donald Albery then ran the co. for three years, being succeeded by B. Grey 1968–79, followed by J. Field 1979–84, since when P. Schaufuss has taken over. Apart from the above-mentioned dancers its most popular dancers have incl. Arova, B. Wright, Briansky, Polajenko in early days, with Chauviré, Danilova, Slavenska, Toumanova, Verdy, and Miskovitch as guests; later T. Lander, Burr, Borowska, Aldous, Fulton, D. Richards, Samsova, Miklosy, Flindt, Musil, Dubreuil, Schaufuss; and most recently Evdokimova, Gielgud, Ruanne, Breuer, Clarke, with Terabust and P. Bart as frequent guests. The repertory is based on the standard classics. Remarkable successes have been Charnley's *Symphony for Fun* (1952), Lander's *Etudes* (1954), J. Carter's *The Witch Boy* (1957), and Dolin's *Variations for Four* (1957). A speciality of the repertory is the staging of full-length bs. such as Charnley's *Alice in Wonderland* (1953), Beriozoff's *Esmeralda* (1954), Bourmeister's *The Snow Maiden* (1961—the first version for any western co. by Sov. ch. & designers), Orlikowsky's *Peer Gynt* (1963), J. Carter's *Beatrix* (or *La jolie fille de Gand*, 1966), W. Borkowski's *Don Quixote* (1970), Nureyev's *The Sleeping Beauty* (1975), and Schaufuss's *La Sylphide* (1979).
BIBL.: J. Braunsweg, *Braunsweg's Ballet Scandals* (London, 1973).

Lopez, Pilar (*b* San Sebastian, 4 June 1912). Span. dancer and choreographer. Studied with Julia Castelão in Madrid, dancing with the co. of her sister (Argentinita) until 1945. Formed her own co. B. Español, in 1946, with J. Greco and M. Vargas among its dancers (who later started troupes of their own). She has toured extensively with the co. Much admired as a d. for her nobility, vitality, musicality, and stylishness. She is also an important ch.; bs. include de Falla's *Le Tricorne* and *El amor brujo*, E. Halffter's *L'Espagnolade* and *El Cojo enamorado,* J. Rodrigo's *Concierto de Aranjuez*, and Debussy's *Préludes et images.*

Lopokov, Andrei Vasilievich (also Lopukhov; *b* St. Petersburg, 8 Aug. 1898, *d* Leningrad, 23 May 1947). Russ. dancer and teacher. Brother of Lydia and Fyodor L. Studied at the Imperial B. School, graduating in 1916. Member of the

Maryinsky Th. until 1945; became one of its outstanding character dancers. Espada (*Don Quixote*), Nur-Ali (*Fountain of Bakhchisaray*), and Mercutio were his best roles. Started to teach in 1927. Co-author of *Fundamentals of Character Dancing* (Leningrad, 1934). Merited Artist of the R.S.F.S.R., (1939).

Lopokov, Fyodor Vasilievich (also Lopukhov; *b* St. Petersburg, 19 Oct. 1886, *d* Leningrad, 28 Jan. 1973). Russ. dancer, choreographer, and teacher. Brother of Lydia and Andrei L. Studied at the Imperial B. Academy, graduating in 1905. Joined the Maryinsky Th. and became one of its outstanding character dancers. Studied further with Gorsky in Moscow in 1909. D. with his sister and with Pavlova in America in 1910. Rejoined Maryinsky Th. and remained with the co. until 1970; dir. 1922–30, 1944–7, and 1955–8. Started Evenings of Young B. with Slonimsky in 1921. First dir. of Leningrad Maly Th. B. 1931–6. Started to ch. in 1916 and became one of the leading avant-garde choreographers of his generation. His experimental prods. caused much controversy, but he was also much admired as 'a choreographer for choreographers', and as a custodian of the classical tradition through his prods. of such bs. as *Sleeping Beauty, Raymonda, Nutcracker, Harlequinade, Coppélia,* and *Swan Lake.* His b. creations include *Firebird* (mus. Stravinsky, 1921), *Dance Symphony* (mus. Beethoven's Fourth Symphony, 1923), *The Red Whirlwind* (mus. V. Deshevov, 1924), *The Ice Maiden* (mus. Grieg, 1927), *The Bolt* (mus. Shostakovich, 1931), *The Bright Stream* (mus. Shostakovich, 1935), *Taras Bulba* (mus. Soloviev-Sedoy, 1940), and *Pictures from an Exhibition* (mus. Mussorgsky, 1963). Dir. of the ch. faculty at Leningrad Conservatory 1962–7. Author of 'The Greatness of Creation' (*Dance Symphony,* 1923), *Paths of Ballet* (1925), *Sixty Years in Ballet* (1966), and *Choreographic Confessions* (1971). Father of the d. Vladimir L. Merited Artist of the R.S.F.S.R. (1939); Merited B. Master.
BIBL.: L. Yoffe, 'The L. Dynasty', *Dance Magazine* (1967/1); N. Roslavleva, in *Era of the Russian Ballet* (London, 1966); M. G. Swift, in *The Art of the Dance in the U.S.S.R.* (Notre Dame, Ind., 1968).

Lopokova, Lydia Vasilievna (also Lopukhova; *b* St. Petersburg, 19 Oct. 1891, *d* Seaford, 8 June 1981). Russ.-Brit. dancer. Sister of Andrei and Fyodor L. Studied at the Imperial B. School, graduating in 1909. Joined the Diaghilev co. in 1910 and remained until it was disbanded, apart from individual tours with Volinine, Mordkin, Massine, Sokolova, de Valois, and Woizikovsky. A brilliant demicaractère ballerina, she created roles in Massine's *Les Femmes de bonne humeur, Parade* (both 1916), and *Boutique Fantasque* (1919)—also *Beau Danube* (1924); one of the Auroras of the *Sleeping Princess* prod. in 1921. A founding member of the Camargo Society. Created the Tango in Ashton's *Façade* (1931), and

d. Swanilda with the Vic-Wells B. in 1932. Founded the Cambridge Arts Th. with her husband Lord Keynes (the economist), in 1936. BIBL.: L. Yoffe, 'The L. Dynasty', *Dance Magazine* (1967/1).

Lorca, Federico García. See *García Lorca, Federico.*

Lorcia, Suzanne (*b* Paris, 18 Dec. 1902). Fr. dancer and teacher. Studied with Zambelli. Joined the Opéra and became étoile in 1931. Created roles in many Lifar bs., incl. *Creatures of Prometheus* (1929), *Salade* (1935), *Le Roi nu* (1936), *Alexandre le Grand* (1937), *Aeneas* (1938), *Boléro* (1941), *Les Animaux modèles* (1942), and *Guignol et Pandore* (1944). Retired in 1950, but continued to teach at Opéra School.

Loring, Eugene (*b* Milwaukee, 1914, *d* Kingston, N.Y., 30 Aug. 1982). Amer. dancer, choreographer, and teacher. Studied at School of Amer. B.; began dancing with Fokine's co. in 1934. Joined Amer. B. in 1936 and created roles in Balanchine's *Alma Mater* and *Card Game*. Started to ch. for B. Caravan in 1936; *Yankee Clipper* (mus. P. Bowles, 1937) and *Billy the Kid* (mus. Copland, 1938) were his biggest successes. Created *The Great American Goof* (mus. H. Brant) for B. Th's inaugural perf., 1940. Formed his own group, D. Players, in 1941. After a period on Broadway he went to Los Angeles in the mid-1940s, where he opened his Amer. School of D. He contributed the ch. to many films, incl. *Meet Me in Las Vegas* (1955), *Funny Face* (1956), and *Silk Stockings* (1956). His later bs. include *Capital of the World* (mus. Antheil, Amer. B. Th. 1953) and several musical prods. Sold his school in 1974 to concentrate on his duties as chairman of the d. dept. at Univ. of Cal., Irvine. D. Magazine Award (1967). BIBL.: 'To E.L.', *Dance Magazine* (1968/4); see also *Dance Magazine* (1968/6, p. 90/92).

Lorrayne, Vyvyan (*b* Pretoria, 20 Apr. 1939). S. A. dancer. Studied with Salamon, Faith de Villiers, and Royal B. School. Joined Cov. Gdn. Op. B. in 1957 and Royal B. in the same year; appointed principal d. in 1967. Created roles in Ashton's *Monotones* (1965), *Jazz Calendar*, and *Enigma Variations* (both 1968), Layton's *The Grand Tour* (1971) and *O. W.* (1972), Hynd's *In a Summer Garden* (1972) and *Charlotte Brontë* (1974), Wright's *Arpège* and *El amor Brujo* (both 1975), and D. Bintley's *Meadow of Proverbs* (1979). Resigned in 1979.

Los Angeles Ballet. The co. first performed in 1974. J. Clifford is its Artistic Dir., principal ch., and star d. He ch. many of its bs; the rest of the repertory consists of bs. by Balanchine and others. Principal dancers incl. Johnna Kirkland and Polly Shelton. No longer active.

Losch, Tilly (*b* Vienna, 15 Nov. *c.* 1904, *d* New York, 24 Dec. 1975). Austrian dancer and actress. Studied at Court Op. B. School. Member of Vienna State Op. B. 1921–8; created her first solo-role in Kröller's *Schlagobers* (1924). Also appeared in straight plays at the Burg Th., and in Reinhardt's Salzburg prod. of *A Midsummer Night's Dream* in 1927, for which she also did the ch. Toured with Reinhardt and Kreutzberg. Married an Englishman, Edward James, who financed Les Bs. 1933. Created the leading roles in Balanchine's *Errante* and *The Seven Deadly Sins* with this co. Later concentrated on acting in plays and films, and on painting. Was subsequently married to the Earl of Carnarvon.

Lost Illusions (orig. Russ. title: *Utrachennye illyuzii*). Ballet in 3 acts and 13 scenes; libr. and déc. V. Dmitriev; ch. Zakharov; mus. Asafiev. Prod. 31 Dec. 1935, GATOB, Leningrad, with Ulanova, Vetcheslova, Sergeyev, Chaboukiani. Inspired by Balzac's novel *Splendeurs et misères des courtisanes*, the b. is centred on the poor Fr. comp. Lucien, who loves a ballerina, but leaves her for a rival in order to get his b. performed. A different version by Jacobson for Sverdlovsk (1936). BIBL.: M. G. Swift. in *The Art of the Dance in the U.S.S.R.* (Notre Dame, Ind., 1968).

Louis, Murray (*b* New York, 4 Nov. 1926). Amer. dancer, choreographer, and teacher. Educated New York Univ. Studied with Halprin and Nikolais. Nikolais' closest collaborator at Henry St. Playhouse from 1949. Since the mid-1950s he has also taught and ch., and now has his own co. which toured Europe for the first time in 1972. A very witty and often comic ch. who likes to work with isolated movements of the individual limbs. His bs. include *Calligraph for Martyrs* (1962), *Junk Dances* (1964), *Proximities* (1969), *Index to Necessary Neuroses* (1973), *Porcelain Dialogues* (1974), *Sheherazade* (full-length version, 1975), *Moment* (mus. Ravel, String Quartet, Scottish B., 1975), and *The City* (1980). Has also produced film series *Dance as an Art Form* (1972) and *The Body as an Instrument*. Contributed 'Forward is not Always Going Ahead' to *Dance Perspectives* 38. Author of *Inside Dance* (New York, 1980). BIBL.: T. Tobias, 'Nikolais and L.: A New Space', *Dance Magazine* (1971/2); interview with M.L., *Dance and Dancers* (1972/5); M. Hodgson, 'M.L. Silver Anniversary', *Dance News* (1975/1).

Loup, Le. Ballet in 1 act; libr. Anouilh and G. Neveux; ch. Petit; mus. Dutilleux; déc. Carzou. Prod. 17 Mar. 1953, Bs. de Paris, Théâtre de l'Empire, Paris, with Petit, Verdy, Sombert, Reich. The b. tells of a bride who is tricked by her deceitful bridegroom into marrying a wolf; she falls in love with it and follows it into the forest, where they are hunted to death. Revived for Royal Dan. B. (1967) and for Paris Opéra (1975). Many individual versions in Ger. (Georgi, Walter, Keres, Cintolesi, etc.). BIBL.: C. Beaumont, 'L.L.', in *Ballets of Today* (London, 1954).

Louther, William (*b* New York, 22 Jan. 1942). Amer. dancer, choreographer, and teacher. Studied at High School of Performing Arts, Juilliard School, and with Graham. Started to d. in O'Donnell's co. in 1958. Appeared on Broadway. D. with the cos. of Ailey, Graham, and McKayle; created roles in McKayle's *District Storyville* (1959), Graham's *Circe* (1964) and *Archaic Hours* (1969). Joined London Contemporary D. Th. in 1969; created further roles in Cohan's *Side Scene* (1969) and *Stages* (1971), B. Moreland's *Kontakion* (1972). Ch. *Versalii Icones* (mus. Maxwell Davies, 1970) and *Divertissements: In the Playground of the Zodiac* (mus. G. Quincey), and taught. Dir. of Batsheva D. co. 1972–4, then of Welsh D. Th. 1975–6. Has since worked as a freelance.
BIBL.: G. Gow, 'Beyond the Mirror Image', *Dancing Times* (1970).

Løvenskjold, Herman Severin (*b* Holdenjernvärk, 30 July 1815, *d* Copenhagen, 5 Dec. 1870). Norweg.-Dan. composer. Wrote the mus. for Bournonville's *La Sylphide* (1836) and *The New Penelope* (1847), and was one of the composers of his *Fantasies* (1838).

Loves of Mars and Venus, The. Ballet d'action in 6 scenes; libr. and ch. J. Weaver; mus. Symonds and Firbank. Prod. 2 Mar. 1717, Drury Lane Th., London, with L. Dupré, Hester Santlow, and Weaver. The b., after introducing the gods individually, shows how Vulcan forges the net in which the Cyclops finally ensnares the two lovers. This is considered the first recorded b. d'action 'wherein the Passions were so happily expressed, and the whole story so intelligently told by the mute narration of gesture only, that even thinking Spectators allowed it both a pleasing and rational entertainment' (Colley Cibber). Extracts from it were recreated by M. Skeaping for 'The Twelfth Rose' programme of B. for All (1969).
BIBL.: L. Kirstein, 'T.L.o.M.a.V.' in *Movement & Metaphor* (New York, 1970).

Love, the Magician. See *Amor brujo, El.*

Lowski, Woytec (orig. Woiciech Wiesidlowski; *b* Brzesc, 11 Oct. 1939). Pol. dancer. Studied at Warsaw Op. B. School, also Leningrad Ch. School. Joined Warsaw Op. B. 1958; member of Ballet of the 20th Century 1966–71, Cologne 1972–3, and Boston B. since 1973. Created roles in Béjart's *Romeo and Juliet* (1966), *Baudelaire, Ni fleurs, ni couronnes* (both 1968), and *Actus tragicus* (1969), and L. Monreal's *Hamlet* (1975). Silver Medal (Varna, 1964).
BIBL.: N. McLain Stoop, 'W.L.', *Dance Magazine* (1976/6).

Lubitz, Monika (*b* Berlin, 3 June 1943). Ger. dancer. Studied at East Berlin State B. School and Leningrad Ch. School. Joined Leipzig Op. b. 1965 and was soon dancing leading roles in the bs. of Köhler-Richter. To Berlin Comic Op. 1969,

creating roles in Schilling's *Cinderella* and *Moor of Venice*. Appointed prima ballerina East Berlin Ger. State Op. in 1972.

Lubovitch, Lar (*b* Chicago, 1943). Amer. dancer and choreographer. Started to study painting, then d. at Juilliard School and with Sokolow, Danielian, and Graham. D. with the cos. of P. Lang (1964), Tetley, Butler, with Manhattan Festival B. and Harkness B. (1967–9). After working as a cost. and lighting designer for Falco and Ailey, formed his own group in 1968, while continuing to work as a guest ch. for Bat-Dor D. Co., Gulbenkian B., Dutch National B., B. Rambert, and Amer. B. Th. A very prolific ch., his list of bs. includes *Whirligogs* (mus. third movement of Berio's Sinfonia, 1970), *Some of the Reactions of Some of the People Some of the Time upon Hearing the Reports of the Coming of the Messiah* (mus. Handel, 1971), *Considering the Lilies* (mus. Bach, 1972), *Three Essays* (mus. Ives, 1974), *Marimba* (mus. St. Reich, 1977), *North Star* (mus. Ph. Glass, 1978), *Cavalcade* (mus. Reich, 1981).
BIBL.: N. McLain Stoop, 'A Human Being who Dances—L.L.', *Dance Magazine* (1972/4); interview with L.L., *Dance and Dancers* (1972/10); J. Gruen, 'L.L.', in *The Private World of Ballet* (New York, 1975); E. R. Luger, 'L.L.', *Dance Magazine* (1981/3).

Lucifer. Ballet in 1 act; libr. and ch. Graham; mus. Halim El-Dahb; set Leonardo Locsin; cost. Halston. Prod. 19 June 1975, M. Graham D. Co., Uris Th., New York, with Nureyev and Fonteyn. 'When Lucifer fell from the heavens, he became half god, half man, and he came to know man's fear and challenges' (Graham). The hero is seen not as Satan but as the bringer of light, paralleling the role of the artist.
BIBL.: R. Philp, 'The Graham Gala: An Historic Collaboration', *Dance Magazine* (1975/6).

Lüders, Adam (*b* Copenhagen, 16 Feb. 1950). Dan. dancer. Studied at Royal Dan. B. School. Joined Royal Dan. B. 1968. Principal d. of London Festival B. 1973–5. Principal d., New York City B., since 1975.

Lüdin, Fritz (*b* Switzerland, *c.* 1934). Swiss dancer. Studied with Chladek, L. Schubert, V. Gsovsky, K. Waehner, Limón, Tudor, Craske, and A. Hitchins. Performed with the J. Limón D. Co. 1963–8; created roles in Limón's *Choreographic Offering* (1964), *My Son, My Enemy* (1965), *The Winged* (1966), and *Psalm* (1967). Has toured with B. Jones and their joint *Dances we Dance* programme since 1964. Has taught at various Amer. colleges and univs. as well as in Eur; teaches at Jones-Lüdin school in Honolulu, Hawaii.

Ludlow, Conrad (*b* Hamilton, Mont. 1935). Amer. dancer. Studied at San Francisco B. School. Joined San Francisco B. 1953, and appointed principal d. 1955. Joined New York City B. 1957; promoted soloist 1960 and leading soloist 1961–

73. Created roles in Balanchine's *Liebeslieder Walzer, Monumentum pro Gesualdo, Tchaikovsky Pas de deux* (all 1960), *A Midsummer Night's Dream* (1962), *Brahms-Schoenberg Quartet* (1966), *Jewels* (1967), and *Suite No. 3* (1970). Appointed artistic dir. of Oklahoma City Met. B. in 1973. Married to the d. Joyce Feldman.

Luigi (orig. Eugene Louis Facciuto; *b* Steubenville, 20 Mar. 1925). Amer. dancer and teacher. Studied with Bolm, Nijinska, Caton, Loring, and Panaieff. Originally a tap d., appearing in ths., films, night-clubs, TV prods. 1949–61. Began to teach in 1951; developed his own system of jazz d. technique, from which the L. Jazz Center emerged in New York.
BIBL.: N. McLain Stoop, 'L.', *Dance Magazine* (1973/1).

Luipart, Marcel (orig. M. Fenchel; *b* Mulhouse, 8 Sep. 1912). Ger.-Austrian dancer, choreographer, b. master, and teacher. Studied with Eduardova, V. Gsovsky, and Legat. Début Düsseldorf in 1933. D. with the cos. in Hamburg, Berlin, and Munich. Joined B. Russe de Monte Carlo in 1938/9. Continued to d. in Milan and Rome and during World War II with the co. of Derra de Moroda. B. master Munich State Op. 1946–8, where he ch. many bs., incl. first prod. of Egk's *Abraxas* (1948). D. with the cos. in Frankfurt, Wiesbaden, and Düsseldorf. B. master Bonn 1957–8, Essen 1958–9, Cologne 1959–61. Taught in Vienna at the d. dept. of the Academy of Mus. and Th.; became dir. 1973. Ch. the first prods. of bs. written by the Ger. novelist G. Grass: *Die bösen Köche* (1957), *Stoffreste* (1959), and *Die Vogelscheuchen* (1970.)

Luisillo (orig. Luis Perez Davila; *b* Mexico City, 1928). Mexican dancer and choreographer. Studied classical and Span. d.; joined Amaya's co. in 1948. Formed his own co., with Teresa, which disbanded in 1954. Founded his second co., L. and his Th. of Span. D., in 1956, touring the world. A splendid stylist as a d., he is also a ch. of dramatically highly charged bs., including *Llanto por un torero,* inspired by García Lorca.

Lukin, Serge (*b* Kiev, 6 Feb. 1953). Sov. dancer. Studied at Kiev B. School, graduating 1971. Joined Kiev b. co., subsequently appointed soloist. Gold Medal (Tokyo, 1978).

Lukom, Yelena Mikhailovna (*b* St. Petersburg, 5 May 1891, *d* Leningrad, 27 Feb. 1968). Sov. dancer and b. mistress. Studied at Imperial B. School, graduating in 1909. Became soloist of the Maryinsky Th. in 1912 and ballerina in 1920 and d. with the co. until 1941. Toured extensively with Boris Shavrov as her partner; they became the first couple to introduce the spectacular and athletic pas de deux which became so popular with the Sov. school of ch. B. mistress for the Kirov repertory 1953–65. Author of *My Work in*

Ballet (Leningrad, 1940). Merited Artist of the R.S.F.S.R. (1925).

Lully, Jean Baptiste (orig. Giambattista Lulli; *b* Florence, 29 Nov. 1632, *d* Paris, 22 Mar. 1687). Ital.-Fr. dancer, composer, conductor, and supervisor. Came to the court of Louis XIV as a d. and violinist. Appeared as a d. with the King in several bs., for which he comp. individual instrumental pieces. Became the King's favourite, and was appointed supervisor of the royal mus. in 1661 and dir. of the Académie Royal de Musique in 1672. He wielded enormous influence on all sorts of royal entertainment; he collaborated closely with de Benserade, Bérain, Beauchamp, Racine, and Molière, for whose plays he comp. numerous entrées. His works include: *La Nuit* (with the famous *B. de la nuit,* 1653), *Les Nopces de Pelée et de Thétis* (1654), *La Puissance de l'amour* (1656), *La Naissance de Vénus* (1665), *George Dandin* (1668), *Monsieur de Pourceaugnac* (1669), *Le Bourgeois gentilhomme* (1670), *Psyché* (1671), *Les Festes de l'Amour et de Bacchus* (1672), *Le Triomphe de l'amour* (1681), *Phaéton* (1683), *Amadis de Gaule* (1684), and *Le Temple de la paix* (1685).
BIBL.: M.-F. Christout, in *Le Ballet de cour de Louis XIV* (Paris, 1967).

Lumbye, Hans Christian (*b* Copenhagen, 2 May 1810, *d* there, 20 Mar. 1874). Dan. composer. Wrote the mus. for many Bournonville bs. (some with other composers), incl. *Napoli* (1842), *Conservatory* (1849), *La Ventana* (1854), *Far from Denmark* (1860), and *The Life Guards on Amager* (1871). Was called 'the Nordic Strauss'.

Lutry, Michel de (*b* 1924). French dancer, teacher, and b. master. Studied with Egorova. D. at Paris Th. du Châtelet. Joined International B. 1946. Member of various cos., with his wife, Domini Callaghan; also appeared on TV. B. master Munich Th. am Gärtnerplatz 1958–60, Zurich 1960–3, Dortmund 1963–6. In charge of Munich State Op. B. School 1966–75. Co-dir. of b. dept. at Munich State Academy of Mus., 1975.

Lynham, Deryck (*b* Maisons Laffitte, Fr., 1913, *d* Lausanne, 2 Nov. 1951). Brit. historian and writer on dance. Worked with B. Guild and was one of the founders of the London *Archives of the Dance.* Author of *Ballet Then and Now* (London, 1947) and *The Chevalier Noverre* (London, 1950).

Lynne, Gillian (*b* Bromley, 1926). Brit. dancer and choreographer. Studied at Royal Academy of Dancing and Cone-Ripman School. Started to d. with Arts Th. B. 1940, then with B. Guild and Sadler's Wells B. 1943–51. Joined Palladium Th. as principal d.; also appeared in films and musicals. Now works mainly as producer-ch. of musicals, operettas, etc. (*Cats,* 1981).

Lyon, Annabelle (*b* New York). Amer. dancer and teacher. Studied with M. and L. Fokine, Balanchine, Vilzak, Fedorova, Vladimirov. Joined Amer. B. 1935, and B. Th. 1940–3; created roles in Fokine's *Bluebeard,* de Mille's *Three Virgins and a Devil* (both 1941), and Tudor's *Pillar of Fire* (1942). Has also appeared on Broadway and taught in New York.

Lyric Suite. Ballet in 6 movements; ch. Sokolow; mus. Berg. Prod. 1953, B. de Bellas Artes, Mexico City. 'An abstract work in the modern idiom which explores the emotions in terms of dance' (A. Chujoy). New York première 1954, with McKayle, J. Duncan, B. Seckler, M. Anthony. A different version by J. Ulrich, Munich State Op., 1974.

Lysistrata Ballets. Aristophanes' comedy, about the Athenian wives who go on strike, has inspired various bs., e.g. by Tudor (mus. Prokofiev, London, 1932), R. Brada (mus. L. Lajhta, Budapest, 1937), G. Blank (mus. Blacher, Municipal Op. Berlin, 1951), and Darrell (mus. J. Dankworth, Western Th. B., 1964).

M

Maar, Lisl (*b* Vienna, 29 Sep. 1942). Austrian dancer. Studied at State Op. B. School, joining State Op. B. in 1956, appointed soloist in 1965. Created role in Nureyev's *Tancredi* (1966).

Macbeth Ballets. Shakespeare's tragedy has inspired various bs., e.g. by Le Picq (mus. Locke, London, 1785), Galeotti (mus. Schall, Copenhagen, 1816), Henry (mus. Pugni, Milan, 1830), Pistoni (mus. R. Strauss, Milan, 1969), and Vasiliev (mus. Molchanov, Moscow, 1980). Also a solo d. by O'Donnell, *The Queen's Obsession*.

McBride, Patricia (*b* Teaneck, N.J., 23 Aug. 1942). Amer. dancer. Studied with Ruth A. Vernon and School of Amer. B. D. with A. Eglevsky B. Co. 1958. Joined New York City B. 1959; appointed soloist 1960, principal d. 1961. Created roles in Balanchine's *Figure in the Carpet* (1960), *A Midsummer Night's Dream* (1962—also in the film version of 1966), *Tarantella* (1964), *Harlequinade* (1965), *Brahms-Schoenberg Quartet* (1966), *Jewels* (1967), *Who Cares?* (1970), *Divertimento from 'Le Baiser de la Fée'* (1972), *Coppélia* (1974), *The Steadfast Tin Soldier* and *Pavane pour une Infante défunte* (both 1975), and *Vienna Waltzes* (1977), and Robbins's *Dances at a Gathering* (1969), *The Goldberg Variations* (1971), *Dybbuk Variations* (1974), *The Four Seasons* and *Opus 19* (both 1979). Dance Magazine Award 1980. Married to the d. J. P. Bonnefoux.
BIBL.: A. Murphy, 'The M. Magic', *Ballet News* (1981/2).

McCabe, John (*b* Liverpool, 1939). Brit. composer, wrote mus. for S. Hywel's *The Teachings of Don Juan* (Northern D. Th., Manchester, 1973), P. Darrell's *Mary, Queen of Scots* (Scottish B., Glasgow 1976).

McDonagh, Don (*b* New York, 6 Feb. 1932). Amer. dance critic. Studied at Fordham Univ. D. reviewer *New York Times* 1967–77. Assoc. editor, *Ballet Review* since 1968. Contributor (Amer. section) to *Ballet for all* (London, 1970). Author of *The Rise and Fall and Rise of Modern Dance* (New York, 1970), *Martha Graham* (New York, 1973), and *The Complete Guide to Modern Dance* (New York, 1976).

Macdonald, Brian (*b* Montreal, 14 May 1928). Can. dancer, choreographer, and b. director. Educated Univ. of Montreal. Started to work as a mus.-critic while studying d. with Gerald Crevier and Elizabeth Leese. One of the orig. members of National B. of Canada 1951–3. After an injury concentrated on ch., first for TV and music-halls, then for Royal Winnipeg B. (*The Darkling*, mus.

Britten, 1958; *Les Whoops-de-Doo*, mus. D. Gillis, 1959; *Rose Latulippe*, mus. H. Freedman, 1966; *The Shining People of Leonard Cohen*, mus. Freedman, 1970); also worked for various other cos. (*Aimez-vous Bach?*, Banff School Festival B., 1962; *Time Out of Mind*, mus. P. Creston, Joffrey B., 1963; *Prothalamion*, mus. Delius, Norweg. B., 1963). Dir. of Royal Swed. B. 1964–66 (*While the Spider Slept*, mus. Karkov, 1965; *Firebird*, mus. Stravinsky, 1966), Harkness B. 1967–8 (*Zealous Variations*, mus. Schubert, 1967), Batsheva D. Co., 1971–2 (*Martha's Vineyard*, mus. Dello Joio, 1971). Artistic Dir. of Les Grands Bs. Canadiens since 1974. Recent bs. include *The Lottery* (mus. Stravinsky's *Sacre du printemps*, Harkness B., 1974) and *Variations on a Simple Theme* (mus. Beethoven's 'Diabelli Variations', Paris Opéra, 1974). Has also ch. mus. Married to the d. Annette av Paul-Wiedersheim.

McDonald, Elaine (*b* Tadcaster, 2 May 1943). Brit. dancer. Studied with Olivia Morley, Louise Brown, and Royal B. School. D. with Gore's London B. 1962. Joined Western Th. B. in 1964 and became principal d., continuing when it became Scottish B. Created roles in Darrell's *Sun Into Darkness* (1966), *Ephemeron* (1968), *Beauty and the Beast* (1969), *Herodias* (1970), *Tales of Hoffman* (1972), Wright's *Dance Macabre* (1968), Neumeier's *Frontier* (1969), Van Schayk's *Ways of Saying Bye Bye*, Prokovsky's *Vespri*, and Moreland's *Intimate Voices* (all 1973). Moved briefly to New London B. in 1974, returned to Scottish B. same year and created title-role in Darrell's *Mary, Queen of Scots* (1976), followed by *Five Rückert Songs* (1978) and *Cinderella* (1979). O.B.E. 1983.

McDowell, John Herbert (*b* Washington, 21 Dec. 1926, *d* Scarsdale, N.Y., 3 Sep. 1985). Amer. composer. Started to write mus. for modern dancers and groups in 1954. By 1976 had comp. over 150 b. scores and himself ch. 16 works, mostly for Judson D. Th. Mus. dir. for P. Taylor and C. Keuter D. Cos. and has also collaborated with G. Solomons, E. Summers, D. Wagoner, and J. Waring. Teaches mus. for d. in New York (Pratt Institute), and Amer. D. Fest., also mus. faculty for Gulbenkian National Ch. Summer Schools in Britain, 1976–9.
BIBL.: 'Busy Man', *Dance and Dancers* (1973/1).

McDowell, Norman (*b* Belfast, 26 Sep. 1931, *d* London, 5 July 1980). Brit. dancer, director, and costume designer. Studied at Sadler's Wells B. School, with M. Lake, G. Goncharov, and Volkova. D. with Original B. Russe in 1951, B. Rambert, London Festival B. Joined B. der Lage Landen,

Amsterdam, with J. Carter; created title role in Carter's *Witch Boy* (1956), which he designed. Formed London D. Th. in 1964; created role in Carter's *Agrionia*. Artistic dir. of London Festival B. during 1965. Has designed costs. for *The Life and Death of Lola Montez* for B. Rambert (1954), *London Morning* (1959) for London Festival B., *Swan Lake* for Teatro Colón, *Three Dances to Japanese Music* (1973) and *The Dancing Floor* (1974) for Scottish B., *Shukumei* (1975) and *Calm* (1976) for Royal B., etc.

McGehee, Helen (*b* Lynchburg, Va.). Amer. dancer, choreographer, and teacher. Studied at Randolph-Macon Women's Univ. and Graham School. Joined Graham Co., in 1944 and became one of the leading soloists. Created roles in Graham's *Clytemnestra* (1958), *Acrobats of God* (1960), *Phaedra* (1962), and *The Archaic Hours* (1969). Now has her own group and teaches at Graham and Juilliard Schools.

McGrath, Barry (*b* Dartford, 15 Mar. 1941). Brit. dancer. Studied at Sadler's Wells B. School and Legat School. Joined London Festival B. 1958; appointed soloist in 1961. Principal d. Zurich B. 1964–8, Royal B. 1968–74; created parts in Ashton's *Siesta* (1972 version) and Hynd's *In a Summer Garden* (1972). D. with Scottish B. 1974–5; moved briefly to New London B. in 1975, then to PACT B., Johannesburg. Married to d. Dianne Richards.

Machov, Saša (orig. František Matha; *b* Zhoř, 16 July 1903, *d* Prague, 23 June 1951). Czech dancer, choreographer, b. master, and teacher. Studied with J. Nikolská. D. with various Czech cos. 1927–39, also in Athens, and op. dir. in Brno. Staged Smetana's *The Bartered Bride* for Sadler's Wells Op. (London, 1946). B. dir. of Prague National Th. 1946 until his suicide in 1951.

McKayle, Donald (*b* New York, 6 July 1930). Amer. dancer, choreographer, and teacher. Studied with Graham, Shook, and Primus. Started dancing 1948; appeared with many modern groups (e.g. Graham, Sokolow, Erdman, Dudley-Maslow). Also appeared on Broadway (*House of Flowers*, *West Side Story*). Ch. *Golden Boy* (1965), *Tale of Two Cities* (1967), *Black New World*, (co-ch., 1967), *Raisin in the Sun* (1973), and *Sophisticated Ladies* (1981) for Broadway. Formed his own group in 1951, for which his main works were *Rainbow 'Round My Shoulder* (trad. mus., 1959) and *District Storyville* (New Orleans jazz, 1962). Head of the Los Angeles-based Inner City D. Co., Artistic Dir. of School of D., California Institute of Arts, 1975. Contributed 'The Act of Theatre' to *Modern Dance* (Middletown, Conn., 1965). Capezio Award (1963).
BIBL.: P. W. Manchester, 'Meet D.M.', *Dancing Times* (1967/1); M. Hodgson, 'D.M.', *Dance News* (1979/12).

Mackerras, Sir Charles (*b* Schenectady, N.Y., 17

Nov. 1925). Austral. conductor. As conductor of Sadler's Wells Th. B. arr. the mus. for Cranko's *Pineapple Poll* (based on Sullivan, 1951) and *The Lady and the Fool* (Verdi, 1954), and for W. Gore's *Night and Silence* (Bach, 1958). Mus. dir. Eng. Nat. Op. 1970–8. CBE 1974, knighted 1979.

McLain Stoop, Norma (*b* Panama Canal Zone, 20 July *c*.1910). Amer. writer and editor. Studied cost. design and singing. Ballroom d. training with Harold Halliday and Henry Bateman. Demonstrated and taught ballroom d. (especially Intern. Style) at Albert Butler School, New York, D. Masters of Amer., D. Educators of Amer., D. Teachers Club of Boston, and D. Caravan. Has worked as a d. film and TV critic, d. photographer and poet. Started to write for *Dance Magazine* 1969 (assoc. editor from 1971, now senior editor) and *After Dark* 1969 (senior editor from 1978).

MacLeary, Donald (*b* Glasgow, 22 Aug. 1937). Brit. d. and b. master. Studied with Sheila Ross and Sadler's Wells B. School. Joined Sadler's Wells Th. B. 1954. Appointed soloist 1955 and principal d., Royal B., 1959. Became Beriosova's favourite partner. Created roles in Cranko's *Antigone* (1959) and *Brandenburg 2 & 4* (1966), and MacMillan's *The Burrow* (1958), *Baiser de la Fée* (1960), *Diversions* (1961), *Symphony* (1963), *Images of Love* (1964), *Checkpoint* (1970), *The Poltroon* (1972), and *Elite Syncopations* (1974). B. master, Royal B., 1976–9. Répétiteur to principal ds. Royal B. 1984.
BIBL.: S. Goodman, 'D.M.', *Dance Magazine* (1960/11); 'Dressage for dancers—D.M. talks to d & d', *Dance and Dancers* (1976/2).

MacMillan, Sir Kenneth (*b* Dunfermline, 11 Dec. 1929). Brit. dancer, choreographer, and b. director. Studied at Sadler's Wells School. Joined Sadler's Wells Th. B. 1946 as one of its original members. To Sadler's Wells B. 1948. Returned to Sadler's Wells Th. B. 1952. Worked for both cos.; appointed resident ch. of the Royal B. 1965. B. dir. of Ger. Op. Berlin 1966–9. Dir. of Royal B. (at first with J. Field, who soon left the co.) from 1970–7, and its principal ch. since 1977; art. assoc. Amer. B. Th. 1984. Ch.—for Ch. Group: *Somnambulism* (mus. S. Kenton, 1953), and *Laiderette* (mus. F. Martin, 1954); for Sadler's Wells Th. B.: *Danses concertantes* (mus. Stravinsky), *House of Birds* (mus. F. Mompou, arr. Lanchbery, both 1955), and *Solitaire* (mus. M. Arnold, 1956); for Sadler's Wells B.: *Noctambules* (mus. H. Searle, 1956) and *Playground* (for Sadler's Wells Royal B., mus. G. Crosse, Edinburgh, Aug. 1979); for Royal B.: *The Burrow* (mus. Martin), *Agon* (mus. Stravinsky, both 1958), *Le Baiser de la Fée* (mus. Stravinsky), *The Invitation* (mus. M. Seiber, both 1960), *Diversions* (mus. Bliss, 1961), *Sacre du printemps* (mus. Stravinsky, 1962), *Symphony* (mus. Shostakovich, 1963), *Images of Love* (mus. P. Tranchell), *La Création du monde* (mus. Milhaud, both 1964), *Romeo and Juliet* (mus. Prokofiev, 1965), *Checkpoint* (mus. R. Gerhard, 1970), *Anas-*

tasia (second version, mus. Tchaikovsky and Martinů, 1971), *Side Show* (mus. Stravinsky), *Ballade* (mus. Fauré), *The Poltroon* (mus. R. Maros), *Triad* (mus. Prokofiev, all 1972), *Pavane* (mus. Fauré), *The Sleeping Beauty, The Seven Deadly Sins* (mus. Weill, all 1973—the Weill also in 1961 for Western Th. B.), *Manon* (mus. Massenet, arr. Lucas), *Elite Syncopations* (mus. S. Joplin, both 1974), *The Four Seasons* (mus. Verdi), *Rituals* (mus. Bartók, both 1975), *Mayerling* (mus. Liszt/Lanchbery, 1978), *La Fin du jour* (mus. Ravel, 1979), *Gloria* (mus. Poulenc, 1980), and *Isadora* (mus. R. R. Bennett, 1981); for Amer. B. Th.: *Journey* (mus. Bartók) and *Winter's Eve* (mus. Britten, both 1957); for Stuttgart B.: *Las Hermanas* (mus. Martin, 1963), *Song of the Earth* (mus. Mahler, 1965), *The Sphinx* (mus. Milhaud, 1968), *Miss Julie* (mus. Panufnik, 1970), *Requiem* (mus. Fauré, 1977) and *My Brother, My Sisters* (mus. Schoenberg and Webern, 1978); for Ger. Op. Berlin: *Valses nobles et sentimentales* (mus. Ravel), *Concerto* (mus. Shostakovich, both 1966), *Anastasia* (mus. Martinů), *Sleeping Beauty* (both 1967), *Olympiad* (mus. Stravinsky), *Cain and Abel* (mus. Panufnik, both 1968), and *Swan Lake* (1969). Has often revived his bs. for other cos. 'He is the poet of passion, of dark, unhappy desires and frustrations and self-deceits. He can show us the gnawing appetites and needs, the loneliness, that polite Society masks behind its superficial behaviour. . . . M.'s only means of expression is movement; his classical training has mercifully provided him with a built-in formal equipment that shapes, canalizes and guides his dance imagination. All his ballets are classical in that they are clear developments . . . of the academic dance' (P. Brinson and C. Crisp in *Ballet for All*, London, 1970). Hon. Dr. (Edinburgh Univ., 1975). Knighted 1983.
BIBL.: Interview with K.M., *About the House* (1963/2 and 1966/6), and *Royal B. Yearbook, 1979–80*.

McRae, Edna (*b* Chicago). Amer. teacher. Studied with B. Hazlitt, Pavley-Oukrainsky, Bolm, also in London and Paris. Taught at various schools in Chicago before establishing her own School of the D. in 1923, which became one of the best in the country. Retired in 1964, but continues as a guest-teacher all over the U.S.

MacRae, Heather (*b* Melbourne, 1940). Austral. dancer and b. mistress. Studied with Laurel Martyn. Joined Borovansky B. in 1960, Gore's London B. in 1962, Australian B. in 1963; appointed b. mistress in 1969.

Mademoiselle Angot. See *Mam'zelle Angot*.

Madsen, Egon (*b* Ringe, 24 Aug. 1942). Dan. d. Studied with Thea Jolles, Bartholin, and Frandsen. Joined Copenhagen Tivoli Th.; d. with von Rosen's Scandinavian B. in 1959. Joined Stuttgart B. in 1961. Appointed soloist in 1962, becoming one of its principal ds. Created roles in Cranko's *Jeu de cartes, Onegin* (both 1965), *Nutcracker*

(1966), *The Interrogation* (1967), *Taming of the Shrew* (1969), *Poème de l'extase, Brouillards* (both 1970), *Carmen* (1971), and *Initials R.B.M.E.* (1972), MacMillan's *Song of the Earth* (1965) and *The Sphinx* (1968), Tetley's *Daphnis and Chloe* (1975), and Neumeier's *Lady of the Camellias* (1978). Appointed artistic dir. of Frankfurt B. in 1981. Art. dir. R. Swed. B. 1984–6, then to Teatro Comunale, Florence. Married to the d. L. Montagnon.
BIBL.: S. Goodman, 'E.M.', *Dance Magazine* (1969/10).

Mad Tristan. Ballet in 2 scenes; libr. and déc. Dali; ch. Massine; mus. Wagner. Prod. 15 Dec. 1944, B. International, International Th., New York, with Moncion. A surrealist b. showing the feverish dreams of T., in with Isolde turns into a praying mantis.

Maeda, Kumiko (*b* 26 Feb. 1960). Jap. dancer. Studied in Minoru Ochi B. Academy, joining M. Ochi B. Co. 1974 as a soloist and now its prima ballerina. A. Pavlova Prize (1976); third prize Moscow B. Competition 1977, third prize Jap. World B. Competition 1978.

Magallanes, Nicholas (*b* Camargo, Mexico, 27 Nov. 1922, *d* North Merrick, L.I., 1 May 1977). Amer. dancer. Studied at School of Amer. B. D. with B. Caravan in 1941, Littlefield B. in 1942, B. R. de Monte Carlo 1943–6, and B. Society and New York City B. 1946–73; became one of its principal dancers. Created roles in Balanchine's *Night Shadow* (1946), *Orpheus* (1948), *La Valse* (1951), *Western Symphony* (1954), *Episodes* (1959), *Liebeslieder Walzer* (1960), and *A Midsummer Night's Dream* (1962), Robbins' *The Guests* (1949), *The Cage* and *The Pied Piper* (both 1951), Ashton's *Illuminations* (1950), and Butler's *The Unicorn, the Gorgon and the Manticore* (1957).

Magic Flute, The (orig. Russ. title: *Volshebnaya fleita*). Ballet in 1 act; libr. and ch. Ivanov; mus. Drigo. Prod. 22 Mar. 1893, Imperial B. School, St. Petersburg. The b. has nothing to do with the op. *Die Zauberflöte*. It centres on Lise, the daughter of a wealthy countrywoman, who loves Luc, a poor peasant boy. A hermit gives Luc as reward for his kindness, a flute which makes everyone d. This enrages the Marquis, who is intended to marry Lise. He condemns Luc to death, but the hermit reveals himself as Oberon, and saves him. The b., created for a school display perf., entered the repertory of the Maryinsky Th. on 23 Apr. 1893, with S. Belinskaya, M. Fokine, C. Christerson, and N. Legat. Later it became a favourite item in the co. of Pavlova; she, Volinine, and Cecchetti shared the leading roles. New version by P. Martins, School of Amer. B., 1981.
BIBL.: C. W. Beaumont, 'T.M.F.' in *Complete Book of Ballets* (London, 1951).

Magri, Gennaro. Ital. choreographer and writer of the second half of the 18th century. He worked

as a ch. in Venice (1760–61), Vienna (1763–4), and Modena (1765). His *Trattato Teoretico-Prattico di Ballo* was published in Naples in 1779: 'the most invaluable 18th century treatise on ballet technique ... pages which manifest his knowledge and his eagerness to show future dancers how to accomplish the wealth of steps he recorded for their benefit' (M.H. Winter).
BIBL.: M. H. Winter, in *The Pre-Romantic Ballet* (London, 1974).

Mahalli Dancers of Iran. A co. based in Teheran, attached to a school which was started by Robert and Jacqueline de Warren in 1971. It is dedicated to the presentation of Persian folklore, offering stage adaptations of dances and rituals from Kurdistan, Baluchistan, Kuzestan, and other regions of the country, including those of the Whirling Dervishes of the Moulavi order. They first appeared in the U.S. at Washington, D.C., in 1971, and in London in 1972. Nothing is known of what happened to them after the revolution of 1978.
BIBL.: 'Discovery in Persia', interview with R. de Warren, *Dance and Dancers* (1973/1).

M'ahesa, Sent (*d* Stockholm, 19 Nov. 1970). Estonian dancer. She gave many solo recitals before the First World War, and became a European equivalent of St. Denis, since she too was mainly concerned with Egyptian and oriental subjects and forms.
BIBL.: H. Brandenburg, 'S.M.' in *Der moderne Tanz* (Munich, 1931).

Mahler, Gustav (*b* Kalischt, 7 July 1860, *d* Vienna, 18 May 1911). Austrian composer. Wrote no b. mus., but his concert mus. has often been used for d. purposes, incl. Tudor's *Dark Elegies* (*Kindertotenlieder*, 1937) and *Shadow of the Wind* (*Song of the Earth*, 1948—also by MacMillan, 1965), Feld's *At Midnight* (*Rückert Songs*, 1967, also Darrell's *Five Rückert Songs*, 1978), Béjart's *Le Chant du compagnon errant* (1971) and *Ce que l'amour me dit* (last 3 movements of Third Symphony, 1974; the whole symphony also by Neumeier, 1975—see *Third Symphony by G.M.*), Petit's *La Rose malade* (Adagietto from the Fifth Symphony, 1973 also Maldoom's *Adagietto No. 5*, 1975), Cranko's *Traces* (Adagio from the Tenth Symphony, 1973), Ulrich's *Des Knaben Wunderhorn* (1974, also Smuin's *Songs of Mahler*, 1976), and Neumeier's *First and Tenth Symphony*, 1980). A check-list of many bs. to mus. by M. was published on the occasion of Neumeier's Nijinsky-M. Gala, in the programme book of the second Hamburg Ballet Days, 1976.

Mahler. B. in 3 parts; ch. Béjart; mus. Mahler; déc. Judith Gombar; light. Alan Burett. First prod. in its complete form 19 Dec. 1978, B. of the 20th Century, Th. Royal de la Monnaie, Brussels. The 3 individual parts are: *Ce que la mort me dit* (mus. from Rückert Lieder and *Des Knaben Wunderhorn*, created Tokyo, 1978), *Chant du*

compagnon errant (*Song of the Wayfarer*, Brussels, 1971), and *Ce que l'amour me dit* (last 3 movements of Third Symphony, Monte Carlo, 1974).

Mahler, Roni (*b* New York, 1942). Amer. dancer. Studied with Swoboda and School of B. Russe de Monte Carlo. Joined B. Russe de Monte Carlo in 1960 and Washington National B. as a soloist in 1962. Member of Amer. B. Th. 1968–71. Since 1974 assistant professor of d., Kansas City Univ.

Maids, The. Ballet in 1 act; ch. Ross; mus. Milhaud. Prod. 13 May 1957, B. Th. Workshop, Phoenix Th., New York, with Loren Hightower, Paul Olson. Inspired by J. Genet's play *Les Bonnes*, and set to Milhaud's concerto for percussion and small orchestra. The b. tells of two maids—played by men—who enact a sinister charade, alternately trying to impersonate their mistress, until one finally suffocates the other. Revived for B. of Two Worlds (1960) and Royal B. (1971). A different treatment of the same story by M. Taubert (mus. Bartók, Brunswick, 1968).

Maillot. The tights favoured by dancers, named after a 19th century costumier of the Paris Opéra.

Maiorano, Robert (*b* Brooklyn, 29 Aug. 1946). Amer. dancer. Studied at School of Amer. B., joining New York City B. in 1962, promoted soloist in 1969. Created roles in Robbins's *Dances at a Gathering* (1969) and *The Goldberg Variations* (1971).
BIBL.: S. Goodman, 'R.M.', *Dance Magazine* (1971/6).

Maiorov, Genrik Alexandrovich (*b* Ulan-Ude, 6 Sep. 1936). Sov. d., ch., and b. master. Studied at Kiev State School of Choreography and Leningrad Conservatory. Member of Lvov Th. of Op. and B. 1957–9, then Kiev Tsevtshenko Th. 1960–7. Appointed b. master Leningrad Maly Th. in 1968 and now of the Kiev Tsevtshenko Th. Has ch. several frequently performed recital dances, incl. *We* and *Cranes*. His bs. include *Poem at Sunrise* (mus. V. Vsenko, 1973) and *Cippolino* (Mus. Karen Khachaturian, 1974). Has also taught at Kiev School for Variety and Circus Professionals and Kiev State School of Ch. Now at Stanislavsky and Nemirovich-Danchenko Th., Moscow. Second Prize at Third All-Union Competition of New Dance Miniatures (for *We*, Moscow, 1969); First Prize with Laureate Title at All-Union Competition of B. Masters (Moscow, 1972); Ballet Master Prize (Varna, 1972).

Maître de ballet. See *Ballet Master*.

Makarov, Askold Anatolevich (*b* Novo-Mossalskoye, 3 May 1925). Sov. dancer and teacher. Studied at Leningrad Ch. School; graduated in 1943. Joined Kirov B., becoming one of its outstanding soloists; created title roles in B. Fenster's *Taras Bulba*, Jacobson's *Spartacus* (both 1956), and Belsky's *Coast of Hope* (1959). Retired in 1970. Now teaches at the Leningrad Conservatory. Stalin Prize (1951); Hon. Artist of the R.S.F.S.R. (1954). Married to the d. Ninel Petrova.

Makarova, Natalia Romanovna (*b* Leningrad, 21 Oct. 1940). Sov. dancer. Studied at Leningrad Ch. School; graduated in 1959. Joined Kirov B. and became one of its outstanding ballerinas. When the co. was in London in 1970 she decided to stay in the West, and she has since pursued a freelance career, mostly dancing with Amer. B. Th., but often performing as a guest with other cos., incl. Royal B., with which she d. for the first time in 1972. Was considered one of the best Giselles of the 1970s. Created role in Neumeier's *Epilogue* (1975). Staged *La Bayadère* for Amer. B. Th. (1974—full version in 1980). Appeared with her own co. on Broadway in 1980. Gold Medal (Varna, 1965); Merited Artist of the R.S.F.S.R. Author of *A Dance Autobiography* (New York, 1979).
BIBL.: D. Makarova, 'Beyond Giselle?', *Dance Magazine* (1972/1); var. articles in *Ballet News* (1980/3).

Malagueña. A d. song from Malaga, not unlike the fandango. Ravel uses it in his *Rhapsodie espagnole*.

Maldoom, Royston (*b* London, 1943). Brit. choreographer. Worked as farmer until age 22, then studied b. with Stella Mann, and Rambert School. D. in musicals and on TV. Began to ch. for workshop programmes in 1970. Resident ch. B. San Marcos, Peru, 1973–4. Studied Alvin Ailey D. Center, New York, 1974, and ch. for First Chamber D. Co, New York. His *Adagietto No. 5* (to slow movement from Mahler's Fifth Symphony) won grand prix, Seventh International Ch. Competition, Bagnolet, 1975, was revived later that year for Northern D. Th. and for Harlem D. Th. in 1977. Also ch. *The Four Seasons* (slow movements from each of Vivaldi's *4 Seasons* concertos), Pont-à-Mousson 1975 and revived for Northern D. Th. 1976. Has worked since for various cos., incl. Scottish B. (*Ursprung*, 1979) Now teaching in Scotland.
BIBL.: L. Brunel, interview with R.M., *Les saisons de la danse* (1975/6).

Malinche, La. Ballet in 1 act; libr. and ch. Limón; mus. N. Lloyd; cost. P. Lawrence. Prod. 31 Mar. 1949, J. Limón Co., Ziegfeld Th., New York, with Limón, Koner, Hoving. The b. shows Cortez's conquest of Mexico. The title role is an Indian princess, who served Cortez as an interpreter; she can find no rest after her death, as she feels that she has betrayed her people.

Mallek, Peter (*b* Vienna, 30 Jan. 1948). Austrian dancer. Studied at Vienna State Op. B. School. Member of Vienna State Op. B. 1963–71; created role in Adama's *Don Juan* (1969). Has since d. with Marseille B., B. Guatemala, Niagara Frontier B., Australian B., Scottish B., London Festival B, and now with his own Vienna Festival B.

Maly Ballet. The co. of the Maly (Small) Th. of Op. and B. in Leningrad, based on the former Imperial Mikhailovsky Th. Today the Th. serves as the city's municipal op. house (as opposed to the state Kirov Th.). Founded in 1915, though the first b. perf. was in 1933. This was *Harlequinade* by Lopokov, the cos. first b. dir. 1933–5. He also staged *Coppélia* (1934) and Shostakovich's *The Bright Stream* (1935). He was succeeded by Lavrovsky 1936–8, who was responsible for *Fadetta* (Delibes's *Sylvia*, 1936), *La Fille mal gardée* (1937), and Asafiev's *Prisoner of the Caucasus* (1938). Many subsequent bs. were ch. by B. Fenster, e.g. Chulaki's *The False Bridegroom* (1946) and *Youth* (1949), Liadov's *The Dead Princess and the Seven Knights* (1949), and Strauss's *Blue Danube* (1956). Other choreographers included Anisimova (*Sheherazade*, 1950, and Yevlachov's *Ivushka*, 1957), Gusev (Karayev's *The Seven Beauties*, 1953, and *Le Corsaire*, 1955), Lopokov (*Ballad of Love*, mus. Tchaikovsky, 1959), and Boyarsky (Stravinsky's *Petrushka*, *Orpheus*, and *Firebird*, 1962, and *The Lady and the Hooligan*, mus. Shostakovich, 1962). Belsky was chief ch. 1963–72; he mounted new prods. of *Humpbacked Horse* and *Nutcracker*, and ch. the first prods. of Shostakovich's *Ninth Symphony* (1966) and Tchernov's *Ovod* (1967). Younger choreographers have also contributed important prods., e.g. Boyartchikov (Basner's *The Three Musketeers*, 1964) Tchernishov (Lazarev's *Anthony and Cleopatra*, 1968), and Vinogradov (Yaroslavna, 1974). Artistic dir. is now Boyartchikov (since 1978), adding to the repertory *Tsar Boris* (mus. Prokofiev, 1978) and *Orpheus and Eurydice* (1979).
BIBL.: N. Roslavleva, in *Era of the Russian Ballet* (London, 1966); M. G. Swift, in *The Art of the Dance in the U.S.S.R.* (Notre Dame, Ind., 1968).

Mam'zelle Angot. Ballet in 3 scenes; libr. and ch. Massine; mus. Lecocq (arr. R. Mohaupt); déc. M. Doboujinsky. Prod. 10 Oct. 1943 (as *Mademoiselle Angot*), B. Th., Met. Op. House, New York, with Massine, N. Kay, Eglevsky, Hightower, Semenoff. Based on Lecocq's light opera *La Fille de Madame Angot* (1872). The b. shows a string of characters, all in love with somebody who unfortunately loves somebody else; finally Mam'zelle Angot discovers that she really loves the Barber, who had pursued her all along. Revived for Sadler's Wells B. (with new mus. arr. by G. Jacob, déc. by Derain, 1947) and Austral. B. (1971).
BIBL.: C. Beaumont, 'M.A.', in *Ballets Past & Present* (London, 1955).

Manchester, Phyllis Winifred (*b* London, *c.* 1910). Eng. b. critic and writer on d. B. critic for *Theatre World* 1941–3. Secretary to Rambert 1944–6. First editor of *Ballet Today* 1946–51. Managing editor of *Dance News*, New York, 1951–69. Author of *Vic-Wells: A Ballet Progress* (London, 1942) and *The Rose and the Star* (with I. Morley, London, 1948). Co-editor with A. Chujoy of

Dance Encyclopedia (1967 edition). Now teaches d. history at Univ. of Cincinnati. Visiting Professor North Carolina School of the Arts and Univ. of Utah.

Manège (Fr., circus-ring). Designates in b. an imaginary wide circle which the d. traverses in tours en manège.

Manen, Hans van (*b* Amstelvee, 11 July 1932). Dutch dancer, choreographer, and b. director. Studied with Gaskell, Adret, and Kiss. Joined B. Recital 1951, Amsterdam Op. B. and Petit's co. 1959. One of the orig. members of Netherlands D. Th. in 1960. Became one of its outstanding choreographers and its artistic dir. (first with Harkarvy, later with Tetley). Left the co. 1970, Joined Dutch National B. as ch. and b. master 1973. Has worked occasionally for Royal B. since 1972, and for Scapino B., Düsseldorf B., Cologne Tanz-Forum, Munich State Op. B., Pennsylvania B, and Basle B. Has ch. many bs., e.g. for Netherlands D. Th.: *Symphony in Three Movements* (mus. Stravinsky, 1963), *Essay in Silence* (mus. Messiaen), *Metaphors* (mus. D. Lesur, both 1965), *Five Sketches* (mus. Hindemith, 1966), *Solo for Voice 1* (mus. Cage, 1968), *Squares* (mus. Satie, 1969), *Situation* (sound-collage), *Mutations* (with Tetley, mus. Stockhausen, both 1970), *Grosse Fuge* (mus. Beethoven, 1971), *Opus Lemaitre* (mus. Bach, 1972), *Septet Extra* (mus. Saint-Saëns, 1973), *Noble et sentimentale* (mus. Ravel, 1975), and *Songs Without Words* (mus. Mendelssohn, 1977); for Dutch National B.: *Twilight* (mus. Cage), *Daphnis and Chloe—Suite No. 2* (mus. Ravel, both 1972), *Adagio Hammerklavier* (mus. Beethoven, 1973), *Sacre du printemps* (mus. Stravinsky, 1974), *Ebony Concerto* (mus. Stravinsky, 1976), *5 Tangos* (mus. Piazzolla, 1977), and *Klaviervariationen* (mus. Bach, Dallapiccola, 1980); for Düsseldorf B.: *Keep Going* (mus. Berio, 1971); for Royal B.: *Four Schumann Pieces* (mus. Schumann, 1975). Officer of Oranje Nassau (1970); prize of Dutch Th. Critics (1974); Jan-Reinink Penny (1976).

BIBL.: interview with H.v.M., *Dance and Dancers* (1969/6); G. Loney, 'H.v.M.: Setting the Record Straight on Netherlands Dance Theatre', *Dance Magazine* (1974/2).

Manipuri. A dance style originating from the north-eastern corner of India, from the valley of Manipur, the Jewelled City. It derives from folklore sources, and its uncomplicated technique lends its perfs. an easy, light, and lyrical grace. Its dramas, supported by dialogue and song, are performed by many dancers; they deal mostly with the Gopis, the milkmaids, Radha, and Krishna.

BIBL.: R. Singha & R. Massey, 'M. Dance' in *Indian Dances* (London, 1967).

Manon. Ballet in 3 acts; libr. and ch. MacMillan; mus. Massenet, arr. Leighton Lucas, déc. Georgiadis. Prod. 7 Mar. 1974, Royal B., Cov. Gdn., London, with Sibley, Dowell, Wall, Rencher,

Mason, Drew. The b. follows roughly the plot of the Abbé Prévost's *Histoire du Chevalier des Grieux et de Manon Lescaut* (1731). An earlier *Manon Lescaut*, libr. Scribe, mus. Halévy, ch. Aumer, scenery Ciceri, cost. Lecomte, E. Lami, and H. Duponchel, had its first prod. 30 Apr. 1830, Opéra, Paris, with P. Montessu, J. Ferdinand, and Taglioni; also a b. M. by Golinelli, mus. Strebinger, Vienna, 1852.

BIBL.: I. Guest, 'M in 19th Century Ballet', and L. Lucas, 'M. and Massenet's Music', *About the House* (Spring 1974).

Manor, Giora (*b* Prague, 23 June 1926). Israeli dance critic and editor. After working for many years as dir. and artistic dir. of several ths. in Israel became journalist and editor of the cultural and arts page of a daily paper in Tel Aviv in 1970. D. critic of Al-Hamishmar and Israeli Radio, editor of *Israeli Dance Annual*, correspondent of *Dance News* and of Ger. b. annual. Author of *Inbal— Quest for a Movement Language* (Tel Aviv, 1975), *Ehud Ben-David, Israeli Dancer* (Tel Aviv, 1978), *The Life and Dance of Gertrud Kraus* (Tel Aviv, 1978), *The Gospel According to Dance* (New York, 1980).

Manzotti, Luigi (*b* Milan, 2 Feb. 1835, *d* there, 15 Mar. 1905). Ital. mime dancer and choreographer. Was very successful in Rome as a mime. Ch. his first b. in 1858: *La Morte di Masaniello*. His special gifts for spectacular effects were evident in his early bs.; they culminated in such works as *Moro delle Antille*, *Michelangelo e Rolla*, *Cleopatra*, and *Pietro Micca*. Went to Milan in 1872, surpassing his Roman successes with *Sieba* (Turin, 1878), *Excelsior* (Milan, 1881), *Amor* (Milan, 1886), and *Sport* (Milan, 1897). His prods. were staged in many of the capitals of the world, and he became enormously famous; but 'M.'s ballets were not ballets in the present understanding of the term, but a succession of related episodes expressed in mime, varied with simple but effective ensembles by dancers, and striking processions by well-drilled supers' (Beaumont, in *Complete Book of Ballets*, London, 1952).

BIBL.: entry 'M., L.' in *Enciclopedia dello spettacolo*.

Mara, Thalia (*b* Chicago). Amer. dancer, teacher, and writer on dance. Studied with A. Maximova, Bolm, Preobrajenska, Legat, and Fokine. Début Chicago 1926. D. with C. Ari co. in Europe; toured U.S. and Canada and appeared in musicals. Opened School of B. Repertory with her husband in New York in 1948, and National Academy of B. in 1963. Author of *First Steps in B.*, *Second Steps in B.*, and *Third Steps in B.*

Maracci, Carmelita (*b* Montevideo, 1911). Amer. dancer and teacher. Studied academic and Span. dance in Cal. Début Los Angeles in 1930. Toured the States with her own group, presenting her very individual brand of Span. dances. Opened a school for academic d. in Los Angeles. Was considered for many years one of the outstanding teachers on the West Coast.

BIBL.: J. W. Knowles, 'Lessons with C. M.', *Dance Magazine* (1964/5).

Marble Maiden, The. Ballet by Vernoy de Saint Georges; ch. Albert; mus. Adam; Prod. 27 Sep. 1845, Drury Lane Th., London, Dumilâtre, L. Petipa. An Eng. version of *La Fille de marbre*.

BIBL.: C. W. Beaumont, in *Complete Book of Ballets* (London, 1952).

Marceau, Marcel (*b* Strasbourg, 22 Mar. 1923). Fr. mime. Studied with Dullin and Decroux. Début as Harlequin in Barrault's prod. of *Baptiste* in 1947. Formed his own group in 1947, with which he toured world-wide. Acclaimed as the outstanding mime of our time; the figure of Bip is his most personal creation. His most ambitious prod. so far has been *Candide* (mus. M. Constant, déc, Daydé), realized with the b. co. of the Hamburg State Op., 1971.

BIBL.: N. McLain Stoop, 'The Interior Music of M.M.', *Dance Magazine* (1975/7).

Marcel (*d.* 1759). Famous Fr. mime dance-master in the first half of the 18th century. His first success was in Campra's *Fêtes Venétiennes* (1710), singing and dancing a minuet. He was the authority on the minuet. Noverre was one of his pupils.

Marcel Proust Remembered. See *Intermittences du coeur, Les.*

Marchand, Colette (*b* Paris, 1925). Fr. dancer. Studied at Paris Opéra School and with V. Gsovsky and Volinine. D. with Opéra B., Met. B. 1947. Won special acclaim as a Petit ballerina; created roles in his *L'Oeuf à la coque* (1949), *Deuil en 24 heures*, *Ciné-Bijou*, and *Lady in the Ice* (all 1953). Appeared in J. Huston's film *Moulin Rouge* (1953). Has since d. with various cos. (Petit, Miskovitch, B. Th. Contemporain). Now works mainly in revues, musicals, and TV prods.

BIBL.: A Livio, in *Etoiles et Ballerines* (Paris, 1965).

Marchiolli, Sonja (*b* Zagreb, 1 May 1945). Yugosl. dancer. Studied at Zagreb State B. School; graduated in 1965. Member of Zagreb B. 1965–7 and Dutch National B. since 1967; appointed first soloist in 1969. Created roles in Van Dantzig's *Ramifications* (1973) and *Blown in a Gentle Wind* (1975) and Van Manen's *Adagio Hammerklavier* (1973). Married to the b. master Ivan Kramar.

Marco Spada ou La Fille du bandit. Ballet in 3 acts and 6 scenes; libr. Scribe; ch. Mazilier; mus. Auber; sets Cambon, Thierry, Despléchin, Nolau, Rubé; cost. Albert, Lormier. Prod. 1 Apr. 1857, Paris Opéra, with C. Rosati, A. Ferraris, L. Petipa. The plot revolves around Count Frederici who loves Angela, without being aware that she is the daughter of the bandit chief M.S., while in reality he is betrothed to the Marchesa Sampietri, niece

of the Governor of Rome, who in her turn is loved by Pepinelli, Captain of the Dragoons. However, after the battle between the dragoons and the bandits the dying M.S. declares that Angela is not his daughter, so that there is no hindrance any more for Frederici to marry her, while Pepinelli finally gets his Marchesa. Revived by P. Lacotte for Rome Opera (1981).

BIBL.: C. W. Beaumont, in *Complete Book of Ballets* (London, 1951).

Maré, Rolf de (*b* Stockholm, 9 May 1898, *d* Barcelona, 28 Apr. 1964). Swed. art patron; member of a wealthy family, and a collector of primitive art. Founded Les Bs. Suédois in Paris 1920; he was dir. and Börlin star-d. and ch. Like Diaghilev he developed a special flair for adapting contemporary trends to b.; he too collaborated with some of the most interesting avant-garde artists of his time. The bs. he prod. during 1920–24—all ch. by Börlin—include *Jeux* (mus. Debussy, déc. Bonnard), *El Greco* (mus. D. E. Inghelbrecht), *L'Homme et son désir* (libr. Claudel, mus. Milhaud, déc, A. Parr), *Les Mariés de la Tour Eiffel* (libr. Cocteau, mus. Les Six, déc. I. Lagut and J. Hugo), *Skating-Rink* (mus. Honegger, déc. Léger), *La Création du monde* (libr. Cendrars, mus. Milhaud, déc. Léger), *La Giara* (libr. Pirandello, mus. Casella, déc. de Chirico), and *Relâche* (mus. Satie, déc. Picabia, film entr'actes René Clair). His co. was disbanded in 1925; he then concentrated on other th. enterprises. Established Les Archives Internationales de la Danse with P. Tugal in Paris in 1931, which organized the first international choreographers' competition in 1932. After his death, part of his rich collection went to the museum of the Paris Opéra and the rest to Stockholm Dansmuseet. See also *Archives Internationales de la Danse* and *Ballets Suédois, Les.*

BIBL.: R.d.M. (editor), *Les Ballets Suédois dans l'art contemporain* (Paris, 1931).

Margalit Dance Theatre Company. See *Oved, Margalit.*

Marguerite and Armand. Ballet in 1 act; libr. and ch. Ashton; mus. Liszt (arr. H. Searle); déc. Beaton. Prod. 12 Mar. 1963, Royal B., Cov. Gdn., with Fonteyn, Nureyev, Somes. Set to an orchestral version of Liszt's Piano Sonata in B minor and *Lugubre Gondole*. The b. tells the famous story of M. Gautier, as a series of feverish flashbacks from her death-bed. The b. is incl. in the film *I Am A Dancer* (1972). For other b. treatments of the same story see *Dame aux camélias, La.*

BIBL.: D. Vaughan, *Frederick Ashton and his Bs* (London, 1977).

Marie Jeanne (orig. M.-J. Pelus; *b* New York, 1920). Amer. dancer. Studied at School of Amer. B. D. with B. Caravan 1937–40, where she created roles in Loring's *Billy the Kid* and Christensen's *Filling Station* (both 1938). B. Russe de Monte Carlo 1940; Amer. B. 1940–1, where she created roles in Balanchine's *Concerto Barocco* (1940) and

Ballet Imperial (1941). Original B. Russe 1942; Marquis de Cuevas' B. International 1944, where she created further roles in Dollar's *Constantia* and Eglevsky's *Colloque Sentimental* (both 1944). B. Russe de Monte Carlo 1945–7; B. Society 1948; then with Grand B. du Marquis de Cuevas and, briefly, with New York City B. Retired in 1954.

Mariemma (orig. Emma Martinez; *b* Valladolid, 1920). Span. dancer. Studied with Estampio and with Goncharova in Paris; d. with the children's b. of the Th. du Châtelet. Toured world-wide and became known as an exceptional stylist of Span. d. Ch. de Falla's *El amor brujo* for Paris Opéra Comique in 1947.

Mariés de la Tour Eiffel, Les. Ballet in 1 act; libr. Cocteau; ch. Börlin; mus. Auric, Milhaud, Tailleferre, Honegger, Poulenc; set Irène Lagut; cost. J. Hugo. Prod. 18 June 1921, Bs. Suédois, Th. des Champs-Elysées, Paris, with C. Ari, J. Figoni, K. Vahlander. The b. farce is set on the 14th of July, on the first platform of the Eiffel Tower, where the attempts of a hunchbacked photographer to photograph a wedding party are constantly frustrated. The work was considered the manifesto of the composers who had banded together as Les Six, though one (L. Durey) did not participate. A later prod. by M. van Hoecke for the B. of the 20th Century (1972).

Markó, Iván (*b* Ballasagyarmatom, 1947). Hung. dancer, choreographer, and director. Studied at Budapest State B. Inst.; graduated in 1967. Joined Budapest State Op. B. Has also d. regularly with B. of the 20th Century since 1972. Created roles in A. Fodor's *The Victim* (1971), Seregi's *Sylvia* (second première, 1972), Béjart's *Le Marteau sans maître* (1973) and *Seraphita* (1974). Appointed artistic dir. of Györ B. 1979, since when he has started to ch. too.
BIBL.: N. McLain Stoop, 'Budapest Knows I.M.', *Dance Magazine* (1973/1).

Markova, Dame Alicia (orig. Lillian Alicia Marks; *b* London, 1 Dec. 1910). Eng. dancer. Studied with Astafieva, Legat, Cecchetti, and Celli. Member of Diaghilev's Bs. Russes 1925–9; became ballerina, and created title-role in Balanchine's *Le Rossignol* (1926). After individual appearances in Monte Carlo and London, became ballerina of Camargo Society in 1931. Ballerina of B. Rambert and Vic-Wells B. until 1935, where she not only d. the ballerina roles in the first Eng. prods. of the classics, but also created a great number of roles in the early bs. of Ashton, e.g. *La Peri* and *Façade* (1931), *Foyer de danse* (1932), *Les Rendezvous* (1933), and *Mephisto Valse* (1934), Tudor's *Lysistrata* (1932), and de Valois' *Bar aux Folies-Bergère* and *The Haunted Ballroom* (1934), and *The Rake's Progress* (1935), etc. Formed Markova-Dolin Co. with Dolin in 1935, and was its prima ballerina until 1938. Ballerina of B. Russe de Monte Carlo 1938–41; created roles in Massine's *Seventh Symphony* (1938), *Capriccio Es-*

pagnol, and *Rouge et noir* (1939), and *Vienna 1814* (1940). Ballerina of B. Th. 1941–5; created further roles in Massine's *Aleko* (1942) and Tudor's *Romeo and Juliet* (1943), but principally appeared in the traditional ballerina roles. Acknowledged as one of the outstanding Giselles of her time. Later returned occasionally to B. Th. Re-formed Markova-Dolin Co. in 1945. Guest ballerina with Mexican B. in 1947, Sadler's Wells B. in 1948. A Markova-Dolin group toured England in 1949; it became London Festival B. in 1950, and M. was prima ballerina until 1952. Continued to appear as guest ballerina with many cos. (incl. Grand B. du Marquis de Cuevas, Royal Winnipeg B., Royal Dan. B., B. of La Scala, R. Page's Chicago Op. B.). At her farewell perfs. in 1962 she was still much admired for 'her extraordinary lightness and her ability to glide through the air, the perfect stress with which she brings each movement to its climax, and the superb manner by which she dissipated her impetus' (A. H. Franks). B. dir. of the N.Y. Met. Op. House 1963–9. Visiting Professor of B., Univ. of Cincinnati, since 1971. Governor of the Royal B. since 1973. First President Lond. Fest. B. 1986. Author of *Giselle and I* (London, 1960). D. Magazine Award (1957); C.B.E. (1958); D.B.E. (1963); D. Mus., Leicester Univ. (1966).
BIBL.: G. Anthony, *A.M.* (London, 1951); A. Dolin, *M.—Her Life and Art* (London, 1953); '30 Years of M.—1925–55', M.-issue of *Dance and Dancers* (1955/1); check-list of roles and activities, *Les Saisons de la danse* (1975/4).

Markova-Dolin Ballet. Formed by M. and D. in London in 1935. Toured England and the continent until 1938 and was briefly revived in Amer. in 1945. Its repertory offered the classics, and such bs. as *Les Biches* and *Pas de quatre*. Dancers included K. Lester, Franklin, Algeranoff, Crofton, D. Gould.

Marks, Bruce (*b* New York, 31 Jan. 1937). Amer. dancer and choreographer. Studied at High School of Performing Arts, Juilliard School, and with Tudor and Craske. Joined Met. Op. B. in 1956; become soloist in 1958. D. with the co. of H. Ross in Spoleto 1959. Leading d. with Amer. B. Th. 1961–71; created leading role in Feld's *At Midnight* (1967). D. as a guest with Royal Swed. B., London Festival B., Feld's Amer. B. Co., and Royal Dan. B., which he joined for a while as a principal d. in 1971. Has ch. several bs., e.g. *Dichterliebe* (mus. Schumann, 1972) and *Asylum* (mus. C. Ruggles, 1974). Artistic co-dir. of B. West since 1976. Contributed to 'The Male Image', *Dance Perspectives* 40. Art. dir. Boston B. since 1985. Was married to the d. Toni Lander.
BIBL.: 'Toni Lander and B.M. On and Off Stage', *Dance Magazine* (1969/8).

Marseillaise, La. Solo d. by Isadora Duncan. Prod. 9 Apr. 1915, Trocadéro, Paris. This was her war contribution, which she d. in a red-stained tunic and red shawl, with great pathos. 'With proud, wide gestures, the d. beckoned to a great unseen army that seemed to fill the stage at her magnetic command. At the end, she stood filled with patriotic fury, her left breast bare as in the statue by Rude on the Arc de Triomphe which had been her inspiration, the auditorium shook with the cheers of the audience' (A. R. Macdougall). Gardel ch. a b. *L.M.*, *Offrande à la liberté* at the Paris Opéra in 1792.

BIBL.: *The Dance Writings of Carl van Vechten* (New York, 1974).

Marsicano, Merle (née M. Petersen; *b* Philadelphia). Amer. dancer and ch. Studied with Ethel Philipps, Mordkin, St. Denis, Graham, and Horst. Début with Pennsylvania Op. Co. Has given solo recitals since 1952; Cage, Feldman, and Wolpe have comp. special pieces for her. Typical titles of hers include *Images in the Open, How Calm the Hour Is, Yellow Night, Eyes of Mauve, Amphibian Memories*, and *Arcana*.

Marteau sans maître, Le. Ballet in 1 act; ch. Béjart; mus. Boulez. Prod. 18 Jan. 1973, B. of the 20th Century, La Scala, Milan, with Poelvoorde, Donn. An abstract work. It is performed by 1 female soloist, 6 male soloists, and 6 Black Persons. Earlier versions by P. Taylor (in *Meridian*, New York, 1960) and Stere Popescu (Bucharest Op. B., Paris, 1965).

Martello, Jacopo (1665–1727). A Bolognese doctor and poet, who wrote several op. libretti. His *Della Tragedia Antica e Moderna* was published in Rome in 1715; it gives a detailed description of the Fr., Span., and Ital. dancing styles at the turn of the century.

BIBL.: M. H. Winter, in *The Pre-Romantic Ballet* (London, 1974).

Marteny, Fred (orig. Feodor Neumann; *b* Prague, 12 Sep. 1931). Czech-Austrian dancer, choreographer, and b. master. Studied at Prague Conservatory. D. with Dia Luca B. 1949–54. Worked in Strasbourg, Marseilles, Hildesheim, and Koblenz. B. master in Graz 1965–70 and Marseilles (under Hightower) 1970–1. Guest b. master of B. Th. Contemporain 1972; Klagenfurt 1974–6. Has ch. many bs. Now working as a freelance b. master and teacher, often in the Far East.

Martin, Frank (*b* Geneva, 15 Sep. 1890, *d* Naarden, Netherlands, 21 Nov. 1974). Swiss composer. Wrote no b. mus., but his concert mus. has often been used for b. purposes, e.g. MacMillan's *Laiderette* (Petite symphonie concertante, 1954), *The Burrow* (Concerto for 7 Brass Instruments, Timpani, Percussion, and String Orchestra, 1958; another version by Darrell, *The Scarlet Pastorale*, 1975) and *Las Hermanas* (Concerto for Harpsichord and Orchestra, 1963) and W. Gore's *Sweet Dancer* (8 preludes for piano and part of suite for guitar, arr. G. Corbett, 1964).

Martin, John (*b* Louisville, 2 June 1893, *d*

Saratoga, N.Y. 19 May 1985). Amer. b. critic and writer on dance. The very influential d. critic of the *New York Times* 1927–62. Also the author of several books, e.g. *The Modern Dance* (New York, 1933), *Introduction to the Dance* (New York, 1939), *The Dance* (New York, 1945), and *World Book of Modern Ballet* (New York, 1952). Has also taught at Univ. of Cal. at Los Angeles.

BIBL.: 'Walter Terry Interviews J.M', *Dance Magazine* (1956/1).

Martin, Keith (*b* Doncaster, 15 June 1943). Brit. d. Studied with Louise Browne and at Royal B. School. D. with Royal B. 1962–71; appointed soloist. Created Puck in Ashton's *The Dream* (1964). Joined Pennsylvania B. as a principal d. in 1971. Founded Keith Martin Ballet Oregon, art. dir. to 1987.

Martinez, Menia (*b* Havana, 27 Sep. 1938). Cub. dancer. Studied with F. Alonso and Parés. D. with B. Alicia Alonso 1952–5. Continued to study in Moscow and Leningrad, appearing as a guest with the Bolshoi and Kirov B. Ballerina of National B. of Cuba 1960–69, B. of the 20th Century 1969–73. Now guest ballerina and teacher of B. de Wallonie.

Martinez, Enrique (*b* Havana, 1926). Cub.-Amer. dancer and b. master. Studied with Alicia Alonso and Schwezoff. Joined Amer. B. Th. in 1950; appointed soloist in 1954. Was b. master of the co., for which he ch. *Coppélia* in 1968. Has worked as guest b. master with the cos. of Alonso and Cuevas and in Denver, Detroit, Rome, West Berlin, and Caracas.

Martiníková, Marcela (*b* Opava, 31 Oct. 1940). Czech dancer. Studied at Prague State Conservatory and in Leningrad. Début Ostravá in 1958. Danced with Prague Studio B. 1964–70, Basle 1970–2. Now principal d. with Prague National Th. Has created many roles in bs. by Smok and Ogoun.

Martins, Peter (*b* Copenhagen, 27 Oct. 1946). Dan. d. Studied at Royal Dan. B. School. Joined Royal Dan. B. in 1965; apptd. solo d. in 1967. Joined N.Y. City B. as a principal d. in 1969; created roles in Robbins' *In the Night* (1970), *The Goldberg Variations* (1971), and *Piano Concerto in G* (1975), Balanchine's *Violin Concerto* and *Duo concertant* (both 1972), *Davidsbündlertänze* (1980), and others. Appeared as guest with London Festival B. in 1970 and 1972. Has ch. many bs. since *Calcium Light Night* (mus. Ives, 1978). Joint b. master-in-chief, N.Y. City B. 1983; retired from d. 1984. Author of *Far From Denmark* (Boston, 1982); Knight of the Order of Dannebrog (1983).

Martinů, Bohuslav (*b* Polička, 8 Dec. 1890, *d* Liestal, Switzerland, 28 Aug. 1959). Czech composer. Wrote the mus. for R. Remislawsky's *Istar* (Prague, 1924), and *Who Is the Mightiest in the World?* (Prague, 1927), Psota's *The Riot* (Brno, 1928), Joe Jenčík's *Spaliček* (Prague, 1933), and

Erick Hawkins' *The Strangler* (New London, 1948). In addition he left several b. scores which have not yet been performed. Concert mus. of his was used in Tudor's *Echoing of Trumpets* (*Symphonic Fantasies*, 1963—also for MacMillan's *Anastasia*, 1967), Smok's *Frescoes* (Fresques de Piero della Francesca, 1965—also for Cauley's *La Symphonie pastorale*, 1970); Tetley's *Sphinx* (Double Stg. Conc., 1979), Corder's *Day into Night* (Sinfonietta 'La Jolla', 1980), and Kylián's *Field Mass* (1980).

Martyn, Laurel (*b* Brisbane, 1916). Austral. dancer, teacher, and b. director. Studied at Sadler's Wells School; d. with Sadler's Wells B. (as L. Gill) 1935–8. Went to Australia and joined Borovansky B. as a principal d. 1947. From 1946 prod. bs. in Melbourne, initially for Melbourne B. Club, from which grew Victorian B. Guild and eventually B. Victoria, of which she was dir. and chief ch. until it disbanded 1976. The co. prod. the classics and many new bs. Awarded OBE (1976).
BIBL.: J. Carger, in *Opera and Ballet in Australia* (Sydney, 1977).

Martyre de Saint-Sébastien, Le. Mystery in 5 acts; text d'Annunzio; mus. Debussy; ch. Rubinstein; déc. Bakst. Prod. 22 May 1911, Th. du Châtelet, Paris, with Rubinstein. A mixture of cantata, op., and b., the work tries to blend elements of the Adonis cult and the Christian religion. Lifar's 1957 prod. at the Paris Opéra (with Tcherina) established the piece in the repertory.

Maryinsky Theatre. See *Kirov Ballet*.

Mary, Queen of Scots. Ballet in 2 acts; libr. N. Goodwin; ch. P. Darrell; mus. J. McCabe; déc. P. Docherty; light. J. B. Read. Prod 3 March 1976, Scottish B., Th. Royal, Glasgow, with McDonald, Haig, Bart, Tyers. M.'s progress from teenage Queen of France to execution at Fotheringhay, the men she attracted, and her relations with Elizabeth of England. M. Graham's contribution to *Episodes* was an earlier treatment of the final scenes.

Maslow, Sophie (*b* New York). Amer. dancer, teacher, and choreographer. Studied with Blanche Talmud and Graham, whose co. she joined. Appeared with J. Dudley and W. Bales in the Dudley-Maslow-Bales Trio 1942–54, for which she ch. extensively. Founding member of the Amer. D. Festival at Connecticut College, 1948. Has also done ch. for op. and play prods. Her pieces are often inspired by Jewish subjects; *The Dybbuk* (mus. R. Starer, 1964) is one of her best known bs. Teaches at the New York D. Group Studio.

Mason, Monica (*b* Johannesburg, 6 Sept. 1941). S.A. d. Studied with Ruth Inglestone, Nesta Brooking, and at Royal B. School. Joined Royal B. in 1958; apptd. soloist in 1961 and principal d. in 1967. Created roles in MacMillan's *Sacre du*

printemps (1962), *Manon* (1974), *Elite Syncopations* (1974), *Rituals* (1975), and *Isadora* (1981), and Van Dantzig's *Ropes of Time* (1970). Principal répétiteur Royal B. 1984.
BIBL.: S. Goodman, 'M.M.', *Dance Magazine* (1968/7); J. Gruen, 'M.M.', in *The Private World of Ballet* (New York, 1975).

Masque. Festive displays, popular at the Eng. court of the 16th and 17th century. They originated in mummings and traditional masked processions. Like their Fr. equivalent, the bs. de cour, they were mostly performed by the nobility. They consisted of allegorical or mythological scenes, with mus., d., mime, declamation, singing, and rich décor. Special emphasis was put on the dancing: in the entrées, in the central grand masque d., and in the concluding ballroom dances. The best known text authors were Ben Jonson, John Milton, Samuel Daniel, and Thomas Campion; composers incl. J. Coperario, A. Ferrabosco II, and R. Johnson; the most famous designer was the architect Inigo Jones, and the producers incl. Thomas Giles and Hieronimus Herne. It was predominantly orientated towards literature rather than mus. and reached its apogee with Jonson and Jones's *Masque of Blackness* (1605) and *Masque of Beauty* (1608). Jonson introduced the anti-m. in 1609—a grotesque interlude. In some of Purcell's works (*The Fairy Queen, King Arthur, Dido and Aeneas*) and Handel's b.-orientated ops., *Alcina* and *Ariodante*, one can see the late successors of the masque. Helpmann attempted to revive Milton's *Comus* mainly in d. form for Sadler's Wells B. (1942), as did Inglesby, with the complete text, for International B. (1946).
BIBL.: L. Kirstein, 'The English Court Masque' in *Movement & Metaphor* (New York, 1970).

Masques, Les. Ballet in 1 act; libr. and ch. Ashton; mus. Poulenc; déc, Fedorovitch. Prod. 5 Mar. 1933, B. Club, Mercury Th., with Ashton, Markova, Argyle, Gore. Set to Poulenc's Trio for Piano, Oboe, and Bassoon. The b. is costumed and set entirely in black and white. A husband and wife meet at a masked ball and fail to recognize each other; when the masks are removed they are covered with confusion.
BIBL.: D. Vaughan, *Frederick Ashton and his Bs.* (London, 1977).

Mass. Th. piece for players, singers, and dancers; mus. Bernstein; ch. Ailey; déc. O. Smith. Prod. 8 Sep. 1971, John F. Kennedy Center, Washington, D.C. The official inauguration work for the new Washington op. house. The dancers came from Ailey's co. and the lead-part was performed by J. Jamison. Revived for Vienna State Op. (1981). Also modern-d. work by R. Cohan for London Contemporary D. Th. (1973, revised 1977).

Mass for Our Time (orig. Fr. title: *Messe pour le temps présent*). Ceremony in 9 episodes, dedicated to the memory of P. Belda, by Béjart. Prod. 3

Aug. 1967, B. of the 20th Century, Palais des Papes, Avignon, with L. Proença, Bortoluzzi, Donn, Lowski, Carrié, Dobrievich. Déc. J. Roustan and R. Bernard. Texts were taken from Buddha, the Song of Songs, Nietzsche's *Also sprach Zarathustra*, and nursery rhymes. The sound effects were prod. by Béjart himself; Venugopal Mukunda played the vina and P. Henry comp. the rock music. Preceded by Nietzsche's 'I can only believe in a god who can dance', the 9 episodes are entitled: The Breath, The Body, The World, The Dance, The Couple, 'Mein Kampf', The Night, The Silence, The Waiting.

Massine, Léonide Fedorovich (*b* Moscow, 8 Aug. 1895, *d* Weseke bei Borken, Westphalia, 15 Mar. 1979). Russ.-Amer. dancer, choreographer, b. master, and teacher. Studied at Moscow Bolshoi School; graduated in 1912 and joined Bolshoi B. Joined Diaghilev's Bs. Russes in 1914; created title role in Fokine's *Legend of Joseph*. Ch. his first b. (*Soleil de nuit*, mus. Rimsky-Korsakov) in 1915. Continued to study with Cecchetti, while Diaghilev guided his development as a ch. Made a double career as d. and ch.; created *Les Femmes de bonne humeur* (mus. D. Scarlatti), *Parade* (mus. Satie, both 1917), *Boutique fantasque* (mus. Rossini, arr. Respighi), *Le Tricorne* (mus. de Falla, both 1919), *Song of the Nightingale*, *Pulcinella*, new version of *Sacre du printemps* (all mus. Stravinsky, 1920). He often took the leading male role. Left Diaghilev in 1921 to tour with some of his d. colleagues. Ch. Milhaud's *Salade*, Satie's *Mercure*, and J. Strauss/Desormière's *Le Beau Danube* in 1924 for Soirées de Paris. With Diaghilev again 1925–8; ch. *Zéphire et Flore* (mus. V. Dukelsky), *Les Matelots* (mus. Auric, both 1925), *Le Pas d'acier* (mus. Prokofiev, 1927), and *Ode* (mus. Nabokov, 1928). Also worked for the London Cochrane revues 1925–6. Solo-d. and b. master of the Roxy Th., New York, 1927–30. Revived *Sacre du printemps* with Graham in 1930. Ch. Sauguet's *David* (1929) and Honegger's *Amphion* (1931) for Rubinstein's co. Started to work for B. Russe de Monte Carlo in 1932; became b. master in 1933. Ch. *Jeux d'enfants* (mus. Bizet, 1932), *Choréartium* (mus. Brahms's Fourth Symphony, 1933), *Les Présages* (mus. Tchaikovsky's Fifth Symphony, 1934) and *Symphonie fantastique* (mus. Berlioz, 1936). Was artistic dir. of R. Blum's rival B. Russe de Monte Carlo 1938–43; ch. *Gaîté Parisienne* (mus. Offenbach-Rosenthal), *Seventh Symphony* (mus. Beethoven), Hindemith's *Nobilissima Visione* (all 1938), *Capriccio espagnol* (with Argentinita, mus. Rimsky-Korsakov), *Rouge et noir* (mus. Shostakovich's First Symphony), *Bacchanale* (mus. Wagner, all 1939), and *Labyrinth* (mus. Schubert's Seventh Symphony, 1941). With B. Th. 1942–3 (*Aleko*, mus. Tchaikovsky, 1942; *Mademoiselle Angot*, mus. Lecocq, 1943). For B. International: *Mad Tristan* (mus. Wagner, 1944). Toured with his own co., B. Russe Highlights, 1945–6 (*Leningrad Symphony*, mus. Shostakovich). Worked

principally in Europe after 1947; further bs. incl. *Clock Symphony* (mus. Haydn, Sadler's Wells B., 1948), *Le Peintre et son modèle* (mus. Auric, Bs. des Champs-Elysées, 1949), *Harold in Italy* (mus. Berlioz, B. Russe de Monte Carlo), *Donald of the Burthens* (mus. I. Whyte, Sadler's Wells B., both 1951), *Laudes Evangelii* (mus. Bucchi, Perugia, 1952), *Mario and the Magician* (mus. F. Mannino, Milan, 1954), and *Don Juan* (mus. Gluck, Milan, 1959). Studied the dances of the Amer. Indians and presented many lecture demonstrations with his son Léonide (now Lorca). Set up B. Europeo for the Nervi Festival in 1960, for which he ch. Rossini's *Barber of Seville*, Anouilh-Auric's *Le Bal des voleurs*, and the full-length *La Commedia umana* (14th-century mus.). Visited the U.S.S.R. as a tourist in 1961; he had not been there since 1914. During the next few years he travelled all over the world to revive his bs. for various cos. He also worked for films: *The Red Shoes* (1946), *Tales of Hoffmann* (1951), and *Carosello Napoletano* (1954). Worked for years on a theoretical study of the essentials of ch. Became guest teacher of ch. at Royal B. School in 1969. As a d. he had his greatest success in character roles, and he has rarely been surpassed in roles he created for himself. As ch. he is one of the most important figures in b. history, mainly through his contributions to the comedy genre, but also as the originator of the Symphonic b., which undoubtedly paved the way for concert mus. on the b. stage. Author of *My Life in Ballet* (London, 1960). He was married to the dancers Vera Savina, Eugenia Delarova, and Tatiana Orlova, and is the father of the d. Tatiana M. and the d.-ch. Lorca M.

BIBL.: A. L. Haskell, 'L.M.: An Appreciation', *Dance Magazine* (1969/11); interview with L.M., *Dance and Dancers* (1971/4); J. Gruen, 'L.M.', in *The Private World of Ballet* (New York, 1975).

Massine, Lorca (orig. Léonide M.; *b* New York, 25 July 1944). Amer. dancer and choreographer. Studied with his father Léonide M., Y. Brieux, and V. Gsovsky. Début Nervi 1960. Created Puck in Britten's *A Midsummer Night's Dream* (Aldeburgh, 1960). Acted in several Paris plays, and occasionally worked as a ch. Formed European B. with his sister Tatiana M. in Paris; they toured 1964–7. Soloist and ch. of B. of the 20th Century 1968–70, where one of his bs. was Mahler's *Tenth Symphony* (1968). Soloist of New York City B. 1971–3, where he ch. *Four Last Songs* (mus. R. Strauss, 1971), and *Ode* (mus. Stravinsky, 1972). Has also ch. *Ondine* (mus. Henze, Hamburg, 1972), *Fête dansée* (mus. Theodorakis, co. of A. Beranger, 1973), and *Esoteric Satie* (Milan, 1978).

Mata and Hari. Amer. dance-duo. Ruth Mata and Eugene Hari studied b. with Volkhart, modern d. with Wigman and Laban, and pantomime with T. Schoop in Zurich. They came to the U.S. with Schoop's d. co. in 1937, and have stayed there ever since. They married, and toured extensively, mostly as a duo, but occasionally with a small group. Frequent TV and film appearances; their most popular numbers include *Carnegie Hall*, *Circus Acrobats*, *Apache Dance*, *Woman on the Couch*, *Kiss Me My Love*, *Have Gun*, *Get Gold*, all ch. by themselves. In 1962 they opened their New York Pantomime Studio.

Match. D. Duo; ch. Schilling; mus. S. Matthus; cost. E. Kleiber. Prod. Varna B. Competition 1970, with M. Lubitz and I. Chmelnitzky. Official first perf. 9 May 1971, Comic Op., Berlin. A pas de deux in the form of a tennis match. It has been revived for many d.-couples. Maximova and Vassiliev perform it in the 1974 Sov. TV film *The Duet*.

Matelots, Les. Ballet in 5 scenes; libr. Kochno; ch. Massine; mus. Auric; déc. Pedro Pruna. Prod. 17 June 1925, Bs. Russes de Diaghilev, Coliseum, London, with Sokolova, Nemchinova, Woizikovsky, Lifar. Before returning to sea, a sailor gets engaged to his girl. He comes back in disguise, with three comrades, to test her faithfulness; but she remains steadfast, so everything ends happily. BIBL.: C. W. Beaumont, 'L.M.' in *Complete Book of Ballets* (London, 1951).

Mathé, Carmen (orig. Margaretha Matheson; *b* Dundee, 3 Nov. 1938). Brit. dancer. Studied at Cone-Ripman (Arts Educational) School and with Craske. Joined Grand B. du Marquis de Cuevas in 1956, New York City B. in 1961, Amer. B. Th. in 1962. Ballerina with London Festival B. 1962–70, Washington National B. 1971–4, Chicago B. since 1974.

Mathis, Bonnie (*b* Milwaukee, Wisc., 8 Sep. 1942). Amer. dancer. Studied with Roberta Reberg, Stone-Camryn, at Juilliard School, and with Vilzak and Slavenska. D. at Radio City Music Hall, with P. Taylor, and in the Broadway prod. of *Hello, Dolly*. Member of Harkness B. 1965–70, then a principal d. with Amer. B. Th. until she joined Netherlands D. Th. in 1976. BIBL.: S. Goodman, 'B.M.', *Dance Magazine* (1970/3).

Mathilde. Ballet in 1 act; libr. and ch. Béjart; mus. Wagner; déc. Thierry Bosquet. Prod. 14 Jan. 1965, B. of the 20th Century, Th. Royal de la Monnaie, Brussels, with Casado, Maryse Patris (singing role), Dobrievich. Set to Prélude and Liebestod from *Tristan und Isolde* and the *Wesendonck Lieder*. Two different levels are interlaced: the first is reserved for 5 dancers going through their daily classroom routine, the second has Le Voyageur, Elle (a singing role), and Lui— referring obviously to Wagner, Mathilde and Otto Wesendonck and their triangular affair. The b. was part of a programme called *Wagner ou L'amour fou*, the other 2 bs. being *Le 'Venusberg'* (ch. Béjart) and *Siegfried-Idyll* (ch. Sparemblek). A novel by Béjart, *M. ou le temps perdu* appeared in 1963.

Matisse, Henri (*b* Le Cateau, 31 Dec. 1869, *d*

Nice, 3 Nov. 1954). Fr. painter. Designed the déc. for Massine's *The Song of the Nightingale* (1920) and *L'Etrange farandole* (alias *Rouge et noir*, 1939).

Matteo (orig. M. Marcellus Vittucci; *b*. Utica, 2 May 1919). Amer. dancer, teacher, choreographer, and director. Studied at Cornell Univ., New York Ethnologic D. Center, Springfield College, and with leading masters of ethnic d. throughout the world. D. with Met. Op. B. 1946–50; then toured the U.S. and abroad as a concert d. artist, presenting ethnic dances, lecturing, and giving master classes under the title of 'A World of Dancing'. Established Indo-Amer. D. Co. with Carola Goya in 1967; this developed into the Indo-Amer. Performing Arts Center of New York in 1970 (now the Foundation for Ethnic Dance and the Ethno Amer. Dance Th.). CBS and WNYC have prod. several TV programmes with him. Contributor on ethnic d. to *Enciclopedia dello spettacolo*. Author of 'Woods That Dance' (on castanets) to *Dance Perspectives* 33. BIBL.: T. Crowder, 'Namaste: M. and the Indo-American Dance Company', *Dance Magazine* (1972/2).

Mattox, Matt (*b* Tulsa, Okla., 18 Aug. 1921). Amer. dancer and teacher. Studied with E. Belcher, N. Charisse, Loring, Cole. Début Broadway, 1946. D. in many musicals, films (e.g. *Seven Brides for Seven Brothers*), revues, and TV prods.; became one of the outstanding teachers of jazz d. Came to London in 1970; taught at the D. Centre and appeared occasionally with his group Jazzart; now teaching in Paris. BIBL.: H. Flatow, 'M.M. Offstage', *Dance Magazine* (1956/2).

Maule, Michael (*b* Durban, 31 Oct. 1926). S.A. dancer. Studied with V. Celli in New York. Début in *Annie Get Your Gun*, 1946. D. with B. Th., co. of A. Alonso, New York City B. 1950–53, Danilova's co. in 1954 (also partnered Danilova as guest with London Festival B.), Robbins's Bs.: U.S.A. in 1959, B. Ensemble 1960–61, and with his own touring group in 1964. Now teaches at M. Hayden's N.Y. studio.

Mauri, Rosita (*b* Tarragona, 15 Sep. 1849, *d* Paris, 1923). Span. dancer. Début Teatro Principal, Barcelona, 1868. D. at La Scala and then with Paris Opéra 1878–1907, where she became a much admired étoile. Created the ballerina roles in Mérante's *La Korrigane* (1880) and *Les deux pigeons* (1886), and in Hansen's *La Maladetta* (1893). Taught at the Opéra until 1920.

Maximova, Yekaterina Sergeyevna (*b* Moscow, 1 Feb. 1939). Sov. dancer. Studied at Bolshoi B. School; graduated in 1958. Joined Bolshoi B. and became one of its most popular ballerinas during her first season, as Katerina in Grigorovich's Moscow prod. of *The Stone Flower*. She was coached by Ulanova, and soon d. Giselle, and had a sensational success as Kitri. Created Masha in

Grigorovich's *Nutcracker* (1966), Phrygia in his *Spartacus* (1968) and Aurora in his *Sleeping Beauty* (1973). London début 1963. Appears with her husband Vladimir Vassiliev in the Sov. TV film *The Duet* (1974). Gold Medal (Varna, 1964).
BIBL.: I. Lidova, 'M.', *Les Saisons de la danse* (1972/11); interview with M., *Dancing Times* (1974/8).

Mayerling. Ballet in 3 acts, with prologue and epilogue; scenario Gillian Freeman; ch. Mac-Millan; mus. Liszt, arr. and orch. by Lanchbery; déc. Georgiadis. Prod. 14 Feb. 1978, Royal B., Cov. Gdn., London, with Wall, Seymour, Wendy Ellis, Parkinson, Park, Connor, Somes, Graham Fletcher. Framed by the burial of the 17 year-old Baroness Mary Vetsera at Heiligenbluth nr. Vienna, the plot centres upon Crown Prince Rudolph of Austria-Hungary, following the events from his wedding to Princess Stephanie of Belgium via his gradual moral and physical decline to his and Mary Vetsera's suicide in 1889 at the hunting lodge of M. London Weekend TV prod. (Prix Italia, 1978). An earlier M. ballet by E. Bernhofer (mus. Dürr, Vienna 1966).
BIBL.: Scenario and list of characters, *Dancing Times* (Feb. 1978).

May, Pamela (*b* Trinidad, 30 May 1917). Brit. dancer and teacher. Studied with Freda Grant and de Valois. Début Vic-Wells B., 1934; became soloist, and eventually ballerina. Created roles in de Valois' *Checkmate* (1936), *The Prospect Before Us* (1940), and *Orpheus and Eurydice* (1941), Ashton's *Horoscope* (1936), *The Wanderer* (1941), and-*Symphonic Variations* (1946). Since 1952 appeared mainly in the mime roles of the classics. Taught at Royal B. School 1954–78.
BIBL.: G. Anthony, 'P.M.', *Dancing Times* (1971/1).

Maynard, Olga (*b* Brazil, 16 Jan. 1920). Amer. writer on dance. Began lecturing and writing professionally in 1956. Lecturer in Fine Arts at Univ. of Cal. at Irvine. Contributing Editor of *Dance Magazine*. Author of *The Ballet Companion* (1957), *The American Ballet* (1959), *Bird of Fire: Biography of Maria Tallchief* (1961), *American Modern Dancers* (1965), *Children and Dance and Music* (1968).

Maywood, Augusta (*b* New York, 1825, *d* Lvov, 3 Nov. 1876). Amer. d. Studied with Hazard at Philadelphia. Début there in *Le Dieu et la Bayadère* in 1837, followed by *La Sylphide* (1838). Continued to study in Paris with Mazilier and Coralli. Was very successful as a guest ballerina in the Opéra's *La Tarentule* 1839. Had a much publicized love-affair with the d. Charles Mabille, whom she accompanied to Lisbon and to Vienna, and married. She stayed in Vienna, for 3 years, after her divorce, as a member of the Kärntnertor Th. She was much admired in *Giselle*, *Le Diable amoureux*, *La Gypsy*, and *La Bayadère*. Went to La Scala in 1848, where she studied with Blasis; she shared the ballerina-roles with Elssler, incl. Perrot's *Faust* and Cortesi's *La Silfide*. Performed

at many Ital. ths. and returned to Vienna, where she enjoyed her greatest success in Filippo Termanini's *Rita Gauthier* (1864). After her retirement as a d. opened a school in Vienna. Spent her last years at Lago di Como. The first Amer. ballerina to win international acclaim.
BIBL.: M. H. Winter, 'A.M.', *Dance Index* (II,1); I. Guest, in *The Romantic Ballet in Paris* (London, 1966); P. Migel, 'A.M.' in *The Ballerinas* (New York, 1972).

Mazilier, Joseph (orig. Giulio Mazarini; *b* Marseilles, 13 Mar. 1801, *d* Paris, 19 May 1868). Fr. dancer, choreographer, and b. master. Début at Paris Th. de la Porte Saint-Martin in 1822. Joined the Opéra and became a much admired character d. Created roles in F. Taglioni's *La Sylphide* (1832), and *La Fille du Danube* (1836), Coralli's *Le Diable boîteux* (1836) and *La Tarentule* (1839), and Guerra's *Les Mohicans* (1837). Appointed b. master in 1839; ch. many bs., e.g. *La Gypsy* (mus. F. Benoist and T. Marliani, 1839), *Le Diable amoureux* (mus. Benoist and H. Reber, 1840), *Lady Henriette, ou la Servante de Greenwich* (mus. Flotow, Burgh-müller, and Deldevez, 1844), *Le Diable à quatre* (mus. Adam, 1845), *Paquita* (mus. Deldevez, 1846), *Griseldis, ou les cinq sens* mus. Adam, 1848), *Vert-Vert* (mus. Deldevez and J. B. Tobecque, 1851), *Jovita, ou les Boucaniers* (mus. T. Labarre, 1853), *Le Corsaire* (mus. Adam, 1856), and *Marco Spada, ou la Fille du bandit* (mus. Auber, 1857).
BIBL.: entry 'M., J.' in *Enciclopedia dello spettacolo*; I. Guest, in *The Romantic Ballet in Paris* (London, 1966); Guest, *The Ballet of the Second Empire 1847–1858* (London, 1955).

Mazowsze. Pol. State D. Co., founded by Tadeusz Sygietynski and his wife Mira Ziminska as a folk d. ensemble in 1948, now with 100 members. The name comes from the central province around Warsaw, were the co. has its residence and school in Karolin. Its aim is to collect Pol. folk-songs and dances and to adapt them to the stage. Since the death of her husband, Ziminska-Sygietynska has been the dir., in charge of the mus. adaptations, the costumes, and the general prod., while Witold Zapala is the chief ch. The co. made its London début in 1957, followed by New York in 1961.

Mazurka. A Pol. folk-d. from Mazovia, first recorded in the 16th century. Originally a peasant d. for 8 or 16 couples in lively 3/4 or 3/8 time; the music is characterized by dotted rhythms, melodic leaps, and accents on the second beat of the bar, and the d. by its proud bearing, stamping, clicking the heels, and a special turning step, the holubiec. It was introduced as a ballroom d. throughout Eur. in the second half of the 19th century.

Mazzo, Kay (*b* Chicago, 17 Jan. 1946). Amer. dancer. Studied with Bernardene Hayes and School of Amer. B. Début with Robbins' Bs.: U.S.A. in 1961 in *Afternoon of a Faun.* Joined New

York City B. in 1962; became soloist in 1965 and principal d. 1969. Created many roles, incl. Balanchine's *Jewels* (1967), *Suite No. 3* (1970), *Violin Concerto, Duo concertant* (both 1972), and *Davidsbündlertänze* (1980), Robbins' *Dances at a Gathering* (1969) and *In the Night* (1970). Now retired from d.; teaches at Sch. of Amer. B.
BIBL.: W. Boggs, 'K.M.', *Dance News* (1973/1); J. Gruen, 'K.M.', in *The Private World of Ballet* (New York, 1975).

Mead, Robert (*b* Bristol, 17 Apr. 1940). Brit. dancer and b. master. Studied with Lillian Houlden and at Sadler's Wells B. School. Joined Royal B. Touring Section in 1958. Moved to Cov. Gdn. section in 1962; appointed principal d. in 1967. Created roles in Ashton's *Two Pigeons* (1961), *Monotones* (1965), *Jazz Calendar*, and *Enigma Variations* (both 1968). Principal d. Hamburg B. 1971–3. Joined Hanover B. as asst. b. master in 1974. Has repeatedly staged Ashton and Nijinska bs. for cos. in Ger., the U.S., and Australia. Asst. art. dir. Northern B. Th. 1983.

Meadowlark. Ballet in 1 act; ch. Feld; mus. attributed to Haydn; set Robert Prévost; cost. Stanley Simmons. Prod. 3 Oct. 1968, Royal Winnipeg B., Centennial Hall, Winnipeg, with D. Frances, R. Rutherford, S. Mackinnon, M. Lewis, D. Hoppmann. Set to individual movements from the Flute Quartets op. 5, attributed to Haydn, and the Finale from his String Quartet op. 74, no. 1. The b. depicts a *fête champêtre* for 6 couples. Revived for London Festival B. (1968), Amer. B. Co. (1969), and City Center Joffrey B. (1972).

Medea. Ballet in 1 act and 5 scenes; libr. and ch. Cullberg; mus. Bartók (arr. H. Sandberg); déc. Alvar Grandstrom. Prod. 31 Oct. 1950, Riksteatern, Gaevle, Sweden, with Lagerborg, Béjart, Inga Noring. Set to selected pieces from Bartók's *Mikrokosmos*. The b. deals with M.'s revenge when her husband Jason deserts her for his new wife Creusa. Revived for Royal Swed. B. (1953), New York City B. (1958), Munich State Op. B. (1965). An earlier b. *Médée et Jason* by Noverre, mus. Rodolphe, Stuttgart, 1763. A modern d. drama under the title *Cave of the Heart by Graham, mus. Barber, New York, 1947. Barber's music also ch. by Butler for Fracci and Baryshnikov (Spoleto, 1975).
BIBL.: G. Balanchine, 'M.' in *Balanchine's New Complete Stories of the Great Ballets* (Garden City, N.Y., 1968).

Meditation. D. for 2 people; ch. Balanchine; mus. Tchaikovsky; cost. Karinska. Prod. 10 Dec. 1963, New York City B., City Center, N.Y., with Farrell and d'Amboise. Set to Tchaikovsky's Op. 42, no. 1 for violin and piano. A dramatic pas de deux in a contemplative mood.
BIBL.: G. Balanchine, 'M.' in *Balanchine's New Complete Stories of the Great Ballets* (Garden City, N.Y., 1968).

Meditation from 'Thaïs'. Pas de deux; ch. Ashton; mus. Massenet. Prod. 21 Mar. 1971 at the Gala in aid of Friends of Fatherless Families, Adelphi Th., London, with Sibley and Dowell. An oriental dream sequence. An earlier version was a very popular piece in Pavlova's rep., d. with Mordkin.

Meehan, John (*b* Brisbane, 1 May 1950). Austral. d. Studied at Austral. B. School, joined Austral. B. in 1970, promoted soloist in 1972, principal d. in 1974. Created roles in Tetley's *Gemini* (1973), Helpmann's *Perisynthion* (1974), Butler's *Night Encounter*, and Hynd's *Merry Widow* (both 1975). Occasionally worked as a ch. Joined Amer. B. Th. 1977–80 and returned 1985; now freelance.
BIBL.: J. Gruen, 'The Public Person of J.M.', *Dance Magazine* (1979/9).

Meister, Hans (*b* Schaffhausen, 13 Oct. 1937). Swiss dancer and b. director. Studied at Zurich Op. B. School and Sadler's Wells B. School. Joined National B. of Canada in 1957, appointed principal d. in 1961. Soloist Met. Op. B. 1962–6, Zurich B. 1967–8. Studied further in Leningrad, where he d. occasionally with the Kirov B. Appeared with various cos. in Switzerland. Principal d. of National B. of Finland 1972–5. B. dir. of Zurich Op. House 1975–8.
BIBL.: interview 'A Swiss in Rossi Street', *Dance and Dancers* (1969/11).

Melville, Kenneth (*b* Birkenhead, 1929). Brit. dancer and teacher. Studied at Sadler's Wells B. School. Joined Sadler's Wells B. in 1946 and eventually became a soloist. Member of London Festival B. 1955–7, Borovansky B. 1957–8. Toured with Svetlova in 1959. Member of National B. of Canada 1960–63, Zurich B. 1963–5. Now teaches at Indiana Univ., Bloomington.

Mendelssohn Bartholdy, Felix (*b* Hamburg, 3 Feb. 1809, *d* Leipzig, 4 Nov. 1847). Ger. composer. Wrote no b. mus., but his concert pieces have often been adapted to d. purposes—e.g. *Songs Without Words*, used by many recital dancers (especially by M. Allan, also as a b. by Van Manen, Den Haag, 1977), the incidental mus. to *A Midsummer Night's Dream (M. Petipa, St. Petersburg, 1877; Fokine, St. Petersburg, 1906, and in *Les Elfes*, New York, 1924; Balanchine, New York, 1962; Ashton, London, 1964; Spoerli, Basle, 1975; Neumeier, Hamburg, 1977, with addl. mus. Ligeti; de Warren, Manchester, 1981), *Scotch Symphony* (Balanchine, New York, 1952), and *Italian Symphony* (Nahat, New York, 1971).

Mendez, Josefina (*b* Havana, 1940). Cub. dancer. Studied at the Sociedad Pro-Arte Mus. with the Alonsos and J. Parés. Joined B. de Cuba in 1955 and National B. of Cuba in 1959. Appointed prima ballerina 1962; now an artistic dir. Bronze Medal (Varna, 1964); Silver Medal (Varna, 1965); *L'Etoile d'or* (Paris, 1970).

BIBL.: I. Lidova, 'J.M.', *Les Saisons de la danse* (1972/4); complete check-list of roles and activities in *Cuba en el ballet* (vol. 3, no. 2).

Ménéstrier, Claude-François (*b* Lyons, 1631, *d* Paris, 1705). A Fr. Jesuit, choreographer, diplomat, chronicler, and pioneer theorist of the *b. d'action*. He was in charge of arranging fêtes and public celebrations both in Italy (Turin) and France; published 2 books in which he describes his work and ideas: *Traité des Tournois, Joustes, Carrousels et autre Spectacles publics* (Lyons, 1669) and *Des Ballets anciens et modernes selon les règles du théâtre* (Paris, 1682).
BIBL.: M. H. Winter, in *The Pre-Romantic Ballet* (London, 1974).

Mengarelli, Julius (*b* Stockholm, 1920, *d* Västanvik, 1960). Swed. dancer. Brother of Mario M. Studied at Royal Swed. B. School. Joined Royal Swed. B., appointed principal d. in 1945. Created leading roles in Cullberg's *Miss Julie* (1950) and Cramér's *The Prodigal Son* (1958).

Mengarelli, Mario (*b* Stockholm, 11 Jan. 1925). Swed. dancer. Brother of Julius M. Studied at Royal Swed. B. School. Joined Royal Swed. B. 1943; appointed principal d. 1960. Created roles in Åkesson's *Sisyphus* (1957) and Tudor's *Echoing of Trumpets* (1963). Resigned 1971.

Menotti, Gian-Carlo (*b* Cadegliano, 7 July 1911). Ital.-Amer. composer. Wrote the mus. for Caton's *Sebastian* (International B., 1944), Graham's *Errand Into the Maze* (New York, 1947), and Butler's *The Unicorn, the Gorgon, and the Manticore* (New York City B., 1956).

Menuett. See *Minuet*.

Menyhárt, Jacqueline (*b* Lens, France, 25 Oct. 1937). Hung. dancer. Studied at the Budapest State B. Inst. and in Moscow. Joined Budapest State Op. B. 1954; appointed principal d. Liszt Award (1968).

Mephisto Valse. Ballet in 1 act; libr. and ch. Ashton; mus. Liszt; déc. Fedorovitch. Prod. 13 June 1934, B. Club, Mercury Th., with Markova, Gore, Ashton. A sombre piece of romanticism, centering on Marguerite, Faust, and Mephistopheles, accompanied by a small corps de b. A revised version as *Vision of Marguerite* for London Festival B. (1952).
BIBL.: D. Vaughan, *Frederick Ashton and his Bs* (London, 1977).

Mer, La. Ballet in 1 act; libr. and ch. Schilling; mus. Debussy; cost. Gottfried Reinhardt. Prod. Varna B. Competition, 1968, with Bey and Gawlik. Two young lovers on the beach are trapped by the rising tide. Won prize for best ch. Extended version taken into the repertory of the East Berlin Comic Op. with déc. by Erich Geister (1969).

Mérante, Louis (*b* Paris, 23 July 1828, *d* Courbevoie, 17 July 1887). Fr. dancer, choreographer and b. master. Member of an Ital. family of dancers; he d. in Liège when 6 years old. Studied with L. Petipa in Paris and soon succeeded him in his roles at the Opéra. Became one of the best premiers danseurs of his time. Created many leading roles between 1853 and 1866 in such bs. as Mazilier's *Marco Spada*, L. Petipa's *Sacountala*, M. Taglioni's *Le Papillon*, Saint-Léon's *Diavolina* and *La Source*; also in Petipa's *Namouna* (1882), and in many divertissements and op. bs. He was much sought-after as a partner by all the leading ballerinas. Appointed b. master 1853. Made his début as a ch. with *Gretna Green* (mus. E. Guiraud), followed by Delibes' *Sylvia* (1876), C. M. Widor's *La Korrigane* (1880), and Messager's *Les deux pigeons* (1886). Married to the d. Zinaida Josefovna Richard, who after ending her stage-career in 1879 became a much respected teacher.
BIBL.: I. Guest, in *The Ballet of the Second Empire* (2 vols., London, 1953 and 1955).

Mercandotti, Maria (*b* Spain, *c.* 1801). Span. dancer. Started as a child d. in Cadiz. Came to London 1814, and studied with Armand Vestris. Gave a much acclaimed single perf. at the King's Th. in July 1814, and then gave a few private perfs. in Brighton. Studied further with Coulon in Paris; d. at the Opéra 1821–2, and was acclaimed as 'the Andalusian Venus'.
BIBL.: I. Guest, in *The Romantic Ballet in Paris* (London, 1966).

Mercure. Tableaux in 3 scenes; libr. and ch. Massine; mus. Satie; déc. Picasso. Prod. 15 June 1924, Soirées de Paris, Th. de la Cigale. The 3 tableaux were intended to evoke various aspects of M.'s mythological personality; the god of fertility, the messenger of the gods, the cunning thief, the magician, and the attendant of the Underworld. It was considered Picasso's rather than Massine's b., because the strikingly cubist déc. completely overshadowed the rather statuesque ch. Diaghilev acquired the prod. for his co. in 1927, but there, too, only very few perfs. took place.
BIBL.: D. Cooper, in *Picasso Theatre* (1967).

Mercury Theatre. Originally a mid-19th-century church hall in Notting Hill Gate in London, which Ashley Dukes and his wife M. Rambert bought in 1927, and turned into a small th. and adjacent b. school. Opened as a th. in 1931 with a perf. by the B. Club. It housed many premières of the slowly emerging Eng. b. It was given its name in 1933, and functioned until 1955, when it was turned into a b. studio.
BIBL.: M. Clarke, *Dancers of Mercury* (London, 1962).

Meri, La. See *La Meri*.

Meridian. Ballet in 1 act; ch. P. Taylor; mus. Boulez; cost. Louise Thompson. Prod. 13 Feb. 1960, P. Taylor and D. Co., Hunter College

Playhouse, New York, with Akiko Kanda, Taylor, and Wagoner. Set to Boulez' *Le Marteau sans maître*. 'A gentle, almost lyric trio, though the manipulation of the girl by her two partners comes close to acrobatics at times' (A. Chujoy). Other bs. to the same mus. by S. Popescu (Bucharest Op. B. in Paris, 1965) and Béjart (B. of the 20th Century, 1973).

Merry, Hazel (*b* Edgware, 20 July 1938). Brit. dancer. Studied at Sadler's Wells School. One of the founder members of Western Th. B. 1957, where she created many leading roles. Also d. with London Festival B. in 1961, B. of the 20th Century in 1963, Netherlands Dance Th. in 1964, B. Rambert in 1966, and Touring Royal B. 1967–73.

Merry Widow, The. Ballet in 3 acts; scenario and staging Helpmann; ch. Hynd; mus. Lehár, arr. Lanchbery; déc. Heeley. Prod. 13 Nov. 1975, The Austral. B., Palais, Melbourne, with M. Rowe, J. Meehan, L. Aldous, K. Coe. The b. follows the plot of Lehár's popular operetta (1905). An earlier b. version of the same operetta was R. Page's *Vilia* (London Festival B., 1953).

Merry Wives of Windsor, The (orig. Russ. title: *Vindzorskiye prokaznitsy*). Ballet in 3 acts and 7 scenes; libr. and ch. V. Bourmeister and I. Kurilov; mus. V. Oransky; déc. B. Volkov. Prod. 10 June 1942, Stanislavsky and Nemirovich-Danchenko Mus. Th., Moscow, with Kurilov as Falstaff. The b. follows Shakespeare's comedy closely, and has been given in various versions throughout the U.S.S.R.

Messac, Magali (*b* Toulon, 1951). Fr. dancer. Studied at local b. school in Toulon, dancing at the op. there. Joined Hamburg B. 1969, promoted soloist 1972. Created roles in Neumeier's *Third Mahler Symphony* (1975), *Swan Lake* (1976), and *Midsummer Night's Dream* (1977). Joined Pennsylvania B. 1978. Principal d. Amer. B. Th. 1980.
BIBL.: N. McLain Stoop, 'M.M.', *Dance Magazine* (1979/5).

Messel, Oliver (*b* Cuckfield, 13 Jan. 1905, *d* Bridgetown, Barbados, 13 July 1978). Eng. painter and designer. Designed Lichine's *Francesca da Rimini* (de Basil's B. Russe de Monte Carlo, 1937), and Helpmann's *Comus* (1942), the Sergeyev-Ashton-de Valois prod. of *Sleeping Beauty* (1946), and Ashton's *Homage to the Queen* (1953, all Sadler's Wells B.). Author of *Stage Designs and Costumes* (London, 1934). C.B.E. (1958).

Messe pour le temps présent. See *Mass for Our Time*.

Messerer, Asaf Michailovich (*b* Vilna, 19 Nov. 1903). Sov. dancer, b. master, and teacher. Studied with Mordkin, Gorsky, and at Moscow Bolshoi B. School. Graduated in 1921 and joined the Bolshoi B. Became one of the co.'s most individual and forceful principal dancers; continued to perform until 1954. His occasional chs. include *La Fille mal gardée* (together with Moiseyev, Bolshoi Filial Th., 1930), fourth act of *Swan Lake* (1937) and *Leçon de Danse* (Brussels, 1961; revised form, *Ballet School*, for Bolshoi B., 1962), and such concert pieces as *Melody* (mus. Gluck) and *Spring Waters* (mus. Rachmaninov). Started to teach at Bolshoi School in 1923; has been in charge of the *classe de perfection* since 1942. Frequently sent abroad, dancing with his sister Sulamith M. and his wife I. Tikhomirnova during the 1920s, and after 1945 as a guest b. master (B. of the 20th Century, 1961–2) and teacher. Author of *Classes in Classical Dance* (Moscow, 1967—Eng. language version, New York, 1975). Brother of the d. Sulamith M., father of the designer Boris M. and uncle of M. Plisetskaya. Merited Artist of the U.S.S.R. (1933); Stalin Prize (1941 and 1947); People's Artist of the R.S.F.S.R. (1951).
BIBL.: N. Roslavleva, in *Era of the Russian Ballet* (London, 1966).

Messerer, Sulamith Michailovna (*b* Moscow, 27 Aug. 1908). Sov. dancer and teacher. Sister of Asaf M. Studied at Moscow Bolshoi B. School; graduated in 1926. Ballerina of the Bolshoi B. 1926–50; especially admired as Jeanne (*Flames of Paris*), Tao-Hoa (*The Red Poppy*), and Zarema (*Fountain of Bakhchisaray*). Began teaching in 1938; became full-time teacher after her dancing career ended. Has often been sent abroad as a teacher (Ceylon, Tokyo, etc.). Decided to stay in the West with her d. son Mikhail M. in Tokyo 1980. Teacher with Royal B. and independently in London, 1981.

Messiaen, Olivier (*b* Avignon, 10 Dec. 1908). Fr. composer. Wrote no b. mus. Although he has repeatedly declared that he dislikes having his concert pieces used for d. purposes, several bs. have been based on his compositions, incl. Van Dyk's *Turangalîla* (the 3 movements 'Solitude', 'Chant d'amour', and 'Danse joyeuse', Hamburg, 1960; the complete symphony by Petit, Opéra, Paris, 1968), Van Manen's *Essay in Silence* (M.'s *Dessins éternels*, Netherlands D. Th., 1965), Tetley's *Chronochromie* (Jacob's Pillow, 1967), Cranko's *Oiseaux exotiques* (Stuttgart, 1967), and Bohner's *Quatuor pour la fin du temps* (Berlin, 1969).

Metamorphoses. Ballet in 4 parts; ch. Balanchine; mus. Hindemith; cost. Karinska. Prod. 25 Nov. 1952, New York City B., City Center, N.Y., with LeClercq, Bolender, Magallanes. Set to Hindemith's Symphonic Metamorphoses on Themes of Carl Maria von Weber. 'A musical ballet with costumes and settings that change from one part of the ballet to the next. The costumes do not represent any particular type of people, or even a particular type of animal. They are merely intended, like the movement of each part, to symbolize the metamorphoses of the different parts of the score. The ballet has nothing to do with Kafka's short story "Metamorphosis"

(Balanchine in *Balanchine's Complete Stories of the Great Ballets*). Different versions of the same mus. by Skibine (Buenos Aires, 1961), Keres (Wiesbaden, 1968), and Danovschi (Bucharest, 1968).

Metastaseis & Pithoprakta. Ballet in 2 parts; ch. Balanchine; mus. Xenakis; light. R. Bates. Prod. 18 Jan. 1968, New York City B., State Th., N.Y., with Farrell, Mitchell. The 2 parts are really 2 different bs., though given together. The first part is for a completely anonymous ensemble—like a machine that slowly starts to work and then returns to its initial position. In the second part a pair of soloists confront a corps of 7 girls and 5 boys.

Metropolitan Ballet. This London-based co., founded by Cecilia Blatch and Leon Hepner, existed 1947–9 and performed in London as well as in the Eng. provinces and abroad. Its first b. master was V. Gsovsky, who was succeeded by Beriozoff and C. Franca. It was this co. which introduced such dancers as Beriosova, Marchand, Bruhn, and S. Perrault to Eng. audiences; other dancers included Arova, Franca, David Adams, and Gnatt. The repertory was made up of classics and works from the Diaghilev repertory together with new bs. by Staff, Howard, Franca, Gsovsky, and Taras, who ch. *Designs with Strings* for the co.
BIBL.: J. Percival, 'The M.B.', *Dance and Dancers* (1960/2–3).

Metropolitan Opera House. New York's leading lyric th. opened in 1883. It was bounded by Broadway and 7th Ave., 39th and 40th Str. The activities of the op. ho.'s own b. co. were always overshadowed by visiting foreign cos., except 1935–8, when Balanchine's Amer. B. was the resident co. The house was closed in 1966, when the M.O.H. moved to its new building at Lincoln Center for the Performing Arts.

Metzger, Márta (*b* Budapest, 29 Sep. 1947). Hung. dancer. Studied at Budapest State B. Inst. Joined Budapest State Op. B. in 1965; appointed principal d. in 1972. Created roles (second premières) in Seregi's *Sylvia* (1972), and Fodor's *Bach Concerto* (1974). Liszt Prize (1974).

Mexican National Ballet. See *National Ballet of Mexico*.

Meyer, Laverne (*b* Guelph, 1 Feb. 1935). Can. dancer, choreographer, and b. director. Studied with B. Volkoff, Graham, at Rambert School, and at Sadler's Wells School. D. with Welsh National Op. in 1956 and Western Th. B. 1957–68; appointed b. master and associate artistic dir. in 1964. Founded *Northern D. Th. in Manchester in 1969. Has ch. many bs., incl. *The Web* (mus. Webern, 1962), *The Trojans* (mus. Berlioz, Scot. Op., 1969), *Schubert Variations* (1972), *Cinderella* (mus. Robert Stewart, 1973), *Aladdin* (mus. E. Tomlinson, 1974). Resigned in 1975; now working as a freelance teacher and ch.

Meyerbeer, Giacomo (*b* Tasdorf, 5 Sep. 1791, *d* Paris, 2 May 1864). Ger. composer. Wrote the mus. for Lauchery's b. *The Fisher and the Milkmaid* (Berlin, 1810). From the b. divertissements of his ops. *Le Prophète* and *Etoile du Nord*, C. Lambert arr. the mus. for Ashton's *Les Patineurs* (1937). Neumeier introduced him as a character in *Meyerbeer-Schumann* (Hamburg, 1974).

Mezentzeva, Galina Sergeevna (*b* Stavropole, 8 Nov. 1952). Sov. dancer. Studied at Leningrad B. School, graduating 1971. Joined Kirov B. 1971, eventually promoted soloist. Silver Medal (Moscow, 1977), First Prize (Tokyo 1980).

Mezinescu, Alexa Dumitrache (*b* Buzau, 7 Mar. 1936). Rum. dancer. Studied at the Bucharest State B. School; graduated in 1954. Joined Bucharest State Op. B.; appointed soloist in 1955. Has often appeared abroad (Royal Winnipeg B., Cullberg B., etc.). Merited Artist (1964); Cultural order of Merit (1969).

Michaut, Pierre (*b* Paris, 1895, *d* there, 16 Sep. 1956). Fr. critic and writer on b. Author of *Histoire du Ballet* (Paris, 1945) and *Le Ballet Contemporain* (Paris, 1950). President of L'Association des Ecrivains et Critiques de la Danse from its foundation in 1945 until his death.

Michel, Marcelle (*b* Verdun, 3 Aug. 1926). Fr. b. critic. Studied at Nancy univ. and at Paris Sorbonne (Docteur ès lettres with 'L'Apogée et la décadence du Ballet classique sous la Révolution et l'Empire'). D. critic of *Le Monde* since 1972.

Middleton, Marjory (*b* Edinburgh, 1908, *d* Haddington, 6 Jan. 1985). Brit. dancer, teacher, and choreographer. Studied with Karsavina, Idzikowsky, and Craske. Opened a school in Edinburgh, where she taught until 1972. Ch. many bs. M.B.E. (1964).

Midinet, Max (*b* Mainz, 16 July 1948). Ger. dancer. Studied at Stuttgart B. School. D. with Stuttgart B. 1967–70 and as a soloist in Frankfurt 1970–73; principal d. of the Hamburg State Op. since 1973. Has created leading roles in many Neumeier bs., incl. *Romeo and Juliet*, *Nutcracker* (both 1971), *Don Juan*, *Le Sacre* (both 1972), *Meyerbeer-Schumann* (1974), *Third Symphony by Mahler* (1975), *Swan Lake* (1976), and *St. Matthew Passion* (1981).

Midsummer Night's Dream, A. Ballet in 2 acts and 6 scenes; ch. Balanchine; mus. Mendelssohn; sets and light. D. Hays; cost. Karinska. Prod. 17 Jan. 1962, New York City B., City Center, N.Y., with Mitchell, Hayden, Villella. The b., which follows roughly the plot of Shakespeare's play, uses Mendelssohn's incidental mus. of the same title and other pieces by him. It was filmed under Balanchine's supervision; the film had its première in 1967. Other bs. using the same mus.: by M. Petipa (1877), Fokine (1902, both St. Petersburg), Ashton (*The Dream*, London, 1964), Spoerli

(Basle, 1975), Neumeier (Hamburg, 1977), and de Warren (Manchester, 1981). A different version, entitled *A New Midsummer Night's Dream* by Schilling (mus. G. Katzer, East Berlin Comic Op., 1981).

BIBL.: G. Balanchine, 'A.M.N.D.' in *Balanchine's New Complete Stories of the Great Ballets* (Garden City, N.Y., 1968).

Milan. The most famous d. master at the court of the Sforzas during the 15th century was Pompeo Diobono, but he soon moved on to Paris. Cesare Negri, one of his pupils, published *Le gratie d'amore* in M. in 1602. During the 1770s Angiolini and Noverre had a bitter dispute about the theory of the b. d'action and its importance. At the Teatro alla Scala, opened in 1778, b. came into its own with the arrival of S. Viganò; his *Gli Strelizi* (1809), *Prometeo, Dedalo* (1813), *Otello, La Vestale* (both 1818), and *I Titani* (1819) were rapturously acclaimed by Stendhal. Other important b. masters of the th.'s early decades were Giovanni Monticini, F. Clerico, and G. Gioja, but they were all overshadowed by Blasis, dir. of the Imperiale Regia Accademia di danze (founded 1813). He built it up into one of the most important schools of the 19th century, and it prod. such dancers as Cerrito, Fuoco, Cucchi, Boschetti, Ferraris, Rosati, and Legnani. During the 1830s and 1840s La Scala became one of the world centres of the romantic b. movement. Luigi Henry's *La Silfide* was seen in 1828 (4 years earlier than Taglioni's in Paris). Cerrito, Elssler, Taglioni, and Grisi often appeared as guests. A. Cortesi ch. a 5-act *Giselle* (with new mus. by Bajetti, 1843). M. Taglioni staged her notorious version of Perrot's *Pas de quatre* (with herself, Fuoco, Galletti (alias Rosati), and C. Vente, 1846). Perrot ch. *Faust* (1848). During the second half of the 19th century P. Taglioni, G. Rota, P. Borri, and H. Monplaisir were some of the better known b. masters who worked here, while Fuoco, Ferraris, Rosati, Zucchi, Brianza, Beretta, and Legnani were the star ballerinas. Towards the end of the century the spectacular prods. of Manzotti's *Excelsior* (1881), *Amor* (1886), and *Sport* (1897) took place. Brianza appeared in *The Sleeping Beauty*, which she had created in St. Petersburg; but a decline had started, and even the appointment of Cecchetti as head of the co. during the mid-1920s did not halt it. The school continued to prod. first-class ballerinas, such as Fornaroli and Radice. Since 1945 there has been a rapid turnover of b. masters and chs. including Milloss, Wallmann, Lifar, Massine, Balanchine, Ashton, Petit, Cranko, Nureyev, Beriozoff, and J. Field, who collaborated with such ds. as Radice, Novaro, Colombo, Cosi, Kovacs, dell'Ara, Pistoni, Amodio, Fascilla, and Fracci, who has become Italy's most important touring ballerina. Dobrievitch was followed by G. Carbone as art. dir. 1980, P. Neary 1986, and R. de Warren 1987.

BIBL.: L. Ross, *Il Ballo alla Scala* (Milan, 1972); F. Pitt, 'Capriccio Italien', *Ballet News* (1981/7).

Milhaud, Darius (*b* Aix-en-Provence, 4 Sep.

The Teatro alla Scala Ballet in dell'Ara's *Excelsior*.   Photo Enrico Pagani.

1892, *d* Geneva, 22 June 1974). Fr. composer. Wrote the mus. for Cocteau's *Le Boeuf sur le toit* (1920), Börlin's *L'Homme et son désir* (1921), *Les Mariés de la Tour Eiffel* (with Honegger, Auric, Poulenc, and Tailleferre, 1921), and *La Création du monde* (1923—numerous later versions incl. K. MacMillan, Royal B., 1964, and J. Taylor, *Almost an Echo*, B. Rambert, 1974), Massine's *Salade*, Nijinska's *Le Train bleu* (both 1924), Balanchine's *Les Songes* (1933), Page's *The Bells* (1946), Charrat's *'adame miroir* (1948), and Petit's *La Rose des vents* (1958). H. Ross based *The Maids* (1957) on M.'s Concerto for Percussion and Orchestra, Darrell based *Chiaroscuro* (1959) on M.'s *Saudades do Brasil* and *Ephemeron* (1968) on M.'s suites *L'album de Madame Bovary, Trois Valses,* and *Joys of Life*; J. Carter's *Lulu* (1976) used *Le Boeuf sur le toit* and *Concertino d'hiver*, and Bintley's *Meadow of Proverbs* (1979) used M.s *Carnaval d'Aix* and other pieces.

Milié, William (*b* Pittsburgh, 27 Nov. 1929). Amer. dancer, choreograher, and teacher. Studied with Tudor, Craske, F. Wagner, Shawn, Limón, and Kinch. Début 1949 in a Pittsburgh mus. prod. D. with various cos. (Kinch, Holder, Butler). Went to Europe 1959, and joined Amer. Festival B. Founded his Munich-based Broadway Jazz B. in 1961. Has since ch. many TV films and mus. prods. and worked as a guest-teacher of jazz d. Now runs his Depot D. Studio in Munich, where jazz, tap, gymnastics, singing, and dancing are taught. First Prize Munich Ch. Competition (1960); Bronze Rose (Montreux, 1961).
BIBL.: J. MacGregor-Smith, 'Spotlight on W.M.', *Dance Magazine* (1974/7).

Mille, Agnes de (*b* New York, 18 Sep. 1909). Amer. d. and ch. Daughter of the film prod. William C. d. M. and niece of the film dir. Cecil B. d. M. Educated at Univ. of S. Cal.; studied d. with Kosloff and Rambert, in whose co., she d. in the early Tudor bs. Appeared in Eng. mus. prods. and toured on the continent as a solo performer and with a group 1929–40. Assoc. with Tudor's first d. co., D. Th., in 1937. Her first important ch. was *Black Ritual* (Milhaud's *Création du monde*, Amer. B. Th., 1940), followed by *Three Virgins and a Devil* (mus. Respighi, 1941). Her further bs. included *Rodeo* (mus. Copland, B. Russe de Monte Carlo, 1942), *Fall River Legend* (mus. Gould, B. Th., 1948), *The Harvest According* (mus. V. Thomson, Amer. B. Th., 1952), *The Four Marys* (mus. T. Rittman, Amer. B. Th., 1965), *A Rose for Miss Emily* (mus. Hovhaness, Amer. B. Th., 1970), and *Summer* (mus. Schubert, Boston B., 1975). On Broadway she ch. *Oklahoma!* (1943), *Carousel* (1945), *Gentlemen Prefer Blondes* (1949), *Paint Your Wagon* (1951) and *110 in the Shade* (1963). Has also often worked for film and TV. An extremely skilled speaker; her lecture demonstrations have won her wide acclaim. The U.S. government often consults her on national d. matters. Her A. d. M. D. Th. lasted 1953–4; she founded the

Heritage D. Th. in 1973, based at the North Carolina School of the Arts. A brilliant writer; her publications include *Dance to the Piper* (New York, 1952), *And Promenade Home* (N.Y., 1956), *To A Young Dancer* (N.Y., 1962), *The Book of the Dance* (N.Y., 1963), 'Russian Journals' (*Dance Perspectives* 44), *Speak to Me, Dance with Me* (N.Y., 1973) and *America Dances* (N.Y., 1981). D. Magazine Award (1956); Capezio Award (1966). BIBL.: J. Gale, 'Spirit of '76: The A.d.M. Heritage Dance Theatre', *Dance Magazine* (1974/6).

Miller, Patricia (*b* Pretoria, 1927). S.A. dancer. Studied with Cecily Robinson. D. with S. A. B. and Cape Town B. Club. Went to London in 1947 and studied at Sadler's Wells B. School. Joined Sadler's Wells Th. B.; became principal d. Created roles in Cranko's *Beauty and the Beast* (1949), *Harlequin in April* (1951), and *The Lady and the Fool* (1954). Returned to S.A. 1956, and opened a school in Cape Town. Has directed the NAPAC B. with her husband Dudley Davies since 1969. BIBL.: G. Anthony, 'P.M.', in *A Camera at the Ballet* (Newton Abbot, 1975).

Millions d'Arlequin, Les. Ballet in 2 acts; ch. M. Petipa; mus. Drigo; sets Allegri; cost. Ponomarov. Prod. 10 Feb. 1900, Hermitage Th., St. Petersburg, with Kschessinska. A good fairy helps Harlequin to get hold of huge sums of money so that he can marry his beloved Columbine. One of Petipa's last bs.; it has been newly ch. from time to time, mostly in abbreviated form—e.g. by Brenaa for Royal Dan. B. where it is still in the Tivoli Th. repertory. See also *Harlequinade*.

Milloss, Aurel von (orig. A.M. de Miholy; *b* Ozora, 12 May 1906). Hung.-Ital. dancer, choreographer, and b. director. Studied with Smeraldi, N. Guerra, Romanowsky, Laban, V. Gsovsky, and Cecchetti. Joined Berlin State Op. in 1928. Appeared in recital perfs., and as soloist and ch. Subsequently b. master in Hagen, Duisburg, Breslau, Augsburg, and Düsseldorf, with occasional visits to Budapest. B. master of the Hung. National Th. 1936–8. Has lived in Rome since 1938. B. dir. of Teatro dell'Opera, Rome, 1938–45 and 1966–9, of Teatro all Scala, Milan, 1946–50, in Cologne 1960–3, of Vienna State Op. 1963–6 and 1971–4. Has also often worked for Maggio Musicale Fiorentino, Teatro Fenice, Venice, Bs. des Champs-Elysées, in Rio de Janeiro, and in São Paulo. He has ch. many works, often to the music of Bartók and Stravinsky and with sets by di Chirico, Clerici, Afro, *et al*. His first prods. include Petrassi's *La follia di Orlando* (Milan, 1947) and *Le Portrait de Don Quichotte* (Bs. des Champs-Elysées, 1947), Dallapiccola's *Marsyas* (Venice, 1948), and the European first perf. of Stravinsky's *Orpheus* (Venice, 1948). D. and b. advisor for *Enciclopedia dello Spettacolo*. BIBL.: entry 'M., A.v.' in *Enciclopedia dello spettacolo*.

Milon, Louis-Jacques (*b* 1766, *d* Neuilly, 25 Nov. 1845). Fr. dancer, choreographer, b. master, and teacher. Studied at Paris Opéra B. School. Joined Opéra B. 1787 and became a very popular d. in bs. by P. and M. Gardel. Started to teach 1789 and to ch. 1799; b. master 1800–26. *Nina ou La Folle par amour* (mus. Persuis after Dalayrac, 1813) is his best known b.

Mime. The art 'of telling a story, expressing a mood or an emotion, or describing an action, without resorting to words. Instead, the artist uses movements and gestures made with every part of his body, which thus becomes an instrument of expression, guided by imagination and knowledge of the way people behave, feel, and work or play' (J. Lawson). Over the centuries b. has developed its own language of m., with a fixed set of gestures and expressions, culminating in such 19th-century bs. as *La Sylphide, Giselle, Coppélia, Swan Lake,* and *Sleeping Beauty.* In such bs. mime alternates with dancing, in the same sort of way as in 18th-cent. op. recitative alternates with arias etc. In the 1970s acquired new status as an independent th. act in the wake of M. Marceau, J. Lecoq., *et al,* with an annual London M. Festival, featuring internat. m. artists, from 1977.

BIBL.: J. Lawson, M., *The Theory and Practice of Expressive Gesture With a Description of its Historical Development* (London, 1957).

Mimodrame. M. Marceau coined this term for his dramatically orientated ensemble pantomimes, culminating in his *Candide* (Hamburg, 1971).

Minkus, Alois Louis (also Léon, orig. Aloisius Ludwig M.; *b* Vienna, 23 Mar. 1826, *d* there 7 Dec. 1917). Austrian composer. Appointed mus. inspector of the Imperial Ths. of St. Petersburg 1861. Official b. comp. of the Moscow Bolshoi Th. 1864–71, then of the St. Petersburg Maryinsky Th. 1872–86; wrote the mus. for M. Petipa's *Don Quixote* (1869), *Camargo* (1872), *Le Papillon* (1874), *La Bayadère* (1877), *Roxana or the Beauty from Montenegro* (1878), *The Daughter of the Snow* (1879), *Night and Day* (1883), *The Magic Pills* (1886), and *Kalkabrino* (1891), and also parts of the mus. for *Paquita* (1881) and for Saint-Léon's *La Source* (with Delibes, 1866).

BIBL.: B. L. Scherer, 'Maligned Minstrel', *Ballet News* (1980/5).

Minuet (also Menuet, Minuetto, or Menuett). Fr., from *pas menu,* small step. Originally a rustic d. from Poitou; became the most popular court d. under Louis XIV, spread all over Europe to become the principal d. of the aristocracy prior to the revolution of 1789. In triple time; a highly stylized terre à terre d., unhurried, with strictly symmetrical figures and elaborate curtseys and bows.

Miracle in the Gorbals. Ballet in 1 act; libr. Michael Bentall; ch. Helpmann; mus. Bliss; déc. Burra. Prod. 26 Oct. 1944, Sadler's Wells B.,

Princes Th., London, with Helpmann, Clayden, Shearer, Rassine. The b. is a morality play set in the slums of Glasgow. It centres on Christ reborn in modern (1944) society, experiencing again the events of his Passion and death.

BIBL.: C. Beaumont, 'M.i.t.G.' in *Ballets Past & Present* (London, 1955).

Miraculous Mandarin, The (original Hung. title: *A csodálatos mandarin*). Pantomime in 1 act; libr. Menyhért Lengyel; mus. Bartók; direction Hans Strohbach. Prod. 28 Nov. 1926, Cologne, with Wilma Aug, Ernst Zeiller. A lurid melodrama about 3 pimps who force a prostitute to rob her customers. A rich Chinese mandarin appears, and they try to kill him, but he cannot die until the girl finally yields to his desire. The b. was immediately banned on moral grounds by the then Lord Mayor of Cologne, Konrad Adenauer. Not until Milloss's Milan La Scala prod. of 1942 did the work really enter the repertory. It has since been given various ch. treatments, incl. those of Harangozó (Budapest, 1945—new version 1956), Bolender (New York City B., 1951), Rodrigues (Sadler's Wells B., 1956), Lavrovsky (under the title *Night City*, Bolshoi B., 1961), Flindt (Copenhagen, 1967), Seregi (Budapest, 1970), and Pistoni (Milan, 1981). TV prods. of the versions by Hangorozó (Hung. TV, 1965), Ogoun (Cologne TV, 1967), Flindt (Dan. TV, 1967), and Eck (Hung. TV).

BIBL.: G. Balanchine, 'T.M.M.' in *Balanchine's New Complete Stories of the Great Ballets* (Garden City, N.Y., 1968).

Mirandolina. Ballet in 3 acts and 6 scenes; libr. P. Abolimov and V. Varkovitsky; ch. Vainonen; mus. S. Vasilenko; déc. H. Shifrin. Prod. 16 Jan. 1949, Bolshoi Filial Th., Moscow, with Lepeshinskaya, Kondratov. The b. is based on Goldoni's comedy of the same title. The pretty hostess of a rural inn deludes her three aristocratic suitors, and finally succumbs to the advances of her waiter. The b. has been given in various ch. versions throughout the Eastern Bloc. A different b. on the same plot by Milloss (mus. V. Bucchi, Rome, 1957).

Mir Iskusstva. The *World of Art* magazine, founded in St. Petersburg by Diaghilev, Benois, Bakst, and Nouvel in 1899. It lasted until 1904 and became the leading Russ. platform for the discussion of all progressive movements in painting, literature, and mus. The men who became the guiding spirits of the B. Russes collaborated on this magazine.

Mirk, Shonach (*b* Westport, Conn., 21 Oct. 1954). Amer. dancer. Studied with Joanne de Berghm, School of Amer. B. and Royal B. School. Joined B. of the 20th Century in 1974 as a soloist, now a principal d. Created roles in Béjart's *Notre Faust* (1975), *Molière imaginaire* (1976), and *Heliogabal* (1976). Now with Zürich B.

Miró, Joán (b Montroig, 20 Apr. 1893, d Mallorca, 25 Dec. 1984). Span. painter and designer, who did the décor for Nijinska's and Balanchine's *Roméo et Juliette* (with M. Ernst, 1926) and for Massine's *Jeux d'enfants* (1932).

Mirror for Witches, A. Ballet with prologue and in 5 scenes; libr., ch., and cost. Howard; mus. D. Aplvor; sets Norman Adams. Prod. 4 Mar. 1952, Sadler's Wells B., Cov. Gdn., London, with Heaton, Farron, Edwards, Hart, Chatfield. Based on the novel by Esther Forbes, the b. deals with witch-hunting and burning in Brittany and New England.
BIBL.: C. Beaumont, 'A.M.f.W.' in *Ballets of Today* (London, 1954).

Mirror Walkers, The. Ballet in 1 act; libr. and ch. P. Wright; mus. Tchaikovsky. Prod. 27 Apr. 1963, Stuttgart, with Cardus, Barra, Cragun, Haydée. Set to Tchaikovsky's first Suite for Orchestra in D major, op. 43. Two dancers who are working in their studio pass through the mirror into a dream world of ideal perfection. Pas de deux only revived for Touring Royal B. (1971).

Miskovitch, Milorad (b Voljevo, 26 Mar. 1928). Yugosl. dancer. Studied with Kirsanova, and in Paris with Kniaseff and Preobrajenska. D. with Bs. des Champs-Elysées, International B., and de Basil's Original B. Russe (all 1947), Grand B. de Monte Carlo 1948, and Petit's Bs. de Paris 1949. Toured with Darsonval and Chauviré. D. with Charrat co. and London Festival B. 1952. Toured with Markova (1954) and Marchand (1955). Founded his own co. 1956. Joined Massine's B. Europeo 1960 and Page's Chicago Op. B. 1961. Appeared as guest with many cos. in Britain, S. Amer., Italy, and Yugosl.; created numerous roles, in bs. e.g. by Béjart (*Haut voltage*, 1956), D. Sanders (*L'Echelle*, 1957), Howard (*La Belle dame sans merci*, 1958), Massine (*Commedia umana*, 1960), Page (*Die Fledermaus*, 1961), and Gai (*The Seagull*, 1968). Started to ch. 1970 (Beethoven's *Creatures of Prometheus*, Genoa). Guest-teacher at various schools and colleges throughout the U.S.A.
BIBL.: 'M.M.', with complete check-list of roles and activities, *Les Saisons de la danse* (1976/6).

Missa Brevis. Ballet in 11 parts; ch. Limón; mus. Kodály; déc. Ming Cho Lee. Prod. 11 Apr. 1958, J. Limón and D. Co. Juilliard D. Th., New York, with Limón, Currier, B. Jones. Set to Kodály's *Missa Brevis in Tempore Belli*, performed in front of a projection of a ruined cathedral. A man struggles alone to survive the chaos and despair which surround him. Revived for Ailey's City Center D. Th. 1973.

Miss Julie (orig. Swed. title: *Fröken Julie*). Ballet in 1 act and 4 scenes; libr. and ch. Cullberg; mus. Ture Rangström; déc. A. Fridericia. Prod. 1 Mar. 1950, Riksteatern, Västeras (Sweden), with von Rosen, J. Mengarelli, Cullberg. The b. follows Strindberg's play closely. Revived for many cos., incl. Royal Swed. B. (with new déc. by Sven Erixson, 1950), Amer. B. Th. (1958), Royal Dan. B. (1959), and Düsseldorf (1965). A different b. with the same plot by MacMillan (*Fräulein Julie*, mus. Panufnik, Stuttgart, 1970, with Haydée, F. Frey, Keil, and Clauss).
BIBL.: C. Beaumont, 'M.J.' in *Ballets of Today* (London, 1954).

Mitchell, Arthur (b New York, 27 Mar. 1934). Amer. dancer, b. director, and choreographer. Studied at High School of Performing Arts and School of Amer. B. D. on Broadway, with the cos. of McKayle and Butler. Joined New York City B. 1956; became one of its most popular soloists. Created many roles in Balanchine bs., e.g. *A Midsummer Night's Dream* (1962), *Agon* (1967), *Metastaseis & Pithoprakta* (1968), and in Taras' *Ebony Concerto* (1960) and Butler's *The Unicorn, the Gorgon and the Manticore* (1963). Founded the *D. Th. of Harlem with K. Shook in 1968 (official début in 1971); he has since created several chs. for it. Capezio Award (1971); D. Magazine Award (1975).
BIBL.: O. Maynard, 'A.M. & The Dance Theatre of Harlem', *Dance Magazine* (1970/3); interview with A.M., *Dance and Dancers* (1974/10).

Mitchell, Jack (b Key West, 13 Sep. 1925). Amer. photographer. Contributing photographer to *Dance Magazine* since 1952. Works with Amer. B. Th., Les Grands Bs. Canadiens, Pennsylvania B. Co., and Arts and Leisure section of the Sunday *New York Times*. Author of *American Dance Portfolio* (New York, 1964) and *Dance Scene U.S.A.* (New York, 1967).

Mlakar, Pia (née P. Scholz; b Hamburg, 28 Dec. 1908). Ger.-Yugosl. dancer and choreographer. Studied with Laban in Berlin and Poljakova in Belgrade, where she met Pino Mlakar, whom she married. For her further career see M., Pino.

Mlakar, Pino (b Novo Mesto, 2 Mar. 1907). Yugosl. dancer, choreographer, and b. director. Studied with Laban in Berlin and Poljakova in Belgrade, where he met and married *Pia M. They went to Darmstadt and Dessau; b. directors in Zurich 1934–8. Their bs. included *Devil in the Village* and *The Ballad of Medieval Love* (mus. both F. Lhotka, 1935; for an earlier version of *Ballad* they were awarded the Bronze Medal of the Paris A.I.D. Competition 1932). B. directors of the State Op. Munich 1939–44; their new bs. included *Der Bogen* (mus. Lhotka, 1939—a full-length chamber b. for a solo couple), an attempt to reconstruct Taglioni-Lindpaintner's *Danina or Jocko the Brazilian Ape* (1940), and *Verklungene Feste* (mus. R. Strauss, 1941). They have lived in Ljubljana since 1945, apart from a return to Munich, as directors of the State Op. b., 1952–4. In Yugosl. they have worked in Ljubljana, Belgrade, Dubrovnik, and Zagreb. They were among the first choreographers to use *Labanotation. Parents of *Veronika M.

Mlakar, Veronika (*b* Zurich, 8 Dec. 1935). Yugosl.-Amer. dancer. Studied with her parents Pia and Pino M. and at the Belgrade State B. School. D. in her parents' *Danina* (Munich, 1941), and made her professional début in H. Rosen's *The Lady and the Unicorn* (1953). Appeared with Bs. de Paris, Chicago Op. B., J. Butler, Robbins's B.: U.S.A., Amer. B. Th., and Cullberg. Created roles in Petit's *La Chambre* (1955) and *La Dame dans la lune* (1958), and Béjart's *Promethée* (1956).

Modern Dance. The Amer. term is used to designate a variety of contemporary th. d. styles, which are not based on (and originally emerged in opposition to) the classic-academic *danse d'école.*

Mohr von Venedig, Der. See *Moor of Venice, The.*

Moiseyev, Igor Alexandrovich (*b* Kiev, 21 Jan. 1906). Sov. dancer, choreographer, and b. director. Studied privately in Moscow, and at Bolshoi B. School 1921–4. D. with Bolshoi B. 1924–39; created title-role in Vasilenko's *Joseph the Beautiful* (1925). His first chs. were *The Footballer* (mus. V. Oransky, 1930), which demonstrated his particular gift for humour and satire, *Salammbô* (mus. A. Arends, 1932), and *Three Fat Men* (mus. Oransky, 1935). Appointed dir. of the ch. section at the Moscow Th. for Folk Art 1936, from which the first Sov. folk-d. ensemble emerged 1937. Its amateur dancers were gradually replaced by highly qualified professionals from the affiliated school. Has toured the world with the M. Folk D. Ensemble (London début 1955, New York 1958), enjoying enormous popularity everywhere and thus stimulating other countries to form their own folk d. cos. As a ch. he is at his best in genre pieces and scenes from daily life; *The Partisans, Football, Moldovenskaya, Pictures from the Past, Dance of Fools,* and *Poem from the Surroundings of Moscow* are some of his most popular bs. Also ch. Khatchaturian's *Spartacus* for Bolshoi B. (1958 version). Founded the classically orientated Young B. (now Classical B. Comp.) 1967. People's Artist of the R.S.F.S.R.; Lenin Prize (1967); D. Magazine Award (1960). His wife Tamara Zeifert and his daughter Olga M. are both members of his Ensemble.

Moiseyeva, Olga Nicolayevna (*b* Leningrad, 25 Dec. 1928). Sov. dancer. Studied at Leningrad Ch. School; graduated 1947. Joined Kirov B.; appointed ballerina 1953. Created Mekhmeneh Banu in Grigorovich's *Legend of Love* (2nd premiere, 1961). Merited Artist of the R.S.F.S.R. (1955); People's Artist of the R.S.F.S.R. (1973).

Molière (stage name of Jean Baptiste Poquelin; *b* Paris, Jan. 1622, *d* there, 17 Feb. 1673). Fr. actor and playwright. Collaborated with Lully on the comédie bs. *L'Amour médecin* (1665), *M. de Pourceaugnac* (1669), and *Le Bourgeois gentilhomme*

(1670). Also wrote the librs. for Beauchamp's *Les Fâcheux* (1661) and Lully's *Le Mariage forcé* (1664), and collaborated with Lully and Beauchamp on *Les Festes de l'Amour et de Bacchus* (1672).
BIBL.: M.-F. Christout, 'M. et la Comédie-Ballet', *Les Saisons de la danse* (1973/11).

Molière imaginaire, Le. Ballet Comedy by Béjart; mus. Nino Rota; déc. J. Roustan and R. Bernard. Prod. 3 Dec. 1976, B. of the 20th Century and Yantra, Comédie Française, Paris, with Robert Hirsh, B. Pié, Donn, M. Gascard, E. Cooper, S. Mirk, C. Verneuil, Poelvoorde. A colourful and spectacular revue about the vicissitudes of Molière's life, identifying some of the most important figures of his plays with real life events. The title role is played by an actor.

Mollajoli, Gustavo (*b* Buenos Aires, 9 Aug. 1935). Argent. dancer, teacher, and b. master. Studied with G. Tomin, Ruanova, Tupin, A. Lonzano, M. Borowsky, and E. de Galantha. Joined Teatro Colón B., of which he is now chief b. master, teacher, and principal d. Has also worked for S.O.D.R.E. (Montevideo B.), La Plata Th., Dallas Civic B., and B. de Wallonie.

Monahan, James (*b* Arrah, India, 1912, *d* London, 23 Nov. 1985). Brit. b. critic and former B.B.C. administrator. Educated Oxford Univ. B. critic of the *Manchester Guardian* (now *Guardian*) since 1935, under the name of James Kennedy. Regular contributor to *Dancing Times*. Dir. Royal B. School 1978–83. Author of *Fonteyn: a Study of the Ballerina in her Setting* (London, 1958) and *The Nature of Ballet* (1976). C.B.E. (1962). His second wife was the d. Merle Park and his third the former d. Gail Thomas.

Moncion, Francisco (*b* Las Vega, Dominican Rep., 6 July 1922). Amer. dancer. Studied at School of Amer. B. Début with New Op. Co. 1942. Joined International B., and created the title-role in Caton's *Sebastian* and Massine's *Mad Tristan* (both 1944). Joined B. Society 1946 and then New York City B., of which he is still a soloist member. Created roles in Balanchine's *Four Temperaments* (1946), *Divertimento* (1947), *Orpheus* (1948), *Firebird* (1949), *La Valse* (1951), *Ivesiana* (1954), *Episodes* (1959), and *A Midsummer Night's Dream* (1962), Ashton's *Picnic at Tintagel* (1952), and Robbins' *The Guests* (1949), *Age of Anxiety* (1950), *Afternoon of a Faun* (1953), and *In the Night* (1970). Has also ch. some bs. and exhibited several of his paintings. Retired 1985.
BIBL.: K. Sandler, 'In the Beginning—F.M.,' *Ballet News* (1979/6).

Monk, Meredith (*b* Lima, 20 Nov. 1943). Amer. dancer and choreographer. Studied with Slavenska, M. Cunningham, Graham, and Mata and Hari. Début 1963. Has become one of the leading figures of Amer. avant-garde d. Performs, with her group, primarily in non-theatrical settings (e.g. Judson Memorial Church, Chicago Museum of Contemporary Art, Guggenheim Museum, Whitney Museum of Amer. Art). Also a singer and composer; has recorded albums of her own music; in 1968 founded The House, 'a co. dedicated to an interdisciplinary approach to performance' (programme note). Her first piece was called M (1963); more recent works incl. *Blueprint* (1967), *Title: Title* (1969), *Needle Brain Lloyd and the System's Kid* (1970), *Education of the Girlchild* (1973), *Quarry* (1979), and *Recent Ruins* (1980).

BIBL.: M. B. Siegel, in *At the Vanishing Point* (New York, 1972), and in *Watching the Dance Go By* (Boston, 1977); S. Banes, in *Terpsichore in Sneakers* (Boston, 1980).

Monotones. Ballet in 3 movements; ch. and cost. Ashton; mus. Satie. Prod. 24 Mar. 1965, Royal B., Cov. Gdn., London, with Lorrayne, Dowell, and Mead. Set to Satie's *Trois Gymnopédies* (orchestrated by Debussy and Roland-Manuel). A pas de trois. Originally planned for one perf. only at the occasion of a Royal B. Benevolent Fund Gala, it proved so successful that Ashton decided to add a second part (for which Lanchbery orchestrated Satie's *Trois Gnossiennes*) for its première on 25 Apr. 1966, with Sibley, Parkinson, and B. Shaw. The two parts are now usually given together; M. II precedes M.I. BBC TV prod. 1968. Revived for City Center Joffrey B. and Chicago B. in 1974.

BIBL.: D. Vaughan, *Frederick Ashton and his Bs.* (London, 1977); P. Brinson and C. Crisp, in *Ballet & Dance* (Newton Abbot, 1980).

Montagnon, Lucia (*b* L. Isenring, Ilanz, 7 Feb. 1952). Swiss dancer. Studied at Stuttgart B. School, joining Stuttgart B. 1971, eventually appointed soloist. Created roles in Forsythe's *flore subsimplici* (1977) and MacMillan's *My Brother, My Sisters* (1978). Joined Frankfurt B. as a principal d. in 1981. Was married to the ch. Patrice M., is now married to the d. and dir. E. Madsen.

Montagnon, Patrice (*b* Menthon St. Bernard, 4 Mar. 1952). Fr. dancer and choreographer. Studied at Geneva conservatory, joining the b. co. of the Grand Th. 1967. D. with Munich State Op. B. 1967–72, after which he joined Stuttgart B., first as a d. and 1977–80 as one of its resident chs. Was married to the d. Lucia M.

Montessu, Pauline (née Paul; *b* Marseilles, 4 June 1805, *d* Amiens, 1 Aug. 1877). Fr. dancer. Studied with her brother Antoine Paul. Début Lyons 1813; joined Paris Opéra 1820. Married the d. François M. in Paris 1822. D. Lise in the first prod. of *La Fille mal gardée* with new mus. by Herold (1828). Created title role in Aumer's *Manon Lescaut* (1830). Left Opéra 1836.

BIBL.: I Guest, in *The Romantic Ballet in Paris* (London, 1966).

Monteux, Pierre (*b* Paris, 4 Apr. 1875, *d* Hancock, Maine, 1 July 1964). Fr. conductor. Diaghilev's chief conductor 1911–14 (and occasionally guest conductor of the Bs. Russes until 1917). Conducted the first prods. of Stravinsky's *Petrushka* (1911), *Sacre du printemps* (1913), and *Le Rossignol* (1914), Ravel's *Daphnis and Chloe* (1912), and Debussy's *Jeux* (1913).

Montez, Lola (orig. Marie Dolores Eliza Rosanna Gilbert; *b* Limerick, 1818, *d* New York, 16 Jan. 1861). Irish dancer and adventuress. The daughter of a Scottish officer and a Creole mother. One of her numerous love-affairs took her to Seville, where she had a few dancing-lessons. She then toured Europe as a genuine Span. d. with varying success (she made little impression when she appeared at Her Majesty's Th. London, in 1843). In Munich she became the mistress of Ludwig I in 1846, caused a government crisis, was made Countess Landsfeld, and brought about the abdication of the King in 1848. After further scandals in Paris, London, and Sydney, she settled in New York; she ended her days as a reformed character helping fallen women. Has inspired many novels, plays, and films. Appears as a character in several bs., e.g. Massine's *Bacchanale* (1939), Caton's *L.M.* (1946), and J. Carter's *The Life and Death of L.M.* (1954).

BIBL.: P. Migel, 'The Legend of Lola', *Ballet Review* (vol. 4, no. 3).

Month in the Country, A. Ballet in 1 act; ch. Ashton; mus. Chopin, arr. Lanchbery; déc. J. Trevelyan Oman. Prod. 12 Feb. 1976, Royal B., Cov. Gdn., London, with Seymour, Dowell, Grant, Rencher, Denise Nunn, Sleep. Based upon Turgenev's eponymous play (first perf. 1872), the b. is a distillation of the central love-triangle between Natalia Petrovna, her ward Vera, and the freshly arrived tutor, Beliaev. The mus. is made up of Chopin's Variations on 'Là ci darem la mano', 'Fantasia on Polish Airs', Andante Spianato, and Grande Polonaise brillante in E Flat.

BIBL.: D. Vaughan, *Frederick Ashton and his Bs.* (London, 1977); P. Brinson and C. Crisp, in *Ballet & Dance* (Newton Abbot, 1980).

Montplaisir, Hippolyte Georges (*b* Bordeaux, 1821, *d* Besana, Italy, 10 June 1877). Fr. dancer, b. master, and choreographer. Studied with Guillemin in Brussels and Blasis in Milan, where he and his wife Adèle (née Bartholomin) d. as 'primi ballerini di rango francese' 1844–6. They went to Trieste, Barcelona, and Lyons, and then joined the French B. Co. (dir. by Adèle's father, Victor Bartholomin) and went to New York 1847. This was the first N.Y. appearance of a large European b. co.; they presented the classics from *Fille mal gardée* to *Esmeralda*, and then toured the States. To Lisbon 1856, where a foot injury ended his career as a dancer. Continued as a choreographer, with particular success from 1861 at La Scala; his most popular bs. include *La Devâdâcy* (1866), *La Camargo* (1868), *Brahma* (1869), *L'Almea*

(1872), and *La Semiramide del Nord* (1889—all his bs. had mus. by C. Dall'Argine).

BIBL.: entry 'M., I.G.' in *Enciclopedia dello spettacolo.*

Monument for a Dead Boy (orig. Dutch title: *Monument voor een gestorven Jongen*). Ballet in 1 act; libr. and ch. Van Dantzig; mus. Jan Boerman; déc. Van Schayk. Prod. 19 June 1965, Dutch National B., Stadsschouwburg, Amsterdam, with Van Schayk, José Lainez. The b. shows in flashback the isolated life of a homosexual boy which finally destroys him. Cologne TV prod. 1967. Revived for Harkness B. (1969), Amer. B. Th. (1973), Royal Dan. B., Ger. Op., Berlin (1976).

BIBL.: G. Balanchine, in *Balanchine's Complete Stories of the Great Ballets* (Garden City, N.Y., 1977).

Monumentum pro Gesualdo. Ballet in 3 parts; ch. Balanchine; mus. Stravinsky; set D. Hays. Prod. 16 Nov. 1960, New York City B., City Center, N.Y., with D. Adams, C. Ludlow. A plotless b., performed by one solo couple and six accompanying couples. Now always performed with Balanchine's *Movements.

BIBL.: G. Balachine, 'M.p.G.' in *Balanchine's New Complete Stories of the Great Ballets* (Garden City, N.Y., 1968).

Moon Reindeer (orig. Dan. title: *Maanerenen*). Ballet in 1 act; libr. and ch. Cullberg; mus. K. Riisager; déc. P. Falk. Prod. 22 Nov. 1957, Royal Dan. B., Copenhagen, with Vangsaae, Kronstam, Bjørnsson. A Lapp girl is turned by a magician into a white reindeer which lures young men to their death; but one of the chosen victims fights the magician and breaks the spell, thus enabling her to resume her own form. Revived for Royal Swed. B. (1959), Amer. B. Th. (1962).

BIBL.: G. Balanchine, 'M.R.' in *Balanchine's New Complete Stories of the Great Ballets* (Garden City, N.Y., 1968).

Moor of Venice, The (orig. Ger. title: *Der Mohr von Venedig*). Ballet in 8 scenes, with prologue and epilogue; libr. and ch. Hanka; mus. Blacher; déc. Wakhevitch. Prod. 29 Nov. 1955, State Op., Vienna, with Dirtl, Zimmerl, Adama. The b. opens with Othello killing Desdemona; the story of their love, leading up to this event, is then told. Specially commissioned for the opening week of the rebuilt Vienna State Op.; it was prod. all over Germany, by T. Gsovsky (Municipal Op., Berlin, 1956), Georgi (Hanover, same year), Rosen (Munich State Op., 1962), and others. Lifar ch. a different b. *Le Maure de Venise* to mus. by M. Thiriet for The Netherlands B. (1960). See also *Othello.*

Moor's Pavane, The. Ballet in 1 act; ch. Limón; mus. Purcell; cost. P. Lawrence. Prod. 17 Aug. 1949, J. Limón D. Co., Connecticut College, New London, with Limón, B. Jones, Hoving, and Koner. A formal, stylized account of the Othello story for 4 people. Now in the repertory of many cos. (e.g. Amer. B. Th., Royal Dan. B., Royal Swed. B., National B. of Canada) and in Nureyev's concert repertory. Filmed by W. Strate in 1950. TV prods. by Amer. Omnibus (1953), BBC (1957), and Swedish TV (1973).

BIBL.: G. Balanchine, in *Balanchine's Complete Stories of the Great Ballets* (Garden City, N.Y., 1977); P. Koner, The Truth about 'The Moor's Pavane', in *Ballet Review* (1980/4).

Moore, Geoff (b Wales, 28 Dec. 1944). Brit. choreographer and producer. Studied Fine Art in Newcastle upon Tyne and at Leeds College of Art. Staged his first ch. and started to work in multimedia prods. in the mid-1960s. Set up his own co., Moving Being, in Sep. 1968; it consisted of dancers, actors, film-makers, and designers. It first appeared at the London I.C.A. during the 1968–9 season, then at The Place 1969–72, and later at the Chapter Arts Centre in Cardiff, S. Wales. Has since scripted, designed, ch., and prod. some 20 different prods. for Moving Being. His wife Pamela M. has been leading d. and cost. designer throughout.

Moore, Jack (b Monticello, Ind., 18 Mar. 1926). Amer. dancer and teacher. Studied at Graham School, School of Amer. B., Conn. College, and with Cunningham. Has appeared with N. Fonaroff, H. McGehee, P. Lang, K. Litz, Graham, and Sokolow. Has taught at Conn. College, Juilliard School, Bennington, Univ. of Calif. at Los Angeles.

Moore, James (b Muncie, Ind., 12 Dec. 1930). Amer. dancer and b. director. Studied with Stone-Camryn, Schwezoff, Craske, and Tudor. D. with Stone-Page B. 1949–50, Robbins' Bs.: U.S.A., and Amer. B. Th., where he was b. master 1966–72. Appeared in many Broadway shows and TV prods. Artistic dir. of Royal Swed. B. 1972–5.

Moore, Lillian (b Chase City, Va., 20 Sep. 1911, d New York, 28 July 1967). Amer. dancer, teacher, and writer on b. Studied with Balanchine, Vladimiroff, M. Curtis, Galli, and Weidman. D. with Amer. B. 1935–8 and numerous other cos. until 1954; then became a much respected teacher, principally at Joffrey's Amer. B. Center. Became the foremost Amer. d.-historian; contributed to the international d. press, encyclopedias, etc. Author of *Artists of the Dance* (New York, 1938—now a D. Horizons reprint), 'The Duport Mystery' (*Dance Perspectives* 7), *Bournonville and Ballet Technique* (with E. Bruhn, London, 1965), and *Images of the D.* (New York, 1965). Editor of *The Memoirs of Marius Petipa* (London, 1958).

Morales, Hilda (b New York, 17 June 1948). Amer. dancer. Studied with Ana Garcia, Gilda Navarra, and at School of Amer. B. Début New York City B. 1965. D. with Pennsylvania B. 1966–73; soloist with Amer. B. Th. since 1973. Retired 1986; now teaching.

BIBL.: S. Goodman, 'H.M.', *Dance Magazine* (1970/7).

Mordkin, Mikhail Mikhailovich (b Moscow,

21 Dec. 1880, d Milbrook, N.J., 15 July 1944). Russ.-Amer. dancer, choreographer, teacher, and b. director. Studied at Moscow Bolshoi B. School; graduated 1899. Immediately joined Bolshoi B. as a soloist; appointed b. master soon afterwards. Participated in Diaghilev's 1909 Paris season; then left to tour with Pavlova. Separated from her and established his All-Star Imperial Russ. B. for an Amer. tour 1911–12; co. included Geltzer, Lopokova, Idzikowsky, and Volinine. Returned to Bolshoi B. 1912; also collaborated with Tairoff's Chamber Th. 1913–17. Appointed dir. of the Bolshoi B. in 1917. Danced and ch. in various towns, left Russia in 1923. After working in Lithuania settled in the U.S.A. 1924, where he became one of the most important pioneers of the slowly emerging Amer. b. Founded M.B. 1926, for which he ch. several bs., incl. a complete prod. of *Swan Lake* (1927). His co., which included Butsova, Doubrovska, Vladimiroff, and Zvereff, also gave guest perfs. in Europe; it then disbanded. Continued to work as a freelance ch. for op. and mus. prods. From the students of his New York school he re-established the M.B. Co. in 1937, and this became the nucleus of the B. Th. co., founded 1939. His pupils included Bowman, Haakon, Danielian, L. Chase, K. Nijinsky, K. Hepburn, and J. Garland.

Moreau, Jacqueline (*b* Bandol, 7 May 1926). Fr. dancer and teacher. Studied at Paris Opéra B. School and with Kiss. Joined Paris Opéra B.; appointed première danseuse 1948. Left the co. 1951. D. with R. Page B. and Bs. des Champs-Elysées. Ballerina of Grand B. du Marquis de Cuevas 1952–9. Now teaches at Paris Opéra B. School.

Moreland, Barry (*b* Melbourne, 1943). Austral. d. and ch. Studied at Austral. B. School; joined Austral. B. 1962. Studied further at School of Contemporary D., London, and d. with its co. Resident ch. of London Festival B. 1971–5. Ch. *Nocturnal Dances* (mus. P. M. Davies), *Summer Games* (mus. S. Barber, both 1970), *Kontakion* (medieval mus.—all for London Contemporary D. Th.), *Summer Solstice* (mus. J. Field, both 1972), *Dark Voyage* (mus. Satie), *In Nomine* (mus. Davies, both 1973), *Prodigal Son* (mus. Scott Joplin, 1974—all for London Festival B.), *Sacred Space* (mus. Bach, 1974, for Australian B.) *Infinite Pages* (mus. Vivaldi, 1973, for New London B.), *Dancing Space* (mus. Mozart, 1975, for London Festival B.), *Triptych* (mus. Albinoni, 1975, for Welsh D. Th.), and *Journey to Avalon* (mus. P. M. Davies, London Festival B., 1980). Art. dir. Western Australian B. 1984.

BIBL.: G. Gow, 'B.M.'s Progress', *Dancing Times* (1973/1).

Moresca. See *Morris Dance*.

Moreton, Ursula (*b* Southsea, 13 Mar. 1903, d London, 24 June 1973). Brit. dancer and teacher. Studied with Cecchetti. Début in the London

prod. of *The Truth About the Russian Dancers* (a play with Karsavina in the central role, 1920). Appeared in the Diaghilev prod. of *The Sleeping Princess* (1921). D. with Massine's co. Started to teach at de Valois' school 1926. Became one of the most active members of the Camargo Society and the Vic-Wells B.; appointed b. mistress 1931. Asst. dir. of Sadler's Wells Th. B. 1946–52. Dir. of Royal B. School 1952–68. O.B.E. (1968).

BIBL.: G. Anthony, 'U.M.', in *A Camera at the Ballet* (Newton Abbot, 1975).

Morini, Elettra (*b* Milan, 27 May 1937). Ital. dancer. Studied at La Scala B. School; graduated 1957. Joined La Scala B.; became soloist 1958 and ballerina 1965.

Morishita, Yoko (*b* Hiroshima, 7 Dec. 1948). Jap. dancer. Studied at Tachitana B. School with Asami Maki and Schwezoff. Joined Asami Maki B. aged 16; début as Odette/Odile. Prima ballerina of Matsuyama B. Co. since 1971. Guest star, Amer. B. Th., Stuttgart, and many other cos. Gold Medal (Varna, 1974).

BIBL.: O. Maynard, 'The Girl Who Loves Jerome Robbins', *Dance Magazine* (1970/7); Y.M., *World's Eminent Prima Ballerinas* (picture book, Tokyo 1980).

Mørk, Ebbe (*b* Skørping, 2 Dec. 1940). Dan. dance and drama critic. Studied at Aarhus univ. D. critic at *Politiken* since 1968. Dan. correspondent of Swed. *Dans* magazine. Author of *Conservatoriet* (Bournonville-monograph), *Behind Many Masks* (biography of Niels Bjørn Larsen), a book on The Royal Dan. Th. and Peter Martins; has often appeared on Dan. TV, introducing or commenting on various d. programmes. Guest lecturer at various Amer. univs. and colleges.

Morlacchi, Giuseppina (*b* Milan, 1843, *d* Millerica, Mass. 1886). Ital. dancer. Studied with Blasis and Augusto Hus. Went to U.S. 1867 and starred in extravaganzas and op. bs.; acclaimed as a prime exponent of the pure Ital. school.

Moroda, Derra de. See *Derra de Moroda, Friderica*.

Morrice, Norman (*b* Agua Dulce, Mexico, 10 Sep. 1931). Brit. dancer, choreographer, and b. director. Studied locally in Mansfield, Notts., and then at Rambert School. Joined B. Rambert 1952; became principal d., asst. b. dir. 1966 (with prime responsibility for the co.'s new policy), joint b. dir. 1970–4, when he resigned to devote himself to ch. Strongly influenced by his visit to the U.S.A. 1961–2, where he studied contemporary techniques and with Graham. First ch. *Two Brothers* (mus. von Dohnányi, 1958). Has also worked for Batsheva D. Co. Has created many bs., including *Hazaña* (1959), *A Place in the Desert* (both mus. Surinach, 1961), *Conflicts* (mus. Bloch, 1962), *The Travellers* (mus. Bloch), *Hazard* (1967), *1–2–3* (1968, all mus. Salzedo), *Them and Us* (mus. Xenakis, 1968), *Blind-Sight* (mus. Bob Downes, 1969), *The Empty Suit* (mus. Salzedo, 1970), *That*

Is the Show (mus. Berio, 1971), *Spindrift* (mus. J. Lewis, 1974). Also important in developing new chs. within B. Rambert. An ITV programme on him called 'People for Tomorrow' was prod. in 1971. Dir. second Gulbenkian National Ch. Summer Course, 1976. Dir. Royal B. since 1977. Contributed various statements to C. Crisp and M. Clarke, *Making a Ballet* (London, 1975). R.A.D. Elizabeth II Coronation Award (1974).

BIBL.: G. Gow, 'Cheerful Breaks In—N.M.', *Dancing Times* (1970/12); Interview with N.M. in *The Royal Ballet: A Souvenir* (London, 1979).

Morris, Margaret (*b* London, 1891, *d* Glasgow, 29 Feb. 1980). Brit. dancer and teacher. Studied with John d'Auban and Raymond Duncan. Developed her own system of free style dancing, which she taught at her London school (opened 1910), and propagated through her group and through the publications of the M.M. Movement, established 1925. Started Celtic B. in Glasgow 1947, a Scottish National B. in Glasgow 1947, and another Scottish National B. in Pitlochry 1960, each short-lived. Author of *Margaret Morris Dancing* (1925), *Notation of Movement* (1928), and *My Life in Movement* (1969).

Morris, Marnee (*b* Schenectady, N.Y., 2 Apr. 1946). Amer. dancer. Studied with Cornelia Thayer, Phyllis Marmein, Dokoudovsky, and at School of Amer. B. Joined New York City B. 1961; appointed soloist 1965. Created parts in Balanchine's *Don Quixote* (1965), *Who Cares?* (1970), and *Symphony in Three Movements* (1972). Married to the d. Roger Peterson.

Morris Dance. Eng. folk d., probably derived from the Moresca, a d. found in Burgundy *c.* 1420. The name may come from Span. *morisco* (Moor) or Greek *moros* (fool). It appeared in England in the 15th century; it has intricate steps, and is usually in 2/4 (but also in 3/4) time. The participants wore bells tied to the legs, and a number of them were usually disguised to represent certain characters such as Fool, Maid Marian, or the Queen of May, while a cardboard horse was also frequently introduced. One of the characters would often have his face blackened' (G. B. L. Wilson). Ashton has adapted some of its ensemble forms for his *La Fille mal gardée*.

Morse, David (*b* Hitchin, 1943). Brit. dancer. Studied at Royal B. School, joined Royal B. 1961, appointed soloist 1970. Created roles in Hynd's *Charlotte Brontë* (1974) and Bintley's *The Outsider* (1978). Ch. *Pandora* (mus. R. Gerhard and D. Atherton, 1976) and *Birdscape* (mus. Martinů, 1977).

Mort du cygne, La. See *Dying Swan, The.*

Mosaval, Johaar (*b* Cape Town, 8 Jan. 1928). S.A. dancer. Studied with D. Howes and at Sadler's Wells B. School. Joined Sadler's Wells Th. B. 1952. Became principal d. of the Royal B. Created roles in Cranko's *The Lady and the Fool* (1953) and

Layton's *The Grand Tour* (1971). Resigned 1974. Since 1976 working in a Cape Town government office to promote d. in S.A.

Moscow. See *Bolshoi Ballet* and *Stanislavsky and Nemirovich-Danchenko Theatre Ballet.* The city has held a 4-yearly International Ballet Competition since 1969.

Moscow Ballet School. In 1773 the Ital. dancing master Filippo Beccari was granted permission to train professional dancers from the inmates of the Moscow Orphanage. The standard of the school improved considerably when it came under the control of the Russ. Imperial Ths. in 1806, with I. Valberkh (from 1807), A. Gluzhkovsky (from 1811), and F. Hullin-Sor (1823–38) as its most prominent teachers. By the end of the 1860s, with the move to the new building at Neglinnaya street, the full course of b. education at Moscow's Th. School lasted up to 7 years. The school however, was always overshadowed by the St. Petersburg Th. School. During the 1930s some Leningrad teachers started to teach in Moscow, incl. Gerdt, Kozhukhova and Gusev. S. Golovkina was appointed dir. 1960. The school opened its magnificent new building 1967, which through its sheer size dwarfs every other b. school in the world, offering 20 studios and an impressive th., equipped with all the necessary technical facilities plus a dormitory for no less than 300 boarders. The film *Secret of Success* (1967) dedicates part of its content to showing the working of the school.

Mosolova, Vera Ilyinishna (*b* Moscow, 19 Apr. 1875, *d* there, 29 Jan. 1949). Russ. dancer, teacher, and b. mistress. Studied at Bolshoi B. School; graduated 1893. Joined Bolshoi B. D. at the Maryinsky Th., St. Petersburg, 1896–1903. Returned to Moscow; d. the ballerina roles until 1918. Appeared at London Alhambra Th. 1911. Taught at Moscow Bolshoi School 1920–40; her pupils included Moiseyev and the Messerers.

Motte, Claire (*b* Belfort, 21 Dec. 1937, *d* Paris, 15 July 1986). Fr. dancer. Studied at Paris Opéra B. School. Joined Paris Opéra B. 1952; appointed première danseuse 1956 and étoile 1960. Has often appeared abroad. Created roles in Lifar's *Chemin de la lumière* (1957), Descombey's *Sarracenia* (1964) and *Bacchus and Ariadne* (1967), Petit's *Notre-Dame de Paris* (1965) and *Turangalîla* (1968), and Blaska's *Concerto pour piano* (1970).

BIBL.: I. Lidova, 'C.M.' with complete check-list of roles and activities, *Les Saisons de la danse* (1972/2).

Mottram, Simon (*b* Woodford, 3 July 1937). Brit. dancer. Studied at Rambert School. Joined B. Rambert 1954, and Touring Royal B. 1956; appointed soloist 1959. D. with London Festival B., London B., Grand B. du Marquis de Cuevas, Western Th. B. 1962–5 (and 1966–8), Royal Swed. B., Netherlands D. Th. 1968–70, Northern D. Th. 1971–2, New London B. 1973–5. B.

Master, Netherlands D. Th. 1975–9. Has ch. some bs. Now freelance b. master.

Mounsey, Yvonne (b Pretoria, 1921). S.A. dancer. Studied with Schwezoff, Preobrajenska, Egorova, and at School of Amer. B. Joined B. Russe de Monte Carlo 1939. Later also d. with de Basil's Original B. Russe and with a co. of her own in S.A. Joined New York City B. 1949; appointed soloist 1950. Created roles in R. Boris' *Cakewalk*, Robbins' *The Cage* (both 1951) and *The Concert* (1956), Ashton's *Picnic at Tintagel* (1952), and Balanchine's *Nutcracker* (1954). The Siren in Balanchine's *Prodigal Son* was one of her best roles. Returned to S.A. 1959 and assisted in the launching of the Johannesburg B.

Movements for Piano and Orchestra. Ballet in 5 parts; ch. Balanchine; mus. Stravinsky; déc. and light. D. Hays and Peter Harvey. Prod. 9 Apr. 1963, New York City B., City Center, N.Y., with Farrell, d'Amboise. Set to Stravinsky's *Movements for Piano and Orchestra*. The plotless b. is a double concerto for male and female solo dancers, both identified with the solo piano, accompanied by 6 girls. It is now almost always given after *Monumentum pro Gesualdo*.
BIBL.: G. Balanchine, 'M', in *Balanchine's New Complete Stories of the Great Ballets* (Garden City, N.Y., 1968).

Moves. Ballet without mus. by Robbins. Prod. 3 July 1959, Bs.: U.S.A., Spoleto. 'A ballet in silence about relationships … between people—man and woman, one and another, the individual and the group' (Robbins). Revived for City Center Joffrey B. (1968), Netherlands D. Th. (1973).
BIBL.: G. Balanchine, 'M.' in *Balanchine's New Complete Stories of the Great Ballets* (Garden City, N.Y., 1968).

Moving Being. A Brit. avant-garde group of actors and dancers, under the direction of Geoff Moore. Début, Work in Progress programme, 17/18 Mar. 1969 at Liverpool Univ. Their aim was 'to create a context for the development of a theatre language capable of expressing a range of ideas not accessible to existing forms of d., theatre or event. … In April 1972 the co. moved to Cardiff's Chapter House arts centre with the aim of setting up a "Bauhaus" situation where the elements that concern us can be explored in closer and more continuous relation.'
BIBL.: Interview with G. Moore, 'A Very Moving Being', *Dance and Dancers* (1969/7).

Mozart, Wolfgang Amadeus (b Salzburg, 27 Jan. 1756, d Vienna, 5 Dec. 1791). Austrian composer. Wrote the mus. for Noverre's *Les petits riens* (Paris, 1778); Pick and Fabier were the choreographers of his Azione teatrale *Ascanio in Alba* (Milan, 1771). The b. divertissements for his op. *Lucio Silla* were ch. by Charles LePiq and Giuseppe Salomoni (Milan, 1772). His most important b. mus. is that for the op. *Idomeneo*, ch.

by Peter Legrand (Munich, 1781). He wrote a great many individual dances and sets of dances. A manuscript, discovered in Graz in 1928, entitled *Die Rekrutierung, oder Die Liebesprobe*, was attributed to him; Fokine ch. it as *L'Epreuve d'amour* (R. Blum's B. Russe, 1936). A. Einstein showed, however, that it was by several lesser composers. His concert mus. is often used for b. purposes: e.g. in Balanchine's *Symphonie concertante* (K 364, B. Society, 1947; a school perf. 1945) and *Caracole* (K 287, New York City B., 1952; a revised version as *Divertimento No. 15*, 1956), Cranko's *Konzert für Flöte und Harfe* (K 299, Stuttgart, 1966), Smuin's *Gartenfest* (K 63, Amer. B. Th., 1968), Arpino's *Secret Places* (Andante K 467, City Center Joffrey B., 1968), and Van Manen's *Quintet* (3 Adagios from K 410, 375, and 361, Dutch National B., 1974).
BIBL.: P. Nettl, *Mozart und der Tanz* (Zurich, 1960).

Mozartiana. Ballet in 1 act; ch. Balanchine; mus. Tchaikovsky; déc. Bérard. Prod. 7 June 1933, Les Bs. 1933, Th. des Champs-Elysées, Paris, with Toumanova, Jasinsky. A plotless b. set to Tchaikovsky's 4th Suite for Orchestra. New version for N.Y. City B., 1981, with Farrell, C. d'Amboise, and I. Andersen. Another b. by R. Hynd (London Festival B., 1973).

Mudra. 'Bodily gesture, especially of hands, which accent the ritual act and the mantric word, as well as the inner attitude which is emphasized and expressed by this gesture' (Lama Anagarika in *Foundations of Tibetan Mysticism*). Most often used in connection with Hindu dancing. Béjart named his Brussels school 'M.'; it is attached to the B. of the 20th Century. All kinds of movements are taught, and its official title is European Centre For Perfection and Research For Artists Taking Part In The Productions.
BIBL.: N. McLain Stoop, 'M.', *Dance Magazine* (1971/11).

Muller, Jennifer (b Yonkers, N.Y., 16 Oct. 1944). Amer. dancer and choreographer. Studied at Juilliard School. D. with various cos. incl. L. Falco's; became his assoc. dir 1972. Her first b. was *Rust—Giacometti Sculpture Garden* (1971), followed by *Tub* (1973), *An American Beauty Rose* (1974), and her full-length *Strangers* (1975—the last two for Netherlands Dance Th.). Formed her own co. 1975.

Multigravitational Aerodance Group. A small co. of Amer. dancers, assembled and directed by Stephanie Evanitsky, who perform on a scaffolding, using trapezes, ropes, etc. as a means of dancing in the air. First perf. in June 1970; has since appeared in museums, galleries, at open air occasions, and at the Paris Grand Palais.
BIBL.: Interview with S. Evanitsky, 'How I Got Up There', *Dance and Dancers* (1973/1).

Munich. The city has a long tradition of popular

dances, incl. the *Schäfflertanz* and *Moresca*, which are still performed today. During the 16th and 17th century court bs. were usually arranged by Fr. or Ital. b. masters. Peter Legrand ch. the first prod. of Mozart's *Idomeneo*, 1781; Crux and Lauchery were active, and the Viganòs were accused of obscenity for appearing in *La Fille mal gardée* 1795. A th. b. school was founded 1792. The Duports d. at the opening of the National Th. 1818, and at its reopening 1825 (after being burned down) and the Taglionis were much acclaimed. The most successful b. master of the first half of the 19th century was Friedrich Horschelt (1820–9 and 1839–47). He was followed by Johann Fenzl (1848–61), Franz Hoffman (1861–4), and Giovanni Golinelli (1864–9). Lucile Grahn (b. mistress 1869–75) ch. the Bacchanale from *Tannhäuser* and helped Wagner with *Meistersinger*; she was also in charge of the local first prods. of *Coppélia* and *Sylvia*. Franz Fenzl was b. master 1876–90. The b. school was particularly successful under Flora Jungmann (1891–1917). Standards declined around the turn of the century, but b. at the State Op. improved under the directorship of H. Kröller (1917–30). Another period of intense b. activity followed when the Mlakars took over 1939–44; the State Op. was one of the very few ths. at that time with its own d.-notator (A. Knust). M. Luipart was b. dir. of the State Op. 1945–8; he gave the controversial first prod. of Egk's *Abraxas*, 1948. R. Kölling followed 1948–50; he gave the local first prod. of Stravinsky's *Sacre du printemps*, 1949. V. Gsovsky (1950–52) gave the first prod. of Blacher's *Hamlet*, 1950, and Auric's *Chemin de la lumière*, 1952. A. Carter (1954–9) gave the Ger. first prods. of Britten's *Prince of the Pagodas*, 1958, and Henze's *Ondine*, 1959. H. Rosen was b. dir. 1959–68. Since then there has been a quick succession of b. directors, incl. R. Hynd, D. Gackstetter, L. Seymour and since 1980 E. Gleede. The repertory of the State Op. is now completely international; it includes both the classics and bs. by Balanchine, Ashton, Robbins, Cranko, Seregi, Van Manen, Neumeier, and Bruce. Munich's second op. house, the Th. am Gärtnerplatz, has also followed its own b. ambitions from time to time, under such b. masters as G. Hess, F. Baur-Pantoulier, I. Keres, and (since 1973) I. Sertic.

BIBL.: various authors, *Ballett Theater* (Munich, 1963).

Muravyeva, Marfa Nicolayevna (*b* Moscow, 29 June 1838, *d* St. Petersburg, 15 Apr. 1879). Russ. dancer. Studied at the St. Petersburg Imperial B. School. Became a member of the Bolshoi Th. there; much admired in the ballerina roles of the romantic repertory. Also very successful in Moscow. One of the first Russ. ballerinas to d. at the Paris Opéra (1863–4).

BIBL.: I. Guest, in *The Ballet of the Second Empire 1858–70* (London, 1953).

Murdmaa, Mai-Esther (*b* Tallinn, 31 Mar. 1933).

Sov. dancer and choreographer. Studied at Tallinn B. School, graduating 1956, then at GITIS (Moscow, faculty of choreographers), 1965. Since 1965 ch. of Estonia Th. in Tallinn. Started to ch. 1964 with *Ballet Symphony* (mus. Tamberg). Further bs. incl. *Cinderella* (mus. Prokofiev), *Medea* (mus. Barber, both 1965), *Daphnis and Chloe* (mus. Ravel, 1968), *The Miraculous Mandarin* (mus. Bartók, 1969), *Johanna, the Possessed* (mus. Tamberg, 1971), *Romeo and Juliet* (mus. Prokofiev, 1972), *Labyrinth* (mus. Bach. Pärt, Tormis, and Prokofiev), *The Prodigal Son* (mus. Prokofiev, 1973), *Prometheus* (mus. Beethoven), and *The Seasons* (mus. Vivaldi, both 1976). Has also worked for Moscow Young B., Finnish TV etc.

Musette (Fr., bagpipe). A very popular d. at the court of Louis XIV and XV, in 2/4, 3/4, or 6/8 time; a rustic form of the gavotte, with persistent bass drone like a bagpipe.

Musil, Karl (*b* Vienna, 3 Nov. 1939). Austrian dancer. Studied at Vienna State Op. B. School. Joined State Op. B. 1953; appointed soloist 1958 and principal d. 1965. Has often appeared abroad, incl. London Festival B., Royal B., and Charrat B. Co.; has also toured with Beriosova and Fonteyn. Has created many roles in bs. by Georgi, Parlić, Walter, Milloss, Orlikowsky, Adama, and Charrat. Brother of the d. Ludwig M. M., and married to the d. Irina Borowska.

BIBL.: S. Goodman, 'K.M.' *Dance Magazine* (1965/3).

Musil, Ludwig M. (*b* Vienna, 23 Mar. 1941). Austrian dancer. Studied at the State Op. B. School. Joined the State Op. B. 1956; appointed soloist 1962; principal d. 1972. Created several roles in bs. by Milloss. Brother of Karl M., and married to the d. Irmtraud Haider.

Mussorgsky, Modest Petrovich (*b* Karevo, 21 Mar. 1839, *d* St. Petersburg, 28 Mar. 1881). Russ. composer. Wrote no b. mus., but several choreographers have used his *Night on the Bare Mountain* (Gorsky, Moscow, 1918; Nijinska, Bs. Russes de Diaghilev, 1924. Lichine, B. Th., 1943) and *Pictures at an Exhibition* (Nijinska, 1944; Hanka, Vienna, 1947; Lopokov, Moscow, 1963; Neumeier, Frankfurt, 1972).

Mutations. Ballet by Tetley (ch.) and Van Manen (film ch.); mus. Stockhausen; set Baylis; cost. Emmy van Leersum and Gijs Bakker; film realization J.-P. Vroom; light. J. B. Read. Prod. 3 July 1970, Netherlands D. Th., Circus Th., Scheveningen, with J. Meyer, Flier, Sarstädt, Lemaitre, A. Licher. The film and live d. fit together; parts of the b. are performed in the nude.

BIBL.: G. Loney, 'Dutch Mutations', *Dance Magazine* (1971/2).

Muzzarelli, Antonio (*b* 1744, *d* Vienna, 7 Aug. 1821). Ital. dancer, choreographer, and b. master. D. in Florence, Venice, Milan, and Vienna and worked as b. master with Viganò (towards whom he became very hostile) 1791–6. Ch. a great number of bs.

My Brother, My Sisters (orig. Ger. title, *Mein Bruder, meine Schwestern*). Ballet in 1 act, ch. MacMillan; mus. Schoenberg and Webern; déc. Y. Sonnabend. Prod. 21 May 1978, Stuttgart, with Cragun, Keil, Montagnon, R. Anderson *et al.* Set to Schoenberg's op. 16 and Webern's op. 10 plus op. 6, the b. shows the partly playful, partly murderous relationships between a brother and his five sisters who are living cut off from any environment and society, acting out their weird fantasies, with a mysterious He appearing in the background. Revived for Royal B. 1980.

Myers, Carl (*b* Loughborough, 28 Mar. 1950).

Brit. d. Studied with Cissie Smith and Hightower, and then at Royal B. School. Joined Royal B. 1968, where Ashton ch. *Lament of the Waves* (1970) for him and M. Trounson. Created further roles in D. Bintley's *Meadow of Proverbs* and *Punch and the Street Party* (1979), and Corder's *Day into Night* (1980). Principal d. of tour. co. from 1976. Left Royal B. 1986.

Mythical Hunters. Ballet in 1 act; ch. Tetley; mus. Oedoen Partos; cost. Anthony Binstead. Prod. 25 Nov. 1965, Ohel-Shem, Batsheva D. Co. The b. deals with the archetypal situation of hunter becoming hunted. Revived for Netherlands D. Th. (1968), Stuttgart B. (1972). W. Berlin TV prod. with Tetley's own co. (1969).

N

Nabokov, Nicolas (*b* Lubsha, 17 Apr. 1903, *d* New York, 6 Apr. 1978). Russ.-Amer. composer. Wrote the mus. for Massine's *Ode* (1928) and *Union Pacific* (1934), T. Gsovsky's *The Last Flower* (Berlin, 1958), and Balanchine's *Don Quixote* (1965). Author of *Old Friends and New Music* (Boston, 1951).

Nachevnaya, Ludmila Petrovna. See *Petrovna, Ludmila.*

Nachteiland. See *Night Island.*

Nádasi, Ferenc (*b* Budapest, 16 Oct. 1893, *d* there, 20 Feb. 1966). Hung. dancer, teacher, and b. master. Studied with Jakob Holczer and Henriette Spinzi and later with Cecchetti and N. Guerra. Toured Russia 1909–21. Solo d. of Budapest Op. B. 1913–21. After extensive tours abroad returned to Budapest State Op. in 1936; became b. master and eventually b. dir. First dir. of the Budapest State B. School 1949–62, where he trained almost all the leading Hung. d. of the generation after World War II. After his resignation appointed head of the committee which produced the *Method of Classic Dance* (1963), a standard work of academic b. training. Kossuth Prize (1958); Merited Artist of the Republic; Order of Merit first Class.
BIBL.: G. Körtvélyes and G. Lörinc, in *Budapest Ballet* (Budapest, 1971).

Nadezhdina, Nadezhda Sergeyevna (*b* St. Petersburg, 3 June 1908, *d* Moscow, 11 Oct. 1979). Sov. dancer, choreographer, and b. director. Studied at Leningrad Ch. School. Joined Moscow Bolshoi B.; excelled as a character d. Resigned rather early. Ch. for mus. halls and for amateur groups; founded and dir. *Beryozhka in 1948.
BIBL.: N. Roslavleva, in 'Beryozka' (Moscow, 1960).

Nagata, Mikifumi (*b* Sapporo, 21 Sep. 1949). Jap. dancer. Studied with Yaoko Kaitani, H. Kitahara, A. Varlamov, Messerer, and Chaboukiani. Joined Kaitani B. 1957. Principal d. of Tokyo B. since 1967.

Nagrin, Daniel (*b* New York, 22 May 1917). Amer. dancer and choreographer. Studied with Tamiris (to whom he was married), Graham, Holm, Sokolow, Caton, and Anderson-Ivantzova. Début on Broadway 1945. D. with various modern cos. Became known through his solo-recitals; his dances have a strong emphasis on social criticism; e.g. *Strange Hero, Man of Action, Indeterminate Figure*, and *The Peloponnesian War*. Founded Tamiris-Nagrin D. Co., with Tamiris

1960, for which he created several group works. Contributed 'War Diary' to *Dance Perspectives* 38.
BIBL.: G. Loney, 'D.N.'s Magnet: The Peloponnesian War', *Dance Magazine* (1970/8); J. Gruen, 'Spotlight on D.N.', *Dance Magazine* (1976/6).

Nagy, Ivan (*b* Debrecen, 28 Apr. 1943). Hung. d. Studied at Budapest State B. Inst., with I. Bartos and Lepeshinskaya. Joined Budapest State Op. in 1960, Washington National B. in 1965, then N.Y. City B. Principal d. with Amer. B. Th. 1968–78. Created leading parts in Smuin's *Gartenfest* (1968) and *Eternal Idol*, Nahat's *Brahms Quintet* (both 1969), and Ailey's *The River* (1970). Now retired. Bronze Medal (Varna, 1965). Art. dir. B. Teatro Municipal, Santiago, and since 1986 of Cincinnati/New Orleans City B. Married to the d. Marilyn Burr.
BIBL.: J. Gruen, 'I.N.', in *The Private World of Ballet* (New York, 1975).

Nahat, Dennis (*b* Detroit, 20 Feb. 1946). Amer. d. and ch. Studied at Juilliard School, Amer. B. Center, and School of Amer. B. Début Joffrey B. 1965. Joined Amer. B. Th. in 1968–71, and became soloist. Started to ch. in 1967; his bs. include *Brahms Quintet* (1969) *Mendelssohn Symphony* (Ital. Symphony, 1971), *Some Times* (mus. Claus Ogerman, 1972). Has also worked for Royal Swed. B. and London Festival B. Artistic adviser and resident ch. of Cleveland B. since 1974, became sole dir. 1984.
BIBL.: W. Salisbury, 'The Dennis and Ernie Show', *(Ballet News*, 1981/1).

Naiade, La. See *Ondine.*

Naila. See *Source, La.*

Namouna. Ballet in 2 acts; libr. C. Nuitter and L. Petipa (also ch.); mus. Lalo; sets Rubé, Chaperon and J. B. Lavastre; cost. E. Lacoste. Prod. 6 Mar. 1882, Opéra, Paris, with Sangalli, Mérante. The b. is set on Corfu. The Lord Adriani stakes all he has, including his ship and Namouna, his favourite slave, in a wager with Count Ollario, and loses. New version with adapted libr. by P. Wright (Stuttgart, 1967). Parts of the mus. were used by Lifar for his *Suite en blanc* (1943).
BIBL.: C. W. Beaumont, 'N.' in *Complete Book of Ballets* (London, 1951).

Nana. Ballet in 1 act and 9 scenes; libr. Edmonde Charles-Roux; ch. Petit; mus. Constant; déc. Ezio Frigerio. Prod. 6 May 1976, Opéra, Paris, with K. Kain, C. Atanassoff, P. Marty, V. Descoutures, O. Patey. The b. summarizes several scenes from Zola's famous novel (1880), materializing as a 'dance of death' of the Second Empire.

NAPAC Ballet. The co., backed by the Natal Performing Arts Council, was founded in 1969 in Durban, S.A. Its directors are Dudley Davies and Patricia Miller.

Naples. At the Teatro di San Carlo (opened 1737), individual bs. were given between and after the op. acts. About 1760 fierce rivalry between the dancers Beccari and Sabatini split the audience into two factions. Noverre's reforms were brought to N. by LePicq. In 1799 Gaspare Ronzi created a *Romeo and Juliet* b. The first quarter of the 19th century was dominated by Gaetano Gioia, who created 44 bs. A B. school attached to the San Carlo was opened in 1812; Pietro Hus was its first dir. followed by Louis Henry and Salvatore Taglioni. It had an excellent reputation, but it was closed again in 1841. Taglioni was much acclaimed as a ch. and it was during his reign that Grisi started her career here in 1835. In the second half of the 19th century there was a rapid decline of b. standards here as everywhere; Manzotti's *Excelsior* dominated the first decades of the 20th century. Individual ballerinas were more notable than chs or bs.: Rosina Galli (especially in *Brahama*), Ettorina Mazzucchelli (*Excelsior*) and Bianca Gallizia (*La Fata delle bambole*, or *The Fairy Doll*). Gallizia was also in charge of reorganizing the co. after 1945, and she reopened the school in 1950. Compared with the international reputation of op. at the San Carlo, its b. co., has been insignificant; b. masters and choreographers have come and gone, without establishing any continuity.
BIBL.: entry 'Napoli' in *Enciclopedia dello spettacolo.*

Napoli, or The Fisherman and His Bride (orig. Dan. title: *Napoli, eller Fiskeren og hans Brud*). Ballet in 3 acts; libr. and ch. Bournonville; mus. H. S. Paulli, E. Helsted, N. W. Gade, and H. Lumbye. Prod. 29 Mar. 1842, Royal Dan. B., Copenhagen, with Bournonville, Caroline Fjeldsted, Stramboe. The fisherman Gennaro's bride, Teresina, is swept overboard in a storm. She is saved by the sea-sprite Golfo, who takes her to his blue grotto on the Island of Capri. Gennaro finds her there at last, and in the third act they celebrate their wedding with a divertissement, finishing with a lively Tarantella. The most popular of all Bournonville bs. Usually only the third act is now performed (solo variations ch. by H. Beck), but the complete b. is still in the repertory of the Royal Dan. B.; Lander made a condensed version for London Festival B. (1954). More recent full-length prods. by von Rosen in Gothenburg (1971), P. Gnatt for Scottish B. (1978), its first full prod. by a Br. co., and P. Schaufuss for National B. of Canada (1981). E. Bruhn mounted the divertissement from the last act for the Royal B. (1962), as did H. Brenaa for Amer. B. Th. (1974).
BIBL.: C. W. Beaumont, 'N' in *Supplement to Complete Book of Ballets* (London, 1952); A.

Fridericia, 'Bournonville's Ballet "N."' in *Theatre Research Studies II* (Copenhagen, 1972).

Naranda, Ludmilla (*b* Zagreb, 17 Sep. 1936). Yugosl. dancer. Studied at Zagreb State B. School; joined Zagreb B. in 1954. Soloist in Frankfurt, Heidelberg, Lübeck, then prima ballerina Wuppertal (1965–73), and Munich Th. am Gärtnerplatz (since 1973). Married to the ch. Ivan Sertić.

Näslund, Eric (*b* Ramsjö 20 Nov. 1948). Swed. dance critic and editor. Studied at Univ. of Stockholm (B.A., 1971). D. critic Dagens Nyheter 1972–6, and Svenska Dagbladet since 1976 as well as for other Swed. papers. Editor of *Dans* magazine since its foundation in 1973. Swed. correspondent of *Dance News* and *Les Saisons de la danse*. Author of *Birgit Cullberg—A Biography* (Stockholm, 1978). Works also as dramaturge for th. department of Swed. TV2.

Nathalie, ou La Laitière Suisse (orig. Ger. title: *Das Schweizer Milchmädchen*). Ballet in 2 acts; libr. and ch. F. Taglioni; mus. A. Gyrowetz. Prod. 8 Oct. 1821, Th. am Kärntnertor, Vienna. N., a peasant girl, is abducted by Oswald, the brother of the lord of the manor. She awakens in a castle where there is a life-size statue of Oswald. Much confusion ensues, but at last she agrees to marry him. The b. was very popular with contemporary audiences, and the title-role became one of Elssler's biggest successes. She d. it first in Berlin 1830; the b. was revived in Vienna 1831. A new version by Taglioni on 7 Nov. 1832, Opéra, Paris with Marie Taglioni and Mazilier. Revived by D. Lacotte for Moscow Classical B. in 1980.
BIBL.: C. W. Beaumont, 'N.,o.L.L.S.' in *Complete Book of Ballets* (London, 1951).

National Ballet. The comp., based in Washington, D.C., emerged from the school founded by the N.B. Society 1962; F. Franklin was dir. of both. Début Washington, 1963; it developed into an ambitious touring co. Its repertory offered Franklin and Stevenson prods. of the classics, numerous Balanchine bs., works from the international standard repertory, and creations by Franklin, Stevenson and other guest choreographers. Appeared regularly in New York; disbanded for financial reasons, summer 1974.
BIBL.: O. Maynard, in 'Frederic Franklin: A Life in the Theatre', *Dance Magazine* (1974/6).

National Ballet of Canada. The Toronto-based co. was founded in 1951, as the E. Can. equivalent of the W. Can. Royal Winnipeg B. Its dir. until 1974 was C. Franca. With K. Ambrose as her art. adviser (1952–61), she modelled the co., strictly on the Sadler's Wells B.; she herself was in charge of the classics. Apart from bs. by Ashton, Tudor, de Valois, Howard, Cranko, and MacMillan, there are several Balanchine works in the repertory. Recent chs. include Bruhn, Petit, Flindt, P. Wright, Nureyev, and Neumeier plus resident chs. J. Kudelka and C. Patsalas. The co. tours

regularly, and now has an annual N.Y. season. It visited Eur., incl. London, for the first time in 1972. After Franca's resignation Alexander Grant was dir. 1976–83 with B. Oliphant assistant dir., and E. Bruhn assoc. prod. Bruhn dir. 1983–6; L. Wallis and V. Wilder joint art. dirs. from 1986, with G. Tetley as art. adviser from 1987.
BIBL.: C. Franca, *'The N.B.o.C., A Celebration'* (Toronto, 1978).

National Ballet of Cuba. The first professional Cuban b. co., based on Havana, was founded in 1948, as Ballet Alicia Alonso, dir. by Alicia and Fernando Alonso, with Alberto Alonso as ch. The work was extremely hard, but the co., soon undertook tours in South Amer. and the U.S. The next step was the foundation of a b. academy 1950 for the education of young dancers. In 1955 the name was changed to Ballet de Cuba, and again in 1961 to Ballet Nacional de Cuba. After the Cuban revolution of 1959 the co., became one of the top international showpieces of the Castro government, with official State backing, and was often sent abroad as an ambassador of Cuban culture—not only to Eastern countries, but also to the West (to the U.S. for the first time only in 1978). Though Alicia Alonso still reigns as the undisputed prima ballerina of the co., its younger soloists have dazzled their audiences everywhere by their technical brilliance, winning medals at all the important international competitions. In Havana it performs about four times a week at the Teatro García Lorca. The repertory offers the standard classics, folklore-based works, and modern bs. The co., has been enormously successful all over the world with its *Giselle*, produced by Alicia Alonso, and was awarded the Grand Prix of the Paris Dance Festival 1964. Some of the more important bs. which have been specially created for the co., include Alberto Alonso's *El Güije* and *Un retablo para Romeo y Julieta*, J. García's *Majismo*, J. Parés's *Un concierto en blanco y negro*, J. Lefèbre's *Edipo Rey*, and A. Mendez' *Nos veremos ayer noche*, *Margarita*, together with Alberto Alonso's *Carmen* (originally created for the Bolshoi B.). Several highlights of the co.'s achievement are preserved in films or TV prods. Br. debut at 1979 Edinburgh Festival.
BIBL.: Summary of the history of the co., with a complete list of all its prods. and dancers in *Cuba en el ballet* (1973/9).

National Ballet of Mexico. The comp., based in Mexico City, was founded in 1949 by Guillerma Bravo, who is still its dir.-ch. It aims for a contemporary repertory with a distinctive national character. Most of its bs. are ch. by Bravo; other contributions have been made by some of its dozen dancers, e.g. Luis Fandiño and Fererico Castro. London début 1974.

National Choreographic Summer School. Founded in 1975 by the UK branch of the Gulbenkian Foundation as the first of its kind to bring together, free of charge, 6–8 choreographers, 6–8 composers, and 24 professional or graduate dancers for 2 weeks of intense creative collaboration. The first course was held at Elmhurst B. School, Camberley, with Glen Tetley as dir., and a faculty consisting of Dame Peggy van Praagh (classical b.), Mary Hinkson (modern d.), and Norma Dalby (mus.). From 1976 the school moved to the Univ. of Surrey, Guildford, with Norman Morrice as dir., Mary Hinkson (modern d.), John Herbert McDowell and Adam Gatehouse (mus.). Dir. 1977–8 was Robert Cohan, after which it became the *International Dance Course for Professional Chs. and Composers.

Nationale Ballet, Het. See *Dutch National Ballet*.

Nault, Fernand (*b* Montreal, 27 Dec. 1921). Can. dancer, choreographer, b. master, and teacher. Studied with Maurice Morenoff and Elizabeth Leese, also with Caton, Craske, Nemchinova, Vilzak, Pereyaslavec, Volkova, Preobrajenska, and Luigi. Member of B. Th. 1944–65, originally as a d.; became b. master and co-dir. of the school 1958. Joined Grands Bs. Canadiens 1965 as artistic adviser and chief ch. Has ch. many bs., including *La Fille mal gardée* (Joffrey B., 1960), *Carmina Burana* (1962), and *Tommy* (mus. The Who, 1970).
BIBL.: D. Leddick, 'Conversation with F.N.', *Dance Magazine* (1960/4).

Navarro, Armando (b. Buenos Aires, 1930). Argent. dancer, choreographer, and b. director. Studied with Bulnes, M. Borowski, and Gema Castillo. D. with Teatro Colón B., B. Alicia Alonso, and Grand B. du Marquis de Cuevas 1956–62. Joined Scapino B. as teacher 1962; became b. master 1963 and artistic dir. 1970. Started to ch. 1946—has ch. several bs. for Scapino B., incl. *Coppélia* (1972), *Halve Symfonie* (mus. Tchaikovsky, 1974), and *Nutcracker* (1975). Married to the dancer Marian Sarstädt.

Neary, Colleen (*b* Miami, Fl., 23 May, 1952). Amer. dancer. Studied at School of Amer. B. and Harkness House. Joined New York City B. in 1969, promoted soloist in 1974. Created roles in Balanchine's *Kammermusik no. 2* and P. Martin's *Tricolore* (both 1978). To Zurich in 1980 as an assistant to her sister Patricia N.

Neary, Patricia (*b* Miami, Fl., 27 Oct. 1942). Amer. d. and b. mistress. Studied with Georges Milenoff and at School of Amer. B. Début National B. of Canada 1959. Joined N.Y. City B. 1960; became soloist 1962. Created leading parts in Balanchine's *Raymonda Variations* (1961) and *Jewels* (1967). Left the co. 1968. Has since mounted many Balanchine bs. for European cos., e.g. Geneva, Vienna, West Berlin, Stuttgart, Rome, and Dutch National B. B. mistress Ger. Op. Berlin 1971–3. Dir. of Geneva B. 1973–8 and of Zurich B. 1978–85, art. dir. B. of La Scala di Milano 1986–7.

BIBL.: J. Gruen, 'Close-Up: P.N.', *Dance Magazine* (1975/9).

Nebrada, Vicente (*b* Caracas, 31 Mar. 1932). Amer. dancer and choreographer. Studied with various teachers locally and in the U.S. D. with Bs. de Paris, R. Joffrey B., and Harkness B. Became b. master and eventually resident ch. of Harkness B. His best known bs. include *Percussions for Six, Schubert Variations*, and *Gemini*. Appointed resident ch. of B. Intern. of Caracas in 1977.

Nederlands Ballet, Het. Became *Dutch National B. in 1961.

Nederlands Dans Theater. See *Netherlands Dance Theatre*.

Negri, Cesare (*b* Milan, *c.* 1536, *d* after 1604). Ital. dancer, dance master, and dance theorist. One of the earliest writers on d.; published *Le Gratie d'Amore* ('di Cesare Negri Milanese, detto il Trombone', 1602) and *Nuove Inventioni di Balli* (1604).

Neil, Sandra (*b* Wellington, 1932). N.Z. dancer. Studied at London Royal Academy of Dancing. Joined Sadler's Wells Th. B. 1951; appointed principal dancer 1955. Returned to New Zealand 1959; appointed principal d. of the United B. Co. Teacher at the Royal B. School, London, 1968–81. Married to the d. and teacher Walter Trevor.

Nelidova, Lydia Richardovna (*b* 1863, *d* 1929). Russ. dancer and teacher. Studied at Moscow Bolshoi B. School; graduated 1884. Joined Bolshoi B., where she danced the ballerina roles (also as a guest at the London Empire Th., 1890) but resigned when she was refused the title of prima ballerina. Opened a school in Moscow in 1908, from which Diaghilev recruited some of his dancers, incl. Nemchinova and N,'s daughter Lydia N., who created the nymph in Nijinsky's *L'après-midi d'un faune* (1912).

Nemecek, Jiří (*b* Říčany, nr. Prague, 12 Apr. 1924). Czech dancer, choreographer, and b. director. Studied with J. Nikolská, I. V. Psota, B. Szynglarski, and at School of Prague National Th. Joined Prague National Th. 1939. B. master of Pilsen B. 1951–7. B. director of Prague National Th. 1957–70 and of Brno B. since 1973. Has ch. many bs., incl. the first prods. of Z. Vostřák's *Snow White* (1956), Burghauser's *The Servant of Two Masters* (1958) and Hanuš's *Othello* (1959). Has often collaborated with the producers of the Prague Laterna Magica programmes. Merited Artist of C.S.S.R. (1963).

Nemtchinova, Vera Nicolayevna (*b* Moscow, 26 Aug.1899, *d* N.Y., 22 July 1984). Russ. d. and teacher. Studied with Nelidova. Joined Diaghilev's Bs. Russes 1915; appointed principal d. 1924. Created roles in Massine's *Boutique fantasque* (1919), *Pulcinella, le Astuzie femminili* (both 1920), *Les Matelots* (1925), and Nijinska's *Les Biches* (1924). D. with Mordkin B., London. Cochrane

revues, Teatro Colón B., N.–Dolin B., Kaunas Op. B. 1930–5 (where her husband A. Oboukhoff was b. master), B. Russe de Monte Carlo (creating role in Fokine's *L'Epreuve d'Amour*, 1936), Markova-Dolin B., Original B. Russe, and B. Th. Also taught in New York. Author of 'In the Shadow of Russian Tradition', *Dance Magazine* (1972/2).

Nerina, Nadia (*b* Cape Town, 21 Oct. 1927). S.A. dancer. Studied with E. Keegan, D. McHair, and H. Grinter. Went to London 1945, and studied at Rambert School and Sadler's Wells B. School. Joined Sadler's Wells B. 1946; became soloist 1947 and ballerina 1951. Created leading roles in Howard's *Mardi Gras* (1946), Cranko's *Bonne Bouche* (1952), Ashton's *Homage to the Queen* (1953), *Variations on a Theme of Purcell* (1955), *Birthday Offering* (1956), and *La Fille mal gardée* (Lise; 1960), MacMillan's *Noctambules* (1956), Helpmann's *Elektra* (1963), and Darrell's *Home* (1965). A brilliant virtuoso and a mesmeric personality; often d. abroad as a guest ballerina. Retired 1966.

BIBL.: C. Swinson, *N.N.* (London, 1954); C. Crisp (ed.), *Ballerina* (London, 1975).

Nervi International Ballet Festival. Established in 1955 as an open-air festival at this seaside resort near Genoa, Mario Porcile is artistic dir. Many of the world's leading cos. have performed here; Massine's B. Europeo was especially assembled for the 1960 festival.

Netherlands. See *Amsterdam, Dutch National B., The Hague , Netherlands Dance Theatre*, and *Scapino Ballet*.

Netherlands Dance Theatre. The co. was established in The Hague by B. Harkarvy 1959, and Carel Birnie gen. dir. since then, as a breakaway group of dancers from Het Nederlands B. Some of the original members soon returned to their former co., but W. de la Bye, J. Flier, and A. Vestegen stayed and formed the nucleus of the N.D.T. Van Manen joined 1960 as artistic co-dir. and the formative ch. of the co. Together they built up the co. and the repertory; they abandoned the classics from the start, and laid particular emphasis on specially created works. Regular collaboration with Americans, such as J. Butler, G. Tetley, and A Sokolow, made clear the need for a modern d. training; so N.D.T. became the first European b. co. to have regular modern d. classes, and one of the foremost European platforms for contemporary ch. When Harkarvy resigned in 1969, Van Manen and Tetley took over as joint artistic directors. Important prods. of these years incl.—1962: *Carmina Burana* (Butler), *Pierrot lunaire* (Tetley); 1963: *Symphony in Three Movements* (Van Manen); 1964: *The Anatomy Lesson* (Tetley), *Recital for Cello and Eight Dancers* (Harkarvy); 1965: *Essay in Silence* and *Metaforen* (Van Manen); 1966: *Screen Play* (J. Sanders), *Five Sketches* (Van Manen); 1968: *Mythical Hunters* and *Circles* (Tetley), *Nouvelles Aventures*

(Flier); 1969: *Arena* and *Embrace Tiger and Return to Mountain* (Tetley), *Catulli Carmina* (Butler), *Squares* (Van Manen); 1970: *Situation* (Van Manen), *Mutations* (Tetley and Van Manen); 1971: *Grosse Fuge* (Van Manen), *Journaal* (Falco); 1972: *Tilt* and *Opus Lemaitre* (Van Manen), *Small Parades* (Tetley); 1973: *Septet Extra* (Van Manen); 1974: *An American Beauty Rose* (J. Muller); 1975: *Caterpillar* (Falco) and *Strangers* (Muller). After the resignation of Van Manen (1970) standards declined until J. Kylián was appointed artistic dir. (collaborating with H. Knill) in 1975, since when the co. has enjoyed an enormous intern. success. More recent important creations incl. Van Manen's *Songs Without Words* (1977) and from Kylián *Transfigured Night* (1975) *Symphony in D* (1976), *Children's Games*, *Symphony of Psalms*, *Sinfonietta* (all 1978) *Glagolitic Mass* (1979), and *Field Mass* (1980).

Neubauer, Henrik (*b* Golnik, 17 Apr. 1929). Yugosl. dancer, teacher, choreographer, and artistic director. Studied at Ljubljana B. School, Moscow GITIS (ch. faculty) and at New York Dance Notation Bureau (teacher's certificate). Joined Ljubljana B. Co. in 1946, promoted soloist in 1953, dir. and ch. 1960–72. Teacher at Ljubljana B. School since 1957. Director of Ljubljana Festival since 1972. Temporary jobs as ch. and op. dir. with various cos. Vicepresident of Yugosl. national centre Intern. Th. Inst. Author of *Labanotation and its Signs* (1958), *Ballet Dictionary* (1963), *A Short History of the Slovene Ballet* (1970).

Neumeier, John (*b* Milwaukee, 24 Feb. 1942). Amer. dancer, choreographer, and b. director. Studied with Sheila Reilly, Stone–Camryn, Volkova, and at Royal B. School. Danced with S. Shearer and Stuttgart B. 1963–9. B. dir. Frankfurt 1969–73, Hamburg State Op. since 1973; regular guest dir. Royal Winnipeg B. since 1973. Started to ch. for Stuttgart Noverre matinées; his best known bs. include *Separate Journeys* (mus. Barber, 1968), *Frontiers* (mus. Bliss, Scottish Th. B., 1969), *Rondo* (various composers, 1970), *Romeo and Juliet*, *Nutcracker* (both 1971), *Dämmern* (mus. Scriabin), *Baiser de la Fée* (mus. Stravinsky), *Daphnis and Chloe* (mus. Ravel), *Don Juan* (mus. Gluck), *Le Sacre*, (mus. Stravinsky, all 1972), *Meyerbeer/Schumann* (1974), *Gustav Mahler's Third Symphony* (1975), *Swan Lake* (1976), *Hamlet Connotations* (mus. Copland, 1976). *Gustav Mahler's Fourth Symphony* (Royal B. London, 1977), *Legend of Joseph* (mus. Strauss, Vienna 1977), *A Midsummer Night's Dream* (mus. Mendelssohn and Ligeti, Hamburg, 1977), *Dreamers* (mus. Strauss; *Don Quixote*, Hamburg, 1979), *Songfest* and *Age of Anxiety* (mus. Bernstein, Hamburg, 1979), and *St. Matthew Passion* (mus. Bach, Hamburg, 1981). Has also worked for Harkness B., Amer. B. Th., Stuttgart B., Royal Dan. B. et al.
BIBL.: various authors, *J.N. Unterwegs* (Frankfurt, 1972); *J. N. und das Hamburger Ballett* (Hamburg,

1977); *J. N. Traumwege* (Hamburg, 1980—incl. Eng. texts).

Neuvième Symphonie. See *Ninth Symphony*.

New Dance. Variations and Conclusions; ch. Humphrey; mus. Wallingford Riegger; cost. P. Lawrence. Prod. 27 Oct. 1935, Humphrey Weidman co., Guild Th., New York, with Humphrey, Weidman. One of Humphrey's major works; part of a trilogy with *Theatre Piece* and *With My Red Fires*. The b. 'represents the world as it should be, where each person has a clear and harmonious relationship to his fellow beings' (Humphrey). Filmed in 1972. Revived for Welsh Dance Th. in 1975.

New Dance Group. During the Depression of 1932, several New York dancers banded together and established the Workers' Dance League, which survived for several decades. They worked either as a studio, or as a number of modern d. groups sharing a single programme or series of perfs. Choreographers included Dudley, Maslow, Sokolow, McKayle, Primus, Erdman, Nagrin, and Weidman.

New London Ballet. Small chamber-size b. co. founded in 1972 by G. Samsova and A. Prokovsky after several successful guest-perfs. abroad. Has toured extensively; London début Mar. 1974. Choreographers incl. Darrell, J. Carter, Moreland, and Prokovsky. Disbanded in 1979.

Newton, Joy (*b* Wimbledon, 1913). Brit. dancer and teacher. Studied with de Valois. One of the earliest members of the Vic-Wells B. B. mistress of Sadler's Wells B. 1942–6. Established Turkish B. School in Istanbul and was its first dir. 1947–51. Returned to London and taught at Royal B. School 1963–9. Now retired.
BIBL.: G. Anthony, 'J.N.', in *A Camera at the Ballet* (Newton Abbot, 1975).

New York. The Eng. dance master Holt gave the first dance perf. in N.Y. on 12 Feb. 1739 at the Long Room: *Harlequin and Scaramouche* or *The Spaniard Trick'd*. An anonymous d. performed *Harlequin Dance*, *Pierrot Dance*, and *The Drunken Peasant* in 1751. Pietro Sodi, Barberina's Berlin partner, appeared with his daughter in Mr. Hull's Assembly Room in 1774. Louis Roussel, from the Paris Opéra, performed in 1783; John Durang, the first professional Amer. male d., performed in 1785. Real b. perfs. started with the small co. of Alexandre Placides 1792–4. Jean-Baptiste Francisquy, from Charleston, performed such bs. as *The Whims of Galatea*, *The Two Hunters and the Milkmaid*, and *The Independence of America* or *The Ever Memorable Fourth of July 1776*. Eng. hornpipes were specially popular in the early 19th century (usually during the entr'actes of plays). Edward Conway, d. at the Park Th., published *Le Maître de danse* or *The Art of Dancing Cotillons*. Claude Labassé, from La Scala, Milan, became b. master at the Park Th. 1821. In 1827 Francisque Hutin, 'pioneer of the striptease', made her début at the Bowery Th., presenting 'the new French style'. Charles Vestris and his wife came from Naples in 1828; Mlle Celeste gave *La Sylphide* at the Park Th. 1835. Elssler was enormously successful in N.Y. 1840–2. Local first prod. of *Giselle* (with Mme Augusta) 1846. The most popular Amer. dancers of these years were Julia Turnbull and George Washington Smith. The Montplaisirs, led by Victor Batholomin, were the first larger Europ. co. to come, in 1847. Domenico Ronzani brought a troupe in 1858, which included the Cecchetti parents and their seven-year-old son Enrico. M. Bonfanti and R. Sangalli brought the extravaganza *The Black Crook* in 1866, which started the vogue for musicals. Genuine b. activity then declined, though *Sylvia* was first prod. at the Academy of Music in 1886. St. Denis and Fuller brought the beginnings of what was to grow into the modern dance movement at the turn of the century. A. Genée and I. Duncan made their débuts in 1908. Pavlova gave her first local perf. in 1910 (with Mordkin as her partner), and the Diaghilev co. appeared at the Century Th. in 1916, giving the first prod. of Nijinsky's *Till Eulenspiegel*. After 1926 there was an increase in modern dance activities. Many dancers and cos. from abroad performed; the majority were presented by Hurok. the B. Russe de Monte Carlo, established in 1933, inspired the formation of several Amer. cos. incl. Mordkin's, the Amer B. of Balanchine in 1934 (which became the New York City B.), and L. Chase's B. Th. in 1940. Since 1945 the city has increasingly become the hub of international b. activity. The Royal B. has appeared regularly since 1949, Dan. B. since 1956, the Bolshoi B. since 1959, the Kirov B. since 1961, the Royal the Stuttgart B. since 1969, and the B. of the 20th Century since 1971. Since the 2nd World War the Joffrey B., the Harkness B., the E. Feld B., and (on the modern d. side) the cos. of Graham, Humphrey, Weidman, Limón, Nikolais, Cunningham, P. Taylor, Ailey, Falco, and Tharp have all been founded or based in N.Y. Theatrical d. has, of course, also played an important role on Broadway, culminating in Robbins' *West Side Story* (1957). See also *American Ballet, American Ballet Company, American Ballet Theatre, Joffrey Ballet, Harkness Ballet, New York City Ballet*, and the individual names mentioned above.

BIBL.: G. Amberg, *Ballet in America* (New York, 1949); entry 'Ballet in America' in *Dance Encyclopedia* (New York, 1967); M. G. Swift, *Belles and Beaux on their Toes: Dancing Stars in Young America* Washington, D.C., 1980).

New York City Ballet. The co. received its present name in 1948, when it became the resident b. co. of the New York City Center for Music and Drama, after a series of highly successful perfs. (as B. Society) at the house on 55th St., led by Kirstein and Balanchine. Kirstein invited Balanchine to come to the States as director of the School of Amer. B. in 1934, and this gave birth to the Amer. B., which made its New York début in 1935. It became B. Caravan in 1936, and B. Society in 1946. Kirstein was general manager, Balanchine artistic dir., and Robbins artistic co.-dir.; the co. rapidly became one of the world's great troupes, successfully combining the Eur. tradition and Amer. contemporaneity. Frequent Eur. appearances since 1950. Its visits, and the Balanchine works mounted by European cos., have considerably influenced the development of ch. in Eur. The co. moved to the New York State Th. at the Lincoln Center in 1964, where its crowning achievement so far was an all-Stravinsky week in 1972. The company's most important prods. include—1949: Balanchine's *Firebird* and *Bourrée fantasque*; 1950: Balanchine's *Prodigal Son* (new version), Robbins' *Age of Anxiety*, and Ashton's *Illuminations*; 1951: Balanchine's *La Valse* and *Swan Lake*, Robbins' *The Cage* and *The Pied Piper*, 1952: Balanchine's *Caracole, Scotch Symphony*, and *Metamorphoses*, Ashton's *Picnic at Tintagel*; 1953: Robbins' *Afternoon of a Faun* and *Fanfare*; 1954: Balanchine's *Opus 34, Nutcracker, Western Symphony*, and *Ivesiana*; 1955: Balanchine's *Pas de dix*; 1956: Balanchine's *Allegro Brillante* and Robbins' *The Concert*; 1957: Balanchine's *Agon*; 1958: Balanchine's *Stars and Stripes* and *The Seven Deadly Sins* (new version); 1959: Balanchine's and Graham's *Episodes*; 1960: Balanchine's *Monumentum pro Gesualdo* and *Liebeslieder Walzer*; 1962: Balanchine's *A Midsummer Night's Dream*; 1963: Balanchine's *Bugaku* and *Movements for Piano and Orchestra*; 1965: Balanchine's *Harlequinade* and *Don Quixote*; 1966: Balanchine's *Variations* and *Brahms-Schoenberg Quartet*; 1967: Balanchine's *Jewels*; 1968: Balanchine's *Metastaseis & Pithoprakta* and *Slaughter on Tenth Avenue*; 1969: Robbins' *Dances at a Gathering*; 1970: Balanchine's *Who Cares?* and Robbins' *In the Night*; 1971: Robbins' *The Goldberg Variations*; 1972: Stravinsky Festival; 1975: Ravel festival; 1978: Balanchine's *Ballo della Regina*, 1979: Robbins' *The Four Seasons* and *Opus 19*; 1980: Balanchine's *Davidsbündlertänze*; 1981: Tchaikovsky Festival. Balanchine d 1983 since when P. Martins and J. Robbins have been appointed b. masters-in-chief.

BIBL.: L. Kirstein, *The N.Y.C.B.* (N.Y., 1973, new ed. 1978), N. Reynolds, *Repertory in Review* (N.Y., 1977).

New York Export: Op. Jazz. Ballet in 5 parts; ch. Robbins; mus. Robert Prince; cost. Florence Klotz and Ben Shahn (also set). Prod. 8 June 1958, Bs. U.S.A., Spoleto, with P. Dunn, J. Norman, W. Curley, J. Jones. 'A formal ballet based on the kinds of movements, complexities of rhythms, expressions of relationships, and qualities of atmosphere found in today's dances' (Robbins). Revived for City Center Joffrey B. (1969).

BIBL.: G. Balanchine, 'N.Y.E.: O.J.' in *Balanchine's*

The New York City Ballet in Robbins's *Dances at a Gathering*.   Photo Martha Swope.

New Complete Stories of the Great Ballets (Garden City, N.Y., 1968).

New Zealand Ballet Company (became Royal New Zealand Ballet 1984). The N.Z. B. Inc. group toured the country in 1953; a series of perfs. was given in 1957 by such dancers as R. Kerr, R. Jackson, P. Chatfield, S. Neil, and W. Trevor, who had returned from London to Auckland. The N.Z. B. co. was founded in Wellington in 1961: Kerr was art. dir., and some backing was given by the N.Z. Arts Council. During subsequent years individual perfs. were given, with guest stars such as Beriosova, Burr, Musil, and Comelin Y. Shabelevsky was appointed b. master in 1967. B. Ashbridge staged *Swan Lake* for the Auckland Festival of 1971 and *Coppélia* in 1972. A National School of B. was established in Wellington 1967; Kerr and Neil were the dirs., succeeded by Jackson and Chatfield in 1973 (Jackson left in 1976).

Nichols, Kyra (*b* Berkeley, Cal., 1958). Amer. dancer. Studied with her mother, the former Sally Streets (member of the New York City B. during the 1950s), then with Alan Howard and at School of Amer. B., joining New York City B. 1974, promoted soloist 1978, principal 1979.

Created role in Robbins's *The Four Seasons* (1979).

Nicks, Walter (*b* Pittsburgh, 26 July 1925). Amer. dancer and teacher. Studied with I. Hawthorn, Orloff, Shook, Schwezoff, Limón, Humphrey, and Dunham. Began dancing in Dunham's co. and taught at her New York school; also appeared in many Broadway prods. and on TV. Gradually concentrated on teaching jazz d. Has performed with a group of his own. Now mainly based in New York, Paris, and Stockholm.

Niehaus, Max (*b* Wesel, 17 Dec. 1888, *d* Munich, 8 Apr. 1981). Ger. writer on b. Author of *Ballett* (1954), *Junges Ballett* (1957 and 1972), *Heinrich Heine und das Ballett* (1959), *Nijinsky* (1961), and *Heinz Bosl* (ed., 1975), *Peter Breuer* (1978—all Munich). Editor of Ger. *Ballett Kalender*, 1958–82.

Nielsen, Augusta (*b* 1822, *d* 1902). Dan. dancer. Studied at Royal Dan. B. School; succeeded Grahn as solo dancer of the Royal Dan. B. Also appeared in Stockholm, Berlin, Paris, and Oslo. Her most popular dance was *La Lithuanienne*.

Night and Silence, The. A Ballet of Jealousy in 1 act; ch. Gore; mus. Bach (arr. Mackerras); déc.

Ronald Wilson. Prod. 28 Aug. 1958, Edinburgh International B., Empire Th., Edinburgh, with Hinton and Poole. Set to various orchestrated pieces of Bach. The girl 'stole happily away from a Ball at the Castle to meet her true love' (programme note). Revived for other cos. (B. Rambert, 1961; Northern Dance Th., 1972). BBC TV prod. 1958.
BIBL.: P. Brinson and C. Crisp, '*T.N.A.S.*' in *Ballet for all* (London, 1970).

Night City. See *Miraculous Mandarin, The.*

Night Island (orig. Dutch title: *Nachteiland*). Ballet in 1 act; libr., ch., and cost. Van Dantzig; mus. Debussy. Prod. 20 Jan. 1955, Netherlands B., Royal Th., The Hague, with Hannie van Leeuwen, Vella Colcher, Van Dantzig, P. P. Zwartjes. Van Dantzig's first b. The 'fight of man with the powers of his ego for the purity, the ideals and dreams, which are escaping with his youth' (programme note). Revived for B. Rambert (1966).

Night Journey. Ballet in 1 act; ch. Graham; mus. W. Schuman; set Noguchi. Prod. 3 May 1947, M. Graham Group, Cambridge, Mass., with Graham, Hawkins, M. Ryder. Commissioned by the E. Sprague Coolidge Foundation. A version of the Oedipus myth, with 'Queen Jocasta as the protagonist. The action of d. turns upon that instant of her death when she relives her destiny, sees with double insight the triumphal entry of Oedipus, their meeting, courtship, marriage, their years of intimacy which were darkly crossed by the blind seer Tiresias until at last the truth burst from him' (programme note). Amer. film prod. of the b. (1960).

Night Shadow (also *La Somnambule* and *La Sonnambula*). Ballet in 1 act; libr. and mus. V. Rieti (after Bellini); ch. Balanchine; déc. Dorothea Tanning. Prod. 27 Feb. 1946, B. Russe de Monte Carlo, City Centre, New York, with Danilova, Magallanes, Maria Tallchief. A poet and a sleep-walker meet at a masked ball in the garden of a manor. Although the b. uses some of the mus. of Bellini's op. of the same title (and from others of his ops.), it has nothing to do with the plot of the op. Revived for many cos., including Grand B. du Marquis de Cuevas (1948—a BBC prod. of this version was televised in 1958), Royal Dan. B. (1955), New York City B. (1960), B. Rambert (1961), London Festival B. (1967), Amer. B. Th. (1981). An earlier b. *La Somnambule* by J. Aumer (mus. Hérold, Paris, 1827); an even earlier rural divertissement *Die Nachtwandlerin* by F. Taglioni (mus. Gyrowetz, Vienna, 1826).
BIBL.: G. Balanchine, '*N.S.*' in *Balanchine's Complete Stories of the Great Ballets* (Garden City, N.Y., 1977).

Nijinska, Bronislava Fominitshna (properly Nijinskaya; *b.* Minsk, 8 Jan. 1891, *d* Los Angeles, 22 Feb. 1972). Russ.-Pol.-Amer. d., ch., b. mistress,

and teacher. Daughter of the dancers Eleonora Bereda and Foma Nijinsky and the sister of Vaslav N.; she was born while her parents were on tour. Studied with Cecchetti; entered St. Petersburg Imperial B. School 1900 and graduated 1908. Joined the Maryinsky Th. Went to Paris with Diaghilev in 1909 and on numerous occasions in the next few years. Created roles in Fokine's *Carnaval* (1910) and *Petrushka* (1911). Left Maryinsky Th. with her brother in 1911; continued to appear with Diaghilev's co. D. with her brother's co. in London 1914, but returned to Petrograd at the outbreak of the 1st World War; choreographed her first b. *La Tabatière* (mus. Liadov). Went to Kiev 1915; danced at the op. house and opened a school. Lifar was her most famous pupil. Left Russ. in 1921 and rejoined Diaghilev's Bs. Russes as a d., prod., and ch. (*Three Ivans*) in the London prod. of *The Sleeping Princess* (1921); further b. creations included Stravinsky's *Renard* (1922) and *Les Noces* (1923), Poulenc's *Les Biches*, Auric's *Les Fâcheux*, and Milhaud's *Le Train bleu* (all 1924). She then worked as a ch. at the Paris Opéra, the Buenos Aires Teatro Colón, and with the I. Rubinstein co., for which she ch. Stravinsky's *Le Baiser de la Fée*, Ravel's *Bolero* (both 1928), and *La Valse* (1929), and Poulenc's *Aubade* (for a Soirée of the Vicomte de Noalles, 1929). Worked for Opéra Russe à Paris, 1930–31, and established her own co. in 1932; revived some of her earlier bs., incl. *Etude* (mus. Bach), and created *Les Variations* (mus. Beethoven, 1932) and *Hamlet* (mus. Liszt, 1934), in which she herself d. the title role, and *Les cent baisers* (mus. F. d'Erlanger) for B. Russe de Monte Carlo (1935). Artistic dir. of the Paris-based B. Polonais 1937; ch. *Chopin Concerto*, R. Palester's *Le Chant de la terre*, and M. Kondracki's *La Legende de Cracovie* (all 1937). Worked for Max Reinhardt in Berlin (*Tales of Hoffmann* and film *A Midsummer Night's Dream*) and Markova-Dolin co. Opened a school in Los Angeles 1938. Worked as a guest ch. with individual cos.; her prods. include *La Fille mal gardée* (mus. Hertel, B. Th., 1940), *The Snow Maiden* (mus. Glazunov, B. Russe de Monte Carlo, 1942), *Ancient Russia* (mus. Tchaikovsky, same co., 1943), *Brahms Variations* and *Pictures from an Exhibition* (mus. Mussorgsky, B. International, 1944), and *Harvest Time* (mus. H. Wieniawski, B. Th., 1945). After 1945 worked principally as b. mistress for the Grand B. du Marquis de Cuevas. During her last years her prods. of *Les Biches* (1964) and *Les Noces* (1966) at the Royal B. confirmed her reputation as one of the formative chs. of the 20th century. Author of *B.N.: Early Memoirs* (N.Y., 1981).
BIBL.: entry 'N., B.' in *Enciclopedia dello spettacolo*; J. Anderson, 'The Fabulous Career of B.N.', *Dance Magazine* (1963/8); P. Brinson and C. Crisp, in *Ballet for all* (London, 1970); G. Schüller, *B.N.* (thesis, Vienna, 1974).

Nijinsky, Vaslav Fomich (*b* Kiev [according to

the birth-certificate at his Warsaw baptism, 17 Dec. 1889; R. Buckle says 12 Mar. 1888, B. Nijinska 1889], d London, 8 Apr. 1950). Like his sister Bronislava N, he was born on a tour of his dancer-parents Eleonora Bareda and Foma Nijinsky. Entered St. Petersburg Imperial B. School 1898; graduated 1907. Joined Maryinsky T., where he had already appeared as a pupil in Fokine's *Acis et Galathée* (1905), *A Midsummer Night's Dream* (1906), and with Pavlova in his *Pavillon d'Armide* (1907). A sensational success, he soon became the partner of Kschessinska, Preobrajenska, and Karsavina. Met and became a close friend of Diaghilev, who made him the star performer of his Paris seasons. He was idolized for his perfs. in the classics and in Fokine's *Pavillon d'Armide*, *Les Sylphides*, and *Cléopâtre* (1909), *Carnaval* and *Sheherazade* (1910), *Spectre de la rose*, *Narcisse*, and *Petrushka* (1911), *Le Dieu bleu* and *Daphnis and Chloe* (1912). The costume he wore for Giselle at the Maryinsky th. was considered indecent, and the ensuing scandal made him resign from the co. in 1911. Diaghilev then established his co. as a permanent touring ensemble, with Nijinsky as the star attraction. He encouraged N. to attempt ch.; the outcome was Debussy's *L'après-midi d'un faune* (1912) and *Jeux*, and Stravinsky's *Le Sacre du printemps* (1913). His bs. were rejected at the time for their daring break with tradition; but they are now considered to foreshadow many developments of later avantgarde ch. While on tour to South Amer., he married the Hung. d. Romola de Pulszky; Diaghilev thereupon severed all connection with him. This was the beginning of his decline. He tried to establish a co. of his own in 1914, but it failed after only 16 days in London. Went to Madrid and Vienna, where his daughter Kyra was born (who became a d. and the wife of the conductor Igor Markevitch); then to Budapest, where he was interned as a Russian when the 1st World War broke out. Diaghilev succeeded in getting him out of Hungary, for a North Amer. tour of D.'s co. in 1916; N. ch. R. Strauss's *Till Eulenspiegel* for this tour. During a subsequent South Amer. tour he showed increasing signs of *dementia praecox*. Settled in St. Moritz in Switzerland in 1916 and gave his last solo perf. in a hotel there in 1919. Worked on his system of dance notation, wrote down his plans for a b. school, designed new bs., and started to draw, while moving from one mental hospital to another. The family moved to London in 1947, where he died after 2½ years of great suffering. His body was taken to Paris in 1953, and buried in the cemetery of Montmartre, beside the graves of G. Vestris, T. Gautier, and E. Livry. As a d. he had exceptional technical virtuosity (he had sensational *ballon* and *élévation*, and could effortlessly execute entrechats huit and occasionally even dix), and instinctive dramatic gifts. One of the greatest artists of b. history; his pioneering role as ch. is only now becoming known, thanks to

the persuasive campaigning of M. Rambert, who was engaged by Diaghilev to help N. with the preparations for the *Sacre du printemps* prod. There have been many plans to make N. films, but so far only H. Ross's *N.* (1980) has materialized. Béjart made a b. about him in 1971: *N., Clown de Dieu*. BBC TV prod. *N.—God of the Dance* in 1975.

BIBL.: R.N., *N.* (London, 1933); *Journal de N.* (Paris, 1953); R. Buckle, *N.* (London, 1971); V. Krasovskaya, *N.* (Leningrad, 1974—Amer. version in 1980); *N.* portfolio in *Dance Magazine* (1974/12; see also Readers' Letters in 1975/2); L. Kirstein, *N. Dancing* (New York, 1975).

Nijinsky, Clown de Dieu. Ballet in 2 parts; idea and ch. Béjart; mus. P. Henry and Tchaikovsky; cost. Joëlle Roustan and Roger Bernard; set and light. R. Bernard. Prod. 8 Oct. 1971, B. of the 20th Century, Forest National, Brussels, with Donn, Bortoluzzi, Lommel, Lanner, Van Hoecke, Farrell, Albrecht, Ullate, Gray-Cullert. Based on a collage of mus. and quotations from N.'s diary. Not strictly a reconstruction of N.'s life; more a series of pictures of a young man continually searching for the truth of life; his four most important roles (*Spectre de la rose*, the Golden Slave from *Sheherazade*, *Petrushka*, and the Faun) form part of the structure.

BIBL.: M.-F. Christout, 'N., C.d.D.', *Dance Magazine* (1971/12).

Nikitina, Alice (*b* St. Petersburg, 1909, *d* Monte Carlo, June 1978). Russ. dancer, singer, and teacher. Studied at the Imperial B. School; left Russia with her parents after the October Revolution. Danced in Ljubljana; went to Vienna, then joined B. Romanoff's Romantic B. in Berlin. Joined Diaghilev's Bs. Russes 1923, and eventually became a ballerina. Created roles in Massine's *Zéphyr et Flore* (1925), Balanchine's *Apollon musagète* (1928) and *Le Bal* (1929). After Diaghilev's death appeared in London Cochrane revues and Balanchine's London seasons of Les Bs. 1933, and later with Vilzak and with B. Russe de Monte Carlo. She then studied singing for 3 years in Milan and Rome and started her new career as a coloratura soprano at Ital. op. houses in 1938. Opened a b. school in Paris in 1949. Author of *N. by Herself* (London, 1959).

Nikolais, Alwin (*b* Southington, Conn., 25 Nov. 1912). Amer. dancer, choreographer, teacher, and b. director. Started his career as a pianist for silent films: then worked as puppet master. Studied dance with Truda Kaschmann and Holm, and later with Graham, Humphrey, Weidman, and Horst. Produced his first full-length work, *Eight Column Line* (Mus. E. Křenek), in Connecticut, 1939. After military service became Holm's assistant. Appointed director of New York Henry Street Playhouse in 1948. This was an experimental th. centre, and he completely reorganized the school and performing co. and began to develop his ideas of a new d. th.; the d. simply provides the kinetic energy for a stage play which consists of abstract forms, patterns, colours, and sounds. His prods. are increasingly closely integrated; he himself is not only author, dir., and ch., but also composer, designer, and—very important—in charge of the lighting. His works are one-man prods. of a ch. total th., defined by himself as 'sound and vision pieces'. Has appeared regularly in Europe since 1968–9 (London début 1969). His most important prods. include *Masks, Props and Mobiles* (1953), *Kaleidoscope* (1956), *Totem* (1959), *Imago* (1963), *Sanctum* (1964), *Somniloquy* and *Triptych* (1967), *Tent* and *Limbo* (1968), *Echo* (1969), *Structures* (1970), *Scenario* (1971), *Grotto* (1973), *Scrolls, Cross-Fade* (1974), *Temple, The Tribe* (1975), *Tryad and Styx* (1976), *Arporisms* (1977), *Gallery* and *Castings* (1978), and *Schema* (1980 for Paris Opéra). Dir. Centre de danse contemporaine à Angers, 1978–81. Contributed 'No Man from Mars' to *The Modern Dance* (Middletown, Conn., 1965). Dance Magazine Award (1967); Chevalier, Légion d'Honneur (1984).

BIBL.: M.B. Siegel, 'Nik', *Dance Perspectives* 48; M. B. Siegel, in *At the Vanishing Point* (New York, 1972); M. B. Siegel, in *Watching the Dance Go By* (Boston, 1977); M. Louis, in *Inside Dance* (New York, 1980).

Nikonov, Vladimir Leonidovich (*b*. Moscow, 28 Nov. 1937). Sov. dancer. Studied at Moscow Bolshoi B. School; graduated 1957. Joined Bolshoi B. and eventually became a soloist. Married to the d. Ludmilla Bogomolova.

Nimura, Yeichi (*b* Suwa, Japan, 25 Mar. 1897, *d* New York, 3 Apr. 1979). Jap.-Amer. dancer, choreographer, and teacher. Studied at Denishawn and with K. Kobeleff, Katharine Edson, Tarasoff, Aurora Arriaza, and Angel Cansino. Danced in ops., operettas, and musicals; then embarked on a career as a concert d. and toured extensively with his partner Lisan Kay from 1932 to the 1940s. Worked as a ch. at the Roxy Th. and Radio City Music Hall. Established B. Arts School at Carnegie Hall in 1940; this gave rise to his N. and B. Arts Co., a workshop performing unit which lasted until 1963. Author of an autobiography, published in Japan 1972. Order of the Sacred Treasure (Tokyo, 1969).

Nina, ou La Folle par amour. Ballet in 2 acts; libr. and ch. Milon; mus. Persius. Prod. 23 Nov. 1813, Opéra, Paris, with Bigottini, F.D. Albert. The b. is based on the then very popular comedy by Marsollier and Dalayrac (1786), used by Paisiello as an op. libr. in 1789. N. goes mad when her father tells her that she must marry somebody other than Germeuil, whom she loves; her sanity is restored when her father at last allows her to marry Germeuil. The b. was a great success, and rapidly appeared all over Eur. An earlier b. version by Galeotti (mus. Schall, Copenhagen, 1802).

BIBL.: C. W. Beaumont, 'N.o.L.F.p.a.' in *Complete Book of Ballets* (London, 1951).

Ninth Symphony (original Fr. title, *Neuvième Symphonie*). Ch. prod. by Béjart; mus. Beethoven; light T. Skelton. prod. 28 Oct. 1964, B. of the 20th Century, Cirque Royal, Brussels, with Höfgen, Pinet, Sifnios, Bortoluzzi, Bari, Lefèbre, Casado. Preceded by a prologue of texts from Nietzche's *Birth of Tragedy*, accompanied by percussion rhythms. The b. follows the 4 movements of Beethoven's symphony, attempting to project its emotional content. 'The dance simply accompanies the composer on his slow path, leading from anger to joy, from darkness to light' (Béjart). An earlier version of the choral movement only, *Ode to Peace*, by Irma Duncan (New York, 1934).

Nobili, Lila de (*b* Lugano, 3 Sep. 1916). It al. painter and designer. Among her b. designs were Milloss's *Mario e il mago* (Milan, 1956), Babilée's *Sable* (Bs. J. Babilée, Paris, 1956), Ashton's *Ondine* (Royal B., London 1958) and the costs. for P. Wright's 1968 prod. of *Sleeping Beauty* (with M. Dobujinsky as designer of the sets, Royal B., London).

Nobilissima Visione. Choreographic Legend in 1 act and 5 scenes; libr. and mus. Hindemith: ch. Massine; déc. Tchelitchev. Prod. 21 July 1938, B. Russe de Monte Carlo, Drury Lane Th., London, with Massine, Theilade, F. Franklin. The b. deals with Francesco Bernadone, who became St. Francis of Assisi. In America the b. was given as *Saint Francis*.

BIBL.: C. W. Beaumont, 'N.V.' in *Supplement to Complete Book of Ballets* (London, 1952).

Noblet, Lise (*b* Paris, 24 Nov. 1801, *d* there, Sep.1852). Fr. dancer. Studied at Paris Opéra B. School; joined Opéra B 1816 and became soloist. Danced as a guest in London 1821–4 at the King's Th.; especially successful as Nina. Created roles in Aumer's new versions of Dauberval's *Le Page inconstant* (1823) and *La Fille mal gardée*, in his *La Belle au bois dormant* (both 1829) and *Manon Lescaut* (1830), F. Taglioni's *La Sylphide* (Effie, 1832), *La Révolte au Sérail* (1833), and *La Fille du Danube* (1836). She was the first Fenella in Auber-Aumer's *La Muette de Portici* (1828) and danced in the first prods. of Rossini-Gardel's *The Siege of Corinth* (1826) and *Moses* (1827), Auber-Taglioni's *Le Dieu et la bayadère* (1830), and Halévy-Taglioni's *La Juive* (1835). She was a rival of Elssler as a performer of Span. dances; *El Jaleo de Jerez* was her speciality. She had a tempestuous temperament, but was much admired for her elegance, virtuosity, and dramatic expressiveness.

BIBL.: I. Guest, in *The Romantic Ballet in Paris* (London, 1966).

Noces, Les (orig. Russ. title: *Svadebka*). 4 Russ. Dance Scenes with Singing and Mus. by Stravinsky; ch. Nijinska; déc. Gontcharova; cond. Ansermet. Prod. 13 June 1923, B. Russe de Diaghilev, Th Gaîté-Lyrique, Paris, with Doubrovska, Semenov. A Russ. wedding ritual—The Blessing of the Bride, The Blessing of the Bridegroom, The Bride's Departure from her Parents' House, and The Wedding Feast. Revived for de Basil's Bs. Russes (1936), Royal B. (1966), Stuttgart b. (1974), Paris Opéra (1976). Different versions by Béjart (B. of the 20th Century, Salzburg, 1962—revived for Paris Opéra, 1965), Robbins for Amer. B. Th., 1965—revived for Royal Swed. B., 1969, and Lubovitch for his own co. (1976).

BIBL.: P. Brinson and C. Crisp, in *Ballet & Dance* (Newton Abbot, 1980); L. Kirstein, in *Movement & Metaphor* (New York, 1970); B. Nijinska, 'Creation of L.N.', *Dance Magazine* (1974/12).

Noctambules. Ballet in 1 act and 2 scenes; libr. and ch. MacMillan; mus. Searle; déc. Georgiadis. Prod. 1 Mar. 1956, Sadler's Wells B., Cov. Gdn., London, with L. Edwards, Lane, Nerina, Linden, Doyle, Shaw. MacMillan's first b. for Cov. Gdn. The perf. of a demonic hypnotist goes wrong, and his audience turns against him.

Nocturne. Ballet in 1 act; libr. E: Sackville-West; ch. Ashton; mus. Delius; déc. Fedorovitch. Prod. 10 Nov. 1936, Vic-Wells B., Sadler's Wells Th., London, with Fonteyn, Brae, Helpmann, Ashton. The b. brings together various characters at a ball, without following a continuous story-line.

BIBL.: C. W. Beaumont, 'N.' in *Complete Book of Ballets* (London, 1951). D. Vaughan, *Frederick Ashton and his Bs.* (London, 1977).

Noguchi, Isamu (*b* Los Angeles, 7 Nov. 1904). Jap.-Amer. sculptor. Designed the sets for Graham's *Frontier* (1935), *Appalachian Spring* and *Herodiade* (1944), *Dark Meadow*, and *Cave of the Heart* (1946), *Errand into the Maze* and *Night Journey* (1947), *Diversion of Angels* (1948), *Seraphic Dialogue* (1955), *Clytemnestra* and *Embattled Garden* (1958), *Acrobats of God* and *Alcestis* (1960), *Phaedra* (1962), *Circe* (1963), and *Cortege of Eagles* (1967), Page's *The Bells* (1946), M. Cunningham's *The Seasons* (1947), and Balanchine's *Orpheus* (1948).

BIBL.: A. Fatt. 'Designers for the Dance; I.N.', *Dance Magazine* (1967/2).

Noir et blanc. See *Suite en blanc*.

Nomos Alpha. Solo Dance; ch. Béjart; mus. Xenakis; Prod. 2 Apr. 1969, Royan, with Bortoluzzi. A succession of dance sequences allowing the performer to demonstrate a wide range of technical virtuosity and dramatic expressiveness. Cologne TV prod. 1969.

Nono, Luigi (*b* Venice, 29 Jan. 1924). Ital, composer. Wrote the mus. for T. Gsovsky's *The Red Cloak* (Berlin, 1954). Several Ger. and Ital. choreographers, incl. G. Bohner and G. Urbani, have used some of his concert mus. for b. purposes.

Nordi, Cleo (*b* Kronstadt, 1899, *d* London, 20 Mar. 1983). Finnish dancer and teacher. Studied with Legat in St. Petersburg and modern d. in Germany, and with a pupil of Duncan in Finland. Début Paris Opéra 1925. Joined Pavlova's co. 1926 and remained until its disbanding in 1931. Taught in London since the 1940s, e.g. at Sadler's Wells B. School and for London Contemporary Dance Th., and at Essen Folkwang School.

BIBL.: 'Conversations with C.N.', *Dance Magazine* (1979/7).

Norman, Gary (*b* Adelaide, 15 Nov. 1951). Austral. dancer. Studied at Floyd and B'Nay School of Dancing and Austral. B. School. Joined Austral. B. 1970; became soloist 1971 and principal d. 1972. Created roles in Tetley's *Gemini* (1973) and Moreland's *Sacred Space* (1974). Joined National B. of Canada as principal d. in 1975.

Norske Ballet, Den. See *Norwegian National Ballet*.

North, Robert (*b* Charleston, S.C., 1 June 1945). Amer. dancer and choreographer. Studied with Crofton, at Royal B. School and London School of Contemporary Dance, and with Graham and M. Cunningham. Began to d. with London Contemporary D. Th. 1967, then for several seasons with Graham co., rejoined L.C.D. Th. as a principal 1969. Began to ch. for London Festival B. Workshop; his bs. incl. *One Was the Other* (mus. M. Finnissy, 1974), *Troy Game* (mus. B. Downes), *Dressed to Kill* (mus. H. Miller and D. Smith, 1974), *Still Life* (mus. Downes, 1975), and *David and Goliath* (with W. Sleep; mus. C. Davis, London, 1975), *Just a Moment* (mus. Downes, 1976), *Scriabin Preludes and Studies* and *Dreams with Silences* (mus. Brahms, 1978), *Reflections* (mus. Blake, 1979), and *Songs and Dances* (1981). Has also worked for Scottish B., B. Rambert, Dance Umbrella and his wife's Janet Smith D. Group. Appointed associate ch. in 1975, art. dir. of B. Rambert 1981–6.

Northcote, Anna (*b* Southbourne, 1907). Brit. dancer and teacher. Studied with Euphan Maclaren, Craske, Legat, and Preobrajenska. Danced in Oumansky B. (as A. Severskaya) 1930, Levitoff-Dandré Bs. Russes 1934, Bs. Russes de Paris 1936, de Basil co. 1937–9. Had her own London studio 1941–69, and has since taught at D. Centre. Has also worked as a guest-teacher for many cos. abroad. Retired 1980.

Northern Ballet Theatre. Manchester-based co. formed under the name Northern Dance Th. in 1969 by Laverne Meyer to tour smaller ths. London début, 1973. At first a repertory of original works by Meyer and other young chs., with J. Thorpe becoming res. ch., and a co. of about 16 dancers. Meyer resigned in 1975 and was succeeded from 1976 by R. de Warren, under whom the name was changed to emphasize classical basis, the co. enlarged to 27 dancers (in 1981). Warren added more full-length bs. incl.

his own *Cinderella* (1979) and *A Midsummer Night's Dream* (1981), A. Prokovsky's *Nutcracker* (1980), and R. Glasstone's *Sylvia* (1981).

BIBL.: *Northern Ballet Theatre, 1969–79*, compiled by R. Southern (Manchester, 1979), with full list of dancers and bs.

Norwegian National Ballet. Oslo-based co. founded in 1948, as Ny Norsk B., by Gerd Kjølaas and Louise Browne, who both functioned as solo dancers and choreographers. The co. toured continuously; after a hard struggle it was disbanded in 1952, and Kjølaas and Rita Tori became artistic directors of the newly established Norske B. in 1953. N. Orloff became its b. master in 1960; he was succeeded by J. Harris 1961–5, who resigned as the company's dir. and became dir. of the new b. school attached to the co. S. Arova took over 1966–70; A. Borg was in charge 1971–6. Over this period the numbers have grown from six to now almost forty dancers. The repertory offers the standard classics, works by contemporary choreographers, and specially created bs. by Barthold Halle, Kari Blakstad, Donya Feuer, Tetley, and others. First U.S. appearance 1974. D. Blair was appointed dir. from 1976, but died before taking up the post, then B. Last, 1977–80. Artistic dir. since 1980 is Jens Graff.

Notre-Dame de Paris. Ballet in 2 acts; libr. and ch. Petit; mus. M. Jarre; sets R. Allio; cost. Y. St. Laurent. Prod. 11 Dec. 1965, Opéra, Paris, with Motte, Petit, Atanassoff, Bonnefous. The b. is based on Victor Hugo's novel *N.-D.d.P.* (1831). In Perrot's version of the same story (*Esmeralda*, 1844), the protagonist is the poet Gringoire, but he does not appear at all in the Petit b., and Quasimodo, the crippled bell-ringer of the Paris cathedral, is the protagonist. Revived for Marseille B. 1974, Kirov B. 1978.

Notre Faust. Spectacle in two parts; libr. and ch. Béjart; mus. Bach and Argent. tangos; déc. T. Bosquet. Prod. 12 Dec. 1975, B. of the 20th Century, Th. Royal de la Monnaie, Brussels, with J. Donn, B. Pie, P, Touron, Béjart, Y. Le Gac, M. Robier. Set to sections of Bach's B Minor Mass, interpolated with tangos, freely quoting Goethe in Ger. and Fr., the b. treats the familiar story as a black mass, presided over by the 3 archangels Lucifer, Satan, and Beelzebub; Faust transforms himself into Mephistophe, while Mephistopheles becomes the young Faust. See also *Faust Ballets*.

BIBL.: N. McLain Stoop, 'Maurice Béjart's 'N.F.', *Dance Magazine* (1976/6).

Nouveau Ballet de Monte Carlo. The co. was founded in 1942; its dancers were recruited partly from former members of the Paris Opéra who had left the city when the Ger. troops were approaching, and partly from pupils of the local schools and from Nice (J. Sedova). Marcel Sablon was dir. and Zvereff b. master. Its repertory consisted of some Diaghilev bs. and some new

works. It was disbanded in 1944 and re-founded by Eugene Grünberg in 1946; Lifar, as artistic dir., revived some of his earlier works and also created *La Péri* (mus. Dukas), *Salomé* (mus. R. Strauss), *Nautéos* (mus. J. Leleu), *Dramma per musica* (mus. Bach), and *Chota Roustaveli* (mus. Honegger *et al.*) for the co. Chauviré, Charrat, Jeanmaire, Tcherina, Adabache, Skouratoff, Kalioujny, Bon, and Algaroff were its most notable dancers. Lifar took most of these dancers back with him to the Paris Opéra in 1947. The Marquis de Cuevas bought the co., with its remaining dancers, in 1947 and called it Grand B. de Monte Carlo; W. Dollar was appointed b. master in 1948.

Novaro, Luciana (*b* Genoa, 3 Mar. 1923). Ital dancer and choreographer. Studied at La Scala B. School; graduated 1941. Joined La Scala B. and became prima ballerina 1946. Started to ch. in São Paolo and has since ch. many bs. in Italy; now works mainly for La Scala and Verona and also for TV.

Noverre, Jean-Georges (*b* Paris, 29 Apr. 1727, d. St.-Germain-en-Laye, 19 Oct. 1810). Fr. dancer, choreographer, ballet master, choreographer, ballet master, and dance-theorist. Studied with Dupré; influenced early on by Sallé. Début at Paris Opéra Comique 1743. Went to Berlin 1744, Dresden 1747, Strasbourg 1749 (where he probably met his future wife, the actress Marguerite Sauveur), Marseilles, Lyons (where he d. with Camargo and ch. his first bs.), and back to Strasbourg 1753–4. B. master at Paris Opéra Comique 1754; staged his very successful *Les Fêtes Chinoises* (which he had created for Lyons, or possibly earlier). There followed his more dramatic bs. *La Fontaine de Jouvence* (1754) and *Réjouissances flamandes* (1755). Mounted his *Fêtes Chinoises* at the London Drury Lane Th. 1755, at Garrick's invitation, but the prevailing dislike for everything French prevented him from working further in London, though Garrick saw in him 'the Shakespeare of the dance'. He stayed, however, for a while as a secret b. master; it is probably during this time that he wrote his *Lettres sur la danse*, published simultaneously in Lyons and Stuttgart at the end of 1759 (dated 1760; English translation 1930). Returned to Lyons 1758–9, where his theories about the b. d'action gave rise to such works as *Les Caprices de Galathée* and *La Toilette de Vénus*. Then went to Stuttgart as b. master, where he worked until the end of 1766; created some of his best bs., e.g. *Admète et Alceste* (1761), *La Mort d'Hercule* and *Psyché et Amour* (1762), *Medée et Jason* and *Orpheus and Eurydice* (1763), *Hypermnestra* (1764), *Cleopatra* (1765), *The Feast of Hymen*, and *The Rape of Proserpine* (1766). His theories about the b. d'action were very controversial. He went to Vienna 1767, where Hilverding and Angiolini had already introduced similar ideas to his own. He remained until 1774, and staged about 50 bs. at the Burg Th. and the

Kärntnertor Th. Some were revivals, but there were also such important creations as *L'Apothéose d'Hercule* (1767), *Don Chischott* (1768), *Der gerächte Agamemnon* and *Roger et Bradamante* (1771), *Vénus et Adonis, Apelles et Campaspe* and *Adèle de Ponthieu* (1773), and *Gli Orazi e i Curiazi* (1774). Considered in Vienna the greatest ch. of his time, in both lyric and heroic bs., and also an excellent teacher. Worked in Milan 1774–6; his fierce controversy with Angiolini about the principles and importance of the b. d'action attracted international attention. His most important new b. was *La Prima età dell'innocenza ossia La Rosaia de Salency* (1775). Returned to Vienna; then to Paris as b. master of the Opéra in 1776, where he was bitterly opposed by M. Gardel and Dauberval (who had themselves hoped to succeed Vestris as b. master). Remained until 1780; his most successful bs. were *Annette et Lubin* and Mozart's *Les petits riens* (1778). He then retired with a pension, but went on to work at the London King's Th., where he formed an excellent co., with P. Gardel and Antoine Bournonville among its dancers, and later M. Guimard, A. Vestris, and Didelot. His new bs. included *Le Triomphe de l'amour conjugal, Le Temple d'amour,* and *Apollo et les Muses* (1782), *Les Offrandes à L'Amour* (1787), *Les Fêtes provençales* (1789), *Pas de trois et de quatre* (mus. *God Save The King*), *Iphigenia en Aulide,* and *Les Noces de Thétis* (1793), and *Adelaide ou La Bergère des Alpes* (1794). Then settled in St. Germain-en-Laye; had to fight for continuation of his pension. His *Lettres sur les Arts Imitateurs en Général et sur la Danse en particulier* was published Paris 1807, demonstrating his continuing interest in the discussion of topical b. questions. One of the most cultivated and intelligent men of b. history. His *Letters on Dancing* and his work in Stuttgart, Vienna, Paris, and London made a considerable contribution to the emancipation of the dramatic b. from its former position as mere divertissement. He overshadowed his forerunners, e.g. Hilverding and Angiolini. A great reformer of the b.; later choreographers who stressed the dramatic mission of the b. often referred to him as their model, e.g. Fokine, Laban, and Jooss. BIBL.: D. Lynham, *The Chevalier N.* (London, 1950; reprinted 1973); M. Krüger, *J.-G. N. und sein Einfluss auf die Ballettgestaltung* (Emsdetten, 1963); M. H. Winter in *The Pre-Romantic Ballet* (London, 1974).

Noverre Society. Founded in May 1958 to promote the Stuttgart B. Organizes lecture-demonstrations, film evenings, matinée perfs. for aspiring choreographers (it was here that A. Killar, G. Veredon, J. Neumeier, and J. Kylián made their first bs.), helps gifted dancers with scholarships, and arranges excursions for its members to other b. cities. Fritz Höver, one of its founders, is still the dir.

Novikoff, Laurent (*b* Moscow, 3 Aug. 1888, *d* New Buffalo, Mich., 18 June 1956). Russ-Amer. dancer, choreographer, b. master, and teacher. Studied at Moscow Bolshoi B. School; graduated 1906. Joined Bolshoi B., became soloist 1909 and principal d. 1910. D. with Diaghilev's co. in Paris 1909 and with Pavlova's co. 1911–14. Returned to Bolshoi B. 1914, and began to ch. Rejoined Diaghilev's Bs. Russes 1919–21 and Pavlova co. 1921–8. Opened a school in London. B. master at Civic Op., Chicago, 1929–33. Opened another school in Chicago. B. master Met. Op. Ho., New York, 1941–5.

Novosibirsk. Siberia's first op. house opened in 1945; dancers from local studios participated in the op. perfs. The b. co. was strengthened by the addition of dancers who left the Moscow Bolshoi B. School. Mikhail Moiseyev, b. master 1946–9, staged the standard works and also the first prod. of I. Morosov's *Doctor Aibolit* (1947). He was succeeded by Vainonen (1950–2), Mikhail Satunovsky, Y. Matcheret (*Aladdin and the Magic Lamp,* 1956, and—with Li Tshen Len and Wan Si San— the Chinese b. *The Priceless Lotus Lamp,* 1959), Serge Pavlov, and Zinaida Vassilyeva. A b. school was opened in 1957, with A. Nikiforova and S. Ivanov as directors. P. Gusev was artistic dir. of the co. 1963–6. He staged *The Ice Maiden* and *The Three Musketeers,* and under his direction Vinogradov ch. his controversial versions of Prokofiev's *Cinderella* (1964) and *Romeo and Juliet* (1965); N. Dolgushin and N. Alexandrova were the most popular dancers. The co. visited Moscow and Paris in 1967 and its artistic standards improved rapidly; it was awarded the title 'Academic', and is now called the N. State Academic Th. of Op. and B. Alexander Dementyev is its artistic dir., and the co. has now more than 100 dancers.

Nuitter, Charles-Louis-Etienne (*b* Paris, 24 Apr. 1828, *d* there, 24 Feb. 1899). Fr. writer and librettist. Wrote for the libr. for many of Offenbach's operettas and vaudevilles, and also for some bs., incl. Mérante's *Les Jumeaux de Bergame* (1866) and *Gretna Green* (1873), *La Source* (1866) and *Coppélia* (1870, both with Saint-Léon) and *Namouna* (with L. Petipa, 1882).

Nureyev, Rudolf Hametovich (*b* on a train journey between Lake Baikal and Irkutsk, 17 Mar. 1938). Sov.-Brit. d. and ch. Started as an amateur dancer at folk-dance courses; participated in some perfs. of the Ufa op. house. Studied at Leningrad Choreographic School under A. Pushkin 1955–8; joined Kirov B. as a soloist. Came into continuous conflict with the authorities and decided, on a visit of the co. to Paris, where he had a sensational success in *Sleeping Beauty,* not to return to Leningrad; demanded political asylum at Le Bourget on 17 June 1961. Has since stayed in the West. Appeared with the Grand B. du Marquis de Cuevas, then at London R.A.D. Gala at Fonteyn's invitation; returned soon afterwards and became Fonteyn's principal partner for several years. Regular guest artist of the Royal B. from

1962 to mid-1970's, but has also danced with many other cos. all over the world. Considered the greatest international male dancer of the 1960s and early 1970s; an artist of dazzling virtuosity, controlled expressiveness, and electrifying charisma. As well as dancing the leading roles of the classics and standard works of the modern repertory, has created roles in Ashton's *Marguerite and Armand* (1963), Petit's *Paradise Lost* (1967), *L'estasi* (1968), and *Pelléas et Mélisande* (1969), Van Dantzig's *The Ropes of Time* (1970), Béjart's *Songs of a Wayfarer* (1971), Tetley's *Tristan* (1974), Graham's *Lucifer* (1975), Van Dantzig's *Blown in a Gentle Wind* (1975), Murray Louis's *Moment* (1975), Van Dantzig's *Ulysses* (1979), Balanchine's *Le Bourgeois gentilhomme* (1979), and Lacotte's *Marco Spada* (1981). Began ch. with pas de deux from the Sov. repertory. His first major prod. was *La Bayadère* (Royal B., 1963), followed by *Raymonda* (Touring Royal B., Spoleto, 1964—also Austral. B., 1965, Zurich B., 1972, and Amer. B. Th., 1975), *Swan Lake* (Vienna, 1964), first prod. of Henze's *Tancredi* (Vienna, 1966), *Don Quixote* (Vienna, 1966—also Austral. B., 1966; this prod. filmed in 1973), *Sleeping Beauty* (Milan, 1966—also National B. of Can., 1972 and London Festival Ballet, 1975), *Nutcracker* (Royal Swed. B., 1967—also Royal B., 1968), *Romeo and Juliet* (London Festival B., 1977), and *Manfred* (mus. Tchaikovsky, Paris Opéra, 1979). Has often appeared on TV; full-length film *I am a Dancer* 1972 (showing him in class and in the bs. *La Sylphide, Field Figures, Marguerite and Armand*, and *Sleeping Beauty*). Author of *N., An Autobiography* (edited by A. Bland, London, 1962). Dance Magazine Award (1973). Had his own Broadway programme *N. and Friends* in Dec.–Jan. 1974–5. Austrian citizen from 1982. B. dir. Paris Opéra since 1983.

BIBL.: C. Barnes, *N.* (New York, 1982).

Nutcracker (orig. Russ. title: *Shchelkunchik*, also Fr. *Casse-Noisette*). Ballet in 2 acts and 3 scenes; libr. Petipa; ch. Ivanov; mus. Tchaikovsky; déc. Botcharov, K. Ivanov, I. Vsevolojsky. Prod. 18 Dec. 1892, Maryinsky Th., St. Petersburg, with dell'Era, Gerdt, Legat, Preobrajenska. The b. is based on E. T. A. Hoffmann's *Der Nussknacker und der Mäusekönig*. Its central character is the girl Klara (in Russ. Marie or Masha), who is given a nutcracker by her godfather Drosselmeyer for Christmas. She falls asleep, and dreams that she defends it against the King of the Mice. The nutcracker then changes into a handsome Prince, who takes her on a fabulous journey; after passing through a snow-storm, they come to the Kingdom of Sweets, where the Sugar-Plum Fairy honours them with a Grand Divertissement. Petipa wanted to produce the b. himself, but illness compelled him to hand it over to Ivanov, of whose ch. only the grand pas de deux of the Sugar-Plum Fairy and her Cavalier has survived. The loose dramatic structure has led to many individual adaptations. The first London prod. of the complete b. was by N. Sergeyev for the Sadler's Wells B. in 1934, and in the U.S.A. by W. Christensen for the San Francisco B. in 1944 (a shortened version had been presented by the B. Russe de Monte Carlo in New York in 1940). Vainonen ch. one of the Sov. standard versions (Kirov B., 1934). The b. has more recently been staged by Balanchine for New York City B. (1954), Grigorovich for Moscow Bolshoi B. (1966), Cranko for Stuttgart B. (1966), Nureyev for Royal Swed. B. (1967, also Royal B., 1968), Flindt for Royal Dan. B. (1971), Neumeier for Frankfurt B. (1971), Baryshnikov for Amer. B. Th. (1976), and others. Full scenario of orig. version in C. Crisp and M. Clarke, *Making a Ballet* (London, 1975). Various TV prods. of the b., incl. Balanchine's (CBS-TV, 1958) and Neumeier's versions (Canadian CBC-TV, 1974).

BIBL.: C. Swinson, *T.N.* (London, 1960); O. Maynard, 'T.N.' *Dance Magazine* Portfolio (1973/ 12); J. Anderson, *T.N. Ballet* (New York, 1979).

Nuyts, Jan (*b* Antwerp, 1949). Belg. dancer. Studied at Antwerp B. School; joined B. of Flanders 1967 and eventually became soloist. Member of Netherlands D. Th. 1969–72, and since then soloist with the B. of the 20th Century. First Prize (junior class, Varna, 1968).

N.Y. Export, Op. Jazz. See *New York Export: Op. Jazz*.

O

Oboukhoff, Anatole Nicolaievich (*b* St. Petersburg, 1896, *d* New York, 25 Feb. 1962). Russ.-Amer. dancer and teacher. Studied at Imperial B. School; graduated 1913. Joined Maryinsky Th.; became soloist 1917. Left Sov. Union 1920. D. at Bucharest Op., then as principal d. with B. Romanoff's Romantic B. Went to South America (with his wife Vera Nemtchinova). Joined Kaunas co. 1935, and appeared with it on a guest visit to London. D. with B. Russe de Monte Carlo 1936–7, and again during its Austral. tour 1939. Taught at New York School of Amer. B. from 1940 until his death. Was considered one of the best danseurs noble of his time.

O'Brien, John (*b* Hopetown, Austral., 29 Aug. 1933). Brit. dancer, teacher, and bookseller. Studied with Xenia Borovansky, at Royal B. School, with Goncharov, Crofton, Preobrajenska, and Rousanne. Joined Sadler's Wells Op. B. 1957. Principal d. Rambert 1957–66; has also taught for the co. since 1963. Has taught regularly at London D. Centre since 1968 and as a guest abroad. Took over Pocketbooks Ltd. in Cecil Court, London; this became B. Bookshop 1966 and then D. Books Ltd. 1974, of which he is now co-dir. (with David Leonard).

O'Conaire, Deirdre (*b* Colwyn Bay, 1938). Brit. dancer. Studied with Mme. Legat and A. Roje in Split; became soloist of Split B. 1954. Joined London Festival B. 1957; appointed soloist 1960. Joined London B. 1962 and Royal B. 1962; later became soloist. Retired 1972.

Ode. Ballet-oratorio in 2 acts; libr. Kochno; ch. Massine; mus. Nabokov; déc. Tchelitchev and Pierre Charbonnier. Prod. 6 June 1928, Bs. Russes de Diaghilev, Th. S. Bernhardt, Paris, with Ira Beliankina, Lifar. The b. was based on a hymn by Lomonosov, dedicated to the Russ. Empress Elizabeth. It is a meditation on the beauty and harmony of nature, which is destroyed by a progressive student. Within an irregular framework of white cords the dancers moved in tight-fitting costumes, while coloured projections and film-sequences bathed them in a continually changing flood of light.

O'Donnell, May (*b* Sacramento, Cal., 1909). Amer. dancer, choreographer, and teacher. Studied with Estelle Reed and Graham, in whose co. she d. 1932–8 and 1944–52. Created roles in Graham's *Appalachian Spring* and *Herodiade* (1944), *Dark Meadow* and *Cave of the Heart* (1946). First solo-recital San Francisco 1939; established the San Francisco D. Th. with G. Shurr. Member of Limón co. 1941–3. Has had her own New York

co. since 1949. Teaches at her own school and School of Performing Arts, and various U.S. univs. and colleges. Worked for London Contemporary D. Th. 1972.

BIBL.: T. Tobias, 'A Conversation with M. O'D.', *Ballet Review* (IX, 1).

Odysseus Ballets. There have been many bs. about the wanderings of the legendary King of Ithaca, from Hilverding's *Ulisses und Circe* (Vienna, *c.* 1740), Lauchery's *O.* (mus. Cannabich, Kassel, 1765), A. Muzzarelli's *Ulisse al monte Etna* (Venice, 1787), G. Gioia's *Il ritorno d'Ulisse* (Naples, 1804), and Milon's *Le Retour d'Ulysse* (Paris, 1807), to Hanka's *Homerische Sinfonie* (mus. T. Berger, Vienna, 1950), Gruber's *Neue Odyssee* (mus. V. Bruns, E. Berlin State Op., 1957), M. Louis' *Odyssey* (mus. I. Fiedel, New York, 1960), Walter's *Die Irrfahrten des O.* (mus. H. Eder, Bregenz, 1965), and Van Dantzig's *Ulysses* (mus. Haubenstock-Ramati, Vienna, 1979).

Oedipus and the Sphinx. See *Rencontre, La*.

Offenbach, Jacques (*b* Cologne, 20 June 1819, *d* Paris, 5 Oct. 1880). Ger.-Fr. composer. Comp. the mus. for several harlequinades; then wrote the mus. for M. Taglioni's b. *Le Papillon* (Paris, 1860; first modern prod. von Rosen's *Utopia*, Gothenburg, 1974; another b. by R. Hynd, *Papillon*, Houston B., 1979, revived for Sadler's Wells Royal B., 1980). Much of his th. mus. has been adapted for b. purposes, e.g. by M. Rosenthal for Massine's *Gaîté Parisienne* (1938), Dorati for Fokine's *Bluebeard* (1941), and Fokine-Lichine's *Helen of Troy* (1942), G. Crum for Tudor's *O. in the Underworld*, and L. Aubert for Cranko's *La Belle Hélène* (both 1955). Béjart staged a ch. prod. of O.'s op. *Tales of Hoffmann* in Brussels 1961, and Lanchbery arranged the score for Darrell's full-length b. *Tales of Hoffmann* (1972).

Offenbach in the Underworld. Ballet in 1 act; libr. and ch. Tudor; mus. Offenbach (arr. G. Crum); déc. K. Ambrose. Prod. 17 Jan. 1955, Palace Th., St. Catherine's, Ontario, with L. Smith, David Adams, E. Kraul. The definitive version of a b. first ch. by Tudor for the Philadelphia B. Co., 1954. It deals with the flirtations between the customers of a fashionable café in the 1870s—a famous operetta star, a grand duke, a penniless painter, a dashing officer, and a débutante. Revived for Amer. B. Th. 1956, and for City Center Joffrey B. 1975.

BIBL.: C. W. Beaumont, 'O.i.t.U.' in *Ballets Past & Present* (London, 1955).

Ogoun, Luboš (*b* Prague, 18 Feb. 1924). Czech

dancer, choreographer, and b. director. Studied with S. Machov. Joined Prague National Th. 1953. D. dir. of Czech Army Ensemble 1953–6. Ch. and teacher Prague National Th. 1956–7; b. dir. Pilsen Op. 1957–61 and Brno Op. 1961–4. Founded B. Prague with P. Smok, 1964, for which he ch. many bs., incl. W. Bukový's *Hiroshima* and Bartók's *Miraculous Mandarin*. Since the co. was disbanded in 1968, has worked with several cos. (Brno, Basle, etc.) and for Laterna Magica. Merited Artist of C.S.S.R. (1966).

Ohman, Frank (*b* Los Angeles, 7 Jan. 1939). Amer. dancer. Studied at San Francisco B. School, joined San Francisco B., then New York City B. 1962; appointed soloist 1965. Established New York D. Th. 1974.

Oiseau de feu, L'. see *Firebird*.

Oliphant, Betty (*b* London, 1918). Brit. dancer, teacher, and b. mistress. Appeared in London musicals; arranged dances for the prods. of Emile and Prince Littler. Opened a school in Toronto 1949. Appointed b. mistress of National B. of Can. 1951 and dir. of its school 1967. Now asst. dir. of National B. of Can.

Olympiad (orig. Ger. title: *Olympiade*). Ballet in 3 movements; ch. MacMillan; mus. Stravinsky. Prod. 11 Mar. 1968, Ger. Op. Berlin, with Seymour, K. Jahnke, H. Peters, Holz, Beelitz, Kapuste. Set to Stravinsky's Symphony in Three Movements. A plotless b., with athletic overtones. Revived for Royal B. 1969.

Olympics. Ballet in 1 act; ch. Arpino; mus. T. Mayuzumi; déc. Ming Cho Lee. Prod. 31 Mar. 1966, R. Joffrey B., City Center, New York, with L. Fuente. An abstract b., inspired by the classical ideals of athletic performance, d. by an all-male cast. The individual events (running, leaping, wrestling, etc.) are unified by the runner with his torch.

Ombre, L'. Ballet in 3 acts; libr. and ch. F. Taglioni; mus. L. Wilhelm Maurer; sets Fedorov, Serkov, Shenian, and Roller; cost. Mathieu. Prod. 10 Dec. 1839, Bolshoi Th., St. Petersburg, with M. Taglioni, A. Guerra. The shade of the title is the ghost of a murdered woman who returns to d. with her lover. Revived in a 2-act version at Her Majesty's Th. London, 1840.
BIBL.: C. W. Beaumont, 'L'O.' in *Complete Book of Ballets* (London, 1951).

Ondine (also Ger. *Undine*). Ballet in 3 acts and 5 scenes; libr. and ch. Ashton; mus. Henze; déc. Lila de Nobili. Prod. 27 Oct. 1958, Royal B., Cov. Gdn., London, with Fonteyn, Somes, Farron, A. Grant. A Mediterranean version of the famous water-nymph story by Friedrich de la Motte Fouqué. The prod. was filmed by P. Czinner in 1959. First Ger. prod. by A. Carter (Munich, 1959); also prod. by T. Gsovsky (Berlin, 1959), Walter (Wuppertal, 1962), Beriozoff (Zurich,

1965), and Eck (Budapest, 1969). Earlier versions by L. Henry (mus. Gyrowetz, Vienna, 1825), P. Taglioni (mus. H. Schmidt, Berlin, 1836) and J. Perrot (mus. Pugni, London, 1843).
BIBL.: H. W. Henze, *Undine—Tagebuch eines Balletts* (Munich, 1959); P. Brinson and C. Crisp, 'O.' in *Ballet for all* (London, 1970); D. Vaughan, *Frederick Ashton and his Ballets* (London, 1977).

Onegin. Ballet in 3 acts and 6 scenes; libr. and ch. Cranko; mus. Tchaikovsky (arr. K. H. Stolze); déc. Rose. Prod. 13 Apr. 1965, Stuttgart, with Barra, Haydée, Cardus, Madsen. The b. follows the plot of Pushkin's famous verse novel *Eugene O.*, but uses none of Tchaikovsky's mus. for the opera *E.O.* In its original form it was preceded by a prologue. Revived for Munich State Op. B. 1972 Royal Swed. B. and Austral. B. (both 1976). Second Channel Ger. TV prod., 1975.
BIBL.: P. Brinson and C. Crisp, in *Ballet & Dance* (Newton Abbot, 1980).

One in Five. Ballet in 1 act; ch. Ray Powell; mus. Joseph and Johann Strauss; cost. Rencher. Prod. 12 June 1960, Sunday B. Club, Lyric Th., London, with Bergsma, Rencher, Newton. Five clowns, one of them a girl, give an impromptu entertainment. Revived for various cos., incl. Western Th. B., Austral. B. and National B. of Canada.

Opéra-Ballet. A mus. prod. with singing, dancing, and splendid décors; very popular in France during the late 17th and first half of the 18th centuries. Emerged from the divertissements, which took up more and more time in the course of the tragédies lyriques. Early examples were Lully's *Triomphe de l'amour* (1681) and *Le Temple de la paix* (1685). The first fully developed example was Campra's *L'Europe galante* (1697). Important works were Campra's *Les Muses* (1703), *Les Fêtes vénitiennes* (1710), and *Les Amours de Vénus et de Mars* (1712), J. J. Mouret's *Les Festes ou le Triomphe de Thalie* (1714), M. P. Montéclair's *Les Fêtes de l'été* (1716), M. R. Delande's and A. C. Destouche's *Les Eléments* (1721), C. de Blachemont's *Les Fêtes grecques et romaines* (1723), and Destouche's *Les Stratagèmes de l'amour* (1726). J. P. Rameau's *Les Indes galantes* (1735), *Les Fêtes d'Hébé ou les talents lyriques* (1739), and *Le Temple de la gloire* (1745) represented the apogee of op.-b. See also *Ballet Opera*.

Opus 1. Ballet in 1 act; ch. Cranko; mus. Webern. Prod. 7 Nov. 1965, Stuttgart, with Cragun, Keil. Set to Webern's Passacaglia op. 1. The life-story of a man striving in vain to reach the ideal. BBC TV prod. as part of the film *Cranko's Castle* (1967). Revived for Ger. Op. Berlin (1968), Frankfurt (1969), Royal Dan. B. (1971), and City Center Joffrey B. (1975).

Opus V (also *Webern Opus 5*). Ballet in 5 movements; ch. Béjart; mus. Webern. Prod. 26 Mar. 1966, B. of the 20th Century, Th. de la Monnaie, Brussels, with Carrié and Donn. Set to

Webern's String Quartet Op. 5. A plotless piece for two dancers. Revived for many couples. Van Dantzig used the same mus. in his *Moments* (1968).

Opus 34. Ballet in 2 parts; ch. Balanchine; mus. Schoenberg; cost. E. Francés. Prod. 19 Jan. 1954, New York City B., City Center, N.Y., with LeClercq, Bliss. The b. is set to Schoenberg's *Begleitmusik zu einer Lichtspielszene*, played twice. 'The first part of the ballet . . . had no story. It was about the music and attempted to look as it sounded . . . The second part . . . showed what the music might be accompanying. Using the key words *threat, danger, fear,* and *catastrophe,* a brother and sister (or lovers?) were shown in a series of events that overpower them' (Balanchine). The same mus. used by Tetley in *Imaginary Film* (1970) and Bohner in *Ballett ohne Titel* (1974). BIBL.: G. Balanchine, 'O. 34' in *Balanchine's New Complete Stories of the Great Ballets* (Garden City, N.Y., 1968).

Opus '65. Ballet in 1 act; ch. Sokolow; mus. T. Macero. Prod. 11 Sep. 1965, R. Joffrey B., Delacorte Th., New York. A vivid portrait of, and comment on, the younger generation of the mid-1960s. Revived for B. Rambert 1970.

Orbs. Ballet in 6 parts; ch. P. Taylor; mus. Beethoven; déc. A. Katz. First New York prod. 26 Dec. 1966, P. Taylor and D. Co., ANTA Th., N.Y., with de Jong, C. Adams, Wagoner, Taylor. Set to movements from Beethoven's last 3 string quartets. An hour-long ceremonial about the planets revolving around the sun. First Amer. perf. 8 Nov. 1966, Harper Th., Chicago.

Orchésographie. The Greek word for d. notation, the title of a book by T. Arbeau (1588). He describes the dances of the 16th century, in the form of a dialogue between himself and his pupil Capriol (*Capriol Suite*), and also gives an account of the history of dancing.

Ordman, Jeannette (*b* Germiston, S.A., 8 Nov. 1935). Brit. dancer, teacher, and b. director. Studied with R. Berman, M. Sturman, Northcote, and Ward. D. with Johannesburg Festival B., appointed soloist in 1954. Went to London; d. for TV, with Sadler's Wells Op. B., and elsewhere. Went to Israel as a teacher in 1965. Founded Bat-Dor D. Co. with Baroness Batsheva de Rothschild 1968; now its artistic dir. and principal d. Dir. of Bat-Dor Studios of Dance.

Orff, Carl (*b* Munich, 10 July 1895, *d* Munich, 29 Mar. 1982). Ger. composer. Though he wrote no genuine bs., d. is often important in his th. works, especially in his great triptych: *Carmina Burana* (ch. I. Hertling, Frankfurt, 1937), *Catulli Carmina* (ch. T. Gsovsky, Leipzig, 1943), and *Trionfo di Afrodite* (ch. T. Gsovsky, Milan, 1953). Each has been variously ch. by others since.

Original Ballet Russe. The B. Russe de Monte Carlo, founded in 1932, became Colonel de Basil's B. Russe in 1936, and changed its name to Covent Garden Russian B. in 1938. The co. was bought up by Educational B. Ltd. in 1939, and called O.B.R. It was disbanded in 1947. De Basil was dir. throughout. From Eur. the co. went to Austral. where Lichine gave the première of his *Graduation Ball* in 1940; then toured N. and S. Amer. and returned to London in 1946. G. Kirsta and the Grigorievs revived it briefly in 1951–2. See also *Ballets de Monte Carlo, Ballets Russes de Monte Carlo,* and *Nouveau Ballet de Monte Carlo.*

Orlando, Mariane (*b* Stockholm, 1 June 1934). Swed. dancer. Studied at Royal Swed. B. School. Joined Royal Swed. B. 1948; became soloist 1952 and ballerina 1953. Studied further in Leningrad. D. with Amer. B. Th. 1961–2. Resigned in 1974. Order of G. Vasa (1967).

Orlikowsky, Vaslav (*b* Kharkov, 8 Nov. 1921). Sov.-Swiss dancer, choreographer, and b. director. Studied with V. Sulima and V. Preobrajensky. D. with cos. in Kharkov, Tiflis, Prague, and Lvov. Came to W. Eur. Formed with the co. of Antonia Tumkovskaya. Formed his Classic Russ. B. in Munich 1950. B. Master in Oberhausen 1952–5; ch. first full-length post-war Ger. prod. of *Swan Lake* in 1955. B. master in Basle 1955–67; b. activity flourished there under his direction, and culminated in his prods. of *Swan Lake, Sleeping Beauty, Nutcracker, Giselle, Romeo and Juliet, The Stone Flower, Abraxas, Prince of the Pagodas, Peer Gynt,* and *Fountain of Bakhchisaray.* Guest ch. for London Festival B. (*Peer Gynt,* 1963; *Swan Lake,* 1965), co. of R. Larrain (*Cinderella,* 1963), and Vienna State Op. (*Sleeping Beauty,* 1963), and for Bregenz and Salzburg Festivals. B. Dir. of Vienna State Op. 1966–71. Now b. dir. Graz op.-house. Ch. Adam's *Le Corsaire* for Bregenz Festival 1975. BIBL.: S. Enkelmann and R. Liechtenhan, in *Ballett in Basel* (Basle, n.d.).

Orloff, Nicholas (*b* Moscow, 1914). Russ.-Amer. dancer and b. master. Studied in Paris with Preobrajenska and V. Gsovsky. Joined Original B. Russe 1939; created Drummer in Lichine's *Graduation Ball* 1940. D. with B. Th. 1941–4, Colonel de Basil again 1947, and Grand B. du Marquis de Cuevas 1950. Now b. master of the Denver Civic B. Married to the d. and teacher Nina Popova.

Orosz, Adél (*b* Budapest, 17 Mar. 1938). Hung. d. Studied at Budapest State B. School. Joined Budapest State Op. B. 1954; became soloist 1957. Studied further in Leningrad. Became dir. Budapest State Op. B. 1984. Created roles in Seregi's *Spartacus* (second première, 1968) and *The Wooden Prince* (1970), and Eck's *Ondine* (1969). Principal role in full-length b. film *Girl Danced into Life* (1964). First Prize (Moscow, 1957).

Orpheus. 1) Ballet in 3 scenes; ch. Balanchine; mus. Stravinsky; déc. Noguchi. Prod. 28 Apr.

1948, B. Society, City Center, New York, with Magallanes, Maria Tallchief, Moncion. 'The b. is a contemporary treatment of the ancient myth of O., the Greek musician who descended into Hades in search of his dead wife, Eurydice ... We saw it as the eternal domestic tragedy of an artist and his wife, with love himself a male angelic embodiment' (Balanchine). Revived for various cos. Other versions using the same mus. by Milloss (Venice, 1948), Walter (Wuppertal, 1954), Cranko (Stuttgart, 1970), and Van Dantzig (Amsterdam, 1974).—2) Ballet in 6 scenes; libr. E. Bond; ch. Forsythe; mus. Henze; sets Axel Manthey; cost. Joachim Herzog. Prod. 17 Mar. 1979, Stuttgart B., Stuttgart, with Cragun, Keil, R. Anderson, M. Witham, O. Neubert. This is a full-length treatment of the ancient myth, interpreting O. as the artist who through his struggle leads human mankind from chaos to civilization and culture, but is opposed by the gods, whom he finally overcomes by smashing his Apollo-given lyre and from its one remaining string assembling the first really human melody, which makes the dead rise from their tombs to participate in the utopian finale of a classless society which has no need for any gods whatsoever.—Earlier b. treatments of the same myth by H. Schütz (Dresden, 1638), Hilverding (Vienna, 1752), Noverre (mus. Deller, Stuttgart, 1763), and Ballon (Turin, 1791). Other b. treatments by Laban (mus. Gluck, 1927), de Valois (mus. Gluck, London, 1941), Charrat (mus. R. Lupi, Venice, 1951), and Béjart (mus. P. Henry, Liège, 1958). There have also been a number of b. prods. of the O. ops. by Monteverdi (Milloss, Florence, 1957; Walter, Wuppertal, 1961; Sparemblek, Brussels, 1960) and Gluck (Balanchine, New York, 1936; Wigman, Leipzig, 1947; Ashton, London, 1953; Bausch, Wuppertal, 1975; Neumeier, Hamburg, 1978).

BIBL.: G. Balanchine, 'O.', in *Balanchine's Complete Stories of the Great Ballets* (Garden City, N.Y., 1977); L. Kirstein, 'O.', in *Movement & Metaphor* (New York, 1970).

Orr, Terry (*b* Berkeley, Cal., 12 Mar. 1943). Amer. dancer. Studied at San Francisco B. School; joined San Francisco B. 1959. Joined Amer. B. Th. as a soloist 1965; became principal d. 1972. Created roles in Nahat's *Brahms Quintet* (1969) and T. Ruud's *Polyandrion* (1973). Now b. master there. Was married to the d. Cynthia Gregory.

Orta, Carlos Enrique (*b* Caracas, 28 March 1947). Venezuelan dancer and choreographer. Studied at Escuela Superior de Teatro in Caracas, modern d. at Scuola Cantorum in Paris and at Essen Folkwang School. D. with Folkwang B. 1970–3, Wuppertal D. Th. 1973–4, Cologne D. Forum 1974–9 and since with J. Limón co. Started to ch. in 1975. Award of Cologne Choreographer's Competition for *The Mistake* (mus. Héctor Capos Parsi, 1976).

Osato, Sono (*b* Omaha, Nebr., 29 Aug. 1919). Jap.-Amer. dancer. Studied with Egorova, Oboukhoff, Caton, Bolm, and B. Holmes. Joined B. Russe de Monte Carlo 1934; principal d. 1936–40. Then d. with B. Th. 1940–43; created a role in Tudor's *Pillar of Fire* (1942). Continued to appear in Broadway musicals. Author of *Distant Dances* (New York, 1980).

BIBL.: J. Gruen, 'S.O.', in *The Private World of Ballet* (New York, 1975).

Osipenko, Alla Yevgenyevna (*b* Leningrad, 16 June 1932). Sov. dancer. Studied at Leningrad Ch. School; graduated 1950. D. with Kirov B. 1954–71; eventually became soloist. Has since joined L. Jacobson's co. Created roles in Grigorovich's *The Stone Flower* (Mistress of the Copper Mountain, 1959), Belsky's *Coast of Hope* (1959), and Sergeyev's *Hamlet* (1970). Pavlova Prize (Paris, 1956); Merited Artist of the R.S.F.S.R. (1957); People's Artist of the R.S.F.S.R. (1960).

Oslo. See *Norwegian National Ballet*.

Østergaard, Solveig (*b* Skjern, 7 Jan. 1939). Dan. dancer. Studied at Royal Dan. B. School; graduated 1957. Joined Royal Dan. B. 1958; became solo d. 1962. Created roles in Feld's *Winter's Court*, Marks' *Dichterliebe* (both 1972), and Flindt's *Felix Luna* (1973).

Oswald, Genevieve (*b* Buffalo, 24 Aug. 1923). Amer. librarian. Educated Univ. of N. Carolina, Juilliard School of Mus., and Columbia School of Library Service. Curator of the D. Collection of the New York Public Library since 1947, which under her energetic direction became an independent division of the library in 1964 and since 1965 has been part of the Library-Museum of the Performing Arts at Lincoln Center. Capezio Award (1956); Amer. D. Guild Award (1970).

Othello. Ballet in 4 acts; libr. and ch. Chaboukiani; mus. A. Machavariani; déc. S. Virsaladze. Prod. 29 Nov. 1957, Op. House, Tiflis, with Chaboukiani, Vera Tsignadze. The b. follows Shakespeare's play closely. Revived for Leningrad Kirov Th. 1960. The Tiflis prod. was filmed in 1960. Other b. treatments of Shakespeare's play by S. Viganò (Milan, 1818), Limón (in *The Moor's Pavane*, mus. Purcell, New London, Conn., 1949), Hanka (in *Der Mohr von Venedig*, mus. Blacher, Vienna, 1955), Němeček (mus. J. Hanuš, Prague, 1959), Lifar (in *Le Maure de Venise*, mus. M. Thiriet, Amsterdam, 1960), d'Amboise (in *Prologue*, mus. arr. R. Irving, New York, 1967), Darrell (mus. Liszt, Samsova's and Prokovsky's co., Trieste, 1971), and Butler (in *La Voix*, mus. G. Crumb, B. du Rhin, 1972).

Other Dances. Dance for two; ch. Robbins; mus. Chopin; cost. Santo Loquasto. Prod. 9 May 1976, Met. Op. House, New York, with Makarova and Baryshnikov at a Gala for the benefit for the Library of the Performing Arts at Lincoln Center. This is a plotless piece d. to 4 mazurkas and a waltz. Later performed on other occasions, e.g. by McBride and Baryshnikov in the rep. of the New York City B.

Ottolenghi, Vittoria (*b* Rome, 8 Apr. 1924). Ital. dance critic and TV producer-director. Studied at Univ. of Rome (degree in Eng. literature). Worked for 10 years as sub-editor of *Enciclopedia dello spettacolo* and since 1958 as D. critic of *Paese sera*, also since 1963 as dir.-producer (mainly for b. and mus.) at Ital. TV (RAI). Correspondent *Dance Magazine* since 1977. Contributor to Milan monthly *Musica Viva* and other magazines. Premio Positano 1972 (for promotion of b. in Italy).

Oukrainsky, Serge (*b* Odessa). Russ.-Amer. dancer, choreographer, and teacher. Started as a mime at the Paris Th. du Châtelet 1911. Toured with Pavlova 1913–15. Principal d. ch., and dir. of Chicago Op. B. 1915–27. Formed a school in Chicago with Andreas Pavley in 1917; this gave rise to the Pavley-Oukrainsky B. B. master of Los Angeles and San Francisco op. houses 1927–30. Founded Serge Oukrainsky B. after Pavley's death 1931. Started to teach in Hollywood 1934. Author of *My Two Years with Anna Pavlova* (1940). BIBL.: A. Barzel, 'S.O.', *Dance Magazine* (1979/6).

Ouvert. (Fr., open). Designates an open position of the feet (opposite of fermé).

Oved, Margalit (*b* Aden, *c.* 1931). Isr. dancer, teacher, and choreographer. Studied with S. Levi-Tanai. Was one of the founding members of Inbal in 1959 and rapidly became its foremost d. Later went to Cal., and joined the d. faculty at UCLA. Now has her own M. D. Th. Co. for which her chs. include *Through the Gate, Aden, Landscape, Yemenite Wedding, Cinderella, In the Beginning*, works representing 'a modern dance expression which integrates drama, mime, rhythm, and music' (Oved).

Ozaï, ou l'Insulaire. Ballet in 2 acts and 6 scenes; libr. and ch. Coralli; mus. Casimir Gide; sets Ciceri; cost. Lormier. Prod. 26 Apr. 1847, Opéra, Paris, with A. Plunkett, Desplaces. A variant of the then very popular subject of the noble savage; the b. is based on the adventures of the Fr. explorer M. de Bougainville (1729–1814).
BIBL.: C. W. Beaumont, 'O.' in *Complete Book of Ballets* (London, 1951).

P

PACT Ballet. S.A., co., orig. called Transvaal B., formed when the Johannesburg City B. merged with the Performing Arts Council of Transvaal in 1963. Johannesburg Festival B. Society, founded in 1944 by Marjorie Sturman as an amateur co., consisting of pupils from her own and other local schools, became the Johannesburg B. and then the Johannesburg City B. First dir. of the PACT B. was Faith de Villiers 1963–71, followed by John Hart 1971–5. The co. has always maintained a close relationship with the Royal B., which has often sent some of its best dancers as guests; its repertory is based upon the classics.

Paganini. Ballet in 1 act and 3 scenes; libr. Rachmaninov (also mus.) and Fokine (also ch.); déc. Soudeikine. Prod. 30 June 1939, Colonel de Basil's B. Russe, Cov. Gdn., London, with Dmitri Rostoff, Baronova, Riabouchinska. The b. shows the struggles of the mus. genius to overcome his conflicts with the world in order to gain immortality. Lavrovsky used the same Rachmaninov Rhapsody for a b. of the same title based on a different libr. (written by himself, Bolshoi B., 1962) as did Ashton for his b. *Rhapsody* (1980).

Pagava, Ethéry (*b* Paris, 1931). Fr. dancer. Studied with Egorova. Appeared in pas de deux with Petit in 1942; joined his Bs. des Champs-Elysées as a soloist 1945. Created roles in his *Les Forains* (1945) and *Les Amours de Jupiter* (1946). Joined Grand B. de Monte Carlo (later Grand B. du Marquis de Cuevas) 1947; her best role was in Balanchine's *La Somnambule*. Later d. with various smaller Fr. cos. and abroad (Amsterdam, Nervi, etc.). Has also ch. some bs.

Page, Annette (*b* Manchester, 18 Dec. 1932). Brit. dancer. Studied at Sadler's Wells B. School. Joined Sadler's Wells Th. B. 1950; became soloist 1954. Joined Sadler's Wells B. 1955; became ballerina 1959. Created roles in Rodrigues's *Café des sports* (1954), MacMillan's *Danses concertantes* (1955), and *Agon* (1958). Resigned 1967. Member of Arts Council of Great Britain, 1976–8, and of its Dance Advisory Panel to 1982. Married to the ch. Ronald Hynd.

Page, Ruth (*b* Indianapolis, 22 Mar. 1900). Amer. dancer, choreographer, and b. director. Studied with Clustine, Bolm, and Cecchetti. Toured S. Amer. with Pavlova 1918. Appeared in Bolm's *Birthday of the Infanta* in Chicago 1919; joined his B. Intime for its London guest season 1920. Prima ballerina of Music Box Revue in Berlin and New York 1923–4. D. with Bolm in Buenos Aires, with Diaghilev's Bs. Russes 1925, and with Met. Op. B. in New York 1926–8. Created Terpsichore

in Bolm's first prod. of Stravinsky's *Apollon musagète* (Washington, 1928). Toured Japan and U.S.S.R. Prima ballerina and b. mistress at Chicago Summer Op. 1929–33; created her first chs there. Toured with Kreutzberg 1932 and 1934. Prima ballerina and b. mistress of the Op. of Chicago 1934–7. Toured Scandinavia 1937. Ch. *Frankie and Johnny* (mus. J. Moross) for Chicago Federal Th. 1938. Formed Page-Stone B. Co. with B. Stone 1938, with which she toured widely (Paris in 1950). Guest ch. of *Revanche* (based on *Il trovatore*, Bs. des Champs-Elysées, 1951), and *Vilia* (or *The Merry Widow*, London Festival B., 1953). During the next few years she worked as a ch. at the Chicago Lyric Op. and for her own co. which appeared under various names and is now called Chicago B. One of the most dynamic personalities of the Amer. b. scene; the extensive tours of her various cos. have made her one of the best known b. artists in the U.S. She ch. *La Guiablesse* 1933 in Chicago (libr. Lafcadio Hearn, mus. William Grant Still), in which she appeared as the only white amidst 50 coloured dancers. As a ch. she became especially well known through her b. adaptations of ops. and operettas, e.g. *Susanna and the Barber* (Rossini's *Il barbiere di Siviglia*, 1955), *Camille* (Verdi's *La traviata*, 1957), *Die Fledermaus* (1958), *Carmen* (1959; an earlier version as *Guns and Castanets*, 1939), *Pygmalion* (Suppé's *Die schöne Galathée*, 1961), and *Bullets and Bonbons* (O. Straus's *The Chocolate Soldier*, 1965). Other important bs. include *The Bells* (based on E. A. Poe, mus. Milhaud, Chicago Univ., 1946), *Mephistophela* (after Heine's *Faust* libr., mus. Berlioz, Boito, and Gounod, 1966), *Carmina Burana* (mus. Orff, 1966), and *Alice in the Garden* (mus. I. van Grove, Jacob's Pillow, 1970). Honorary doctor Columbia College, Chicago, 1974. D. Magazine Award 1980.
BIBL.: J. Martin, *R.P.-An Intimate Biography* (New York, 1977); *Page by Page* (New York, 1980).

Palais de cristal, Le. See *Symphony in C*.

Pallerini, Antonia (*b* Pesaro, 25 June 1790, *d* Milan, 11 Jan. 1870). Ital. dancer. Member of a well-known family of dancers. First appeared under G. Gioia at La Scala, Milan. Created there all the leading ballerina roles in S. Vigano's bs., from *Prometeo* (1813) to *Didone* (1821). Ritorni called her not only the 'prima ballerina seria assoluta' but also 'la più gloriosa delle attrici italiane d'ogni genere'.

Palley, Xenia (*b* Chicago, 17 Apr. 1933, *d* 25 Apr. 1980). Fr. dancer. Studied with Sedova, Kniaseff, and Rousanne. Début with Grand B. du Marquis de Cuevas 1948. Prima ballerina Stuttgart B. 1957–61, after which she d. with various touring cos. Prix René Blum (1952).

Paltenghi, David (*b* Christchurch, 1919, *d* Windsor, 1961). Brit. dancer and choreographer Studied with Tudor and Rambert. Joined London B. 1939; remained with the co. when it merged with B. Rambert. Created Young Nobleman in Howard's *La Fête étrange* (1940). Joined Sadler's Wells B. 1941, and became principal d. Created roles in Helpmann's *Comus* (1942), *Hamlet* (King, 1942), and *Miracle in the Gorbals* (1944). With B. Rambert again 1947–51; began to ch. (*Eve of St. Agnes*, etc.). Appeared in Kelly's film *Invitation to the Dance* (*Ring Around the Rosy*, 1952). Directed and ch. films and TV commercials after his retirement.

Palucca, Gret (*b* Munich, 8 Jan. 1902). Ger. dancer and teacher. Studied with Kröller and Wigman; joined Wigman's group 1923. Gave her first solo-recital 1924; then toured extensively in Ger. and abroad. Opened a school in Dresden 1925; appeared with her pupils in numerous concerts. Was considered one of the most lyrical and charming of modern Ger. dancers. In 1939 her Dresden school was closed by the Nazis, but she was able to reopen it in 1945. It has since become one of the leading State-sponsored schools in E. Germany; its summer courses draw pupils from all over the world. She still teaches. National Prize of the G.D.R. (1960).
BIBL.: G. Schumann, *P.* (E. Berlin, 1972).

Panaieff, Michel (*b* Novgorod, 21 Jan. 1913, *d* Los Angeles, 10 Feb. 1982). Russ.-Amer. dancer and teacher. Studied in Belgrade and with Egorova, Volinine, Kniaseff, and Rousanne. Principal d. Belgrade Op. 1935. Joined B. Russe de Monte Carlo 1936; created roles in Massine's *Capriccio Espagnol* and *Rouge et noir* (1939). D. with original B. Russe 1940–1. Opened a school in Los Angeles 1946. Was artistic dir. of D. Th. of Orange County until 1974.
BIBL.: V. H. Swisher, 'Franz, Otherwise Known as M.P.', *Dance Magazine* (1967/12).

Panov, Valeri Matyevich (*b* Vitebsk, 12 Mar. 1938). Sov. dancer. Studied at Leningrad Ch. School; graduated 1957. Joined Maly B. 1957–64, then Kirov B. 1963–72, where he was admired as one of the most brilliant virtuoso dancers of his generation; created roles in Boyarsky's *The Lady and the Hooligan* (1962), Boyartchikov's *The Three Musketeers* (1964), Vinogradov's *Gorianka* (1968), Sergeyev's *Hamlet* (title-role, 1970), and Kasatkin-a's and Vasilyov's *Creation of the World* (1971). When he applied in 1972 for an exit visa to Israel for himself and his wife, d. Galina Ragozina, he was expelled from the co. and temporarily imprisoned. His fight for a permit to emigrate drew world-wide attention, and many appeals for him and his wife were made in the capitals of the Western world; in June 1974 they were allowed to leave the country, since when they were based

in Israel, but made many guest appearances abroad, in which P.'s self-willed and individual talent found difficulty in adapting to Western artistic standards. His chs. for Ger. Op. Berlin B. incl. *Cinderella* (mus. Prokofiev, 1977), *Sacre du printemps* (mus. Stravinsky, 1978), *The Idiot* (mus. Shostakovich, 1979), and *War and Peace* (mus. Tchaikovsky, 1981). Author of *To Dance* (New York, 1978). Lenin Prize (1969); Merited Artist of the R.S.F.S.R. (1970). Art. dir. Royal B. of Flanders 1984–6.

Pantomime. (Greek, all-imitating). General term for all kinds of stage shows with action, but without words or song, though sometimes accompanied by mus. Also for its Eng. variant, 'a traditional . . . entertainment (now usually performed at Christmas) dating from the early eighteenth century, of music, d., and mime, usually following set lines and ending with a transformation scene and a harlequinade, though of recent years its character has greatly changed' (G. B. L. Wilson).

Pan Twardowski (orig. Pol. title). Ballet-pantomime in 3 acts and 8 scenes; libr. and mus. Ludomir Różycki; ch. Piotr Zajlich; déc. Wincent Drabik. Prod. 9 May 1921, Warsaw, with Zygmunt Tokarski, Zajlich, Halina Szmolcówna. Based on a Pol. variant of the Faust legend. Has been mounted in many different versions all over Poland and in some other E. bloc countries; a one-act version (mus. arr. by V. Launitz, ch. Czeslaw Konarski, 1941) was one of the most popular works of the Anglo-Polish B. An earlier version with ch. by Virgilio Calori and mus. by Adolph Sonnenfeld, Warsaw, 1871. A different b. on the same subject by Nijinska (*La Légende de Cracovie*, mus. M. Kondracki, B. Polonais, 1937).
BIBL.: B. Mamontowicz-Lojek, in 'Pologne', *Les Saisons de la danse* (1973/10).

Papillon, Le. Ballet in 2 acts and 4 scenes; libr. de Saint-Georges; ch. Marie Taglioni; mus. Offenbach; set Martin, Despléchin, Nolau, Rubé, Cambon, Thierry; cost. Albert. Prod. 26 Nov. 1860, Opéra, Paris, with Livry, Mérante. The complicated plot centres on Farfalla, a beautiful young girl. She falls into the hands of the Bad Fairy Hamza and is turned into a butterfly. E. M. von Rosen used the same mus. for her b. *Utopia* (Gothenburg, 1974). Another new version by R. Hynd for Houston B. 1979, revived for Sadler's Wells Royal B., 1980.
BIBL.: C. W. Beaumont, 'L.P.' in *Complete Book of Ballets* (London, 1951).

Papillons, Les. Ballet in 1 act; ch. Fokine; mus. Schumann (arr. Tcherepnin); set Doboujinsky; cost. Bakst. Prod. 10 Mar. 1913, Maryinsky Th., St. Petersburg, with Karsavina, Fokine. Pierrot, strolling in a park at night during carnival time, meets a group of young girls, whom he takes for butterflies. At its first perf. the b. was called

Papillon. Fokine then staged it for Diaghilev's Bs. Russes, 16 Apr. 1914, Monte Carlo.

BIBL.: C. W. Beaumont, in *Michel Fokine & His Ballets* (London, 1935).

Pâquerette. Ballet in 3 acts and 5 scenes; libr. Gautier; ch. Saint-Léon; mus. Benoist; sets Despléchin, Cambon, and Thierry; cost. Lormier and Marchal. Prod. 15 Jan. 1851, Opéra, Paris, with Cerrito, Saint-Léon. P., a Flemish girl, accompanies her beloved François when he has to join the army, and helps him to escape from prison.

BIBL.: C. W. Beaumont, 'P.' in *Complete Book of Ballets* (London, 1951).

Paquita. Ballet in 2 acts and 3 scenes; libr. Paul Foucher; ch. Mazilier; mus. E. Deldevez; sets Philastre, Cambon, Diéterle, Séchan, and Despléchin; cost. Lormier and H. de B. d'Orschwiller. Prod. 1 Apr. 1846, Opéra, Paris, with Grisi, L. Petipa. The b. is set in Spain under Napoleonic occupation; P., a Span. gipsy, saves the life of the Fr. officer Lucian, who falls in love with her—but they have to surmount numerous obstacles, until it is finally revealed that she is really of noble birth, so that they can marry after all. M. Petipa prod. it for his St. Petersburg début in 1847; he later asked Minkus to compose new mus. for a Pas de trois and a Grand Pas in 1881, and it is these two pieces which have survived in the repertory—e.g. of the Kirov B. Balanchine ch. two different versions of the Pas de trois for the Cuevas co. in 1948 and for New York City B. in 1951. Danilova staged a 1-act version for B. Russe de Monte Carlo in 1949. Nureyev mounted the Grand Pas for the 1964 R.A.D. Gala at Drury Lane; he d. it himself with Fonteyn and some young soloists and students. This version was reproduced by M. Besobrasova at La Scala, Milan (1970), for dancers of the Vienna State Op. B. (Salzburg, 1970), and for Amer. B. Th. (1971). Casenave mounted it for London Festival B. in 1967 and Scottish B. in 1975, as did Samsova in another version for Sadler's Wells Royal B., 1980. Act II was staged by Makarova for her own co., New York (1980). Sov. TV prod.

BIBL.: C. W. Beaumont, 'P.' in *Complete Book of Ballets* (London, 1951).

Parade. Realistic Ballet in 1 act; libr. Cocteau; ch. Massine; mus. Satie; déc. Picasso. Prod. 18 May 1917, Bs. Russes de Diaghilev, Th. du Châtelet, Paris, with Lopokova, Massine, Woizikowski, Zvereff. A group of Fr. music-hall artists performs on a Sunday afternoon in the street outside their theatre to attract an audience. The décor became one of the most discussed examples of cubist art in the th. Revived for B. of the 20th Century (1964), City Center Joffrey B. (1973), London Festival B. (1974), and Zurich B. (1981). A different version by Gray Veredon for Met. Op. B. (New York, 1981).

BIBL.: L. Kirstein, 'P.' in *Movement & Metaphor* (New York, 1970).

Paradise Lost. Ballet in 1 act; libr. Jean Cau; ch. Petit; mus. Constant; déc. Martial Raysse. Prod. 23 Feb. 1967, Royal B., Cov. Gdn., London, with Fonteyn, Nureyev; also given that year at the Paris Opéra. A modern treatment of the Adam and Eve story. Georgi ch. the first Ger. prod. (Hanover, 1968).

BIBL.: G. Balanchine, 'P.L.' in *Balanchine's New Complete Stories of the Great Ballets* (Garden City, N.Y., 1968).

Parés, José (*b* Puerto Rico, 11 Dec. 1926). Amer. dancer, teacher, b. master, and choreographer. Studied with Caton, Craske, Nemchinova, and Fedorova. D. with Teatro de Danza 1956–9 and National B. of Cuba 1952–70. B. master of Teatro di Danza and National B. of Cuba, also permanent guest teacher for B. of the 20th Century. Has ch. a number of bs. for Teatro de Danza, National B. of Cuba, B. of the 20th Century, and Ger. Op. Berlin.

Paris. The Académie royale de danse was founded 1661. In 1671 it amalgamated with the Académie royale de musique P. Beauchamp was in charge of the dances for the first prod. of *Pomone.* Lully was dir. 1672–78; he collaborated closely with Beauchamp. The first ballerina to appear on its stage was Mlle La Fontaine in *Triomphe de l'Amour*, 1681. Beauchamp was succeeded as b. master by L. Pécour (1687–1703) and N. Blondy. Its associated school (which still exists) was founded in 1713; Balon, La Prévost, La Camargo, and La Sallé were its first famous students. J.-P. Rameau's ops. (1733–60) considerably improved artistic standards. Dupré was appointed b. master in 1739; G. Vestris and Noverre were among his pupils. The improvement continued with Gluck's ops. (from 1774). Sallé and Vestris (1770–6) paved the way for Noverre's reforms; he led the co. 1776–80, and staged the first prod. of Mozart's *Les petits riens* in 1778. The best-known dancers of these years were Guimard, Thérèse, and Auguste Vestris. Noverre was succeeded by M. Gardel (1781–7) and Pierre Gardel (1787–1817; he ch. the usual mythological and anacreontic bs., and also *La Marseillaise* and *Offrande à liberté*, both 1792). B. was also an important part of the ops. of Spontini, the later Rossini, Auber, Adam, Meyerbeer, and Halévy. F. Taglioni's *La Sylphide* 1832 was an important landmark, in which his daughter Marie introduced Romantic b. Elssler made her local début 1834; Coralli ch. *Le Diable boîteux* for her 1836. Coralli's and Perrot's *Giselle*, with Grisi, was performed in 1841. Saint-Léon then became b. master in 1850, followed by Mazilier in 1853. L. Petipa made his début in 1858 and was appointed b. master in 1860. During the 1840s and 50s the city attracted the world's best choreographers and dancers. Towards the end of the 1860s, however, decline set in; the last climax was Saint-Léon's *Coppélia*, in 1870. The present building (Palais Garnier) was opened 1875; Mérante's *Sylvia* (1876), L. Petipa's *Namouna*

The Paris Opera Ballet in Nureyev's *Manfred*.   Photo Serge Lido.

(1882), and Mérante's *Les deux pigeons* (1886) were among its early successes. Mérante was b. master 1869–87, followed by Joseph Hansen and L. Staats (1907). In the years before the First World War all else was overshadowed by the success of the Diaghilev seasons. These continued into the late 1920s; another serious competitor for the public's favour was Les Bs. Suédois. The Opéra's b. activities gradually stabilized when Lifar was appointed b. master and principal d. in 1930. He strengthened the co. and contributed a number of new works to the repertory; he also established b. performances on the same day each week. After a short interruption for political reasons, he returned to the Opéra in 1947. After 1945, however, the numerous small cos. of Petit, Charrat, and later Béjart, *et al.*, were doing the most interesting work. Lifar resigned 1959; the Opéra has since had a succession of directors, incl. G. Skibine, V. Verdy, and, since 1980, R. Hightower. Bs. have, of course, also been shown in other ths. in the city. During the second quarter of the 19th century, perfs. at the Th. de la Porte-Saint-Martin enjoyed great popularity. The Opéra Comique had a considerable number of b. perfs. 1922–72. Though it has perhaps been less creative in recent years, P. is still one of the world centres of b.; traditional and modern cos. from all over the globe are eager to perform here. The annual Festival International de Danse de P. began in 1963 and has continued each autumn since, with some variations in format. See also *Ballet de France, Ballet des Etoiles de P., Ballet National Jeunesses Musicales de France, Ballets de la Jeunesse, Ballets de l'Etoile, Ballets de P., Ballets des Champs-Elysées, Ballets 1933, Ballets Modernes de P., and Ballet-Théâtre de P.*
BIBL.: L. Vaillat, *Ballets de l'Opéra de P.* (P., 1947); I. Guest, *The Ballet of the Second Empire (1847–70)* (2 vols., P., 1953 and 1955); Guest, *The Romantic Ballet in P.* (London, 1966); Guest, *Le Ballet de l'Opéra de P.* (P., 1976).

Park, Dame Merle (*b* Salisbury, Rhodesia, 6 Oct. 1937). Brit. d. Studied with Betty Lamb and at Elmhurst School. Joined Sadler's Wells B. 1954; apptd. soloist 1958 and principal 1962. Created roles in Tudor's *Shadowplay* (1967), Ashton's *Jazz Calendar* (1968) and *The Walk to the Paradise Garden* (1972), Nureyev's London *Nutcracker* (1968), MacMillan's *Elite Syncopations* (1974), *Mayerling* (1978), *La Fin du jour* (1979), and *Isadora* (1981), J. Carter's *Lulu* (1976) and Bintley's *Adieu* (1980). She also danced all the ballerina roles in the classical repertory. Dir. Royal Ballet Sch. from 1983. C.B.E. (1974); D.B.E. (1986).
BIBL.: J. Gruen, 'M.P.', in *The Private World of Ballet* (New York, 1975). C. Rigby, 'M.P.', in *Royal Ballet Yearbook 1979–80* (London, 1979).

Parkes, Ross (*b* Sydney, 17 June 1940). Austral. dancer. Studied with Valrene Tweedie, Peggy Watson, Audrey de Vos, and Graham. Début with B. Français 1959. Has d. with many modern groups in the U.S. and with Pennsylvania B. Was a soloist with Graham's co.

Parkinson, Georgina (*b* Brighton, 20 Aug. 1938). Brit. dancer. Studied at Sadler's Wells B. School. Joined Royal B. 1957; became soloist 1959, and principal d. in 1962. Created roles in MacMillan's

Symphony (1963), Ashton's *Monotones II* (1966) and *Enigma Variations* (1968), and Chloe in Cranko's *Daphnis and Chloe* (Stuttgart, 1962). One of her best roles was La Garçonne in Nijinska's *Les Biches*. Left Royal B. in 1978. Now b. mistress of Amer. B. Th.

BIBL.: G. Gow, 'G.P.', *Dancing Times* (1975/12).

Parlić, Dimitrije (*b* Salonika, 23 Oct. 1919). Yugosl. dancer, choreographer, and b. director. Studied with Poliakova and Boskovitch. Joined Belgrade Op. 1938; became principal d. 1941. D. in Berlin, Vienna, and Zagreb; returned to Belgrade 1946 and was appointed ch. 1949. Has remained with the co. for which he ch. numerous bs. During leave of absence he has repeatedly worked abroad (Paris, Edinburgh, b. dir. of Vienna State Op. 1958–61, of National B. of Finland 1970–1).

Parmain, Martine (orig. Hemmerdinger; *b* Parmain, Val d'Oise, 14 Oct. 1942). Fr. dancer. Studied at Paris Opéra B. School. Joined Paris Opéra B. 1960; became première danseuse 1964. Ballerina of B. Th. Contemporain. She has also d. at Paris Opéra Comique and Zurich Op. House. Married to the ch. Michel Descombey; has created roles in many of his bs.

BIBL.: M. Netter, 'M.P.', *Les Saisons de la danse* (1969/10).

Parnel, Ruth (*b* Belgrade, 1928). Yugosl. dancer and teacher. Studied with M. Jovanović and Kirsanova. Joined Belgrade Op. 1941; became ballerina 1946. Has created many roles in bs. by Parlić. Now a teacher.

Pártay, Lilla (*b* Budapest, 25 Nov. 1941). Hung. dancer. Studied at Budapest State B. Inst. Joined Budapest State Op. 1961 and later became principal d. Created roles (second premières) in Seregi's *Miraculous Mandarin* (1970) and *The Cedar* (1975). Bronze Medal (Varna, 1968).

Partisans' Days (orig. Russ. title: *Partisanskie dni*). Ballet in 4 acts and 6 scenes; libr. Vainonen (also ch.) and V. Dmitriev (also déc.); mus. Asafiev. Prod. 10 May 1937, Kirov Th., Leningrad, with Anisimova, Chaboukiani, Koren. An episode in the Civil War; the partisans in the North Caucasus are fighting the White Guard Cossacks; the beautiful but poor peasant-girl Nastia is forced to marry a rich Cossack. This was the first Sov. character d. b. without point shoes.

BIBL.: N. Roslavleva, in *Era of the Russian Ballet* (London, 1966).

Pas (Fr., step). In b. terminology, generally used with certain characterizations—e.g. p. de bourrée, p. de chat (see Bourrée, Chat, etc.); also used to specify a certain form—e.g. in P. d'action for a dramatic scene, and in connection with numerals—P. seul, P. de deux, P. de trois—meaning a d. for that number of dancers. The most famous is the P. de deux for the ballerina and her cavalier; it usually consists of the entrée and adagio for both partners, a variation for the danseur, a variation for the ballerina, and ends with the coda for both partners.

Pas d'acier, Le (orig. Russ. title: *Stalnoi skok*). Ballet in 2 scenes; libr. and déc. G. Yakulov; ch. Massine; mus. Prokofiev. Prod. 7 June 1927, Bs. Russes de Diaghilev, Th. S. Bernhardt, Paris, with Tchernicheva, Danilova, Massine, Lifar, Woizikowski. The b. has no continuous plot; it shows scenes from daily Sov. life, ending with machine dances in a factory. It was intended as a tribute to the constructivist art of the young U.S.S.R. Diaghilev originally wanted it to be prod. by Tairov, Meyerhold, and Goleizovsky.

Pas de deux. See *Pas*.

Pas de dix. Ballet in 1 act; ch. Balanchine; mus. Glazunov; cost. E. Francés. Prod. 9 Nov. 1955, New York City B., City Center, N.Y., with Maria Tallchief, Eglevsky. Set to mus. from the last act of *Raymonda*. A b. for 10 dancers; 'there is no attempt here to approximate Petipa's original [ch. of *Raymonda*] . . . What I have done instead is to try to make an entertaining spectacle with no story, simply a series of dances for a ballerina, her partner, and a small ensemble' (Balanchine). Revived for Hamburg State Op. B., Stuttgart B., Cologne, Dutch National B., and other cos.

BIBL.: G. Balanchine, 'P.d.d.' in *Balanchine's New Complete Stories of the Great Ballets* (Garden City, N.Y., 1968).

Pas de Duke. D. for two; ch. Ailey; mus. Duke Ellington; déc. Ter-Arutunian. Prod. 11 May 1976, A. Ailey City Center D. Th. at City Center, New York, with Jamison and Baryshnikov. Created for a gala occasion this pas de deux, which thrives upon the contrasting styles of a modern d. and a star of classical b. was later performed on numerous other occasions.

Pas de quatre. Ballet divertissement; ch. Perrot; mus. Pugni. Prod. 12 July 1845, Her Majesty's Th., London, with Taglioni, Grisi, Cerrito, and Grahn. The plotless b. epitomizes the Romantic cult of the ballerina. Lumley, the dir. of the th., managed to persuade 4 of the most famous ballerinas of his time to appear together. Four perfs. were given—at two later perfs. in 1847, the part created by Grahn was handed over to Rosati. A probably very similar version was staged by Taglioni at Milan's La Scala in 1846, as an insert in *Le Diable à quatre*, with herself, Fuoco, C. Galetti (i.e. Rosati), and C. Vente. Later reconstructions were staged by K. Lester for Markova-Dolin B. in 1936 (with Molly Lake, D. Gould, Prudence Hyman, and Crofton) and by Dolin for B. Th. in 1941 (with Gollner, Stroganova, Alonso, and Sergava; the latter version was revived for many cos. incl. Kirov B., 1966). A. Fr. TV prod. of the Dolin version with Markova, Hightower, Moreau, and Bourgeois was televised in 1953. Cuban film prod. 1971. Lester's version is still in use at the annual summer courses of the Royal Academy of Dancing.

BIBL.: I. Guest, *The P.d.Q.* (London, 1968).

Pas des déesses. See *Jugement de Pâris, Le.*

Passacaglia (Ital., from Span. pasacalle, passing through a street). Used to describe a band of musicians marching through the street, playing pasodobles and other march-like pieces. During the 16th century the P. came to Italy as a Span. d. It is a d.-song in measured 3/4 time with variations over an ostinato bass. Performed at the court of Louis XIV of France at the beginning or end of Lully's bs.

Passacaglia in C Minor. Ballet in 1 act; ch. Humphrey; mus. Bach; set Arch Lauterer; cost. P. Lawrence. Prod. 5 Aug. 1938, Humphrey-Weidman D. Co., Armory, Bennington, Vt., with Humphrey and Weidman. A group work for 12 co. members and 11 apprentices, 'an abstraction with dramatic overtones. . . . The d. was inspired by the need for love, tolerance, and nobility in a world given more and more to the denial of these things.' (Humphrey).

Passamezzo. (Ital., half step.) A 16th-century Ital. promenading d., originally accompanied by singing, in slow duple time. Often followed by a saltarello.

Passé. (Fr., passed.) In b., the transitional movement of the leg from one into the next position.

Passepied. (Fr., pass feet.) Orig. a rapid d. for sailors, not unlike the branle; first mentioned in Paris in 1587. Performed by couples or groups of 4 men, accompanied by singing or bagpipes. Under Louis XIV it became a very popular court-d. in 3/8 or 6/8 time; it also appeared in the bs. of that time.

Passo d'addio. The farewell perf. of the students at Ital. b. schools attached to the op. houses, after they have passed their graduation.

Path of Thunder, The (orig. Russ. title: *Tropoyu groma*). Ballet in 3 acts; libr. Slonimsky; ch. Sergeyev; mus. K. Karayev; déc. V. Dorrer. Prod. 4 Jan. 1958, Kirov Th., Leningrad, with Sergeyev, Dudinskaya. Inspired by the novel of the same title by the S.A. writer Peter Abraham. The negro Lenny loves the white girl Sari, and this brings about their death. Revived for Bolshoi B. 1959. Many newly ch. versions have been presented throughout the U.S.S.R.

BIBL.: M. G. Swift, in *The Art of the Dance in the U.S.S.R.* (Notre Dame, Ind., 1968).

Patineurs, Les. Ballet in 1 act; ch. Ashton; mus. Meyerbeer (arr. Lambert); déc. Chappell. Prod. 16 Feb. 1937, Vic-Wells B., Sadler's Wells Th., London, with Turner, Honer, Miller, Fonteyn, Helpmann. Lambert took the mus. from Meyerbeer's ops. *Le Prophète* and *L'Etoile du Nord*; Ashton ch. a divertissement, characterized by steps simulating the movements of ice-skaters. The b. has frequently been revived, e.g. for B. Th. 1946, with new déc. by C. Beaton.

BIBL.: D. Vaughan, *Frederick Ashton and his Ballets* (London, 1977).

Patsalas, Constantin (b Thessaloniki, 1 Aug. 1943). Greek dancer and choreographer. Studied at Essen Folkwang School, joining Düsseldorf B. 1969, then National B. of Canada 1972, appointed second soloist 1976, first soloist 1979 and co. ch. 1980. Before winning the first Boston B. Ch. Showcase 1979 with *Piano Concerto* (mus. Ginastera), had already ch. *Inventions* (mus. Miloslav Kabelac, 1974), *Black Angels* (mus. G. Crumb, 1976), and *The Rite of Spring* (mus. Stravinsky, 1978), followed since by *Nataraja* (mus. Charpentier, 1981) as well as some more bs. for other cos. and groups plus a pas de deux for E. Bruhn and Karyn Tessmer, *In the Mist* (mus. Janaček, Spoleto 1978).

Paul, Annette av (also Wiedersheim-Paul; b Stockholm, 1944). Swed. dancer. Studied at Royal Swed. B. School; joined Royal Swed. B. 1961. Created Katerina in Grigorovich's Stockholm prod. of *The Stone Flower* (1962), and roles in Tudor's *Echoing of Trumpets* (1963) and Macdonald's *While the Spider Slept* (1965). Married ch. Macdonald; has often appeared as guest in his bs. for the Royal Winnipeg B. (e.g. *Rose La Tulippe*, 1966) and other cos. Principal d. of the Royal Swed. B. until 1972, and then with his Grands Ballet Canadiens, of which her husband is artistic dir. Retired from d. 1984; now dir. of Vancouver B.

BIBL.: S. Goodman, 'A.a.P', *Dance Magazine* (1968/1).

Paul, Mimi (b Nashville, Tenn., 3 Feb. 1942). Amer. dancer. Studied with L. Gardiner, M. Day, Franklin, and at School of Amer. B. D. with Washington B. 1955–60, New York City B. 1960–8; principal d. of Amer. B. Th. 1969–74. Created roles in Balanchine's *Don Quixote* (1965), *Divertimento No. 15* (1966 version), *Jewels* (1967), and Nahat's *Quintet* (1969) and *Ontogeny* (1970). Had one of her best roles in Balanchine's *Bugaku*.

Paulli, Holger Simon (b Copenhagen, 22 Feb. 1810, d there, 23 Dec. 1891). Dan. conductor and composer. Wrote the mus. for a great number of Bournonville bs., incl. *Napoli* (with Helsted, Gade, and Lumbye, 1842), *Konservatoriet* (1849), *Kermesse in Bruges* (1851), *The Wedding in Hardanger* (1853), and *Flower Festival at Genzano* (with Helsted, 1858).

Pavane. Either from Ital. Padovana, Paduan, or Span. pavo, peacock. A stately court d. in simple duple time; specially popular in Italy, France, and Spain during the 16th and 17th centuries. Ravel's *Pavane for a Dead Infanta* has often been ch. as has Fauré's *P.*

Pavillon d'Armide, Le. Ballet in 1 act and 3 scenes; libr. and déc. Benois; ch. Fokine; mus. N.

Tcherepnin. Prod. 25 Nov. 1907, Maryinsky Th., St. Petersburg, with Pavlova, Gerdt, Nijinsky. Based on Gautier's story *Omphale*; the Vicomte de Beaugency looks at a tapestry of Armida and her court and dreams that he is Rinaldo, succumbing to her charms. Fokine originally created the b. for the graduation perf. of the St. Petersburg Imperial B. Academy 1907 and revived it in somewhat extended form for the Maryinsky Th. When the Diaghilev troupe presented it on its first night at the Paris Th. du Châtelet on 19 May 1909 (with Karalli, Nijinsky, and Mordkin) its artistic unity created a sensation.
BIBL.: L. Kirstein, 'L.P.d'A.' in *Movement & Metaphor* (New York, 1970).

Pavlova, Anna Pavlovna (b St Petersburg, 12 Feb. 1881, d The Hague, 23 Jan. 1931). Russian d. Entered St. Petersburg Imperial B. Academy 1891; studied with Oblakhov, Legat, Vazem, and Gerdt. While at the school, and in her first th. appearances, her exceptionally poetic way of moving and her refined sensibility of style attracted special attention. Graduated 1899 and joined Maryinsky Th.; became second soloist in 1902, first soloist in 1903, ballerina (after further studies with Cecchetti) in 1905, and prima ballerina in 1906. By that time she had already d. all the traditional ballerina roles and had a considerable following. In 1907 she created Fokine's *Dying Swan*, which became her most famous solo d. She then created her first great solo roles in Fokine's *Pavillon d'Armide* (1907), *Egyptian Nights*, and the second version of his *Chopiniana* (both 1908). In 1908 she began to tour abroad, visiting Scandinavia, Leipzig, Prague, and Vienna. D. with the Diaghilev co. in Paris 1909. Remained a member of the Maryinsky Th. until 1913, but appeared there increasingly seldom as she spent most of her time on her tours abroad, with Mordkin as her partner. Berlin début 1909, New York and London 1910. Appeared with the Diaghilev co. for the last time in 1911 in London. Bought Ivy House in Golders Green, and took up residence there. Assembled her own co. and embarked on numerous world tours, organized by her reputed husband, Victor Dandré. After her partnership with Mordkin ended, Novikov became her partner in 1911, then Volinine in 1914, and Vladimiroff in 1927. Her indefatigable tours made her a pioneer of classical b. all over the world, incl. S.A. and Austral. Adhered to strictly conservative aesthetic principles, and showed little sympathy for the reforms advocated by Diaghilev and his followers. Her repertory consisted mainly of the classics (often in abbreviated form) by Coralli-Perrot, Petipa, and Ivanov, and her Fokine dances, together with bs. ch. by Legat, Clustine (e.g. *The Fairy Doll*) and U. Shankar, and her own character pieces, of which *Autumn Leaves* (mus. Chopin—the only complete b. ever ch. by her) and *Gavotte* (mus. P. Lincke) were the most popular. As a d. her most impressive qualities were her unique lightness, grace, poetry, and spirituality; she became a legend and a household name in her own lifetime. In a 90-minute silent film, prod. in Hollywood in 1915, she played Fenella in *The Dumb Girl of Portici*. Test shots, made in Hollywood in 1924, including excerpts from *Christmas*, *Dying Swan*, *Oriental Dance*, *Rose Mourante*, *Fairy Doll*, *The Californian Poppy*, and *Colombine*, were newly arranged for the film *The Immortal Swan*, released in 1956. The London Museum staged a notable P. exhibition in 1956 for the 25th anniversary of her death. At Ivy House one room, furnished with some of her personal belongings, is open to the public at certain times.
BIBL.: V. Krasovskaya, *A.P.* (Leningrad, 1964—in Russ.); O. Kerensky, *A.P.* (London, 1973). See also the souvenir issues of *Dance and Dancers* and *Dance Magazine* (both 1956/1) and the portfolio in *Dance Magazine* (1976/1).

Pavlova, Nadezhda Vasilyevna (b Tsheboksari, 15 May 1956). Sov. dancer. Studied at Perm State B. School; graduated in 1974. Won All-Sov. B. Competition, Moscow, 1972, and Grand Prix of International B. Competition, Moscow, 1973. D. for the first time in the W. in New York, Summer 1973, and again with the Perm co. in Bregenz, in the same year. Appeared in the Amer. film *The Blue Bird* (1976). Joined Bolshoi B. in 1975. Married to the d. V. Gordeyev.
BIBL.: K. Sandler, 'Moscow's favourites' (N. P. and V. Gordeyev), *Ballet News* (1979/11).

Paxton, Steve (b Tucson, Ariz., 1939). Amer. dancer and choreographer. Started as an amateur in religious ds., morality plays, and Jewish folk ds. Studied with M. Cunningham and Rob. Dunn, becoming a member of Cunningham's co., working also with Y. Rainer, R. Rauschenberg, D. Hay, L. Childs, T. Brown *et al.* One of the founder-members of Judson D. Th. in 1962. Started to explore commonplace objects and their relationship to the body, trying to connect d. to outside world experiences and progressing from there to *'Contact Improvisation'* with its inter-actions passing to and fro between partners in their myriad varied choices and possibilities.
BIBL.: S. Banes, in *Terpsichore in Sneakers* (Boston, 1980).

Peasant Pas de deux. An insert in the first act of *Giselle*, ch. Coralli, mus. Burgmüller, performed at the b.'s first night on 28 June 1841, Opéra, Paris, by N. Fitzjames and Auguste Mabille. The standard version (amended by M. Petipa) is also often given on gala occasions. P. Wright distributed it among 6 dancers, when he prod. *Giselle* in Stuttgart, 1966 (also occasionally performed by 4, when given by the Royal B. touring co.).

Pécourt, Louis (also Pécour; b Paris, 10 Aug. 1653 [1651?] d there, 22 Apr. 1729). Fr. dancer, choreographer, and dance master. Studied with Beauchamp. Début 1674 in the op. *Cadmus et*

Hermione; became one of the best known dancers in the Lully ops., most successful in *Le Triomphe de l'Amour* (1681) and *Le Temple de la paix* (1685). He succeeded Beauchamp as b. master 1687–1703; continued to appear as a d. until 1710. Ch. many bs. in the ops. of P. Colasse, H. Desmaret, A. C. Destouches, T. Bertin, and Lully.

Pécs Ballet. See *Ballet Sopianae.*

Peer Gynt. Ballet in 3 acts and 10 scenes; libr. Eugen Wigeliew; ch. Orlikowsky; mus. Grieg; déc. Lec Bothas; cost. S. Schröck. Prod. 30 Oct. 1956, Basle, with D. Christensen, M. Parnitzki, H. Sommerkamp, Deege. The b. follows the plot of Ibsen's play. Revived for London Festival B. 1963. Other b. versions of the same play, based on Grieg's mus., by G. Tregubov (Lvov, 1955—in the repertory of many Sov. ths.), Tomaszewski for Cramér B. 1972, and G. Buch, Dresden Landesbühne, 1974.

Pelléas et Mélisande Ballets. Several bs. have been inspired by Maeterlinck's play, (1893), incl. those by P. van Dyk (mus. Schoenberg, Wiesbaden, 1952), J.-J. Etchevery (mus. Fauré, Enghien, 1953), T. Gsovsky (mus. M. Baumann, Berlin, 1954), Walter (mus. Schoenberg, Wuppertal, 1955), Petit (mus. Schoenberg, Royal B., 1969), and Menegatti and Gai for Fracci (mus. Sibelius, La Scala, 1972).

Peña, George de la (*b* New York, 9 Dec. 1955). Amer. dancer. Studied at School of Amer. B. and High School of Performing Arts. D. with St. Paul Civic Op. and André Eglevsky B. Co. Joined Amer. B. Th. 1974, promoted soloist 1977. Starred in the title role of 20th Century Fox's *Nijinsky* film (1979).

Penché. Fr., bent forward.

Penderecki, Krzysztof (*b* Deciba, 23 Nov. 1933). Pol. composer. Wrote no b. mus., but his concert pieces have often been used for b. purposes, particularly in Ger.; e.g. L. Höfgen's *Polymorphia* (Bonn, 1966—same mus. by Chesworth in *H*, B. Rambert, 1968, and Jerzy Makarowski, Warsaw, 1971), Butler's *Ceremony* (based on *Anaklasis* and *Fluorescences*, Pennsylvania B. Co., 1968), Doutreval's *Sonate per Violoncello* (Frankfurt, 1969), and Borg's *De natura sonoris* (Swed. TV, 1969).

Penitente, El. Ballet in 1 act; ch. Graham; mus. Horst; set Arch Lauterer; cost. E. Gilfond (déc. later redesigned by Noguchi). Prod. 11 Aug. 1940, M. Graham and Co., Bennington College Th., Bennington, Ver., with Graham, Hawkins, and M. Cunningham. Three strolling players enact a primitive morality play, with Graham performing as the Virgin, Magdalen, and the Madonna, Hawkins as the Penitent, and Cunningham as Christ. Revived for London Contemporary D. Ths., 1969.

Penney, Jennifer (*b* Vancouver, 5 Apr. 1946). Can. dancer. Studied with Gweneth Lloyd and Betty Farrally and at Royal B. School. Joined Royal B. 1963; became soloist 1966 and principal d. 1970. Created roles in MacMillan's *Anastasia* (1971), *Seven Deadly Sins* (1973), *Elite Syncopations* (1974), *Four Seasons* (1975), *La Fin du jour* (1979), and *Gloria* (1980); Van Manen's *Four Schumann Pieces* (1975), and Neumeier's *Fourth Symphony* (1977). She also dances all the ballerina roles in the classical repertory.
BIBL.: J. Gruen, 'J.P.', in *The Private World of Ballet* (New York, 1975).

Pennsylvania Ballet. The Philadelphia-based co. emerged from the regional b. co. and b. school led by B. Weisberger, with the aid of a Ford Foundation grant, in 1963. It maintains a close contact with New York City B. The repertory consists mainly of Balanchine works, but also includes bs. by Rodham (its b. master), Butler, J. Sanders, Comelin, Dollar, Smuin, Moncion, Harkarvy, and Van Manen. Its direction was shared between Weisberger and Harkarvy and since 1982 dir. by Robert Weiss.
BIBL.: E. Palatsky, 'The P.B.', *Dance Magazine* (1967/11).

Percival, John (*b* Walthamstow, 16 Mar. 1927). Brit. critic and writer on b. Educated Oxford Univ. Co-ed. (with C. Barnes) of Oxford B. Club magazine *Arabesque* 1950. Has contributed to *Dance and Dancers* since 1950; became assoc. ed. in 1965 and editor from 1981. B. critic of *The Times* since 1965. London correspondent of *Dance Magazine*, and Ger. *Ballett* annual. Author of *Antony Tudor (Dance Perspectives* 17), *Modern Ballet* (new edn. 1980), *The World of Diaghilev, Experimental Dance* (both 1971), *Nureyev—Aspects of the Dancer* (1975), and *Facts about a Ballet Company* (1979), *Theatre in my Blood*, biog. of J. Cranko (London, 1983).

Peretti, Serge (*b* Venice, 28 Jan. 1910). Fr. dancer and teacher. Studied at Paris Opéra B. School. Joined Paris Opéra B.; became premier danseur at the age of 20, and in 1931 was the first d. to be given the title of étoile at 21. His first great success was in Lifar's *Creatures of Prometheus* (1929); created roles in Lifar's *Bacchus et Ariane* (1931), *Salade* (1935), *Le Chevalier et la damoiselle* (1941), and *Joan de Zarissa* (1942). Appointed provisional b. master in 1945; ch. several works, notably Honegger's *L'Appel de la montagne*. Then opened a school of his own; taught at the Paris Opéra B. School 1963–70, in charge of the class of étoiles.

Pereyaslavec, Valentina (*b* Ukraine, 1907). Russ.-Amer. dancer and teacher. Studied at Moscow Bolshoi B. School; graduated 1926. D. with the cos. in Kharkov and Sverdlovsk; created the ballerina role in Jacobson's *Lost Illusions* (1936). Studied further with Vaganova in Leningrad; became her asst. Went to Lvov as ballerina in 1940. Deported by the Germans to Leipzig as a factory worker. Opened a b. school in Ingolstadt 1945. Went to America in 1949 and started to teach in T. Semeyonova's Philadelphia studio;

moved to New York and has taught at Amer. B. Th. School since 1951. Still in great demand as guest teacher all over the world (Royal B., Vienna State Op. B., Cologne Summer Academy, etc.).
BIBL.: interview with V.P., *Dance and Dancers* (1964/4).

Perez, Rudy (*b* New York, 24 Nov. 1929). Amer. dancer, choreographer, and teacher. Studied with New D. Group, Graham, and Cunningham. Début 1963 with his solo piece *Take Your Alligator (Coat) with You* at Judson Workshop. Further pieces of his include *Count Down* (1964), *Center Break* (1967), *Loading Zone* (1968), *Transit* (1969), *Coverage* (1970), and *Asparagus Beach* (1972). Most of his bs. are set to sound-collages arr. by himself. Artist-in-residence at Marymount College, N.Y. since 1969.
BIBL.: M. B. Siegel, in *At the Vanishing Point* (New York, 1972).

Péri, La. Ballet in 2 acts and 3 scenes; libr. Gautier; ch. Coralli; mus. Burgmüller; sets Séchan, Diéterle, Philastre, and Cambon; cost. Lormier. Prod. 17 July (Castil-Blaze says 22 Feb.) 1843, Opéra, Paris, with Grisi, L. Petipa. The complicated plot centres on the poet Sultan Achmet who meets the Queen of the Fairies in one of his opium dreams, and is taken to her heavenly kingdom. The b. was very popular, and rapidly reached tths. all over Eur.; London première Sep. 1843, St. Petersburg and Vienna 1844. A different b. *L.P.* by Clustine to mus. by Dukas, Paris, 1912 (individual later versions, using the same mus., by Staats, Paris, 1921; Ashton, B. Club, London, 1931 and another version, Royal B., 1956; Lifar, Nouveau B. de Monte Carlo, 1946; Darrell, London Festival B., 1973).
BIBL.: C. W. Beaumont, '*L.P.*' in *Complete Book of Ballets* (London, 1951).

Per la dolce memoria di quel giorno. See *'I trionfi' di Petrarca*.

Perm. Sov. city on the edge of the Urals. The first serf th. was opened in 1821; first op. perfs. in 1870, regular op. seasons with b. from 1895. A b. studio was organized in 1925, and from 1926 separate b. perfs. of the classics began to be given: *Giselle*, followed by *Coppélia* and *The Red Poppy*. Second State Urals Op. founded 1931; during the next 10 years there was much b. activity. The repertory included the classics and contemporary works such as *The Red Poppy* and *Fountain of Bakhchisaray*. During the Second World War the Leningrad Kirov B. was evacuated to the city, now called Molotov; they performed at the op. house, while the local co. visited nearby cities. The city's special enthusiasm for b. dates from this period; a strongly Leningrad-orientated Ch. School was founded in 1945. The Kirov B. returned to Leningrad in 1944, and the local co. returned to the op. house. During the following decades, particularly after 1958 when the th.

building was considerably enlarged and renovated, b. made rapid progress under the energetic direction of GITIS graduate Murat Gaziev. The Ch. School was directed for many years by former Maly ballerina Ksenia Yesaulova; the directors are now Ludmila Sacharova and Pyotr Kolovratsky. It has prod. numerous brilliant young dancers; Nadezhda Pavlova won the Grand Prix of the Moscow B. Competition 1973. The co. first visited the West for the Bregenz Festival of 1973. Artistic dir. N. Boyartchikov was succeeded in 1977 by I. A. Shapovalov.

Perrault, Serge (*b* 1920). Fr. dancer and teacher. Studied at Paris Opéra B. School; joined P. Opéra B. 1946. Left 1947 to pursue a freelance career, d. with many smaller cos. Created Toreador in Petit's *Carmen* (1949). Now teaches in Paris.

Perrot, Jules Joseph (*b* Lyons, 18 Aug. 1810, *d* Paramé, 24 Aug. 1892). Fr. dancer, choreographer, and b. master. Studied in Lyons. D. at Th. de la Gaîté, Paris 1823, then at Th. de la Porte-St.-Martin 1826. Studied further with A. Vestris. Appointed first soloist at London's King's Th. 1830. Paris Opéra début same year; soon became Taglioni's regular partner. Dissatisfied with his contract, he left the Opéra; appeared in London 1833–6, and in Naples 1834, where he met Grisi and subsequently became her b. master, partner, and lover. Though his physique was rather awkward, he was considered the greatest d. of his time, 'with the perfect legs of a Greek statue, somewhat feminine in their roundness' (Gautier). Began to ch.; his first major b. was *Le Nymphe et le Papillon* for the Vienna Kärntnertor Th. (1836). Further guest appearances with Grisi in Milan and Naples; returned to Paris 1840 and ch. (probably) all Grisi's solos for the *Giselle* first prod. in 1841. To London, where he appeared with Grisi in *Giselle* in 1842 and ch. *Alma ou la Fille de feu* with Deshayes and Cerrito. B. master at Her Majesty's Th. until 1848; ch. *L'Aurore* and *Ondine* (1843), *La Esmeralda* (1844), *Eoline ou la Dryade* and *Pas de quatre* (1845), *Caterina ou la Fille du bandit* and *Le Jugement de Pâris* (1846), *Les quatre saisons* (1848 all mus. Pugni), *Lalla Rookh ou la Rose de Lahore* (mus. P. and F. David, 1846) and *Les Eléments* (mus. Bajetti, 1847). His next important b. was *Faust* (mus. Panizza, La Scala, Milan, 1848). B. master at St. Petersburg 1851–8; revived some of his former bs. and ch. *Le Angustie d'un maître de ballet* (1851), *La Guerre des Femmes ou les Amazones du XIXe siècle* (1852), *Gazelda ou les Tziganes* (1853), *Markobomba* (1854, all mus. Pugni). Meanwhile also worked in Berlin, Warsaw, Brussels, Lyons, and Paris (*La Filleule de fées*, mus. Adam and Saint-Julien, 1849). Retired to a village in France with his wife, the Russ. ballerina Capitoline Samovskaya, and died there. One of the most dramatic and expressive choreographers of the Romantic movement.
BIBL.: J. Slonimsky, '*J.P.*', *Dance Index* (IV, 12); I. Guest in *The Romantic Ballet in England* (London,

1954); M.-F. Christout, 'P., génie méconnu', *Les Saisons de la danse* (1972/11).

Persephone. Melodrama in 3 scenes; text A. Gide; ch. Jooss; mus. Stravinsky; déc. A. Barsacq. Prod. 30 Apr. 1934, Rubinstein co., Opéra, Paris, with Rubinstein. P., daughter of the Fertility Goddess Demeter, wanders eternally between the earth and the underworld, where she must join Pluto every winter. Perfs. of the work have been relatively rare, since the performer must both recite the text and d. Wallmann prod. it with Zorina for the Salzburg Festival 1955, Ashton with Beriosova for the Royal B. in 1961.

Persia. See *Iran* and *Mahalli Dancers of Iran*.

Perugini, Giulio (*b* Rome, 1927). Ital. dancer. Studied at B. School of Teatro dell'Opera, Rome. Joined La Scala B., Milan; became principal d. 1949. Has often appeared abroad. Appointed b. master at La Scala 1959.

Peter and the Wolf (orig. Russ. title: *Pyotr i volk*). Mus. fairy-tale by Prokofiev; ch. Bolm; déc. Lucinda Ballard. Prod. as a b. in 1 act, 13 Jan. 1940, B. Th., Center Th., New York, with Loring, Dollar, V. Essen, K. Conrad, Stroganova. The work was conceived for narrator and orchestra (first perf. Moscow, 1936); Peter, despite his grandfather's warnings, catches the dangerous wolf, with the help of his animal friends, and takes it to the zoo. Later b. versions by F. Staff for B. Rambert (1940, revived for PACT B. and Northern D. Th.), G. Blank (Berlin, 1954), A. Varlamov for Bolshoi B. (1959), and P. Belda for B. of the 20th Century (1966).
BIBL.: C. W. Beaumont, '*P.a.t.W.*' in *Supplement to Complete Book of Ballets* (London, 1952).

Peters, Kurt (*b* Hamburg, 10 Aug. 1915). Ger. dancer, teacher, and dance publicist. Studied with Mariska Rudolph and Fedorova. D. with the cos. of Saarbrücken and Hamburg. From 1945 concentrated on a teaching career in Hamburg; founded *Tanzarchiv*, which started as a collection of books, etc., and in 1953 became the name of the Ger. monthly d. magazine, of which he was publisher and chief editor until 1980. In 1966 the collection and the magazine moved to Cologne; P. was one of the directors of the Institute for Stage D. there (which also houses the collection). Author of *Lexikon der klassischen Tanztechnik* (Hamburg, 1961).

Peterson, Kirk (*b* New Orleans, 1951). Amer. dancer. Studied with Lelia Haller; d. with her B. Jeunesse. Joined Harkness Youth Dancers, N.Y., 1970; principal d. of Washington National B. 1971–4, then with Amer. B. Th., and since 1981 with San Francisco B. Guest artist with London Festival B. in 1973.
BIBL.: S. Goodman, 'K.P.', *Dance Magazine* (1972/5).

Petipa, Jean Antoine (*b* Paris, 1796, *d* St. Petersburg, 1855). Fr. dancer, choreographer, and teacher. D. in Paris; moved with his family to Marseilles and then to Brussels, where he was b. master 1819–32, 1833–5, 1841–2, and 1843 (and the founder of Conservatoire de la Danse). Also worked as a ch. in Bordeaux and Madrid; settled in St. Petersburg 1848 and became a teacher at the Imperial B. Academy. Father of Lucien and Marius P.

Petipa, Lucien (*b* Marseilles, 22 Dec. 1815, *d* Versailles, 7 July 1898). Fr. dancer, choreographer, and b. master. Studied with his father Jean Antoine P. and d. under his guidance in Brussels and Bordeaux. Moved to Paris 1839; début in *La Sylphide* and created Albert in *Giselle* 1841. Much admired for his elegance and style; became Grisi's regular partner. Created leading roles in Coralli's *La Péri* (1843) and *Eucharis* (1844), Mazilier's *Le Diable à quatre* (1845), *Paquita* (1846), *Jovita, ou les Boucaniers* (1853), *Les Elfes* (1856), and *Marco Spada* (1857), Mabille's *Griseldis* and Perrot's *La Filleule des fées* (1849), and Cerrito's *Gemma* (1854). Ch. op. bs. for Verdi's *Les Vêpres siciliennes* (1855) and Auber's *Le Cheval de bronze* (1857); his first genuine b. was *Sakountala* (mus. E. Reyer, 1858). B. master of the Opéra 1860–8; ch. the bs. *Graziosa* (1861) and *Le Roi d'Yvetot* (both mus. T. Labarre, 1865) and collaborated in the first prods. of Rossini's *Sémiramis* (1860), Wagner's *Tannhäuser* (1861), Gounod's *La Reine de Saba* (1862), Verdi's *Don Carlos* (1867), and Thomas' *Hamlet* (1868). A hunting accident ended his dancing career, but he returned to the Opéra to ch. Lalo's *Namouna* (1882). One of the best danseurs nobles of his time, though as a ch. he was overshadowed by his brother Marius.
BIBL.: I. Guest, in *The Romantic Ballet in Paris* (London, 1965); Guest, in *The Ballet of the Second Empire* (2 vols., London, 1953 and 1955).

Petipa, Maria Mariusovna (*b* St. Petersburg, 29 Oct. 1857, *d* Paris, 1930). Russ. dancer. Studied with her father Marius P. and Johannson. Début as the Blue Dahlia in the b. of the same title 1875. She developed into a much admired character d., creating many national dances in bs. and ops. and the Lilac Fairy in her father's *Sleeping Beauty* (1890). Her mother was Maria Surovshchikova P.

Petipa (Surovshikova), Maria Sergeyevna (*b* 1836, *d* Novocherkassk, 1882). Russ. dancer. Studied at St. Petersburg Imperial B. Academy; graduated 1854. Married Marius P. 1854 and entered the Bolshoi Th.; created many roles in her husband's bs. Her en travestie numbers, *Le petit Corsaire* and *The Little Mujik* were her most popular pieces. Divorced in 1869; then rapidly declined as a d. Mother of Maria Mariusovna P.

Petipa, Marius (*b* Marseilles, 11 Mar. 1818, *d* Gurzuf, Crimea, 14 July 1910). Fr. dancer, choreographer, and b. master. Son of Jean Antoine P., the brother of Lucien P., the husband of Maria Surovshchikova and later of Liubov Leonidovna

Savitskaya, and the father of Maria Mariusovna P. Studied with his father. Début Brussels in P. Gardel's *Dansomanie* 1831. Went to Bordeaux with his family. Principal d. in Nantes 1838; ch. his first bs. *Le droit du Seigneur, La petite bohémienne*, and *La Noce à Nantes*. Toured North America with his father 1839. Studied further with A. Vestris; principal d. in Bordeaux, where he appeared in *Giselle, La Fille mal gardée*, and *La Péri*, and ch. *La jolie Bordelaise, La Vendange, L'Intrigue amoureuse*, and *Le Langage des fleurs*. Appeared at the Teatro del Circo, Madrid, 1845, studied Span. d. and ch. *Carmen et son Toréro, La Perle de Séville, L'Aventure d'une fille de Madrid, La Fleur de Grenade*, and *Départ pour la course des taureaux*. Principal d. in Paris and then in St. Petersburg, 1847, where he was much acclaimed in such bs. as *Paquita, Giselle, La Péri, Armida, Catarina, Le Délire d'un peintre, Esmeralda, Le Corsaire*, and *Faust*; often appeared with Elssler. When *Giselle* was revived in 1850, he made some changes in the Wilis scenes, which became the Grand Pas des Wilis of 1884. Perrot's asst. for a while; then created his first b. for St. Petersburg, *The Star of Granada* (mus. various, 1855). Appointed first b. master there in 1862. His first really successful b. was *La Fille du Pharaon* (mus. Pugni, 1862). Ch. about 50 bs. for the Imperial Ths. in St. Petersburg and Moscow, incl. *Don Quixote* (mus. Minkus, Moscow, 1869) and *La Camargo* (mus. Minkus, 1872), *Bayaderka* (mus. Minkus, 1877), *The Talisman* (mus. Drigo, 1889), *The Sleeping Beauty* (mus. Tchaikovsky, 1890), *Kalkabrino* (mus. Minkus, 1891), *Cinderella* (with Cecchetti and Ivanov, mus. Baron Shell, 1893), *Swan Lake* (with Ivanov, mus. Tchaikovsky, 1895), *Halte de Cavalerie* (mus. J. Arnsheimer, 1896), *Raymonda* (1898), *Ruses d'amour* (1900), *The Seasons* (1900—mus. all Glazunov), *Les Millions d'Arlequin* (mus. Drigo, 1900), and his last b. *The Magic Mirror* (mus. Koreshenko, 1903—all St. Petersburg). He also newly ch. large sections of such successful contemporary bs. as *La Fille du Danube* and *Le Corsaire* (1880), *Paquita* (1881), *Coppélia* (1884), *Le Diable à quatre* (1885), *Esmeralda* (1886), and *La Sylphide* (1892). He collaborated closely with Tchaikovsky, on the *Nutcracker*, but had to hand over the first prod. to Ivanov in 1892, because of illness. Towards the end of his career he faced growing opposition from the younger generation who wanted to strengthen the dramatic content of b. He was retired on full b. master's salary 1903. P. was undoubtedly responsible for leading the Tsarist b., based upon the best traditions of the Fr. and Ital. school, to its magnificent climax. His noble classicism and consciousness of form was considered old-fashioned at the turn of the century. However, it was vindicated by Diaghilev's prod. of *The Sleeping Princess* 1921. The prods. of the Sadler's Wells and Royal B. and the Leningrad Kirov B's visits to the West have caused a reappraisal of his oeuvre, which is now considered one of the greatest achievements of b. history.

BIBL.: L. Moore (ed.), *Russian Ballet Master—The Memoirs of M.P.* (London, 1968); Moore, 'The P. family in Europe and America', *Dance Index* (Vol. VI, no. 5); check-list of his works in *Les Saisons de la danse* (1968/6); *M.P.—Materiali, Vospominania, Stati* (Leningrad, 1971—a comprehensive selection of articles and commentaries, in Russ.; Ger. ed., E. Berlin, 1976); V. Krasovskaya, 'P. and "The Sleeping Beauty"', *Dance Perspectives* 49.

Petit, Roland (*b* Villemomble, 13 Jan. 1924). Fr. dancer, choreographer, and b. director. Studied at Paris Opéra B. School; joined Paris Opéra B. 1940. Appeared with M. Bourgat and Charrat in various recitals. Left the Opéra 1944. D. at the Vendredis de la Danse at the Th. S. Bernhardt. Formed Bs. des Champs-Elysées 1945, which he left to form the Bs. de Paris in 1948; he was star d. and chief ch. of each co. Toured extensively in France and abroad with both cos. B. de Paris was disbanded, and reassembled for various seasons, when he presented his new bs. Also worked as a dir. and ch. of revues, for Hollywood and TV. Bought Casino de Paris and directed it 1970–75, where he staged several revues with his wife, Zizi (i.e. Renée) Jeanmaire. Dir. of his B. de Marseille since 1972. A d. of great personal magnetism; his bs. are often choreographically slight, but derive a certain attractiveness from his close collaboration with fashionable writers and designers. One of the most fertile Fr. post-war choreographers; he combines chic, sex, and theatricality in his own unique way. His best known prods. incl. (for his own co. unless otherwise stated) *Les Forains* (mus. Sauguet, 1945), *Les Amours de Jupiter* (mus. Ibert), *Le jeune homme et la mort* (mus. Bach) and *Bal des blanchisseuses* (mus. V. Duke, 1946), *Les Demoiselles de la nuit* (mus. Français, 1948), *Carmen* (mus. arr. after Bizet, 1949), *Ballabile* (mus. Chabrier, Sadler's Wells B., 1950), film *Hans Christian Andersen* (1951), *Le Loup* (mus. Dutilleux), *Deuil en 24 heures* (mus. M. Thiriet, both 1953), films *Daddy Long Legs* and *Glass Slipper* (1954) and *Anything Goes* (1955), *La Chambre* (mus. Auric, 1955), film *Folies Bergère* (1956), revue *Zizi au music-hall* (1957), *Cyrano de Bergerac* (mus. Constant, 1959), film *Un-deux-trois* (with *Cyrano, Carmen, La Croqueuse de diamants*, and *Deuil en 24 heures*, 1960), *Maldoror* (mus. M. Jarre, 1962), *Notre-Dame-de-Paris* (mus. Jarre, Opéra, 1965), *Eloge de la folie* (mus. Constant, 1966), *Paradis perdu* (mus. Constant, Royal B., 1967), *Turangalîla* (mus. Messiaen, Opéra) and *L'estasi* (mus. Scriabin, La Scala, Milan, 1968), *Pelléas et Mélisande* (mus. Schoenberg, Royal B.) *Kraanerg* (mus. Xenakis, National B. of Can., both 1969), *Allumez les Etoiles* (various composers, 1972), *La Rose malade* (mus. Mahler, 1973), *Les Intermittences du coeur* (various composers, 1974), *Symphonie fantastique* (mus. Berlioz, 1975), *Coppélia* (new version, 1975), *Nana* (mus. Constant, 1976), *La Dame de pique* (mus. Tchaikovsky, 1977), *Le Fantôme de l'Opéra* (mus. M. Landowski, 1980), *La Chauve souris* (mus. Joh.

Strauss, 1980). Has revived several of his works for other cos. Father of the d. Valentine P. (b 1955). Chevalier dans l'ordre des arts et des lettres (1962); Chevalier de la Légion d'Honneur (1974).
BIBL.: I. Lidova, 'R.P.' with complete check-list of roles and activities, *Les Saisons de la danse* (Summer, 1968); *Ballet National de Marseille*—R.P. (Paris, 1981).

Petits rats. The children of the Paris Opéra B. School.

Petits riens, Les. Ballet Divertissement in 3 scenes; libr. and ch. Noverre; mus. Mozart. Prod. 11 June 1778, Opéra, Paris, with Guimard, Dauberval. The original libr. has been lost. According to a review in the *Journal de Paris* (12 June 1778), in the first scene Amor is caught by a shepherdess and imprisoned in a birdcage; in the second a shepherdess and a shepherd play blind man's buff; in the third Amor acts as matchmaker. Mozart's manuscript was rediscovered in the library of the Opéra in 1872, and has occasionally been rechoreographed, e.g. by Ashton (B. Rambert, 1928) and de Valois (Vic-Wells B., 1931).
BIBL.: P. Brinson and C. Crisp, 'L.p.r.' in *Ballet for all* (London, 1970).

Petroff, Paul (b Elsinore, 1908, d Antwerp, 27 Apr. 1981). Dan.-Amer. dancer and teacher. Studied with Katja Lindhart in Copenhagen. Début 1930. Became premier danseur of B. Russe de Monte Carlo, and later of Original B. Russe, B. Th., and International B. Then taught in Cal. Was married to the d. and teacher Nana Gollner.

Petrov, Nicolas (b Novi Sad, 13 Dec. 1933). Yugosl. dancer, choreographer, and b. director. Studied at Novi Sad Th. Academy D. Dept., Belgrade State B. Academy, and with various teachers in Paris, Geneva, and London. Member of National Popular Th., Novi Sad, 1946–51, Belgrade National Popular Th., 1951–4. Went to France in 1954; he d. with the cos. of Charrat, Grjebina, A. Galina, and Tcherina, with Massine's B. Europeo di Nervi, and on Fr. TV. B. master of Pittsburgh Playhouse School of the D. 1967–9; founder and artistic dir. of Pittsburgh B. Th. 1969. Has since ch. many bs. for the th., incl. the first Amer. full-length prod. of Prokofiev's *Romeo and Juliet*, Stravinsky's *Sacre du printemps*, and Beethoven's *Ninth Symphony*. Chairman of D. Dept. of Point Park College.
BIBL.: O. Maynard, 'Art and Academy—The Pittsburgh Ballet and Point Park College', *Dance Magazine* (1972/4).

Petrova, Ninel Alexandrovna (b Leningrad, 16 Mar. 1924). Sov. dancer and teacher. Studied at Leningrad Ch. School; graduated 1944. Joined Kirov B. and later became soloist. Retired 1968, and became a teacher at the Leningrad Ch. School. Merited Artist of the R.S.F.S.R. Married to the d. Askold Makarov.

Petrowa, Ludmila (b Ludmila Petrovna Nachey-

evna, Komsomolsk, 14 Feb. 1942). Sov. dancer and teacher. Studied at Leningrad B. School. Member of Bolshoi B. 1962–9. Further studies at Moscow GITIS with N. Tarasov, N. Kapustina, and O. Jordan. Teacher at Budapest State B. Inst. 1969–77 and since at Vienna State Op. B. and assoc. school, of which she became artistic dir. 1979.

Petrushka. Burlesque in 4 scenes; libr. Benois (also déc.) and Stravinsky (also mus.); ch. Fokine; cond. P. Monteux. Prod. 13 June 1911, B. Russe de Diaghilev, Th. du Châtelet, Paris, with Nijinsky, Karsavina, Orlov, Cecchetti. The b. is set in Admiralty Square, St. Petersburg, during Butterweek Fair 1830; the owner of a puppet theatre brings P. (the Russ. harlequin), the Ballerina, and the Moor to life; P. falls in love with the Ballerina; but she prefers the Moor, who kills P. Fokine revived the b. for many cos., incl. the B. Th. prod. of 1942. The Grigorievs staged his version for the Royal B. in 1957 and the BBC prod. a TV film of it in 1962. There have been many other versions, particularly in Germany, where the b. has been ch. e.g. by Georgi, Milloss, T. Gsovsky, and Walter.
BIBL.: C. W. Beaumont, 'P.' in *Complete Book of Ballets* (London, 1951); L. Kirstein, 'P.' in *Movement & Metaphor* (New York, 1970); P. portfolio, *Dance Magazine* (1970/2).

Phèdre. Tragedy in Choreography; libr. and déc. Cocteau; ch. Lifar; mus. Auric. Prod. 14 June 1950, Opéra, Paris, with Toumanova, Lifar, Darsonval, Roger Ritz (earlier perf. in May at Maggio Musicale Fiorentino). Cocteau based his libr. on Racine's version of the Greek legend of Theseus' wife, who fell in love with her stepson Hippolytus. Other b. treatments of the same subject by Angiolini (Milan, 1789), Didelot (mus. Cavos and Turik, St. Petersburg, 1825), Graham (mus. R. Starer, New York, 1962), and Cullberg (Swed. TV prod., *I Am not You*, mus. B. Brustad, 1966).
BIBL.: C. W. Beaumont, 'P.' in *Ballets Past & Present* (London, 1955).

Philadelphia Ballet. See *Littlefield, Catherine.*

Philippines. First accounts of dancing on the P. islands date back to Magellan's landing there 1521. Dances of the natives ranged from religious ceremonies to pure entertainment. Systematic research into folklorist traditions, however, started only during the 1920s, due to Francisca Reyes Aquino, who presented her finds in programmes arranged as part of the Physical Education syllabus. From these emerged the Filipino Folk Song and D. Troupe, based on the campus of the Univ. of the P., which in itself brought forth the P. Folk D. Society, established 1949. While Aquino concentrated on original research, Leonor Orosa-Goquingco used the material found for theatrical stylization, at first thought rather daring but now a common

practice, with *Filipinescas: Philippine Life, Legend, and Lore in Dance* as its model prod. From this came the Filipinescas Co., organized 1962. Even more successful was the *Bayanihan Philippine D. Co. which had its intern. breakthrough at the 1958 Brussels Expo. It was and still is the co. which has attracted the world's attention to the beauty, richness, dignity, colourfulness, and sensuousness of the P. d. lore. When the Americans took over from the Spanish at the turn of the last century, Amer. social d. was introduced to the islands and readily assimilated by the Filipinos. 1915 saw the first Manila presentation of classical b. by a troupe, calling itself Imperial Russ. B. This was followed by the Pavlova co. 1922, while the Denishawn co. made its local bow 1926. Various local schools were founded during the 1920s, incl. the Cosmopolitan B. and Dancing School of Luva Adameit. First attempts at establishing small-scale cos. of more or less amateur status resulted in the forming of the Hariraya D. Co., which later became the Hariraya B. Co. In addition Manila now counts among its top cos. the D. Th. P., Cultural Center of the P. D. Co., D. Concert Co., and Manila Metropolis B. Modern d. has caught on steadily since the 1930s. During the 1970s d. has spread vigorously to the provinces, too. April 1976 saw the establishment of the B. Federation of the P. as a pool organization of all the native personalities and institutions engaged in furthering the cause of b. in the islands. A first National B. Festival was held in Manila 1976 and has since become an annual event. In 1979 the restored Manila Metropolitan Th. opened its doors to the until then homeless 5 major Manila cos. Today visiting guests from abroad, incl. teachers, choreographers, individual dancers, and classical and modern cos. from all over the world are a regular part of the P. d. scene, while the Filipinos themselves have started to send abroad, not only the world-famous Bayanihan co., but also other ensembles like the C.C.P.D. Co. (headed by Alice Reyes) and individuals, of whom Reynaldo G. Alejandro has been the most influential pioneer in the dissemination of Filipino d. culture in the US.
BIBL.: R. G. Alejandro, *Philippine Dance* (Manila, 1976).

Phillips, Ailne (*b* Londonderry, 1905). Brit. dancer and teacher. Began to d. in the Carl Rosa Op. Co., directed by her father M. B. Phillips; eventually became première danseuse. D. with Vic-Wells B. 1931–7; then returned to Carl Rosa co., and later joined Inglesby's International B. Began teaching at Sadler's Wells B. School 1940. Became de Valois' personal asst. when the Sadler's Wells B. took up residence at Cov. Gdn. in 1946. Went to Turkey to teach in 1960. Retired in the mid-1960s, but still gives occasional classes at the Royal B. School.
BIBL.: G. Anthony, 'A.P.', *Dancing Times* (1971/6).

Picasso, Pablo Ruiz (*b* Malaga, 23 Oct. 1881, *d*

Mougins, 8 Apr. 1973). Span. painter. As a b. designer collaborated on Massine's *Parade* (1917), *Tricorne* (1919), *Pulcinella* (1920), and *Mercure* (1924), and the *Cuadro flamenco* prod. (1924). Designed the curtain for Nijinska's *Le Train bleu* (an enlargement of one of his paintings, 1924), Petit's *Le Rendez-vous* (1954), and Lifar's *L'après-midi d'un faune* (1960 for Paris Opéra, first used in Toulouse, 1965), and the déc. for Lifar's new version of *Icare* (1962).
BIBL.: P. issue, *Dance Index* (vol. V, no. 11); D. Cooper, *P.: Theatre* (Paris and London, 1967).

Pichler, Gusti (*b* Vienna, 10 Oct. 1893, *d* Vienna, 13 Apr. 1978). Austrian dancer. Studied at Vienna Court Op. B. School. Joined Court Op. B. 1908; prima ballerina 1925–35. Created roles in Kröller's *Josephslegende* (1922) and *Schlagobers* (1924), and Wallmann's *Fanny Elssler* (1934). Honorary member of Vienna State Op. (1935).

Pick, Günter (*b* Roetgen, 4 Nov. 1943). Ger. d., ch. and b. director. Studied with L. Renoldi in Aachen, then at Essen Folkwang School. Joined Folkwang Ballet 1965, d. with National B. of Canada 1966–8, Gelsenkirchen b. 1968–9, Düsseldorf b. 1969–71 and as guest soloist with various cos. B. dir. and chief ch. at Ulm th. 1973–8. Augsburg 1979–81. Since then freelancing as teacher and ch. Has collaborated several times with the comp. P. Henry (*Metamorphoses*, Paris Opéra, 1979; *Les Noces chymiques*, Paris Opéra, Comique, 1980, *Woyzeck*, Augsburg, 1981). Since 1985 b. dir. Munich Th. am Gärtnerplatz.

Picnic at Tintagel. Ballet in 1 act and 3 scenes; libr. and ch. Ashton; mus. Bax; déc. Beaton. Prod. 28 Feb. 1952, New York City B., City Center, N.Y., with Diana Adams, Moncion, and D'Amboise. The story of Tristan and Isolde, set at Tintagel in 1916, the year Bax comp. the mus., *The Garden of Fand*.
BIBL.: G. Balanchine, 'P.a.T.' in *Balanchine's New Complete Stories of the Great Ballets* (Garden City, N.Y., 1968); D. Vaughan, *Frederick Ashton and his Ballets* (London, 1977).

Picture of Dorian Gray. O. Wilde's novel (1890) has inspired several bs., e.g. by Bico von Larsky (mus. Scriabin, Augsburg, 1955), Orlikowsky (mus. M. Lang, Basle, 1966) and Layton (*Double Exposure*, mus. Scriabin and Pousseur, City Center Joffrey B., 1972). A prod. for the Sadler's Wells B. was planned by Helpmann in 1943 (libr. M. Benthill, déc. S. Fedorovich) but abandoned because the music proved unsatisfactory.

Pictures at an Exhibition. Mussorgsky's suite of piano pieces (1874) has inspired several bs. (mostly based upon Ravel's orchestral version), e.g. by Nijinska (B. International, New York, 1944), Hanka (Vienna State Op., 1947), Lopokov (Stanislavsky Th., Moscow, 1963), Neumeier (in a collage of the original, the orchestral arr., and the rock version of Emerson, Lake & Palmer, under the title *Unterwegs*, Frankfurt, 1972), and von Rosen (the Emerson, Lake & Palmer version, Gothenburg, 1972).

Pied Piper, The. Ballet in 2 parts; ch. Robbins; mus. Copland. Prod. 4 Dec. 1951, New York City B., City Center, N.Y., with D. Adams, Magallanes, Jillana, Bolender, Robbins. Set to Copland's Concerto for Clarinet and String Orchestra. The b. 'has nothing to do with the famous Pied Piper of Hamelin and refers instead to the clarinet soloist' (programme note). The dancers fall under the on-stage clarinettist's spell one after another, and become his puppets.
BIBL.: G. Balanchine, 'T.P.P.' in *Balanchine's New Complete Stories of the Great Ballets* (Garden City, N.Y., 1968).

Piège de lumière. Ballet in 1 act; libr. Philippe Hériat; ch. Taras; mus. J.-M. Damase; set Félix Labisse; cost. A. Levasseur. Prod. 23 Dec. 1952, Grand B. du Marquis de Cuevas, Th. de l'Empire, Paris, with Hightower, Golovine, Skouratoff. A group of escaped prisoners live in a tropical forest, catching butterflies; one of them catches the Queen of the Morphides, which poisons him, and in his madness he thinks he is a butterfly. Revived for various cos., incl. New York City B. (1964) and London Festival B. (1969).
BIBL.: C. W. Beaumont, 'P.d.l.' in *Ballets of Today* (London, 1954).

Pierrot lunaire. A cycle of melodramas by A. Schoenberg, set to poems by Albert Giraud. A highly mannerist work for speech-song and chamber group, about the Artist-Clown figure, comp. in 1912. Massine wanted to ch. it in 1922, omitting the vocal line, but Schoenberg refused, and a planned Cranko prod. in 1958 for Edinburgh International B. was forbidden by the Schoenberg estate. The first d. version was apparently ch. by Joffrey (R. Joffrey B. Concert, New York, 1955), but the version which entered the repertory was Tetley's, created for his first recital evening, with L. Hodes and R. Powell as the other dancers (déc. Ter-Arutunian, New York, 5 May 1962) and revived for several cos., incl. Netherlands D. Th. (1962), B. Rambert (1967), Royal Dan. B. (1968), Munich State Op. B. (1972), Stuttgart B. (1976).
BIBL.: P. Brinson and C. Crisp, in *Ballet & Dance* (Newton Abbot, 1980).

Piletta, Georges (*b* Paris, 13 Feb. 1945). Fr. dancer. Studied with his mother, Anna Stéphane, and then at Paris Opéra B. School. Joined Paris Opéra B. 1963; became premier danseur 1968 and étoile 1969. Created roles in Petit's *Turangalîla* (1968) and *Kraanerg* (1969), Blaska's *Deuxième concerto* (1970) and *Arcana* (1973), and Keuten's *Ionisation* (1973). Prix René Blum (1962) and Prix Printemps de Suède (1969).
BIBL.: O. Maynard, 'Spotlight on G.P.', *Dance Magazine* (Mar. 1973).

Pillar of Fire. Ballet in 1 act and 2 scenes; libr. and ch. Tudor; mus. Schoenberg; déc. Jo. Mielziner. Prod. 8 Apr. 1942, B. Th., Met. Op. House, New York, with Kaye, Chase, Lyon, Tudor, Laing. Based on Schoenberg's *Transfigured Night* (inspired by a poem by Richard Dehmel). The young woman Hagar fears that she will lose the man she loves to her flirtatious young sister; in desperation she gives herself to a stranger, but is forgiven by her real lover who shows her nothing but sympathy and understanding. Revived for Royal Swed. B. (1962) and Vienna State Op. B. (1969). Other prods. under the music's orig. title by Walter (Wuppertal, 1961), Kylián (Netherlands D. Th., 1975), and Petit (Opéra, Paris, 1976).
BIBL.: C. W. Beaumont, 'P.o.F.' in *Ballets Past & Present* (London, 1955).

Pilobolus Dance Theater. Amer. co. from Lochlyndon Farm, Verm., founded in 1971 by Moses Pendleton and Jonathan Wolken, later joined by Lee Harris and Robby Barnett and in 1973 by Alison Chase and Martha Clarke. Completely self-sufficient: its dances are conceived, ch., d., managed, and publicized by its members. Its energetic and dynamic style aims at a purely body-orientated synthesis of athletics, gymnastics, acrobatics, and modern d. movements, in the form of an 'energy circus'. First appeared in Eur. at the 1973 Edinburgh Festival.
BIBL.: I. M. Fanger, 'P.', *Dance Magazine* (July 1974); T. Mason, *P.* (New York, 1978).

Pineapple Poll. Ballet in 1 act and 3 scenes; libr. and ch. Cranko; mus. Sullivan (arr. Mackerras); déc. O. Lancaster. Prod. 13 Mar. 1951, Sadler's Wells Th. B., Sadler's Wells Th., London, with Fifield, Blair, Poole. Inspired by W. S. Gilbert's Bab Ballad *The Bumboat Woman's Story*. The girls of Portsmouth find Captain Belaye so irresistible that they disguise themselves as sailors and go on board H.M.S. Hot Cross Bun, where they discover that he has just married Blanche. BBC TV prod. 1959. Cranko revived the b. for many cos. incl. Borovansky B., Austral. B., National B. of Can., City Center Joffrey B., and Stuttgart B.
BIBL.: C. Beaumont, 'P.P.' in *Ballets of Today* (London, 1954).

Piollet, Wilfride (*b* Drôme, 28 Apr. 1943). Fr. dancer. Studied at Paris Opéra B. School. Joined Paris Opéra B. 1960; became soloist 1966 and étoile 1969. Created roles in Descombey's *Zyklus* (1968), Cunningham's *Un jour ou deux* (1973), Macdonald's *Variations on a Simple Theme* (1974). Guest ballerina of Bs. F. Blaska. Retired 1983. Married to the d. Jean Guizerix.
BIBL.: S. Dupuis, 'W.P.', with complete check-list of roles, *Les Saisons de la danse* (1978/4).

Piper, John (*b* 13 December 1903). Brit. painter. Designed the déc. for Ashton's *The Quest* (1943), de Valois' *Job* (revival 1948), and Cranko's *Sea Change* (1949), *Harlequin in April* (1951), *The*

Shadow (1953), and *Prince of the Pagodas* (sets only, 1957).

Piqué (Fr., pricked). Designates in b. a step directly on to the point, without bending the knee.

Pirouette (Fr., spinning-top). Designates in b. one or more turns of the body on one leg (on half or full point), with the point of the working leg generally touching the knee of the supporting leg. It can be executed à la seconde, en attitude, en arabesque, or sur le coup-de-pied.

Pistolets. See *Ailes de pigeon*.

Pistoni, Mario (*b* Rome, 11 Jan. 1932). Ital. dancer and choreographer. Studied at B. School of Teatro dell'Opera, Rome. Joined Teatro dell'Opera B. 1948; became soloist 1950 and principal d. 1951. Joined La Scala, Milan, 1951. Has ch. many bs., incl. *La Strada* (mus. N. Rota, 1966), *The Macbeths* (mus. R. Strauss, 1969), *Romeo and Juliet* (mus. Prokofiev, 1974), and *The Miraculous Mandarin* (mus. Bartók, 1981). Married to the d. Fiorella Cova.

Pitrot, Antoine Bonaventura (*b* Marseilles, probably in the 1720s, *d* after 1792). Fr. dancer and choreographer. A strikingly handsome and much sought-after performer; travelled all over Europe, continually involved in scandalous love affairs, brawls, and duels, so that the police records of the various cities give a clear account of his career! Though not a ch. of marked individuality, he was considered by his contemporaries as one of the pioneers of the b. d'action; he was apparently able to adapt quickly the discoveries of his more creative colleagues.
BIBL.: M. H. Winter, in *The Pre-Romantic Ballet* (London, 1974).

Pittsburgh Ballet Theatre. Founded in 1970 by N. Petrov, who was dir. and ch. the greater part of its repertory, incl. first Amer. full-length prod. of Prokofiev's *Romeo and Juliet*, Stravinsky's *Sacre du printemps*, and Beethoven's *Ninth Symphony*. Art. dir. since 1982 is P. Wilde.
BIBL.: O. Maynard, 'Art and Academe—The P.B. and Point Park College', *Dance Magazine* (1972/4); M. Hodgson, 'P.B.T.: Educating the Public', *Dance Magazine* (1975/2).

Pla, Mirta (*b* Havana *c.* 1940). Cub. dancer. Studied with the Alonsos, Fedorova, L. Fokine, Skeaping, Ivanova, and Parés. Début, co. of A. Alonso, 1953; appointed prima ballerina of National B. of Cuba 1962. D. Myrtha in Cuban film *Giselle* (1963), Cerrito in film *Grand Pas de quatre* (1971), and Sphinx in film *Edipo Rey* (1971). Silver Medals (Varna 1964 and 1966); Etoile d'or (Paris, 1970).
BIBL.: Complete check-list of roles and activities, *Cuba en el ballet* (vol. 3, no. 3).

Place, The. The former London headquarters of the Artists' Rifles Regiment, adjacent to St. Pancras Church, W.C.1; acquired in 1969 by *Contemporary D. Trust as the residence of the London School of Contemporary D. and its co., the London Contemporary D. Th. It houses a th., adaptable to various seating arrangements, several studios, and a canteen, and has since been enlarged and adapted to further d. use.
BIBL.: J. Percival, 'A Place for Dancing', *Dance Magazine* (1972/5).

Place, sur (Fr., on the spot). Not moving away from one's original position on the stage.

Placing. Perfect balance of carriage, according to the rules of the danse d'école.

Planets, The. Holst's orchestral suite (op. 32, 1915) has inspired several bs., incl. those of H. Kreutzberg (Berlin State Op., 1931), Tudor (Mars, Venus, Mercury, and Neptune, B. Rambert, 1934), and Walter (Vienna State Op., 1961).

Platoff, Marc (also M. Platt; *b* Seattle, Wash., 1915). Amer. dancer and choreographer. Studied with M. A. Wells. D. with de Basil's Bs. Russes de Monte Carlo and the Massine-Blum B. Russe de Monte Carlo. Original cast member *Oklahoma!* (1943). D. and ch. for many Hollywood films. Was d.-dir. of Radio City Music Hall B.

Playford, John (*b* Norwich, 1623, *d* London, 1686). Brit. mus. publisher. In 1651 published *The English Dancing Master: or, Plaine and easie rules for the Dancing of Country Dances, with the tunes to each dance*, the standard work of its time. Many editions up to 1728. Reprint London, 1957.

Playground. Ballet in 1 act; libr. and ch. MacMillan; mus. Gordon Crosse; déc. Y Sonnabend. Prod. 24 Aug. 1979, Sadler's Wells Royal B., The Tent, The Meadows, Edinburgh, with D. Kelly, M. Tait *et al.* 'The young man is attracted by "games" in a playground. He involves himself only to become captive' (MacMillan in his programme note).

Pleasant, Richard (*b* Denver, Col., 1906, *d* New York, 5 July 1961). Amer. b. director and artists' agent. Trained as an architect; worked in Hollywood as an artists' agent. Went to New York as manager of the Mordkin B., 1937. Organized B. Th. with the co.'s ballerina L. Chase; first perf. in 1940. Resigned as the co.'s dir. after its second season in 1941. After the war collaborated with I. Bennett in her public relations firm.

Plié (Fr., bent). In b. designates the bending of the knees, for instance before commencing or on landing from any jump; also particularly the exercise in which the knees are bent slowly, with the feet turned right out, heels firmly planted on the ground. It is the opening exercise of the daily class-routine and serves to loosen the muscles and tendons and to strengthen the dancer's balance.

Pli selon pli. Ballet in 5 parts; ch. Béjart; mus. Boulez; déc. J. Roustan and R. Bernard. Prod. 22

Oct. 1975, B. of the 20th Century, Th. Royal de la Monnaie, Brussels, with K. Kharkevitch, A. Ziemski, I. Marko, L. Glauber, L. Bouy, D. Gray-Cullert, A. Albrecht, G. Wilk, R. Poelvoorde, B. Pie, J.-M. Bourvron, D. Lommel. The b. is based on Boulez' *Portrait de Mallarmé*. Of its 5 parts 'Mallarmé III' was first shown at the 1973 Shiraz Festival, while 'Tombeau' was premièred by the co. on a guest visit to Milan in Dec. 1973; 'Don', 'Mallarmé I', and 'Mallarmé II' were added for the first complete Brussels prod. Béjart has described it as 'a non-figurative work based exclusively upon the relationship of music and gesture, while the poetry which originally inspired the music transforms constantly the abstract universe of the d. and lends it a special splendour.' Part of the same mus. was used by D. Mendel in *Improvisations sur Mallarmé* (Ger. Op. Berlin, 1961) and D. Reiter-Soffer in *Women* (Irish B., 1974). Béjart's 'Mallarmé III' also appears as the centrepiece of his TV film *Je t'aime, tu danses* (1973).

Plisetskaya, Maya Michailovna (*b* Moscow, 20 Nov. 1925). Sov. dancer. Niece of Asaf and Sulamith Messerer, cousin of their designer son Boris Messerer, sister of the d. Azari Plisetsky. Studied at Moscow Bolshoi B. School; appeared as a student in some perfs. at the Bolshoi B.'s Filial Th., where her exceptional virtuosity attracted immediate attention. Graduated in 1943; joined the Bolshoi B. as a soloist, and became ballerina in 1945. During the following years she d. all the standard ballerina roles; particularly admired as Odette-Odile, Kitri, Raymonda, the Tsarevna in *The Humpbacked Horse* (also in the film of 1961) and the Dying Swan. A dazzling technician, to whom nothing seems impossible; her arms and hands are uniquely supple. Also a spellbinding actress (appeared in several straight film roles, e.g. *Anna Karenina*, 1968). She created the Mistress of the Copper Mountain in Lavrovsky's *Stone Flower* (1954), Aegina in Moiseyev's *Spartacus* (1958), and—the role with which she has been most closely identified—Carmen in A. Alonso's *Carmen* (1967); also Petit's *La Rose malade* (Paris, 1973) and Leda (ch. Béjart, 1979). Her first ch. was *Anna Karenina* (with N. Ryzhenko and V. Smirnov-Golovanov, mus. Shchedrin, 1972), followed by *The Seagull* (after Tchechov, mus. Shchedrin, 1980); Sov. film version, with herself in the title role, 1974. Appears as d. and actress in the Sov. film *Vernal Floods* (1975). Sov. TV film about her, *P. Dances*, 1966. B. dir. Rome Op. 1983–6. Lenin Prize (1964); D. Magazine Award (1965); awarded Hero of Socialist Labour (1985). Married to the comp. Rodion Shchedrin.
BIBL.: N. Roslavleva, *M.P.* (Moscow, 1956—in Eng.); J. Baril, 'M.P.' with complete check-list of roles and activities, *Les Saisons de la danse* (1968/10); G. Feifer, 'P. Portrait', *Dance News* (1971/11–1972/3); interview with M.P., *Dancing Times* (1972/2).

Plucis, Harijs (*b* Riga, 1900, *d* Vienna, 21 Feb. 1970). Latvian dancer and teacher. Studied at the local b. school. Joined Riga Op. B. 1920 and eventually became principal d. Studied further with Legat in Paris; joined Rubinstein's co. 1928. Returned to Riga 1931; founded State B. School 1932, and directed it until 1944. B. master of Sadler's Wells B. 1947–56. Teacher at Zurich B. Academy 1957–61; then in charge of the Vienna State Op. B. School until his death. His son Andris P. is now dancing with the Frankfurt B.

Plunkett, Adeline (*b* Brussels, 31 Mar. 1824, *d* Paris, 8 Nov. 1910). Belg. dancer. Studied in Paris with Barrez. Appeared in Trieste and in London at Her Majesty's Th. and Drury Lane Th. Became a principal d. at the Opéra, Paris, 1845; created roles in Coralli's *Ozaï, ou l'insulaire* (1847), Mabille's *Nisida, ou les Amazones des Açores* (1848), and Mazilier's *Vert-Vert* (1851). Retired 1857.
BIBL.: I. Guest, in *The Romantic Ballet in Paris* (London, 1965).

Poelvoorde, Rita (*b* Antwerp, 23 Feb. 1951). Belg. dancer. Studied at Royal Flemish B. School; member of Netherlands D. Th. 1969–71. Joined B. of the 20th Century and later became soloist; created roles in Béjart's *Le Marteau sans maître* (1973), 'I trionfi'di Petrarca (1974). Appeared with Béjart in the Belg. TV film *Je t'aime, tu danses* (1973). Second Prize, junior category (Varna, 1968).
BIBL.: L. Gordon, 'Profil de R.P.', *Les Saisons de la danse* (May 1973).

Poème de l'extase. Ballet in 2 parts; libr. and ch. Cranko; mus. Scriabin and Fortner; déc. Rose. Prod. 24 Mar. 1970, Stuttgart, with Fonteyn, Madsen, Stripling, Berg, Clauss, Cragun. 'Among the guests at a soirée given by a famous Diva there is a young man who falls in love with her. Although she is at first flattered by his attentions, she gradually recalls her former loves. Finally she realises that her life has already been fulfilled and she rejects the young man' (programme note). Inspired by Colette's novel *La Naissance du jour* and visually by the Vienna *Jugendstil* painter Gustav Klimt. Fortner orchestrated Scriabin's 9th piano sonata as a prologue. Revived for Fonteyn with Royal B. 1972. Other b. versions, using the same mus., by Sokolow (New York, 1956), R. Wagner (New York, 1963), Petit (Milan, 1968), Keres (Wiesbaden, 1969), and Beatty (Cullberg B., 1971).

Pointe (or Point). To d. on point means at the extreme tip of the toe; b. terminology differentiates between *sur la pointe* (on full point), *à trois quarts* (raised on the flexed toes), *à demi* (on the ball of the foot), and *à quart* (on the full ball of the foot, with hardly raised heels). Historians disagree about who was the first d. to appear on full point. The Fr. critic Castil-Blaze quotes contemporary accounts of Mlle. Gosselin (*d* 1818) standing up 'for a full minute' on point. Istomina is also said to have d. 'fully on points' before 1820.

A Waldeck etching of 1821 shows F. Bias in *Flore et Zéphyre* on point. A. Brugnoli was much admired for her point technique in the 1820s in Milan and Vienna. M. Taglioni raised dancing on points from a virtuoso stunt to a feat of sublime artistry and poetry. It was a marvellous means for the expression of the aims of the Romantic movement, starting with Taglioni's appearance in *La Sylphide* 1832. It also made possible the perfection of the pirouette technique. During its early years no special point shoes existed; the dancers padded their shoes with cotton wool and darned their points, to give them more stability. Modern point shoes, with their toes stiffened with glue ('blocked'), began to appear during the 1860s. They are still darned by the dancers themselves, who also sew on the ankle ribbons. Point d. is rare for men, but it was used by Nijinsky in *Les Fâcheux* (1924) and Ashton in *The Dream* (1964) to characterize certain roles. The cossacks of Georgia and the Ukraine have practised it for centuries, wearing soft boots—although they most often d. with their toes bent under, so that they really land on the 'knuckles' of the toes.

Poker Game. See *Jeu de cartes.*

Polajenko, Nicholas (*b* New York, 15 Dec. 1932). Amer. dancer and b. master. Studied with Schollar and Vilzak. Début Ottawa B. Co. 1947. Came to Europe; joined Met. B. 1948. Later d. with Bs. des Champs-Elysées, Bs. de Paris, Met. Op. B., and London Festival B.; then as principal d. with Grand B. du Marquis de Cuevas, 1956–62. Also d. with Harkness B. and Golovine's Geneva B. Asst. professor at D. Dept., Point Park College, Pittsburg. Appointed b. master Houston B. 1974.

Poland. Before 1918 there was little b. apart from the *Warsaw Grand Th. Among the first cos. established outside the capital was that attached to the Poznań Grand Th. in 1919; Maksymilian Statkiewicz (*b* 1889) ch. the first Pol. prod. of K. Szymanowski's b. *Harnasie* (1938). Another co. was attached to the Grand Th. in Lvov, and J. Cieplinski led an independent co. 1922–4. Between the two World Wars Duncan, E. Jaques-Dalcroze, and Wigman had a strong influence and there were many private schools where their different systems were taught, especially those of Janina Mieczyńska and Stefan and Tacjana Wysocki in Warsaw. Today there are 6 cos. of between 50 and 100 dancers, attached to the op. houses, 2 smaller cos. attached to mus. ths., 7 attached to operetta ths., and 1 independent co. Furthermore the Mazowsze, Slask, and Central Ensemble of the Pol. Army have their own d. groups. Outside Warsaw there are b. cos. attached to the National Op. at Poznań (founded 1945, b. dir. Barbara Kasprowicz), Op. of Silesia at Bytom (founded 1946, Henryk Kowiński), National Op. of Wroclaw (founded 1946, Teresa Kujawa 1971–4, vacant in 1975), Baltic Op. of Gdańsk (founded

1950, Janina Jarzynówna Sóbczak), National Op. of Łódź (founded 1954, since 1967 called Grand Th., Witold Borkowski). The Pol. d. Th. of Poznań was founded in 1973 (dir. Conrad Drzewiecki). The National B. Schools were reorganized in 1949; there are now 4, in Warsaw, Poznań, Bytom, and Gdańsk. They are free of charge, and they run 9-year courses, after which the students get their baccalaureate and professional diploma. Since 1972 the Warsaw High School of Mus. has run a special department for future d. teachers, headed by Zbigniew Korycki. There is close collaboration with the Moscow GITIS and the Ch. Faculty at the Leningrad Conservatory.

Poliakova, Yelena Dimitrievna (*b* St. Petersburg, 1884, *d* Santiago, 25 July 1972). Russ. dancer, teacher, and b. mistress. Studied at St. Petersburg Imperial B. Academy; graduated 1902. Joined Maryinsky Th.; also appeared with Diaghilev in Paris 1909. Prima ballerina of the Op. B., Belgrade, 1920. Started to teach while in Russia (where Nikitina was among her pupils) and continued in Belgrade; her students included Youskevitch, Roje, and Parlić. Went to Chile 1949; appointed b. mistress of National B. of Chile 1958. Presented her library to Santiago's Teatro Municipal, which, on the initiative of C. Robilant, named its d. archive after her in 1965.

Polka. From Czech *tanec na polo*, half-step d. A popular Bohemian d., originating from the early 19th century, in quick duple time, with steps on the first 3 half-beats and a hop on the 4th. As a round d. it quickly spread through the ballrooms of Eur., and entered the Paris Opéra in 1844, when Maria and Eugene Coralli d. a p. specially comp. by Burgmüller. There is also a mixture of p. and mazurka, called p.-mazurka, in 3/4 time.

Poll, Heinz (*b* Oberhausen, 18 Mar. 1926). Ger.-Amer. dancer, teacher, choreographer, and b. director. Studied at Essen Folkwang School and with T. Gsovsky, E. Poliakova, and N. Kiss. Started to d. at Göttingen Municipal Th.; d. with East Berlin State Op. B. 1948–50, then National B. of Chile 1951–61, since when he has worked with various Fr., Can., and Amer. cos. Taught at the Chilean Instituto de Extensio Mus. and the New York National Academy of B.; became founder-dir. of the Ohio Chamber Ballet in 1967, now the Ohio B., and teacher at the affiliated D. Institute of the Univ. of Akron, Ohio.

Polonaise. A festive Polish national d. in 3/4 time, with a rhythm not unlike the Bolero. Originally possibly a triumphal d. of homecoming warriors or a choral d. of peasants; certainly d. when August the Strong was crowned as King of Poland in 1697. Specially popular as the opening processional d. of a ball, led by a couple who initiate the patterns to be executed (snail, spiral, shell, fan, star, etc).

Polovtsian Dances. See *Prince Igor.*

Pomare, Eleo (*b* Cartagena, Colombia, 22 Oct. 1937). Amer. dancer and choreographer. Studied with Limón, Horst, Curtis James, and Jooss. Founded his own modern d. co. in 1958. His works incl. *Narcissus Rising* (tape-collage, 1968), *Las Desenamoradas* (after García Lorca's *The House of Bernarda Alba*, mus. J. Coltrane, 1970), *Burnt Ash* (mus. collage M. Levy), and *Black on Black* (poems, 1971).
BIBL.: R. Estrada, 'E.P.', *Dance Magazine* (1968/11).

Pomarès, Jean (*b* L'Alma, Algeria, 12 Dec. 1943). Fr. dancer, choreographer, teacher, and notator. Studied in Paris with Diane Blake, Amala Devi, and Waehner, and in London with Guru Kelu Nayar and at Institute of Choreology. D. with Bs. Contemporains de K. Waehner. Appeared with his own group Askew in London and France 1972–3. Now works mainly as a freelance ch. of fringe events, often collaborating with Giovanni di Testa as designer and Jean-Yves Bosseur as comp. Prize for best co. (Bagnolet, 1973).

Pomiès, Georges (*b* Paris, 27 July 1902, *d* Dreux, 7 Oct. 1933). Fr. actor and dancer. Started as a parodist of music hall stars and became known as France's first self-taught modern d. during the late twenties. Appeared in recitals together with Lisa Duncan, performing contemporary characters (*Rugby, Tennis, Boxe*), also d. without mus. Participated in various films and established a school in Versailles. A highly versatile artist with widely varied talents.
BIBL.: var. authors, *Danser c'est vivre—G.P.*, Paris, no year).

Pomona. Ballet in 1 act; ch. Ashton; mus. Lambert; déc. John Banting. Prod. 19 Oct. 1930, Camargo Society, Cambridge Th., London, with Anna Ludmila, Dolin. Revived for Vic-Wells B. 1933 and 1937. An earlier version by Nijinska (Buenos Aires, 1927).
BIBL.: D. Vaughan, *Frederick Ashton and his Ballets* (London, 1977).

Pongor, Ildikó (*b* Budapest, 17 Jan. 1953). Hung. dancer. Studied at Budapest State B. Inst. and Leningrad Ch. School. Joined Budapest State Op. B. 1972, becoming soloist 1974. Third Prize, junior category (Varna, 1970 and 1972).

Ponomaryov, Vladimir Ivanovich (*b* St. Petersburg, 22 July 1892, *d* Budapest, 21 Mar. 1951). Sov. dancer and teacher. Studied at St. Petersburg Imperial B. Academy; graduated 1910 (having previously appeared in perfs. of the Maryinsky Th.). Joined Maryinsky Th.; became principal d. 1912. D. with Diaghilev's co. 1911–2. Began teaching in 1913; became one of the most admired teachers of the young generation of Sov. male dancers. His pupils include Gusev, K. Sergeyev, Chaboukiani, Lavrovsky, and Zakharov. Merited Artist of R.S.F.S.R. (1934).

Pontois, Noëlla (*b* Vendôme, 24 Dec. 1943). Fr.

dancer. Studied at Paris Opéra B. School. Joined Paris Opéra B. 1960; became première danseuse 1966 and étoile 1968. Frequently appears as guest ballerina abroad (London Festival B. 1967, Vienna State Op., etc.). Prix Pavlova (1969); Chevalier de la Légion d'Honneur (1975). Retired 1983, now makes guest appearances. Married to the d. Daïni Kudo.
BIBL.: J. C. Diénis, 'N.P.', with complete check-list of roles and activities, *Les Saisons de la danse* (1973/1).

Poole, David (*b* Cape Town, 17 Sep. 1925). S.A. dancer and b. director. Studied with D. Howes and C. Robinson, then at Sadler's Wells B. School. Joined Sadler's Wells Th. B. 1947; became principal d. 1948. Created roles in Cranko's *Sea Change* and *Beauty and the Beast* (both 1949), *Pineapple Poll* (1951), and *The Lady and The Fool* (1954), Rodrigues's *Blood Wedding* (1953) and MacMillan's *Danses concertantes* and *House of Birds* (both 1955). Left Sadler's Wells B. 1955; later d. with B. Rambert (1956) and Edinburgh International B. (1958), creating roles in Gore's *The Night and the Silence* and Wright's *The Great Peacock*. Returned to S.A. as a teacher. Appointed b. master of Cape Town Univ. B. 1963 and dir. 1969.

Popa, Magdalena (*b* Bucharest, 19 June 1941). Rum. dancer. Studied at Bucharest State B. School and Leningrad Ch. School. Joined Bucharest State Op. B. 1961; later became prima ballerina. Has also appeared as guest ballerina abroad (B. Th. Contemporain, Grand B. Classique de France, etc.). Silver Medal (Varna, 1964); Etoile d'or (Paris, 1965).

Popescu, Gabriel (*b* Bucharest, 15 Mar. 1932). Rum. dancer and b. master. Studied at Bucharest State B. School. Joined Bucharest State Op. B. 1951. Principal d., Zurich Op. B., 1965–75; has also ch. some bs.

Popko, Nicolai Mikhailovich (*b* 1911, *d* 1966). Sov. dancer, choreographer, and b. master. Studied at Moscow Bolshoi B. School; graduated 1930. D. with Bolshoi B. 1930–56. Ch. *The Little Stork* (mus. Klebanov, 1937), *Svetlana* (mus. Klebanov, 1939) and *Red Sails* (mus. Yurovsky, 1942), all with Pospekhin and Radunsky.

Popova, Nina (*b* Novorossisk, 20 Oct. 1922). Sov.-Amer. dancer, teacher, and b. director. Studied with T. Wassilieff, Preobrajenska, Egorova, Vilzak, Oboukhoff, and Schwezoff. Started to d. with B. de la Jeunesse 1938, later with Original B. Russe (1940–1), B. Th. (1941–3), and B. Russe de Monte Carlo (1943–5). Worked for TV and on Broadway. Supervisor of B. Dept. and principal teacher at New York High School of Performing Arts 1954–67. Founder and art. dir. of the Houston B. and chairman and teacher at its B. Academy 1968–75.

Porcile, Mario (*b* Genoa, 29 Aug. 1921). Ital. dance promoter. Artistic director of Nervi B.

Festival since 1955. Dir. of Genoa Academy of Classic D. since 1964. Coordinator of the d. activities at Nervi Festival, Arena di Verona, Teatro Regio di Torino, and Teatro La Fenice of Venice. Member of numerous intern. d. committees. L'Ordre des Arts et des Lettres (1984).

Port de bras. (Fr., carriage of the arms). There are 5 positions, corresponding to those of the feet.

Porter, Marguerite (b Doncaster, 1950). Brit. dancer. Studied locally, joining Royal B. School in 1965 and graduating two years later. Joined Royal B. 1967, switching over to its touring section 1972, but returning as a soloist to the Cov. Gdn. co. 1973, promoted principal d. 1978. Created roles in MacMillan's *Manon* (1974), *The Four Seasons* (1975), and *Mayerling* (1978), Van Manen's *Four Schumann Pieces* (1975), and Ashton's *Month in the Country* (1976). She danced the ballerina roles of the classical repertory. Resigned 1985, but continued guest appearances.
BIBL.: Interview *Dance and Dancers* (1979/4).

Portugal. See *Gulbenkian Ballet* and *Lisbon*.

Pose. A stationary position of the d.

Posé. (Fr., placed). Designates in b. stepping from one foot to the other, with a straight knee, onto a flat foot; also on half or full point, either forwards, sideways, or backwards.

Positions. See *Five Positions*.

Pospekhin, Lev Alexandrovich (b Moscow, 23 Mar. 1909). Sov. dancer, choreographer, and b. master. Studied at Moscow Bolshoi B. School; graduated 1928. Joined Bolshoi B. and became one of its best character dancers. Ch.—with Radunsky and Popko—*The Little Stork* (mus. Klebanov, 1937), *Svetlana* (mus. Klebanov, 1939) and *Red Sails* (mus. Yurovsky, 1942). After ending his career as a d., became repetiteur at the Bolshoi B. Merited Artist of the R.S.F.S.R. (1966).

Potts, Nadia (b London, 20 Apr. 1948). Can. dancer. Studied at National B. of Can. School. Joined National B. of Canada 1966; became soloist 1969 and principal d. 1972. Bronze Medal (Varna, 1970). Retired 1986.

Poulenc, Francis (b Paris, 7 Jan. 1899, d there, 30 Jan. 1963). Fr. composer. With his colleagues of Les Six, contributed to Börlin's *Les Mariés de la Tour Eiffel* (1921). Wrote the mus. for Nijinska's *Les Biches* (1924) and *Aubade* (1929), and Lifar's *Les Animaux modèles* (1942). P. Wright used his Sinfonietta for *Summer's Night* (1964), Cauley his Sonata for Clarinet and Piano and Sonata for Oboe and Piano for *In the Beginning* (1969), E. Walter his Organ Concerto for *Gravité* (1969—also Tetley for *Voluntaries*, 1973) and MacMillan his *Gloria* (1980).

Poulsen, Aage (b Copenhagen, 4 July 1943). Dan. dancer. Studied at Royal Dan. B. School. Joined Royal Dan. B.; became solo d. 1968.

Poulsen, Ulla (b Copenhagen, 2 May 1905). Dan. dancer and teacher. Studied at Royal Dan. B. School. Joined Royal Dan. B. 1921; became solo d. 1923. Left the co. in 1927 to d. as guest ballerina with various cos. in Scandinavia, France, and Germany; returned 1934–9, and continued to work as a teacher until 1947.

Poupon, Michèle (b Biel, 27 July 1940). Swiss dancer. Studied with Erna Mohar, Pilato, Lifar, Olga Stens, and Léon Anlen. D. with the cos. in Bonn 1955–6, Lübeck 1956–8, Oberhausen 1959–60, Gelsenkirchen 1960–7; prima ballerina in Essen 1967–81.

Pourfarrokh, Ali (b Kermanshah, 27 Nov. 1938). Iranian dancer, b. master and b. director. Studied at Teheran D. Academy and in the U.S. at Metropolitan Op. B. School, School of Amer. B. Th. and Graham School. Started to d. with Alicia Alonso's California Group, joined Amer. B. Th. 1959–63, continuing with Metropolitan Op. B., Harkness B., Frankfurt B., and Joffrey B. Appointed assoc. dir. and b. master of A. Ailey D. Th. 1972–6, then artistic dir. of Iranian National B. 1976–9. B. master Essen (Ger.) and since 1986 art. dir. Dance Th. of Long Island.

Powell, Ray (b Hitchin, 1925). Brit. dancer and b. master. Studied at Sadler's Wells B. School. Member of Sadler's Wells B. 1941–4; rejoined 1947 after military service, becoming soloist 1948. Created roles in Ashton's *The Quest* (1943) and *Madame Chrysanthème* (1955), de Valois's *Promenade* (1943) and *Don Quixote* (1950), A. Howard's *Veneziana* (1953), and Cranko's *Prince of the Pagodas* (1957). Ch. *One in Five* (mus. Johann and Joseph Strauss, 1960) and some later works. Appointed b. master Austral B. 1962, and later the co.'s associate dir. (with B. Ashbridge).

Powell, Robert (b Hawaii, 1941 d New York, 24 Oct. 1977). Amer. d. Studied at High School of Performing Arts. Began dancing with Graham co. 1958; later became soloist. Created roles in Graham's *Acrobats of God* (1960), *Secular Games* (1962), *Circe* (1963), *Plain of Prayer, A Time of Snow*, and *The Archaic Hours* (all 1968). Has also d. with G. Tetley (created Brighella in *Pierrot Lunaire*, 1962), and with the cos. of P. Taylor, J. Limón, L. Falco, D. McKayle, B. Ross, Ailey, and with London Contemporary D. Th., where he created leading role in Cohan's *Cell* (1969). Was Assoc. Dir. of Graham co.
BIBL.: M. Last, 'He's Got Feet Down Below His Knees', *Dance Magazine* (1970/11).

Praagh, Dame Peggy van (b London, 1 Sep. 1910). Brit. dancer, teacher, and b. director. Studied with Aimée Phipps, Craske, Sokolova, Volkova, Karsavina, Bodenwieser, and de Mille. D. as soloist with B. Rambert 1933–8, then with Tudor's London B. Created roles in his bs. *Jardin aux Lilas* (1936), *Dark Elegies* (1937), *Soirée Musicale, Gala Performance* (both 1938), and *The*

Planets (extended version, 1939). At the beginning of the war became joint dir. with M. Lloyd of the London B., revived initially for lunch-time performances during the Blitz. Principal d., Sadler's Wells B., 1941. Appointed b. mistress of the newly established Sadler's Wells Th. B. 1946; Asst. Dir. 1951–5. Then did some freelance work (also for TV); mounted bs. of the Royal B. repertory for Eur. and overseas countries. Directed the Edinburgh International B. 1958. Became Artistic Dir. of Borovansky B. (Austral.) 1963; Artistic Dir. of Austral. B. 1963–74. Author of *How I Became a Dancer* (London, 1954) and—with P. Brinson—*The Choreographic Art* (London, 1963). C.B.E. (1966); D.B.E. (1970); Hon Dr. of Letters, Univ. of New South Wales, Armidale (1974); Distinguished Artist Award of Austral. Art Circle (1975).

BIBL.: K. S. Walker, 'A Sort of Dedication', *Dancing Times* (1974/12).

Prague. Dance perfs. are first mentioned in the second half of the 16th century. B. perfs. at Czech and Moravian castles were given either by foreign troupes or by groups of serfs. Some Ital. dancers came to Bohemia during the later 17th century. Strolling comedians from Italy and Germany had bs. and pantomimes in their repertory. The city opened its first regular b. in 1724; ops. and occasionally bs. were performed. At the th. in Kotce, opened 1737, bs. and pantomimes were given; during the second half of the 18th century excerpts from Noverre bs. were mounted there by the Noverre pupil Vojtech Moravec (Alberti). Bs. by Czech composers, e.g. Jírovec, Koželuh, Vranický and others, however, were mostly prod. abroad. During the first half of the 19th century the city was visited by a number of guest cos. and individual artists. In 1838 Johann Raab gave the first stage perf. of the polka. The Romantic b. arrived in P. rather late. *La Sylphide* was first perf. at the Tyl Th. in 1850; Grahn visited the city, dancing in several Romantic bs., in the same year. The first independent Czech th., the Prozatímni divadlo, opened in 1862 with Václav Reisinger (who later created *Swan Lake* in Moscow) as b. master. He became the first b. master of the National Th., inaugurated 1881, and ch. the first prod. of Karel Kovařovic's *Hashish* in 1884. He was succeeded by Augustin Berger, who ch. the second act of *Swan Lake* (which Tchaikovsky saw when he visited P. in 1888) and the first prod. of Janáček's *Rákoš Rakoczy* (1891). Towards the end of the 19th century the dominance of Ital. influence culminated in the prod. of Manzotti's *Excelsior*. Achille Viscusi, an excellent teacher, was the b. master in charge of the first local complete perf. of *Swan Lake* (1907), and ch. many of N. O. Nedbal's bs. Berger was b. master again 1912–22, followed by Remislav Remislavský 1922–7, who ch. the first prods. of Martinů's *Istar* and F. Skvor's *Doktor Faust*. Diaghilev's Bs. Russes visited P. in 1927. National composers became

more interested in b. during the 1920s and 1930s; Jaroslav Hladík ch. Novák's *Signorina Gioventù* and *Nikotina* (both 1930), and Josef Jenčík created Martinů's *Spaliček* (1933) and Bořkovec's *The Pied Piper* (1942). After 1945 the Sov. school of teachers and choreographers became increasingly influential. B. masters of the National Th. were Saša Machov (1946–51; Prokofiev's *Romeo and Juliet* and Vostřák's *Viktorka*, both 1950), Vlastimil Jílek (1951–3), Antonín Landa (1953–7), Jiří Němeček (1957–70; Burghauser's *Servant of Two Masters*, 1958, and Hanuš's *Othello*, 1959), Emerich Gabzdyl (1970–73; Stravinsky's *Sacre du printemps*, 1972), and now J. Němeček again. The Royal B. visited P. in 1947 and 1966, the Kirov B. in 1959, the Budapest State Op. B. in 1964, the Merce Cunningham co. in 1964, and the Bolshoi B. in 1967 and 1975. See also *Prague Ballet*.

BIBL.: L. Schmidová, *Ceskoslovenský Balet* (Prague, 1962).

Prague Ballet (Czech: Balet Praha). The co. was founded in autumn 1964 by the 2 chs. Ogoun and Smok and critic Vladimír Vašut; début 23 Apr. 1965, Prague Th. of Nusle. Planned as a chamber-size troupe with experimental ambitions; became a workshop of contemp. Czech ch., with a repertory dominated by the bs. of Ogoun and Smok. Frequent foreign tours; first appeared in Britain 1969. Disbanded 1970. Revived gradually during the mid-1970s as P. Chamber B., with Šmok as dir.-ch. Obtained govt. funding 1983.

Prebil, Zarko (*b* Split, 1934). Yugosl. dancer, choreographer, and b. master. Studied at Zagreb State B. School. D. with Zagreb Op. B. 1951–5 and Belgrade State Op. B. 1955–65. Studied further at GITIS, Moscow; graduated as a teacher and ch. Has mounted several prods. of the b. classics for various cos. since 1968 (e.g. Rome Teatro dell'Opera, Naples Teatro San Carlo, Dutch National B.)

Premier danseur. (Fr., leading [male] dancer). The female equivalent is première danseuse. The hierarchy of the Paris Opéra has one higher rank: premier danseur (première danseuse) étoile (star d.).

Preobrajenska, Olga Josifovna (properly Preobrajenskaya; *b* St. Petersburg, 2 Feb. 1870, *d* Saint-Mandé, 27 Dec. 1962). Russ.-Fr. dancer and teacher. Studied at St. Petersburg Imperial B. Academy; graduated 1889. Joined Maryinsky Th.; became soloist 1896 and prima ballerina 1900. Appeared in about 700 perfs.; a splendid technician. Her best roles were in *Coppélia*, *Raymonda*, *The Seasons*, *Le Corsaire*, *Sleeping Beauty*, *Paquita*, *Nutcracker*, *The Talisman*, *Sylvia*, and *Don Quixote*. Frequently appeared abroad after 1895. Began teaching in 1914. Left Sov. Union in 1921; taught in Milan, London, Buenos Aires, and Berlin. Settled permanently in Paris 1923; became one of the most respected teachers at the Studio

Wacker. Baronova, Toumanova, Youskevitch, Skibine, Golovine, and Miskovitch were among her most famous students. Retired 1960. As a ballerina she dominated the b. in Russia during the first 2 decades of the 20th century; as a teacher she formed several generations of Europe's best dancers.

Preobrajensky, Vladimir Alexeievich (*b* St. Petersburg, 21 Jan. 1912, *d* Moscow, 24 Feb. 1981). Sov. dancer and teacher. Studied at Leningrad B. School; graduated 1931; d. with Kirov Th. until 1935. Went to Sverdlovsk as a teacher. Principal d. Kiev 1939–43, then Bolshoi B. until 1963; became Lepechinskaya's partner. Became head of the d. dept. of the Moscow concert organization. Stalin Prize (1946).

Préparation. (Fr., preparation). Designates in b. getting into position for a movement requiring special effort, e.g. a pirouette.

Présages, Les. Ballet in 4 movements; libr. and ch. Massine; mus. Tchaikovsky; déc. André Masson. Prod. 13 Apr. 1933, Colonel de Basil's B. Russe, Monte Carlo, with Verchinina, Baronova, Riabouchinska, Lichine, Woizikovsky. Set to Tchaikovsky's Fifth Symphony. Massine's first symphonic b. It depicts man's struggle with his destiny; the 4 parts are entitled: Action—Passion—Frivolity—War.
BIBL.: C. W. Beaumont, 'L.P.' in *Complete Book of Ballets* (London, 1951).

Présence. Ballet in 1 act; libr. and ch. Cranko; mus. B. A. Zimmermann; déc. Jürgen Schmidt-Oehm. Prod. 16 May 1968, Stuttgart B., Schwetzingen Festival, with Haydée, Cragun, Clauss. Set to Zimmermann's *Concerto scénique pour violon, violoncello et piano*. Relationships are explored between Molly (Bloom), Roy (Roi Ubu), and Don (Quixote), symbols of sex, power, and idealism. Second Channel Ger. TV prod. 1970. Revived for Munich State Op. B. 1970. Different prod. of the same b. by Bohner (Darmstadt, 1972).
BIBL.: J. Percival, 'P.' in P. Brinson and C. Crisp, *Ballet for all* (London, 1970).

Prévost, Françoise (*b* probably Paris, c. 1680, *d* Paris 1741). Fr. dancer. Début in Lully's *Atys*, Opéra, 1699. The foremost Fr. prima ballerina for 30 years; her lightness, elegance, and expressiveness were much admired. One of the first dancers to use mus. not specially comp. for dancing.

Price. A Dan. family of Eng. extraction, which prod. a number of dancers, mimes, actors, and music-hall artists from the end of the 18th to the beginning of the 20th century. Juliette P. (1831–1906) was one of the leading ballerinas of the Dan. b. She created Bournonville's *Konservatoriet* in 1849; Bournonville cast her in the most important roles in his bs. In 1862 she became the first Dan. Giselle. Her brother Waldemar P. (1836–1908) began studying with Bournonville

in 1849. Joined Royal Dan. B. 1857; became the leading Dan. premier danseur of his time. An artist of impeccable taste and an excellent actor; resigned 1901. Julius P. (1833–93), their cousin, was first solo d. of the Vienna Court Op. 1855–93 and became a professor at the Vienna Conservatory and teacher at the Court Op. B. School. He was very popular with Vienna audiences; appeared in 2480 perfs. in 25 years. Ellen P. (1878–1968), great-niece of Juliette and Waldemar, was very successful as a solo d. of the Royal Dan. B. 1903–12; created the title role in H. Beck's *The Little Mermaid* (1909).
BIBL.: T. G. Venle, 'The Dancing P.s of Denmark', *Dance Perspectives* 11.

Priest, Josias (*d* London, 20 Apr. 1734). Brit. dancer, choreographer, and teacher. Appeared as d. and ch. in masques and plays at Lincoln's Inn Fields. Opened an unlicensed d.-school 1669. Became dir. of the School for Young Gentlewomen which prod. Purcell's *Dido and Aeneas* in 1689, for which he ch. the dances. He then ch. Purcell's *The Prophetess or The History of Dioclesian* (1690), *King Arthur or The British Worthy* (1691), *The Fairy Queen* (1692), and *The Indian Queen* (1695).

Prima ballerina (Ital., first d.). The female d. at the top of a co. In Russia at the turn of the century the even higher title of P. B. Assoluta was very occasionally awarded, as it was by the Royal B. to Fonteyn in 1979, the year of her 60th birthday.

Primitive Mysteries. Ballet in 3 sections; ch. and cost. Graham; mus. Horst. Prod. 2 Feb. 1931, M. Graham and Group, Craig Th., New York. A work dealing with religious feeling in generalized, stark simplicity; the 3 sections were called Hymn to the Virgin, Crucifixus, and Hosannah. This was Graham's first major group work.

Primus, Pearl (*b* Trinidad, 29 Nov. 1919). Amer. dancer, choreographer, teacher, and anthropologist. Studied medicine and anthropology in New York and d. with the New D. Group, with which she made her début 1941. First solo recital 1943; first appearance with her own group 1944, for which she ch. *African Ceremonial*. Concentrated on research into and presentation of West Indian, African, and other primitive d. forms with her husband Percival Borde. Made several research expeditions to Africa. Dir. of the Art Centre of Black African Culture in Nigeria. Teaches at New York Hunter College. Has ch. for various groups, incl. A. Ailey D. Th. (*Congolese Wedding*, 1974).
BIBL.: R. Estrada, 'P.P.', *Dance Magazine* (1968/11).

Prince Igor. (Orig. Russ. title: *Knyaz Igor*). Opera by Borodin, which includes the *Polovtsian Dances*, staged by Khan Konchak to entertain his royal captives, Prince Igor and his son Vladimir. At the op.'s first prod., 4 Nov. 1890, St. Petersburg Maryinsky Th., these dances were ch. by Ivanov.

Fokine revised them for presentation in Diaghilev's first Paris season; Paris audiences found them startlingly wild and vigorous (déc. Roerich, first prod. 19 May 1909, Th. du Châtelet, with Fedorova, Smirnova, Bolm). Fokine's version has been often revived (e.g. Grigoriev prod. for Royal B., 1965); there have also been numerous individually ch. versions.

BIBL.: C. W. Beaumont, 'P.I.' in *Complete Book of Ballets* (London, 1951).

Prince of China, The. See *Chinese Orphan Boy, The.*

Prince of the Pagodas, The. Ballet in 3 acts; libr. and ch. Cranko; mus. Britten; sets Piper; cost. D. Heeley. Prod. 1 Jan. 1957, Royal B., Cov. Gdn., London, with Beriosova, Farron, Blair. A fairytale b. about the Emperor of the Middle Kingdom and his 2 daughters. The modest Princess Belle Rose is banished by her evil sister, Princess Belle Epine. On her journey through air, fire, and water, Belle Rose meets the frightening Green Salamander in the Kingdom of Pagodas. She helps him to regain his original form as a handsome Prince; he then helps her and her imprisoned father to get back their kingdom. The first specially composed full-length Brit. b. of modern times. Cranko revived it for Milan (1957) and Stuttgart (1960). Other versions by A. Carter (Munich State Op., 1958), Orlikowsky (Basle, 1961), and S. Wilson (Genoa and Venice, 1980).

BIBL.: D. Mitchell, 'T.P.o.t.P.' in *The Decca Book of Ballet* (London, 1958).

Princess and the Seven Knights, The (orig. Russ. title: *Skaska o mertvoi tsarevne i sjemi bogatirjakh*). Ballet in 3 acts and 10 scenes; libr. G. Jagdfeld; ch. A. Andreiev and B. Fenster; mus. Liadov (arr. V. Deshevov); déc. G. Melnikov, T. Subkova, and A. Katuchina. Prod. 16 June 1949, Maly Th., Leningrad. An adaptation of the Snow White story, as retold by Pushkin in *The Fairy Tale of the Dead Princess and the Seven Knights.* The Evil Queen becomes the vain Tsarevna in this version, and the seven dwarfs are seven knights.

Prinz, John (b Chicago, 14 May 1946). Amer. d. Studied at Amer. B. Center, Sch. of Amer. B., and B. Th. School. Début N. Y. City B. 1964; later became soloist. Joined Amer. B. Th. 1970. Has created roles in Balanchine's *Don Quixote* (1965), *Jewels* (1967), and *Pas de deux: La Source* (1968), Robbins's *Dances at a Gathering* (1969), and Smuin's *Schubertiade* (1970). Founded Illinois B. Th., Chicago, 1979. B. master Cleveland B., 1980. B. master B. Nacional Classico, Madrid since 1985.

BIBL.: S. Goodman, 'J.P.', *Dance Magazine* (1968/5); J. Gruen, 'J.P.', in *The Private World of Ballet* (New York, 1975).

Prisoner of the Caucasus, The. Pushkin's poem (orig. Russ. title: *Kavkazsky plennik*) has inspired several bs., incl. those by Didelot (in 4 acts, mus.

Cavos, prod. 27 Jan. 1823, Bolshoi Th., St. Petersburg, with Istomina, Goltz), Lavrovsky (in 3 acts and 7 scenes, mus. Asafiev, déc. Khodasevich, prod. 14 Apr. 1938, Maly Th., Leningrad), and Skibine (in 1 act, mus. Khachaturian from *Gayane*, prod. 4 Dec. 1951, Grand B. du Marquis de Cuevas, Th. de l'Empire, Paris, with Skibine, Marjorie Tallchief).

BIBL.: (the Lavrovsky version) C. W. Beaumont, 'T.P of t.C.' in *Supplement to Complete Book of Ballets* (London, 1952).

Private Lesson, The. See *Lesson, The.*

Prodigal Son, The (orig. Fr. title: *Le Fils prodigue*, also Russ. *Bludny syn*). Ballet in 1 act; libr. Kochno; ch. Balanchine; mus. Prokofiev; déc. Rouault. Prod. 21 May 1929, Bs. Russes de Diaghilev, Th. S. Bernhardt, Paris, with Lifar, Doubrovska. This ballet tells the parable dramatically, with certain necessary omissions from and additions to the original story, but with the central theme (St. Luke, 15:11–24) preserved (Balanchine). Revived for various cos., e.g. New York City B. (1950), Royal B. (1973), Paris Opéra, and Washington National B. (1974). Other versions of the same b. by Jooss (Essen, 1931), Milloss (Düsseldorf, 1934), and Lichine (Original B. Russe, Sydney, 1938). A different b., orig. Swed. title, *Den Förlorade Sonen*, based on traditional art from the Dalekarlia area of Sweden, by I. Cramér (mus. H. Alfvén, déc. R. Linstrom, prod. 27 Apr. 1947, Royal Swed. B., Stockholm, with Holmgren, Rhodin, von Rosen, J. Mengarelli). Another b., *P.S. (In Ragtime)*, by B. Moreland (mus. S. Joplin and others, London Festival B., 1974).

BIBL.: G. Balanchine, 'P.S.' in *Balanchine's New Complete Stories of the Great Ballets* (Garden City, N.Y., 1968).

Prokofiev, Serge Sergeyevich (b Sonzowska, 23 Apr. 1891, d Moscow, 5 Mar. 1953). Sov. composer. Wrote the mus. for *Ala and Lolly* (comp. 1914; ch. Terpis, Berlin State Op., 1927), *Chout* (comp. 1915; ch. Slavinsky and Larionov, Bs. Russes de Diaghilev, Paris, 1921), *Le Pas d'acier* (ch. Massine, Bs. Russes de Diaghilev, Paris, 1927), *The Prodigal Son* (ch. Balanchine, Bs. Russes de Diaghilev, Paris, 1929), *Sur le Borsythène* (ch. Lifar, Opéra, Paris, 1932), *Romeo and Juliet* (ch. Psota, Brno, 1938), *Cinderella* (ch. Zahkarov, Bolshoi B., Moscow, 1945), and *The Stone Flower* (ch. Lavrovsky, Bolshoi B., Moscow, 1954). Bs. based on his concert mus. incl. Tudor's *Gala Performance* (to Classical Symphony and first movement of 3rd Piano Concerto, London B., 1938), Bolm's *Peter and the Wolf* (B. Th., New York, 1940; also many other versions), Fokine's *Russian Soldier* (to film mus. for *Lieutenant Kijé*, B. Th., New York, 1942; same mus. also for *L.K.*, ch. Lapauri and Tarasova, Bolshoi B., Moscow, 1963), Milloss's *Estro arguto* (to 3rd Piano Concerto, Rome, 1957), Lichine's *Image chorégraphique* (to Fifth Symphony, Ger. Op. Berlin, 1962), Blaska's *Deuxième Concerto* (to

2nd Piano Concerto, Marseilles, 1970), dell'Ara's *Egyptian Nights* (to incidental mus. for *Anthony and Cleopatra*, La Scala, Milan, 1971), MacMillan's *Triad* (to 1st Violin Concerto, Royal B., 1972— also Robbins's *Opus 19*, New York City B., 1979) J. Sanders' *Fugitive Visions* (Netherlands D. Th., 1973), Grigorovich's *Ivan the Terrible* (to film mus. and excerpts from the symphonies, Bolshoi B., Moscow, 1975), and Boyartchikov's *Tsar Boris* (various pieces, Perm, 1975).

BIBL.: various authors in *S.P.—Autobiography, Articles, Reminiscences* (Moscow, n.d.—in Eng.); S. Vasilenko, *Baleti Prokofieva* (Moscow, 1965—in Russ.); G. Dorris, 'P. and the Ballet', *Ballet Review* (vol. IV, no. 6).

Prokovsky, André (*b* Paris, 13 Jan. 1939). Fr. dancer, choreographer, and b. director. Studied with Egorova, Kiss, Peretti, and Zverev. Début Comédie Française 1954. D. with the cos. of Charrat (1955), Petit (1956); principal d. with London Festival B. (1957–60 and 1966–73), Grand B. du Marquis de Cuevas (1960–2), and New York City B. (1963–6). Created roles in Dolin's *Variations for Four* (1957), J. Carter's *The Unknown Island* (1969), and Hynd's *Dvorak Variations* (1970). Started his own group with his then wife Galina Samsova in 1972; this later became New London B. Created title-role in Darrell's *Othello* (1971). Ch. several bs. for his co., incl. *Scarlatti and Friends* (mus. A. Scarlatti, 1972), *Bagatelles, opus 126* (mus. Beethoven, 1972), *Vespri* (mus. Verdi, 1973), *Piano Quartet No. 1* (mus. Beethoven, 1974), *Elégie* (mus. Fauré, 1975), *Commedia I* (mus. R. R. Bennett, both 1975), *Anna Karenina* (mus. Tchaikovsky, for Austral. B., 1979). *The Three Musketeers* (mus. Verdi/Woolfenden, for Austral. B., 1980), *The Storm* (mus. Shostakovitch), and *Verdi Variations* (mus. Verdi), both for London Festival B., 1981.

Promenade. (1) Designates in b. a slow turn on one foot, with the body held in a set position, e.g. an arabesque or attitude. Also a slow turn in a pas de deux, with the danseur holding the ballerina, who is on points, and walking around her. (2) Ballet in 1 act; libr. and ch. de Valois; mus. Haydn (arr. E. Evans and G. Jacob); déc. Stevenson. Prod. 25 Oct. 1943, Sadler's Wells B., King's Th., Edinburgh, with G. Hamilton, P. Clayden, Fonteyn, Paltenghi. 'A very slight suite of dances, linked by the person of a quavery old lepidopterist who continued his singleminded pursuit of butterflies no matter what was going on around him' (M. Clarke).

Prometheus. See *Creatures of Prometheus, The.*

Prospect Before Us, The. Ballet in 7 scenes; libr. and ch. de Valois; mus. William Boyce (arr. Lambert); déc. Roger Furse. Prod. 4 July 1940, Vic-Wells B., Sadler's Wells Th., London, with Helpmann, C. Newman, May. The b. derives its title from T. Rowlandson's engraving of the same name. Its plot, based on J. Ebers' *Seven Years of the*

King's Theatre (1828), tells of 2 rival London th. managers, Mr. Taylor of the King's Th. and Mr. O'Reilly of the Pantheon; they try to lure away each other's dancers, who include Noverre, Didelot, and Vestris. Mainly notable for Helpmann's outrageously funny portrait of Mr. O'Reilly.

BIBL.: C. W. Beaumont, 'T.P.B.U.' in *Supplement to Complete Book of Ballets* (London, 1952).

Psota, Ivo Váňa (*b* Kiev, 1 May 1908, *d* Brno, 16 Feb. 1952). Czech dancer, choreographer, and b. master. Studied with A. Berger; joined Prague National Th. B. 1924. Soloist and ch. in Brno 1926–32, with B. Russe de Monte Carlo 1932–6; b. master Brno 1936–41, régisseur B. Th. 1941, b. master de Basil's Original B. Russe 1942–7, b. dir. Brno 1947–52. Ch. the first prod. of Prokofiev's *Romeo and Juliet* (Brno, 1938, with himself as Romeo). His other bs. include *Slavonica* (mus. Dvořák's *Slavonic Dances*, B. Th., 1941).

Pugni, Cesare (*b* Genoa, 31 May 1802, *d* St. Petersburg, 26 Jan. 1870). Ital. composer. Wrote his first b. for La Scala, Milan, in 1823: *Il castello di Kenilworth* (ch. G. Gioja). Worked for Paris, London, and Berlin; appointed b. comp. in St. Petersburg in 1851. He comp. 312 bs.; the most successful were in collaboration with Perrot: *Ondine* (1843), *Eoline ou la Dryade*, and *Pas de quatre* (1845), *Catarina ou la Fille du bandit* (1846— all for London), and *Faust* (St. Petersburg, 1854); with Saint-Léon: *La Fille de marbre* (Paris, 1847) and *The Humpbacked Horse* (St. Petersburg, 1864); with Mazilier: *Le Corsaire* (St. Petersburg, 1858); with M. Petipa *La Fille du Pharaon* (1862) and *Le Roi Candaule* (1868, both St. Petersburg). For Grisi's St. Petersburg début he composed a pas de cinq for *Giselle* (1850).

Pulcinella. Ballet with song in 1 act; libr. and ch. Massine; mus. Stravinsky (after Pergolesi); déc. Picasso. Prod. 15 May 1920, Bs. Russes de Diaghilev, Opéra, Paris, with Karsavina, Tchernicheva, Nemchinova, Massine, Idzikowsky, Zverev, Cecchetti. Massine based his libr. on the Neapolitan play *The Four Pulcinellas* (c. 1700); he centred the commedia dell'arte characters on the popular Neapolitan figure of P. in a complicated love-story; fathers oppose their children's marriage choices. Stravinsky used various Pergolesi manuscripts which he and Diaghilev had discovered in Ital. libraries. Massine ch. a completely revised version for Milan's La Scala in 1971 (revived for City Center Joffrey B., 1974). There have been many different ch. treatments of the b., e.g. by Lopokov (Leningrad, 1925), Georgi (Hanover, 1926), Jooss (Essen, 1932), Woizikowsky (own co. London, 1935), E. West (Western Th. B., 1957), Balanchine and Robbins (New York City B., 1972; second Channel Ger. TV prod. 1974), and D. Dunn (Paris Opéra, 1980). Bolender used the suite—without any reference to the plot—for his *Commedia Ballettica* (B. Russe

de Monte Carlo, New York, 1945), as did Smuin for his *P. Variations* (Amer. B. Th., New York, 1968).
BIBL.: C. W. Beaumont, 'P.' in *Complete Book of Ballets* (London, 1951).

Puppenfee, Die. See *Fairy Doll, The.*

Purcell, Henry (*b* London, 1659, *d* there, 21 Nov. 1695). Brit. composer. His mus. for plays and masques was usually ch. by John Priest: *Dido and Aeneas* (1689), *The Prophetess or The History of Dioclesian* (1690), *King Arthur or The British Worthy* (1691), *The Fairy Queen* (1692), and *The Indian Queen* (1695). Modern bs. have been ch. to arrangements of his mus., e.g. Ashton's *Dances for 'The Fairy Queen'* (B. Rambert, 1927), de Valois'*The Birthday of Oberon* (Vic-Wells B., 1933), Tudor's *Suite of Airs* (B. Rambert, 1937), Helpmann's *Comus* (Sadler's Wells B., 1942), J. Limón's *The Moor's Pavane* (1949), Walter's *Orpheus Britannicus* (Wuppertal, 1957), Varkovitsky's *La Tale of a Priest and his Labourer Balda* (to *Dido and Aeneas*, Schwetzingen Festival, 1966), and part of Van Dantzig's *Ramifications* (Dutch National B., 1973). A complete *Fairy Queen* (ch. Ashton, déc. M. Ayrton, 1946) was the first postwar op. prod. at Cov. Gdn., in collaboration with the Sadler's Wells B.; a revival in 1951 had new ch. by Cranko.

Push Comes to Shove. Ballet in 1 act; ch. Tharp; mus. Haydn and Jos. Lamb, arr. by David E. Bourne; cost. Santoloquasto. Prod. 9 Jan. 1976, Amer. B. Th., Uris Th., New York, with Baryshnikov, Tcherkassky, Van Hamel, C. Tippett, Aponte. 'A mix of old and new music, time past and present, new and old dance, *P.C.t.S.* displays the genius of the contemporary dancer in rare and droll combinations' (Balanchine). D. Hering, in *Dance Magazine* wrote: as 'It's like a giant Euclidian doodle with a form undercurrent of pure ballet logic'.
BIBL.: G. Balanchine, 'P.C.t.S.' in *Balanchine's Complete Stories of the Great Ballets* (Garden City, N.Y., 1977).

Pushkin, Alexander Ivanovich (*b* Mikulino, 7 Sep. 1907, *d* Leningrad, 20 Mar. 1970). Sov. dancer and teacher. Studied at Leningrad B. School; graduated 1925. D. with GATOB and Kirov B. 1925–53. Became one of the best teachers of male dancers at the Ch. School; his pupils included Semyonov, Makarov, Soloviev, Nureyev, Panov, and Baryshnikov.

Pushkin Ballets. The works of the writer Alexander Pushkin (1799–1837) inspired several bs. during his own lifetime, e.g. Adam Glushkowsky's *Ruslan and Ludmila* (Moscow, 1821) and Didelot's *The Prisoner of the Caucasus* (St. Petersburg, 1823). These were followed by Saint-Léon's *The Goldfish* (St. Petersburg, 1867) and F. Nijinsky's *A Victim of Jealousy* (based on *The Fountain of Bakhchisaray*, Kiev, 1892). A number of P. bs., were prod. in the U.S.S.R., e.g. Zakharov's *The Fountain of Bakhchisaray* (mus. Asafiev, Leningrad, 1934), Lavrovsky's *The Prisoner of the Caucasus* (mus. Asafiev, Leningrad, 1938), Zakharov's *The Aristocratic Peasant Girl* (mus. Asafiev, Moscow, 1946) and *The Bronze Horseman* (mus. Glière, Leningrad, 1949), Varkovitsky's *The Tale of a Priest and his Labourer Balda* (mus. M. Chulaki, Leningrad, 1940), Kholfin's *The Gypsies* (mus. S. Vasilenko, Moscow, 1937), and A. Andreiev's and B. Fenster's *The Princess and the Seven Knights* (mus. Liadov, Leningrad, 1949). Outside Russia there have been Massine's *Aleko* (mus. Tchaikovsky, B. Th., New York, 1942), Skibine's *Le Prisonnier du Caucase* (mus. from Khachaturian's *Gayane*, Grand B. du Marquis de Cuevas, Paris, 1951), Lifar's *La Dame de pique* (mus. Tchaikovsky, arr. Annenkov, Monte Carlo, 1960—also by R. Petit, mus. Tchaikovsky, 1977), Cranko's *Onegin* (mus. Tchaikovsky, arr. K. H. Stolze, Stuttgart, 1965), and Boyartchikov's *Tsar Boris* (mus. Prokofiev, Perm, 1975).
BIBL.: N. Elyash, *P. i baletny teatr* (Moscow, 1970); Y. Slonimsky, *Baletnye stroki Pushkina* (Leningrad, 1974; both in Russ.).

Pygmalion Ballets. Ovid's *Metamorphoses* tell of P., the king of Cyprus, who fell in love with a beautiful statue; Aphrodite answered his prayers and brought it to life. The story has inspired many bs., incl. those by Sallé (London, 1734), J. P. Rameau (as an op. b., Paris, 1748), Hilverding (St. Petersburg, 1763), Angiolini (Vienna, 1776), Dauberval (London, 1784), Milon (Paris, 1800), Therese Elssler (Berlin, 1835), Telle (Vienna, 1881), A. Howard (London, 1946), V. Gsovsky (London, 1947), and Etchevery (Brussels, 1957).
BIBL.: L. Kirstein, 'P.' in *Movement & Metaphor* (New York, 1970).

Q

Qarrtsiluni. Ballet in 1 act; libr. K. Riisager (also mus.) and Lander (also ch.); déc. Svend Johansen. Prod. 21 Feb. 1942, Royal Dan. B., Copenhagen, with N. B. Larsen. The title is the Eskimo word for the transition between winter and spring. The spirit of spring is ritually invoked by a tremendous drum crescendo. First perf. during the Ger. occupation of Denmark; the audience saw an unmistakable political message in the b.
BIBL.: C. Beaumont, 'Q.' in *Ballets Past & Present* (London, 1955).

Quadrille. 'A square dance which first became popular at the court of Napoleon I and then in France generally, and was imported in 1816 into Britain, where it soon became the rage. The music fell in 5 sections in different kinds of time. Independently of dancing, multitudes of quadrilles were composed often based on airs from some opera, or the like. The *Lancers*, introduced about 40 years later, was a variant of the Quadrille' (*The Concise Oxford Dictionary of Music*). Offenbach's qs. enjoyed special popularity. Used to designate the square formations of couples in the Amer. Square D.; also defines the corps de b. dancers in the hierarchy of the Paris Opéra (premiers and seconds qs.).

Quaternaria (also Quadernaria). One of the 4 basic dances of the 15th century, it consists of 2 steps, repeated after beating the feet together.

Quatre Saisons, Les. Ballet Divertissement in 1 act; ch. Perrot; mus. Pugni. Prod. 13 June 1848, Her Majesty's Th., London, with Cerrito, Grisi, Rosati, and Taglioni. See also *Four Seasons, The*.

Quatrième. (Fr., 4th). The 4th position of the feet.

Quest, The. Ballet in 5 scenes; libr. Doris Langley Moore; ch. Ashton; mus. Walton; déc. Piper. Prod. 6 Apr. 1943, Sadler's Wells B., New Th., London, with Fonteyn, Helpmann, Edwards. Inspired by Edmund Spenser's *Faerie Queene*; the b. shows the victory of St. George over the forces of evil.
BIBL.: D. Vaughan, *Frederick Ashton and his Ballets* (London, 1977).

Quica, La (née Francisca Gonzalez; *b* Seville, *c.* 1907, *d* Madrid, 1967). Span. dancer and teacher. Made her début as a child in a *café chantant*; studied classical d. and then flamenco d. with her husband Frasquillo. Became a sought-after authority on flamenco and national Span. dances. First d. in London 1951.

Quinault, Philippe (*b* Paris, 1635, *d* there, 26 Nov. 1688). Fr. dramatist and librettist. A member of the Académie française. Wrote the libr. for the first b. op. *Les Fêtes de l'Amour et de Bacchus* in 1672; this began his collaboration with Lully, which lasted until 1686. Further important b. librs. of his were *Le Triomphe de l'Amour* (1681) and *Le Temple de la paix* (1685).

Quintet. Ballet in 1 act; ch. P. Wright; mus. Ibert; cost. Walter Gayer. Prod. 13 July 1963, Stuttgart, with Heinrich, Barra, Cragun, Griffith, and Sutherland. Set to Ibert's Quintet for Woodwind. The b., in the style of a divertissement, draws its charm from the correspondences between the dancers and the musicians who are placed on the stage. Revived for Touring Royal B. (1964). A different b., *Q.*, ch. Van Manen; mus. Mozart; déc. J. P. Vroom. Prod. 3 Oct. 1974, Dutch National B., Amsterdam, with A. Radius, E. Greyling, D. Loring, J. Petty, B. Pleines.

R

Rabovsky, István (orig. I. Rab; *b* Szeged, 1930). Hung.-Amer. dancer and teacher. Studied with Nádasi at Budapest State Op. B. School; joined Budapest State Op. B. in 1948. Escaped from E. Berlin to the West with his d. wife *Nóra Kovach in 1953. Appeared with London Festival B. and then went to the U.S., where they toured widely with a small co., presenting their virtuoso display pieces; later also performed in nightclubs and luxury hotels. They now have a school in Beechhurst, N.Y. Authors of *Leap through the Curtain* (London, 1955).

Rachmaninov, Serge Vasilievich (*b* Oneg, govt. Novgorod, 1 Apr. 1873, *d* Beverly Hills, Cal., 28 Mar. 1943). Russ.-Amer. composer. Wrote no b. mus., but his *Rhapsody on a Theme of Paganini* has often been used for b. purposes, incl. Fokine (Cov. Gdn. Russ. B., London, 1939), Lavrovsky (Bolshoi B., Moscow, 1960), and Ashton (Royal B., London, 1980). W. Gore ch. *Winter Night* to the Second Piano Concerto (B. Rambert, 1948). Christian Holder used some of R.'s piano pieces for his *Five Dances* (City Center Joffrey B., New York, 1975), as did B. Stevenson in *Three Preludes* (Harkness B., 1969; revived for London Festival B., 1973), R. Duse his *Isle of the Dead* (Lucerne, 1976), and P. Montagnon ch. R.'s choral symphony *The Bells* (Stuttgart B., 1978).

Radice, Attilia (*b* Taranto, 8 Jan. 1914, *d* Capranica, 14 Sep. 1980). Ital. dancer and teacher. Studied at La Scala B. School; graduated in 1932. Joined La Scala B.; soon became prima ballerina. Also prima ballerina of the Rome Teatro dell'Opera. Created many roles in bs. by Milloss. Resigned 1957; became Dir. of Rome Op. B. School.

Radius, Alexandra (*b* Amsterdam, 3 July 1942). Dutch dancer. Studied with Nel Ross. Début Netherlands B. in 1957. D. with Netherlands D. Th. 1959–69, Amer. B. Th. 1969–70, and as principal, Dutch National B. since 1970. Created many roles, especially in bs. by Van Manen, e.g. *Symphony in Three Movements* (1963), *Metaforen* (1965), *Five Sketches* (1966), *Twilight* (1972), *Adagio Hammerklavier* (1973), *Sacre du printemps*, and *Quintet* (both 1974). Order of Orange Nassau (1975). Married to the d. Han Ebbelaar.

BIBL.: E. Huf, *A.R. and Han Ebbelaar Dancing* (Haarlem, 1979).

Radojevic, Danilo (*b* Sydney, 8 Sep. 1957). Austral. dancer. Studied with Estella Nova and Jeffrey Kovel and at Austral. B. School. Joined Austral. B. 1975, appointed soloist 1977, creating title role in W. Bourke's *Super Boy* (1977). Joined

Amer. B. Th. as a soloist 1978, later principal. Gold Medal (Moscow, 1977).

BIBL.: J. Gruen, 'D.R.' *Dance Magazine* (1978/5).

Radshenko, Serge Nikolaievich (*b* Shdanov, 12 Feb. 1944). Studied at Moscow Bolshoi B. School; graduated in 1964. Joined Bolshoi B. and later became soloist. Created Toreador in Alonso's *Carmen Suite* (1967).

Radunsky, Alexander Ivanovich (*b* Moscow, 2 Aug. 1912). Sov. dancer, choreographer, b. master, and teacher. Studied at Moscow Bolshoi B. School; graduated in 1930. Joined Bolshoi B.; became one of its most brilliant character soloists. Ch. *The Little Stork* (mus. D. Klebanov, 1937), *Svetlana* (mus. Klebanov, 1939), *Crimson Sails* (mus. V. Yurovsky, 1942, all with Popko and Pospekhin), and the Shchedrin version of *The Humpbacked Horse* (1960). Retired from dancing in 1962; became chief ch. of the Red Army Song and D. Ensemble. Merited Artist of the R.S.F.S.R.

Ragozina, Galina (*b* Archangel, 17 Mar. 1949). Sov. dancer. Studied at Perm State B. School; graduated in 1967. D. with Perm B. 1967–70 and as a soloist with Kirov B. 1970–2. Dismissed with her husband *Valeri Panov when he applied for emigration visas to Israel in 1972. Created She-Devil in Kasatkina-Vassiliov's *Creation of the World* (1971). To Israel in 1974, now performing mostly with her husband as G. Panova. Gold Medal (Varna, 1968).

Ragtime Ballets. See *Joplin, Scott*.

Rainbow 'Round My Shoulder. Ballet; ch. McKayle; mus. traditional prison songs, arr. Robert de Cormier and Milton Okun; cost. Ursula Reed, Prod. 10 May 1959, D. McKayle Dance Co., YM-YWHA, New York, with McKayle, Hinkson. The work deals with the experiences of a Southern chain gang—their interminable labour, their dreams, and their sorrows.

Rainer, Yvonne (*b* San Francisco, 1934). Amer. dancer and choreographer. Studied with Graham, M. Cunningham, Halprin, and E. Stephen. D. in the cos. of Waring, Pasloff, B. Schmidt, and J. Dunn. Founder-member of Judson D. Workshop in 1962, which soon became the foremost platform of experimental dance in New York. Became a film-maker with *Lives of Performers* (1972) and *A Film About a Woman Who . . .* (1974). 'She is post-modern dance's most dedicated iconoclast' (D. McDonagh). Author of *Work 1961–73.*

BIBL.: D. McDonagh, in *The Rise and Fall and Rise of Modern Dance* (New York, 1970); M.B. Siegel, in *At the Vanishing Point* (New York, 1972); S. Banes, 'Y.R.', in *Terpsichore in Sneakers* (Boston, 1980).

Raines, Walter (*b* Braddock, Pa. 16 Aug. 1940). Amer. dancer and teacher. Studied at d. dept. of Pittsburgh Playhouse and School of Amer. B. D. with Pennsylvania B. 1962–4, Stuttgart b. 1964–7; principal d. with D. Th. of Harlem 1968. Also works as a teacher and occasional ch.

Rainò, Alfredo(*b* Rome, 4 Dec. 1938). Ital dancer. Studied at Rome Op. B. School and with Kniaseff, Besobrasova, and Bruhn. Joined Rome Teatro dell'Opera B. 1956; became primo ballerino in 1961 and primo ballerino extra in 1971. Has appeared with many other Ital cos. and also danced abroad. Silver Slipper (1964); Positano prize (1971); Golden Spear (1974).

Rainoldi, Paolo (*b* Milan, 18 Apr. 1781 or 1784, *d* Prague, 1 Jan. 1853). Ital dancer, choreographer, and b. master. Studied with Francesco Sedini, who sent him to Vienna, where he became a favourite of the b. masters S. Gallet and F. Taglioni. One of his most popular numbers was a parody of Duport in *Flore et Zéphire*. He also appeared at the Th. an der Wien, Th. in der Josephsstadt, and Th. in der Leopoldsstadt. To Prague 1840–6. He was a much sought-after teacher and left a very revealing account of the harrassing social situation of the dancing profession of his time in an autobiographical sketch, kept in Vienna Municipal Library.
BIBL.: M. H. Winter, in *The Pre-Romantic Ballet* (London, 1974).

Rake's Progress, The. Ballet in 6 scenes; libr. and mus. Gavin Gordon; ch. de Valois; déc. Rex Whistler. Prod. 20 May 1935, Vic-Wells B., Sadler's Wells Th., London, with Gore, Markova. The b. was inspired by the Hogarth series of paintings, which are in Sir John Soane's Museum, London. Frequently revived for the Sadler's Wells and Royal B., and also mounted abroad, e.g. Munich State Op. B. (1956), B. of Flanders (1972), Zurich B. (1976).
BIBL.: C. W. Beaumont 'T.R.P.' in *Complete Book of Ballets* (London, 1951).

Rall, Tommy (*b* Kansas City, Mo., 27 Dec. 1929). Amer. dancer and choreographer. Studied with Lichine, Maracci, and Oboukhoff. Appeared as a child d. and actor with B. Th. 1944–7. Subsequently appeared in musicals, films (*Invitation to the Dance, Seven Brides for Seven Brothers*, etc.) and TV prods., for which he also occasionally choreographs.

Ralov, Børge (*b* Copenhagen, 1908). Dan. dancer, teacher, and choreographer. Studied at Royal Dan. B. School. Joined Royal Dan. B. in 1927; became solo d. in 1933, b. instructor in 1934. First solo d. 1942–57. He was Margot Lander's favourite partner and a much admired Petrushka.

Ch. *Widow in the Mirror* (mus. B. Christensen, 1934). Began teaching in 1945.

Ralov, Kirsten (*née* Gnatt; *b* Baden Austria, 1922). Dan. dancer. Sister of Paul Gnatt; studied at Royal Dan. B. School. Joined Royal Dan. B. in 1940; solo d. 1942–62. Prod. of Bournonville Bs. Since 1978 Assistant B. Dir. of Royal Dan. B. Knight of the Order of Dannebrog (1952). Married first to the d. Børge R. and then to the d. and b. master Fredbjørn Bjørnsson.

Rambert, Dame Marie (orig. Cyvia Rambam, then Miriam Ramberg; *b* Warsaw, 20 Feb. 1888, *d* London, 12 Jun. 1982). Pol.-Brit. dancer, teacher, and b. director. Studied d. in Warsaw, then medicine in Paris; but main interest was d.; went to Duncan-style d. perfs. Studied further with Jaques-Dalcroze in Geneva 1910; accompanied him to Dresden-Hellerau and became his assistant teacher. Diaghilev saw her and engaged her as Nijinsky's rhythmic adviser for the first prod. of Stravinsky's *Le Sacre du printemps* (1913). Danced in the corps of the Bs. Russes and studied with Cecchetti. Went to London; worked with Astafieva, married the dramatist Ashley Dukes in 1918, and opened her b. school in 1920. It produced most of the dancers and choreographers with whom she performed from 1926; the co. was orig. called M.R. Dancers, then B. Club from 1930, and B. Rambert from 1935. Considered, with de Valois, one of the great pioneer personalities of modern Brit. b., as a teacher, producer of the classics, and dir. of her co. Also an indefatigable discoverer and promoter of young choreographers; those who have especially profited from her enthusiasm and advice include Ashton, Tudor, Howard, Staff, Gore, Morrice, and Cranko. Her school, based on the *Mercury Th., produced such eminent dancers as Argyle, Gould, Lloyd, Franca, Gilmour, Aldous, and Turner. Author of autobiography *Quicksilver* (London, 1972). C.B.E. (1954); Chevalier de la Légion d'Honneur (1957); D.B.E. (1962); D.Litt. Sussex Univ. (1964). See *Ballet Rambert*.
BIBL.: Anniversary Issue, *Dance and Dancers* (1955/10); check-list of her activities and b. prods., *Les Saisons de la danse* (1971/11); Interview in *Ballet Rambert: 50 Years and On* (London, 1981).

Rambert Academy, The. Established in 1979 as a collaboration between B. Rambert and the West London Inst. of Higher Education to provide dance training of the highest professional standards. Eligible are pupils of 16+ years. Course Directors were J. Chesworth and C. Bruce, with G. Sherwood as Course Tutor. The inst. merged with the Rambert School in 1982.

Rameau, Jean-Philippe (*b* Dijon, 24/25 Sep. 1683, *d* Paris, 12 Sep. 1764). Fr. composer. Wrote many b. ops., incl. *Les Indes galantes* (1734), *Castor et Pollux* (1737), *Les Fêtes d'Hébé* (1739), *Platée* (1745), and *Pygmalion* (1748), most of which were ch. by Cahusac.

Rameau, Pierre. Early 18th-century Fr. b. master and dance theorist. Started his career as dancing master to the pages of the Queen of Spain; later became dancing master to the queen's household. Published *Le Maître à danser* in Paris, 1725, 'which teaches the manner of executing all the different d. steps with all the regularity of Art, and the manner of holding the arms for every step.' It became the standard work of its time, and appeared in many editions. Six months later he published *Abrégé de la nouvelle méthode de l'art d'écrire ou de tracer toutes sortes de danses de ville.* Eng. edition of *The Dancing Master*, translated and published by C. W. Beaumont (London, 1931—*Dance Horizon* reprint).

Rao, Shanta (*b* Managalore, 1930). Indian dancer. Studied Kathakali with Ravunni Menon, then Mohini Attam with Shri Pannikar, and Dasi Attam with Minakshisundaram Pillai. Her unusually large repertory, spell-binding personality, and very individual, almost masculine style of wide leaps and springs have made her world-famous.
BIBL.: F. Bowers, 'The Mystery and the Wonder', *Dance Magazine* (1963/10).

Rasch, Albertina (*b* Vienna, 1896, *d* Hollywood, 1967). Austrian dancer. Studied at Vienna Court Op.B. School. Went to America; formed the A.R. Girls' troupe in 1924, based on a solid academic technique. They later appeared in Europe. Began teaching in New York in 1925. Ch. for musicals and films.

Rassadin, Konstantin Alexandrovich (*b* Leningrad, 27 Oct. 1937). Sov. dancer and teacher. Studied at Leningrad State B. School; graduated in 1956. Joined Kirov B.; became one of its leading character dancers. Created roles in Jacobson's *Choreographic Miniatures* (1958) and *The Bedbug* (1961). Merited Artist of the R.S.F.S.R. (1971). Married to the d. Margarita Zagurskaya.

Rassine, Alexis (orig. Rays; *b* Kaunas, 26 July 1919). Lithuanian-Brit. dancer. Studied in Cape Town, then with Preobrajenska, Volkova, and Idzikowsky. Début at the Paris Bal Tabarin. D. with B. Rambert in 1938, Three Arts B. 1939–40, Anglo-Polish B. 1940–2, Sadler's Wells B. 1942–55, and later as a guest soloist (Gore's London B., etc.). Created roles in Helpmann's *Hamlet* (1942), *Miracle in the Gorbals* (1944), and *Adam Zero* (1946), Ashton's *The Quest* (1943), *Les Sirènes* (1946), and *Homage to the Queen* (1953), and de Valois' *Promenade* (1943) and *Don Quixote* (1950).

Rauschenberg, Robert, (*b* Port Arthur, Tex., 22 Oct. 1925). Amer. painter and designer. Has frequently collaborated with M. Cunningham (e.g. *Antic Meet, Summerspace* (both 1958), *Field Dances* (1963), and *Winterbranch* (1964)) and P. Taylor (e.g. *Three Epitaphs* (1956), *The Tower* (1957), *Images and Reflections* (1958), and *Tracer* (1962)).
BIBL.: A. Fatt, 'R.R.', *Dance Magazine* (1967/4).

Ravel, Maurice (*b* Cibourne, 7 Mar. 1875, *d* Paris, 28 Dec. 1937). Fr. composer. Wrote the mus. for *Ma Mère l'Oye* (ch. Staats, Th des Arts, Paris, 1912), *Adelaïde ou le Langage des fleurs* (ch. Clustine, Th. du Châtelet, Paris, 1912), *Daphnis and Chloe* (ch. Fokine, Bs. Russes de Diaghilev, Paris, 1912), *Boléro* (ch Nijinska, Rubinstein co., Paris, 1928), and *La Valse* (ch. Nijinska, Rubinstein co., Monte Carlo, 1929); also collaborated in *L'Eventail de Jeanne* (Paris, 1928). His lyric fantasy *L'Enfant et les sortilèges* (libr. by Colette) has been produced by several choreographers, incl. Balanchine, Milloss, and Charrat. In addition much of his concert mus. has been used for b. purposes, particularly *Pavane pour une infante défunte, Alborada del grazioso,* and *Le Tombeau de Couperin.* Cranko based his *Beauty and the Beast* (Western Th. B., 1966; Royal B., 1971) on the suite *Mother Goose,* and *Quatre Images* (Stuttgart, 1967) on various R. pieces, Russillo his *Rêves* (Paris, 1973) on the 2 piano concertos, Murray Louis his *Moment* (Scottish B., 1975) on the String Quartet, and Hynd ch. *Valses Nobles et Sentimentales* for New London B. (1975). In May 1975 the New York City B. staged an 'Hommage à R,', consisting of 3 different programmes, offering Balanchine's *Sonatine, Gaspard de la Nuit, Rhapsodie espagnole, Le Tombeau de Couperin, Tzigane, L'Enfant et les sortilèges,* and *La Valse,* Robbins's *Piano Concerto in G, Introduction and Allegro, Chansons Madegasses,* and *Ma Mère l'Oye,* Taras' *Daphnis and Chloe,* and d'Amboise's *Alborada del grazioso* and *Sarabande et Danse.* MacMillan ch. *Fin. du jour* to R.'s piano concerto in G (Royal B., 1979).
BIBL.: J.-L. Dutronc, 'M.R. et le ballet', *Les Saisons de la danse* (1975/11).

Rayet, Jacqueline (*b* Paris, 26 June 1932). Fr. dancer. Studied at Paris Opéra B. School. Joined Opéra B. in 1946; became première danseuse in 1956 and étoile in 1961. Frequently appeared as a guest ballerina with the Hamburg State Op. during the early 1960s. Created roles in Lifar's *Blanche-Neige* (1951) and *Les Noces fantastiques* (1955), Van Dyk's *Unfinished Symphony* (1957), *La Peau de chagrin, Turangalîla* (both 1960), and *Romeo and Juliet* (1961), and Petit's *Turangalîla* (1968). Chevalier dans l'Ordre des Arts et Lettres (1957); Légion d'Honneur (1973).
BIBL.: J.-P. Hersin, 'J.R.', with complete check-list of activities and roles, *Les Saisons de la danse* (1969/11).

Raymonda. Ballet in 3 acts and 4 scenes; libr. Lydia Pashkova and M. Petipa (also ch.); mus. Glazunov; déc. O. Allegri, K. Ivanov, and P. Lambin. Prod. 19 Jan. 1898, Maryinsky Th., St. Petersburg, with Legnani, S. Legat, Gerdt. Raymonda is to marry Jean de Brienne; but the Saracen knight, Abderakhman, forces his attentions on R. while de Brienne is on a crusade. At the last moment de Brienne returns, fights his rival, and thus sets the seal on the preparations for the marriage festivities, which start with a lavish Hungarian divertissement. The b. has been constantly revived in the U.S.S.R. and is still kept in the repertory of the more ambitious cos. It came to the West in N. Zverev's prod. for the National B. of Lithuania, given in London in 1935; the first U.S. prod. was Danilova's and Balanchine's abbreviated version for B. Russe de Monte Carlo (1946). A complete prod. was staged by Nureyev for Touring Royal B. in 1964, but this was shown only at the Spoleto and Baalbek Festivals; thereafter only the 3rd act was kept in the repertory. Further complete versions were mounted by Nureyev for the Austral. B. (1965), Zurich Op. B. (1972), and Amer. B. Th. (1975), and by T. Gsovsky (1st 2 acts) and Beriozoff (3rd act) for Ger. Op. Berlin (1975). Balanchine ch. a b. *Pas de dix* in 1955 (most of the mus. was from the Grand pas hongrois), *Raymonda Variations* in 1961 (to a different set of musical numbers), and *Cortège Hongrois* (1973).

BIBL.: C. W. Beaumont, 'R.' in *Complete Book of Ballets* (London, 1951); I. Guest. 'R.'s History', *Dancing Times* (1965/12).

Red Detachment of Women. Modern revolutionary ballet. Prod. 1 Oct. 1964, Peking. Orig. an op. (a film of which won a prize at the Moscow Film Festival, 1961); converted into a full-length b. in Peking 1964. This was filmed in 1970 with the China B. Troupe, with Pai Shu-hsiang and Liu Chingtang in the leading roles. The film was widely broadcast by Western TV stations. It deals with a Red company of women on Hainan Island during the period of civil war 1927–37, and shows the liberation of the peasant slave girl Wu Ching-hua, who becomes the Party Representative and finally the Leader of the company. The script and score were published by Foreign Languages Press, Peking, 1972.

Red Flower, The. See *Red Poppy, The*.

Redlich, Don (*b* Winona, Minn., 17 Aug. 1933). Amer. dancer, choreographer, and teacher. Studied with Holm and Humphrey. Began dancing on Broadway in 1954; later danced with the cos. of Holm, Humphrey, Sokolow, Louis, and Butler. Established D.R. Dance Co., with which he performs. Has taught at Sarah Lawrence College and Adelphi Univ. Contributed 'Reflections on "Reacher"' to *Dance Perspectives* 38.

BIBL.: D. Hering, 'D.R. Dance Comp.', *Dance Magazine* (1969/4).

Redowa. The name derives from the Czech Rejdovák (rej is Czech for round dance); a social d. in rapid 3/4 or 3/8 time, not unlike the Mazurka, which entered the Paris ballrooms about 1840.

Red Poppy, The (orig. Russ. title: *Krasny mak*). Ballet in 3 acts and 8 scenes; libr. M. Kurilko (also déc.); ch. Lashchilin and Tikhomirov; mus. Glière. Prod. 14 June 1927, Bolshoi Th., Moscow, with Geltzer, Tikhomirov, Messerer. The b. is set in a port in Kuomintang China in the 1920s; the dancer Tao-Hoa is exploited by the vicious capitalist Li Shan-fu, and gives her life to save the leader of the revolutionary crowd of coolies from the bullet of an assassin. She thus paves the way for the liberation of the Chinese people, and their Sov. comrades. It was frequently revived in the U.S.S.R. (though not recently), with the title changed to *The Red Flower* (to avoid associations with opium) and often with new ch.; e.g. Zakharov, for the Kirov B., and Lavrovsky, for the Bolshoi B., both 1949. An abbreviated version was ch. by Schwezoff for B. Russe de Monte Carlo in 1943.

BIBL.: C. W. Beaumont, 'T.R.P.' in *Complete Book of Ballets* (London, 1951); M. G. Swift, in *The Art of the Dance in the U.S.S.R.* (Notre Dame, Ind., 1968).

Red Sails. See *Crimson Sails*.

Red Shoes, The. Hans Andersen's fairy-tale inspired a b. by Hassreiter (mus. R. Mader, Vienna Court Op., 1898). It became a world success in 1948 as the central b. of the Eng. film *T.R.S.*, ch. by Helpmann and Massine, with M. Shearer, Helpmann, and Massine in the leading roles.

BIBL.: J. Cardiff, 'T.R.S. and Ciné-Choreography', *Ballet Annual* (III, 1949).

Red Whirlwind, The (orig. Russ. title: *Krasny vikhr*). Ballet in 2 Processes, with prologue and epilogue; libr. and ch. Lopokov; mus. V. Deshevov; déc. K. Tshupiatov. Prod. 29 Oct. 1924, GATOB, Leningrad, with Victor Semenov, Gerdt. Subtitled *Bolsheviki*; the 'synthetic production' of speech, song, acrobatics, and dance was intended as an allegory of the events of the October Revolution. The prologue showed the victory of the red five-cornered star over the cross of Christ. 'The First Process presented the idea of socialism, its paths, schisms, and continual affirmation ... In the Second Process, the inhabitants of a city, dreaming of their old cross, are unable to understand the revolution.... The epilogue attempted "scenically to reveal the idea of the Soviet Republic as the logical completion of the October Revolution".' (M. G. Swift). The b. was attacked as a prime example of Proletkult and was only performed twice.

BIBL.: M. G. Swift in *The Art of the Dance in the U.S.S.R.* (Notre Dame, Ind., 1968).

Reed, Janet (*b* Tolo, Ore., 15 Sep. 1916). Amer. dancer and b. mistress. Studied with W. Christensen, Balanchine, and Tudor. D. with San Francisco B. 1937–41 (Odette-Odile in first Amer. full-length prod. of *Swan Lake*), Dance Players in 1942, B. Th. 1943–6 (creating roles in Robbins' *Fancy Free*, 1944, and *Interplay*, 1945, and in Kidd's *On Stage!*, 1945), then on Broadway, and with New York City B. 1949–60; created further roles in Balanchine's *Bourrée fantasque* (1949) and *Western Symphony* (1954), Robbins' *The Pied Piper* (1951), and Butler's *The Unicorn, the Gorgon, and the*

Manticore (1957). B. mistress of New York City B. 1959–64. Now teaches.

Reel. Old Eng. dance in common time, probably of Celtic origin, which spread from England to Ireland, Scotland, and Scandinavia. A rapid dance, performed by 2 or more couples; the Highland Fling is a variant.

Regional Ballet Movement. During the last 2 decades there has been an enormous growth of non-professional b. cos. in the U.S., based on the local schools of individual cities. They call themselves Regional B. or Civic B. and work on a non-profit-making basis, giving 1 or more perfs. during the year. They belong to a regional organization, which holds an annual festival once a year, to which the cos. of the district are invited. Standards vary widely, from purely amateur level to almost professional competence. Guest stars are often specially flown in. The first Regional B. Festival took place in Atlanta in 1956. Ten years later Chujoy estimated that there were considerably more than 200 cos., of which 70 to 80 belonged to the 4 leading organizations (there are now 5).
BIBL.: D. Hering, 'A Kind of Oneness—Regional ballet and its festivals, what do they mean to American dance?', *Dance Magazine* (1970/10).

Regitz, Hartmut (*b* Stuttgart, 22 Apr. 1943). Ger. b. critic. Studied Tübingen Univ. Dance editor of *Stuttgarter Nachrichten*, writes regularly also for *Abendzeitung, Basler Zeitung*, and *Das Tanzarchiv*. Co-editor of the Ger. b. annual *Ballett* since 1968.

Reiman, Elise (*b* Terre Haute, Ind.). Amer. dancer and teacher. Studied with Bolm and at School of Amer. B. Created Calliope in Bolm's first prod. of Stravinsky's *Apollon musagète* (1928). Soloist with Amer. B. 1935–6; then danced on Broadway, in films, and on TV. D. with B. Society 1946–8; created roles in Balanchine's *The Four Temperaments* and *Divertimento*. School of Amer. B. faculty 1945–53 and 1964 to present.

Reinhart, Charles Lawrence (*b* Summit, N.J., 5 Dec. 1930). Amer. writer on dance, manager, and dance-director. Has been a contributor on d. to various newspapers and magazines. Now President of C.R. Management, which has been in charge of various New York modern d. series, sent individual troupes abroad, and directed the Jacob's Pillow Dance Festival. Now dir. of Amer. D. Festival.

Reinholm, Gert (*b* Chemnitz, 20 Dec. 1926). Ger. dancer, teacher, and b. director. Studied at Berlin State Op. B. School and with T. Gsovsky. Joined Berlin State Op. in 1942; became soloist in 1946. Danced at the Buenos Aires Teatro Colón 1951–3. Returned to Berlin; became soloist at the Municipal Op. in 1953. When the co. moved to its new building and became the Ger. Op. Berlin in 1961, he became b. director; continued as b. administrator when MacMillan took over in

1966, but was reinstated as artistic dir. of the co. in 1972. Formed Berlin B. with T. Gsovsky in 1955; continued to perform and travel with the co. well into the 1960s. Created leading roles in many bs. by T. Gsovsky, incl. *Hamlet* (1953), *The Moor of Venice* (1956), *The Lady of the Camellias* (1957), *Joan of Zarissa* (1958), and *Tristan* (1965). Established Berliner Tanzakademie in 1967. Ger. Critics' Prize (1958); Art Prize of the City of Berlin (1962); Golden star (Paris, 1962); Diaghilev Prize (1963).
BIBL.: H. Kellermann, *G.R.* (Berlin, 1957).

Reise, Die. See *Journey, The*.

Reisinger, Wenzel (*b* Prague, 14 Feb. 1828, *d* Berlin, 1892). Austrian choreographer. Little is known about the controversial ch. of the first prod. of Tchaikovsky's *Swan Lake* (Moscow, 1877). During the early 1860s a certain Václav R. was working in Prague. R. was probably the ch. of M. Kredler's *Mephistophela*, Hamburg, 1856. He was b. master in Leipzig 1864–72. Ch. (probably as a guest) W. K. Mühldörfer's *The Magic Slipper* at the Moscow Bolshoi Th. in 1871. B. master of the Bolshoi Th. 1873–8. Returned to Prague; appointed b. master at the newly opened National Th. for the 1883–4 season. Ch. the first prod. of K. Kovařovic's *Hashish*.

Reiter-Soffer, Domy (*b* Tel Aviv, 24 Oct. 1948). Israeli dancer and choreographer. Studied with Mia Arbatova, Frandsen, de Vos, R. Gluck, and Sokolow. Danced with Israeli Op. B. in 1959, as a soloist with Irish Th. B. 1962–3, Irish National B. 1963–4, London Dance Th. 1964–5. Appeared as an actor at London Royal Court Th. 1965–6; danced with Western and Scottish Th. B. 1966–70. Began ch. in 1962; resident ch. of the Irish National B. Co. since 1974. His bs. include *I Shall Sing to Thee* (mus. Zvi Avni, Bat-Dor Dance Co., 1971), *Song of Deborah* (own mus., Bat-Dor, 1972), *Mirage* (mus. M. Seter, Bat-Dor, 1973), *Phases* (mus. A. Jansen, Bat-Dor, 1973), *Timeless Echoes* (mus. Vivaldi, Irish B. Co., 1973), *Women* (mus. Boulez, Irish B. 1973), *Jingle Rag* (mus. J. Novak, Irish B., 1974), *Other Days* (mus. B. Downes, Irish B., 1975), *Love Raker* (mus. I. Yun, Irish B., 1975). and *Equus* (mus. Wilfred Josephs, Maryland B., 1980).
BIBL.: Interview and checklist, *Dance and Dancers* (1979/7).

Rejdovák. Bohemian d. in 2/4 time; the Redowa is a variant. A dashing character d. which was very popular in the bs. of the 1840s.

Rekrut, Der. See *Epreuve d'amour, L'*.

Relâche. Instantaneous b. in 2 acts, a cinematographic entr'acte, and a 'queue de chien' by René Clair; libr. and déc. F. Picabia; ch. Börlin; mus. Satie. Prod. 4 Dec. 1924, Bs. Suédois, Th. des Champs-Elysées, Paris, with Edith Bonsdorff, Börlin, Kaj Smith. A Dadaist fantasy, described by Picabia as 'life as I like it; life without a

morrow, the life of to-day, everything for to-day, nothing for yesterday, nothing for to-morrow. Motor headlights, pearl necklaces, the rounded and slender forms of women, publicity, music, motor-cars, men in evening dress, movement, noise, play, clear and transparent water, the pleasure of laughter, that is Relâche . . .' Revived by Moses Pendleton for Joffrey B. (1980).
BIBL.: C. W. Beaumont, 'R.' in *Complete Book of Ballets* (London, 1951).

Relevé. (Fr., lifted.) Designates the rising of the body from the flat foot to half or full-point.

Remington, Barbara (*b* Windsor, Ont., 1936). Can. dancer. Studied with Sandra Severo and at School of Amer. B., B. Th. School, and Royal B. School. Joined Amer. B. Th. in 1958, and Royal B. in 1959; became soloist in 1961. Returned to Amer. B. Th. in 1964; danced with City Center Joffrey B. 1966–9, Harkness B. 1969–72.

Renard, Le (orig. Russ. title: *Baika*). A burlesque story about the fox, the cock, the cat, and the goat, to be sung and played on the stage; text and mus. Stravinsky; ch. Nijinska; déc. Larionov, cond. Ansermet. Prod. 18 May 1922, Bs. Russes de Diaghilev, Opéra, Paris, with Nijinska, Idzikowsky, Jazvinsky, and Federov. 'To be played by clowns, dancers, or acrobats, preferably on a trestle stage with the orchestra placed behind'; based on 2 episodes from Afanasiev's collection of Russ. stories about the exploits of the Fox. Later prods. by Lifar (Bs. Russes, 1929), Balanchine (B. Society, 1947), Rodrigues (Western Th. B., 1961), Rosen (Munich State Op., 1962), and Béjart (Opéra, Paris, 1965)—also 2 concert versions by D. Drew and A. Killar, using Royal B. casts.
BIBL.: E. W. White, in *Stravinsky, The Composer and His Works* (London, 1966; rev. edn., 1979).

Renault, Michel (*b* Paris, 1927). Fr. dancer and teacher. Studied at Paris Opéra B. School. Joined Opéra B. in 1944; became the co.'s, youngest-ever étoile in 1946. Created roles in Balanchine's *Palais de cristal* (1947), Lifar's *Mirages* (1947), *Nautéos* (1945), and *Romeo and Juliet* (1955), and Cranko's *La Belle Hélène* (1955). Left the Opéra in 1959; worked as a freelance ch. for nightclubs and revues. Now teaches at Paris Opéra B. School.

Rencher, Derek (*b* Birmingham, 6 June 1932). Brit. dancer. Studied at London Royal College of Art and with B. Vernon, J. Gregory, Goncharov, Schwezoff, and Pereyaslavec. Joined Sadler's Wells B. in 1952; became principal d. of Royal B. in 1969. Created roles in Ashton's *Persephone* (1961), *The Dream* (1964), *Enigma Variations* (1968) and *A Month in the Country* (1976), Helpmann's *Elektra*, MacMillan's *Romeo and Juliet* (1965), *Anastasia* (new version 1971), *Manon* (1974), and *Isadora* (1981), and Tudor's *Shadowplay* (1967). Has also designed several bs.

Rencontre, La, ou Edipe et le Sphinx. Ballet in 1 act; libr. Kochno; ch. Lichine; mus. Sauguet;

déc. Bérard. Prod. 8 Nov. 1948, B. des Champs-Elysées, Th. des Champs-Elysées, Paris, with L. Caron and Babilée. Oedipus' encounter with the Sphinx is set in a circus; the Sphinx is placed on a high platform.
BIBL.: C. Beaumont, 'L.R.' in *Ballets Past & Present* (London, 1955).

Rendezvous, Le. Ballet by Petit, libr. Prévost, mus. J. Kosma, photos Brassai, backdrop Picasso. Bs. des Champs-Elysées. Prod. Paris, 1945, with Petit, Babilée. An atmospheric drama in the streets of Paris. Contained the song which became famous as 'Autumn Leaves'.

Rendez-vous, Les (later *Les Rendezvous*). Ballet in 1 act; ch. Ashton; mus. Auber; déc. Chappell. Prod. 5 Dec. 1933, Sadler's Wells B., Sadler's Wells Th., London, with Markova, Idzikowsky, de Valois, S. Judson, Helpmann. Set to the b. mus. from the op. *L'Enfant prodigue*. A suite of light-hearted dances for young people in a park. Revived for several cos., incl. National B. of Can. (1956) and Munich State Op. B. (1972); BBC TV prod. 1962.
BIBL.: D. Vaughan, *Frederick Ashton and his Ballets* (London, 1977).

René, Natalia (*b* Kiev, 22 Feb. 1907, *d* Moscow, 2 Jan. 1977). Sov. writer on dance. Educated Moscow Univ. and Lunacharsky Choreographic Institute. Regular contributor to *Dance and Dancers* and *Dancing Times*. Author of *English Ballet* (1959), *Beryozka* (1960), *Maya Plisetskaya* (1964; enlarged ed. 1968), 'Stanislavsky and the Ballet' (*Dance perspectives* 23), and *Era of the Russian Ballet* (London, 1966). Also writes under the pen-name N. Roslavleva.

Renversé. (Fr., overturned.) Designates the bending of the body while turning, deliberately disturbing normal balance without loss of equilibrium.

Repertory Dance Theatre. The resident performing co. attached to the Univ. of Utah in Salt Lake City; originally consisted of 12 dancers. Established in 1966; soon gained the reputation of being the best Amer. modern d. co. outside New York. It is collectively directed, without any individual artistic dir. or chief ch.; B. Evans is chairman, and the repertory includes works by Limón, McKayle, Butler, Farber, Sanasardo, Tetley, Muller, Sokolow, Kuch, Evans. *et al.*
BIBL.: M. Woodworth, 'R.D.T.—Democracy in Dance', *Dance Magazine* (1972/3).

Requiem. Ballet in 1 act; ch. MacMillan; mus. Fauré; déc. Yolanda Sonnabend. Prod. 28 Nov. 1977, Stuttgart, with Haydée, Keil, Cragun, Madsen, Andersen. Dedicated to the memory of Cranko, the b., using the whole co., reflects the shifting elegiac moods of Fauré's 1886/7 R. Earlier b. treatments of the same mus. in the same year by Russillo and Casado.

Requiem Canticles. Ballet in 6 movements; ch. Robbins; mus. Stravinsky; light. R. Bates. Prod. 25 June 1972, New York City B., State Th., New York, with M. Ashley, S. Hendl, B. Wells, R. Maiorano. An abstract setting of Stravinsky's 1966 score. Revived for Royal B. (1972) and Munich State Op. B. (1974). An earlier b. version by Balanchine 1968 (a single perf., dedicated to the memory of Martin Luther King).
BIBL.: P. Brinson and C. Crisp, in *Ballet & Dance* (Newton Abbot, 1980).

Revelations. Ballet in 3 sections; ch. Ailey; mus. traditional Negro folklore, arr. Howard Roberts; déc. Ves Harper. Prod. 31 Jan. 1960, A. Ailey Dance Th., YM-YWHA, New York. 'This suite explores motivations and emotions of American Negro religious music, which, like its heir the blues, takes many forms—true spirituals with their sustained melodies, song-sermons, Gospel songs, and holy blues—songs of trouble, of love, of deliverance' (programme note). The 3 sections are: Pilgrim of Sorrow—Take Me to the water—Move, Members, Move. One of Ailey's most popular works; usually given at the end of a programme.

Révérence. (Fr., curtsey). The formal bow of the dancers at the end of a class or perf.

Revolt. TV ballet film by Cullberg, mus. Bartók, directed by Mans Reuterswärd for Swed. TV, produced 1973, with N. Ek. Set to Bartók's Music for Strings, Percussion and Celesta, and danced within a setting of Piranesi's 'Carceri d'invenzione'. Prison inmates rise up against their oppressors. Cullberg later adapted it for the stage.

Rhapsody. Ballet in 1 act; ch. and set Ashton; mus. Rachmaninov; cost. W. Chappell. Prod. 4 Aug. 1980, Royal B., Cov. Gd., London, with Baryshnikov, Collier *et al.* Dedicated to Her Majesty Queen Elizabeth the Queen Mother, based upon the composer's R. on a theme of Paganini for Piano and Orch., and set for a soloist couple and 6 accompanying couples with no suggestion of a plot or a subject. This is a display piece of virtuosity and technical wizardry at its most dazzling. Earlier bs. to the same mus. by Fokine (Col. de Basil's B. Russe, London 1939) and Lavrovsky (Bolshoi B., 1960).

Rhapsody in Blue. See *Gershwin, George.*

Rhodes, Lawrence (*b* Mount Hope, W. Va., 24 Nov. 1939). Amer. dancer. Studied with Violette Armand in Detroit and at B. Russe School. Joined B. Russe de Monte Carlo in 1958. Danced with R. Joffrey B. 1960–4; created roles in Arpino's *Incubus* and Macdonald's *Time Out of Mind* (1962). Principal d. with Harkness B. 1964–70; became Artistic Dir. in 1968. D. with Dutch National B. 1970–1; created leading role in Van Dantzig's *On the Way.* Member of Pennsylvania B. since 1972. Has frequently appeared as a guest star with other cos. Chmn. N.Y. Univ. Sch. of Dance 1981.

BIBL.: J. J. O'Connor, 'Another Try at the "Inevitable" Direction', *Dance Magazine* (1969/11). J. Gruen, 'Close-Up; L.R.', *Dance Magazine* (1975/2).

Rhodin, Teddy (*b* Stockholm, 1919). Swed. dancer, choreographer, and teacher. Studied at Royal Swed. B. School. Member of Royal Swed. B. 1937–64; became principal d. in 1942. One of his best roles was Jean in Cullberg's *Miss Julie.* B. master Malmö Op.B. 1967–70. Has ch. many op. and TV bs. Carina Ari Medal (1964).

Rhythme et Structure. Fr. modern d. co. of about 8, established in Paris 1969 by Aline Roux who functions as artistic dir., and chief ch. and soloist. Apart from her, other contributing choreographers incl. L. Bewley, M. Mattox, and Gilbert Mayer. New York début 1979.

Riabouchinska, Tatiana (*b* Moscow, 23 May 1916). Russ.-Amer. dancer and teacher. Studied with Volinine and Kschessinska. Début in the Paris *La Chauve-Souris* revue. Joined B. Russe de Monte Carlo as one of the 3 baby ballerinas in 1932; remained with the co. until 1942. Created roles in Balanchine's *La Concurrence*, Massine's *Jeux d'enfants* (1932), *Les Présages, Scuola di ballo, Beach,* and *Choreartium* (1933), Lichine's *Francesca da Rimini* (1937) and *Graduation Ball* (1940), Fokine's *Cendrillon* (1938) and *Paganini* (1939). Guest d. with B. Th. in 1944, and in occasional perfs. thereafter—e.g. with Original B. Russe, Bs. des Champs-Elysées, and London Festival B. Married Lichine in 1943; they opened a school in Los Angeles, where she still teaches.
BIBL.: V. H. Swisher, 'The Real Mirror—A Portrait of T.R.', *Dance Magazine* (1972/4).

Riabinkina, Yelena Lvovna (*b* Sverdlovsk, 21 Aug. 1941). Sov. dancer. Studied at Moscow Bolshoi B. School; graduated in 1959. Joined Bolshoi B.; eventually became soloist. Created roles in Kasatkina-Vassiliov's *Vanina Vanini* (1962) and Messerer's *Snow Queen* (1969). Her sister, Xenia R., also dances with the Bolshoi B.

Rianne, Patricia (*b* Palmerston North, N.Z., 1943). Brit. dancer. Studied with her mother. Joined N.Z. B. in 1959. Studied further at Royal B. School. D. with Marseilles Op. B. 1963–5, then with B. Rambert 1966–9, and with Scottish B. since 1969; has created roles in Darrell's *Herodias* (1970), *Tales of Hoffmann* (1972), *Scorpius* (1973), and *The Scarlet Pastorale* (1975), Gore's *Embers of Glencoe,* and Van Schayk's *Ways of Saying Bye-Bye* (both 1973).

Ricarda, Ana (*b* San Francisco). Amer. dancer, teacher, and choreographer. Studied with Minnie Hawke, Celli, Vladimiroff, Escudero, Argentina, and la Quica. D. with Markova-Dolin co. in America. Joined Grand B. du Marquis de Cuevas 1949, becoming ballerina and ch. Her bs. always have a Spanish flavour; best known are *Del Amor y de la Muerte* (mus. Granados, 1949), *Doña Inès* *de Castro* (mus. J. Serra), and *La Tertulia* (mus. M. Infante, both 1952). Has taught at Royal B. School and ch. for its public perfs.

Ricaux, Gustave (*b* Paris, 20 Aug. 1884, *d* Aubagne, 24 Oct. 1961). Fr. dancer and teacher. Studied at Paris Opéra B. School. Became principal d. at the Opéra; was Spessivtzeva's partner. He then opened a school in Paris and became a much respected teacher; his pupils included Brieux, Peretti, Petit, and Babilée.

Ricercare. Ballet in 1 act; ch. Tetley; mus. M. Seter; déc. Ter-Arutunian. Prod. 15 Jan. 1966, Amer. B. Th., State Th., New York, with Hinkson and S. Douglas. A duo ballet about a woman and a man after an emotional and sexual relationship; Ter-Arutunian's huge concave sculpture is the one stable element in their shifting relationships. Revived for B. Rambert (1967), Royal Swed. B. (1970).

Rich, John (*b c*. 1682, *d* Hillingdon, 1761) Eng. mime and impresario; built the th. at Cov. Gdn. in 1732. He was a very popular author, producer, and actor of harlequinades. Brought Sallé, Noverre, and La Barberina to England. He succeeded his father as owner of the Lincoln's Inn Th., where he produced Gay's *The Beggar's Opera* in 1728.
BIBL.: S. Vince, 'England's Dancing Harlequin', *Dance and Dancers* (1965/12).

Richards, Dianne (*b* Luanshya, Northern Rhodesia, 13 Nov. 1934). Brit. dancer. Studied with Marjorie Sturman. Member of London Festival B. 1951–68; became soloist in 1955 and ballerina in 1959, creating title-role in J. Carter's *Beatrix* (1966). Guest ballerina Amer. B. Th. 1963–4. Ballerina of Scottish Th. B. 1970–5, also guest-ballerina with New London B. Married to the dancer Barry McGrath.

Richardson, Larry (*b* Minerva, Ohio, 6 Jan. 1941). Amer. dancer, teacher, and choreographer. Studied at Ohio State Univ. School of Dance. Appeared with the cos. of Tetley and Lang and on Broadway. Now teacher, d., ch., and dir. of L.R. and Dance Co.

Richardson, Philip John Sampey (*b* Winthorpe, 17 Mar. 1875, *d* London 17 Feb. 1963). Eng. d. publicist. Founder (with T. N. Middleton) of the *Dancing Times* and chief editor 1910–51. Co-founder of Association of Operatic Dancing in Britain in 1920 (now the Royal Academy of Dancing). Founded the Camargo Society with Haskell in 1930. In addition he organized many charity perfs., incl. the Sunshine Matinées and the Dancers' Circle Dinners. He was chairman of numerous committees and societies and built up one of the most comprehensive private b. libraries. Author of *The Art of the Ballroom* (with V. Silvester, 1936), *A History of English Ballroom Dancing* (1948), and *Social Dances of the 19th Century* (1960). His profound knowledge, his

indefatigable activity, and his persuasiveness made him one of the most influential personalities in the Brit. dance world of his time.
BIBL.: A. H. Franks, 'P.R.' in *Ballet Annual 18*.

Riccoboni, François (orig. Francesco R.; *b* Mantua, 1707, *d* Paris, 1772). Fr. author, actor, and choreographer. His was a well-known Ital. theatrical family; his father was Luigi R., the famous 'Lelio' of Ital. comedians. Principally associated with the Paris Th. Italien, where he collaborated closely with M. Sallé before her departure for London. He staged his version of *Pygmalion* only a couple of months after Sallé's London prod. in 1734, and this was an important event in furthering the cause of the b. d'action. Author of *L'Art du Théâtre* (1750).
BIBL.: M. H. Winter, in *The Pre-Romantic Ballet* (London, 1974).

Riegger, Wallingford (*b* Albany, Ga., 29 Apr. 1885, *d* New York, 1961). Amer. composer. Wrote the mus. for Humphrey's *New Dance* (1935), *Theatre Piece*, and *With My Red Fires* (1936), Graham's *Chronicle* (1936), and E. Hawkins's *The Pilgrim's Progress*—also (with Geneviève Pitot) for Weidman's *Candide* (1933) and (with Varèse) for Holm's *Trend* (1937).

Rieti, Vittorio (*b* Alexandria, 28 Jan. 1898). Ital. composer. Composed or arranged the mus. for Balanchine's *Barabau* (Bs. Russes de Diaghilev, 1925), *Le Bal* (Bs. Russes de Diaghilev, 1929), *Waltz Academy* (B. Th., 1944), *Night Shadow* (B. Russe de Monte Carlo, 1946), *Triumph of Bacchus and Ariadne* (B. Society, 1948), and *Native Dancers* (New York City B., 1959), Lifar's *David triomphant* (Opéra, Paris, 1935), and A. Cobos's *The Mute Wife* (B. International, 1944).

Riga. A Ger. op. house was opened in 1863. It was rebuilt after being burned down in 1887 and is now called Latvian Academic Opera and Ballet Theatre. During the 19th century it had its own group of dancers, headed by the Ital. M. Balbo (*d* Riga, 1943), who became the first teacher of Latvian dancers. The National Opera Theatre was founded in 1919, with Voldemar Kommissaris (1899–1931), a pupil of Mordkin, as b. master. He built up the first national co., with Klara Gentele (1894–1959) as ballerina. Individual b. perfs. started with *La Fille mal gardée* in 1922, followed by *Paquita* and *Magic Flute* in the Maryinsky Th. version, staged by N. Sergeyev. The co. was then directed by A. Fedorova (Fokina) 1925–32, who staged further bs. from the Maryinsky repertory. In the studios of Sergeyev and Fedorova, who later joined forces, the first generation of genuine Latvian dancers was raised, incl. O. Lemanis and H. Plucis. Y. Tangijeva-Birzniek (1907–65) was appointed prima ballerina in 1927. Fokine came here in 1929, and staged *Chopiniana* and *Prince Igor* in the early 1930s; L. Zhukov, Vilzak, M. Pianovsky, and Tikhomirov (*Red Poppy*, 1933) worked here.

Lemanis became the first Latvian b. master in 1934; he started with *Swan Lake*, and followed it with Latvian-inspired bs. such as *The Song of Love, Ilga, The Nightingale and the Rose,* and *Autumn* (during these years E. Frandsen was prima ballerina). The th. opened its own b. school in 1932, which absorbed the pupils from the Fedorova-Sergeyev studio. After the 2nd World War the former prima ballerina Tangijeva-Birzniek became b. dir. (she died in 1965); she built up a solid and balanced repertory of classics, contemporary Sov. standard works, and specially created bs., which were ch. either by her or by Eugene Tshanga (*b* 1920). The co. is now headed by A. Lemberg. Dancers who have come from the Riga State B. School (with Tamara Vitina as its present director) include Liepa, Baryshnikov, Markovsky, and Godunov.

Rigaudon. A lively dance in common time, deriving from Provence about 1485, and called after a dancing master from Marseilles. Somewhat faster than the Bourrée and accompanied by singing; it is performed by couples who d. side by side, without holding hands.

Riisager, Knudage (*b* Port Kunda, Estonia, 6 Mar. 1897, *d* Copenhagen, 26 Dec. 1974). Dan. comp. Wrote the mus. for Ralov's *Twelve by the Mail* (1942), H. Lander's *The Land of Milk and Honey* (1942). *Qarrtsiluni* (1942), *The Phoenix* (1946), and *Etudes* (1948), Cullberg's *Moon Reindeer* (1957) and *The Lady from the Sea* (1960).

Rimsky-Korsakov, Nicolai Andreievich (*b* Tikhvin, 18 Mar. 1844, *d* Lubensk, 21 June 1908). Russ. composer. Wrote no b. mus., but some of his scores have been used for b. purposes—especially by Fokine (*Sheherazade*, 1910; b. prod. of his op. *The Golden Cockerel*, 1914; *Igrouchi* for *Russian Toys*, 1922; and *Capriccio Espagnol* for *Ole Toro*, 1924).

Rinaldo and Armida. Ballet in 1 act; ch. Ashton; mus. M. Arnold; déc. Rice. Prod. 6 Jan. 1955, Sadler's Wells B., Cov. Gdn., London, with Beriosova, Somes. One of the many b. accounts of the encounter of the enchantress and the warrior, taken from Tasso's *Gerusalemme Liberata*. Earlier versions by Noverre (Stuttgart, 1761), LePicq (Venice, 1769), O. Viganò (Venice, 1778), Angiolini (Milan, 1780), and Fokine's *Le Pavillon d'Armide (St. Petersburg, 1907).*
BIBL.: C. Beaumont, 'R.a.A.' in *Ballets Past & Present* (1955). D. Vaughan, *Frederick Ashton and his Ballets* (London, 1977).

Rio de Janeiro. Though some kind of theatrical dancing is mentioned towards the end of the 17th century, and individual European cos. paid occasional guest visits during the 19th century, little is known of genuinely Brazilian b. activities. Thus one can easily imagine the impact created by the appearance of Diaghilev's Bs. Russes in Oct. 1913. However, its lasting influence was very slight. A school was opened at the Teatro Municipal in 1931, with Maria Olenewa as director, succeeded by Schwezoff (who also worked at the op. house) and Veltchek. The best Brazilian dancers emerging from the school preferred to work abroad—e.g. Consuelo, Meyer, and Haydée. The situation has not changed during recent years. Cos. from abroad make rare guest appearances, but the frequent attempts to build up a workable b. co. at the city's op. house have so far always proved abortive. The B. do R.d.J. was established under the direction of Dalal Achcar in 1975.

Rio Grande. Ballet in 1 act; ch. Ashton; mus. Lambert; déc. Burra. Prod. 29 Nov. 1931, Camargo Society, Savoy Th., London, with Lopokova, Gore, Markova, Chappell. Originally called *A Day in a Southern Port*, the exotic b. is freely based on S. Sitwell's poem of the same title, which Lambert set for chorus and orchestra, solo contralto, and solo pianist. It was a hotly debated work, and Beaumont called it 'an orgy of sailors and their doxies'. Revived for Sadler's Wells B. in 1935; Fonteyn had her first important role as the Creole Girl (created by Markova).
BIBL.: D. Vaughan, *Frederick Ashton and his Ballets* (London, 1977).

Ripman, Olive (*b* Teddington, 1886, *d* Moreton-hampstead, 29 Apr. 1981). Brit. dancer and teacher. Studied with Miss Wordsworth in London. Founded her own school in London; in 1944 she joined Grace Cone and they created the Cone-Ripman School, which later became the Arts Educational Trust. Retired in 1969.

Rite of Spring, The. See *Sacre du printemps, Le.*

Ritterballet. Ballet with mus. by Beethoven, conceived by Count Ferdinand Waldstein in collaboration with the dancing master Habich from Aix-la-Chapelle and first performed on 6 Mar. 1791 at the Bonn Redoutensaal. Obviously a portrait of the aristocrats in the Palatinal Cologne Palace, taking part in an old Ger. ball. It may have been accompanied by a text, but none survives. The mus. consists of 1, March; 2, German song; 3, Hunting Song; 4, Romance; 5 War Song; 6, Drinking Song (mihi est propositum); 7, German Dance; and 8, Coda. Later perfs. have been very rare—Laban ch. one for the Magdeburg Dancers Congress in 1927, followed by Urbani (Bonn, 1962), and Dia Luca (Vienna, 1970).

Rituals. Ballet in 3 movements; ch. MacMillan; mus. Bartók; déc. Y. Sonnabend. Prod. 11 Dec. 1975, Royal B., Cov. Gdn., London, with Drew, Eagling, S. Beagley, Derman, Rencher, Seymour, Mason. The b., inspired by Japanese rituals and set to Bartók's Sonata for 2 Pianos and Percussion, shows in the first movement 'Preparation for combat and self defence', in the second 'Puppets'

(in a wedding ceremony), and in the third 'Celebration and prayer' (after having given birth).
BIBL.: P. Brinson and C. Crisp, in *Ballet & Dance* (Newton Abbot, 1980).

Rivera, Chita (*b* Washington, D.C., 23 Jan. 1933). Amer. dancer and actress. Studied at School of Amer. B. Appeared in the Broadway prods. of *Call Me Madam* and *Guys and Dolls*, and created Anita in Robbins' *West Side Story* (1957), which she also performed in London. Further leading roles in *Bye Bye, Birdie* (1960), *Sweet Charity* (1966), and *Chicago* (1975).

Rivoltade. A turning step; the d. turns as he jumps, with one leg passing over the other, and lands facing the opposite way.

Road of the Phoebe Snow, The. Ballet in 1 act; ch. Beatty; mus. Ellington and Billy Strayhorn; light. N. Cernovich. Prod. 28 Nov. 1959, YM-YWHA, New York, with Candace Caldwell, Georgia Collins, Tommy Johnson, Hermann Howell. 'The Phoebe Snow is a train of the Lackawanna Railroad Line which still passes through the mid-western section of the United States. Legend has it that its name came from a meticulous named Phoebe Snow who travelled this line dressed in white satin and lace and looked out on the surrounding countryside with high disdain.... This ballet deals, first abstractly, then dramatically, with some incidents that may have happened on or near these railroad tracks' (programme note). Revived for A. Ailey Dance Th. and for London Contemporary Dance Th. (1971.)

Robbins, Jerome (*b* New York, 11 Oct. 1918). Amer. dancer, choreographer, and director. Studied with Ella Daganova, Helena Platova, Loring, and Tudor—also Span. d. with Helene Veola, Oriental d. with Nimura, and modern d. with his sister Sonya R. and with Alice Bentley. Also studied acting with E. Kazan, violin, and piano. Début as an actor with the Yiddish Art Th. in 1937; as a dancer at the Dance Center of Felia Sorel and Gluck-Sandor. Did his first chs. for summer stock repertory. Appeared in several Broadway musicals 1938–40. Joined B. Th. in 1940; soloist 1941–4. Created roles in Fokine's *Bluebeard* (1941), Lichine's *Helen of Troy* (1942), Tudor's *Romeo and Juliet* (1943). His first b., *Fancy Free* (mus. Bernstein, 1944), was so sensationally successful that he and Bernstein adapted it in the same year as a musical (*On the Town*). He then ch. the bs. *Interplay* (mus. Gould, 1945) and *Facsimile* (mus. Bernstein, 1946) for B. Th., and the 2 musicals *Billion Dollar Baby* (1946) and *High Button Shoes* (1947). Associate artistic dir. and d. of New York City B. 1949–59; he ch. *Age of Anxiety* (mus. Bernstein, 1950), *The Cage* (mus. Stravinsky), *The Pied Piper* (mus. Copland, 1951), *Fanfare* (mus. Britten), *Afternoon of a Faun* (mus. Debussy, 1953), and *The Concert* (mus. Chopin, 1956), for the co., and appeared as a d. in some of these and other

bs. His musical *West Side Story* (mus. Bernstein, 1957), which he conceived, directed, and ch., gained world-wide attention. Formed his own co., Bs.: U.S.A., for the Spoleto Festival of 1958; ch. the new bs. *Moves* (no. mus.) and *New York Export: Op. Jazz* (mus. R. Prince). Though the subsequent European tour was very successful, the co. did less well in the U.S. and had to be disbanded. It was re-established for the Spoleto Festival of 1961, with the new b. *Events* (mus. Prince); again a highly successful European tour followed, and a very short-lived Amer. one. During these years he continued to be enormously successful as a ch. and dir. on Broadway; his prods. (most of them filmed) incl. *The King and I* (1951), *Peter Pan* (1954), *Bells Are Ringing* (1956), *Gipsy* (1959), *Funny Girl* (1964), and *Fiddler on the Roof* (1964). He also directed some plays, incl. Brecht's *Mother Courage* and A. Kopit's *Oh Dad, Poor Dad, Mama's Hung You in the Closet and I'm Feelin' so Sad*. Ch. Stravinsky's *Les Noces* for Amer. B. Th. in 1965. Returned to New York City B. as b. master in 1969; ch. *Dances at a Gathering* (mus. Chopin, 1969), *In the Night* (mus. Chopin, 1970), a new prod. of *Firebird* (with Balanchine; mus. Stravinsky, 1970), *The Goldberg Variations* (mus. Bach, 1971), *Watermill* (mus. Teiji Ito, 1972), and (for the Stravinsky Festival of 1972) *Scherzo fantastique, Circus Polka, Dumbarton Oaks, Requiem Canticles*, and *Pulcinella* (with Balanchine), followed by *An Evening's Waltzes* (mus. Prokofiev, 1973), *Dybbuk Variations* (mus. Bernstein, 1974), and *Piano Concerto in G, Introduction and Allegro, Ma Mère l'oye*, and *Chansons Madecasses* (all for 'Hommage à Ravel' Festival, 1975). *Opus 19* (mus. Prokofiev), *The Four Seasons* (mus. Verdi, both 1979), and, for the Tchaikovsky Festival of 1981, *Piano Pieces, Pas de Deux* and *Allegro con grazia*. As a ch. R. has developed a highly individual demi-caractère idiom, which effortlessly absorbs influences from such different sources as academic and modern d., jazz, show, and social d. In addition he has become, through his musicals, one of the most influential personalities not only of b., but of the contemporary world th. scene. Many of his bs. have been filmed either for the cinema or for TV and an Amer. TV film *Ballets: U.S.A.* was produced in 1961, another one *An Evening with J. R.* by NBC TV in 1980. Since 1983 he has been joint b. master-in-chief of N.Y. City B. Two Hollywood Oscars for *West Side Story* (direction and ch., 1962); Chevalier de l'Ordre des Arts et lettres (1964); Capezio Award (1976), Kennedy Center Honors (1981).
BIBL.: I. Lidova, 'J.R.', with complete check-list of bs. and activities, *Les Saisons de la danse* (1969/12).

Robert le Diable (*Robert the Devil*). Opera in 5 acts by Scribe (libr.) and Meyerbeer (mus.). Prod. 21 Nov. 1831, Opéra, Paris. The 'Ballet of Nuns' from this op. was the beginning of the Romantic b. movement. The wicked hero, in search of a talisman to help him win the princess he desires, comes to the medieval cloister of Sainte-Rosalie, where the nuns who violated their vows are buried. They are summoned from their graves, and Helena, their abbess, commands them to waltz, and to wallow in their voluptuous pleasures. The first prod. was ch. by F. Taglioni and the role of the abbess was danced by his daughter Marie.

BIBL.: L. Kirstein, 'R.l.D.', in *Movement & Metaphor* (New York, 1970).

Robilant, Claire H. de (*b* Breslau, Ger., 24 Jan. 1915). Chilean writer on dance and archivist. Started to study with Kschessinska, then specialized in the history of d. and op. Was the first to teach the Cecchetti System in Chile. Dance critic of various Chilean publications 1959–75 and contributor to a number of foreign d. publications, incl. *Dance News, Les Saisons de la danse*, and the Ger. b. annual *Ballett* from 1971 onwards. Founder-Director of Archivo Municipal e Internacional de Danza, Ballet y Opera 'Elena Poliakova' at the Santiago Teatro Municipal 1965–74, closed by the political authorities in 1974. Now lives in London.

Robinson, Bill (known as 'Bojangles'; *b* Richmond, Vir., 1878, *d* New York, 25 Nov. 1949). Amer. tap dancer. Started in vaudeville as a boy. Went to New York in 1898; danced in various restaurants, played vaudeville, and toured abroad. His th. reputation dates from 1928, when he appeared in the revue *Blackbirds*. Hailed as 'The Dark Cloud of Joy', he d. in most of the leading ths. and night clubs in the U.S., participated in several films, and was featured in *The Hot Mikado* prod. of 1939. 'B.R.'s contribution to tap dancing is exact and specific: He brought it up on the toes, dancing upright and swinging ... with a hitherto-unknown lightness and presence' (M. and J. Stearns).

BIBL.: M. and J. Stearns, 'B.R.' in *Jazz Dance* (New York, 1968).

Rock ballets. Bs. to rock mus., commenting on the hard reality of life for contemporary youth, became popular with the rise of this musical movement during the 1960s, integrating all the appropriate kinds of dances. A select list must incl. Darrell's *Mods and Rockers* (1963), Joffrey's *Astarte* (1967), Van Manen's *Twice* (1970), Nault's *Tommy* (1970), Arpino's *Trinity*, and Flindt's *The Triumph of Death* (both 1971) and more recently by K. Armitage, L. Seymour, *et al.*

BIBL.: S. W. McDermott, 'From the Wonderful Folk Who Gave You the Swan Queen—Rock-Ballet as Synthesis of Forms', *Dance Magazine* (1971/10); J. Rockwell, 'Rock, Dance, and Rock Dancing', *Ballet Review* (vol. 4, no. 2).

Rockettes. The name of the female group of precision dancers who appear at New York's Radio City Music Hall since 1931.

Rode, Lizzie (*b* Copenhagen, 1933). Dan. dancer and b. mistress. Studied at Royal Dan. B. School. Joined Royal Dan. B. in 1952; later became soloist, and is now b. mistress of the co.

Rodeo. Ballet in 2 scenes; libr. and ch. de Mille; mus. Copland; sets O. Smith; cost K. Love. Prod. 16 Oct. 1942, B. Russe de Monte Carlo, with Kasimir Kokitch, Franklin, de Mille, Milada Mladova. The b. is subtitled *The Courting at Burnt Ranch*. The cowboys on a Texan ranch chase every woman in sight, but are unaware of the charms of a cowgirl working at the ranch; this is remedied, however, when she appears dressed up for a Saturday night ball. The work, which introduced square d. forms to b., was an immediate hit, and is still in the repertoire of Amer. B. Th. (which first staged it in 1949). Revived for Wuppertal B. (with new déc.) in 1974.

BIBL.: G. Balanchine, 'R', in *Balanchine's New Complete Stories of the Great Ballets* (Garden City, N.Y., 1968).

Rodgers, Rod (*b* Detroit, *c.* 1938). Amer. dancer, choreographer, and teacher. Studied in Detroit. Danced in the co. of Hawkins. D. supervisor of the Mobilization for Youth project. Now has his own co. for which he choreographs extensively.

BIBL.: M. B. Siegel, in *At the Vanishing Point* (New York, 1972).

Rodham, Robert (*b* Pittston, Pa., 2 Sep. 1939). Amer. dancer, b. master, and choreographer. Studied with Weisberger, E. V. Williams, and at School of Amer. B. Danced with New York City B. 1960–3; then joined Pennsylvania B. as principal dancer, b. master, and occasional ch.

Rodolphe, Johann Joseph. See *Rudolph, J.J.*

Rodrigues, Alfred (*b* Cape Town, 18 Aug. 1921). Brit. dancer and choreographer. Studied with C. Robinson and participated in several B. Club prods.; ch. his first b. in 1938. Went to London in 1946; studied further with Volkova. Appeared in the musical *Song of Norway*. Joined Sadler's Wells B. in 1947; became soloist in 1949; b. master 1953—4. Ch. *Blood Wedding* (mus. ApIvor, 1953) and *Café des Sports* (mus. A. Hopkins, 1954) for Sadler's Wells Th. B., and *The Miraculous Mandarin* (mus. Bartók, 1956) and *Jabez and the Devil* (mus. A. Cooke, 1961) for Sadler's Wells and Royal B. Has worked as a freelance ch. for many cos., incl. La Scala di Milano (Prokofiev's *Romeo and Juliet*, Verona, 1955, *Cinderella*, 1955, and *Nutcracker*, 1956), Royal Dan. B. (*Vivaldi Concerto*, 1960), Warsaw Grand Op. (Ravel's *Daphnis and Chloe*, Stravinsky's *Le Sacre du printemps* and *Orpheus*; TV prod. of the last 2 for second Ger. Channel in 1964), Ankara, and Bonn. Now mainly ch. for musicals. Married to the former d. Julia Farron.

Rodriguez, Zhandra (*b* Caracas, 17 Mar. 1947). Venezuelan dancer and dir. Studied at Academia Interamericana de Ballet and Amer. B. Th. School.

D. with National B. of Venezuela 1964–7. Joined Amer. B. Th. in 1968; became soloist in 1970 and principal d. 1973–4. Created leading role in Neumeier's *Third Symphony by Gustav Mahler* (Hamburg, 1975). Dir. and prima ballerina of B. Intern. de Caracas since 1977.

BIBL.: S. Goodman, 'Z.R.', *Dance Magazine* (1972/1).

Rogers, Ginger (*b* Independence, Mo., 16 July 1911). Amer. dancer and actress. Appeared on Broadway; then made highly successful film career as a dancer and Astaire's partner in *Flying Down to Rio* (1933), *The Gay Divorcee* (1934), *Roberta* and *Top Hat* (1935), *Follow the Fleet* and *Swing Time* (1936), *Shall We Dance?* (1937), *Carefree* (1938). *The Story of Vernon and Irene Castle* (1939), and *The Berkeleys of Broadway* (1949). After the partnership broke up, she continued to appear mainly as a straight actress, although she has also occasionally performed in musicals (e.g. *Hello, Dolly!* and *Mame*).

BIBL.: A Croce, *The Fred Astaire & G.R. Book* (New York, 1972).

Rogge, Lola (*b* Altona, 20 Mar. 1908). Ger. dancer, choreographer, and teacher. Studied with Laban and Knust. Became head of the Hamburg Laban School when Knust left in 1934; under her it developed into one of the city's most active d. centres. Has ch. for many prods. at the city's ths.

BIBL.: K. Peters, 'L.R.—eine musikalische Insel der Tanzkultur', *Tanzarchiv-Reihe* (no. 3).

Roi Candaule, Le. Ballet in 4 acts; libr. de Saint-Georges and M. Petipa (also ch.); mus. Pugni; déc. David. Prod. 29 Oct. 1868, Maryinsky Th., St. Petersburg, with Henriette d'Or, Gyges. King of Lydia (King Candaule), and his wife Nisia both fall victims to their own pride. The 22 perfs. of the first run were completely sold out; the Pas de Vénus, in which Mlle d'Or performed a series of 5 pirouettes sur la pointe, was a sensation.

BIBL.: C. W. Beaumont, 'L.R.C.' in *Complete Book of Ballets* (London, 1951).

Roi nu, Le. Ballet in 1 act and 4 scenes; libr. and ch. Lifar; mus. Françaix; déc. P. Pruna. Prod. 15 June 1936, Opéra, Paris, with Chauviré, Lifar, Goubé. The Andersen fairy-tale of *The Emperor's New Clothes*. Later versions by Inge Herting (Cologne, 1937), de Valois (Sadler's Wells B., 1938), and many others.

BIBL.: C. W. Beaumont, 'L.R.N.' in *Supplement to Complete Book of Ballets* (London, 1952).

Roje, Ana (*b* Split, 1909). Yugosl. dancer and teacher. Without having studied d., made her début as a d. at the Split Op. House in 1926. Then studied with Froman in Zagreb, where she danced at the Op. House until 1930. Moved to Belgrade with her husband, the d. Oskar Harmoš, and studied further with Poliakova; d. as a soloist at the Op. House. Went to London in 1933; worked with N. Legat and became his assistant.

Became b. mistress B. Russe de Monte Carlo in 1938; then joined de Basil's Original B. Russe. Returned to Yugoslavia during World War II and worked in Split and Zagreb; opened a b. school in Split in 1953. Since 1954 has also worked in the U.S. Now teaching in Bermuda, Boston, and Split.

Roleff, Peter (*b* Quadrath, 18 Dec. 1906). Ger. dancer, b. master, and teacher. Studied with V. Gsovsky and Berthold Schmidt. Début Berlin Municipal Op. D. with various Ger. th. cos.; worked as a b. master in Bonn and Bielefeld after the Second World War. Opened the Ballet-Schule Roleff-King with K. H. King in Munich in 1956; it soon became one of the city's most flourishing schools. Has ch. many bs.

Romanesca. An old Ital. folk-dance in triple time with gliding steps and leaps, not unlike the Galliard, deriving from the Romagna. In b. the first act of *Raymonda* offers an example.

Romanoff, Dimitri (*b* Tzaritzin, nr. St. Petersburg, 1907). Russ.-Amer. dancer, b. master, and régisseur. Studied with Koslov, Bolm, Mordkin, and Fokine, Début in M. Reinhardt's *Midsummer Night's Dream* film in 1935. Toured with Theilade; then soloist San Francisco Op. B., Mordkin B. 1937–9, and from 1940 for many years with B. Th. Became régisseur in 1946. Now teaches in Cal.

Romanov, Boris Georgievich (*b* St. Petersburg, 22 Mar. 1891, *d* New York, 30 Jan. 1957). Russ-Amer. dancer, choreographer, and b. director. Studied at St. Petersburg Imperial B. School; graduated in 1909. Joined Maryinsky Th. and became a much admired character soloist. A member of Diaghilev's Bs. Russes. Started to ch. with F. Schmitt's *La Tragèdie de Salomé* (1913) and Stravinsky's *Le Rossignol* (1914). Continued to ch. many op. prods. for Petrograd, where he also created some experimental bs. with Yelena Smirnova (whom he later married), at the Letni Th. Miniatur. Left Russia in 1921. Went to Bucharest and then to Berlin, where he founded the Russ. Romantic B. with Elsa Krüger. Toured Middle and Western Eur. with the co. for 5 years. He then joined the Pavlova co. as b. master; b. master of the Teatro Colón 1928–34. Also worked in Monte Carlo and Yugoslavia. Then concentrated on working in Rome and Milan; b. master of the New York Met. Op. House 1938–42 and 1945–50.

BIBL.: T. Mara, 'B.R.', *Dance Magazine* (1957/3).

Rome. B. has followed a rather chequered course in the Ital. capital. Though the appearance of Vincenzo Trenti and Onorato Viganò, and of the 'giovanissimo Salvatore Viganò, applauditissimo, in vesti muliebri' is mentioned in 1783, there seems to have been little b. activity until the romantic era, when Cerrito (1833), Grisi (1834), Elssler (1845), Taglioni, and Grahn (1846) all performed here. *Una Silfide a Pechino* was produced in 1860, Manzotti's *Excelsior* in 1883, Saint-Léon's *Coppélia* in 1885, and Montplaisir's *Brahma* in 1887. Diaghilev's Bs. Russes appeared at the Teatro Costanzi in 1911 and 1917 (when it gave the first prod. of Massine's *Les Femmes de bonne humeur*). It became the Teatro Reale dell' Opera in 1928 (now the Teatro dell' Opera), and at the same time the attached school was founded, under the direction of Ileana Leonidoff and Dimitri Rostoff (now headed by Radice). B. Romanov was b. director 1934–8; he presented *Histoire d'un Pierrot* and *Volti la laterna!* (1934), *Il Drago rosso* (1935), *Gli Uccelli* and *Lunawig e la saetta* (1937), and the first local prod. of *Swan Lake*. Milloss was b. director 1938–45, and under him there was a certain stabilization and an extension of the repertory. Romanov returned 1945–54, on leave of absence from his Amer. obligations; he staged further prods. of such classics as *Giselle* (1952), *Nutcracker* (1953), and *Sleeping Beauty* (1954). He was succeeded once again by Milloss, who was in charge of the b. premières 1955–60. Since then the directors of the th. have mostly engaged b. masters for 1 or 2 seasons only (more recent ones have included Claude Newman, Dolin, Bruhn, Parlić, Prebil, Plisetskaya, and William Carter).

Romeo and Juliet (orig. Russ. title: *Romeo i Dzhulyetta*). Ballet with prologue, 3 acts and 13 scenes, and epilogue; libr. Lavrovsky, Prokofiev (also mus.), and S. Radlov; ch. Psota: déc. V. Skrušny. Prod. 30 Dec. 1938, Brno., Czechoslovakia, with Psota, Zora Semberová. The b. follows Shakespeare's tragedy closely; special emphasis is laid on the social conflict of the 2 feuding families, who are finally reconciled over the tombs of the star-crossed lovers. The music had been commissioned for the Sov. prod., which became the model prod. for many years, with ch. by Lavrovsky, déc. by P. Williams; premièred 11 Jan. 1940 at the Kirov Th., Leningrad, with Ulanova and Sergeyev (revived for Moscow Bolshoi B. in 1946, and later mounted for many E. Bloc cos.—the Bolshoi prod. was filmed in 1954 and again for TV in 1976). Individual Sov. versions were ch. by Vinogradov (Novosibirsk, 1967) and Boyartchikov (Perm, 1972; revived for West Berlin Ger. Op., 1974). The first prod. to reach the West was M. Froman's for the Zagreb B. (London, 1955). Western prods. of the b. were ch. e.g. by Ashton (Royal Dan. B., 1955, rev. London Fest. B. 1985), Cranko (first with ds. from La Scala di Milano at Venice 1958; then his famous Stuttgart prod. of 1962, revived for various cos., incl. Austral. B. and Nat. B. of Can.— TV prod. for second Ger. Channel, 1974), MacMillan (déc. Georgiadis, 9 Feb. 1965, Royal B., Cov. Gdn., London, with Fonteyn and Nureyev, revived for Royal Swed. B., 1969—a film prod. of the Royal B. version was released in 1966), Van Dantzig (Dutch National B., 1967 and

a later version in 1974). Neumeier (Frankfurt, 1971; revived for Hamburg State Op. B., 1973 and Royal Dan. B., 1974), Smuin (San Francisco B., 1976), Nureyev (London Festival B., 1977), and Araiz (Joffrey B., 1977). Earlier bs. on R. and J. by Eusebio Luzzi (Venice, 1785), Galeotti (mus. C. Schall, Copenhagen, 1811), Nijinska and Balanchine (mus. Lambert, Bs. Russes de Diaghilev, 1926); also various b. versions of Tchaikovsky's Fantasy Overture (Bartholin, Harangozó, T. Gsovsky, etc.—Lifar's is the version best known in Britain). Tudor ch. a R. and J. b., to mus. by Delius, for B. Th. in 1943 (with Markova and Laing). There have also been several b. versions of Berlioz's Dramatic Symphony, incl. those by Skibine (Grand B. du Cuevas, 1955), Walter (Wuppertal, 1959), Béjart (B. of the 20th Century, 1966—RAI TV prod., 1971), and Veredon (Cologne, 1976).

Ron, Rahamim (*b* Cairo, 15 Nov. 1944). Israeli dancer and teacher. Studied in Israel and at Graham School. D. with Batsheva Dance Co. 1963–6 and as a principal d. 1969–73, also with the co. of Graham and McKayle 1967–8 and the Swiss Chamber B. Teaches at his own studio in Tel Aviv. Etoile d'or (with R. Schenfeld, for best couple, Paris, 1971).
BIBL.: S. Goodman, 'R.R.', *Dance Magazine* (1971/2).

Róna, Viktor (*b* Budapest, 17 Aug. 1936). Hung. dancer and b. master. Studied at Budapest State B. Inst., then with Pushkin in Leningrad. Joined Budapest State Op. in 1955; became principal d. in 1956. Has appeared with many cos. abroad; d. as Fonteyn's partner at R.A.D. Gala in 1963. Dances the premier danseur roles of the standard repertory. Created leading roles in Charrat's *Tu auras nom ... Tristan* (1963), Eck's *Ondine* (1969), Seregi's *Spartacus* (second première, 1968), *The Wooden Prince* (1970), and *Sylvia* (1972). Has also appeared as an actor in Hung. films. Guest principal d. and b. master of various cos. since (Norwegian Nat. B., Paris Opéra, La Scala di Milano). Liszt Prize (1963); Kossuth Prize (1965).
BIBL.: G. Körtvélyes and G. Lörinc, in *The Budapest Ballet* (1971).

Rond de jambe. (Fr., circle of the leg.) Designates in b. a circular movement of the leg, which can be performed à terre or en l'air (i.e. with the foot raised—if during a jump it is r.d.j. en l'air sauté).

Rooms. Ballet in 1 act; ch. Sokolow; mus. K. Hopkins. Prod. 24 Feb. 1955, YM-YWHA, New York, with B. Seckler, E. Beck, McKayle, J. Duncan. The b. deals with loneliness in a big city. Its sections are entitled: Alone—Dream—Escape — Going — Desire — Panic — Daydream — The End?—Alone. Revived for various cos. (e.g. Netherlands Dance Th., A. Ailey Dance Th., City Center Joffrey B.).

Roope, Clover (*b* Bristol, 1937). Brit. dancer,

choreographer, and teacher. Studied at Sadler's Wells B. School. Joined Sadler's Wells B. in 1956. Début as a ch. with *Le Farceur* for Sunday B. Club in 1958. Ch. for Bristol Old Vic. Joined Western Th. B. in 1960, for which she ch. several bs.; further study in U.S.A. 1964–6 with Graham, Cunningham, and Nikolais, also perfs. at Jacob's Pillow and Montreal; returned to Britain and joined B. Rambert as d. and teacher, 1966–8. Since then has taught and ch. for London School of Contemp. Dance and in France; now at *Rambert Academy of which she was deputy dir. 1985–7.

Ropes of Time, The. Ballet in 1 act; ch. Van Dantzig; mus. Jan Boerman; déc. Van Schayk. Prod. 2 Mar. 1970, Royal B., Cov. Gdn., London, with Nureyev, Vere, Mason. 'Every journey we make is an adventure into the unknown; each arrival a birth and each departure a death' R. Buckle (programme note). Revived for Dutch National B. (1970).

Rosario (née Florencia Pérez Podilla; *b* Seville, 11 Nov. 1918). Span. dancer. Studied with Realito. Début with her cousin *Antonio in Liège in 1928; then danced in Seville in 1930. They became the most famous Span, d. couple of their generation and performed all over the world. After their partnership broke up, she collaborated with R. Iglesias 1953–4; rejoined Antonio for his 1964 seasons in London and New York. Continued to perform with various groups of her own, for which she ch. several bs., incl. *Ritmo gracia y sentimiento* (mus. Infante), *Capriccio espagnol* (mus. Rimsky-Korsakov), *Sortilegio de la luna* (mus. M. Salvedor), *El Diablo en la playa*, and *Café de Burrero* (Andalusian folk. mus.). Gold Medal (Circulo de Bella Artes, 1952); Croce di Isabella la Cattolica (1956).
BIBL.: E. Brunelleschi, in *Antonio and Spanish Dancing* (London, 1958).

Rosati, Carolina (née C. Galletti; *b* Bologna, 13 Dec. 1826, *d* Cannes, May 1905). Ital. dancer. Studied with Blasis. First appeared aged 7; d. in Rome in 1841, in Trieste and Parma. D. with her husband Francesco R. at La Scala from 1846, at Her Majesty's Th. in London in 1847, where she succeeded Grisi in *Pas de quatre*, created a role in Perrot's *Les quatre saisons* (1848), and was especially successful in P. Taglioni's *Coralia, Thea, Fiorita, La Prima Ballerina* and *Les Plaisirs d'hiver*. Début at the Paris Opéra in 1853 in Mazilier's *Jovita*; then created the leading roles in Mazilier's *Le Corsaire* (1856) and *Marco Spada* (1857). Performed in St. Petersburg 1859–60 and again in 1862, when she created M. Petipa's *La Fille du Pharaon*. Afterwards returned to Paris and retired. Spent the rest of her life in Cannes. She was a distinct terre à terre d. of rare dramatic projection. Jouvin said of her: 'If La Rosati no longer had feet, she would continue to dance with her smile or a curl of her hair.'

BIBL.: I. Guest, in *The Ballet of the Second Empire* (London, 1955).

Rose, Jürgen (*b* Bernburg, 25 Aug. 1937). Ger. th. designer. Designed prods. at Ulm; Cranko then invited him to design the Stuttgart *Romeo and Juliet* prod. (1962). They became close friends and R. designed Cranko's *Swan Lake* (1963), *The Firebird* (1964), *Onegin* (1965), *Poème de l'extase* (1971), *Initials R.B.M.E.* (1972), and his Stuttgart prod. of *The Merry Widow* (1971). He also designed Tudor's *Giselle* (Ger. Op. Berlin, 1963), Franca's *Nutcracker* (National B. of Canada, 1964) and *Cinderella* (1968), MacMillan's *Concerto* (Ger. Op. Berlin, 1966), Neumeier's *Baiser de la Fée* and *Daphnis and Chloe* (Frankfurt, 1972), *Nutcracker* (Royal Winnipeg B., 1972), *Romeo and Juliet* (Royal Dan. B., 1974), *Swan Lake* (Hamburg, 1976), *Sleeping Beauty* (Hamburg, 1978), and *Lady of the Camelias* (Stuttgart, 1978).

Rose Adagio. The pas d'action from the first act of Tchaikovsky-Petipa's *Sleeping Beauty*, danced by Princess Aurora with her 4 suitors, each of whom presents her with 2 roses.

Rose Latulippe. Ballet in 3 acts; libr. W. Solly and Macdonald (also ch.); mus. H. Freeman; déc. R. Prevost. Prod. 16 Aug. 1966, Royal Winnipeg B., Shakespeare Festival Th., Stratford, Ont., with Wiedersheim-Paul, Rutherford, Sheila McKinnon. The first full-length Can. b.; based on an old Fr.-Can. legend, published in 1837, which has some similarity to the *Giselle* story.

Rose malade, La. Ballet in 3 parts; ch. Petit; mus. Mahler; cost. Saint-Laurent. Prod. 10 Jan. 1973, Saison des Bs. de Marseille, Palais des sports, Paris, with Plisetskaya and Bryans. A duo for 2 lovers, accompanied by a small group of men; inspired by W. Blake's *Marriage of Heaven and Hell*, and performed to the Adagietto from Mahler's 5th Symphony. Fr. TV prod.

Rosen, Elsa Marianne von (*b* Stockholm, 21 Apr. 1927). Swed. dancer, choreographer, teacher, and b. director. Studied with Vera Alexandrova, Albert Kozlovsky, J. Hasselquist, and at Royal Dan. B. School. Début in various d.-recitals. D. with B. Russe de Monte Carlo in 1947. Founded The Swedish B. with her husband, the Dan. b. critic A. Fridericia, in 1950; created the title-role in Cullberg's *Miss Julie* (1950) and *Medea* (1951). Ballerina of the Royal Swed. B. 1951–9; d. all the roles of the standard repertory. Toured with her Scandinavian B. 1960–1; then worked as a freelance ballerina, producer of Bournonville bs., and ch. (*La Sylphide* for B. Rambert, 1960; *Irene Holm*, mus. Lumbye, Royal Dan. B., 1960; *Helios*, mus. Nielsen, Scandinavian B., 1960; *Virgin Spring*, mus. Alfven, Royal Dan. B., 1965; *Jenny von Westfalen*, mus. Bentzon, Scandinavian B., 1965; *Don Juan*, mus. Gluck, Royal Dan. B., 1967). She then opened a school in Copenhagen, and was b. director of the Gothenburg B. 1970–6; her

prods. there include *Napoli* and *Swan Lake* (1971), Beethoven's *Prometheus* and Prokofiev's *Romeo and Juliet* (1972), *Utopia* (mus. Offenbach's *Le Papillon*, 1974) and *A Girl's Story* (mus. Emerson, Lake and Palmer, 1975). Produced *La Sylphide* for the Maly B. (Leningrad, 1975). Freelance ch. since 1976. Carina Ari Medal (1962).
BIBL.: A. Fridericia, *E.M.v.R.* (1953).

Rosen, Heinz (*b* Hanover, 3 July 1908, *d* Kreuzlingen, 25 Dec. 1972). Ger. dancer, choreographer, and b. director. Studied with Laban, Jooss, and V. Gsovsky. D. with Bs. Jooss. B. master in Basle from the end of the Second World War until 1951. Ch. the Cocteau-Chailley *Lady and the Unicorn* for Munich Th. am Gärtnerplatz in 1953; then directed musicals, ops., and plays. Ch. Strauss's *Legend of Joseph* (1958) and Orff's *Carmina Burana* and *Catulli Carmina* (1959) for Munich State Op. B. Director of the Munich State Op. 1959–69; ch. many further bs., incl. Egk's *Joan von Zarissa* and Orff's *Trionfo di Afrodite* (1960), W. Killmayer's *La Buffonata* (1961), Blacher's *Moor of Venice*, Stravinsky's *Les Noces* and *Renard* (1962), and Berlioz's *Symphonie fantastique* (1967).
BIBL.: various authors, in *Ballett Theater* (Munich, 1963).

Rosenthal, Jean (*b* New York, 1912, *d* there, 1 May 1969). Amer. lighting designer. One of the pioneer personalities of modern stage lighting for the Amer. th. Worked mainly on Broadway, but also collaborated closely with B. Society and New York City B. 1946–57, M. Graham Dance Co. from 1958, and Robbins's Bs.: U.S.A. 1959–60.
BIBL.: S. Goodman, 'Meet J.R.', *Dance Magazine* (1962/2).

Roslavleva. See *René, Natalia.*

Ross, Bertram (*b* Brooklyn, 13 Nov. 1920). Amer. dancer, teacher, and choreographer. Orig. studied painting; then went to Graham School. Joined Graham's co. in 1954 as her partner; created leading roles in her *Seraphic Dialogue* (1955), *Embattled Garden* and *Clytemnestra* (1958), *Acrobats of God* and *Alcestis* (1960), *Samson Agonistes* (1961), *A Look at Lightning, Phaedra,* and *Legend of Judith* (1962), *Circe* (1963), *Lady of the House of Sleep* and *A Time of Snow* (1968), and *The Archaic Hours* (1969). Teaches at Graham and Juilliard Schools. Had his own group, for which he ch. extensively. Now a singer.
BIBL.: B. J. Stein, 'B.R.', *Dance Magazine* (1976/8).

Ross, Herbert (*b* Brooklyn, 13 May 1926). Amer. dancer, choreographer, and director. Studied with Platova and Humphrey. Danced on Broadway. His early chs., for New York Choreographers Workshop, include *Caprichos* (mus. Bartók, 1950). Ch. the musicals *House of Flowers* (1954), *Body Beautiful* and *Wonderful Town* (1958), and *Finian's Rainbow* (1960), the dances for the *Carmen Jones* film (1954), and for Amer. B. Th. *Paean* (mus.

Chausson) and *The Maids* (mus. Milhaud, 1975), *Tristan* (mus. Wagner) and *Ovid Metamorphoses* (mus. Schoenberg, 1958), *Dark Songs* (mus. Křenek), *Serenade for Seven Dancers* (mus. Bernstein) and *Angel Head* (various jazz mus.; the last three for the Spoleto Festival of 1959). Established B. of Two Worlds with his ballerina wife Nora Kaye in 1960; it made its début at Spoleto and toured Germany, with the new bs. *Persephone* (mus. Bartók) and *The Dybbuk* (mus. R. Starer). Since the co. was disbanded he has pursued a career as dir. of films and musicals. Dir. of the films *The Turning Point* (1977) and *Nijinsky* (1980).
BIBL.: L. Joel, 'H.R Talks Shop', *Dance Magazine* (1967/12).

Ross-Ballette. For the Vienna species of bs. on horseback see *Ballet de chevaux.*

Rossini, Gioacchino (*b* Pesaro, 29 Feb. 1792, *d* Passy, 13 Nov. 1868). Ital. composer. Comp. no bs., but his ops., written or adapted for Paris, contain large b. divertissements, e.g. *Le Siège de Corinthe* (ch. Gardel, 1826). *Moïse* (ch. Gardel, 1827) and *Guillaume Tell* (ch. Aumer, 1829); some of these have occasionally been performed separately. During the 19th century some of his arias were interpolated in b. scores, for instance for Viganò's *I Titani* (Milan, 1819) and for the Hérold version of *La Fille mal gardée* (1828). Special arrangements of R. compositions were made for Massine's *La Boutique fantasque* (1919), Howard's *Selina* (1948), L. Christensen's *Con amore* (1953), and Arpino's *Confetti* (1970). Many different bs. have been set to Britten's R. adaptations of *Soirées musicales* and *Matinées musicales*, e.g. by Tudor and Cranko. P. Darrell ch. *Cinderella*, for which Bramwell Tovey adapted mus. from R.'s op. *La Cenerentola* (Scottish B., 1979).

Rosson, Keith (*b* Birmingham, 21 Jan. 1937). Brit. dancer. Studied at Priory School and Sadler's Wells School. Joined Sadler's Wells B. in 1955; became soloist in 1959 and principal d. in 1964. Created roles in Ashton's *Persephone* (1961) and Petit's *Pelléas et Mélisande* (1969). Principal d. of the Johannesburg PACT B. 1971–5, then briefly joined New London B., and Northern Dance Th. from 1976.

Rota, Giuseppe (*b* Venice, 1822, *d* Turin, 23 May 1865). Ital. dancer, choreographer, and b. master. He started as a self-taught ch. in Turin at about the middle of the century; went on to Milan and Vienna, where he was enormously successful with his spectacular *azione mimo-danzante*.
BIBL.: entry 'R.,G.' in *Enciclopedia dello spettacolo.*

Rotardier, Kelvin (*b* Trinidad, 23 Jan. 1936). West Indian dancer. Studied with Leeder in London and at International School of Dance in New York. D. with the cos. of Primus, African Carnival, Shawn, Holder, and McKayle; joined A. Ailey Dance Theatre in 1964 and became one of its principal dancers.

Rothschild, Bethsabee (Batsheva) de (*b* London, 1914). Isr. dance promoter and director. Studied at Sorbonne Univ. in Paris and Columbia Univ. in New York, where she became interested in d., studying with Graham and later sponsoring perfs. of her co. and tours abroad. Settled in Israel in 1958. Established Batsheva Dance Co. in Tel Aviv, 1964, Bat-Dor Studios of Dance, ibid., 1967, and Bat-Dor Dance Co., ibid. 1968. Author of *La Danse artistique aux USA* (Paris, 1949).

Rouge et noir. See *Etrange farandole, L'*.

Roussel, Albert (*b* Tourcoing, 5 Apr. 1869, *d* Royan, 23 Aug. 1937). Fr. composer. Wrote the mus. for Staats' *Le Festin de l'araignée* (1913), Lifar's *Bacchus et Ariane* (1931) and *Aeneas* (1938), and for the b. op. *Padmâvatî* (ch. Staats, 1923). P. Darrell used his Petite Suite pour Orchestre in *Francesca* (1967).

Rousanne, Madame (née R. Sarkissian; *b* Baku, 1894, *d* Paris, 19 Mar. 1958). Armenian-Fr. teacher. Studied with Clustine and Volinine; gave very few perfs. because she started her training so late. Opened her Paris studio in 1928 and became one of the city's most famous teachers; her pupils included Darsonval, Peretti, Brieux, Chauviré, Verdy, Algaroff, Kalioujny, van Dyk, Babilée, Petit, and Béjart.

Roux, Aline (*b* Brest, 22 Aug. 1935). Fr. dancer, choreographer, and teacher. Studied with K. Waehner and at Kansas Univ. Began dancing with Waehner's Bs. Contemporains in 1960. Formed her own group, Rhythme et Structure, in 1969, for which she has ch. extensively. Teaches in Paris. Second Prize (Cologne Young Choreographers Competition, 1968); first Prize (Ballet pour demain, Bagnolet, 1970).
BIBL.: L. Rossel, 'Profil d'A.R.', *Les Saisons de la danse* (1968/11).

Rowe, Marilyn (*b* Sydney, 20 Aug. 1946). Brit. d. Studied with Frances Letl and at Austral. B. School. Joined Austral. B. in 1965; became principal d. in 1970. Created leading roles in Moiseyev's *The Last Vision* (1969), Tetley's *Gemini* (1973), and Hynd's *Merry Widow* (1975). Deputy art. dir. Austral. B. 1983–4; became dir. Austral. B. Dancers Co. 1985. Silver Medal (Moscow, 1973); O.B.E. (1984).

Rowell, Kenneth (*b* Melbourne, 1922). Austral. painter and designer. Designed Gore's *Winter Night* (B. Rambert, 1948), *Carte Blanche* (Sadler's Wells B., 1953), and *Light Fantastic* (W. Gore's B., 1953), Charnley's *Alice in Wonderland* (London Festival B., 1953), MacMillan's *Laiderette* (B. Rambert, 1954), *Baiser de la Fée* (Royal B., 1960), and *Solitaire* (Royal Dan. B. prod., 1961), and for Austral. B. *Coppélia* (1960), *Giselle* (1965), Helpmann's *Sun Music* (1968), and *Sleeping Beauty* (1973). Author of *Stage Design* (1972). Contributed 'The Designer Speaks' to C. Crisp and M. Clarke, *Making a Ballet* (London, 1975).

Roy, Alexander (orig. Udo Badstübner; *b* Magdeburg, 16 Oct. 1935). Ger. dancer, choreographer, and b. director. Studied with G. Steinweg, T. Gsovsky, Blank, Kiss, and Northcote. Began dancing in Leipzig in 1951; then with E. Berlin Comic Op. from 1954, Bremen B. from 1957, Amer. Festival B. in 1960, Amsterdam B. in 1961, Teatro del Balletto in 1962, and Netherlands Dance Th. in 1963. Formed International B. Caravan with his ballerina wife Christine Gallea in 1965; has since ch. extensively, occasionally also working for B. of Flanders. Re-named his co. The A. R. London Ballet Theatre in 1976.

Royal Academy of Dancing. Founded by Genée, Karsavina, Bedells, E. Espinosa, and Richardson in London on 31 July 1920 as Association of Operatic Dancing in Great Britain. In 1936 it was granted a Royal Charter and took its present name. Genée was its first President, succeeded by Fonteyn in 1954. Its aim is to further the cause of artistic dancing throughout Great Britain and the Commonwealth, especially classic-academic dancing, and the continuous improvement of its teaching standards. Examinations are held every year for dancers and teachers, a comprehensive programme of lectures, demonstrations, qualification courses, and conferences is offered in addition to the teacher's Training Course, which was started in 1947, and diplomas are awarded. Various scholarships are available, and since 1954 the Queen Elizabeth II Coronation Award has been made for distinguished services to Brit. b.; the recipients include de Valois, Karsavina, Rambert, Dolin, Bedells, Helpmann, Moreton, Beaumont, Richardson, Idzikowski, Gilpin, van Praagh, K. Gordon, Louise Browne, Ruth French, and Haskell. John Field was apptd. art. dir. in 1975 and dir. 1976–9, followed by Alan Hooper as art. dir. 1979–82 and dir. to 1983, J. Farron dir. since 1983, with D. Wall assoc. dir. since 1984.

Royal Ballet, The. The name given by Royal Charter on 31 Oct. 1956 to the former Sadler's Wells B. and Sadler's Wells Th. B. (at that time based respectively at the Royal Op. Ho., Cov. Gdn., and Sadler's Wells Th., London) and the former Sadler's Wells B. School. The organization is descended from the Academy of Choreographic Art, started by de Valois in London in 1926. Its pupils appeared occasionally in the bs. which de Valois ch. for the Old Vic prods. She was invited by Lilian Baylis to move her school to the newly built Sadler's Wells Th. in Jan. 1931. A 'first full evening of ballet' was given on 5 May 1931 (at the Old Vic), with *Les petits riens, Danse sacrée et profane, Hommage aux Belles Viennoises, The Jackdaw and the Pigeons, Scène de ballet* from Faust, Bach Suite of Dances, and *The Faun*, all with ch. by de Valois, and a *Spanish Dance* by Dolin; the dancers included de Valois, Moreton, Sheila McCarthy, Beatrice Appleyard, and Joy Newton, and guest

The Royal Ballet in Ashton's *Symphonic Variations*.   Photo Edward Griffiths.

artists Dolin, Leslie French, and Stanley Judson. The first perf. at Sadler's Wells Th. followed on 15 May, and in the autumn season fortnightly perfs. were given by what was now called the Vic-Wells B., with Lambert as musical dir. (until 1948). De Valois' *Job*, created for the Camargo Society, was the most ambitious and successful early prod. (1931). Apart from de Valois the first Brit. ch. working for the co. was Ashton, who contributed *Regatta* as guest ch. in 1931 and *Les Rendezvous* on joining the co. in 1933. Markova appeared with the co. from 1932 and Helpmann from 1933. First prod. of a classic was the second act of *Swan Lake* (1932), followed by *Coppélia* (with Lopokova as guest, 1933), *Giselle*, *Nutcracker*, and the complete *Swan Lake* (1934)—all mounted by N. Sergeyev. In 1935 Fonteyn had her first substantial role in Ashton's *Rio Grande*. Further important dancers during these early years included May, Brae, Honer, Turner, Gore, Chappell, and Somes; the more important b. creations included de Valois' *The Haunted Ballroom* (1934), *The Rake's Progress* (1935), and *Checkmate* (1937), Ashton's *Baiser de la Fée* (1935), *Apparitions* (1935), *Nocturne* (1936), *Les Patineurs* and *A Wedding Bouquet* (1937), and *Horoscope* (1938). *The Sleeping Princess* was first given in 1939. During the war (from 1940) activity increased, with tours and appearances at London's New Th. and Princes Th. The co. first visited Paris in 1937; on a second Eur. visit they were almost trapped by the Ger. troops invading Holland in 1940. Helpmann ch. *Comus* (1941), *Hamlet* (1942), and *Miracle in the Gorbals* (1944). After the Second World War the co. became the resident co. of the Royal Op. House, Cov. Gdn., opening with a new prod. of

Sleeping Beauty on 20 Feb. 1946. This marked a new stage of development, which brought enormous international reputation. The first internationally famous ch. to work for it was Massine, who staged *La Boutique fantasque*, *Mam'zelle Angot*, and *Le Tricorne* (1947), followed by Balanchine with *Ballet Imperial* and Petit with *Ballabile* (both 1950). Ashton's *Symphonic Variations* (1946) summed up the stylistic virtues of the co.; it was followed by *Cinderella* (1948), his first full-length b. Important dancers at the end of and immediately after the war included Grey, Shearer, Elvin, Hart, Rassine, and Field. The Sadler's Wells Op. B. was formed in 1946 as a second co. for young dancers and aspiring choreographers. It changed its name to Sadler's Wells Th. B., and was based on the th. in Rosebery Ave., with extensive provincial tours. Here Nerina, Beriosova, Lane, Page, Blair, Holden, and MacLeary first became known to a wide public; such choreographers as Cranko, MacMillan, and Rodrigues created their first bs. for this co. During the next few years the Cov. Gdn. co. and its repertory were steadily strengthened and the co. started regular foreign tours; its first New York appearance in 1949 was triumphantly successful. The school was reorganized and a boarding school was attached. Further important prods. of the 2 cos. up to 1956 were Ashton's *Scènes de ballet* (1948), *Daphnis and Chloe* (1951), *Sylvia* (1952), *Homage to the Queen* (1953), and *Birthday Offering* (1956), Cranko's *Pineapple Poll* and *Harlequin in April* (1951) and *The Lady and the Fool* (1954), and MacMillan's *Danses concertantes* and *House of Birds* (1955) and *Solitaire* (1956—all Cranko's and MacMillan's bs. for Sadler's Wells Th. B.) It then became the Royal B. in 1956; the difficulty for the general public since then in differentiating between the 2 cos. led to some complaints. De Valois resigned in 1963 and was succeeded by Ashton as dir., with MacMillan as chief ch. B. for All group was founded in 1964 under the direction of Brinson, with the aim of travelling with its B. Plays to places which cannot be visited by the larger cos. The co. was reorganized when MacMillan became its dir. in the autumn of 1970 (with Field, and then Wright as associate dir.). The initial intention was to have one large co., with a rotating group of selected dancers who would tour as the 'New Group' with many new prods. and no classics, but this policy was never fully implemented. Since 1975 the pattern has again been of 2 large cos., one of about 80 dancers based at Cov. Gdn. and undertaking some major tours, the other of about 50 dancers, mostly on tour with London seasons at Sadler's Wells (now called Sadler's Wells Royal B.). N. Morrice was art. dir. 1977–86, since when A. Dowell has taken over. New prods. of the classics have always been held in special esteem; new bs. to enter the repertory include Cranko's *Prince of the Pagodas* (the first specially commissioned full-length Brit. b. score, 1957) and *Antigone* (1959), Ashton's *Ondine* (1958), *La Fille mal gardée* (1960), *The Two Pigeons* (1961), *Marguerite and Armand* (1963), *The Dream* (1964), *Monotones* (1965), *Sinfonietta* (1967), *Jazz Calendar*, *Enigma Variations* (both 1968), *A Month in the Country* (1976), and *Rhapsody* (1980); MacMillan's *The Burrow* (1958), *Baiser de la Fée* and *The Invitation* (1960), *The Rite of Spring* (1962), *Images of Love* (1964), *Romeo and Juliet* (1965), *Song of the Earth* (1966), *Concerto* (1967), *Anastasia* (1971), *Manon* (1974), *Rituals* (1975), *Mayerling* (1978), *La Fin du jour* (1979), *Gloria* (1980), and *Isadora* (1981); Nijinska's *Les Biches* (1964) and *Les Noces* (1966); Tudor's *Shadowplay* (1967) and *Knight Errant* (1969); Balanchine's *Serenade* (1964), *Apollo* (1966), *The Four Temperaments*, *Agon*, and *Prodigal Son* (1973); Robbins's *Dances at a Gathering* (1970) and *Afternoon of a Faun* (1971); Tetley's *Field Figures* (1971) and *Laborintus* (1972); Van Manen's *Grosse Fuge* (1972) and *Four Schumann Pieces* (1975); J. Carter's *Shukumei* (1975) and *Lulu* (1976), together with bs. by younger choreographers such as Drew, Cauley, Killar, Morse, Bintley, and Corder. The co. received a tremendous boost when Nureyev joined it as a permanent guest in 1962. The younger generation of dancers emerging during the 1960s included Sibley, Seymour, Park, Wells, Barbieri, Mason, Penney, Collier, Dowell, Wall, and Coleman. The R.B. is now considered among the foremost b. cos. of the world, and because of its large and supremely balanced repertory and its wealth of highly individual first class dancers many people consider that it is the leading co. in international terms. Many of its bs. are presented in TV or film prods. BIBL.: A. Bland, *The R.B.—The first 50 Years* (London, 1981).

Royal Ballet School, The. This began as the Sadler's Wells School, founded by de Valois 1931 (a precursor had been her London Academy of Choreographic Art, opened 1926). With Haskell's appointment as dir. and its move to Baron's Court in 1947, the school was much expanded, incl. full academic education. The Lower School, run as a boarding and day school, with grammar school education and b. training for girls and boys aged 11–16, was established at White Lodge, Richmond Park, 1955, while the Upper School, offering full b. curriculum and education courses for girls and boys over 16, continues at its Talgarth Rd. base. School perfs. and the participation of senior pupils in the perfs. of the Royal B. provide th. experience. Haskell was succeeded as dir. by M. Wood 1966–78, J. Monahan 1978–83, and M. Park since then, with B. Fewster as dir. of B. Studies (since 1968). The Upper School also runs a Teacher's Training Course, dir. by Valerie Adams. Members of the 2 cos. of the Royal B. are, almost without exception, ex-students of the school.

Royal Danish Ballet. Court bs. are recorded in Copenhagen in the second half of the 16th century. At the Lille Grønnegade Th. (built 1722) and the Royal Th. at Kongens Nytorv (1748) b. was run by Ital. and Fr. b. masters for many years. Under the Florentine Galeotti b. flourished between 1775 and 1811; his *The Whims of Cupid* (1786) is still performed today, but his bs. after Voltaire and Shakespeare and his excursions into Scandinavian history were equally popular at the time. The Fr. d. Antoine Bournonville came to Copenhagen in 1792; his more distinguished son August Bournonville (1805–79) was the greatest ch. ever produced by the country and also an unusually successful teacher. He reorganized the system of b. education completely. From 1829 almost until his death he controlled the school and the co., both of which owe to him their world-wide reputation. Of the 50-odd bs. he created, 10 have survived, and still form the backbone of the company's repertory, e.g. *La Sylphide* (1836), *Napoli* (1842), *Konservatoriet* (1849), *Kermis in Bruges* (1851), *A Folk Tale* (1854), and *Far from Denmark* (1860). His pupils H. Beck and V. Borchsenius tried to preserve his heritage, but there was a marked decline. Fokine and Balanchine worked with the co. during the late 1920s and early 1930s, but there was little creative output. In the 1940s b. flourished again under the inspired leadership of H. Lander. For the first time Dan. b. gained international recognition, and the co. made its first visits abroad; Lander's *Etudes* (1948) became a world-wide hit, and the wealth of the Bournonville repertory at last received its due appreciation. Lander left for Paris in 1951 and a period of instability followed; directors changed frequently, but the school continued its steady course under Volkova. Guest choreographers included Balanchine, Robbins,

Ashton, Petit, Cullberg, and MacMillan. Flindt was appointed b. dir. in 1966, and the situation improved as he attempted to build up a carefully balanced repertory of Bournonville classics, the standard classics of the world repertory, bs. by choreographers of international repute (incl. some modern-dance-orientated ones, e.g. Tetley, P. Taylor, and M. Louis), and a strong contingent of his own bs., always very ambitious contemporary creations. The co. has always had interesting d. personalities; Margot Lander and Børge Ralov, the stars of the 1930s and 40s, were followed by Mona Vangsaae, Kirsten Ralov, Margrete Schanne, Kirsten Simone, Frank Schaufuss, Niels Bjørn Larsen, Fredbjørn Bjørnsson, and Henning Kronstam. Toni Lander and Erik Bruhn have embarked on international careers, as have Flindt, Niels Kehlet, Peter Martins, Peter Schaufuss, and Ib Andersen. The present generation of Dan. dancers incl. Anna Laerkesen, Solveig Østergaard, Vivi Flindt, Mette Hønningen, Sorella Englund, Dinna Bjørn, Flemming Halby, Flemming Ryberg, Palle Jakobsen, Johnny Eliasen, and Hans Jakob Kølgaard. H. Kronstam was art. dir. 1979–85, succeeded by Frank Andersen.
BIBL.: S. Kragh-Jacobsen, *The R.D.B.* (Copenhagen and London, 1955); D. Fog, *The R.D.B. 1760–1958* (check-list of prods.; Copenhagen, 1961); Kragh-Jacobsen, *20 Solo Dancers of the R.D.B.* (Copenhagen, 1965).

Royale. An entrechat with two crossings of the legs; really an entrechat-deux. Named after Louis XIV, who was unable to perform the asked-for entrechat-quatre.

Royal New Zealand Ballet. See *New Zealand Ballet Company*.

Royal Swedish Ballet. The first court b. perf. in Sweden took place in 1638, arranged by the Fr. b. master Antoine de Beaulieu. When the new Stockholm op. house opened in 1773 the Fr. Louis Gallodier was appointed b. master of the co., which consisted of 24 dancers. 10 years later there were 72 dancers, some of Swed. origin. Under Gustavus III b. flourished; Antoine Bournonville (the father of the Dan. August B.) and Marcadet were choreographers. Didelot was born in Stockholm, but made his career abroad. Filippo Taglioni became b. master in 1818; his daughter Marie also worked abroad, returning only rarely as a guest to the city of her birth. The brilliantly gifted premier danseur and later famous teacher Christian Johansson d. as Taglioni's partner in Russia and stayed there. The first well-known Swed. b. master was Anders Selinder, a contemporary of August Bournonville, who based his bs. on folklore material. August Bournonville also worked as a guest in Stockholm. The co. suffered a severe decline during the second half of the 19th century, although it recovered slightly when the two Fokines came to Stockholm in 1913. They staged some Fokine bs. and generated new enthusiasm among the young dancers; but the best of these left the country to appear with the Paris-based Bs. Suédois 1920–5. Fokine returned several times, but there was no b. continuity. Jan Cieplinski was appointed b. master in 1928, followed by Julian Algo in 1931, and by George Gé in 1940; b. activity was still very limited. The public had meanwhile turned increasingly to modern d., since Duncan's first triumphant success in Stockholm. Such dancers as Jooss, Wigman, and Kreutzberg found an enthusiastic audience, and it was their example which inspired younger Swedes such as Cullberg and Cramér to set up their own groups. A new start was made with the appointment of Tudor as b. dir. in 1950, succeeded by Skeaping in 1953, who concentrated on cultivating the classics; the modern repertory also improved, through the work of Cullberg (*Miss Julie, Medea*), Cramér (*The Prodigal Son*), and Åkesson. Tudor returned occasionally, the repertory was enlarged with bs. by Massine and Balanchine, and in more recent years also bs. by such choreographers as Robbins, Limón, Tetley, MacMillan, Nureyev, Feld, Cranko, and Kylián. Macdonald was b. dir. 1964–6, Bruhn 1967–71; James Moore 1972–5 and Ivo Cramér 1975–80; Gunilla Roempke 1980–4, E. Madsen 1984–6, and N. A. Häggbom since. The principal dancers incl. Anneli Alhanko, Yvonne Brosset, Kerstin Lidström, Viveka Ljung, Berit Sköld, Astrid Strüwer, Niklos Ek, Nils-Ake Häggbom, István Kisch and Per-Arthur Segerström.

Royal Winnipeg Ballet. The oldest of Canada's 3 top b. cos. is descended from the Winnipeg B. Club, which was founded by Gweneth Lloyd and Betty Farrally in 1938 and gave its first perf. as Winnipeg B. in 1939. It continued on a semi-professional basis until 1949, when it became fully professional. The first b. co. to be granted a (Brit.) Royal Charter in 1953. Lloyd was succeeded as Director by Arnold Spohr in 1958; he was responsible for the considerable build-up of the co. and its repertory during the next few years and the increasing number of foreign tours. The present repertory offers a solid basis of classics, supplemented by bs. by Balanchine, de Mille, Macdonald, Neumeier, Vesak, and others. The list of leading soloists incl. Evelyn Hart, Susan Bennet, Patti Caplette, Kathleen Duffy, Margaret Slota, Michael Bjerknes, Joost Pelt, Baxter Branstetter, David Herriott, and David Peregrine.
BIBL.: M. Wyman, 'The R.W.B.: 35 Years of Pioneering', *Dance Magazine* (1975/9); M. Wyman, *The R.W.B.: The First Forty Years* (New York, 1978).

Ruanne, Patricia (*b* Leeds, 3 June 1945). Brit. dancer. Studied with Jean Pearce, Louise Brown, and at Royal B. School. Joined Royal B. touring co. in 1962; became soloist in 1966, principal d. in 1969. Left for London Festival B. in 1973, and became b. mistress 1983–5; created leading role in Moreland's *Prodigal Son* (1974), Hynd's *The*

Sanguine Fan (1976), and Prokovsky's *The Storm* and *Verdi Variations* (both 1981). Joined Paris Op. 1986 as a teacher.

Ruanova, Maria (*b* Buenos Aires, 1912). Argent. dancer, b. mistress, and teacher. Studied with Y. Smirnova, B. Romanov, and Nijinska. Joined Teatro Colón B. in 1926; became ballerina in 1932. Joined Blum's B. Russe de Monte Carlo in 1936. Also danced with Grand B. du Marquis de Cuevas in 1956; then retired and took up teaching at the Buenos Aires National B. School. Director of Teatro Colón B. for several years until 1972.

Rubinstein, Ida Lvovna (*b* St. Petersburg, *c.* 1885, *d* Vence, 20 Sep. 1960). Russ. dancer and actress. Studied recitation and mime, and, stimulated by Duncan, for a short while privately with Fokine; he ch. a *Salome* dance for her, which was performed only once because the censor intervened. As a member of the Diaghilev co. 1909–11, she was much admired for her exceptional beauty as Fokine's *Cléopâtre* and *Zobeide*. She then tried to form a rival ensemble to the Diaghilev troupe, with herself as protagonist, for which she commissioned a number of works: from d'Annunzio and Debussy *Le Martyre de Saint Sébastien* (ch. Fokine, 1911), from D. de Sévérac and E. Verhaeren *Hélène de Sparte* (prod. A. Sanine, 1911), and from d'Annunzio and Pizzetti *La Pisanelle* (ch. Fokine, 1913). After the First World War she appeared in various plays, and d. in Staats' *Istar* at the Paris Opéra in 1924. Fromed another co. 1928–9, revived in 1931 and 1934; created the leading role in specially commissioned works such as *Les Noces de Psyché et d l'Amour* (mus. Bach), *Boléro* (mus. Ravel), *Le Baiser de la Fée* (mus. Stravinsky—all ch. Nijinska), *David* (mus. Sauguet, ch. Massine—all 1928), *La Valse* (mus. Ravel, ch. Nijinska, 1929), *Amphion* (mus. Honegger, ch. Massine, 1931), *Diane de Poitiers* (mus. Ibert, ch. Fokine), *Perséphone* (mus. Stravinsky, ch. Jooss), and *Sémiramis* (mus. Honegger, ch. Fokine, all 1934). Retired in 1935, and handed over to the Paris Opéra the further works she had commissioned, incl. Milhaud's and Claudel's *La Sagesse,* Honegger's and Claudel's *Joan of Arc at the Stake* (in which she appeared for a single perf. in Basle in 1938 and in Orleans in 1939), F. Schmitt's *Oriane la Sans-Egale,* and Ibert's *Le Chevalier errant.* Her exceptional, highly individual, and very complex fascination has been defined by d'Annunzio as '. . . l'artiste dont la tête voilée de rêve et de doleur à la charpente osseuse de l'Athéna de Lemnos, dont le corps a la ligne la plus austère qui se puisse trouver et dont toute la personne respirait l'ardeur mystique.'
BIBL.: entry 'R.,I.' in *Enciclopedia dello spettacolo.*

Rudner, Sara (*b c.* 1945). Amer. dancer and choreographer. Studied with Sanasardo and d. with his co. until branching out with various other cos. and finally becoming a principal in Tharp's co. 1966–74. Now working as a solo performer and choreographing for her own S.R. Performing Ens. Married to the d. Bob Clifford.
BIBL.: interview with S.R., *Dance and Dancers* (1978/11).

Rudolph, Johann Joseph (also Jean-Joseph Rodolphe; *b.* Strasbourg, 14 Oct. 1730, *d* Paris, 18 Aug. 1812). Fr. comp. Wrote a number of bs. for Noverre while he was in Stuttgart, incl. *Rinaldo und Armida* (1761), *Psyché et l'Amour* (1762), *Medea und Jason* (1763). In Paris he wrote the b. op. *Ismenor* (1773) and the b. *Apelles et Campaspe* (1799).

Ruins and Visions. Ballet in 1 act; ch. Humphrey; mus. Britten; set Paul Trautvetter; cost P. Lawrence. Prod. 20 Aug. 1953. J. Limón D. Co., 6th Amer. Dance Festival, Connecticut College, New London, with Limón, Koner, Hoving, Lavinia Nielsen. Set to Britten's String Quartet; its title is taken from that of a book of Stephen Spender's poems. 'From the shelter of a garden we move into the extravagant atmosphere of the actor's stage, on into the raucousness of the street, then into the hideousness of a war-shattered place. As the action closes, the Actor leads a Litany of Survival' (programme note).

Ruses d'amour, Les. Ballet in 1 act; libr. and ch. Petipa; mus. Glazunov. Prod. 29 Jan. 1900, Hermitage Th., St. Petersburg, with Legnani, Gerdt. The b., also called *The Trial of Damis,* brings a Watteau *fête champètre* to life. Isabella, the daughter of a Duchess, dresses as a chamber-maid to test the love of her betrothed, the Marquis Damis. Only when he is prepared to elope with her in her disguise is she convinced that he loves her for herself and not for her title. An earlier b. *La Toilette de Vénus ou L.R.d'a.* by Noverre, Lyons, 1760.
BIBL.: C. W. Beaumont, 'L.R.d'a.' in *Complete Book of Ballets* (London, 1951).

Ruskaja, Jia (*née* Eugenia Borisenko; *b* Kerch, 1902 *d* Rome, 19 Apr. 1970). Russ.-Ital dancer and teacher. Studied d. as a child, then medicine in Geneva. Went to Rome in 1923, where she d. at the Teatro degli indipendenti. Began working as a d. and ch. in various Ital cities in 1924, collaborating on many open air drama prods. Director of the Milan La Scala B. School 1932–4, where she taught her own system (based on Jaques-Dalcroze) which she called Orchestica and for which she developed her own system of notation. Opened a private school in Rome in 1934, with considerable support from the Fascist government. This became the Accademia nazionale di danza, which enabled her to exert great influence in teaching classic b., though she was herself a modern d. Wrote *La danza come modo d'essere* (1928).
BIBL.: entry 'R.,J.' in *Enciclopedia dello spettacolo.*

Russell, Paul (*b* Texas, 2 Mar. 1947). Amer. dancer. Studied at School of Amer. B. and Dance

Th. of Harlem School. Début with Hartford B. in 1970. Joined Dance Th. of Harlem in 1971, Scottish B. in 1978, and later became principal d. San Francisco B. 1980.

BIBL.: R. Greskovic, in 'Dance Theatre of Harlem', *Ballet Review* (vol. 4, no. 6).

Russia. See *Soviet Union.*

Russian Soldier. Ballet in 4 scenes; libr. and ch. Fokine; mus. Prokofiev; déc. Doboujinsky. Prod. 6 Apr. 1942, B. Th., Met. Op. House, New York, with Lazowski. Based on Prokofiev's Suite from *Lieutenant Kijé,* Fokine dedicated the b., the last one he completed. to the Russ. soldiers of World War II. A soldier, dying on the battlefield, remembers some of the events of his home and his life. A completely different b. version of the same mus. by Lapauri and Tarasova in *Lieutenant Kijé* for Bolshoi B., 1963.

Russillo, Joseph (*b* New York, 1941). Amer. dancer, choreographer, and teacher. Studied with Mattox. Danced with several Amer. cos. Went to Spoleto Festival 1968, where he also worked as ch. Then went to Turin, Milan, and eventually Paris, where he formed a co. with A. Béranger in 1971, of which he is now the sole dir. and ch. His bs. include *Momente* (mus. Stockhausen), *Il etait une fois comme toutes les fois* (mus. W. Carlos), *Rêves* (mus. Ravel's 2 piano concertos) and *Mémoires pour demain* (mus. Berlioz and J. Lejeune). His co.

first visited London in Mar. 1973. As a jazz d. teacher has worked mainly at Chauviré's Paris B. Academy. Resident ch. of Paris Nouveau Carré Th. since 1975.

BIBL.: L. Rossel, 'J.R.', *Les Saisons de la danse* (1971/ 1); N. McLain Stoop 'J.R.', *Dance Magazine* (1979/ 5).

Rutherford, Richard (*b* Augusta). Amer. dancer and b. régisseur. Studied with Joffrey, Caton, and at Amer. B. Th. School. Joined Royal Winnipeg B. in 1957 and later became principal d.; b. régisseur and assistant to the director A. Spohr since 1970.

BIBL.: E. Herf, 'R.R.', *Ballet Today* (1966/9).

Ruud, Tomm (*b* Pasadena, Cal., 25 May 1943). Amer. d. and ch. Studied with W. Christensen, M. Gavers, S. Williams, Pereyaslavec, et al. Charter member of B. West 1963–75; became soloist in 1965, principal d. in 1969. Since 1975 with San Francisco B. Has ch. several bs., incl. *Polyandrion* (mus. Copland) for Amer. B. Th. in 1973. Married to the d. Mary Bird.

BIBL.: R. Baker, 'Spotlight on T.R.', *Dance Magazine* (1972/2).

Ryberg, Flemming (*b* Copenhagen, 24 Nov. 1940). Dan. dancer Brother of Kirsten Simone. Studied at Royal Dan. B. School. Joined Royal Dan. B. in 1959; became solo-dancer in 1966. An outstanding Bournonville dancer.

S

Sabirova, Malika (*b* Dushanbe, 1942, *d* 27 Feb. 1982). Sov. dancer. Studied at Leningrad Ch. School; graduated in 1961. Returned to Dushanbe and became ballerina of the S. Aini Th. for Op. and B. of Tajikistan. D. in London with the Bolshoi B. in 1965. A film *Malika* was produced with her. Silver Medal (Varna, 1964); Gold Medal (Moscow, 1969).

Sacharoff, Alexander. See *Sakharoff, Alexander.*

Sachs, Curt (*b* Berlin, 29 June 1881, *d* New York, 5 Feb. 1959). Ger.-Amer. musicologist. Author of *Eine Weltgeschichte des Tanzes* (Berlin, 1933), published in Eng. as *World History of the Dance* in 1937, still considered the standard work of its kind.

Sacountala. Ballet in 2 acts; libr. Gautier; ch. L. Petipa; mus. Ernest Reyer; sets Martin, Nolau, and Rubé; cost. Albert. Prod. 14 July 1858, Opéra, Paris, with Ferraris and Petipa. The b. is based on the 4th-century Sanskrit drama of the same name by Kalidasa; it tells of the love of King Dushmata for the humble maid Sacountala who is of divine origin.
BIBL.: C. W. Beaumont, 'S.' in *Complete Book of Ballets* (London, 1951).

Sacre du printemps, Le (orig. Russ. title: *Vesna suyashchennaya*, also Eng. *The Rite of Spring*). Pictures from Pagan Russia in 2 Parts by Stravinsky and Roerich; ch. Nijinsky; cond. Monteux. Prod. 29 May 1913, Bs. Russes de Diaghilev, Th. des Champs-Elysées, Paris, with Maria Piltz. The b. represents a fertility rite, during which a girl is sacrificed. At its Paris première the b. caused an enormous scandal and was given only six times afterwards. A different prod. by Massine, using the same Roerich déc., same co., with Sokolova as the Chosen Girl, in 1920. Massine staged it again with Graham in Philadelphia in 1930 and revived it for several cos. Later versions by Horton (Hollywood, 1937), Milloss (Rome, 1941), Georgi (Düsseldorf, 1953), Wigman (Municipal Op. Berlin, 1957), Béjart (Brussels, 1959; later prod. for Belgian TV), MacMillan (Royal B., London 1962; déc. Nolan, with Mason), Kasatkina and Vassiliov (Bolshoi B., 1965), Walter (Düsseldorf, 1970), Neumeier (Frankfurt, 1972), Tetley (Munich State Op., 1974), and Van Manen (Dutch National B., 1974). The b. also features in Disney's film *Fantasia* (1940). A completely different version, in cartoon style, to the four-hand piano adaptation, by P. Taylor (1980)—the same musical adaptation also by R. Alston (1981).
BIBL.: *The R. of S. Sketches 1911–1913*, with autograph facsimiles, commentary by the comp. on Nijinsky's original ch., and essays and commentary by R. Craft (London/New York, 1969); L. Kirstein, 'L.S.d.p.' in *Movement & Metaphor* (New York, 1970); R. Buckle, in *Nijinsky* (London, 1971).

Saddler, Donald (*b* Van Nuys, Calif., 24 Jan 1920). Amer. dancer and choreographer. Studied with Maracci, Dolin, and Tudor. Began dancing in Cal. in 1937; d. with B. Th. 1939–43, 1946–7. Established himself as a ch. of musicals with Bernstein's *Wonderful Town* (1953); his greatest success was *No, No, Nanette* (1971). Asst. to dir. then assoc. dir. Harkness B. 1964–9.

Sadler's Wells Royal Ballet. The present name for the Royal B. touring co. came into force when the troupe, previously known as the Royal B. touring Co., started its London autumn 1976 season at the Rosebery Ave. th. with a regular rehearsal base there.

Sadoff, Simon (*b* Hoboken, 1919). Amer. pianist and conductor. Has been pianist and conductor of the New York City B. for many years, and also with the cos. of Limón, Taylor, and Graham.

Sagan, Gene Hill (*b* Emporia, Virg., 28 Sep. 1936). Amer. dancer, choreographer, teacher, and b. master. Studied with Michael Brigante and M. Panaieff, at B. Th. School, and with Vyroubova and Corvino. Began dancing with First Negro Classical B. in 1959, subsequently with L. Johnson D. Co., C. de Lavallade and G. Holder, Puerto Rican B., Amer. Festival B., Israel National Op. B., Jazz B. of Stockholm, and Cologne B. Started to ch. for his own Munich-based co. in 1963. Has since worked mainly in Israel, where he has ch. for various cos. Has also taught for various Israeli schools and academies.

Sailor's Return, The. Ballet in 2 acts and 6 scenes; libr., ch., and déc. Howard; mus. Arthur Oldham. Prod. 2 June 1947, B. Rambert, Sadler's Wells Th., London, with Gilmour, Gore, Staff, Gilpin. The b. is based on David Garnett's well-known short novel. A sailor returns to his native fishing village with his Afr. bride. The population is at first completely enchanted by her, but eventually prejudice and race hatred take their tragic course.
BIBL.: C. Beaumont, 'T.S.R.' in *Ballets of Today* (London, 1954).

St. Denis, Ruth (orig. R. Dennis; *b* New Jersey, 20 Jan. 1879, *d* Hollywood, 21 July 1968). Amer. dancer, choreographer, and teacher. Studied recitation, social d., and Delsarte mime with her

mother; then briefly studied b. with Bonfanti. Appeared in the New York music-hall prods. of David Belasco. A cigarette poster showing the Egyptian goddess Isis inspired her first oriental b. in 1904; she presented it in 1906 in the series of New York Sunday Night Smoking Concerts: *Radha, the Dance of the Five Senses* (mus. from Delibes's *Lakmé*). During the same year created *The Incense* and *The Cobras* for her first d. recital programme, with which she embarked on her first Eur. tour in July. This lasted for 3 years and was triumphantly successful, especially in Berlin and Vienna. Her next dances were *The Nautch* and *Yogi*. In 1909 created *Egypta* for her first big Amer. tour followed by her first Jap. b. *O-Mika* (with spoken text) in 1913. Established Denishawn D. School with Shawn in Los Angeles in 1915; this became the first Amer. platform of modern d., and had its own co., which toured extensively until 1932. One of their major prods. was *A Dance Pageant of Egypt, Greece, and India* (mus. by W. Myrowitz, Horst, and A. Nevins, 1916) and Gluck's *Orpheus and Eurydice* (1918). After her separation from Shawn and the disbanding of Denishawn, she concentrated on the study and execution of religious dances. Presented *Masque of Mary* at New York Riverside Church in 1932; then founded the Society of Spiritual Arts, which aimed to synthesize religious motivation and artistic decoration. Established New York School of Natya with La Meri in 1940, and continued to perform in demonstrations, lectures, films, and TV prods. until shortly before her death. Published a book of poems, *Lotus Light*, in 1932, and her autobiography *An Unfinished Life* in 1939. As d., ch., teacher, and theorist she attempted to make mus. visible through d. (rather as did Jaques-Dalcroze). She drew her main inspiration from Eastern art, though she had a rather imprecise idea of the various oriental d.-styles. Her dances had a refined preciosity which is apparent in many of her titles; e.g. *Japanese Flower Arrangement, White Jade, The Peacock, The Dance of the Black and Gold Sari, Kwannon, Chrysanthemum, Thirteenth-Century Poetess*, and *Ishtar of the Seven Gates*. There are several films about her art, incl. *Ruth St. Denis* by Baribault (1940s and early 50s), *First Lady of American Dance* (Skipper Prods., 1957), and *Ruth St. Denis and Ted Shawn* (NBC, 1958); there is also a film of her b. *Radha*, shot in 1941, but not edited until 1973. In recent years there have been several attempts at reviving her bs.
BIBL.: C. L. Schlundt, *The Professional Appearances of R. St. D. & Ted Shawn—A Chronology and an Index of Dances 1906–32* (New York, 1962); Schlundt, 'Into the Mystic with Miss Ruth', *Dance Perspectives* 46; J. Sherman *The Drama of Denishawn Dance* (Middletown, Connecticut, 1979); S. Shelton, *Divine Dancer* (New York 1981)..

Saint Francis. See *Nobilissima Visione.*

Saint-Léon, Arthur (*b* Paris, 17 Sep. 1821, *d*

there, 2 Sept 1870). Fr. dancer, choreographer, b. master, and teacher. Studied with his father, a b. master at the courts of Tuscany and Stuttgart. Début as a violinist in Stuttgart in 1834, and as a d. in Munich in 1835. Studied further in Paris with Albert. Appointed premier danseur de demi-caractère in Brussels in 1838. Went to Turin, Milan, Vienna, and eventually London, where he appeared as Matteo with Cerrito—to whom he was married 1845–51—in the creation of Perrot's *Ondine* (1843). Ch. his first b. *Vivandiera ed il postiglione* (mus. E. Rolland) for Rome in 1843. Created Phoebus in Perrot's *Esmeralda* (London, 1844). Toured extensively all over Europe, mostly with Cerrito. Ch. his first great b. successes for Paris: *La Fille de marbre* (1847), *Le Violon du diable* (1849), and *Stella ou Les Contrebandiers* (1850); all to mus. by Pugni). Appointed teacher of the classe de perfectionnement at the Paris Opéra, where he was in charge of the b. divertissements for many op. prods. Succeeded Perrot as b. master of the St. Petersburg Imperial Ths. 1859–69, where he ch. *Graziella ou La Querelle amoureuse* (1860), *La Perle de Séville* (1861), *Fiammetta*, and *The Humpbacked Horse* (both 1864; all mus. Pugni). Also b. master of the Paris Opéra 1863–70, where he revived *La Fille mal gardée* (1866) and ch. *La Source* (mus. Minkus and Delibes, 1866) and *Coppélia* (1870). Developed his own system of d. notation, which he published as *La Sténochorégraphie ou Art d'écrire promptement la danse* in 1852. He was one of the best dancers of his time, famous for his remarkable ballon and élévation. He occasionally appeared as a violinist and d. simultaneously (e.g. in *Le Violon du diable*). He sometimes comp. the mus. to his bs., e.g. for *Saltarello*, (Lisbon, 1855) and was much admired as a ch. for his skilful b. adaptations of national dance.
BIBL.: I. Guest, in *The Ballet of the Second Empire* (2 vols., London, 1953 and 1955).

Saisons, Les (orig. Russ. title: *Vremena goda*). Ballet in 1 act and 4 scenes; libr. and ch. M. Petipa; mus. Glazunov; déc. P. Lambin and I. Ponomariov. Prod. 20 Feb. 1900, Hermitage Th., St. Petersburg, with Pavlova, Preobrajenska, Kschessinska, Legat. A grand divertissement, starting with a winter scene, followed by spring, summer, and autumn, after which a nocturnal apotheosis of the stars concludes the b. Later versions by Legat (1907), L. Leontiev (GATOB, 1924), A. Varlamov (Bolshoi B., 1959), and Cranko (Stuttgart, 1962). Its Bacchanale became world famous through the perfs. of the Pavlova co. Ashton used part of the mus. in his *Birthday Offering* (1956). For other bs. dealing with the seasons see *Four Seasons, The*.
BIBL.: C. W. Beaumont, 'L.S.' in *Complete Book of Ballets* (London, 1951).

Saisons de la danse, Les. A Paris magazine, covering all aspects of th. dancing. Edited by André-Philippe Hersin, its first issue appeared in

Feb. 1968, since when 10 issues have been published per year.

Sakharoff, Alexander (orig. Zuckermann; *b* Mariupol, 26 May 1886, *d* Sienna, 25 Sep. 1963). Russ. dancer and teacher. Studied law and painting in Paris; saw Sarah Bernhardt performing a minuet in a drama prod., and decided to become a d. Trained as an acrobat in Munich; gave his first dance concert there in 1910, inspired by subjects from ancient mythology and renaissance paintings. On his world-wide tours with his partner *Clothilde von Derp—whom he married in 1919—he developed a personal form of modern d. which he called 'abstract pantomime'. Cultivated a style of refined preciosity; he himself designed his luxurious costumes. Went to Rome in 1953, where he and his wife established a school at the Palazzo Doria, moving to Sienna for their annual summer courses
BIBL.: H. Brandenburg, in *Der moderne Tanz* (Munich, 1931).

Salade. Ballet chanté; text Albert Flamand; mus. Milhaud; ch. Massine; déc. Braque. Prod. 17 May 1924, Comte Etienne de Beaumont's Soirées de Paris, Th. de la Cigale, Paris, with Massine, Eleanora Manna. The b. shows the most famous characters from the Ital. commedia dell'arte in their usual highly involved plots. Later versions by Terpis (Berlin State Op., 1929), Lifar (Opéra, Paris, 1935), Darrell (Western Th. B., 1961), and Milloss (Vienna State Op., 1963).
BIBL.: C. W. Beaumont, in *Complete Book of Ballets* (London, 1951).

Salammbô. Ballet in 5 acts and 7 scenes; libr. and ch. Gorsky; mus. A. Arends; déc. K. Korovin. Prod. 10 Oct. 1910, Bolshoi Th., Moscow, with Geltzer, Mordkin. The b. was inspired by Flaubert's novel *S.*, about the war between the Carthaginians and their own mercenaries and the tragic love affair between the Princess of Carthage and the Libyan Matho. This was one of Gorsky's most important reform bs., told in what he himself called 'mimodrame'. Some of the corps de b. d. in sandals to heighten the realistic effect of the prod.
BIBL.: N. Roslavleva, in *Era of the Russian Ballet* (London, 1966).

Saland, Stephanie (*b* Brooklyn, N.Y., 1954). Amer. dancer. Studied with local teachers in Massapequa, then with Mme Eglevsky and at School of Amer. B., graduating 1972 and joining New York City B., promoted soloist 1979. Created roles in Balanchine's *Ballo della Regina* (1978) and Robbins's *The Four Seasons* (1979). Principal d. 1984.

Salavisa, Jorge (*b* Lisbon). Port. dancer. Studied with Anna Mascolo, V. Gsovsky, and Egorova. D. with Grand B. du Marquis de Cuevas 1959–62, Petit's Bs. de Paris in 1962, London Festival B.

1963–71 (soloist from 1965), Scottish Th. B. 1971–3. Art. dir. Gulbenkian B. since 1977.

Salem Shore. Solo d. by Graham; mus. Paul Nordoff; set Arch Lauterer; cost. Edythe Gilfond. Prod. 26 Dec. 1943, 46th St. Th., New York. A lyric d., set in the past but with strong reference to the then current war; it expressed 'the longings and frustrations of women left at home while their men were away' (D. McDonagh).

Sallé, Marie (*b* 1707, *d* Paris, 27 July 1756). Fr. dancer. The daughter of an acrobat. Appeared with her brother as a child in the London pantomimes of John Rich; Paris début at the Foire Saint-Laurent in *La Princesse de Carisme* in 1718. Then studied with Prévost; début at the Opéra in 1727. Became a fierce rival of Camargo (who was the better technician, while S. was admired for her dramatic sensitivity). Also appeared regularly in London; created a sensation when she wore a muslin tunic in *Pygmalion* in 1734, instead of the voluminous baroque skirts and panniers. Her friends included Garrick, Voltaire, Noverre, and Handel (who comp. for her the *Terpsichore* prologue for *Pastor fido*, 1734, and the 3 b. ops. *Oreste* (1734), *Ariodante*, and *Alcina* (1735). In Paris her greatest successes were in the comedy bs. of Molière and Lully; also in Campra's *Fêtes vénitiennes* and *L'Europe galante*, and Rameau's *Les Indes galantes*. Resigned in 1740, but continued to appear occasionally in Paris and London at court balls; probably her last appearance was in *Tyrsis et Doristée* in Fontainebleau in 1752. Noverre wrote about her: 'Elle ne possédait ni le brillant ni les difficultés qui règnent dans celles de nos jours, mais elle remplaçait ce cliquant par des grâces simples et touchantes; exempte d'affèterie, sa physiognomie était noble, expressive et spirituelle.' She is considered one of the pioneers of the b. d'action. Voltaire, Pope, and Gay wrote poems about her.
BIBL.: S. Vince, 'S. in London', *Dance and Dancers* (1962/5); P. Migel, 'M.S.' in *The Ballerinas* (New York, 1972).

Salome. Ballet in 2 acts; libr. and ch. Flindt; mus. P. M. Davies; déc. Daydé. Prod. 10 Nov. 1978, Circus Th., Copenhagen, with V. and F. Flindt, J. Eliasen, L. Rhode. Flindt's first b. prod. since his resignation as artistic dir. of the Royal Dan. B., a full-length work, realized with a specially assembled co., uses the story of the daughter of King Herod, who asks to be rewarded for her d. with the head of John the Baptist (Mark 6, 17–29), adding some political aspects and finishing with a visionary sequence of S. and John, liberated from their chains, in a gorgeous landscape of love. Earlier d. treatments of the story, most of them based upon O. Wilde's homonymous tragedy, incl. those by M. Allan (mus. Marcel Remy, Vienna, 1907), Fuller (mus. F. Schmitt, Paris, 1907); the mus. was also used by Romanov for *La Tragédie de S.*, Bs. Russes de Diaghilev,

Paris, 1913, Gorsky (mus. R. Strauss, Moscow 1921); same mus. from the op. also used by Abramowitsch, Warsaw, 1933, Lifar, Monte Carlo, 1946, J. Lefèbre, East Berlin State Op., 1970; L. Leontiev (mus. Glazunov, Leningrad, 1922). Horton (own percussion mus., Los Angeles, 1938), Cullberg (mus. H. Rosenberg, Stockholm, 1964), Lazzini (mus. Francis Miroglio, Amiens, 1968), Darrell (mus. Hindemith, Scottish Th. B., 1970), Leclair (mus. Walton, B. of Flanders, 1971), and L. Kemp (mus. collage, New York, 1975).

Salon Mexico, El. Ballet in 1 act; ch. Humphrey; mus. Copland; cost. Elizabeth Parsons. Prod. 11 Mar. 1943, J. Limón D. Co., Studio Th., New York, with Limón, Florence Lessing. A sequence of short sketches; the protagonist is a Mexican peasant, who dreams of his encounters with various women.
BIBL.: R. Lawrence, 'E.S.M.' in *The Victor Book of Ballets and Ballet Music* (New York, 1950).

Saltarello. A vivacious Roman jumping d. in 3/4 or 6/8 time, not unlike the Tarantella, but d. accelerando. It dates from the 14th century and enjoyed its greatest popularity in the 16th century, when it was mostly performed after a Passamezzo or a Pavane. Entered the symphonic repertory in the final movement of Mendelssohn's Italian Symphony (1833), and the b. repertory in Perrot's *Catarina ou La Fille du bandit* (London, 1846).

Salvioni, Guglielma (*b* Milan, 1842, *d* ?). Ital. dancer. Studied at La Scala B. School; graduated in 1856. D. at various Ital. ths. and at the Paris Opéra 1864–7, where she created Naïla in Saint-Léon's *La Source* in 1866 and the ballerina role in his Pushkin-inspired *The Little Goldfish* in St. Petersburg in 1867. Prima ballerina of Vienna Court Op. 1870–3; created Myrrha in Taglioni's *Sardanapal* in the inaugural b. perf. of the new op. house on the Ring in 1869.

Salzedo, Leonard (*b* London, 24 Sep. 1921). Brit. conductor and composer. Educated at Royal College of Music, London. Mus. Dir. of B. Rambert 1966–72, Principal Conductor of Scottish Th. B. 1972–4, and conductor of New London B. in 1974. Comp. the mus. for many bs., e.g. Howard's *The Fugitive* (1944) and *Mardi Gras* (1946), J. Carter's *The Witch Boy* (1956) and *Agrionia* (1964), Morrice's *The Travellers* (1963), *The Realms of Choice* (1965), and *Hazard* (1967). Morrice used his Concerto for Percussion for *Percussion Concerto* (Batsheva D. Co.—later staged as *The Empty Suit* for B. Rambert, 1970).

Samaropoulo, Persephone (*b* Cairo, 28 Jan. 1941). Greek dancer. Studied with Sonia Iwanowa, H. Remus, C. Molina, Y. Metsis, and Kniaseff, then in London with W. Edwards, E. Ward, Fay, and Rambert. D. with Cairo TV B. 1959–64, Athens Op. B. 1964–6, Stuttgart B. 1966–7, again in Athens 1968–70, Zurich Op. B. 1968–70,

Frankfurt B. 1970–3, and a principal d. of the Hamburg State Op. B. 1973–80.

Samsova, Galina (formerly spelt Samtsova; *b* Stalingrad, 17 Mar. 1937). Sov.-Can. dancer. Studied at Kiev State B. School; graduated in 1956. Joined Kiev B. and later became soloist. Married the Can. Alexander Ursuliak and went to Canada; joined the National B. of Canada as ballerina in 1961. Created title-role in Orlikowsky's Paris *Cinderella* prod. in 1963. Ballerina of London Festival B. 1964–73; then founded the New London B. with her second husband, André Prokovsky, with which she toured extensively. Principal d. Sadler's Wells Royal B., 1979 for whom she staged a version of the Grand Pas from *Paquita*, also teaching for the co. and the school Created roles in J. Carter's *The Unknown Island* (1969) and *Pythoness Ascendant* (1973), Hynd's *Dvorak Variations* (1970) and *Valses Nobles et sentimentales* (1975), Darrell's *Othello* (1971), *La Péri* (1971), and *Chéri* (1980), and Prokovsky's *Bagatelles Op. 26* (1972), *Vespri* (1973), *Piano Quartet No. 1* (1974), *The Seven Deadly Sins*, and *Simorgh* (1975). Fr. TV prod. *Portrait d'une Etoile* 1973. B. principal Legat Sch., Kent, since 1986. Now divorced from Prokovsky. Gold Medal (Paris, 1963); Pavlova Prize (Paris, 1963).
BIBL.: E. Herf, 'G.S.', *Ballet Today* (1966/3–4); Interview in *Dance and Dancers*, 1981/4 (Dec.).

Samtsova. see *Samsova*.

Sanasardo, Paul (*b* Chicago, 15 Sep. 1928). Amer. dancer, choreographer, and teacher. Studied with Tudor, Erika Thimey, Graham, and Slavenska. Début with E. Thimey D. Th. in 1951. D. with the cos. of Sokolow and Lang, on Broadway, and with New York City Op. Established the S. D. Co. with D. Feuer in 1957, and the Studio for D. in 1958. Artistic dir. Batsheva Dance Co. 1977–81. Now Dir. of Modern D. Artists in New York and School of Modern D. in Saratoga, N.Y.
BIBL.: D. Hering, 'A Darkening Pond', *Dance Magazine* (1971/8); T. Gruen, 'Close-Up: P.S.', *Dance Magazine* (1975/6).

Sand, Monique (*b* Dakar, Senegal, 24 June 1944). Fr. d. Studied at Ecole de Danse Tanëeff in Toulon; joined Toulon Op. B.; went to Geneva; soloist at Hamburg State Op. B. in 1966. Created roles in van Dyk's *Pinocchio* (1969) and Tetley's *Chronochromie* (1971). Principal d. of the Dutch Nat. B. from 1971; created roles in Van Dantzig's *Ramifications* and Van Manen's *Adagio Hammerklavier* (1973) and *Sacre du printemps* (1974). Retired 1983; now teaching in The Hague. Married to the d. Francis Sinceretti.

Sanders, Dick (also Dirk; *b* Djakarta, 1933). Dutch dancer and choreographer. Studied with Jooss. Settled in Paris in 1952 and began working as a freelance d. and ch.; appeared in many film and TV prods. Ch. *L'Echelle* (mus. Zdenko Turjac) for Miskovitch co. in 1956 and Henze's *Maratona di danza* for West Berlin Municipal Op. in 1957.

Has since worked mainly for Fr. TV (often collaborating with J. C. Averty).

BIBL.: S. Goodman 'D.S.', *Dance Magazine* (1958/8).

Sanders, Job (*b* Amsterdam, 21 July 1929). Dutch dancer, choreographer, and teacher. Studied with A. Gavrilov and at School of Amer. B. Début with B. Society. D. on Broadway, with B. Russe de Monte Carlo, Amer. B. Th., R. Page's Chicago Op., B., and Amer. Festival B. Dancer and choreographer of Netherlands D. Th. 1961–7; has since returned to the co. several times as a ch. Dir. of Mex. B. Clásico 1971–3. Now teaches in The Hague.

San Diego Ballet Company. Cal. co., founded by Richard Carter in 1961. Début in the summer of 1962; at that time the co. collaborated closely with the San Francisco B. On Carter's resignation in 1969, Jillana was apptd. art. dir.; she continued as a guest artist and art. adviser when Dame Sonia Arova and Thor Sutowski took over as artistic directors in 1971. Originally a concert-size ensemble; the co. grew to 40 ds. and has professional status, with a repertory based upon a choice of classics (most of which have been staged by Arova) and various 20th-century bs. (many ch. by Sutowski). First U.S. tour in 1975. Ceased 1980; revived as shared co. with Hartford B., 1984.

Sandonato, Barbara (*b* Harrison, N.Y., 22 July 1943). Amer. dancer. Studied with Lorna London and at School of Amer. B. Début at Radio City Music Hall. Joined Pennsylvania B. 1963; later became principal d. Frequently appeared with National B. of Canada. Bronze Medal (Varna, 1970). Married to the d. Alexei Yudenich.

BIBL.: S. Goodman, 'B. S. and Alexei Yudenich', *Dance Magazine* (1968/11).

San Francisco Ballet, The. America's oldest b. co. was founded as S.F. Op. B. in 1933, together with the S.F. B. School; Bolm was its first ch. At first it appeared mainly in op. prods. and occasionally in b. perfs., ch. by Bolm. S. Oukrainsky took over in 1937, and under him the co. became more independent; W. Christensen was premier danseur. He succeeded Oukrainsky as dir. in 1938; he staged the early productions of *Coppélia*, *Swan Lake*, and *Nutcracker*. H. Christensen became the dir. of the affiliated school. W. Christensen's brother L. Christensen became dir. of the co. in 1951. He established a close link with the New York City B., which was maintained throughout the 1950s. Since 1957 it has made several foreign tours. It is now jointly directed by L. Christensen and M. Smuin, with R. Gladstein as asst. dir. and b. master. Its present repertory is dominated by Christensen and Smuin bs., together with bs. by Balanchine, Butler, Carvajal, Gladstein, and others. Better-known dancers to emerge from the co. incl. J. Reed, J. Vollmar, H. Lang, S. Bailey, C. Gregory, and S. Douglas.

British début 1981 in Edinburgh. Jointly d. by L. Christensen and M. Smuin to 1984, then solely by Smuin 1984–5; now dir. by H. Tomasson.

BIBL.: See Christensen portfolio, *Dance Magazine* (1973/6); S. von Buchau, 'The Biggest Game in Town', *Ballet News* (1980/10).

Sangalli, Rita (*b* Milan, 1850, *d* Carpesino d'Arcellasco, 1909). Ital dancer. Studied with A. Hus. Début in P. Taglioni's *Flick and Flock* at La Scala in 1865. Toured extensively in Italy, Austria, England. Went to the U.S. in 1866, where her first appearance was in the New York prod. of *The Black Crook*. Début at Paris Opéra in *La Source* in 1872; then created the ballerina roles in Mérante's *Sylvia* (1876) and *Yedda* (1879), and L. Petipa's *Namouna* (1882). Married Baron de Saint-Pierre in 1886. Was one of the great Paris beauties of the Belle Epoque. Author of a charming little book, *Terpsichore* (1875), in which she shows herself to be remarkably intelligent, reasonable, and kind.

Sanguine Fan, The. Ballet in 1 act by E. Elgar. first prod. as a mimed play at London's Chelsea Palace in aid of war charities in 1917. First prod. as a legitimate b. (under the title *L'Eventail*), ch. Hynd, déc. Docherty, 6 July 1976, London Festival B., Th. de l'Opéra de Monte Carlo, with P. Clarke, D. von Loggenburg, M. Asensio, P. Ruanne. The b. revolves around a mislaid fan, very much in the manner of a Wilde comedy of social manners, though carefully avoiding any direct suggestion of Lady Windermere. For its home perfs. the co. restored its original Eng. title.

Sankovskaya, Yekaterina Alexandrovna (*b* Moscow, 1816, *d* there, 28 Aug. 1878). Russ. dancer. Studied at Moscow Bolshoi B. School; appeared as a student in b. and drama perfs. Graduated in 1836 and became the most popular Moscow ballerina of her time. In 1837 she was the city's first La Sylphide; later famous roles included Giselle, Esmeralda, and La Fille du Danube. She was especially admired for her stirring and dramatically engaged interpretations. Resigned in 1854, after which she earned a living by teaching social d. in the families of wealthy Moscow merchants (K. Stanislavsky was one of her pupils).

BIBL.: N. Roslavleva, in *Era of the Russian Ballet* (London, 1966).

San Martín Ballet (Ballet de Teatro Municipal General San Martin de Buenos Aires). The co. was founded in 1968 by O. Araiz, with the aim of counterbalancing the classically-orientated Teatro Colón B., and as a platform for modern b. Most of its repertory works were ch. by Araiz, together with bs. by Alejandro Genert, Lia Labaronne, Gloria Contreras, D. Hoyer, G. Urbani, and R. Schottelius. In 1969 the co. embarked on its first Eur. tour; in London they performed at The Place. Disbanded in 1973.

Santestevan, Maria (*b* Morón, 1933). Argent.

dancer and b. mistress. Studied with Bulnes; joined Teatro Colón B. in 1946. D. in La Plata, with Grand B. du Marquis de Cuevas 1956–9, Stuttgart B., and with various Fr. cos. Joined Bordeaux B. in 1961; eventually became b. mistress.

Santiago de Chile. The first b. perfs. were given at the Teatro Principal in 1850, where the group of M. Ponçot and the ballerinas Mlles Dimier and Solidni appeared in the romantic standard repertory. The co. of the Roussets then introduced *Giselle* in 1856. However, there was no continuous cultivation of b., and the next important guest season was that of the Pavlova co. in 1917–18. The former Pavlova d. Jan Kaweski founded a b. school in 1921, which served as the basis of the city's b. activities. Another important teacher was Doreen Young, a pupil of Astafieva, who later became b. mistress of the National B. of Chile. De Basil's Original B. Russe de Monte Carlo came to Chile, as did the Bs. Jooss in during the 1940s; the latter created a strong impression, and 2 of its dancers, E. Uthoff and Lola Botka, returned to the city in 1942, when the tour was over, and founded a school, with the backing of the State Univ. This served as the basis of occasional perfs.; the dancers became increasingly professional and the co. took the name of the National Chilean B. Most of its repertory was ch. by Uthoff and Jooss. In 1952 the Russ.-trained E. Poliakova became b. mistress, and the co. was able to offer some more interesting work for classically-trained dancers, who had previously mostly gone abroad. Regular b. seasons were given at the Teatro Municipal, until the co. moved to the smaller Teatro Victoria in 1957. Gradually its perfs. spread to neighbouring countries and in 1964 the co. paid its first visit to the U.S. Uthoff resigned in 1964. In more recent years there has been a rapid turnover of b. directors; they have included C. Dickson, D. Carey, V. Roncal, and P. Bunster. The associated school of the Teatro Municipal, established in 1949 by the Sov. dancers Vadim Sulima and Nina Gritsova, gave rise to the Ballet Clásico Nacional, which was based on a repertory of classics. In 1959 O. Cintolesi founded Ballet de Arte Moderno; he was a former pupil of Uthoff who had worked for a long time in Europe, and he was able to achieve a considerable improvement of standards of the co., now called Ballet Municipal de Santiago. It attracted many dancers and choreographers of international repute. He was succeeded in 1966 by Dickson, followed by Blanchette Hermansen (1974–6), Rosario Llansol (1976–9), and Cintolesi again (since 1979). After the political coup in 1973 2 cos. continued to function: the Ballet Nacional Chileno, based on the Univ. of Chile, with Nora Arriagada as b. dir.; and the Teatro Contemporaneo de la Danza, with Ingeborg Krusell as its head, now disbanded. The most important schools are now the Escuela Coreográfica Nacional de Ministerio de Educación (not functioning at the present), the Departamento de Danza de la Universidad de Chile, and the Teatro Municipal B. School. Since 1965 there has been a b. archive, named after Poliakova, built up by C. de Robilant now in charge of Hilda Sato.

Santlow, Hester (*b c.* 1690, *d* 1773). Brit. dancer and actress. Gave her dancing début at London's Drury Lane Th. 1706: acting début as Miss Prue in Congreve's *Love for Love* at the same th. 1709. Pursued a double career, creating Venus in Weaver's *Loves of Mars and Venus* (1717) as well as Eurydice in his *Dramatick Entertainment of Dancing* (1718) and Helen in his *Judgment of Paris* (1733). Further dancing roles in bs. and masques by John Thurmond. Mistress of James Cragg (later Secretary of War) and wife of the actor Barton Booth, upon whose death in 1733 she retired from the stage. James Thompson praised her dancing as 'so delicious, has such melting lascivious motions, airs and postures . . '
BIBL.: S. J. Cohen, 'H.S.' in *Famed for Dance* (New York, 1960).

Sappington, Margo (*b* Baytown, Tex., 30 July 1947). Amer. dancer and choreographer. Studied with Camille Hill, Mattox and at Amer. B. Center. Appeared in musicals. Became known as ch. of *Oh! Calcutta!* in 1969. Has since ch. *Weewis* (mus. Stanley Walden, City Center Joffrey B., 1971) *Rodin, mis en vie* (mus. Michael Kamen, Harkness B., 1974), and *Juice* (mus. Kamen, Netherlands D. Th., 1975).
BIBL.: N. McLain Stoop, 'Not a "Swan Lake" Swan', *Dance Magazine* (1972/1).

Sarabande. A dignified d. in triple time, which probably came from Middle Amer. to Spain, from where it spread during the 17th and 18th century all over Europe. Its accent is on the second beat, which is often dotted. Originally a distinctly improper and lascivious d.; it was forbidden by Philip II in 1598 and only accepted as a court d. after modification in 1618.

Sarabhai, Mrinalini (*b* Madras, 1923). Ind. dancer, choreographer, and teacher. Studied at Devis Kalakshetra Academy of Dramatic Art. Début in Madras in 1939. Has frequently appeared with R. Gopal and with her own co. all over the world. Founded the Darpana Academy of D., Drama, Mus., and Puppetry in Ahmedabad in 1949 and is still its dir. Appointed State D. in 1955; she became dir. of the newly established Sangit Natak Academy at the same time. Author of *This Alone Is True* (1952).
BIBL.: Interview with M.S., *Dance and Dancers* (1971/9).

Sardanapal. Ballet in 4 acts and 6 scenes; libr. and ch. P. Taglioni; mus. Paul Hertel. Prod. 24 Apr. 1865, Royal Op. House, Berlin. The b. dealt with the legendary King of Assyria. Revived for Vienna Court Op., where it was the opening b.

prod. of the newly built op. house in 1869. An earlier b. version by D. Ballon in Venice (1788).

Sarry, Christine (*b* Long Beach, 1947). Amer. dancer. Studied with Silver, Maracci, Oumansky, Fallis, and Thomas. Joined Joffrey B. in 1963 and Amer. B. Th. in 1964; became principal d. in 1973. Left the co. to d. as ballerina with Feld's Amer. B. 1969–71 and again in 1974. Left Feld B., 1981.

BIBL.: J. Gale. 'A Romantic from Lilliput: C.S.', *Dance Magazine* (1972/10).

Sarstädt, Marian (*b* Amsterdam, 11 July 1942). Dutch dancer and b. mistress. Studied with Ann Sybranda, Kiss, and de Vos. Début with Scapino B. in 1957; became soloist in 1958. D. with Grand B. du Marquis de Cuevas 1960–1, then with Netherlands D. Th. 1962–72; became one of its most distinguished soloists, and created many parts in bs. by Harkarvy and Van Manen. Retired in 1972, b. mistress of the Scapino B. to 1983, and now teaches in The Hague. Married to the Scapino B.'s artistic dir., Armando Navarro.

Satanella oder Metamorphosen. Ballet in 1 act; libr. and ch. P. Taglioni; mus. Paul Hertel. Prod. 28 Apr. 1852, Royal Op. House, Berlin. The b. was based on Cazotte's *Diable amoureux*: the Heidelberg student Karl becomes ensnared by the she-devil S., who causes him to leave his betrothed. An earlier version by Taglioni, with Grisi in the title-role, at Her Majesty's Th., London, in 1850.

BIBL.: C. W. Beaumont, 'Les Metamorphoses' in *Complete Book of Ballets* (London, 1951).

Satie, Erik Alfred Leslie (*b* Honfleur, 17 May 1866, *d* Paris, 1 July 1925). Fr. composer. Wrote the mus. to the Cretan b. *Uspud* (no details known), Massine's *Parade* (1917) and *Mercure* (1924), Börlin's *Relâche* (1924), and Balanchine's *Jack in the Box* (1926). His *Trois Gymnopédies* have been often used for b. purposes, mostly in the orchestral version arr. by Debussy and Roland-Manuel—e.g. by Ashton in *Monotones* (1965—supplemented by *Trois Gnossiennes*, arr. Lanchbery, 1966) and Van Manen in *Squares* (1969—later replaced, for copyright reasons, by very similar-sounding mus. by Z. Silassy). M. Cunningham has frequently used his mus., e.g. for *Idyllic Song* (1944), *The Monkey Dances* (1948), *Two Step* (1949), *Waltz* and *Rag Time Parade* (1950), *Septet* (1953), *Nocturnes* (1956), and *Second Hand* (planned in 1970 to his *Socrate*, but because of legal objections finally performed to mus. by Cage). A number of his pieces were used by B. Moreland in *Dark Voyage* (1973), and another anthology by P. Taylor in *Sports and Follies* (1974). L. Massine ch. *Esoteric S.*, Milan (1978).

Sauguet, Henri (*b* Bordeaux, 18 May 1901). Fr. composer. Orchestrated mus. by Metra for Massine's *Les Roses* (1924), *David* (1928), and *Les Saisons* (1951), Balanchine's *La Chatte* (1927) and *Fastes* (1933), Lifar's *La Nuit* (1930) and *Les Mirages* (1947), Petit's *Image à Paul et Virginie* (1943) and *Les Forains* (1945), Lichine's *La Rencontre, ou Edipe et le Sphinx* (1948), Charrat's *Le dernier jugement* (1951) and *Paris* (1966), Taras' *Cordelia* (1952), Babilée's *Le Caméléopard* (1956), T. Gsovsky's *Die Kameliendame* (1957), and Orlikowsky's *Fünf Etagen* (1960).

Saunders, James (*b* Wilmington, Del., 14 July 1946). Amer. dancer. Studied sculpturing and painting at Philadelphia College of Arts plus dancing at School of Pennsylvania B. and with Caton and Zaraspe. D. with Pennsylvania B., B. of the 20th Century. Principal d. with Cologne D. Forum 1973–7 and from 1977–8 with Frankfurt B., creating roles in bs. by Veredon and Howald. Started to ch. in 1976 and has since worked regularly for various workshops.

BIBL.: H. Koegler, 'J.S.' in *Ballett 1978*.

Saut. (Fr., leap.) Designates in b. a jump off both feet, and landing in the same position.

Saut de basque. See *Basque, Pas de*.

Savignano, Luciana (*b* Milan, 30 Nov. 1943). Ital dancer. Studied at La Scala B. School. Joined La Scala B. in 1961; became soloist in 1965 and principal d. in 1972. Has often appeared abroad (Bolshoi B., Lyric Op. Chicago, B. of the 20th Century). Created leading role in Béjart's *Ce que l'amour me dit* (1974).

Savino, Jo (*b* St. Paul, 30 Dec. 1935). Amer. dancer and teacher. Studied with Franklin, Kiss, Franchette, and Gonta. D. with Slavenska-Franklin B. in 1953, B. Russe de Monte Carlo 1954–6, Amer. Festival B. 1956–9, Zurich Opera B. 1960–2, and several other cos., incl. Grand B. Classique de France, PACT B., and B. de Wallonie. Now Instructor of the B. at Univ. of Minnesota. Dir. of Classical B. Academy of Minnesota, and of Rochester B. Center. Has his own J.S. Ballet National.

Sawicka, Olga (*b* Poznan, 7 Feb. 1932). Pol. dancer. Studied at Poznan State B. School. Joined Warsaw Op. B. in 1953; later became prima ballerina. Prima ballerina of Poznan State Op. since 1963. Golden Cross (1954 and 1956); Order of Renaissance (1959); Medal of 30th Anniversary (1974).

Scala, Ballet of Teatro alla. See *Milan*.

Scandinavian Ballet, The (orig. Den Scandinaviske Ballet). The co., founded by E. M. von Rosen and her husband A. Fridericia in 1960, operated under the aegis of the Swed. Riksteatern and the Dan. Andelsteatret. It opened in Waxjö in Sweden on 2 Feb. 1960, and toured Scand. and Ger. until the autumn of 1961, when it was disbanded. The repertory consisted of bs. by Bournonville, Rosen, and Cramér; Rosen was prima ballerina, and the other dancers included Skouratoff (guest artist), U. Paulsson, L. Isaksen, and E. Madsen.

Scapino Ballet. The oldest Dutch b. co. was founded by Hans (Johanna) Snoek in Amsterdam in 1945 with the aim of performing for children. It gives regular performances in Amsterdam, the Dutch provinces, and abroad of its repertory, mostly specially created bs. (at first ch. almost exclusively by Snoek, but now also e.g. by Van Manen, Czarny, Howard, Navarro, Hampton); its ds. also frequently visit schools and youth centres for lecture-demonstrations and the co. has a small attached group for smaller centres. Snoek retired in 1970, succeeded by A. Verstegen and A. Navarro as directors and Navarro as sole dir. since 1977.

Scaramouche. Ballet in 3 scenes; libr. Paul Knudsen; mus. Sibelius; ch. Emilie Walbom. Prod. 12 May 1922, Royal Dan. B., Copenhagen. The b. tells of a demonic fiddler who seduces an artistocratic lady; afterwards she sees no alternative to killing him, but she is so haunted by his melody that she dances herself to death. Sibelius composed this his only b. score, in 1913. Later versions by Lemanis in Riga (1936), R. Hightower for de Cuevas B. (1951), and Irja Koskkinen in Helsinki (1955).

Scarlatti, Domenico (*b* Naples, 26 Oct. 1685, *d* Madrid, 23 July 1757). Ital. composer. Wrote no b. music, but some of his harpsichord sonatas have been arranged for b. purposes—e.g. for Massine's *Les Femmes de bonne humeur* (arr. Tommasini, 1917), Loring's *Harlequin for President* (1936), Aveline's *Elvire* (1937), Béjart's *La Mégère apprivoisée* (1954), Cranko's *La Reja* (1959) and *The Taming of the Shrew* (arr. Stolze, 1969), Prokovsky's *Scarlatti and Friends* (1973), J. Scoglio's *The Small Hours* (1976), and P. Martins's *S.* (1979).

Scènes de ballet. Ballet divertissement; mus. Stravinsky; ch. Dolin. Prod. 7 Dec. 1944, in the Billy Rose revue *The Seven Lively Arts*, Ziegfeld Th., New York, with Markova, Dolin. The score consists of 11 numbers, which Stravinsky specified should be performed by 2 soloists and a corps of 4 boys and 12 girls. First prod. was given in abbreviated form, since Stravinsky refused to agree to the alterations asked for by the producers during the Philadelphia trial perfs. The first prod. of the score in its integral form had ch. by Ashton and déc. by A. Beaurepaire, and was given on 11 Feb. 1948 by the Sadler's Wells B., at Cov. Gdn., London, with Fonteyn and Somes. Later versions by Blank (Berlin Municipal Op., 1952) and Taras (Netherlands B., 1954).
BIBL.: G. Balanchine, 'S.d.b.' in *Balanchine's New Complete Stories of the Great Ballets* (Garden City, N.Y., 1968); D. Vaughan, *Frederick Ashton and his Ballets* (London, 1977).

Schall, Claus (*b* Copenhagen, 28 Apr. 1757, *d* Kongens Lyngby, 10 Aug. 1835). Dan. composer. The son of a dancing teacher. Started as an élève at the Royal Dan. B.; became violinist, répétiteur, concert master, and from 1817 music dir. He wrote about 20 b. scores, most of which were ch. by Galeotti, e.g. *Lagertha* (1801), *Romeo and Juliet* (1811), and *Macbeth* (1816). His sister-in-law was the d. Anna Margrethe S. (1775–1852), a pupil of Galeotti and a principal d. of the Royal Dan B. 1802–24; she created the title role in Galeotti's *Nina* (1802).

Schanne, Margrethe (*b* Copenhagen, 21 Nov. 1921). Dan. dancer. Studied at Royal Dan. B. School. Member of the Royal Dan. B. 1940–66; appointed solo d. in 1943. She d. the ballerina roles of the Bournonville and international standard repertory, and was much admired for her airiness and soulful sensitivity, especially as La Sylphide. She often appeared abroad and also d. with the Grand B. du Marquis de Cuevas. Since her resignation has continued to coach younger dancers in her roles, and to teach at her school. The first Dan. d. to be portrayed on a postage stamp (1957). Knight of Dannebrog (1953); Th. Trophy (1955). Married to the d. Kjeld Noak.
BIBL.: S. Kragh-Jacobsen, *Vor sidste Sylfide* (Copenhagen, 1966); Kragh-Jacobsen, 'M.S.' in *20 Solodancers of The Royal Danish Ballet* (Copenhagen, 1965).

Schaufuss, Frank (*b* Copenhagen, 13 Dec. 1921). Dan. dancer, choreographer, and teacher. Studied at Royal Dan. B. School and with Bartholin. D. with N. B. Larsen B. 1940–1 and with the Royal Dan. B. 1941–70; appointed solo-dancer in 1949, and b. master 1956–8. Ch. *Idollon* (1953), *Opus 13* (1959), and *Garden Party* (1963). After his resignation founded Dan. Academy of B. in Copenhagen with his wife Mona Vangsaae in 1970, from which came the Dan. B. Th; both existed until 1973. Knight of Dannebrog. He is the father of Peter S.
BIBL.: S. Kragh-Jacobsen, 'F.S.' in *20 Solo-dancers of The Royal Danish Ballet* (Copenhagen, 1965).

Schaufuss, Peter (*b* Copenhagen, 26 Apr. 1949). Son of Frank S. and M. Vangsaae. Dan. dancer. Studied at Royal Dan. B. School. Joined Royal Dan. B. in 1965, with which he now has a guest contract. Has d. guest seasons with the National B. of Canada, Zagreb B., London Festival B., Pittsburgh B., Frankfurt B., San Francisco B. Principal New York City B. 1974–77, same position National B. of Canada ever since with numerous guest perfs. all over the world, often appearing with R. Petit's co. After choreographing various smaller bs., scored a major hit with his prod. of Bournonville's *La Sylphide* for London Fest. B. (1979), succeeded by *Napoli* for Nat. B. of Canada (1981). Apptd. art. dir. London Fest. B. 1984.
BIBL.: 'Interview with P.S.' *Dance and Dancers* (1978/7).

Schayk, Toer van (*b* Amsterdam, 28 Sep. 1936). Dutch dancer, designer, and choreographer. Studied with Gaskell; d. with her co. 1955–9. Worked as a painter and sculptor. Returned to

Dutch National B. in 1965, where he created leading parts in many of Van Dantzig's bs., and was frequently also in charge of the déc. As a ch. he started with *Past Imperfect* (mus. Ligeti, 1971), followed by *Before, During, and After the Party* (mus. Gilius Bergeik, 1972), *The Art of Saying Bye-Bye* (mus. Purcell, 1973), *Pyrrhic Dances* (mus. Geoffrey Grey, 1974), *8 Madrigals* (mus. Gesualdo, 1975), *Jeux* (mus. Debussy. 1977), *Eerste Lugtige Plaatsing* (mus. L. Spohr, 1976), *Pyrrhic Dances II* (mus. Lully etc., 1977), *Pyrrhic Dances III* (mus. Berg), and *Neglected Garden* (mus. Mozart, both 1980).

Schéhérazade. See *Sheherazade*.

Schenfeld, Rina (*b* Tel-Aviv, 16 Dec. 1938). Israeli dancer and choreographer. Studied with Graham and at Juilliard School. Formed her own group in Israel. Also d. with Sokolow's Lyric Th. A leading member of the Batsheva D. Co. since 1963, for which she has ch. several bs., e.g. *Jephthah's Daughter* (mus. M. Seter, 1964), *Blind-man's Buff* (mus. E. Carter, 1966), *Curtains* (mus. N. Sherriff, 1968), and *Corners* (no mus., 1973).

Schermerhorn, Kenneth D. (*b* Schenectady, N.Y., 1929). Amer. conductor. Educated at New England Conservatory. Started his long association with Amer. B. Th. as conductor and mus. dir. in 1957. Has been guest conductor for many other cos., incl. B. Russe de Monte Carlo and J. Limón D. Co. Was married to the d. Lupe Serrano.

Scherzer, Steffi (*b* Stollberg, 14 July 1957). Ger. dancer. Studied at East Berlin State B. School 1968–75. Joined East Berlin State Op. B. in 1975, appointed soloist in 1978. Bronze Medal (Varna, 1978).

Scherzo fantastique. Ballet in 1 act; ch. Robbins; mus. Stravinsky; light. R. Bates. Prod. 18 June 1972, New York City B., State Th., N.Y., with G. Kirkland, B. Cook. A scintillating display piece for 2 soloists and 3 accompanying boys. Revived for Paris Opéra (1974). An earlier version of the same mus. by Staats (in *Abeilles*, Opéra, Paris, 1917.)

Scheuermann, Lilly (*b* Vienna, 13 Nov. 1945). Austrian dancer. Studied at Vienna State Op. B. School. Joined its co. in 1961; became soloist in 1970 and principal d. in 1972. Created roles in several Milloss bs.

Schiafino, Carlos (*b* Buenos Aires, 1932). Argent. dancer. Studied at Teatro Colón B. School. Joined its co.; became soloist in 1955 and principal d. in 1961.

Schilling, Tom (*b* Esperstedt, 23 Jan. 1928). Ger. dancer, choreographer, and b. director. Studied at Dessau Op. B. School and with Hoyer, Wigman, and Olga Ilyina. D. with the cos. in Dresden, Leipzig (1946–52), and Weimar (1953–6), where he began to ch. B. Dir. and chief-ch. of Dresden

State Op. 1956–64, and of the East Berlin Comic Op. since 1965. Ch. the first Ger. prod. of Asafiev's *Fountain of Bakhchisaray* (Weimar, 1955), Prokofiev's *The Stone Flower* (Dresden, 1960), Bernstein's *Fancy Free* (East Berlin, 1971); in Weimar: Khachaturian's *Gayane* (1953) and Asafiev's *Flames of Paris* (1954); in Dresden: Griesbach's *Snow White* (1956), Egk's *Abraxas* (1957), Reinhold's *The Nightingale* (1958), *Swan Lake* (1959), Weill's *The Seven Deadly Sins* (1962), and *Sleeping Beauty* (1963); in East Berlin: Berlioz' *Symphonie fantastique* (1967), Prokofiev's *Cinderella* (1968) and *Romeo and Juliet* (1972), Debussy's *La Mer* (1968), Blacher's *Moor of Venice* (1969), Henze's *Ondine*, Matthus' *Match* (both 1970) and *Black Birds* (mus. G. Katzer, 1975), *Pastorale* (mus. Beethoven's Pastoral Symphony 1979), and Katzer's *A New Midsummer Night's Dream* (1981). Has also worked as a guest ch. for Grand B. Classique de France, B. de Wallonie, Norwegian National B., Vienna State Op. B, and Stanislavsky and Nemirovich-Danchenko Music Th. B. Choreographer's Prize (Varna, 1968); Berlin Critics' Prize (1970).

Schlagobers. Ballet in 2 acts; libr. and mus. R. Strauss; ch. Kröller; déc. Ada Nigrin. Prod. 9 May 1924, State Op., Vienna, with G. Pichler, H. Pfundmayr, T. Losch, T. Birkmeyer, W. Fränzl. The title means 'whipped cream', and refers to the dreams of a little boy who has eaten too much pastry at his confirmation party. Austrian TV prod. by Dia Luca in 1964.
BIBL.: C. W. Beaumont, 'S.' in *Complete Book of Ballets* (London, 1951).

Schlemmer, Oskar (*b* Stuttgart, 4 Sep. 1888, *d* Baden-Baden, 13 Apr. 1943). Ger. painter, dancer, th. theorist, and designer. One of the pioneers of Central Eur. *Abstrakter Tanz, which he approached by way of painting and sculpture, and which materialized in its purest form in his *Triadic Ballet* (Stuttgart, 1922). He researched into the relationship between figure, movement, and space at the Bauhaus in Weimar and Dessau where he created his *Dance of Space, Dance of Gestures*, and *Dance of Forms*, and also his dances with technical materials such as the *Stick Dance, Metal Dance, Glass Dance, Hoop Dance*, etc. Also designed several b. prods. for Magdeburg, Dresden, Hagen, and Breslau.
BIBL.: E. Scheyer, 'The Shapes of Space: The Art of Mary Wigman and O.S.', *Dance Perspectives* 41.

Schmidt, Jochen (*b* Borken, 22 Sep. 1936). Ger. dance critic. Educated Univs. of Münster, Munich, and Cologne. D. critic of *Frankfurter Allgemeine Zeitung* since 1968. Also a frequent broadcaster.

Schmucki, Norbert (*b* Bobo-Dioulasso, 22 Feb. 1940). Swiss dancer and choreographer. Studied at Paris Opéra B. School; d. with its co. 1957–71, and returned as répétiteur in 1972, after a season as assistant b. master in Zurich. Began to ch. in 1964 and has ch. many bs.

BIBL.: J.-C. Diénis, 'N.S.', *Les Saisons de la danse* (1969/6).

Schnee, Joel (*b* New Jersey, 23 Mar. 1935). Amer. dancer, choreographer, and b. master. Studied with Lewitzky, Maracci, and at Juilliard School and Amer. B. Center. D. in various Amer. groups; came to Eur. in 1963, and worked as teacher, b. master, or ch. for cos. in Berlin, Cologne, Oslo, Helsinki, and from 1966 in Stockholm, where he has also ch. many TV prods. Has also ch. many musicals. B. master of St. Gall Municipal Th. 1974–6, then Kassel State Th. 1976–80. Winner of 1980 Boston B. Choreographers' Competition with *Figures in a Revue*.
BIBL.: W. Sorrell, 'An American Choreographer Working in Switzerland', *Dance News* (1976/3).

Schneider, Alexander (*b* Timisoara, 15 June 1941). Rum. dancer, choreographer and b. director. Studied at Cluj B. School, graduating 1965. D. with Temesburg State Op. B. eventually becoming ch. and b. master. Artistic dir. and ch. Cluj State Op. B. 1975/9, also working as guest ch. at Bucharest State Op, and West Berlin Ger. Op. Has ch. numerous bs. (also for TV). Provisional b. dir. Frankfurt 1980–81, now in Linz/ Austria.

Schneider, Jürgen (*b* Berlin, 2 May 1936). Ger. dancer, teacher, and b. master. Studied in East Berlin, with Tarasov in Moscow, and with Pushkin in Leningrad. D. with the cos. in Weimar and with East Berlin Comic Op. from 1958; b. master 1968–71. B. master of Stuttgart B. 1971– 3, then Munich State Op. B. 1973–4; now b. master Amer. B. Th.

Schneitzhoeffer, Jean-Madeleine (*b* 1785, *d* 1852). Fr. conductor and composer. He was second chorus-conductor at the Paris Opéra and wrote the mus. for 6 bs., incl. Albert's *Le Séducteur du village* (1818), Deshayes' *Zémire et Azor* (1824), Taglioni's *La Sylphide* (1832), and Coralli's *La Tempête* (1834).
BIBL.: I. Guest, in *The Romantic Ballet in Paris* (London, 1966).

Schoenberg, Arnold (*b* Vienna, 13 Sep. 1874, *d* Los Angeles, 13 July 1951). Austrian composer. Wrote no b. mus. except the *O*. Around the Golden Calf as part of his op. *Moses and Aaron* (ch. by e.g. J. Berger, Zurich, 1957; Hoyer, Berlin Municipal Op., 1959; Walter, Düsseldorf, 1968; Vienna State Op., 1973; Araiz, Buenos Aires, 1970; Neumeier, Frankfurt, 1970; Macdonald, Nuremberg, 1970; Veredon, Hamburg State Op., 1974; H. Wandtke, Dresden, 1975). Some of his concert mus. has been adapted to b. purposes: e.g. *Transfigured Night* (Tudor, *Pillar of Fire*, 1942; Van Dyk, Paris, 1958; Walter, Wuppertal, 1961; Cauley, Milan, 1972; Catá, Geneva, 1973; Kylián, The Hague, 1975; Petit, Paris, 1976), First Chamber Symphony (by Limón, *The Exiles*, 1950), *Pelleas and Melisande* (Van Dyk, Wiesbaden, 1952;

Walter, Wuppertal, 1955; Petit, Royal B., 1969), Begleitmusik zu einer Lichtspielszene (Balanchine, *Opus 34*, 1954; Tetley, *Imaginary Film*, Scheveningen, 1971; Bohner, *Ballet Without Title*, Darmstadt, 1974), *Pierrot lunaire* (Joffrey, New York, 1955; Tetley, New York, 1962; Taubert, Brunswick, 1968), Variations for Orchestra op. 31 (Milloss, *Wandlungen*, Cologne, 1960), *Serenade* op. 24 (Furtwängler, Münster, 1964), adaptation of Brahms' Piano Quartet (Balanchine, *Brahms-Schoenberg Quartet*, 1966), Second Chamber Symphony (by Waring, in *Figures in a Landscape*, Scheveningen, 1971), and 5 Pieces for Orchestra op, 16 (by Catá, Frankfurt, 1974). Catá staged a programme of bs. to mus. by S. for Frankfurt in 1974; it consisted of *Transfigured Night, Within Time* (orchestral arr. of works by Bach and Brahms), and *Cult of Night* (Five Pieces for Orchestra, op 16, ch. Butler).

Schollar, Ludmila Franzevna (also Shollar; *b* St. Petersburg, 1888, *d* San Francisco, 11 July 1978). Russ.-Amer. dancer and teacher. Studied at Imperial B. School; graduated in 1908. Entered Maryinsky Th. D. with Diaghilev's co. 1909–14; created roles in Fokine's *Carnaval* (1910), *Petrushka* (1911), *Papillon* (1914), and Nijinsky's *Jeux* (1913). A Red Cross sister during the First World War; returned to Maryinsky and GATOB Th. 1917– 21, then to Diaghilev's Bs. Russes 1921–5. Went to Buenos Aires with Vilzak, whom she later married; d. with the cos. of Rubinstein, Karsavina-Vilzak, and Nijinska. They began to teach in New York in 1936, first at School of Amer. B., then at B. Th. School. Taught at Washington School of B. 1963–5, and then at San Francisco B. School. She was especially admired in the character ballerina roles of the Fokine bs.

Scholz, Uwe (*b* Jugenheim, 31 Dec. 1958). Ger. d. and ch. Studied at John Cranko School, Stuttgart. Member of Stuttgart B. since 1979 as d. and the co.'s. youngest ch. Has also worked as a ch. for Frankfurt and in Israel. Art. dir. Zurich B. since 1985.

School of American Ballet. Founded by Kirstein, Balanchine, Dimitriev, and Warburg in 1933 in Hartford; moved to New York City in 1934, until its home in the Juilliard School building of Lincoln Center was opened in 1970. The Amer. B. was recruited from its pupils, and it now serves as the official school of the New York City B. Noted teachers have incl. Danilova, Doubrovska, M. Stuart, Vladimirov, Eglevsky, and S. Williams. A film, *S. of A.B.*, was made by Virginia Brooks (1972) and is described in *Dance Magazine* (1976/5).

School of Ballet (orig. title: *Leçon de danse*). Ballet in 1 act; ch. A. Messerer; mus. Liadov, Glazunov, Rubinstein, Liapunov, Shostakovich, arr. by A. Zeitlin. Prod. 6 May 1961, B. of the 20th Century, Th. Royal de la Monnaie, Brussels. In front of plain curtains, with a *barre* the b. opens with children at class and proceeds in crescendo style, via the class-work of the co. members, towards the climax when the soloists exhibit their bravura techniques. Messerer reworked the b. completely when he mounted it for the Bolshoi B., which first presented it 17 Sep. 1962 at the New York Met. Op. Ho. Later on Shostakovich adapted some of his former b. mus. for it.

Schoop, Trudi (*b* 1903). Swiss-Amer. dancer and choreographer. Studied in Vienna and Zurich. Became known as a cabaret d.; created many comic bs., with which she toured Europe during the 1930s. Won second prize for her *Fridolin en route* (mus. Kruse and Kasics) at the Paris Choreographers' Competition of 1932. Went to the U.S., and continued to tour until 1947. Since her retirement has concentrated on d. therapy.
BIBL.: S. Roberts, 'T.S.', *Dance Magazine* (1979/10).

Schorer, Suki (*b* Cambridge, Mass., 11 Mar. 1939). Amer. dancer. Studied at San Francisco B. School; joined its co. 1957. D. with New York City B. 1959–71; became soloist in 1963 and principal d. in 1969. Created roles in Balanchine's *Harlequinade* and *Don Quixote* (both 1965). On the faculty of Sch. of Amer. B. since 1972.

Schottelius, Renate (*b* Flensburg, 1921). Ger.-Argent. dancer, choreographer, and teacher. Studied in Berlin and Buenos Aires, also with Miriam Winslow, in whose co. she appeared. Started to tour from Argent. as a concert d. in 1945; formed her own modern d. co. in Buenos Aires in 1955. Has also worked with Limón, Humphrey, Holm, and New York D. Notation Bureau, and ch. for Teatro San Martin B. Now teaches at Boston Conservatory of Music.

Schottische. Ger. couple d. in 2/4 time which was very popular in the mid-19th century. It succeeded the Ecossaise and was also called Ger. Polka, though it is d. at a slower tempo.

Schubert, Franz (*b* Liechtenthal, 31 Jan. 1797, *d* Vienna, 19 Nov. 1828). Austrian composer. Wrote no b. mus., but some of his concert mus. has been adapted to b. purposes, notably by the Viennese *Wiesenthal sisters. His *Rosamunde* mus. has been particularly popular with choreographers (Leontiev, Vienna State Op., 1928; Adama, Hanover, 1968; Catá, Geneva, 1968; Gerster, Vienna, 1978). Other bs. to his mus. by Hassreiter and Lehnert in *Jahreszeiten der Liebe* (Vienna Court Op., 1911), I. Duncan in *Unfinished Symphony* (Paris, 1927; also Knust, Hamburg, 1931; Van Dyk, Paris, 1957; Van Dantzig in *Here Rests: A Summer Day*, Dutch National B., 1973), Nijinska in *La Bien Aimée* (mus. partly by S., Rubinstein co., 1928), Balanchine in *Errante* (the 'Wanderer' Fantasy, Les Bs. 1933; also Ashton, *The Wanderer*, Sadler's Wells B., 1941), Howard in *Death and the Maiden* (last movement only, B. Rambert, 1937; complete quartet, Walter, Wuppertal, 1964), Massine in *Labyrinth* (Seventh Symphony, B. Russe de Monte

Carlo, 1941), H. Lander in *Printemps à Vienne* (Second Symphony, Opéra, Paris, 1954), Macdonald in *Octet* (Royal Swed. B., 1965), Drew in *Intrusion* (the F minor Fantasy, Royal B., 1969), Smuin in *Schubertiade* (various waltzes, San Francisco B., 1970), L. Meyer in *S. Variations* (Trio in B flat major, Northern D. Th., 1972), Catá in *Scharaden* (arr. Jacques Guyonnet, Frankfurt, 1973), de Mille in *Summer* (5 Lieder, Sonata in A major, *Death and the Maiden*, Boston B., 1975), Van Manen in *Grand Trio* (in B major, Vienna, 1978), North in *Songs and Dances* (Quartet-movement in C minor plus 7 Lieder; London Contemporary D. Th., 1981). Lichine's *The Enchanted Mill* (de Cuevas co., 1949) was based on a S. potpourri.

Schubert, Lia (*b* Vienna, 1926). Austrian-Swed. dancer and teacher. Studied in Zagreb and with Preobrajenska, Egorova, Kiss, and V. Gsovsky. D. with various Fr. cos. and in Malmö. Began teaching in Stockholm in 1953; dir. of her own B. Academy 1957–69. Went to Israel and opened a school in Haifa; dir. of the co. The Dancers' Stage.

Schuhplattler. A Bavarian folk d. in 3/4 time; the girls waltz round the room and the men d. round their partners and then slap thighs, buttocks, heels, knees, chest, and cheeks, while snapping fingers, clapping hands, and performing high jumps or hops on alternate feet.

Schuman, William (*b* New York, 4 Aug. 1910). Amer. composer. Wrote the mus. for Tudor's *Undertow* (1945) and for Graham's *Night Journey* (1947), *Voyage*, and *Judith* (both 1950).

Schumann, Robert (*b* Zwickau, 8 June 1810, *d* Endenich 29 July 1856). Ger. composer. Wrote no b. mus., but several of his concert pieces have been adapted to b. purposes: Fokine, *Le Carnaval* (Berlin, 1910) and *Les Papillons* (St. Petersburg, 1913); Nijinska, *Schumann Concerto* (Piano Concerto in A Minor, New York, 1951); Schwezoff, *Eternal Struggle* (Symphonic Etudes, Sydney, 1940; also T. Gsovsky, Berlin, 1956); Marks, *Dichterliebe* (Copenhagen, 1973); Thorpe, *A Woman's Love* (Manchester, 1974); Neumeier, *Meyerbeer-Schumann* (various works, Hamburg, 1974); Van Manen, *Four Schumann Pieces* (String Quartet no. 3, Royal B., 1975), Spoerli *Ein Faschingsschwank aus Wien* (Vienna, 1977); Balanchine, *Davidsbündlertänze* (New York City B., 1980).

Schumann Concerto. Ballet in 3 movements; ch. Nijinska; mus. Schumann; déc. Stewart Chaney. Prod. 27 Sep. 1951, B. Th., Met. Op. House, New York, with Alonso and Youskevitch. An abstract setting of Schumann's Piano Concerto in A minor; the b. follows the shifting romantic moods of the mus.
BIBL.: G. Balanchine, 'S.C.' in *Balanchine's New Complete Stories of the Great Ballets* (Garden City, N.Y., 1968).

Schwaarz, Heidrun (*b* Munich, 15 Aug. 1943). Ger. dancer. Studied at Munich State Op. B. School; joined its co. in 1960. Principal d. of Frankfurt Op. B. 1965–70; soloist of the West Berlin Ger. Op. 1970–81—now b. dir. Essen. Married to the d. Igor Kosak.

Schwartz, Sheldon (*b* Montreal, 27 Oct. 1954). Can. dancer. Studied at Julliard School with Tudor, Zaraspe, Limón, McGehee, Winter, and M. Hill. Joined Basle B. 1973, eventually appointed soloist and creating roles in numerous Spoerli bs. Has also started to ch.

Schwarz, Josephine Lindeman (*b* Dayton, Ohio, 8 Apr. 1908). Amer. dancer, teacher, and choreographer. Studied at Dayton Bott Dancing Academy, with Bolm, at School of Amer. B. and modern d. with Wigman, Laban, and Chladek. D. with Bolm's B. Intime, R. Page Ravina Op. B., Weidmann Th. D. Co., in various Broadway musicals and with her sister Hermene S. on tour. Became founder, dir and ch. of Dayton B. Co. in 1937. Has worked as guest ch. for many Regional b. cos. throughout the US. Dancers who were trained by her incl. R. Wright, Daniel and Joseph Duell, Donna Wood, and Jeffrey Gribler. Hon. Doctor of Fine Arts, University of Dayton (1974), Ohio Arts Council Award for Arts Management (1977).

Schwarz, Solange (*b* Paris, 1910). Fr. dancer. The daughter of Jean A.S. (1884–1936), a famous Paris b. teacher. Studied at Paris Opéra B. School; joined Paris Opéra B. in 1930. Appointed étoile at Opéra Comique in 1933. Returned to Opéra in 1937 and became étoile in 1940. Her most famous role was Swanilda, which she d. for her farewell perf. in 1957. Created roles in Lifar's *Bacchus et Ariane* (1931), *Alexandre le Grand* (1937), *Entre deux rondes* (1940), *Le Chevalier et la damoiselle* (1941), *Les Animaux modèles* (1942), and in his versions of *Sylvia* (1941) and *Joan de Zarissa* (1942). She and Lifar left the Opéra in 1945. Performed as a guest with Bs. de Champs-Elysées; created Bellastriga in Liupart's *Abraxas* (Munich, 1948). D. again at the Opéra Comique, with Grand B. du Marquis de Cuevas, and with Béjart's B. de l'Etoile. Now retired.

Schweizer Milchmädchen, Das. See *Nathalie, ou la Laitiére Suisse.*

Schwezoff, Igor (*b* St. Petersburg, 1904, *d* N.Y., 28 Oct. 1982). Russ.-Amer. dancer, choreographer, and teacher. Studied at Leningrad Ch. School and with Fedorova. D. in Leningrad, then at various Ukrainian ths., in China in revues 1930–1, as principal d. at Teatro Colón in Brazil. Made a film in Berlin in 1932; appeared at Paris Opéra Comique and with co. of Nijinska. Opened a sch. in The Hague and Amsterdam, from which the B.I.S. emerged 1933–6, for which he ch. several bs. D. and ch. in Monte Carlo 1936–7; then opened school in London. Soloist of Original B.

Russe 1939–41. Ch. of New Op. Co. in 1941. Military service in the U.S. 1942–3. B. dir., ch., and d. of Teatro Municipal in Rio de Janeiro in 1945. Ch. of New York City Op. in 1946. Founder-Dir. of Rio de Janeiro B. da Juventude in 1947. Opened school in New York in 1949. Formed a further co. of his own in 1953. Teacher at B. Th. School in New York 1956–62; has since taught intermittently at various schools in New York. Ch. *Eternal Struggle* (mus. Schumann, Sydney, 1940), *The Red Poppy* (mus. Glière, B. Russe de Monte Carlo, 1943) and *Concerto dansante* (mus. Saint-Saëns, Rio de Janeiro, 1945). Author of *Borzoi* (London, 1935).
BIBL.: N. Russell, 'Around the World with I.S.', *Dance Magazine* (1969/6).

Scoglio, Joseph (*b* New York, 2 June 1943). Amer. dancer. Studied at School of Amer. B. and Amer. B. Center. D. with the cos. of Hoving, Goslar, and with Les Grand Bs. Canadiens, with which he came to London. Joined B. Rambert in 1969; created roles in J. Taylor's *'Tis Goodly Sport* (1970), *Listen to the Music* (1972), Bruce's *There was a Time* and *Duets* (1973), Chesworth's *Project 6354/9116* (1974), and North's *Running Figures* (1975). Ch. *Stop-Over* (mus. Takemitsu, 1972), *Les Saltimbanques* (mus. Cowie, 1973), *The Night Dances* (mus. Downes, 1974), and *The Small Hours* (mus. Scarlatti, 1976). Assistant Artistic Dir. of Austral. D. Th. since autumn 1976.

Scotch Symphony. Ballet in 3 movements; ch. Balanchine; mus. Mendelssohn; set H. Armistead; cost. Karinska and David Ffolkes. Prod. 11 Nov. 1952, New York City B., City Center, N.Y., with Maria Tallchief, Eglevsky, Wilde, Hobi, Maule. A classic b. with a slightly Scottish atmosphere (especially so in the second movement with its references to *La Sylphide*), to all but the first movement of Mendelssohn's A minor Symphony. Revived for Munich State Op. B. (1964).
BIBL.: G. Balanchine, 'S.S.' in *Balanchine's New Complete Stories of the Great Ballets* (Garden City, N.Y., 1968).

Scott, Colleen (*b* Durban, 6 Sep. 1945). South Afr. dancer. Studied with Eileen Keegan and at Royal B. School. D. with Johannesburg B. 1962–64, Düsseldorf B. 1967–74, appointed soloist in 1970, Munich State Op. B. 1974–77, and since 1977 as a first soloist with Hamburg State Op, B. Created roles in Walter's *Pelleas and Melisande* (1969) and Neumeier's *Orpheus and Eurydice* (1977). Married to the d. Ivan Liška.

Scott, Margaret (*b* Johannesburg, 1922). Brit. dancer and teacher. Studied at Sadler's Wells School and Rambert School. D. with Sadler's Wells B. 1941–3 and B. Rambert 1943–8. Stayed in Australia after one of the co.'s tours. Co-founder of Australian National Th. B. Co. and dir. of Australian B. School since 1964.

The Scottish Ballet in Darrell's *Chéri*

Scottish Ballet, The. In May 1956 some members of the Bristol School of Dancing, the Old Vic Th. School, and interested Bristol citizens founded the Western Th. B. as a small b. co. with theatrical aspirations. The initiative came from Elizabeth West, who until her early death in 1962 was the decisive force behind it. The co. started work in May 1957, and gave its first perf. at Dartington on 24 June 1957 with bs. by West and Darrell, who gradually became its chief ch. and is now its dir. The early years were extremely hard, and the co. faced bankruptcy more than once. During the early 1960s the situation improved. Invitations from abroad (to participate in Béjart's Brussels *Sacre du printemps* prod.) and to festivals (Edinburgh, 1961; Jacob's Pillow, 1963) attracted wider attention. Important b. creations at this period included Darrell's *The Prisoners* (1957), *Chiaroscuro* (1959), *A Wedding Present* (1962), *Jeux*, and the first Beatles b., *Mods and Rockers* (1963). In 1965 the co. was invited to d. in the op. prods. of the Sadler's Wells Op., for which it moved to London, where it premiered the first full-length Brit. b. with a contemporary subject, Darrell's *Sun Into Darkness*, in 1966. The co. favoured strongly dramatic bs., such as Béjart's *Sonate à trois*, MacMillan's *Las Hermanas*, and Flindt's *The Lesson*; J. Carter contributed *Cage of God* (1967) and P. Wright *Dance Macabre* (1968). The co. moved to Glasgow in April 1969, and took the name Scottish Th. B. (since 1974 The Scottish B.). The classics entered the co.'s repertory, together with further full-evening works by Darrell: *Beauty and the Beast* (1969), *Tales of Hoffmann* (1972), *Mary Queen of Scots* (1976), and *Cinderella* (1979), with various shorter works. Darrell remained art. dir. to 1987, then became founder-choreographer. The co. numbers about 40 dancers
BIBL.: N. Goodwin *A Ballet for Scotland* (Edinburgh, 1979).

Scriabin, Alexander Nicolaievich (*b* Moscow, 6 Jan. 1872, *d* there, 27 Apr. 1915). Russ. composer. Wrote no b. mus., but several of his concert pieces have been adapted for b. purposes, particularly *Le Poème de l'extase* (Sokolow, New York, 1956; R. Wagner, New York, 1963; Petit, Milan, 1968; Keres, Wiesbaden, 1969; Cranko, Stuttgart, 1970; Beatty, Stockholm, 1972). Other bs. include Goleizovsky's *Scriabiniana* (Bolshoi B. 1962), Neumeier's *Dämmern* (*Twilight*, Frankfurt, 1972), Walter's *Third Symphony* (Düsseldorf, 1974), North's *S. Preludes and Studies* (London Contemporary D. Th.), and Howald's *Prometheus* (Frankfurt, 1979). A Sokolow ch. a full-length *Hommage à S.* in 1977.

Scribe, Eugène (*b* Paris, 24 Dec, 1791, *d* there, 20 Feb. 1861). Fr. playwright. Though b. librettos constitute only a small fraction of his oeuvre, he wrote the libr. for some of the most important works of the pre-romantic b. era; e.g. Aumer's *La Somnambule* (1827), *La Belle au bois dormant* (1829), and *Manon Lescaut* (1830), Coralli's *L'Orgie* (1831)

and *La Tarentule* (1839), and F. Taglioni's op. b. *Le Dieu et la Bayadère* (1830).

Scuola di ballo. Ballet in 1 act; libr. and ch. Massine; mus. Boccherini (arr. J. Français); déc. Comte E. de Beaumont. Prod. May 1924, Soirées de Paris, Th. de la Cigale, Paris. The b. is based on Goldoni's comedy *S. d. B.* An impresario visits a b. school, looking for a new prima ballerina; the teacher tries to sell him the least talented of all the girls. Revived for B. Russe de Monte Carlo in 1933.

Scythian Suite. Commissioned by Diaghilev, Prokofiev composed a b. *Ala and Lolly* in 1914 on the subject from Scythian mythology, dealing with the rivalry between the sun god Veles and the wooden idol Ala (libr. Gorodetzky). When Diaghilev rejected the finished score, Prokofiev adapted it, as *S.S.*, for a concert perf. in Petrograd in 1916. First prod. by Terpis as *Die Erlösten (The Saved Ones)*, based on Dante, on 7 May 1927 at the Berlin State Op. Later versions by Nijinska (Teatro Colón, 1927), K. Tóth (Bratislava, 1964), and G. Alexidze (Kirov B., 1969).

Seasons, The. See *Four Seasons, The.*

Sebastian. Ballet in 1 act and 3 scenes; libr. and mus. G.-C. Menotti; ch. Caton; set O. Smith; cost, Milena. Prod. 31 Oct. 1944, B. International, International Th., New York, with Moncion. Set in Venice at the end of the 17th century; a Moorish slave substitutes himself for a wax figure, and dies from the arrows shot into it. Different versions by de Mille (Amer. B. Th., 1957) and Butler (Netherlands D. Th., 1963).
BIBL.: G. Balanchine, 'S.' in *Balanchine's New Complete Stories of the Great Ballets* (Garden City, N.Y., 1968).

Seconde, A, la. Fr., in the second position.

Secular Games. Ballet in 3 movements; ch. Graham; mus. R. Starer; set J. Rosenthal. Prod. 17 Aug. 1962, M. Graham D. Co., Amer. D. Festival, New London, Conn., with Powell, Wood, Kuch, Gain, C. Thompson. Set to Starer's Concerto a Tre. The 3 movements are entitled: Play with thought—on a Socratic island; Play with dream—on a Utopian island; Play—on any island.

Sedova, Julie (née Julia Nicolaievna S.; *b.* St. Petersburg, 21 mar 1880, *d* Cannes, 23 Nov. 1969). Russ.-Fr. dancer and teacher. Studied at Imperial B. Academy; graduated in 1898. Member of the Maryinsky Th. 1898–1911 and 1914–16 (after guest appearances in W. Eur. and the U.S.). Left Russia after the October Revolution and went to France; she opened a studio in Nice, which produced many eminent Fr. dancers, incl. Palley, Golovine, Skibine, Melikova, and E. Carroll.

Segarra, Ramon (*b* Mayaguez, 26 Nov. 1939, *d* Miami, Fl., 23 Sep. 1984). Puerto Rican dancer, teacher, and b. master. Studied with Chaffée,

Pereyaslavec, Zaraspe, and O'Donnell. Début with G. Chaffée B. in 1953; d. with O'Donnell co. 1956–8, B. Russe de Monte Carlo 1958–61, New York City B. 1961–4. Then worked freelance. Began teaching in 1965 (Ger. Op. Berlin, Harkness House, Univ. of California at Irvine, Pennsylvania B., Hamburg State Op., A. Ailey Amer. D. Th., Eglevsky B. Co.). Ch. *Misa Criolla* (mus. Ariel Ramirez) for B. Hispanico (New York, 1974).

Segerström, Per Arthur (*b* Stockholm, 1952). Swed. dancer. Studied at Royal Swed. B. School and with Hightower and Franchetti. Joined Royal Swed. B. in 1970; later became soloist. Award for best couple (with Alhanko, junior category, Varna, 1972).

Segovia, Rosita (*b* Barcelona, 1926). Span. dancer. Studied with La Tanginesa and Verchinina. Joined co. of Barcelona Teatro Liceo in 1938, Morosova b. in 1949, and Antonio's co. in 1953.

Seguidilla. A very old Span. d., known by different names in the various provinces, and d. with slight variations. The popular version is a lively d. for couples in 3/4 time, accompanied by guitar and sung coplas. A slower form is called Seguidilla Manchega; a faster version is Seguidilla Bolera; and a sentimental one Seguidilla Gitana. Glinka and Albeniz introduced it to concert mus., and its most prominent example is in the first act of Bizet's *Carmen*.

Seigneuret, Michéle (*b* Paris, 1934). Fr. dancer. Studied with Jeanne Schwarz. Début with Béjart's Bs. de L'Etoile in 1954; later became his main ballerina, and created many leading roles in his early bs.—e.g. *Symphonie pour un homme seul* (1955), *Le Teck* (1956), and *Sonate à trois* (1957). Afterwards appeared only very rarely. René Blum Prize (1956).

Seillier, Daniel (*b* Villiers-sur-Marne, 1926). Fr. dancer and b. master. Studied with Ricaux, Egorova, and V. Gsovsky. Member of Paris Opéra B. until 1946. Soloist and b. master of Grand B. du Marquis de Cuevas 1951–61. B. master Lisbon San Carlos Opera B. in 1961, Les Grand Bs. Canadiens 1963, and National B. of Canada since 1965.

Sekh, Yaroslav (*b* Ukraine, 1 Oct. 1930). Sov. dancer and teacher. Early training in the folk dance movement; studied at Lvov Op. B. School and at Moscow Bolshoi School. Graduated in 1951 and has been a soloist of the Bolshoi B. since then. Especially good in character roles. Created title role in Lavrovsky's *Paganini* (1960) and a leading role in Vinogradov's *Asel* (1967). Now teacher at GITIS.

Selina. Ballet in 1 act by Howard (libr., ch., and cost.) and P. Williams (libr. and déc); mus. Rossini (arr. Guy Warrack). Prod. 16 Nov. 1948, Sadler's Wells Th. B., Sadler's Wells Th., London, with

Züllig, Fifield, Trecu, Holden. A b. satire on the absurdities of the romantic convention.

Selinder, Anders (*b* Stockholm, 1806, *d* there, 1874). Swed. dancer and b. master. Appointed solo d. of the Royal Swed. B. in 1829; the co.'s first native b. master 1833–45 and 1851–6. In his bs. his frequent use of Swed. folk dances, adapted for the stage, helped to conserve them. Retired from the Stockholm Op. in 1871 and opened a b. school.

Semberová, Zora (*b* Vyškov, 13 Mar. 1913). Czech dancer and teacher. Studied with J. Hladík, then with Preobrajenska, Chladek, and T. Gsovsky. D. in Brno 1922–8, at Prague National Th. 1928–30, in Brno again 1932–42 (created Juliet in Psota's world première of Prokofiev's *Romeo and Juliet*, 1938), and at Prague National Th. again 1943–60. Staff member of the d. department at Prague Conservatory 1946–68.

Semenoff, Simon (*b* Liepaja, 1908). Latv.-Amer. dancer, teacher, and inpresario. Studied with Fedorova, Messerer, Tikhomirov, Preobrajenska, Egorova, and Fokine. D. with Riga National Op. B. 1922–30, then with many Western cos., e.g. R. Blum's B. Russe de Monte Carlo, B. Th., B. International, San Francisco B., London Festival B. Opened a b. school in Santa Monica, Calif., in 1947, and another in Stamford, Conn., in 1954. From 1958 worked for Hurok Attractions. Made guest appearances with Marseilles and Austral. Bs. as Don Gamache in Nureyev's prod. of *Don Quixote*.

Semenyaka, Ludmila Ivanovna (*b* Leningrad, 16 Jan. 1952). Sov. dancer. Studied at Leningrad Ch. School; graduated in 1970. D. with Kirov B. 1970–2; has since been soloist of the Moscow Bolshoi B. Second Prize All-Sov. B. Competition (Moscow, 1972); First Prize (Tokyo, 1976). BIBL.: T. Tobias, 'Bolshoi Profiles: L. S.', *Dance Magazine* (1975/8).

Semiramis Ballets. Bs. about the legendary Assyrian queen and her famous hanging gardens were ch. by Angiolini (mus. Gluck, Vienna, 1765), S. Viganò (own mus. arr., Venice, 1792), and Fokine (text P. Valéry, mus. Honegger, I. Rubinstein Co., Paris, 1934).

Semizorova, Nina (*b* Krivoy Kog, 15 Oct. 1956). Sov. dancer. Studied at Kiev B. School. Upon graduation in 1975 joined Kiev B., now a principal d. of the Moscow Bolshoi B. Gold Medal (Moscow, 1977).

Semyonov, Victor Alexandrovich (*b* St. Petersburg, 25 Dec. 1892, *d* Moscow, 13 Apr. 1944). Sov. dancer and teacher. Studied at Imperial B. Academy; graduated in 1912. Joined Maryinsky Th.; became principal dancer in 1917. Frequently appeared with Spessivtseva and his wife Marina Semyonova. Retired in 1931; moved to Moscow and became principal teacher at Bolshoi B. School.

His pupils included Lepeshinskaya and Golov-kina.

Semyonov, Vladilen Grigorievich (b Samara, 12 Nov. 1932). Sov. dancer. Studied at Leningrad Ch. School; graduated in 1950. Joined Kirov B. and later became principal d. Chairman of the choreographers collective 1970–2. Now a repetiteur of the co. Merited Artist of the R.S.F.S.R. (1962); People's Artist of the R.S.F.S.R. (1972). Married to the d. Irina Kolpakova.

Semyonova, Marina Timofeyevna (b St. Petersburg, 12 June 1908). Sov. dancer and teacher. Began studying with Vaganova, whose most famous pupil she was, in 1919. Appeared in 1923 at the GATOB; graduated in 1925. Joined GATOB; became ballerina in 1926. Admired for her charm and distinguished nobility. Went to Moscow and was prima ballerina of the Bolshoi B. 1930–52. First Sov. ballerina to d. Giselle (with Lifar) at the Paris Opéra, 1935. Began teaching in 1925; taught the classe du perfectionnement of the Bolshoi B. from 1946. Retired from the stage, but continued to teach at the Moscow Bolshoi School. People's Artist of the R.S.F.S.R. (1951). Married to the d. and teacher Victor Semyonov.

Sentimental Colloquy. Ballet in 1 act; ch. G. Balanchine, credited to A. Eglevsky; mus. Paul Bowles; déc. Dali. Prod. 30 Oct. 1944, B. International, International Th., New York, with Eglevsky, Marie Jeanne. The b. was based on a poem by Verlaine, but was completely dwarfed by Dali's gigantic backdrop of a great number of bicyclists.

Sent M'ahesa. See M'ahesa, Sent.

Septet Extra. Ballet in 5 movements; ch. Van Manen; mus. Saint-Saëns; déc. Vroom. Prod. 2 July 1973, Netherlands D. Th., Circus Th., Scheveningen, with Lemaitre, Venema. Set to Saint-Saëns' Septet for Strings, Piano, and Trumpet and his Etude in Waltz Form, op. 52 no. 6. A humorous essay for 10 dancers; the 'extra' refers to movements which the ch. could not use in his previous bs., as well as to the added Etude. Revived for Royal B. New Group (1974) Düsseldorf B. (1975), and Royal Dan. B. (1977). BIBL.: P. Brinson and C. Crisp, in Ballet & Dance (Newton Abbot, 1980).

Septième Symphonie, La. See Seventh Symphony.

Sept péchés capitaux, Les. See Seven Deadly Sins, The.

Seraphic Dialogue. Ballet in 1 act; ch. Graham; mus. Dello Joio; set Noguchi; light. Rosenthal. Prod. 8 May 1955, M. Graham D. Co., ANTA Th., New York, with Linda Margolies, Patricia Birch, Hinkson, Turney, Ross. 'A drama about Joan of Arc at the moment of her exaltation. In a dialogue with Saint Michael, Saint Catherine, and Saint Margaret, whose voices had guided her towards her destiny, she looks back upon herself

as a maiden, a warrior, and a martyr and, transfigured, is taken to her place of honour' (programme note). An earlier solo d. by Graham on the same subject was Triumph of St. Joan (same mus., 1951). U.S. film version (1969). See also Joan of Arc.

Seregi, László (b Budapest, 12 Dec. 1929). Hung. dancer and choreographer. As a member of the Hung. Army Ensemble, studied with Nádasi and Harangozó. Joined Budapest State Op. B. in 1958 as a character d. Began choreographing op. bs. in 1965; his first major b. prod. was Khachaturian's Spartacus, 1968, followed by Bartók's The Wooden Prince and The Miraculous Mandarin in 1970, Delibes's Sylvia in 1972, F. Hidas' The Cedar in 1975, Hindemith's Kammermusik No. 1, Bernstein's Serenade and On the Town (all 1977), and Dohnányi's Variations on a Nursery Song (1978). Has also worked in W. Germany, Zurich, and Vienna. Erkel Prize.
BIBL.: G. Körtvélyes and G. Lörinc, in Budapest Ballet (Budapest, 1971).

Serenade. Ballet in 4 parts; ch. Balanchine; mus. Tchaikovsky; cost. Jean Lurçat. Prod. 10 June 1934 by students of the School of Amer. B. at the estate of Felix M. Warburg, White Plains, N.Y. 'Named after its music—Tchaikovsky's Serenade in C major for String Orchestra—Serenade tells its story musically and choreographically, without any extraneous narrative' (Balanchine). There are 28 dancers in blue costumes in front of a blue background; the third and fourth movements of Tchaikovsky's score are exchanged. First public perf. 8 Dec. 1934, Producing Co. of the School of Amer. B., Avery Memorial Th., Hartford, Conn.; first professional perf., 1 Mar. 1935, Amer. B., Adelphi Th., New York. New costs. were designed for later prods.; the latest ones were by Karinska, for the 1964 prod. Revived for many cos., incl. B. Russe de Monte Carlo (1940), Paris Opéra B. (1947), Royal Dan. B. (1957), La Scala di Milano (1960), and Royal B. (1964). Various TV prods. of the b., incl. New York City B., Berlin, 1973.
BIBL.: G. Balanchine, 'S.' in Balanchine's New Complete Stories of the Great Ballets (Garden City, N.Y., 1968). D. Daniels, 'The New World of S', Ballet Review (vol. 5, no. 1).

Sergeyev, Konstantin Mikhailovich (b St. Petersburg, 5 Mar. 1910). Sov. dancer, choreographer, and b. director. Studied at the evening courses of the Leningrad B. School; graduated in 1928. Participated as principal d. in an extensive tour of the co. of Joseph Kschessinsky. Studied further at the Leningrad Ch. School 1929–30; joined GATOB on graduation and became admired as one of the most elegant soloists. Created many roles in such bs. as Vainonen's Flames of Paris (1932), Zakharov's Fountain of Bakhchisaray (1934), Lost Illusions (1935), and The Bronze Horseman (1949), Anisimova's Gayane (1942), Lopokov's Spring Fairytale (1947), Jacobson's

Shuraleh (1950), and Fenster's *Taras Bulba* (1955). Also created Romeo in Lavrovsky's *Romeo and Juliet* (1940) and d. all the danseur noble roles of the standard repertory, usually as the partner of Ulanova or his wife Dudinskaya. Ch. Leningrad première of Prokofiev's *Cinderella* 1946, with himself as the Prince (also created the male lead role in many of his later bs.); new prods. of *Raymonda* (1948), *Swan Lake* (1950), and *Sleeping Beauty* (1952), and the first prods. of K. Karayev's *Path of Thunder* (1958), B. Maizel's *The Distant Planet* (1963), and Chervinsky's *Hamlet* (1970). Artistic Dir. of the Kirov B. 1951–6 and 1960–70; led the co. on its first Western tours. He has run into political difficulties more than once, but always remained with the Kirov B. in some capacity, and is still a member of its executive committee. Father of the d. Nicolai S. Stalin Prize (1946, 1947, and 1949); Merited Artist of the R.S.F.S.R. (1939); People's Artist of the R.S.F.S.R. (1957); Lenin Prize (1970).

Sergeyev, Nicholas Grigorievich (*b* St. Petersburg, 15 Sep. 1876, *d* Nice, 23 June 1951). Russ. dancer, b. master, and director. Studied at Imperial B. Academy; graduated in 1884. Joined Maryinsky Th.; became soloist and dir. in 1904, and was dir.-general 1914–18. Left Russ. after the October Revolution with Stepanov notation (in varying degrees of detail, from rough outlines to complete scripts) of 21 of the Maryinsky b. prods. From these he mounted prods. of the standard classics in the West; they formed the basis of most later Western prods. He produced *The Sleeping Princess* for Diaghilev's Bs. Russes in 1921, *Giselle* for Paris Opéra (1924; also for London Camargo Society, 1932), and *Coppélia* (1933), *Giselle, Nutcracker*, and *Swan Lake* (1934), and *Sleeping Beauty* (1939) for Vic-Wells and Sadler's Wells B. B. master in Riga 1922–4; also had a school in Paris. Appointed dir. of Inglesby's International B. School, and mounted the classics for International B. from 1941 onwards. Sov. b. historians accuse him of an almost dictatorial régime at the Maryinsky Th., but there can be no doubt that he laid the foundations of Western knowledge of the Maryinsky classics. He bequeathed his Stepanov scores to Inglesby, who sold them to the Harvard Library.
BIBL.: entry 'S.,N.' in *Enciclopedia dello spettacolo*.

Sergievsky, Orest (*b* Kiev, 21 Aug. 1911, *d* N.Y., 16 Oct. 1984). Russ.-Amer. d. and teacher. Studied with Fokine, Mordkin, and Haakon. Started to perform in supper clubs. Joined Metropolitan Op. B. 1938 and B. Th. 1939, then de Basil's Original B. Russe. Drafted into the Army 1942–5. Started to teach in New York, opening a studio of his own 1950. During the mid-50s had a co., called D. Varieties.
BIBL.: J. Gruen, 'Character Dancer with Russian Roots: O.S.', *Dance Magazine* (1979/2).

Serrano, Lupe (*b* Santiago, 7 Dec. 1930). Chilean-Amer. dancer. Studied with Nelsy Dambre in Mexico City, Schwezoff, and Tudor. Appeared as a child. Official début with B. of Mexico City in 1944. D. with various Mex. cos., B. Alicia Alonso in 1949, B. Russe de Monte Carlo 1949–51, in a weekly TV show in Mexico City 1952–3, with Schwezoff's B. Concerts in 1953, and as ballerina with Amer. B. Th. from 1953 until early 1970s (also guest ballerina with numerous cos.). Joined Pennsylvania B. School 1975. Created title role in Cullberg's *Lady from the Sea* (1960). Considered one of the most brilliant technicians of her generation. Now teaches in Illinois and Pennsylvania. Was married to the conductor Kenneth Schermerhorn.

Sert, José Maria (*b* Barcelona, 1876, *d* Paris, 1945). Span. painter and designer. Designed the sets for Fokine's *Legend of Joseph* (1914), Massine's *Las Meniñas* (1916) and *Le Astuzie femminili* (1924), and Lifar's *Pavane* (1940).

Sertić, Ivan (*b* Zagreb, 13 Jan. 1927). Yugosl. dancer, choreographer, and b. director. Studied at Zagreb State B. School; d. with the cos. in Zagreb and Belgrade. Soloist in Frankfurt 1956–61, b. master in Heidelberg 1961–3, Lübeck 1963–5, Wuppertal 1965–73 (becoming b. dir. in 1968), and b. dir. of the Munich Th. am Gärtnerplatz B. 1973–85. Has ch. many bs., and occasionally worked as a guest in Basle and with various Yugosl. cos. Married to the d. Ludmilla Naranda.

Servant of Two Masters (orig. Czech title: *Sluha dvou pánu*). Ballet with prologue, in 3 acts and 4 scenes; libr. J. Rey; mus. J. Burghauser; ch. Němeček; déc. V. Heller. Prod. 9 May 1958, Tyl Th. Prague, with Kúra. Based on Goldoni's popular comedy. It became one of the most performed post-war Czech bs., and was given in many different versions in various Eastern Bloc countries. An earlier b. version of the same play was Fenster's *The False Bridegroom* (mus. M. Chulaki, Maly Th., Leningrad, 1946).

Seven Deadly Sins, The (orig. Ger. title; *Die sieben Todsünden der Kleinbürger*, first prod. in Fr. as *Les sept péchés capitaux*). Ballet with songs, with prologue, 7 scenes, and epilogue; text Brecht; mus. Weill; ch. Balanchine; déc. C. Neher. Prod. 7 June 1933, Les Bs. 1933, Th. des Champs-Elysées, Paris, with Losch, Lenya. 'The ballet is the story of two Annas, a singing Anna who narrates the progress of a silent dancing Anna in her search for enough money to build a home for her family back in Louisiana. Anna travels to seven American cities, in each of which she encounters a sin. Anna I is the experienced alter-ego of the innocent Anna II' (Balanchine). Revived for New York City B. in 1958 with new Balanchine ch. Numerous other prods., e.g. those by H. Lander (Copenhagen, 1936), T. Gsovsky (Frankfurt, 1960), Béjart (Brussels, 1961), MacMillan

(Edinburgh Festival, 1961; also for Royal B., 1973), and Prokovsky (PACT B., 1975).
BIBL.: G. Balanchine, 'T.S.D.S.' in *Balanchine's New Complete Stories of the Great Ballets* (Garden City, N.Y., 1968).

Seventh Symphony (original Fr. title: *La septième symphonie*). Ballet in 4 movements; ch. Massine; mus. Beethoven; déc. Bérard. Prod. 5 May 1938, B. Russe de Monte Carlo, Monte Carlo, with Markova, Theilade, Franklin, Youskevitch. An abstract b. dealing with the creation and destruction of the earth. The 4 movements are entitled: The Creation—The Earth—The Sky—Bacchanale. An earlier d. version by I. Duncan (New York, 1908).
BIBL.: C. W. Beaumont, in *Supplement to Complete Book of Ballets* (London, 1952).

Seyffert, Dietmar (*b* Reichenberg, 7 Apr. 1943). Ger. dancer and choreographer. Studied at Dresden Palucca School and in Leipzig. Joined East Berlin State Op. B. in 1962. B. master and ch. in Cairo 1967–9. Rejoined East Berlin State Op. B.; ch. *Le Roi nu* (mus. Françaix, 1971), *David and Goliath* (mus. Tilo Medek, 1972), *Flight of Birds* (mus. Martinů, 1973, and *The Three Musketeers* (mus. B. Basner, 1975). Has also ch. for other cos., incl. Tokyo B. Chief ch. Leipzig op. house since 1980; ch. Stravinsky *Sacre du printemps* (1981).

Seymour, Lynn (orig. Springbett; *b* Wainwright, 8 Mar. 1939). Can. dancer. Studied in Vancouver with Jean Jepson and Nicolai Svetaloff, then at Sadler's Wells School. Joined Cov. Gdn. Op. B. in 1956, Touring Royal B. in 1957, Royal B. as a soloist in 1958; became principal dancer in 1959. Went with MacMillan to Ger. Op. Berlin as prima ballerina 1966–9. Then returned to Royal B. Has also been guest ballerina with various other cos., incl. London Festival B., National B. of Canada, A. Ailey Amer. D. Th., London Contemporary D. Th., Amer. B. Th. A ballerina of rare dramatic projection. Created leading roles in MacMillan's *The Burrow* (1958), *Baiser de la Fée* and *The Invitation* (1960), *Images of Love* (1964), *Concerto* (1966), *Anastasia* (1967 and 1971), *Olympiade* (1968), and *Mayerling* (1978), and in his Berlin prods. of *Sleeping Beauty* (1967) and *Swan Lake* (1969); he also modelled his Juliet upon her, though this role was first performed by Fonteyn. Created further roles in Ashton's *Les deux pigeons* (1961), *Brahms Waltzes*, and *A Month in the Country* (both 1975), Petit's *Kraanerg* (1969), and Ailey's *Flowers* (1971). Her first ch. was for Royal B. Ch. Group, followed by *Gladly, Sadly, Badly, Madly* (with R. North) for London Contemporary D. Th. (1975), Artistic Dir. Munich State Op. B. 1978–80. Rejoined Royal B. for a short while in 1981. C.B.E. (1976).
BIBL.: A. Crickmay and C. Crisp, *LS.* (London, 1980); R. Austin, *LS.* (London, 1980).

Shabelevsky, Yurek (*b* Warsaw, 1911). Pol.-Amer. dancer and b. master. Studied at Warsaw

Op. B. School and with Nijinska. D. with Rubinstein's co. in 1928, as a soloist with de Basil's B. Russe de Monte Carlo 1932–9, as a guest with B. Th. in 1940, and later with various South Amer. and Ital. cos. Became b. master of New Zealand B. in 1967.
BIBL.: G. Anthony, 'Y.S.', *Dancing Times* (1976/4).

Shadow of the Wind. Ballet in 6 movements; ch. Tudor; mus. Mahler; déc. Jo Mielziner. Prod. 14 Apr. 1948, B. Th., Met. Op. House, New York, with Alonso, Gollner, Bentley, Youskevitch, Laing, Koesun. The first b. treatment of Mahler's *Song of the Earth* (also ch. by MacMillan, Stuttgart, 1965). 'The choreographer has said that this ballet symbolizes the impermanence of existence, the Chinese philosophy of accepting the mutations of life and bowing before them' (Balanchine).
BIBL.: G. Balanchine, 'S.o.t. W.' in *Balanchine's New Complete Stories of the Great Ballets* (Garden City, N.Y., 1968).

Shadowplay. Ballet in 1 act; libr. and ch. Tudor; mus. Koechlin; déc. Michael Annals. Prod. 25 Jan. 1967, Royal B., Cov. Gdn., London, with Dowell, Rencher, Park. Based on Koechlin's *Les Bandar Log* (with an excerpt from *La Course de printemps* interpolated). An allegory: the Boy with Matted Hair grows up in the jungle, and meets the Arboreals and Aereals. He is confronted by the dominating male figure of The Terrestrial and subjected to the charms of the beautiful Celestial goddess. Like the mus., the ch. seems to be partly inspired by Kipling's *Jungle Book*. Revived for Amer. B. Th. in 1975.
BIBL.: G. Balanchine, 'S.' in *Balanchine's New Complete Stories of the Great Ballets* (Garden City, N.Y., 1968).

Shakers, The. Ballet in 1 act; libr. and ch. Humphrey; mus. and cost P. Lawrence. Prod. 12 Nov. 1930, Humphrey Weidman co., Hunter College, New York. Originally called *Dance of the Chosen* and performed to the accompaniment of a drum, an accordion, and a wordless soprano. An evocation of a religious meeting of the Shaker sect in the pioneer days of Amer. history; they got their name from the habit of trembling violently in a kind of trance-d. during worship. First professional perf. 1 Feb. 1931, Craig Th., New York. Revived on numerous occasions, incl. Welsh D. Th. (1975). A silent film of the b. was made by Thomas Bouchard.

Shakespeare Ballets. The plays of the Brit. dramatist (1564–1616) have always been a source of inspiration for choreographers. The most important bs. include: *The Taming of the Shrew* by Béjart (mus. D. Scarlatti, Paris, 1954), Vera Untermüllerová (mus. O. Flosman, Litoměřice, 1961), Cranko (mus. D. Scarlatti, arr. Stolze, Stuttgart, 1969), and L. Falco in *Kate's Rag* (1980), *Romeo and Juliet* by Eusebio Luzzi (Venice, 1785), Galeotti (mus. C. Schall, Copenhagen, 1811), Nijinska (mus. Lambert, Monte Carlo, 1926),

Bartholin (mus. Tchaikovsky, Paris, 1937), Psota (mus. Prokofiev, Brno, 1938; also Leningrad, ch. Lavrovsky, 1940), T. Gsovsky (mus. L. Spies, Leipzig, 1942), Tudor (mus. Delius, New York, 1943), Skibine (mus. Berlioz, Paris, 1955), and many others; *A Midsummer Night's Dream* by M. Petipa (mus. Mendelssohn, St. Petersburg, 1877), Balanchine (Same mus., New York, 1962), Ashton (in *The Dream*, same mus., London, 1964), Neumeier (Mendelssohn and Ligeti, Hamburg, 1977) R. de Warren (Mendelssohn, Manchester, 1981), and T. Schilling (in *A New Midsummer Night's Dream*, mus. G. Katzer, East Berlin, 1981); *Twelfth Night* by Tudor (in *Cross-Gartered*, mus. Frescobaldi, London, 1937) and Howard (mus. Grieg, Liverpool, 1942); *Hamlet* by Francesco Clerico (mus. by himself, Venice, 1788), L. Henry (mus. W. R. Gallenberg, Paris, 1816), Nijinska (mus. Liszt, Paris, 1934), Helpmann (mus. Tchaikovsky, London, 1942), V. Gsovsky (mus. Blacher, Munich, 1950), Sergeyev (mus. Chervinsky, Leningrad, 1970), Chaboukiani (mus. R. Gabikhvadze, Tiflis, 1971), and Neumeier (in *H.: Connotations*, mus. Copland, Amer. B. Th., New York, 1976); *The Merry Wives of Windsor* by Bourmeister and I. Kurilov (mus. V. Oransky, Moscow, 1942); *Much Ado About Nothing* by V. Boccadoro (mus. T. Khrennikov, Moscow, 1976); *Othello* by S. Viganò (various composers, Milan 1818), Limón (in *The Moor's Pavane*, mus. Purcell, New London, Conn., 1949), Hanka (in *Der Mohr von Venedig*, mus. Blacher, Vienna, 1955), Chaboukiani (mus. V. Machavariani, Tiflis, 1957), Němeček (mus. J. Hanuš, Pargue, 1959), Lifar (in *Le Maure de Venise*, mus. M. Thiriet, Amsterdam, 1960), Darrell (mus. Liszt, Trieste, 1971), and Bonnefous (Louisville Civic B., 1981); *Macbeth* by Le Picq (mus. Locke, arr. Barthelémon, London, 1785), Galeotti (mus. Schall, Copenhagen, 1816), H. Henry (mus. Pugni, Milan, 1830), and Pistoni (mus. R. Strauss, Milan, 1969); *Antony and Cleopatra* by Noverre (Stuttgart or Ludwigsburg, after 1761), Aumer (mus. Kreutzer, Paris, 1808), I. Chernyshov (mus. E. Lazarev, Leningrad, 1968), and dell'Ara (mus. Prokofiev, Milan, 1971); *Coriolanus* by S. Viganò, (mus. Weigl, Milan, 1804); *The Tempest* by Coralli (mus. Schneitzhoeffer, Paris, 1834), F. Taglioni (in *Miranda*, London 1838), Howard (mus. Tippett, London, 1964), Eck (mus. Sibelius, Helsinki, 1974), Tetley (mus. A. Nordheim, B. Rambert, 1979), and Smuin (mus. Chihara after Purcell, San Francisco, 1981). Other bs. based on subjects taken from S. incl. Lacotte's *Such Sweet Thunder* (mus. Ellington, Berlin, 1959) and MacMillan's *Images of Love* (mus. P. Tranchell, London, 1964).
BIBL.: P. Hartnoll (editor), in *S. in Music* (London 1964).

Shane, Gillian (*b* Malden, 14 Dec. 1943). Brit. dancer. Studied with Letty Littlewood. First appeared as a d. in pantomime, aged 12. Joined London Festival B. in 1960; became soloist in 1961. Resigned 1971; appeared 1972–3 with New London B. Now retired. Twin sister of the d. Jeremy Sutcliffe; married to the d. Alain Dubreuil.

Shankar, Uday (*b* Udaipur, 8 Dec. 1900, *d* Calcutta, 26 Sep. 1977). Ind. d. Produced Hindu plays with his father; Pavlova saw them and invited him to collaborate on her b. *Radha Krishna*, in which he appeared. Then embarked on a career as a d.; appeared as a soloist, and later with his own co. He introduced many people, all over the world, to Ind. dancing. Established a d. school in India in 1938 and continued to appear with members of his family until the early 1960s.
BIBL.: R. Singha & R. Massey, 'U.S. and his Dance', in *Indian Dances* (London, 1967).

Sharaff, Irene. Amer. costume designer. Works for Broadway and Hollywood; also designed the costs. for Massine's *Union Pacific* (1934), Balanchine's *Card Game* (also *Jeu de cartes*, New York, 1937), and Robbins' *Interplay* (1945), *Fanfare* (déc., 1953), and *The Concert* (1956).

Shaw, Brian (orig. Earnshaw; *b* Huddersfield, 28 June 1928). Brit. dancer and teacher. Studied with Mary Shaw, R. French, and at Sadler's Wells School. Joined Sadler's Wells B. in 1944; later became soloist and principal d. Principal teacher of the co. since 1972. His best roles were Blue Bird and Blue Skater; created roles in Ashton's *Symphonic Variations* (1946), *Ondine* (1958), and *Monotones* (1966), Cranko's *Bonne-Bouche* (1952) and *Prince of the Pagodas* (1957), Howard's *Veneziana* (1953), and MacMillan's *Noctambules* (1956). Queen Elizabeth II Coronation Award (1975).
BIBL.: J. Percival, 'Musicality with Bravura: B.S.', *Dance and Dancers* (1958/12); 'Dancer to Teacher', interview with B.S., *Dance and Dancers* (1972/4).

Shawn, Ted (*b* Kansas City, 21 Oct. 1891, *d* Orlando, Florida, 9 Jan. 1972). Amer. dancer, teacher, and choreographer. Studied with Hazel Wallack; first appeared as a d. in Denver in 1911. Opened a d. school in Los Angeles, where he appeared in one of the very first d. films, *Dance of the Ages*, and then embarked with a small co. on his first coast-to-coast tour in 1914. In New York he met St. Denis, whom he married in Aug. 1914. Together they made many tours and founded *Denishawn in 1915, which, as a school and a d. co., became one of the pillars of the Amer. modern d. scene. They then extended their tours to Europe and Asia. After the disbanding of Denishawn and their separation in 1932, he established an All-Male Dancers Group in 1933, with which he toured the country for many years; the co. was influential in overcoming the prejudices against male dancing in the U.S. In 1933 he acquired *Jacob's Pillow, a farm in Mass., which he turned into a d. studio; this eventually became the most important Amer. d. festival, which still attracts dancers, teachers, and observers

from all over the world. It offers a unique blend of teaching courses and perfs. He continued to perform well into the 1960s. As a d., ch., and teacher, he was extremely versatile although his main concern was always the cause of the male d. In this area he was the most important pioneer of the Amer. d. scene. NBC TV film *Ruth St. Denis and T.S.* (1958). Author of *Ruth St. Denis: Pioneer and Prophet* (1920), *The American Ballet* (1926), *Gods Who Dance* (1929), *Fundamentals of a Dance Education* (1935), *Dance We Must* (1940), *Every Little Movement* (1954), *33 Years of American Dance* (1959), *One Thousand and One Night Stands* (with Gray Poole, 1960), and 'Remember: Jacob's Pillow Was a Stone', *Dance Magazine* (July 1970).
BIBL.: C.L. Schlundt, *The Professional Appearances of Ruth St. Denis & T.S.* (New York, 1962); Schlundt, *The Professional Appearances of T.S. & his Men Dancers* (New York, 1967); W. Terry, 'The Anniversaries of T.S.' *Dance Magazine* (1971/11).

Shchedrin, Rodion Konstantinovich (*b* Moscow, 16 Dec. 1932). Sov. composer. Wrote the Mus. for Radunsky's new version of *The Humpbacked Horse* (1960), Alb. Alonso's *Carmen Suite* (1967), and his wife Plisetskaya's *Anna Karenina* (1972) and *The Seagull* (1980).

Shearer, Moira (orig. King; *b* Dunfermline, 17 Jan. 1926). Brit dancer. Studied in N. Rhodesia and from 1936 in London with Flora Fairbairn, Legat, and at Sadler's Wells School. Début with International B. in 1941. Joined Sadler's Wells B. in 1942; became soloist, and ballerina in 1944. Created roles in Ashton's *The Quest* (1943), *Symphonic Variations* (1946), *Don Juan*, and *Cinderella* (1948), de Valois' *Promenade* (1943), Helpmann's *Miracle in the Gorbals* (1944), and Massine's *The Clock Symphony* (1950). Guest ballerina of Bs. de Paris in 1950. Her biggest international success was in the film *The Red Shoes* (1948); also appeared in *Tales of Hoffmann* (1951), *The Man Who Loved Redheads* (1955), *Black Tights* (1960), etc. Guest ballerina of the Sadler's Wells B. from 1952. Played Titania in the *Midsummer Night's Dream* prod. of the 1954 Edinburgh Festival, where she also appeared with Helpmann in *The Soldier's Tale*. Now retired. Married to the author and broadcaster Ludovic Kennedy.
BIBL.: P. Crowle, *M.S.* (London, 1949).

Shearer, Sybil (*b* Toronto, *c* 1918). Amer. dancer. Studied with Humphrey. D. with Humphrey-Weidman co. With several other dancers, formed the Th. D. Co. in 1938. Made her début as a solo recital-d. in New York in 1941. Moved to Chicago; undertook numerous tours as a concert-d. all over the States, although she appeared only rarely in New York. Has always collaborated closely with Helen Morrison, who is a designer and lighting dir. of her prods. Started the S.S. Co. in 1959, with which she moved to Winnetka (nr. Chicago); now has her own studio and th. there. Her perfs. elsewhere are very rare, though she has been a guest-teacher at various colleges. She gives an annual series of perfs. which draws an audience from all over the U.S. She has always been considered an outsider in Amer. modern d. Her programmes are usually in cyclical form. Walter Terry has said that 'she dances as if she were a part of nature, innocent and free and strangely worshipful of the miracles of life which surround her. Technically, she can probably outdance almost anyone. Sometimes she chooses to disclose her incredible command of movement; again she will merely stand and move a lifted hand as if she were parting branches so as to look at the sky. Either way, she is remarkable, for although she tries the patience of her many admirers with fruitless ch. digressions, her sense of dedication is unarguable and her command of movement enviable' (in *The Dance in America*, New York, 1956).
BIBL.: M. Lloyd, in *The Borzoi Book of Modern Dance* (New York, 1949).

Sheherazade (also Schéhérazade). Ballet in 1 act; libr. Benois; ch. Fokine; mus. Rimsky-Korsakov; déc. Bakst. Prod. 4 June 1910, co. of Diaghilev, Opéra, Paris, with Rubinstein, Nijinsky, Cecchetti. The libr. is based on the first story from *Thousand and One Nights*; Zobeide, the favourite concubine and leader of the harem of Shariar, betrays him with the Golden Slave when she thinks he is away hunting. Shariar returns, the Golden Slave dies by the scimitar of Shah Zeman, and Zobeide finally stabs herself. The b. uses only 3 of the 4 movements of Rimsky-Korsakov's Symphonic Suite (which is associated with a completely different story). Frequently revived; several versions by Beriozoff for London Festival B. Anisimova ch. a different version, in which she retained the original programme, for the Leningrad Maly Th. in 1950. The Ind. d. Lilavati ch. a Kathakali prod. for the Malmö Municipal Th. in 1969. Another *S.*, using Ravel's song-cycle, by G. Murphy for Sydney D. Co., 1979.
BIBL.: L. Kirstein, '*S.*' in *Movement & Metaphor* (New York, 1970).

Shelesnova, Eleonora (*b* Moscow, 9 Jan. *c* 1932). Sov. dancer and teacher. Studied in Baku; joined Baku Op. House B. Went to Sofia, then to East Berlin in 1966; d. as a soloist at the Comic Op. Married to an orchestral musician; succeeded in reaching West Berlin, where she worked as a teacher at the Ger. Op. Berlin 1971–3. Now a teacher at the Munich State Op. B.

Shelest, Alla Jakovlevna (*b* B. Smolensk, 26 Feb. 1919). Sov. dancer and b. mistress. Studied at Leningrad B. School; graduated in 1937. Joined Kirov B. and became one of its most popular ballerinas. A splendid technician and unusually expressive dramatically. Appeared in all the standard ballerina roles of the repertory, and created Aegina in Jacobson's *Spartacus* (1956). Concert appearances in London, 1953. B. mistress

SHERWOOD 380

of the co. since 1970. Merited Artist of the R.S.F.S.R. (1953); People's Artist of the R.S.F.S.R. (1957). Was married to the ch. Yuri Grigorovich.

Sherwood, Gary (b Swindon, 24 Sep. 1941). Brit. dancer and b. master. Studied at Sadler's Wells and Royal B. School. Joined Cov. Gdn. Op. B. in 1959, Touring Royal B. in 1961 (became soloist in 1962), Western Th. B. in 1965, London Festival B. in 1966, and Royal B. again in 1967 (principal d. 1970–3). A d. of unusual versatility; created roles in Morrice's *The Tribute* (1964), Darrell's *Sun Into Darkness* (1966), and Layton's *The Grand Tour* (1971). B. master of B. Rambert 1974–9; course dir. at * Rambert Academy until 1984; now a freelance teacher. Married to the d. Diana Vere.

Sheta, Reda (b Cairo, 1 Apr. 1949). Egypt. dancer. Studied at Cairo State B. School and in Leningrad, where he participated in some perfs. of the Kirov B. D. with the Cairo B. 1966–9, eventually becoming premier danseur, then in Palermo 1970–3, Ger. Op. Berlin 1973–5, and since 1975 as a principal d. with the Zurich Op. B. Created Abderakhman in T. Gsovsky's *Raymonda* (1975), and Narziss in Spoerli's eponymous b. (1981). His younger brother Hassan S. is a premier danseur of the Cairo B.

Shirah. Ballet in 1 act; ch. and cost. Lang; mus. Hovhaness; light. T. Skelton. Prod. 16 Aug. 1960, Amer. D. Festival, Conn., with Lang, B. Marks. Dedicated to the memory of Margaret Lloyd; an ecstatic essay on the theme of mortality, in a mood of uplift and reassurance. Revived for Dutch National B. in 1962.

Shollar, Ludmila. See *Schollar, Ludmila*.

Shook, Karel (b Renton, Wash., 8 Aug. 1920, d Englewood, N.J., 25 July 1985). Amer. dancer, teacher, and b. master. Studied with D. Fisher, Caton, Fornaroli, Noviloff, Stone, and Camryn, and at School of Amer. B. D. with Seattle Civic Op. B. in 1938, B. Russe de Monte Carlo 1939–40, on Broadway in several musical prods., with New York City B. in 1949, and with B. Russe de Monte Carlo again 1950–2. Dir. of the b. dept. of the K. Dunham School in New York 1952–4. Had his own school in New York 1954–7. Dir. of b. dept. at J. Taylor School 1957–9. B. Master of Netherlands B. 1959, transferred to Het Nationale B. 1961–8; then associate art. dir. of the D. Th. of Harlem. Author of *Elements of Classical Ballet Technique* (Brooklyn, N.Y., 1977).
BIBL.: T. Tobias, 'Talking with K.S.', *Dance Magazine* (1973/1); O. Maynard, in 'Dance Theatre of Harlem', *Dance Magazine* (1975/5).

Shostakovich, Dmitri Dmitrievich (b St. Petersburg, 25 Sep. 1906, d Moscow, 9 Aug. 1975). Sov. composer. Wrote the mus. for Kaplan and Vainonen's *The Golden Age* (1930), Lopokov's *The Bolt* (1931) and *The Bright Stream* (1935). Bs. based on his concert mus. incl. Massine's *L'étrange farandole* (First Symphony, Monte Carlo, 1939;

also MacMillan's *Symphony*, London, 1963), Massine's *Leningrad Symphony* (Seventh Symphony, New York, 1945; also by Belsky, Leningrad, 1961), Morrice's *The Wise Monkeys* (Concerto for Piano, Trumpet and String Orchestra, London 1960; also Cranko's *The Catalyst*, Stuttgart, 1961, and Mottram's *In Concert*, Manchester, 1974), Boyarsky's *The Lady and the Hooligan* (Concert Suites, Leningrad, 1962), Van Dyk's *Ninth Symphony* (Hamburg, 1964), Belsky's *Eleventh Symphony* (Leningrad, 1966), MacMillan's *Concerto* (Second Piano Concerto, West Berlin, 1966; also Mitchell's *Fête noire*, New York, 1971), A. Carter's *Tenth Symphony* (Wuppertal, 1967), and Drew's *Sacred Circles* (Piano Quintet op. 57, London, 1973). V. Panov based his b. *The Idiot* on a selection of S. works (West Berlin, 1979), and A. Prokovsky based *The Storm* on a selection of S. film music and other works (London Festival B., 1981).

Shuraleh. Ballet in 3 acts and 4 scenes; libr. A. Faysi and Jacobson (also ch.); mus. Farid Yarullin; déc A. Ptushko, L. Miltchin, and I. Vano. Prod. 12 Jan. 1945, Kazan; definitive version 28 June 1950, Kirov Th., Leningrad, with Belsky, Dudinskaya, Sergeyev. S. is a wood-demon of Tartar folklore; Suimbike, a girl who is turned into a bird, and Ali-Batyr, a hunter, fall in love with each other, but Shuraleh interferes, and only when they decide to die together is the spell broken. Revived for many cos. in Eastern Bloc countries.
BIBL.: N. Roslavleva, in *Era of the Russian Ballet* (London, 1966).

Shurr, Gertrude (b Riga). Latvian-Amer. dancer and teacher. Studied at Denishawn, with Humphrey, Weidman, and Graham. D. with Denishawn group 1925–7, Humphrey-Weidman co. 1927–9, and Graham co. 1930–8. Has taught at many schools and colleges, with O'Donnell at their New York studio, High School of Performing Arts, and summer courses at Utah State Univ.
BIBL.: D. McDonagh, 'A Conversation with G.S.', *Ballet Review* (vol. 4, no. 5).

Sibelius, Jean (b Hämeenlinna, 8 Dec. 1865, d Jävenpää, 21 Sep. 1957). Finn. composer. Wrote the mus. for the b. *Scaramouche* in 1913; it received its first prod. in 1922 (ch. E. Walbom, Copenhagen. Bs. based upon his concert mus. incl. Kniaseff's *Obsession* (Monte Carlo, 1931), Ashton's *Lady of Shalott* (London, 1931), Gore's *Confessional* (Oxford, 1941), *Antonia* (London, 1949), and *Ginevra* (The Hague, 1956), Franca's *Khadra* (London, 1946), Cranko's *Sea Change* (Dublin, 1949), Gai's *Pelleas and Melisande* (Milan, 1970), Helpmann's *Perisynthion* (Sydney, 1974), Eck's *The Tempest* (Helsinki, 1974), numerous versions of his *Swan of Tuonela* (e.g. by Dolin and Ulbrich), U. Gadd's *Kalevala* (Gothenburg, 1975), P. Montagnon's *Sleepwalkers* (mus. *Tapiola*, Stuttgart 1979).

Sibley, Antoinette (*b* Bromley, 27 Feb. 1939). Brit. dancer. Studied at Cone-Ripman School and Sadler's Wells School. Joined Sadler's Wells B. in 1956; became soloist in 1959 and principal d, in 1960. Has appeared in all the ballerina roles of the standard repertory. A marvellous stylist of exceptional musicality. Created roles in Rodrigues's *Jabez and the Devil* (1961), MacMillan's *Symphony* (1963), *Anastasia* (1971 version), *Triad* (1972), *Pavane* (1973), *Manon* (1974), and Aurora in his *Sleeping Beauty* prod. (1973), Ashton's *The Dream* (1964), *Monotones* (1966), *Jazz Calendar* and *Enigma Variations* (1968), and *Meditation from Thaïs* (1971). Announced resignation in May 1979, returned in Helpmann's *Hamlet* 1981 and gradually resumed dancing career. Was married to Michael Somes. C.B.E. (1973).
BIBL.: O. Maynard, 'Pas de deux par excellence . . .', *Dance Magazine* (1970/4); N. Dromgoole, *Sibley and Dowell* (London, 1976).

Siciliano (also Siciliana or Sicilienne). A gently rocking pastoral folk-d. from Sicily in a slow 6/8 or 12/8 time; very popular in the 18th century.

Siegel, Marcia B. (*b* New York, 17 Sep. 1932). Amer. writer on dance. Educated Connecticut College. D. critic of the *Hudson Review* and *The Soho Weekly News*. Regular contributor to *Dance Magazine*. Founder-editor of *Dance Scope* 1964–6. Dir. of West Coast Institute for D. Criticism, Mills College, Oakland, Cal. Contributed 'American Dance' to *Ballet & Modern Dance* (London 1974). Author of *At the Vanishing Point* (New York, 1972), *Watching the Dance Go By* (Boston, 1977), and *The Shapes of Change* (Boston, 1979).

Sifnios, Duska (*b* Skopje, 15 Oct. 1934). Yugosl. dancer. Studied with Kirsanova, Lavrovsky, Messerer, and V. Gsovsky. Joined Belgrade State Op. B. in 1951 and later became prima ballerina. Has appeared with various cos. abroad, incl. Miskovitch B. in 1959, Massine's B. Europeo in 1960; permanent guest with B. of the 20th Century 1961–72. Created roles in Béjart's *Bolero* and *Webern* (1960), *Les Noces* (1962), and *Ninth Symphony* (1964).

Silvain, James (orig. J. Sullivan; *d* Paris, 1856). Brit. dancer and b. master. Brother of the actor Barry Sullivan. First appeared in pantomime; later progressed to b., and d. at London's King's Th. in 1824 and 1826 and during the 1830s and 40s, and at Paris Opéra 1831–3. Toured America as Elssler's partner and b. master of her co. 1840–2.
BIBL.: I. Guest, in *Fanny Elssler* (London, 1970).

Silver, Mark (*b* Kingston-upon-Hull, 20 June 1955). Brit. dancer. Studied with Gillian Quinn, Elizabeth Kennedy and at Royal B. School 1965–73. Joined Royal B. 1973, appointed soloist 1977, and principal in 1979. Left co. in 1981, joined Pittsburgh B.

Simone, Kirsten (*b* Copenhagen, 1 July 1934).

Dan. dancer. Studied at Royal Dan. B. School. Joined Royal Dan. B. in 1952; became solo-d. in 1956, and first solo-d. (unofficial prima ballerina) in 1966). Has frequently appeared as a guest ballerina abroad. A coolly elegant and slightly aloof ballerina. Dances all the standard roles of the Dan. Bournonville and international repertory; created roles in Flindt's *The Three Musketeers* (1966), von Rosen's *Don Juan* (1967), and Lander's *Festpolonaise* (new version, 1970).
BIBL.: E. Aschengreen, 'K.S.' with complete checklist of roles and activities, *Les Saisons de la danse* (1971/3).

Sinceretti, Francis (*b* Grasse, 18 July 1942). Fr. dancer. Studied in Nice and with Golovin and V. Gsovsky. Began dancing at the Nice Op.; then went to Toulon and Geneva. Soloist at Hamburg State Op. 1966–71, and since then principal d. of Dutch National B. Created leading parts in Petit's *24 Préludes* (1967), Van Dyk's *Pinocchio* (1969), Tetley's *Chronochromie* (1971), Van Dantzig's *Ramifications*, and Van Manen's *Adagio Hammerklavier* (1973) and *Sacre du printemps* (1974). Married to the d. Monique Sand.

Sinfonietta. Ballet in 3 movements; ch. Ashton; mus. M. Williamson; sets (projections) Hornsey Coll. of Art; cost. Peter Rice. Prod. 10 Feb. 1967, Touring Royal B., Royal Shakespeare Th., Stratford-upon-Avon, with Last, Cooke, Anderton, Farley, Wells, Wall, Clarke. A plotless b., reflecting the moods of the 3 movements, Toccata, Elegy (an ingenious adagio for Wells with a group of partners), and a spirited Tarantella, with moving projections, the colours of which were echoed in the costumes. Revived 1981 for Sadler's Wells Royal B. with different static decor by Rice.
BIBL.: D. Vaughan, *Frederick Ashton and his Ballets* (London, 1977).

Sinfonietta. Ballet in 5 movements; ch. Kylián; mus. Janáček; déc. Walter Nobbe. Prod. 9 June 1978, Netherlands D. Th., Charleston, S.C. The b., set to Janáček's exuberant work of 1926 and d. by 7 couples, is an ebullient hymn to life and the conquering of space, though not without some undertones of sorrow and nostalgia. An earlier version by P. Smok (Basle, 1971).

Sirènes, Les. Ballet in 1 act; ch. Ashton; mus. Lord Berners; déc. Beaton. Prod. 12 Nov. 1946, Sadler's Wells B., Cov. Gdn., London, with Fonteyn, Helpmann, Ashton. Loosely based on Ouida's novel *Moths*, with the heroine modelled on La Belle Otero. Set on the beach at Trouville at the height of the 1904 season. The scene is peopled with various eccentric Edwardian characters, incl. a Span. dancer La Bolero, an Oriental Potentate, and an Austral. tenor. The collaborators wanted 'to create an atmosphere that was mysterious and vaguely sinister; it was to be a foggy day on the beach and there should be a sense of desolation behind all the *mondaine* high-jinks' (Beaton).

BIBL.: D. Vaughan, *Frederick Ashton and his Ballets* (London, 1977).

Sissonne. Fr., from ciseaux, scissors; a scissor-like movement.

Situation. Ballet in 1 act; ch. Van Manen; sound-collage; déc. Vroom. Prod. 20 Apr. 1970, Netherlands D. Th., Circus Th., Scheveningen with Lemaitre, Sarstädt, Vervenne, Hampton. A series of aggressive and brutal encounters in an enclosed room. Revived for Dutch Nat. B. and Cologne D.-Forum (1980). Cologne TV prod. 1971.

Sizova, Alla Ivanovna (b Moscow, 22 Sep. 1939). Sov. dancer. Studied at Leningrad Ch. School; graduated in 1958. Joined Kirov B., becoming one of its most popular ballerinas. Her best role is Aurora, which she also d. in the 1965 film of *Sleeping Beauty*. Created Girl in Belsky's *Leningrad Symphony* (1961) and Ophelia in Sergeyev's *Hamlet* (1971). Gold Medal (Varna, 1964). Merited Artist of the R.S.F.S.R. (1966).
BIBL.: S. Goodman 'Meet A.S.' *Dance Magazine* (1962/1).

Skálová, Olga (b Brno, 25 Apr. 1928). Czech dancer. Studied with Psota in Brno and at Moscow Bolshoi School. Joined Brno B.; moved to Prague and became ballerina of the National Th. Created leading roles in Němeček's *Servant of Two Masters* (1958) and *Othello* (1959). B. mistress, Brno. since 1974. Merited Artist (1958); People's Artist (1968).
BIBL.: K. V. Burian, *O.S.* (Prague, 1973).

Skating Rink. Ballet in 1 act; libr. Riciotto Canudo; ch. Börlin; mus. Honegger; déc. Léger. Prod. 20 Jan. 1922, B. Suédois, Th. des Champs-Elysées, Paris, with Yolande Figoni, Kay Smith, Börlin. Grotesque caricatures of the people at a skating rink.
BIBL.: C. W. Beaumont, 'S.R.' in *Complete Book of Ballets* (London, 1951).

Skeaping, Mary (b Woodford, 15 Dec. 1902, d London, 9 Feb. 1984). Brit. dancer, choreographer, and b. director. Studied with Novikov, Trefilova, Egorova, and Craske. Début w. Pavlova co. in London 1925. D. with Nemtchinova-Dolin B. and other cos. B. mistress at Sadler's Wells B. 1948–51. Guest producer of various prods. of b. classics in Can. and Cuba 1952–4. B. director of Royal Swed. B. 1953–62; prod. the standard classics of the 19th century and also revived some historic Swed. court bs., e.g. *Cupid out of his Humour*, Drottningholm Court Th., 1956. Directed a series of Swed. TV prods. on historic d. styles. Then worked as a freelance producer; staged new prod. of *Giselle* for London Festival B. in 1971. Acknowledged as an international authority on the technique and style of the *b. de cour* in the 17th century. Participated in several programmes of the B. for All group, incl. *The World of Giselle* (1963). Author of 'Ballet under the Three Crowns' (history of Royal Swed. B.

1637–1792, *Dance Perspectives* 23). M.B.E. (1958); Order of Gustav Vasa (1961); C. Ari Medal (1971).

Skibine, George Borisovich (also d. as Yura S.; b Yasnaya Poliana, 30 Jan. 1920, d Dallas, Tex. 14 Jan. 1981). Russ.-Amer. dancer, choreographer, and b. director. Son of Boris S., a corps de ballet d. of the Diaghilev co. Studied with Preobrajenska, Eduardova, Lifar, Fokine, Volinine, and Sedova. Début as a can-can dancer at the Bal Tabarin and as a b. d. with B. de la Jeunesse in 1937. D. with B. de Monte Carlo 1938–9, de Basil's B. Russe 1939–41, B. Th. 1941–2. After his military service joined Markova-Dolin B. in 1946; d. with Original B. Russe, and with Grand B. du Marquis de Cuevas 1947–56, where he began to ch. Appeared as guest, with his wife Marjorie Tallchief, with R. Page's Chicago B.; they were then appointed danseurs étoiles at the Paris Opéra in 1957. He was b. dir. there 1958–62. A short period as a freelance ch.; artistic dir. of the newly founded Harkness B. 1964–6. Artistic dir. of Dallas Civic B. and at its affiliated Academy since 1969. As a d. he was especially admired for his romatic good looks and poetic elegance. As a ch. his début was with *Tragédie à Vérone* (mus. Tchaikovsky) in 1950. Then ch. many bs., incl. *Annabel Lee* (mus. B. Schiffmann) and *Prisoner of the Caucasus* (mus. Khachaturian, 1951), *Idylle* (mus. F. Serette, 1954), *Romeo and Juliet* (mus. Berlioz, 1955), *Daphnis and Chloe* (mus. Ravel, 1959), *Les Noces* (mus. Stravinsky, 1962), *Bacchus and Ariadne* (mus. Roussel, 1964), *The Firebird* (mus. Stravinsky, 1967), *Les Bandar Log* (mus. Koechlin, 1969), and *Carmina Burana* (mus. Orff, 1970). Chevalier dans l'ordre des Arts et Lettres (1967).
BIBL.: L. Nemenschousky, *A Day With Marjorie Tallchief and G.S.* (London, 1960); I. Lidova, 'G.S.', with complete check-list of roles and activities, *Les Saisons de la danse* (1970).

Sköld, Berit (b Stockholm, 15 Jan. 1939). Swed. dancer. Studied at Royal Swed. B. School; joined the co. in 1956 and became soloist. Created Juliet in Tudor's Stockholm prod. of *Romeo and Juliet* (1962).

Skorik, Iréne (b Paris, 27 Jan. 1928). Fr. dancer. Studied with Zambelli, Preobrajenska, V. Gsovsky, and Brieux. Debut with B. Recitals at the Th. S. Bernhardt in 1944. D. with Bs. des Champs-Elysées 1945–50; prima ballerina at Munich State Op. 1950–2. Then d. as freelance ballerina with many cos., incl Miskovitch's. Prima ballerina of Basle B. 1960–5, then guest ballerina. Created roles in Charrat's *Jeu de cartes* and Petit's *Le Déjeuner sur l'herbe* (1945) and *Les Amours de Jupiter* (1946), V. Gsovsky's *Hamlet* (1950), *Cinderella* (1951), and *Chemin de la lumière* (1952), T. Gsovsky's *Fleurenville* (1956), and Orlikowsky's *Prince of the Pagodas* (1961), *The Stone Flower* (1962), and *Abraxas* (1963). Has taught at

Chauviré's Paris Académie Internationale de Danse since 1971.

BIBL.: A. Haskell, 'I.S.' in *Dancers and Critics* (London, 1950).

Skouratoff, Vladimir (*b* Paris, 12 Mar. 1925). Fr. dancer, choreographer, and b. master. Studied with Preobrajenska, Volinine, and Kniaseff. Began dancing in the corps of the Lido; joined Nouveaux B. de Monte Carlo as a soloist in 1946, Original B. Russe in 1947, Bs. de Paris in 1948. Toured with Chauviré and Toumanova; d. with Bs. des Champs-Elysées in 1951, with Grand B. du Marquis de Cuevas 1952–7, in the Sagan prod. of *Le Rendezvous manqué* in 1958, then as a guest with London Festival B., in Nice, and with Scandinavian B. B. master in Strasbourg 1966–7 and, since 1970, in Bordeaux, where he has ch. a number of bs. Created leading parts in Lifar's *Dramma per musica* and *Chota Roustaveli* (1946), Charrat's *La Femme et son ombre* and 'adame miroir (1948), Dollar's *Le Combat* (1949), Taras' *Piège de lumière* (1952) and *Le Rendezvous manqué* (1958), and Skibine's *Idylle* (1954).
BIBL.: J. Percival, 'He Can Bring a Poor Ballet to Success', *Dance and Dancers* (1959/12).

Skroblin, Gislinde (*b* Ballenstedt, 23 July 1944). Ger. dancer. Studied in Saarbrücken and at Munich State Op. B. School; joined the co. in 1959 and became soloist in 1966. Created roles in Charrat's *Casanova in London* (1969), Cranko's *Ebony Concerto* (1970), and Ashton's Munich prod. of *La Fille mal gardée* (Lise; 1971).

Slansk. The Pol. State Folklore B., founded by Stanislaw Hadyna in 1954. Chief ch. is Elwira Kaminska; the repertory offers a wide selection of dances and songs based on folklore material. The co. has toured the world, and made its London début in 1958, going to New York in the following year.

Slaughter on Tenth Avenue. Ballet from the mus. comedy *On Your Toes*; ch. Balanchine; mus. R. Rodgers; set Jo Mielziner; cost. Sharaff. Prod. 11 Apr. 1936, Imperial Th., New York, with Ray Bolger, Geva, George Church. The b. is the climax of the musical, which tells of the adventures of a young Amer. member of a touring Russ. b. co.; he is followed by some gangsters, and has to d. for his life; the police arrive at the last moment and arrest the gangsters. Produced as a separate b. on 2 May 1968 by New York City B., State Th., N.Y., with Farrell, Mitchell.
BIBL.: G. Balanchine, 'S.o.T.A.' in *Balanchine's New Complete Stories of the Great Ballets* (Garden City, N.Y., 1968).

Slavenska, Mia (orig. Corak; *b* Slavenski-brod, 1914). Yugosl.-Amer. dancer, choreographer, and teacher. Studied in Zagreb with Josephine Weiss and Froman, then in Vienna with Leo Dubois, Gertrud Kraus, and Lily von Weiden, and in Paris with Egorova, Kschessinska, and Preobrajenska.

Prima ballerina Zagreb Op. B. 1930–3; d. with Paris Opéra Russe 1933–4, then again in Zagreb, in Paris with Lifar, in London with Dolin, several times in Berlin, and with B. Russe de Monte Carlo 1938–42. Settled in the U.S. and formed her own group, B. Variante, and founded a school in Los Angeles. Continued to appear with various cos. in Amer. and Eur.; established S.-Franklin B. in 1952, and created Blanche Dubois in Bettis' *A Streetcar Named Desire*. Starred as ballerina in J. Benoît-Lévy's film *La Mort du cygne* (1938). Currently on the staff of School of D. at California Inst. of the Arts.
BIBL.: portfolio on M.S., *Dance Magazine* (1973/3).

Sleep, Wayne (*b* Plymouth, 17 July 1948). Brit. dancer. Studied at Royal B. School. Joined Royal B. in 1966. Became soloist in 1970; principal d. 1973–83. Created roles in Ashton's *Jazz Calendar*, *Enigma Variations* (1968), *Tales of Beatrix Potter* (film; 1971) and *A Month in the Country* (1976), MacMillan's *Anastasia* (1971), *Sleeping Beauty* (1973), *Manon*, *Elite Syncopations* (both 1974), and *The Four Seasons* (1975). Ch. *David and Goliath* (with R. North; mus. C. Davis, London, 1975), and for his own d. group, Dash, formed in 1980. Has also appeared as a stage and film actor and with special success in the G. Lynne ch. musical *Cats* (1981). Now freelancing.

Sleeping Beauty, The (orig. Russ. title: *Spyashchaya krasavitsa*; also Fr. *La Belle au bois dormant*; formerly in Eng. also *The Sleeping Princess*). Ballet with prologue, in 3 acts and 4 scenes; libr. M. Petipa and Ivan Vsevolojsky; ch. Petipa; mus. Tchaikovsky; sets G. Levot, I. Andreyev, M. Botcharov, K. Ivanov, and M. Shishkov; cost. Vsevolojsky. Prod. 15 (public dress-rehearsal) and 16 (première) Jan. 1890, Maryinsky Th., St. Petersburg, with Brianza, Gerdt, Cecchetti, Maria Petipa, Nikitina. Based on Perrault's fairy-tale. It is considered the climax of the Tsarist b. culture of the 19th century. Petipa's variations for the fairies in the prologue, the rose adagio for Aurora and 4 princes and Aurora's variation in the first act, the character dances, the pas de deux of princess Florine and the Blue Bird, and the grand pas de deux in the finale embody some of his most precious ch. ideas, which have been carefully conserved. A prod. of the complete b. was given at La Scala, Milan in 1896 (staged by Giorgio Savocco, with Brianza in the title-role), and Pavlova d. a 48-minute version (staged by Clustine) in New York in 1916, but the enormous reputation of the b. in the western world dates from Diaghilev's prod., under the title of *The Sleeping Princess*, in London in 1921. In spite of its tremendous artistic success it was too expensive to be kept in the repertory, so Diaghilev produced a shortened version, based mainly on the last act, called *Le Mariage de Belle au bois dormant*, for Paris in 1922. Other cos. staged their own versions in more or less shortened form (in Amer., Mordkin in 1936 and Littlefield in 1937). After Diaghilev

the first real attempt to revive the original Petipa version was by Sergeyev in 1939, for the Sadler's Wells B. A new, more lavish prod. (also by Sergeyev) was given when the co. transferred to Cov. Gdn. in 1946, and the co. opened its first New York season with it in 1949 at the Met. It served as a basis for later new prods. at the Royal B. (by P. Wright in 1968, with additional ch. by Ashton, and by MacMillan in 1973—most recently with some Ashton and de Valois ch. restored, in 1977). It also served as a model for many other prods. in the West; e.g. Beriozoff's for Stuttgart in 1957 and MacMillan's for the Ger. Op. Berlin in 1967. Nureyev staged his first prod. of *S.B.* in 1966 for La Scala, Milan, revived in 1972 for the National B. of Canada and in 1975 for London Festival B. Other recent prods. incl. Nijinska-Helpmann's for the Grand B. du Marquis de Cuevas in 1960, P. Wright's intimate one for Cologne in 1967, Grigorovich's for the Moscow Bolshoi B. in 1973, Helpmann's for the Australian B. in 1973, and Neumeier's for Hamburg B., 1978, Béjart's *Ni fleurs, ni couronnes*, based on ch. subjects from Petipa's *S.B.*, was premièred in 1968 for the B. of the 20th Century in Grenoble. A chamber b. adaptation by H. W. Henze was produced by Alfredo Bortoluzzi in 1951 in Essen. There are various films and TV prods. of the b., e.g. BBC, Royal B., 1959, and K. Sergeyev, Leningrad, 1965. Various films reviewed in *Dance Magazine* (Dec. 1975). Other b. versions incl. Aumer's *La Belle au bois dormant* (mus. Hérold, Paris, 1829) and Laban's *Dornröschen* (mus. J. Strauss, Berlin State Op., 1934).
BIBL.: C. W. Beaumont, 'T.S.P.' in *Complete Book of Ballets* (London, 1951); L. Kirstein, 'T.S.B.' in *Movement & Metaphor* (New York, 1970); V. Krasovskaya, 'Marius Petipa and T.S.B.', *Dance Perspectives* 49; O. Maynard, portfolio on 'T.S.B.', *Dance Magazine* (1972/12); complete scenario in C. Crisp and M. Clarke, *Making a Ballet* (London, 1975).

Sleeping Princess, The. The title of *The Sleeping Beauty* when the Diaghilev co. premièred its prod. in London in 1921, also used for the 1939 Sadler's Wells prod.

Slingsby, Simon. Brit. dancer, of whose life little is known. Studied with R. Aldridge; d. with Baccelli and A. Vestris at the London King's Th. during the 1780s, and was probably the first Brit. d. to make a career at the Paris Opéra, where he was quite successful during the last decade of the century.

Slonimsky, Yuri Josifovich (*b* St. Petersburg, 12 Mar. 1902, *d* Moscow, 23 Apr. 1978). Sov. writer on b. and librettist. Began writing b. criticism in 1919. One of the founders of the Young B. group in 1921. Taught b. history in Moscow and Leningrad during the 1930s and 40s; became the founder of the Sov. school of analytical b. criticism. Author of many books, incl. *Masters of the Ballet in the 19th Century* and *Classics of Choreography* (1937), *Tchaikovsky and the Ballet Theatre of his Time* (1956), *Didelot* (1958), *Seven Ballet Stories* (about his experiences as a b. librettist; 1967), and *Pushkin's Ballet Verses* (1973). Ed. of the Sov. *Petipa* vol. (1971). Contributed the libr. for Fenster's *Youth* (1949), Gusev's *The Seven Beauties* (1952), Sergeyev's *Path of Thunder* (1958), and Belsky's *Coast of Hope* (1959).

Smirnova, Yelena Alexandrovna (*b* St. Petersburg, 1888, *d* Buenos Aires, 15 Jan. 1934). Russ. d. Studied at Imperial B. Academy; graduated in 1906. Joined Maryinsky Th.; became ballerina in 1916. Left Russ. with her husband Boris Romanov after the October Revolution; became ballerina of his Berlin-based Romantic B., and later in Buenos Aires of his Th. Romantique Russe.

Smith, George Washington (*b* Philadelphia, *c* 1820, *d* there, 18 Feb. 1899). Amer. dancer, b. master, and teacher. Known as a clog-d. while a child. Joined the co. of Elssler in 1840; studied with J. Silvain, and became Amer.'s first Albrecht in *Giselle* (Boston, 1846). Appointed principal d. and b. master at the New York Bowery Th. in 1847 and at Brougham's Lyceum Th. in 1850; staged several romantic bs., in which he also appeared as a d. Toured U.S. with L. Montez; then worked freelance with various cos., incl. the Ronzani B., where he became a colleague of E. Cecchetti. Became b. master at Fox's Amer. Th. in Philadelphia; opened a school there and taught until his death. His son Joseph S. (1875–1932) became one of the best known Amer. choreographers of musicals.
BIBL.: L. Moore, 'G.W.S.', *Dance Index* (vol. IV. no. 6).

Smith, Lois (*b* Vancouver, 8 Oct. 1929). Can. dancer. Studied at June Roper Studio in Vancouver and Rosemary Deveson School. Began dancing in operetta and musical prods. in 1945. Joined National B. of Canada in 1951; prima ballerina 1955–69. Appeared in many TV prods. After her retirement as a d. opened a school in Toronto. Was married to the d. David Adams.

Smith, Oliver (*b* Waupun, Wis., 1918). Amer. designer. Co-director of Amer. B. Th. since 1945; designed de Mille's *Rodeo* (1942) and *Fall River Legend* (1948), Robbins' *Fancy Free* (1944), *Interplay* (1945), *The Age of Anxiety* (1950), *West Side Story* (1957), and *Les Noces* (1965), Caton's *Sebastian* (1944), Kidd's *On Stage!* (1945), and D. Blair's prod. of *Swan Lake* for Amer. B. Th. (1967). Handel Medallion (1975).
BIBL.: A. Fatt, 'Designers for the Dance', *Dance Magazine* (1967/3).

Smok, Pavel (*b* Levoča, 22 Oct. 1927). Czech dancer, choreographer, and b. director. Studied at Prague State Conservatory. D. with Army Ensemble 1952–5 and in Plzen 1955–8; b. master in Usti nad Labem 1958–60 and Ostrava 1960–4.

Co-founder of Prague B. (with Ogoun), and b. master 1964–70. B. dir. of Basle B. 1970–3. Now a freelance ch. in Czechoslovakia. Has ch. many bs. and TV prods., incl. *Rossiniana* (1961), *Frescoes* (mus. Martinů, 1966), *Intimate Letters* (mus. Janáček, 1968), *Glagolitic Mass* (mus. Janáček, 1969), *The Servant of Two Masters* (mus. J. Burghauser, 1970), and *Sinfonietta* (mus. Janáček, 1971).

BIBL.: L. Joel, 'Art Must Say Something', *Dance Magazine* (1969/10).

Smorgacheva, Ludmila Ivanovna (*b* Kiev, 29 Nov. 1950). Sov. dancer. Studied at Kiev B. School. Upon graduation in 1969 joined Kiev B., eventually appointed soloist. Silver Medal (Moscow, 1973), Gold Medal (Tokyo, 1978).

Smuin, Michael (*b* Missoula, Mont., 13 Oct. 1938). Amer. d. and ch. Studied with the Christensen brothers in Utah and at San Francisco B. School. D. with Univ. of Utah B. 1955–7, San Francisco B. 1957–62; then worked with his wife Paula Tracy as a freelance d-couple, and as a ch. in night clubs and for TV. Joined Amer. B. Th. as a principal d. and ch. 1969–73; became co-dir. (with L. Christensen) of San Francisco B. to 1984, sole dir. 1984/5. Has ch. many bs., e.g. *Pulcinella Variations* (mus. Stravinsky) and *Gartenfest* (mus. Mozart, 1968), *The Eternal Idol* (mus. Chopin, 1969), *Schubertiade* (1970), *Harp Concerto* (mus. Boïeldieu), *Shinju* (mus. Paul Chihara, 1975), *Romeo and Juliet* (mus. Prokofiev, 1976), *A Song for Dead Warriors* (mus. C. Fox, 1977), and *The Tempest* (mus. Paul Chihara, 1980). Ch. and dir. the Broadway musical, *Sophisticated Ladies* (mus. Ellington), 1981.

BIBL.: O. Maynard, 'San Francisco Ballet's M.S.', *Dance Magazine* (1976/5); S. von Buchau, 'M.S.' *Ballet News* (1980/10).

Snoek, Hans (orig. Johanna S.; *b* Geertruidenberg, 29 Dec. 1910). Dutch dancer, choreographer, and b. director. Studied with Jooss and Leeder. Founder-dir. of Scapino B. in 1945, for which she ch. many bs.; the pioneer of the b. for youth movement in Holland. Author of *Dance and Ballet* (1955). Retired in 1970. Knight of Order of Orange-Nassau (1960). Married to the TV producer Erik de Vries.

Snow Maiden, The. Ballet in 3 acts; libr. and ch. Bourmeister; mus. Tchaikovsky; déc. Yuri Pimenov and Gennadi Epishin. Prod. 17 July 1961, London Festival B., Royal Festival Hall, London, with B. Wright, Burr, Briansky. Inspired by Ostrovsky's fairy-tale play *Snegurochka* (earlier adapted by Rimsky-Korsakov as an opera), for which Tchaikovsky wrote the incidental mus. Bourmeister used this mus. and the first 2 movements from Tchaikovsky's First Symphony. The S.M. falls in love with the peasant Mizgir and plans to marry him; but she becomes a victim of the spring sun and melts away under its rays. Other bs., using the same subject, by

Nijinska (mus. Glazunov, B. Russe de Monte Carlo, 1942) and Varkovitsky (mus. Tchaikovsky, Bolshoi B. School, 1946).

Snow White Ballets. A Russ. version was ch. by A. Andreiev and B. Fenster as *The Princess and the Seven Knights*, based on Pushkin's story, with mus. by Liadov, for Maly Th., Leningrad, in 1949. Lifar ch. *Blanche-Neige* to mus. by M. Yvain for the Paris Opéra in 1951.

Sobeka. The pen name of Kochno as a librettist for several bs. he wrote for the Diaghilev co.

Sodi, Pietro (*b* Rome(?), *d* Charleston(?), after 1775). Ital. dancer, choreographer, and b. master. Possibly studied with R. Fossano. Appeared in Naples during the 1741–2 season; his varied career then took him to London, Paris, Berlin, Vienna, and Venice. He frequently returned to Paris; worked at the Opéra (1748–52), Th. Français (1753), and Th. Italien (1758–60, with De Hesse). From 1761 he was a d. and probably ch. at London's Cov. Gdn. In 1774 he went to New York and from there to Philadelphia and Charleston, offering his services as a dancing master to the local society. 'An exceptional gift for the composition and execution of pantomime dances' (Parfaict); much acclaimed by his contemporaries as one of the pioneers of the b. d'action.

BIBL.: M. H. Winter, in *The Pre-Romantic Ballet* (London, 1974).

Sofia. Though Bulgaria has a rich folk song and d. tradition, the b. dancing is of relatively recent origin. Anastas Petrov, who had studied with Eduardova in Berlin, founded the b. co. attached to the city's National Th. in 1927 and directed it until 1961. He ch. *Coppélia* in 1927, followed by other b. classics and the main works of the Diaghilev repertory, as well as Bulgarian bs. such as *The Dragon and Jana* (mus. Hristo Manolov, 1937) and *Nestinarka* (mus. Marin Goleminov, 1942). The first really qualified Bulgarian ballerina was Maria Dimova. After the Second World War Russia helped b. in Bulgaria by providing teachers, choreographers, and bs., and inviting gifted young dancers to study in Leningrad and Moscow. A State Ch. School was established in 1951, with N. Isow as dir. With the opening of the city's new op. house in 1953, the scope of the co. was extended. Nina Kirdaschikewa, who had been a d. and b. mistress, succeeded Petrov as b. dir. 1961–73; the co. is now directed by G. Abrachev. A smaller touring co., Arabesque, under L. G. Goranov, supplements the State Op. B. and serves as a platform for contemporary ch.

Soft Shoe Dance. Related to the tap d., but performed in shoes with soft soles and without metal taps. Ray Bolger was one of its most persuasive practitioners.

Soir de fête. Ballet divertissement; ch. Staats; mus. Delibes (arr. Busser); déc. Valdo Barbey. Prod. 30 June 1925, Opéra, Paris, with Spessivtseva, Ricaux. Performed to an arr. from *La Source*, became one of the most successful bs. of the co.'s repertory. 300th perf given in 1961. Revived in 1974.

Soirées musicales. Britten's concert suite of Rossini melodies (1936) has frequently been used for b. purposes, occasionally with his *Matinées musicales*. First b. version by Tudor, 26 Nov. 1938, Cecchetti Society Matinée, Palladium Th. London, with Larsen, Lloyd, Laing, Tudor, Van Praagh. Later versions by Zolov (Met. Op. House, 1955), H. Heiden (Mannheim, 1960), Cranko (in *Bouquet garni*, Stuttgart, 1965), etc.

Soirées de Paris, Les. A season of b. perfs., organized by Comte Etienne de Beaumont, 17 May—30 June 1924, Th. de la Cigale, Paris. Its first prods. incl. *Mercure* (mus. Satie, déc. Picasso), *Salade* (mus. Milhaud, déc. Braque), *Le beau Danube* (mus. J. Strauss, arr. Désormière, déc. V. Polunin), *Gigue* (déc. Derain), and *Scuola di ballo* (mus. Boccherini, arr. Françaix, déc. Comte de Beaumont; all with ch. by Massine). A Cocteau prod. of *Romeo and Juliet* was also given (déc. J. Hugo).

Sokolov, Oleg Germanovich (*b* Leningrad, 5 Oct. 1936). Sov. dancer. Studied at Leningrad Ch. School; graduated in 1954. Joined Kirov B. and later became a principal dancer. Created leading role in Belsky's *Leningrad Symphony* (second première, 1961). Married to the d. Irina Gensler.

Sokolova, Evgenia Pavlovna (*b* St. Petersburg 1 Dec. 1850, *d* Leningrad, 2 Aug. 1925). Russ. dancer and teacher. Studied at Imperial B. Academy; graduated in 1869. Joined St. Petersburg Bolshoi Th.; was one of its most popular ballerinas of the Petipa era (1869–86). She then became a famous teacher; her pupils included Pavlova, Karsavina, Egorova, Spessivtseva, and Trefilova.

Sokolova, Lydia (orig. Hilda Munnings; *b* Wanstead, 4 Mar. 1896, *d* Sevenoaks, 5 Feb. 1974). Brit. dancer. Studied at London Stedman B. Academy and with Pavlova, Mordkin, Clustine, and Cecchetti. Toured with Mordkin's co. in 1911; d. with Diaghilev's Bs. Russes 1913–22 and 1923–9, and with Massine in London and with her husband Nicholas Kremnev in music halls 1922–3, The first Eng. ballerina of Diaghilev's co. A spirited and vivacious d. with great dramatic gifts. Created roles in many Massine bs., incl. *Las Meniñas* and *Contes Russes* (1916), *Boutique fantasque* (1919), *Le Chant du rossignol*, *Le Astuzie femminili*, and *Sacre du printemps* (1920), and *Les Matelots* (1925). Massine also ch. for her the role of the Miller's Wife in *Le Tricorne* (1919), though this was first performed by Karsavina. Created roles in Nijinsky's *Till Eulenspiegel* (1916), Nijinska's *Les Biches* and *Le Train bleu* (1924), and *Romeo and Juliet* (1926), and Balanchine's *Le Bal* (1929). Also an excellent Fokine d. After the disbanding of the

Diaghilev co. she appeared in the London season of Woizikovsky's co. in 1935, and in Massine's Royal B. prod. of *The Good-Humoured Ladies* in 1962. Buckle edited her memoirs *Dancing for Diaghilev* (London, 1960).

Sokolow, Anna (*b* Hartford, Conn., 1912). Amer. dancer, choreographer, and teacher. Studied with Blanche Talmud, Graham, Horst, Margaret Curtis, and at School of Amer. B. D. with Graham's co. 1930–9; was Horst's assistant. Gave own recitals from 1934 and appeared with a group; her dances stressed her social commitment (*Ballad in a Popular Style*, *Slaughter of the Innocents*, both to mus. by Alex North). In 1939 she began working as ch. and teacher in Mexico City; she frequently returned there and created some of her most important works; e.g. *Lament for the Death of a Bullfighter* (poems by Garcia Lorca, mus. S. Revueltas), *Lyric Suite* (mus. Berg, 1953), *Opus '60* (mus. T. Macero, 1960), *Dreams* (mus. Bach and Webern), and *Musical Offering* (mus Bach, 1961). After 1954 (when she ceased to appear as a d.) she ch., for her own co. in the U.S., *Rooms* (mus. K. Hopkins, 1955), *Poem* (mus. Scriabin's *Poème de l'extase*, 1956), *Metamorphosis* (after Kafka, no mus., 1957), and *Sessions '58* (mus. Macero, 1957). Since 1960 she has occasionally worked for Netherlands D. Th. (Weill's *The Seven Deadly Sins*, 1967), B. Rambert (Varèse's *Deserts*, 1967), London Contemporary D. Th. (*Scenes from the Music of Charles Ives*, 1972), Batsheva D. Co. (T. Baird's *In memoriam No. 52436*, 1973), etc. Ch. full-length *Hommage to A. Scriabin* in 1977. One of the most uncompromising representatives of the modern d. scene; she deals mostly with contemporary subjects of social criticism. Contributed 'The Rebel and the Bourgeois' to *The Modern Dance* (Middletown, Conn., 1965).

BIBL.: M. Lloyd, 'A.S.' in *The Borzoi Book of Modern Dance* (New York, 1949); J. Gales, 'Odyssey Continued', *Dance Magazine* (1970/2).

Soldier's Tale, The. See *Histoire du soldat, L'*.

Soleil de Nuit, Le. Ballet in 1 act; ch. Massine; mus. Rimsky-Korsakov; déc. Larionov. Prod. 20 Dec. 1915, Bs. Russes de Diaghilev, Grand Théâtre, Geneva, with Massine, Zverev. This was Massine's first b., a series of Russ. dances and scenes, set to mus. from Rimsky-Korsakov's op. *Snegurochka*.

Solitaire. Ballet in 1 act; ch. MacMillan; mus. M. Arnold; déc. D. Heeley. Prod. 7 June 1956, Sadler's Wells Th. B., Sadler's Wells Th., London, with M. Hill, S. Neil, A. Page, M. Boulton, D. Britton. 'A kind of game for one' (MacMillan); the mus. is Arnold's two Suites of English Dances. A girl tries repeatedly to join in the activities of her friends, but always finds herself left alone. Revived for Stuttgart B. and Royal Dan. B. (1961), and Ger. Op. Berlin (1967).

BIBL.: G. Balanchine, 'S.' in *Balanchine's New*

Complete Stories of the Great Ballets (Garden City, N.Y., 1968).

Solo-dancer. The highest rank in the hierarchy of the Royal Dan. B.; the equivalent of danseur étoile or principal d. in other cos. The Dan. co. very occasionally bestows the title of first solo-d. (e.g. K. Simone); the rank of prima ballerina has been granted only once, to Margot Lander.

Solomons, Gus, Jr. (*b* Boston, *c* 1940). Studied with Jan Veen and E. V. Williams. Joined Boston D. Makers in 1960. Went to New York in 1962 and d. with the cos. of Graham, Lang, McKayle, Trisler, and Cunningham. Began appearing in his own pieces at Clark Center and Kaufmann Concert Hall. Has had his own group since 1971. Is now Artistic Dir. of Cal. Arts School of D. at Los Angeles.
BIBL.: H. M. Simpson, 'G.S.', *Dance Magazine* (1980/9).

Solov, Zachary (*b* Philadelphia, 1923). Amer. dancer, choreographer, and b. director. Studied with Littlefield, Preobrajenska, Holm, Humphrey, and at School of Amer. B. Début with Littlefield B. in 1939. D. with Amer. B., Loring's D. Players, B. Th., and on Broadway. B. master and ch. at Met. Op. Ho. 1951–8; his bs. incl. *Mlle Fifi* (mus. Lajarte, 1953—revived for London Festival B., 1955), *Vittorio* (mus. Verdi), and *Soirée* (mus. Britten, 1955). He then toured with his own co. Returned to the Met. 1965–6; has since ch. several of its op. prods. In recent years has occasionally worked for Kansas City B.
BIBL.: G. Loney: 'Ballets for Bing', *Dance Magazine* (1973/4).

Soloviev, Yuri Vladimirovich (*b* Leningrad, 10 Aug. 1940, *d* Sosnora nr. Leningrad, 15 Jan. 1977). Sov. dancer. Studied at Leningrad Ch. School; graduated in 1958. Joined the Kirov B. and soon became one of its most brilliant principals. Endowed with a phenomenal élévation. One of his best roles was the Blue Bird, but also danced all the standard danseur noble roles, incl. the Prince in the film of Kirov's *Sleeping Beauty* prod. (1965). Created roles in Belsky's *Leningrad Symphony* (1961), Sergeyev's *The Distant Planet* (1963), Boyarsky's *The Pearl* (1965), Jacobson's *Land of Miracles* (1967), Alexidze's *Orestie* (1968), and Kasatkina–Vassiliov's *Creation of the World* (1971). Merited Artist of the R.S.F.S.R. (1964); People's Artist of the R.S.F.S.R. (1967). Was found shot in his dacha, in rather mysterious circumstances. Was married to the d. Tatiana Legat.

Solveig. Ballet Suite in 3 acts and 5 scenes, with prologue and epilogue; ch. Jacobson; mus. Grieg (arr. B. Asafiev and E. Kornblit); dec. V. Khodasevich. Prod. 25 Dec. 1952, Maly Th., Leningrad. Not the same as Lopokov's *The Ice Maiden* or *Solveig* (mus. Grieg, GATOB, Leningrad, 1927), with which it is often confused.

Sombert, Claire (*b* Courbevoie, 1935). Fr. dancer and teacher. Studied with Brieux, V. Gsovsky, Rousanne, and Preobrajenska. Debut Lausanne, 1950. D. with Bs. J. Charrat 1951–2, Bs. R. Petit 1953—4, co. of Miskovitch in 1956, Bs. J. Babilée 1957–9, then with various other cos., in the Larrain prod. of *Cinderella* in 1964, and on a Russ. tour with Michel Bruel in 1968. Associate artistic dir. and étoile of B. du Rhin 1972–4. Also took part in Kelly's film *Invitation to the Dance* (1962). Created roles in Petit's *Le Loup* (1953), Béjart's *Promethée* (1956), and Lifar's *Pique Dame* (1960). Inspectrice de la danse à Paris (1979). Prix René Blum (1952).
BIBL.: I. Lidova, 'C.S.' with complete check-list of roles and activities, *Les Saisons de la danse* (1973/4).

Somes, Michael (*b* Horsley, 28 Sep. 1917). Brit. dancer and b. director. Studied with Katherine Blotz at Weston-super-Mare and Espinosa and Bedells in Bristol; also Sadler's Wells School from 1936. Soon joined Sadler's Wells B. and became a principal d. in 1938; career interrupted by war service and an injury, but on Helpmann's retirement in 1949 became the co.'s leading male d., and the regular partner of Fonteyn. D. the danseur noble roles in all the prods. of the classics and created roles in many bs., e.g. Ashton's *Horoscope* (1938), *Dante Sonata* and *The Wise Virgins* (1940), *The Wanderer* (1941), *Symphonic Variations* (1946), *Scènes de ballet* and *Cinderella* (1948), *Daphnis and Chloe* and *Tiresias* (1951), *Sylvia* (1952), *Homage to the Queen* (1953), *Rinaldo and Armida* (1955), *La Péri* and *Birthday Offering* (1956), *Ondine* (1958), and *Marguerite and Armand* (1963), also in Massine's *Clock Symphony* (1948), Cranko's *Antigone* (1959), MacMillan's *Romeo and Juliet* (1965), and the title role in Layton's *O.W.* (Oscar Wilde, 1972). Assistant dir. of Royal B. 1963–70; principal répétiteur and teacher until 1984. Ch. one b., *Summer Interlude* (mus. Respighi, Sadler's Wells Th. B., 1950). C.B.E. (1959). Was married to the dancers Deirdre Dixon and Antoinette Sibley.
BIBL.: H. Fisher, *M.S.* (London, 1955); J. Gruen, 'M.S.', in *The Private World of Ballet* (New York, 1975).

Somnambule ou l'Arrivée d'un nouveau Seigneur, La. Pantomimic Ballet in 3 acts; libr. Scribe and Aumer (also ch.); mus. Hérold; sets Ciceri. Prod. 19 Sep. 1827, Opéra, Paris, with Montessu, Legallois, Ferdinand. The b. is set in a village in Provence, where Thérèse causes a scandal when she appears in her nightdress in the guest-room of the inn; her fiancé renounces her in public. Thérèse is then suddenly seen sleepwalking on the edge of a roof, which explains everything and so the wedding between Thérèse and Edmond can take place. It was this b. which caused Bellini to write his op. *La Sonnambula* (1831). For Balanchine's b., which is given in Fr. mostly as *La Somnambule*, see *Night Shadow*.

BIBL.: L. Kirstein, 'L.S.' in *Movement & Metaphor* (New York, 1970).

Somnambulism. Ballet in 1 act; ch. MacMillan; mus. Stan Kenton; Prod. 1 Feb. 1953, Sadler's Wells Ch. Group, Sadler's Wells Th., London, with Lane, MacMillan, Poole. MacMillan's first b.; it deals with the neuroses and frustrations of three dancers who suffer from anxiety, monotony, and premonition, but eventually find, to their relief, that they have all been dreaming. First public perf. 29 May 1956, Sadler's Wells B., Sadler's Wells Th., London, with Hill, Britton, Heaton.
BIBL.: H. Fisher, in *The Sadler's Wells Theatre Ballet* (London, 1956).

Sonate à trois. Ballet in 1 act; ch. Béjart; mus. Bartók; cost. H. Bert. Prod. 27 Apr. 1957, B. de l'Etoile, Essen, with Bari, Seigneuret, Béjart. Set to Bartók's Sonata for Two Pianos and Percussion; inspired by Sartre's *Huis clos*. Two women and one man who have to live together in a closed room from which there is no escape. The Paris first perf. took place on 19 June 1957. Revived for various cos., incl. Western Th. B. in 1960.
BIBL.: P. Brinson and C. Crisp, 'S.à.t.' in *Ballet for all* (London, 1970).

Song of a Wayfarer (orig. title *Chant du compagnon errant*). Ballet in 1 act; ch. Béjart; mus. Mahler. Prod. 11 Mar. 1971, B. of the 20th Century, Forest National, Brussels, with Bortoluzzi and Nureyev. Set to Mahler's song-cycle, *Lieder eines fahrenden Gesellen*. A romantic student (Nureyev) rages against himself, until fate (Bortoluzzi) takes him by the hand, soothing and placating him. Revived for various pairs of dancers since.

Song of the Earth (orig. Ger. title: *Lied von der Erde*). Ballet in 6 movements; ch. MacMillan; mus. Mahler; no déc. Prod. 7 Nov. 1965, Stuttgart B., Stuttgart, with Madsen, Barra, Haydée, Cardus. The Messenger of Death links the 6 episodes, which are atmospheric rather than literal interpretations of the texts from Hans Bethge's *The Chinese Flute*, on which Mahler based his score. Revived for Royal B. in 1966, with designs by Georgiadis (initially anonymous, but later acknowledged). Earlier versions by Tudor (*Shadow of the Wind*, Amer. B. Th., 1948) and Koner (last movement only, *Farewell*, 1962).
BIBL.: G. Balanchine, 'S.o.t.E.' in *Balanchine's New Complete Stories of the Great Ballets* (Garden City, N.Y., 1968).

Song of the Nightingale. See *Chant du rossignol, Le.*

Sopianae Ballet. See *Ballet Sopianae.*

Sorcerer's Apprentice, The (orig. Fr. title: *L'Apprenti sorcier*). Dukas' *Scherzo d'après une Ballade de Goethe* (1897) has inspired several bs., e.g. by Fokine (Maryinsky Th., Petrograd, 1916),

and H. Lander (Royal Dan. B., Copenhagen, 1940).

Sorel, Ruth. See *Abramowitsch, Ruth.*

Sorley Walker, Kathrine (*b* Aberdeen). Scot. critic and writer on b. Studied at Univ. of London (King's College), Besançon Univ., and Trinity College of Mus. Ballet critic *Playgoer* 1951–6 and *Daily Telegraph* from 1962. Contributor to *Dancing Times, The Stage, Encyclopedia Britannica, Enciclopedia dello Spettacolo, The Encyclopedia of Dance & Ballet* (London, 1977), etc. London Editor and contributor to Amer. *Dance Encyclopedia*. Editor of the collected criticisms of A. V. Coton. Author of *Brief for Ballet* (London, 1948), *Robert Helpmann* (Rockliff, 1957), *Eyes on the Ballet* (London, 1963), *Eyes on Mime* (New York, 1969), *Dance and its Creators* (New York, 1972), and, with S. Woodcock, *The Royal Ballet: A Picture History* (London, 1981).

Sorrell, Walter (*b* Vienna, 2 May 1905). Austrian–Amer. writer on dance. Educated Univ. of Vienna and Columbia Univ. Contributor to *Dance Magazine* and *Ballet Today*. Contributing editor of *Dance Scope*. Feature writer for *Dance News*. Lecturer at Barnard College. Author of *The Dance Through the Ages* (London, 1967), *Hanya Holm* (Middletown, Conn., 1969), *The Dancer's Image* (New York, 1971), *The Mary Wigman Book* (Middletown, Conn., 1975, and *Dance in its Time* (New York, 1981). Author–Editor of *The Dance Has Many Faces* (New York, 1951).

Sorokina, Nina Ivanovna (*b* 13 May 1942). Sov. dancer. Studied at Moscow Bolshoi School; graduated in 1961. Joined Bolshoi B. and bacame one of its most popular ballerinas. Created roles in Kasatkina–Vassiliov's *The Geologists* (1964) and *Sacre du printemps* (1965), Vinogradov's *Asel* (1967), and Vassiliev's *Icarus* (1971). Gold Medal (Varna, 1966, and Moscow, 1969). Married to the d. Yuri Vladimirov.

Soubresaut. (Fr. sudden leap.) Executed upward and forward, from fifth position with straight knees and well pointed toes, and with the front foot hiding the back foot, landing in the same position.

Soudeikine, Serge (*b* Smolensk, 19 Mar.1882, *d* Nyack, N.Y., 12 Aug. 1946). Russ.–Amer. painter and designer. His many b. designs incl. B. Romanov's *La Tragédie de Salomé* (Bs. Russes de Diaghilev, 1913), Clustine's *The Fairy Doll* (Pavlova co., 1914), Novikoff's *Coppélia* (Pavlova co., 1923), Bolm's *Petrushka* (Met. Op. Ho., New York, 1925), *Dionysus, La Fille mal gardée, Giselle, The Goldfish, Trepak,* and *Fair at Sorochintsy* (all for Mordkin B., 1937–8), Fokine's *Paginini* (de Basil's B. Russe, 1939), Nijinska's *La Fille mal gardée* (B. Th., 1940), and Massine's *Moonlight Sonata* (B. Th., 1944).

Source, La. Ballet in 3 acts and 4 scenes; libr.

Nuitter and Saint-Léon (also ch.); mus. Minkus (first and fourth scene) and Delibes (second and third scene); sets Desplechin, Lavastre, Rubé, and Chapéron; cost. Loumier and Albert. Prod. 12 Nov. 1866, Opéra, Paris, with Guglielmina Salvioni, Eugénie Fiocre, Mérante. The b. is set in a fictitious Persia. Naïla, Spirit of the Spring, is protected by Djemil, a hunter, from the gipsy Morgab, who threatens to poison her waters; N. therefore helps him to win his beloved Nouredda, to whom she gives a magic flower which protects her life. The b. was originally intended for Grantzow, but she was injured during rehearsals. Saint-Léon ch. a completely new version for Grantzow under the title *Le Lys* for St. Petersburg in 1869. He revived it as *Naïla* for the Vienna Court Op. in 1878. Later versions by A. Koppini (St. Petersburg, 1902), N. Sergeyev as farewell perf. for Vaganova (Petrograd, 1916), and Ponomariev and Vaganova (Leningrad, 1925). Staats ch. his *Soirée de fête* to the mus. of this b., arr. H. Busser (Opéra, Paris, 1928). Separate pas de deux versions by Cranko (Stuttgart, 1964) and Balanchine (New York City B., 1968; he added ensemble 1969).
BIBL.: C. W. Beaumont, 'L.S.' in *Complete Book of Ballets* (London, 1951).

Souritz, Elizabeth (orig. Yelizaveta Yakovlevna Suritz; *b* Berlin, 25 Feb. 1923). Sov. writer on b. Educated at Moscow Lunacharsky State Institute of Th. Art. Worked at the Bakhrushin Museum 1951–60 and Moscow Th. Library 1960–4. Head of the d. section at the Moscow Inst. of History of the Arts since 1964. Writes regularly for Sov. *Theatre* magazine and *Soviet Encyclopedia*. Compiled *All About Ballet* (dictionary, Moscow, 1966). Author of *Choreograficheskoye iskusstvo dvadtsatykh godov* (Moscow, 1979). Contributor to *Balet: entsiklopediya* (Moscow, 1981). Was married to the ch. Vladimir Varkovitsky (1916–74).

Soutenu. (Fr., sustained.) Designates in b. a sustained or drawn-out movement.

South Africa. See *CAPAB Ballet* (Cape Town); *NAPAC Ballet* (Durban); *PACT Ballet* (Johannesburg).

Souvenirs. Ballet in 1 act; libr. and ch. Bolender; mus. Barber; déc. Ter–Arutunian. Prod. 15 Nov. 1955, New York City B., City Center, N.Y., with Mitchell, Bolender, Larsson, Tobias, Jillana, Watts. The b. (for which Barber orchestrated his 2-piano suite) is set in a fashionable pre-1914 hotel with a smart but eccentric clientele. Revived for many cos., incl. Cologne B. (1963), Th. an der Wien B. (1968), and Harkness B. (1969).
BIBL.: G. Balanchine, 'S', in *Balanchine's New Complete Stories of the Great Ballets* (Garden City, N.Y., 1968).

Soviet Union. B. in the U.S.S.R. is inseparably linked to its origins in Tsarist Russia. The Fr. Jean-Baptiste Landé was summoned to St. Peters-burg as a teacher of ballroom dancing in 1734. He opened the first Russ. b. school there for the children of palace servants in 1738, and this became eventually the present Leningrad Ch. School and the Kirov B. The first foreign choreographers invited to stage their bs. included Fusano, Angiolini, Hilverding, and Le Picq. In 1773 a d.-wing was attached to the Orphanage in Moscow with Filippo Beccari as dir.; this developed into the present Bolshoi School and B. At the same time many wealthy landowners had their own troupes of serf dancers on their vast estates; they performed not only national dances but also genuine bs. B. flourished in St. Petersburg under its first Russ. b. master Ivan Valberkh, who was appointed Dir. of the St. Petersburg School and Inspector of the b. co. of the local Bolshoi Th. in 1794. The school and the co. were further consolidated, and the repertory strengthened, under the Frenchman Didelot (1801–11 and 1816–33); this was an era of unprecedented b. activity, and Pushkin wrote of 'the Russian Terpsichore's soul-inspired flight'—a phrase which still describes the genuine quality of Russ. dancing. Adam Gluszkowski was one of the first to base his bs. on Pushkin and other national literature. Marie Taglioni's St. Petersburg début as La Sylphide in 1837 introduced the romantic b. movement; a stream of guest ballerinas and b. masters followed from the West, and the country prod. its own first Romantic ballerinas, Yelena Andreyanova and Yekaterina Sankovskaya. Perrot worked in St. Petersburg 1848–59, staging all his Paris and London hit prods., and was succeeded by Saint-Léon 1859–69; *The Humpbacked Horse* (1864) was his biggest success, and Marfa Muraieva his favourite Russ. ballerina. Russ. Tsarist b.'s most glorious era was under M. Petipa, who was first a d. and then b. dir. 1847–1903; he was responsible for the first prods. of *Don Quixote* (1869), *La Bayadère* (1877—the year of Reisinger's Moscow *Swan Lake* first prod.), *Sleeping Beauty* (1890), *Swan Lake* (1895, with Ivanov, whose first prod. of *Nutcracker* took place in 1892), and *Raymonda* (1898). There was a splendid array of ballerinas and premier danseurs, many of them trained by Christian Johansson, and b. flourished in Russia while steadily declining in the W. The Moscow Bolshoi B. was always more realistically inclined than the St. Petersburg Maryinsky B., and under Gorsky it became the stronghold of dramatic b. in the early 20th century; St. Petersburg lost many of its best dancers, incl. Pavlova, Karsavina, and Nijinsky, and the ch. Fokine, to the West. Diaghilev's Bs. Russes dazzled Western audiences with their high artistic standards; they revolutionized the international b. scene from 1909. The October Revolution of 1917 created a completely new situation. The new Soviet ballet, under such choreographers as Lopokov and Goleizovsky, was subject to all kinds of modern influences, and there was much discussion about the course Soviet ballet was to take; in 1932 Socialist Realism was introduced as the sole criterion of art. Lashilin's and Tikhomirov's *The Red Poppy*, the first big story b. with a revolutionary plot to hold its place in the repertory, was created in 1927. Ballet education was thoroughly reorganized and centralized under the supervision of Vaganova, who developed her own method which was made obligatory for all ballet teaching in the U.S.S.R. (and after 1945 for most other countries in the Eastern Bloc). New companies were formed throughout the country; there had been a few companies outside St. Petersburg and Moscow in Tsarist times, e.g. in Kiev and Tiflis (and of course in Russian-occupied Warsaw), but they were relatively unimportant compared with the Maryinsky and the Bolshoi. Leningrad maintained its leading position during the 1930s. Vainonen's *Flames of Paris* (1932), Zakharov's *Fountain of Bakhchisaray* (1934), and Lavrovsky's *Prisoner of the Caucasus* (1938) and *Romeo and Juliet* (1940) contributed enormously to the strengthening of the new repertory (though the classics were never abandoned). The Bolshoi Ballet's *Cinderella* première in 1945 (Zakharov), however, marked a shift of emphasis to Moscow, and the country's leading ballerina Ulanova was transferred from the Kirov to the Bolshoi B. The leading Soviet companies have paid frequent visits to the West since the mid-1950s, and the major Soviet cities have been visited in return by many of the leading Western cos. (incl. some modern dance troupes; the general influence of Western trends on Soviet ballet has, however, been negligible. There are some middle-aged choreographers such as Vinogradov (Kirov Theatre, Leningrad), Boyartchikov (Maly Theatre, Leningrad), Dolgushin (Maly Theatre, Leningrad), and Maiorov (Kiev), and such established choreographers as Moiseyev, Grigorovich, and Kasatkina-Vassiliov continue to produce new works. The creative situation is so stale, however, that some of the best dancers have decided not to return from foreign tours—e.g. Nureyev, Makarova, Baryshnikov, and Godunov—and others, such as the Panovs, chose to emigrate, although the schools all over the country, and especially in Leningrad and Moscow, continue to produce scores of tremendously gifted and brilliantly equipped dancers. Clearly some assistance from the West in ch. development would be valuable. See also *Bolshoi Ballet, Kiev, Kirov Ballet, Maly Ballet, Novosibirsk, Perm, Riga, Stanislavsky and Nemirovich-Danchenko Music Theatre Ballet, Tallinn Tiflis*, and all the individuals and ballets mentioned above.

BIBL.: N. Roslavleva, *Era of the Russian Ballet* (London, 1966); M. G. Swift, *The Art of the Dance in the U.S.S.R.* (Notre Dame, Ind., 1968); *Enziklopedia Balet* (Moscow, 1981).

Sowinski, John (*b* Scranton, Pa., 19 Aug. 1947). Amer. dancer. Studied at School of Amer. B. and with W. Griffith, R. Thomas, B. Fallis, and F.

Jhung. D. with Amer. B. Th. 1966–9; principal d. of Feld's Amer. B. Co. 1969–71, soloist of Amer. B. Th. 1972–4, and then leading dancer of E. Feld B. Created leading roles in Feld's *Intermezzo* and *Cortège Burlesque* (1969), *Early Songs, Cortège Parisien*, and *The Consort* (1970), and *Tzaddik* (1974).

BIBL.: S. Goodman, 'J.S.', *Dance Magazine* (1970/10).

Spain. Classically trained dancers are occasionally assembled under a b. master to contribute d. sequences for the op. seasons (e.g. at Barcelona's Teatro Liceo), but the abundance of cos. specializing in Span. d. seems effectively to have prevented the growth of a national b. culture, and the increasingly frequent guest visits of foreign b. cos. do not seem to have stimulated a desire to build up similar native cos. until B. Classico de Madrid in the 1980s.

Sparemblek, Milko (*b* Farnavas, 1 Dec. 1928). Yugosl. dancer, choreographer, and b. director. Studied with Roje. D. with Zagreb National Op. B. 1949–53. Studied further in Paris with Preobrajenska and Peretti. D. with many cos.—principally with Miskovitch, but also with Charrat, Béjart, and Tcherina (with whom he continued to collaborate for many years, notably for her appearances in Debussy's *Martyre de Saint Sébastien* and in the b. and film versions of *Les Amants de Teruel*). B. master of the Brussels Th. de la Monnaie from 1960; deputy dir. of the B. of the 20th Century 1963–4. Then made many Fr. TV prods.; dir. of the Lisbon Gulbenkian B. 1970–5. Also b. dir. of New York Met. Op. Ho. 1970–2. Has ch. many bs., incl. *Quatuor* (mus. R. Banfield, 1957), *The Mirror* (mus. M. Kelemen, 1959), *The Seven Deadly Sins* (mus. Weill, 1962), *Orfeo* (mus. Monteverdi), *Siegfried-Idyll* (mus. Wagner, 1965), *Cantate profane* (mus. François Bayle, 1968), *L'Absence* (mus. Ivo Malec, 1969), *Symphony of Psalms* (mus. Stravinsky), and *Ancient Voices of Children* (mus. G. Crumb, 1972). Prix Italia for his TV film *Phèdre* (mus. Auric, 1968).

Spartacus (orig. Russ. title: *Spartak*). Ballet in 4 acts and 9 scenes; libr. Nicolai Volkov; ch. Jacobson; mus. Khatchaturian; déc. Valentina Khodasevich. Prod. 27 Dec. 1956, Kirov Th., Leningrad, with A. Makarov, Zubkovskaya, Shelest. The story of the slave S. and his wife Phrygia, who are brought by the Roman general Crassus to Rome; S. incites his fellow slaves to revolt against their oppressors, but is eventually killed by his enemies. The b. was not successful, and even less so in Moiseyev's prod. for the Moscow Bolshoi B. in 1958; Grigorovich staged the definitive prod. on 9 Apr. 1968 for the Bolshoi B., with Vassiliev, Maximova, Liepa, and Timofeyeva (déc. S. Virsaladze). This was first shown in the West in London in 1969. Other versions by Blažek (Prague, 1957), Seregi (Budapest, 1968), and Labis (Charleroi 1977).

BIBL.: G. Balanchine and F. Mason, in *Balanchine's Complete Stories of the Great Ballets* (Garden City, N.Y., 1977).

Spectre de la rose, Le. Ballet in 1 act; libr. Jean-Louis Vaudoyer; ch. Fokine; mus. Weber; déc. Bakst. Prod. 19 Apr. 1911, co. of Diaghilev, Monte Carlo, with Karsavina and Nijinsky. The duo b. tells of a girl who brings home a rose from a ball; she falls asleep in her chair, and dreams that the spirit of the rose is dancing with her—until the spirit disappears with a spectacular leap through the window and she awakes, still under the spell of her dream. Fokine set it to Weber's *Invitation to the Dance*, originally a piano piece, orchestrated by Berlioz as a supplementary d.-number in 1841, ch. Saint–Léon. Revived for London Festival B. in 1962, Royal B. in 1972.
BIBL.: C. W. Beaumont, L.S.d.l.r.' in *Complete Book of Ballets* (London, 1951).

Spessivtseva, Olga Alexandrovna (also O. Spessiva; *b* Rostov, 18 July 1895). Russ.-Amer. dancer. Studied at St. Petersburg Imperial B. Academy; graduated in 1913. Joined Maryinsky Th.; became soloist in 1916, and was soon one of the most admired ballerinas of the co. Went to Amer. with Diaghilev's Bs. Russes; returned to Maryinsky Th. and became prima ballerina in 1918. Appeared as guest ballerina with Diaghilev's co. in the London prod. of *Sleeping Princess* (1921). Returned to Petrograd, and worked with Vaganova; finally left Russ. in 1923. Went to Buenos Aires; étoile at Paris Opéra 1924–32. Created roles in Staats's *Soir de fête* and Nijinska's *Les Rencontres* (1925), N. Guerra's *Salomé*, and Lifar's *Creatures of Prometheus* (1930) and *Bacchus and Ariadne* (1931); her most important role was undoubtedly Giselle, of which she was one of the outstanding interpreters of b. history. D. again with the Diaghilev co. in 1927 and 1929; created a further role in Balanchine's *La Chatte* (1927). Visited the Teatro Colón in 1931; then d. with the London Camargo Society, the co. of V. Landré and A. Levitov, and the Opéra Comique B. in 1935. Gave her farewell perf. at the Teatro Colón in 1939. Went to U.S.A. in 1939 and became an advisor for the foundation of B. Th. Had a nervous breakdown in 1943 and remained in a mental hospital until 1963, when Dolin with the help of Dale Fern and Doubrovska managed to secure her a place at the Tolstoy Farm in Valley Cottage, N.Y. An immaculate stylist of the classic St. Petersburg school tradition and a perfect technician, she radiated an air of pure spirituality; she is considered one of the greatest classical ballerinas of all time.
BIBL.: L. Vaillat, *O.S.* (Paris, 1944); 'S.: A Tribute from Her Colleagues', *Dance and Dancers* (1960/7); A. Dolin, *The Sleeping Ballerina* (London, 1966).

Spider's Banquet, The. See *Festin de l'araignée, L'*.

Spira, Phyllis (*b* Johannesburg, 18 Oct. 1943).

S.A. dancer. Studied with Renée Solomon and Reine Berman, then at Royal B. School. Joined Touring Royal B. in 1960; became soloist in 1962. Returned to S.A. and became ballerina of PACT B. (Johannesburg); since 1965 ballerina of CAPAB B. (Cape Town).

Spoerli, Heinz (*b* Basle, 8 July 1941). Swiss dancer, choreographer, and b. master. Studied with Walter Kleiber, also at School of Amer. B., Amer. B. Center, and London D. Centre. D. with Basle B. 1960–3, Cologne B. 1963–6, Royal Winnipeg B. 1966–7, Grands Bs. Canadiens 1967–9 and 1970–1, and Geneva B. 1971–3. Since 1973 b. master in Basle, where he has ch. a number of bs., incl *Firebird* (mus. Stravinsky, 1973), *Petrushka* (mus. Stravinsky, 1974), a full-length *Midsummer Night's Dream* (mus. Mendelssohn and Shakespeare texts, 1976), *Giselle* (1976), *Romeo and Juliet* (mus. Prokofiev, 1977), *Ondine* (mus. Henze, 1978), and *Nutcracker* (1980) plus *La Fille mal gardée* (1981 for Paris Opéra), and *Child Harold* (mus. Berlioz, 1981 for Ger. Op. Berlin).

Spohr, Arnold (*b* Rhein, Saskatchewan, *c.* 1915). Can. dancer, choreographer, and b. director. Studied in London, New York, Hollywood, and Leningrad; his most important teachers included A. de Vos, Volkova, and Pushkin. D. with Winnipeg B. 1945–54; eventually became principal d. Worked for Can. TV and d. with Markova in the London prod. of *Where the Rainbow Ends* 1956–7. Dir. of Royal Winnipeg B. since 1958. Has ch. several bs. Also a professional pianist. Centennial Medal (Can., 1967); Hon. Dr. of Univ. of Manitoba.
BIBL.: O. Maynard, 'A.S. and the Royal Winnipeg B.' *Dance Magazine* (1971/4). M. Wyman, 'The Royal Winnipeg B.: 35 Years of Pioneering', *Dance Magazine* (1973/9).

Spotting. Means in b. fixing one's eyes on a spot in the auditorium or wings for as long as possible while turning to ensure one's sense of orientation and prevent giddiness.

Square Dance. (1) 'Any type of American folk dance in which an even number of couples participate, arranged so that they form a square, as in the square set and quadrille, or in two lines facing each other as in the longway set, or in a circle as in the running set.... The square dance is made up of many figures which are called out by the caller' (A. Chujoy). (2) Ballet in 1 act; ch. Balanchine; mus. Corelli and Vivaldi. Prod. 21 Nov. 1957, New York City B., City Center, N.Y., with Elisha C. Keeler (Caller), P. Wilde, Magallanes. 'Within a framework of an American square dance (complete with square dance caller), the dancers perform a classical ballet to the elegant strains of Renaissance music played by a string ensemble on stage' (programme note). The mus. is in fact the first movement of Vivaldi's Concerto in E Major for Violin, op. 3, no. 12, and the Concerto Grosso in B Minor, op. 3., no. 10, and

Corelli's *Gigg* and *Badinerie*. Revived for City Center Joffrey B. in 1971.

BIBL.: (2) G. Balanchine, 'S.D.' in *Balanchine's New Complete Stories of the Great Ballets* (Garden City, N.Y., 1968).

Squares. Ballet in 2 parts; ch. Van Manen; mus. Satie; déc. Bonies. Prod. 24 June 1969, Netherlands D. Th., Th. de la Ville, Paris. A plotless b., in which 5 plus 5 dancers relate to the various square forms (a platform, a square of neon lights) which define the space. For copyright reasons the Satie mus. (*Gymnopédies*, played first on the piano, and then in an orchestrated version) was later replaced by a specially composed but rather similar score by Zoltan Szilassy. Cologne TV prod. (1972). Revived for Düsseldorf B. (with Satie mus.) in 1972, and for Basle B., in 1979.

Staats, Léo (*b* Paris, 26 Nov. 1877, *d* there 15 Feb. 1952). Fr. dancer, choreographer, b. master, and teacher. Studied at Paris Opéra B. School; joined its co. in 1893. Was the partner of Zambelli; maître de b. between 1907 and 1936. Ch. many bs., incl. *Javotte* (mus. Saint-Saëns and Cruze, 1909), *Contes de ma mère l'oie* (mus. Ravel, 1912), *Cydalise et le Chèvre Pied* (mus. G. Pierné, 1923), and *Soir de fête* (mus. Delibes, arr. H. Busser, 1925). He also did prods. of the classics: *Namouna* (after L. Petipa, 1909), *Les deux pigeons* (after Mérante, 1912), *Sylvia* (after Mérante, 1919 and 1941), and *La Péri* (after Coralli, 1931). Invented in 1926 the *Défilé du corps de ballet*, which is now a tradition of the co. Had his own school.

Staff, Frank (*b* Kimberley, S.A., 15 June 1918, *d* Bloemfontein, 7 May 1971). S.A. dancer and choreographer. Studied with Helen Webb and Maude Lloyd in Cape Town, then with Rambert and Tudor. D. with B. Rambert, Vic-Wells B., and London B.; created the Boy in Howard's *La Fête étrange* (1940). Began choreographing in 1940; his bs. include *Czernyana* (1939), *Peter and the Wolf* (mus. Prokofiev), and *Enigma Variations* (mus. Elgar, both 1940, all for B. Rambert). Returned to S.A. in 1953, and worked for Cape Town Univ. B., PACT B. (Johannesburg); became dir. of PACOFS B. (Orange Free State) in 1970. His last bs. included *Transfigured Night* (mus. Schoenberg), *Apollo* (mus. Britten, *Variations on a Theme by Frank Bridge*), *Romeo and Juliet* (mus. Prokofiev), and a 3-act b. on S.A. themes, *Raka* (mus. Newcater).

BIBL.: L. Kersley, 'F.S.', *Dancing Times* (1971/6).

Stages. Production by Cohan; mus. for Stage 1 by Arne Nordheim, for Stage 2 by Bob Downes; déc. Farmer; light. J. B. Read; films and projections Anthony McCall. Prod. 22 Apr. 1971, London Contemporary D. Th., The Place, London, with Louther, Lapzeson, North. 'In the first stage the world is seen as the underworld. From the conscious choice of trying to see it as it is, all loneliness, meetings with illusion or Maya, and selfquestionings occur. In the second stage the myths or trials that once might have helped us seem to be of little use. They have become the subject of technicolour movies and comic books. We are left solely with our humanity at whatever stage it may be . . .' (programme note). The mixed media prod. took place on the area normally occupied by the tiers of seats, while the audience was seated in the stage area.

BIBL.: P. Brinson and C. Crisp, in *Ballet & Dance* (Newton Abbot, 1980).

Stahle, Anna Greta (*b* Stockholm, 31 Jan. 1913). Swed. dance critic. Educated at Stockholm Univ. D. critic of *Dagens Nyheter* 1951–75, and still a contributor. Scandinavian correspondent of *Dance News* Has also written for *Ballet Annual*, *Dance Perspectives*, and *Dance Encyclopedia*. Taught at Stockholm Univ., State D. School, and Royal Swed. B. School.

Stanislavsky and Nemirovich-Danchenko Music Theatre Ballet (generally referred to as Stanislavsky B.). The b. co. of Moscow's second op. house (a kind of municipal op.) is descended from the Art B. founded by V. Krieger in Moscow in 1929; it places special emphasis on the dramatic projection of the prods. It was joined in 1933 by a group of former d. students from the Lunacharsky State Institute of Th. Art. They gave perfs. in Moscow and toured the provinces; the co. was absorbed into the newly formed S.a.N.-D. Music Th. in 1939. Under Krieger and Bourmeister, the co.'s dir. and chief-ch. 1930–71, the repertory always stressed dramatic truth, according to the principles of realistic th. prod. taught by Stanislavsky. The first prod. was *The Rivals* (alias *La Fille mal gardée*, new ch. N. Kholfin and P. Markov, 1933). Further important prods. included *The Gipsies* (ch. Kholfin, mus. Vasilenko, 1937), *Christmas Eve* (ch. Lopokov, mus. Asafiev, 1938). *Straussiana* (ch. Bourmeister, 1941), *The Merry Wives of Windsor* (ch. Bourmeister and I. Kurilov, mus. V. Oransky, 1942), *Lola* (ch. Bourmeister, mus. Vasilenko, 1943), *Coast of Happiness* (ch. Bourmeister, mus. A. Spadavecchia, 1948, *Esmeralda* (ch. Bourmeister, mus. Pugni, 1950), *Swan Lane* (ch. Bourmeister, 1953), *A Daughter of Castilia* (ch. Alexei Tchitchinadze, mus. Glière, 1955), *Joan of Arc* (ch. Bourmeister, mus. N. Peiko, 1957), *The Corsair* (ch. Nina Grishina, mus. Adam and Delibes, 1958), *Masquerade* ch. Igor Smirnov, mus. Mikhail Laputin, 1961), *Pictures from an Exhibition* (ch. Lopokov, mus. Mussorgsky, 1963), and *Appassionata* (ch. Bourmeister, mus. Beethoven, 1971). The co. was headed by Tchitchinadze as b. dir. and chief ch. Its first appearance in the West was in Paris in 1956. Dmitri Alexandrevich Briantzev dir. from 1985.

Stars and Stripes. Ballet in 5 campaigns; ch. Balanchine; mus. John Philip Sousa, arr. H. Kay; set D. Hays; cost. Karinska. Prod. 17 Jan. 1958, New York City B., City Center, N.Y., with Kent, Diana Adams, Hayden, Barnett, d'Amboise. 'The ballet is a kind of balletic parade, led by four "regiments". The five campaigns or movements feature each regiment in turn and at the end they all combine' (Balanchine). Second Channel Ger. TV prod. (1973).

BIBL.: G. Balanchine, 'S.a.S.' in *Balanchine's New Complete Stories of the Great Ballets* (Garden City, N.Y., 1968).

Starzer, Joseph (*b* Vienna, 1726, *d* there, 22 Apr. 1787). Austrian composer. Wrote the mus. for many Noverre bs., e.g. *Diana and Endymion* (1770), *Roger and Bradamante* (1771), *Adèle of Ponthieu* (1773), and *The Horatians and the Curatians* (1774); also some bs. for Angiolini.

Stefanschi, Sergiu (*b* Komrat, 2 Mar. 1941). Rum. dancer. Studied at Bucharest State B. School and Leningrad Ch. School. Début Bucharest State Op. B. in 1962. D. with various Sov. cos. and with Charrat and Lazzini; principal d. of National B. of Canada since 1971. Silver Medal (Varna, 1964).

Stefanescu, Marinel (*b* Bucharest, 1 Jan. 1947). Rum. dancer. Studied at Bucharest State B. School 1957–66; joined Bucharest State Op. B. and eventually became principal d. Has also been principal d. of Zurich Op. House B. First Prize (Junior category, Varna, 1966).

Stepanov, Vladimir Ivanovich (*b* 29 June 1866, *d* St. Petersburg, 28 Jan. 1896). Russ. dancer and teacher. Studied anatomy at St. Petersburg Univ. Then developed his system of d. notation with the assistance of Prof. Lesgaft, based on the principles of musical notation, which he published as *Alphabet des Mouvements du Corps Humain* in Paris in 1892. After his return to St. Petersburg, his notation was accepted into the syllabus of the Imperial B. Academy. In 1895 he moved to Moscow to introduce it to the Bolshoi School. Gorsky first had prods. of classics notated; he worked from these notes when he mounted the same bs. in Moscow. His system was not published in Russ. until after his death, and was never commonly used. N. Sergeyev brought the St. Petersburg notations of the Maryinsky classics to the West and worked from them when he produced these for Diaghilev, in Eng. and Fr.

Stevenson, Ben (*b* Southsea, 4 Apr. 1937). Brit. dancer, choreographer, teacher, and b. director. Studied with Mary Tonkin and at Arts Educational School. Joined Th. Arts B. in 1953 and Sadler's Wells Op. B. in 1956; d. with Sadler's Wells B. 1957–9, and soloist, later principal and b. master, at London Festival B. 1959–68. Mounted *Sleeping Beauty* with B. Grey for London Festival B. in 1967 (and for Washington National B., 1971). Has since worked mostly in the U.S.; appointed dir. of Harkness Youth co. in 1969, for which he ch. *Bartók Concerto* and *Three Preludes* (mus. Rachmaninov). Produced Prokofiev's *Cinderella* for Washington National B. in 1970 (and for London Festival B., 1973); assistant dir. 1971–

4. Artistic Dir. of R. Page's Chicago B. 1974–5; Artistic Dir., Houston B., from 1976.

BIBL.: V. Huckenpahler, '. . . give the public what sells, but . . .', *Dance Magazine* (1972/5).

Stevenson, Hugh (*b* 1910, *d* London, 16 Dec. 1946). Brit. designer. Designer of Tudor bs., e.g. *The Planets* (1934), *Jardin aux lilas* (1936), *Soirée musicale* (1938), and *Gala Performance*. Also designed de Valois' *The Gods Go a-Begging* (1936) and *Promenade* (1943), Howard's *The Fugitive* (1944) and *Mardi Gras* (1946), Cranko's *Pastorale* (1950), and *Swan Lake* for Sadler's Wells B. (1934) and *Giselle* for B. Rambert (second act, 1945) and for London Festival B.

Still Point, The. Ballet in 1 act; ch. Bolender; mus. Debussy. Prod. 3 Aug. 1955, D. Drama Co., Jacob's Pillow Festival, Lee, Mass., with Frankel, Ryder. Based on the first 3 movements of Debussy's String Quartet; the growing pains of a young girl, who always feels rejected by her friends, until at last she finds fulfilment with a boy who returns her love. First prod. New York City B. on 13 Mar. 1956, with Hayden and d'Amboise. Revived for Munich State Op. B. in 1956, Cologne B. (1963), and several other cos.

BIBL.: G. Balanchine and F. Mason, in *Balanchine's Complete Stories of the Great Ballets* (Garden City, N.Y., 1977).

Stimmung. Ballet in 1 act; ch. Béjart; mus. Stockhausen; set Roger Bernard; cost. Joëlle Roustan. Prod. 19 Dec. 1972, B. of the 20th Century, Free Univ., Brussels, with H. Asakawa, R. Denvers, Donn, Ek, Gray-Cullert, D. Hughes, Lanner, Lommel, B. Pie, M. Robier, C. Verneuil. A b. for 11 dancers which tries to project the different 'climates' of the mus. into space, in the form of a slow-motion ritual, with the dancers partly improvising on the given ch. material.

BIBL.: G. Balanchine and F. Mason, in *Balanchine's Complete Stories of the Great Ballets* (Garden City, N.Y., 1977).

Stockhausen, Karlheinz (*b* Mödrath, 22 Aug. 1928). Ger. composer. Has written no b. mus., but his concert mus. has increasingly been used for d. purposes—e.g. Electronic Study no. 1 by J. Cébron in *Structure* (Hamburg, 1960), *Gesang der Jünglinge* and part of *Kontakte* by Tetley in *Ziggurat* (B. Rambert, 1967), *Mixtur* and *Tele Music* by Tetley and Van Manen in *Mutations* (Netherlands D. Th., 1970), 2 pieces from *Aus den sieben Tagen* by Tetley in *Field Figures* (Royal B., 1970), *Zyklus* by Descombey (Opéra, Paris, 1968; also by Adret, B. Th. Contemporain, 1973), *Hymnen* by a group of choreographers under the direction of Descombey (B. Th. Contemporain, 1971), and *Stimmung* by Béjart (B. of the 20th Century, 1972).

Stockholm. See *Royal Swedish Ballet* and *Cullberg, Birgit.*

Stone, Bentley (*b* Plankinton, S. Dak., *c* 1908, *d* Chicago, 10 Feb. 1984). Amer. dancer and teacher.

Studied with Margaret Severn, G. M. Caskey, L. Albertieri, Novikoff, and Rambert. D. in musicals, with various Chicago Op. B. Cos., B. Rambert in 1937, Page–S. B. 1938–41, and B. Russe de Monte Carlo in 1945. Ch. several bs. with Page. Together with W. Camryn in charge of S.-Camryn School in Chicago until 1981.

Stone Flower, The (orig. Russ. title: *Kamenny tsvetok*). Ballet with prologue, in 3 acts and 8 scenes; libr. Mira Mendelson-Prokofieva and Lavrovsky (also ch.); mus. Prokofiev; déc. T. Starzhentsky. Prod. 12 Feb. 1954, Bolshoi Th., Moscow, with Ulanova, Plisetskaya, Preobrajensky, Yermolayev, Koren. The b. is based on fairytales from the Urals, collected by Pavel Bazhov, under the title of *The Malachite Casket*. It 'tells of the fate of the stone carver Danila who wishes to see the full power of stone and show its beauty to the people. The creative urge which possesses Danila and the desire to create more perfect art is the leitmotif of the ballet' (Grigorovich). Danila is in love with Katerina and he has to overcome the power of the Mistress of the Copper Mountain. While he is away, working in the Copper Mountain on his malachite vase, Katerina has to defend herself against the approaches of the bailiff Severyan. The Moscow prod. was not a success. Grigorovich ch. a new prod. for the Kirov B. (27 Apr. 1957, déc. Virsaladze, with Kolpakova, Osipenko, Gribov, Gridin), which became the standard version (revived for Bolshoi B., then for Royal Swed. B., 1962). Other versions by Schilling (Dresden, 1960), Orlikowsky (Basle, 1962), Sertič (Wuppertal, 1972), Gai (Bologna, 1973), and Walter (Düsseldorf, 1976).

BIBL.: G. Balanchine 'T.S.F.' in *Balanchine's New Complete Stories of the Great Ballets* (Garden City, N.Y., 1968).

Stoop, Norma McLain. See *McLain Stoop, Norma.*

Stowell, Kent (*b* Idaho, 1939). Amer. dancer and b. master. Studied at d. dept. of Univ. of Utah and School of Amer. B. D. with Univ of Utah B. 1955–7, San Francisco B. 1957–62, New York City B., 1962–8; assistant professor of b. at Univ. of Indiana 1969–70, soloist, Munich State Op. B., 1970–3, and b. master of the Frankfurt B. 1973— and since artistic dir. of Pacific North-west B. in Seattle, Wash. Has ch. several bs. Married to the d. and b. mistress Francia Russell, who has mounted many Balanchine prods. for Eur. cos.

Strate, Grant (*b* Cardston, Alberta, 1927). Can. dancer, choreographer, and teacher. Studied with Laine Mets, Franca, and Oliphant. Joined National B. of Can. in 1951. Became soloist in 1953; resident ch. 1958–69. Has ch. a number of bs.; *House of Atreus* (mus. Harry Somers, 1964) is the best known. Since 1970 he has been associate professor and dir. of the Programme in D., York Univ., Toronto.

Strauss, Johann, Jr. (*b* Vienna, 25 Oct. 1825, *d* there, 3 June 1899). Austrian composer. His only b., *Cinderella*, was discovered after his death; it was adapted by J. Bayer and ch. by E. Graeb (Berlin, 2 May 1901); Hassreiter (Vienna Court Op., 1908), and R. de Warren (Manchester, 1979). Many bs. have been based on arrangements of his mus., but few have remained long in the repertory. The more lasting incl. Kröller's *Tales from the Vienna Woods* (1926), Massine's *Le beau Danube* (1924), Lichine's *Graduation Ball* (1940), Hanka's *Titus Feuerfuchs* (1941), Bourmeister's *Straussiana* (1941), Harangozó's *Promenade Concert* (1948), Fenster's *On the Blue Danube* (1956), Page's *Fledermaus* (1958), Luca's *Vienna Merry-Go-Round* (1959), Ray Powell's *One in Five* (1960), and Balanchine's *Vienna Waltzes* (with other mus. by Lehár and R. Strauss, New York, 1977). The Wiesenthal sisters were famous interpreters of his waltzes.

Strauss, Richard (*b* Munich, 11 June 1864, *d* Garmisch, 8 Sep. 1949). Ger. composer. Wrote the mus. for *The Legend of Joseph* (ch. Fokine, Bs. Russes de Diaghilev, Paris 1914) and *Schlagobers* (*Whipped Cream*, ch. Kröller, Vienna State Op., 1924). His *Couperin Dance Suite*, which Kröller had ch. at S.'s special request in 1923, was later extended for the b. *Verklungene Feste*, ch. by the Mlakars for Munich State Op. B. in 1941. Gorsky ch. a b. *Salome's Dance* to an arrangement from the op. for the Moscow Bolshoi Th. in 1921. Among the bs. ch. to his mus. are Nijinsky's *Tyl Ulenspiegel* (Bs. Russes de Diaghilev, New York, 1916—later also Babilée, 1949, and Balanchine, 1951), Irene Lewison's *Ein Heldenleben* (New York, 1929), Balanchine's *Le Bourgeois gentilhomme* (B. Russe de Monte Carlo, 1932—later also by Maudrik, Berlin State Op., 1936, and Tudor in *Knight Errant*, Royal B., 1968), Milloss's *Death and Transfiguration* (Augsburg, 1934; also Van Dantzig in *Blown in a Gentle Wind*, Dutch National B., 1975), T. Gsovsky's *Don Juan* (Berlin, 1938—later also by Milloss, Rome, 1944, Ashton, Sadler's Wells B., 1948, and Luipart, Bonn, 1957), Tudor's *Dim Lustre* (the Burlesque for Piano, B. Th., 1943; also by Feld in *Theatre*, Amer. B. Co., 1971), Georgi's *Metamorphoses* (Hanover, 1962—also by G. Cauley, London Festival B., 1978), Macdonald's *Four Last Songs* (Royal Swed. B., 1966; also by Béjart in *Serait-ce la mort?*, Marseilles, 1970, and Van Dantzig, Dutch National B., 1977), Pistoni's *Macbeth* (Milan, 1969), and Feld's *Early Songs* (Amer. B. Co., 1970).

BIBL.: A. Jefferson, 'R.S. and Ballet', *Dancing Times*, (1969/4–5).

Stravinsky, Igor Fedorovich (*b* Oranienbaum, 18 June 1882, *d* New York, 6 Apr. 1971). Russ.–Fr.–Amer. composer. Of all the composers who have dedicated a major part of their oeuvre to b., S. has been the most influential, surpassing even Tchaikovsky, with whom he has often been compared. His preoccupation with b. lasted all his life. Diaghilev discovered his b. potential when he heard his *Fantastic Scherzo* and *Fireworks* at a St. Petersburg concert in 1909. After moving to the U.S. he maintained a close friendship with Balanchine (whom he had known when he worked with Diaghilev) until his death. He wrote the mus. to the bs. *The Firebird* (ch. Fokine, Paris, 1910), *Petrushka* (ch. Fokine, Paris, 1911), *Le Sacre du printemps* (ch. Nijinsky, Paris, 1913), *Le Chant du rossignol* and *Pulcinella* (ch. Massine, Paris, 1920), *Les Noces* (ch. Nijinska, Paris, 1923—all Bs. Russes de Diaghilev), *Apollon musagète* (ch. Bolm, Washington, D.C., 1928), *Le Baiser de la fée* (ch. Nijinska, Rubinstein co., Paris, 1928), *Jeu de cartes* (ch. Balanchine, Amer. B., New York, 1937), *Scènes de ballet* (ch. Dolin, Billy Rose Prods., New York, 1944), *Orpheus* (ch. Balanchine, B. Society, New York, 1948), and *Agon* (ch. Balanchine, New York City B., 1957). In addition the following works show strong ch. leanings: *L'Histoire du soldat* (prod. L. and G. Pitoëff, Lausanne, 1918), *Renard* (ch. Nijinska, Bs. Russes de Diaghilev, Paris, 1922), *Perséphone* (ch. Jooss, Rubinstein co., Paris, 1934), and *The Flood* (ch. Balanchine, CBS TV, New York, 1962). He comp. a *Circus Polka* for the elephants of the Ringling Brothers Circus (ch. Balanchine, 1942). Other bs. have frequently been created to his concert mus., especially by Balanchine, e.g. *Balustrade* (Violin Concerto, Original B. Russe, New York, 1941; also by Milloss in *Les Jambes Savantes*, Vienna, 1965, and a new version by Balanchine in *Violin Concerto*, New York City B., N.Y., 1972), *Danses concertantes* (B. Russe de Monte Carlo, New York, 1944; also by MacMillan, Sadler's Wells Th. B., London, 1955), *Monumentum pro Gesualdo* (New York City B., N.Y., 1960), *Movements for Piano and Orchestra* (New York City B., N.Y., 1963), *Variations* (New York City B., N.Y., 1966), *Jewels* (the second part, Rubies, set to Capriccio for Piano and Orchestra, New York City B., N.Y., 1967), *Requiem Canticles* (New York City B., N.Y., 1968—later also by Robbins, New York City B., 1972), *Duo Concertant* (New York City B., N.Y., 1972), *Scherzo à la Russe* (New York City B., N.Y., 1972), *Symphony in Three Movements* (New York City B., N.Y., 1972), and *Choral Variations on Bach's 'Vom Himmel hoch'* (New York City B., N.Y., 1972). Milloss, Walter, Béjart, MacMillan, and Spoerli have all ch. numerous bs. to mus. by S. Other pieces which have repeatedly been used for b. purposes incl. *Little Suites* (ch. Terpis, Berlin State Op., 1927), the Concerto in D (ch. Hoyer, Hamburg, 1950; also in Robbins' *The Cage*, New York City B., N.Y., 1951, and Van Manen's *Tilt*, Netherlands D. Th., Rotterdam, 1972), *Ebony Concerto* (ch. Taras, New York City B., N.Y., 1960; also by Cranko, Munich State Op., 1970 and Van Manen, Dutch National B., 1976), the Concerto for Piano and Brass Instruments (in *Arcade*, ch. Taras, New York City B., 1963), and *Dumbarton Oaks* (ch. Robbins, New York City B., N.Y., 1972). The New York City B. held a S. Festival, in which 31 bs. to his mus. were performed, from 18 to 25 June 1972 at the New York State Th.; a 2nd S. Festival was held in 1982. S. comments extensively on his bs. in his *Chronicle of My Life* (London, 1936), *Conversations with I.S.* (New York and London, 1959), *Memories and Commentaries* (New York and London 1960), *Expositions and Developments* (New York and London, 1962), and *Dialogues and a Diary* (New York, 1963).

BIBL.: M. Lederman. 'S. in the Theatre', *Dance Index* (vol. VI, nos. 10–12; later also as a book, New York, 1949); catalogue *S. and the Dance* (New York Public Library, 1962); portfolio on S., *Dance Magazine* (1972/6); N. Goldner, *The S. Festival* (New York, 1973).

Streetcar Named Desire, A. Ballet in 1 act; libr. and ch. Bettis; mus. Alex North, arr. Rayburn Wright; cost. Saul Bolasni. Prod. 9 Oct. 1952, Slavenska-Franklin B., Her Majesty's Th., Montreal, with Slavenska, Franklin, Lois Ellyn. The b. follows closely the plot of Tennessee Williams' play *A.S.N.D.* (1947). Revived for Amer. B. Th. (1954) and Washington National B. (1974).

BIBL.: G. Balanchine, 'A.S.N.D.' in *Balanchine's New Complete Stories of the Great Ballets* (Garden City, N.Y., 1968).

Street Games. Ballet in 1 act; libr. and ch. Gore; mus. Ibert; déc. Ronald Wilson. Prod. 11 Nov. 1952, New B. Co., Wimbledon Th., London, with Angela Bayley, Constance Garfield, Margaret Kovac, Jack Skinner. Set on a wharfside near Blackfriars Bridge; children play at hopscotch, writing on the wall, skipping, etc. Revived for many cos.

BIBL.: P. Brinson and C. Crisp, in *Ballet & Dance* (Newton Abbot, 1980).

Strider. The London-based co. was started in 1972 by several dancers from the London Contemporary D. Th., headed by Richard Alston. Working on the basis of Cunningham technique, its aim was to perform new works and try new approaches. Disbanded in 1975.

Strike, Lois (*b* Sydney, 3 Dec. 1948). Brit. dancer. Studied at Scully-Borovansky School and Royal B. School. Joined Royal B. in 1966; became soloist in 1972 and principal d. in 1973. B. mistress Sydney Op. from 1984.

Stroganova Nina (*b* Copenhagen, 31 Oct. 1920). Dan.–Amer. dancer and teacher. Studied with Jenny Moller, later also with Preobrajenska and Dokoudovsky. D. with B. Russe de l'Opéra Comique in Paris 1935–6, Mordkin B. 1937–40, B. Th. 1940–2, de Basil's Original B. Russe 1942–50, then as guest ballerina with Royal Dan. B. and B. Russe de Monte Carlo. Now teaches at New York Conservatory of Dance and School of Classic B., Englewood, N.J.

Struchkova, Raissa Stepanovna (*b* Moscow, 5 Oct. 1925). Sov. dancer. Studied at Bolshoi B. School; created title role in Popko's, Pospekhin's, and Radunsky's *The Little Stork* in 1937 (while still at school); graduated in 1944. Has been a member of the Bolshoi B. ever since; her heartwarming friendliness has made her one of the most popular ballerinas of the co. Created roles in her husband Lapauri's and Tarasova's *Song of the Woods* (1961) and *Lieutenant Kijé* (1963), and Lavrovsky's *Pages of Life* (1961). Much admired with Lapauri in such display pieces as *Spring Waters* and *Moszkowski Waltz*. Title role in the film of the Bolshoi *Cinderella* prod. (1961). Retired in 1978. Now a professor at GITIS and an editor of a Soviet b. magazine. People's Artist of the U.S.S.R.

Strüwer, Astrid (*b* The Hague, 3 Dec. 1942). Dutch-Swed. dancer. Studied with Gaskell, Damianov, Lepeshinskaya, Preobrajenska, Kiss, and P. Leontieff. D. with Dutch National B. 1958–62, Cullberg B. 1962–71; soloist with Royal Swed. B. since 1972.

Stuart, Muriel (*b* London, 1903). Brit. dancer and teacher. Studied with Pavlova, Cecchetti, Graham, and others. D. with Pavlova co. 1916–21. Established school in San Francisco in 1927; taught there until 1934. Then moved to the School of Amer. B. Author of *The Classic Ballet: Basic Technique and Terminology* (with Kirstein, London, 1953).
BIBL.: J. Gruen, 'M.S.', in *The Private World of Ballet* (New York, 1975).

Studio Ballet Prague. See *Prague Ballet.*

Studio Wacker. The building at 69 rue de Douai, near Place Clichy, for many years housed the busiest d. studios in Paris. Preobrajenska taught here, and so did Rousanne, V. Gsovsky, and Kiss. Its notice board and restaurant served as a sort of market-place for dancers, teachers, b. masters, and choreographers from all over the world until the house was demolished in 1974.

Stukolkin, Timofei Alexeievich (*b* 6 May 1829, *d* St. Petersburg, 1894). Russ. dancer. Member of the Maryinsky Th. 1848–94 and one of its greatest character dancers. The first Russ. Coppelius (1884); also created Catalabutte in *Sleeping Beauty* (1890) and Drosselmeyer in *Nutcracker* (1892).

Sturman, Marjorie (*b* London, 1902). Brit. teacher. Studied with Ray Espinosa (Mme Ravodna) in Johannesburg and with Edouard Espinosa and Volkova in London. Began teaching in Pretoria in 1922; opened her own school in Johannesburg in 1934. Formed Pretoria B. Club in 1943 and Festival B. Society (with Ivy Commee and Poppy Frames) in 1944; this started the first Johannesburg b. prods., and later prod. the PACT B. Principal b. teacher at Art B. and Mus. School in Johannesburg since 1953.

Stuttgart. Local court bs. date back to 1609. Under Jacques Courcelles the so-called 'Sing-Ballette' flourished 1684–1709. The city first became internationally known for its bs. when Duke Carl Eugen of Württemberg invited Noverre to come to S. in 1759. Noverre's *Rinaldo und Armida, Admet und Alkeste, Medea und Jason, Der Sieg des Neptun, Der Raub der Proserpina, Die Danaiden*, etc. pioneered the b. d'action (as opposed to the b. divertissement, which was cultivated almost exclusively until then). He extended the co. to 7 female and 7 male principal dancers, and 21 female and 21 male figurants. During his stay the most famous dancers appeared regularly as guests—e.g. G. Vestris, Gardel, Dauberval, Heinel, Miss Nancy-Levier, and N. Sauveur. When finances were drastically reduced in late 1766 he left for Vienna. The co. continued on a much smaller scale under Louis Dauvigny; but a Ducal B. School, opened in 1771 and functioned until 1794. A new era of promise started when Filippo Taglioni and his daughter Marie worked in S. 1824–8; *Jocko or the Brazilian Ape* (1826) was the most successful b. prod. of this period. Later the city satisfied its b. needs by importing visiting cos.; the Court Th. always maintained a small group for its op. needs. August Brühl's prod. of *The Fairy Doll* was uniquely successful; it was given consecutively from 31 Jan. until 18 Mar. 1891. Fritz Scharf ch. the dances for the first prod. of Strauss's *Der Bürger als Edelmann* and *Ariadne auf Naxos* (1912). Parts of Schlemmer's *Triadisches Ballett* were performed in 1916; the first complete prod. took place in S. in 1922. Lina Gerzer was ch. of the Württemberg State Th. during the 1930s, succeeded by Gertrud Pichl and Mascha Lidolt during the war years. After the second World War the first b. masters were Anneliese Mörike, Robert Wosien, Osvald Lemanis, and Robert Mayer; Beriozoff arrived in 1958, and his prods. of the classics laid the foundations for the remarkable progress made by the B. of the Württemberg State Th. under Cranko's directorship 1961–73. He built up a solid repertory of classics, new full-length bs. (*Romeo and Juliet, Onegin, The Taming of the Shrew*), specially created shorter bs. by himself and guest-choreographers (MacMillan's *Las Hermanas* and *Song of the Earth*), and a selection of Balanchine bs.; he also laid great emphasis on the improvement of technical standards of the co., which was continuously expanded. Haydée, Barra, Cardus, Keil, Madsen, Cragun, and Clauss were the top soloists. He also watched carefully over the school, which was able to open a full-time residential wing in 1971. When foreign tours became more extensive a second co., the Noverre B., was formed in 1970 to d. in the op. prods. and give occasional perfs. of its own; this was abandoned, however, in 1973. The Noverre Society was formed by Fritz Höver as a platform for the public discussion of the new b. activities; it regularly organizes matinées for young choreographers, at which e.g. A. Killar, G. Veredon, J. Neumeier, and J. Kylián presented their first bs. Cranko died in 1973 on a return flight from the U.S. with his co. Tetley was his successor 1974–6, since when Haydée has become Artistic Dir. The Stuttgart Ballet now ranks among the youngest and most lively b. cos. of the

The Stuttgart Ballet (Haydée and Cragun) in Cranko's *Onegin*.   Photo Myra Armstrong.

world. It paid its first visit abroad to the Edinburgh Festival in 1953, followed by many other foreign tours; it first visited New York in 1969, Leningrad and Moscow in 1971, and London in 1974.

BIBL.: H. Kilian, *Stuttgarter Ballett* (Weingarten, 1980). See also *Cranko, John*.

Stuyf, Koert (*b* Amsterdam, 6 June 1938). Dutch dancer, choreographer, and teacher. Studied in Holland, at Jacob's Pillow, Connecticut College, Juillard School, Graham School, and with M. Cunningham. D. with Netherlands B., Scapino B., and B. of the Netherlands Op., and with the cos. of Lang, Tudor, Limón, and Butler. Returned to Holland in 1962 with his wife, the d. Ellen Edinoff; they founded a co. and a sch. in Amsterdam, the Foundation Contemporary Dance, for which he ch. a number of works 1964–75. Has also worked as a teacher and ch. for Dutch National B.

Subligny, Marie-Thérèse (*b* 1666, *d* after 1735). Fr. dancer. Ballerina at the Paris Opéra 1688–1707; thus bridged the gap between La Fontaine and La Prévost. She appeared mostly in the op. bs. of Lully and Campra; the first professional ballerina to appear in Eng. (1700–2).

Sugihara, Sara (*b* Boston, Mass., 21 Nov. 1953). Amer. dancer, teacher, and choreographer. Studied at New York School of Arts, Sarah Lawrence College, with D. Howard, S. Stackhouse, J. Muller, D. Wagoner, and R. Kuch. Ch. *Window* (various mus., 1976) and *Sleeping Birds* (mus. Brahms, 1977, both for B. Rambert), *F.* (mus. Scarlatti, Austral. D. Th., 1977), and *Gathering Water* (own mus., Kibbutz D. Co., 1978). Has taught widely for various cos. in the U.S. and Europe. Works now as a free-lance ch., teacher, and comp.

Suite en blanc. Ballet in 1 act; ch. Lifar; mus. Lalo; déc. Dignimont. Prod. 19 June 1943, Paris Opéra B., Zurich, with Schwarz, Chauviré, Darsonval, Lifar. A brilliant display piece of the technical resources of the co., ch. to a Suite from *Namouna*. Revived for many cos., incl (as *Noir et blanc*) Nouveau B. de Monte Carlo (1946) and London Festival B. (1966).

BIBL.: P. Brinson and C. Crisp, 'N.e.B.' in *Ballet & Dance* (Newton Abbot, 1980).

Suite No. 3. Ballet in 4 movements; ch. Balanchine; mus. Tchaikovsky; déc. N. Benois. Prod. 3 Dec. 1970, New York City B., State Th., N.Y., with Aroldingen, Blum, Mazzo, Ludlow, Morris, Clifford, G. Kirkland, Villella. The plotless b. adds the first 3 movements of the Tchaikovsky Suite to the *Theme and Variations* (4th movement) already ch. by Balanchine in 1947.

Sulich, Vassili (*b* Puscice, 29 Dec. 1929). Yugosl.-Amer. dancer and choreographer. Studied with Roje and Kniaseff. D. with Zagreb National B. 1946–9. Studied further in Paris and d. with various cos. incl. those of Miskovitch, Charrat, Petit, and Tcherina, and with Massine's Eur. B.

Went to U.S. in 1962 and finally settled in Las Vegas; became dir. of the local Folies Bergère troupe. D. Instructor at Univ. of Nevada since 1972. Artistic dir. of Nevada D. Th. since 1978.

Sultzbach, Russell (*b* Gainsville, Fla., 13 Aug. 1952). Amer. dancer. Studied at Orlando Royal School of B. and Amer. B. Center. D. with the Joffrey II co., joined City Center Joffrey B. in 1971 and created roles in Layton's *Double Exposure* and Arpino's *Sacred Grove on Mount Tamalpais* (1972), Feld's *Jive* (1973), and Arpino's *The Relativity of Icarus* (1974).

BIBL.: R. Baker, 'Spotlight on R.S.', *Dance Magazine* (1973/9).

Sümen, Meric (*b* Istanbul, 1943). Turk. dancer. Studied with Molly Lake and Beatrice Appleyard in Istanbul and Ankara and at Royal B. School. Joined Ankara Devlet B. in 1963; the first Turk. prima ballerina, and the first Turk ever to dance at the Moscow Bolshoi Th.

Summers, Elaine (*b* Perth, Australia, 20 Feb. 1925). Amer. dancer, choreographer, and film-maker. Studied with Graham, Erdman, J. and R. Dunn, M. Cunningham, Horst, at Russakoff School of B., with Mme Cassan, and B. Circle. Taught d. and kinetic awareness at various schools and Clark Center. One of the founder members of the New York Judson Church d. movement. Created New York's first multi-media dance prod., *Fantastic Garden*, in 1964; has since concentrated on 'intermedia research exploring the potential of technologies for multi-media spatial interaction', with film, videotape, photography, sculpture, and painting as additional media. Is now Dir. of the Experimental Intermedia Foundation, which made its London début at The Place in 1972.

BIBL.: M. Harriton, 'E.S.: New Forms, New Ideas!', *Dance Magazine* (1970/9).

Summerspace. Ballet for 6 dancers; ch. M. Cunningham; mus. M. Feldman; déc. R. Rauschenberg. Prod. 17 Aug. 1958, M. Cunningham D. Co., Connecticut College, N.L., with Cunningham, Brown, Farber, C. Stone, M. Wood, R. Charlip. A plotless work 'about changing tempos. . . . At one point all six dancers are leaping across the stage, all at different speeds. Often a dancer picks up a gesture and carries on with it at a different pace after the first dancer has left the stage' (M. B. Siegel). New York première 16 Feb. 1960, Phoenix Th. Revived for New York City B. with the dancers wearing shoes and dancing on point (1966), Cullberg B. (1967), and Boston B. (1974).

BIBL.: G. Balanchine and F. Mason, in *Balanchine's Complete Stories of the Great Ballets* (Garden City, N.Y., 1911).

Sumner, Carol (*b* Brooklyn, 24 Feb. 1940). Amer. dancer. Studied with Eileen O'Connor and at School of Amer. B. Joined New York City B. in

1959; became soloist in 1963. Has also taught at School of Amer. B. and throughout the U.S.

BIBL.: J. Gruen, 'C.S.', in *The Private World of Ballet* (New York, 1975).

Sunday Ballet Club. Founded by James Ranger and Francis Sitwell (from Oxford Univ. B. Club) in London in 1958 to take the place of the former B. Workshop. Its aim was to offer a professional platform for aspiring young choreographers. Those who worked here included Worth, Dixon, Roope, Carey, Darrell, Charnley, P. Wright, and Macdonald. Powell's *One in Five* (1960), Lynne's *The Owl and the Pussycat* (1962), and L. Meyer's *The Web* (1963) were first produced here, and were later taken into the repertory of regular cos. Disbanded in 1966.

Sunshine Matinées. Established by Mrs. Dorothy Claremont (from the Sunshine Home for Blind Babies) and P. J. S. Richardson in London in 1919 as an annual occasion to review the Eng. situation of stage dancing. The first took place on 25 Nov. 1919 at the London Queen's Th. There were ten such matinées altogether; the dancers included Wigman, Trefilova, Dolin, Bedells, de Valois, and Astafieva. The series ended in 1930, when its functions were taken over by the Camargo Society. In 1924 the All England Sunshine Dancing Competition was started, open to young dancers up to the age of 22. This gave rise to the Sunshine Galas; the first was held in 1965. The Beryl Grey Award has been given every year since then to the best classical d.

Surinach, Carlos (*b* Barcelona, 14 Mar. 1915). Span.–Amer. composer. Wrote the mus. for some modern dance pieces, incl. Humphrey's *Ritmo Jondo* (1953), Graham's *Embattled Garden* (1958) and *Acrobats of God* (1960), and Lang's *Apasionada* (1962). Bs. based on his concert mus. include Butler's *The Sybil* (1959), Morrice's *Hazaña* and *A Place in the Desert* (1961), Ailey's *Feast of Ashes* (1962), and P. Taylor's *Agathe's Tale* (1967). Contributor to 'Composer / Choreographer', *Dance Perspectives* 16.

Surmejan, Hazaros (*b* Skopje, 1943). Yugosl. dancer and ballet master. Studied with A. Dobrohotov in Skopje, and with Hightower. Joined Skopje B. in 1960; later became soloist. Danced with Mannheim B. in 1962 and Cologne B. 1963–6; principal dancer with National B. of Can. since 1966 and now one of its b. masters..

Sur place. Fr., on the spot.

Susana. See *Audeoud, Susana.*

Sutherland, David (*b* Santa Ana, Cal., 18 Sep. 1941). Amer. dancer and b. master. Studied with Panaieff, Aaron Girard, and F. Alonso. D. with B. de Cuba 1959–61 and since 1963 with Stuttgart B.; has also occasionally choreographed for the Noverre matinées and TV. B. master Netherlands

Dance Th. 1977–79, Munich State Op. 1979–82. Married to the d. Gudrun Lechner.

Sutherland, Paul (*b* Louisville, Ky., 1935). Amer. dancer. Studied with Ross Hancock and Dollar. D. in Dollar's Concert Group with Royal Winnipeg B., Amer. B. Th. 1957–9, with R. Joffrey B. 1959–64 and since 1967 (with Met. Op. B. and Amer. B. Th. 1964–7). Created roles in Arpino's *Incubus* (1962) and *Sea Shadow* (1963), Ailey's *Feast of Ashes* (1962), and Joffrey's *Gamelan* (1963). Married to the d. Brunilda Ruiz.

Sutowski, Thor (*b* Trenton, N.J., 21 Jan. 1945). Amer. dancer and b. director. Studied with A. Howard, Caton, W. Griffith, Swoboda, Pereyaslavec, and Franchetti. D. with San Diego B. 1960–3, San Francisco B. 1963–4, National B. of Washington 1964–5, Hamburg State Op. 1965–6 and 1970–1, and Norwegian National B. 1966–70, then, together with his wife S. Arova, dir. and ch. of San Diego B. 1971–6, since when they have moved to Alabama Fine Arts School and Alabama B.

Sutton, Valerie J. (*b* New York, 22 Feb. 1951). Amer. dancer and teacher. Studied with various teachers in Cal. and in Copenhagen, becoming an authorized teacher of the Bournonville system. D. with Laguna Beach B. and various other cos. Researched the entire Bournonville training system, writing it down in her own Sutton Movement Shorthand, a system designed to notate all forms of movement, which she has published in book form and teaches in the U.S. as well as in Europe.

Svedin, Lulli (*b* Danderyd, 24 Nov. 1906). Dancer, teacher and writer. Studied with Valborg Franchi, A. and N. Kozlovsky, T. Rauser, M. Wigman, H. Kreutzberg et al. Advanced Teachers Certificate of Royal Academy of Dancing. Freelance concert d. during the 1930s and early 40s. Teacher at Koreografiska Institutet Stockholm. Correspondent of Dance Magazine since 1967. Now retired but still active as part-time teacher. Author of *Den Klassiska Balettens Byggstenar* (1978). Carina Ari Medal (1976).

Svetlana. Ballet in three acts with prologue; ch. Radunsky, Pospekhin, and Popko; mus. D. Klebanov; déc. R. Makarov. Prod. 20 Dec. 1939, Bolshoi Filial Th., Moscow, with Lepeshinskaya, Kondratov, Messerer. The b. tells of S., the daughter of a forester, who lives in the distant Taiga; she sets her own house on fire to let the frontier-guards know that there is a saboteur in the Taiga. The b. has been produced in many different versions throughout the U.S.S.R.

BIBL.: M. G. Swift, in *The Art of the Dance in the U.S.S.R.* (Notre Dame, Ind., 1968).

Svetlova, Marina (*b* Paris, 3 May 1922). Fr.-Amer. dancer and teacher. Studied with Trefilova, Egorova, Vilzak, and V. Gsovsky. D. with Original B. Russe 1939–41, B. Th. 1942–3, Met. Op. B.

1943–50, and New York City Op. B. 1951–2. Had her own group from 1953, with which she toured Eur. and the U.S. Guest ballerina with many Eur. comps., incl. London Festival B., Royal Swed. B., and Finn. National B. Was Artistic Director of Dallas Civic B. and is now Chairman of B. Dept. at Univ. of Indiana at Bloomington.

BIBL.: P. Rawlings, 'M.S.', *Dance Magazine* (1960/12).

Swaine, Alexander Freiherr von (*b* Munich, 28 Dec. 1905). Ger. dancer and teacher. Studied with Eduardova. Had his first success as Puck in Max Reinhardt's prod. of *A Midsummer Night's Dream*. Began touring in 1928 and became one of the best known Ger. concert dancers, often appearing with Darja Collin or Chladek and later with Czobel. Has also occasionally been a member of resident comps. (e.g. Berlin Municipal and State Op., Heidelberg, Cologne). Has been teaching since 1960 at the Bellas Artes School in Mexico City.

Swan Lake (orig. Russ. title: *Lebedinoe ozero*; Fr., *Le Lac des cygnes*). Ballet in four acts; libr. V. P. Begitchev and V. Geltser; mus. Tchaikovsky; ch. V. Reisinger; sets H. Shangin, K. Valts, and H. Groppius; cost. H. Simone and Vormenko. Prod. 4 Mar. 1877, Bolshoi Th., Moscow, with Pelageia Karpakova, S. Gillert. The B. is based on motives from J. K. A. Musäus' *Der geraubte Schleier* (*The Stolen Veil*) published in his collection of *Volksmärchen der Deutschen*. The central character is Princess Odette, who is turned into a swan by the magician Rothbart. At midnight she and her companions regain their human form for a few hours. On one such occasion she is met by Prince Siegfried who falls in love with her and swears to rescue her. At a ball in the castle Siegfried is expected to choose his bride; the knight Rothbart appears with his daughter Odile in the form of a Black Swan, so that she looks exactly like Odette. She bewitches Siegfried, who becomes betrothed to her; Odette then appears. Siegfried now recognizes that he has broken his oath and he rushes off to the lake, where Odette and her companions are mourning their fate. Siegfried acknowledges his faithlessness and is forgiven by her. Rothbart then conjures up a storm and the two lovers are drowned. In some versions there is a happy ending: Siegfried fights Rothbart, breaks the spell, and rescues Odette and her companions. Other versions have a prologue in which Rothbart surprises Odette and her companions when they are gathering flowers at the shore of the lake, and transforms them into swans. The Moscow first prod. was not a success (though not, as is often stated, a complete disaster). The St. Petersburg Maryinsky Th. gave the second act in a Tchaikovsky Memorial Matinée on 1 Mar. 1894 with ch. by Ivanov, and with Legnani and Gerdt; a complete prod. was given on 27 Jan. 1895 with ch. by Petipa (first and third act) and Ivanov (second and fourth act), for which major changes

were made in the mus. sequence, déc. M. Botcharov and M. Levogt, again with Legnani (in the double role of Odette–Odile) and Gerdt. Gorsky then mounted the b. with his own revisions at the Moscow Bolshoi Th. in 1901; this became the basis for the later Bolshoi prods. with amendments by Messerer in 1937. The prod. is still seen in the Kremlin Palace perfs. of the co. Other important Sov. versions by Vaganova (Kirov Th., 1933), Lopokov (Kirov Th., 1945), K. Sergeyev (Kirov Th., 1950), Bourmeister (Stanislavsky and Nemirovich–Danchenko Music Th., 1953), and Grigorovich (Bolshoi Th., 1969). Sov. film prods. were *Trio Ballet* (continuous excerpts only, with Ulanova, Dudinskaya, and Sergeyev, 1953), a Bolshoi *S.L.* (with Plisetskaya and Fadeyechev, 1957), and a Kirov *S.L.* (with Yevteyeva and Markovsky, 1968). Tchaikovsky himself saw the second act only in a perf. at the Prague National Th., ch. by A. Berger, in 1888. The first prod. of the complete b. outside Russ. was ch. by Achille Viscusi at Prague National Th. in 1907. The first London prod. of the second act was at the Hippodrome in 1910 (with Preobrajenska), followed by the première of the prod. by Diaghilev's co. (two acts, three scenes, with Kschessinska and Nijinsky, at Cov. Gdn. in 1911). In New York it was first prod. at the Met. Op. House in 1911 (with Geltser). The first Western prod. of the complete Petipa-Ivanov version was staged by N. Sergeyev for Vic-Wells B. in 1934; this became the basis for all the later prods. by the co. (and by many other cos. throughout the world). Further important prods. incl. Balanchine's (extended version of second act, New York City B., 1951), Bourmeister's (Moscow, 1953, the first to return to Tchaikovsky's original mus. sequence) Cranko's (Stuttgart B., 1963), Nureyev's (Vienna State Op. B., 1964), MacMillan's (Ger. Op. Berlin, 1964) Neumeier's (Hamburg, 1976), and Darrell's (Scottish B., 1977). Nureyev's Vienna prod. was filmed in 1966 (with Fonteyn and himself). In addition there are numerous film and TV prods. of the second act and other extract versions.

BIBL.: C. W. Beaumont, *The Ballet Called 'S.L.'* (London, 1952); Y. Slonimsky, in 'Writings on Lev Ivanov', *Dance Perspectives* 2; L. Kirstein, 'S.L.' in *Movement & Metaphor* (New York, 1970).

Swan of Tuonela. Sibelius' Legend for Orchestra (1896) has been used several times for b. purposes, e.g. by A. Saxelin (Helsinki, 1948), W. Ulbrich (Leipzig, 1958), and Dolin (Guatemala, 1965).

Sweden. See *Cramér, Ivo; Cullberg, Birgit; Gothenburg; Royal Swedish Ballet; Scandinavian Ballet*. In addition there is the Malmö Municipal Th. B., directed by E. M. von Rosen.

Sweeney Todd. Ballet in one act; libr. and ch. Cranko; mus. M. Arnold; déc. Alix Stone. Prod. 10 Dec. 1959, Royal B., Stratford-upon-Avon, with Britton, Doyle, Anderton. Based on George

Dibdin Pitt's melodrama *The Demon Barber of Fleet Street*; S.T. procures human victims to fill Mrs. Lovett's delicious meat pies.

Swinson, Cyril (*b* London, 1910, d. St. Albans, 3 Jan. 1963). Brit. publisher and writer on b. Director of A. & C. Black, London, who thanks to his initiative became one of the pioneering publishers of b. books in Eng. and Amer. For 17 years Associate Editor of the *Ballet Annual*; he was the vital force behind the first books of I. Guest, Bruhn's and Moore's book on Bournonville technique, Clarke's histories of the B. Rambert and Sadler's Wells B., and Van Praagh's and Brinson's book on ch. In addition he was the author (sometimes under the pen-names of Joseph Sandon or Hugh Fisher) of *The Story of the Sadler's Wells Ballet* (London, 1954), *The Sadler's Wells Theatre Ballet* (London, 1956), and several vols. in the series *Dancers of Today*.
BIBL.: 'C.S.', *Dancing Times* (1963/2).

Switzerland. The country attracted first some intern. attention when Laban worked here. He set up his so-called 'Dance Farm' as part of the colony of life-reformers and artists at the Ascona Monte Verità (nr. Locarno), and established a modern d. tradition which he continued at his Zurich school (and later on there through his pupil Suzanne Perrotet, while Charlotte Bara, a modern d. had a th. built at Ascona for herself, the Teatro San Martino, where she for many years continued to give perfs.). For individual cities see the entries on *Basle*, *Geneva*, and *Zurich* plus the entry *Lausanne*, *Prix de*. Other cities with b. cos. attached to the local municipal th. incl. Berne (directed in 1981 by R. Duse), Lucerne (D. Ammann), and St. Gall (Taubert). Jean Deroc established the Swiss Chamber B. based in Windisch, 1968. At Nyon on Lake Geneva an annual 'Concours internationale de choréographie' was established by Francisco Miranda 1977.

Swope, Martha (*b c.* 1933). Amer. photographer. Official photographer of New York City B., Martha Graham D. Co., and D. Th. of Harlem. Has also worked for many other cos. Co-author of *Mourka* (with T. LeClercq; New York, 1964), *Martha Graham* (with L. Leatherman; New York, 1967), and *New York City Ballet* (with L. Kirstein; New York, 1973).

Sydney Dance Company. Austral. modern-d. co. formed as educ. group in 1965, and on a professional basis as The Dance Co. of New South Wales from 1971. Under J. Flier as artistic dir. 1975–6, the co. perf. works by himself, Butler, Sokolow, Tetley and Austral. chs. G. Murphy appointed artistic dir. in 1976, since when the repertory has become more adventurous incl. his own full-length bs., *Poppy* (1978), *Rumours* (1979) and *An Evening* (1981). Co. now numbers 20 ds. and made its Eur. début 1980, with an Italian tour, followed by New York and London in 1981.

Sylphide, La. Ballet in 2 acts; libr. Adolphe Nourrit; ch. F. Taglioni; mus. Schneitzhoeffer; sets P.L.C. Ciceri; cost. E. Lami. Prod. 12 Mar. 1832, Opéra, Paris, with M. Taglioni, Noblet, Mazilier, L. Elie. The b. was based on Charles Nodier's *Trilby, ou le Lutin d'Argail* (1822). It is set in Scotland. The young farmer James is visited by the S. on the eve of his marriage to Effie. He leaves his bride and his friends and follows her to the woods. To bind her forever to him, he accepts a magic shawl from the witch Madge. When he puts it around her shoulders, however, her wings fall off and she dies. In the finale one sees the wedding party on its way to the church: Effie is now marrying Gurn, whom she had previously rejected. There had been the romantic B. of Nuns in Meyerbeer's op. *Robert Le Diable* (1831); but this was the first fully fledged romantic b. It introduced spirits and elemental beings, which dominated b. for the next decades. The b. was soon seen all over Eur. and the U.S.; London and Berlin in 1832, New York and St. Petersburg in 1835, and Vienna in 1836. An earlier version was L. Henry's *La Silfide* in Milan (1828). Bournonville staged his own version with mus. by Løvenskjold in Copenhagen on 28 Nov. 1836 (with Grahn and himself). This prod. has been frequently revived and is still kept in the repertory of the Royal Dan. B. (foreign prods. of the Bournonville version include von Rosen's for B. Rambert, 1960, and Maly B., 1975, Bruhn's for National B. of Can., 1964, Lander's for Amer. B. Th., 1964, Brenaa's for Scot. Th. B., 1973, and Schaufuss's for London Festival B. 1979). More recent prods. using the orig. Schneitzhoeffer score have been staged by V. Gsovsky (Bs. des Champs-Elysées, 1946), Adama (the first to go back to the original sources, Bremen, 1964), and Lacotte (Opéra, Paris, 1972). BBC TV prod. (of the Bournonville version) in 1961; Fr. TV prod. (of the Lacotte version) in 1971.
BIBL.: I. Guest. in *The Romantic Ballet* (London, 1966); L. Kirstein, '*L.S.*' in *Movement & Metaphor* (New York, 1970).

Sylphides, Les (orig. Russ. title: *Chopiniana*); Ballet in 1 act; ch. Fokine; mus. Chopin. Prod. 23 Feb. 1907, Maryinsky Th., St. Petersburg, with Pavlova, Fokina, Oboukhoff. In this earliest version the b., which used 5 Chopin piano pieces orchestrated by Glazunov, had a strong Pol. character: the introductory Polonaise in A major (op. 40, no. 1) was set in a ballroom; the Nocturne in F major (op. 15, no. 1) showed Chopin's feverish dreams in Majorca; in the Mazurka in C sharp minor (op. 50, no. 3) a Pol. wedding was celebrated; the Valse in C sharp minor (op. 64, no. 2) was a pas de deux, in which the ballerina wore the traditional romantic cost. (otherwise Pol. national costs. were worn); the final Tarantella in A flat major (op. 43) showed a Neapolitan folk scene. A revised version, based on the pas de deux, which attempted to revive the spirit of the romantic b., was ch. by Fokine on 21 Mar. 1908 at Maryinsky Th., St. Petersburg, with Preobrajenska, Pavlova, Karsavina, and Nijinsky; Maurice Keller orchestrated some additional Chopin pieces. This version is still performed. It consists of the Polonaise in A major (in Western perfs. the Prélude in A major, op. 28, no. 7, is now usually substituted—it reappears later in the b.), the Nocturne in A flat major, op. 32, no. 2 (ensemble for 3 female soloists, 1 male soloist, and group), the Valse in G flat major, op. 70, no. 1 (for the première danseuse), the Mazurka in D major, op. 33, no. 2 (usually d. by the prima ballerina), the Mazurka in C major, op. 67, no. 3 (for the premier danseur), the Prélude in A major (as above—for another première danseuse), the Valse in C sharp minor, op. 64, no. 2 (the pas de deux of the original version), and the Grande Valse in E flat major, op. 18, no. 1 (for the whole ensemble). For a later prod. Fokine ch. the Mazurka in C major, op. 33, no. 3, as an alternative variation for the premier danseur—it is still d. in the Kirov prod., but rarely in Western prods. The b. received its final form when Fokine staged it for the Diaghilev co., with déc. by Benois, on 2 June 1909, Th. du Châtelet, Paris, with Pavlova, Karsavina, Baldina, and Nijinsky. Fokine, who wrote in great detail about his conception of the b. in his *Memoirs of a Ballet Master* (Boston, 1961), revived it for many cos. all over the world, incl. the prod. for B. Th. in 1940. The Royal B.'s present prod. goes back to Markova's staging for the Vic-Wells B. in 1932. Danilova staged a prod. in practice dresses for New York City B. in 1972. The b. is still kept in the repertory of b. cos. throughout the world. There are numerous film and TV prods., incl. the BBC prod. of 1958 and that in the film *An Evening With the Royal Ballet* (1965).

BIBL.: L. Kirstein, 'L.S.' in *Movement & Metaphor* (New York, 1970); O. Maynard, 'L.S.', *Dance Magazine* (1971/12).

Sylvia, ou La Nymphe de Diane. Ballet in 3 acts and 5 scenes; libr. Barbier and Baron de Reinach; ch. Mérante; mus. Delibes; sets Chéret, Rubé, and Chaperon; cost. Eugène Lacoste. Prod. 14 June 1876, Opéra, Paris, with Sangalli, Sanlaville, Mérante. The b. tells of the love of the shepherd Amyntas for S., who is a nymph of Diana. He is however, rejected, as is Orion, the Black Hunter. When Eros intervenes she changes her mind, but first Amyntas' love is put to the test. Then even Diana forgives her faithless nymph, and gives her blessing to their wedding. The b. is based on Ariosto's pastoral drama *Aminta*. The role of Eros was given *en travestie*. The b. has often been revived and newly ch. at the Paris Opéra, e.g. by Staats (1919) and Lifar (1941). First prod. in Vienna in 1877, Berlin in 1884, St. Petersburg in 1901 (the prod. in which Diaghilev was involved, and which caused his resignation from the staff of the Maryinsky Th.), and London in 1911 (at the Empire Th., staged by C. Wilhelm

and Fred Farren, with Kyasht, Bedells, Unity More, Mossetti, Farren). Among more recent prods. 2 stand out: Ashton's for the Sadler's Wells B. (déc. R. and C. Ironside, 3 Sep. 1952, Cov. Gdn., London, with Fonteyn, Somes, Hart, Grant, Farron—reduced to a 1-act version in 1967) and Seregi's for the Budapest State Op. B. (1972). Balanchine ch. the third act pas de deux for Maria Tallchief and Eglevsky in 1951. Lavrovsky ch. his first major b., *Fadetta*, to mus. from this b. (and other compositions by Delibes), for a Leningrad Ch. School matinée in 1931.

BIBL.: C. W. Beaumont, 'S.o.L.N.d.D.' in *Complete Book of Ballets* (London, 1951); on the Ashton version: Beaumont, 'S.' in *Ballets of Today* (London, 1954).

Symons, Oliver (*b* London, 6 Aug. 1936). Brit. dancer and b. master. Studied with N. Robinson and at Sadler's Wells School. D. with Sadler's Wells Op. B. 1956–7. One of the founder members of Western Th. B. 1957–64; created many roles. D. with Zurich Op. B. 1964–5. Appointed b. master of B. for All in 1965. Has also been b. master for the TV series *Ballet for All*.

Symphonic Ballets. The term was coined during the 1930s, when Massine presented his first bs. to symphonic mus. He claimed that these projected the purely mus. content and formal development by means of the d. Some extra-mus. message was, however, usually conveyed in *Les Présages* (Tchaikovsky's 5th Symphony, 1933), *Choreartium* (Brahms's 4th Symphony, 1933), *Symphonie fantastique* (Berlioz, (1936), *La Septième Symphonie* (Beethoven, 1938), and *Rouge et noir* (Shostakovich's 1st Symphony, 1939). Balanchine, in contrast, generally avoided telling a story when he tackled such mus. In the U.S.S.R. b. historians nowadays like to talk of a 'symphonization' of the ch. form, which they trace back to Ivanov's second act of *Swan Lake*. However, choreographers before Massine created S.B., though they were not so-called: e.g. A. J. J. Deshayes (Beethoven's 6th Symphony, London 1829), Duncan (Beethoven's 7th Symphony, New York, 1908), Gorsky (Glazunov's 5th Symphony, Moscow, 1915), and Lopokov (Beethoven's 4th Symphony, in *Dance Symphony*, Leningrad, 1923).

Symphonic Variations. Ballet in 1 act; ch. Ashton; mus. C. Franck; déc. Fedorovitch. Prod. 24 Apr. 1946, Sadler's Wells B., Cov. Gdn., London, with Fonteyn, May, Shearer, Somes, Shaw, and Henry Danton. A plotless b. for 6 dancers, reflecting the flow and the mood of the score. Widely considered one of Ashton's greatest masterpieces and the truest reflection of the co.'s style. It has never been performed by any other co. Ashton commented on his concept in a conversation with Buckle, published in *Ballet* (Nov. 1947). Granada TV prod. in 1973.

BIBL.: D. Vaughan, *Frederick Ashton and his Ballets* (London, 1977).

Symphonie Concertante. Ballet in 3 movements; ch. Balanchine; mus. Mozart; cost. James Stewart Morcom. Prod. 12 Nov. 1947, B. Society, City Center, New York, with Maria Tallchief, LeClercq, Bolender. 'Set to Mozart's Sinfonia Concertante in E flat major for Violin and Viola (K.364), this ballet follows closely the design of the music. It has no story. Its gold backdrop represents the formal classical frame into which both music and dancing fit. The three parts correspond to the three movements of the score. There are two ballerinas, corresponding to the solo instruments, a danseur, a group of six secondary soloists, and a corps de ballet of sixteen dancers' (Balanchine).
BIBL.: G. Balanchine, 'S.C.' in Balanchine's *New Complete Stories of the Great Ballets* (Garden City, N.Y., 1968).

Symphonie fantastique. Ch. Symphony in 5 scenes; libr. (after Berlioz) and ch. Massine; mus. Berlioz; déc. Bérard. Prod. 24 July 1936, de Basil's co., Cov. Gdn., London, with Massine, Toumanova, Platov, Zoritch, Koslov, Shabelevsky. According to Berlioz' programme the b. tells the story of a romantic young musician, who in a fit of love-sickness takes a dose of opium; he then embarks on a journey through the landscapes of his visions, always striving to reach his unattainable Beloved. Revived for several cos., sometimes as *Episodes in the life of an Artist*. Ashton's treatment of a very similar subject in *Apparitions*, about the same time, helped to win recognition of the Young Vic-Wells B.'s artistic progress. Version by R. Petit for the Paris Opéra, Dec. 1975, with Zizi Jeanmaire, M. Denard.
BIBL.: C. W. Beaumont, 'S.f.', in *Complete Book of Ballets* (London, 1951).

Symphonie inachevée. See *Unfinished Symphony*.

Symphonie pour un homme seul (*Symphony for a Lonely Man*). Ballet in 1 act; ch. Béjart; mus. P. Henry and P. Schaeffer. Prod. 26 July 1955, B. de l'Etoile, Paris, with Béjart and Seigneuret. The central figure is modern man trapped between technology and sex, manipulated by anonymous forces, and trying in vain to escape. This was Béjart's first b. success. Fr. TV prod. 1956. Revived for his various cos. and for Cologne B. in 1963. Part of the mus. had already been used by Cunningham in his *Collage* (1952).
BIBL.: G. Balanchine and F. Mason, in *Balanchine's Complete Stories of the Great Ballets* (Garden City, N.Y., 1977).

Symphony. Ballet in 4 movements; ch. MacMillan; mus. Shostakovich; déc. Yolanda Sonnabend. Prod. 15 Feb. 1963, Royal B., Cov. Gdn., London, with Sibley, Parkinson, MacLeary, Doyle. Set to Shostakovich's First Symphony, this is a plotless b. which, however, subtly reflects the emotional tensions between the 4 soloists, 3 couples of secondary soloists, and 6 couples of corps de ballet dancers. Massine used the same mus. for his b. *Rouge et noir* (*L'étrange farandole*, Monte Carlo, 1939).

Symphony for a Lonely Man. See *Symphonie pour un homme seul*.

Symphony in C (orig. *Le Palais de cristal*). Ballet in 4 movements; ch. Balanchine; mus. Bizet; déc. L. Fini. Prod. 28 July 1947, Opéra, Paris, with Darsonval, Toumanova, Bardin, Lafon, Kalioujny, Ritz, Renault, Bozzoni. A plotless b.; a different team of dancers dances each of the first 3 movements and states its individual ch. subject; a fourth team opens the fourth movement, and the 3 other teams later join in. Second Channel Ger. TV prod. (with New York City B., 1972). Revived for many cos. Howard used the same mus. for her b. *Assembly Ball* in 1946.
BIBL.: G. Balanchine 'S.i.C.', in *Balanchine's New Complete Stories of the Great Ballets* (Garden City, N.Y., 1968).

Symphony in Three Movements. Ballet in 3 movements; ch. Balanchine; mus. Stravinsky; light. R. Bates. Prod. 18 June 1972, New York City B., State Th., N.Y., with Leland, Villella, Tomasson. A plotless b. of bustling energy and many asymmetrical patterns. Other versions incl. Van Manen's (Netherlands D. Th., 1963).
BIBL.: G. Balanchine and F. Mason, in *Balanchine's Complete Stories of the Great Ballets* (Garden City, N.Y., 1977).

Symphony of Psalms (orig. *Psalmensymfonie*). Ballet in 1 act; ch. Kylián; mus. Stravinsky; set W. Katz; cost. J. Stokvis. Prod. 24 Nov. 1978, Netherlands D. Th., Circustheater, Scheveningen. The b., set for 8 pairs of dancers, emerges as a dark and stark rendering of Stravinsky's 1930 symphony in clear and concise, energetically driven formal patterns. An earlier version by Sparemblek (Gulbenkian B., 1972).

Szönyi, Nora (*b* Budapest, 23 Apr. 1953). Hung. dancer. Studied at Budapest State B. Inst. and Leningrad Ch. School. Joined Budapest State Op. B. as a soloist in 1973.

Szumrák, Vera (*b* Budapest, 28 Oct. 1938). Hung. dancer. Studied at Budapest State B. Inst; joined Budapest State Op. B., and became soloist in 1965. Created Girl in Seregi's *The Miraculous Mandarin* (1970) and leading role in his *The Cedar* (1975) Liszt Award (1968). Married to the d. Imre Dózsa.

Szymanski, Stanislaw (*b* Krakow, 17 June, 1930). Pol. dancer. Studied with Woizikovsky and Janina Jarzynówna. Début with Woizikovsky's co. in Krakow in 1948. D. with Warsaw Teatr Nowy B. 1948–50, Poznan Op. B. 1950–1, Pol. Army Ensemble 1951–6, and since 1956 with Warsaw Teatr Wielki B.; became principal d. in 1965. Created many roles in bs. by Woizikovsky, Gruca, Adret, and Lazzini. Appeared in several TV b. prods.
BIBL.: T. Wysocka, in *Dzieje Baletu* (Warsaw, 1970).

T

Taconeo. (Span., noise of heels.) Designates in flamenco dancing the heel technique.

Taglioni. Famous Ital. family of dancers and choreographers during the eighteenth and nineteenth century. Carlo T. was born in the mid-eighteenth century in Turin and worked from 1782 until the turn of the century in Venice, Rome, Sienna, and Udine. Two of his sons are especially important in the history of b.: Filippo T. (1777–1871) and Salvatore T. (1789–1868). Filippo T. was the father of Marie T. (1804-84) and Paul (Paolo) T. (1808–84). Paul T.'s daughter was Marie T. the younger (1833–91).

Taglioni, Filippo (*b* Milan, 5 Nov. 1777, *d* Como, 11 Feb. 1871). Ital. dancer and choreographer. He was the son of Carlo T. and the father of Marie and Paul T. Appeared first in female roles in Pisa (1794); moved to Livorno, Florence, and Venice, then to Paris in 1799, where he studied with Coulon and d. at the Opéra. Appointed principal d. and b. master in Stockholm in 1803, where he married the daughter of a singer. During the following years he travelled all over Europe, sometimes with his family; he worked in Vienna, Cassel, Munich, Milan, Turin, Stuttgart, and Paris, and dedicated himself increasingly to furthering his daughter's career. He also worked in Berlin, St. Petersburg, Warsaw, and again in Stockholm; he retired to Como, and spent his last years there, after the death of his wife, in worsening mental decline. As a ch. made his début in Vienna with *Atalante und Hippomenes* in 1805, followed by *Das Schweizer Milchmädchen* (mus. Gyrowetz), *Lodoïska* (mus. Umlauff and Gyrowetz), *Jaconde* (after Vestris—all 1821), *Margaretha, Königin von Catanea* (mus. Graf von Gallenberg), *La Réception d'une jeune nymphe à la cour de Terpsichore* (for the début of his daughter Marie—both 1822), etc. His most important Stuttgart b. creation was *Danina, oder Jocko der brasilianische Affe* (mus. P. von Lindpaintner, 1826). His creativity reached its peak in Paris, where he did the first prods. of the ops. *Le Dieu et la Bayadère* (1830) and *Gustave III* (both mus. Auber, 1833), *Robert le Diable* (1831) and *Les Huguenots* (both mus. Meyerbeer, 1836), and *La Juive* (mus. Halévy, 1835)—and the bs. *La Sylphide* (mus. Schneitzhoeffer), *Nathalie ou La Laitière suisse* (definitive version of *Das Schweizer Milchmädchen*, both 1832), *La Révolte au Sérail* (mus. Labarre, 1833), *Brézilia, ou La Tribu des femmes* (mus. von Gallenberg, 1835), and *La Fille du Danube* (mus. Adam, 1836). He then ch. *La Gitana* (mus. Schmidt and Aumer, 1838), *L'Ombre* (mus. Maurer, 1839), and *Aglaë ou L'Eléve d'amour* (mus.

Keller, 1841) for St. Petersburg. He was much admired by his contemporaries as the creator of a new style of gracious lightness, légèreté, and élévation, and for the chaste purity of his bs. and their mystic and even religious quality.
BIBL.: I. Guest, in *The Romantic Ballet in Paris* (London, 1966); M. H. Winter, in *The Pre-Romantic Ballet* (London, 1974).

Taglioni, Marie (*b* Stockholm, 23 Apr. 1804, *d* Marseilles, 22 Apr. 1884). Swed.–Ital. dancer. Daughter of Filippo T., and sister of Paul T. Studied mainly with her father in Vienna and Cassel, and also with Coulon in Paris. Made her début in her father's *La Réception d'une jeune nymphe à la cour de Terpsichore*, 10 June 1822, in Vienna; during the following years he gradually moulded her, while he was engaged in Munich and Stuttgart, into the ballerina of his stylistic ideals. Created the title-role in his *Danina oder Jocko der brasilianische Affe* (1826). Introduced herself to the Paris audience in a variation inserted in the b. *Le Sicilien* in 1827. Her highly individual technique created a sensation at every perf. Her greatest successes included the creations of *La Belle au bois dormant* and *Guillaume Tell* (op. by Rossini, both ch. Aumer, 1829), *Le Dieu et la Bayadère* (op by Auber, 1830), *Robert le Diable* (op by Meyerbeer, 1831), and *La Sylphide* (1832; all ch. by her father). In the title-role of the last-mentioned b., she established herself as a ballerina of perfect spirituality and poetic transfiguration. Her further important creations during the next years included *Nathalie ou La Laitière suisse* (1832), *La Révolte au Sérail* (1833), and *La Fille du Danube* (1836). She married Comte Gilbert de Voisins in London in 1832, but the marriage was very unhappy, and they were divorced in 1844. In Paris she had to struggle to maintain her position against the up-and-coming Elssler, but elsewhere in Eur. she triumphed—e.g. Berlin, London, St. Petersburg (where she was enormously popular 1837–42), Warsaw, Milan, and Turin, and on return visits to Vienna, Munich, and Stockholm. During the last years of her career, created further leading roles in her father's *La Gitana* (1838) and *L'Ombre* (1839), and Perrot's *Pas de quatre* (1845) and *Le Jugement de Pâris* (1846). She gave her farewell perf. in this last-mentioned b. in London in 1847. Retired for a while to her parents' home in Como, and to Venice; returned to Paris in 1860 to ch. her only b., *Le Papillon*, to mus. by Offenbach for Emma Livry. Inspectrice des classes et du service de la danse at the Opéra until 1870; took great personal care of the careers of Boschetti, Salvioni, and Laurati. Initiated the system of

examinations which still continues at the Opéra. In the war of 1870–1 she lost her whole fortune and was obliged to earn her living in London as a teacher of ballroom dancing and deportment. Her last 4 years were spent with her son in Marseilles. She is considered one of the greatest ballerinas of b. history, and she is one of the very few ballerinas who have asst. in creating a new style. An ethereal ballerina of immaculate purity, she transformed the d. on points, which had previously been a technical tour de force, into a means of sublime poetry. A genuine lyricist, she became the most important ballerina of the romantic movement.
BIBL.: A Levinson, *M.T.* (Paris, 1929); L. Vaillat, *La T. ou La vie d'une danseuse* (Paris, 1942); I. Guest, in *The Romantic Ballet in Paris* (London, 1966); P. Migel, 'M.T.' in *The Ballerinas* (New York, 1972).

Taglioni, Marie, the younger (*b* Berlin, 27 Oct. 1833, *d* Neu-Aigen, nr. Vienna, 27 Aug. 1891). Ger. dancer. Studied with her father Paul T. and made her début in his London b. *Coralia* in 1847, followed by his *Théa ou La Fée aux fleurs* (1847) and Perrot's *Les quatre saisons* (1848). She d. in Vienna 1853–6 and then until her marriage to the Prinz of Windisch-Grätz (1866) as ballerina at the Berlin Court Op.; created roles in her father's *Flick und Flocks Abenteuer* (1858), *Des Malers Traumbild* (1859), and *Sardanapal* (1865). J. Strauss comp. the Taglioni-Polka for her, based on melodies from her bs.

Taglioni, Paul (also Paolo; (*b* Vienna, 12 Jan. 1808, *d* Berlin, 6 Jan. 1884). Ger. dancer and b. master. He was the son of Filippo T., the brother of Marie T., and the father of Marie T. the younger; another daughter, Augusta T. (1831–1911) became a much admired Berlin actress. Studied with his father and with Coulon in Paris. Made his début in a pas de deux with his sister in Stuttgart in 1824 and was then her partner for several years; married the ballerina Anna Galster in Berlin in 1829, with whom he made an Amer. tour in 1839. Settled in Berlin, where he ch. his first 2 bs. in 1835: *Amors Triumph* and *Der arme Fischer* (both mus. H. Schmidt). From Berlin he often paid guest visits to other cities, mostly to Vienna (solo d. 1826–9, regular guest ch. 1853–74), but also to Naples (b. master 1853–6) and Milan (b. master 1861–2). B. master at Berlin Court Op. 1856–83, where he enjoyed great popularity. Mounted about 40 bs., in which he showed himself a solid craftsman; he enjoyed trying out new technical means (e.g. electric lights in his b. *Electra* and roller-skates in *Les Plaisirs de l'hiver*, both in 1849). He also commissioned P. L. Hertel to write new mus. for the Berlin prod. of *La Fille mal gardée* in 1864 (this is still used in Russ. prods. of the b.). His most important Berlin bs. included *Undine, die Wassernymphe* (mus. Schmidt, 1836—a revised version as *Coralia*, London, 1847), *Don Quixote* (mus.

Gährich, 1839), *Thea oder Die Blumenfee* (mus. Pugni, 1847—first prod., London, same year, called *Théa ou La Fée aux fleurs*), *Santanella, oder Metamorphosen* (mus. Hertel, 1852; the original version of this was *Les Metamorphoses*, mus. Pugni, London, 1850), *Flick und Flocks Abenteuer* (1858), *Sardanapal* (1865—revived for the opening of the new Vienna Court Op., 1869), *Fantasca* (1869), *Militaria* (1872—all mus. Hertel), and his own version of *Coppélia* (1882). His daughter took the leading ballerina role in most of his bs. up to 1866. The final Seguidilla in Bournonville's *La Ventana* he ch. after P.T.
BIBL.: C. W. Beaumont, 'P.T.', in *Complete Book of Ballets* (London. 1951).

Taglioni, Salvatore (*b* Palermo 1789, *d* Naples 1868). Ital. dancer and choreographer. He was the son of Carlo T., the brother of Filippo T., and the father of Luisa T. (1823–93), who made her career as a ballerina at the Paris Opéra, and of Fernando T. (1810–74?), who became a well respected composer. He studied in Paris with Coulon d. in Lyons and Bordeaux, and established a very successful b. school with L. Henry in Naples. Ch. a great number of bs. there, in Milan, and in Turin, in which he usually appeared with his wife, Adélaide Perraud.

Tait, Marion (*b* London, 7 Oct. 1950). Brit. dancer. Studied at Royal B. School, graduating into touring co. 1968, promoted principal dancer 1974. Created roles in A. Killar's *The Entertainers* and C. Bruce's *Unfamiliar Playground* (both 1974), J. Carter's *Shukumei* (1975), D. Morse's *Pandora* (1976), D. Bintley's *Meadow of Proverbs*, and *Punch and the Street Party* (both 1979), and *Night Moves* (1981), MacMillan's *Playground* (1979), and Corder's *Day into Night* (1980).
BIBL.: C. Crisp, 'M.T.', a Profile, in *The Royal B. 1980/81* (London, 1980).

Takei, Kei (*b* Tokyo). Jap. dancer, choreographer, and teacher, Studied at Sakaki Bara Dance School, Kaitani B. School, and Kenji Hinoki School, where she started to choreograph modern dance works. To New York in 1966; studied further at Juilliard School and with Nikolais, Graham, Cunningham, Halprin, and T. Brown. Formed her Moving Earth comp., for which she has ch. extensively; her main work is a cycle of 15 pieces, collectively called *Light*, started in 1969 and first given in a single programme in 1975. 'Essentially *Light* consists of vignettes showing people confronting adversities, never overcoming them, but never wholly succumbing to them, either' (J. Anderson).

Tales of Beatrix Potter. An EMI Film Production; dir. Reginald Mills; ch. Ashton; mus. Lanchbery; déc. Christine Edzard; masks K. Doboujinsky; with dancers of the Royal B., incl. Ashton, A. Grant, K. Martin, Mead, Last, Coleman, Sleep, Collier, L. Edwards. Released in 1971. This is a b. film in which the best-loved of Beatrix

Potter's characters, incl. Mrs. Tiggy-Winkle, Peter Rabbit, Mrs Tittlemouse, Johnny Town-Mouse, Jemima Puddle-Duck, Pigling Bland, Black Berkshire Pig, Jeremy Fisher, Hunca Munca, Tom Thumb, and Squirrel Nutkin are performed by dancers.

Tales of Hoffmann. Ballet in 3 acts; libr. and ch. Darrell; mus. Offenbach (arr. Lanchbery); déc. Alistair Livingstone. Prod. 6 Apr. 1972, Scot. Th. B., King's Th., Edinburgh, with Cazalet, Aitken, Hilary Debden, Marian St Claire, E. Mcdonald. The b. roughly follows the course of Offenbach's op., with the Antonia act placed between the Olympia and the Giulietta acts, and with Antonia having ambitions to dance rather than sing. Revived for Amer. B. Th. with new déc. by P. Docherty in 1973 (in this version 1 ballerina dances all 3 heroines). A b. prod. of the op. was ch. by Béjart for the Brussels Th. de la Monnaie in 1961. The Powell and Pressburger film of the op. was ch. by Massine (1951).
BIBL.: (the Darrell version) P. Brinson and C. Crisp, in *Ballet & Dance* (Newton Abbot, 1980).

Tallchief, Maria (b Fairfax, Okla., 24 Jan. 1925). Amer. dancer of Amer. Indian descent; sister of Marjorie T. Studied with E. Belcher, Nijinska, Lichine, and at School of Amer. B. At first undecided whether to pursue a career as a concert pianist or a dancer. Member of B. Russe de Monte Carlo 1942–7; created roles in Balanchine's *Danses concertantes* (1944) and *Night Shadow* (1946). Was married to Balanchine (1946–52), and accompanied him to the Paris Opéra in 1947, where she appeared in his *Serenade*, *Apollon musagète*, and *Baiser de la Fée*. Joined B. Society in the autumn of 1947 and became the leading ballerina of the New York City B. (with brief interruptions, when she danced with B. Russe de Monte Carlo and R. Page's Chicago Op. B.). She appeared in almost all Balanchine's bs., and created leading parts in his *Symphonie concertante* (1947), *Orpheus, Firebird*, and *Bourrée fantasque* (1948), *Caracole* and *Scotch Symphony* (1952), *Pas de dix* (1955), *Allegro brillante* (1956), and *Gounod Symphony* (1958), and his versions of *Sylvia Pas de deux* (1950), *Swan Lake* (1951), and *Nutcracker* (1954). Left New York City B. in 1965; created title role in Van Dyk's *Cinderella* (Hamburg, 1965). During her best years she was considered the most technically accomplished ballerina America had ever produced. Founder and head of Chicago City B. 1981. D. Magazine Award (1960); Capezio D. Award (1965); Prize for the Best Couple (with Van Dyk, Paris, 1965).
BIBL.: O. Maynard, *Bird of Fire, The Story of M.T.* (New York, 1961); E. Myers, *M.T.* (New York, 1966).

Tallchief, Marjorie (b Fairfax, Okla., 19 Oct 1927). Amer. dancer of Amer. Indian descent; sister of Maria T. Studied with Nijinska and Lichine. Member of B. Th. 1944–6, Original B.

Russe 1946–7. Married the d. and ch. George Skibine in 1947; they both joined the Grand B. du Marquis de Cuevas. She remained until 1957 and became one of its leading ballerinas; created roles in Skibine's *Annabel Lee* (1951) and *Le Prisonnier du Caucase* (1951), *L'Ange gris* (1953), *Idylle* (1954), and *Romeo and Juliet* (1955). Guest ballerina of R. Page's Chicago Op. B. in 1956 and 1958; created leading role in Page's *Camille* (1958). Première danseuse étoile at Paris Opéra 1957–62 (the first American ever to hold this title); created roles in Skibine's *Concerto* (1958), *Conte Cruel* (1959), and *Pastorale* (1961). Appeared as guest ballerina with various Eur. and Amer. comps. Member of Harkness B. 1964–6; created title role in Ailey's *Ariadne* (1965). Was admired as a ballerina of great expressive powers and for her exceptional acrobatic elasticity. Dir. of the Sch. of the Chicago City B.
BIBL.: L. Nemenschousky, *A Day with M.T. and George Skibine* (London 1960).

Tallinn. Th. d. in Estonia started when the first national ths. were opened during the 1870s in Tartu and T., but it served only as a decoration for op., operetta, and drama prods. Development of b. as an art form did not materialize until the early years of the twentieth century, when it came under the influence of both the Russ. classical school and the Central Eur. modern d. movement. First professional d. was Ella Ilbak, a former student of Duncan. Of greater importance was the establishment of a studio by Gerd Neggo, a pupil of Laban, in 1926. Classical b. in Estonia was propagated through the studio of Y. Litvinova, a former d. of the Maryinsky Th., and it is from her pupils that the present b. comp. of the Academic Th. for Op. and B. 'Estonia' developed. Under Rahel Olbrei, 1926–44, the position of b. was strengthened, especially through her prods. of *Giselle* (1929 and 1942), *Nutcracker* (1936), *Red Poppy* (1939), *Swan Lake* (1940), and the national b. *Kratt* (mus. Eduard Tubin, 1944). After 1944 a new development took place, with Anna Ekston (1944–51) producing *Fountain of Bakhchisaray, The Merry Wives of Windsor*, and *Swan Lake*, while Helmi Tohvelman created *Kalevipoeg* (mus. Eugen Kapp, 1948). Bourmeister and Fenster came as guest-choreographers. Subsequent choreographers were Viktor Päri (1956–65), Nina Ulanova, and Enn Suve, but the most important b. prods. were contributed during the last 15 years by Mai Murdmaa (b. 1933), a highly talented woman, whose bs. include *Medea* (mus. Barber, 1966), *The Miraculous Mandarin* (mus Bartók, 1968), *Joanna Tentata* (same subject as *Devils of Loudon*, mus. E. Tamberg, 1971), *Labyrinth* (mus. A. Pärt, 1973), *The Flight of the Swans* (mus. V. Tormis, 1973), and *Prodigal Son* (mus. Prokofiev, 1973). Estonian dancers of today include Helmi Puur, Tiiu Randviir, Juta Lehiste (all female), and Tiit Härm (male).

Tally-Ho! or the Frail Quarry. Ballet in 1 act;

libr. and ch. de Mille; mus. Gluck (arr. Mottl-
Nordoff); déc. Motley. Prod. 25 Feb. 1944, B. Th.,
Los Angeles, with de Mille, Laing, Dolin, Chase,
Karnilova, M. Bentley. The b. is set in a Fr. rococo
park; a young lady tries in vain to inspire the
jealousy of her brilliant husband, who is absorbed
in his books. The New York première took place
on 11 Apr. 1944 at the Met. Op. House.
BIBL.: W. Terry, 'T.-H.!' in *Ballet* (New York,
1959).

Talvo, Tyyne (*b* Helsinki, 25 Aug. 1919). Finn.
dancer and choreographer. Studied b. and modern
dance technique; became a dancer in the comps.
of her husband, Ivo Cramér. Has ch. several bs.
for Cramér B., incl. *Sauna* (mus. Pokela–Ernryd)
and *Bright Night* (mus. Lars Dahlberh).

Tambourin. A vivid Provençal d. in 2/4 time, in
which the tambourin (tabor) is used. It was very
popular during the eighteenth century, and many
examples were composed by J. P. Rameau.

Taming of the Shrew, The. Ballet in 2 acts; libr.
and ch. Cranko; mus. Scarlatti–Stolze; déc.
Elisabeth Dalton. Prod. 16 Mar. 1969, Stuttgart
B., Stuttgart, with Haydée, Cragun, Hanke,
Madsen, Neumeier, Clauss. The b. roughly
follows the plot of Shakespeare's play. Revived
for Munich State op. B. in 1976 (with new décor
by J. Rose) and for Royal B. in 1977. Second
Channel Ger. TV prod. 1971. Earlier b. versions
of the same Shakespeare play by Béjart (mus.
Alwyn–Scarlatti, B. des Etoiles de Paris, 1954)
Vera Untermüllerová (mus. Olderich Flosman,
Liberec, 1961), later also by L. Falco in *Kate's Rag*
(1980).
BIBL.: P. Brinson and C. Crisp, in *Ballet & Dance*
(Newton Abbot, 1980).

Tamiris, Helen (née H. Becker; b. New York, 24
Apr. 1905, *d* there 4 Aug. 1966). Amer. dancer,
choreographer, and teacher. Studied with I.
Lewinson, Fokine, and Galli. Danced with Met.
Op. B., changed to modern d. in 1927. Became
known through her d. recitals in the U.S. and
Eur.; appeared with various groups from 1930.
Her works clearly reflect her concern with social
criticism (*Walt Whitman Suite, Cycle of Unrest,
Salut au monde, How long Brethren?*, etc.). Taught
at her New York School of Amer. D. and for
many other schools elsewhere, specializing in
modern stage movement. Began choreographing
for Broadway in 1945; her prods. include Kern's
Showboat, Berlin's *Annie Get Your Gun*, and Rome's
Fanny. During her last years she co-directed the
T.-Nagrin Dance Comp. and Workshop with her
husband Daniel Nagrin.
BIBL.: C. L. Schlundt, *T.: A Chronicle of Her Dance
Career 1927–1955* (New York, 1973).

Tango. Central Amer. dance in slow 2/4 time
with dotted rhythm. It was brought by slaves to
Argentine and Uruguay, where it absorbed certain
features of the habanera and the bolero, gradually
crystallizing in its present ballroom form. In b. it
appears prominently in Ashton's *Façade*, Bolender's *Souvenirs*, Flindt's *Tango Chicane*, Van Manen's *5 Tangos*, and Araiz's full-length *Tango*
(Geneva, 1981).

Tanner, Richard (*b* Phoenix. Ariz., 28 Oct.
1948). Amer. dancer, choreographer, and b.
director. Studied with R. and S. Lindgren,
W. Christensen, and at School of Amer. B. D.
with B. West and New York City B., for which
he ch. several bs. Appointed Artistic Director of
Denver Civic B. in 1972.

Tanzarchiv, Das. Ger. monthly d. magazine,
founded by Kurt Peters in Hamburg in 1953 and
published 1966–80 in Cologne. Also refers to the
collection and library which Peters started to
build up during the 1940s in Hamburg, and
which was transferred to Cologne in 1966.

Tanzblätter. The magazine, published by the b.
direction of the Vienna State Op. and destined
mainly for the dancers of the co. and the pupils
of the associated school plus specially interested
people to provide background material of forthcoming local activities and of the city's b. history,
is edited by Gunbild Schüller and Alfred Oberzaucher. The first issue appeared in Sep. 1976,
since when it has been published mostly (but not
always) on a monthly base during the season of
the Vienna State Op.

Tanz-Forum Köln. The official name of the d.
comp. attached to the Cologne Municipal Stages
since 1971, when it was reorganized with a
tripartite directorship of Helmut Baumann,
Jochen Ulrich, and Gray Veredon. Made its Brit.
début 1976 at Th. Royal, Norwich. See *Cologne*.

Tanzsynfonia. See *Dance Symphony.*

Tap Dancing. Derived from the Irish and
Lancashire clog dancing; its distinguishing feature is the rapid tapping of the toes and heels on
the floor—for which the shoes are specially fitted
with metal cleats. It gained great popularity on
the variety stage and through the early musical
films; Bill Robinson, Eleanor Powell, Fred Astaire,
Paul Draper, Ray Bolger, and Ann Miller were
among its most distinguished performers. In
Germany it is called 'Steptanz'.

Taqueté. (Fr., pegged.) Designates steps with
accentuated points such as piqués, pas de bour-
rées—i.e. the pizzicato variant of dancing on
points.

Tarantella. The most popular of all South Ital.
folk dances, executed mainly by couples, in
accelerating 6/8 time. It derives its name from
the city of Taranto, the citizens of which in the
fourteenth century were said, when bitten by a
tarantula spider, to dance until they had sweated
out the spider's poison. In 1839 Coralli ch. a b.
*La Tarentule, and Milloss ch. *La Tarantola*, mus.
G. Piccioli, in 1942, but most famous example is

undoubtedly to be found in the third act of *Swan Lake*. Others are found in Bournonville's *Napoli* and Massine's *La Boutique fantasque*. Balanchine ch. a *T.* to mus. by Gottschalk, arr by H. Kay, for McBride and Villella in 1964.

BIBL.: R. Taborr, 'Wolf Spider—The Beast That Lent Its Name to Dance', *Dance Magazine* (1973/1).

Taras Bulba. Ballet in 3 acts; lib. Semyon Kaplan; ch. Lopokov; mus. Soloviev–Sedoy; déc. Rindin. Prod. 12 Dec. 1940, Kirov Th., Leningrad, with Dudinskaya, Chaboukiani. The b. is based on Gogol's short story about the fight of the Cossack general and the Ukrainians against their Pol. oppressors. Individual later versions by Zakharov (Bolshoi B., 1941) and Fenster (Kirov Th., 1955).

BIBL.: C. W. Beaumont, '*T.B.*' in *Supplement to Complete Book of Ballet* (London, 1952).

Taras, John (*b* New York, 18 Apr. 1919). Amer. dancer, choreographer, and b. master. Started to dance when 9 years old in an Ukrainian folk dance ensemble; choreographed his first b. when 13. Started to study d. in 1936 with Fokine, Vilzak, Schollar, Anderson–Ivantzova, and at School of Amer. B. Joined B. Caravan in 1940, Littlefield B. in 1941; member of B. Th. 1942–6 where he ch. *Graziana* (mus. Mozart 1945). Worked with various comps.; ch. *Camille* (mus. Schubert, arr. Rieti, Original B. Russe, 1946), *The Minotaur* (mus. E. Carter, B. Society, 1947), and *Designs with Strings* (mus. Tchaikovsky, Met. B., 1948). Member of Grand B. du Marquis de Cuevas 1948–59 (with brief interruptions); ch. *Piège de lumière* (mus. J. M. Damase, 1952) and *La Forêt romantique* (mus. Glazunov, 1957). Intermittently worked as a guest with many comps. all over the world; also in charge of the ch. for the first and third act of the Sagan b. *Le Rendezvous manqué* (mus. M. Magne, Monte Carlo, 1958). B. master of New York City B. since 1959, with occasional leave of absence to assume other b. master posts (Paris Opéra, Ger. Op. Berlin, etc.). Has ch. many bs., incl. *Ebony Concerto* (mus. Stravinsky, 1960), *Arcade* (mus. Stravinsky's Concerto for Piano and Brass Instruments, 1963), *Jeux* (mus. Debussy, 1966), *Danses concertantes* (mus. Stravinsky, 1971), *Le Sacre du printemps* (mus. Stravinsky, Milan, 1972), *Daphnis and Chloe* (mus. Ravel, 1975) and *Souvenir de Florence* (mus. Tchaikovsky,1981). Left N.Y. City B. 1984, apptd. assoc. dir. Amer. B. Th.

Tarasov, Nicolai Ivanovich (*b* Moscow, 19 Dec. 1902 *d* there, 8 Feb. 1975). Sov. dancer and teacher. Son of the eminent dance teacher Ivan T. (1878–1954); studied at Moscow Bolshoi B. School and graduated in 1920. Joined Bolshoi B.; became one of its leading dancers. His eminence, however, rests with his work as a teacher; he taught from 1923–61 at the Bolshoi School and was especially admired for his boys' classes. Since 1946 he had also been professor at the ch. faculty of GITIS. Co-

author (with V. Moritz and A. Chekrygin) of the textbook *Method of Classical Training* (1940) and of *Classical Dance—The School of the Male Dancer* (1971).

Tarentule, La. Ballet in 2 acts and 3 scenes; libr. Scribe; ch. Coralli; mus. Casimir Gide; sets Séchan, Diéterle, Feuchères, and Despléchin; cost. Lormier. Prod. 24 June 1839, Opéra, Paris, with Elssler, Mazilier. Luigi and Lauretta are in love, but when Luigi is bitten by a tarantula Dr Omeopatica agrees to heal him only in return for Lauretta's hand. She agrees, but then pretends that she too has been bitten by the dangerous spider. This causes much confusion, but in the end everything is happily sorted out and Dr. Omeopatica is reunited with his own wife, who had been abducted by robbers. The b. contributed immensely to the popularization of the Tarantella, which became one of Elssler's famous show pieces.

BIBL.: C. W. Beaumont, '*L.T.*' in *Complete Book of Ballets* (London, 1951).

Taubert, Gottfried (*b* Ronneburg, *c.* 1680). Ger. dancing master and writer on dance. Maître de danse in Leipzig, where he published his *Rechtschaffener Tantzmeister* (*The Worthy Dancing Master*) in 1717, a lengthy work containing the first Ger. translation of Feuillet's *Chorégraphie*, and some dances by Feuillet and Pécour. The book is of special interest as it reflects the Fr. dominance on the Eur. dancing scene of its time, and for the wealth of information on Fr. and Ger. dancing masters.

BIBL.: M. H. Winter, in *The Pre-Romantic Ballet* (London, 1974).

Taubert, Karl Heinz (*b* Stettin, 16 Dec. 1912). Ger. professor and teacher of historic dances. Educated Berlin Academy of Music. Now in charge of the historic d. classes at the Berlin Academy of Arts; frequently conducts guest-courses abroad. Author of *Höfische Tänze* (Mainz, 1968) and (with Fritz Feldmann) of 'Historische Tänze der Musikalischen und Choreographischen Weltliteratur', *Die Tanzarchiv Reihe* 15.

Taubert, Manfred (*b* Berlin, 27 Dec. 1935, *d* St. Gallen, 7 Mar. 1986). Ger. dancer, choreographer, and b. master. Studied at West Berlin Op B. School and with T. Gsovsky and Kiss. Member of Berlin Municipal Op. B. 1952–63; eventually became soloist. B. master Salzburg Th. 1963–4, Brunswick State Th. 1964–74, Karlsruhe State Th. 1974–6, and St. Gall since 1980. Ch. many bs., incl the first prod. of G. Humel's *Herodias* (1967), Schoenberg's *Pierrot lunaire* (1968), and the first complete Ger. prod. of Glazunov's *Raymonda* after the Second World War (1969).

Taverner, Sonia (*b* Byfleet, 1936). Brit. dancer. Studied at Elmhurst B. School and Sadler's Wells School. Member of Sadler's Wells B. 1955–6, Royal Winnipeg B. 1956 (also guest ballerina with Les Grand Bs. Canadiens) and principal d. with the Pennsylvania B. Comp. 1971–2.

BIBL.: S. Goodman, 'S.T.', *Dance Magazine* 1967/10.

Tayakina, Tatiana Alexeievna (*b* Kiev. 12 Jan. 1951). Sov. dancer. Studied at Kiev B. School, graduating 1969. Joined Kiev T. Shevtchenko Th. of Op. and D. co., where she dances ballerina roles. Bronze Medal (Varna, 1970).

Taylor, Burton (*b* White Plains, N.Y. 19 Aug. 1943). Amer. dancer. Danced with Amer. B. Th. 1962–8, then with Atlanta B. and New York City Op.; joined Joffrey City Center B. 1969. A stage accident in 1970 forced him to retire for 3 years; rejoined Joffrey B. as a principal d. in 1973. Married to the d. Diana Cartier.

BIBL.: J. Gruen, 'Close-Up: B.T.', *Dance Magazine* 1975/11.

· **Taylor, Jonathan** (*b* Manchester, 2 May 1941). Brit. dancer and choreographer. Studied with Lloyd and A. Hardie. Started as a d. in London prod. of musicals. Member of Massine's B. Europeo in 1960, Amsterdam B. 1960–1, and B. Rambert 1961–73; eventually became principal d. Created leading parts in Morrice's *Conflicts* (1962), *The Travellers* (1963), *The Realms of Choice* (1965), *Hazard* (1967), and *Blind Sight* (1969); Chesworth's *Time Base* (1966), *Pawn to King 5* (1968), and *Four According* (1970); and Tetley's *Ziggurat* (1967), *Embrace Tiger and Return to Mountain* (1968), and *Rag Dances* (1971). Ch. *Diversities* (mus. Badings, 1966), *'Tis Goodly Sport* (Elizabethan mus., 1970), *Listen to the Music* (mus. arr. A. Hymas, 1972), and *Almost an Echo* (mus. Milhaud, 1974; all for B. Rambert). Since leaving the B. Rambert has mainly concentrated on choreographing musicals (*Cockie*, 1973; *The Good Companions*, 1974), but has also ch. bs. in Australia and for Netherlands D. Th. Artistic dir. of Austral. D. Th. 1977–85. Married to the d. and teacher Ariette Taylor.

BIBL.: G. Gow, 'From Rambert to Musicals', *Dancing Times* (1974/3); 'J. T. Talks to Dance and Dancers', *Dance and Dancers* (1979/11).

Taylor, June (*b* Chicago, 1918). Amer. dancer, choreographer, and teacher. Studied with Merriel Abbott. Performed in night clubs and revues until stricken with tuberculosis in 1938. Then formed the J. T. Dancers and gained nation-wide popularity through their participation in the Jackie Gleason TV Show. Now dir. of the J.T. School in New York City.

BIBL.: D. Boroff, 'Schoolmistress J.T.', *Dance Magazine* (1957/2).

Taylor, Paul (*b* Alleghany County, Pa., 29 July 1930). Amer. dancer, choreographer, and b. director. Started as a student of sports, then studied with Graham, Humphrey and Limón, Tudor and Craske. Danced with various modern

comps. (incl. those of Cunningham in 1954, Lang in 1955), in Graham's *Clytemnestra* and *Embattled Garden* (1958), *Alcestis* (1960), and *Phaedra* (1962), and participated in the first prod. of *Episodes* (1959), in which Balanchine ch. a solo for him. His first ch. was *Hobo Ballet* (mus. Ponchielli, Syracuse, 1953). Has had his own comp. since 1954, with which he has appeared all over the world (Spoleto Festival, 1960; Berlin Festival 1963; London début 1964). He is not only one of the most fertile, imaginative, and musical choreographers of his generation, but also possesses a rare sense of humour. The best known of his many bs. include *3 Epitaphs* (mus. Laneville-Johnson Union Brass Band, 1956), *Duet* (mus. Cage, 1957), *Meridian* (mus. Boulez, later replaced by Feldman, 1960), *Insects and Heroes* (mus. J. H. McDowell) and *Junction* (mus. Bach, 1961), *Aureole* (mus. Handel, 1962—revived for several comps.), *Scudorama* (mus. C. Jackson) and *Party Mix* (mus. Haieff, 1963), *Duet* (mus Haydn, 1964), *Post Meridian* (mus. E. Lohoeffer) and *From Sea to Shining Sea* (mus. McDowell, 1965), *Orbs* (mus. Beethoven, 1966), *Agathe's Tale* (mus. Surinach) and *Lento* (mus. Haydn, 1967), *Public Domain* (mus-collage McDowell, 1968), *Churchyard* (mus. Cosmos Savage, 1969), *Foreign Exchange* (mus Subotnik, 1970), *Big Bertha* (mus. Band Machines from the St Louis Melody Museum) and *The Book of Beasts* (various composers 1971), *American Genesis* (various composers, 1973), *Sports and Follies* (mus. Satie, 1974) and *Esplanade* (mus. Bach, 1975), *Cloven Kingdom* (mus. J. H. McDowell) and *Polaris* (mus. Donald York, 1976), *Diggity* (mus. D. York) and *Nightshade* (mus. Scriabin, 1979), *The Rehearsal* (mus. Stravinsky's *Sacre du printemps*, 1980), and *Arden Court* (mus. W. Boyce, 1981). Contrib. 'Down with choreography' to *The Modern Dance* (Middletown, 1965). Best Ch. (Paris D. Festival, 1962); Premio de la Critica (Chile, 1965); Capezio D. Award (1967); Dance Magazine Award (1980); L'Ordre des Arts et des Lettres (1984).

BIBL.: D. McDonagh, 'P.T.—Advanced Ideas and Conventional Theatre' in *The Rise and Fall and Rise of Modern Dance* (New York, 1970); J. Baril, 'P.T.', with complete check-list of roles and activities, *Les Saisons de la danse* (1973/7); L. E. Stern, 'P.T.': Gentle Giant of Modern Dance, *Dance Magazine* (1976/2); J. Anderson, 'Choreographic Fox: P.T.', *Dance Magazine* (1980/4).

Tblisi. See *Tiflis*.

Tchaikovsky, Piotr Ilyich (*b* Votkinsk, 7 May 1840, *d* St Petersburg, 6 Nov. 1893). Russ. composer. Wrote the mus. for 3 bs.: *Swan Lake* (ch. Reisinger, Moscow, 1877—version Petipa and Ivanov, St. Petersburg, 1895), *Sleeping Beauty* (ch. Petipa, St. Petersburg, 1890), and *Nutcracker* (ch. Ivanov, St. Petersburg, 1892). In addition much of his concert mus. has been used for b. purposes, incl. his Serenade for String Orchestra (by Fokine in *Eros*, Petrograd, 1915—also by

The Paul Taylor Dance Company (Gillis and Andrien) in Taylor's *The Rehearsal*.

Photo Lois Greenfield.

Balanchine in *Serenade*, White Plains, N.Y., 1934), *Francesca da Rimini* (by Fokine, Petrograd, 1915—also by Lichine, B. Russe de Colonel de Basil, London, 1937; Lifar, Opéra, Paris 1958), *Romeo and Juliet* (by Bartholin, Paris, 1937—also by Harangozó, Budapest, 1939; Lifar, Monte Carlo, 1946; Skibine in *Tragédie à Vérone*, Grand B. du Marquis de Cuevas, 1950), *Hamlet* (by Helpmann, Sadler's Wells B., London, 1942), the first Suite for Orchestra (by P. Wright in *Mirror Walkers*, Stuttgart, 1963), the third Suite for Orchestra (at first only the last movement by Balanchine in *Theme and Variations*, B. Th., New York, 1947—later the whole score in *Suite No. 3*, New York City B., N.Y., 1970), the fourth Suite for Orchestra (by Balanchine in *Mozartiana*, Les Bs. 1933, Paris, 1933—later also by Hynd, London Festival B., London, 1973), the first Piano Concerto in B flat minor (by Nijinska in *Ancient Russia*, B. Russe de Monte Carlo, Cleveland, 1943), the second Piano

Concerto in G major (by Balanchine in *Ballet Imperial*, Amer. B. Caravan, New York, 1941), the unfinished third Piano Concerto (by Balanchine in *Allegro Brillante*, New York City B., N.Y., 1956), the Rococo Variations for Violoncello and Orchestra (by Harkarvy, Netherlands D. Th., 1968; also by Arpino in *Reflections*, City Center Joffrey B., New York, 1971), the Valse Scherzo for Violin and Orchestra (by Balanchine in *Waltz Scherzo*, New York City B., N.Y., 1958), the first Symphony (the first 2 movements by Bourmeister as part of *Snow Maiden*, London Festival B., London, 1961—the whole score by MacMillan as first act of *Anastasia*, Royal B., London version, 1971; P. Martins, New York City B., 1981), the third Symphony (by MacMillan as second act of *Anastasia*), the fifth Symphony (by Massine in *Les Présages*, B. Russe de Colonel de Basil, Monte Carlo, 1933), the sixth Symphony (by Lifar in *L'Amour et son destin*, Grand B. du Marquis de

Cuevas, Vienna, 1957—parts also by Béjart in *Nijinsky, Clown de Dieu*, B. of the twentieth Century, Brussels, 1971) the Manfred Symphony (by Nureyev, Paris, 1979), the Piano Trio (by Massine in *Aleko*, B. Th., Mexico City, 1942— later the Theme and Variations only by Taras in *Designs with Strings*, Metropolitan B., Edinburgh, 1948), the incidental mus. to Ostrovsky's play *Snow Maiden* by Bourmeister, with other mus. by T., in his b. of the same name, London Festival B., London, 1961), the Pas de deux from the *Swan Lake* Supplement (by Balanchine in *Tchaikovsky Pas de deux*, New York City B., N.Y., 1960—also used in many recent *Swan Lake* prods.). From various lesser known pieces Stolze arr. the score for Cranko's *Onegin* b. (Stuttgart, 1965); full-length b. 'T' (by Horst Mueller, mus. various T., Nuremberg, 1979—another *T*. by D. Vamos (various B., Munich, 1980). V. Panov used various individual movements for his *War and Peace* b. (Ger. Op. Berlin, 1981). In June 1981 the New York City B. held a ten days' T. Festival, with contributions by Balanchine, Robbins, Martins, Taras, d'Amboise, and J. Duell, incl. 12 new bs. to T. mus.

BIBL.: J. Warrack, *T*. (London, 1973); J. Warrack, *T. Ballet Music* (BBC Music Guides, London, 1979). R. J. Wiley, *Tchaikovsky's Bs.* (New York, 1985).

Tchaikovsky Memorial Ballet. The orig. name of the Tokyo-based classical b. comp., now called *Tokyo Ballet Company.

Tchelitchev, Pavel (*b* district of Moscow, 21 Sep. 1898, *d* Rome, 31 July 1957). Russ.–Amer. painter and designer. His b. designs included Massine's *Ode* (B. Russes de Diaghilev, 1928) and *Nobilissima Visione* (B. Russe de Monte Carlo, 1938), and Balanchine's *Errante* (Les Bs. 1933), *Orpheus and Eurydice* (Amer. B., 1936), *Balustrade* (Original B. Russe, 1941), and *Apollon musagète* (Buenos Aires, 1942).

BIBL.: D. Windham, 'The Stage and Ballet Designs of P.T.', *Dance Index* (vol. 3, no. 1).

Tcherepnin, Nicolai Nicolaievich (*b* St. Petersburg, 15 May 1837, *d* Issy-les-Moulineaux, 26 June 1945). Russ. composer. Conductor of the Diaghilev comp. 1909–14; wrote the mus. for Fokine's *Le Pavillon d'Armide* (St. Petersburg, 1907), *Cléopâtre* (with several other composers, Diaghilev comp., 1909), and *Narcisse* (Bs. Russes de Diaghilev, 1912); *Dionysus* (1922), *Russian Fairy Tale* (1923), and *The Romance of a Mummy* (1924) for Pavlova; and *The Goldfish* (1937) for Mordkin. Collaborated with Rimsky-Korsakov on orchestration of Schumann's *Carnaval* (ch. Fokine, Diaghilev's comp., 1910). The father of the comp. Alexander N.T. (*b* 1899, *d* 1977), who wrote the mus. for Pavlova's *Ajanta Frescoes* (1923), Petit's *Déjeuner sur l'herbe* (1945), Lifar's *Chota Roustaveli* (1946), and Charrat's *La Femme et son ombre* (1948).

Tcherina Ludmila (orig. Monique Tchemerzina; *b* Paris, 10 Oct, 1924). Fr. dancer. Studied with Blanche d'Alessandri, Preobrajenska, and Clustine, later also with Ricaux. First appeared when 8 years old. Official début in Lifar's *Roméo et Juliette* in 1942. D. with Kniaseff's comp., at the Opéra de Marseilles, in various Paris d. concerts (with her husband Edmond Audran, who was killed in a car accident in 1951), and with Nouveaux Bs. de Monte Carlo (where she created the ballerina roles in Lifar's *A la memoire d'un héros* and *Mephisto Valse*, 1946). Then appeared as a guest ballerina, notably as Giselle (which she also danced in Moscow) and Dying Swan, but principally in Sparemblek's prod. of *Le Martyre de Saint Sébastien*. Appeared with her own comp. in the Rouleau–Sparemblek prod. of *Les Amants de Teruel* in 1959, which was later filmed. D. with the B. of the Twentieth Century in the Dali–Béjart prod. of *Gala* in 1961. She has participated in several films (*The Red Shoes, Tales of Hoffmann*) and TV prods., and appeared in Lazzini's *The Miraculous Mandarin* (1967), dell'Ara's *Excelsior* (Florence, 1967), and as Fenella in Auber's *La Muette de Portici* (Palermo, 1972). Held an exhibition of her own paintings in Paris in 1973. An unusually beautiful woman, she excelled as a d. in dramatic roles.

BIBL.: I. and S. Lido, *L.T., Tragédienne de la danse* (Paris, 1967).

Tcherkassky, Marianna (*b* Glen Cove, N.Y., 1955). Amer. d. Studied with her mother Lillian T. and later at Washington School of B. and School of Amer. B. D. with A. Eglevsky Comp.; joined Amer. B. Th. 1970 and became a soloist 1973, later also principal. Created a role in Tharp's *Push Comes to Shove* (1976). Married to d. Terry Orr.

BIBL.: J. Gruen, 'Robert La Fosse, M.T., George de la Pena', *Dance Magazine* (1981/9).

Tchernicheva, Lubov Pavlova (*b* St. Petersburg, 17 Sep. 1890, *d* Richmond, Surrey, 1 Mar. 1976). Russ.–Brit. dancer and b. mistress. Studied at Imperial B. Academy; graduated in 1908. Joined Maryinsky Th.; married the b. régisseur Grigoriev in 1909 and joined the Diaghilev comp. with him in 1911. Became a principal d. and remained with the comp. until it closed in 1929; created roles in Massine's *The Good-Humoured Ladies* (1917), *La Boutique fantasque* (1919), *Pulcinella* (1920), and *Le Pas d'acier* (1927), Nijinska's *Les Noces* (1924), and Balanchine's *Jack-in-the-Box* (1926), *Apollon musagète*, and *The Gods Go a-Begging* (1928). Appointed b. mistress in 1926. Joined B. Russe de Monte Carlo with her husband in 1932; occasionally appeared as a d. (created title-role in Lichine's *Francesca da Rimini*, 1937), but worked mainly as b. mistress, e.g. with Original B. Russe 1937–52. During the following years she and her husband continued to stage individual prods. of bs. from the Diaghilev repertory, incl. *Firebird* (Sadler's Wells B., 1954) and *Petrushka* (Royal B.,

1957). Has also worked as a teacher for Sadler's Wells B. and London Festival B.

BIBL.: G. Anthony, 'L.T.', *Dancing Times* (1976/2).

Tedeyev, Vadim Sergeievich (*b* Moscow, 26 July 1946). Sov. dancer. Studied at Moscow Bolshoi School; graduated in 1965. Joined the Stanislavsky and Nemirovich–Danchenko Music Th., and soon became one of its top soloists. Bronze Medal (Moscow, 1973).

Telle, Karl (*b* Berlin, 12 Oct. 1826, *d* Klosterneuburg, Austria, 4 Jan. 1895). Ger. dancer, choreographer, and b. master. Son of Constantin Michel T., who was b. master at the Berlin Court Op. 1813–30; studied with his father and P. Taglioni. He then went to Vienna; b. régisseur and b. master of the Court Op. until 1890, and dir. of its b. school; ch. many bs., incl. the local first prods. of *Coppélia* (1876) and *Sylvia* (1877).

Telloli, Bruno (*b* 1937). Ital. dancer. Studied at Milan La Scala B. School; graduated in 1957. Joined La Scala B.; became soloist in 1958 and eventually principal d.

Tempest, The. Ballet in 2 parts; ch. Tetley; mus. Arne Nordheim; déc. Baylis. Prod. 3 May 1979, B. Rambert, Schwetzingen, with Chr. Bruce, L. Burge, Gianfranco Paluzi, Thomas Yang, Mark Wraith *et al*. Based upon Shakespeare's play, the b. 'is about voyage and loss, and regaining that which is lost' (Tetley). Revived for Norwegian B. (1980). A different b. *T.T.* by M. Smuin (mus. Paul Chihara after Purcell, San Francisco B., 1980). BIBL.: (the Tetley version) P. Brinson and C. Crisp, in *Ballet & Dance* (Newton Abbot, 1980); interview with Tetley in *Dance and Dancers* (1979/5).

Temps. (Fr., time.) Designates in b. a step or movement without any transfer from one foot to the other. It is also used to describe the division of a step into various movement sections.

Tendu. Fr., stretched or held (as in *battement tendu*).

Tennant, Veronica (*b* London, 1946). Brit. dancer. Studied at Cone-Ripman School and Can. National B. School; graduated in 1963 and joined National B. of Can., and eventually became principal d. Order of Can. (1975).

BIBL.: O. Maynard, 'V.T.', *Dance Magazine* (1972/5).

Terabust, Elisabetta (*b* Varese, 5 Aug. 1946). Ital. dancer. Studied at Rome Op. B. School; joined its comp. in 1964 and became prima ballerina in 1966. Has since d. with many Ital. comps. and abroad, frequently (since 1973) with London Festival B. Premio Positano (1969), Le Noci d'oro (Lecce, 1970).

BIBL.: I. Lidova, 'E.T.', *Les Saisons de la danse* (1974/12).

Ter-Arutunian, Rouben (*b* Tiflis, 24 July 1920). Amer. th. designer. His b. designs incl. Bolender's

Souvenirs (1955), Balanchine's *The Seven Deadly Sins* (1958 version), *The Flood* (CBS TV, 1962), *Ballet Imperial* and *Nutcracker* (1964), *Harlequinade* (1965), *Coppélia* (1974), *Union Jack* (1976), and *Davidsbündlertänze* (1980), Graham's *Visionary Recital* (1961), Tetley's *Pierrot lunaire* (1962), *Sargasso* and *Field Mass* (1965), *Ricercare* (1966), *Chronochromie* (1971), *Laborintus* (1972), and *Voluntaries* (1973), Macdonald's *Time Out of Mind* (1963), and Butler's *Villon* (1969). Author of 'In Search of Design', *Dance Perspectives* 28.

BIBL.: A. Fatt, 'Designers for the Dance', *Dance Magazine* (1967/3).

Teresa (Orig. T. Viera-Romero; (*b* New York, 1929). Amer.–Span. dancer. Studied with Lusillo, and married him. D. with the group of Amaya; formed the T. and Luisillo B. Español with her husband in 1949, and performed all over the world.

Terpsichore. One of the 9 Muses of Greek mythology, responsible for choral d. and song. Her attribute is the lyre. Appears in many bs., from Handel's T. prologue for *Pastor fido* and Beethoven's *Creatures of Prometheus* to Stravinsky's *Apollon musagète*.

Terre à terre. (Fr., down to earth.) Designates in b. movements in which the feet hardly leave the ground (as against the steps of élévation). Also used to characterize a more earth-bound d. (e.g. Elssler as compared with Taglioni, who was considered a danseuse aérienne).

Terry, Walter (*b* New York, 14 May 1913, *d* N.Y., 4 Oct. 1982). Amer. writer on d. Educated Univ. of N. Carolina. Studied d. with Markova, Dolin, Vilzak, Joffrey, Shawn, Graham, Humphrey, Limón, and others. D. critic of *Boston Herald* 1936–9, *New York Herald Tribune* 1939–42 and 1945–67, *World Journal Tribune* 1967–8, and *Saturday Review/World* since 1968. Also worked as a lecturer, instructor, and d. consultant. Dir. of Jacob's Pillow Festival, 1973. Author of many books, incl. *Star Performance* (1954), *Ballet* (1958), *The Dance in America* and *The Ballet Companion* (1968), *Isadora Duncan: Her Life, Her Art, Her Legacy*, and *Miss Ruth—The More Living Life of Ruth St. Denis* (1969), *Ted Shawn—Father of American Dance* (1976), *I Was There* (selected reviews and articles, 1978), *The King's Balletmaster*. (1980). Contributor to *Encyclopedia Britannica*, *Dance Encyclopedia*, etc. Capezio Prize, 1980.

Ter-Weeme, Mascha (*b* Amsterdam, 17 Oct. 1902). Dutch dancer, choreographer, and b. director. Studied with Wigman, Georgi, Schwezoff, V. Gsovsky, and others. Soloist with and asst. to Georgi 1936–44. Founder of B. der Lage Landen 1947–59 and of Amsterdam Op. B. 1959–61.

Testa, Alberto (*b* Torino, 23 Dec. 1922). Ital. dance publicist. Studied with S. Egri and at univ. of Torino. D. with the cos. of Massine (*Laudes*

Evangelii), Wallmann (Salzburg Festival, 1955) and in various bs. by Milloss, Egri, Charrat, Nives Poli, *et al.* Has worked as ch. for op. and in films (Visconti's *The Leopard*, 1962, Zeffirelli's *Romeo and Juliet*, 1967, etc). Teacher of history of d. at Rome National Academy of D. since 1963. D. critic and correspondent of various journals and magazines, incl. *La Repubblica, Il Dramma, Sipario, Les Saisons de la danse, Enciclopedia dello spettacolo,* and *Enciclopedia Musica Ricordi.* Organized exhibitions on Diaghilev (La Scala, 1972, Rome, 1977). Author of *Discorso sulla Danza e sul Balletto* (Rome, 1970). Premio Positano Arte della Danza (1969).

Tetley, Glen (*b* Cleveland, 3 Feb. 1926). Amer. dancer, choreographer, and b. director. Studied medicine, then dance with Holm, Craske, Tudor, and Graham. As Holm's asst. started to d. in mus. prods. and with her comp. 1946–51, then with New York City Op. 1952–4, Butler's comp. in 1955, Joffrey B. 1956–7, Graham comp. in 1958 (creating roles in *Clytemnestra* and *Embattled Garden*), Amer. B. Th. in 1960, and Robbins's Bs.: U.S.A. in 1961. Joined Netherlands D. Th. as a d. and ch. in 1962; eventually became artistic adviser (with Van Manen, until 1970). Had his own comp. in 1969, with which he toured Europe. Succeeded Cranko as dir. of the Stuttgart B. 1974–6. As a ch. he started with uncompromisingly modern works, and it was not until the early 1970's that elements of the academic vocabulary began to show in his bs., which are generally characterized by an unemotional coolness and enigmatic aloofness. Started to choreograph in 1948; made a break-through with *Pierrot lunaire* (mus. Schoenberg) in 1962. Has since ch. a great number of bs., e.g. *The Anatomy Lesson* (mus. M. Landowski, Netherlands D. Th.) and *Sargasso* (mus. Krenek, Netherlands D. Th., 1964), *Mythical Hunters* (mus. O. Partos, Batsheva D. Comp., 1965), *Ricercare* (mus. M. Seter Amer. B.. Th., 1966), *Freefall* (mus. M. Schubel, Univ. of Utah Repertory D. Th.) and *Ziggurat* (mus. Stockhausen, B. Rambert, 1967), *Circles* (mus. Berio, Netherlands D. Th.) and *Embrace Tiger and Return to Mountain* (mus. Subotnik, B. Rambert, 1968), *Arena* (mus. Subotnik, Netherlands D. Th., 1969), *Field Figures* (mus. Stockhausen, Royal B.), *Imaginary Film* (mus. Schoenberg), and *Mutations* (with Van Manen, mus. Stockhausen, both Netherlands D. Th., 1970), *Rag Dances* (mus. A. Hymes, B. Rambert) and *Chronochromie* (mus. Messiaen, Hamburg State Op., 1971—an earlier version at Jacob's Pillow, 1966), *Threshold* (mus. Berg, Hamburg State Op.), *Small Parades* (mus. Varèse, Netherlands D. Th.) and *Laborintus* (mus. Berio, Royal B., 1972), *Voluntaries* (mus. Poulenc, Stuttgart B., 1973), *Le Sacre du printemps* (mus. Stravinsky, Munich State Op.) and *Tristan* (mus. Henze, Opèra, Paris, 1974), *Daphnis and Chloe* (mus. Ravel) and *Greening* (mus. A. Nordheim, both Stuttgart B., 1975), *The Tempest* (mus.

Nordheim, B. Rambert, 1979), *Dances of Albion* (mus. Britten, Royal B., 1980), *Summer's End* (mus. Dutilleux, Netherlands D. Th., 1980). Became art. adviser for Nat. b. of Canada in 1987.
BIBL.: G. Loney, 'Dutch Mutations', *Dance Magazine* (1971/2); J. Percival, 'G.T.' in *Experimental Dance* (London, 1971).

Thaïs Pas de deux. See *Meditation from 'Thaïs'.*

Thamar. Ballet in 1 act; libr. and déc. Bakst; ch. Fokine; mus. Balakirev. Prod. 20 May 1912, Bs. Russes de Diaghilev, Th. du Châtelet, Paris, with Karsavina, Bolm. The b. tells the legend of T., Queen of Georgia, who disposes of her lovers by stabbing them and throwing their corpses from her turret into the waters below.
BIBL.: C. W. Beaumont, 'T.' in *Complete Book of Ballets* (London, 1951).

Tharp, Twyla (*b* Portland, Ind., 1 July 1942). Amer. dancer and choreographer. Studied with Schwezoff, Mattox, Graham, Nikolais, M. Cunningham and P. Taylor; d. in Taylor's comp. 1963–5. Has since worked as a freelance ch. with her own group and with various other comps. One of the most discussed figures of the contemporary d. scene; the flippant and often amusing surface of her bs. conceals the meticulously worked structure of a perfectionist craftsman. Her bs. include *Tank Dive* and *Cede Blue Lake* (1965), *Re-Moves* (1966), *Dancing in the Streets of London, and Paris, Continued in Stockholm and Sometimes in Madrid* (1969), *The Fugue and Eight Jelly Rolls* (1971), *The Bix Pieces* (1972), *Deuce Coupe* and *As Time Goes By* (both for City Center Joffrey B., 1973), *In the Beginning* (1974), *Ocean's Motion* (mus. Chuck Berry, 1975), and *Push Comes to Shove* (mus. Haydn, Amer. B. Th., 1976) and *When We Were Very Young* (own co., 1980). D. Magazine Award, 1981.
BIBL.: M. B. Siegel, in *The Shapes of Change* (Boston, 1979); A. Robertson, 'T. Comes to Shove', *Ballet News* (1980/3); M. Robertson, 'Fifteen Years: T.T.', *Dance Magazine* (1980/3).

That Is the Show. Ballet in 5 movements; ch. Morrice; mus. Berio; déc. Baylis. Prod. 6 May 1971, B. Rambert, J. Cochrane Th., London, with Craig, Bruce. The title is a quotation from the 3rd movement of Berio's *Sinfonia*. The b. has no continuous narrative, but is concerned with various themes suggested to the ch. by the words and mus. of the score, incl. the idea of heroes and especially of their womenfolk, in myth and in modern life. Morrice's b. includes the 5th movement added to the *Sinfonia* by Berio. Revived for Cologne D. Forum in 1975. Other ch. treatments of Berio's orig. 4-movement *Sinfonia* include Butler's *Itinéraire* (B. Th. Contemporain, 1970), Van Manen's *Keep Going* (Düsseldorf B., 1971), and Lubovitch's *Whirligogs* (3rd movement only, Bat-Dor Comp.).

Théâtre du Silence. A Fr. modern d. troupe of

ten-plus dancers, established in 1971 by Brigitte Lefèvre and Jacques Garnier, and based upon the city of La Rochelle. Apart from the 2 artistic directors, other contributing choreographers incl. M. Cunningham, Lubovitch, and Béjart. U.S. début, New York, March, 1978.

Theatre Piece. Dance in 8 parts; ch. Humphrey; mus. W. Riegger; cost. P. Lawrence. Prod. 19 Jan. 1936, Humphrey-Weidman Comp., Guild Th., New York. The centrepiece of a trilogy (the other 2 pieces being *New Dance* and *With My Red Fires*), this group work for 19 dancers 'depicts the world, as it is today: a place of grim competition. Miss Humphrey has called it *Theatre Piece* to stress the fact that, even though this savage competition is dominant at the present time, it is far from being the whole of life. It distorts and kills too much of life that is good and erects symbols and numbers and figures in place of human values. Throughout the d., Miss Humphrey plays the part of one who rebels against this way of life and prophesies a better way of living' (Doris Humphrey papers).

Theilade, Nini (*b* Java, 1916). Dan. dancer and choreographer. Studied with Asta Møllerup, C. Ari, and Egorova. Had her first success in M. Reinhardt's Berlin prods. and then started to tour as a concert d. Ch. he first b. *Psyché* (mus. C. Franck) for Royal Dan. B. in 1936. Member of B. Russe de Monte Carlo 1938–40; created roles in Massine's *Nobilissima Visione* (1938), *Seventh Symphony*, and *Bacchanale* (1939). Then settled in Brazil; appeared occasionally with comps. there and returned to Europe from time to time. Ch. *Cirklen* (mus. Tchaikovsky's Sixth Symphony, 1938), *Concerto* (mus. Schumann's Piano Concerto, 1950), and *Kalkbillede* (mus. K. Høgenhaven, 1968) for Royal Dan. B. Has had a school in Svendborg, Denmark, since 1970.

Theme and Variations. Ballet in 1 act; ch. Balanchine; mus. Tchaikovsky; déc. Woodman Thompson. Prod. 26 Nov. 1947, B. Th., New York, with Alonso, Youskevitch. A plotless b., set to the final movement of Tchaikovsky's Suite for Orchestra, no. 3, in G major. In 1970 Balanchine ch. in addition the first 3 movements; the complete b. is now called **Suite No. 3*.
BIBL.: G. Balanchine, 'T.a.V.' in *Balanchine's New Complete Stories of the Great Ballets* (Garden City, N.Y., 1968).

Théodore, Mlle. (orig. Marie-Madeleine Crépé; (*b* Paris, 6 Oct. 1760, *d* Audenge, 9 Sept. 1796). Fr. dancer. Studied with Lany, début Paris Opéra in 1777, where she was very popular in bs. by Noverre and Gardel. Her outspokenness frequently got her into trouble, and she was even imprisoned in 1782, for campaigning against the administration of the Opéra. She was the wife of Dauberval and created Lise in the Bordeaux first prod. of *La Fille mal gardée* in 1789. She was much admired by Noverre and Rousseau.

There Is a Time. Ballet in 1 act; ch. Limón; mus. Dello Joio; cost. P. Lawrence. Prod. 20 Apr. 1956, J. Limón D. Comp., Juilliard Concert Hall, New York, with Limón, Koner, Currier, B. Jones, L. Nielsen, Hoving. 'To everything there is a season, and a time to every purpose under the heaven' (Ecclesiastes).

There Was a Time. Ballet in 1 act; ch. Bruce; mus. B. Hodgson; déc. Baylis. Prod 10 Jan. 1973, B. Rambert, Young Vic, London, with Avrahami, L. Warren, Blaikie. 'There was a time when the countless tribes of men, though wide-dispersed, oppressed the surface of the deep-bosomed earth, and Zeus saw it and had pity and in his wise heart resolved to relieve the all-nurturing earth of men by causing the great struggle of the Ilian war, that the load of death might empty the world' (Homer). Revived for Munich State Op. B. in the same year.

Thesmar, Ghislaine (*b* Peking, 1943). Fr. dancer. Studied at the Paris Conservatoire. Début with Grand B. du Marquis de Cuevas in 1961. D. mainly with Lacotte's comp., and became his wife in 1968. Also d. with B. Rambert, Petit, Grands Bs. Canadiens, and since 1972 as an étoile at the Opéra. Created title-role in Lacotte's TV. prod. of *La Sylphide* (1971). Jt. dir. B. de Monte C. since 1985.
BIBL.: I. Lidova, 'G.T.', *Les Saisons de la danse* (1971/6); J. Gruen, 'G.T.', *Dance Magazine* (1979/8).

Thibon, Nanon (*b* Paris, 1 Nov. 1943). Fr. dancer. Studied at Paris Opéra B. School. Joined the comp. in 1958, and became première danseuse in 1963 and étoile in 1965. Created several roles in bs. by Adret, Descombey, Lifar, and in Petit's *Turangalîla* (1968), Charrat's *Hyperprism* (1973), and Tetley's *Tristan* (1974). Prix René Blum (1960).
BIBL.: A. P. Hersin, 'N.T.', with complete checklist of roles and activities, *Les Saisons de la danse* (1971/12).

Third Symphony by Gustav Mahler (orig. Ger. title: *Dritte Sinfonie von Gustav Mahler*). Ballet in 6 movements; ch. Neumeier; projections Marco Arturo Morelli. Prod. 14 June 1975, Hamburg State Op. B., with F. Klaus, Z. Rodriguez. The b., which lasts almost 2 hours, has no real plot. It reflects the content of Mahler's 6 movements, retitled by Neumeier Yesterday, Summer, Autumn, Night, Angel, and What Love Tells Me. It shows Man's inextinguishable desire for beauty and the ideal in a world falling to pieces. TV prod. in 1976. For different treatment of the symphony's last 3 movements only see Béjart's *Ce que l'amour me dit* (1974).

Thomas, Robert (*b* Lyon, 3 May 1944). Fr. dancer and choreographer. Studied at Opéra de Lyon B. School. D. with Lyon b. 1964–8, B. of the Twentieth Century 1968–71, Strasbourg b. 1972–8. Started to choreograph for B. of the Twentieth Century, continuing with B. du Rhin (Mulhouse), with *La Chaise* (mus. Charles Chaynes, 1976) and *Carmina Burana* (mus. Orff, 1977) as his most important contributions.

Thompson, Clive (*b* Kingston, Jamaica, 20 Oct. *c*. 1940). Brit. dancer. Studied with Ivy Baxter and d. with her comp. Went to New York in 1960; studied with Graham and joined her comp. in 1961. Created roles in her *One More Gaudy Night* (1961), *Secular Games* (1962), and *Circe* (1963). Has since d. with many modern groups, incl. those of Beatty, Lang, Yuriko, and Ailey. Now dir. C. T. Dance Co.

Thorogood, Alfreda (*b* Lambeth, 17 Aug. 1942). Brit. dancer. Studied with Volkova, Goncharov, Nancy Robinson, and at Sadler's Wells School. Joined Touring Royal B. in 1960; became soloist in 1965 and principal d. in 1968. Left the comp. in 1975 but rejoined the Royal B. in the same year. Created roles in Tudor's *Knight Errant* (1968), Cauley's *In the Beginning* (1969) and *Symphonie pastorale*, and Ashton's *Creatures of Prometheus* (1970). Married to the d. David Wall. Her sister Patricia T. was also a d. with the Royal B.

Thorpe, Jonathan (*b* Birmingham, 12 Oct. 1943). Brit. dancer, choreographer, and b. master. Studied with Dulcie Pyne and at Royal B. School. A. Hardie School, and Folkwang School. Member of Oldenburg B. 1964–5, Lübeck B. 1965–6, Folkwang B. 1966–7, and Düsseldorf B. 1967–9; joined Northern D. Th. in 1970, and was resident ch. to 1979. Began to choreograph with *Tancredi e Clorinda* (mus. Monteverdi, 1970); his further bs. include *Quartet* (mus. Beethoven, op. 130, 1971), *The Wanderer and His Shadow* (mus. Brahms, 1972), *Part Exchange* (no mus. 1973), *A Woman's Love* (mus. Schumann, 1974), *Stamping Ground* (mus. Bach, 1975), *Triptych* (mus. Beethoven, 1975), *Spring Song* (mus. Dvořák, 1976), *Madam Butterfly* (mus. Puccini, 1979).
BIBL.: Interview with J.T. (with complete list of bs.), *Dance and Dancers* (1975/4).

Three-Cornered Hat, The (also *Le Tricorne*). Ballet in 1 act ; libr. Martinez Sierra; mus. de Falla; ch. Massine; déc. Picasso. Prod. 22 July 1919, Bs. Russes de Diaghilev, Alhambra Th., London, with Massine, Karsavina, Woizikovsky, Idzikowski. The b. is based on Pedro Antonio de Alarcon's story *El sombrero de tres picos* (1874), from which Sierra and de Falla had already drawn the pantomime *El Corregidor y la Molinera*. It tells of a highly attractive Miller's Wife, her extremely jealous husband, and the senile Corregidor who pursues her, but is humiliatingly rebuffed. The many revivals personally staged by Massine include those for B. Th. (1943), Sadler's Wells B. (1947), Vienna State Op. B. (1964), City Center Joffrey B. (1969), and London Festival B. (1973). Unitel TV prod. of Antonio version, 1974.
BIBL.: C. W. Beaumont, '*L.T.*' in *Complete Book of Ballets* (London, 1951); anon., 'The Making of *T.T.-C.H.*', *Dance Magazine* (1969/9).

3 Epitaphs. Ballet for 5 dancers; ch. P. Taylor; mus. Laneville–Johnson Union Brass Band; cost. Rauschenberg. Prod. 1956, P. Taylor D. Comp., Henry St. Playhouse, New York. Created in 1953 as *Four Epitaphs*. The b. shows the macabre antics of dancers in coal-black costumes with tiny mirrors; these costs. completely cover the dancers' faces and bodies, making them look completely depersonalized. The movements are often comical. Revived for London Contemporary D. Th. in 1970. Cologne TV prod. 1969.

Three Fat Men, The (orig. Russ. title: *Tritolstyaka*). Ballet in 4 acts and 8 scenes; libr. Yuri Olesha; ch. Moiseyev; mus. V. A. Oransky; déc. B. A. Matrunine. Prod. 1 Mar. 1935, Bolshoi Th., Moscow, with A. Bulgakov, Radunsky, Rudenko, Lepeshinskaya, Messerer. The 3 protagonists are representatives of capitalism at its worst; they throw the revolutionary Prospero into prison, but he teaches them a lesson and, with the help of his lover, the circus artiste Suok, leads the workers to victory against the vicious capitalists.
BIBL.: C. W. Beaumont, '*T.T.F.M.*' in *Complete Book of Ballets* (London, 1951).

Three Ivans. The d. of Innocent Ivan and his Brothers was interpolated by Diaghilev in the last act divertissement of his London prod. of *The Sleeping Princess* in 1921. It was not in Petipa's original St. Petersburg prod. It is performed to the Coda from the final Grand Pas de Deux, reorchestrated by Stravinsky and ch. by Nijinska. De Valois created a new version for the Royal B's. 1964 prod.

Three Musketeers, The. (orig. Dan. title: *De Tre Musketerer*). Ballet in 2 acts; libr. and ch. Flindt; mus. Georges Delerue; déc. Daydé. Prod. 11 May 1966, Royal Dan. B., Copenhagen, with Kronstam, Simone, Laerkesen, Ryberg, Martins, J. Madsen. Based on A Dumas's novel *Les trois mousquetaires* (1844), the b. tells of the adventures of the young Gascon d'Artagnan and his 3 comrades Athos, Aramis, and Porthos in the service of their beautiful queen, and of the obstacles they have to overcome due to the sinister machinations of Cardinal Richelieu and his attractive spy, Milady de Winter. Revived for Munich State Op. in 1967. A Sov. version of the same plot by Boyartchikov (mus. V. Basner, Maly Th., Leningrad, 1964), another version by A. Drokovsky (mus. Verdi/Woolfenden, Austral. B., 1980).

Three Virgins and a Devil. Ballet in 1 act; libr. Ramon Reed; ch. de Mille; mus. Respighi; set Arne Lundborg; cost. Motley. Prod. 11 Feb. 1941, B. Th., Majestic Th., New York, with de Mille, Chase, Lyon, Loring, Robbins. The b. shows how the Devil tricks the Priggish One, the Greedy One, and the Lustful One into going to hell.
BIBL.: G. Balanchine and F. Mason, in *Balanchine's Complete Stories of the Great Ballets* (Garden City, N.Y., 1977).

Tietz, Michael (*b* Grömitz, 28 Aug. 1948). Ger. dancer. Studied with G. Blank, R. Franchetti, E. Ward, and H. Zaraspe. Joined Basle co. 1967, Dutch National B. 1968, and Ger. Op. Berlin as a soloist 1973. With his wife, the dancer Yvonne Vendrig, opened b. school in West Berlin 1974. Has occasionally ch. for West Berlin Academy of Arts.

Tiflis (now called Tbilisi). During the nineteenth century b. perfs. were restricted to guest appearances of groups from St. Petersburg. The city's op. house—now called the Georgian Academic Opera and B. Th. S.P. Paliashvili—was opened in 1896, with a b. comp. of 12 dancers. For many years Maria Petrini was prima ballerina. The b. repertory offered works by Tchaikovsky, Glazunov, and others, and guests included the Fokines, Kschessinska, Preobrajenska, and Geltzer. During the pre-revolutionary era the troupe was led by S. Vakaretz and M. Bauersacks and (1920–2) by Mordkin. During these years the comp. had 38 members, and the first bs. on national subjects included *Iranian Pantomime* (1914), *The Love Potion* (1920), *Msetamze* (1926), and *Chandzari* (1930)—all composed by Tamara Vakhvakhisvili. During the later 1920s bs. were ch. e.g. by M. Dyskovsky, M. Moiseyev (*Swan Lake*, *Giselle*), S. Sergeyev (*Carnaval*, *Firebird*, *Sheherazade*, etc.), V. Zaplin (*Red Poppy*), L. Lukin (*Carmencita*), and R. Balanotti. In the 1930s Chaboukiani started his meteoric career; he was the first local d. to win international renown. In 1936 he ch. the first really important national b.: *Msetchabouki* (later the revised version was called *The Heart of the Hills*), followed by the first national b. with a contemporary subject, *Maltakva*, in 1938. By this time the comp. had grown to 70 dancers. Chaboukiani was appointed b. master and principal d. in 1941, and ch. the repertory's backbone of bs.: *The Heart of the Hills* (1938), *Sinatle* (1947), *Gorda* (1949), *For Peace* (1953), *Othello* (1957—filmed in 1960), *Demon* (1961), and *Ballet Poem* (1963), but he was also in charge of all the big. prods. of classics. Other bs. were ch. by Gulbat Davitashvili, S. Kikaleishvili, and R. Zulukidze. Chaboukiani led the comp. on its first visits to the West (Vienna, 1958, Paris, 1966). After Chaboukiani's resignation in 1972, the comp. was directed by Georgi Alexidze, and then for a time by M. L. Lavrovsky. The first local dance studio was opened in 1902, and Perini established a b. school in 1916, which became the official op. b. school in 1921. It became the State Ch. School in 1925 and was completely reorganized by D. Dsharvrishvili in 1934.

Tights. The tight-fitting garment of wool, cotton, silk, or nylon which covers the dancer's body from the waist down.

Tikhomirnova, Irina Victorovna (*b* Moscow, 18 July 1917). Sov. dancer and teacher. Studied at Bolshoi School, graduating in 1936. Joined Bolshoi B. as a soloist the same year and soon came to d. the ballerina roles. Created Asol in Popko's, Pospekhin's, and Radunsky's *Crimson Sails* (1942). Toured extensively with her husband A. Messerer; also collaborated with him as a b. mistress and asst. B. mistress of Moiseyev's Young B. Stalin Prize (1947); Merited Artist of the R.S.F.S.R. (1951).

Tikhomirov, Vassili Dimitrievich (*b* Moscow, 30 Mar. 1876, *d* there, 20 June 1956). Russ. dancer, choreographer, and teacher. Studied at Bolshoi School; graduated in 1891. Studied further with Gerdt and Johansson in St. Petersburg; d. at the Maryinsky Th. Joined Bolshoi B. in 1893, and was soon acknowledged as its leading principal d. His best roles were in *Raymonda*, *Le Corsaire*, and *Esmeralda*. Appeared in London in Gorsky's *Dance Dream* in 1911, and became Pavlova's partner during her 1914 tour. Appeared mostly with Geltzer, who was his pupil and later his wife. As a d. he possessed a singular athletic plasticity which he tried to pass on to his pupils. Started to teach in 1896 and became one of the most famous teachers of his time; his pupils included Novikov, Volinine, T. and A. Koslov, Messerer, and the ballerinas Karalli, Balashova, and Krieger. After the October Revolution he fought courageously for the preservation of the classics. Succeeded Gorsky as dir. of the Bolshoi B. and its school 1925–30. He staged the classics and the first prod. of Glière's *Red Poppy* with Lastshilin in 1927. Continued to teach until 1937 and is considered one of the greatest teachers in the history of the Russ. b.
BIBL.: various authors, *V.D.T.—Artist, Ballet-Master, and Teacher* (Moscow, 1971—in Russ.).

Tikhonov, Vladimir Petrovich (*b* Kishinev, 24 Oct 1935). Sov. dancer. Studied at Leningrad Ch. School. Joined Kishinev B. in 1957; transferred to Bolshoi B. as a soloist in 1960. Created a role in Kasatkina-Vassiliov's *Vanina Vanini* (1962). Gold Medal (Varna, 1965).

Till Eulenspiegel (also Til or Tyl E. or Ulenspiegel). R Strauss's op. 28, *T.E.'s Merry Pranks* (1895), has inspired several bs., e.g. by Nijinsky (Bs. Russes de Diaghilev, New York, 1916), V. Kratina (Berlin, 1940), Babilée (Bs. des Champs-Elysées, Paris, 1949), and Balanchine (New York City B., N.Y., 1951).
BIBL.: the Nijinsky version, R. Buckle, in *Nijinsky* (London, 1971); the Balanchine version G. Balanchine, '*T.E.*' in *Balanchine's New Complete Stories of the Great Ballets* (Garden City, N.Y., 1968).

Tiller Girls. Troupes of English dancing girls trained by Mrs John Tiller for mus. and variety shows; their name is proverbial for precision of ensemble work.

Tilt. Ballet in 2 parts; ch. Van Manen; mus. Stravinsky; déc. Vroom. Prod. 14 Dec. 1971,

Netherlands D. Th., Rotterdam, with Lodewijk, Lemaitre, Van Boven, Benoit, Westerdijk, and Tipton. The purely formal b. for 3 couples, performed to Stravinsky's Concerto in D (to which Robbins ch. his b. *The Cage*), is given twice over, but the second time with the boys and girls exchanging parts. Revived for Royal B. and Cologne D. Forum in 1973.

Time Out of Mind. Ballet in 1 act; ch. MacDonald; mus. P. Creston; déc. Ter-Arutunian. Prod. 5 Sep. 1963, R. Joffrey B., Delacorte Th., New York, with M. Mercier, L. Rhodes. A modern fertility rite, in which man's primitive instincts are released. Revived for Harkness B. in 1965, later also for Royal Swed. B. and Dutch National B.
BIBL.: G. Balanchine, 'T.O.o.M.' in Balanchine's *New Complete Stories of the Great Ballets* (Garden City, N.Y., 1968).

Timofeyeva, Nina Vladimirovna (*b* Leningrad, 11 June 1935). Sov. dancer. Studied at Leningrad Choreographic School; graduated in 1953 and became a member of the Kirov Th. Joined Bolshoi B. as a soloist in 1956; soon became one of the co.'s best known ballerinas. Created title-role in Vinogradov's *Asel* (1967), Aegina in Grigorovich's *Spartacus* (1968), and another role in Boccadoro's *Love for Love* (1976). Was married to the conductor Gennadi Rozhdestvensky. People's Artist of the R.S.F.S.R. (1969).
BIBL.: B. Lwow-Anochin, 'N.T.', *Ballet Today* (1960/7).

Tippet, Clark (*b* Parsons, Kan., 5 Oct. 1954). Amer. dancer. Studied at Amer. B. Th. School. Joined Amer. B. Th. 1972, appointed soloist, 1975, principal d., 1976. Created part in Tharp's *Push Comes to Shove* (1976). Appears in the film *The Turning Point* (1977). Joined Cleveland B. in 1979, has since returned to Amer. B. Th.
BIBL.: N. MacLain Stoop, 'C.T.', *Dance Magazine* (1977/5); W. Salisbury, 'T.: Comeback in Cleveland,' *Dance Magazine* (1979/11).

Tiresias. Ballet in 3 scenes; libr. and mus. C. Lambert; ch. Ashton; déc. Isabel Lambert. Prod. 9 July 1951, Sadler's Wells B., Cov. Gdn., London, with Fonteyn, Somes, Field. The b. shows T's double life as a man and woman; he is struck blind by Hera when he proves her wrong in her argument with Zeus that a man's life is the happier one, and Zeus thereupon bestows on him the gift of prophecy.
BIBL.: C. W. Beaumont, 'T.' in *Ballets of Today* (London, 1954); D. Vaughan, *Frederick Ashton and his Ballets* (London, 1977).

Titus, Antoine. Fr. b. master and choreographer. He was b. master at the Berlin Court Op. 1824–32, where he staged many of the b. successes of the international repertory. Then went to St. Petersburg, where he succeeded Didelot as b. master (with Blache) of the Bolshoi Th. 1832–49.

Sov. b. historians have treated him rather harshly, blaming him with the failure of the first prods. of Glinka's *Ivan Susanin* (orig. *A Life for the Tsar*, 1836) and *Ruslan and Ludmila* (1842), for which he created the bs. Staged the St. Petersburg first prods. of Taglioni's *La Sylphide* and *Révolte au Sérail* in 1839, and the first Russ. *Giselle* prod. in 1842.

Tivoli Pantomime Theatre. Opened in 1874 as part of the Copenhagen Tivoli Gardens. Not only mime plays but also small bs. are regularly performed there, based upon commedia dell'arte characters.

Tobias, Tobi (*b* New York, 12 Sep. 1938). Amer. writer and editor. Studied at Barnard College (B.A., 1959) and New York Univ. (M.A., 1962). Joined *Dance Magazine* as contributing editor, becoming associate editor and editor of criticism 1976. Teaches d. criticism at Barnard College; other professional activities incl. lecturing, adjudicating, and editorial consultation. Has written various books for children, d. subjects incl. *Maria Tallchief* (1972) and *Arthur Mitchell* (1975).

Tokyo Ballet Company (orig. Tchaikovsky Memorial Ballet). The co. emerged from the city's first classical b. school, the Tokyo Ballet Gakko, which was founded by Koichi Hayashi in 1960 and, from its very beginnings, strongly dominated by Sov. teachers and teaching methods. The school and troupe were completely reorganized by Tadatsugu Sasaki in 1964, their activities vastly expanded, and a solid repertory of classics built up, mostly based upon Sov. models supplemented by contemporary works by such choreographers as Descombey, Petit, Blaska, Hynd, and A. Alonso. The co., now under the artistic direction of its star-dancer Hideteru Kitahara, performs all over Japan; it paid its first visit to the U.S.S.R. in 1966 and to Western Eur. in 1970 (Brit. in 1975).

Tokyo Ballet Concours. Officially termed World Ballet Concours, but always referred to as Tokyo Concours, the intern. competition was started 1976 and first repeated 1978. Entry is for pas de deux couples only and each participant must be over 17 years of age. There are gold, silver, and bronze medals (with prize money) and special prizes and nominations. Winners so far incl. L. Smorgacheva, J. Kurova, S. Lukin, and L. Kafka.
BIBL.: O. Maynard, 'A Dance Agon in Japan', *Dance Magazine* (1978/7).

Tomasson, Helgi (*b* Reykjavik, 1942). Icelandic dancer. Studied with Sigridur Arman, Erik Bidsted, Volkova, and at School of Amer. B. Début with Copenhagen Tivoli B. in 1958. Joined R. Joffrey B. in 1961, Harkness B. as a soloist in 1964, and New York City B. as a principal d. in 1970. Created roles in Walker's *Night Song* and Butler's *A Season in Hell* (1967), Neumeier's *Stages and Reflections* (1968), Harkarvy's *La Favorita* (1969), Robbins' *The Goldberg Variations* (1971) and *Dybbuk Variations* (1974), and Balanchine's *Symphony in Three Movements, Divertimento from 'Le Baiser de la Fée'* (1972), *Coppélia* (1974), and *Vienna Waltzes* (1977). Contributor to 'The Male Image', *Dance Perspectives* 40. Has worked as a ch. since 1982; retired from dancing 1985. Now art. dir. of San Francisco B. Married to the former d. Marlene Rizzo. Silver Medal (Moscow, 1969); Knight of the Order of the Falcon (Iceland, 1974). BIBL.: J. Gruen, 'H.T.', in *The Private World of Ballet* (New York, 1975); E. Taub, 'Just About Perfect', *Ballet News* (1980/7).

Tomaszewski, Henryk (*b* Poznan, 20 Nov. 1925). Pol. dancer, choreographer and director of his pantomime troupe. Studied at Cracow B. School. D. with the co. of F. Parnell and at Warsaw Teatr Wielki. Established the Pol. Mime B. Th. in Wroclaw in 1956, with which he has since toured the whole world, developing a strongly dance-orientated from of pantomime. Has occasionally ch. some bs., incl. *Bagage* (mus. Pergolesi, Royal Dan. B., 1969) and *Before Five Years Passed* (mus. J. Luciuk, Dutch National B., 1972).

Tombé. (Fr., fallen.) Designates in b. the fall from one leg to the other, or from both feet to one, with knees bent on landing.

Tomsky, Alexander Romanovich (*b* Moscow, 3 Jan. 1905, *d* Milan, 27 Sep. 1970). Sov. dancer, choreographer, b. master, and b. director. Studied at Moscow Bolshoi B. School; joined Bolshoi B. in 1923, and later became soloist (until 1954). Started to work as a ch. in 1929; frequently sent to other cities to stage such bs. as *Red Poppy, Le Corsaire, Svetlana, Fountain of Bakhchisaray,* and *The Stone Flower.* B. master of Bolshoi B. 1948–51, artistic dir. 1957–9. Artistic dir. of the b. co. at Stanislavsky and Nemirovich–Danchenko Music Th. 1962–4, and b. master of the Bolshoi B. from 1964 until his death. BIBL.: O. Maynard, interview with A.T., *Dance Magazine* (1968/8).

Toreadoren. Idyllic b. in 2 acts; libr. and ch. August Bournonville; mus. comp. and arr. E. Helsted. Prod. 27 Nov. 1840, Royal Dan. B., Royal Th., Copenhagen. The plot centers upon Maria, the beautiful daughter of a Span. inn-keeper, and the handsome toreador Alonzo, who love each other deeply but have to undergo some trials when the pretty Fr. ballerina Céleste turns up, seducing every male through her charms, including the two visiting Eng. tourists Mr. Arthur and Mr. William. It enjoyed enormous popularity and survived in different prods. until 1929. It was again revived on 17 Mar. 1978, ch. and prod. F. Flindt (Span. dances with the collaboration of J. Udaeta), mus. Erling D. Bjerno after Helsted, déc. Hans Chr. Molbech, Royal Dan. B., Copenhagen, with I. Andersen, L. Hindberg, M. Hoenningen, N. Kehlet, H. Kronstam (another revival for Royal Swed. B., Stockholm, same year).

Toronto. In addition to the *National B. of Canada, the city houses the modern-dance-orientated Toronto D. Th., founded in 1969 and led by Peter Randazzo, Patricia Beatty, and David Earle, which made its London début in 1972. BIBL.: S. Landen Odom, 'At the Frontier of Canada's Modern D.: T.D. Th.', *Dance Magazine* (1975/11).

Toth, Edra (*b* Budapest, 18 Sep. 1952). Hung. dancer. Came to the U.S. when 4 years old. Studied with Alda Marova in Dorchester and with E. Virginia Williams. Joined Boston B. as an apprentice in 1964; eventually became a principal d. BIBL.: S. Goodman, 'E.T.', *Dance Magazine* 1969/12.

Toumanova, Tamara (*b* in a train near Shanghai, 1919). Russ.-Amer. dancer. Studied with Preobrajenska. Début as a child prodigy in the 1929 Paris prod. of *L'Eventail de Jeanne.* Balanchine engaged her as one of the 3 'baby ballerinas' for B. Russe de Monte Carlo in 1932, where she created roles in his *Cotillon, Concurrence,* and *Le Bourgeois gentilhomme* (1932). She then joined his Les Bs. 1933 and created roles in his *Songes* and *Mozartiana.* Returned to B. Russe de Monte Carlo and remained until 1937; created roles in Massine's *Union Pacific* (1934), *Jardin public* (1935), and *Symphonie fantastique* (1936—and earlier in his *Jeux d'enfants,* 1932). Appeared in the New York musical prod. of *Stars in Your Eyes* (1939). Joined Original B. Russe in 1939; created ballerina role in Balanchine's *Balustrade* (1941). Moved to Denham's B. Russe de Monte Carlo in 1941; took part in Massine's creation of *Labyrinth* (1941). Made her first Hollywood film, *Days of Glory,* in 1943. Ballerina of B. Th. 1944–5; created roles in Massine's *Moonlight Sonata* (1944) and Nijinska's *Harvest Time* (1945). During the following years she pursued a career as a freelance ballerina, dancing with many cos. in America and Europe; created roles in Balanchine's *Le Palais de cristal* (Paris, 1947), Lifar's *Phèdre* (Paris, 1950), Wallmann's *Legend of Joseph* (Milan, 1951), Charrat's *The Seven Deadly Sins* (mus. Verretti, Milan, 1956), and Taras' *Fanfares pour le Prince* (Monte Carlo, 1956). For years she continued to appear in individual perfs., mostly with Vladimir Oukhtomsky as her partner. Her latest appearances include Hitchcock's *The Torn Curtain* (1966) and B. Wilder's *The Private Life of Sherlock Holmes* (1970—earlier films were *Tonight We Sing,* 1953, in which she played Pavlova, and G. Kelly's *Invitation to the Dance,* 1956). Undoubtedly the most glamorous of the Russ. emigré ballerinas. BIBL.: V. H. Swisher, 'T.T.: A Unique Career', *Dance Magazine* (1970/9).

Tour en l'air. (Fr., turn in the air.) Designates in b. a movement in which the d. turns while leaping vertically into the air. It is usually a prerogative of the male d. and can be performed several times (double, very rarely triple t.e.l'a.).

Touron, Patrice (*b* Dakar, Senegal, 21 Aug. 1952). Fr. dancer. Studied at Conservatoire de la Danse in Bordeaux and 2 years with R. Hightower in Cannes. Joined B. of the Twentieth Century, 1972, now principal d. Created roles in Béjart's *Trionfi* (1974), *Notre Faust* (1975), *Heliogabal*, *Molière imaginaire* (both 1976), *Claire de lune* (solo, 1977), *Spectre de la rose*, and *Dichterliebe* (both 1978).
BIBL.: A. Ph. Hersin, 'P.T.', *Les Saisons de la Danse* (1976/7).

Toye, Wendy (*b* London, 1917). Brit. dancer, choreographer, and director. Started to appear in London mus. prods. Toured with Markova Dolin B. 1934–5 and then embarked on a career as a ch. and dir. of musicals and pantomimes.

Tragédie de Salomé. See *Salome Ballets.*

Tragedy of Fashion, A, or The Scarlet Scissors. Ballet in 1 act; ch. Ashton; mus. E. Goossens; déc. Fedorovitch. Prod. 15 June 1926 in the revue *Riverside Nights*, Lyric Th., London, with Ashton, Rambert. Set to Goossens's *Kaleidoscope*, the b. tells of a dressmaker who commits suicide when his dress is rejected by a wealthy customer. This was Ashton's first b.
BIBL.: D. Vaughan, *Frederick Ashton and his Ballets* (London, 1977).

Traguth, Fred (*b* Stuttgart, 6 Feb. 1932). Ger. dancer, choreographer, and teacher. Studied at Essen Folkwang School and in New York with Oboukhoff, Vladimiroff, F. Wagner, and Graham. Returned to Ger. in 1959 and worked in Ulm and Cologne; then became professor of modern d. at the Univ. Bahia (Brazil). Founder-dir. of the Bonn International D. Workshop in 1973. Often teaching abroad.

Trailine, Boris (*b* Lemnos, Greece, 13 June 1921). Fr. dancer, teacher, and impresario. Studied with Sedova, Clustine, and Volinine. Started to d. with B. de Cannes in 1941; joined Nouveau B. de Monte Carlo in 1943 (creating roles in Lifar's *Chota roustaveli*, 1946, and *Dramma per musica*, 1950). Then pursued a career as a freelance d.; frequently appeared with Chauviré and Toumanova. Created the Knight in Rosen's *The Lady and the Unicorn* (Munich, 1953). After Volinine's death in 1955 he took over his studio, where he taught until 1970. Now an impresario in Paris. He is the brother of the d. Hélène T.

Trailine, Hélène (*b* Bombas, Lorraine, 6 Oct. 1928). Fr. dancer. Studied with Sedova and Egorova. Début with Nouveau B. de Monte Carlo in 1946. D. with Bs. des Champs-Elysées 1949–50, then with the comps. of Charrat, Milloss, Miskovitch, and Béjart. Created roles in Béjart's *Haut voltage* (1956) and Charrat's *Electre* (1960).

She is the sister of the d. Boris T. and married to the d. Juan Giuliano.

Train Bleu, Le. Ballet in 1 act; libr. Cocteau; ch. Nijinska; mus. Milhaud; curtain Picasso; set Henri Laurens; cost. C. Chanel. Prod. 20 June 1924, Bs. Russes de Diaghilev, Th. de Champs-Elysées, Paris with Nijinska, Sokolova, Dolin, Woizikovsky. The 'T.b.', the express between Paris and the Côte d'azur, does not actually appear; the b. is an operetta dansée of a chic and flippant society which pursues its foibles and follies on a Mediterranean beach.
BIBL.: C. W. Beaumont, 'L.T.b' in *Complete Book of Ballets* (London, 1951).

Training. The term used in Germany for the daily b. class.

Traitor, The. Ballet in 1 act; libr. and ch. Limón; mus. G. Schuller; set Paul Trautvetter; cost P. Lawrence. Prod. 19 Aug. 1954, J. Limón D. Co., Connecticut College, with Limón, Hoving. A modern d. retelling of the story of Jesus Christ and his betrayal by Judas. Revived for Amer. B. Th. in 1970.

Transfigured Night. (Orig. Ger. title: *Verklärte Nacht*). String Sextet by A. Schoenberg, op. 4 (1899). Either in its orig. version or arr. for orchestra, the mus. has inspired several bs. Tudor's *Pillar of Fire* (B. Th., New York, 1942) is its most famous realization; later versions include those by E. Walter (Wuppertal, 1961), P. Van Dyk (Hamburg, 1965), J. Kylián (Netherlands D. Th., The Hague, 1975) and R. Petit (Opéra, Paris, 1976).

Travestie, En. Fr. term for a woman in male dress, but also used for a man in female dress. Famous b. roles performed e.t. include Widow Simone in *La Fille mal gardée*, Franz in the orig. Paris prod. of *Coppélia*, Carabosse in *Sleeping Beauty*, the Head Mistress in *Graduation Ball*, and also Madge, the Witch, in Bournonville's *La Sylphide*.

Trecu, Pirmin (orig. Pirnon Aldabaldetrecu; *b.* Zaraus, Spain 1930). Span. dancer and teacher. Came to England as a refugee of the Span. Civil War. Studied at Sadler's Wells School. Joined Sadler's Wells Th. B. in 1947: principal d. in 1948. D. with Sadler's Wells B. 1955–61; a leg injury then compelled him to give up his career as a d. Created roles in Howard's *Selina* (1948), Cranko's *Sea Change* (1949), *Pastorale* (1950), *Reflection* (1952), *The Lady and the Fool* (1954), and *The Prince of the Pagodas* (1957), Somes's *Summer Interlude*, and Balanchine's *Trumpet Concerto* (1950), MacMillan's *Anon* (1958), and Ashton's *Ondine* (1958). Had his best role as the Boy in *La Fête étrange*. Now has a school in Oporto.

Trefilova, Vera Alexandrovna (*b* St. Petersburg, 8 Oct. 1875, *d* Paris, 11 July 1943). Russ. dancer. Studied at Imperial B. Academy; graduated in

1898. Joined Maryinsky Th. and became soloist in 1901 and prima ballerina in 1906. Fierce intrigues against her (mainly instigated by Kschessinska and her followers) made her resign prematurely in 1910. Left Russia in 1917 and opened a b. school in Paris. Diaghilev invited her to d. Aurora in his London prod. of *The Sleeping Princess* In 1921, and these were her farewell perfs., though she continued to make individual appearances for some time. A ballerina of exceptional virtuosity and great expressive means; Aurora was her best role. Her pupils included Vyroubova and Svetlova. Her third husband was the eminent critic Valerian Svetlov, whose book *Contemporary Ballet* (St. Petersburg, 1911) is one of the standard works of international b. literature.

Trend. Ballet in 6 parts; libr. and ch. Holm; mus. W. Riegger and Varèse; set Arch Lauterer; cost. Betty Joiner. Prod. 13 Aug. 1937, Bennington College. In addition to the specially comp. mus. by Riegger, Varèse's *Ionization* and *Octandre* were used for this colossal work, which deals with the survival of society through decadence and collapse.
BIBL.: W. Sorell, in *Hanya Holm* (Middletown, Conn., 1969).

Trepak. A lively Ukranian d. in 2/4 time for males only, with squatting steps and split leaps. The most famous example in b. is the Russ. D. in the final divertissement of *Nutcracker*.

Trevor, Walter (*b* Manchester, 1931). Brit. dancer and teacher. Studied at Manchester B. Club and Sadler's Wells School. Joined Sadler's Wells Th. B. in 1951; became soloist in 1956. Went to N.Z. with his wife, d. Sara Neil, in 1959, and founded the United B. Comp. Returned to London in 1968; teachers at the Royal B. School until 1981.

Triad. Ballet in 1 act; ch. MacMillan; mus. Prokofiev; déc. Peter Unsworth. Prod 19 Jan. 1972, Royal B., Cov. Gdn., London, with Sibley, Dowell, Eagling. Set to Prokofiev's Violin Concerto No. 1 in D major, the b. is about a girl who intrudes on the very close relationship of two brothers. A different b. to the same mus. is *Opus 19* by Robbins (1979).
BIBL.: P. Brinson and C. Crisp, in *Ballet & Dance* (Newton Abbot, 1980).

Triadic Ballet. (orig. Ger. title: *Triadisches Ballett*). By Oskar Schlemmer. Prod. 30 Sep. 1922, Landes Th., Stuttgart, with Schlemmer, Albert Burger, and Elsa Hötzel. An abstract work which explores the relationship between the moving figure and space, the b. offered 'a structure of stylized d. scenes, developing from humorous to serious'. It was in 3 parts—Lemon yellow: a gay burlesque; Pink: a solemn ritual; Black: a mystical fantasy. 'The twelve different dances in eighteen different costumes are d. alternately by three persons, two male, one female. Costumes are partly of padded

cloth, partly of stiff papier-maché coated with metallic or coloured paint.' Earlier versions in 1911 and 1916. For later perfs. Hindemith comp. mus. for mechanical organ. Ger. TV reconstruction by Margarethe Hasting in 1970. Revived with the same costs., to mus. by H. J. Hespos, by G. Bohner (Berlin, 1977).
BIBL.: L. Kirstein, 'T.B.' in *Movement & Metaphor* (New York, 1970).

Tricorne, Le. See *Three-Cornered Hat, The.*

Trio Ballet. Ballet film from the Leningrad Studio Lenfilm, released in the West in 1954, showing the Bolshoi and Kirov B. in continuous excerpts from *Swan Lake* (prod. by Sergeyev, with Ulanova, Dudinskaya, and Sergeyev), *The Fountain of Bakhchisaray* (with Ulanova, Plisetskaya, Gusev, Zhdanov, and Belsky), and *Flames of Paris* (with Chaboukiani, M. Gotlieb, V. Zaplin, Y. Sangovich, and V. Smolzov).

Triomphe de l'amour, Le. Ballet de cour in 20 entrées; text I. de Benserade and P. Quinault; mus. Lully; prod. and ch. Beauchamp and Pécour; déc. J. Bérain. Prod. 21 Jan. 1681, Château de Saint-Germain-en-Laye, with Beauchamp as Mars and Pécour in various entrées, and with the ladies and gentlemen of the Fr. court. A fabulous baroque spectacle; the entrées start with Venus, followed by Peace. They summon the Graces, Dryads, and Naiads, and the work builds up to the climax, when all the participants pay homage to Love as the ruler of gods and men. At a perf. 4 months later at the Paris Palais Royal, Mlle. Lafontaine, Reine de danse, made the first appearance of a professional ballerina. Later versions by Hilverding (Vienna, 1765) and H. Lander (Royal Dan. B., 1962).

Trionfi di Petrarca, I. See *'I trionfi' di Petrarca.*

Trionfo di Afrodite. Concerto scenico by Orff; prod. and cond. H. von Karajan; ch. T. Gsovsky; déc. J. Fenneker. Prod. Teatro alla Scala, Milan, 13 Feb. 1953. The final part of Orff's triptych (also incl. *Carmina Burana* and *Catulli Carmina*); it uses poems by Catullus and Sappho and a chorus from Euripides's *Philoctetes* for the dramatic presentation of an antique marriage ritual. Later prods. have stressed the ch. aspects of the work, especially those by Rosen at the Munich State Op. (1960) and Walker for Les Grands Bs. Canadiens (1965).

Trisler, Joyce (*b* Los Angeles, 1934, *d* New York, 9 Oct. 1979). Amer. dancer, choreographer, and teacher. Studied with Horton, Maracci, Tudor, Holm, Joffrey, and Caton. D. with L. Horton D. Th. 1951–4 and Juilliard D. Th. 1955–9; also presented individual perfs. with her own group and d. in Ailey co.'s first Eur. tours in 1964. She also worked as a ch. for plays and musicals. Was considered one of the foremost teachers of L. Horton technique. Contributed 'The Magic and the Commitment' (on Horton) to *Dance Perspectives* 31.

Tristan. Ballet in 1 act; ch. Tetley; mus. Henze; déc. Baylis. Prod. 13 Nov. 1974, Opéra, Paris, with Nureyev, Carlson. This is a semi-abstract version of the legend of T. and Isolde. Other b. treatments of the same subject incl. Massine's (in *Mad T.*, mus. Wagner, déc. Dali, B. International, New York, 1944), Ashton's (in *Picnic at Tintagel*, mus. Bax, New York City B., 1952), Ross's (in *T.*, mus. Wagner, Amer. B. Th., New York, 1958), Charrat's (in *Tu auras nom ... T.*, mus. Jef Maes, Geneva, 1963), T. Gsovsky's (in *T.*, mus. Blacher, Ger. Op. Berlin, 1965), Béjart's (in *Les Vainqueurs*, Tibetan mus. and Wagner, Brussels, 1969), Morrice's (in the third movement of *That is the Show*; also in *Isolde*, mus. John Lewis, B. Rambert, 1973), and Cohan's (in the second part of *Dances of Love and Death*, mus. C. Davis and C. Nancarrow, London Contemporary D. Th., 1981).

Triumph of Death. (orig. Dan. title: *Dødens Triumf*). TV Ballet by Flindt; mus. Thomas Koppel; sets Poul Arnt Thomsen; cost. Søren Breum; prod. Jørgen Mydtskov. Premiered 23 May 1971, Dan. TV, with Flindt, F. Schaufuss, Eliasen, V. Flindt. Based upon Ionesco's *Jeu de massacre*; a lavish 'dance-of-death' revue, showing in individual episodes how modern man tries to escape the grim consequences of the plague. First perf. of the stage prod. 19 Feb. 1972, Royal Dan. B., Copenhagen.

Triumph of Neptune, The. Eng. Pantomime in 12 scenes; libr. S. Sitwell; ch. Balanchine; mus. Lord Berners; déc. Prince A. Shervashidze. Prod. 3 Dec. 1926, Bs. Russes de Diaghilev, Lyceum Th., London, with Danilova, Tchernicheva, Sokolova, Lifar, Balanchine. The b. was inspired by designs by G. and R. Cruikshank, Tofts, Honigold, and Webb for Pollock's toy ths. It is really a parodistic revue of the mythological op., from the perspective of the Eng. children's th., with its leanings towards commedia dell'arte. A different b. using the same mus. by D. Bintley, *Punch and the Street Party*, Sadler's Wells Royal B., 1979. BIBL.: B. Kochno, 'T.T.o.N.' in *Diaghilev* (New York, 1970).

Triumph of St. Joan. See *Seraphic Dialogue*.

Trockadero Gloxinia Ballet Company. The New York-based co. was formed in 1973 by Ekaterina Sobechanskaya (alias Mr. Larry Rhee); it consists of 9 men who d. as women, on point, and perform a repertory of excerpts from the b. classics. Eur. début in 1975.

Trommler, Birgitta (*b* Munich, 29 Jan. 1944). Ger. dancer, teacher, and choreographer. Studied with M. Lex in Cologne, then with Truitte, Pomare, Limón, Cunningham, and Faber. D. with the cos. of Lex, Dunham, Limón, and with Boston D. Circle, Tunis National Institute co., and Philadelphia D. Th. Started to choreograph 1967,

has since worked for many Amer. cos. and since 1976 for Tanzprojekt Munich, of which she is founder and artistic dir. plus teaching at its assoc. schools. Also guest teacher for various schools in the U.S. and all over Eur.

Trouhanova, Natalia Vladimirovna (*b* Kiev, 1885, *d* Moscow, 25 Aug. 1956). Russ.–Fr. dancer. Started to d. in Russ. variety ths. Went to Paris and d. at the Opéra in 1907; she was admired above all for her striking beauty but failed to gain a place in Diaghilev's Bs. Russes. Developed her own free d. style under the influence of Duncan, which she presented in many solo recitals. Her greatest perf. was the première, in one programme, of d'Indy's *Istar*, Dukas' *La Péri*, Schmitt's *La Tragédie de Salomé*, and Ravel's *Adélaïde ou La Langage des fleurs*, all ch. Clustine, conducted by their respective composers, in 1912. Retired upon her marriage to Count Ignatiev. Wrote 'Anna Pavlova, a Reminiscence', *Dance Magazine* (1976/1).

Trounson, Marilyn (*b* San Franciso, 30 Sep. 1947). Amer.–Brit. dancer. Studied at San Francisco Conservatory of B. and Royal B. School. Joined Royal B. in 1966; created roles in Ashton's *Jazz Calendar* (1968) and *Lament of the Waves* (1970), and MacMillan's *Anastasia* (London version, 1971). D. with J. Russillo's co. and with Stuttgart B. 1974–6.

Troy Game. Ballet in 1 act; ch. R. North; mus. B. Downes/Batucada; cost. P. Farmer. Prod. 7 Oct. 1974, London Contemporary D. Th., Stoke-on-Trent. An all-male display, poking fun at muscle-flexing macho athleticism. Revived for D. Th. of Harlem 1979, for Royal B. 1980.

Truitte, James (*b* Chicago, *c.* 1925). Amer. dancer and teacher. Studied with A. Savage, J. Collins, Maracci, and Horton; joined Horton's co. in 1950 and took over his school when he died in 1953. Joined Ailey's co. as a principal d. in 1960 and eventually became associate artistic dir. (until 1968). Has since specialized in teaching Horton technique. Joined faculty of d. at Univ. of Cincinnati College-Conservatory of Music in 1970; appointed Associate Professor of D. in 1973.

Trunoff, Vassilie (*b* Melbourne, 14 Sep. 1929, *d* London, 11 Jan. 1985). Austral. dancer, teacher, and b. master. Studied with Borovansky and Kirsova; joined Borovansky B. and later became soloist. D. (as Basil Truro) with B. Rambert in Australia 1948. Joined London Festival B. as a principal d. in 1950. Returned to Borovansky B. in 1953. Rejoined London Festival B. in 1959; appointed b. master in 1962. Has also taught for Washington National B., PACT B., and the cos. in Naples and Venice and ch. some bs. Married to the b. mistress Joan Potter.

Truyol, Antonio (*b* Buenos Aires, 1933). Argent. dancer and b. director. Studied at Teatro Colón B.

School; joined the b. co. Became principal d. in 1953; is now general dir.

Tsinguirides, Georgette (*b* Stuttgart, 1933). Ger. dancer and choreologist. Studied at Stuttgart B. School. Joined Stuttgart B. in 1947; became soloist in 1955. Studied choreology in London; returned to Stuttgart B. as a notator in 1966. Has staged many of the cos. bs. for other troupes in Ger. and abroad.

Tudor, Antony (orig. William Cook; *b* London, 4 Apr. 1908, *d* N.Y., 19 April 1987). Brit. d., ch., and teacher. Began studying with Rambert in 1928; then also with Argyle, Turner, and Craske. Joined B. Rambert as d., asst., and sec. to Rambert in 1930; ch. his first bs., in most of which he participated as a d., e.g. *Cross-Garter'd* (mus. Frescobaldi, 1931), *Lysistrata* (mus. Prokofiev) and *Adam and Eve* (mus. Lambert, 1932), *The Planets* (mus. Holst, 1934), *The Descent of Hebe* (mus. Bloch, 1935), *Jardin aux lilas* (mus. Chausson, 1936), and *Dark Elegies* (mus. Mahler, 1937). Established his D. Th. with de Mille in 1937, with Laing as principal d. (for whom he ch. almost all his early bs.). Ch. *Gallant Assembly* (mus. Tartini) for the co. It was disbanded after a 1 week engagement in Oxford; he then ch. *Judgment of Paris* (mus. Weill) for an ad hoc troupe in 1938. Formed London B. with Laing in Dec. 1938; ch. *Gala Performance* (mus. Prokofiev). In 1939 he and Laing moved to New York, where he worked for 10 years as a staff ch. of the newly founded B. Th. He d. with the co., revived his earlier b. successes, and ch. *Goyescas* (mus. Granados, 1940), *Pillar of Fire* (mus. Schoenberg, 1942), *Romeo and Juliet* (mus. Delius) and *Dim Lustre* (mus. R. Strauss, 1943), *Undertow* (mus. W. Schuman, 1945), and *Shadow of the Wind* (mus. Mahler, 1948). Worked for Royal Swed. B. 1949–50 and for New York City B. 1951–2; ch. *Lady of the Camellias* (mus. Verdi, 1951) and *La Gloire* (mus. Beethoven, 1952). Appointed dir. of Met. Op. B. School in 1950; concentrated on teaching for the next few years. Ch. *Offenbach in the Underworld* and other works for National B. of Can. in 1954. Became faculty member of the teaching staff at Juilliard School; ch. some smaller bs. for its performing co. B. dir. of Royal Swed. B. 1963–4; ch. *Echoing of Trumpets* (mus. Martinů, 1963). Since the second half of the 1960s has often travelled abroad, staging his existing bs. and occasionally new ones, incl. *Shadowplay* (mus. Koechlin, Royal B., 1967), *Knight Errant* (mus. R. Strauss, Royal B., 1968), *The Divine Horseman* (mus. Egk, The Austral. B., 1969), *Fandango* (mus. Soler, National B. of Can., 1972), and *Cereus* (mus. G. Grey, Pennsylvania B., 1972). Joined Amer. B. Th. as Associate Dir. in 1974; ch. *The Leaves Are Fading* (mus. Dvořák, 1975), *The Tiller in the Fields* (mus. Dvořák, 1978). He is considered one of the foremost choreographers of the twentieth century and has been called 'the ch. of human sorrow' because of his sympathy for suffering. Through

him b. has acquired new psychological insight into man's heart and soul, and he has enriched the psychology of ch. with a wealth of nuances b. had never known before. He is the subject of an Amer. educational TV film *Modern Ballet*. Carina Ari Gold Medal (1973); D. Magazine Award (1974); R.A.D. Q. Elizabeth II Coronation Award (1985).
BIBL.: J. Percival and S. J. Cohen, 'A.T.', *Dance Perspectives* 17/18; S. Ames 'A.T.: From Freud to Zen', *Dance Magazine* (1973/10).

Tugal, Pierre (*b* Russia, 1883, *d* Paris, 1964). Fr. writer on b. Curator of the Archives Internationales de la Danse in Paris 1931–50. Author of many books, incl. *Initiation à la Danse* (1947) and *La Danse Classique Sans Maître* (with L. Legrand, 1956).

Tulip of Harlem, The. Ballet in 3 acts and 4 scenes; ch. Ivanov, mus. Baron Fitingoff-Shell. Prod. 4 Oct. 1887, Maryinsky Th., St. Petersburg, with Bessone, Legat, Gerdt. In this b. Legnani performed her sensational 32 fouettés for the first time in Russia.

Tune, Tommy (*b* Wichita Falls, Tex., 28 Feb. 1939). Amer. dancer and actor. Studied with Camille Hill, Emma Mae Horn, and Shirley Dodge. Started to perform in musicals all over the U.S. Became known as an actor-d. (and a brilliant tap d.) in such films as *Hello, Dolly* (1969) and *The Boy Friend* (1971), and as the ch.-performer of the mus. *Seesaw* (1973). Later prods. of his incl. *The Club* (1977) and *A Day in Hollywood/A Night in the Ukraine* (1980).
BIBL.: R. Roman, 'T.T. Dancing in the Clouds to a Beat of Three . . . ', *Dance Magazine* (1973/9).

Tupine, Wasil (*b* Tyrnova, Bulg., 4 Apr. 1922). Bulg.–Argent. dancer and teacher. Studied with Egorova and Oboukhoff. D. with Bs. de la Jeunesse 1937–9, B. Russe du Colonel de Basil 1939–43, Teatro Colón B. 1944–56, Grand B. du Marquis de Cuevas, 1957–60, and again with Teatro Colón B. 1960–72. Now a teacher at The Teatro Colón B. School.

Turangalîla. Symphony in 10 movements by O. Messiaen. Van Dyk ch. the 3 movements 'Solitude', 'Chant d'amour', and 'Danse joyeuse', with déc. by A. Siercke, 22 June 1960, Hamburg State Op. B., with Lihn, Kempf, Rayet, Schmiedel, Clauss, Van Dyk. The complete symphony was first ch. by Petit, déc. M. Ernst, 21 June 1968, Opéra, Paris, with Motte, Vlassi, Rayet, Thibon, Piletta. A later version by N. Vesak for Marin Civic B. (San Francisco, 1971).

Turkey. De Valois visited T. to examine the b. situation, and a national b. school was then established in Istanbul in 1947, with Joy Newton as dir. This was transferred to Ankara in 1950, where Beatrice Appleyard was installed as dir. She was assisted by Lorna Mossford and Robert Lunnon from the Sadler's Wells B., and in 1963 Mossford staged the first prod. of *Sleeping Beauty* in Ankara, with Meriç Sümen as Aurora. R. Glasstone (dir. 1965–9) mounted *Sylvia* and *Prince of the Pagodas* (1967). A second b. school was established in Istanbul in 1970, with A. Carter as dir.; he left when the Istanbul op. house burnt down the same year. Links with the Royal B. have meanwhile been strengthened: Rodrigues has staged some bs. and Ankara acquired Ashton's *La Fille mal gardée*. There are now 2 b. cos., the Ankara Devlet B., with Nevit Kodalli as dir., and the Istanbul Devlet B., with Aydin Gün as dir.

Turnbull, Julia (*b* Montreal, 18 June 1822, *d* Brooklyn, 11 Sep. 1887). Amer. dancer Studied with Mme. LeComte and Jules Martin. D. with Mary Ann Lee in *The Sisters* in 1839, and then in the co. of Elssler 1840–2; studied further with J. Sylvain. During the following years she became one of the foremost Amer. ballerinas, dancing all the major roles of the romantic standard repertory. Retired in 1857.
BIBL.: L. Moore, in 'George Washington Smith', *Dance Index* (vol. 4, nos 6–8).

Turner, Harold (*b* Manchester, 2 Dec. 1909, *d* London, 2 July 1962). Brit. dancer and teacher. Studied in Manchester with Alfred Haines and d. in his co. Studied further with Rambert; appeared, during the early years of Brit. b., with various groups and cos., incl. those of Dolin, Karsavina, and B. Club. Created roles in Ashton's *Les petits riens* (1928) and *Capriol Suite* (1930). A brilliant virtuoso, especially in the demi-charactère roles of the classic repertory (Blue Bird, etc.). Appeared as a guest with Sadler's Wells B.; joined the co. in 1935 and became one of its principal dancers. Remained (with 2 brief interruptions) until 1951; created roles in de Valois' *The Rake's Progress* (1935) and *Checkmate* (1937), Ashton's *Les Rendez-vous* (1933), *A Wedding Bouquet*, and *Les Patineurs* (1937). Principal d. of International B. 1941–2. During his later career he enjoyed particular success in Massine's *Boutique fantasque* and *The Three-Cornered Hat*. After ending his career as a d., continued to teach at Sadler's Wells School and as b. master of Cov. Gdn. Op. B. He was married first to the d. Mary Honer and then to Gerd Larsen.
BIBL.: G. Anthony, 'Pioneers of the Royal Ballet: H.T.', *Dancing Times* (1971/8).

Turney, Matt (*b* Americus, Ga.). Amer. dancer. Studied dance at Univ. of Wisconsin. Joined Graham's co. in 1951; became one of her outstanding soloists. Remained until 1964, and created leading roles in *Seraphic Dialogue* (1955), *Embattled Garden* (1958), *A Look at Lightning*, and *Samson Agonistes* (1962). Has also appeared with the cos. of McKayle, Ailey, P. Taylor, Lang, and in recitals with R. Cohan.

Turning Point, The. Twentieth Century Fox feature film about two former d. colleagues, one of which has become an ageing ballerina (Anne Bancroft as Emma), while the other one (Shirley MacLaine as Deedee) has quit to raise a family, with a dancing daughter (Leslie Browne as Emilia) who sets out to fulfil her mother's ballerina dreams. The plot revolves around the daily routine of a b. co. (Amer. B. Th.), with a lot of classroom and perf. shots, and with Emilia having an affair with the co.'s star (M. Baryshnikov as Yuri). The film was scripted by Arthur Laurents and directed by H. Ross (asst. by N. Kaye), featuring in other roles A. Sibley, A. Danilova, S. Danias, S. Douglas, D. Levans, J. Schneider, D. Nahat *et al.*, and, as gala guests, L. Aldous, F. Bujones, R. Cragun, S. Farrell, M. Haydée, and P. Martins. Released in New York, 1977.
BIBL.: N. McLain Stoop, 'Drama Defines Dance: T.T.P.', *Dance Magazine*, (1977/10).

Turnout. The Eng. equivalent of the Fr. *en dehors*. One of the basic requirements of the academic d. The 90° turnout position (with the feet at right-angles from a forward-facing line) was introduced by Blasis into b. teaching, to enable the d. to move freely in every direction. It needs careful development in suitable exercises over several years. A. Levinson has written about its aesthetic aspects in 'The Spirit of the Classic Dance' (reprinted in S. J. Cohen's *Dance as a Theatre Art*, New York, 1974).

Turska, Irena (*b* Warsaw, 26 Oct. 1912). Pol. writer on b. Educated at J. Mieczýnska's Warsaw School of Eurhythmics and Artistic Dance and Paris Ecole Superieure d'Etudes Chorégraphiques. D. contributor to *Ruch Muzyczny*. Taught at the d. educational dept of Warsaw Academy of Music. Author of numerous books. e.g. *Leon Wójcikowski* (contributor, 1958), *Dance in Poland* and *A Short Outline of the History of Dance and Ballet* (both 1962), *About the Dance* (1965), and *Ballet Guide* (1973). Has also written some b. librs., incl. *The King's Fool* (mus. T. Kiesewetter, Bytom, 1958), *Mazepa* (mus. T. Szeligowski, Warsaw, 1958), and *Pinocchio* (mus. J. Szajina-Lewandowska, Wrocaw, 1964).

Tutu. (Fr., bottom). The b. skirt, made from several layers of tarlatan, silk, or nylon, which has become the standard female b. wear since Taglioni's appearance in *La Sylphide* (1832). In its romantic form it reaches halfway between the knee and the ankle; the classic form is much shorter, reaching at most to the knee. The almost horizontal t. at hip-length is a later variant.
BIBL.: G. Chaffee, 'The Birth of the T.', *Dance Index* (vol. 3, no. 9).

Twilight. (1) Ballet in 1 act; ch. Van Manen; mus. Cage; déc. Vroom. Prod. 20 June 1972. Dutch National B., Stadsschouwburg. Amsterdam, with Radius and Ebbelaar. Set to Cage's *Perilous Night*; a dramatic b. for a woman and a man, who fight out their precarious relationship with unrelenting provocation and aggression. Revived for Royal B. (1973). (2) A completely different b., under the Ger. title *Dämmern*, by

Neumeier, mus. Scriabin, 3 May 1972, Frankfurt B., Frankfurt, with L. Benedict, Cordua, Kruuse, M. Barra, Finney, Howald, Midinet, as the opening part of *Bilder I, II, III (Pictures I, II, III)* showing a team of dancers who become united through their work. Revived, as *Scriabin*, for Royal Winnipeg B. (1973).

BIBL.: (Van Manen version) P. Brinson and C. Crisp, in *Ballet & Dance* (Newton Abbot, 1980).

Two Pigeons, The. See *Deux pigeons, Les.*

Tyl Eulenspiegel. See *Till Eulenspiegel.*

Tzivin, Mikhail (*b* Moscow, 19 Mar. 1949). Sov. dancer. Studied at Moscow Bolshoi B. School. Joined Bolshoi B. upon graduation in 1967. Gold Medal (Varna, 1974).

U

Udaeta, José (*b* Barcelona, 27 May 1919). Span. dancer, choreographer, and teacher. Studied in Madrid and became b. master at Barcelona's Teatro Liceo, where he and prima ballerina *Susana Audeoud prepared a concert programme of Span. dances which they first performed in Geneva in 1948. Their partnership became highly successful and they toured the world for the next 20 years. He has been on the teaching staff of the Krefeld–Cologne Summer Academy 1958–79, and has also taught at many other places and regularly, since 1973, at his own Summer School in Sitges. Has also ch. for various cos. (Hanover B., Royal Swed. B., Harkness B., etc.). Contributed 'Flamenco' to *Die Tanzarchiv-Reihe 5*.
BIBL.: G. Zacharias, *Susana y José* (Vienna, 1970—in Ger.).

Ugray, Klotild (*b* Budapest, 15 Nov. 1932). Hung. dancer. Studied with Edith Jármay and Nádasi. Joined Budapest State Op. B. in 1950, and was principal d. 1952–73. Now works as a teacher and b. mistress at Budapest State Op. B. Liszt Award (1964).

Ulanova, Galina Sergeyevna (*b* St. Petersburg, 8 Jan. 1910). Sov. dancer and teacher. Daughter of the b. régisseur Serge U. and the d. and teacher Maria Romanova. Studied for 4 years from 1919 with her mother, then with Vaganova at Petrograd State B. School; graduated in 1928. Joined GATOB and soon d. the ballerina roles of the traditional repertory; much admired for her poetry and dramatic projection. From 1930 also appeared in roles of the contemporary Sov. repertory; her first major part was Maria in Zakharov's *Fountain of Bakhchisaray* (1933). Started to d. at Moscow Bolshoi B. in 1935. Created Coralie in Zakharov's *Lost Illusions* (1935) and Julia in Lavrovsky's *Romeo and Juliet* (1940). Evacuated to Perm/Molotov with the Kirov B. Joined Bolshoi B. in 1944. Here she created Tao-Hoa in Lavrovsky's new version of *Red Poppy* (1949) and Katerina in his *Stone Flower* (1954), but not, as is often stated, the title role in Zacharov's *Cinderella*, 1945 (this was Lepeshinskaya). In 1945 she made her first appearance in the West, in Vienna; she then visited Rome (1949) and Florence and Venice (1951). D. with the Bolshoi B. from 1956 on its first tours in the West (London, 1956; New York, 1959); she was universally admired as the prima ballerina assoluta of the Sov. b. In 1959 she began to reduce the number of her appearances, and she gave her farewell perf. in 1962. However, she still works with the Bolshoi B. as a b. mistress and coach for young ballerinas. As a ballerina she is one of the great personalities of b. history. Her role interpretations were especially distinguished by her warm and radiant humanity. She had the rare gift of not only thrilling her audiences, but actually moving them to tears. Some films have conserved her essential qualities, e.g. *Trio Ballet* (excerpts from *Swan Lake* and *Fountain of Bakhchisaray*, 1953), *Romeo and Juliet* (1954), and *Giselle* (Brit., 1957—this includes her *Dying Swan*). She has also frequently been a spokeswoman of Sov. b. and has written about its problems. She is still chairman of committees and juries (regularly at the Varna competition). Contributed to *U., Moiseyev and Zakharov on Soviet Ballet* (London, 1954), 'The Author of My Favourite Ballets' to *S.S. Prokofiev: Autobiography, Articles, Reminiscences* (Moscow, 1956, in Eng.), and 'The Making of a Ballerina' to *The Bolshoi Ballet Story* (New York, 1959). Stalin Prize (1941, 1946, 1947, and 1950); People's Artist of the R.S.F.S.R. (1951); Lenin Prize (1957); Hero of Socialist Work and Lenin Order (1974). Was married to the stage dir. Y. Zavadsky and later to the designer Vadim Ryndin.
BIBL.: A. Kahn, *Days with U.* (New York and London, 1962).

Ullate, Victor (*b* Saragossa, 9 May 1947). Span. dancer. Studied with Maria de Avila and Hightower. D. with Antonio's co., 1962–5. Joined B. of the 20th Century in 1965, and later became principal d.; created roles in Béjart's *Ni Fleurs, ni couronnes* (1967), *Offrande chorégraphique* (1970), *Nijinsky, Clown de dieu* (1971), *Golestan* (1973), and 'I trionfi' di Petrarca (1974). Commissioned to form a new Span. Nat. B., 1979.
BIBL.: N. McLain Stoop, 'V.U.', *Dance Magazine* (1975/12).

Ullmann, Lisa (*b* Berlin, 17 June 1907, *d* Chertsey, 25 Jan. 1985). Ger.-Brit. dance and movement teacher. After studying painting, concentrated on d. training at the Berlin Laban School; gained Laban Diploma in 1929. Taught in Nuremberg and at Essen Folkwang School. Emigrated to Eng. with Jooss in 1934; taught at Dartington Hall until 1940 and became Laban's closest collaborator from 1938 until his death in 1958. Lectured, taught, and ch. extensively 1940–5; co-founder of Laban Art of Movement Guild in 1945 and Art of Movement Studio in Manchester in 1946 (incorporated in the Laban Art of Movement Centre Trust, Addlestone, Surrey, in 1954) which she dir. until 1973. Has constantly revised and added to several books originally written by Laban. Currently engaged in researching and cataloguing the Laban Archives.

BIBL.: A. Turnbull, in 'The Art of Movement Studio', *Dance and Dancers* (1969/6).

Ulrich, Jochen (*b* Osterode, 3 Aug. 1944). Ger. dancer, choreographer, and b. director. Studied at Cologne Institute for Th. D. Joined Cologne Op. B. in 1967 and became one of its leading soloists. One of the 3 founder-directors of the Cologne D. Forum in 1971. Has ch. many bs., incl. *Des Knaben Wunderhorn* (mus. Mahler, 1974), *Für Maurice Ravel* (1975), *Die Regel war unabänderlich* (mus. J. G. Fritsch, 1976), *Walzerträume* (mus. K. Schwertsik, 1977), *Der blaue Mantel* (mus. Britten/Debussy, 1979), *Der grosse Gesang* (mus. Fritsch), *The Miraculous Mandarin* (mus. Bartók, 1980), and *Canto General* (mus. Fritsch, verse Neruda, 1981).

Ulysses Ballets. See *Odysseus Ballets*.

Undertow. Ballet in 1 act, with prologue and epilogue; libr. and ch. Tudor; mus. W. Schuman; déc. Raymond Breinin. Prod. 10 Apr. 1945, B. Th., Met. Op. House, New York, with Laing, Gollner, A. Alonso, Kriza. The b. 'attempts to show us why a young man, called the transgressor, commits murder. It shows us where he was born, the people he grew up with, and the people who influenced his life. All the characters in the ballet, except the hero, have names derived from mythology . . . The time is present' (Balanchine). BIBL.: G. Balanchine, '*U.*', in *Balanchine's New Complete Stories of the Great Ballets* (Garden City, N.Y., 1968).

Undine. See *Ondine*.

Unfinished Symphony. Schubert's post-humously published Symphony No. 8, in B Minor, has been ch. by I. Duncan (Paris, 1927), Knust (Hamburg, 1931), and Van Dyk (Paris and Lyons, 1957).

Unicorn, the Gorgon, and the Manticore, The (or *The Three Sundays of a Poet*). Madrigal Fable for Chorus, Dancers, and Nine Instruments by Menotti; ch. Butler; set Rosenthal; cost. Robert Fletcher. Prod. 15 Jan. 1957, New York City B., City Center, N.Y., with Magallanes. On three successive Sundays the poet strolls through the city, with one of his favourite pets. The citizens at first think he is crazy, but soon they find themselves imitating him. Other versions by Darrell (Western Th. B., 1958) and Georgi (Hanover, 1959). BIBL.: W. Terry, '*T.U.,t.G.,a.t.M.*' in Ballet (New York, 1959).

Union Jack. Ballet in 3 parts; ch. Balanchine; mus. folk, military, naval, and music-hall themes, arr. H. Kay; déc. Ter-Arutunian. Prod. 13 May 1976 (preview 12 May), New York City B., New York State Th., N.Y., with d'Amboise, von Aroldingen, Bonnefous, Farrell, Leland, McBride, Martins, Mazzo, Tomasson. '*U.J.*' acknowledges those ritual aspects of Britain as alive today in military ceremony and in theatrical vitality as they were in the 18th century' (information notice). The co.'s contribution to Amer.'s Bicentennial festivities. BIBL.: G. Balanchine, in *Balanchine's Complete Stories of the Great Ballets* (Garden City, N.Y., 1977).

University of Utah Repertory Dance Theatre. See *Repertory Dance Theatre*.

United States. Ballet was brought to Amer. by Eur. artists and small cos., incl. such celebrities as Elssler, P. Taglioni, and the Petipas. The first important Amer. dancers emerged during the Romantic period—e.g. Augusta Maywood, Mary Ann Lee, and George Washington Smith. B. in Amer. dates back to 1735, when the Eng. Henry Holt d. in *The Adventures of Harlequin and Scaramouch* and *The Burgo'master Trick'd*, in Charleston. Alexandre and Mme Placide presented a whole b. season in New York in 1792, during which they showed *The Bird Catcher, The Return of the Labourers,* and *The Philosophers, or The Merry Girl*; John Durang, Amer.'s first professional d., was a member of their co. Later the Fr. Mme Placide became prima ballerina of the New Orleans th., where she put on bs. inspired by Noverre and Dauberval, as well as some original bs. The first serious b., *La Forêt noire* (imported from Fr. by Mme Anna Gardie, with newly comp. mus. by Alexander Reinagle), was given in Philadelphia in 1794. *Sophia of Brabant, The Danaides,* and *The Caledonian Frolic* were also seen there. 34 different bs. were presented by the Fr. ch. Jean Baptiste Francisqui during the 1794–5 season at the Charleston Th., incl. works after Noverre's *The Whims of Galatea* and Gardel's *Le Déserteur*. Later Francisqui went to New York with a group of dancers, incl. Mme Gardie and Durang; they appeared in *Pygmalion,* adapted from Rousseau, *The Milkmaid or The Death of the Bear,* and *The American Heroine* (a 'Grand Historic and Military Pantomime'). Towards the turn of the century, the Eng. James Byrne's harlequin pantomimes in Philadelphia became famous. During the early 1820s the Fr. b. master Claude Labasse and Francisque Hutin, the ballerina of his troupe, introduced the 'New French style of dancing', i.e. much greater virtuosity than had been seen before. In the next decade *La Muette de Portici and Le Dieu et la Bayadère* were produced in New York with Fr. dancers, and enthusiastically received. In 1835 Mlle Celeste gave *La Sylphide*, and M. A. Lee d. Giselle in Boston in 1846. P. Taglioni (from Berlin) appeared in *La Sylphide, Le Dieu et la Bayadère,* and *Nathalie, ou La Laitière Suisse* at the New York Park Th. in 1839. Elssler's Amer. tours (1840–2) were enormously successful. Hermine Blangy, the Ravel family, the Monplaisir B., Les Petites Danseuses Viennoises, and the Ronzani B. (which included the Cecchettis and their little son Enrico) also brought the Romantic repertory to Amer. *The Black Crook,* an extravaganza, opened in 1866, and during its very long run it introduced generations of Amers. to the art of b. (though in rather crude form). The opening of the Met. Op. House in 1883 did little to further the cause of b. in the U.S.— dancers were imported for its op. prods., and its school did not open tunil 1909. The Amer. Op. Co. of Theodore Thomas introduced *Coppélia* and *Sylvia*. Genée, Fornaroli, and Pavlova visited the country, and Mordkin first appeared in 1910. Diaghilev's Bs. Russes came in 1916; Pavlova visited the country almost every year until 1925 and left a lasting impression. Smaller cos. flourished very briefly; not until the arrival of the B. Russe de Monte Carlo in 1933 was first class b. regularly available. During the 1930s the School of Amer. B. and the Amer. B. of Kirstein and Balanchine were founded; the latter was for 2 years the resident co. of the Met. Op. House, where it staged its ambitious Stravinsky B. Festival in 1937. During the 1930s professional cos. also began to emerge outside New York, such as Littlefield's in Philadelphia, Page and Stone's in Chicago, and the Christensens' in San Francisco. The representatives of modern d. also had enormous influence; the movement was started before the turn of the century by such inspiring dancers as I. Duncan and St. Denis, and it reached its peak with the appearance of such great artists as Graham, Humphrey, Weidman, and Limón. The present-day Amer. B. Th. was founded in 1940. In the post-war period there was a massive increase in interest, and the N.Y. City B. and many other cos. in N.Y. and throughout the country were set up.

BIBL.: L. Moore, 'Ballet in America', in *Dance Encyclopedia* (N.Y., 1967—also gives an invaluable list of further bibliographical references); Portfolio on d. in U.S. in *Dance Magazine* (1976/7); L. Moore, *Echoes of American Ballet* (Brooklyn, N.Y., 1976); E. Kendall, *Where She Danced* (N.Y., 1979); M. G. Swift, *Belles and Beaux on Their Toes: Dancing Stars in Young America* (Washington, D.C., 1980); M. B. Siegel, *The Shapes of Change: Images of American Dance* (Boston, 1979).

University of Cape Town Ballet. The co., emerged from the private b. school which Dulcie Howes founded in Cape Town in 1930. It became the University of Cape Town School of B. in 1932, from which came the U.o.C.T.B. in 1934. This was the first S.A. b. co., and performed all over S.A., with Howes as its dir. It has been State subsidized since 1963 and was taken over by the Cape Performing Arts Board in 1965; it has since been called CAPAB Ballet.

Un jour ou deux. Ballet in 1 act; ch. M. Cunningham; mus. Cage; déc. J. Johns. Prod. 6 Nov. 1973, Opéra, Paris, with Piollet, Denard, Guizerix. The work lasts an evening; it offers 'a number of separate d. events—solos, duets, trios, quintets, and larger groups—sometimes seen as a single entity, and sometimes in multiple, with

several going on at once. There are no predetermined characters and there is no prearranged story, so the characters of the d. become characters of the individual dancers themselves, and the story is the continuity of events as they succeed each other' (Cunningham).

Urbain, James (*b* Paris, 6 Dec. 1943). Fr. dancer. Studied with Clémence Louis, Peretti, Hightower, and Besobrasova. D. in Petit's *Cyrano de Bergerac* in 1959, with Grand B. du Marquis de Cuevas 1960–2, co. of Golovine 1962–3, Grand B. Classique de France from 1965, B. Th. Contemporain since 1968, and various cos. in Italy. Has created many roles in bs. by Descombey, Adret, Butler, and in Italy by Gai and dell'Ara. Gold Medal (Paris, 1966); Prix Nijinsky (1966).
BIBL.: A. P. Hersin, 'J.U.', *Les Saisons de la danse* (1968/12); S. Goodman, 'J.U.', *Dance Magazine* (1973/1).

Urbani, Giuseppe (*b* Rome, 30 Dec. 1928). Ital. dancer, choreographer, and b. master. Studied at Rome Op. B. School. D. in many b. seasons of Ital. op. houses and with Milloss in Cologne 1959–62. B. master of Bonn B. 1962–9; ch. many bs. Now a freelance ch. in Italy. Positano Prize (1969).

Urseanu, Tilde (*b* Bucharest, 9 Nov. 1923). Rum. dancer, choreographer, b. mistress, and teacher. Studied with Paul Sybill, Karalli, and Anton Romanian, later also in Moscow. Joined Bucharest State Op. B. in 1945, and later became soloist. Started to ch. in 1957; created many bs. for various Rum. cos. Also teaches at the Bucharest State B. School.

Ursuliak, Alexander (*b* Edmonton, 1 Oct. 1937). Can. dancer, teacher, and b. master. Studied with Fred Seychuk in Can. and with Kliavin, Zaytsev, and Vakulin in Kiev; graduated at Kiev State B. School as b. master and ch. Member of Can. National B. 1961–3. Taught at London Arts Educational School 1963–5, then at Vienna State Op. B. 1966–73 (also became assistant b. dir. and dir. of State Op. B. School). B. master of Stuttgart B. since 1973. Was married to the d. Galina Samsova and is now married to the d. Christl Himmelbauer.

U.S.A. See *United States*.

U.S.S.R. See *Soviet Union*.

Utah Repertory Dance Theatre. See *Repertory Dance Theatre*.

Uthoff, Ernst (*b* Duisburg, 28 Dec. 1904). Ger.-Chilean dancer, choreographer, teacher, and b. master. Studied with Jooss and Leeder. Joined Folkwang B. in 1927; created Standard Bearer in *The Green Table* (1932). Emigrated with Jooss. When the Bs. Jooss went to S. Amer. in 1941, he and his d. wife Lola Botka stayed in Santiago de Chile, where they opened a school at the univ., from which came the Chilean National B. He was thus the pioneer in S. Amer. of the Jooss-Leeder technique. He based the repertory of his co. on some of Jooss's best bs. and some of his own, incl. Gluck's *Don Juan*, Stravinsky's *Petrushka*, and Orff's *Carmina Burana*. Retired in 1965. He is the father of Michael U. Gold Medal 'por su relevante labor en favor de danza en Chile' (1971).

BIBL.: H. Ehrmann-Ewart, 'A Descendant of the Jooss Ballet Thrives in Chile', *Dance Magazine* (1957/4).

Uthoff, Michael (*b* Santiago, 5 Nov. 1943). Chil. dancer, choreographer, and b. director. The son of Ernst U., he studied at Juilliard School, School of Amer. B., and with Graham. Début with Limón's co. in 1964. Member of Joffrey B. 1965–9; created leading roles in Arpino's *Olympics* and *Nightwings* (1966). Member of First Chamber D. Co. 1970–3 with his d. wife Lisa Bradley, where he started to ch., and produced the d. film *Seafall* (after Poe's *Annabel Lee*, mus. Albinoni, with himself and Bradley, 1970). Artistic Dir. of Hartford B. Co. since 1973. His bs. incl. *Aves Mirabiles* (mus. L. Foss), *Brahms Variations,* and *Cantata* (mus. A. Ginastera).

BIBL.: M. Marks, 'M.U.', *Dance Magazine* (1968/10); N. Laroche, in 'Hartford Ballet', *Dance Magazine* (1975/2).

V

Vaculík, Libor (b Prague, 10 Mar. 1957). Czech dancer. Studied at b. dept. of Prague State Conservatory. Joined National Th. Bratislava b. as a soloist in 1976. Bronze Medal (Varna, 1978).

Vaganova, Agrippina Jacovlevna (b St. Petersburg, 24 June 1879, d Leningrad, 5 Nov. 1951). Sov. dancer, teacher, and b. director. Studied at St. Petersburg Imperial B. Academy, graduating in 1897. Joined Maryinsky Th.; her career progressed extremely slowly, in spite of her superb technical gifts, and she did not become ballerina until 1915. Retired in 1916. Taught at Volynsky's private School of Russ. B. from 1919; moved to Petrograd State Ch. School in 1921 and became its most famous teacher, and its dir. in 1934. She mainly taught the perfection classes and the pedagogic courses, gradually developing her teaching system, which was named after her, and now forms the basis of b. education in the Eastern Bloc countries and in many schools of the Western world. She is considered one of the most important teachers of b. history; her pupils included Semyonova, Ulanova, Vetcheslova, Dudinskaya, Shelest, Kolpakova, and Volkova. Her system, which she published in *Fundamentals of the Classic Dance* (Leningrad, 1934; Eng. translation by A. Chujoy, New York, 1937) is an unusually harmonious synthesis of the most important schools and individual styles from all over the world, incl. the Cecchetti system and the technique of Preobrajenska, which she meticulously analysed. Thanks to her teaching system the new Sov. b. was able to develop its exceptional virtuosity. Appointed ass. b. dir. at the GATOB in 1927; b. dir. of the GATOB and Kirov B. 1931–7. She actively furthered the first prods. of Vainonen's *Flames of Paris* (1932) and Zakharov's *Fountain of Bakhchisaray* (1934), and was herself responsible for the highly individual prods. of *Swan Lake* (1933) and *Esmeralda* (1935) and various display pieces. In 1957 the Leningrad Ch. School was named after her. Merited Artist of the R.S.F.S.R. (1936); Stalin Prize (1946).

BIBL.: N. Rene, 'She Linked the Generations', *Dance and Dancers* (1962/1); various authors, *A.J.V.* (Leningrad-Moscow, 1938—in Russ.).

Vagaries of the Human Heart, The. See *Intermittences du coeur, Les.*

Vaillat, Léandre (b Publier, 1876, d Paris, 1 Oct. 1952). Fr. writer on b. For many years doyen of Fr. b. critics; wrote *Histoire de la danse* (1942), *La Taglioni* (1942), *Olga Spessivtseva* (1945), *Ballets de l'Opéra* (1947), and *La Danse à l'Opéra de Paris* (1951).

Vainonen, Vasily Ivanovich (b St. Petersburg, 21 Feb. 1901, d Moscow, 23 Mar. 1964). Sov. dancer and choreographer. Studied at Imperial B. Academy; graduated in 1919. Joined GATOB and became an excellent character d. As a ch. he started with smaller pieces for the Evenings of Young B., for which he created his spectacular *Moszkowski Waltz*. His first professional b. was Shostakovich's *The Golden Age* (1930), which aroused great controversy because of its acrobatic daring. His first prod. of Asafiev's *Flames of Paris* (1932) was a more lasting success and so, especially, was his *Nutcracker* (1934—still in the Sov. repertory), while his *Raymonda* (with a new libr. by Slonimsky, 1938—all GATOB and Kirov Th.) was soon taken out of the repertory. His futher bs. included *Partisan Days* (mus. Asafiev, 1937, GATOB and Kirov Th.), *Mirandolina* (mus. V. Vasilenko, Bolshoi Filial Th., Moscow, 1949), *Coast of Happiness* (mus. A. Spadavecchia, Novosibirsk, 1952—also a brilliantly successful prod. of *Sleeping Beauty*), and *Gayane* (mus. Khachaturian, Bolshoi Th., Moscow, 1957). Worked for Budapest State Op. B. 1950–1, reviving *Flames of Paris* and *Nutcracker*. He was one of the guiding spirits of the new Sov. ch. Stalin Prize (1947 and 1949); Merited Artist of the R.S.F.S.R. (1939). Married to the d. and b. mistress Klavdia Armashevskaya.

BIBL.: Armashevskaya and Nikita V., *Ballet Master* (Moscow, 1971—in Russ.).

Vainqueurs, Les (Eng. *The Victors*). Ceremony in 5 scenes after an idea by Wagner; mus. Wagner (excerpts from *Tristan and Isolde*) and classic Indian and Tibetan mus.; ch. Béjart; déc. Yahne le Toumelin. Prod. 10 Dec. 1969, B. of the 20th Century, Th. Royal de la Monnaie, Brussels, with Donn, Bari. The scenes are entitled Mandala—The Forest—The Vessel—On the Way to the Other Coast—The Ocean. Béjart attempts to create a synthesis of Indian initiation rites and the *Tristan and Isolde* story, referring to some Wagner letters, his mention of Bournof's *Introduction à l'histoire du Buddhisme* in the third part of his autobiography, and the *Tibetan Book of the Great Liberation,* which says 'The victors are the Buddhas'.

BIBL.: G. Balanchine, in *Balanchine's Complete Stories of the Great Ballets* (Garden City, N.Y., 1977).

Valberkh, Ivan Ivanovich (b Moscow, 14 July 1766, d St. Petersburg, 26 July 1819). Russ. dancer, choreographer, b. master, and teacher. Studied at St. Petersburg Th. School with Angiolini and Canzani, graduating in 1786. He d. under LePicq and became the first Russ. b. master of renown. Succeeded Canziani as b. inspector of the co. of the St. Petersburg Bolshoi Th. and dir. of the school in 1794; later he also reorganized the Moscow school. He became a fierce partisan of Russ. dancers and assisted Eugenia Kolosova in her career. As a ch. he preferred literary subjects, and plots from popular ops. and plays. Ch. *The New Werther* (mus. Serge Titov, 1799), *Romeo and Juliet* (a tragic b. with choruses, 1809) and various bs. on patriotic subjects (e.g. *Love for the Fatherland,* mus. Catarino Cavos, 1812, which was said to have inflamed the spectators to such a degree that they went from the th. to the recruiting offices to enlist for the Army fighting Napoleon).

BIBL.: N. Roslavleva, in *Era of the Russian Ballet* (London, 1966).

Valkyrien. Ballet in 4 acts; libr. and ch. A. Bournonville; mus. J. P. E. Hartmann; déc. Edvard Lehmann. Prod. 13 Sep. 1861, Royal Dan. B., Copenhagen, with J. Price, V. Price, A. Füssel, H. Scharff, L. Gade. The b. interweaves the Valkyrie theme with the story of Harald Hildetand's death; Odin takes the shape of the king's counsellor to save him from the ignominy of dying in his bed.

BIBL.: S. Jacobsen, 'Bournonville's Ballet *Valkyrien*' in *Theatre Research Studies* (Copenhagen, 1972).

Valois, Dame Ninette de (orig. Edris Stannus; *b* Baltiboys, Ireland, 6 June 1898). Brit. dancer, choreographer, teacher, and b. director. Studied with Lila Field, then in London with E. Espinosa and Cecchetti. Appeared in revues and pantomimes in 1914, in the Cov. Gdn. op. season of 1919, with the Massine-Lopokova co. in 1922, and with Diaghilev's Bs. Russes 1923–5 (also in 1926). Opened her London Academy of Ch. Art in 1926 and began her collaboration with Lilian Baylis of the Old Vic; she taught movement to actors, and appeared with her pupils in the play prods. Also worked at the Cambridge Festival Th. and with Yeats at the Abbey Th., Dublin. Ch. Mozart's *Les petits riens* (her first b.) as the opening b. for a perf. of *Hansel and Gretel* at the Old Vic in 1928, the first of various b. perfs. at this th. Closed her private school in 1931 and moved to the official b. school of the newly opened Sadler's Wells Th., where her reorganized co., now called Vic-Wells B., appeared in regular b. perfs. The co. grew steadily and became the Sadler's Wells B., with which she moved to the Royal Op. House, Cov. Gdn., in 1946; it became the Royal B. in 1956. In addition she founded a second co. in 1946, the Sadler's Wells Op. B., which soon changed its name to Sadler's Wells Th. B. During these years she was also in charge of the rapidly expanding school. She continued to d. occasionally until 1937, mostly in demi-caractère roles, and d. Webster in *A Wedding Bouquet* in a gala at Sadler's Wells in 1930. As a ch. her most successful years were the 1930s, when she created *Danse sacrée et danse profane* (mus. Debussy, Camargo

Society, 1930), *La Création du monde* (mus. Milhaud) and *Job* (mus. Vaughan Williams; both Camargo Society, 1931), *Bar aux Folies-Bergère* (mus. Chabrier, B. Rambert), *The Haunted Ballroom* (mus. G. Toye) and *La Jarre* (mus. Casella, 1934), *The Rake's Progress* (mus. G. Gordon, 1935), *The Gods Go a-Begging* (mus. Handel, arr. Beecham), *Barabau* (mus. Rieti) and *Prometheus* (mus. Beethoven 1936), *Checkmate* (mus. Bliss, 1937), *La Roi nu* (mus. Françaix, 1938), and *The Prospect Before Us* (mus. Boyce, arr. Lambert, 1940), succeeded by *Orpheus and Eurydice* (mus. Gluck, 1941), *Promenade* (mus. Haydn, arr. Evans, 1943), and *Don Quixote* (mus. R. Gerhard, 1950). Resigned as dir. of the Royal B. in 1963, but continued to work actively for the school until 1971 and then became a Life Governor. Together with Rambert she is one of the great pioneers of the new Brit. b., thanks to whom the Royal B. and the Royal B. Sch. have gained worldwide renown. She still continues to lecture and advise in numerous capacities at home and abroad. BBC *Omnibus* TV portrait (1974). Author of *Invitation to the Ballet* (1937) and *Come Dance with Me* (1957). C.B.E. (1947); D.B.E. (1951); C.H. (1981); Chevalier de la Légion d'Honneur (1950); honorary degrees from London (1947), Reading (1951), Oxford (1955), and Aberdeen (1958) Univs.; Erasmus Prize (1974).

BIBL.: A. Bland, in *The Royal Ballet—The first Fifty Years* (London, 1981).

Valse, La. Poème chorégraphique in 1 act; ch. Nijinska; mus. Ravel; déc. A. Benois. Prod. 12 Jan. 1929, I. Rubinstein Co., Monte Carlo, with Rubinstein, Vilzak. Ravel imagined the b. as 'a sort of apotheosis of the Viennese waltz ... At first the scene is dimmed by a kind of swirling mist, through which one discerns, vaguely and intermittently, the waltzing couples. Little by little the vapours disperse, the illumination grows brighter, revealing an immense ballroom filled with dancers.' Often revived in individual versions; the most famous was by Balanchine, cost. Karinska, light. Rosenthal, 20 Feb. 1951, New York City B., City Center, N.Y., with LeClercq, Magallanes, Moncion; this version used Ravel's *Valses nobles et sentimentales* as an introduction. 2nd channel Ger. TV prod. (of the Balanchine version) in 1972. Another version by Ashton (La Scala di Milano, 1958, revived for Royal B., 1959; this prod. is part of the film *An Evening with the Royal Ballet,* (1965).

BIBL.: G. Balanchine, 'L.V.' in Balanchine's *New Complete Stories of the Great Ballets* (Garden City, N.Y., 1968).

Valses nobles et sentimentales. Ravel composed his group of 8 short waltzes for piano 'after the example of Schubert' in 1911. They were first performed anonymously by the Paris Societé Indépendante. Trouhanova commissioned Ravel to orchestrate the pieces in 1912, and in this form they were first prod. as *Adélaide, ou Le Langage des* *fleurs*, ch. Clustine, déc. M. Drésa, 22 Apr. 1912, Th. du Châtelet, Paris, with Trouhanova. Later versions by Lifar (Opéra, Paris, 1938), Ashton (Sadler's Wells B., London, 1947), MacMillan (Ger. Op. Berlin, 1966), and Hynd (New London B., 1975). Balanchine used them as an introduction to his version of *La Valse* (New York City B., N.Y., 1951).

Vamos, György (now Youri V.; *b* Budapest, 21 Nov. 1946). Hung. dancer. Studied at Budapest State B. Inst.; graduated in 1967. Joined Budapest State Op. B. in 1968. Went to Munich State Op. B. in 1972 and later became principal d. Later worked as a ch.; dir. Dortmund B. since 1985.

Van. All names preceded by 'van' (or 'von') are listed under the family name (e.g. Beethoven, Dantzig, Dyk, Manen, Praagh, Schayk, etc.).

Vangsaae, Mona (not Vangsaa, though she appeared thus spelt; *b* Copenhagen, 29 Apr. 1920, *d* there, 17 May 1983). Dan. dancer and teacher. Studied at Royal Dan. B. School and in Paris. Joined Royal Dan. B. in 1938; solo d. 1942–63. Created Juliet in Ashton's *Romeo and Juliet* (1955) and title-role in Cullberg's *Moon Reindeer* (1957). Co-dir. of the Dan. b. Academy and B. Th. with her former husband Frank Schaufuss until it disbanded in 1974. Mother of the d. Peter Schaufuss. Knight of Dannebrog.

Vanina Vanini. Ballet in 1 act and 7 scenes; libr. and ch. Kasatkina-Vassiliov; mus. N. Karetnikov; déc. A. Goncharov. Prod. 25 May 1962, Bolshoi Th., Moscow, with Riabynkina, Tikhonov. The first b. of the Sov. wife and husband team of choreographers was based on Stendhal's story *V.V.* The title-figure is an Ital. princess, who hides a wounded Carbonaro in her father's house. They fall in love, but the patriotic consciousness of the Carbonaro makes him return to his comrades.

Vantaggio, Giancarlo (*b* Rome, 11 Oct. 1936). Ital. dancer and choreographer. Studied at Rome Op. B. School. Joined Rome Op. B. and later became principal d.; created roles in many Milloss bs. Has also d. with various other Ital. cos., in Bonn and Bordeaux. Started as a ch. for the Fogli d'Album programme at the Spoleto Festival of 1961. Has often collaborated with S. Bussotti. Petit's assistant and répétiteur for Bs. de Marseille since 1974, for which he ch. *Bizet'isme* (1974).

Varèse, Edgard (*b* Paris, 22 Dec. 1883, *d* New York, 6 Nov. 1965). Fr.-Amer. composer. Wrote no b. mus., but his concert mus. has often been used for d. purposes, incl. *Intégrales* by Graham (New York, 1934), *Ionisation* and *Octandre* by Holm (in *Trend*, Bennington College, 1937), various pieces by T. Gsovsky (in *Labyrinth of Truth*, Ger. Op. Berlin, 1964), *Déserts* by Milloss (in *Einöde*, Vienna State Op., 1965—also by Sokolow, B. Rambert, 1967, and Descombey, B.-Th. Contemporain, 1968), *Intégrales, Densité 21.5, Octandre, Hyperprism,* and *Ionisation* by Tetley (in

Small Parades, Netherlands D. Th., 1972). A programme *Hommages à V.* was premiered by the Paris Op. B. on 24 May 1973, consisting of *Octandre, Le Poème électronique, Arcana* (all ch. Blaska), *Hyperprism, Offrandes* (both ch. Charrat), *Intégrales, Amériques* (both ch. Butler), *Ionisation* (ch. S. Keuten), and *Densité 21.5* (ch. Carlson).

Variation. Designates in b. every solo d. not otherwise specified.

Variations. Ballet in 3 parts; ch. Balanchine; mus. Stravinsky; light. R. Bates. Prod. 31 Mar. 1966, New York City B., State Th., N.Y., with Farrell. The plotless b. is set to Stravinsky's Variations for Orchestra, dedicated to the memory of Aldous Huxley, which are played three times for a set of three dances, the first d. by 12 girls, the second by 6 boys, and the third a solo for the ballerina.
BIBL.: G. Balanchine, 'V.' in *Balanchine's New Complete Stories of the Great Ballets* (Garden City, N.Y., 1968).

Variations for Four. Divertissement; ch. Dolin; mus. Marguerite Keogh; cost. Tom Lingwood. Prod. 5 Sep. 1957, London Festival B., Royal Festival Hall, London, with Gilpin, Flindt, Godfrey, Prokovsky. A brilliant display piece of male virtuosity—a sort of modern male equivalent to the historic *Pas de quatre.* ITV prod. in 1958. Revived for many cos. Dolin later ch. a female supplement—in this version the b. is called *V.f.F. plus Four.*
BIBL.: G. Balanchine, in *Balanchine's Complete Stories of the Great Ballets* (Garden City, N.Y., 1977).

Varkovitsky, Vladimir Alexandrovich (*b* Odessa, 1 Jan. 1916, *d* Moscow, 9 Oct. 1974). Sov. dancer, b. master, choreographer, and teacher. Studied at Leningrad B. School. Upon graduation in 1936 joined Kirov B., then Maly Th. 1941–3. Teacher and ch. Moscow B. School 1944–53. B. master Yerevan 1953–4. His bs. incl. *Christmas Eve* (mus. Asafiev, Leningrad B. School, 1938), *The Story of the Pope and his Worker Balda* (mus. Chulaki, Maly Th., 1940), *The Snowmaiden* (mus. Tchaikovsky, Moscow B. School, 1946), *The Dawn* (mus. Zagorsky, Kishinev, 1960), *Gavroche* (mus. Bitov, Maly Th., 1958) etc. Was known for his concert dances (*The Monument, Fly, Pigeons, The Swanmaiden*) and programmes for children. Was married to the d. writer and lexicographer E. Souritz.

Varna, International Ballet Competition. The Bulg. Ministry of Culture staged the first competition for dancers at the seaside resort of Varna in 1964. The second was held in 1965, and the third in 1966; it has since been held every second year. An international jury, with Ulanova as chairman, judges the competitors, who come in 2 classes: juniors aged 15–19, and seniors aged 20–28. Gold, silver, and bronze medals are awarded. It is one of the most prestigious competitions, and many of today's star dancers became known to a wider international public through it. Apart from the U.S.S.R., Cuba has provided the most medallists.

Vasiliev, Vladimir Victorovich (*b* Moscow, 18 Apr. 1940). Sov. dancer. Studied at Moscow Bolshoi School; graduated in 1958. Joined Bolshoi B.; became soloist and soon an internationally popular star. He frequently appears in the West (usually with his d. wife, Yekaterina Maximova). A d. of unshakable heroic optimism, exceptional virtuosity, and irresistible dynamism. Created leading roles in Radunsky's new version of *The Humpbacked Horse* (1960), Tarasova's and Lapauri's *Song of the Forests* (1961), Lavrovsky's *Pages of Life* (1961), Goleizovsky's *Leili and Medshnun* (1964), and Grigorovich's *Nutcracker* (1966), *Spartacus* (1968), *Sleeping Beauty* (1973), *Ivan the Terrible* (second premiere, 1975), and *Angara* (1976). His first ch. was *Icarus* (mus. S. Slonimsky, 1971), followed by *Macbeth* (mus. K. Molchanov, 1980). He appears in the b. films *The Humpbacked Horse* (1961) and *Secret of Success* (1967), and in the Sov. TV film *The Duet* (1974). Gold Medal (Varna, 1964); Nijinsky Prize (Paris, 1964); Merited Artist of the R.S.F.S.R. (1964); Lenin Prize (1970).
BIBL.: A. Iloupina, 'V.', with complete check-list of roles and activities, *Les Saisons de la danse* (1970/6); T. Tobias, 'Bolshoi Profiles: V.V.', *Dance Magazine* (1975/6).

Vasiliov, Vladimir Yudovich (*b* Moscow, 8 Feb. 1931). Sov. dancer and choreographer. Studied at Bolshoi B. School; graduated in 1949. Studied further at GITIS; graduated as ch. in 1953. Joined Bolshoi B. in 1949. Established a successful ch. partnership with his wife Natalia Kasatkina. Their bs. include *Vanina Vanini* (mus. N. Karetnikov, 1962), *Heroic Poem* (mus. Karetnikov, 1964), *Le Sacre du printemps* (mus. Stravinsky, 1965), *Preludes and Fugues* (mus. Bach, 1968; all for Bolshoi B.), *Creation of the World* (mus. A. Petrov, Kirov B., 1971), and *Seeing the Light* (mus. Yuri Buzko, Stanislavsky and Nemirovich-Danchenko Music Th., 1974).

Vašut, Vladimír (*b* Dolní Marklovice, 26 Mar. 1931). Czech. writer. Studied at Prague Univ. and Academy of Arts, joining the dance dept. of the latter in 1974. Has worked as a d. critic for various publications since 1956. Has written so far 16 b. librettos, incl. the much performed *Hiroshima*. Works as a d. specialist at the Prague Theatre Institute.

Vaughan, David (*b* London, 17 May 1924). Brit. dancer, administrator, and writer on dance. Studied with Rambert, de Vos. School of Amer. B., Tudor, M. Cunningham, and others. D. with the cos. of Waring, P. Taylor, L. Johnson, Litz, and others. Administrator of M. Cunningham Studio 1959–72, and for some of the overseas tours of the co. Associate editor of *Ballet Review*. Contributor to *Dancing Times* and *Dance Magazine*. Author of *Frederick Ashton and his Ballets* (London, 1977), co-author (with M. Clarke) of *The Encyclopedia of Dance & Ballet* (London, 1977).

Vaussard, Christiane (*b* Neuilly-sur-Seine, 1923). Fr. dancer and teacher. Studied at Paris Opéra B. School. Joined its co. and became première danseuse in 1945; étoile 1947–61. Created roles in Lifar's *Le Chevalier errant* (1950), *Firebird* (1954), and *Pas de quatre* (1960). Now retired, but continues to teach at the Opéra.

Vazem, Yekaterina Ottovna (*b* Moscow, 13 Jan. 1848, *d* Leningrad, 1937). Rus. dancer. Studied at St. Petersburg Imperial B. Academy; graduated in 1876. Joined St. Petersburg Bolshoi B.; Petipa's favourite ballerina 1864–84. He ch. for her *Le Corsaire* (1868), *The Butterfly* (1874), *The Bandits* (1875), *La Bayadère* (1877), *The Daughter of the Snows* (1879), *Zoraya* (1881), *Night and Day* (1883) and the Grand Pas in his new version of *Paquita* (1881). She was technically brilliant, but cool. Appeared as a guest in Amer. and created a sensation when she participated in some classes at the Paris Opéra. Retired in 1884, but continued to teach at the Academy, where her pupils included Pavlova and Vaganova. Author of *Memoirs of a Ballerina of the St. Petersburg Bolshoi Theatre* (Leningrad, 1937).

Vechten, Carl van (*b* Cedar Rapids, 1880, *d* New York, 21 Dec. 1964). Amer. critic and writer. As mus. critic of the *New York Times* became the first influential d. critic of the U.S., minutely reporting on the d. events of the 1910s in Amer. and elsewhere (especially on Pavlova, Nijinsky, the Diaghilev co., and Duncan)—later contributed individual d. pieces to various magazines.
BIBL.: P. Padgette, *The Dance Writings of C.v.V.* (New York, 1974).

Veigl, Eva Maria. See *Violette, Eva Marie.*

Venema, Mea (*b* Haarlem, 22 June 1946). Dutch dancer. Studied at Kennemer B. Studio of J. L. Zielstra and T. and M. Tschernoff. Joined Netherlands D. Th. in 1963; became soloist in 1970. Created leading parts in Tetley's *Circles* (1968) and *Imaginary Film* (1970), Van Manen's *Grosse Fuge* (1971), and Falco's *Eclipse* (1974). Joined Dutch National B. in 1975.

Veneziana. Ballet in 1 act; ch. Howard; mus. Donizetti (arr. ApIvor); déc. Fedorovitch. Prod. 9 Apr. 1953, Sadler's Wells B., Cov. Gdn., London, with Elvin, Ray Powell. Set to b. mus. mainly taken from Donizetti's ops. *La Favorita* and *Dom Sebastian*. A lavish divertissement, suggesting a masked ball in Venice during Carnival.
BIBL.: C. Beaumont, 'V.' in *Ballets of Today* (1954/11).

Ventana, La. Ballet in 1 act; ch. Aug. Bournonville; mus. Lumbye. Prod. 19 June 1854 by the Price family, Casino, Copenhagen. The title means 'The Window'. The b. is a divertissement with a Spanish flavour; the mirror d. is its most famous number. The first perf. at the Royal Th. took place in 1854. Bournonville revised it in 1856, and it has been in the repertory ever since; the final Seguidilla is credited as 'after Paul Taglioni'. Revived for various cos. abroad, incl. Western Th. B. in 1968.

BIBL.: P. Brinson and C. Crisp, in *Ballet & Dance* (Newton Abbot, 1980).

Venza, Jac (*b* Chicago, 23 Dec. 1926). Amer. TV producer. Studied at Chicago Goodman Th. and Chicago Arts Inst. Has produced many d. films for various TV cos. Now Dir. of Cultural Programming, WNET-TV, New York. AADC Award in 1979 for TV series 'Dancer in America'.

Verchinina, Nina (*b* Moscow). Russ.-Amer. dancer, teacher and choreographer. Studied with Preobrajenska and Nijinska, later also Laban technique. Début with Rubinstein co. in 1928. Joined B. Russe de Monte Carlo in 1933: created roles in Massine's *Les Présages* and *Choreartium* (1933), and *Symphonie fantastique* (1936). Ballerina of San Francisco B. 1937–8, Original B. Russe 1939–41. Has since worked in Rio de Janeiro and Buenos Aires. Now teaches at her school in Copacabana.

Verde Gaio. A Lisbon-based Portuguese folklore b. co., formed in 1940; Francis Graça was its first dir., chief ch., and principal d. It later extended its repertory to include some classically based bs., but returned to its original aim of presenting national works based on national subjects in 1968. Ivo Cramér was at one time dir. of the co.

BIBL.: J. Sasportes, in *História da Dança em Portugal* (Lisbon, 1970).

Verdi, Giuseppe (*b* Le Roncole, 10 Oct. 1813, *d* Milan, 27 Jan. 1901). Ital. composer. Wrote no bs., but some of his ops., especially the revised versions he prepared for Paris, contain substantial b. sequences: *Jérusalem* (or *I lombardi*, Paris, 1847), *Les Vêpres Siciliennes* (Paris, 1855), *Le Trouvère* (or *Il trovatore*, Paris, 1857), *Macbeth* (Paris, 1865), *Don Carlos* (Paris, 1867), *Aida* (Cairo, 1871), and *Otello* (Paris, 1894). The *Four Seasons* b. from *Vêpres Siciliennes* has often been performed individually; recent versions include Verdy's (for Cincinnati B., 1970), Prokovsky's (for New London B., 1973), MacMillan's (Royal B., 1975), Smuin's *Quattro à Verdi* (San Francisco B., 1978, with Le Trouvère), and Robbins's for New York City B. (1979). During V.'s lifetime several bs. were concocted to potpourris from his ops., incl. Filippo Termanini's *Rita Gauthier* (*La traviata*, Turin, 1857). Page based her bs. *Revanche* (after *Il trovatore*, 1951) and *Camille* (after *La traviata*, 1957) on arrangements from the ops. Bs. using mus. from various of his ops. incl. J. Carter's *The Life and Death of Lola Montez* (B. Workshop, London, 1954), Cranko's *The Lady and the Fool* (arr. Mackerras, Sadler's Wells Th. B., 1954), Solov's *Vittorio* (Met. Op. House, New York,

1955). Prokovsky's *The Three Musketeers* (arr. G. Woolfenden, The Austral. B., 1980), and *Verdi Variations* (London Festival B., 1981). Petit ch. his String Quartet (Opéra, Paris, 1976).

BIBL.: A. Porter, 'V.'s Ballets', *Opera News* (vol. 36, no. 20).

Verdon, Gwen (*b* Culver City, Cal., 13 Jan. 1926). Amer. dancer and musical performer. Studied with Ernest Belcher and Maracci. Started to appear in night-club acts with J. Cole. Her great breakthrough came with Cole Porter's *Can-Can* in 1953 (ch. Kidd), since when she has made a highly successful Broadway and Hollywood career; her successes include *Damn Yankees* (1955), *Sweet Charity* (1966), and *Chicago* (1975). Was married to the ch. and dir. Bob Fosse.

BIBL.: W. Hawkins, 'Something About G.V.', *Dance Magazine* (1958/8).

Verdy, Violette (orig. Nelly Guillerm; *b* Pont-l'Abbé, 1 Dec. 1933). Fr. dancer and b. director. Studied with Rousanne and V. Gsovsky. Début with Bs. des Champs-Elysées in 1945. Starred in L. Berger's and Georgi's film *Ballerina* in 1949. Acted with the co. of M. Renaud and J.-L. Barrault. Joined Petit's Bs. de Paris in 1950. D. with co. of Maggio Musicale Fiorentino in 1951, with Chauviré's B. Marigny in 1952, Bs. de Paris again 1953–4 (also in Petit's film *The Glass Slipper*), London Festival B. 1954–5, as a freelance ballerina, with Amer. B. Th. 1957–8, and 1958–77 as a principal d. with New York City B. Has frequently appeared with other Amer. cos., and occasionally abroad. Her quicksilver effervescence and inimitable charm have won her a great following in Eur. as well as in Amer. Has created many leading parts, incl. Petit's *Le Loup* (1953), Rodrigues' *Romeo and Juliet* (Verona, 1955) and *Cinderella* (Milan, 1955), Balanchine's *Episodes* (1959), *Tchaikovsky Pas de deux, Figure in the Carpet,* and *Liebeslieder Walzer* (1960), *Electronics* (1961), *A Midsummer Night's Dream* (1962), *Jewels* (1967), *La Source* (1968), and *Sonatine* (1975), Robbins' *Dances at a Gathering* (1969), *In the Night* (1970), and *A Beethoven Pas de deux* (1973), and Balanchine's and Robbins' *Pulcinella* (1972). Artistic dir. of Paris Op. B. 1977–80, then assoc. dir. Boston B., becoming sole dir. 1983/4. Principal teacher N.Y. City B. Dance Magazine Award (1967); Chevalier dans l'Ordre des Arts et Lettres (1973).

BIBL.: I. Lidova and N. Goldner, 'V.V.', with complete check-list of roles and activities, *Les Saisons de la danse* (1971/1); M. Marks 'V.V.', *Dance Magazine* (1972/2); R. Greskovic, in 'Some Artists of the New York City Ballet', *Ballet Review* (vol. 4, no. 4). V. Huckenpahler 'V.V.' (New York, 1979).

Vere, Diana (orig. D. Fox; *b* Trinidad, 28 Sep. 1942). Brit. dancer. Studied at Elmhurst B. School and Royal B. School; joined Royal B. in 1962. Became soloist in 1968; principal d. 1970–4. Since retired. A. Genée Gold Medal (1961). Married to the d. and b. master Gary Sherwood.

Veredon, Gray (b Tauranga, N.Z., 5 Apr. 1943). Brit. dancer and choreographer. Studied with P. Gnatt, then at Royal B. School, with Idzikowsky and Hightower. Début in N.Z. in 1960. Joined Cov. Gdn. Op. B. in 1963; member of Stuttgart B. 1964–8. Went to Cologne in 1968; co-founder of Cologne D. Forum (with Baumann and Ulrich) in 1971, and one of its directors until 1978. Started to ch. for the Stuttgart Noverre matinées; his bs. include *Collage* (mus. Berio's Sinfonia, 1970), *Allmende* (mus. L. Fišer, 1972), *Chapter* (pop mus., 1973), *One Day* (mus. Brahms), *The Ragtime Dance Company* (mus. S. Joplin), *Dance Around the Golden Calf* (in the Hamburg prod. of Schoenberg's *Moses und Aron*, 1974), *Pelleas and Melisande* (mus. Schoenberg, 1975), and *Romeo and Juliet* (mus. Berlioz, 1976)—also *Parade* (mus. Satie—1981 for Metrop. Op.). Married—to the d. Svenbjörg Alexanders.

Vernon, Konstanze (orig. K. Herzfeld; b Berlin, 2 Jan. 1939). Ger. dancer. Studied with T. Gsovsky, Kiss, and Peretti. Joined Municipal Op. Berlin in 1954; became soloist in 1956. Joined Munich State Op. B. as a principal in 1962; created roles in Rosen's *Triptych* (1963) and *Symphonie fantastique* (1967), Cranko's *Encounter in Three Colours* (1968) and *Triplum*, Tetley's *Sacre du Printemps* (1974), and title role in Bohner's Munich prod. of *The Torturings of Beatrice Cenci* (1972). Resigned 1980. Co-dir. of b. department at Munich Music Academy since 1975.

Verso, Edward (b New York, 25 Oct. 1941). Amer. dancer. Studied at High School of Performing Arts and with R. Thomas and B. Fallis. Appeared in the *West Side Story* prod. and with Robbins' Bs. U.S.A. Joined Amer. B. Th. in 1962 and City Center Joffrey B. in 1969. Created roles in Robbins' *Les Noces* (1965) and Feld's *Harbinger* (1967).

Verstegen, Aart (b Rotterdam, 23 Aug. 1920). Dutch dancer and b. director. Studied with Els Keezer and Gaskell. D. with Bs. Jooss 1947–8, London Met. B. 1948–9, Oslo B. 1949–51, Düsseldorf B. 1951–3, Netherlands B. 1953–9, then with Netherlands D. Th., of which he was a founder member 1959–70 (with K. Birnie). Co-dir. of Scapino B. (with A. Navarro) 1959–70.

Vesak, Norbert (b Vancouver, 22 Oct. 1936). Can. dancer and choreographer. Studied with M. Cunningham, J. Slater, Craske, La Meri, Volkova, G. Holder, Koner, and others. D. as a guest artist with various cos. in Can. Started to work as a ch. for Vancouver Playhouse Th. Co. in 1964. Ch. numerous bs. incl. *The Ecstasy of Rita Joe* (mus. Mortifee, 1971) and *What to Do Till the Messiah Cometh* (mus. Chilliwack, Werren, and Syrinx, 1972; both for Royal Winnipeg B.), *Whispers of Darkness* (mus. Mahler, National B. of Can., 1974),

and *In Quest of the Sun* (mus. G. Martindale, Royal Winnipeg B., 1975). Dir. of Metrop. Op. B., N.Y., since 1976.

Vesalii Icones. Solo D. by and with W. Louther; mus. P. Maxwell Davies. Prod. 9 Dec. 1969, Queen Elizabeth Hall, London. Based on the anatomical engravings of Andreas Vesalius from his *De Humani Corporis Fabrica* of 1543; the d. relates these images of a man, almost completely naked, to the Stations of the Cross. The work was conceived by the comp. for cello solo, small instrumental group, and d. After its first perf. it was taken into the repertory of London Contemporary D. Th.

Vescovo, Bruno (b Lodi, 5 Feg. 1949). Ital. dancer. Studied at La Scala B. School. Joined its co. in 1968 and became soloist in 1971.

Vespri. Divertissement; ch. Prokovsky; mus. Verdi; déc. N. McDowell. Prod. 11 Aug. 1973, New London B., La Coruña (Spain), with Samsova, Prokovsky. A display piece, set to the *Four Seasons* b. mus. from Verdi's *Les Vêpres siciliennes* (1855). Other recent versions by Verdy (Cincinnati B., 1970), MacMillan (Royal B., 1975), and Robbins (New York City B., 1979).

Vessel, Anne Marie (b Copenhagen, 1 May 1949). Dan. dancer. The daughter of the d. and régisseur Poul V. (b Copenhagen, 1914). Studied at Royal Dan. B. School: joined the co. in 1967 and eventually became soloist.

Vestris. Famous Ital.-Fr. family of dancers, originating in Florence. Tommaso Maria Ippolito V. had 7 children, 3 of whom contributed to b. history: Teresa V. (1726–1808), Gaetano V. (1728–1808), and Angiolo V. (1730–1809). Gaetano V. was the father of Auguste V. (1760–1842), who was the father of Armand V. (1786–1825).
BIBL.: G. Capon, *Les V.—Le Dieu de la Danse et Sa Famille 1730–1808 d'après des Rapports de Police et des Documents inédits* (Paris, 1908).

Vestris, Angiolo Maria Gasparo (b Florence, 1730, d Paris 1809). Ital. dancer and actor. Son of Tommaso V. and brother of Gaetano V. D. at various Ital. ths.; studied in Paris with Dupré. Became a soloist at the Opéra in 1753 and appeared as a guest for 4 years at several Eur. ths. Noverre's principal d. during his Stuttgart era. Returned to Paris in 1767, where he became an actor at the Comédie Italienne. Was married to the actress Rose Gourgaud.

Vestris, Armand (b Paris, 1786, d Vienna, 17 May 1825). Fr. dancer and choreographer. Son of Auguste V. Studied with his grandfather, Gaetano V., and appeared with his father and grandfather, when 4 years old, on the stage of the Opéra. He worked in Italy and Port., but mainly in London (1809–16): ch. at the King's Th. 1813–16, later also in Italy and Vienna until his death. He was married to Eliza Bartholozzi, the famous Mme V. of Eng. th. history.

Vestris, Auguste (orig. Marie-Jean Augustin—the public called him Vestr'Allard; *b* Paris, 27 Mar. 1760, *d* there 5 Dec. 1842). Fr. dancer and teacher. The illegitimate son of Gaetano V. and the d. Marie Allard; studied with his father. Début in the divertissement *La Cinquantaine* in 1772; immediately recognized to be extraordinarily gifted. His first big success came as Amor in his father's b. *Endymion* (1773). Appointed soloist at the Opéra in 1776, premier danseur in 1778, and premier sujet de la danse in 1780. Danced in the first prod. of Noverre's *Les petits riens* and of Gluck's *Alceste* (1778). Appeared with his father in London in 1781; they were so successful that Parliament interrupted its sessions when they were dancing. The favourite male d. of Gardel's bs. 1781–7. He was highly conceited, rather short, and knock-kneed; but he also had a sensational élévation and was such a dazzling virtuoso that he was soon considered the first d. in Eur. In the aftermath of the Fr. Revolution he fled to London in 1789, where he d. in Noverre's bs. until 1793. Returned triumphantly to the Opéra, where he had to fight the rivalry of the younger Duport; continued to d. until 1816. For a while he had financial difficulties and even went to prison, but then the situation improved. He became one of the most famous teachers of his time; his pupils included Didelot, Perrot, Aug. Bournonville, and Marie Taglioni, with whom he appeared in a stately minuet at the Opéra in 1835. B. technique owes to him a considerable improvement of virtuoso resources. He had a formidable ballon; his batterie and pirouette technique were also considered almost miraculous. He was extremely vain and difficult (he left his first wife a few days after the birth of his son Armand); but he was the undisputed star d. of his time. Noverre admired his expressiveness and called him the 'nouveau Protée de la danse.'
BIBL.: S. Lifar, *A.V.* (Paris, 1950).

Vestris, Gaetano Apolline Baldassare (*b* Florence, 18 Apr. 1728, *d* Paris, 23 Sep. 1808). Ital. dancer and choreographer. Son of Tommaso V., brother of Angiolo V., and father of Auguste V. D. at various Ital. and Ger. ths., studied with Dupré in Paris. Made his début at the Opéra in 1748; appointed premier danseur in 1751. Highly conceited; went to Turin and Berlin for personal reasons 1754–5. Returned to the Opéra in 1755, and enjoyed one triumph after another. Appointed co-ch. (with Dauberval) in 1761. The first d. to appear without a mask (in *Médée et Jason*); considered the most modern d. of his time. Known as 'le beau V.', later 'l'homme à la belle jambe', and finally 'le dieu de la danse' (as Dupré had been). He succeeded Lany as chief ch. in 1770, but was only moderately successful; he handed over the job to Noverre in 1776, with whom he had already collaborated in Stuttgart.

He continued to d. until 1782, but concentrated increasingly on directing the affiliated b. school and on the career of Auguste, his son by the d. Marie Allard. He met the d. Anna Heinel in Stuttgart, and married her in 1792. When he appeared with his son in London in 1781 Parliament interrupted its sessions. Of himself he said 'Il n'y a que trois grands hommes en Europe: le Roi de Prusse, M. de Voltaire et moi.' Obviously he must have been not only a formidable technician, but also a great artist, of whom Noverre spoke with the greatest respect; Castil-Blaze called his d. 'un chef d'oeuvre de noblesse et de grâce.'
BIBL.: L. Moore, in *Artists of the Dance* (New York, 1938).

Vestris, Teresa (also Thérèse; *b* Florence, 1726, *d* Paris, 1808). Ital. dancer. Daughter of Tommaso V., sister of Angiolo and Gaetano V. Studied in Naples; made her début in Palermo. D. in Vienna; there became the mistress of Prince Esterhazy. This aroused the jealousy of Empress Maria Theresia, who ordered her immediate transfer to Dresden. She appeared there and in Florence and came to Paris in 1746, where she prepared the ground for the entrée of her brothers at the Opéra. She made her Opéra début with them in 1751 and was in great demand as a soloist until 1766; she shared the glamour of the meteoric career of her brothers.

Vetcheslova, Tatiana Mikhailovna (*b* St. Petersburg, 10 Feb. 1910). Sov. dancer and b. mistress. Daughter of the ballerina Yevgenia Snietkova. Studied with Ulanova at the Petrograd State Ch. School; graduated in 1928. Member of the GATOB and Kirov B. 1929–53; d. the standard ballerina roles. Esmeralda, in Vaganova's new version of 1935, was her greatest success. Created roles in Zakharov's *Fountain of Bakhchisaray* (Zarema, 1934), Chaboukiani's *Heart of the Hills* (1938) and *Laurencia* (1939), Anisimova's *Gayane* (1942), Sergeyev's *Cinderella* (1946), and the title role in Bourmeister's *Tatiana* (1947). Toured Amer. with Chaboukiani 1933–4. Retired as a d., and dir. Leningrad Ch. School until 1954. Later b. mistress of the Kirov B. Author of *I am a Ballerina* (Leningrad, 1966). Merited Artist of the R.S.F.S.R. (1939); Stalin Prize (1946). Was married to the d. Sviatoslav Kusnetzov.

Vic-Wells Ballet. See *Royal Ballet*.

Vienna. Bs. on horse-back were very popular around the middle of the 17th century and still continue at the Hofreitschule. At the court of the Habsburgs b. was strictly controlled by Ital. and to a lesser degree Fr. b. masters. Hilverding (1743–68) was one of the earliest pioneers of the b. d'action, which gained considerable ground under Angiolini (Gluck's *Don Juan* 1761; *Semiramis*, 1765), and Noverre (1767–74), who ch. an enormous number of works. Salvatore Viganò was important at the turn of the century; his first prod. of Beethoven's *The Creatures of Prometheus* (1801) was the climax of his career. The b. monopoly of the Kärntnertor Th. (the op. house) was challenged when the Th. auf der Wieden started to give b. perfs. of its own; Horschelt's fairy-tale bs. were a popular success, and so was his Children's B. The parodistic pantomimes staged by Rainoldi at the Th. in der Leopoldstadt were hardly less popular. In the 1820s Fanny Elssler, the city's greatest d., rose to fame, and Marie Taglioni, who was to become her fiercest rival, made her début in 1822. During the 1830s and 40s the great stars of the romantic b. visited V. regularly and appeared in *La Sylphide* (1836), *Le Diable boîteux* and *La Fille du Danube* (1839), *La Gitana* (1840), *The Revived Sylphide* (by Bernard Vestris, 1841), *Giselle* (1842), *La Tarentule* (1843), *La Péri* (1844), *Beatrice from Ghent* (1845—the year of the local débuts of K. Lanner and A. Maywood), *Esmeralda*, and *Le Diable à quatre* (1846)—staged after the Paris model prods. From 1853 Paul Taglioni regularly came from Berlin as a guest-ch. Aug. Bournonville was b. master 1855–6; he staged *The Gazelle from Bassora* (1855) and *Napoli* (1856). J. Rota's *A Sylphide in Peking* (1862) was a local curiosity. The first b. prod. at the new Court Op. House on the Ring was P. Taglioni's *Sardanapal* (1869). Telle then produced the local first prods. of *Coppélia* (1876) and *Sylvia* (1877). He was succeeded by Hassreiter (1891–1920), who made his début as a ch. with the enormously popular *The Fairy Doll* in 1888 (still in the repertory). Hassreiter ch. 48 bs., mostly collaborating with the comp. J. Bayer, and contributed one of the most successful chapters to the city's b. history. The Wiesenthal sisters embarked from here with their programmes of Viennese waltzes. After Hassreiter's retirement the next important b. masters were Kröller (1922–8; first prod. of R. Strauss's *Couperin Suite*, 1923, and *Schlagobers*, 1924) and Wallmann (1934–9; first prod. of F. Salmhofer's *Oesterreichische Bauernhochzeit*, 1934). Hanka's appointment in 1942 began a new period of relative stability; the highlights were her prods. of T. Berger's *Homeric Symphony* (1950), Blacher's *The Moor of Venice* (1955), Hellmesberger-Schönherr's *Hotel Sacher* (1957), and von Einem's *Medusa* (1957). When the State Op. reopened after the war in its rebuilt house on the Ring in 1955, Hanka got G. Hamilton to take care of the classic side of the repertory; *Giselle* was his début prod. in 1955. After Hanka's death in 1958 a new period of unrest began with a rapid turnover of b. masters and directors: Parlić (1958–61), Milloss (1961–6 and 1971–4), and Orlikowsky (1966–71), with very few outstanding events such as Nureyev's prod. of *Swan Lake* (1964) and Grigorovich's *Nutcracker* (1973). G. Brunner was appointed Artistic Dir. of the State Op. B. and its affiliated school in 1976. While Dia Luca was its b. mistress, the Volksoper also offered regular b. programmes. The Th. an der Wien, which presents musicals and operetta prods., also started

to pursue b. ambitions when Alois Mitterhuber became b. dir. of the house. The city's d. education is now taken care of by the large State Op. B. School.

BIBL.: G. Winkler, *Das Wiener Ballet von Noverre bis Fanny Elssler* (dissertation, Univ. of Vienna, 1967); catalogue of the anniversary exhibition *100 Jahre Wiener Oper am Ring* (Vienna, 1969); various articles in *Almanach der Wiener Festwochen 1969*.

Vienna Children's Ballet. Bs. performed by children have always enjoyed great popularity in V.; Hilverding and Noverre ch. some. Horschelt's Children's B. of the Th. an der Wien then attracted enormous attention 1815–17; the Emperor ordered the disbanding of the co. for moral reasons. It was the springboard for the talents of Therese Heberle, Wilhelmina Schröder-Devrient, and Anton Stuhlmüller; Fanny Elssler denied that she had ever been a member. The scandal did not prevent the formation of a new b., consisting exclusively of girls, by Josephine Weiss, b. mistress of the Th. in der Josephsstadt; she travelled with her 48 Danseuses Viennoises not only to Paris and London, but also to Can. and Amer. 1845–8. They were very successful everywhere and the regime was so strict and morally upright that all attempts to accuse her of irregularities failed.

BIBL.: I. Guest, 'The Viennese Children' in *The Romantic Ballet in England* (London, 1954, reprint 1974); F. Crisp, 'Scandalous and Delightful', *Dance Magazine* (1969/8); M. H. Winter, in *The Pre-Romantic Ballet* (London, 1974).

Vienna Waltzes. Ballet in 5 parts; ch. Balanchine; mus. Joh. Strauss jr., Lehár, R. Strauss; sets Ter-Arutunian; cost. Karinska. Prod. 15 (Gala Preview) and 23 June 1977, New York City B., State Th., New York, with von Aroldingen and Lavery, McBride and Tomasson, Leland and Cook, Mazzo and Martins, Farrell and Donn. Set to 'Tales from the Vienna Woods', 'Voices of Spring', 'Explosion Polka', 'Gold and Silver Waltz' and the waltzes from *Rosenkavalier*, the b., which uses the whole co., follows the mus. closely in a nostalgic revue from Vienna's 19th-century past.

Viganò, Giulio. Ital. dancer, choreographer, and composer. Son of the d. and ch. Onorato V. (*b* 1739, *d* 1811) and brother of Salvatore V. D. in Venice 1788–94 and then in Vienna. He composed a number of bs. for his father and brother and ch. various bs. in Vienna.

Viganò, Salvatore (*b* Naples, 25 Mar. 1769, *d* Milan, 10 Aug. 1821). Ital. dancer and choreographer. Son of the d. and ch. Onorato V. (*b* 1739, *d* 1811) and nephew of the comp. L. Boccherini, with whom he started to study composition, in addition to studying painting and dancing. Made his début in Rome in a female role. D. in Madrid in 1788. Married the Span. d. Maria Medina (not to be confused with Josepha Meyer, *b* Vienna, 1756, who was married to Anton Viganò who worked for many years in Vienna). They went to Fr. and Eng. with the Daubervals, then to Brussels and Venice, where they d. in the bs. of V.'s father in 1790. He ch. his first b., *Raoul, Signor de Crequi*, in 1791; (he usually comp. the mus. for his bs. himself, or arr. the works of other composers). They appeared 1793–5 in Vienna with great success; the male members of the audience were fascinated by her daring costs. which made her look naked. He ch. a succession of bs., incl. *Raoul* and *Die Tochter der Luft, oder: Die Erhöhung der Semiramis* (1793), *La Fille mal gardée* (1794), *Richard Löwenherz, König von England* (mus. Weigl) and *Das gefundene Veilchen* (1795). They toured Eur., and d. in Venice again 1798–9; they then separated (M. Medina died in Paris, 1833). He worked in Vienna again 1799–1803; his bs. include *Clothilde, Herzogin von Salerno* (after Gozzi, 1799), *The Creatures of Prometheus* (mus. Beethoven, 1801), and *I Giuocchi Istmici* (mus. Weigl, 1803). Continued to work in Italy; ch. *Coriolano* (mus. Weigl, 1804), his first Shakespeare b., for Milan. His next important b. was *Gli Strelizzi* for Venice (1809). From 1813 until his death in 1821 he was b. master at la Scala di Milano, where he ch. his masterworks, which Stendhal enthusiastically admired: *Prometeo* (in 6 acts, with only 4 of Beethoven's original numbers kept, 1813), *Gli Ussitti* and *Numa Pompilio* (1815), *Mirra* and *Psammi, re d'Egitto* (1817), *Otello, Dedalo*, and *La Vestale* (1818), *I Titani* (mus. mostly by Rossini, 1819), *Alessandro nelle Indie* (1820), *Giovanna d'Arco* and *Didone* (1821—mus. for the last 3 G. Ayblinger). He was considered by his contemporaries the creator of the 'coreodramma'. His tombstone calls him 'sommo tra i coreografi'. 'His single greatest characteristic was his use of rhythmic pantomime halfway between normal imitative gesture and traditional dancing, with a complete subordination of both to the music' (Kirstein).

BIBL.: C. Ritorni, *Commentari della vita e delle opere coreodrammatiche di S.V.* (Milan, 1838); L. Kirstein, in *Dance* (New York 1935, reprint 1969); H. M. Winter, in *The Pre-Romantic Ballet* (London, 1974).

Vikulov, Serge Vasilievich (*b* Leningrad, 11 Nov. 1937). Sov. dancer. Grandson of A. Gorsky. Studied at Leningrad Ch. School: graduated in 1956. Joined Kirov B. and later became soloist. Gold Medal (Varna, 1964); Nijinsky Prize (1965); Merited Artist of the R.S.F.S.R. (1966); People's Artist of the R.S.F.S.R. (1970). Married to the d. Tatiana Udalenkova.

Vilimaa, Ülo (*b* Tallinn, 13 July 1941). Sov. dancer and choreographer. Graduated from the Tallinn b. school 1962 (pupil of K. Saareke), continued to study at Leningrad Ch. School 1964–5. Started to d. with the b. co. of the Vanemuine th. in Tartu (Estonia) 1962, appointed chief ch. 1973. Has ch.: *Le Rossignol* (mus. Stravinsky), *Contrasts* (mus. Bach, Ravel, Brubeck, both 1967), *Pictures* (mus. Debussy, Saint-Saëns, Yamada,

Rogers, 1969), *Romeo, Juliet and the Darkness* (mus. Auster), and *The Hands* (mus. of the 12th–18th centuries, both 1973). Has d. in many of his bs.

Villanella. A light-hearted 16th-century Neapolitan madrigal or gay rustic d. in 3/4 time.

Villella, Edward (*b* Bayside, N.Y., 10 Jan. 1936). Amer. dancer. Studied at School of Amer. B. and High School of Performing Arts. Joined Maritime College and then New York City B. in 1957. Became soloist and principal d. and one of the top stars of the co.; a d. of irresistible virile energy and dynamism. Created roles in Balanchine's *Electronics* (1961), *A Midsummer Night's Dream* (1962), *Bugaku* (1963), *Tarantella* (1964), *Harlequinade* (1965), *Brahms-Schoenberg Quartet* (1966), *Jewels* (1967), *Suite No. 3* (1970), Robbins' *Dances at a Gathering* (1969), *Watermill* (1972), and Balanchine-Robbins' *Pulcinella* (1972). One of his best roles was Balanchine's *Prodigal Son*. Has also starred in musicals (*Brigadoon*, 1962) and ch. bs., e.g. *Narkissos* (mus. R. Prince, 1966). NBC produced a TV film on him: *Man Who Dances* (1968). Contributed to 'The Male Image', *Dance Perspectives* 40. Appointed artistic coordinator of the Eglevsky B., 1979–84; dir. B. Oklahoma, 1983–5; founder and dir. Miami City B. 1986.

BIBL.: O. Maynard, 'A Dancer's Phases: V. in '72' *Dance Magazine* (1972/12); R. Greskovic, in 'Some Artists of the New York City Ballet', *Ballet Review* (vol. 4, no. 4).

Vilzak, Anatole Josifovich (*b* Vilna, 1898). Russ.-Amer. dancer and teacher. Studied at Imperial B. Academy; graduated in 1915. Joined Maryinsky Th.; became principal d. in 1917. Joined Diaghilev's Bs. Russes with his wife Ludmila Schollar in 1921; d. all the danseur noble roles. Staged the short version of *Swan Lake* (1924 version) with Schollar; created roles in Nijinska's *Les Biches* and *Les Fâcheux* (1924). D. with Rubinstein's co. in the first prods. of Nijinska's *Le Bien-Aimée, Baiser de la Fée*, and *Bolero* (1928), Jooss's *Persephone* (1934), and at the Paris Th. Mogador. B. master in Riga 1934. Joined B. Russe de Paris in 1935 and B. Russe de Monte Carlo in 1936; created a role in Fokine's *Don Juan* (1936). D. one season with Amer. B., then began teaching at School of Amer. B., then at V.-Schollar School in New York 1940–6, later also at B. Russe de Monte Carlo School, Washington School of B., and since 1965 at San Francisco B. School.

Vinogradov, Oleg Mikhailovich (*b* Leningrad 1 Aug. 1937). Sov. dancer, choreographer, and b. master. Studied at Ch. School (also studied painting); graduated in 1958. Joined Novosibirsk co.; soon began to ch. for op. prods. under the careful guidance of P. Gusev, who allowed him to stage the Waltz from the first act of *Swan Lake* and the third scene from Karaiev's *The Seven Beauties*. His first major b. prod. was Prokofiev's *Cinderella* (1964). followed by *Romeo and Juliet* (1965); both were very unorthodox stagings. His

next bs. were *Asel* (mus. V. Vlasov, Bolshoi Th., 1967), *Gorianka* (mus. M. Kashlaiev, Maly Th., 1968), *Two* (mus. A Melikov, Kirov Th., 1969), *La Fille mal gardée* (mus. Hérold, Maly Th., 1970), *Prince of the Pagodas* (mus. Britten, Kirov Th., 1972), and *Yaroslavna* (mus. B. Tishenko, Maly Th., 1974). Chief ch. of Maly Th. 1972, and since Artistic Dir. of Kirov B. Merited Artist of the R.S.F.S.R. (1968); Lenin Prize (1970).
BIBL.: N. Rene, 'The Cause of Controversy', *Dance and Dancers* (1967/11); P. Bohlin, 'O.V.', *Dans* (1976/3).

Violette, Eva Maria (orig. Faigel, also Faigl and Veigl; *b* Vienna, 29 Feb. 1724, *d* London 16 Oct. 1822). Austrian dancer. Studied with Sellier and Hilverding; appeared in Hilverding's bs. in Vienna 1734–44. Went to London in 1746; equally successful as a d. and as a society lady. Married the actor David Garrick in 1749. Contrary to expectation it proved an unusually happy marriage, and she was buried at her husband's side in Westminster Abbey.
BIBL.: F. Derra de Moroda, 'The Dancer in Westminster Abbey', *Dancing Times* (1967/6).

Violin Concerto. B. in 4 movements; ch. Balanchine; mus. Stravinsky; light R. Bates. Prod. 18 June 1972, N.Y. City B., State Th., N.Y., with von Aroldingen, Mazzo, Bonnefoux, Martins. A plotless b. for 2 couples and a corps of 9 girls and 7 boys. Second Channel Ger. TV prod. in 1973. An earlier version of the same mus. was Balanchine's *Balustrade* (1941), and another version Milloss's *Les Jambes savantes* (Vienna, 1965). Now called *Stravinsky Violin Concerto.*
BIBL.: G. Balanchine and F. Mason, in *Balanchine's Complete Stories of the Great Ballets* (Garden City, N.Y., 1977).

Violon du Diable, Le. Ballet in 2 acts; libr. and ch. Saint-Léon; mus. Pugni; sets Despléchin and Thierry; cost. Lormier. Prod. 19 Jan. 1849, Opéra, Paris, with Cerrito, Saint-Léon. The young violinist Urbain falls in love with the beautiful Hélène. However, a sinister doctor bewitches the tone of his violin; but Pater Anselm intervenes, his violin regains its beautiful sound, and everything ends happily. Saint-Léon not only ch. and d., but also played the violin so brilliantly that he was much admired by the comp. Adam. An earlier version, *Tartini il violinista* (libr. after Gavarni by Saint-Léon; mus. Saint-Léon, Felis, and Pugni; ch. Emmanuele Viotti, Venice, 1848).
BIBL.: C. W. Beaumont, 'L.V.d.D.' in *Complete Book of Ballets* (London, 1951).

Virsaladze, Simon Bargatovich (*b* Tiblisi, 24 Jan. 1909). Sov. designer. Chief designer of Tiflis Opera and B. Th. 1932–6, Leningrad Kirov Th. 1945–62. After collaborating on many prods. with Chaboukiani became internationally known as Grigorovich's designer, collaborating with him on his prods. of *The Stone Flower* (1957), *Legend of Love* (1961), *Sleeping Beauty* (1965 and 1973),

Nutcracker (1966), *Spartacus* (1968), *Swan Lake* (1969), *Ivan the Terrible* (1975), *Angara* (1976), and *Romeo and Juliet* (1978). Lenin Prize (1970).
BIBL.: V. Vanslov, *S.V.* (Moscow, 1969).

Vision of Marguerite. See *Mephisto Valse.*

Vivandière, La. Ballet in 1 act; libr. and ch. Saint-Léon; mus. Pugni; déc. W. Grieve. Prod. 23 May 1844, Her Majesty's Th., London, with Cerrito, Saint-Léon. The b. is set in a little village in Hungary; Kathi, the camp-follower, loves Hans, the son of a tavern-keeper, but they have to overcome the jealousy of the Burgomaster and the Baron, who are both pursuing Kathi, before they can get married. The b. became famous because it introduced London to 'the *Redowa,* or Original Polka of Bohemia'. An earlier version—without Redowa—by Saint-Léon for Rome in 1843.
BIBL.: C. W. Beaumont, 'L.V.' in *Complete Book of Ballets* (London, 1951).

Viva Vivaldi! Ballet in 1 act; ch. Arpino; mus. Vivaldi. Prod. 10 Sep. 1965, R. Joffrey B., Delacorte Th., Central Park, New York, with Blankshine, Fuente, Horvath, Singleton. A plotless b., with a slight Span. flavour, set to the Violin Concerto in D Major, P. 151 (arr. for orchestra with solo classic guitar). Became for many years the co.'s 'signature b.'.

Vlaanderen, Ballet van. See *Ballet of Flanders.*

Vláčilová, Hana (*b* Prague, 25 Nov. 1956). Czech dancer. Studied at Prague Conservatory. Joined Prague National Th. B., and eventually became soloist. First Prize (junior category, Varna, 1972); Silver Medal (Tokyo, 1976).

Vladimiroff, Pierre (orig. Piotr Nicolaievich; *b* St. Petersburg, 1893, *d* New York, 25 Nov. 1970). Russ.-Amer. dancer and teacher. Studied at Imperial B. Academy; graduated in 1911. Joined Maryinsky Th. and soon d. the Nijinsky roles. D. with Diaghilev's Bs. Russes in 1912 and 1914, but remained with the Maryinsky Th. until 1918; became principal d. in 1915 and created roles in Fokine's *Francesca da Rimini* and *Eros* (1915). He then joined Diaghilev's Bs. Russes and d. the Prince in the London prod. of *Sleeping Princess* (1921). Toured with Karsavina, then with Mordkin B. 1926–7, and with Pavlova B. 1928–31. Went to New York and taught at School of Amer. B. 1934–67. Was married to the d. and teacher Felia Doubrovska.
BIBL.: F. Doubrovska, 'P.V.', *Dance Magazine* (1971/2).

Vladimirov, Yuri Kuzmich (*b* Kosterovo, 1 Jan. 1942). Sov. dancer. Studied at Bolshoi B. School; graduated in 1962. Joined Bolshoi B. and became one of its most energetic and forceful soloists; created leading roles in Kasatkina-Vasiliov's *Heroic Poem* (1964) and *Sacre du printemps* (1965), Vasiliev's *Icarus*, title role in Grigorovich's *Ivan* *the* Terrible (1975), and a further role in Boccado-ro's *Love for Love* (1976). Gold Medal (Varna, 1966; Moscow, 1969). Married to the d. Nina Sorokina.

Vlassi, Christiane (*b* Paris, 5 June 1938). Fr. dancer. Studied at Paris Opéra B. School (Zambelli's last pupil); joined the co. in 1952 and became première danseuse in 1961 and étoile in 1963. Created roles in her husband A. Labis's *Entrelacs* (1963), *Arcades* (1964) and *Romeo and Juliet* (1967), Béjart's *Damnation de Faust* (1964), and Petit's *Turangalîla*. Fr. TV prod. *Portrait d'une Etoile* (1975).
BIBL.: A.-P. Hersin, 'C.V.', *Les Saisons de la danse* (1970/4).

Vlassova, Eleanora Evgenia (*b* nr. Moscow, 1 July 1931). Sov. dancer. Studied at Moscow Bolshoi B. School; graduated in 1949. Joined Stanislavsky and Nemirovich-Danchenko Music Th.; became ballerina in 1955. Merited Artist of the R.S.F.S.R. (1957).
BIBL.: A. Livio, 'E.V.' in *Etoiles et Ballerines* (1965).

Vodehnal, Andrea (*b* Oak Park, Ill., 1938). Amer. dancer. Studied at B. Russe de Monte Carlo School, School of Amer. B., and with T. Semenova and Danilova. Joined B. Russe de Monte Carlo 1957 and later became soloist; ballerina with Washington National B. 1962–8. Now dances with Houston B. Married to the d. Eugene Collins.

Volé. (Fr., flown). Designates in b. a movement performed in the air, e.g. Brisé volé.

Volinine, Alexander Yemelianovich (*b* Moscow, 17 Sep. 1882, *d* Paris, 3 July 1955). Russ.-Fr. dancer and teacher. Studied at Bolshoi B. School; graduated in 1901. Joined Bolshoi B. and later became principal d. D. with Diaghilev's co. in 1910, then toured with Geltzer, Kyasht, Lopokova, and Genée. Pavlova's partner 1914–25. Then opened a well known school in Paris; Jeanmaire, Lafon, and Eglevsky were among his pupils.
BIBL.: J. V. Cross, 'A.V. Vignette', *Dance Magazine* (1957/2).

Volkov, Boris (*b* Tula, 1902). Russ.-Can. dancer, teacher, and choreographer. Studied with Jan-Janowicz Domaratski-Novakowski in Moscow. D. with Baku B., Mordkin B., and Moscow State B. Worked as a d.-ch. in Shanghai and toured the Far East. Arrived in the U.S. in 1927; joined Bolm B. as a leading soloist in 1928. Settled in Toronto in 1929 and opened a school, from which the V. Can. B. emerged, for which he ch. the entire repertory. Melissa Hayden was one of his pupils.

Volkova, Vera (*b* St. Petersburg, 1904, *d* Copenhagen, 5 May 1975). Russ.-Brit. dancer and teacher. Studied at Imperial B. Academy and with Vaganova at Volynsky's Russ. Ch. School. D. at the GATOB, then toured Japan and China with several colleagues. Settled in Shanghai in 1929; d.

with G. Goncharov's co. and taught in the school he opened. Went to London with her husband, the painter and architect Hugh Williams, in 1936; opened another school and taught at Sadler's Wells B. and its School 1943–50. Became the leading Western authority on the Vaganova system and perhaps the most formative teacher of the Brit. dancers who came to public attention in the post-war years. Went to La Scala di Milano (1950) and then to Copenhagen in 1951; became artistic adviser to the Royal Dan. B. Has also been guest teacher for cos. abroad and was on the staff of the Essen Folkwang School. Knight of Dannebrog (1956); Carlsberg Memorial Legacy (1974).
BIBL.: D. Hering, 'America Meets V.V.', *Dance Magazine* (1959/9).

Vollmar, Jocelyn (*b* San Francisco, 25 Nov. 1925). Amer. dancer and teacher. Studied at San Francisco B. School and School of Amer. B. D. with San Francisco B., B. Society, Amer. B. Th., Grand B. du Marquis de Cuevas 1951–3, Borovansky B. 1954–6, and San Francisco B. as prima ballerina 1956–72; created numerous roles in the bs. of L. Christensen. Retired in 1972, since when she has been assistant dir. of San Francisco B. School.

Volta (also Volte or Lavolta). (Ital. and Fr., turn.) A fast d. in simple triple time, probably derived from the Galliard. It is characterized by daring jumps and quick turns in the air, in which the lady is lifted by her partner. Though some people considered it indecent, it was much loved by Queen Elizabeth I, who is depicted dancing it with the Earl of Essex in a painting at Penshurst Place, Kent. It is mentioned by several Elizabethan writers, incl. Shakespeare, and is d. by Elizabeth I and her court in Britten's op. *Gloriana*.

Volynsky, Akim Lvovich (*b* Zhitomir, 3 May 1863, *d* Leningrad, 6 July 1926). Russ. critic and school dir. One of the most influential and respected St. Petersburg-Petrograd b. critics. Wrote two very important books: *Problems of Russian Ballet* (1923) and *The Book of Exultations* (1925), in which he tried to formulate his d. philosophy. Established a private Russian Ch. School, where Vaganova first taught.

Voluntaries. Ballet in 1 act; ch. Tetley; mus. Poulenc; déc. Ter-Arutunian. Prod. 22 Dec. 1973, Stuttgart B., Stuttgart, with Haydée, Cragun, Keil, R. Anderson, Stripling. Set to Poulenc's Concerto in G minor for Organ, Strings, and Timpani. 'The ballet is conceived as a linked series of voluntaries' (Tetley), i.e. the free-ranging organ or trumpet improvisations, often played before, during, or after religious services; the Latin root of the word also suggests flight or desire. The b. was conceived as a memorial to Cranko. Revived for Royal B. (1976) and Amer. B. Th. (1977).
BIBL.: P. Brinson and C. Crisp, in *Ballet & Dance* (Newton Abbot, 1977).

Vondersaar, Jeanette (b Indianapolis, Ind., 17 May 1951). Amer. dancer. Studied at Jordan College of Music with Jack Copeland, Karl Kaufmann, George Verdak, and Gay Besser Shields, then at School of Amer. B. and Harkness House for B. Arts. Joined Harkness Youth Dancers in 1970 and eventually became a member of the Harkness B. and one of its principal dancers. Joined Zurich Op. B. in 1975 and Dutch National B. in 1977.

Vondruška, Petr (b Hradec Králová, 15 June 1943). Czech. dancer. Studied at Prague Conservatory. D. with B. Praha 1964–7, Prague National Th. 1967–9, and with Düsseldorf B as a principal d. since 1969; has created roles in many bs. by Walter. Also working as a teacher.

Vooss, Hanna (b Houdeng-Goegnies, 1916). Belg. dancer, choreographer, and b. director. Studied with Mme Cannès and with Jooss and Leeder at Dartington Hall. B. mistress at Mons 1945–56 and Charleroi 1956–9. Founded B. du Hainaut in 1959; it became the B. de Wallonie in 1966, since when she has been its artistic dir. as well as head of the teaching staff at the Conservatoire de Charleroi. Has ch. a number of bs. Retired in 1976.

Vsevolojsky, Ivan Alexandrovich (b 1835, d 1909). Russ. diplomat, th. dir., and designer. Dir. of the Russ. Imperial Ths. 1881–99; commissioned the great bs. of Petipa-Tchaikovsky and Petipa-Glazunov. Also designed the costs. for about 25 bs., incl. *Sleeping Beauty, Nutcracker,* and *Raymonda.*

Vtorushina, Olga Mikhailovna (b Leningrad, 1947). Sov. dancer. Studied at Leningrad Ch. School; graduated in 1966. Joined Kirov B.; became soloist in 1969. Has frequently appeared with Baryshnikov. Gold Medal (Varna, 1966).

Vulpian, Claude de (b Paris, 29 Dec. 1952). Fr. dancer. Studied at Paris Opéra B. School 1964–8. Joined Paris Opéra B.1969, appointed première danseuse 1975 and danseuse étoile 1978.

Vyroubova, Nina (b Gurzuf, 4 June 1921). Russ.-Fr. dancer and teacher. Studied with her mother and with Trefilova, Preobrajenska, Kniaseff, Egorova, V. Gsovsky, Brieux, and Lifar. Début as Swanilda in Caen in 1937. D. with B. Russe de Paris in 1940, Bs. des Champs-Elysées 1945–7, Bs. de Paris in 1949, as étoile at the Opéra 1949–56, Grand B. du Marquis de Cuevas 1957–62 and then as guest ballerina with various cos. A ballerina of delicate lyrical sensitivity; created roles in Petit's *Les Forains* (1945), V. Gsovsky's *La Sylphide* (possibly her best role, 1946), Lifar's *Blanche-Neige* (1951), *Nôces fantastiques* (1955), *Hamlet* (1957), and *L'Amour et son destin* (1957), Ricarda's *Chanson de l'éternelle tristesse* (1957), Golovine's *Mort de Narcisse* (1958), and Van Dyk's *Abraxas* (1965). Also appeared in the films *Le Spectre de la danse* (1960 and *L'Adage* (1965). Now teaches in Paris at the Opéra and in her own studio. Mother of the d. Youra Kniazeff (b 1951). Prix Pavlova (1957).

BIBL.: I. Laurent, *N.V. et ses visages* (Paris, 1958); S. Goodman, 'Meet N.V.', *Dance Magazine* (1962/6). 'Hommage à V.' and list of roles in *Les Saisons de la danse* (1980/11).

W

Wacker, Studio. See *Studio Wacker.*

Waehner, Karin (*b* Gleiwitz, 12 Mar. 1926). Ger. dancer, choreographer, and teacher. Studied with Wigman in Berlin. Taught modern d. in Buenos Aires 1950–3. Opened a school in Paris in 1953; appeared together with Jerome Andrews as Les Compagnons de la danse. Co-founder of the experimentally orientated Th. d'Essai de la Danse in 1955. Formed Les Bs. Contemporains de K.W., with which she has frequently toured Fr. and abroad. Has ch. many works, and is one of the foremost personalities of modern d. in France.

Wagner, Frank (*b* St. Mary's, 4 Jan. 1922). Amer. dancer and teacher. Studied with Dunham, Limón, Sokolow, Kinch, Holm, Anderson-Ivantzova, Starbuck, and Hawthorne. Started to appear as a d.-actor on Broadway in 1948. Dir. and ch. a great number of d. numbers in musicals, shows, revues, and for TV. Has taught modern jazz d. at New York International School of D. since 1955.

Wagner, Richard (*b* Leipzig, 22 May 1813, *d* Venice, 13 Feb. 1883). Ger. composer. Wrote no b. mus., but choreographers have based some bs. on his op. and concert mus.; e.g. Massine's *Bacchanale* (*Tannhäuser*, overture and Bacchanale, B. Russe de Monte Carlo, New York, 1939; also Béjart's separate b. ch. after his collaboration with Wieland W. at the Bayreuth *Tannhäuser* prod. of 1961, B. of the 20th Century, Brussels, 1963) and *Mad Tristan* (excerpts from *Tristan and Isolde*, International, New York, 1944; also H. Ross's *Tristan*, Amer. B. Th., New York, 1958, and Béjart's *Les Vainqueurs*, B. of the 20th Century, Brussels, 1969), Sparemblek's *Siegfried Idyll* (B. of the 20th Century, Brussels, 1965), and Béjart's *Mathilde* (*Wesendonck Lieder* and excerpts from *Tristan*, B. of the 20th Century, Brussels, 1965; the *Wesendonck Lieder* only in Joffrey's *Remembrances*, City Center Joffrey B., New York, 1973, also in Spoerli's *Dreams*, Stuttgart B., 1980).

Wagoner, Dan (*b* Springfield, Mass. 31 July 1932). Amer. dancer and choreographer. Studied with Ethel Butler and Graham. Début with Graham co. in 1958; then d. with M. Cunningham and, for many years, with P. Taylor. Created roles in many bs. incl. *Insects and Heroes* (1961), *Aureole* (1962), *Scudorama* (1963), and *Orbs* (1966). Started to ch. in 1968; has had his own group since 1969, which has toured the U.S., S. Amer., and Eng. Has also ch. for London Contemporary D. Th. and the Brit. group, Mantis.
BIBL.: K. Duncan, 'D.W., a Dancer turns Choreographer', *Dance Magazine* (1974/11).

Wakhevich, Georges (*b* Odessa, 18 Aug. 1907, *d* Paris, 11 Feb. 1984). Russ.-Fr. th. designer. Designed many b. prods., e.g. Petit's *Le jeune homme et la mort* (Bs. des Champs-Elysées, 1946) and *La Croqueuse de diamants* (Bs. de Paris, 1950), Page's *Vilia* (London Festival B., 1953), Dollar's *The Combat* (Amer. B. Th., 1953), Lifar's *Firebird* (Opéra, Paris, 1954) and *L'Amour et son destin* (Grand B. du Marquis de Cuevas, 1957), Hamilton's *Giselle* (Vienna State Op., 1958), Hanka's *Moor of Venice* (1955) and *Hotel Sacher* (1958; both Vienna State Op.), Parlić's *Romeo and Juliet* (Vienna State Op., 1960), and Taras' *Petrushka* (Ger. Op. Berlin, 1971). Father of Igor W. (*b* 1948), who has comp. several bs. for N. Schmucki.

Walker, David Hatch. See *Hatch Walker, David.*

Walker, Norman (*b* New York, 21 June 1934). Amer. dancer, choreographer, and teacher. Studied with O'Donnell, Shurr, Graham, Pereyaslavec, and Joffrey. Début with O'Donnell co. in 1953; then d. with the cos. of Yuriko, Koner, and Lang. Started to teach at High School of Performing Arts in 1956. Has occasionally appeared with a group of his own, but mostly works as a freelance ch. (Grands Bs. Canadiens, Harkness B., Batsheva D. Co., Cologne D. Forum, D. Wayne's Dancers' Co., etc.). Currently Chairman of D. Dept. at Adelphi Univ., Garden City, N.Y. Has also been in charge of Jacob's Pillow Festival.
BIBL.: K. Cunningham, 'A Romantic Poet . . . A Sculptor in Space', *Dance Magazine* (1969/12).

Walk to the Paradise Garden, The. Ballet in 1 act; ch. Ashton; mus. Delius; déc. Chappell. Prod. 15 Nov. 1972. Royal B. Benevolent Fund Gala, Cov. Gdn., London, with Park, Wall, Rencher. Set to the prelude to the last act of the op. *A Village Romeo and Juliet*. The b. shows two ecstatic lovers who finally meet the Angel of Death.
BIBL.: G. Balanchine and F. Mason, in *Balanchine's Complete Stories of the Great Ballets* (Garden City, N.Y., 1977); D. Vaughan, *Frederick Ashton and his Ballets* (London, 1977).

Wall, David (*b* Chiswick, 15 Mar. 1946). Brit. dancer. Studied in Windsor and at Royal B. School; joined Royal B. in 1963 and became soloist in 1964 and principal in 1966. One of the most virile and expressive dancers of the co.; created roles in Ashton's *Sinfonietta* (1967) and *The Walk to the Paradise Garden* (1973), Cauley's *In the Beginning* (1969), and MacMillan's *Anastasia* (London version, 1971), *Manon* and *Elite Syncopations* (1974), *The Four Seasons* and *Rituals* (1975), and *Mayerling* (1978), and Bintley's *Adieu* (1980). Tudor ch. *Knight Errant* (1971) for him, and the male lead in Ashton's *Creatures of Prometheus* (1979) was also made for him, but injuries prevented him from dancing on the first nights. Was a frequent partner to Fonteyn. Married to the former d. Alfreda Thorogood. Retired 1984. Now assoc. dir. Royal Academy of Dancing. C.B.E. (1985).

BIBL.: O. Maynard, 'D.W.', *Dance Magazine* (1974/8); D. Dougill, 'D.W.' in *The Royal Ballet: A Souvenir* (London, 1978).

Wallmann, Margarethe (also Margarita W.; b Vienna, 22 July 1904). Austrian dancer, choreographer, teacher, b. mistress, and op. prod. Studied with Eduardova, Preobrajenska, and Wigman; joined Wigman group and became dir. of the Berlin branch of the Wigman School in 1927. Went to Amer. in 1928 to teach Wigman technique. Returned to Eur. and performed with her own group. Prod. Gluck's *Orpheus and Eurydice*, her first op., for Salzburg Festival in 1933; unofficial chief ch. for all Salzburg Festival prods. until 1939. B. dir. of Vienna State Op. and its affiliated school 1934–9; her bs. included *Oesterreichische Bauernhochzeit* (mus. F. Salmhofer), *Fanny Elssler* (mus. M. Nador, 1934), and *Der liebe Augustin* (mus. A. Steinbrecher, 1936). Started to work as a ch. for La Scala, Milan, Hollywood, and Buenos Aires Teatro Colón, where she became b. dir. during the Second World War. Formed a chamber b. troupe in 1943, which gave an especially successful prod. of Honegger's *Joan of Arc at the Stake*. After the war settled in Italy and ch. some more bs. for Rome, Milan, and Salzburg, but concentrated increasingly on op. prods.

Wallonie, Ballet de. See *Ballet de Wallonie*.

Walpurgis Night. B. Divertissement from the last act of Gounod's op. Faust, ch. Henri Justament, prod. 3 Mar. 1869, Opéra, Paris. Has often been performed as a separate b., especially the version ch. by Lavrovsky for Bolshoi B. (Moscow, 1941—this is part of the Brit. film *Giselle*, with the Bolshoi B., 1956). Balanchine first ch. it within the *Faust* prod. of the Paris Opéra (1975) and revived his ch. for New York City B. (1980).

Walter, Erich (b Fürth, 30 Dec. 1927, d Herdecke, 23 Nov. 1983). Ger. d., ch., and b. director. Studied with Olympiada Alperova in Nuremberg. D. with Nuremberg Op. B. 1946–50, Göttingen B. 1950–1, and Wiesbaden B. 1951–3. B. master in Wuppertal 1953–64; began to ch. and by close collaboration with the designer Heinrich Wendel made it one of the most interesting Ger. b. cos., with a musically unusually ambitious repertory (many bs. to mus. by Stravinsky, Monteverdi, Bartók, Schoenberg, Henze, etc.). Appointed b. dir. of Düsseldorf's Ger. Op. on the Rhine in 1964; built it up into one of the foremost Ger. cos. A second co. had to be founded in 1970 to perform in the op. prods., of which he was also dir. Also worked as a ch. for Municipal Op. and Ger. Op. Berlin, Vienna State Op., Zurich Op.,

Munich State Op., Scala di Milano, and Bregenz Festival. His numerous bs. incl. *Pelleas and Melisande* (mus. Schoenberg, 1955), *Die weisse Rose* mus. Fortner, 1956), *Jeux* (mus. Debussy, 1958), *Romeo and Juliet* (mus. Berlioz, 1959), *The Planets* (mus. Holst, 1961), *L'Orfeo* (b. prod. of Monteverdi's op., 1961), *Ondine* (mus. Henze, 1962), *Death and the Maiden* (mus. Schubert, 1964), *String Quartet No. 1* (mus. Janáček, 1966), *Dance Around the Golden Calf* (as part of the Düsseldorf prod. of Schoenberg's *Moses und Aron* 1968), *Le Sacre du printemps* (mus. Stravinsky, 1970), *Third Symphony* (mus. Scriabin, 1974) and *Fantaisies* (mus. Tchaikovsky, 1980); he also prod. some of the classics: *Swan Lake* (1969), *Giselle* (1971), and *Sleeping Beauty* (1974).

BIBL.: various authors, *Ein Ballett in Deutschland* (Düsseldorf, 1971).

Waltz (also Ger. Walzer or Fr. Valse). A Ger.-Austrian turning d. in swift 3/4 or 3/8 time, probably derived from the Ländler, which has been d. in Austria and Bavaria for centuries and which Mozart, Beethoven, and Schubert called the Deutsche. The name appeared in the late 18th century, but the d. gained widespread popularity through the Viennese ballroom Ws. of Lanner and the Strausses. On the stage it was first seen in Martín y Soler's op. *La cosa rara* (Vienna, 1786); the first b. to include it was Gardel's *La Dansomanie* (Paris, 1800). It reached its climax in the 3 Tchaikovsky bs. *Swan Lake* (Moscow, 1877), *Sleeping Beauty* (St. Petersburg, 1890), and *Nutcracker* (St. Petersburg, 1892). More recent W. bs. have been Ravel's *Adelaïde, ou Le Langage des fleurs* (ch. Clustine, Paris, 1912) and *La Valse* (ch. Nijinska, Monte Carlo, 1929), and Balanchine's *Liebeslieder Walzer* (mus. Brahms, New York, 1960), Ulrich's *Walzertraüme* (mus. K. Schwertsik, Cologne) and Balanchine's *Vienna Waltzes* (mus. Strauss jr., Lehár, and R. Strauss, New York City B., 1977).

BIBL.: P. Nettl, 'Birth of the Waltz', *Dance Index* (vol. 5, no. 99).

Wanderer, The. Ballet in 4 scenes; libr. and ch. Ashton; mus. Schubert; déc. Graham Sutherland. Prod. 27 Jan. 1941, Sadler's Wells B., New Th., London, with Helpmann, Fonteyn. Set to Schubert's *Wanderer Fantasie*. A man recapitulates in his imagination several episodes from his life. Balanchine used the same mus. (arr. Liszt) for his b. *Errante* (Paris, 1933).

Wandtke, Harald (b Schönehr, 26 Sep. 1939). Ger. dancer and choreographer. Studied with J. Weidt and at Dresden Palucca School. D. with the cos. in Karl-Marz-Stadt, Weimar, and Dresden State Op. Joined East Berlin Comic Op. in 1966. Started to ch. in 1970; *Triptych* (mus. Françaix, Ohana, Stravinsky, 1974), the ch. for the Dresden prod. of Schoenberg's *Moses und Aron* (1975), and a full-length b. to mus. by C. M. von Weber

(1980) are his major works so far. Now chief ch. of Dresden State Op.

Ward, Charles (*b* Los Angeles, 24 Oct. 1952, *d* Downey, Ca., 11 July 1986). Amer. dancer. Studied with Audrey Share, S. Holden, M. Lland, G. Marinaccio, and Amer. B. Th. School. Joined Houston B. 1970, Amer. B. Th. 1972, appointed soloist 1974 and principal d. 1976. Appeared in B. Fosse's mus. *Dancin'* (1978).

Ward, Eileen (*b* Camberley). Brit. dancer and teacher. Studied at Elmhurst School, Rambert School, and with Volkova. Joined International B. in 1940, and later became soloist; joined B. Rambert in 1946. Started to teach at Elmhurst School in 1951, then with Rambert School and B. Rambert, London Festival B., and 1965–75 with Royal B. and Royal B. School. Now a freelance guest teacher.

Waring, James (*b* Alameda, Cal., 1 Nov. 1922, *d* New York, 2 Dec. 1975). Amer. dancer, choreographer, and teacher. Studied with Raoul Pausé, at School of Amer. B., and with Vilzak, Tudor, M. Cunningham, Halprin, and Horst. D. with his own co. 1949–66 and was then artistic dir. of The B. Stage Co., choreographing many bs. (also for other cos. such as Manhattan Festival B., New England D. Th., and Netherlands D. Th.) and solos for various performers. Described as the most paradoxical of all Amer. choreographers. Contributed 'Theater Lecture' to *Ballet Review* (vol. 4, no. 3).
BIBL.: J. Anderson, 'The Paradoxes of J.W.', *Dance Magazine* (1968/11).

Warren, Robert de (*b* Montevideo, 1933). Brit. dancer and b. director. Studied with Goncharov, Grigorieva, and at Royal B. School. Joined National B. of Uruguay in 1954; d. with Cov. Gdn. Op. B., Royal B. 1958–60, Stuttgart B. 1960–2, and Frankfurt B. 1962–4. Dir. of National B. of Iran 1968–70; has since concentrated on studying Persian folklore. Formed *Mahalli troupe of folk dancers in 1971, which he directed until 1976. Ch. full-length b. *Simorgh* (mus. Tjeknavorian, 1975). Artistic dir. of Northern B. Th. since the end of 1976, for which his bs. incl. *Romeo and Juliet ... Tragic Memories* (mus. Tchaikovsky, 1978), *Cinderella* (mus. Joh. Strauss, 1979) and *A Midsummer Night's Dream* (mus. Mendelssohn arr. Salzedo, 1981). Homayoun Medal (first class, 1975).
BIBL.: 'R.d.W. Talks to *Dance and Dancers*' (1973/1).

Warsaw. Bs. given at the th. of the Royal Palace (which opened in 1643) included the *B. de la Reine* (1654) and *B. à la occasion du sacre de Sa Majesté le Roi Jean III* (1676). An op. house was built in 1724, where the b. *Proserpine* caused a scandal in 1727 because of its licentiousness. The National Th. started to perform in 1765. Early Ital. b. masters included Giovanni Antonio Sacco and

Daniel Kurtz; G. Vestris appeared as a guest during the 1777–8 season. François Gabriel Le Doux (1755–1823) founded a b. school in 1782 (it started in Grodno, was then transferred to Postawy and again, in 1785, to W.), from which emerged La Compagnie des Danseurs de Sa Majesté le Roi, which continued until 1794. This co. prod. the first Pol. national b., *Wanda, Queen of Polonia* (1788). Le Doux taught at his private school in W. and his pupils appeared in the occasional perfs. given at the National Th. A few years later Franciszek Szlancowski (1751–1827) took over. Julia Mierzyńska (1801–31) was the first Pol. b. mistress of renown. During the 19th and 20th century up to the end of the First World War, when Poland was occupied by Russia, Prussia, and Austria, there was little artistic development. B. was mostly controlled by foreign b. masters. A resident b. co. was formed at the National Th. in 1818, with Louis Thierry as its dir.; he ch. (with Mierzyńska) *Marriage at Ojców* (mus. Karol Kurpiński, 1823), based on the folklore of the Cracow province. He was succeeded by another Frenchman, Maurice Pion; during his regime (1826–43) the technical standard of the co. was raised. The co. moved to the newly opened Teatr Wielki (Grand Th.) in 1833; the affiliated b. school was opened in 1834. F. Taglioni was b. dir. 1843–53, and during this period the first native Pol. ch., Roman Turczynowicz (1813–82), after studying in Paris, staged the famous bs. of the Romantic repertory: *Giselle* and *La jolie fille de Gand* (1848), *Le Diable boîteux* (1849), *Paquita* (1854), *Catarina ou la fille du bandit* (1850), *Esmeralda* (1851), and *Le Corsaire* (1857). Turczynowicz was b. master 1853–66, but his patriotism brought him into conflict with the Russ. authorities. Blasis staged his *Faust* in 1856; Marie Taglioni, the Paul Taglionis, and Grisi appeared during this period. Distinguished Pol. dancers of these years included Konstancja Turczynowicz (the wife of the ch.), Ann and Karolina Strauss, Teodora Gwozdecka, Marie Freitas, and Felix Krzesinski (better known as Kchessinsky, the spelling he adopted when he moved to Russia). Foreign b. masters continued to dominate the local b. scene; Virgilio Calori (1869–74; in charge of the first prod. of A. Sonnenfeld's *Pan Twardowski*, 1871), Pasquale Borri (1875–8), José Mendez (1879–89; first prod. of *Coppélia*, 1882), Raffaelle Grassi (1892–1902; first prod. of *Swan Lake*), and E. Cecchetti (1902–5). Important Pol. dancers included Helena Cholewicka (1848–83; the first Pol. prima ballerina), Matylda Dylewska, Michalina Rogińska, Aleksander and Antoni Tarnowski, Jan Popiel, and Aleksander Gillert. A new development started with the country's liberation and reunification in 1918. Under Piotr Zajlich (1884–1948) the Grand Th. reorganized its b. co. and numerous 20th-century works entered the repertory. The soloists were led by Halina Szmolcówna (1892–1939), Irena Szymańska (*b* 1899), and Zygmunt Dabrowski (1896–

1973). In 1937 an independent Balet Polski was formed, with Nijinska as ch.; she mounted an all-Pol. programme, with which the co. appeared at the Paris World Exhibition. Woizikovsky joined the co. for the 1938–9 season and staged some bs. (as did Jan Cieplinski) in Fr., Brussels, and New York. The city was totally destroyed during the Second World War and a fresh start had to be made in 1945; the op. house had been destroyed, so the b. co. worked under makeshift conditions until the newly built Grand Th. was opened in 1965. But even while the op. co. was performing at the Roma cinema, the repertory was carefully built up to present a balanced choice of works from the classics and the 20th century. Pol. choreographers who worked here and at the new Grand Th. included Stanisław Miszszyk (*b* 1910), Eugeniusz Papliński (*b* 1908), Woizikovsky, and Witold Gruca (*b* 1927); foreign guest choreographers included K. Sergeyev and Dudinskaya, A. Tomsky, A. Rodrigues, F. Adret, A. Tsitsinadze, J. Lazzini, and A. Messerer. The Grand Th. also acts as an experimental platform, and such young choreographers as Jerzy Makarowski, Marta Bochenek, and Mariquita Compe showed their first bs. there. The co's. present dir. is Elzbieta Jaron.

BIBL.: entry 'Polonia' in *Enciclopedia dello spettacolo*; I. Turska, *Dance in Poland* (Warsaw, 1962); J. Pudetek, *Warszawski Balet Romantyczny* (Cracow, 1968).

Washington National Ballet. See *National Ballet*.

Watermill. Ballet in 1 act; ch. Robbins (also déc., with David Reppa); mus. Teiji Ito; cost. P. Zipprodt. Prod. 3 Feb. 1972, New York City B., State Th., N.Y., with Villella. The b., which is strongly influenced by Jap. Noh techniques, shows a man summing up his life, which reflects the phases of the moon and the cycle of seasons.

BIBL.: G. Balanchine and F. Mason, in *Balanchine's Complete Stories of the Great Ballets* (Garden City, N.Y., 1977).

Water Study. Ballet in 1 act; ch. Humphrey; no mus.; cost. P. Lawrence. Prod. 28 Oct. 1928, Humphrey-Weidman Group, Civic Repertory Th., New York. Set in silence for a group of 14 dancers, *W.S.* 'is a collection of images of water . . . , using movement that does not *describe* the movement of water but corresponds to its energies and spatial configurations' (M. B. Siegel).

BIBL.: M. B. Siegel, in 'Four Works by Doris Humphrey', *Ballet Review* (vol. 7, no. 1).

Watts, Heather (*b* Los Angeles, 21 Sep. 1953). Amer. dancer. Studied at School of Amer. B., joining New York City B. 1970, promoted soloist 1978 and principal d. 1980. Created roles in P. Martins's *Calcium Light Night* (1978), Robbins's *The Four Seasons* (1979), *Piano Pieces* (1981), and Balanchine's *Davidsbündlertänze* (1980).

BIBL.: J. Gruen, 'H.W.', *Dance Magazine* (1980/2).

Watts, Jonathan (orig. John B. Leech; b. Fort Warren, Wyo., 8 Nov. 1933). Amer. dancer and teacher. Studied with Joffrey and O'Donnell. Début with Joffrey group. Joined New York City B. in 1954 and became soloist in 1957; principal d. 1959–62. Created roles in Balanchine's *Divertimento No. 15* (1956), *Agon* (1957), *Episodes* (1959), *Donizetti Variations*, and *Liebeslieder Walzer* (1960). Rejoined R. Joffrey B. in 1962. D. with Austral. B. 1962–3 and Cologne B. 1965–8. Returned to the U.S., taught at Amer. B. Center, and became dir. of Joffrey II B., for which he has ch. several bs. Has held various teaching jobs since.

Wayne, Dennis (orig. D. W. Wendelken; *b* St. Petersburg, Fla., 19 July 1945). Amer. dancer. Studied with N. Walker, Shurr, and Graham. Début with N. Walker Co. 1962. Joined Harkness B. in 1964 and became one of its leading soloists. Principal d. of Joffrey B. 1972–4, and soloist with Amer. B. Th. 1974–5. Has toured with his own 'Dancers' group since 1975.

BIBL.: J. Gruen, 'D.W.', in *The Private World of Ballet* (New York, 1975).

Weaver, John (*b* Shrewsbury, 21 July 1673, *d* 24 or 28 Sep. 1760). Brit. dancer, choreographer, teacher, and dance theorist. Known as 'the father of English pantomime' and one of the pioneers of the b. d'action. The son of a dancing master; appeared mainly in character and comic roles. D. and ch. at the London ths. of Drury Lane and Lincoln's Inn Fields 1700–36, where he staged such important works for the development of the action b. as *The Tavern Bilkers* (1702) and *The Loves of Mars and Venus* (1717). He was his own librettist and became one of the most distinguished d. writers of his time. Published the first Eng. edition of Feuillet's *Chorégraphie* in 1706, followed by *An Essay towards a History of Dancing* (1712), *Anatomical and Mechanical Lectures upon Dancing* (1721), and *History of Mimes and Pantomimes* (1728).

BIBL.: S. Vince, 'The Amazing Weaver', *Dance and Dancers* (1967/3); L. Kirstein, 'The Loves of Mars and Venus' in *Movement & Metaphor* (New York, 1970); M. H. Winter, in *The Pre-Romantic Ballet* (London, 1974).

Weber, Carl Maria von (*b* Eutin, 18 Dec. 1786, *d* London 5 June 1826). Ger. composer. Wrote no b. mus., but incidental dances, waltzes, and polonaises, and his *Invitation to the Dance*, arr. for orchestra by Berlioz, have frequently been ch.; e.g. by Telle in *Rokoko* (Berlin, 1876). The best known b. version is undoubtedly Fokine's *Le Spectre de la rose* (Bs. Russes de Diaghilev, 1911). Massine his *Vienna—1814* to various of his pieces (B. Russe de Monte Carlo, 1940), Van Dyk his *Konzertstück* (for piano in F minor, Hamburg State Op., 1965; also by K. Stowell, Bonn, 1972), and Walter his *Piano Concerto No. 2, E flat major* (Düsseldorf, 1971). A full-length b. to various pieces by W. was ch. by H. Wandtke for Dresden B. in 1980.

Webern, Anton (von) (b Vienna, 3 Dec. 1883, d Mittersill, 15 Sep. 1945). Austrian composer. Wrote no b. mus., but his concert mus. has frequently been used for b. purposes; e.g. Graham's and Balanchine's *Episodes* (Graham: Passacaglia, op. 1, 6 Pieces for Orchestra, op. 6; Balanchine: Sinfonie, op. 21, 5 Pieces for Orchestra, op. 10, Concerto for Orchestra, op. 24, Variations for Orchestra, op. 30, and Ricercar from Bach's *Musical Offering*; M. Graham D. Co. and New York City B., 1959), Béjart's *Temps* (Pieces for Orchestra, op. 6 and 10, as part of his *Suite Viennoise*, B. of the 20th Century, 1960, also as part of MacMillan's *My Brother, My Sisters*, Stuttgart B., 1978), *Cantates* (op. 29 and 31, B. of the 20th Century, 1965), and *Webern—opus 5* (B. of the 20th Century, 1966), L. Meyer's *The Web* (String Quartet, op. 5, Western Th. B., 1962), Cranko's *Opus 1* (Passacaglia, op. 1, Stuttgart B., 1965), Van Dantzig's *Moments* (6 Bagatelles, op. 9, and String Quartet, op. 5, Dutch National B., 1968), and Butler's *Transitions* (op. 5 arr. for string orchestra and 6 Pieces for Orchestra, op. 6, Cologne B., 1969).

Webster, Clara (b Bath, 1821, d London 17 Dec. 1844). Brit. dancer. Studied with her father Benjamin W. in Bath. Début with her brother Arthur W. in a pas de deux in 1830. Went to London in 1836 and appeared at the Haymarket Th., and later in Dublin, Liverpool, and Manchester. One of the first Eng. dancers to d. the *Cachucha*, *Cracovienne*, and (with her brother) the *Tyrolienne*. Died from burns suffered when her costume caught fire during the perf. of *The Revolt of the Harem* at Drury Lane Th.
BIBL.: I. Guest, *Victorian Ballet Girl* (London, 1957).

Wedding Bouquet, A. Ballet in 1 act; libr., mus., and déc. Lord Berners (with words by G. Stein); ch. Ashton. Prod. 27 Apr. 1937, Sadler's Wells B., Sadler's Wells Th., London, with Honer, Helpmann. This is a comic b. about a wedding, set in provincial France at the turn of the century; the groom is embarrassed by the presence among the guests of various former mistresses, incl. Julia, who has gone mad with grief. Phrases from Stein's play, *They Must Be Wedded to their Wife*, are spoken by a narrator seated at a table on the stage and inspire or comment on the various incidents. Revived for Joffrey B., 1979.
BIBL.: P. Brinson and C. Crisp, in *Ballet & Dance* (Newton Abbot, 1980); D. Vaughan, *Frederick Ashton and his Ballets* (London, 1977).

Weidman, Charles (b Lincoln, Neb., 22 July 1901, d New York, 15 July 1975). Amer. dancer, choreographer, and teacher. Studied with Eleanor Frampton and at Denishawn; became a member of its co., and appeared with it for 8 years. Formed a co. with Humphrey in 1928, which survived in various forms until 1945, and for which he ch.

extensively; his best pieces were those in light satirical vein such as *And Daddy Was A Fireman* (1943). Also worked for Broadway and founded a school, from which emerged the C. W. D. Co.; his bs. for the co. included *A House Divided* (about Lincoln, 1945), *Fables for Our Time* (after Thurber, 1947), *The War Between Men and Women* and *Lysistrata* (1954), and *Is Sex Necessary?* (1959). Then worked as a ch. for New York City Op. and various drama prods., and taught on the West Coast. Established the Expression of Two Arts Th. in New York with the sculptor Mikhail Santaro in the early 1960s. Continued to perform until his death. His pupils incl. S. Shearer, Limón, J. Cole, and B. Fosse.
BIBL.: M. B. Siegel, in *At the Vanishing Point* (New York 1972); D. W. Wynne, 'Three Years with C. W.', *Dance Perspectives* 60.

Weidt, Jean (b Hamburg, 7 Oct. 1904). Ger. dancer and choreographer. Studied with Leeder and d. in his group. Went to Berlin in 1929 and formed the Red Dancers group, which performed at many communist rallies. He was the first Ger. exponent of a strictly politically orientated d. Emigrated to Moscow, Paris, and Algeria after 1933. Returned to East Berlin in 1948, where he ch. for a group of young women; became b. master in Schwerin and Karl-Marx-Stadt, and still works as a b. master at the Komische Oper. Author of *Der Rote Tänzer* (East Berlin, 1968). First Prize, Copenhagen Ch. Competition (for his b. *The Cell*, 1947).

Weigl, Joseph (b Eisenstadt, 28 Mar. 1766, d Vienna, 3 Feb. 1846). Austrian composer. Wrote many bs. for Muzzarelli, Viganò, Traffieri, and Clerico, which were performed in various Viennese ths.

Weisberger, Barbara (orig. B. Linshen; b Brooklyn c. 1926). Amer. dancer, teacher, and b. director. Studied with Marian Lehman, at School of Amer. B., and with D. Littlefield in Philadelphia. Opened a school in Wilkes-Barre, from which derived a regional b. co. Moved to Philadelphia in 1962, where she opened another studio, from which emerged the Pennsylvania B., which started to perform in 1963, and of which she was dir. until 1982.
BIBL.: O. Maynard, 'B.W. and the Pennsylvanian B.' *Dance Magazine* (1973/3).

Weiss, Josephine (b 1805, d Vienna, 18 Dec. 1852). Austrian dancer and b. mistress. Soloist of the Viennese Kärntnertor Th. 1820–6 and 1841, subsequently becoming b. mistress at the Josephstädter Th., where she formed Les Danseuses Viennoises (see *Vienna Children's Ballet*), with which she toured extensively after 1845.
BIBL.: I. Guest, in *The Romantic Ballet in England* (London, 1954).

Weiss, Robert (b N.Y., 1 Mar. 1949). Amer. d. Studied at B. Th. School and Sch. of Amer. B.

Started as a child d. in the *Nutcracker* perfs. of the N.Y. City B.; joined the co. in 1966, later became soloist, and principal in 1977. Created roles in Balanchine's *Symphony in Three Movements* (1972) and *Coppélia* (1974). Became art. dir. of Pennsylvania B. 1982.

BIBL.: J. Gruen, 'R.W.', *Dance Magazine* (1979/1).

Welch, Garth (*b* Brisbane, 14 Apr. 1936). Austral. dancer, choreographer, and b. director. Studied with Phyllis Danaher, V. Gsovsky, Northcote, Van Praagh, and Kellaway. D. with Borovansky B. 1952–8, Western Th. B. 1958–9, Grand B. du Marquis de Cuevas 1961–2. Returned to Australia; principal d. of Austral. B. 1962–74. His first ch., *Othello* (mus. Jerry Goldsmith, 1971), has been his greatest success so far. Appointed artistic dir. of B. Victoria in 1974. Married to the d. Marilyn Jones.

BIBL.: N. McLain Stoop, 'Up On Top From Down Under', *Dance Magazine* (1971/1).

Wells, Bruce (*b* Tacoma, Wash., 17 Jan. 1950). Amer. dancer and choreographer. Studied with Patricia Cairns and at School of Amer. B. Joined New York City B. 1967, soloist from 1970. To Connecticut B. 1975 as resident ch., for whom he ch. several bs. incl. the full-length *Coppélia* (1977), *A Midsummer Night's Dream* (1978), and *Beauty and the Beast* (mus. Debussy, 1979). To Boston B. 1979 as resident ch., principal d. and teacher. Ch. there *La Fille mal gardée* (1980), and Acts 1 and 3 of *Swan Lake* (V. Verdy the others, 1981). Ch. *The Hunchback of Notre Dame* (mus. Bartók) for Austral. B. 1981.

BIBL.: S. Goodman, 'B.W.', *Dance Magazine* (1972/9).

Wells, Doreen (*b* Walthamstow, 25 June 1937). Brit. dancer. Studied at Bush-Davies School and Royal Ballet School. Joined Sadler's Wells Th. B. in 1955, and Sadler's Wells B. in 1956; later became soloist. Ballerina of Touring Royal B. 1960–74 (also d. with the main co.). Created title role in Nureyev's *Raymonda* prod. (Spoleto, 1964) and further roles in Ashton's *Sinfonietta* and *The Creatures of Prometheus* (1970), Layton's *The Grand Tour* and Cauley's *Ante Room* (1971). Retired in 1974 but returned occasionally as guest ballerina, also with London City B. in 1981. Became Marchioness of Londonderry on her marriage in 1972

BIBL.: P. Buckley, 'D.W.', *Dance Magazine* (1971/3).

Wells, Kenn (*b* Durban, 28 Oct. 1942). S. A. dancer. Studied with D. McNair. Member of PACT B. 1964–7, Western Th. B. 1968–72 (eventually as soloist), and London Festival B. since 1972 where he was promoted principal d. in 1978. He created a notably successful role as the M.C. in Moreland's *Prodigal Son in Ragtime* and in 1981 appeared in the musical, *Cats*.

Wells, Mary Ann (*b* 1896). Amer. teacher.

Started to teach at Cornish School Art Center in Seattle, in 1916; soon became one of the most respected teachers in the West. Her pupils include Margaret Petit (Leslie Caron's mother), F. Hobim, M. Platt, Joffrey, Arpino, T. Rall, R. Englund, and W. Weslow. Contributed 'Some Notes About Teaching' to *Dance Magazine* (1962, 9 and 11). Retired in 1962.

Welsh Dance Theatre. Based in Cardiff, the small group of dancers, most of whom had been recruited from the London School of Contemporary D. started to perform in October 1974. Artistic dir. was then David Nicholas, who was succeeded by W. Louther. The repertory included works by R. Charlip, B. Moreland, Tamara McLorg, D. Humphrey, and Louther. Disbanded in Mar. 1976 after a London season, for financial reasons.

BIBL.: P.W., 'The W. D. Th.', *Dance and Dancers* (1975/7).

Wengerd, Tim (*b* Boston, 4 Jan. 1945). Amer. dancer. Studied with Elizabeth Waters, Petrus van Muyden, then as a d.-ch. with Utah Repertory Th. and 1973–82 as a soloist with the Graham Co. Now freelance ch. and solo concert dancer.

BIBL.: L. Draegin, 'T.W.', *Dance Magazine* (1977/9).

Wennergren, Lena (*b* Karlstadt, 1947). Swed. dancer. Studied with L. Schubert, Holmgren, and B. Ross. Joined Schubert's Stockholm Jazz B. in 1965, and Cullberg B. (as soloist) in 1967.

West, Elizabeth (*b* Alassio, 1927, *d* nr. Matterhorn, 28 Sep. 1962). Brit. dancer, choreographer, and b. director. Studied with E. Espinosa, Muriel Carpenter, and at Bristol Old Vic Th. School. Started to work at Bristol Old Vic in 1946; ch. occasionally. Eventually became th. ch. for Bristol Old Vic and Shakespeare Festival in Stratford-upon-Avon. Founded Western Th. B. (now Scottish B.) with Darrell in 1957; ch. Stravinsky's *Pulcinella* and Prokofiev's *Peter and the Wolf* (1957). Became Artistic Dir. It was thanks to her indefatigable initiative and zest that the co. survived its very hard early years.

Westerdijk, Lenny (*b* Amsterdam, 14 Feb. 1946). Dutch dancer. Studied with Karel Poons at Scapino D. Academy; joined Scapino B. Member of Netherlands D. Th. 1965–8, and B. Rambert 1968–9; then returned to Netherlands D. Th. Rejoined B. Rambert 1972–7. Created roles in J. Sanders' *Screenplay* (1966), Tetley's *Embrace Tiger and Return to Mountain* (1969) and *Small Parades* (1972), Van Manen's *Squares* (1969), *Grosse Fuge* (1971), *Tilt* (1972), and *Opus Lemaitre* (1972), Falco's *Journal* (1971), and Chesworth's *Project 6354/9116 Mk. 2* (1974). Ch. *5-4-3-2-1* (mus. N. Hooper, B. Rambert, 1976) and other bs. for cos. in Brit. and Holland. Appointed Rehearsal Dir.

London Contemporary D. Th. 1980–4. With Austral. Dance Th. since 1985.

Western Symphony. Ballet in 3 movements; ch. Balanchine; mus. H. Kay; set John Boyt; cost. Karinska. Prod. 7 Sep. 1954, New York City B., City Center, N.Y., with Diana Adams, Bliss, Reed, Magallanes, P. Wilde, LeClercq, d'Amboise. 'My idea in this ballet was to make a formal work that would derive its flavour from the informal American West, a ballet that would move within the framework of the classical school, but in a new atmosphere ... I wanted to do a ballet without a story in an unmistakably native American idiom' (Balanchine). At its première the b. had 4 movements and was d. in practice dress. There is an Amer. film of the b.
BIBL.: G. Balanchine, 'W.S.' in *Balanchine's New Complete Stories of the Great Ballets* (Garden City, N.Y., 1968).

West Side Story. Amer. mus. Libr. Arthur Laurents; mus. Bernstein; prod. and ch. Robbins; sets O. Smith; cost. I. Sharaff. Prod. 26 Sep. 1957, Winter Garden Th., New York. A mus. ch. almost throughout, based on the *Romeo and Juliet* plot translated into modern New York gang warfare terms. Revived all over the world. Amer. film prod. 1961. J. Neumeier produced and ch. it for Hamburg State Op. in 1978.
BIBL.: D. Boroff, 'W.S.S', *Dance Magazine* (1957/8).

What Love Tells Me. See *Ce que l'amour me dit.*

Whims of Cupid and the Ballet Master, The (orig. Dan. title: *Amors og Balletmesterens Luner*). Ballet in 1 act; libr. and ch. Galeotti; mus. Jens Lolle. Prod. 31 Oct. 1786, Royal Dan. B., Copenhagen. Cupid blindfolds lovers of many lands who have paid tribute to him, and mismatches the couples, which causes great confusion when the blindfolds are removed. The oldest b. to survive with its original ch. It has frequently been revived by the Royal Dan. B. and occasionally also by foreign cos. (Paris Opéra, 1952; Netherlands B., The Hague, 1957).
BIBL.: C. Beaumont, 'T.W.o.C.' in *Ballets Past & Present* (London, 1955).

Whipped Cream. See *Schlagobers.*

White, Onna (*b* Inverness, Nova Scotia, 24 Mar. 1922). Amer. dancer and choreographer. Studied at San Francisco B. School and Frieda Marie Shaw B. School. Joined San Francisco B., and later became ballerina. Worked as asst. to M. Kidd; became ch. for Broadway and Hollywood. Her musicals include *Music Man* (also film), *Irma la douce, Half a Sixpence, Mame* (also film), *1776* (also film), *Ilya Darling, Billy,* and films *Bye, Bye, Birdie* and *Oliver.* Academy Award (Oscar) for *Oliver* (1968).

White-Haired Girl, The. Ballet in 8 acts. Prod. 1964, Shanghai School of Dancing. 'Hsi-erh's father, unable to pay his debts, is beaten to death and she is taken by force to work in the home of the landlord, Huang Shih-jen. Her fiancé joins the People's Army, determined to liberate the village and rescue the girl ... In the course of time she endures such suffering that her long black hair turns white. The Eighth Red Army frees the village, and Hsi-erh's fiancé finds the nearly wild girl in a cave. Reunited with the people, she has the triumph of seeing her oppressor liquidated ... Along with the young villagers, Hsi-erh joins the army and goes forth to carry on the revolution' (L. Wheeler Snow). The b. derives from a Chinese folk opera of 1945. Orig. a half-hour version, which was extended to a one-hour prod. and then to the full-length version. The title-role is so extremely strenuous that it is d. by several ballerinas in the course of one perf. Filmed by Shanghai Film Studio and released for general exhibition on the 13th anniversary of Mao's talks on literature and art at Yenan (15 Feb. 1972).
BIBL.: L. Wheeler Snow, in *China on Stage* (New York, 1972).

Who Cares? Ballet in 1 act; ch. Balanchine; mus. Gershwin (arr. H. Kay); cost. Karinska; light. R. Bates; piano Gordon Boelzner. Prod. 5 Feb. 1970, New York City B., State Theater N.Y., with von Aroldingen, McBride, M. Morris, d'Amboise. 'Who cares / If the sky cares to fall in the sea? / Who cares / What banks fail in Yonkers? / Long as you've got a kiss that conquers, / Why should I care? / Life is one long jubilee, / So long as I care for you / And you care for me' (Gershwin). Balanchine uses the Gershwin songs not as a facile recapitulation of a lost epoch, but simply as songs or melodies for classic, undeformed, traditional academic dances, which are reflected in the balance of phrasing, dynamics, and emotion.
BIBL.: G. Balanchine and F. Mason, in *Balanchine's Complete Stories of the Great Ballets* (Garden City, N.Y., 1977); R. Sealy, 'Mr. Robbins, Mr Balanchine, Mr. Boelzner', *Ballet Review* (vol 3, no. 3).

Widerberg, Tommy (*b* Stockholm, 25 June 1946). Swed. dancer. Studied at Royal Swed. B. School; joined Royal Swed. B. in 1964, and became soloist in 1969.

Wiedersheim-Paul, Annette av. See *Paul, Annette av.*

Wiedmann, Ilse (*b* Buenos Aires, 1933). Argent. dancer and b. mistress. Studied with Bulnés. Joined Teatro Colón B. in 1955. D. with Stuttgart B. 1959–67 and eventually became soloist. Returned to Buenos Aires; b. mistress of San Martin B. 1968–73 and subsequently of Hamburg State Op. B.

Wiesenthal, Grete (*b* Vienna, 9 Dec. 1885, *d* there 22 June 1970). Austrian dancer, choreographer, and teacher. Studied at Vienna Court Op. B. School. Member of the co. 1901–7, which she left to start her own career. Created what seems to be the ultimate interpretation of the Viennese waltz, going beyond its normal sweetish image. Started to d. with her sisters Elsa and Berta, later at her worldwide tours mainly with Tony Birkmeyer. Also appeared occasionally in films and pantomimes written specially for her by poets like Hugo von Hofmannsthal. Collaborated from 1908 with Max Reinhardt in Berlin, Munich, and Stuttgart (creating Kitchen Boy in the first prod. of R. Strauss's *Ariadne auf Naxos*, 1912). During the 1920s, 30s, and 50s ch. for Salzburg Festival. Her few bs. incl. *Der Taugenichts in Wien* (mus. F. Salmhofer, Vienna State Op., 1930). Developed a special technique based upon classical b., but enriched by her own idiom of suspense and balance. Taught at her private school since 1919 and at the d. dept. of the Academy of Mus. and Perf. Arts in Vienna 1934–52 (dir. 1945–52). Formed a small co. after World War 2, which existed until the early 50s. Some of her waltzes were revived successfully for the Vienna State Op. B., 1977.

Wiesenthal Sisters. They numbered 6, *Grete the most important, but Elsa and Berta enjoyed a smaller reputation of their own. D. together 1908–10, later on touring without Grete, whose place was taken by Marta.

Wigman, Mary (orig. Marie Wiegmann; *b* Hanover, 13 Nov. 1886, *d* Berlin, 18 Sep. 1973). Ger. dancer, choreographer, and teacher. Studied with Jaques-Dalcroze in Hellerau/Dresden and from 1913 with Laban in Munich and Zurich; later became his asst. Made her début as a recital d. in 1914. Her real career as Ger.'s most famous modern d. started after the First World War. After overwhelming successes in Zurich and Hamburg in 1919, she opened a school in Dresden in 1920, which soon became the focal point of Ger. modern d. Holm, Georgi, Palucca, Wallmann, and Kreutzberg were among her pupils and also appeared in her group. During the following years she toured extensively; made her London début in 1928, and her U.S. début in 1930. Created numerous solo dances and group chs., which were landmarks of Ger. expressionist dancing. Offshoots of her Dresden Central School were set up everywhere, incl. the U.S. (Holm's); in the early 1930s there were almost 2000 pupils in all. The Nazi authorities had little sympathy for her, and her appearance at the Berlin Olympic Games of 1935 was one of her last. They took the school away from her, but friends secured her a post at the Leipzig Mus. Academy. She started again after 1945, and opened a school in Leipzig, but moved to West Berlin in 1949. There her school was once again, a meeting point for modern d. enthusiasts from all over the world well into the 1960s. She also worked as a guest ch. for Ger. op. houses; her most important prods. incl. Gluck's *Orpheus and Eurydice* (ch. throughout, Leipzig, 1947), Handel's *Saul* (Mannheim, 1954), Orff's *Catulli Carmina* and *Carmina Burana*

(Mannheim, 1955), Stravinsky's *Sacre du printemps* (Municipal Op., Berlin, 1957), and Gluck's *Alcestis* (Mannheim, 1958). Author of *Deutsche Tanzkunst* (Dresden, 1935), *Die Sprache des Tanzes* (Stuttgart, 1963; Amer. ed. *The Language of the Dance*, Middletown, Conn., 1966), and the posthumous *M.W. Book* (ed. W. Sorrell, Middletown, Conn., 1973). Schiller Prize (Mannheim, 1954); Ger. Critics' Prize (1961).

BIBL.: E. Scheyer, 'The Shapes of Space: The Art of M.W. and Oskar Schlemmer', *Dance Perspectives* 41; M. B. Siegel, 'M.W.: A Tribute', *Dance Magazine* (1973/11); W. Sorell, *The M.W. Book* (Middletown, Conn., 1975); J. Mueller, 'Films: A Glimpse of M.W.', *Dance Magazine* (1976/3).

Wilde Ballets. Ballets based on the literary output of Oscar Wilde (1856–1920) include Bolm's *Birthday of the Infanta* (mus. J. A. Carpenter, Chicago, 1919; earlier version by O. Zöbische, mus. M. Radnai, Budapest, 1918; later versions by W. Fortner in *Die weisse Rose*, ch. Keith, Municipal Op., Berlin, 1951, and by G. Burne, mus. H. Partsch, Cape Town, 1971), Dolin's *The Nightingale and the Rose* (mus. H. Fraser-Simson, Nemtchinova-Dolin B., London, 1927), Etchévery's *Ballade de la geôle de Reading* (mus. Ibert, Opéra Comique, Paris, 1947), *The Picture of Dorian Gray* (ch. B. von Larsky, mus. Scriabin, Augsburg, 1955; ch. Orlikowsky, mus. M. Lang, Basle, 1966; also in *Double Exposure*, ch. Layton, mus. Scriabin and H. Pousseur, City Center Joffrey B., New York, 1972). A biographical b., *O.W.*, by Layton, mus. Walton, Royal B., London, 1972. There have also been countless solo dances and bs. based upon his play *Salome*; see *Salome Ballets*.

Wilde, Patricia (*b* Ottawa, 16 July 1928). Can. dancer and teacher. Studied with Gwendolyne Osborn, D. Littlefield, and at School of Amer. B. Début with Amer. B. Concert in 1943. D. with various cos. (B. International, B. Russe de Monte Carlo, etc.); joined New York City B. in 1950 and became one of its best known principal dancers. Created roles in Balanchine's *La Valse* (1951), *Caracole* and *Scotch Symphony* (1952) *Opus 34*, *Western Symphony*, and *Ivesiana* (1954), *Divertimento No. 15* (1956), *Square Dance* (1957), and *Raymonda Variations* (1961), Boris's *Cakewalk* (1951), and Robbins's *Quartet* (1954). Resigned in 1965. Principal of Harkness School of B. 1965–7. Has also taught for Geneva B. and since 1969, at Amer. B. Th. School, where she was art. dir. 1979–82, since when she has been art. dir. Pittsburgh B.

BIBL.: T. Tobias, 'P.W.', *Dance Magazine* (1971/9); J. Gruen, 'P.W.', in *The Private World of Ballet* (New York, 1975).

Wilhelm, Franz (*b* Bilin, 14 Apr. 1945). Austrian dancer. Studied at Vienna State Op. B. School. Joined the co. in 1960 and became a soloist in 1967 and principal d. in 1972.

William the Jew of Pesaro. See *Ebreo, Guglielmo*

Williams, Andrés (b Havana, 1952). Cub. dancer. Studied at Cub. National B. School with Ramona de Saa and Joaquin Banegas. Joined National B. of Cuba in 1970, eventually promoted principal d. Bronze Medal (Moscow, 1973).

Williams, Daniel. See *Grossman, Daniel Williams*.

Williams, Dudley (b New York, Aug. 1938). Amer. dancer. Started taking tap-dancing lessons. Studied at High School of Performing Arts and also with Shook, Chaffee and O'Donnell, and Tudor. Appeared with O'Donnell's co. Joined Graham D. Co. in 1961. Has also d. with the cos. of Ailey, Beatty, and McKayle.
BIBL.: S. Goodman, 'D.W.', *Dance Magazine* (1967/3).

Williams, Ellen Virginia (b Melrose, Mass. 12 Mar. 1914, d Malden, Mass. 8 May 1984). Amer. dance teacher, choreographer, and b. director. Studied with Geraldine Cragin, Dana Sieveling, and with D. Teachers Club of Boston. Occasionally appeared as a d. in San Carlo op. prods. Started a school of her own in Boston, from which came the dancers of the New England Civic B., formed in 1958. This became the Boston B. in 1963, of which she was artistic dir. until 1983 (since 1980 jointly with V. Verdy). Ch. *Stephen Foster Suite*, *The Green Season*, and *Sea Alliance*. Has also taught at Walnut Hill School, Boston Univ., and for numerous teacher organizations. Contributed 'What Makes a Great Teacher of Classical Ballet?' to *Dance Magazine* (1963/8). D. Magazine Award 1976.
BIBL.: T. Tobias, 'E.V.W. and the Boston Ballet', *Dance Magazine* (1976/6).

Williams, Peter (b Burton Joyce, 12 June 1914). Brit. writer on dance. Educated at London Central School of Art and Design. Founded *Dance and Dancers* in 1950 and was editor until 1980. D. critic of *Daily Mail* 1950–3. Deputy d. critic of *The Observer* since 1970. Member of the Arts Council of Great Brit. 1972–5 (and of its D. Advisory Committee 1965–80, Chmn. 1973–80), also of Brit. Council (Drama and D. Advisory Committee since 1961, Chmn. 1975–81). Founder-Chmn. Dancers' Pensions and Resettlement Fund since 1975. Has occasionally worked as a designer, e.g. for Taras's *Designs with Strings* (Met. B., 1948) and Howard's *Selina* (also libr., Sadler's Wells Th. B., 1949). Author of *Masterpieces of Ballet Design* (London, 1981). O.B.E. (1971).

Williams, Stanley (b Chappel, Eng., 1925). Anglo-Dan. dancer and teacher. Grew up in Copenhagen and studied at Royal Dan. B. School. Joined the co. and became solo d. in 1949 and teacher at the school in 1950. Left Royal Dan. B. in 1963. Taught for Kirsta's London B. Comique and New York City B.; joined the teaching staff of the School of Amer. B. in 1964 and became one of its most respected members. D. Magazine Award 1981.

BIBL.: T. Tobias, 'The Quality of the Moment: S.W.', *Dance Magazine* (1981/3).

Williams Yarborough, Lavinia (b Philadelphia, Penn., 2 July 1926). Amer. dancer and teacher. Started to d. when still a very young child. Studied drawing and only then dancing with Sokolow, at Graham School and with L. Kay. D. with Eugene von Grona's Negro Ballet, later joined A. de Mille's co., teaching at her school. Appeared in various musicals and films. In 1953 went to Haiti, where she set going various schools and d. academies and the Haitian Institute of Folklore and Classic D. Now based on the Bahamas, where she founded the National School of D. and established the National D. Troupe of Jamaica, West Indies. She is the mother of the d. Sarah Yarborough.

Wilson, Billy (b Philadelphia, 21 Apr. 1935). Amer. d., ch., teacher, and b. director. Studied with Tudor, Shook, Nicks, and Cole; d. with Philadelphia B. Guild Co., in various Broadway musicals, and with Netherlands B., transferred to Dutch Nat. B. 1959–63. Worked as a ch. for several Dutch, Ger., and Amer. TV prods.; also for op. and musicals. Taught at Brandeis Univ., National Center of Afro-Amer. Artists, and Harvard Univ. Now Artistic Dir. of the D. Th. of Boston, for which he choreographs regularly. D. Award of Association of Performing Artists (1974); Emmy Award for *Zoom* (WGBH-TV). Married to the d. Sonja van Beers.
BIBL.: I. M. Fanger, 'B.W.', *Dance Magazine* (1976/6).

Wilson, George Bulkeley Laird (b Kew Gardens, 22 Mar. 1908, d Roehampton, 20 Aug. 1984). Brit. engineer and writer on dance. Educated at Cambridge Univ. Member of Grand Council of R.A.D. Founder of the Association of B. Clubs in 1947, and chairman ever since. Asst. editor of *The Ballet Annual* 1946–63. Contributor to *The Dancing Times* from 1957. London correspondent of Amer. *Dance News* since 1969. Contributor to *Encyclopaedia Britannica* and *Enciclopedia dello spettacolo*. Author of *Dictionary of Ballet* (London, 1957; new enlarged ed., 1974).

Wilson, Lester (b New York, c. 1942). Amer. dancer and choreographer. Studied at Juillard School. Started as a d. in musicals in 1964. Went to Ger. in 1966, and became one of the most prolific choreographers for TV and musicals.

Wilson, Robert M. (b Waco, Tex., 4 Oct. 1941). Amer. artist. Orig. embarked on a painting career. Completely unconventional in his working methods and artistic aims; his prods. offer a certain amount of dancing, but it is impossible to call them d. or even b. prods. Nonetheless he has attracted a great number of d. enthusiasts to his slow-motion prods., which are generally extremely long (sometimes more than 12 hours). His first prod. was a *Dance Event* at the 1965 New

York World's Fair; the most important so far include *ByrdwoMAN* (New York, 1968), *The Life and Times of Sigmund Freud* (New York, 1969), *Deafman Glance* (Iowa City, 1970). *KA MOUNTAIN AND GUARDenia TERRACE* (Shiraz, 1972), *The Life and Times of Joseph Stalin* (New York, 1973), *The Life and Times of Dave Clark* (São Paulo, 1974), *The $ Value of Man* (New York, 1975), and *Einstein on the Beach* (Avignon, 1976). Has conducted many workshops in Amer. and Eur. Also works as a painter and film-maker. Is now dir. of Byrd Hoffman Foundation. Drama Desk Award for Direction (New York, 1971); Guggenheim Fellowship Award (New York, 1971).
BIBL.: M. B. Siegel, in *At the Vanishing Point* (New York, 1973).

Wilson, Sallie (*b* Fort Worth, Tex., 18 Apr. 1932). Amer. dancer. Studied with Dorothy Colter Edwards, Craske, Tudor, and Caton. Joined B. Th. in 1949; d. with Met. Op. B. 1950–5. Returned to Amer. B. Th. in 1955 and became soloist in 1957 and ballerina in 1961, specializing in dramatic roles. Has also been a member of New York City B.; created Mary Stuart in Graham's *Episodes* (1959). Her other creations incl. Robbins' *Les Noces* (1965).
BIBL.: J. Gruen 'S.W.', in *The Private World of Ballet* (New York, 1975).

Wilson, Zane (*b* Elkton, Md., 25 Feb. 1951). Amer. dancer. Started to perform in amateur prods. at his home town and only then moved on to study at Harkness School. Joined Harkness Youth Dancers 1970, creating immediately a part in Nebrada's *Percussion for Six*. After disbanding of the Harkness co. joined Ballet Internacional de Caracas as a foundation member 1975, creating further roles in bs. by Nebrada and in Neumeier's *Ariel* duo (with Z. Rodriguez, Hamburg, 1977).
BIBL.: N. McLain Stoop, 'The Ballet Internacional de Caracas and Two of Its Dancers', *Dance Magazine* (1978/1).

Wings. Ballet in 1 act; ch. Bruce; mus. Bob Downes; déc. Dieter Rose. Prod. 7 Nov. 1970, D. Forum, Cologne, with S. Alexanders, M. Montiva, H. Tegeder, J. Burth, J. Ulrich, G. Veredon. A plotless b., inspired by birdlike movements. Revived for B. Rambert, 1974.

Winnipeg Ballet. See *Royal Winnipeg Ballet*.

Winter, Ethel (*b* Wrentham, Mass., 18 June 1924). Amer. dancer, choreographer, and teacher. Studied at Bennington College and with Graham. Joined Graham's co. in 1945 and succeeded her in her roles in *Herodiade* and *Frontier*. Also d. with other cos.; created title role in Maslow's *The Dybbuk* (1964). Has appeared with her own co. and ch. for Batsheva D. Co. and Repertory D. Th. of Utah.

Winter, Marian Hannah (*b* New York, 20 Mar. 1910, *d* Paris, 15 Dec. 1981). Amer. writer. Attended Radcliffe, various univs., finally Sor-

bonne (doctorate, 1951). Her numerous articles (*Musical Quarterly, Dance Index et al.*) and books, especially *Le Théâtre du Merveilleux* (Paris, 1962) and *The Pre-Romantic Ballet* (London, 1974), contain a wealth of d. information.

Winterbranch. Ballet for 6 dancers; ch. M. Cunningham; mus. LaMonte Young; cost. R. Rauschenberg. Prod. 21 Mar. 1964, M. Cunningham D. Co., Wadsworth Atheneum, Hartford, Conn., with Cunningham, Brown, Farber, B. Lloyd, W. Davis, Paxton. A plotless b.: 'the dancers are alternately confined by deep darkness and exposed by glaring light coming from sharp angles. They're like insects or some other helpless creatures beating out their existence against inexorable, uncontrollable forces—or like man living under the hand that stays the Bomb' (M. B. Siegel). New York première, 4 Mar. 1965, N.Y. State Th. Revived for Boston B. (1974).
BIBL.: M. B. Siegel, in *The Shapes of Change* (Boston, 1979).

Witch Boy, The. Ballet in 1 act and 3 scenes; libr. and ch. J. Carter; mus. Salzedo; déc. N. McDowell. Prod. 24 May 1956, B. der Lage Landen, Amsterdam, with McDowell, Angela Bayley, Carter. The b. is based on an Amer. version of the ballad of Barbara Allen. Revived for London Festival B. (27 Nov. 1957, Manchester, with Gilpin) and other cos.
BIBL.: P. Brinson and C. Crisp, in *Ballet & Dance* (Newton Abbot, 1980).

With My Red Fires. Ballet in 2 parts; libr. and ch. Humphrey; mus. W. Riegger; cost. P. Lawrence. Prod. 13 Aug. 1936, Humphrey-Weidman Co. Bennington College. The final section of a trilogy (preceded by *New Dance* and *Theatre Piece*); the title is taken from Blake's poem *Jerusalem II*: 'For the Divine appearance is Brotherhood, but I am Love / Elevate into the Region of Brotherhood with my red fires.' Its 2 parts are entitled 'Ritual' and 'Drama'. and it evolves as a choral drama; 2 Lovers fight to maintain themselves against the oppressiveness of the Matriarch. Filmed in 1972.
BIBL.: M. Lloyd, in *The Borzoi Book of Modern Dance* (New York, 1949).

Woizikovsky, Leon (orig. Wójcikowski; *b* Warsaw, 20 Feb. 1899, *d* there, 23 Feb. 1975). Pol. dancer, b. master, and teacher. Studied at Warsaw Imperial B. School and with Cecchetti. Joined Diaghilev's Bs. Russes in 1916, and became one of its outstanding character dancers; created roles in Massine's *Las Meninas* (1916), *Les Femmes de bonne humeur* and *Parade* (1917), *La Boutique fantasque*, and *Le Tricorne* (1919), *Les Matelots* (1925), and *Le Pas d'acier* (1927), Nijinska's *Les Noces* (1923), *Les Biches*, and *Le Train bleu* (1924), Balanchine's *Barabau* (1925), *The Gods Go a-Begging* (1928), *Le Bal*, and *Prodigal Son* (1929). Also much admired in the Fokine bs. Remained with the co. until it disbanded. Member of Pavlova co. 1929–

31, and of B. Russe de Monte Carlo 1932–4. Created roles in Balanchine's *Cotillon* and *Le Concurrence* (1932), and Massine's *Jeux d'enfants, Les Présages, Beach,* and *Choreartium* (1933). Had his own co. Les Bs. de L.W., with which he toured Eur. 1935–6. Rejoined B. Russe de Colonel de Basil and remained with it throughout the war. Returned to Warsaw in 1945, and taught at the op. b. school. Went to London and staged and ch. *Petrushka* in 1958 and *Sheherazade* in 1960 for London Festival B. Member of Massine's B. Europeo 1960–1, then b. master of London Festival B. Taught at Cologne Institute for Th. D. until the mid-1960s and at Bonn Univ. until 1974; occasionally staged Diaghilev repertory bs. for such cos. as the Cologne B. and The Royal Flemish B. Returned to Warsaw in 1974.

Wood, Donna (*b* New York, 21 Nov. 1954). Amer. dancer. Studied with Josephine Schwarz at Dayton, starting to perform with Dayton Contemporary D. Co., then as a scholarship student with D. Th. of Harlem, before joining A. Ailey Amer. D. Th. 1972, of which she is now one of the top soloists, a guest also of various regional cos. throughout the US, in Canada, and at Hamburg and Vienna.
BIBL.: L. Small, 'D.W.', *Dance Magazine* (1979/12).

Wood, Michael (*b* Sunderland, 1912). Brit. b. school director and former publicist and administrator. After military service was press officer of Royal Op. House, Cov. Gdn., London, 1946–58. Appointed General Manager of Royal B. in 1958. Succeeded Haskell as Dir. of the Royal B. School 1966–78. Chmn. *Council for D.Educ. and Training 1979–81.

Wood, Roger (*b* Madras, 1920). Brit. photographer. Started to photograph b. in 1944; became one of the best known b. photographers in Eng. Published a number of books, e.g. *Katherine Dunham* (with R. Buckle, London, 1949), *The Sadler's Wells Ballet at the Royal Opera House* (London, 1951), and *The Theatre Ballet of Sadler's Wells in Photographs* (London, 1952). Now works mainly as a photographer of archaeology.

Wooden Prince, The (also *The Woodcut P.*; orig. Hung. title: *A fából faragott királyfi*). Ballet in 1 act; libr. Béla Balász; mus. Bartók; ch. Otto Zöbisch; déc. Count Bánffy. Prod. 12 May 1917, Budapest, with Anna Palley (en travestie as the Prince), Emilia Nirschy, Ede Brada, and Boriska Hormat. A fairy tale about a prince, whose love for a princess is unrequited; he carves a wooden prince to win her admiration. She, however, falls in love with the carved prince, and only when she gets tired of his mechanical movements does she begin to appreciate the humanity of the real prince, and repentantly returns to him. Later prods. by Harangozó (Budapest, 1939), Milloss (Venice, 1950), Walter (Wuppertal, 1962), Seregi (Budapest, 1970—also for Hung. TV), and Cauley (London Festival B., 1981).

BIBL.: C. Mason, 'Béla Bartók' in *The Decca Book of Ballet* (London, 1958).

Woolliams, Anne (*b* Folkestone, 3 Aug. 1926). Brit. dancer, teacher, and b. mistress. Studied with J. Espinosa and Volkova. D. with Kyasht B. in 1943, Russian Op. B., and St. James's B., and in the film prod. of *The Red Shoes*. Taught at Essen Folkwang School 1958–63 and d. with its co. B. mistress Stuttgart B. 1963–75; also Dir. of Cranko B. School. Artistic dir. Austral. B., 1976–77 and since then Dean of D. at Victoria College of the Arts, Melbourne. Author of *Ballettsaal* (Stuttgart, 1973). Married to the ex-d. and ch. Jan Stripling.

Worth, Faith (*b* Scarborough. 1938). Brit. dancer and dance notator. Studied with Brownlie, Tweedy, and at Royal B. School, then studied Benesh Notation at Institute of Choreology. Joined Royal B. as notator in 1960. Has since mounted a number of its bs. for cos. abroad.

Wranitzky, Paul (*b* Neu-Reisch, 30 Dec. 1756, *d* Vienna, 28 Sep. 1808). Austrian composer. Wrote the mus. for a great number of bs. performed at the Vienna ths. for such choreographers as Muzzarelli, Trafieri, Clerico, and Gioja.

Wright, Belinda (orig. Brenda W.; *b.* Southport, 18 Jan. 1927). Brit. dancer. Studied with Dorothea Halliwell, Preobrajenska, and Crofton. Joined B. Rambert in 1945; then d. with Bs. de Paris, London Festival B., Grand B. du Marquis de Cuevas, and as ballerina with London Festival B. 1955–7 and occasionally later. D. the premiere of Ashton's *Vision of Marguerite* (1952) when Markova withdrew, and created roles in Charnley's *Alice in Wonderland* (1953), Beriozoff's *Esmeralda* (1954), and Bourmeister's *Snow Maiden* (1961). She then pursued a career as guest artist (incl. Royal B., 1963), undertaking world-wide tours with her d.-husband Jelko Yuresha.
BIBL.: E. Herf, 'B.W.', *Ballet Today* (1963/2).

Wright, Peter (*b* London, 1926). Brit. dancer, choreographer, b. master, and director. Studied with Jooss, Volkova, and Van Praagh. D. with Bs. Jooss 1945–6 and 1951–2, Met. B. in 1947, St. James's B. in 1948, and Sadler's Wells Th. B. 1949–51 and 1952–5, where he became asst. b. master. Taught at Royal B. School 1957–9. Occasionally worked as a ch.-his bs. incl. *A Blue Rose* (mus. Barber, Royal B., 1957), *The Great Peacock* (mus. Searle, International B., Edinburgh, 1958), and *Musical Chairs* (mus. Prokofiev, Western Th. B., 1959). B. master of Stuttgart B. 1961–7; ch. *The Mirror Walkers* (mus. Tchaikovsky, 1963), *Quintet* (mus. Ibert, 1963), and *Namouna* (mus. Lalo, 1967), and staged *Giselle* (1966), which he has since mounted for several other cos. He then joined the BBC as b. master for its TV b. prods. Staged *Sleeping Beauty* (Cologne, 1967; Royal B., 1968). Ch. *Danse Macabre* (mus. J. McCabe, Western Th. B., 1968), *Arpège* (mus. Boïeldieu, Royal B. School, 1974; Touring Royal

B., 1975), and *El amor brujo* (mus. de Falla, Touring Royal B., 1975). Has also worked for Bat-Dor D. Co., National B. of Canada, and taught at Royal B. and Royal B. School. Associate Dir. of the Royal B. since 1970 and Resident Dir. of the Touring Co. (now Sadler's Wells Royal B.) since 1975. C.B.E. (1985).

BIBL.: C. Crisp, 'P.W.', *About the House* (vol. 3, no. 7).

Wright, Rebecca (*b* Springfield, Ohio, 5 Dec. 1947). Studied with Jorg Fasting, Honor Thompson, Josephine and Hermine Schwarz, and at School of Amer. B. and Amer. B. Center. Joined Joffrey City Center B. in 1966 and became one of its principal dancers. Joined Amer. B. Th. as a soloist in 1975, left 1981; now teaching. Created roles in Arpino's *Cello Concerto* (1967), *Confetti* and *Trinity* (1970), *Valentine* and *Kettentanz* (1971), and Layton's *Double Exposure* (1972).

BIBL.: R. A. Thom, 'R.W.: Pineapple Poll Turns Titania', *Dance Magazine* (1974/5); J. Gruen, 'R.W.', in *The Private World of Ballet* (New York, 1975).

Wührer, Ully (*b* Vienna, 30 Oct. 1940). Austrian dancer. Studied at Vienna State Op. B. School and with W. Fränzl, E. Vondrak, Royal B. School, Hightower, and Pereyaslavec. Joined Vienna State Op. B. in 1955; became soloist in 1965.

Wyckoff, Bonnie (*b* Natick, Mass., 20 Nov. 1945). Amer. dancer. Studied at Boston School of B. Joined Boston B. Co. 1967; became soloist in 1970 and principal d. in 1972. Joined Royal Winnipeg B. in 1973 and became principal d. in 1974. Since 1980 with Geneva, B.

X

Xenakis, Iannis (*b* Braila, Rumania, 1 May 1922). Greek-Fr. architect and composer. Wrote the mus. for Petit's *Kraanerg* (National B. of Canada, Ottawa, 1969). Bs. ch. to his concert mus. include P. Taylor's *Private Domain* (based on *Atrées*, New York, 1967), Morrice's *Them and Us* (on *Eonta*, B. Rambert, 1968; also by Adret, B. Th. Contemporain, 1969), Balanchine's *Metastaseis & Pithoprakta* (New York City B., 1968), Béjart's *Nomos Alpha* (B. of the 20th Century, 1969; also by Bohner in *Frustration–Aggression*, Berlin, 1969), and Schmucki's *Oresteia* (Marseilles, 1971).

Y

Yacobson, Leonid. See *Jacobson, Leonid.*

Yarborough, Sara (*b* New York, *c.* 1950). Amer. dancer. Daughter of the d. teacher Lavinia Williams. Started to study at her mother's Academy of D. in Haiti, then at School of Amer. B. and Harkness B. School. Joined Harkness B. in 1967; d. with Ailey's City Center D. Th. from 1971; joined City Center Joffrey B. in 1975.
BIBL.: M. Marks, 'S.Y. of Harkness Ballet', *Dance Magazine* (1968/11); S. Goodman, 'S.Y.', *Dance Magazine* (1972/11).

Yaroslavna. Ballet in 3 acts; libr., ch. and déc. Vinogradov; mus. B. Tishenko. Prod. 30 June 1974, Maly Th., Leningrad, with Tatiana Fesenko, Dolgushin, O. Oushinsky. Based on the 13th-century *Tale of Igor's Campaign*, as is Borodin's op. *Prince Igor*, but it views the expedition of Igor Svyatoslavich against the Polovtsians from the angle of the suffering women at home. The prod. benefited considerably from Vinogradov's close collaboration with the eminent drama dir. Yuri Lubimov from the Moscow Taganka Th.

Yermolayev, Alexei Nicolaievich (*b* St. Petersburg, 23 Feb. 1910, *d* Moscow, 12 Dec. 1975). Sov. dancer and teacher. Studied at Petrograd State B. Academy; graduated in 1926. Joined GATOB; eventually became soloist. Principal d. with Moscow Bolshoi B. 1930–53. D. Tybalt in the Sov. film of *Romeo and Juliet* (1954). Has occasionally worked as a ch. Has taught the boys' graduate class at Bolshoi School since 1961. Stalin Prize (1944, 1947, and 1949); Merited Artist of the R.S.F.S.R. (1940, 1951, and 1970).

Yevdokimov, Gleb (*b* Moscow, 1923). Sov. dancer and teacher. Studied at Bolshoi School; graduated in 1941. Joined Bolshoi B.; became soloist in 1944. Since his retirement in 1962 has taught at Bolshoi School and for Stanislavsky and Nemirovich-Danchenko Music Th.

Yevteyeva, Yelena Victorovna (*b* Leningrad, 14 Mar. 1947). Sov. dancer. Studied at Leningrad Ch. School; graduated in 1966. Joined Kirov B. and later became soloist. D. Odette-Odile in the Kirov *Swan Lake* film of 1968. Silver Medal (Varna, 1970).

YMHA. Abbr. for Young Men's (and Young Women's) Hebrew Association. A social centre and th., on East 92nd St., New York, which has served since 1937 as one of the city's most active platforms for all kinds of d. recitals. Dr William Kolodney was in charge of the Educational Department for many years, and he was the inspiring force for the many different perfs. at the Kaufmann Concert Hall.

Young, Gayle (*b* Lexington, Ky., 7 Nov. *c.* 1938). Amer. dancer. Studied with Dorothy Pring, then at Amer. B. Th. School. D. with Joffrey B. and New York City B. before joining Amer. B. Th. in 1960; became principal d. in 1964.

Youskevitch, Igor (*b* Piriatin, 13 Mar. 1912). Russ.-Amer. dancer and teacher. Grew up in Belgrade and became an athlete; participated in the Prague Olympic Games of 1932 as a member of the Yugosl. team. Started to study d. with Xenia Grunt in the same year; later became her partner. Studied further with Preobrajenska in Paris. Début with B. Russe de Paris in 1934; then d. with co. of Woizikovsky in 1935/6, and de Basil's 2nd co. in Austral. 1936/7. Principal d. with B. Russe de Monte Carlo 1938–44; created roles in Massine's *Gaîté Parisienne* and *Seventh Symphony* (1938), *Rouge et noir* (1939), *Vienna 1814* and *The New Yorker* (1940), Nijinska's *Snow Maiden* (1942) and *Ancient Russia*, and Schwezoff's *Red Poppy* (1943). After military service d. with Massine's B. Russe Highlights in 1946 and B. Th. 1946–55; created roles in Balanchine's *Theme and Variations* (1947), Tudor's *Shadow of the Wind* (1948), and Nijinska's *Schumann Concerto* (1951). Continued to d. with other cos. from time to time and with Alicia Alonso in special perfs. until he finally retired in 1962. Appeared in the *Circus* and *Ring Around the Rosy* episodes of G. Kelly's film *Invitation to the Dance* (1952). Returned to the B. Russe de M.C. as principal d. and art. adviser 1955–7, and continued to make guest appearances. Now art. dir. of N.Y. Ballet Competition. As a d. he was much admired for the nobility and elegance of his style, which made him an ideal interpreter of the great danseur noble roles of the traditional repertory; he became Alonso's regular partner. With his wife, the ex-d. Anna Scarpova, he taught at his school in Massapequa, L.I., N.Y., 1962–80, which served as the home of the semi-professional Y.B. Romantique. Contributed to the issue 'The Male Image', *Dance Perspectives* 40. Father of Maria Y. (*b* New York, 11 Dec. 1945), a d. of Amer. B. Th.
BIBL.: S. J. Cohen, 'Prince Igor', *Dance Magazine* (1953/5; repr. in *25 Years of American Dance*, New York, 1954). On Maria Y.: M. Marks, 'M.Y.', *Dance Magazine* (1969/9).

Youth (orig. Russ. title: *Yunost*). Ballet in 4 acts and 6 scenes; libr. Slonimsky; ch. Fenster; mus. Chulaki; déc. T. Bruni. Prod. 9 Dec. 1949, Maly Th., Leningrad, with Sheina, Shishkin, Tulubiev,

Isayeva. Based on Nikolai Ostrovsky's novel *How the Steel Was Tempered*; the first successful b. dealing with events in the Civil War. The children Petia, Dasha, and Dima live in a southern Russ. city, from which the Red Army has withdrawn under pressure from the White Army; they join two revolutionaries who have remained in the city, and help them to accomplish heroic deeds against the local bourgeoisie.

BIBL.: M. G. Swift, in *The Art of the Dance in the U.S.S.R.* (Notre Dame, Ind., 1968).

Yudenich, Alexei (*b* Sarajevo, 7 July 1943). Yugosl. dancer. Studied at the local op. b. school; joined the co. in 1961, then d. with the co. of the Zagreb National Op. Joined Pennsylvania B. in 1964; became principal d. and the regular partner of his wife, Barbara Sandonato. Created roles in Rodham's *Gala Dix* (1967) and *Cavalier Variations* (1969), Butler's *Ceremony* (1968) and *Journeys* (1970). Has often performed as a guest with other cos., incl. National B. of Canada. Silver Medal (Varna, 1970).

BIBL.: S. Goodman, 'Barbara Sandonato and A.Y.', *Dance Magazine* (1968/11).

Yugoslavia. Large b. cos. perform in such cities as *Belgrade and *Zagreb; b. cos. are attached to the local op. house in Ljubljana (48 dancers, dir.; Breda Smid), Maribor (17, Iko Otrin), Novi Sad (35, Zarko Milenković), Osijek (8, Mirta Dinter), Priština (23, Abdurahman Nokšići; this is a co. attached to a playhouse), Rijeka (23, Joža Komljenović), Sarajevo (50, Slavko Pervan), Skopje (44, Olga Milosavljeva), and Split (16, Luciano Perić).

Yuresha, Jelko (*b* Zagreb, 1937). Yugosl. dancer. Studied with Roje. Joined Split B. in 1954 and later became soloist. Joined London Festival B. in 1960 and Royal B. in 1962, but left the co. to start a freelance career; has since undertaken several world tours with his d. wife Belinda Wright.

Yuriko (orig. Y. Kikuchi; *b* San Jose, Cal., 2 Feb. 1920). Amer. dancer, teacher, and choreographer. Grew up in Japan; d. with the cos. of K. Ishii and Y. Amanaya. Returned to the U.S. and was a member of the Dorothy S. Lyndall Junior D. Group in Los Angeles until 1941. She then went to New York to study with Graham; a member of her co. 1944–67. Created roles in *Canticle for Innocent Comedians* (1952), *Clytemnestra* and *Embattled Garden* (1958), and succeeded Graham in many of her roles. Has frequently appeared in solo-recitals and, since 1968, with her own co., for which she has ch. extensively. Now teaches in New York, and again working with the Graham co.

BIBL.: L. Joel, '*The Dark Time*, and *The New Spring*', *Dance Magazine* (1968/3).

Z

Zagreb. Visiting b. cos. began to appear in 1862. Irene Freisinger was d. and ch. for the co. attached to the local op. house 1876–89 (when the op. closed), but it only appeared in the op. prods. A prod. of *The Fairy Doll*, performed by actors, was ch. by L. Gundlach in 1892. The first truly professional co. was formed in 1894, with Otokar Bartik as b. master, Freisinger as teacher, Emma Gordone from Milan as prima ballerina, and 12 dancers. The repertory consisted mainly of bs. to mus., by Delibes or Bayer. The op. house was again temporarily closed, and b. only began to flourish in 1921, when M. Froman and her brother Max were engaged; such soloists as A. Roje, Oskar Harmoš, M. Slavenska, Olga Orlova, and Zlata Lanović appeared in perfs. of *Swan Lake* and *Coppélia* (1921), *Sheherazade, Polovtsian Dances*, and *The Fairy Doll* (1922) *Petrushka* and *Thamar* (1923), and *Carnaval* (1924). The first Yugosl. bs. to be staged were Zajc and Baranović's *Wedding Dance* (1922), *The Gingerbread Heart* (1925), and *Imbrek with the Nose* (1935). B. perfs. were suspended during World War II.; immediately after 1945 a new co. and repertory began to be built up, under such b. masters as Roje, Milena Jovanović, Cintolesi, Kastl, Nevenka Horvat-Bidjin, Frano Jelinčić, Silvio Pavletić and now Damir Novak. The repertory grew to an impressive selection of the traditional classics, the Diaghilev classics, the standard works of the contemporary Sov. repertory, and such native bs. as *The Legend of Lake Ochrid, Devil in the Village,* Kelemen's *Man in the Mirror* and *Abbandonate*. The co. now consists of 25 soloists and 37 corps dancers and has often performed abroad (London, 1955). There has been a State B. School since 1949, and a special b. studio attached to the op. house was opened in 1970.

Zakharov, Rostislav Vladimirovich (*b* Astrakhan, 7 Sep. 1907, *d* Moscow, 15 Jan. 1984). Sov. dancer, choreographer, b. director, and teacher. Studied at Petrograd State B. School; graduated in 1925. Joined Kharkov B.; then d. with Kiev B. 1926–9. Returned to Leningrad to continue his studies at the Th. Technicum; graduated in 1932. Joined GATOB; ch. *The Fountain of Bakhchisaray* (mus. Asafiev, 1934) and *Lost Illusions* (mus. Asafiev, 1935). Artistic dir. of Moscow Bolshoi B. 1936–9; ch. *The Prisoner of the Caucasus* (mus. Asafiev, 1938), *Cinderella* (mus. Prokofiev, 1945), and *The Young Lady Peasant Girl* (mus. Asafiev, 1946), and for Leningrad *The Bronze Horseman* (mus. Glière) and a new version of *The Red Poppy* (both Kirov B., 1949). Ch. *Under Italian Skies* (mus. V. Yurovsky) with S. Sergeyev for Kiev B. in

1952. As a ch. he was one of the first to apply the Stanislavsky method to b., emphasizing strongly the dramatic texture of each of his works. Professor of Ch. at Lunacharsky Institute of Theatrical Art in Moscow 1942–6, Dir. of Bolshoi School 1946–9, and since 1956 a teacher (professor since 1958) at GITIS. Author of *The Art of the Choreographer* (Moscow, 1954). Though his bs. have been strongly criticized in the West (because of their poor d. invention), he was highly regarded in the U.S.S.R. and considered one of the pioneers of the new Sov. b. Was married to the d. Maria Smirnova. Stalin Prize (1942 and 1945).
BIBL.: N. Roslavleva, in *Era of the Russian Ballet* (London, 1966).

Zambelli, Carlotta (*b* Milan, 4 Nov. 1875, *d* there, 28 Jan. 1968). Ital. dancer and teacher. Studied at La Scala B. School. Début at Paris Opéra in 1894; later became prima ballerina, and succeeded R. Mauri in her roles. Created ballerina part in Staats' *Cydalise et le Chèvre pied* (1923). The last foreign ballerina at the St. Petersburg Maryinsky Th., 1901; much admired in *Coppélia, Giselle*, and *Paquita*. Retired in 1930 and became senior teacher at the Paris Opéra B. School, where she was addressed as 'Grande Mademoiselle'.
BIBL.: Portfolio on Z., *Dance Magazine* (1974/2–3).

Zambra. Span., a perf. of gipsy dances. Also used to designate a d. performed together with the recitation or singing of 'romances', known to Moors and Spaniards since the 14th century.

Zapateado. A Span. flamenco d., d. by men only and characterized by staccato footwork and rhythmic stamping.

Zappolini, Walter (*b* Florence, 1930). Ital. dancer. Studied at Rome Op. B. School; joined its co. in 1946 and became principal d. in 1947.

Zarabanda. See *Sarabande*.

Zaraspe, Hector (*b* Tucumán, 1931). Argent. dancer and teacher. Studied folk d. and later, b. with Bulnés in Buenos Aires. D. with Teatro Colón B. 1949–52; began to teach there in 1951. Went to Spain in 1954 and taught for the cos. of Mariemma and Antonio. Settled in New York in 1964; now teaches at Joffrey's Amer. B. Center. Has often taught as a guest abroad (Vienna State Op. B., Dutch National B., Cologne Summer Academy, etc.). B. dir. of Rio de Janeiro Teatro Municipal 1971–3.
BIBL.: A. Fatt, 'Flamboyant Maestro', *Dance Magazine* (1969/10).

Zéphire et Flore. Ballet in 1 act; libr. Kochno; ch. Massine; mus. Vladimir Dukelsky; déc. Braque. Prod. 28 Apr. 1925, Bs. Russes de Diaghilev, Monte Carlo, with Lifar, Nikitina, Dolin. A modern attempt to reconstruct Didelot's famous b. *Flore et Zéphire* of 1796. Boreas was Lifar's first important solo role.

BIBL.: B. Kochno, in *Diaghilev and the Ballets Russes* (New York, 1970).

Zhdanov, Yuri Timofeievich (*b* Moscow, 29 Nov. 1925, *d* Moscow, 9 April 1986). Sov. dancer and b. director. Studied at Bolshoi School; graduated in 1944. Joined Bolshoi B.; later became principal d. Ulanova's partner from 1951. D. Romeo in the Bolshoi B. film *Romeo and Juliet* (1954). Dir. of the Moscow Classic B. Ensemble 1972–6, for which he ch. some bs. Merited Artist of the R.S.F.S.R. (1964).

Ziggurat. Ballet in 1 act; ch. Tetley; mus. Stockhausen; déc. Baylis. Prod. 20 Nov. 1967, B. Rambert, Cochrane Th., London, with Chesworth, Curtis, Smith, Taylor, Craig. The b. is performed to Stockhausen's *Gesang der Jünglinge* and part of *Kontakte*. 'The *Ziggurat* was a mighty temple-tower of ascending rectinlinear terraces built by the Assyrians and worshipped as the earth-soul. It is said to have been the Hanging Gardens of Babylon, perhaps the stairway of Jacob's dream, and the origin of the Tower of Babel' (programme note).

BIBL.: P. Brinson and C. Crisp, in *Ballet & Dance* (Newton Abbot, 1980).

Zimmerl, Christl (*b* Vienna, 27 Feb. 1939, *d* there, 19 Mar. 1976). Austrian dancer. Studied at Vienna State Op. B. School. Joined its co. in 1953 and became soloist in 1957 and principal d. in 1965. Created roles in Hanka's *Moor of Venice* (1955) and *Medusa* (1957), and Milloss' *Deserts* (1965) and *Orpheus Loses Eurydice* (1966). Was married to the then mus. and d. critic (now b. dir.) Gerhard Brunner.

BIBL.: E. Herf, 'C.Z.', *Ballet Today* (1959/3).

Zimmermann, Bernd Alois (*b* Bliesheim, 20 Mar. 1918, *d* Gross-Königsdorf, 10 Aug. 1970). Ger. composer. Wrote the b. *Alagoana* (ch. Roleff, Bielefeld, 1954). Several of his concert pieces were comp. with an eventual b. prod. in mind, e.g. *Kontraste* (ch. Roleff, Bielefeld, 1954; also by Bolender, Cologne, 1964), *Présence* (ch. Cranko, Schwetzingen-Stuttgart, 1968; also by Bohner, Darmstadt, 1972), *Concerto pour violoncelle et orchestre en forme de pas de trois* (ch. Sertić, Wuppertal, 1968), and *Musique pour les soupers du Roi Ubu* (ch. Walter, Düsseldorf, 1968). Other concert mus. of his which has been adapted for b. purposes includes *Giostra Genovese* (in *La Chatelaine*, ch. Urbani, Bonn, 1962), Sonata for Violoncello Solo (in *Die Befragung*, ch. Cranko, Stuttgart, 1967), and *Tratto* (ch. Bohner, Berlin, 1969).

Zlocha, Erika (*b* Vienna, 8 Feb. 1939). Austrian dancer. Studied at Vienna State Op. B. School; joined its co. in 1953 and became soloist in 1958. Created Mizzi in Hanka's *Hotel Sacher* (1957).

Zolan, Miro (orig. Miroslav Zlochovsky; *b* Prague, 1926). Czech-Brit. dancer, choreographer and b. master. Studied with Nikolska. Début at Prague National Th. Left Czechoslovakia in 1941; d. with various cos. and studied further with T. Gsovsky and Egorova. Joined International B. in 1947 and later became soloist; then d. in Australia, N.Z., and with B. Rambert and Borovansky B. Joined Sadler's Wells Th. B. as a soloist in 1953; became principal d. in 1954. B. master Royal Winnipeg B. 1957–9. Went to Tehran with his wife, d. Sandra Vane, in 1960 to form a b. co. Has since worked as a b. master and ch. all over the world, e.g. with Mexican National B., in Tokyo, with B. San Carlo, Naples, and now in London.

BIBL.: J. Percival, 'A Dancer with Expression', *Dance and Dancers* (1958/4).

Zorina, Vera (orig. Eva Brigitte Hartwig; *b* Berlin, 2 Jan. 1917). Ger.-Amer. dancer and actress. Studied with Eduardova and T. and V. Gsovsky. Début in M. Reinhardt's *A Midsummer Night's Dream* prod. Went to London in 1933 and studied further with N. Legat and Rambert and appeared as an actress. Member of B. Russe de Monte Carlo 1934–6. Appeared in the London prod. of *On Your Toes* (1937). Went to Hollywood as a film-d. Started to appear in Broadway musicals in 1938 (début in the Balanchine prod. of *I Married an Angel*). D. with B. Th. in 1943. Continued to appear as an actress; specialized in such works as Honegger's *Joan of Arc at the Stake* (1948), Stravinsky's *Persephone* (1955), and Debussy's *Le Martyre de Saint-Sébastien*. Her films include *The Goldwyn Follies* (1938), *On Your Toes* (1939), and *Star Spangled Rhythm* (1943). Contributed 'The Inward and the Outward Eye', *Dance Magazine* (Dec. 1959). Was married to Balanchine 1938–46; was married to the CBS producer Goddard Lieberson.

BIBL.: J. Gruen, 'V.Z.', in *The Private World of Ballet* (New York, 1975).

Zoritch, George (*b* Moscow, 6 June 1919). Amer. dancer and teacher. Studied with Preobrajenska, Vilzak, Oboukhoff, and Nijinska. Début with Rubinstein's co. in 1933. Joined de Basil's B. Russe in 1936; created roles in Massine's *Jardin public* (1935) and *Symphonie fantastique* (1936); then d. with Blum's B. Russe de Monte Carlo from 1938. Appeared in various films and musicals and with several b. cos., e.g. Grand B. du Marquis de Cuevas, Teatro Colón B., B. Russe de Monte Carlo again, and cos. of the Amer. Regional B. movement. His most famous role was in *L'Après-midi d'un faune*. Opened a studio in Hollywood in 1964. Has been guest professor at Arizona Univ.

Zorn, Friedrich Albert. Ger. dance teacher and writer. Little is known about his life. He was a d. teacher at the Richelieu Gymnasium in Odessa in

1846. Published his standard work, *Grammatik der Tanzkunst*, in Leipzig in 1887, after thorough research and consultation with P. Taglioni and Sain-Léon. This was a textbook on dancing which used his own system of notation. Among the annotated dances is a *Cachucha*, which may be the one d. by Elssler.

Zubkovskaya, Inna Borisovna (*b* Moscow, 29 Nov. 1923). Sov. dancer and teacher. Studied at Bolshoi School; graduated in 1941. Joined the Kirov B. in Perm, created Phrygia in Jacobson's *Spartacus* (1956) and Mekhmene-Banu in Grigorovich's *Legend of Love* (1961). Retired in 1970, but still teaches at Leningrad Ch. School. Stalin Prize (1951); People's Artist of the R.S.F.S.R. (1957). Married to the d. Sviatoslav Kusnetzov.

Zucchi, Virginia (*b* Parma, 10 Feb. 1849, *d* Monte Carlo, 12 Oct. 1930). Ital. dancer and teacher. Studied with Blasis and Lepri in Milan. Began dancing in the Ital. provinces in 1866; then d. in Rome, Milan, Berlin, London, and in St. Petersburg 1885–92, where she first appeared at a café-concert. Her brilliant Ital. virtuosity was a great success there; she was commanded to d. before the Tsar and then invited to d. at the Maryinsky Th., where she was very influential in perfecting the technique of the St. Petersburg school. However, she was not only a dazzling technician, but also a fascinating actress; her greatest successes were in Manzotti's *Brahma* and the Petipa versions of *La Fille mal gardée, La Fille du Pharaon, Esmeralda, Paquita,* and *Coppélia*. After her return from Russia she appeared only on rare occasions. Ch. bs. for op. prods. (some for the Teatro Colón) and later opened a school in Monte Carlo, where she taught until her death.

Züllig, Hans (*b* Rorschach, 1 Feb. 1914). Swiss dancer, choreographer, and teacher. Studied with Jooss and Leeder in Essen and Dartington. D. as a soloist with Bs. Jooss 1935–47, Sadler's Wells Th. B. 1948–9, Folkwang D. Th. 1949–52, and Zurich B. 1953–4. Taught at Essen Folkwang School 1954–6; at the same time b. master with Jooss at Düsseldorf B. Went to Santiago; teacher, ch. and soloist at Chilean Univ. 1956–61. Rejoined teaching staff of Folkwang School in 1961; appointed dir. of its d. department in 1969. Created roles in Jooss's *Ballade* and *Johann Strauss, Tonight!* (1935), *A Spring Tale* (1939), *Company at the Manor* (1943), and *Pandora* (1944), Leeder's *Sailor's Fancy* (1943), his own b. *Le Bosquet* (1945), Howard's *Sélina* (1948), and Cranko's *Sea Change* (1949).

Zumbo, Francesca (*b* Paris, 28 Apr. 1944). Fr. dancer. Studied at Paris Conservatoire and Paris Opéra B. School. D. with Grand B. du Marquis de Cuevas 1961–2; then joined Paris Opéra B., and became première danseuse in 1969. Created a sensation when she performed a pas de deux

from Béjart's *Bhakti* with P. Bart at the Moscow Dancers' Competition in 1969, with which she won a Gold Medal. Has also been a guest ballerina with the Bolshoi B. and the Royal Winnipeg B. Retired 1984.
BIBL.: L. Rossel, 'Profil de F.Z.', *Les Saisons de la danse* (1969/12).

Zurich Through Laban's School, the city became one of the focal points of the Central Eur. modern d. movement in the years immediately preceding and during the First World War. At the Municipal Th. of Switzerland's biggest city b. served mainly to decorate the op. and operetta prods. It attracted some attention of its own when the Mlakars worked here as b. directors 1934–8, choreographing the first prods. of Lhotka's *Devil in the Village* (1935) and *Ballad of Medieval Love* (1936), later mounted by many continental cos. After the Second World War Hans Macke, Jaroslav Berger, and Robert Mayer were the b. masters (Berger ch. a *Sacre du printemps* version 1951, and he was also in charge of the ch. for the 1957 first prod. of Schoenberg's *Moses and Aaron*). However, it was only with N. Beriozoff's appointment as artistic dir. 1964–71 that the foundations were laid for a regular repertory, based firmly upon the classics plus some modern full-length works, most of which were ch. by himself, with G. Fulton as prima ballerina. Nureyev then mounted *Raymonda* in 1972. The following years saw instability return under such b. directors as M. Descombey (1971–3), G. Cauley (1973–5), and the combined b. directorship of H. Meister and J. Burth (1975–8). Stability returned with P. Neary 1978–85, when the repertory was based mainly upon Balanchine revivals. Uwe Scholz has been in charge of the co. since 1985/6.

Zvereff, Nicholas (*b* Moscow, 1888, *d* St. Raphael, June 1965). Russ.-Fr. dancer, b. master, and teacher. D. with Diaghilev's Bs. Russes 1912–26, where he excelled in character roles. Toured various countries with his wife, d. V. Nemchinova (they were later divorced), and Oboukhoff. B. dir. at Kaunas op. house 1930–6. Soloist and b. master of B. Russe de Monte Carlo 1936–45. Had his own studio in Paris 1946–52; staged revivals of bs. from the Diaghilev repertory at the Opéra and at La Scala, Milan. Reorganized the b. co. of the Brussels Th. de la Monnaie in 1952. Taught at Kniaseff's B. Academy in Lausanne 1953–5, and was b. master at the Buenos Aires Teatro Colón 1957–60; also continued to work occasionally in Paris.

Zviagina, Suzanna Nicolaievna (*b* Moscow, 1918). Sov. dancer, teacher, and b. mistress. Studied at Bolshoi School; graduated in 1937. Joined Bolshoi B. and later became soloist. B. mistress Novosibirsk Op. House 1961–70. Dir. and first b. mistress of Moscow Music Hall 1971–5.

OXFORD

MORE OXFORD PAPERBACKS

This book is just one of nearly 1000 Oxford Paper-backs currently in print. If you would like details of other Oxford Paperbacks, including titles in the World's Classics, Oxford Reference, Oxford Books, OPUS, Past Masters, Oxford Authors, and Oxford Shakespeare series, please write to:

UK and Europe: Oxford Paperbacks Publicity Manager, Arts and Reference Publicity Department, Oxford University Press, Walton Street, Oxford OX2 6DP.

Customers in UK and Europe will find Oxford Paperbacks available in all good bookshops. But in case of difficulty please send orders to the Cash-with-Order Department, Oxford University Press Distribution Services, Saxon Way West, Corby, Northants NN18 9ES. Tel: 0536 741519; Fax: 0536 746337. Please send a cheque for the total cost of the books, plus £1.75 postage and packing for orders under £20; £2.75 for orders over £20. Customers outside the UK should add 10% of the cost of the books for postage and packing.

USA: Oxford Paperbacks Marketing Manager, Oxford University Press, Inc., 200 Madison Avenue, New York, N.Y. 10016.

Canada: Trade Department, Oxford University Press, 70 Wynford Drive, Don Mills, Ontario M3C 1J9.

Australia: Trade Marketing Manager, Oxford University Press, G.P.O. Box 2784Y, Melbourne 3001, Victoria.

South Africa: Oxford University Press, P.O. Box 1141, Cape Town 8000.

OXFORD LETTERS AND MEMOIRS
RICHARD HOGGART

A Local Habitation
Life and Times: 1918–1940

With characteristic candour and compassion, Richard Hoggart evokes the Leeds of his boyhood, where as an orphan, he grew up with his grandmother, two aunts, an uncle, and a cousin in a small terraced back-to-back.

'brilliant . . . a joy as well as an education' Roy Hattersley

'a model of scrupulous autobiography' Edward Blishen, *Listener*

A Sort of Clowning
Life and Times: 1940–1950

Opening with his wartime exploits in North Africa and Italy, this sequel to *A Local Habitation* recalls his teaching career in North-East England, and charts his rise in the literary world following the publication of *The Uses of Literacy*.

'one of the classic autobiographies of our time' Anthony Howard, *Independent on Sunday*

'Hoggart [is] the ideal autobiographer' Beryl Bainbridge, *New Statesman and Society*

OXFORD BOOKS

THE OXFORD BOOK OF ENGLISH
GHOST STORIES

Chosen by Michael Cox and R. A. Gilbert

This anthology includes some of the best and most
frightening ghost stories ever written, including
M. R. James's 'Oh Whistle, and I'll Come to You,
My Lad', 'The Monkey's Paw' by W. W. Jacobs,
and H. G. Wells's 'The Red Room'. The important
contribution of women writers to the genre is represented by stories such as Amelia Edwards's 'The
Phantom Coach', Edith Wharton's 'Mr Jones', and
Elizabeth Bowen's 'Hand in Glove'.

As the editors stress in their informative introduction, a good ghost story, though it may raise
many profound questions about life and death,
entertains as much as it unsettles us, and the best
writers are careful to satisfy what Virginia Woolf
called 'the strange human craving for the pleasure of
feeling afraid'. This anthology, the first to present
the full range of classic English ghost fiction, simi-
larly combines a serious literary purpose with the
plain intention of arousing pleasing fear at the
doings of the dead.

'an excellent cross-section of familiar and unfamiliar stories and guaranteed to delight' *New
Statesman*

OXFORD POETS

Winner of the 1989 Whitbread Prize for Poetry

SHIBBOLETH

Michael Donaghy

This is Michael Donaghy's first full-length collection. His work has a wit and grace reminiscent of the metaphysical poets, and his subjects range widely, responding in unexpected ways to his curiosity and inventiveness. Among the varied pieces collected here are a number of love poems remarkable for their blend of tenderness and irony; a terse 'news item'; playful 'translations' of a mythical Welsh poet; and an 'interview' with Marcel Duchamp.

As the American critic Alfred Corn says:

'Michael Donaghy's poems have the fine-tuned precision of a ten-speed bike, the wit of a streetwise don, a polyphonic inventiveness . . . Poems so original, wry, and philosophical as these are hard to come by. Don't think of passing them up.'

PAST MASTERS

General Editor: Keith Thomas

SHAKESPEARE

Germaine Greer

'At the core of a coherent social structure as he viewed it lay marriage, which for Shakespeare is no mere comic convention but a crucial and complex ideal. He rejected the stereotype of the passive, sexless, unresponsive female and its inevitable concommitant, the misogynist conviction that all women were whores at heart. Instead he created a series of female characters who were both passionate and pure, who gave their hearts spontaneously into the keeping of the men they loved and remained true to the bargain in the face of tremendous odds.'

Germaine Greer's short book on Shakespeare brings a completely new eye to a subject about whom more has been written than on any other English figure. She is especially concerned with discovering why Shakespeare 'was and is a popular artist', who remains a central figure in English cultural life four centuries after his death.

'eminently trenchant and sensible . . . a genuine exploration in its own right' John Bayley, *Listener*

'the clearest and simplest explanation of Shakespeare's thought I have yet read' Auberon Waugh, *Daily Mail*

HISTORY IN OXFORD PAPERBACKS
TUDOR ENGLAND
John Guy

Tudor England is a compelling account of political and religious developments from the advent of the Tudors in the 1460s to the death of Elizabeth I in 1603.

Following Henry VII's capture of the Crown at Bosworth in 1485, Tudor England witnessed far-reaching changes in government and the Reformation of the Church under Henry VIII, Edward VI, Mary, and Elizabeth; that story is enriched here with character studies of the monarchs and politicians that bring to life their personalities as well as their policies.

Authoritative, clearly argued, and crisply written, this comprehensive book will be indispensable to anyone interested in the Tudor Age.

'lucid, scholarly, remarkably accomplished . . . an excellent overview' *Sunday Times*

'the first comprehensive history of Tudor England for more than thirty years' Patrick Collinson, *Observer*

OPUS

General Editors: Walter Bodmer,
Christopher Butler, Robert Evans,
John Skorupski

CLASSICAL THOUGHT

Terence Irwin

Spanning over a thousand years from Homer to Saint Augustine, *Classical Thought* encompasses a vast range of material, in succinct style, while remaining clear and lucid even to those with no philosophical or Classical background.

The major philosophers and philosophical schools are examined—the Presocratics, Socrates, Plato, Aristotle, Stoicism, Epicureanism, Neoplatonism; but other important thinkers, such as Greek tragedians, historians, medical writers, and early Christian writers, are also discussed. The emphasis is naturally on questions of philosophical interest (although the literary and historical background to Classical philosophy is not ignored), and again the scope is broad—ethics, the theory of knowledge, philosophy of mind, philosophical theology. All this is presented in a fully integrated, highly readable text which covers many of the most important areas of ancient thought and in which stress is laid on the variety and continuity of philosophical thinking after Aristotle.

THE OXFORD AUTHORS

General Editor: Frank Kermode

THE OXFORD AUTHORS is a series of authoritative editions of major English writers. Aimed at both students and general readers, each volume contains a generous selection of the best writings—poetry, prose, and letters—to give the essence of a writer's work and thinking. All the texts are complemented by essential notes, an introduction, chronology, and suggestions for further reading.

THE WORLD'S CLASSICS
THE WIND IN THE WILLOWS

Kenneth Grahame

The Wind in the Willows (1908) is a book for those 'who keep the spirit of youth alive in them; of life, sunshine, running water, woodlands, dusty roads, winter firesides'. So wrote Kenneth Grahame of his timeless tale of Toad, Mole, Badger, and Rat in their beautiful and benevolently ordered world. But it is also a world under siege, threatened by dark and unnamed forces—'the Terror of the Wild Wood' with its 'wicked little faces' and 'glances of malice and hatred'—and defended by the mysterious Piper at the Gates of Dawn. *The Wind in the Willows* has achieved an enduring place in our literature: it succeeds at once in arousing our anxieties and in calming them by giving perfect shape to our desire for peace and escape.

The World's Classics edition has been prepared by Peter Green, author of the standard biography of Kenneth Grahame.

'It is a Household Book; a book which everybody in the household loves, and quotes continually; a book which is read aloud to every new guest and is regarded as the touchstone of his worth.' A. A. Milne

Oxford Reference

The Oxford Reference series offers authoritative and up-to-date reference books in paperback across a wide range of topics.

Abbreviations
Art and Artists
Ballet
Biology
Botany
Business
Card Games
Chemistry
Christian Church
Classical Literature
Computing
Dates
Earth Sciences
Ecology
English Christian
   Names
English Etymology
English Language
English Literature
English Place-Names
Eponyms
Finance
Fly-Fishing
Fowler's Modern
   English Usage
Geography
Irish Mythology
King's English
Law
Literary Guide to Great
   Britain and Ireland
Literary Terms

Mathematics
Medical Dictionary
Modern Quotations
Modern Slang
Music
Nursing
Opera
Oxford English
Physics
Popes
Popular Music
Proverbs
Quotations
Sailing Terms
Saints
Science
Ships and the Sea
Sociology
Spelling
Superstitions
Theatre
Twentieth-Century Art
Twentieth-Century
   History
Twentieth-Century
   World Biography
Weather Facts
Word Games
World Mythology
Writer's Dictionary
Zoology